The McGraw-Hill

Homeland Security Handbook

**STRATEGIC GUIDANCE FOR A
COORDINATED APPROACH TO EFFECTIVE
SECURITY AND EMERGENCY MANAGEMENT**

Second Edition

David G. Kamien, Editor
CEO & Founder of Mind-Alliance Systems

With a Foreword by the Honorable Michael Chertoff
*Principal of The Chertoff Group and
former Secretary of Homeland Security*

New York • Chicago • San Francisco • Lisbon • London •
Madrid • Mexico City • Milan • New Delhi • San Juan •
Seoul • Singapore • Sydney • Toronto

1 2 3 4 5 6 7 8 9 10   DOC/DOC   1 8 7 6 5 4 3 2

ISBN: 978-0-07-179084-0
MHID: 0-07-179084-5

e-ISBN   0-07-179085-3
e-MHID   978-0-07-179085-7

McGraw-Hill books are available at special quantity discounts to use as premiums and sales promotions or for use in corporate training programs. To contact a representative, please e-mail us at bulksales@mcgraw-hill.com.

This book is printed on acid-free paper.

CONTENTS

Foreword   *xix*
Preface   *xxi*
Acknowledgements   *xxv*
List of Contributors   *xxvii*

PART 1   **INTRODUCTION TO PART I: TERRORIST AND CRIMINAL THREATS**   **1**

CHAPTER 1   **The Legacy of Osama bin Laden's Strategy**   **5**

Introduction   5
Bin Laden and the Afghan–Soviet War   7
Terrorist Attacks and the Economy   9
Bleeding Wars   10
The War on Oil   12
The Thousand Cuts   15
Conclusion   18
Notes   19

CHAPTER 2   **The Terrorist Threat to Surface Transportation: The Challenge of**
                 Securing Public Places   **21**

Introduction   21
The Threat is Real   21
Bombings Account for the Most Casualties   23
Terrorist Campaigns   23
Chemical and Biological Attacks Were An Initial Fad   24
Will Terrorists move Toward Derailment?   25
An Aviation Security Model Will Not Work   26
Surface Transportation Security must be Realistic   28
Enlisting Staff and Public Participation Saves Lives   29
Notes   30

CHAPTER 3   **Geostrategy of Criminality: Highly Intensive Criminality** **33**

Contemporary Criminal Chaos   33
Notes   43

CHAPTER 4 **The Psychology of Terrorism: Current Understanding and Vital Next Steps** **45**

Introduction 45
The Terrorist 47
The Next Steps 49
Conclusion 56
Notes 57

CHAPTER 5 **Twenty-First Century Biological Threats** **59**

Introduction 59
A National Security Perspective 61
Assessing the Threat 62
Notes 67

PART 2 **INTRODUCTION TO PART II: POLICY, GOVERNANCE, AND LEGAL RESPONSES** **69**

CHAPTER 6 **Homeland Security: The Advancing National Strategic Position** **71**

Introduction 71
The Strategic Position Documents: The Formative Years 72
The Overarching Goal and Policy and Operational System 75
Implementing the Preparedness Goal and Further Goal Updates 77
A New National Strategy for Homeland Security 79
The Strategic Position Documents: The Refinement Years 80
The Quadrennial Review and New Strategy 81
Restatement and Revitalization of the Presidential National
   Preparedness Directive, Goal, and System 82
The New National Preparedness Goal and System 85
Current Themes and Additional Challenges 89
Conclusion 95
References 96

CHAPTER 7 **Prosecuting the Financiers of Terror** **99**

I. Why Go After the Money? 99
II. Material Support Statutes, 18 U.S.C. §§ 2339A and 2339B 101
III. Terrorist Financing Prosecutions and Convictions 110
IV. Conclusion 114
Notes 115

CHAPTER 8 **Counterterrorism Legislation** **121**

Introduction 121
First Steps 122

Sanctions and State Sponsors   123
The Long-Arm Statute   126
Aviation and Maritime Security   127
The Newer Focus: Non-State Terrorist Groups and Actors   128
Foreign Terrorist Organizations   129
Administrative Record   131
Weapons of Mass Destruction   132
The Patriot Act   133
Civil Suits   135
Prosecution and Detention of Terrorists   138
Implementation and Challenges   143
Notes   146

CHAPTER 9   **Intelligence and Information Sharing for Homeland Security and Counterterrorism**   **149**

Introduction   149
The Impetus to Improve Terrorism-Related Information Sharing   150
Major Information Sharing Initiatives from 2001 to 2011   151
Assessment of Progress on Information Sharing Initiatives   160
Information Sharing Issues and Challenges for the Next Decade   161
Notes   166

CHAPTER 10   **Developing Information Sharing Protocols and Planning Policy to Support Homeland Security Missions**   **169**

Introduction   169
Information Sharing is a Central Aspect of Homeland Security   170
Information Sharing is Essential for Joint-Planning and
    Operational Coordination   171
The Importance of Information Sharing Recognized in Policy   172
Information Sharing and National Intelligence Reform   172
Critical Infrastructure Protection   174
Private Sector Business Continuity and Enterprise Resilience   177
Emergency Management and Whole Community Resilience   177
Information Sharing and the Military's Comprehensive Approach   180
Information Sharing and Communication
    Technology Cannot Replace Planning   182
The Need to Develop Information Sharing Protocols   183
Leadership and Management Are Accountable for
    Driving the Improvement of Information Sharing   185
National Information Sharing Planning Policy   186
Conclusion   188
Acknowledgements   189
Notes   189

PART 3   **INTRODUCTION TO PART III: INTEROPERABILITY,**
                    INFORMATION SHARING, AND COLLABORATION   **191**

CHAPTER 11   **Why We Fail—And How to Succeed**   **195**

                    An Historical Perspective   195
                    Conventions   197
                    The Pearl Harbor Deficiencies   205
                    Intelligence   221
                    Summary   248
                    Acknowledgements   249
                    Notes   249

CHAPTER 12   **Key Requirements for Enabling Information Sharing Planning**
                    and Policy Audits   **253**

                    Introduction   253
                    Requirements for an Information Sharing Planning Process   254
                    Implications for the ISP Process   255
                    Towards an ISP Methodology   259
                    ISP Software Requirements   261
                    Conclusion   268
                    Acknowledgements   268
                    Notes   268

CHAPTER 13   **The Information Sharing Environment (ISE)**   **271**

                    Introduction   271
                    Background of the Information Sharing Environment (ISE)   271
                    Purpose and Scope of the ISE   273
                    ISE Mission Partners   275
                    Maturing and Strengthening the ISE   276
                    Case Study: NIEM   278
                    Leveraging Standards-Based Data Exchanges for Suspicious
                        Activity Reporting   278
                    Fusion Centers and Information Sharing between
                        States and Regional Stakeholders   280
                    Conclusion and Future of the ISE   281
                    About the Author   281
                    Notes   282

CHAPTER 14   **Fusion Centers: Touchpoints that Promote National**
                    Preparedness and Intelligence-Led Policing   **283**

                    Introduction   283
                    Foundational Concepts: The Evolution of the Fusion Process   287
                    National Preparedness   290

Intelligence-Led Policing 294
Key Considerations for Fusion Center Operations 297
Advancing Fusion Centers to Underpin Homeland
   Security and Intelligence-Led Policing 314
Conclusion 317
Study Resources Section 318
Notes 319

CHAPTER 15   **The Necessity of Interagency Collaboration**   **323**

Introduction 323
Case Studies 325
DHS and Collaboration 327
How to Collaborate 328
Conclusion 331
References 331

PART 4   **INTRODUCTION TO PART IV: RISK MANAGEMENT,
DECISION MAKING, AND COMMUNICATION**   **333**

CHAPTER 16   **Integrating Risk Management with Homeland Security and
Counterterrorism Resource Allocation Decision Making**   **335**

The Impact of Terrorism on National, State, and Local Community
   Resource Allocation 335
Counterterrorism (CT) Decision-Making Framework 336
Three Counterterrorism Resource Allocation Approaches 337
Lessons from Other Important Risk Applications 339
Comparison of CT with Other Risk Applications 341
Discussion of Analysis Tools and Techniques 342
Selection of Risk Analysis Techniques 357
Conclusions 362
Acknowledgements 363
References 363

CHAPTER 17   **Pervasive Readiness: Pipedream or Possible?**   **367**

Overview 367
A Framework for Pervasive Readiness 371
Quantifying Risk—Beyond Basic Risk Analysis 376
A Focus on All-Hazards Readiness 379
Measuring Readiness—Putting It All Together 382
Driving Change—Budgets and Performance Measures 386
Public Safety Ecosystems 389
Conclusion 391
Notes 394

CHAPTER 18   **The Psychological Perception of Risk**   **397**

Introduction   397
Creating Appropriate Communication Channels   400
Delivering Decision-Relevant Information
     Concisely and Comprehensibly   407
Managing Risks Well, So as to Have a Credible
     Message to Communicate   412
Conclusions   416
Bibliography   417
Appendix: A Strategy for the Content of Risk Communications   419
Notes   421

CHAPTER 19   **National Terrorism Advisory System**   **425**

Effective Risk Communication and Responding to Terrorism   425
Principles of Effective Risk Communication   426
Failures of the Homeland Security Advisory System   426
The National Terrorism Advisory System   427
An Evolving System: From HSAS to NTAS   428
Risk Communication: The Next Decade and Beyond   432
Notes   433

PART 5   **INTRODUCTION TO PART V: PROTECTING CRITICAL
INFRASTRUCTURE**   **435**

CHAPTER 20   **Critical Infrastructure and Interdependency Revisited**   **437**

Critical Infrastructure and Its Security   437
Interdependencies Among Infrastructures   443
Factors Contributing to Interdependence   445
Analyzing Interdependence   447
Institutional Interdependence   449
Technology and Interdependence   452
Reducing Vulnerability by Modifying Interdependency   453
Conclusion   455
Notes   455

CHAPTER 21   **Homeland Security for Drinking Water and Wastewater
Utilities**   **461**

Threats to Drinking Water and Wastewater Utilities   464
Vulnerability Assessment   479
Mitigation of Risk   480
Emergency Response   484
References   487

CHAPTER 22   **Civil Aviation Security: On the Ground and In the Air**   **489**

The Psychological Battle of Aviation Security   489
Pre-9/11 History   490
The Response of Government, Industry, and the Traveling Public to 9/11   492
Innocence Lost: A New Paradigm   496
An Explosion of Threat Vectors: Chasing Yesterday   497
Bag Screening, Passenger Searches, FAMS, and Public Safety   501
Technological Solutions vs. Risk Management—
  Approaches to Passenger Screening   504
Insider Threat   508
Cargo Security in the International Distribution Stream   510
Public Education, Aviation Security, and Civil Liberties   511
Shared Responsibility for Security   514
Better Intelligence and Layers of Security   518
Protecting the Travel Experience   519
Notes   521

CHAPTER 23   **Creating Disaster Resilient Regions through**
Whole Community Engagement   **523**

Regional Disaster Resilience:A Guide to Develop an Action Plan 2011 Edition   525

PART 6   **INTRODUCTION TO PART VI: DISASTER PREPAREDNESS AND**
EMERGENCY MANAGEMENT   **587**

CHAPTER 24   **Learning from History: The Evolution of Emergency**
Management in the United States   **593**

Importance of Knowing the History of Emergency Management   594
Key Concepts in Disaster and Emergency Management   595
Evolution of Disaster Response in the United States over the Past Century   597
Policy, Political, and Organizational Context in Which Emergency
  Management Exists   599
Developing an Effective Emergency Management System   601
The Likely Future of Emergency Management in the United States   602
Conclusion   604
Notes   605

CHAPTER 25   **A City Once Underwater: Lessons Learned and the**
Story of the New Orleans Evacuation Plan   **607**

Introduction   607
The 2005 New Orleans Mindset   610
Conclusion   635
Notes   635

CHAPTER 26   **From Response to Resilience: State Emergency Preparedness**
                   Priorities   **637**

                   The Evolution of Homeland Security   637
                   Lesson 1: You Will Be Good at What You Do Every Day   638
                   Lesson 2: Use Clear, Plain Language, Set Goals,
                       and Understand That What Gets Measured Gets Done   647
                   Lesson 3: Homeland Security Is an All Hazards, All the Time Job   648
                   Lesson 4: It Is Not a Matter of If, but When—
                       The Question Is How We Respond and Recover   649
                   Lesson 5: We Are All in This Together,
                       and No one Has a Monopoly on Expertise   649
                   Conclusion: Homeland Security Is Hometown Security   650

CHAPTER 27   **Emergency Response: An Overview**   **653**

                   Who Does What?   653
                   Normal Operations   657
                   Coordination of Activities   658
                   Large-Scale Events   659
                   Weapons of Mass Destruction   662
                   Technology: Interoperable Communications   662
                   A Practical Guide to Preparing for Incidents   665
                   Notes   666

CHAPTER 28   **Understanding and Preparing for the Psychological**
                   Consequences of Terrorism   **667**

                   Introduction   667
                   What Are we Worried About?   668
                   Who Will most Probably be Affected?   669
                   Strategies for Preparedness and Response   672
                   What Works? Developing and Evaluating Interventions   673
                   Who Can Respond?   674
                   How Can We Ensure that the Responders Are Ready?   675
                   Conclusion   676
                   Notes   676

CHAPTER 29   **Crisis Preparedness and Crisis Response: The Meta-Leadership**
                   Model and Method   **679**

                   The Demands of Crisis Leadership   680
                   The Model of Meta-Leadership: Origins and Extensions   682
                   The Five Dimensions of Meta-Leadership: Design, Concept, and Practice   684
                   Dimension One: The Person of the Meta-Leader   685
                   Dimension Two: Diagnosing the Challenge, Change, or Crisis   688
                   Dimension Three: Leading the Base   692
                   Dimension Four: Leading Up   694

Dimension Five: Leading Across the System   696
Unity of Effort: The Outcome and Effect of Meta-Leadership   699
On Being a Meta-Leader   702
Conclusion   704
Notes   706

**CHAPTER 30   Advice in Crisis: Leaders, Lawyers, and the Art of Disaster
                 Management   711**

Introduction   711
Disasters are Different   713
What Do Leaders Need from their Lawyers?   715
How Can Lawyers most Effectively
    Advise their Leaders in Disasters?   716
How Can Leaders get the Most from their Lawyers?   733
Concluding Thoughts   734
Appendix: What Is "SALT"?   735
Notes   736

**PART 7   INTRODUCTION TO PART VII: PRIVATE SECTOR
                 SECURITY AND RESILIENCE   739**

CHAPTER 31   Role of Corporate Security   743

Introduction   743
Security Risk Assessments   745
Baseline Security   747
Emergency Planning   751
Crisis Management   754
Sources and Contacts   758
Conclusion   761
Notes   761

CHAPTER 32   Corporate Emergency Management   763

Introduction   763
Program Management   768
Threat Assessment   769
Mitigation   770
Resources   772
Emergency Organization   772
Incident Command System   775
Emergency Response Plan   779
Alerting, Warning, and Communications   780
Protective Actions   781
Threat-Specific Emergency Procedures   785

Training, Drills, and Exercises 798
Critiques, Audits, and Evaluations 799
Notes 799

CHAPTER 33 **Operational Resilience for Private and Public Sector Organizations** **801**

Operational Risk in Homeland Security: Current Concepts, Capabilities, and Challenges 802
Operational Resilience: A Framework for Integrating Capabilities to Manage Risk 806
Notes 809

CHAPTER 34 **Building A Resilient Nation** **811**

Resilience as a Counterterrorism Imperative 813
Resilience as Disaster Mitigation 815
Building Infrastructure Resilience 816
Building Community Resilience 820
Conclusion 822

CHAPTER 35 **The Community Resilience System: Operationalizing a Whole Community Approach** **825**

Introduction 825
Whole Community Approaches 826
Community Resilience 828
Development of the Community Resilience System 829
The Community Resilience System 830
Piloting the CRS 840
Implementing a Whole Community Approach 840
Conclusion 841
Appendix: Description of Community Services 842
Notes 846

CHAPTER 36 **Collaboration Not Isolation: A Joint Approach to Business Continuity and Resilience** **847**

PART 8 **INTRODUCTION TO PART VIII: THINKING, EDUCATION, AND TRAINING** **857**

CHAPTER 37 **A Systems Perspective on Homeland Security** **861**

Introduction 861
Homeland Security as a Complex System 863
Fundamentals of a Systems Perspective 866
Identifying Components, Relationships, and Wholes 866

Identifying and Leveraging System Structure and Patterns   866
Understanding Emergence and Unintended Consequences   867
Leveraging Stakeholder Participation   867
Systems Thinking Applied to Mass Transit Security   868
Conclusion   874
Notes   875

CHAPTER 38   **Perceptual Framing of Homeland Security**   **877**

Introduction   878
Building a Theory of Homeland Security
  Using Multiple Frame Analysis   881
Lens I: Homeland Security as a Criminal
  Justice Problem/Terrorism as a Crime   883
Lens II: Homeland Security as an International
  Relations Problem/Terrorism as War   887
Lens III: Homeland Security as an Organizational Design Problem/
  Terrorism as a Network   893
Conclusion   898
Notes   900

CHAPTER 39   **Emergency Exercise Design Principles and Objectives**   **905**

Exercise Design Objectives   907
Exercise Design Principles   908
Looking at Tabletop Exercises   911
References and Resources   916

CHAPTER 40   **Higher Education in Homeland Security: Current State
                   and Future Trends**   **917**

Introduction   917
Existing Frameworks for HS Curricula Offerings   919
Acknowledgements   934
Bibliography   934
Notes   935

PART 9   **INTRODUCTION TO PART IX: SCIENCE AND TECHNOLOGY**   **939**

CHAPTER 41   **Information Technology and Information Sharing**   **943**

Executive Overview   943
Homeland Security Is a Success   944
Performance Throughput: Considerations   954
Maximize Availability: Considerations   956
Predictive Analytics (Situation Awareness) Solutions   956
The Importance of Events   957

Architectural Insights—Summarized   958
The Future of Homeland Security Technology   960
What Did Who Know and When?   969
Predictive Analysis and Staging System   970
The VISION: Assertions   977
VISION: Scenario   979

CHAPTER 42   GIS Technology for Public Safety, Emergency Management,
              and Homeland Security   983

              Introduction   983
              Geographic Information System Technology   983
              The Evolution of GIS Technology   984
              Emergency Call Handling/Dispatch   986
              Situational Awareness   990
              Crime Analysis   993
              Fire & Rescue Station Location Analysis   996
              Emergency/Disaster Management   998
              Hazard and Risk Analysis   998
              Response Exercises   1001
              Intelligence Analysis   1004
              Critical Infrastructure Protection   1007
              Mobile GIS for Public Safety   1009
              Special Events   1011
              Case Studies   1011
              Summary   1017

CHAPTER 43   Technology Foraging: A Novel Approach to Technology
              Problem Solving within the DHS Science and Technology
              Directorate   1019

              Executive Summary   1019
              Background   1021
              Technical Approach   1024
              Methodology   1025
              Down-Select to Projects   1029
              Recent Implementation   1030
              Lessons Learned   1031
              Summary   1031

CHAPTER 44   Social Media and Crowdsourcing to Help Disaster
              Management   1033

              Introduction   1033
              Definitions   1034
              How Do Social Media, Crowdsourcing, and Crowdsensing Work?   1036
              What Can the Crowd Do?   1037

How to Harness Social Media and the Crowd   1041
Concerns   1044
Future Tools   1045
Crowd Sentiment Detection During Disasters and Crises:
    A Case Study of the San Bruno Fire   1046
Further Reading   1047

CHAPTER 45   **EIS: Goals, Progress, and Challenges for the Unified**
                 Incident Command and Decision Support National
                 Middleware   **1049**

Overview   1049
Background   1050
The Problem   1051
DHS Steps Forward to Seek a Solution   1052
A Concept of Information Sharing   1053
UICDS Integration Across the Integration Layer   1055
The UICDS Architecture   1058
UICDS Real-World Deployment   1060
Making It Work: UICDS Core Web Services   1062
Transporting Content: Fractional Data, Standards,
    UCore Digests, and UICDS Work Products   1065
Getting to the Right Data: National
    Doctrine Drives the UICDS Vision   1067
Local ConOps Drive Information Sharing Requirements   1069
It's All About the Right Content   1070
Common Operational Data: The Right Content   1071
Working with Other Sharing Programs as COD Sources   1076
Conclusion   1080
Notes   1082

CHAPTER 46   **The Challenging Realities of Homeland Security**
                 Technology Business   **1083**

Introduction   1083
Market Size   1084
Diversity of Needs   1086
Federal Technology Priorities   1087
State and Local Technology Priorities   1089
Why Some Make It and Others Don't   1089
Increasing Chances for Success   1091
Summary   1111
Acknowledgements   1111
Further Reading   1112

PART 10	INTRODUCTION TO PART X: CIVIL LIBERTIES AND OTHER LEGAL ISSUES	1113

CHAPTER 47	Vigilance on Two Fronts: Civil Liberties & the Homeland Security Professional	1117
	Introduction	1117
	The Debate	1118
	Applying These Considerations	1121
	Conclusion	1129
	Notes	1129

CHAPTER 48	GOVERNMENT DATA MINING	1133
	Introduction	1133
	The Broad and Changing Definition of "Data Mining"	1134
	Information Privacy and Its Protection from Intrusion by the Government	1136
	Recommendations for Regulating Government Data Mining	1153
	Notes	1160

PART 11	INTRODUCTION TO PART XI: INTERNATIONAL CHALLENGES AND APPROACHES	1169

CHAPTER 49	The Hyogo Framework for Action	1173
	Gaps and Challenges in Early Warning Systems	1178
	Understanding Risks	1180
	From Words to Investment	1181
	Incorporating DRM into National Planning and Investment	1182
	Urban and Land Use Planning	1184
	Environmental Planning and Management	1185
	Social Protection	1186
	Strengthening Institutional and Legislative Arrangements	1187
	Limited Local Capacity and Action	1188
	Very Limited Progress in Public Awareness and Education for DRM	1188
	Regional Progress	1189
	Global Gender Blindness	1191
	Further Information and Reading	1192

CHAPTER 50	International Homeland Security	1195
	Introduction	1195
	Counterterrorism and Policing Models	1197
	Emergency Management	1204
	The Role of the Military in Homeland Security	1209

	Conclusion	1213
	Notes	1214

CHAPTER 51   ISO Security Management Standards   1215

Introduction   1215
ISO's Solution to the Supply Chain Security Problem   1217
Who's Using ISO 28000? Examples of Recent, Diverse ISO 28000
    Certifications   1225
The Road Ahead   1231
ISO 28000 Supports Regional, Domestic, and Sector-Specific Programs   1233
Audit, Accreditation and Certification   1243
International Accreditation Forum (IAF)   1245
Conclusion   1247
Resources and Suggested Reading   1249
Notes   1250

CHAPTER 52   Why Fukushima Was Preventable   1253

Introduction   1255
The Accident Sequence   1256
Identifying Key Questions   1259
Underestimating the Threat   1262
Predicting Disaster   1264
A Missed Opportunity   1269
How Could the Plant Have Been Protected?   1271
International Best Practices   1273
Why Weren't These Practices and Actions Carried Out at
    Fukushima Daiichi?   1279
Conclusion   1286
Notes   1289

CHAPTER 53   Whole-of-Society Disaster Resilience: The Swedish Way   1295

Introduction   1295
Societal Security   1296
The Engine that Drives the Enterprise in Sweden   1299
Towards an All-Hazards Plus Approach   1306
Flow Security   1307
Sweden's Holistic Philosophy—A Balancing Act   1309
Cooperation in the Nordic Area and in the Near-Abroad   1310
Developing the Common EU Capacity   1312
Euro-Atlantic Cooperation   1314
Notes   1317

CHAPTER 54   Evolution of Counterterrorism and Security in India   1321

Notes   1334

CHAPTER 55   156 Chileans Dead: How the Impact of the 2010 Tsunami
                  Could Have Been Minimized   1337

                  Introduction   1337
                  Saturday February 27th, 2010   1338
                  Where Did It Go Wrong?   1340
                  Who Assumes Responsibility?   1349
                  What Improvements Have Been Made to Reduce
                     The Risk of This Happening Again?   1350
                  Summary   1352
                  Notes   1354

CHAPTER 56   International Cooperation in Counterterrorism   1357

                  Introduction   1357
                  Importance of a Strategic Approach,
                     Including the Respect of Human Rights   1358
                  EU Achievements   1359
                  International Cooperation   1362
                  EU–U.S. Counterterrorism Cooperation   1364
                  Conclusion   1365
                  Note   1365

Afterword   Homeland Security—The Organizational Challenge   1367

Index   1369

FOREWORD

Michael Chertoff

More than a decade has passed since the world witnessed the horrifying events of Tuesday, September 11, 2001. After that long ago fateful morning, the United States government put into place new policies and programs that significantly transformed the way we protect our nation from acts of terror. While the initial purpose was to implement a new regime of anti-terrorism measures, new programs that took into account threats involving both man-made and natural disasters were also developed. Whether it is increased information sharing among law enforcement and intelligence agencies, stronger border security, a layered aviation security regime, or stronger capabilities and more frequent and uniform training across all levels of government, today we are better prepared to prevent and protect against urgent threats and we have an enhanced ability to respond and quickly recover should another disaster occur.

Critical to helping us maintain this momentum is sharing our hard-won experiences with others. This handbook serves as an important contribution to this collaborative effort so that we may learn, practice and identify new ways to manage our risk and be prepared for the next generation of threats likely to emerge.

Of course, completely eliminating risk is not possible without compromising the freedoms and liberties we hold so dear. For example, we could stop all potential danger or risk from boarding a commercial airliner if we simply stopped flying. Keeping every possible danger from crossing our nation's borders could be accomplished if we halted all imports and stopped all travel and commerce from entering our country. But these draconian scenarios are both unrealistic and undesirable. Therefore, homeland security is about risk management and not risk elimination. It is about determining what layers of security we can put in place to get the best possible protection at a reasonable cost.

Most recently, the U.S. was able to demonstrate success at reducing our risk of another potential terrorist attack on our shores with the death of Osama Bin Laden. However, this victory does not eliminate the threat of terrorism and should not foster complacency. Our adversaries are evolving; we will confront a new set of leaders who may think differently and develop novel tactics and technologies to carry out their threats.

In addition to terrorism, other actors threaten not only our homeland security but our economic well-being as well. Today's persistent cyber threat represents an increasing highly disruptive threat to our national security; perhaps the biggest game changer since the onset of the nuclear age more than 65 years ago. Information technologies and network operations are essential to our daily lives as well as our global commerce. As a result, they continue to be targeted and attacked daily by a variety of actors ranging from today's modern-day criminals interested in pure financial gain, to nation states seeking stronger advantages for their own global competitiveness and dominant warfighting powers. Despite various government initiatives to help mitigate our risk to cyber-attack, there is in place no comprehensive strategy for cyber defense and security. To be blunt, we lack a unified vision of the problem and a comprehensive set of solutions to tackle it.

Today more than ever, we need a knowledgeable and skilled security community to meet these challenges and others that we will certainly face. This handbook serves as an important resource so that we may learn from what has been accomplished, even in only the last few years, while building and expanding a new generation of leaders with new thinking, decision making, and strategies. We must be prepared to constantly retool our approach and adapt new plans and tactics that protect our nation without unreasonable financial and social costs.

As you read through this unique guide of critical homeland security issues, you can begin to identify where the future threats are likely to be. Through your own contributions, you can help identify the planning and tools necessary to help us best confront them.

Michael Chertoff
Chairman of The Chertoff Group
Secretary of the U.S. Department of Homeland Security (2005–2009)

PREFACE

The 2012 edition of *The McGraw-Hill Homeland Security Handbook* aims to foster an integrated and coordinated approach to homeland security, emergency management, and enterprise resilience. The *Handbook* has several important features:

- The 2012 edition of the *Handbook* provides extensive thematic coverage, offering an opportunity to understand how homeland security challenges are interconnected. As pointed out in the Foreword to the 2006 edition, only a team of individuals with genuine crosscutting knowledge and practical experience will be able to understand the complexity of any particular homeland security challenge, devise an efficient and viable strategy for dealing with the problem, and implement this strategy effectively.
- The contributors include distinguished members of government, industry, and academia, many of whom combine theory with practical experience in homeland security and are active in educating the next generation of national security leaders.
- As no country has a monopoly on best practices, this edition has an expanded section on international approaches, with perspectives and insights from past disasters.
- This edition includes management principles, models, concepts, and specific practical guidance. Many chapters present practical steps that security, emergency preparedness, and business continuity professionals can apply immediately to create vigilant, prepared, and resilient communities and business enterprises.
- The book emphasizes the importance of systems thinking, holistic interoperability, and information sharing protocol development. The need for this emphasis stems from the reality that, since the last edition was published, the world has witnessed numerous occasions when poor information sharing and coordination undermined counterterrorism defenses and crisis consequence management following catastrophic natural disasters.

- The book covers recent homeland security policy developments, such as Presidential Policy Directive 8 (PPD-8) with National Frameworks for Prevention, Protection, Mitigation, Response, and Recovery.
- The website at www.HomelandSecurityBook.com provides valuable resources for further study.

ORGANIZATION

This book is divided into 11 sections that group subject matter into thematic units, providing a framework for study and discussion.

Section I on "Terrorist and Criminal Threats" discusses the threat from Islamist Jihadists, inspired by bin Laden and Al-Qaida, who want to impact Western adversaries by combining smaller attacks to drive up security costs—for example, against surface transportation, with occasional large-scale plots, possibly using weapons of mass destruction (WMD). A chapter on the psychology of terrorists raises the question of whether there is such a thing as a terrorist personality or profile, and warns that this notion can have dangerous consequences and implications for counterterrorism. The section also examines highly intensive criminality—crime that has morphed into a chaotic phenomenon so endemic and severe that it should be considered a national security matter.

Section II on "Policy, Governance, and Legal Responses" chronicles the major changes in national preparedness policy, counterterrorism legislation, and efforts to prosecute the financing of terrorism since September of 2001. The section addresses the evolution of federal intelligence information sharing policy and initiatives in this area. The section also describes a critical gap in U.S. homeland security—the lack of policy governing information sharing planning (ISP)—a policy needed to motivate agencies to develop documented information-sharing protocols vital to enhance cross-organizational integration and operational coordination, and support performance improvement and governance.

Section III on "Interoperability, Information Sharing, and Collaboration" emphasizes the importance of holistic interoperability, information sharing, and collaboration for national security. The section offers a deep analysis of the various types of historic interoperability and information-sharing failures. It then presents efforts to enable terrorism-related information to flow vertically and horizontally between partners in different levels of government, including the establishment of an Information Sharing Environment (ISE) and state and local intelligence fusion centers.

Section IV on "Risk Management, Decision Making, and Communication" explains that the key to risk analysis is to use a systematic and tailored process to identify critical system assets, assess risks, and make smart risk-management decisions. The section also discusses fundamental aspects of the psychological perception of risk and risk communication issues and initiatives such as the National Terrorism Advisory System, designed to communicate clear, timely, and specific information about the nature of the terrorist threat.

Section V on "Protecting Critical Infrastructure" discusses the evolution of civil aviation security, strategies to enhance cybersecurity, and methods for protecting critical infrastructure such as water utilities. It also provides in-depth examination of the topic of interdependency between infrastructures. The section includes a Regional Infrastructure Protection Guide developed by and for practitioners.

Section VI on "Disaster Preparedness and Emergency Management" addresses key fundamentals of emergency response and the challenges associated with communications and radio systems interoperability. In this section, homeland security leaders from New Orleans share the lessons their city learned from Hurricane Katrina. The section also presents the importance of "meta-leadership," a framework and practice method designed for the challenges of leading in complex situations. The final chapter in the sections addresses the need for emergency managers and other leaders to access expert legal advice when confronting real-time dilemmas in crisis situations fraught with uncertainty and grave consequences for the public.

Section VII on "Private Sector Security and Resilience" presents successful approaches to corporate security, emergency management, and business continuity as well as models for public–private sector initiatives dealing with community preparedness and regional resilience. It also offers valuable guidance about the international ISO–28000 standard for supply chain security and resilience.

Section VIII on "Thinking, Education, and Training" explains why coping with the dynamic complexity of the homeland security area requires systems thinking, and why no single discipline can achieve a comprehensive understanding of terrorism or homeland security. The section offers a theoretical foundation for interdisciplinary study and homeland security education. Also included in this section is a chapter on emergency exercise design and evaluation.

Section IX on "Science and Technology" covers a range of topics—it presents information technology solution architecture and technology to support emergency incident command and information sharing among disparate organizations. The section also discusses the importance of Geographical Information Systems (GIS) and how to leverage crowdsourcing and social media tools in disaster response. The section includes practical guidance for technology vendors interested in selling technology to government homeland security buyers, and a promising new model that the Department of Homeland Security (DHS) Science & Technology Directorate is using to actively seek out relatively mature technology solutions that can be modified to rapidly address defined operational capability needs or problems.

Section X on "Civil Liberties and Other Legal Issues" discusses topics related to the law—civil liberties questions, the evolution of counterterrorism legislation, and government data mining.

Section XI on "International Challenges and Approaches" emphasizes the importance of comparative analysis and covers counterterrorism policy in the European Union and India, Sweden's approach to whole-of-society disaster resilience, Chile's response to the 2010 earthquake and tsunami, the Fukushima Nuclear disaster in Japan, and the status of global commitment to disaster risk management under the United Nations' Hyogo Framework for Action (HFA).

The book concludes with a brief call-to-action chapter meant to guide leaders in the homeland security community.

ACKNOWLEDGEMENTS

This book would not have been possible without the generous contributions of the participating authors and their staff, the editorial support of Bev Weiler, and the valuable suggestions from Claire B. Rubin. I deeply appreciate their help and the support and encouragement provided by: Felice Maranz, Roger Kamien, Anita Kamien, Stuart Friedman, Jean-François Cloutier, Howard Steinberg, Romit Chatterjee, Andy Mazzeo, Jan Ithier, Kiki Lawal, Stephen Rodriguez, Ron Krakower, David Steiner, Mike Horsefield, John Voeller, Andy Lauland, Randall Larsen, Cal Downs, Ray Bjorklund, Dennis Quinn, Chad Sweet, and many others who willingly provided advice, reviews, and moral support during this year-long endeavor. I would also like to thank Mary Glenn and the excellent publishing staff at McGraw-Hill for their patience and willingness to support this project. In closing, the editorial team regrets the passing of R.V. Raju, former Director General, National Investigation Agency of India who contributed to this text.

LIST OF CONTRIBUTORS

David G. Kamien
CEO & Co-Founder
Mind-Alliance Systems

Hon. Michael Chertoff
Chairman of The Chertoff Group
Former Secretary of the U.S. Department of Homeland Security

Daveed Gartenstein-Ross
Senior Fellow, The Foundation for Defense of Democracies
Lecturer in World Politics, The Catholic University of America

Brian Michael Jenkins
Director of the National Transportation Security Center at
The Mineta Transportation Institute

Jean-François Gayraud
High Council for Strategic Education and Research (CSFRS)

Dr. John F. Morrison
School of Law and Social Sciences
University of East London, United Kingdom

Bob Graham
Bipartisan WMD Terrorism Research Center

Randy Larsen
Bipartisan WMD Terrorism Research Center

Lynne Kidder
Bipartisan WMD Terrorism Research Center

Sharon L. Caudle, Ph.D.
The Bush School of Government and Public Service
Texas A&M University

James Gurulé
Professor of Law
Notre Dame School of Law
Notre Dame University

Michael Kraft
Counterterrorism Consultant and Writer

Brent Davidson, J.D.
Director of Program Development for
the International Security and Biopolicy Institute

Christian Beckner
Congressional Staff Member

Robert I. Desourdis, Jr.
Science Applications International Corporation

Jean-François Cloutier
Mind-Alliance Systems

Mr. Kshemendra Paul
Program Manager
Information Sharing Environment

W. Ross Ashley, III
Executive Director
National Fusion Center Association

Ray Guidetti
Captain
New Jersey Regional Operations Intelligence Center

Steven Pugh
Captain
United States Air Force

Dr. Gregory S. Parnell
Professor of System Engineering at the
U.S. Military Academy at West Point

Dr. Robin Dillon-Merrill
Associate Professor
McDonough School of Business
Georgetown University

Terry A. Bresnick
Senior Principal Analyst
Innovative Decisions, Inc.

Ari Vidali
Chief Executive Officer
Envisage Technologies Corporation

Jason D. Hutchens
Director, Planning and Assessment
Indiana Department of Homeland Security

Baruch Fischhoff
Howard Heinz University Professor
Carnegie Mellon University

James Carafano
Deputy Director
The Kathryn and Shelby Cullom Davis
Institute for International Studies
The Heritage Foundation

Jessica Zuckerman
Research Associate
The Heritage Foundation

Rae Zimmerman
Professor of Planning and Public Administration
Director, Institute for Civil Infrastructure Systems (ICIS)
Wagner Graduate School of Public Service
New York University

Stanley States, Ph.D.
Director of Water Quality and Production
Pittsburgh Water and Sewer Authority

Rafi Ron
CEO
New Age Security Solutions (NASS)

Robert Faber
Former Senior Oversight Counsel
House Transportation Committee

Paula L. Scalingi, Ph.D.
Executive Director
Bayarea Center for Regional Disaster Resilience

Claire B. Rubin
President
Claire B. Rubin & Associates LLC

Jude Colle
Principal
at JZ Colle & Associates

J.W. Sneed
LtCol USMC (Retired); Deputy Mayor of Public Safety
Director of the Office of Homeland Security and Emergency Preparedness
City of New Orleans

Stephen A. Murphy
Former Planning Section Chief
New Orleans Office of Homeland Security & Emergency Preparedness
Current Director of Emergency Management
Loyola University

Matthew A. Kallmyer
Former Deputy Director
New Orleans Office of Homeland Security & Emergency Preparedness
Current Director
Atlanta–Fulton County Emergency Management Agency

Martin O'Malley
Governor Maryland

Ray Lehr
Statewide Interoperability Director
State of Maryland

Terri L. Tanielian, M.A.
Senior Research Analyst, Rand Corporation

Bradley D. Stein, M.D.
Natural Scientist, Associate Rand Corporation

Dr. Leonard J. Marcus
Founding Co-Director
National Preparedness Leadership Initiative
Harvard University

Dr. Barry C. Dorn
Associate Director
National Preparedness Leadership Initiative
Harvard University

Dr. Isaac Ashkenazi
Director of Urban Terrorism Preparedness
National Preparedness Leadership Initiative
Harvard University

Joseph P. Henderson, M.A.
Senior Executive
Centers for Disease Control and Prevention

Eric J. McNulty
Senior Editorial Associate
National Preparedness Leadership Initiative
Harvard University

Eric Stern
Co-Chairman of the Critical Incident Analysis Group
University of Virginia

Gregory Saathoff, M.D.
Executive Director of the Critical Incident Analysis Group
University of Virginia

Brad Kieserman
Chief Counsel
Federal Emergency Management Agency

Ronald J. Kelly
Director, IBM Corporation Security

Donald L. Schmidt
Vice President, Chief Security Officer, and
Chief Technology Officer, Worldwide Government
TIBCO Software Inc.

William A. Gouveia, Jr.
Managing Director, Consulting
SunGard Availability Services

Stephen Flynn
Co-Director of the Kostas Research Institute for Homeland Security
Professor of Political Science
Northeastern University

Sean Burke
Associate Director
Kostas Research Institute for Homeland Security

M. J. Plodinec
Community and Regional Resilience Institute

W.C. Edwards
Community and Regional Resilience Institute

Richard Stones
MSc CSyp FSyI

Sibel McGee, Ph.D.
Principal Analyst
Applied Systems Thinking Institute
Analytic Services, Inc.

Linda Kiltz, Ph.D.
Assistant Professor of Public Administration

Robert McCreight
George Washington University

Irmak Renda-Tanali, D.Sc.
Collegiate Associate Professor
Director of Homeland Security and Emergency Management
Master's Programs
University of Maryland, University College

Donald S. Adams
Vice President, Chief Security Officer,
& Chief Technology Officer, Worldwide Government
TIBCO Software, Inc.

Russ Johnson
Director, Public Safety Industry Solutions
Esri

Michael Hopmeier
President
Unconventional Concepts, Inc.

Jeannie Stamberger, Ph.D.
Researcher
Peace Innovation Lab
Stanford University

Ahmed Nagy
Doctoral Candidate
IMT Institute for Advanced Studies
Lucca, Italy

James W. Morentz, Ph.D.
JWMorentz, LLC

Rick Wimberly
Chief Executive Officer
Government Selling Solutions/Galain Solutions, Inc.

Laura W. Murphy
Director, Washington Legislative Office
American Civil Liberties Union

Newton N. Minow
Senior Counsel
Sidley Austin LL.P.

Fred H. Cate
Distinguished Professor and C. Ben Dutton Professor of Law
Indiana University Maurer School of Law

Margareta Wahlstrom
UN Secretary General's Special Representative for Disaster Risk
Reduction
Head of UNISDR
UN Office for Disaster Risk Reduction

Captain. Charles H. Piersall
Chairman
(ISO/TC8) Committee on Ships and Marine Technology

James M. Acton
Washington, D.C.; Carnegie Endowment for International Peace 2012

Mark Hibbs
Washington, D.C.; Carnegie Endowment for International Peace 2012.

Helena Lindberg
Director General
Swedish Civil Contingencies Agency

Bengt Sundelius
Professor of Government
Swedish National Defense College

R.V. Raju
Former Director General
National Investigation Agency of India

Nick Lavars
Journalist
The Santiago Times

Gilles De Kerchove
European Union Counterterrorism Coordinator

William J. Bratton
Chairman
Kroll Advisory Solutions, Inc.

John G. Voeller
Senior Vice President
Black & Veatch

Joseph Nimmich
Retired Admiral, U.S. Coast Guard
Raytheon Homeland Security

Gregory T. Brunelle
Deputy Director of Operations
New York State Office of Emergency Management

Ira Tannenbaum
Director of Public/Private Initiatives
New York City Office of Emergency Management

Daniel Stevens
Training Coordinator and National Planning Cadre Manager
Department of Homeland Security
FEMA, Response Directorate

K.A. Taipale
Founder and Executive Director
Stillwell Center

Nadav Morag
Author of *Comparative Homeland Security: Global Lessons*
(New York: John Wiley & Sons, 2011)

1

INTRODUCTION TO PART I: TERRORIST AND CRIMINAL THREATS

This section examines strategic aspects of the evolution of terrorist and hybrid criminal-terrorist threats. This strategic understanding is vital to the success of the homeland security effort.

In the last decade, the terrorist threat has evolved, making it more difficult for law enforcement or the intelligence community to detect and disrupt plots. The jihadist threat is clearly now not limited to the al-Qaeda core group, or organizations with close operational links to al Qaeda. Al Qaeda actions and activities have inspired affiliates (such as al-Shabaab in Somalia, the Tehrik-e Taliban, and al Qaeda in the Arabian Peninsula) and other groups and individuals who share its violent ideology to launch attacks. Several countries have experienced attacks and foiled plots by homegrown, self-radicalized terrorists who were exposed to online propaganda. In some cases, these terrorists have had limited discernible links to terrorist organizations—they learned terrorist tactics online or in training camps in places such as the Federally Administered Tribal Areas of Pakistan. These operatives are familiar with Western and American culture and security practices, which can increase the likelihood that an attempted attack could be successful.

Daveed Gartenstein-Ross explains the broad contours of al Qaeda's strategy, and shifts and adaptations that the group made in response to challenges it confronted and opportunities that were presented to it. In the past, poor strategic understanding of al Qaeda's strategic thinking has contributed to expensive errors, both large (Iraq) and small, in the fight against jihadi foes.

The discovery of notes in Osama bin Laden's compound indicating that the terrorist leader was contemplating attacking trains in the United States on the tenth anniversary of 9/11 underscores the continuing terrorist threat to public surface transportation. In his chapter, Brian Michael Jenkins discusses the very real terrorist threat to surface transportation and the challenge of securing such public places from attacks using improvised explosive devices (IEDs).

Despite the fact that attacks with explosives are more prevalent than attacks with chemical, biological, or nuclear weapons, we must be prepared for those modes of attack. Senators Graham and Talent offer insights into biological threats. Although naturally occurring disease remains a serious threat, a thinking enemy armed with these same pathogens, or with multi-drug-resistant or synthetically engineered pathogens, could produce catastrophic consequences. Traditional deterrence may not be effective against non-state actors; therefore, the primary means of defending the American homeland against bioterrorism is the capability to effectively respond after an attack has occurred, with appropriate public health, medical countermeasures, and hospital preparedness.

According to Jean-François Gayraud, organized crime and terrorism are converging in such a way that should give rise to deep concern. The real danger of Osama bin Laden's followers, underestimated before 9/11, was subsequently overestimated. Al Qaeda and the Salafi Jihad Movement have never had the level of organization and menace that the media and some public administrations have thought it necessary to depict. The obsession with Osama bin Laden blinded authorities to emerging and much more pernicious threats from highly intensive criminality from hybrid entities: partly political, predatory, sectarian, religious, and terrorist. Because of their many complex facets and activities, entities such as the Lebanese Hezbollah or the Tamil Tigers from the LTTE, and Sahelian armed groups such as "Al Qaeda in the countries of the Islamic Magrheb" (AQIM) are ever-more dangerous, resilient, and difficult to understand. This lack of understanding allows them to fall through the cracks of the administrative divisions (the police, the law, intelligence services, customs, etc.) and to blur their true nature in the eyes of the media. They wield the tool of terrorism to exert influence over states that are hindering their activities or being too inquisitive.

John Morrison, too, observes that terrorism can be utilized by politically violent organizations in combination with other tactics. In his chapter on the psychology of terrorism, Morrison suggests that in order to strengthen the foundation for counterterrorism policies and initiatives researchers must study the heterogeneity of roles and other elements of terrorist involvement, from initial engagement right up to disengagement, and everything in between. They must look at both the legal and illegal activities involved in terrorist membership, and at the changing internal and external influences, as well as the fluctuating roles of individual members.

1

THE LEGACY OF OSAMA BIN LADEN'S STRATEGY

Daveed Gartenstein-Ross

Senior Fellow, The Foundation for Defense of Democracies
Lecturer in World Politics, The Catholic University of America

INTRODUCTION

Despite numerous reassuring proclamations from pundits and U.S. officials, Osama bin Laden's death and other recent setbacks that the jihadi group al Qaeda has experienced do not herald the end of this threat. As a UPI special report noted in March 2012, numerous signs suggest that al Qaeda is beginning to rebound, including its geographic gains in Yemen that a U.N. envoy described as "alarming," its resurgence in Iraq and North Africa, and reports of an al Qaeda presence in such diverse locales as Syria, Lebanon, Egypt, and Ethiopia.[1] Other factors, such as the diffusion of weaponry from Muammar Qaddafi's former caches in Libya, provide al Qaeda with additional opportunities. Indeed, although some Western analysts have declared the series of events popularly known as the "Arab Spring" to be a disaster for al Qaeda, the group's leaders, strategists, and circle of supporters unambiguously believe that the chaos gripping the region provides the organization with new opportunities.[2]

Because jihadi groups expect to have newfound freedom to operate in the Arab world due to the wrenching changes transforming the region, including a greater ability to evangelize for their militant understanding of Islam, in the near term al Qaeda is likely to focus more of its energy on Muslim-majority countries than on attacks against the West. Another reason that its focus on the West is likely to diminish in the near term, frankly, is that the recent losses that al Qaeda suffered *have* in fact damaged its ability to execute attacks against the West. This doesn't mean that the group's strategic defeat is "within reach," as one U.S. official put it.[3] Indeed, al Qaeda has proven in the past to be more resilient than Western analysts expected, and its organizational structure continues to maximize its resiliency.[4]

In the end, neither al Qaeda's current operational weakness nor its growing focus on the Arab world due to the unrest there mean the end of its fight against the West. In addition to the group's already addressed resilience, recent history shows that a predominant focus on the Muslim world does not prevent al Qaeda from striking at Western targets. Prior to the 9/11 attacks its operating budget was also primarily focused on the Muslim world, and this did not stop it from carrying out the most vicious surprise attack in U.S. history.

In the past, the U.S. often blundered in its fight against al Qaeda due to its inability to understand this foe strategically. So long as this formidable adversary remains alive, it is important in this age of austerity to understand al Qaeda's strategy for warfare against the West. A critical core of strategic thinkers associated with al Qaeda has developed concepts of guerrilla warfare and "Fourth Generation Warfare," based in large part on the works of Western scholars.[5] But though these thinkers have had varying degrees of influence, al Qaeda's strategy for its war against America has been primarily codified at top levels, by such individuals as bin Laden and Ayman al Zawahiri. This strategy has had several distinct but overlapping phases, driven both by paradigms forged in the Afghan–Soviet war and the pressures and opportunities created by the West's reactions to the jihadi group.

This chapter begins by illuminating bin Laden's experiences in the Afghan–Soviet war, and how they influenced his understanding of strategic principles for defeating a superpower. The chapter then turns to the development of al Qaeda's strategy for warfare against the West. This strategy went through four phases that, as previously noted, are distinct in conception but overlap in implementation: carrying out terrorist attacks aimed at undermining the enemy's economy; embroiling America and its allies in "bleeding wars" abroad; attacking the global supply of oil; and finally, utilizing a "strategy of a thousand cuts" focused on smaller yet more frequent attacks.

BIN LADEN AND THE AFGHAN–SOVIET WAR

Osama bin Laden was born in the late 1950s to Mohammed bin Laden, who from humble beginnings in Yemen rose to become a multibillionaire construction magnate and confidant of Saudi Arabia's royal family. Osama rose to international prominence after the Soviet Union invaded Afghanistan in December 1979. He traveled to Pakistan in the early 1980s, soon after the Afghan–Soviet war began. Bruce Riedel, a Brookings Institution senior fellow and former CIA officer, notes that once he arrived, bin Laden became "a major financier of the mujahedin, providing cash to the relatives of wounded or martyred fighters, building hospitals, and helping the millions of Afghan refugees fleeing to the border region of Pakistan."[6] But bin Laden's first trip to the front lines in Afghanistan in 1984 left a lasting impression on him and gave him a thirst for more action. In 1986, he established a base for Arab fighters near Khost in eastern Afghanistan, where the Soviets had a garrison.

Bin Laden and his comrades-in-arms were attacked by the Soviets in the spring of 1987. They unexpectedly held their ground for about three weeks in the face of several attacks by Russian special forces (*spetsnaz*), until bin Laden and several companions were able to flee to safety. This intense combat launched bin Laden to prominence in the Arab media as a war hero.[7] Although bin Laden subsequently emphasized his role in the conflict, every serious history concludes that the "Afghan Arabs," fighters from the Arab world who traveled to South Asia, were not a real factor in Russia's defeat. Nonetheless, bin Laden's time on the Afghan battlefield was a formative experience that shaped the approach he would take when running al Qaeda.

Russia didn't just withdraw from Afghanistan in defeat; the Soviet empire itself collapsed soon thereafter, in late 1991. Thus, bin Laden thought he had not only bested one of the world's superpowers on the battlefield, but also played an important role in its demise. From the view that he had played a critical role in causing the Soviet empire to fall, we can discern two further aspects of bin Laden's thought. The first is the centrality of economics to his fight against a superpower. It is indisputable, after all, that the Soviet withdrawal from Afghanistan did not directly collapse the Soviet Union. The most persuasive connection that can be drawn between that war and the Soviet empire's dissolution is through the costs imposed by the conflict. Indeed, bin Laden spoke of how he used "guerrilla warfare and the war of attrition to fight tyrannical superpowers, as we, alongside the mujahedin, bled Russia for ten years, until it went bankrupt."[8]

This may seem like an implausible propaganda piece. But there are reasonable constructions of this argument, holding that that the costs imposed by the Afghan–Soviet war prevented the Soviet Union from adapting to other economic challenges, such as grain shortages and the declining world price of oil (the Soviet Union depended economically on its oil exports).[9] Certainly bin Laden *perceived* economics as central to defeating a superpower based on his experiences in that war. For example, in October 2004, bin Laden said that just as the Afghan mujahedin and Arab fighters had destroyed Russia economically, al Qaeda was now doing the same to the United States, "continuing this policy in bleeding America to the point of bankruptcy."[10] In a September 2007 video, bin Laden claimed that "thinkers who study events and happenings" were now predicting the American empire's collapse. Comparing President Bush to Leonid Brezhnev, the architect of the Soviet invasion of Afghanistan, bin Laden said, "The mistakes of Brezhnev are being repeated by Bush."[11]

A second aspect of bin Laden's strategic thought stemming from his experiences in Afghanistan deals with the breadth of the conflict. The Soviet invasion outraged the Muslim world, including heads of state, clerics, the Arab media, and the man on the street. In January 1980, the foreign ministers of thirty-five Muslim countries, as well as the Palestine Liberation Organization, passed a resolution through the Organization of the Islamic Conference (OIC) declaring the invasion of Afghanistan to be a "flagrant violation of all international covenants and norms, as well as a serious threat to peace and security in the region and throughout the world."[12] The OIC expelled Afghanistan's Soviet-installed regime, and urged all Muslim countries "to withhold recognition of the illegal regime in Afghanistan and sever diplomatic relations with that country until the complete withdrawal of Soviet troops." At the time, the *Christian Science Monitor* described this condemnation of Soviet actions as "some of the strongest terms ever used by a third-world party."[13]

The stream of about ten thousand Arabs who flocked to South Asia to help the Afghan cause was a testament to the widespread outrage caused by the invasion. Mohammed Hafez, an associate professor in the American Naval Postgraduate School's National Security Affairs Department, notes that these Arab volunteers "included humanitarian aid workers, cooks, drivers, accountants, teachers, doctors, engineers, and religious preachers. They built camps, dug and treated water wells, and attended to the sick and wounded."[14] There was, of course, also a contingent of Arab foreign fighters, which bin Laden ultimately joined. Nor were the volunteers who went to South Asia the only Arabs to support the Afghan resistance. The jihad was also aided by a donor network known as the "golden chain," whose financiers came primarily from Saudi Arabia and other Gulf Arab states.[15] Essentially, bin Laden sat at the top of a major multinational organization during the Afghan–Soviet war. Its members included fighters, aid workers, and other volunteers. It enjoyed a media presence, external donors, and widespread support.

Al Qaeda was founded in August 1988, in the waning days of the Afghan–Soviet war.[16] It was created because bin Laden and his mentor, Abdullah Azzam, agreed that the organization they had built during the conflict shouldn't simply dissolve when the war ended, but rather wanted it to serve as "the base" (*al qaeda*) for future mujahedin efforts. The two strategic pillars for fighting a superpower that emerged from that war—the centrality of economics and the importance of broadening the fight—carried over into the organization's later struggle against the United States.[17]

TERRORIST ATTACKS AND THE ECONOMY

Bin Laden's attacks on the United States before 9/11 did not have much of an economic impact. The greatest costs inflicted by al Qaeda attacks before September 2001 came from the August 1998 bombings of U.S. embassies in Kenya and Tanzania, which prompted the State Department to initiate a $21 billion program to replace 201 different facilities that it regarded as either dilapidated or insecure.[18] But the economic damage caused by 9/11 dwarfed that of previous attacks, a fact that was not lost on bin Laden.

Bin Laden's perception of the 9/11 attacks was elucidated at length in an October 21, 2001, television interview that he gave to Al Jazeera's Taysir Allouni. The wide-ranging interview, conducted shortly after the U.S. military campaign in Afghanistan began, is significant contemporaneous evidence of what bin Laden intended to accomplish through the 9/11 attacks.[19] When bin Laden was asked to speak of the attacks' impact, his first observation concerned the economic damage they caused. "According to their own admissions," he said, referring to the Americans, "the share of the losses on the Wall Street market reached 16%. They said that this number is a record, which has never happened since the opening of the market more than 230 years ago."

Bin Laden then provided an extended exposition of the actual economic numbers, as well as associated costs, which shows he had given much thought to the economic implications of 9/11. "The gross amount that is traded in that market reaches $4 trillion," he said. "So if we multiply 16% [by] $4 trillion to find out the loss that affected the stocks, it reaches $640 billion of losses from stocks, with Allah's grace."

He knew, though, that the direct damage to America's stock market was not the only economic impact. He also factored in lost productivity, as well as building and construction losses, and gloated about all the lost American jobs—stating that 170,000 employees were fired from the airline industry, and the InterContinental Hotel chain had been forced to cut 20,000 jobs. So taking into account the second- and third-order consequences, bin Laden calculated that the cost to the United States was "no less than $1 trillion by the lowest estimate." Bin Laden may in fact have been conservative on this point. As former CIA officer Bruce Riedel has noted, the property damage and lost productivity caused by the 9/11 attacks probably cost more than $100 billion. When factoring in lower profits and economic volatility, Riedel writes that the price tag is "as high as $2 trillion according to some estimates."[20]

In a video released in October 2004, bin Laden amplified this analysis by pointing out how much damage 9/11 inflicted upon the U.S. in comparison to the much smaller costs that al Qaeda incurred in executing them. "Al Qaeda spent $500,000 on the event," he said, "while America, in the incident and its aftermath, lost—according to the lowest estimate—more than $500 billion, meaning that every dollar of al Qaeda defeated a million dollars."[21]

BLEEDING WARS

A second facet of al Qaeda's economic strategy for combating the United States has been to embroil it in bleeding wars overseas. Bin Laden also explicitly referred to this in his public speeches.

The U.S. had a clear interest in taking military action in Afghanistan following the 9/11 attacks: to deprive al Qaeda of the sanctuary that the Taliban then provided it. The United States began its bombing campaign on October 7, 2001. When it inserted troops later in the month,

America did not enter Afghanistan with a "heavy footprint." Rather, the U.S. attacked with a light force, consisting of about 300 Special Forces soldiers and 110 CIA officers who liaisoned with tens of thousands of fighters from the Northern Alliance, a group based in northern Afghanistan that opposed the Taliban. The Taliban had no response to American airpower, which devastated their ranks. The combination of U.S. airpower and the light counterattack toppled the Taliban from power within weeks.

But exploration of further military options against Iraq began almost immediately after the 9/11 attacks, and in November 2001 the Pentagon began formally considering plans to attack Iraq. As the United States prepared to topple its then-president Saddam Hussein, CIA specialists and Special Forces units alike were reassigned from Afghanistan to Iraq.

The Iraq war was explicitly portrayed as a part of the "war on terror," and indeed almost certainly would not have occurred absent the 9/11 attacks. As Patrick Clawson, a Middle East expert at the Washington Institute for Near East Policy, has noted, those who argued that the administration came into office determined to attack Iraq—such as former Treasury secretary Paul O'Neill—failed to grasp the actual thrust of President Bush's early policies. "What O'Neill doesn't notice is that those who wanted to go to war lost, and those who supported 'smart sanctions' won," Clawson said.[22]

The U.S. did not possess a proper understanding of al Qaeda's strategy at the time it decided to go to war in Iraq: official documents from the first five years of the war on terror show that top analysts too frequently perceived the jihadi group as simply incapable of strategic thought.[23] But a proper understanding of al Qaeda's strategic thinking would have suggested that invading Iraq was a poor move with respect to the jihadi group, and could prove disastrous. Bin Laden, as outlined above, had two major ideas about how to defeat America, and the Iraq war provided al Qaeda opportunities on both fronts. In terms of al Qaeda's economic strategy, the Iraq war was extremely expensive. It will, when all is said and done, cost the United States more than a trillion dollars in direct budgetary outlays. Moreover, the Iraq invasion helped the other major element of al Qaeda's strategy by feeding its overarching narrative that Islam itself was under attack by the United States and other forces of disbelief.

Long before the financial crisis hit, bin Laden recognized that the invasion of Iraq played into his strategy of economic warfare.

He spoke of this in a major address that Al Jazeera broadcast on October 29, 2004, days before the U.S. presidential election—at a time when many Americans thought that the al Qaeda leader was already dead. Bin Laden stood at a podium in the video, his beard gray, wearing a white turban and white tunic covered by a gold cloak. He addressed the American people directly. The overarching theme was how al Qaeda was succeeding in its strategy of "bleeding America to the point of bankruptcy." He said that it was easy to bait the U.S., that al Qaeda needed only to "send two mujahedin to the furthest point east to raise a piece of cloth on which is written al Qaeda, in order to make the generals race there to cause America to suffer human, economic, and political losses."[24]

But bin Laden said also that al Qaeda alone was not responsible for America's coming defeat. Rather, "the policy of the White House that demands the opening of war fronts to keep busy their various corporations—whether they be working in the field of arms or oil or reconstruction—has helped al Qaeda to achieve these enormous results."[25] Thus, he said, "it has appeared to some analysts and diplomats that the White House and us are playing as one team towards the economic goals of the United States, even if the intentions differ." He referred to America's astronomical budget deficit as "evidence of the success of the bleed-until-bankruptcy plan." So, while al Qaeda had gained since 9/11, bin Laden said the Bush administration had gained too, as can be seen by "the size of the contracts acquired by the shady Bush administration-linked mega-corporations, like Halliburton."

Who has lost? "The real loser," bin Laden said, "is you. It is the American people and their economy."

THE WAR ON OIL

On March 24, 2010, Saudi Arabia announced the arrest of 113 alleged al Qaeda militants whom it claimed were planning attacks on oil facilities. "We have compelling evidence against all of those arrested, that they were plotting terrorist attacks inside the kingdom," Mansour al Turki, a spokesman for Saudi security services, told Reuters.[26]

Initial arrests in Arab states often constitute bloated sweeps, with innocents who were caught in the net quietly released later. Despite this, the report that terrorists in Saudi Arabia had focused on oil targets was unsurprising. Between 2004 and the mass arrests in March 2010, al Qaeda had come to see attacks against oil facilities, particularly in Saudi Arabia, as a critical aspect of their economic warfare strategy—and justifiably so, as the United States is the world's largest oil importer, consuming around 21 million barrels each day. Though the percentage of oil the U.S. imports has declined in recent years, in part due to increased domestic oil and gas production, the U.S. still imports 45% of the petroleum it uses.[27]

Bin Laden did not always see attacks on oil as part of his fight against America. When he first declared war against the U.S. in 1996, bin Laden specified that oil was not one of al Qaeda's targets because the resource was "a large economical power essential for the soon to be established Islamic state."[28] That is, bin Laden was looking toward al Qaeda's ultimate goal of reestablishing the caliphate. When the caliphate was declared, it would benefit from its control of a significant portion of the world's oil.

But the events and reactions that the 9/11 attacks set in motion made clear that the U.S. strategy for fighting al Qaeda was very costly. This may have influenced a change in jihadi strategy pertaining to oil. An early indication that jihadi thinkers were beginning to see oil as a desirable target was a treatise entitled *The Laws of Targeting Petroleum-Related Interests and a Review of the Laws Pertaining to the Economic Jihad,* which was posted online in March 2004. Written by al Qaeda strategist Rashid al Anzi, this document argued for the legitimacy of attacks against oil facilities.[29] After the publication of Anzi's treatise, bin Laden came around to a similar understanding of the permissibility of attacking oil targets, as expressed in an audio address entitled "Depose the Tyrants," which was released in December 2004.

Bin Laden's new call to attack oil targets echoed throughout al Qaeda's ranks. In a December 2005 video, Ayman al Zawahiri asked al Qaeda fighters to "focus their attacks on the stolen oil of the Muslims." Referring to the purchase of oil at then-market prices as history's greatest theft, he continued, "The enemies of Islam are consuming this vital resource with unparalleled greed. We must stop this theft any way we can, in order to save this resource for the sake of the Muslim nation."[30] *Sawt al Jihad,* the now-defunct online magazine of al Qaeda in the Arabian Peninsula (AQAP), claimed in February 2007 that cutting the U.S. oil supply through terrorist attacks "would contribute to the ending of the American occupation of Iraq and Afghanistan."[31]

Jihadi discussions of attacks on the oil supply are not just rhetoric. Of particular concern are Saudi Arabian facilities, which are a point of vulnerability for the entire world economy. Saudi Arabia is critical to world oil markets. It produces almost 10 million barrels per day, and is the only country able to maintain an excess production capacity of around 1.5 million barrels per day (a *swing reserve*) in order to keep world prices stable. Saudi production is vulnerable to attack, however, because it depends on a limited number of hubs.[32]

Several incidents show how jihadi terrorists are attempting to exploit this vulnerability. The first incident occurred in September 2005, when a 48-hour shootout with Islamist militants at a villa in the Saudi seaport of al Dammam ended with Saudi police introducing light artillery. When the police entered the compound to conduct a search in the aftermath of the fight, they found not only what *Newsweek* described as "enough weapons for a couple of platoons of guerilla fighters," but also forged documents that would have given the extremists access to the country's key oil and gas facilities.[33]

The most significant security incident to date targeting Saudi facilities came a few months later, on February 24, 2006. Terrorists affiliated with AQAP attacked the Saudi Aramco–operated refinery at Abqaiq, which processes two-thirds of Saudi Arabia's crude oil. Written evidence submitted to Britain's House of Commons by Neil Partrick, a senior analyst in the Economist Group's Economist Intelligence Unit, claimed that the terrorists—who wore Saudi Aramco uniforms and drove Saudi Aramco vehicles—managed to enter the first of three perimeter fences surrounding the refinery. They were fired upon only as they approached the second fence. Partrick wrote that either the terrorists "had inside assistance from members of the formal security operation of the state–owned energy company" in acquiring the vehicles and uniforms, or else "security was sufficiently [lax] that these items could be obtained and entry to the site obtained."[34] Needless to say, neither possibility is reassuring—although the U.S. has made efforts since then to bolster the security of Saudi facilities.

There have also been several significant arrests since the February 2006 attempt on Abqaiq, including the March 2010 arrest of 113 alleged militants that opened this section. If there were a catastrophic attack on key Saudi oil installations, the impact on the world economy would be tremendous. As former CIA case officer Robert Baer writes, "A single jumbo jet with a suicide bomber at the controls, hijacked during takeoff from Dubai and crashed into the heart of Ras Tanura, would be enough to bring the world's oil-addicted economies to their knees, America's along with them."[35]

THE THOUSAND CUTS

The dramatic collapse of the U.S. economy in September 2008 signaled a new, more perilous era for America. It also ushered in a new phase in al Qaeda's strategy for combating the United States.

Put simply, the collapse made the country seem mortal. When bin Laden declared war on America in 1996, he explained that the U.S. economy was the driver of the country's military dominance—and after September 2008, it seemed that the U.S. economy *had actually been shattered*, dramatically weakening America's global position. The perception that the economic collapse made America mortal is apparent throughout the ranks of jihadi spokesmen, as well as the rank and file. "Due to this jihad, the U.S. economy is reeling today," the late Yemeni-American cleric Anwar al Awlaki said in an interview that posted to the Internet in May 2010. "America cannot withstand this Islamic nation. It is too weak. America's cunning is weaker than a spider web."[36]

Because of this perception of America's mortality, al Qaeda and its affiliates came to believe that their economic strategy could benefit from a relatively simple adaptation. Whereas once the United States wouldn't have been bothered by anything but the most dramatic blows, the weakened economy meant that even smaller attacks could have a large impact. This new phase was described as "the strategy of a thousand cuts" in the November 2010 issue of AQAP's English-language online magazine *Inspire*—an issue commemorating a plot attempted the previous month, in which two bombs disguised as ink cartridges were successfully placed on FedEx and United Parcel Service planes. The bombs were subsequently flown on passenger planes before ultimately being discovered due to a tip from Saudi Arabian intelligence. Although that issue of *Inspire* represents the best articulation of this new phase in al Qaeda's strategy, the basic contours were evident even before November 2010.

The cover of *Inspire*'s November 2010 issue features a photo of a UPS plane and the headline "$4,200." That pithy headline provides deep insight into the direction that al Qaeda's strategy has taken, referring to the great disparity between the cost of executing the ink cartridge plot (and indeed, terrorist attacks more generally) and the cost to Western countries of playing defense. Anwar al Awlaki explains that AQAP settled on the idea of attacking cargo planes because of the principle that "if your opponent covers his right cheek, slap him on his left."[37]

Awlaki explained, "The air freight is a multi-billion dollar industry. FedEx alone flies a fleet of 600 aircraft and ships an average of four million packages per day. It is a huge worldwide industry. For the trade between North America and Europe, air cargo is indispensable and to be able to force the West to install stringent security measures sufficient enough to stop our explosive devices would add a heavy economic burden to an already faltering economy." *Inspire* lucidly explains that large strikes, such as those of 9/11, are no longer required to defeat the United States. "To bring down America we do not need to strike big," it claims. "In such an environment of security phobia that is sweeping America, it is more feasible to stage smaller attacks that involve less players and less time to launch and thus we may circumvent the security barriers America worked so hard to erect."[38]

These attacks do not even have to be carried out by recognizable members of al Qaeda. Al Qaeda the organization is attempting, in this phase of its strategy, to more effectively harness al Qaeda the idea by prompting those who share its ideology to lash out on their own. The organization can harness the idea of al Qaeda by encouraging its self-motivated supporters to focus on targets that will advance the organization's strategy of warfare. Indeed, al Qaeda spokesmen are already doing just that. For example, in a March 2010 video message, Adam Gadahn praised Fort Hood shooter Nidal Hasan and encouraged other Muslims to follow his example. Although Hasan's target was not economic, Gadahn linked this emulation of Hasan by other would-be jihadis to the economy, saying that by copying the Fort Hood attack his audience could "further undermine the West's already struggling economies with carefully timed and targeted attacks on symbols of capitalism which will again shake consumer confidence and stifle spending."[39]

Gadahn continued in this vein in a 100-minute video released in June 2011, urging Muslims to buy guns and attack targets of opportunity in the United States.[40] The video emphasized economic targets, displaying the logos of Exxon, Merrill Lynch, and Bank of America, while encouraging these strikes. Indeed, rank-and-file jihadis and their online supporters seem to have internalized the importance of economic targets, based on a review of their discussions.

In this new strategy of a thousand cuts, whether attacks succeed in killing "infidels" is somewhat, though not completely, beside the point. If an attack breaches the enemy's security, it will significantly drive up costs, even if it kills nobody and inflicts no structural damage.

As Awlaki noted in *Inspire*, blowing up cargo planes in the ink-cartridge plot "would have made us very pleased but according to our plan and specified objectives it was only a plus."[41] The attack could be considered a success, in his estimation, even without killing anybody.

Other jihadi statements also reflect an awareness that even "failed" attacks can achieve their objectives. In March 2010, for example, Gadahn explained that attacks that kill nobody can still "bring major cities to a halt, cost the enemy billions and send his corporations into bankruptcy."[42] The notion that success can be attained solely through driving up security costs, without actually destroying the enemy's targets, has also been embraced by al Qaeda's online supporters. One message making this point at length was posted to the Al Fallujah Islamic Forums in December 2009. The author mockingly addressed the security services monitoring the web forum, asking them to write the following in their reports:

A Very Serious Threat

Source: A Radical Islamist Forum

Warn them that they must protect every federal building and skyscraper, such as: Library Tower (California), Sears Tower (Chicago), Plaza Bank (Washington State), the Empire State Building (New York), suspension bridges in New York, and the financial district in New York.

  Nightclubs frequented by Americans and the British in Thailand, Philippines, Indonesia (especially our dear Bali Island), the oil company owned by the former Secretary of State Henry Kissinger in Sumatra (Indonesia), and U.S. ships and oil tankers in the Strait of Hormuz, Gibraltar, and the Port of Singapore.

  Let us not forget any airport, seaport, or stadium. Tell them to protect [these places] no matter the cost, day and night, around the clock throughout Christmas and the holiday season.[43]

The point is clear: Security is expensive, and driving up costs can wear down Western economies. These economies can be harmed by failed attacks, or even phantom threats. Indeed, the message goes on to encourage the United States "not to spare millions of dollars to protect these targets" by increasing the number of guards, closely searching all who enter and exit the enumerated locations, and even preventing flying objects from approaching the targets. "Tell them to stop anything that moves on land, flies in the air, and swims on or under the river," it says. "Tell them that the life of the American citizen is in danger, and that his life is more significant than billions of dollars. … Hand in hand, we will be with you until you are bankrupt and your economy collapses."

CONCLUSION

Al Qaeda's core has been hammered hard in the past two years and diminished. But its weakened core is complemented by resurgent affiliates, including those that control significant portions of Yemen and Somalia. These affiliates, faced with new opportunities and challenges due to the Arab Spring, will likely devote more of their energies to that region than was previously the case.

Despite this, Western countries will not disappear as operational targets. Al Qaeda and its affiliates will likely continue to pursue a "strategy of a thousand cuts" against their Western adversaries, combining smaller attacks designed to drive up security costs with occasional large-scale plots that could have a bigger impact, but that also have a lesser chance of success. This is the mode of combat against Western states that al Qaeda and its affiliates adopted in the years leading up to bin Laden's death.

In the past, the U.S. has often had a poor strategic understanding of al Qaeda. This contributed to errors, both large (Iraq) and small. Now that we are in an era of severely constrained resources, America cannot afford the kind of blunders that it made during the early parts of its fight against its jihadi foes. This chapter has described the blueprint of al Qaeda's strategic thinking: its major principles prior to the 9/11 attacks, and how its strategic thought has evolved since, in large part as a response to challenges it confronted and opportunities that were presented to it. Certain policy prescriptions can attempt to address al Qaeda's twin reliance on economic attrition-based warfare and broadening its conflict against the United States.[44] But while points of policy can be debated, the importance of knowing this foe's strategy cannot. American planners should understand the broad contours of al Qaeda's strategy, and recognize shifts and adaptations that the group is making, in order to craft better plans for countering it. In fact, devoting more governmental assets to the neglected field of jihadi strategic studies may well be a good investment, one that could pay significant dividends in the long run.

NOTES

1. "Signs Are al Qaeda Is on the Move Again," UPI, March 13, 2012.

2. For examples of commentary declaring the Arab Spring to be a disaster for al Qaeda, see Neal Conan, "Bergen Correctly Predicted bin Laden's Location," interview with Peter Bergen, National Public Radio, May 3, 2011; Fawaz Gerges, "The Rise and Fall of al Qaeda: Debunking the Terrorism Narrative," *Huffington Post*, January 3, 2012; Dan Murphy, "Bin Laden's Death Puts Exclamation Mark on al Qaeda's Demise," *Christian Science Monitor*, May 3, 2011. For an extended look at the opportunities that salafi jihadis see in the events of the Arab Spring, see Daveed Gartenstein-Ross and Tara Vassefi, "Perceptions of the 'Arab Spring' within the Salafi Jihadi Movement" (unpublished manuscript, draft dated February 16, 2012).

3. Elizabeth Bumiller, "Panetta Says Defeat of al Qaeda is 'Within Reach,'" *New York Times*, July 9, 2011.

4. See Derek Jones, *Understanding the Form, Function, and Logic of Clandestine Insurgent and Terrorist Networks: The First Step in Effective Counternetwork Operations*, Joint Special Operations University (forthcoming, 2012).

5. These thinkers include Abd al Aziz al Muqrin, Abu Bakr Naji, Abu Ubayd al Qurashi, and Abu Musab al Suri. See Michael W. S. Ryan, *The Deep Battle: Decoding al Qaeda's Strategy Against America* (unpublished manuscript, December 10, 2011).

6. Bruce Riedel, *The Search for al Qaeda: Its Leadership, Ideology, and Future* (Washington, DC: Brookings Institution Press, 2008), 42.

7. Steve Coll, *Ghost Wars: The Secret History of the CIA, Afghanistan, and bin Laden, from the Soviet Invasion to September 10, 2001* (New York: Penguin Books, 2004), 163.

8. "Bin Laden Addresses American People on Causes, Outcome of 11 Sep Attacks," trans. Open Source Center, Al Jazeera, October 29, 2004.

9. See Yegor Gaidar, "The Soviet Collapse: Grain and Oil," American Enterprise Institute, April 19, 2007.

10. "Bin Laden Addresses American People," Al Jazeera.

11. Osama bin Laden, "The Solution," trans. Nine Eleven Finding Answers (NEFA) Foundation, video, September 7, 2007, http://www.nefafoundation.org/file/FeaturedDocs/2007_09_08_UBL.pdf.

12. Declaration, 1st Extraordinary Session of the Islamic Conference of Foreign Ministers, Islamabad, Pakistan, January 27–29, 1980.

13. James Dorsey, "Islamic Nations Fire Broadsides at Soviet Military Interventions," *Christian Science Monitor*, January 30, 1980.

14. Mohammed M. Hafez, "Jihad after Iraq: Lessons from the Arab Afghans Phenomenon," *CTC Sentinel* (Combating Terrorism Center at West Point), March 2008.

15. *9/11 Commission Report: Final Report of the National Commission on Terrorist Attacks upon the United States* (New York: W. W. Norton, 2004), 55.

16. Indictment, *United States v. Arnaout*, 02 CR 892 (Northern District of Illinois, 2002), 2.

17. For a description of al Qaeda's evolution from an organization focused on the threat that Communism posed to the *umma* into one that primarily targeted the United States, see Daveed Gartenstein-Ross, *Bin Laden's Legacy: Why We're Still Losing the War on Terror* (New York: John Wiley & Sons, 2011), 23–24.

18. U.S. Government Accountability Office, "Embassy Construction: State Has Made Progress Constructing New Embassies, but Better Planning Is Needed for Operations and Maintenance Requirements" (June 2006), 1.

19. Taysir Allouni, "A Discussion on the New Crusader Wars," trans. Open Source Center, Al Jazeera, October 21, 2001.

20. Bruce Riedel, *The Search for al Qaeda: Its Leadership, Ideology and Future* (Washington, DC: Brookings Institution Press, 2008), 1.

21. "Bin Laden Addresses American People," Al Jazeera.

22. Thomas E. Ricks, *Fiasco: The American Military Adventure in Iraq* (New York: Penguin Books, 2006), 28.

23. See discussion in Gartenstein-Ross, *Bin Laden's Legacy*, pp. 40–43.

24. "Bin Laden Addresses American People," Al Jazeera.

25. Ibid.

26. Souhail Karam, "Riyadh Says Arrested Militants Planning Oil Attacks," Reuters, March 24, 2010.

27. Neela Banerjee, "U.S. Report: Oil Imports Down, Domestic Production Highest Since 2003," *Los Angeles Times*, March 12, 2012.

28. Osama bin Laden, "Declaration of Jihad against the Americans Occupying the Land of the Two Holy Mosques," trans. Open Source Center, August 23, 1996.

29. "Al Qaeda in Saudi Arabia: Excerpts from 'The Laws of Targeting Petroleum-Related Interests,'" *GlobalTerrorAlert*, March 2006.

30. "Newly Released Video of al Qaeda's Deputy Leader Ayman al Zawahiri's Interview to al Sahab TV," Middle East Media Research Institute, No. 1044, December 8, 2005.

31. Quoted in "Group Suggests Striking Oil Facilities in Canada, Mexico, and Venezuela," *Jerusalem Post*, February 15, 2007.

32. See Gal Luft and Anne Korin, "Terror's Next Target," *Journal of International Security Affairs*, December 2003.

33. Christopher Dickey, "Saudi Storms," *Newsweek*, October 3, 2005.

34. Neil Partrick, testimony to the House of Commons Select Committee on Foreign Affairs, March 2006. Diplomatic cables subsequently released by WikiLeaks further bolster Partrick's account. See Kevin G. Hall, "WikiLeaks Cables Show Worry about Saudi Oil Security," McClatchy Newspapers, June 15, 2011.

35. Robert Baer, *Sleeping with the Devil: How Washington Sold Our Soul for Saudi Crude* (New York: Three Rivers Press, 2003), xxv.

36. "Yemeni-American Jihadi Cleric Anwar al Awlaki in First Interview with al Qaeda Media Calls on Muslim U.S. Servicemen to Kill Fellow Soldiers," Middle East Media Research Institute, release no. 2480, May 23, 2010.

37. Head of Foreign Operations [Anwar al Awlaki], "The Objectives of Operation Hemorrhage," *Inspire*, November 2010, 7.

38. Editorial, *Inspire*, November 2010, 4.

39. Adam Gadahn, "A Call to Arms," video, March 2010.

40. "'What Are You Waiting For': U.S. Born al Qaeda Spokesman Calls on Americans to 'Buy Guns and Start Shooting People,'" *Daily Mail* (London), June 4, 2011.

41. Awlaki, "The Objectives of Operation Hemorrhage."

42. Gadahn, "A Call to Arms."

43. "Threat Message on Jihadist Forum Names U.S., International Targets," Open Source Center summary in Arabic, December 31, 2009.

44. For my own extended thoughts on this point, see Gartenstein-Ross, *Bin Laden's Legacy*, pp. 201–32.

2

THE TERRORIST THREAT TO SURFACE TRANSPORTATION: THE CHALLENGE OF SECURING PUBLIC PLACES

Brian Michael Jenkins

Director of the National Transportation Security Center at the Mineta Transportation Institute

INTRODUCTION

The discovery of notes in Osama bin Laden's compound indicating that the terrorist leader was contemplating attacking trains in the United States on the tenth anniversary of September 11 underscores the continuing terrorist threat to public surface transportation.

Public surface transportation—trains and stations, buses and bus depots, even groups of people waiting at bus stops—offers terrorists an attractive target: easy access and easy escape, concentrations of people in confined environments that enable an attack to achieve the high body counts terrorists seek, and confined environments that can enhance the effects of explosives and unconventional weapons. This poses enormous challenges for security.

THE THREAT IS REAL

The terrorist threat to public surface transportation is real. While terrorists remain obsessed with attacking commercial aviation, they regard surface transportation as a killing field. Between September 11, 2001 and December 31, 2011, terrorists carried out 75 attacks on airliners and airports worldwide, causing 157 deaths. During the same period, terrorists carried out nearly 1,804 attacks on surface transportation, most of them against bus and train targets, killing more than 3,900 people. (This does not include attacks in war zones like Afghanistan and Iraq.)[1]

While terrorists recently have attacked aviation targets less often, they have been attacking surface transportation more frequently. Between 1970 and 1979, terrorists carried out a total of 15 surface transportation attacks that caused fatalities. (Only incidents with fatalities are included to avoid apparent increases that are due solely to better reporting.) The number grew to 43 attacks with fatalities in the 1980s, 281 in the 1990s, and 465 in the decade between 2000 and 2009.

Many of these attacks involved a few fatalities and did not make headline news, but 11 of them since 9/11 resulted in 50 or more deaths, and three of the attacks (including one carried out by a deranged arsonist) each killed nearly 200 people. The total number of fatalities in these 14 attacks is the approximate equivalent of the fatalities in seven major airline crashes. One can imagine the furor that would have resulted if seven commercial airliners had been brought down by terrorists after 9/11.

The West is not immune. Most of the attacks have occurred in developing countries like India, but there have been attacks on trains and buses in France, Spain, the United Kingdom, Russia, and Japan. Further terrorist plots against surface transportation targets have been uncovered and foiled in the United Kingdom, Germany, Spain, Italy, and Australia.

Attacks on surface transportation could also occur in the United States. Since 9/11, there have been seven reported terrorist plots involving attacks on trains in the United States. Authorities reportedly uncovered a plot in 2003 to release poison gas in New York's subways. In 2004, New York police infiltrated a plot by two men to bomb a mid-Manhattan subway station. In 2006, a terrorist plot was uncovered in Lebanon to blow up train tunnels under the Hudson River. Bryant Vinas, a homegrown recruit to al Qaeda, offered terrorists his assistance in attacking the Long Island Railroad where he once worked, and in 2009, authorities uncovered a mature plot to bomb New York's subways. Faisal Shazad, the Time Square bomber, initially planned to follow up that attack with a bombing at New York's Grand Central Station. In 2010, Farooque Ahmed was arrested in an FBI sting operation for planning to bomb Washington's Metro stations.[2]

BOMBINGS ACCOUNT FOR THE MOST CASUALTIES

Of 3,150 attacks on public surface transportation between 1970 and 2011, 44 percent were directed against rail targets, including trains, subways, train stations, and tracks; while 48 percent were directed against bus targets, including buses of all types, bus depots, and bus stops. Eight percent were directed against infrastructure, including bridges, tunnels, etc.

Improvised explosive devices are the most common tactic, accounting for 57 percent of the total attacks. All types of explosives including improvised explosive devices, grenades, mines, dynamite, etc. account for more than two-thirds of all attacks.[3] Shootings and armed assaults account for 14 percent. Incendiary devices and other forms of arson account for 10 percent of all attacks. Mechanical means of sabotage (mostly of rails) account for less than two percent.

Bombings are generally the most lethal form of attack and account for more than 60 percent of the nearly 8,000 fatalities in surface transportation attacks since 1970. This statistic is underscored by spectacular attacks like the 1980 bombing of the Bologna train station, which killed 85 people; the 2003 Stavropol train bombing in Russia, which killed 40; the 2004 Madrid commuter train bombings, which killed 191; the 2004 Moscow Metro bombing, which killed 41; the 2005 London Transport bombings, which killed 52; the 2006 Mumbai commuter train bombings, which killed 207; the 2009 bombing of the Samjhauta Express in India, which killed 66; and the 2010 Moscow Metro bombing, which killed 40 people.

TERRORIST CAMPAIGNS

These data are informative, but must be seen in their historical context. Many of the attacks on surface transportation targets were components of broader terrorist campaigns. For 25 years, from the 1970s to the 1990s, the Irish Republican Army (IRA) carried out a terrorist campaign attacking rail lines in Northern Ireland and public transportation in England.[4] In the mid–1990s, terrorists in France carried out a series of bombings aimed at surface transportation, among other targets.[5] Spain's Basque separatists (the ETA) were responsible for numerous attempts to derail passenger trains.

Muslim separatists made numerous attempts to derail trains in southern Thailand. The Tamil Tigers carried on a 20-year terrorist campaign in Sri Lanka, frequently targeting public transportation. During the Second Intifada, from 2001 to 2006, Palestinian extremists carried out numerous suicide bombings on Israeli buses.[6] Chechen separatists bombed and derailed trains in Russia and carried out a number of suicide bombings on Moscow's metro. India confronted bombings and sabotage campaigns by Muslim extremists, Maoist insurgents, and separatist tribesmen in the Northeastern states. Jihadist fanatics bombed Pakistan's trains and buses.

Two spectacular terrorist successes—the 2004 Madrid and 2005 London bombings—and most of the foiled terrorist plots in the West during the first decade of the twenty-first century were part of an ongoing global campaign of terrorism directed against a variety of targets in Western nations that were branded by jihadists as enemies. This terrorist campaign was inspired by continuing exhortations from al Qaeda leader Osama bin Laden and other al Qaeda communicators, and it was waged by individuals who subscribed to al Qaeda's ideology, some of whom had trained in its training camps or had learned from information posted on various jihadist websites. This is not to say that the campaign was centrally directed. Some of the terrorist plots were instigated and assisted by al Qaeda or by Pakistan's Taliban. Others were merely inspired by al Qaeda's ideology. All, however, appear to have been the products of local initiative—individuals or small groups determined to be part of the global armed struggle, with or without al Qaeda's direct support. The campaign reached a high point in mid-decade, with three major terrorist attacks on trains in Madrid, London, and Mumbai, and seven foiled plots between 2004 and 2006, after which the activity declined.

This has important implications for security. Protecting vast public systems against terrorist attack is difficult and costly. Much can be achieved by eliminating the source of threat—the terrorists—or at least by degrading their operational capabilities.

CHEMICAL AND BIOLOGICAL ATTACKS WERE AN INITIAL FAD

The early part of the jihadist terrorist campaign (from 2001 to 2004) focused on various forms of chemical attack, reflecting al Qaeda's own exploration of chemical and biological warfare, possibly inspired by the 1995 nerve gas attack on Tokyo's subways, which killed 12 people and sent more than 5,000 to hospitals. Three of the four plots to use chemical–biological weapons involved poison gas and one involved ricin.

Given the difficulty of acquiring chemical or biological substances in large quantities, it seems doubtful that any of the plots would have resulted in mass casualties, but the discovery of laboratories and evidence of chemical-weapon tests having been conducted at al Qaeda's training camps in Afghanistan made it clear that the architects of 9/11 were pursuing an active chemical and biological weapons development effort. It is therefore not difficult to understand official apprehension.

Even if the plots were no more than talk, they say something about terrorist thinking at the time. Al Qaeda's global terrorist campaign was still in its early stages. The 9/11 attacks encouraged imagination and audacity. Armed with superficial knowledge, the plotters understood that the crowded, confined spaces of subway trains offered an ideal venue for the dispersal of poison gas and lethal toxins. Even if only handfuls of people died, the novelty and terrible effects of these invisible weapons would cause panic and widespread alarm.[7]

None of the plots succeeded, and by mid-decade, the poison fad was over. Meanwhile, terrorists in Madrid in 2004 and London in 2005 demonstrated that by using more-reliable explosive devices on trains and subways, terrorists could achieve the slaughter they desired. Multiple bombs became the new prototype for terrorist attack. This pattern continued through the end of the decade.

WILL TERRORISTS MOVE TOWARD DERAILMENT?

Osama bin Laden's later notes urged followers to derail speeding passenger trains in the United States. Guerilla fighters and terrorists have frequently attempted to derail passenger trains either by planting bombs on the tracks or by mechanical means such as removing spikes or sections of rails, or loosening fish plates, sometimes succeeding spectacularly as they did in 2010 in India, where coaches from a derailed passenger train were struck by a freight train going in the opposite direction; 141 people died. Maoist Naxalites claimed responsibility for causing the derailment.

The spread of high-speed rail systems appears to offer terrorists new possibilities. The high-speed trains themselves are iconic targets sought by terrorists, while their higher velocity would seem to make derailments potentially more lethal. (Actually, data from high-speed rail accidents suggests that the more rigidly-connected cars of high-speed trains make them less likely to jack-knife or tip over, which is a major source of casualties.) Still, bombs placed on the tracks are on average twice as lethal for high-speed rail as bombs placed in the passenger compartments of high-speed trains. This may be because passenger loads on high-speed trains—per-car and per-train—are much less than slower-speed commuter trains. Terrorists choose between volume—the possibility of high body counts on crowded subways and commuter trains—and velocity—the possibility of a catastrophic derailment of a high-speed train.

Terrorists have attacked high-speed rail systems in Japan, France, Germany, Spain, Switzerland, and Russia. In 1995, terrorists failed to derail France's TGV between Lyons and Paris, but in 2009, terrorists succeeded in derailing Russia's Moscow–St. Petersburg Nevsky Express, killing 27.[8]

AN AVIATION SECURITY MODEL WILL NOT WORK

Protecting public places that, by their very purpose, must be easily accessible to large numbers of people, is extremely difficult. This does not mean that physical security and other countermeasures have no effect.

In retrospect, the enormous investment in aviation security seems to have worked, at least as a deterrent to many terrorist attacks. Between the late 1960s and the late 1970s, an average of nine to ten terrorist airplane hijackings occurred each year. This dropped to an average of six a year in the 1980s, and to three a year between 1987 and 1996. In the past 15 years, there have been only six airplane hijackings, including the four successful hijackings on 9/11.

Several factors in addition to improvements in aviation security contributed to this decline, including the elimination of some terrorist groups and international agreements to prosecute or extradite hijackers. Increased security after 9/11 and, more importantly, a fundamental change in passenger reactions—from passive acceptance to defiant action—oblige terrorists to think twice before attempting a hijacking today.

Terrorist attempts to sabotage airliners also have declined over time, from three to four attempts a year in the 1960s and 1970s to less than two a year in the late 1980s and 1990s. In the past decade, only six attempts have been made to smuggle bombs onto passenger planes and only two onto cargo planes. Unfortunately, the terrorists succeeded in placing their devices on board all eight planes, although they brought down only two of the passenger planes, both in Russia. Security worked here too, albeit indirectly. By forcing terrorists to build smaller, more easily concealed devices using harder to detect components and ingredients, their bombs became less reliable.

But the aviation security model will not work for surface transportation, given the current and even near-term limits of technology. Screening of all train (let alone bus) passengers would be nearly impossible. Even before airline screening was initiated, passengers boarded airliners in single lines on the tarmac, but trains and their stations use multiple, simultaneous access points. Moreover, the difference in the volume of air and train passengers is staggering. New York's Penn Station alone handles in each morning's rush hours the same number of passengers that O'Hare International Airport in Chicago handles in 60 hours.

And while airline passengers may be willing to wait 15-20 minutes to be screened for a flight to a distant city, train passengers would not be willing to add that time to their daily commute each way. Also, train systems and stations tend to be more diverse than their airport counterparts, making a uniform approach less likely to work.

Moreover, the cost of screening would be prohibitive. Staffing a force of TSA officers to screen subway and commuter train passengers would require adding $7 to $8 to each fare, which would destroy public surface transportation. Finally, the waiting lines at the security checkpoints themselves would make tempting targets, easy for terrorists to access.

The bottom line is that security that shuts down the public surface transportation system—as an airline-style screening regime would if applied to surface transportation—or that even makes it more vulnerable, is not acceptable.

There is another important conceptual difference between protecting airplanes and protecting trains and buses. Airline security is front-loaded, that is, it aims at deterrence, detection, and prevention. In contrast, surface transportation encompasses a broader spectrum of countermeasures, including deterrence, detection, prevention, mitigation of casualties through the design of coaches and stations, and reducing fatalities by facilitating evacuation and rescue. In the case of armed assaults, rapid intervention can prevent further killing. The multitude of entry points and volumes of passengers limit what can be done at the front end, but there are still opportunities to save lives even after a terrorist event.

SURFACE TRANSPORTATION SECURITY MUST BE REALISTIC

Security for surface transportation protection has lagged behind airport security. It did not really become a major concern until after the 2004 Madrid bombing. Even then, security resources remained limited. Increased police patrols in stations and on trains, random passenger screening, explosives-sniffing dogs, and the installation of working cameras came along slowly. More can be done, of course, but security proposals must be realistic.

Protecting public places that, by their very nature require easy access, is difficult and costly. To be worthwhile, security must provide a net security benefit. The result cannot be a mere diversion of the attack to another equally accessible public place where the attacker can achieve the same results in numbers of casualties. One hundred percent security in surface transportation is not possible. Some risk is unavoidable, just as when we drive our automobiles, but the risk to individual citizens from terrorism is minuscule.

Security must be sustainable. We cannot look forward to the end of terrorism when the security structures erected over the past several decades can be dismantled. Security measures put into place today are likely to become a permanent feature of the landscape. Therefore, they must be sustainable in terms of public acceptance, and costs for operations, maintenance, upgrades, evaluation, and replacement.

Despite these difficulties, measures can be taken to make terrorist planning more difficult, to increase deterrence, and to make responses to terrorist threats rapid and flexible, as well as to improve the effectiveness of responses to attacks.

Rail operators and transit systems have increased the presence of security personnel. They have added cameras to improve surveillance, assist in rapid diagnosis if an event occurs, and deter terrorists who want to avoid capture. Smarter camera systems alert monitors to objects that do not move when they should or to movement where there should be none. Some transportation systems have implemented random passenger screening, which introduces uncertainty for attackers and therefore has deterrent value.[9]

The U.S. Transportation Security Administration has deployed VIPR (Visual Intermodal Prevention and Response) teams to randomly reinforce the security presence at busy transportation hubs or during periods of peak traffic. Explosives-sniffing dogs are increasingly being used to search for bombs and detect vapor trails left by explosives. Remote explosives-detection technologies are being deployed on an experimental basis, but there is no near-term technological solution.

Random passenger screening, the deployment of canine units, pilot projects involving explosives-detection technology, and VIPR teams probably are not deployed frequently enough to provide a strong deterrent, but they establish the protocols, allow for training, and thereby provide a foundation for an orderly surge in security, should intelligence provide some warning of imminent attack, or in the immediate aftermath of an event to discourage further planned or copycat attacks. These measures are also flexible and can easily be scaled back when the immediate threat is seen to diminish.

All of these measures enhance security, but local governments and operators, strapped for cash, can do only so much. Whatever security measures are put into place must be sufficient to handle the huge volumes of passengers, must not trample civil liberties, must be economically sustainable, and must offer a net security benefit. Implementing such measures will require intelligence and imagination. The answer is not merely implementing more security, but implementing smart security.

ENLISTING STAFF AND PUBLIC PARTICIPATION SAVES LIVES

Employee and passenger awareness counts. Just as airline passengers have become the last line of defense against terrorists on airplanes, rail passengers can become the first line of defense in ensuring their own security. Daily riders know the environment intimately and are most able to identify suspicious objects or behavior. Sixteen percent of all bomb attacks on surface transportation were prevented because vigilant staff and passengers detected the device. For trains and subways, the figure is more than 20 percent. During the Irish Republican Army's bombing campaign, British authorities depended on alert passengers, already sensitized by IRA bombings, to report suspicious objects within minutes of their being placed. Reports were followed up with visual diagnosis through cameras and personnel on scene. Bomb squads were summoned only when necessary, thereby minimizing disruption. This made London's tubes and trains a hostile environment for terrorist operatives. One can see the results over time, as the terrorists gradually edged away from their preferred targets in crowded central London to more remote venues.

The failure of the British public to detect the al Qaeda-inspired terrorist bombers who killed 52 people on subway trains and a bus in 2005 was due to the fact that the terrorists did not leave their explosives-filled backpacks unattended, but remained attached to them when they detonated. Obviously, it is more difficult to deter suicide bombers, but as suicide bombers are more difficult to recruit, this represents progress in raising the threshold for terrorist plotters.

Passengers can be enlisted as partners in their own security. Current "see something, say something" campaigns are a first step. They need to be evaluated to see if the message is getting through and how better to engage the public. Communications have to be facilitated. Procedures have to be established to ensure rapid diagnosis and response. Callers need to be acknowledged for their efforts, even when it turns out to be a false alarm. Disruptions must be minimized.

Finally, it should be noted that police intelligence operations account for a majority of the terrorist plots foiled by authorities. Similar to degrading the operational capabilities of the terrorists, intelligence collection is a national effort that extends far beyond the security force charged with protecting a particular transportation system. However, transit police forces have developed creative ways to enlist staff, riders, vendors, and nearby merchants as additional eyes and ears. In today's terrorism, the tip that leads to uncovering a terrorist plot may just as easily come from a local source as a foreign intercept.

NOTES

1. The statistics in this report are drawn from the Mineta Transportation Institute's database of attacks on surface transportation from January 1970 to December 2011. The database, which was funded by the Department of Transportation, the Department of Homeland Security, and the Mineta Institute itself contains over 3,000 incidents coded according to more than 100 fields, including country, perpetrator, target, weapons, delivery and concealment methods, fatalities, injuries, etc.

2. For a full account of the various terrorist plots, see Brian Michael Jenkins and Joseph Trella, *Carnage Interrupted: An Analysis of Fifteen Terrorist Plots against Surface Transportation* (San Jose, CA: Mineta Transportation Institute, 2012).

3. See Brian Michael Jenkins and Bruce R. Butterworth, *Explosives and Incendiaries Used in Terrorist Attacks on Public Surface Transportation: A Preliminary Empirical Analysis* (San Jose, CA: Mineta Transportation Institute, 2010).

4. For a detailed account of this campaign, see Brian Michael Jenkins, "The United Kingdom's Response to the IRA's Terrorism Campaign Against Mainland Surface Transportation," in Jenkins and Larry N. Gersten, *Protecting Public Surface Transportation Against Terrorism and Serious Crime: Continuing Research on Best Security Practices* (San Jose, CA: Mineta Transportation Institute, 2001); see also Brian Taylor, et al., *Designing and Operating Safe and Secure Transit Systems: Assessing Current Practices in the United States and Abroad* (San Jose, CA: Mineta Transportation Institute, 2005).

5. For a fuller account of this campaign, see Brian Michael Jenkins, "The Paris Subway Bombing at St. Michel," in Brian Michael Jenkins (ed.), *Protecting Surface Transportation Systems and Patrons from Terrorist Activities: Case Studies of Best Security Practices and A Chronology of Attacks* (San Jose, CA: Mineta Transportation Institute, 1997).

6. For a detailed account of the terrorist campaign against buses in Israel, see Bruce R. Butterworth, Shalom Dolev, and Brian Michael Jenkins, *Security Awareness for Public Bus Transportation: Case Studies of Attacks Against the Israeli Public Bus System* (San Jose, CA: Mineta Transportation Institute, 2012).

7. Jenkins, *Carnage Interrupted*.

8. See Brian Michael Jenkins, Bruce R. Butterworth, and Jean-Francois Clair, *The 1995 Attempted Derailing of the French TGV (High-Speed Train) and a Quantitative Analysis of 181 Rail Sabotage Attempts* (San Jose, CA: Mineta Transportation Institute, 2010); see also James Graebner, "The Derailment of the Sunset Limited," in Jenkins (ed.), *Protecting Surface Transportation Systems and Patrons*.

9. See Brian Michael Jenkins and Bruce R. Butterworth, *Selective Screening of Rail Passengers* (San Jose, CA: Mineta Transportation Institute, 2007), and Jenkins and Butterworth, *Supplement to MTI Study on Selective Passenger Screening in the Mass Transit Rail Environment* (San Jose, CA: Mineta Transportation Institute, 2010).

3

GEOSTRATEGY OF CRIMINALITY: HIGHLY INTENSIVE CRIMINALITY

Jean-François Gayraud

High Council for Strategic Education and Research (CSFRS)

CONTEMPORARY CRIMINAL CHAOS

The strategic order of the planet has drastically changed since the fall of the Berlin Wall. A multipolar and global world has emerged. The ancient order was certainly dangerous, but was nevertheless relatively clear and comprehensible. The enemy was identified without ambiguity. The strategic threat was both military and ideological, embodied by state actors such as the communist regimes. Terrorism represented a true nuisance but remained unable to call into question, in a fundamental way, the states' authority. The different forms of terrorism were either localized and limited in their effects and aims (the fighting communist parties; the Nationalist and Freedom fighters groups) or in effect, at the disposal of the states, used for the sole purpose of circumventing indirect strategies. As for the phenomenon of predatory criminality, its harmfulness was limited by geographic constraints. The danger embodied by organized crime was under control and remained relatively tolerable; as such, the threat was contained by the legal system. In the final analysis, during the Cold War everything that was really perilous turned out to be foreseeable and therefore controllable.

This strategic order has since given way to a chaotic system. A disconcerting confusion (*tohu bohu*) has followed what was previously a comprehensible disorder. This new tumult is not characterized by a greater number of conflicts and violent deaths, but by a lack of predictability and a blurring of the strategic horizon.[1] From now on, the enemy is no longer obvious. Above all, distinctions that were obvious in the past have become blurred: internal or external, civilian or military, peace or war, terrorist or criminal, legal or illegal, etc. Previously, impenetrable groups who operated in relatively distant worlds, have moved closer, converged, and have even intermingled. In this way, different hybridizations have resulted in the genetic mutation of entities, which in the past were classified either in the category of "criminal organizations" or "terrorist organizations." Terrorist groups, like the FARC from Columbia or the PKK in Turkey, buoyed up with political and religious ideals, have degenerated into plain predatory crime and gangsterism. On the other hand, groups that were previously considered gangster organizations have embraced the terrorism weapon and discovered territorial ambitions. Examples include the Columbian and Mexican drug cartels, the Calabrian Ndrangheta, and the Sicilian Cosa Nostra.

Beyond the political masks, hybrid entities have appeared: partly political, predatory, sectarian, religious, and terrorist. Having many facets and activities, these entities reveal themselves to be kaleidoscopic. It becomes ever more difficult to understand them. This new complexity allows them to fall through the cracks of the administrative divisions (the police, the law, intelligence services, customs, etc.) and to blur their true nature in the eyes of the media. Who can, at this time, say precisely what the Lebanese Hezbollah or the Tamil Tigers from the LTTE have become? Who would dare to be fooled by the label "Al Qaeda in the countries of the Islamic Magrheb" (AQIM) when everyone knows how these Sahelian armed groups, hiding behind religious dogma, actually indulge in simple predatory activities (abductions, various forms of trafficking, etc.)?

Not only is the DNA of these groups mutating, but their real status has changed. Many of these criminals are no longer operating just in the underworld, or on the fringes of political and economic developments, but are installing themselves at the very center of the political, economic, and social arenas. This new strategic horizon, born from globalization, puts into perspective threats originating from single nations—without having them disappear—and underscores the new importance of wealthy and evolving transnational criminal entities.

As a matter of fact, the globalization has created the stimulus for the criminal actors to now infiltrate all levels of society. Criminal actions have reached an unprecedented stage in history and markedly changed their nature. It has now become impossible to analyze them with sociological and criminological tools alone. It is necessary to think in terms of macroeconomics (financial and economic crisis; destabilization and contamination of the financial and economic markets; far-reaching frauds) and above all, geopolitics (territories, flows, powers), to figure out the real outlines. We are confronted with criminal powers having deeply staked out their territories, managing financial floods of macroeconomical importance, now being able to compete with state sovereignties.

Terrorism: Diversion, Trivialization, Hybrids

This changing of *nomos* is still difficult for many observers to perceive. Unfortunately, the concept of a global war on terrorism (GWOT) has not helped to clarify the strategic horizon, because it has acted as an illusion for a decade.

The real danger of Osama bin Laden's followers, after having been underestimated for many years (1995–2001), was subsequently overestimated (2001–2011). A bloody, but single event—the September 11 attacks—became the intellectual center, sometimes the pretext indeed, for geopolitical adventures, in this case, two expensive and now-lost wars. Al Qaeda and the Salafi Jihad Movement have never had the level of organization and menace that the media and some public administrations have thought it necessary to depict. The out of proportion reaction to this threat is like a self-fulfilling prophecy, having the effect of creating as many terrorist vocations as the number it has annihilated. Osama bin Laden had become an obsession for Washington—and for a great part of the Western world—even more prejudicial, for it has provoked a real blindness to emerging and much more pernicious threats. The War on Terrorism was based upon a metaphysical view of the enemy—is it possible to fight a concept or a fear?—and it provided the impetus for the proliferation of poorly controlled internal and external security agencies, the efficiency of which remains doubtful in comparison with the amount of money expended. Of course, some metastases and dregs of bin Laden's organization will still have to be monitored, but by-and-large this violent Salafiya is no longer able to durably destabilize states.

Occupied and distracted by this war on terrorism, states lost interest in the ascent of the big criminal phenomena. This virtual war will have given an opportunity of historical importance to all criminal actors, including both the white collar criminals (financiers and kleptocrats) and the blue collar offenders (organized crime). Perhaps the ironic aspect of the September 11th attacks has been neglected: Osama bin Laden wished, with these attacks, to strike America in its symbolic and economic heart—Wall Street and its financial industry. But while this financial body displayed its resilience to terrorist crimes, it almost disappeared not because of an explosion coming from a foreign enemy, but because of an implosion coming from the very heart of the system (the subprimes). The real danger for the survival of the United States was the result of an internal strategic threat but not of an external one. The true peril came from its very heart not from a foreign and distant threat.

This diverting effect generated by the antiterrorist struggle will continue for a long time to produce destroying effects for two reasons. First of all, the public administration inertia is such that is unable to quickly reorient its priorities. The vast public and private complex born from the antiterrorist struggle in the United States—as well as in other places—will not easily abandon an entrenched vision of the world which allows these enterprises to survive.[2] As a consequence, organized crime has been able to take advantage of the opportunity to gain new market shares, taking the place of anemic financial institutions following the subprime crisis. Criminal entities have become shadow bankers, a sort of alternative banking system for firms having financial difficulties. This process has sped up laundering operations, and thereby the undermining of the legal economy. The question now arises: in some countries, as in Italy, has not the point of no return not already been reached?

Terrorism has not disappeared from the strategic horizon. It is only necessary to consider it calmly and dispassionately for what it truly represents. Terrorism is not an essence—as this war strategy would have us believe—but a tool. And this tool is nowadays trivialized. It is no longer wielded by states and political organizations alone. It has become democratic and popular, serving multiple causes. This phenomenon originally surfaced at the end of the Cold War; it is now manifest. Criminal entities do not hesitate to use it to exert influence over states that are hindering their activities or being too inquisitive. Organized crime and terrorism are converging in such a way that should give rise to deep concern. It is obvious that such unions will make these groups more resilient and, above all, more dangerous. Have we really taken into account the importance of such changes?

**Wars and
Criminal Armies**

Terrorist crimes also impose their presence on the battlefield. In fact, twenty-first century warfare will take unprecedented directions. This new face of belligerence certainly upsets a great number of our certitudes and customs. We often tend to prepare for the "next war" with the ideas of the previous one and to choose "comfortable" enemies—those who would be perfectly adapted to our prejudice, our customs, and our institutions! But war is by nature totally unforeseeable. It always takes on an unexpected form, and the enemy will not always have the face that we imagine or prefer.

Great wars between states seem to have no future. Traditional wars have had their day. Wars with abstract or metaphysical aims (war against drugs, against terrorism, etc.) are not true wars and in the end they fail because they have no clearly identified enemies. On the contrary, asymmetrical wars have become the standard. War itself has, simultaneously, a predatory face and a terrorist one. The problem is no longer that of criminal behaviors (war crimes) perpetrated by military units, but now includes the metamorphosis of criminal groups—previously called "organizations"—into real armies. These criminal armies are almost overtly fighting against states, using insurrectionary, asymmetrical, and terrorist tactics. The world of crime is undergoing a profound change towards becoming more or less visible paramilitary entities joining very murderous "little wars."

The emblematic examples of these paramilitary entities are the Mexican drugs cartels, which, beyond their deeply polycriminal real nature, now possess true military capacity, considering the number of their fighters, the nature of their equipment and their modus operandi. That is why Mexico will probably be the biggest strategic focus of the Americas in the twenty-first century. North America will be confronted with a real criminal insurrection for the first time in its history.[3] The Mexican government has lost control of a great part of its country: the North was the historical birthplace of the drug cartels, but now other parts of the country are also becoming more and more important. Northern Mexico has become a grey and chaotic zone, almost out of control. Faced with local and federal police corruption, President Calderon has been forced to call out the Army, with mediocre results. This "war" has resulted in about 50,000 deaths since the end of 2006, not taking into account the thousands of "missing people," probably around 10,000, according to reports made by NGOs and the Mexican press.

Thus, towns like Ciudad Juarez have today become objectively more dangerous than Bagdad or Kabul, which are considered true war zones. Cartels can easily line up 100,000 men—that is to say, as many fighters as there are in the Mexican Army. These cartels have at their disposal an almost infinite number of means of corruption because of the various types of trafficking that result in billions of dollars each year. They also have the capability for military operations—remember that a large part of the membership of these cartels comes from the special forces of the Mexican Army, the Zetas, men trained in the United States, who later joined the criminal side for the lure of money. The cartels have intelligence and police capacities worthy of the Mexican State; they own firms, submarines, etc. This picture would not be complete without a sharp analysis of the battle of wills involved. First, this war cannot be summed up as a mere conflict between two clearly identified sides—the State on one side and the cartels on the other—but is rather a more subtle conflict between state segments, parties, and cartels. It is not about a war "against" drugs but "for" drugs, the aim being to take possession of an income stream which had been under control of a state party, the PRI, for a long time. Moreover, the conflict seems particularly insolvable, in that the Mexican government is less the answer than a part of the problem because of its deep corruption. We can be sure, for the United States, the defense of the Rio Grande in the twenty-first century, will be a longer, more perilous, and more vital war than that on the Durand Line between Afghanistan and Pakistan. Nothing can be worse than a war next door, with unusual rules of the game, without any recognizable faces or uniforms.

Moreover, the smart analysis of insurrectionary wars in Iraq and Afghanistan shows that the belligerents who fought against Western troops were not all politically or religiously motivated. Classical criminality was barely hidden behind community and religious motivations. Many attacks and abductions, both in Iraq and in Afghanistan, have a financial incentive barely covered up by pseudo-political claims.

Increasingly More Criminalized Territories and States

Wealthier and more active criminal entities take root in or conquer new territories, creating an expanded flow of illegal criminal activity, which shows a worrisome resilience to repression, ultimately gaining real power. However, this silent crime globalization manages to go through the radar of the media and the states, as these entities are hypnotized by spectacular terrorism. This creates a major geopolitical consequence—grey areas are multiplying all over the world: 1) out of control territories: northern Mexico (and soon the whole country), the gulf coasts of Guinea, Somalia, East Timor, Haiti, the favelas in Brazil, etc.; 2) failed and collapsed states, where crime is both a cause and a consequence of these collapses; 3) anarchic megalopolies including relegated suburbs and "informal housing" places—shantytowns, in fact; 4) anarchic maritime zones with growing piracy.

This point needs to be explained. Piracy, operating along East African coasts—with Somalia as the epicenter[4]—is symptomatic of the actual chaos because this criminal reality is a merging of terrorism and classical predation with political and religious overtones. These pirates became professional in a very short time, as they had the capability to buy very sophisticated equipment thanks to the money they received from ransoms. Despite the presence of an enormous Western armada trying to protect international trade, these pirates still present a grave danger. Their criminal territory continues to grow, as if the different attempts at international repression had provoked a dispersal of the phenomenon, rather than a containment of it. The reason is simple: Piracy is the consequence of a terrestrial disorder. However, after the lessons learned by the failures of 1990s, no state in the future will dare to send troops in order to restore order in a country where the government has definitively failed.

These anomic territorial realities are not only in the southern hemisphere but are also entrenching themselves in the north. Many territories are now falling under criminal control; these entities appear in the shape of powers like cartels, mafias, megagangs, or street gangs. Therefore, criminality in Central and South America should raise concerns. In these places, megagangs literally control whole areas or districts and they do not hesitate, as in Brazil, to lead urban guerilla operations as soon as the state dares to endanger their existence. At that point, the police become overwhelmed by street gangs acting in a military manner. A brief news item—revealing and not isolated—should be mentioned. In May 2006, in Brazil, the "First Commando of the Capital," a megagang led by Marcos Camacho, went on the offensive in the very center of Sao Paulo to protest against the transfer of more than 700 prisoners from one jail to another. In fact, the FCC, along with other gangs, control the Brazilian jails and will not accept prison administration interventions, such as the dispersal of their incarcerated members. The result of three days of riots, which was in fact urban guerilla warfare, is staggering: 250 official buildings, bank agencies, or buses were attacked; simultaneous mutinies broke out in 73 penitentiaries;

200 guards were taken hostage; and in total, there were 169 deaths, including 32 policemen. On the fourth day, authorities were forced to negotiate with the gang in order to end the conflict. It is obvious that the FCC controls entire districts in Sao Paulo, as well as the prisons, and any time the state tries to do its job, an open war breaks out.

The criminalization of civil societies by organized crime does not sum up the whole contemporary criminal question. A greater number of states throughout the planet have become kleptocratic powers. This phenomenon reaches all forms of governments, as the democratic form of institutions no longer constitutes a lasting immunity in the face of systematical corruption of the political and administrative elite. Even if correlation does not necessarily mean causality, a parallel has to be drawn between this advanced criminalization of societies and states, and one of the biggest (but poorly recognized) geopolitical phenomenon of the twentieth century: that is to say the proliferation of states. From about forty at the end of World War II, there are about 200 separate nations today. The planet has been balkanized and fragmented at an ever-increasing rate, and this process is not yet over. It will last further into the twenty-first century, stirred up by claims for national identity, and sometimes by money-grubbing actors who are primarily concerned with appropriating wealth within their reach. This new global mosaic gives rise to weak states, void of any political, military, judicial, or financial credibility. They are often a sort of "Potemkin state"— states incapable of resisting transnational criminal powers. International life is thus like a shadow play, where ever more numerous states occupy the stage, while negotiations take place backstage among less presentable actors. What can a microstate in the Pacific area, the Caribbean, or Western Africa possibly do in the face of aggressive criminal entities with unlimited means? History tells us that political nature abhors a vacuum. The vacuums existing in these states will more than ever be stealthily filled with criminal actors. This phenomenon is worldwide, occurring even in the most developed nations.

Financial Criminal Crises

Contemporary disorder will also have lasting effects on economic and financial markets. However, economic and financial crimes are less obvious and visible because they are subtle and complex. No financial crime will have the physical, intellectual, legal, or judicial evidence of a homicide or armed robbery. Revelation of financial crimes requires decoding so that the entire *corpus delicti* can be revealed in all of its malfeasance. Some contemporary macroeconomic crises are explained by systematic criminal behaviors. Depending on the circumstances, these financial criminals belong either to the under-world of traditional organized crime, or to the upperworld of white collar criminality. However, the world of crime is characterized by convergences and growing hybridization, where clear distinctions of classical criminology between organized crime, corporate white collar crime, and entrepreneurial crime vanish. For example, we see emerging white collar organized crime (WCOC).

Three financial crime horizons show characteristics of system-atic and routine fraud: 1) Some financial and real estate bubbles are based on the massive flow of drug money, as was the case in Spain during the years 1990–2000; 2) crimes based on megafrauds and swin-dles have proliferated; their profits amounting to billions of dollars or Euros, as was the case with the Madoff pyramid scheme in the United States, or the carbon-tax fraud in Western Europe; and finally and more seriously, 3) financial crises are triggers for repeated frauds.

Therefore, it is advisable to question the public policies of deregula-tion. Since the 1980s, first in the United States, and then elsewhere in the world, these policies have (dis)organized economic and financial mar-kets. Dogmatic deregulation is basically criminogenic, in that it multiplies opportunities for and incitements to fraud.[5] Financial crises resulting from deregulations reveal a criminal depth, as was the case in the 1980s with the Yakuza recession in Japan, or the savings and loan collapses in the United States, and later, in the decade between 1990 and 2000 with the subprimes crisis. To date, most of the defrauders are widely unpun-ished and this provides encouragement for them to repeat their offenses. The most worrisome fact for the future is that no fundamental lesson has been drawn from these financial criminal crises, even though these have highlighted both the power and anomy of the financial markets.

Promising Future for Criminal Middle Classes

This criminal chaos gave rise to a new sociological reality—a bour-geoisie (upper middle class) widely transnational and globalized—the criminal middle class. The phenomenon is not unknown in history. It even is sometimes a part of the development of new socie-ties, as was the case in the second half of the nineteenth century in the United States, or more recently in the ex-Soviet countries when they suddenly discovered the harshness of capitalism. However, this criminal bourgeoisie is growing faster with globalization. It comes from a dual convergence: First, thanks to a large storage of capital, savvy criminals have become real businessmen in legal or illegal activities. They emerged from their ghettos to form social groups in search of respectability and integration within the legal elite. The laundering of illegal benefits has now become a laundering of the criminal actors themselves. This process has actually been made easier by the media, which is always quick to glamorize criminal careers. It is not unusual to find among the biggest world fortunes leaders of criminal organizations or dubious financiers. But the gentrification of the criminal elite must not delude. It is in fact, on the surface, legalization of the superior levels of organized crime, corresponding to a form of internalization of the illegal elite within the legal world.

However, this new social class has another group on its side: a part of the legal and respectable elite, which agrees, out of fear or cupidity, to collaborate with the organized crime world. Where does this profound tendency come from? Organized crime needs to buy impunities and to perpetually find solutions to the demands of the laundering of money coming from criminal enterprises. So, criminal organizations are forced to develop unions and partnerships with new respectable accomplices, who then become partners: lawyers, legal and tax consultants, bankers, politicians, etc. These dubious professionals constitute a new half-world, a gray universe, a necessary bridge between the legal world and criminal endeavors.[6]

Organized crime elite and accomplices from the legal world have common goals and act in symbiosis. This view of the criminal elite would not be complete without the long list of kleptocrats governing many states throughout, the world whose illegally gained goods are hidden in tax havens, new *terrae incognitae* off-shore, and sometimes on-shore, like the City of London.

To Conclude: Crime becomes Systemic

From now on, crime is systemic. It transforms political institutions, social life, economic, and financial markets. Crime becomes an economic and political "model." So, what can possibly be done?

A solution will come from a dual approach. First an intellectual work: it is necessary to emerge from our blindness to the criminal realities by accepting those obvious realities which, as Edgar A. Poe stated in *The Purloined Letter*, "mischievously occupy the place of honor on the desk." Hypervisibility makes us blind. Second, renewed operations based upon a new paradigm: let intelligence work be a priority tool for the fight against crime (organized crime, white collar criminals, entrepreneurial businessmen, etc.), in order to get away from acting in a manner that is purely reactive, piecemeal, and short-sighted.[7] Crime is now a national security matter, which deserves as much interest and attention, if not more, than terrorism or the proliferation of weapons of mass destruction.

NOTES

1. Xavier Raufer, *Quelles guerres après Oussama ben Laden*, Plon, Paris, 2011; *Les nouveaux dangers planétaires, Chaos mondial, décèlement précoce*, CNRS éditions, 2009.

2. Dana Priest and William M. Arkin, *Top Secret America: The Rise of the New American Security State* (New York: Little, Brown, 2011).

3. "Criminal Insurgencies in Mexico and the Americas: The Gangs and Cartels Wage War," *Small Wars & Insurgencies* 22, no. 5 (December 2011).

4. Martin N. Murphy, *Somal: The New Barbary?Piracy and Islam in the Horn of Africa* (New York: Columbia University Press, 2010); Jeffrey Gettleman, "The Pirates Are Winning," *The New York Review of Books*, October 14, 2010.

5. Jean-François Gayraud, *La grande fraude. Crime, subprimes et crises financières*, Odile Jacob, Paris, 2011; *Géostratégie du crime*, avec François Thual, Odile Jacob, Paris, 2012.

6. Seal of the President of the United States, *Strategy to Combat Transnational Organized Crime, Addressing Converging Threats to National Security*, July 2011.

7. Jean-François Gayraud et François Farcy, *Le renseignement criminel*, CNRS éditions, 2011.

4

THE PSYCHOLOGY OF TERRORISM: CURRENT UNDERSTANDING AND VITAL NEXT STEPS

Dr. John F. Morrison

School of Law and Social Sciences, University of East London, United Kingdom

INTRODUCTION

For many, the beginning of the twenty-first century can be defined by the understandable, international preoccupation with terrorism. Within the realms of academia, this has led to a proliferation of 'experts' on terrorism. Across the disciplines, and external from academia, there have been countless individuals putting forward their interpretation of terrorists, their organizations and the violent events they are responsible for. While this has seen many welcoming advances being made in our understanding of terrorism is recent years, much of the research must also be treated with caution.

A significant proportion of the ever-growing terrorism literature has not been based on any prior knowledge, understanding, or research. The work of too many new researchers is built on a weak foundation of assumption and conjecture rather than data and rigorous research, and has in turn failed to acknowledge the findings of those who have gone before them. Consequently, the excess of terrorism-related publications has led to a number of mistakes being made time and again. The most significant of these recent failures has been to continuously treat terrorism as a synonym for religious terrorism, and particularly Islamist terrorism. This blinkered approach has failed to acknowledge the complexity and heterogeneity of terrorism and terrorist actors, which has been to the detriment of this area of study. For many, their research is guided by the desire to find a way to effectively counter terrorism. However, it needs to be acknowledged that before it is possible to even begin to counter terrorism, it is first of all essential that we understand those actors and groups who utilize terrorism as a tactic. Without this understanding it is next to impossible to come close to alleviating the threat of terrorism. This must not be mistaken for a justification of terrorism, as understanding terrorism and terrorists does not proffer any degree of support for the actions. One of the ways that has helped in providing this understanding has been by taking a psychological approach to the study of terrorism. While small but significant advances have recently been made in areas of the psychology of terrorism, there has at times been a failure to adequately connect the theoretical advances with the functional necessity of counterterrorism.[1] This apparent failure may lead some to question the efficacy, or even the capability of developing a worthwhile psychological understanding of terrorism. However, with a good understanding of the past and present research, alongside a clear future research agenda, the true value of a psychological approach to terrorism will become apparent.

The purpose of this chapter therefore is to provide a brief overview of how a psychological approach has, and can continue to, enhance our understanding of terrorism, and in turn how it can aid in counterterrorism. Throughout, there will be an attempt to dispel myths and common misconceptions while outlining the advancements which have been made within this area. The chapter will predominantly focus on outlining some of the perceived gaps in the literature and how we can seek to address them. While this chapter concentrates on the contribution of psychology to terrorism studies, what must be clear throughout is that no one discipline can achieve a comprehensive understanding of terrorism. If the study of terrorism, and therefore our understanding of terrorism, is to make the necessary advances, then it is essential that a multidisciplinary approach be embraced. This must not be based on anecdotes and conjecture. It needs to be led by the generation and analysis of new data, while also testing and retesting previous assumptions and findings. It must also seek to apply and modify, where relevant, existing theoretical approaches from our understanding of individual and group behaviour.

THE TERRORIST

It can at times be too easy to label those who partake in terrorism as 'crazy' or as 'psychopaths.' Why else would they engage in such activity? No 'right-minded' person could possibly be involved in such an action. However, such assumptions display a significant failure to understand the psychological process of being a terrorist. While some early researchers may have believed that all terrorists suffered from some form of psychotic disorder, this was rarely, if ever, based on the rigorous research methods and assessment techniques which good psychological research rightfully prides itself on. Leading researchers in the field of terrorism psychology, people such as Martha Crenshaw,[2] Jerrold Post,[3] Max Taylor,[4] John Horgan,[5] and Clark McAuley and Mary Segal,[6] have each emphasized the psychological normality of terrorists. At the 2004 Madrid Summit on Terrorism, Security, and Democracy, the conclusion of the summit was that "[e]xplanations at the level of individual psychology are insufficient in trying to understand why people become involved in terrorism. The concepts of abnormality or psychopathology are not useful in understanding terrorism."[7]

So why is there this dearth of psychopathy within terrorist groups? And why at times do terrorist groups actively discourage involvement or weed out psychopathic individuals or members with other psychological disorders? The answer can be found within the very characteristics of psychopathy. By their very nature, psychopaths have a pathological egocentricity. This would appear to hinder any significant involvement in a terrorist group which requires "high motivation, discipline and an ability to remain reliable and task-focused in the face of stress, possible capture and imprisonment."[8] In essence, the presence of a psychopath within a terrorist group does not assist the success of operations. On the contrary, they can in fact be a liability. It has been said that there are two ways of looking at terrorism through a psychological lens, as either a syndrome or a tool. The syndrome view posits that terrorism is the result of distinct psychological personalities and has its origins in psychological root causes such as oppression or poverty-related frustration. It goes on to claim, therefore, that the removal of these causes would significantly reduce or even eliminate terrorism. However, research has failed to show any significant support for this viewpoint, and that actually it is the depiction of terrorism as a tool which is a more worthwhile way for both academics and policymakers to view terrorist activity.[9] This is more in line with the understanding that terrorism is a tactic available to all. One need not be a psychopath or have a personality disorder to engage in terrorism. History and research has shown that terrorism has been utilized by state and non-state actors, be they groups or lone individuals in the pursuit of the immediate and ultimate goals. It can be used either consistently or sporadically as a tactic, and can be utilized in combination with other non-terrorism related tactics.

With this denunciation of the syndrome view of terrorism, where does that leave the psychology of terrorism? It actually is in a much healthier position now that the majority of researchers have moved away from this diagnostic form of analysis. One can gain a greater understanding of individual and group involvement in terrorism by accepting the psychological normality of individual actors and their groups. In separate writings, Fathali Moghaddam[10] and Max Taylor and John Horgan[11] have put forward the idea that involvement in terrorism should be viewed as a process. While Moghaddam proposed the metaphor of the narrowing staircase where individuals go from floor to floor, Horgan and Taylor utilized a stage-based process of engagement, terrorist involvement, and disengagement to depict the process of terrorist involvement. Both models assess the relevant psychological processes involved at each stage of terrorist involvement. By assessing each stage of the process, the psychologist can ask both why and how an individual initially becomes involved, actively engages in terrorist activity, and ultimately leaves the organization. However, at times the 'how' questions can provide more worthwhile answers than the 'why' questions,[12] and can be answered by looking at both push and pull factors. By outlining terrorist involvement as the consequence of rational behavioural choices, Taylor and Horgan came to three key findings:

1. There is no generalizable route into terrorism; there are individual routes which can change over time.
2. Terrorism works both at an individual and political level, as a result of "*behaviour* acting on the environment sustained and focused by *ideology,* and the effect of that on subsequent behaviour."
3. Social, political, and organizational context play a significant role in strengthening engagement in terrorism by exerting control over behaviour.[13]

While there was little to no understanding of the final stage of disengagement from terrorism when Taylor and Horgan proposed their conceptualization in 2006, in the past few years there has been a growing interest in this stage of the process from both academics and policymakers alike. With the rising number of known terrorist actors, both incarcerated and free, there has been growing interest in the need to understand the processes by which people leave terrorist groups. With the increasing number of programs developed internationally to deradicalize members of Al Qaeda, increased interest has been paid by researchers to assess their efficacy, as the heightened lack of proper evaluations are noted in their absence.[14]

Researchers are continuously addressing the topic by asking the questions "is deradicalization possible? And is it necessary?" The growing consensus is that deradicalization of individual terrorists, which would involve the "changing of their mindset and ideological beliefs"[15] is increasingly difficult and not as realistic an outcome as physical disengagement. As opposed to deradicalization, the physical disengagement from terrorist activity does not necessarily necessitate a parallel psychological disengagement or a fundamental change in attitudes, and similar to initial engagement, it can have a different meaning for different people[16] even within the same group or movement. Therefore, any attempt to successfully disengage an individual from terrorism must take into consideration the relevant contextual factors for each individual, as well as questioning whether an overall deradicalization is necessary, possible, or even viable.

THE NEXT STEPS

This chapter opened by dispelling some of the common misconceptions about terrorism while also briefly presenting our current understanding of the psychology of terrorism. The purpose of the rest of the chapter, and the focus of the majority of this piece, is to put forward some suggestions for the direction of future research. Before suggesting any new directions, it is clear that the most vital change this area of study must take is in replication and retesting of research and data. In order to assess the validity of the findings, as well as their applicability, it is essential that research is continuously replicated and the findings tested. It is only by doing this across and within groups that we will be able to fully appreciate the full scope of our research findings. Even though there are so many untouched areas within the realms of the psychology of terrorism, this call is vital. This reexamination needs to play a constant role in the continued advancement of our understanding of the individuals and groups who partake in terrorist activity. We need to constantly cast a critical eye over the research which has gone before, and through the utilization of a robust research methodology, constantly test and retest the findings of others. This will allow psychologists, and others, to be more confident in their findings and beliefs. This replication and retesting must not be seen as a necessity for the psychology of terrorism alone, but must be adopted by all those studying terrorism across every discipline.

This necessity of replication and retesting must be the cornerstone for the advancement of research in the psychology of terrorism. However, there are a number of serious gaps in the literature which must also be filled. Chief amongst these is our understanding of terrorist recidivism. While criminology and forensic psychology has for years assessed this issue with respect to common criminals, little to no worthwhile research has been carried out on the issue with respect to terrorism studies. This research can be linked to our growing understanding of the final stage of terrorist involvement, disengagement. In his essential list of fifty "un- and under-researched" topics within terrorism and counterterrorism studies, Alex Schmid cites recidivism as one of these fifty key areas which needs our focus. This was in specific reference to the need for a comparison of the rehabilitation of terrorists and the rehabilitation of "common criminals."[17] At its most basic level, recidivism refers to the conviction of an individual with a prior criminal history. Recidivism research can look at crime in general, or alternatively look at the reconviction for a specific form of criminal activity, e.g., sexual violence. Traditionally, this has been used as a means to assess the success rates of different forms of punishment, most notably prisons, as a means of deterring future crimes and rehabilitating former criminals. However, this has at times come with the failure to appreciate the true role which the external context can have on reoffending behaviour. If recidivism is to be assessed for terrorist activity, this appreciation of context is vital. A failure to fully acknowledge this will lead to an incomplete understanding of the issue at hand. With the ever-growing numbers of individuals being convicted for terrorist activity and ultimately being released, there is a growing need to understand how and why these individuals may recidivate. The questions which need to be answered are numerous. At a basic level we need to ask who recidivates and why? This introduces the researcher to a number of more specific inquiries. What role does the returning terrorist play within the organization post-release? How is this similar or different to their previous role? Are there any significant differences between the recidivism rates and motivations of lone-actor terrorists and those affiliated with a terrorist organization? How are returning convicts perceived by their new and former comrades? What is the time period between release and reconviction? Are there any significant differences across typologies of terrorist groups? The questions are numerous, but ultimately what we need to know is how these former convicts can be deterred from reengaging in terrorist activity.

In his 2008 article, Dennis Pluchinsky attempted to address this issue of terrorist recidivism by "raising a red flag" specifically on the issue of global jihadist recidivism.[18] Within this article he outlined the major stumbling block facing terrorist researchers attempting to address this issue—access to worthwhile data. Without valid and reliable data it is impossible to carry out any worthwhile research in the area. There is, therefore, a necessity for access to detailed imprisonment and re-imprisonment data. However, while his attempts to address this under-researched area must be welcomed, they were fundamentally flawed from the outset. Failing to heed his own warnings Pluchinsky went on to develop hypotheses and put forward far-reaching assumptions based almost exclusively on anecdotal evidence, and rarely, if ever, backed up by previous research or scientific evidence. This is exactly the form of research which terrorism psychologists must avoid if our findings are to be taken seriously. A much more worthwhile guide for those attempting to address the issue of terrorist recidivism is the work of Mats Devernik and colleagues.[19] They set out to address the predictive abilities of psychologists and psychiatrists with respect to terrorist recidivism. While they acknowledged that mental health professionals can "with moderate accuracy" predict violent recidivism in groups of offenders, there was no evidence to suggest that this accuracy could be transferred to the prediction of terrorist recidivism. This is due to the fact that a significant proportion of the predictive value of recidivism among violent offenders is based on the assessment of mentally disordered offenders. Therefore, the lack of a terrorist profile or personality in effect leaves the traditional clinical assessment close to obsolete. They argued that due to the lack of any clear common ground in the rationale and motivations of terrorists and ordinary criminals, a more worthwhile approach to terrorist recidivism would be to look at terrorism through the lens of social movement activism rather than criminality. The overarching theme of their article is that psychological risk assessments are not suitable to be utilized in the risk assessment of terrorists, and that even with suitable tools psychologists would need the assistance of case-specific terrorist experts to assist within the risk assessment process. For anyone attempting to address the vital issue of terrorist recidivism, this brief article, especially the seven recommendations at the end, is essential reading. As any good psychologist should do in preparing their research, Devernik and colleagues address the potential pitfalls in carrying out any research or assessment and outline how these can be avoided.

Any understanding of the psychology of terrorism must show an appreciation for the heterogeneity of terrorist involvement. By only focusing on the broad concept of involvement in terrorism, researchers from psychology as well as from other disciplines will continuously fall into the trap of the over-generalization of their findings. The disparate nature of terrorist involvement takes a number of different forms both within and between terrorist groups, which must be reflected in the research design and assessment of results. While steps have been taken through the assessment of terrorist involvement as a stage-based process, further consideration must be given to the issue of heterogeneity. Researchers must first of all consider whether an individual is a lone-actor terrorist or the member of a broader organization. If they are a member of a broader organization, what role or function do they have within this group? How actively involved are they? What is the overall purpose of the terrorist group and how is this similar or different to the individual member's rationale for membership and active involvement? What is the overall local, national, and international context surrounding their involvement and the continued existence of their group? Are they members of a new group or a longstanding terrorist organization? Is this a splinter or a parent group? These and many other questions need to be asked if we are to gain maximum value from any data collected. In looking at particular groups and movements, we need to constantly be asking ourselves how has the group changed over time? Taking Al Qaeda for example, what may have been true for them at the time of 9/11 was not necessarily true in the years prior or subsequent to the attacks. We therefore need to acknowledge these changes and assess how they have affected the overall workings of the organization and the individuals involved.

The issue of the heterogeneity of roles is one area which is continuously growing. The role of the suicide bomber in particular has become the focus for a number of leading researchers. The growing utilization of this tactic by terrorist organizations has led psychologists to question why any individual would be willing to take their own life for the advancement of the goals of their group. However, the very nature of the activity does not lend itself well to traditional research methods. How do you assess the motivation, personality, and influences of an individual who has already taken their own life? Due to the clandestine nature of terrorism in general, and suicide terrorism in particular, how does one get access to would-be suicide bombers, or is this possible at all? When faced with such problems terrorism researchers, as always, need to develop alternative methods of analysis. In their recent article, the Israeli psychologist Ariel Merari and his colleagues attempted to address this issue and answer the question whether there was anything unique about individuals who partake in suicide terrorism.[20] Within this study, the researchers met with three different groups of individuals to carry out clinical interviews and tests: failed Palestinian suicide bombers, a control group of non-suicide terrorists, and a group of organizers of suicide attacks. The utilization of failed suicide bombers as subjects allowed the researchers to overcome the inherent problems faced by those wishing to attempt any detailed form of analysis of suicide terrorists. Similarly, by utilizing a control group of non-suicide bombers as well as a third group of organizers of suicide attacks, there is the necessary respect for the heterogeneity of roles. The results of the research suggested that while there may not be a significant overall "terrorist personality," or even a single personality of Palestinian would-be suicide bombers, there may in fact be more distinct personality characteristics for those in specific roles within terrorist organizations. Their research found that the failed suicide bombers had significantly lower levels of ego strength than the organizers' group, which in turn led to them being more susceptible to social influence. However, in their analysis the authors are reticent to over-generalize, as their findings related to a very small and specific group of individuals: failed Palestinian suicide bombers and Palestinian suicide terrorism organizers. They acknowledged the possibility of different culture- and situation-dependent psychological characteristics across suicide bombers internationally. These culture- and situation-dependent characteristics do not only refer to different countries and regions, but also to the changing context within one area across time. Therefore, in order to assess the true reliability and validity of these findings, future researchers must replicate and retest these and other bodies of research across time and place. As was stated earlier, it is only then that we can truly appreciate the significance of the findings.[21] This welcome respect for heterogeneity needs to be seen across all levels of terrorism research, and particularly within the psychology of terrorism. By doing so we will gain a more thorough understanding of the individuals and organizations involved.

Adopting the process model of Taylor and Horgan, our understanding of terrorist engagement and disengagement is slowly, but significantly, growing. Small but significant advances have been made in recent years in both regards. However, with respect to the middle stage in the process—involvement in a terrorist group—our understanding has actually stagnated more than one would first anticipate. Yes, there have been significant studies done looking at individuals' involvement in acts of terrorism. However, the majority of a person's involvement in a terrorist group is not actually in the illegal act of terrorism. These acts of terrorist illegality are but the intermittent peaks within the overall membership of, and affiliation with, a terrorist organization. I propose that it is only when we understand an individual's involvement, and a group's continued existence within the troughs of lessened or nonexistent activity, that we will fully understand what it really means to be a terrorist or a terrorist group. The issues of continued membership and organizational survival raise some interesting questions. What does it mean to be a member of a terrorist group? What motivates individuals to remain active within a group? How does the organizational leadership maintain internal and external support for their activities? What causes a breakdown in this support? What causes interorganizational factionalization and splits? Within the factionalization of a group or an organizational split, why do individual members decide to side with one group over the other? By answering these questions and more we will gain a more detailed understanding of terrorist groups and individuals.

The topic of my doctoral research was the analysis of divisions in the Irish Republican Movement from 1969 to 1997. This research looked at splits in both the paramilitary and political sides of Irish Republicanism from both an individual and an organizational viewpoint. Within the dissertation, political organization and social movement theories were adapted so as to develop a process model for splits in terrorist movements. Parallel to this, the question was asked "why did individuals choose which side to stay loyal to within the factionalization and ultimately the splits?" This research was carried out by interviewing members of all the relevant groups from the four divisions under examination. This included semi-structured interviews with individuals from both the rank and file membership and leadership of each of the paramilitary and political groups. The analysis of the data provided an interesting insight into the loyalty choices made. From the utilization of an adaptation of interpretative phenomenological analysis (IPA), an analytical technique which has traditionally been used in health psychology, four keys themes emerged. These were:

1. Timing and context
2. Influential individuals
3. Regionalism
4. Age[22]

As can be seen, none of these factors have any reference to the inherent differences between the groups, or indeed any underlying ideology. They are in fact all in reference to quite normal, even mundane factors, which, similar to an individual's initial engagement with a terrorist group, provide the individuals with an opportunity—in this case an opportunity to stay with one side over the other. To highlight this point of opportunity over ideology, one interviewee when discussing the split in the mid-1970s between the Official IRA and the INLA described that

> "... even at the time of the split in 74–75 all of the Divis Flats unit and 99% of *na Fianna* [the youth wing of the Irish Republican Movement] all went to join the INLA and it was the opposite in Leeson Street, 98–99% stayed and only one or two left."[23]

This importance of regionalism, which was heavily affected by the influential individuals in specific regional locations, was echoed throughout the interview process. This example, and others like it, shows us the importance of normal everyday factors with respect to loyalty choice and other key decisions made by members of terrorist organizations. By assessing these nonviolent aspects of being and remaining a terrorist, we open ourselves up to gaining a greater understanding of the overall function and roles of individual members. Similar to the work of Merari et al. this research showed a clear respect for the heterogeneity of roles and groups, but it also needs to be replicated and retested within and across groups. The question needs to be asked whether these findings are reflected within other terrorist groups around the world, as well as for the violent dissident Irish republicans active today.

CONCLUSION

This chapter has aimed to give a brief insight into the psychology of terrorism, and more importantly pose some vital questions for those going forward in this area of research. The application of psychological tools, methods and theories can and has greatly assisted in the strengthening of our understanding of both the individual terrorist actors and their groups. This chapter has shown that there is no such thing as a terrorist personality or profile, and that any attempts to apply such a notion can end in dangerous consequences. More appropriately, the psychology of terrorism should be more defined by the psychological normality of the individuals involved. For example, it has been shown that there has been no acknowledged over-representation of psychopaths within terrorist groups when compared to the general population. This should not be confused with there being no psychopaths within terrorist groups at all. What it does suggest is that there is not a prevalence of psychopathy within these politically violent organizations. Therefore, what future research needs to address is whether there are specific roles in the terrorist groups where there is a significantly higher proportion of psychopaths or individuals with other distinct psychological characteristics present. By looking more in-depth at the heterogeneity of roles and other elements of terrorist involvement we will achieve a greater understanding of terrorist involvement and activity, and in turn this will lead to a strengthening of the foundation on which counterterrorism policies and initiatives are based. Future researchers must look beyond the traditional aspects of terrorist involvement. They must continue to assess all elements of involvement from initial engagement right up to disengagement, and everything in between. This research must look at both the legal and illegal activities involved in terrorist membership. It must look at the changing internal and external influences, as well as the fluctuating roles of individual members. This chapter should not be considered as a comprehensive evaluation of the psychology of terrorism—to do so would require a much vaster space. It is clear that psychology has a significant role to play in helping the victims and family of victims, as well as aiding in the support of the wider community. However, the guiding principle of this piece has been to give the reader an introduction to the value of assessing terrorist involvement from a psychological point of view, while also introducing some important areas which vitally require further assessment and scrutiny.

NOTES

1. John Horgan, "Disengaging from Terrorism," in *The Faces of Terrorism: Multidisciplinary Perspectives,* ed. David Canter (Oxford: Wiley-Blackwell, 2009) 257–76.

2. Martha Crenshaw, *Explaining Terrorism: Causes, Processes, and Consequences* (London: Routledge, 2011).

3. Jerrold Post, *The Mind of the Terrorist: The Psychology of Terrorism from the IRA to Al-Qaeda* (New York: Palgrave Macmillan, 2007).

4. Maxwell Taylor and Ethel Quayle, *Terrorist Lives* (London: Brassey's, 1994).

5. John Horgan, *The Psychology of Terrorism* (London: Routledge, 2005).

6. Clark R. McAuley and Mary E. Segal, "The Social Psychology of Terrorist Groups," in *Group, Organizational, and Intergroup Relations, Annual Review of Social and Personality Psychology,* ed. C. Hendrick, vol. 9 (Beverly Hills, CA: Sage, 1987).

7. Jerrold Post, "The Psychological Roots of Terrorism," in *Addressing the Causes of Terrorism: The Club de Madrid Series on Democracy and Terrorism,* vol 1 (Madrid: Club de Madrid: 2005), 7–12. Cited in Jerrold Post, *The Mind of the Terrorist: The Psychology of Terrorism from the IRA to Al-Qaeda* (New York: Palgrave Macmillan, 2007), 4.

8. Horgan, 51.

9. Arie W. Kruglanski and Shira Fishman, "The Psychology of Terrorism: 'Syndrome' Versus 'Tool' Perspectives," in *Terrorism and Political Violence* 18 (2006): 193–215.

10. Fathali M. Moghaddam, "The Staircase to Terrorism: A Psychological Explanation," in *American Psychologist* 60 (2005): 161–69.

11. Maxwell Taylor and John Horgan, "A Conceptual Framework for Addressing Psychological Process in the Development of the Terrorist," *Terrorism and Political Violence* 18, no. 4 (2006): 585–601.

12. Horgan, 2005, 104.

13. Taylor and Horgan, 597.

14. Andrew Silke, "Disengagement or Deradicalization: A Look at Prison Programmes for Jailed Terrorists," *CTC Sentinel* (January 1, 2011): 18–21.

15. Ibid., 18.

16. John Horgan, *Walking Away from Terrorism: Accounts of Disengagement from Radical and Extremist Movements* (London: Routledge, 2009).

17. Alex P Schmid, "50 Un- and Under-researched Topics in the Field of (Counter-) Terrorism Studies," in *Perspectives on Terrorism* 5, no. 1 (2011): 76–78. The issue of a lack of research on

terrorist recidivism is mentioned by a number of different authors; see, for example, Neil Ferguson "Disengaging from Terrorism," *The Psychology of Counter-Terrorism*, ed. Andrew Silke (London: Routledge, 2011), 111–22.

18. Dennis A. Pluchinsky, "Global Jihadist Recidivism: A Red Flag," in *Studies in Conflict and Terrorism* 31, no. 3 (2008): 182–200.

19. Mats Dernevik, Alison Beck, Martin Grann, Todd Hogue, and James McGuire, "The Use of Psychiatric and Psychological Evidence in the Assessment of Terrorist Offenders," *The Journal of Forensic Psychiatry and Psychology* 20, no. 4 (2009), 508–15.

20. Ariel Merari, Ilan Diamant, Arie Bibi, Yoav Broshi, and Giora Zakin, "Personality Characteristics of 'Self Martyrs'/'Suicide Bombers' and Organizers of Suicide Attacks," *Terrorism and Political Violence* 22, no. 1 (2009): 87–101. See also Ariel Merari, *Driven to Death: Psychological and Social Aspects of Suicide Terrorism* (Oxford: Oxford University Press, 2010).

21. For further reading on suicide terrorism, see also Mia Bloom, *Dying to Kill* (New York: Columbia University Press, 2005); Diego Gambetta (ed.), *Making Sense of Suicide Missions* (Oxford: Oxford University Press, 2006).

22. John Morrison, "Why Do People Become Dissident Irish Republicans?" In P. M. Currie and Max Taylor (eds.) *Dissident Irish Republicanism* (London: Continuum Press, 2011), 17–41.

23. Denis in Ibid., 31.

5

TWENTY-FIRST CENTURY BIOLOGICAL THREATS

Bob Graham, Jim Talent, Randy Larsen, & Lynne Kidder

Bipartisan WMD Terrorism Research Center
Excerpted with permission from "The Bio-Response Report Card,"
published by The Bipartisan WMD Terrorism Research Center

INTRODUCTION

Today we face the very real possibility that outbreaks of disease, naturally occurring or man-made, can change the very nature of America—our economy, our government, and our social structure.

- Naturally occurring disease remains a serious biological threat; however, a thinking enemy armed with these same pathogens—or with multi–drug-resistant or synthetically engineered pathogens—could produce catastrophic consequences.
- A small team of individuals with graduate training in several key disciplines, using equipment readily available for purchase on the Internet could produce the type of bioweapons created by nation-states in the 1960s.
- Even more troubling, the rapid advances in biotechnology, such as synthetic biology, will allow non-state actors to produce increasingly powerful bioweapons in the future.
- Prevention alone will never be enough to secure America against these 21st century threats.

There is no question America is vulnerable to infectious and contagious diseases. The influenza pandemic of 1918–1919 killed more than
20 million people—more than 600,000 in the United States. That winter, more U.S. soldiers died from influenza than had died on World
War I battlefields (See Figure 5-1).[1]

According to Centers for Disease Control and Prevention (CDC),
nearly 40,000 Americans die annually from seasonal flu. And most
experts agree that the human race is long overdue for an influenza
pandemic far more deadly than the H1N1 pandemic of 2009–2010.
However, the threat from Mother Nature goes far beyond the flu.

An average of 15–20 previously unknown diseases have been
discovered in each of the past few decades—including incurable
diseases like HIV/AIDS, Ebola, hepatitis C, Lyme disease, hantavi-
rus pulmonary syndrome, and Severe Acute Respiratory Syndrome
(SARS). Studies indicate that new strains of influenza and other
newly emerging diseases are likely to spread even more broadly
and quickly due to the mobility of the world's population. Additionally, many of the diseases once managed with medical countermeasures are now re-emerging in strains resistant to drug therapies.[2]
And modern technology threatens to speed the development of such
novel diseases and enhance the threat they pose to the population
at large.

The emergence of such a deadly pandemic, for which the nation
was unprepared to respond, could change America forever.

Naturally occurring disease remains a serious biological threat;
however, a thinking enemy armed with these same pathogens—or

Figure 5-1

Influenza killed more
people in two years
(1918–1919) than
died in all of WWI.

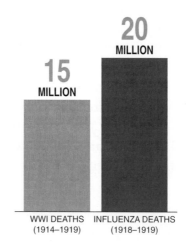

15
MILLION

20
MILLION

WWI DEATHS   INFLUENZA DEATHS
(1914–1919)   (1918–1919)

with multi–drug-resistant or synthetically engineered pathogens— could produce catastrophic consequences.

A NATIONAL SECURITY PERSPECTIVE

The relative threat of bioterrorism has been intensely debated within the national security community for more than a decade, with a focus on the biotech revolution and which capabilities fall within the reach of non-state actors.

In many respects, this debate is reminiscent of previous national security arguments. Shortly after World War I, two junior Army officers began writing articles in military journals about high-speed tanks and how they could revolutionize land warfare. Their ingenuity was severely chastised by the Commander of the Infantry in the War Department. He threatened the young officers with charges of insubordination if they continued to advocate high-speed tanks. The senior officer stated, "There is no reason for a tank to ever exceed three miles per hour, because that is the fastest an infantry unit can move on a battlefield."[3]

Thankfully, Major George S. Patton and Captain Dwight D. Eisenhower were undeterred by the warnings from the War Department. They continued their research and advocacy because they were convinced we could not predict the future by looking to the past.

During World War I, the technology was not available to produce high-speed tanks, so few really considered the possibility of massive armored juggernauts moving at high speed out in front of the infantry. However, on September 1, 1939, 2,400 German tanks raced across the Polish border, far in advance of German infantry units. The armored columns were supported by another rapidly emerging technology— airpower—and a new concept of warfare was introduced: Blitzkrieg (lightening war).

Some national security technologies require decades to mature, such as tanks and airplanes; others require far less time. In June 1941, the U.S. Navy concluded that Pearl Harbor was too shallow for the effective use of air-dropped torpedoes. This was a correct assessment for June 1941. But in September 1941, the Japanese Navy discovered that simple wooden boxes attached to the rear of torpedoes would allow them to operate in shallow water. On December 7, 1941, 27 of these newly modified torpedoes struck U.S. warships in Pearl Harbor.

ASSESSING THE THREAT

Today, some scholars would look to the past to predict the future of bioterrorism. They argue it has proven too difficult for terrorist groups to successfully develop and use sophisticated bioweapons—that the threat is overstated.

A better way to forecast the threat of bioterrorism is by careful examination of three critical questions:

- Can non-state actors produce and deliver biological weapons? (Capability)
- Is there a desire by terrorists to use biological weapons? (Intent)
- Would using biological weapons produce the intended effects? (Vulnerability and Consequences)

Capability

When the Biological Weapons Convention (BWC) was ratified in 1972, the ability of nation-states to produce sophisticated bioweapons was unquestioned. These weapons were capable of killing on the scale of nuclear weapons, but compared to the cost of a nuclear weapons program, they were far less expensive—hence the term, "poor-man's atom bomb."[4]

There was little or no consideration of non-state actors producing such weapons in the 1970s. That changed, however, by the end of the century. Dr. George Poste, then chairman of the Defense Science Board, predicted, "In terms of national security, the 20th century will be remembered as the century of physics, but the 21st century will be remembered as the century of biology."[5]

The first piece of hard evidence regarding the capability of non-state actors to produce sophisticated biological weapons came in 1999 from a Defense Threat Reduction Agency study called Biotechnology Activity Characterization by Unconventional Signature (BACUS).[6] The initial purpose of the study was to determine if a small-scale bioweapons production facility would produce an observable "intelligence signature."

The answer was no. The study concluded that even when using "national technical means," it would be extremely difficult, if not impossible, for the intelligence community to detect a clandestine production facility. This conclusion was somewhat expected. The surprise, however, came from an experiment conducted as part of the study. Individuals, with no background in the development and production of bioweapons and no access to the classified information from the former U.S. bioweapons program, were able to produce a significant quantity of high-quality weaponized Bacillus globigii—a close cousin to the well-known threat, Anthrax.

In spring 2001, the Defense Science Board (DSB) released a report, co-authored by Nobel Laureate Dr. Joshua Lederberg and the former chair of the chemistry department at Harvard Dr. George Whitesides, entitled Biological Defense. The report stated:

> "... major impediments to the development of biological weapons—strain availability, weaponization technology, and delivery technology—have been largely eliminated in the last decade by the rapid global spread of biotechnology."[7]

Unbeknownst to the authors of the DSB report, al Qaeda had already begun its bioweapons programs in Afghanistan and Malaysia in late 1999 under the supervision of Ayman Zawahiri.[8] (Zawahiri is now the leader of al Qaeda.)

Although many initially assumed the anthrax letters of October 2001 came from al Qaeda, the Federal Bureau of Investigation (FBI) is now convinced the anthrax letters came from a U.S. Army civilian employee at Ft. Detrick, Maryland.

This conclusion remains controversial. If the FBI is correct, however, then a single individual with no work experience in the weaponization of pathogens (a vaccine specialist), using equipment that could readily be purchased over the Internet, was able to produce very high-quality, dry-powdered anthrax.

Fortunately, the casualties were limited (22 infected and five died) because the small quantity of material was delivered with warning notes inside the envelopes. But according to Dr. Peggy Hamburg, the current FDA Administrator, an attack releasing the same quantity of dry-powdered anthrax into the ventilation system of the World Trade Center in late August 2001, could have killed far more people than the airplane attacks did on 9/11.[9]

The FBI theory of the attacks is that a single individual, working alone late at night, produced enough dry-powder anthrax to mount the attacks through the mail. A small team could have used the same approach to create enough product to attack a city.

Despite advances in biotechnology, some skeptics continue to ask where terrorists could obtain such pathogens. Unfortunately, most pathogens likely to be used as weapons exist widely in nature.[10] Anyone seeking to develop these pathogens as weapons would not have to look far for sources.

Clearly then, small, disaffected, but technically competent groups could develop credible biothreats to the United States. The next question is whether they could deliver it.

There are three primary means of delivering a bioweapon:

- Putting it in food or water,
- Using vectors (such as fleas, ticks, or infected humans), or
- Pumping it into the air (aerosolization).

All of these approaches are possible, but the most effective method is aerosol release.

The aerosolization of pathogens was perfected during the Cold War by U.S. and Soviet military scientists. Releasing pathogens in 3–5 micron size allows them to enter the lungs and flow immediately into the blood stream. In the 1960s, achieving this effect required sophisticated technology available only to major nation-states. Today, pulmonary drug delivery is used worldwide by the medical and pharmaceutical industries.

In summary, modern biotechnology provides small groups the capabilities for a game-changing bio-attack previously reserved to nation-states. Even more troubling, rapid advances in biotechnology, such as synthetic biology, will allow small teams of individuals to produce increasingly powerful bioweapons in the future.

Intent

Critics who question whether terrorists intend to develop and use bioweapons should consider the following:

- The Aum Shinrikyo cult in Japan attempted to produce both anthrax and botulinum toxin weapons. In 1995 they released large quantities of non-pathogenic Bacillus anthracis in Tokyo.
- A January 2010 Belfer Center Study on Terrorism and WMD by Rolf Mowat-Larssen observed:[11]

> "Another 9/11-scale operational plot managed by the al Qaeda core leadership was the development of anthrax for use in a mass casualty attack in the United States. The sophisticated anthrax project was run personally by al Qaeda deputy chief Ayman Zawahiri, in parallel to the group's efforts to acquire

a nuclear capability; anthrax was probably meant to serve as another means to achieve the same effect as using a nuclear bomb, given doubts that a nuclear option could be successfully procured. Notably, al Qaeda's efforts to acquire nuclear and biological weapons capability were concentrated in the years preceding September 11, 2001. Based on the timing and nature of their WMD-related activity in the 1990s, al Qaeda presumably anticipated using these means of mass destruction against targets in the U.S. homeland in the intensified campaign they knew would follow the 9/11 attack. There is no indication that the fundamental objectives that lie behind their WMD intent have changed over time."

- A video played worldwide on al Jazeera TV in February 2009 featured a Kuwaiti professor talking about bringing four pounds of dry-powdered anthrax to Washington, D.C., and killing several hundred thousand Americans.[12] It has been viewed more than 100,000 times on various web sites.

- The web site of Anders Behring Breivik, the perpetrator of the 2011 terrorist attacks in Norway, talked of using anthrax weapons. There is serious doubt that he had the technical capability to produce any type of bioweapon, but little question he would have used one if available. Clearly, one should not assume that international terrorists are the sole threat for bioterrorism. Had Ted Kaczynski (the Unibomber) been a microbiologist rather than a mathematician, he might have selected a far more deadly form of weapon.[13]

Vulnerability and Consequences

Despite major improvements in public health and medical science, the human race remains vulnerable to infectious diseases. A global economy and highly mobile population make the likelihood and consequences of a disease outbreak even greater. In 2003, a single individual infected with the SARS virus spread the disease to 24 people—who in three days, had traveled to six countries on four continents.[14]

With respect to man-made threats, this vulnerability is also clear. The offensive bioweapons programs of the United States and the former Soviet Union demonstrated, without question, the potential lethality of sophisticated bioweapons.

But 40 years of advancement in biotechnology may now enable development of bioweapons by small nation-states and non-state actors. This growing threat creates significant new vulnerabilities for our nation and the world, as described by President Obama in a foreword to the National Security Council's Strategy for Countering Biological Threats.

"The effective dissemination of a lethal biological agent within an unprotected population could place at risk the lives of hundreds of thousands of people. The unmitigated consequences of such an event could overwhelm our public health capabilities, potentially causing an untold number of deaths. The economic cost could exceed one trillion dollars for each such incident. In addition, there could be significant societal and political consequences that would derive from the incident's direct impact on our way of life and the public's trust in government."[15]

Consider, for example, smallpox, a disease that killed more than 300 million people in the 20th century. Although it was eradicated in its natural form 30 years ago, concerns remain that someone might still hold stores that could have a devastating effect on unvaccinated populations today. Even worse, the causative agent, variola virus, can be synthetically produced in high-tech laboratories. Should the government prove unprepared for either a natural outbreak or an attack, the consequences might shake the very foundations of America.

As technology spreads, the growing challenge of attribution may also make us even more vulnerable than in the past.

Until now, the combination of the Biological Weapons Convention and traditional deterrence has prevented nation-state use of bioweapons. But, deterrence is largely ineffective against non-state actors because they are hard to find and hold accountable. Should rogue nation-states provide sophisticated bioweapons to non-state actors, while remaining "a silent partner" to bioterrorism, the problem would be compounded.

The threat of biological disaster is real and growing. There are people in this world with the capability and the intent to use biological weapons. Americans are vulnerable to such an attack, as we are to a naturally occurring disease pandemic. The consequences of either could harm the fabric of the nation itself.

NOTE: In October 2011, the Bipartisan WMD Terrorism Research Center released a report card on America's capabilities to respond to biological attacks. The purpose was to provide a strategic, end-to-end assessment of America's bioresponse capabilities. Many of the nation's top biodefense, public health, and medical experts guided this project. A Board of Advisors informed project methodology, the seven categories of bioresponse, the scale of potential bioevents, and the proposed metrics by which to assess capabilities in each category (see: www.wmdcenter.org).

NOTES

1. John Barry, *The Great Influenza: The Epic Story of the Deadliest Plague in History* (Viking Adult, September 2004).

2. WHO, *Emerging Diseases*, www.who.int/trade/glossary/story022/en/index.html.

3. Dwight D. Eisenhower, *At Ease: Stories I Tell My Friends* (Eastern Acorn Press, 1981).

4. Committees of the North Atlantic Assembly, Chemical and Biological Weapons: The Poor Man's Bomb (United Kingdom: North Atlantic Assembly, 1996), p.1. http://www.fas.org/irp/threat/an253stc.htm.

5. George Poste, "The Impact of Life Sciences on National Security" (speech presented at Preserving National Security: The Growing Role of the Life Sciences, Center for Biosecurity meeting, Washington, D.C., March 3, 2011).

6. Judith Miller, Stephen Engelberg, and William Broad, Germs: *Biological Weapons and America's Secret War* (New York: Simon & Schuster, 2001).

7. Joshua Lederberg and George Whitesides, *Biological Defense: Report of the Defense Science Board/Threat Reduction Advisory Committee Task Force* (Washington D.C.: Office of the Undersecretary of Defense for Acquisition, Technology, and Logistics, June 2001), p. 18.

8. Rolf-Mowatt Larrsen, *Al Qaeda Weapons of Mass Destruction Threat: Hype or Reality?* (Cambridge, MA: Harvard Kennedy School, Belfer Center for Science and International Affairs, 2010) http://belfercenter.ksg.harvard.edu/files/al-qaeda-wmd-threat.pdf.

9. Peggy Hamburg (presentation at NORTHCOM Homeland Security Conference, Colorado Springs, CO, October 25, 2005).

10. Kunal J. Rambhia, Abigail S. Ribner, and Gigi Kwik Gronvall, *Everywhere You Look, Select Agent Pathogens*, www.upmc-biosecurity.org/website/resources/publications/2011/2011-03-03-select_agent_pathogens.html.

11. Rolf-Mowatt Larrsen, *Al Qaeda Weapons of Mass Destruction Threat: Hype or Reality?*

12. Kuwaiti Professor Anthrax, YouTube video 9:05, Kuwaiti Professor Abdallah Nafisi Dreams about a Biological Attack at the White House and Prays for the Bombing of a Nuclear Plant on Lake Michigan, uploaded by "oppozed1" on February 18, 2009, http://www.youtube.com/watch?v=M32M–2B2mz8.

13. Former National Security Advisor Anthony Lake's book, *Six Nightmares: Real Threats in a Dangerous World and How America Can Meet Them* (New York: Little, Brown & Company, 2000), devoted a chapter to domestic bioterrorism.

14. World Health Organization. *SARS: How a Global Epidemic Was Stopped.* Geneva, Switzerland: World Health Organization, 2006.

15. National Security Council, National Strategy for Countering Biological Threats, November 2009, p. 1, http://www.whitehouse.gov/sites/default/files/National_Strategy_for_Countering_BioThreats.pdf.

2

INTRODUCTION TO PART II: POLICY, GOVERNANCE, AND LEGAL RESPONSES

This section describes some of the policy and legal responses that the U.S. government has and has not taken in the areas of national preparedness and counterterrorism. Sharon L. Caudle chronicles the major changes in national preparedness policy, strategy, and guidance since the September 2001 terrorist attacks, and the actions the federal government has taken to determine national preparedness or readiness goals and priorities. She points out that it is not clear if a capabilities approach is the most effective or efficient, and that the measurement of those capabilities remains a work in progress. In order to achieve security in protecting the nation and its people, vital interests, and way of life, preparedness investments by all members of the homeland security community should be done in ways that emphasize clarity, sustainability, integration, balance, and accountability.

Shutting down the sources of funding that fuels terrorism is critical to preventing terrorist attacks and saving innocent lives. James Gurulé explains the efforts that have been taken to prosecute the financiers of terrorism and expresses concern about the paucity of major terrorist financing prosecutions, jury acquittals, and hung juries in high-profile terrorist financing cases. Gurulé's chapter argues that Congress and the Department of Justice should reexamine the U.S. Government's counterterrorist financing strategy.

Michael Kraft and Brent Davidson survey how counterterrorism laws have and will continue to develop in a complex pattern, mirroring the unpredictable nature of terrorist threats and tactics, with each step building upon existing laws that may or may not be the proper tool for the new challenge. Counterterrorism laws could be consolidated into one comprehensive package to resolve inconsistencies and clarify ambiguity.

Christian Beckner examines the issue of terrorism-related information sharing, discussing a number of policy reforms and activities that were undertaken following the attacks of September 11, 2001. These initiatives were designed to ensure that all information that was potentially related to a terrorist plot was effectively shared among relevant federal agencies and with key nonfederal stakeholders, including state, local, and tribal agencies and the private sector. He surveys key information sharing-related initiatives of the past decade, including legislation, organizational changes, improvements to federal information sharing systems, cultural shifts, and initiatives for information sharing with nonfederal entities. His chapter then assesses the overall progress that has been made in the last decade with respect to terrorism-related information sharing, and discusses several significant ongoing issues and challenges for the next decade.

Effective disaster planning requires that organizations define the kinds of information that they send and receive in an emergency. David Kamien's chapter proposes changes in national homeland security policy that will be necessary to encourage stakeholders to engage in information-sharing planning. Developing information sharing and communication protocols for homeland security missions is critically needed to support strategic and operational coordination with partners, collaborative risk management, and intelligence-informed decision making.

HOMELAND SECURITY: THE ADVANCING NATIONAL STRATEGIC POSITION

Sharon L. Caudle, Ph.D.

The Bush School of Government and Public Service, Texas A&M University

INTRODUCTION

In Congressional testimonies shortly after the September 2001 terrorist attacks, David Walker (2001a, 2001b), then head of the U.S. General Accounting Office (now the U.S. Government Accountability Office), posed a set of fundamental questions to frame decision-making about homeland security:

1. What national vision and objectives will make the homeland more secure?
2. What leadership is needed to guide our efforts and leverage resources within and outside government?
3. What approach to risk management will identify threats, vulnerabilities, and the critical assets that we must protect?
4. What federal tools and programs provide the most cost-effective approaches for homeland security?
5. What organization of the executive branch and the Congress will address these issues?
6. What approach will assess the effectiveness of implementation to address the spectrum of threats?

The answers to Walker's queries are both simple and complex. Certainly in the decade following the terrorist attacks there were major homeland security legislation, policy documents, and guidance. These produced immediate, significant changes in federal, state, and local government security and emergency management organizations and the committee structure of Congress. They became the organizational infrastructure to address homeland security issues.

Separately, the complexity comes from answers about the national vision and objectives, leadership, risk management, federal tools and programs, and assessment of effectiveness found in the evolution of national preparedness doctrine and guidance. The early, formative years of homeland security under President George W. Bush gave way to a refinement of preparedness goals, objectives, and the management system under President Obama.

The refinement is both broad and deep. Homeland security has been firmly placed within national security. The definition of homeland security has expanded from being exclusively concerned with terrorism, to a focus on confronting terrorism and other hazards while protecting national interests and establishing adaptability through resiliency plans. The components of preparedness have solidified into prevention, protection, mitigation, response, and recovery. Extra emphasis is being given to the homeland security responsibility of what is called the whole homeland security community, not just the federal government. Much more focused security objectives to guide action are now apparent, such as effectively controlling air, land, and sea borders instead of the more amorphous border and transportation security. In addition, prescriptive, detailed individual tasks and target capabilities have morphed into guidance about core capabilities and their performance targets. Overall, preparedness is now the policy and operational face of homeland security within the overall construct of national security.

This chapter presents and discusses these developments in national preparedness and identifies preparedness policy and operations challenges in at least two main areas. One is leadership and management of preparedness expectations; another is performance assessment.

THE STRATEGIC POSITION DOCUMENTS: THE FORMATIVE YEARS

In the aftermath of the September 2001 terrorist attacks, the United States government began considering terrorism to be the primary domestic threat to its citizens and infrastructure and anticipated that the threat would be ongoing. Major policy announcements, transformation of federal agencies into a new domestic security department, and the development of a specific national homeland security strategy reflected the criticality of immediate action. Combatting terrorism within the United States was seen as a truly national, not a federal, responsibility; although the federal government assumed control of policy and strategy development, buttressed with federal grants to states and localities. In line with a philosophy of managing for results, homeland security was to have specific goals, performance targets, and performance measures. The emergency management structure would continue its traditional role of anticipating the aftermath of any attack or emergency.

The Administration laid out the homeland security agenda and means quickly. In June 2002, President Bush (2002a) released *Securing the Homeland: Strengthening the Nation.* In the document, the President called the terrorist threat a permanent condition for the nation and homeland security a new national calling. He presented homeland security as critically necessary because of the vulnerability of American society and the uncertainty of when or where the next terrorist attack would occur. He said the federal government did not have a more important mission than fighting terrorism overseas and securing the homeland from future terrorist attacks. He previewed the forthcoming first homeland security national strategy, intended to be the comprehensive, long-term national blueprint for confronting terrorism with clear objectives, benchmarks, and performance measures. It called for the federal government to partner with other levels of government, the private sector, and citizens.

At the same time that the President previewed the first national strategy, he (2002b) presented the organizational structure considered best suited to meet the terrorism threat at the federal level. He proposed a new Department of Homeland Security, whose primary mission was to protect the homeland from terrorist attacks. The proposed department was to have four divisions—border and transportation security; emergency preparedness and response; chemical, biological, radiological and nuclear countermeasures; and information analysis and infrastructure protection. The Federal Emergency Management Agency (FEMA) would be in the department, with its traditional role continuing through what was described as a comprehensive, risk-based, all-hazards emergency management program of preparedness, mitigation, response, and recovery. However, it was anticipated that the emergency management culture would continue to change from reacting to terrorism and other disasters to proactively aiding communities and citizens to avoid becoming victims of such events. The Homeland Security Act of 2002 (P.L. 107-296) authorized the new department.

In July 2002, the Office of Homeland Security issued the first *National Strategy for Homeland Security.* This Strategy was intended to answer four basic questions that were much the same as those raised by David Walker earlier: 1) What is "homeland security" and what missions does it entail? 2) What do we seek to accomplish, and what are the most important goals of homeland security? 3) What is the federal executive branch doing now to accomplish these goals and what should it do in the future? 4) What should nonfederal governments, the private sector, and citizens do to help secure the homeland?

Not surprisingly, answers to the Strategy's four questions at the time concerned terrorism. The Strategy defined homeland security as "a concerted national effort to prevent terrorist attacks within the United States, reduce America's vulnerability to terrorism, and minimize the damage and recover from attacks that do occur (p. 2)." Terrorism prevention, vulnerability reduction, minimizing damage, and recovery were set as homeland security's strategic objectives—the initial definition of what preparedness meant that carried over the decade. It was expected the new department would guarantee greater accountability and unity of purpose among the agencies responsible for the homeland security. The Strategy included actions to prevent or mitigate (reduce vulnerability and respond to and recover from) terrorist attacks within the United States. Prevention meant action at home and abroad to deter, prevent, and eliminate terrorism. Reducing vulnerability meant identifying and protecting critical infrastructure and key assets, detecting terrorist threats, and augmenting defenses, while balancing the benefits of mitigating risk against economic costs and infringements on individual liberty. Response and recovery meant managing the consequences of attacks and building and maintaining the financial, legal, and social systems to more readily recover.

The Strategy's missions were intelligence and warning, border and transportation security, domestic counterterrorism, critical infrastructure protection, catastrophic terrorism defense, and emergency preparedness and response. In addition, the Strategy described four foundations for all mission areas, government levels, and sectors of the society: law, science and technology, information sharing and systems, and international cooperation. Each foundation aided in defining and acting, and in evaluating homeland security investments. For example, legal authority provided the foundation to act within appropriate limits.

THE OVERARCHING GOAL AND POLICY AND OPERATIONAL SYSTEM

These early documents spoke primarily to an overall terrorism threat and strategy. Starting in early 2003, the Bush Administration began issuing a number of directives and guidance documents that accelerated the formation of a national preparedness goal and supporting policy and operational system. The action responded to what was seen as major failures during the September 2001 attacks and the need for overall preparedness to bring together all levels of government assets.

In February 2003, the President (2003a) issued *Homeland Security Presidential Directive 5*, which required the development and administration of a National Incident Management System (NIMS) and a National Response Plan. The Homeland Security Act of 2002 also required the consolidation of existing federal government emergency response plans into a single national response plan. These initiatives were intended to strengthen the nation's ability to manage domestic incidents.

The major policy development for the national preparedness structure at that time, with its influence continuing to the present day, was President Bush's (2003b) December 2003 issuance of *Homeland Security Presidential Directive 8* (HSPD-8). HSPD-8 crafted homeland security's strategic position as national preparedness for all major events—terrorism, major disasters, and other domestic emergencies. It defined preparedness in terms of planning, operations, and equipment at all levels of government to prevent, respond to, and recover from major events. The directive mandated a national domestic all-hazards preparedness goal, established mechanisms to advance federal delivery of preparedness assistance to state and local governments, and described actions to further improve federal, state, and local entity preparedness.

The critical policy requirement in HSPD-8 was the national preparedness goal. The goal was to establish measurable readiness priorities and targets, but with the caveat they balance the potential threat and emergency event with resources. Assessment of preparedness was to be a clear feature of the efforts, with expectations for readiness metrics and elements, standards for preparedness assessments and strategies, and a system to assess the nation's overall preparedness to respond to major events. Nevertheless, the emphasis on assessment of response overshadowed, to a certain extent, the homeland security objectives of prevention and recovery. Subsequently, the fiscal year 2005 Department of Homeland Security appropriations legislation (P.L. 108-234) established a statutory requirement for implementing HSPD-8. The legislation called for nationally accepted first responder preparedness levels by January 31, 2005, state and local adoption of national preparedness standards in fiscal year 2005 as part of federal grant guidance guidelines, and issuance of national preparedness goal final guidance by March 31, 2005.

The Department of Homeland Security (2005a) met the March 2005 deadline with the issuance of the Interim National Preparedness Goal. DHS stated the Interim Goal enabled the nation to answer: "How prepared do we need to be?" "How prepared are we?" and "How do we prioritize efforts to close the gap?" The Interim Goal highlighted a collection of fifteen national planning scenarios and a target capabilities list. The scenarios, issued in 2004 by the Homeland Security Council, described plausible terrorist attacks and natural disasters intended to stretch the nation's prevention and response capabilities for events, such as a nuclear detonation, pandemics, chemical and biological attacks, a major hurricane or earthquake, and a cyber attack. Collectively, the scenarios identified a complete array of preparedness needs.

The target capabilities list identified what was necessary to carry out critical operations and tasks in response to a major disaster or catastrophe based on the combined planning scenarios. It was derived from a universal task list intended to respond to the planning scenario events. For example, an incident management task included the coordination of transportation operations. Further, the Interim Goal included a number of national priorities: expand regional collaboration; implement NIMS and the National Response Plan; implement the National Infrastructure Protection Plan; and strengthen capabilities in three areas—interoperable communication; medical response; and chemical, biological, radiological, nuclear, and explosives detection.

The focus on capabilities was seen as the optimal way to deal with terrorist attacks or natural disasters. This approach characterized preparedness then and still does to the present day. The Interim Goal stated that a capability provided the means to accomplish one or more tasks under specific conditions and to specific performance standards. It also reflected national preparedness as a continuous cycle of activity to develop the necessary elements, such as plans, policies, and equipment, vital to maximizing capabilities. The target capabilities list set forth a set of essential capabilities, stated as necessary in whole or in part by various levels of government to carry out certain tasks to prevent, protect against, respond to, and recover from terrorist attacks and major disasters.

The Interim Goal results were intended to be national, not purely federal products, but clearly governmental. However, efforts would be needed by all levels of government and between government and private-sector and nongovernmental organizations to identify threats, determine vulnerabilities, and identify required resources, all part of capabilities-based planning and operations.

IMPLEMENTING THE PREPAREDNESS GOAL AND FURTHER GOAL UPDATES

With the issuance of the Interim Goal, implementing guidance took center stage. Such guidance would solidify the use of capabilities-based planning and related tools. Initial guidance was included in the fiscal year 2005 Homeland Security Grant Program Guidance (Department of Homeland Security 2005b). In April 2005, the Department of Homeland Security (2005c) issued a companion document to the Interim Goal—the *National Preparedness Guidance*. This document provided a more detailed explanation of the content and use of capabilities-based planning supporting achievement of the interim goal, including the national planning scenarios, the universal task list, and the target capabilities list. It also expanded on the national priorities, standards and strategies for preparedness assessments of capabilities, and included a timeline for HSPD-8 implementation. Hurricane Katrina exposed a number of preparedness gaps, so Subtitle C of the Post-Katrina Emergency Reform Act of 2006 (P.L. 109-295) continued the call for immediate implementation of the HSPD-8 requirements, adding to the institutionalization of capabilities development because of legislative mandates.

Fiscal year 2006 appropriations legislation (P.L. 109-90) called for the Department of Homeland Security to issue a final national preparedness goal by the end of December 2005. That month, the Department of Homeland Security (2005d) issued a new draft of the *National Preparedness Goal*. This draft Goal presented the achievement of capabilities as the central feature in the road from prevention to recovery from domestic incidents. The draft included expanded attention on minimizing the impacts of major events, such as those experienced during the major hurricanes of 2005. DHS defined the goal as "to achieve and sustain risk-based target levels of capability to prevent, protect against, respond to, and recover from major events, and to minimize their impact on lives, property, and the economy, through systematic and prioritized efforts by federal, state, local, and tribal entities, their private and nongovernmental partners, and the general public" (p. 1). As was the case with the use of target levels of capability in the definition of the goal, the definition of preparedness was stated as "the range of deliberate, critical tasks and activities necessary to build, sustain, and improve the operational capability to prevent, protect against, respond to, and recover from domestic incidents" (p. A-2). It called again for the collective efforts at all levels of government and between government and private-sector and nongovernmental organizations.

The December 2005 draft Goal further delved into the specifics of preparedness. Operationally, it meant establishing guidelines, protocols, and standards for planning, training and exercises, personnel qualification and certification, equipment certification, and publication management. As was the case with earlier documents, the draft Goal emphasized major events such as terrorist attacks, major disasters, and other emergencies that required coordinated action by multiple levels of government. Government entities in turn were responsible for leading and prioritizing preparedness efforts within their jurisdictions and involving private-sector, nongovernment organizations, and citizens as appropriate. The draft Goal reiterated previous policy and guidance that the target capabilities list would be the primary source of readiness metrics. Standards to assess national preparedness collectively would be found in the goal and the capabilities-based planning tools, such as the national planning scenarios and the target capabilities list.

In September 2007, the Department of Homeland Security updated the national preparedness goal and its guidance in the *National Preparedness Guidelines*. DHS stated that the publication of the Guidelines actually finalized the national goal and its related preparedness tools. As was the case with earlier preparedness policy, the new Guidelines retained a capabilities-based approach to organize and synchronize national efforts in and investments for prevention, protection, response, and recovery. The Guidelines also incorporated lessons learned from

Hurricane Katrina and a 2006 review of states' and major cities' emergency operations and evacuation plans. Readiness metrics remained a feature of the national goal, although specific metrics and standards remained under development.

The Guidelines contained four critical elements. One was the national preparedness vision, which the Guidelines called a concise statement of the core preparedness goal for the nation: "a nation prepared with coordinated capabilities to prevent, protect against, respond to, and recover from all hazards in a way that balances risk with resources and need" (p. 1). Other elements were the national planning scenarios; the universal task list of some 1,600 unique tasks to prevent, protect against, respond to, and recover from the major events represented by the national planning scenarios; and the target capabilities list containing 37 specific capabilities that communities, the private sector, and the levels of government should collectively have for effective disaster response.

A NEW NATIONAL STRATEGY FOR HOMELAND SECURITY

President Bush's July 2002 national homeland security strategy heavily emphasized the justification for a new federal department for homeland security. In the following five years, the Administration and Congress clarified the scope, mission areas, and responsibilities for homeland security. In October 2007, the Homeland Security Council issued a new *National Strategy for Homeland Security* that reflected the Guidelines. While the first strategy identified terrorism as the central threat, the 2007 Strategy added catastrophic natural disasters and accidents. The rationale was that the country would be more vulnerable to a terrorist attack during the time of a catastrophe.

Consistent with earlier policy documents, the Strategy presented the bedrock principle of a culture of preparedness and partnership that would share responsibility for homeland security across the entire nation—local, tribal, state, and federal governments, faith-based and community organizations, and businesses. Further, its four objectives remained consistent with earlier policies: 1) prevent and disrupt terrorist attacks; 2) protect the American people, critical infrastructure, and key resources; 3) respond to and recover from incidents that do occur; and, 4) continue to strengthen the foundation to ensure long-term success. The fourth objective was targeted directly at homeland security management.

The Strategy presented clear expectations reinforced with capabilities, management, and stakeholders. For example, it included actions such as preventing violent Islamic extremist radicalization in the United States and deterring state sponsors of terrorism, terrorist groups, and other non-state actors who support or facilitate terrorism. Better homeland security management called for strengthening and clarifying roles and responsibilities for response, strengthening doctrines to guide the national response, and a joint planning process to improve response capabilities. The Strategy consistently stated the importance of capabilities to anticipate and handle incidents and the need to create and institutionalize a comprehensive homeland security management system incorporating all stakeholders.

The new Strategy directly discussed the establishment and institutionalization of a comprehensive Homeland Security Management System that would build on the planning and operations detailed in the National Preparedness Guidelines. The System was to have activity in the four phases of 1) guidance (presidential directives and other key policies), 2) planning (family of strategic, operational and tactical plans), 3) execution of operational and tactical level plans, and 4) assessment and evaluation of both operations and exercises.

THE STRATEGIC POSITION DOCUMENTS: THE REFINEMENT YEARS

The change of administrations after the 2008 national election marked a considerable refinement of homeland security policies and strategies. Early in the Obama Administration, the Department of Homeland Security conducted and responded to statutory requirements for a quadrennial review, similar to the statutory requirements for national defense. A fundamental change was the expansion of national security—traditionally focused on international affairs—to encompass homeland security and its domestic emphasis. This was a departure from the previous separation of homeland security and national security into two separate policy arenas. In addition, the objectives of homeland security retained the prominence of the preparedness cycle from prevention to recovery (and resiliency), but added mitigation as another fundamental element.

The expected security outcome was clearer—realizing overall national interests and way of life. The direction also spoke of greatest risk and called for maximum capacity for a catastrophic event—a meta-event—not individual scenarios. Target capabilities gave way to core capabilities across the whole homeland security community. This apparently signaled the end of prescriptive, all-encompassing federal definitions and requirements for capabilities to accomplish specific tasks. The practical result in the Strategy was the massive streamlining of the earlier voluminous universal task list and target capabilities list (based on national planning scenarios) with which state and local governments had to contend to secure federal funding.

THE QUADRENNIAL REVIEW AND NEW STRATEGY

In February 2010, the Department of Homeland Security released the *Quadrennial Homeland Security Review Report: A Strategic Framework for a Secure Homeland.* The Report was the response to the quadrennial homeland security review (QHSR) mandated by the Implementing Recommendations of the 9/11 Commission Act of 2007 (P.L. 110-53). The legislation required that the QHSR outline a homeland security strategy and priorities for the entire homeland security enterprise (federal, state, local, tribal, and territorial governments, nongovernmental organizations, the private sector, communities, families, and individuals). As was the case with earlier policies, the national effort in the Report called for collective efforts and shared responsibilities to build and sustain critical homeland security capabilities. The homeland security vision was "a homeland that is safe, secure, and resilient against terrorism and other hazards where American interests, aspirations, and way of life can thrive" (p. 4).

The Report placed homeland security as an essential element of the nation's security, and thus was made a part of the broader national security. The Report observed that no longer could the four key activities of prevention, protection, response, and recovery, targeted primarily at terrorism, be sufficient for security. Security was to protect the United States and its people, vital interests, and way of life. Further, resilience was necessary for rapid recovery, as was engagement with the rest of the world through exchanges such as trade and travel.

The grave security environment identified in the Report clearly supported a broader security stance. It was expected that violent extremist groups would use terrorism to attack United States targets; social and/or political instability would continue; health threats would be more difficult to prevent; technological developments and cyber threats would pose challenges; climate change would increase weather-related hazards; multiple simultaneous crises were likely;

and complacency would be a danger as major crises receded from memory.

In May 2010, President Obama released a new *National Security Strategy* that reflected the homeland security policies and concepts identified in the Report. The Strategy noted that the nation should no longer make traditional distinctions between homeland and national security. National security, such as prevention of terrorist attacks, it said, required full coordination of actions taken abroad with the actions and precautions taken domestically. A more secure and resilient nation and maintaining the open flows of goods and people were central to national security. The merging of homeland security with national security was consistent with the approach taken by a number of other countries (Caudle 2009).

The Strategy reaffirmed the "whole of government" approach to strengthening national capacity, that retained the notions of a homeland security enterprise and a culture of preparedness. The homeland security section of the national strategy document called for shared efforts to meet a number of security goals reflective of current and emerging threats and the importance of resiliency. These goals were to identify and interdict threats; deny hostile actors the ability to operate within the borders; maintain effective control of physical borders; safeguard lawful trade and travel into and out of the United States; disrupt and dismantle transnational terrorist and criminal organizations; and ensure national resilience in the face of the threat and hazards.

RESTATEMENT AND REVITALIZATION OF THE PRESIDENTIAL NATIONAL PREPAREDNESS DIRECTIVE, GOAL, AND SYSTEM

The quadrennial homeland security review, the subsequent report, and the new national security strategy set the stage for both a restatement and revitalization of the presidential direction for preparedness. President Obama's March 2011 *Presidential Policy Directive 8 National Preparedness* (PPD-8) replaced the 2003 HSPD-8 issued by President Bush. The new directive reaffirmed past policies and direction, calling for the development of 1) a national preparedness goal identifying the core capabilities necessary for preparedness, and 2) a national preparedness system guiding activities enabling the nation to achieve the goal. PPD-8 described security as the protection of the nation and its people, vital interests, and way of life. Building capabilities remained the primary means of achieving security. As was the case with HSPD-8, the national preparedness system was to provide an all-of-nation approach to build and sustain a cycle of preparedness activities with guidance for planning, organization, equipment, training, and exercises. In addition, the system would include an approach with a consistent methodology to assess national preparedness by measuring operational readiness of national capabilities against target capability levels identified in the national preparedness goal.

However, PPD-8 revitalized the policies and direction in a number of ways that built on the existing homeland security foundation but set in motion new emphases and significant changes. First, mitigation was added to the purposes in the national preparedness goal. National preparedness was defined as actions taken to plan, organize, equip, train, and exercise to build and sustain the capabilities necessary to prevent, protect against, mitigate the effects of, respond to, and recover from the threats posing the greatest risk to the nation's security. Mitigation was one component that President Bush (2002a) had earlier included as part of an all-hazards emergency management program.

Second, PPD-8 explicitly defined protection, mitigation, response, recovery, and resiliency in the directive itself and provided details on specific, core capabilities. Prevention capabilities were those necessary to avoid, prevent, or stop a threatened or actual act of imminent terrorism. Capabilities included information sharing and warning, domestic counterterrorism, and preventing the acquisition or use of weapons of mass destruction. The other objectives or mission areas were designed for all-hazards. Protection capabilities were those securing the homeland against acts of terrorism and man-made or natural disasters, such as critical infrastructure protection and border security. Mitigation capabilities were those lessening the impact of disasters and thus reducing loss of life and property, such as community-wide risk reduction projects. Response capabilities were those saving lives, protecting property and the environment, and meeting basic human needs after an incident has occurred. Recovery capabilities were those assisting communities affected by an incident to recover effectively. Although not mentioned as a separate goal mission area, the directive cited resilience capabilities appropriate across the other five mission areas: the ability to adapt to changing conditions, and withstand and rapidly recover from disruption due to emergencies.

Third, PPD-8 required that the new national preparedness goal address specific threats and vulnerabilities, overtly reducing reliance on the national planning scenarios as a yardstick for capabilities. The goal also was to define the core capabilities necessary to prepare for incidents posing the greatest risk to the nation's security. This made concrete a new policy emphasis on maximum capacity for any major disaster or catastrophe.

Fourth, the directive required a new piece to the national preparedness system—system planning frameworks for each of the five preparedness objectives from prevention to recovery. Each planning framework would have a basic plan for all-hazards with roles and responsibilities at the federal level, but annexes would address unique requirements for particular threats or scenarios. In contrast, HSPD-8 had directed only a National Response Plan.

Finally, the directive required what was called a campaign to build and sustain preparedness. This campaign was expected to build a structure that would integrate new and existing community-based, nonprofit, and private sector preparedness programs, research and development activities, and preparedness assistance.

In May 2011, the Administration took another step to facilitate realization of the directive. The Department of Homeland Security (2011a) issued the *Implementation Plan for Presidential Policy Directive 8: National Preparedness*. This further explained the rationale for the national preparedness goal, such as observing that the goal would aid in developing collaborative thinking about strategic needs, and ensure that all levels of government have a common understanding and awareness of threats and hazards and their risk. The implementation plan explained that the forthcoming national preparedness system would provide an all-of-nation and whole community approach, including civic groups and businesses. The Department of Homeland Security would perform a strategic, national-level risk assessment applicable to national, regional, and local levels.

The assessment would lead to identification of where core capabilities should be placed and their associated performance objectives—all hazards and the maximum preparedness capacity required for a catastrophic event. A major departure from earlier homeland security policy was developing whole-of-community or whole community core capabilities for such a catastrophe, not just the constricted threat and hazard scenarios described in the earlier national planning scenarios. In June 2011, FEMA administrator Craig Fugate described the change in approach as planning for a "meta-scenario" (or maximum of maximums) disaster. This is a worst-case scenario that challenges preparedness and overwhelms the response capabilities of every level of government.

The implementation plan also emphasized that evaluating preparedness for all hazards remained a priority. A national preparedness report (required by legislation) was to describe the nation's level of preparedness in developing and maintaining the performance objectives necessary for core capabilities.

THE NEW NATIONAL PREPAREDNESS GOAL AND SYSTEM

In September 2011, the Department of Homeland Security (2011b) issued the *National Preparedness Goal First Edition* in compliance with PPD-8. Success was defined as "a secure and resilient nation with the capabilities required across the whole community to prevent, protect against, mitigate, respond to, and recover from the threats and hazards that pose the greatest risk" (p. 1). The Goal objectives, coverage across the entire community, and greatest risk restated the intent of PPD-8. Achievement of the goal called for core capabilities (p. 1):

- Preventing avoiding, or stopping a threatened or actual act of terrorism.
- Protecting citizens, residents, visitors, and assets against the greatest threats and hazards in a manner that allows our interests, aspirations, and way of life to thrive.
- Mitigating the loss of life and property by lessening the impact of future disasters.
- Responding quickly to save lives, protect property and the environment, and meet basic human needs in the aftermath of a catastrophic incident.
- Recovering through a focus on the timely restoration, strengthening, and revitalization of infrastructure, housing, and a sustainable economy, as well as the health, social, cultural, historic, and environmental fabric of communities affected by a catastrophic incident.

The document made clear that these core capabilities presented an evolution from the target capabilities list developed in response to

HSPD-8. Not only do the core capabilities now include mitigation, they also better define expectations for prevention and protection capabilities. The core capability targets would be the performance thresholds for each core capability and the basis to develop performance measures to evaluate progress in meeting the targets. As was the case with earlier Administration documents, it was expected that meeting the capability targets required the effective actions of the entire homeland community on a national scale. A strategic national risk assessment, the Goal stated, confirmed the necessity for an all-hazards, capability-based approach to preparedness planning.

The Department of Homeland Security (2011d) made available a December 2011 unclassified Strategic National Risk Assessment that grouped threats and hazards into national-level events that could test the nation's preparedness. These included natural, technological/accidental, and adversarial/human caused threat and hazard groups:

- Natural

  Animal disease outbreak; earthquake; flood; human pandemic outbreak; hurricane; space weather; tsunami; volcanic eruption; wildfire

- Technological or Accidental

  Biological food contamination; chemical substance spill or release; dam failure; radiological substance release

- Adversarial or Human-Caused

  Aircraft as a weapon; armed assault; biological terrorism attack (non-food); chemical/biological food contamination terrorism attack; chemical terrorism attack (non-food); cyber attack against data; cyber attack against physical infrastructure; explosives terrorism attack; nuclear terrorism attack; radiological terrorism attack

These were the specific event hazards and attacks included in the Goal. The hazards listed in the Goal did not address emerging or longer-term threats such as climate change identified in documents such as the Quadrennial Homeland Security Review Report. This was purposeful. The unclassified Strategic National Risk Assessment said it evaluated the risk from known threats and hazards. Only those events, it noted, that had a distinct beginning and end and clearly linked to homeland security missions were included. Thus political, economic, environmental, and societal trends possibly contributing to a risk environment but not national events for homeland security were excluded from the assessment, although they will be important for future assessments. Non-national-level threats, such as droughts and heat waves, could pose risk to jurisdictions and thus should be considered in their preparedness planning.

The new Goal included detailed tables with core capabilities for prevention through recovery (called mission areas), as well as their preliminary targets. The prevention mission area capabilities for example, included planning, public information and warning, operational coordination, forensics and attribution, intelligence and information sharing, interdiction and disruption, and screening, search, and detection. Each capability was described: for example, interdiction and disruption was defined as to delay, divert, intercept, halt, apprehend, or secure threats and/or hazards. The targets for interdiction and disruption under the prevention mission area were (p. 6):

1. Maximize the ability to interdict specific conveyances, cargo, and persons associated with an imminent terrorist threat or act in the land, air, and maritime domains to prevent entry into the United States or to prevent an incident from occurring in the Nation.

2. Conduct operations to render safe and dispose of CBRNE hazards in multiple locations and in all environments, consistent with established protocols.

3. Prevent terrorism financial/material support from reaching its target, consistent with established protocols.

4. Prevent terrorist acquisition of and the transfer of CBRNE materials, precursors, and related technology, consistent with established protocols.

5. Conduct tactical counterterrorism operations in multiple locations and in all environments, consistent with established protocols.

The description of the core capabilities and their preliminary targets were significantly streamlined from the task and capability lists issued in response to HSPD-8. While still prescriptive, it can be anticipated that the streamlining should create more room for the other members of the homeland security community to craft capabilities responsive to their own jurisdiction, regional considerations, and national interest.

In November 2011, the Department of Homeland Security (2011c) released a six-page description of the *National Preparedness System.* It presented its own mission area components. These included 1) identifying and assessing risk, 2) estimating capability requirements, 3) building and sustaining capabilities, 4) planning to deliver capabilities, 5) validating capabilities, and 6) reviewing and updating. The ongoing maturing and use of the National Incident Management System was expected to ensure a unified approach across all of the System's mission areas.

The presentation of each area was very straightforward and consistent with a traditional planning approach. As an example, to identify and assess risk, the System document stated that the Strategic National Risk Assessment would analyze the greatest risks to the Nation. The Threat and Hazard Identification and Risk Assessment guidance currently under development would provide a common, consistent approach for identifying and assessing risks and associated impacts. For the second component of estimating capability requirements, it was expected that the results from a risk assessment would define desired outcomes for each area of capabilities, e.g., prevention, and thus the estimate of the required types and levels of capability. These would be compared with the current capability levels and decisions made regarding changes needed; target levels for capabilities then would be set. Capabilities would be put in place, monitored and assessed, and updated as warranted.

The document stated measuring progress toward achieving the National Preparedness Goal could be done through tools such as exercises, remedial action management programs, and assessments. The National Exercise Program was noted as the principal exercise mechanism to measure readiness, supplemented by exercises performed by individual organizations. Training and performance during actual events would also test and validate achievement of desired capabilities. Ongoing sharing of lessons learned and monitoring would also occur through a remedial action management program and a comprehensive assessment system of the whole community. A National Preparedness Report is due in November 2012.

In March 2012, FEMA released working drafts of the revised National Response Framework, the newly developed Prevention, Protection, and Mitigation Frameworks, and an initial draft of an interagency operational plan to implement the already issued National Disaster Recovery Framework. These detailed documents, for example, describe roles and responsibilities, integration of actions across the whole community, planning assumptions, and guidance on developing or revising state, local, and private sector plans. The drafts discuss critical tasks to develop core capabilities. For example, the interdiction and disruption capability under the prevention area calls for tasks such as disrupting terrorist travel, conducting tactical counterterrorism operations, and enhancing the visible presence of law enforcement (p. 14).

CURRENT THEMES AND ADDITIONAL CHALLENGES

Up to this point, this chapter has chronicled the major changes in national preparedness policy, strategy, and guidance since the September 2001 terrorist attacks. It has highlighted a number of major themes in this evolution:

- Homeland security placed within national security.
- All-hazards became the centerpiece for preparedness for threats, including terrorism.
- Preparedness defined with the full coverage of objectives: prevention, protection, mitigation, response, and recovery, with response and recovery no longer the centerpieces of preparedness.
- The whole homeland security community, in addition to the federal government, was given responsibility to protect national interests and way of life.
- Maximum capacity for a catastrophic event—a meta-event— and not individual scenarios stated as the benchmark for preparedness.
- Known threats and hazards with a distinct beginning and end identified as national-level for homeland security missions.
- Core capabilities and targets for a national effort updated prescriptive, detailed individual tasks and target capabilities.
- A homeland security management system, expected to manage homeland security and crafted with specific components, performance expectations, and assessment and adjustment requirements.
- Assessment of preparedness progress expected primarily through exercises and actual events.

The national homeland security strategies, and subsequent broadened national security strategy, set the homeland security roadmap. Other national strategies have emerged over time to guide components of homeland security. For example, the *National Strategy for Counterterrorism* presented the approach to disrupt, dismantle, and eventually defeat al-Qa'ida and its affiliates and adherents. Other national strategies cover aviation security, maritime security, pandemic influenza, biological threats, cyber-security, national infrastructure protection, homeland defense and civil support, and transnational organized crime, among others.

Both Republican and Democratic administrations and Congress have aggressively designed and implemented policies for preparedness. The National Preparedness Goal and other documents are robust in their description of Goal objectives and missions, core capabilities, and the roles and responsibilities of the whole homeland security community. Despite the uncertainty of government funding, it is reasonable to assume that preparedness will retain its importance, although not perhaps to the hoped-for levels of national capabilities for a meta-scenario.

That said, preparedness policy and operations could face challenges in at least two main areas. One is leadership and management of preparedness expectations. Another is performance assessment.

Leadership and Management of Preparedness Expectations

Leadership and management of preparedness expectations, of course, are major parts in the national direction for homeland security. However, there are three leadership and management issues that may raise concerns. One is integrating capabilities-based implementation and management system standards for the whole homeland security community. Another is recognizing the conflict of federal control over the other levels of government composing part of the homeland security community. The final issue is addressing threats that are slower in their emergence as a direct threat to national security, such as economic instability and climate change.

Integrating Capabilities Requirements and Management System Standards

The national preparedness goal and supporting documents, including legislation, have identified building and sustaining specific capabilities for the entire homeland security community. Federal, state, and local governments, nongovernmental organizations, private organizations, and the general public comprise that community. National preparedness comes from capabilities across the whole community.

However, the capabilities approach is not solely what federal legislation and federal rules have practically advocated as preparedness standards for the public sector and state and local entities. There are two national voluntary programs where management system preparedness standards are used as the preparedness requirements, not core capabilities (Caudle 2011a). Legislation implementing many of the 9/11 Commission's recommendations (Section 524 of the August 2007 P.L. 110-53) called for the Department of Homeland Security to create a voluntary private sector preparedness program and standards, including accreditation and certification processes. In June 2010, DHS implemented the legislation through the Private Sector Preparedness Accreditation and Certification Program (PSPrep). Three management system standards were approved for adoption in the program: ASIS SPC.1-2009 *Organizational Resilience: Security Preparedness, and Continuity Management System*; British Standard 25999-2:2007 *Business Continuity Management*; and National Fire Protection Association 1600: 2007/2010 *Standard on Disaster/Emergency Management and Business Continuity Programs*. At the end of September 2010, DHS announced a certification program tailored to the needs of small business.

The other national effort using management system standards is the current Emergency Management Accreditation Program (EMAP), a voluntary review process for state and local emergency management programs. EMAP certifies government programs against standards directly based on NFPA 1600. State and local entities can use federal homeland security grant funding to pay for EMAP activities. At one time, FEMA used the EMAP standards to administer its National Emergency Baseline Capability Assurance Program.

To date, the Department of Homeland Security has not addressed how the management system standard voluntary program is to be reconciled, if at all, with building and sustaining core capabilities. At a minimum metrics identified as part of implementing the National Preparedness Goal should be compared to those in PSPrep and the EMAP standards. If there truly is to be a whole community effort, it would seem to be a necessary condition to have a compatible approach for all the entities involved.

Conflict in Federal Control Over Other Governmental Levels

There likely will be a continual sorting out of the roles and responsibilities of community actors to meet the national homeland security interest. However, a major concern is the apparent conflict between the stated importance and needed leadership of the whole homeland security community, and the actual federal control over other levels of government. An article (Caudle 2011b) discussing federalism and homeland security noted that the September 2001 terrorist attacks created a high demand for national homeland security policy and action. The many federal homeland security directives, mandates, and grant compliance requirements have framed and centralized control of the national homeland security agenda, even if there was collaboration in the development with selected state and local officials. Hurricane Katrina presented another opportunity for an expanded federal government role in disasters because of the failures of individual agencies and weak intergovernmental collaboration.

Both the terrorist attacks and natural disasters have made it difficult to find the appropriate balance between the national interest and its objectives and the flexibility and local discretion under federalism. The homeland security links between the broadened national security strategy and state and local support depend on state and local implementation of national direction. At present, the National Preparedness Goal and its supporting documents have limited language about explicit state and local flexibility and the meeting of specific and direct state and local interests. The streamlining of lists of core capabilities and their preliminary targets is encouraging, but federal approval of state and local implementation will be the proof whether state and local jurisdictions can craft capabilities responsive to their needs as well as what is seen as the national interest. This will be a continuing concern as budgets face fiscal austerity decisions. It is expected that there will be funding constraints at all levels of government for building and sustaining preparedness capabilities.

Address Slowly Emerging Threats

A leadership and management challenge is addressing threats that are more slowly emerging as a direct threat to national security in the Goal and supporting documents. As mentioned earlier, the hazards listed in the National Preparedness Goal reference well-known, specific event hazards and attacks determined by the Strategic National Risk Assessment. Other political, economic, environmental, and societal trends that might impact the national risk environment were not addressed at this time. Non-national level threats such as droughts should be considered in jurisdictional preparedness planning.

However, the National Security Strategy and Quadrennial Homeland Security Review Report explicitly define a strategic threat environment and global trends that appear to have national preparedness implications, although they are not imminent. For example, these include the creeping, gradual emergencies and disasters that result from dependence upon fossil fuels, global climate change, fragile and failing states, global illicit trafficking and related transnational crime, and economic and financial instability.

In other countries, the security environment includes these longer-term threats. However, their national security strategies (including those covering homeland security or domestic security) incorporate these threats into the strategies, follow-on policy, and operational requirements and guidance (Caudle 2009). For example, climate change or environmental change pose dangers that may occur on a national or global scale, such as more frequent heat waves, droughts, flooding, reduced crop yields, and wildfires (Hough 2008). The Goal and supporting documents narrowly target building and sustaining capabilities for the near-term threat of a meta-scenario. It is not clear how these capabilities will prepare the country for the challenges of the longer-term threats.

Performance Assessment

As mentioned at the beginning of this chapter, David Walker asked what approach would assess the effectiveness of implementation to address threats. Certainly performance assessment is another challenge for near-term preparedness policy and operations. Concerns include assessing and reporting on preparedness levels, and determining the cost effectiveness of past and expected preparedness efforts.

Assessing National Preparedness Levels

From HSPD-8 to the National Preparedness System description, perhaps the weakest area of policy and operational implementation is assessing national preparedness levels. Presidential documents and legislation such as the Post Katrina Emergency Reform Act have repeatedly called for specific goals, performance targets, performance measures, and valid reporting of actual preparedness levels. Those responsible for homeland security would utilize a consistent methodology, measuring current capabilities against target (now core) capabilities, and making adjustments as necessary.

After almost a decade, the reality is that assessing preparedness in and of itself remains very elusive. Summing the difficulties, William O. Jenkins of the U.S. Government Accountability Office (2010) found that evaluation efforts which collected data on national preparedness capabilities faced limitations such as data reliability and the lack of standardized data collection. Data was self-reported and was not readily comparable to other states' data because of interpretations by each reporting organization. FEMA had centered its national preparedness assessment efforts on its comprehensive assessment system and streamlining of data-reporting requirements. However, it experienced problems in completing the system and had not developed national preparedness capability requirements based on established metrics. FEMA thus could not report to Congress on preparedness levels, a legislative requirement. Even though the new National Preparedness Goal requires that preparedness levels be assessed, the past history of the Department of Homeland Security of failing to do so, despite numerous mandates, makes it unlikely.

The Cost-Effectiveness of the Capabilities Policy Choice

David Walker also asked what federal tools and programs were providing the most cost-effective approaches for homeland security. What has been lost in the ongoing evolution and rapid issuance of new or updated preparedness policies, strategies, and guidance, and at their core, the reliance on capabilities development, is their cost-effectiveness.

As noted earlier, the first National Strategy for Homeland Security contained the principle that the benefits of mitigating risk must be balanced against economic costs and infringements on individual liberty. HSPD-8 required that a national preparedness goal define measurable readiness (preparedness) priorities and targets, but also contained a caveat about the resource investments. PPD-8 called for actions to achieve a preparedness approach to optimize the use of available resources. However, these documents are amazingly silent about the cost-effectiveness policy choice of preparedness capabilities.

Simply put, cost-effectiveness analysis compares different policy alternatives that can produce wanted benefits in terms of their relative costs. This analytical approach measures costs in monetary values, and effectiveness is measured with valued effects, such as units of goods or services (see, for example, Dunn 2012, Kraft and Furlong 2010, and Weimer and Vining 2011). It is particularly useful for policies or programs where objectives cannot be easily measured—certainly the case for homeland security.

The Bush and Obama Administrations did not publicly issue any cost-effectiveness analysis to justify the selection of capabilities as the central feature of preparedness. The Department of Homeland Security adopted the capabilities approach from the Department of Defense; the approach was used by the defense community of many countries (Caudle 2005). Apparently, federal officials believed that developing capabilities was the best route towards achieving preparedness, but its cost-effectiveness was not made explicit—if, in fact, it was even considered.

In the interim, billions have been spent on preparedness. The Congressional Research Service cites a source which states that the U.S. government has spent $636 billion, adjusted for inflation, on homeland security since the September 2001 attacks (Painter 2011). Using a risk-based methodology, the Department of Homeland Security has provided billions in preparedness grants intended to aid states, urban areas, tribal governments, and nonprofit organizations strengthen their capabilities for threats associated with potential terrorist attacks and other hazards. Over time, the Department has attempted to link dollars spent with the development of capabilities (see, for example, the report of the Local, State, Tribal, and Federal Preparedness Task Force 2010). Left unanswered is the question: What preparedness did the dollars buy? With federal funding constraints for the foreseeable future, this is an opportune time to consider if other policy options might be more cost effective, or, at a minimum, justify the policy of capabilities development.

CONCLUSION

The September 2010 Local, State, Tribal, and Federal Preparedness Task Force report commissioned by Congress underscored the importance of preparedness as a major policy agenda, but also warned of the central difficulty. The Task Force determined, "The basic tenets of preparedness … are relatively uncontroversial within both the emergency management discipline and homeland security policy. What has changed is the realization that preparedness can be only as effective as the goals and priorities for readiness. The challenge is determining what our readiness goals and priorities should be, from which preparedness activities are subsequently derived and then measured against (p. 6).

Over the past decade, the federal government has done much to determine national preparedness or readiness goals and priorities. Recalling Walker's questions at the beginning of this chapter, a national vision and objectives are in place, intended to make the homeland more secure. Leadership is to come from the entire homeland security community, but federal direction may limit the flexibility of other members of the community. Risk management is an integral part of the national preparedness goal. Federal tools and programs are rooted in preparedness capabilities, but it is not clear if a capabilities approach is the most effective or efficient; the measurement of those capabilities remains a work in progress.

In the next decade of homeland security as part of national security, the threat environment—the security environment—is somewhat known, but also uncertain. New threats may emerge and others recede. The larger social and economic environment, such as fiscal austerity and demographic changes, create instability in what can, and should be done. Preparedness investments by all members of the homeland security community should be done in ways that emphasize clarity, sustainability, integration, balance, and accountability. Those ways, should, as PPD-8 states, achieve security in protecting the nation and its people, vital interests, and way of life.

REFERENCES

Bush, George W. 2002a. *Securing the Homeland: Strengthening the Nation*. Washington, DC: The White House (June 17, 2002).

———. 2002b. *The Department of Homeland Security*. Washington, DC: The White House (June 2002).

———. 2003a. *Homeland Security Presidential Directive/HSPD-5 Management of Domestic Incidents*. Washington, DC: The White House (February 28, 2003).

———. 2003b. *Homeland Security Presidential Directive/HSPD-8 National Preparedness*. Washington, DC: The White House (December 17, 2003).

Caudle, Sharon L. 2005. "Homeland Security Capabilities-based Planning: Lessons from the Defense Community." *Homeland Security Affairs* I, no. 2 (Fall 2005). http://www.hsaj.org/?article=1.2.2 (accessed January 4, 2012).

———. 2009. "National Security Strategies: Security from What, for Whom, and by What Means." *Journal of Homeland Security and Emergency Management* 6, no. 1 (Article 22). http://www.bepress.com/jhsem/vol6/iss1/22 (accessed January 4, 2012).

———. 2011a. "National Preparedness Requirements: Harnessing Management System Standards." *Homeland Security Affairs* 7, no. 14 (June). http://www.hsaj.org/?article=7.1.14 (accessed January 4, 2012).

————. 2011b. "Centralization and Decentralization of Policy: The National Interest of Homeland Security." *Journal of Homeland Security and Emergency Management* 8, no. 1 (Article 56). http://www.bepress.com/jhsem/vol8/iss1/56 (accessed January 4, 2012).

Dunn, William N. 2012. *Public Policy Analysis.* 5th ed. Boston: Pearson.

Fugate, Craig. 2011. *Evolution of Emergency Management and Communication.* Statement before the U.S. Senate Committee on Appropriations, Subcommittee on Homeland Security. Washington, DC: FEMA, Department of Homeland Security (June 8, 2011).

Homeland Security Council. 2004. *National Planning Scenarios.* Washington, DC: The White House.

————. 2007. *National Strategy for Homeland Security.* Washington, DC: The White House (October 2007).

Kraft, Michael E., and Scott R. Furlong. 2010. *Public Policy: Politics, Analysis, and Alternatives.* 3rd ed. Washington, DC: CQ Press.

Hough, Peter. 2008. *Understanding Global Security.* 2nd ed. London: Routledge.

Jenkins, William O. 2010. *FEMA Has Made Limited Progress in Efforts to Develop and Implement a System to Assess National Preparedness Capabilities.* Letter to Subcommittee on Homeland Security Committee on Appropriations. Washington, DC: U.S. Government Accountability Office (October 29, 2010).

Local, State, Tribal, and Federal Preparedness Task Force. 2010. *Perspective on Preparedness: Taking Stock Since 9/11,* Report to Congress. Washington, DC: Local, State, Tribal, and Federal Preparedness Task Force (September 2010).

Obama, Barack. 2010. *National Security Strategy.* Washington, DC: The White House (May 2010).

————. 2011a. *Presidential Policy Directive/PPD–8 National Preparedness.* Washington, DC: The White House (March 30, 2011).

————. 2011b. *National Strategy for Counterterrorism.* Washington, DC: The White House (June 2011).

Office of Homeland Security. 2002. *National Strategy for Homeland Security.* Washington, DC: The White House (July 2002).

Painter, William L. 2011. *Issues in Homeland Security Policy for the 112th Congress.* R42025. Washington, DC: Congressional Research Service (September 22, 2011).

U.S. Department of Homeland Security. 2005a. *Interim National Preparedness Goal.* Washington, DC: Department of Homeland Security (March 31, 2005).

————. 2005b. *Fiscal Year 2005 Homeland Security Grant Program, Program Guidelines, and Application Kit.* Washington, DC: Department of Homeland Security.

————. 2005c. *National Preparedness Guidance.* Washington, DC: Department of Homeland Security (April 27, 2005).

————. 2005d. *National Preparedness Goal.* Washington, DC: Department of Homeland Security (draft December 2005).

————. 2007. *National Preparedness Guidelines.* Washington, DC: Department of Homeland Security (September 2007).

————. 2010. *Quadrennial Homeland Security Review Report: A Strategic Framework for a Secure Homeland.* Washington, DC: Department of Homeland Security (February 2010).

————. 2011a. *Implementation Plan for Presidential Policy Directive 8: National Preparedness.* Washington, DC: Department of Homeland Security (May 2011).

————. 2011b. *National Preparedness Goal First Edition.* Washington, DC: Department of Homeland Security (September 2011).

————. 2011c. *National Preparedness System.* Washington, DC: Department of Homeland Security (November 2011).

————. 2011d. *The Strategic National Risk Assessment in Support of PPD 8: A Comprehensive Risk-Based Approach Toward a Secure and Resilient Nation.* Washington, DC: Department of Homeland Security (December 2011).

Walker, David. 2001a. *Homeland Security: A Framework for Addressing the Nation's Efforts.* GAO-01-1158T. Washington, DC: U.S. General Accounting Office (September 21, 2001).

———. 2001b. *Homeland Security: Challenges and Strategies in Addressing Short- and Long-Term National Needs.* GAO-02-160T. Washington, DC: U.S. General Accounting Office (November 7, 2011).

Weimer, David L., and Aidan R. Vining. 2011. *Policy Analysis.* 5th ed. Boston: Longman.

7

PROSECUTING THE FINANCIERS OF TERROR

James Gurulé

Professor of Law, Notre Dame School of Law, Notre Dame University

I. WHY GO AFTER THE MONEY?

Money is the "lifeblood" of terrorist organizations.[1] Money is critical to financing terrorist operations (operational costs) as well as sustaining the terrorist groups' organizational infrastructure (organizational costs).[2] Terrorists cannot pursue sophisticated operations like the 9/11 terror attacks without adequate funding. The 9/11 attacks that resulted in the killing of approximately 3,000 innocent civilians cost as much as $500,000 to stage.[3] Multiple, smaller terrorist attacks may also require significant financial resources. When considered collectively, the operational costs associated with the commission of multiple terrorist attacks may be substantial as well. Prior to the 9/11 attacks, al Qaeda's annual operating budget was estimated at between $30 and $50 million.[4] HAMAS's annual operating budget is even higher and estimated to range between $30 and $90 million.[5] Hizballah's operating budget may be as high as $200 million per year.[6]

At the organizational level, terrorist groups such as al Qaeda, HAMAS, and Hizballah need money to "pay for salaries, recruitment, training camps, a safe haven, vehicles, weapons, ammunition, explosives and precursor chemicals for bombs, communications, travel, false identification documents, safe houses, bribing government officials, buying the support of other terrorist groups, and printing and distributing propaganda materials, including producing audio and video recordings and developing terrorist training manuals."[7] Financial inducements are often used to recruit suicide bombers. Terrorist recruits are promised that if they sacrifice their life in a suicide attack, their families will receive a monthly stipend to compensate them for their loss.[8] It is estimated that HAMAS distributes $2–3 million in monthly payments to the surviving family members of suicide bombers.[9]

Terrorists need money to finance training camps. Between 1996 and 2000, as many as 20,000 al Qaeda terrorists were trained in dozens of training camps in Afghanistan.[10] Terrorists are trained on how to construct deadly roadside bombs, as well as how to use automatic weapons, grenade launchers, shoulder-fired missiles, and other military weaponry. Substantial funding is needed to sustain these camps and train new recruits. Money is also needed to bribe government officials to secure a safe haven for terrorists to plan and launch future terrorist attacks. The FINAL REPORT OF THE NATIONAL COMMISSION ON TERRORIST ATTACKS UPON THE UNITED STATES found that Osama bin Laden paid approximately $10–20 million per year to the Taliban in return for providing al Qaeda a safe haven in Afghanistan.[11] Additionally, terrorist organizations such as al Qaeda distribute money to like-minded terrorist groups to leverage their support and purchase their loyalty.[12] Funding is also essential to developing and sustaining al Qaeda's global propaganda campaign. The Internet has become an effective tool for communicating the terrorist message and recruiting terrorists. Terrorist websites deliver a wide range of products and services, including terrorist training manuals and texts, pamphlets, and video and audio recordings that encourage the growth of home-grown terror cells around the world.[13]

Attacking the financial infrastructure of terrorist organizations is fundamentally a preventive strategy.[14] Starving terrorists of funding is critical to prevent terrorist attacks, especially attacks committed on a large scale. However, going after the money is important for other reasons. First, investigating terrorist financial networks may "expose terrorist financing 'money trails' that may generate leads to previously unknown terrorist cells and financiers."[15] Second, disrupting channels of funding may force terrorists to use more risky and less efficient and reliable means to transfer money globally to finance terrorist activities.[16] Third, arresting terrorist financiers and shutting down their front companies and corrupt charities may deter wealthy donors from providing financial assistance to terrorist groups. "Simply stated, depriving [terrorist organizations] of funding is as important as targeting the operational terror cells themselves."[17] However, while shutting down terrorist financial networks is essential to preventing terrorist attacks, the U.S. Department of Justice has a relatively unimpressive record of prosecuting the financiers of terrorism.

II. MATERIAL SUPPORT STATUTES, 18 U.S.C. §§2339A AND 2339B

The "material support" statutes, 18 U.S.C. §§2339A and 2339B, are the principal criminal statutes used to prosecute terrorist financiers.[18] Sections 2339A and 2339B make it a federal crime to provide "material support or resources" to terrorists or designated foreign terrorist organizations (FTOs).[19] In enacting these statutes, Congress recognized that "[c]utting off 'material support or resources' from terrorist organizations deprives them of the means with which to carry out acts of terrorism and potentially leads to their demise."[20] The material support statutes prevent terrorists and terrorist sympathizers from raising money within the United States, or using the United States as a conduit for the receipt of funds collected in other nations.[21]

1. Legislative Intent and Statutory Framework

Section 2339A was enacted as part of the Violent Crime Control and Law Enforcement Act of 1994.[22] The statute makes it a crime to provide "material support or resources" "knowing or intending" that they be used to prepare for or carry out any of the statute's enumerated terrorism-related predicate offenses, such as plotting to kill an officer or employee of the United States (including any member of the uniformed services) while such officer or employee is engaged in the performance of his official duties, in violation of 18 U.S.C. §1114.[23] To convict under §2339A, the Government must prove four elements: "(1) the defendant knowingly, (2) provided 'material support or resources,' (3) knowing or intending that the provision of 'material support or resources' be used in preparation for, or in carrying out (4) one or more of the violent crimes specified in the statute."[24]

Two years later, Congress enacted 18 U.S.C. §2339B as part of the Anti-Terrorism and Effective Death Penalty Act (AEDPA) of 1996.[25] Section 2339B was designed to cut off monetary and other support for terrorist activities by prohibiting persons from knowingly providing "material support or resources" to foreign terrorist organizations.[26] That prohibition is based on a finding by Congress that terrorist organizations "are so tainted by their criminal conduct that any contribution to such an organization facilitates that conduct."[27] Section 2339B was intended to close a loophole left by §2339A. In *Humanitarian Law Project v. Gonzales*, the court examined the legislative history of the statute, stating:

> Congress enacted §2339B in order to close a loophole left by §2339A. Congress, concerned that terrorist organizations would raise funds "under the cloak of a humanitarian or charitable exercise," sought to pass legislation that would "severely restrict the ability of terrorist organizations to raise much needed funds for their terrorist acts within the United States" [citations omitted]. As §2339A was limited to donors intending to further the commission of specific federal offenses, Congress passed §2339B to encompass donors who acted without the intent to further federal crimes.[28]

The court also noted:

> [T]he AEDPA sought to prevent the United States from becoming a base for terrorist fundraising. Congress recognized that terrorist groups are often structured to include political or humanitarian components in addition to terrorist components. Such an organizational structure allows terrorist groups to raise funds under the guise of political or humanitarian causes. Those funds can then be diverted to terrorist activities.[29]

To sustain a conviction under §2339B, the Government must prove that the defendant acted with knowledge that the foreign group has been designated an FTO, or has engaged in or engages in acts of terrorism.[30] Unlike §2339A, §2339B does not require proof that the defendant provided support or resources with the knowledge or intent that such resources be used to commit an act of terrorism.[31] According to one commentator:

> To prove a violation of section 2339B, the defendant must have knowledge that the organization is a designated [FTO] or engages or has engaged in acts of terrorism. The Government is not required to prove that the defendant intended to further the illegal aims of the FTO by the provision of material support or resources. Under §2339B, the donor is criminally liable even if he intended to fund the humanitarian activities of the organization, if he had knowledge that the group had been designated an FTO or engaged or engages in terrorist activities.[32]

The term "material support and resources" is a legal term of art and prohibits the provision of various types of assistance and support to terrorists and foreign terrorist groups. As defined in the statute, the term "material support or resources" means:

> any property, tangible or intangible, or service, including currency or monetary instruments or financial securities, financial services, lodging, training, expert advice or assistance, safehouses, false documentation or identification, communications equipment, facilities, weapons, lethal substances, explosives, personnel (1 or more individuals who may be or include oneself), and transportation, except medicine or religious materials.[33]

Among other forms of material assistance, the statute bans the knowing provision of "currency," "monetary instruments," "financial securities," and "financial services" to a terrorist or designated FTO.[34]

Upon conviction, both §§2339A and 2339B impose a substantial fine or a term of imprisonment of not more than 15 years, or both, and, if the death of any person results, incarceration for any term of years or for life.[35] Further, assets involved in violations of the material support statutes are subject to forfeiture under 18 U.S.C. §981.[36]

2. FTO Designation Process

For purposes of §2339B, a "foreign terrorist organization" is "an organization designated as a terrorist organization under section 219 of the Immigration and Nationality Act."[37] Section 219 of the Immigration and Nationality Act, which is codified at 8 U.S.C. §1189, authorizes the Secretary of State to designate a group as a "foreign terrorist organization" if the group satisfies the following criteria:

(A) the organization is a foreign organization;
(B) the organization engages in terrorist activity (as defined in section 1182(a)(3)(B) of this title) or terrorism (as defined in section 2656f(d)(2) of Title 22), or retains the capability and intent to engage in terrorist activity or terrorism; and
(C) the terrorist activity or terrorism of the organization threatens the security of United States nationals or the national security of the United States.[38]

Pursuant to 8 U.S.C. §1189, the Secretary of State has designated 49 groups as FTOs.[39] Those groups include: al Qaeda; al Qaeda in Iraq; al Qaeda in the Islamic Maghreb; Jemaah Islamiya; Lashkar-e Tayyiba;

Army of Islam; HAMAS; and Hizballah.[40] The designation of an organization as an FTO lasts two years.[41] The designation process requires the Secretary of State to compile an "administrative record" and make "findings" based on this record.[42] The FTO designation may be based on "classified information" which is unavailable for review by the designated party.[43] Further, while due process requires that the Secretary of State afford entities under consideration notice that the designation is impending, notice may be delayed until after designation where predesignation notice would jeopardize national security or foreign policy.[44] Seven days before designating an organization as an FTO, the Secretary must submit to key Congressional leaders and committee members a "classified communication" detailing the Secretary's findings.[45] A designation "shall take effect upon publication" in the Federal Register.[46] An FTO designation may be revoked in three ways: "(1) Congress blocks or revokes a designation, 8 U.S.C. §1189(a)(5); (2) the Secretary revokes the designation based on a finding that changed circumstances or national security warrants such a revocation, 8 U.S.C. §1189(a)(6)(A); or (3) the D.C. Circuit sets aside the designation under 8 U.S.C. §1189(c)(3)."[47]

Judicial Review of FTO Designations

The D.C. Circuit Court of Appeals has exclusive jurisdiction to review FTO designations.[48] The court may review the Secretary's findings that the entity is a "foreign" organization and that it engages in "terrorist activity."[49] However, the decision of whether the foreign organization "threatens the national security of United States nationals or the national security of the United States" is a non justiciable question.[50] The D.C. Circuit will set aside an FTO designation only if it finds it to be "(1) arbitrary, capricious, an abuse of discretion, or otherwise not in accordance with the law; (2) contrary to constitutional right, power, privilege, or immunity; (3) in excess of statutory jurisdiction, authority, or limitation, or short of statutory right; (4) lacking substantial support in the administrative record taken as a whole or in classified information submitted to the court; or (5) not in accord with the procedures required by law."[51]

The legal consequences of being designated an FTO are severe. Financial institutions are required to freeze the assets of an FTO located in the United States,[52] and representatives and members of the FTO are prohibited from entering the United States.[53] Finally, a person convicted of knowingly providing "material support or resources" to an FTO is subjected to severe criminal penalties, including a term of imprisonment of not more than 15 years.[54]

Collateral Attack of the FTO Designation

Pursuant to 8 U.S.C. §1189(a)(8), defendants being prosecuted for a violation of 18 U.S.C. §2339B are precluded from challenging the validity of the recipient organization's designation as an FTO during the criminal proceedings.[55] Defendants argue that this prohibition deprives them of their constitutional right to a jury determination of guilt on each element of the charged offense. The courts have consistently rejected defendants' constitutional argument on two grounds. First, the courts hold that defendants lack standing to challenge the FTO designation procedure on behalf of the designated foreign organization.[56] Under the standing doctrine, a litigant must assert his own legal rights and cannot rest his claim on the legal rights of others.[57] Thus, for example, a defendant charged with violating the material support statute lacks standing to challenge the validity of an FTO designation on behalf of al Qaeda, HAMAS, or some other designated FTO.[58]

Second, the relevant element of §2339B is the fact of an organization's designation as an FTO, not the validity of the designation.[59] In *United States v. Afshari*, the Ninth Circuit held that "the element of the crime that the prosecutor must prove in a §2339B case is the predicate fact that a particular organization was designated at the time the material support was given, not whether the government made a correct designation."[60] The *Afshari* court stated:

> The defendants are right that §1189(a)(8) prevents them from contending, in defense of the charges against them under 18 U.S.C. §2339B, that the designated terrorist organization is not really terrorist at all. No doubt Congress was well aware that some might claim that "one man's terrorist is another man's freedom fighter." Congress clearly chose to delegate policymaking authority to the President and Department of State with respect to designation of terrorist organizations, and to keep such policymaking authority out of the hands of United States Attorneys and juries. Under §2339B, if defendants provide material support for an organization that has been designated under §1189, they commit the crime, and it does not matter whether the designation is correct or not.[61]

Thus, because the validity of an FTO designation is not an element of the offense, defendant's inability to challenge the validity of the FTO designation does not deprive him of his constitutional rights.[62]

3. Constitutional Challenges

The Intelligence Reform and Terrorism Prevention Act of 2004 (IRTPA) amended 18 U.S.C. §2339B to clarify the mental state necessary to sustain a violation of the statute, requiring knowledge of the foreign group's designation as an FTO or the group's commission of terrorist acts, not intent to further the terrorist objectives of the FTO.[63] Despite the amendment imposed by the IRTPA, defendants have challenged the constitutionality of the material support statute. In the absence of a specific intent element, defendants argue that §2339B violates the First Amendment right of freedom of association. Defendants contend that §2339B impermissibly criminalizes mere membership in, or association with, a terrorist organization. Defendants also maintain that the material support statute violates freedom of speech guaranteed by the First Amendment. Finally, defendants argue that the statute is unconstitutionally vague and imposes criminal liability in the absence of personal guilt in violation of the Fifth Amendment Due Process Clause.

In *Holder v. Humanitarian Law Project*, the United States Supreme Court rejected similar legal challenges raised by plaintiffs to the constitutionality of the material support statute.[64] In that case, two U.S. citizens and six domestic organizations, including the Humanitarian Law Project, claimed that they wished to provide support for the humanitarian and political activities of the Kurdistan Workers' Party (also known as the Partiya Karkeran Kurdistan or PKK) and the Liberation Tigers of Tamil Eelam (LTTE).[65] However, because the PKK and the LTTE had been designated as FTOs, plaintiffs claimed that they could not do so for fear of prosecution under §2339B.[66]

Unconstitutional Vagueness

Plaintiffs maintained that the material support statute was unconstitutionally vague. The vagueness claims focused on the terms "training," "expert advice or assistance," "personnel," and "service."[67] The term "training" is defined under the statute to mean "instruction or teaching designed to impart a specific skill, as opposed to general knowledge."[68] Further, the term "expert advice or assistance" means "advice or assistance derived from scientific, technical or other specialized knowledge."[69] Plaintiffs wanted to train members of the PKK on the use of humanitarian and international law to peacefully resolve disputes, and teach the PKK members how to petition international bodies such as the United Nations for relief.[70] However, they argued whether their proposed conduct violated the material support statute was unclear.[71]

The Supreme Court held that the terms "expert advice or assistance" and "training" were not unconstitutionally vague as applied to plaintiffs. The Court stated:

> A person of ordinary intelligence would understand that instruction on resolving disputes through international law falls within the statute's definition of "training" because it imparts a "specific skill," not "general knowledge." Plaintiffs' activities also fall comfortably within the scope of "expert advice or assistance": A reasonable person would recognize that teaching the PKK how to petition for humanitarian relief before the United Nations involves advice derived from … "specialized knowledge."[72]

Plaintiffs also maintained that they wanted to engage in "political advocacy" on behalf of the Kurds living in Turkey and the Tamils residing in Sri Lanka.[73] Plaintiffs were unclear whether such conduct violated the material support statute under a theory of providing "personnel." The term "personnel" is defined as knowingly providing a person "to work under the terrorist organization's direction or control or to organize, manage, supervise, or otherwise direct the operation of that organization."[74] Further, the statute explicitly provides that "personnel" does not cover independent advocacy.[75] The Court stated that plaintiffs' proposed political advocacy on behalf of the PKK and LTTE would not be barred under the statute for two reasons. First, plaintiffs would not be working under the PKK's or LTTE's direction and control.[76] Second, the statute does not punish independent advocacy.[77] Thus, the Court held that the term "personnel" is not unconstitutionally vague as applied to plaintiffs' proposed conduct.[78]

The Court rejected plaintiffs' vagueness challenge to the term "service." The statute prohibits proving a service "to a foreign terrorist organization."[79] The Court reasoned that the work "to" indicates a connection between the "service" and the FTO.[80] The Court held that "a person of ordinary intelligence would understand that independently advocating for a cause is different from providing a service to a group that is advocating for that cause."[81] Further, "a person of ordinary intelligence would understand the term 'service' to cover advocacy performed in coordination with, or at the direction of, a foreign terrorist organization."[82] However, how much direction and coordination is necessary for an activity to constitute a "service," the Court stated that adjudication of that issue must await a concrete fact situation.[83]

Freedom of Speech

The Court rejected plaintiffs' claim that the material support statute bans "pure political speech." The Court stated that §2339B does not prohibit independent advocacy of any kind. Plaintiffs "may speak and write freely about the PKK and LTTE, the government of Turkey and Sri Lanka, human rights, and international law."[84] Further, §2339B does not prevent the plaintiffs from becoming members of the PKK and LTTE.[85] Rather, "the statute is carefully drawn to cover only a narrow category of speech to, under the direction of, or in coordination with foreign groups that the speaker knows to be terrorist organizations."[86]

Finally, the Court rejected plaintiffs' claim that when applied to speech, §2339B should be interpreted to require proof that a defendant intended to further an FTO's illegal activities. The Court held that plaintiffs' interpretation of §2339B was inconsistent with the text of the statute, which "knowingly" providing material support with "knowledge" that an organization is a designated organization or engages or has engaged in acts of terrorism.[87] The Court posited: "Congress plainly spoke to the necessary mental state for a violation of §2339B, and it chose knowledge about the organization's connection to terrorism, not specific intent to further the organization's terrorist activities."[88] Thus, the Government is not required to prove that the accused provided material support and resources with the specific intent to further or facilitate the terrorist activities of the FTO.

Freedom of Association

The Supreme Court rejected plaintiffs' argument that §2339B violates the First Amendment right of association, claiming that the statute penalizes mere association with an FTO. The Court stated that the statute does not prohibit being a member of a designated group or vigorously promoting the political goals of the group.[89] Instead, the statute prohibits the act of giving material support.[90]

Conclusion

The Court's decision makes clear that for purposes of §2339B, the terms "training," "expert advice or assistance," "personnel," and "service" are not unconstitutionally vague as applied to plaintiffs.[91] Further, independent advocacy is not banned under the material support statute.[92] Finally, to sustain a conviction under the statute, including a conviction for providing monetary assistance to an FTO, the Government does not have to prove that the defendant intended to further the illegal activities of the designated terrorist group.[93]

4. Terrorist Financing Statute, 18 U.S.C. §2339C

In 2002, Congress enacted the Suppression of the Financing of Terrorism Convention Implementation Act ("Suppression of the Financing of Terrorism Act" or "2002 Act"), which criminalizes the act of providing or collecting funds for terrorist purposes.[94] The Suppression of the Financing of Terrorism Act implements the International Convention for the Suppression of the Financing of Terrorism, which was adopted by the United Nations General Assembly on December 9, 1999, and ratified by the U.S. Senate on June 26, 2002.[95] The treaty is aimed at curtailing the flow of financial resources to terrorists and terrorist organizations, and obligates signatory states to criminalize the willful provision and collection of funds to support terrorist activities.[96] The 2002 Act created a new statute, 18 U.S.C. §2339C, which criminalizes unlawfully and willfully "provid[ing] or collect[ing]" funds with the intention or knowledge that the funds are to be used to carry out an offense within the scope of various counterterrorism treaties specified in the statute.[97] Section 2339C is limited to providing or collecting funds for certain predicate acts, including offenses within the scope of nine counterterrorism treaties.[98] However, the statute expressly provides that "[f]or an act to constitute an offense … it shall *not* be necessary that the funds were used to carry out a predicate act."[99] Section 2339C also punishes the provision or collection of funds for any other act intended to cause death or serious bodily injury to a civilian, "when the purpose of such act … is to intimidate a population, or to compel a government or an international organization to do or refrain from doing any act."[100] Anyone convicted under the terrorist financing statue can be fined, imprisoned for not more than 20 years, or both.[101] Further, any property involved in a violation of the statute is subject to forfeiture, as is property that constitutes or is derived from proceeds traceable to a violation of §2339C.[102] Finally, there is extraterritorial jurisdiction for violations of §2339C, which means that federal prosecutors may prosecute terrorist fundraising committed outside of the U.S.[103]

There have been relatively few prosecutions under the terrorist financing statute. Both §§2339C and 2339B punish the financial support of terrorism. However, §2339C requires proof of a more heightened *scienter* than §2339B. To sustain a conviction under §2339C, the Government must prove that the accused acted "with the intention that such funds be used, or with the knowledge that such funds are to be used ... in order to carry out" a statutorily enumerated terrorist offense.[104] The defendant is criminally liable if he either acted with the specific intent to fund acts of terrorism or had knowledge that the funds would be used for such purposes. By contrast, §2339B requires proof that the defendant provided material support or resources with knowledge that the organization is a designated FTO or engages in terrorist activity.[105] Under §2339B, the Government is not required to prove that the accused acted with the specific intent or knowledge that the material support be used for the commission of terrorist acts. The only *mens rea* requirement is knowledge that the recipient is connected to terrorism.[106] Thus, when prosecuting terrorist financing cases, prosecutors prefer charging under §2339B, which only requires proof that the defendant had knowledge of the recipient's status as an FTO or participation in terrorist-related activities.

III. TERRORIST FINANCING PROSECUTIONS AND CONVICTIONS

Prior to the September 11, 2001 terrorist attacks there were few prosecutions under the material support statutes. There were even fewer, if any, prosecutions for providing monetary support and financial services to terrorist groups such as al Qaeda, HAMAS, and Hizballah. Post–9/11, the Department of Justice increased the number of criminal prosecutions under the material support statutes, including prosecutions of the financial supporters of terrorism. However, the Justice Department's record of prosecutions of the financial supporters of terrorism has been checkered.[107] One of the most disappointing legal setbacks involved the prosecution of Sami Al-Arian, a former engineering professor at the University of South Florida. In 2003, Al-Arian and seven other defendants were charged in a fifty-three count indictment alleging violations of racketeering, conspiracy to murder, maim or injure persons outside the United States, money laundering, and conspiracy to provide and providing material support to an FTO, and other serious federal crimes.[108] The indictment alleged that Al-Arian and the other defendants were responsible for operating and directing the fundraising activities for the Palestinian Islamic Jihad (PIJ) in the United States for almost 20 years. The PIJ was designated a Specially Designated Terrorist and an FTO in 1997 because of the threat it posed to the Middle East peace process and its indiscriminate use of violence against Israeli civilians.[109] The Government maintained that Al-Arian was the leader of the PIJ in the United States and Secretary of the "Shura Council," or worldwide governing group of the PIJ.[110] The indictment further alleged that the defendants established a PIJ cell using the structure and facilities of the University of South Florida and two other entities, the World and Islam Studies Enterprise and the Islamic Concern Project, as a cover to conceal their terrorist fundraising activities.[111]

Al-Arian and three co-defendants were tried before a federal jury in Tampa, Florida. After a six-month jury trial, the jury failed to convict the defendants on any of the 53 charges against them.[112] Al-Arian was acquitted on 8 of 17 counts, while the jury remained deadlocked on the other nine counts against him.[113] The jury was unable to reach a verdict on three of the four most serious charges against Al-Arian and co-defendant Hatem Naji Fariz—the RICO conspiracy, conspiracy to provide material support, and conspiracy to violate IEEPA.[114] Al-Arian and Fariz were acquitted of conspiracy to murder persons abroad, and the Travel Act, material support and money laundering charges.[115] The other two defendants were acquitted on all criminal charges.[116]

Rather than pursue a retrial, the Government entered into a plea agreement with Al-Arian, where he was permitted to plead guilty to a lesser charge of conspiracy to make or receive contributions of funds for the benefit of the PIJ, in violation of 50 U.S.C. §1705(b) and 18 U.S.C. §371.[117] In return, the Government agreed to dismiss the remaining counts against him, including the financial support charges, not charge him with any other crimes, and make a recommendation at the low end of the federal sentencing guidelines, 46–57 months.[118] Al-Arian also agreed to deportation, where arguably he could continue raising money for the PIJ.

Another disappointing result involved the prosecution of Enaam Arnaout, the executive director of the Benevolence International Foundation (BIF), a purported Islamic charity. Arnaout was indicted in the Northern District of Illinois and charged with conspiracy to engage in a RICO enterprise; conspiracy to provide material support to al Qaeda, Hezb e Islami, and other related terrorists; providing material support to fighters in Chechnya; conspiracy to launder money; money laundering; and mail and wire fraud.[119] Specifically, the Government alleged that Arnaout used BIF, a Chicago-based charity, as a front to illicitly raise funds from unsuspected donors to support Osama bin Laden, al Qaeda, other associated terrorist groups, and Muslim fighters in Bosnia.[120]

Ultimately, Aranout was never convicted of providing financial assistance to al Qaeda. Instead, the Government permitted Aranout to plead guilty to racketeering conspiracy, admitting that he fraudulently obtained charitable donations and diverted the funds to pay for boots, uniforms, and other equipment to support fighters in Chechyna and Bosnia–Herzegovina.[121] In return, the Government dismissed all terrorist-financing related charges.[122] Thus, what was once hailed by the Department of Justice as a major terrorist financing case was plea-bargained to a fraud case.

In 2007, the Department of Justice suffered another humiliating defeat. A federal jury in Chicago acquitted Muhammad Salah and Abdelhaleem Ashqar of raising money for HAMAS in the United States, in violation of 18 U.S.C. §2339B.[123] The indictment alleged that the defendants operated a racketeering enterprise that recruited and trained members of HAMAS and raised money for the FTO in the United States.[124] Salah was accused of receiving wire transfers totaling approximately $985,000 deposited into his Chicago-based bank account to be distributed to HAMAS in the West Bank and Gaza Strip.[125] After a three-month jury trial, both Salah and Ashqar were acquitted of the most serious charges alleged in the indictment, participating in a RICO conspiracy to provide financial support, training, and other material aid to HAMAS.[126]

One of the first successful terrorist financing prosecutions involved allegations that Mohammed Hammoud raised money in the U.S. for Hizballah and then forwarded the funds to Sheikh Abbas Harake, a senior military commander for Hizballah. In *United States v. Hammoud*, the Fourth Circuit affirmed Hammoud's conviction for providing monetary support to Hizballah, rejecting defendant's vagueness challenge, holding that there was nothing vague about the term "currency."[127] However, the material support count involved a relatively small personal donation of $3,500 to Hizballah.[128]

In 2005, the Justice Department won an important legal victory in curtailing the flow of funds to al Qaeda and HAMAS. Following a five-week trial, a federal jury convicted Mohammed Ali Hasan Al-Moayad, a Yemeni cleric, and his assistant, Mohammed Mohsen Yahya Zayed, of conspiring to provide material support to al Qaeda and attempting to provide material support to HAMAS.[129] The defendants were charged with conspiring to funnel millions of dollars from a Brooklyn mosque to al Qaeda fighters in Afghanistan and Bosnia, and to Palestinian suicide bombers on behalf of HAMAS.[130] Al-Moayad and Zayed were arrested as part of a government "sting" operation involving an undercover FBI agent offering to donate millions of dollars to support terrorist-related activities.[131] Al-Moayad was caught on undercover tape recordings discussing the collection of funds from the Al Farook mosque in Brooklyn and his intent to distribute millions of dollars to al Qaeda and HAMAS to finance violent jihad.[132] During one of the taped conversations, Al-Moayad referred to himself as a spiritual adviser to Osama bin Laden. Al-Moayad and Zayed were sentenced to 75 years and 45 years in prison, respectively.[133]

The most significant terrorist financing prosecution involves the conviction of five leaders of the Holy Land Foundation for Relief and Development (HLF), a purported Muslim charity based in Richardson, Texas. However, it was a long sought victory. The HLF case has been characterized as "the largest and most complex legal effort to shut down American financing for terrorist organizations in the Middle East."[134] The defendants were accused of illegally funneling more than $12 million to zakat committees in the West Bank and Gaza that allegedly served as fronts for HAMAS.[135] In 2001, as the result of HLF's terrorist-related activities, the Treasury Department designated the group a Specially Designated Global Terrorist and blocked its assets.[136]

In 2004, the Department of Justice indicted the HLF and its directors and officers. The five defendants charged with terrorist-financing violations included: Ghassan Elashi, the original HLF Treasurer and former Chairman of the Board; Shukri Abu Baker, the former HLF CEO; Mohammad El-Mezain, the Foundation's original chairman, who became Director of Endowments; Mufid Abdulqader, a top fundraiser and a former city of Dallas public works supervisor; and Abdulrahman Odeh, HLF's New Jersey representative.[137]

In 2005, the Government filed a superseding indictment charging the defendants with 42 counts related to funding terrorism. The indictment involved a combination of 197 counts, including conspiracy to provide material support to an FTO (18 U.S.C. §2339B(a)(1)) by raising funds in the U.S. and sending them to organizations operated on behalf of or under the control of HAMAS; conspiracy to provide funds to a specially designated terrorist (50 U.S.C. §1701–6) by making regular payments to zakat committees who were acting on behalf of HAMAS; conspiracy to commit money laundering (18 U.S.C. §1956(h)); conspiracy to impede the IRS and file false tax returns for an organization exempt from income tax (18 U.S.C. §371); and filing false tax returns or an organization exempt from income tax (26 U.S.C. §7206(1)).[138]

In October 2007, after almost two months of trial testimony, a federal judge declared a mistrial on what was widely seen as the Justice Department's "flagship terrorism financing case."[139] The jury failed to issue a single guilty verdict, acquitting one defendant on all but one count, on which it deadlocked, and failed to reach a unanimous verdict on any of the other criminal counts.[140]

In 2008, a year after the case dissolved in a mistrial, the HLF defendants were retried by the Government. This time around, the prosecutors were successful. A federal jury in Dallas convicted the five defendants of multiple criminal charges for their funding of HAMAS, handing the Justice Department a significant victory in its largest terrorism financing case. Ghassan Elashi, HLF's former chairman, and Shukri Abu-Baker, HLF's chief executive, were convicted of a combined 69 counts, including providing material support to HAMAS, money laundering, and tax fraud.[141] Mufid Abdulqader and Abdulrahman Odeh were convicted of conspiracy to provide material support to an FTO, conspiracy to provide funds to a specially designated terrorist, and conspiracy to commit money laundering, and Mohammed El-Mezain was convicted on one count of conspiracy to support a terrorist organization.[142] A federal judge sentenced Elahsi and Abu-Baker to 65 years in prison.[143] Abdulqader was sentenced to 20 years, while El-Mezain and Odeh were sentenced to 15 years' imprisonment. The sentencing judge also affirmed the jury's $12.4 million money judgment against the defendants with the exception of El Mezain, who was not convicted of money laundering.[144]

IV. CONCLUSION

Shutting down the sources of funding that fuels terrorism is critical to preventing terrorist attacks and saving innocent lives. Simply stated, terrorists need money to terrorize."[145] Given the critical importance of going after terrorist money, the paltry number of terrorism financing convictions by the Justice Department is disturbing. Perhaps going after terrorist money is no longer a priority for the federal government. Alternatively, federal prosecutors and investigators may lack adequate training to investigate complex, international terrorist financing schemes involving corrupt charities who raise terrorist funds under the guise of providing humanitarian relief, sham front organizations, and convoluted international wire transfers. Another possible rationale is that complacency has overtaken the sense of urgency that existed immediately following the 9/11 attacks to deprive terrorists of funding. Whatever the explanation, "the paucity of major terrorist financing prosecutions, and the jury acquittals and hung juries in high-profile terrorist financing cases should cause Congress and the Department of Justice to reexamine the U.S. Government's counterterrorist financing strategy."[146]

NOTES

1. National Strategy for Combating Terrorism, 17 (2003), *available at https://www.cia.gov/ … terrorism/Counter_Terrorism_Strategy.pdf.*

2. Jimmy Gurulé, UNFUNDING TERROR: THE LEGAL RESPONSE TO THE FINANCING OF GLOBAL TERRORISM 279 (Edward Elgar, 2008) [hereinafter "UNFUNDING TERROR"].

3. *See* NATIONAL COMMISSION ON TERRORIST ATTACKS, THE 9/11 COMMISSION REPORT: FINAL REPORT OF THE NATIONAL COMMISSION ON TERRORIST ATTACKS UPON THE UNITED STATES 169 (W.W. Norton & Company 2004), *available at* http://govinfo.library.unt.edu/911/report/911Report.pdf [hereinafter THE 9/11 COMMISSION REPORT].

4. *See* The 9/11 Commission Report, *supra* note 3, at 171. *See also* ROHAN GUNARATNA, INSIDE AL QAEDA: GLOBAL NETWORK OF TERROR 61 (Columbia University Press 2002).

5. *See* MATTHEW LEVITT, HAMAS, POLITICS, CHARITY AND TERRORISM IN THE SERVICE OF JIHAD, 59 (New Haven: Yale University Press 2006) [hereinafter HAMAS].

6. *Hezbollah: Financing Terror through Criminal Enterprise: Hearing Before the S. Comm. on Homeland Sec. and Governmental Affairs,* 109th Cong. 1 (2005) (statement of Matthew Levitt).

7. UNFUNDING TERROR, *supra* note 2, at 24–25. *See also* Financial Action Task Force, Terrorist Financing (Feb. 28, 2008), *available at* http://www.fatf-gati.org/dataoecd/28/43/40285899.pdf.

8. *See* Almog v. Arab Bank, 471 F. Supp.2d 257, 262 (E.D.N.Y. 2007).

9. *See* HAMAS, *supra* note 5, at 54.

10. *See* THE 9/11 COMMISSION REPORT, *supra* note 3, at 67; PETER L. BERGEN, HOLY WAR, INC.: INSIDE THE SECRET WORLD OF OSAMA BIN LADEN 167–68 (New York: Simon & Schuster 2002) (estimating the number of terrorists trained in Afghanistan training camps at 10,000).

11. *See* THE 9/11 COMMISSION REPORT, *supra* note 3, at 171.

12. *Id.* (noting that bin Laden may have used money to create alliances with other terrorist groups).

13. *See* UNFUNDING TERROR, *supra* note 2, at 25; PETER L. BERGEN, HOLY WAR INC.: INSIDE THE SECRET WORLD OF OSAMA BIN LADEN 40 (New York: Simon & Schuster 2002).

14. UNFUNDING TERROR, *supra* note 2, at 21.

15. U.S. Dep't of Treasury, National Money Laundering Strategy 7 (2003), *available at* http://www.treasury.gov/press-center/press-releases/Documents/js10102js1010.pdf.

16. Unfunding Terror, *supra* note 2, at 22.

17. *Id.*

18. 18 U.S.C. §2339A (West 2008); 18 U.S.C. §2339B (2000 & Supp. IV 2004).

19. 18 U.S.C. §2339A(b)(1).

20. Humanitarian Law Project v. Mukasey, 552 F.3d 916, 931 (9th Cir. 2009), *overturned on other grounds*, Holder v. Humanitarian Law Project, 130 S.Ct. 2705, 2728 (2010).

21. Unfunding Terror, *supra* note 2, at 279.

22. Violent Crime Control and Law Enforcement Act of 1994, Pub. L. No. 103–322, §12005(a), 108 Stat. 1796, 2022–23 (1994) (*codified at* 18 U.S.C. §2339A).

23. *See* United States v. Chandia, 514 F.3d 365, 373 (4th Cir. 2008).

24. Unfunding Terror, *supra* note 2, at 279.

25. Antiterrorism and Effective Death Penalty Act of 1996, Pub. L. No. 104–132, §301(a)(7), 110 Stat. 1247 (1996) (AEDPA).

26. 18 U.S.C. §2339B (1996). *See also* United States v. Afshari, 635 F. Supp.2d 1110, 1113 (C.D. Cal. 2009).

27. AEDPA, *supra* note 7, at note following 18 U.S.C. §2339B (Findings and Purpose).

28. Humanitarian Law Project v. Gonzales, 380 F. Supp. 2d 1134, 1146 (C.D. Cal 2005).

29. *Id.* at 1137.

30. 18 U.S.C. §2339B (2000 & Supp. IV 2004).

31. *See* Holder v. Humanitarian Law Project, 130 S. Ct. 2705, 2717 (2010).

32. Unfunding Terror, *supra* note 2, at 281 (citations omitted) (emphasis in original).

33. 18 U.S.C. §2339(b)(1).

34. *Id.*

35. 18 U.S.C. §§2339A, 2339B.

36. 18 U.S.C. §981 (West, 2008).

37. 18 U.S.C. §2339B(g)(6) (2000 & Supp. IV 2004).

38. 8 U.S.C. §1189(a)(1).

39. *See* Foreign Terrorist Organizations, Office of the Coordinator for Counterterrorism, U.S. Dep't of State (Jan. 27, 2012), *available at* http://www.state.gov/j/ct/rls/other/des/123085.htm (last visited Feb. 24, 2012).

40. *Id.*

41. 8 U.S.C. §1189(c) (*See also* 2004 Act, Dec. 17, 2004 amendment).

42. 8 U.S.C. §1189(a)(3)(A).

43. *Id.* at §1189(a)(3)(B). *See also* People's Mojahedin Org. of Iran v. Dept. of State, 327 F.3d 1238, 1240–41 (D.C. Cir. 2003) ("PMOI"); National Council of Resistance of Iran v. Dept. of State, 251 F.3d 192, 209 (D.C. Cir. 2001 ("NCRI").

44. *See National Council of Resistance of Iran v. Dept. of State*, 251 F.3d at 209.

45. 8 U.S.C. §1189(a)(2)(B)(i).

46. *Id.* at §1189(a)(2)(A)(ii).

47. United States v. Taleb-Jedi, 566 F. Supp.2d 157, 163 (E.D.N.Y. 2008).

48. 8 U.S.C. §1189(c)(1).

49. *See* People's Mojahedin Org. of Iran v. Department of State, 327 F.3d 1238, 1240–41 (D.C. Cir. 2003).

50. *Id.*

51. United States v. Taleb-Jedi, 566 F. Supp.2d 157, 163 (E.D.N.Y. 2008) (citing 8 U.S.C. §1189(c)(3)(A)–(E)).

52. *See* 18 U.S.C. §2339B(a)(2).

53. *See* 8 U.S.C. §1189(a)(3)(B)(i).

54. *See* 18 U.S.C. §2339B(a)(1). If death results from the provision of material support, the defendant may be imprisoned for life. *Id.*

55. *See* 8 U.S.C. §1189(a)(8).

56. *See, e.g.,* United States v. Warsame, 537 F. Supp.2d 1005, 1022 (D. Minn. 2008).

57. *See* Valley Forge Christian Coll. v. American United, 454 U.S. 464, 474–75 (1982); *Warsame,* 537 F. Supp.2d at 1022.

58. *Id.* at 1022.

59. *See* JIMMY GURULÉ & GEOFFREY CORN, PRINCIPLES OF COUNTER-TERRORISM LAW 284 (West-Thompson Reuters 2011) [hereinafter PRINCIPLES OF COUNTER-TERRORISM LAW].

60. United States v. Ajshari, 426 F.3d 1150, 1159 (9th Cir. 2005).

61. *Id.* at 1155–56.

62. *See* United States v. Hammoud, 381 F.3d 316, 331 (4th Cir. 2004) (finding that "Congress has provided that the *fact* of an organization's designation as an FTO is an element of §2339B, but the *validity* of the designation is not") (emphasis in the original); United States v. Chandia, 514 F.3d 365, 371 (4th Cir. 2008) (citing *Hammoud* with approval); United States v. Afshari, 412 F.3d 1071, 1076 (9th Cri. 2005); *Warsame,* 537 F. Supp.2d at 1021.

63. Intelligence Reform and Terrorist Prevention Act of 2004 (IRTPA), §6003, 118 Stat. 3762–64.

64. Holder v. Humanitarian Law Project, 130 S. Ct. 2705 (2010).

65. *Id.* at *2713.

66. *Id.* at *2713–14. The PKK was founded in 1974 for the purpose of establishing an independent Kurdish state in southeast Turkey. *Id.* at 2713. The LTTE was established in 1976 for the purpose of creating an independent Tamil state in Sri Lanka. *Id.*

67. *Humanitarian Law Project,* 130 S. Ct., at 2720.

68. 18 U.S.C. §2339A(b)(2).

69. *Id.* at §2339A(b)(3).

70. *Holder v. Humanitarian Law Project,* 130 S. Ct. 2705, at 2720 (2010).

71. *Id.* at *2718–19.

72. *Id.* at *2720.

73. *Id.* at *2721.

74. 18 U.S.C. §2339B(h).

75. *Id.*

76. *Holder v. Humanitarian Law Project,* 130 S. Ct. 2705, at 2721 (2010).

77. *Id.*

78. *Id.*

79. *Id.* at *2721–22 (quoting 18 U.S.C. §2339B(a)(1)).

80. *Id.* at *2722.

81. *Id.*

82. Holder v. Humanitarian Law Project, 130 S. Ct. 2705, at 2722 (2010).

83. *Id.*

84. *Id.* at *2723.

85. *Id.*

86. *Id.*

87. *Id.* at *2717.

88. Holder v. Humanitarian Law Project, 130 S. Ct. 2705, at 2717 (2010).

89. *Id.*

90. *Id.*

91. *Id.* at *2720–21.

92. *Id.* at *2721.

93. *Id.* at *2717.

94. Suppression of the Financing of Terrorism Convention Implementation Act of 2002, Pub. L. No. 107–197, tit. II, 116 Stat. 724 (2002) (*codified at* 18 U.S.C. §2339C (West 2008)).

95. International Convention for the Suppression of the Financing of Terrorism, Dec. 9, 1999, 39 I.L.M. 270, *available* at http://untreaty.un.org/ENGLISH/TreatyEvent2003/treaty_11.htm.

96. *Id.* at art. 4.

97. 18 U.S.C. §2339C.

98. For purposes of section 2339C, the term "treaty" refers to the following international counterterrorism conventions ratified by the United States:

    (A) Convention for the Suppression of Unlawful Seizure of Aircraft, done at The Hague on December 16, 1970;

    (B) the Convention for the Suppression of Unlawful Acts against the Safety of Civil Aviation, done at Montreal on September 23, 1971;

    (C) the Convention on the Prevention and Punishment of Crimes against Internationally Protected Persons, including Diplomatic Agents, adopted by the General Assembly of the United Nations on December 14, 1973;

    (D) the International Convention against the Taking of Hostages, adopted by the General Assembly of the United Nations on December 17, 1979;

    (E) the Convention on the Physical Protection of Nuclear Material, adopted at Vienna on March 3, 1980;

    (F) the Protocol for the Suppression of Unlawful Acts of Violence at Airports Serving International Civil Aviation, supplementary to the Convention for the Suppression of Unlawful Acts against the Safety of Civil Aviation, done at Montreal on February 24, 1988;

    (G) the Convention for the Suppression of Unlawful Acts against the Safety of Maritime Navigation, done at Rome on March 10, 1988;

    (H) the Protocol for the Suppression of Unlawful Acts against the Safety of Fixed Platforms located on the Continental Shelf, done at Rome on March 10, 1988; or

    (I) the International Convention for the Suppression of Terrorist Bombings, adopted by the General Assembly of the United Nations on December 15, 1997.

99. 18 U.S.C. §2339C(a)(3) (emphasis added).

100. *Id.* at §2339C(a)(1)(B).

101. *Id.* at §2339C(d)(1).

102. *See* 18 U.S.C. §981(a)(1)(H) (West 2008).

103. *See* 18 U.S.C. §2339C(b)(2) (West 2008). Section 2339B(d)(1) also authorizes extraterritorial jurisdiction. However, §2339A is silent on the subject.

104. *Id.* at §2339C(a)(1).

105. 18 U.S.C. §2339B(a)(1).

106. *Id.*

107. The following review of the post–911 terrorist financing prosecutions relies in large part on Unfunding Terror, *supra* note 2, at 302–08.

108. *See* United States v. Al-Arian, 308 F. Supp. 2d 1322 (M.D. Fla. 2004); *see also* Press Release, U.S. Dep't of Justice, Members of the Palestinian Islamic Jihad Arrested, Charged with Racketeering and Conspiracy to Provide Support to Terrorists (Feb. 20, 2003), *available at* http://www.justice.gov/opa/pr/2003/February/03_crm_099.htm.

109. *See* Prohibiting Transactions with Terrorists Who Threaten to Disrupt the Middle East Peace Process, Exec. Order No. 12,947, 60 Fed. Reg. 5079, at 5080, *codified at* 3 C.F.R. 319–20 (1995), *reprinted as amended in* 50 U.S.C. §1701 note (2000 & Supp. IV 2004); *see also* Designation of Foreign Terrorist Organizations, 62 Fed. Reg. 52,650 (1997).

110. *See* Press Release, U.S. Dep't of Justice, Members of the Palestinian Islamic Jihad Arrested, Charged with Racketeering and Conspiracy to Provide Material Support to Terrorists, *supra* note 105.

111. *Id.*

112. *See* Verdict, United States v. Al-Arian, 308 F. Supp. 2d 1322 (M.D. Fla. 2004) (8:03-CR-00077-JSM-TBM), ECF Nos. 1463; 1465–67.

113. *Id.*

114. *Id.*

115. *Id.*

116. *Id.*

117. *See Plea Agreement,* United States v. Al-Arian, 308 F. Supp. 2d 1322 (M.D. Fla. 2004) (8:03-CR-00077-JSM-TBM), ECF No.1563.

118. *Id.*

119. *See* Second Superseding Indictment, United States v. Arnaout, 2003 WL 255226 (N.D. Ill. 2003), (1:02-Cr-00892), ECF No. 130; *see also* Prepared Remarks of Attorney General John Ashcroft, Press Conference Announcing Enaam Arnaout Indictment (Oct. 9, 2002), *available at* http://www.usdoj.gov/archive/ag/secches/2002/100902agremarksbifindictment.htm.

120. *Id.*

121. *See* Press Release, U.S. Dep't of Justice, Benevolence Director Pleads Guilty to Racketeering Conspiracy and Agrees to Cooperate with the Government (Feb. 10, 2003), *available at* http://www.usdoj.gov/usao/iln/pr/chicago/2003/pr021003_01.pdf.

122. *See* Edward Alden, *Charity Guilty of Backing Muslim Fighters: Chicago Fraud Case Justice Department Fails to Secure Al-Qaeda Funding Conviction, Lesser Charges Brought After,* Financial Times, Feb. 12, 2003, at 12.

123. Both Salah and Ashqar were convicted of less serious charges, affording some consolation to the Department of Justice. Salah was found guilty of obstruction of justice for lying under oath when questioned in a civil suit filed by the surviving member of an American student killed in a HAMAS-related shooting in Israel. Ashqar was convicted of obstruction of justice and criminal contempt for refusing to testify before a grand jury. *See* Rudolph Bush and Jeff Coen, *Two Found Not Guilty of Supporting Hamas,* Chicago Tribune, Feb. 2, 2007.

124. *See* Second Superseding Indictment, United States v. Marzook et al., 383 F. Supp.2d 1056 (N.D. Il. 2004), (1:03-CR-00978), ECF No. 59.

125. *Id.*

126. *See* Bush & Coen, *supra* note 120.

127. United States v. Hammoud, 381 F.3d 316, 330–1 (4th Cir. 2004) (*en banc*), *vacated on other grounds,* 543 U.S. 1097 (2005), *reinstated in relevant part,* 405 F.3d 1034 (4th Cir. 2005).

128. *Id.*

129. *See* Superseding Indictment, United States v. Al-Moayad, (1:03-cr-01322-DLI) (E.D.N.Y. 2004), ECF No. 94.

130. *Id.*

131. *Id.*

132. *Id.*

133. Sentencing Order, United States v. Al-Moayad, (1:03-cr-01322-DLI) (E.D.N.Y. Aug. 01, 2004), ECF No. 197.

134. Unfunding Terror, *supra* note 2, at 305 (citations omitted).

135. *See* Superseding Indictment, United States v. Holy Land Found. for Relief & Dev., No. 3:04-cr–00240, 2007 WL 2059722 (N.D. Tex. Nov. 30, 2005), ECF No. 233; *see also* Press Release, U.S. Dep't of Treasury, Shutting Down the Terrorist Financial Network (Dec. 4, 2001), *available at* http://www.treas.gov/press/releases/po841.htm.

136. *See* Shutting Down the Terrorist Financial Network, *supra* note. 132.

137. *See* Holy Land Foundation: About the Trial, THE DALLAS MORNING NEWS, Oct. 18, 2007, *available at* http://www.dallasnews.com/sharedcontent/dws/news/longterm/stories/092707dnmethlabout.1127940bf.html. Two other defendants charged in the case remained fugitives. *Id.* A superseding indictment was filed in November 2005, charging HLF and its directors and officers with 42 counts related to terrorist financing. *See* Superseding Indictment, *supra* note 132.

138. *See* Superseding Indictment, *supra* note 132.

139. UNFUNDING TERROR, *supra* note 2, at 306; *see also* Mistrial Order, United States v. Holy Land Found. for Relief & Dev., 2007 WL 2059722 (N.D. Tex. Oct. 22, 2007), (3:04-cr-00240).

140. *See* Mistrial Order, *supra* note 136.

141. *See* Paul J. Weber, *Holy Land retrial ends in sweeping guilty verdicts*, WASH. POST, November 25, 2008; *see also* Press Release, U.S. Dep't of Justice, Federal Judge Hands Down Sentences in Holy Land Foundation Case (May 27, 2009), *available at* http://www.justice.gov/opa/pr/2009/may/09-nsd–519.html.

142. *Id.*

143. *See* Federal Judge Hands Down Sentences in Holy Land Foundation Case, *supra* note 138.

144. *Id.*

145. UNFUNDING TERROR, *supra* note 2, at 21.

146. *Id.* at 309.

8

COUNTERTERRORISM LEGISLATION

Michael Kraft

Counterterrorism consultant and writer, retired Senior Advisor for legislative and budget affairs in the State Department Office of the Coordinator for Counterterrorism, former Staff Director of the Senate, Foreign Relations Committee Middle East Subcommittee, and a former Washington and foreign correspondent

Brent Davidson, J.D.

Director of Program Development for the International Security & Biopolicy Institute (ISBI) and former Fellow at the California Healthcare Institute (CHI), Graduate of the DePaul University College of Law with an emphasis in International and Comparative Law

INTRODUCTION

The terrorism threat has evolved considerably during the past four decades and, in response, the Executive Branch and Congress have drafted and enacted a variety of U.S. laws.

Early in the emergence of modern terrorism threats in the 1970s, most of the terrorist attacks affecting Americans and American interests were overseas, conducted by secular terrorist groups that usually were supported by various rogue states such as Syria and Iran. This prompted the development of U.S. economic sanctions legislation against state sponsors plus international treaties and implementing legislation against various forms of terrorism, such as attacks on aircraft and commercial shipping. In the early 1990s, some major terrorist groups were becoming more independent from state sponsors, developing their own means of funding. The counterterrorism emphasis then shifted to developing laws and regulations aimed at stemming the money and other forms of material support that terrorists receive from non-state actors, so called "charities," and even individuals. Major terrorist attacks overseas, especially in the Middle East, gave impetus to this effort, along with the 1993 World Trade Center attacks and the 1995 Oklahoma City Federal Building bombing. Following 9/11, the Bush Administration's War on Terror and invasions of Afghanistan and Iraq forced the Executive Branch and Congress to grapple with Constitutional, moral, and effective means of prosecuting and detaining relatively large numbers of suspected terrorists and combatants captured in foreign territory. Meanwhile, the United States, working with the U.N and its own training programs, tried to strengthen foreign governments' counterterrorism efforts, including their ability to stem financial contributions to suspect terrorist groups.

Many forms of terrorist attacks, such as murder and assault, were already covered by the criminal code. However, the newer legislation with enhanced penalties for terrorist acts, and the changing nature of terrorism and legislative countermeasures, resulted in a complex web of laws that both authorize a variety of domestic and overseas counterterrorism measures, and try to balance them with civil liberties concerns. This chapter reviews the evolution of these measures, recent highlights, applications to homeland security, and practical issues of enforcement.

FIRST STEPS

In countering international terrorism, the first phase was the development of international treaties against such crimes as hijacking aircraft and taking hostages. By 1971, there were four international conventions dealing with the security of civil aircraft; and in the 1970s, three international conventions against taking hostages were enacted.

After terrorist acts against airports and the hijacking of the Italian cruise ship *Achille Lauro* in the 1980s, international conventions were negotiated to cover attacks on civilian airports, passenger vessels, and offshore platforms. In the 1990s, the United States and other countries, working together at the United Nations, successfully drafted international conventions against terrorist bombings and against funding terrorism.

These treaties usually required implementing legislation. For example, the Anti-Hijacking Act of 1974 prohibits the hijacking of aircraft in the jurisdiction of the United States, and provides jurisdiction over offenders who hijack other civil aircraft in other countries if those hijackers are subsequently found in the United States. Often, the necessary implementing legislation is tacked on as a provision of a broader vehicle bill.

Two themes are clear: although these international treaties did not try to define terrorism, they were responses to the relevant form of terrorist attack such an aircraft hijacking, and they embodied the "extradite or prosecute" principle. That is, parties to the conventions are obligated to extradite suspects to the country that had primary jurisdiction over the crime, or prosecute the suspects in their own courts.

Apart from the Convention for the Suppression of Financing of Terrorism (1999),[1] the conventions do not define terrorism but consider actions such as blowing up aircraft a criminal act—an extraditable offense regardless of motivation. The approach that terrorist acts are criminal regardless of motivation[2] has been reflected in numerous statements by high-level U.S. government officials including President Reagan. It is also indicative of the difficulties in achieving an international consensus on a definition of terrorism.[3]

SANCTIONS AND STATE SPONSORS

In the late 1970s, when Congress began enacting specific counterterrorist laws, it focused on imposing sanctions against countries that supported terrorism. Thus, in the wake of the terrorist killings of Israeli athletes at the 1972 Olympics in Munich and other terrorism overseas, one early law, enacted in 1976, cut off foreign assistance to "any government which aids or abets, by providing sanctuary from prosecution, any group or individual which has committed an act of international terrorism."[4] It was logical for Congress to use foreign aid to exert pressure because of the view that the United States should not give foreign assistance to countries that support terrorism.

The "Terrorism List"

Because the Commerce Department and State Department had approved export licenses to Libya and Syria of militarily useful equipment, Congress also became concerned that tighter scrutiny and controls were needed over the export of dual-use equipment, such as certain heavy duty trucks, aircraft, and boats, to countries supporting terrorism.

Several influential members of the House Committee on Foreign Affairs particularly were concerned that export licensing officials were not giving enough attention to the foreign policy implications of approving licenses for military and dual-use equipment to countries supporting terrorism. They felt that approving export licenses for dual-use equipment without serious consideration at high levels could send the wrong signal—that the United States was willing to conduct business as usual, even with regimes engaged in terrorism or the support of terrorists.

The issue specifically emerged in 1978, when the Commerce Department approved export licenses for exporting dual-use equipment to Libya and Syria. The sale to Libya involved 400 heavy-duty off-road trucks of the type used by the American and Canadian armies for transporting tanks into a battle zone. In Syria's case, Commerce and the State Department's Near East Bureau also approved the export of six so-called civilian versions of the Lockheed C-130 transport plane, at a time that Syria was shelling the Christian suburbs of eastern Beirut.

Representative Millicent Fenwick (Republican, New Jersey), a junior member of the House Foreign Affairs Committee, introduced an amendment to require closer scrutiny of such sales. Working with the Economic subcommittee, she won passage of an important counterterrorism amendment to the pending Export Administration Act of 1979. The amendment required the State Department to notify Congress 30 days before export licenses were issued for goods or services, valued at more than $7 million, that would significantly enhance the military capability or the ability to support acts of international terrorism by governments that the secretary of state determined had repeatedly supported acts of terrorism.[5] This provision was intended to ensure that tentative decisions favoring licenses for dual-use exports to state sponsors of international terrorism would be considered and approved at the top levels of the State Department before notifying Congress and the licenses would be reviewed for foreign policy implications rather than for primarily commercial considerations.

This amendment, originally intended as an export control mechanism, became known as the "terrorism list" or "state sponsors list" and developed into an important counterterrorist tool. The countries initially designated were Libya, Iraq, Syria, and South Yemen, and Iran, Cuba, North Korea, and the Sudan were added in subsequent years. South Yemen was dropped after it merged with North Yemen. Iraq was initially dropped in 1982, but redesignated after Saddam

Hussein's invasion of Kuwait in 1991. On October 20, 2004, after the overthrow of the Saddam Hussein regime, the State Department took Iraq off the list following the advance notification procedures required in a 1989 law (see below). The State Department has also subsequently removed Libya and North Korea leaving Cuba, Iran, Sudan, and Syria as the nations remaining on the list as of the beginning of 2012.

In piecemeal fashion, over the years after the Export Administration Act of 1979 was enacted and later modified to remove the dollar threshold and broaden the requirement for Congressional notification to cover items that "could" enhance the recipient country's terrorist or military capabilities instead of the more narrow assessment that the export "would" do so. Congress also passed half a dozen "piggyback" amendments imposing sanctions on designated countries. One such provision amended the U.S. tax code to discourage American investments in the listed countries by denying American companies and individuals federal income tax credits for income earned from those investments. Other provisions included cutting off military and economic assistance to countries on the list and suspending American assistance to countries that supplied lethal military equipment to the listed countries.

Major legislation also followed the Iran–Contras scandal during the Reagan administration. Congress and the Justice Department investigated whether, as part of efforts to free Americans held hostage by Muslim terrorists in Lebanon, Oliver North, a National Security Council (NSC) staffer, had violated U.S. laws by selling Tube-launched, Optically tracked, Wire-guided missile (TOW) anti-tank missiles to Iran and using the proceeds to finance the Contras in Nicaragua. (He was convicted of three counts in 1988, but the convictions were vacated on appeal on the grounds that North's Fifth Amendment rights may have been violated by the indirect use of his testimony to Congress which had been given under a grant of immunity).

After a series of hearings on the affair, Congress passed the Anti-Terrorism and Arms Export Control Act of 1989, which codified procedures for designating "state sponsors" of terrorism under the foreign assistance and military assistance laws, as well as under the Export Administration Act.

The 1989 law, sponsored by Rep. Howard Berman (Democrat, California), who later became chairman of the House Foreign Affairs Committee, also laid out specific criteria and advance notification procedures that had to be followed before a country could be taken off the terrorism list. The procedures require the President to certify to Congress that the government of the country in question has not supported acts of international terrorism for the previous six months and has given assurances that it will not do so in the future. The rescission cannot take effect until 45 days after Congress is notified, giving it time to challenge the removal if it decides to do so. This advance notification provision was a reaction to the outcry when the State Department removed Iraq from the list in 1982 without consulting or informing Congress in advance.[6]

The second removal of Iraq, in October 2004, followed Congressional procedures and assurances given by the interim Iraqi government. The effect in this case was largely symbolic because after the overthrow of Saddam Hussein, the Bush Administration already used special authorities Congress had enacted a year earlier for Iraq, which permitted the lifting of the pre-war sanctions.

THE LONG-ARM STATUTE

In October 1985, a Palestinian terrorist group boarded the Italian cruise liner *Achille Lauro* in an effort to enter Israel during a port call. The terrorists intended to take hostages after landing and force the Israelis to release other group members who had been arrested for previous terrorist acts, including one in which a terrorist smashed a toddler to death against a rock. However, a crew member accidently discovered the plotters with their weapons in a cabin, and the terrorist's plans quickly changed to hijacking the passenger liner.

During the hijacking, the terrorists threw overboard Leon Klinghoffer, an elderly American passenger who was in a wheelchair. Abu Abbas, the leader of the group, was later arrested after the ship finally docked in Alexandria, Egypt. Italian authorities forced his release when the American military plane transporting him to the United States landed at an Italian air base for refueling. Abu Abbas fled to Yugoslavia, then took refuge in Iraq, was eventually recaptured by U.S. forces after the 2003 invasion, and died of a heart attack while in custody.

In short, the terrorists killed an American overseas and were released by one country to take refuge in another. This prompted the Justice Department to draft a so-called "long-arm statute,"[7] making it a federal crime to murder, attempt to murder, conspire to murder, or cause serious bodily injury to Americans if the Attorney General determined that the violence was terrorism, rather than an ordinary nonpolitical criminal offense.[8] This legislation allows the United States to prosecute terrorists who attack Americans overseas, even if the attack does not take place on American territory, such as an embassy. In singling out terrorist crimes from ordinary crimes, the legislation defined the criteria to be used by the Attorney General as action intended to coerce, intimidate, or retaliate against a government or civilian population.

Following enactment of the long-arm statute, the Justice Department greatly expanded its assignment of legal attachés (LEGATs) abroad. Although this sometimes caused friction with the State Department, whose embassies were already strained to provide logistical support for other agencies, the LEGATs did facilitate U.S, investigations, and in some cases, also helped host countries pursue investigations and improve their own laws. Currently, the FBI has 76 fully operational LEGAT offices and sub-offices, with more than 250 agents and support personnel stationed around the world.[9]

AVIATION AND MARITIME SECURITY

The hijackings of airplanes in the 1970s and 1980s, and the attacks on airports in Rome, Vienna, and Karachi in the mid-1980s, prompted a series of aviation and security-related laws.

Section 1115 of the Federal Aviation Act allows the President to suspend air transportation between the United States and any foreign state that acts "in a manner inconsistent" with the antihijacking convention of The Hague (1970); or permits territory under its jurisdiction to be used by terrorists for operations, training, or sanctuary; or arms, aids, and abets any terrorist organization that "knowingly uses the illegal seizure of aircraft or the threat thereof as an instrument of policy." The President also is authorized to suspend air transportation between the United States and any country that maintains air service between itself and such a state. The United States has banned direct air service to Lebanon because of concerns about terrorist groups within anti-aircraft missile range of flights using Beirut's international airport.

After the hijacking of TWA 847 and other aircraft in the 1980s, Congress enacted Sec. 551 of the International Security and Development Cooperation Act of 1985, which directs the Secretary of Transportation to inspect security at foreign airports with air links to the United States.

Travel advisories are to be issued if the security is substandard and has not been sufficiently improved after airport authorities are given 90 days' notice. Advisories have been issued for airports in cities such as Lagos and Athens. Typically, as in the above cities, the bans are lifted after the State Department Antiterrorism Training Assistance (ATA) program sends aviation security specialists overseas to help the local airport authorities improve their security.

After the bombing of Pan Am 103 in December 1988 with plastic explosives concealed in a radio, an international convention was drafted to require explosives manufacturers to incorporate a detection chemical. About a dozen countries (including Czechoslovakia, which had manufactured the explosive, Semtex, used in the bombing of flight 103) cooperated to identify chemicals that could be mixed into various plastic explosives. The United States passed its implementing legislation as part of the Antiterrorism and Effective Death Penalty Act of 1996 (AEDPA).[10]

One controversial provision of AEDPA required the Federal Aviation Administration (FAA) to impose the same security measures required of American carriers on foreign air carriers serving a U.S. airport. This entailed considerable negotiations, as some countries claimed that their own measures were equivalent, if not exactly identical.

After the hijacking of the *Achille Lauro*, Congress added to the Omnibus Diplomatic Security and Antiterrorism Act of 1986[11] a program for protecting passenger liners against hijacking. This included developing International Maritime Organization security standards, inspecting U.S. and foreign ports, and issuing travel advisories against unsafe foreign ports. The Intelligence Reform Act passed in December 2004, contained a provision requiring that cruise ship crews and passengers be checked against a comprehensive, coordinated database containing information about known or suspected terrorists and their associates.

THE NEWER FOCUS: NON-STATE TERRORIST GROUPS AND ACTORS

In the 1990s, U.S. government terrorist experts began focusing on blocking support for terrorists that did not enjoy state sponsorship. For example, a CIA paper that later was partly declassified, indicated that the Abu Nidal organization had set up front companies in Eastern Europe to raise and transfer funds.

In 1994, Congress enacted a "material support" provision making it a criminal offense to provide funds or other material support for specific acts of terrorism, whether conducted by a terrorist organization or an individual.[12] Material support was defined as "currency or other financial securities, financial services, lodging, training, safe houses, false documentation or identification, communications equipment, facilities, weapons, lethal substances, explosives, personnel, transportation, and other physical assets, except medicine or religious materials." This provision was a refinement of the concept of "aiding and abetting" in criminal law, and became part of the Violent Crime Control and Enforcement Act of 1994.[13]

Because of concern that more extensive proposals might get lost during the Congressional deliberations of that large-scale crime control legislation, the Clinton administration meanwhile began working on a separate, more comprehensive counterterrorist bill to be introduced early the following year. This legislation was prompted by a series of terrorist acts in Israel and the West Bank by Palestinians and a shooting of Arabs at a mosque in Hebron by an Israeli who emigrated from the United States. As an interim measure, on 23 January 1995, the administration issued Executive Order 12947 freezing the assets subject to U.S. jurisdiction of 12 groups, ten Arab and two Jewish, whose support of violence was deemed to undermine the peace process in the Middle East.[14]

FOREIGN TERRORIST ORGANIZATIONS

In January 1995, the Clinton administration submitted to Congress the broad counterterrorism bill its lawyers and State Department counterterrorism specialists had drafted during 1994. The bill contained provisions to designate foreign and domestic terrorist organizations for the purpose of prohibiting the provision of material support. In revising the legislation, which finally passed in April 1996 as the Antiterrorism and Effective Death Penalty Act of 1996 (AEDPA),[15] Congress narrowed the scope to foreign organizations, sidestepping issues of defining the parameters of free speech in the absence of attempted or successful terrorist acts.

AEDPA makes it a criminal offense for an American to knowingly provide funds and other material support to foreign groups formally designated by the Secretary of State (in consultation with the Attorney General and the Secretary of the Treasury) as foreign terrorist organizations (FTOs). A companion provision, modeled after the 1994 Criminal Act provision criminalizes material support for *specific* acts of terrorism, whether committed by an individual or by members of a previously unknown or undesignated group. It dropped a 1994 section that imposed a high requirement for launching an investigation, which, in effect, made it difficult to conduct an investigation until an attack plan was well underway.

Some of the designated FTOs also engaged in non-terrorism activities, such as running health clinics or schools, but Congress declared in Sec. 301(7) of the act ("Findings and Purpose") that: "Foreign organizations that engage in terrorist activity are so tainted by their criminal conduct that any contributions to such an organization facilitates that conduct." Also, even a contribution intended for legitimate charitable purposes would free up funds for terrorist activities, such as buying weapons. Some terrorist groups, such as Hamas and those in Algeria and Egypt, attracted adherents by providing schools and medical facilities, or assisting the families of active members or suicide bombers.

In the provisions regarding FTOs,[16] AEDPA defined material support as it had been defined in the Crime Act of 1994. That definition was expanded in the Intelligence Reform Act of 2004 to include a clarification of the meaning of training to include military-type training from or on behalf of a terrorist organization and training to impart specific skills as opposed to general knowledge.[17] These modifications were enacted in the wake of court cases in which the definition of training was questioned. Overall, these material support provisions in law have been used in cases involving previously unknown and undesignated terrorist groups. By 2011, more than 200 persons had been charged under one or both of the material support provisions, and more than half had been convicted or had pleaded guilty (sometimes to other criminal charges).

The material support provisions do not define terrorism directly, but instead cite U.S. laws implementing various international conventions regarding terrorism, such as those concerned with destroying civilian aircraft and taking hostages, as well as U.S. laws concerning attacks on the President, cabinet officials, members of Congress, and government property. The provision also cites the definitions used in the Immigration and Nationality Act and the Foreign Relations Authorization Act for FY 1988 and 1989 that mandated the State Department's annual global terrorism report to Congress.[18]

AEDPA also authorizes the Treasury Department to seize assets in the United States of a designated FTO. This provision complements executive orders issued under the authority of the International Emergency Economics Powers Act (IEEPA); such orders have been used increasingly since 9/11.

Additionally, the FTO provision tightens the Immigration Nationality Act as regards restrictions on visas for persons involved with terrorist groups. Under AEDPA, mere membership in a designated FTO was added to the grounds for denying a visa, as well as previous restrictions against leaders or representatives of a terrorist group.

ADMINISTRATIVE RECORD

While deliberating on AEDPA, some members of Congress, from both parties, expressed concern that groups might be designated FTOs for political reasons or with insufficient justification. The final legislation compromise required the Secretary of State to base the designations on a detailed administrative record that had to withstand scrutiny and could not be "arbitrary or capricious." As noted above, the Attorney General and the Secretary of the Treasury had to be consulted; also, a group was allowed to challenge its designation within 30 days in the U.S. Court of Appeals for the District of Columbia. Congress also stipulated that a designation would expire after two years unless renewed. A renewal entailed using the same procedure required for the initial designation—including a detailed administration record.

Because the administrative record was the sole basis for the review process, the Justice Department decided that it should be equivalent to a court brief. This proved to be a labor-intensive matter, especially as redesignations had to be automatically reviewed every two years. Preparing administrative records, even for groups that boasted of their terrorist activities, turned out to be time consuming and diverted government officials from other counterterrorism efforts.

Therefore, in 2003, the State Department Counterterrorism Office and Justice Department drafted amendments, which would extend the review requirements to a four–year period. The amendments first passed the House in 2003 and in early 2004, but the vehicle, the State Department Authorization bill, became bogged down in the Senate. Finally, as part of the Intelligence Reform Act of 2004, Congress included an amendment extending the review period for all groups to five years, with a provision allowing for a designated group to seek a review every two years.

The first designations were made in October 1997. As of late 2011, 49 groups are designated FTOs.[19] Most of them were on the original list. Several groups have challenged their designations more than once, including the Mujahedin-e Khalq organization (MEK), an anti-Iranian government group that actively lobbies Congress and conducts an expensive public relations campaign, however U.S. courts have upheld these designations.

WEAPONS OF MASS DESTRUCTION

A growing concern over weapons of mass destruction (WMD) led to the Biological Weapons and Anti-Terrorism Act of 1989.[20] In 1992, the Weapons of Mass Destruction Act called on the Defense and Energy departments to maintain and improve their ability to monitor and respond to the proliferation of WMD and missile delivery systems. Although the nonproliferation effort originally was directed against nations, it has since also been directed against non-state groups such as al-Qaeda that evidently are seeking to obtain or develop chemical and biological agents.

Progressively tighter legislation has strengthened controls over chemical, biological, and radioactive (CBR) agents, or has authorized sanctions against countries that use CBR weapons in violation of international law, as well as against companies that aid in the proliferation of such weapons. For example, provisions in Title V of AEDPA refine and expand the definition of possession of CBR agents to cover unlawful possession of certain substances whether or not the material is in the form of a delivery system, such as a bomb or missile. The Intelligence Reform Act of 2004 also contained additional provisions to tighten controls over CBR agents. The provisions in Title VI include specific prohibitions against possession of CBR agents by persons who are acting on behalf of terrorist organizations The provisions also include prohibitions against the manufacture or possession of the variola virus.

Two years earlier, in 2002, Congress enacted the Public Health and Bioterrorism Preparedness and Response Act[21] to improve the ability of the U.S. to prevent and respond to bioterrorism and other public health emergencies. This was followed by the Project Bioshield Act of 2004,[22] which authorized the purchase of vaccines that would be used in the event of a bioterrorist attack.

THE PATRIOT ACT

The U.S.A. Patriot Act[23] was rushed through Congress and passed on 26 October 2001 in the wake of 9/11. Reflecting the focus of and impetus for the legislation, Title I was called "Enhancing Domestic Security against Terrorism." Many other titles also related to home-land security—for example, by facilitating investigations and surveil-lance. Some provisions had been drafted earlier during the Clinton administration by career officials in the Justice Department and other agencies, but had been rebuffed by Congress before 9/11. One exam-ple is a "roving wiretap" provision (Sec. 206) under which federal officials may get a wiretapping order that would follow a suspect to any phone he uses (previously, a wiretap order had to apply to a specific phone number). Roving wiretaps were already permitted in ordinary criminal cases. The bill also permitted law enforcement to subpoena personal customer records from internet service providers, financial institutions, and credit card companies by issuing "National Security Letters" to those companies without notice to the targeted suspects.

The Patriot Act also permits the sharing of foreign intelligence (including information relating to protection against international terrorism or foreign attack, or concerning foreign activity and the conduct of foreign affairs) with officials of federal law enforcement, protective enforcement, immigration, national defense, and national security, for the performance of official duties. This removal of an earlier legal barrier is considered by some observers a major benefit of the Patriot Act. Others, however, say that the barrier against sharing information across agency lines had resulted not from law but from perceived restrictions and operating practices within the CIA and FBI. Regardless, the Patriot Act enhanced the government's ability to share intelligence with criminal investigators and prosecutors and has facil-itated criminal prosecutions and helped in some court cases.

The Patriot Act also allows the Secretary of State (in order to counter terrorism and other crimes) to share with foreign governments infor-mation in the State Department's visa lookout system. The United States already had a working relationship regarding the sharing of this database of terrorist suspects with Canada, and with Australia in connection with the 2000 Sydney Olympic Games.

Addressing the funding of terrorism, the Patriot Act includes pro-visions on money laundering, including establishing jurisdiction over foreigners who maintain a bank account in the United States. Section

311 of the Patriot Act has been used by the Treasury Department to ban transactions with the Lebanese Bank of Canada which has been used by Hezbollah as a money laundering conduit.

Also, U.S. financial institutions are required to terminate correspondent relationships with foreign banks that ignore U.S. subpoenas for records. Additionally, the money laundering provisions make terrorism subject to RICO (anti-racketeering legislation), and all assets of a person or entity that participates in or plans an act of domestic or international terrorism are subject to forfeiture. This provision includes a procedure for the owner of confiscated property to contest the seizure.

The FTO designations of AEDPA were modified by the Patriot Act, which allows redesignation of a terrorist group after the initial two years even if no terrorist activities have been cited during that period, provided that the group retains the "capability and intent" to engage in terrorism. This change takes account of the fact that terrorist groups sometimes "lie low" and do not conduct an actual attack for a period of time, and that their planning and fundraising may be undetectable. It also conserves the considerable time resources required by repeating the same basic facts and clearing the paperwork for designating groups whose situations have not changed, allowing the government analysts and lawyers to focus on higher priority new developments.

The Patriot Act has critics outside the government and in Congress. Many members of Congress—although they were reluctant to be painted as obstructionists or as weak on terrorism—were perturbed when the voluminous bill was rushed through in the aftermath of 9/11 without enough time to read and study it. Liberals and civil libertarians campaigned against select provisions. The reaction was to some extent fueled by distrust of former Attorney General Ashcroft's leadership of the Justice Department. On the other hand, many people in government counterterrorism work consider the opposition unjustified and sometimes overwrought, such as in the case of concerns about access to library records.

In spite of the controversy, the bill was reauthorized in early 2006, although with sections that had been modified by judicial rulings which invalidated several key provisions. In 2004, the use of National Security Letters to obtain personal email and phone data was ruled to violate the First and Fourth Amendments in *Doe v. Gonzalez*. The bill's domestic "sneak and peek" provisions were similarly found to violate the Fourth Amendment in the 2007 case of *Mayfield v. U.S.*

In that case, a Muslim attorney in Portland, Oregon was incorrectly linked to the 2004 Madrid train bombing and secretly surveilled using the provisions. After ultimately being jailed for several weeks before the case against him was dismissed, Mayfield eventually received an apology from the Justice Department along with a multimillion dollar settlement.[24]

Border Security

Reflecting a concern that terrorists could enter the United States across the land borders with Canada and Mexico, Title IV of the Patriot Act (called "Protecting the Borders") authorized tripling the number of border patrol personnel.

The new law required the Administration to develop a comprehensive strategy for intercepting terrorists and constraining their mobility. Early pilot studies on the use of advanced technology to improve border security, including the use of unmanned aircraft, have transitioned to standard practices.

CIVIL SUITS

A new legal dimension is the filing of civil suits by victims of terrorism against terrorists, their supporters, or both.

An early suit was brought by the family of Leon Klinghoffer, who was killed during the hijacking of *Achille Lauro* in 1985. An Italian court had convicted the terrorist leader Abu Abbas in absentia; but a U.S. warrant was dropped two years after the hijacking when the Justice Department concluded that the available evidence—reportedly intercepts—could not be used under U.S. legal procedures. Because Abu Abbas was a member of the Fatah ruling council, the Klinghoffer family filed suit in 1990 against the Palestine Liberation Organization (PLO), which had property in the United States. The case, brought under the Death on the High Seas Act,[25] was settled out of court in 1996; the terms were never publicly disclosed.

Several changes in the U.S. legal system made it easier to file civil suits against terrorists and their alleged supporters. Legislation initially enacted in 1990 with the support of the State Department, and of the Klinghoffer family and the families of those who died on Pan Am 103, allowed U.S. nationals or their survivors injured by acts of international terrorism to file civil suits to seize terrorists' assets.[26] The measure contained provisions addressing the concerns of the Justice Department about protecting evidence that might be used in criminal prosecutions.

Another development was Sec. 221 of the Antiterrorism and Effective Death Penalty Act of 1996[27] amending the Foreign Sovereign Immunity Act (FSIA) to allow U.S. nationals to bring civil actions against terrorist states. Generally, the FSIA protects nations and their authorized agents from civil suit for actions that take place in the course of their duties—a concept which is interpreted generously and with few exceptions. The enforcement of favorable judgments can be problematic, however, because in some cases, the countries supporting terrorists had no assets in the United States, or these countries' assets had already been frozen and were subject to previous claims and agreements. The State Department has had difficulty persuading families and the public to accept its concerns about previous claims and agreements and about setting precedents that might be used by other countries to seize U.S. assets.

Criminal actions such as murder are one such exception to the FSIA's protections of foreign sovereigns. Families of the victims of Pan Am 103 successfully sued Libya for its complicity in the attack, winning large financial settlements. Americans who were taken hostage in Lebanon during the 1980s by the Iranian-backed organization Hezbollah brought suits against Iran—as have the families of some American citizens killed by Palestinian terrorists affiliated with groups receiving Iranian material support. In July 2004, the U.S. District Court of Rhode Island ruled that the Palestinian Authority and PLO did not have sovereign immunity, because "Palestine" does not constitute a state under U.S. law. It awarded $116 million in damages to the family of Yaron Ungar, who had been shot and killed by Palestinian gunmen.

In July 2004, a civil case was filed against the Arab Bank of Jordan alleging that it had provided material support to terrorists by serving as a conduit for funds from Saudi contributors to families of Palestinian suicide bombers. Several Americans joined in the suit, including the widow of John Linde, one of three U.S. civilian contractors killed by a roadside bomb. Linde had been serving on a protective detail for U.S. diplomats who were visiting the West Bank to interview Palestinian candidates for scholarships. In July 2010, after Arab Bank repeatedly failed to produce court-ordered documents, a federal judge ruled that the jury in the case could infer that the refusal demonstrated that the bank had knowingly and purposefully worked on behalf of the terrorist organizations.[28]

In September 2004, Cantor Fitzgerald Securities, a bond trading firm that lost over 600 employees on 9/11, filed a civil suit against

Saudi Arabia and dozens of banks and Islamic charities, alleging that charities authorized or controlled by the Saudi government provided money, safe houses, weapons, and money laundering to terrorist groups. The Port Authority of New York and New Jersey and numerous other individuals and businesses also filed suits which were ultimately combined into a single case, *In Re Terrorist Attacks on September 11, 2001.* In 2005, a judge ruled to dismiss the Saudi Government and members of its Royal family as defendants in the case based on protections provided by the Foreign Sovereign Immunities Act. The dismissals were upheld on appeal on somewhat different grounds, nonetheless reiterating federal court's historical preference for leaving international matters of this sort to diplomatic rather than judicial measures.[29] The cases against other defendants not protected by principles of sovereign immunity are still pending as of early 2012.

In December 2004, a federal judge in Chicago ordered the Holy Land Foundation and two other American-based Islamic organizations that describe themselves as charities to pay $156 million to the family of David Boim, an American citizen who was fatally shot at an Israeli bus stop by members of Hamas. A jury earlier ruled in favor of the Boim family, which charged the groups and an alleged fundraiser with providing material support to Hamas, a Palestinian group formally designated by the State Department as a foreign terrorist organization.

In a November 2011, a ruling in an FSIA civil suit against Iran and Sudan for indirect support for the 1998 bombings of the U.S. embassies in Kenya and Tanzania cited links between those nations and al-Qaeda for the first time.[30] The case proceeded under a provision in the FSIA that permits foreign national employees of the U.S. to sue for injuries resulting from terrorism.[31] Both Iran and Sudan previously have been accused of being engaged in or supporting terrorist activities; however, this was the first case taken to the trial process, testing evidence presented in a federal court.[32] While the opinion did not find Iran and Sudan directly liable for the attacks, it did find sufficient evidence to satisfy the statute's strong requirement that an extrajudicial killing be "caused by" the defendant's material support. The judge wrote, "Iran's training and technical support was specifically required for the successful execution of al-Qaeda's plot."[33] Some believe the decision could serve as a precedent in holding Iran accountable for a broader range of terrorist activity in the future.[34]

PROSECUTION AND DETENTION OF TERRORISTS

Since 9/11, the U.S. has struggled to develop the laws and procedures that govern both the prosecution and non-criminal detention of terrorists. The unique nature of these cases has proven to be a challenge to constitutional principles of the U.S. and its established criminal law traditions.

Practical challenges inherent to terrorism interdiction and investigation present novel legal problems for both the prosecution and detention of terrorist subjects. Most simply, many suspects are non-citizens apprehended in foreign territory by military rather than civilian personnel. Military personnel are trained as war fighters; they do not patiently investigate or gather evidence on terrorist subjects, and they do not detain witnesses in war zones or take statements for trial purposes. Even if they could do so in the heat and confusion of a battle, such witnesses cannot legally or reliably be summoned to the U.S. at a later date to testify. Further, the military as well as other national security forces do not and cannot operate on the same evidentiary basis as do civil law enforcers. In these combat zones or cities where terrorists are operating, they must have the latitude to operate without warrants and act based on hearsay, fragmented information, or evidence that comes from confidential or unknown origins.

So, while terrorist activity may at one level seem to be simple criminal violations punishable under law, prosecutions of such cases are beset by numerous challenges: Are non-citizen terrorist subjects captured in foreign territory entitled to Constitutional protections during trial? In which courts—civil or military—should the proceedings take place? Whose laws should govern?

Even more vexing, the nature of terrorist threats and the need to interdict terrorists before terrorist crimes and potentially major attacks with large numbers of casualties occur, arguably counsels for a need to detain select suspects indefinitely and without trial. Britain and some other countries allow for preventive detention, though usually for a fixed period of time.

Military and national security personnel cannot risk waiting for incidents to occur in order to launch investigations or detain suspects. The fact that a suspect is a member of a terrorist organization or has attended terrorist training camps, for example, may signal they are a dangerous, if not imminent threat, but there is not yet court admissible evidence that they have committed a criminal violation. Further, the evidence or intelligence used to reach conclusions about terrorist subjects may be sensitive or simply inadequate to obtain a reliable conviction. Therefore, it is argued that despite our inability to successfully convict suspects in these grey areas, their preemptive and potentially indefinite detention is nonetheless essential to U.S. security. A challenge is how to apprehend and detain suspected terrorists without violating the principle of innocent until proven guilty, and without provoking a backlash. In Iraq and Afghanistan in particular, the U.S. and its allies had to face the problem of weeding out persons who may be bit players, caught up in a sweep or victims of false or exaggerated charges leveled by enemies or competitors for political, personal, or financial reasons.

Background

Both criminal prosecution and non-criminal detention policies share a common legal background formed through early sparring between all three branches of the U.S. government. In November of 2001, President Bush issued a military order establishing the right of military courts to try and detain certain non-citizens in the war on terrorism.[35] The Order specified that such persons had no recourse to federal civil courts to challenge their detention or appeal the military courts' decisions. In the landmark 2004 case of *Rasul v. Bush,* the Supreme Court specifically invalidated the provisions of the Order, which denied detainees access to civil courts, holding that non-citizen detainees in military custody at Guantanamo Bay, Cuba, had a right to challenge their detention in civil courts under habeas corpus law.

Congress responded with the Detainee Treatment Act (DTA) of 2005[36], a legislative response to *Rasul* meant to strip federal courts of the ability to hear habeas corpus petitions from suspected terrorist detainees like Rasul. In place of habeas petitions, the DTA instead provided for a special process of limited review, which would be confined to the jurisdiction of the D.C. Circuit Court of Appeals. In a narrow holding meant to avoid direct conflict, the Court answered in *Hamdan v. Rumsfeld* by interpreting DTA's jurisdiction-stripping language as not applicable to *currently pending* detainee habeas petitions. Yet, in a separate portion of its opinion the Court was not shy, ruling to invalidate the military commission system established by President Bush's original Military Order. In doing so, the Court refrained from outlining acceptable procedures, stating only that valid trial procedures must be as similar as possible to those used for military court martials as outlined in the Uniform Code of Military Justice (UCMJ).

Congress countered with the Military Commissions Act of 2006.[37] In conformity with *Hamdan*, the Act established a new military commissions system with procedural rules based upon those provided in the UCMJ (although with significant departures). However, in a direct challenge to the Court's ruling in *Hamdan*, the Act once again reiterated Congress's intent to strip habeas jurisdiction from federal courts for cases involving non-citizen detainees, including jurisdiction for currently pending cases. Subsequent actions in these areas diverged after *Hamdan* and are explained further below.

Prosecution

Following *Hamdan* and the passage of the Military Commissions Act (MCA) of 2006, the Department of Defense released further regulations to guide the military commission process[38] and began using the system. The commissions were used to try and convict several individuals including Salim Hamdan, and Australian citizen, David Hicks. In 2009, President Obama halted the commissions pending a review of their use and the individual cases of those still detained at Guantanamo Bay.

Later in 2009, the Department of Defense modified the Manual for Military Commissions[39], and the Senate passed the Military Commissions Act of 2009 (MCA 2009)[40] making reforms to the process, including some proposed by President Obama. Also in 2009, President Obama's Detention Policy Task Force issued a preliminary report reaffirming that the White House considered military commissions to be an appropriate forum for trying suspected violations of the laws of the war, although civil courts would be the preferred forum.[41] The report also included guiding considerations for disposing of the cases still pending against detainees at Guantanamo Bay, including, in brief, efficiency, the nature and gravity of offenses or underlying conduct, and other prosecution considerations, such as the extent to which the forum permits a full presentation of the wrongful conduct and appropriate sentencing upon conviction. After review of the Guantanamo detainee's cases, approximately 110 were scheduled for release pending the identification of suitable host countries, 40 were to be tried using military commissions, and 50 were ordered to remain in detention without trial. As of this writing, no case challenging the existing military commission system and criminal procedures has reached the Supreme Court.

These significant legal battles and unanswered questions surrounding the use of military commissions has moved the Obama Administration to heavily favor trying terrorist suspects in U.S. federal court. In a 2010 response to the Senate Judiciary Committee, the Assistant

U.S. Attorney General provided reasons why federal courts may be preferred to military commissions.[42] Federal courts have an established track record and a well-developed body of law, including an established plea system that allows for guilty pleas in capital cases. [43] Some cases can only be tried in federal courts because they may not constitute crimes tryable under the Military Commissions Act. Lastly, some foreign nations have expressed concern about extraditing possible defendants if they are to be tried in military courts as opposed to federal courts.

However, in April 2012, the Obama administration changed its mind on one high-profile case, announcing that terrorist mastermind Khalid Sheikh Mohammed and four co-conspirators will be tried in a military commission at Guantanamo Bay. Attorney General Eric Holder said Congress created conditions where the Department of Justice cannot try them in a federal court.[44] Mohammed was to have been tried in New York City, but city officials strongly objected to the move and Congress refused to appropriate funds to house Guantanamo inmates on mainland United States and to provide funds for a trial of extraordinary expense.

"Non-Criminal" Detention

In the Military Commissions Act of 2006, Congress had reiterated its intent to block Federal courts from hearing terrorist detention cases, setting up a showdown which came to a head in the 2008 case of *Boumediene v. Bush*. In *Boumediene*, the Court announced two critical holdings regarding detention cases. First, it held that non-citizens held by the military at Guantanamo were protected by a U.S. Constitutional right to challenge their detention through habeas corpus petitions in federal district courts. By ruling that a *Constitutional* right existed, the Court conclusively invalidated Congress's attempts to strip civil courts of the ability to hear habeas petitions from Guantanamo detainees. Second, the Court held that the alternate judicial review process described in the Detainee Treatment Act was not a constitutionally sufficient substitute for normal habeas review. However, while the Court cited some specific deficiencies, it did not give definitive outlines of what was a sufficient procedure, instead leaving that task explicitly to the lower courts to design in practice.

The Court's decision was perhaps guided by the notion that federal courts are the best, and perhaps only, tool to develop the law around the entirely new body of non-criminal detention law. Such development requires a flexibility, pace of change, and sophistication that Congress simply cannot provide in the often politically charged atmosphere of this subject and the give and take of the legislative process. For this reason, subsequent development has in fact taken place through case-by-case common law actions rather than through sweeping legislative advance.

Lower courts have and will continue to cope with issues such as: Whom can we detain? What is the evidentiary burden of proof that should be used—Substantial certainty? Totality of the evidence? On whom does that burden rest? What evidence is admissible? Hearsay evidence from unavailable witnesses or protected intelligence sources? Involuntary confessions? Once detained, how long can or should indefinite detention last? What is the process to appeal or reverse such a designation?

However, in addition to this more specific development, recent legislation has once again moved to delineate the extent of the Executive's power to detain terrorist suspects. In late December 2011, as part of the National Defense Authorization for Fiscal Year 2012,[45] Congress passed, and the President signed into law, new controversial provisions giving the President powers about which he himself expressed reservations.[46] The provisions authorize the President to detain covered persons pending disposition under the law of war. Covered persons include: 1) Those who planned, authorized, committed, or aided the 9/11 attacks, or harbored those responsible; or 2) those who substantially support al-Qaeda, the Taliban, or associated forces engaged in hostilities against the U.S.[47] The provisions allow the President to: 1) Detain suspects under the law of war without trial until the end of the hostilities authorized by Congress's original 2001 Authorization for Use of Military Force; 2) try them in military commissions; 3) transfer them for trial to an alternative court; or 4) transfer them to their country of origin, any other foreign country, or any other foreign entity.[48]

The continued use of Guantánamo itself has been a major point of contention between President Obama and Republicans in Congress.[49] During his 2008 election campaign, Obama pledged to close the prison which received its first prisoners in January 2001. The prison became and has continued as a focus point of criticism in the Muslim world and among some human rights advocates in the U.S. because of allegations of prisoner abuse including torture and desecration of the Koran by a prison guard. But Congressional Republicans blocked plans to close the prison and move inmates to high security prisons in the U.S. Some members argued that there would be a security risk from housing hard core terrorist prisoners in prisons on U.S. soil, although the Bureau of Prisons has said there have been no escapes of terrorists who have been previously convicted and imprisoned. During the 111th session of Congress 2009–2010, lawmakers led by the Republican-controlled House, passed nine pieces of legislation that contained a ban. Similarly, they inserted into the 2011 Defense Authorization bill—a military funding bill, which is politically virtually impossible for a President to veto— a provision that prohibits the use of funds to transport Guantanamo detainees to the United States.

At its core, the dispute also reflects the stance of some Republicans that military courts and prisons should be used for handling terrorists, not the civilian court system, even though the Justice Department has a had a high success rate using material support and other conspiracy related provisions of law, as well as laws applying to directly committed violence. Ironically, although some members of Congress and writers have criticized the use of civilian courts and prisons instead of a military court to punish terrorists, as noted in the introduction, it was the Reagan administration that emphasized and even established a public diplomacy campaign to brand terrorists as criminals and not freedom fighters.[50]

IMPLEMENTATION AND CHALLENGES

While the United States and many other countries have extensive counterterrorism laws on the books, enactment of legislation and ratification of international conventions is not enough to stem terrorism. Effective implementation of counterterrorist laws and regulations requires commitment by political leaders and the law enforcement community, motivated personnel, training, financial resources, and equipment. With many countries, especially in the developing world, the will and or capability are often weak

Even in the United States where the will and resources are great, there have been shortfalls. For example, as revealed by the 9/11 Commission and Congressional committees, the FBI's antiquated computer system impeded the sharing of information between investigators and thus made it more difficult to "connect the dots." By contrast to the FBI, then Secretary of State Colin Powell made it a priority to upgrade the State Department's computer system; previously, many officers seeking to perform unclassified research, for example on terrorist organizations, found it easier to access the internet on their home computers.

Despite the new focus on counterterrorism even before and especially after 9/11, the government was initially reluctant to provide additional resources toward this effort. Although the FBI has been criticized for being slow to respond to terrorist threats, during a flurry of threats in the summer of 2001 it made efforts to shift resources to counterterrorism, but was rebuffed. In May 2001, according to the 9/11 Commission report, Attorney General Ashcroft testified at a Congressional appropriations hearing that "one of the nation's most fundamental responsibilities is to protect its citizens ... from terrorist attacks"; yet the next day, his department distributed internal guidance for the fiscal year 2003 budget request to Congress that did not list fighting terrorism as a priority. The Commission reported that Dale Watson, the FBI counterterrorism chief, "told us that he almost fell out of his chair when he saw the memo." As the summer wore on, the FBI submitted its request for an increase to the Justice Department for forwarding to the Office of Management and Budget (OMB), but on 10 September, according to the commission's report, Ashcroft turned down the request.

OMB and Congress have also short-changed international counterterrorism programs, even though President Bush repeatedly said the U.S. must fight terrorists overseas before they can hit America at home.[51] The State Department's Antiterrorist Assistance (ATA) program suffered budget-cutting behind the scenes despite the public rhetoric. ATA strengthens the counterterrorism capabilities of foreign law enforcement personnel; it offers courses in subjects such as crisis management, airport security, detecting and defusing explosives, negotiating for the release of hostages, and protecting important individuals. Yet despite widespread terrorist attacks in Kenya, Tanzania, Yemen, Morocco, the Philippines, Indonesia, and elsewhere, OMB cut the State Department's ATA budget request by an average of 20 percent for fiscal years 2003, 2004, and 2005. Several smaller but important related programs, such as the terrorist interdiction program and funding for foreign emergency support teams, were cut even more. Then in November 2004, in a lame-duck session after the elections, Congress finally passed an Omnibus Appropriations Bill that cut the OMB-approved request for ATA training by 9.5 percent, from $128 to $120 million.

Since then funding for key programs has increased, but the battles in Congress to cut the overall government budget have had their impact on counterterrorism programs. For example the Consolidated Appropriation Act passed in December 2011 for Fiscal Year 2012 cut about a billion dollars for grants to state and local governments, to improve their security, reducing the level to $2.37 billion.

In addition to the pressures to reduce the overall federal government, the task of adequately funding counterterrorism programs becomes more difficult because of the way the OMB and Congressional budget specialists usually operate. They tend to look at the previous year's budget as the baseline for the new fiscal year, adding or subtracting a certain percentage, instead of focusing on the actual needs of a program. They may then describe an appropriation as an increase of X percent over last year's budget instead of noting that it is, say, only 75 percent of the program's projected requirement. Furthermore, there is no magic formula for working out a cost-benefit analysis—how much money should be spent on a particular program to deal with a potential attack that may be rated low in probability but high in consequence. The errorists have the initiative in deciding where to strike and there are too many vulnerable potential targets. Meanwhile, there is the challenge inherent of detecting and countering the emergence of "lone wolf" terrorists or would-be terrorists who do not have communications that could be intercepted with known terrorist individuals or groups.

Codifying the Counterterrorism Laws?

Mirroring the unpredictable nature of terrorist threats and tactics, counterterrorism laws have and will continue to develop in a complex pattern, with each step building upon existing laws which may or may not be the proper tool for the new challenge. In an ideal world, the myriad of counterterrorism law would be consolidated and rewritten into one comprehensive package to resolve inconsistencies and clarify ambiguity. Comprehensive legislation could also work out more precise guidelines for determining which suspects should be tried in civil courts and which ones in military courts. However, this would be a tremendously time consuming undertaking and difficult in the increasingly partisan atmosphere that has developed in recent years. At one time—before the political tension between the Clinton administration and the Republican-controlled Congress, and before 9/11—fighting terrorism was mainly a bipartisan effort. That is no longer necessarily true. When the idea of taking a more comprehensive approach was discussed by State Department and Justice Department officials in the past, there was a concern that Congress could write provisions that might be unworkable or counterproductive.[52]

Yet, if there is another large-scale terrorist attack, there will be a scramble to "do something"—and that often involves passing new laws. Lawmakers and the executive branch should collaborate closely to ensure that such legislation is carefully drafted before enactment. The odds of that, however, have declined in recent years.

NOTES

1. United Nations. *International Convention for the Suppression of Terrorism*, 1999, http://www.un.org/law/cod/finterr.htm (accessed January 12, 2012).

2. Reagan, Ronald, Radio Address to the Nation on Terrorism. May 31, 1986, http://www.presidency.ucsb.edu/ws/index.php?pid=37376#ixzz1MpziZAr6 (accessed January 10, 2012).

3. Academic researchers have found at least 110 definitions of terrorism. One reason for the difficulty in obtaining a consensus at the United Nations has been the effort by some third countries to exclude Palestinian groups and other "legitimate national liberation groups" from being covered by the definition. For additional discussion, see Boaz Ganor, *The Counter-Terrorism Puzzle* (New Brunswick, NJ, and London: Transaction Publishers. 2008), 8, 17. Also see Bruce Hoffmann *Inside Terrorism*, revised and expanded (New York: Columbia University Press, 2006), 1, 41.

4. Section 303 of the International Security Assistance and Arms Export Control Act of 1976, which created Sec. 620A of the Foreign Assistance Act (since modified in 2002, Public Law 107–115: Stat. 3147, 2153, 2155).

5. Section 6(j) of the Export Administration Act of 1979 (P.L. 96–72. Codified as 50 U.S.C. App. Sec. 2405). In 1988, "would enhance" was changed to "could enhance." Also, the dollar threshold was lowered, making the provision more stringent. Co-author Michael Kraft was a national security legislative assistant to Mrs. Fenwick at the time and played a role in drafting the legislation.

6. Also see Michael B. Kraft and Edward Marks 2011, *U.S. Government Counterterrorism: A Guide to Who Does What* (Boca Raton, FL: CRC Press, 2008), 33-45.

7. Section 1202 of the Omnibus Diplomatic Security and Antiterrorism Act of 1986, Pub. Law 99–399, later modified as U.S.C. 2332.

8. Section 1202 of the Omnibus Diplomatic Security and Antiterrorism Act of 1986 (P.L. 99–399, 18 U.S.C 2332). Section 60022 of the Violent Crime Control and Law Enforcement Act of 1994 added a death penalty provision.

9. Federal Bureau of Investigation (FBI) website. International Operations: Overview of the Legal Attaché Program, http://www.fbi.gov/about-us/international_operations/overview (accessed January 12, 2012).

10. P.L. 104–132 (28 U.S.C. 1602 et seq.).

11. 46 U.S.C. App. §§1801–1805.

12. 18 U.S.C. Sec. 2339A(a).

13. P.L 103–322, Sec. s12005a.

14. E.O. 2947 and executive orders freezing the assets of other terrorist groups after 9/11 were issued pursuant to the International Emergency Economic Powers Act (P.L. 95–223).

15. The provisions regarding FTOs and material support were signed into law on April 24, 1996 as part of AEDPA (P.L. 104-132, 110 Stat.). Although the bill had been drafted in response to terrorism overseas, it gained impetus after the bombing in Oklahoma City. The precision of the wording of the final draft suffered to some extent because the Clinton administration and the Republican-controlled Congress prodded each other to move quickly before various recesses. For a fuller discussion of the material support provisions, see Charles Doyle, "Terrorist Material Support: An Overview of 18 U.S.C. 2339A and 2339B," Congressional

Research Service Brief R41333, July 19, 2010, http://www.fas.org/sgp/crs/natsec/R41333.pdf (accessed March 20, 2012).

16. 18 U.S.C. Sec. 2339B.

17. Intelligence Reform and Terrorism Protection Act of 2004 (IRTPA), Pub. L. No. 108–458, 118 Stat. 3638, (Dec. 17, 2004), codified at 42 U.S.C. §2000ee, 50 U.S.C. §403-1 et seq., §403-3 et seq. Sec. 2339A and Sec. 2339D.

18. State Department Bureau of Counterterrorism, legislative requirements and definitions for the annual report on international terrorism to Congress, http://www.state.gov/g/ct/rls/crt/2010/170265.htm (accessed January 11, 2012).

19. Department of State website, Foreign Terrorist Organizations, http://www.state.gov/j/ct/rls/other/des/123085.htm (accessed January 12, 2012).

20. P.L. 101–298.

21. P.L. 107–188.

22. P.L. 108–276.

23. See Brian Yoh and Charles Doyle, USA Patriot Improvement and Reauthorization Act of 2005: A Legal Analysis. Updated December 21, 2006. Uniting and Strengthening America by Providing Appropriate Tools Required to Intersect and Obstruct Terrorism Act of 2001 (P.L 107–56). USA PATRIOT is the acronym. http://www.fas.org/sgp/crs/intel/RL33332.pdf. (accessed March 20, 2012).

24. Eric Lichtblau, "U.S. Will Pay $2 Million to Lawyer Wrongly Jailed," *New York Times,* November 30, 2006, http://www.nytimes.com/2006/11/30/us/30settle.html (accessed January 8, 2012).

25. 46 U.S.C. Sec 761.22, 1006 Congressional Research Service http://www.au.af.mil/au/awc/awcgate/crs/rl33332.pdf (accessed January 10, 2012).

26. 18 U.S.C. Sec. 2333.

27. P.L. 104–132, 28 U.S.C. 1602 et seq.

28. A. G. Sulzberger, "Bank Hit with Sanctions in Suit over Terrorist Aid," *New York Times,* July 14, 2010, http://www.nytimes.com/2010/07/14/nyregion/14terror.html (accessed January 4, 2012).

29. Anna Henning, Congressional Research Service (2008). *In Re Terrorist Attacks on September 11, 2001: Dismissals of Claims Against Saudi Defendants Under the Foreign Sovereign Immunities Act,* http://fpc.state.gov/documents/organization/112480.pdf.

30. *Owens et al. v. Republic of Sudan et al.,* Memorandum Opinion, November 28, 2011, http://docs.justia.com/cases/federal/district-courts/district-of-columbia/dcdce/1:2001cv02244/15028/215/0.pdf?1322561421.

31. 28 U.S.C. 1605A(a)2(A)(ii)(III).

32. For example, the 9/11 Commission Report stated that "al-Qaeda operatives, including top military committee members and operatives involved in the Kenya cell's plotting of the embassy bombings, developed the tactical expertise to execute this kind of attack when they attended Hezbollah terrorist training camps in Lebanon sometime in 1993." Hezbollah is in turn linked to heavy Iranian influence and support. National Commission on Terrorist Attacks upon the United States (Philip Zelikow, Executive Director; Bonnie D. Jenkins, Counsel; Ernest R. May, Senior Advisor), *The 9/11 Commission Report* (New York: W. W. Norton & Company, 2004).

33. *Id*. at 30, pp. 34–35.

34. Matthew Levitt, U.S. Court Ruling Links Iran to Al Qaeda, The United States Institute of Peace: The Iran Primer, December 13, 2011, http://iranprimer.usip.org/blog?page=1.

35. Detention, Treatment, and Trial of Certain Non-Citizens in the War Against Terrorism §1(a), 66 Fed. Reg. 57,833 (November 16, 2001).

36. P.L. No. 109–148, §1005, 119 Stat. 2739, 2742 (amending 28 U.S.C. §2241).

37. P.L. 109–366, codified at chapter 47a of title 10, U.S. Code.

38. Department of Defense, The Manual for Military Commissions, January 18, 2007, http://www. defenselink.mil/news/MANUAL%20FOR%20MILITARY%20COMMISSIONS%202007% 20signed.pdf.

39. Letter from Robert M. Gates, Secretary of Defense, to Senator Carl Levin, May 15, 2009, http://www.nimj.org/documents/2009%20DoD%20MMC%20Changes.pdf.

40. P.L. 111–84.

41. Memorandum from the Detention Policy Task Force to the Attorney General and the Secretary of Defense, July 20, 2009, http://www.nimj.com/display.aspx?base=MilitaryCommis sions&ID=255.

42. Written answers to questions posed to Attorney General Eric Holder during testimony given before the Senate Judiciary Committee on April 14, 2010, http://www.fas.org/irp/congress/2010_hr/doj-qfr.pdf.

43. For illustrative an list of federal statutes related to terrorism cases, see Department of Justice U.S. Attorneys' office, Counterterrorism Efforts, http://www.justice.gov/usao/briefing_room/ns/counterterrorism.html (accessed March 20, 2012).

44. ABC News, "In Reversal, Obama Orders Guantanamo Military Trial for 9/11 Mastermind Khalid Sheikh Mohammed," http://abcnews.go.com/Politics/911-mastermind-khalid-sheikh-mohammed-military-commission/story?id=13291750#.T2fDj3mcySo.

45. H.R. 1540, signed into law as P.L. 112–81.

46. Mark Landler, "After Struggle on Detainees, Obama Signs Defense Bill," *New York Times*, December 31, 2011, http://www.nytimes.com/2012/01/01/us/politics/obama-signs-military-spending-bill.html?_r=2&scp=1&sq=obama%20signs%20defense&st=cse (accessed January 6, 2012).

47. *Id.* at 39. Sections 1021(b)(1) and (b)(2).

48. *Id.* Sections 1021(c)(1)–(c)(4).

49. CBS News, *Guiantanamo Closure Hopes Fade as Prison Turns 10,* July 11, 2012, http://www.cbsnews.com/8301-202_162-57356858/guantanamo-closure-hopes-fade-as-prison-turns-10/.

50. Michael B. Kraft and Edward Marks, *U.S. Government Counterterrorism: A Guide to Who Does What* (Boca Raton, FL: CRC Press), 33–34. Also see Ronald Reagan, *Radio Address to the Nation,* May 31, 1986, http://www.reagan.utexas.edu/archives/speeches/1986/53186a. htm (accessed January 10, 2011).

51. In an Oak Ridge, Tennessee, speech July 2004 on the terrorist threat, President Bush said, "We will confront them overseas so we will not have to confront them at home." Available at http://www.presidentialrhetoric.com/speeches/07.12.04.html (accessed January 10, 2011).

52. Co-author Kraft had heard many such discussions during his 19 years in the State Department and previously as a Senate staffer.

9

INTELLIGENCE AND INFORMATION SHARING FOR HOMELAND SECURITY AND COUNTERTERRORISM

Christian Beckner

Congressional Staff Member[1]

INTRODUCTION

This chapter examines the issue of terrorism-related information sharing. The chapter reviews a number of policy reforms and activities that were undertaken following the attacks of September 11, 2001 to ensure that all information that was potentially relevant to a terrorist plot was effectively shared among relevant federal agencies and with key non-federal stakeholders, including state, local, and tribal agencies, and the private sector.

The chapter begins by discussing the impetus to address the issue of information sharing after 9/11, with respect to missed opportunities to detect the terrorist plot due to inadequate information sharing. It then surveys key information sharing-related initiatives of the past decade, including legislation, organizational changes, improvements to federal information sharing systems, cultural shifts, and initiatives for information sharing with non-federal entities. The chapter then assesses the overall progress that has been made in the last decade with respect to terrorism-related information sharing, and discusses several significant ongoing issues and challenges for the next decade.

THE IMPETUS TO IMPROVE TERRORISM-RELATED INFORMATION SHARING

In the days and weeks after the al Qaeda terrorist attacks of September 11, 2001 in New York, Virginia, and Pennsylvania, the media began to report on the missed opportunities for detecting the plot prior to its execution. The Congressional Joint Inquiry released its report on the 9/11 attacks in 2002, and the 9/11 Commission released its report in 2004, providing official narratives of the events leading up to the attacks, and detailing examples of information relevant to the plot that agencies did not fully share—in some cases because they did not understand the relevancy of certain pieces of information, in other cases because of organizational or cultural barriers. The 9/11 Commission Report identified ten missed "operational opportunities" to potentially detect and disrupt the 9/11 plot—nine of which relate to the issue of information sharing. In discussing these missed opportunities, the Commission focused on the ways in which the legacy systems and processes for sharing information were becoming increasingly mismatched with current threats:

> What all these stories have in common is a system that requires a demonstrated "need to know" before sharing. This approach assumes it is possible to know, in advance, who will need to use the information. Such a system implicitly assumes that the risk of inadvertent disclosure outweighs the benefits of wider sharing. Those Cold War assumptions are no longer appropriate. The culture of agencies feeling they own the information they gathered at taxpayer expense must be replaced by a culture in which the agencies instead feel they have a duty to the information-to repay the taxpayers' investment by making that information available....
>
> ... Each agency's incentive structure opposes sharing, with risks (criminal, civil, and internal administrative sanctions) but few rewards for sharing information. No one has to pay the long-term costs of over-classifying information, though these costs—even in literal financial terms—are substantial. There are no punishments for not sharing information. Agencies uphold a "need-to-know" culture of information protection rather than promoting a "need-to-share" culture of integration.[2]

This discussion of missed opportunities, which began in the days and weeks after the attack, prior to the release of the Joint Inquiry and 9/11 Commission reports, elevated the importance of terrorism-related information sharing on the policy agenda. Policymakers took a fresh look at the recommendations of several pre-9/11 national security commissions (Hart–Rudman, Gilmore) that had discussed issues related to information sharing. Starting in 2002, the Markle Task Force for National Security[3] released a series of detailed reports that looked closely at what an effective information sharing regime would look like and considered the technological, governance, policy, and cultural challenges associated with making progress toward that vision of effective information sharing. The 9/11 Commission Report noted its debt to the Markle Task Force in its discussion of the issue in 2004.

The issue also quickly became a matter of official policy for the Executive Branch. For example, the first National Strategy for Homeland Security (released in 2002) highlights the importance of the issue, noting that "to secure the homeland better, we must link the vast amounts of knowledge residing within each government agency while ensuring adequate privacy."[4] In 2007, President George W. Bush issued a detailed National Strategy for Information Sharing that highlighted the key information sharing initiatives and activities underway within the federal government, and in 2012, the Obama Administration is in the process of updating this information sharing strategy.[5]

MAJOR INFORMATION SHARING INITIATIVES FROM 2001 TO 2011

In the last decade, a number of initiatives have been undertaken to respond to the imperative for improved information sharing, to remedy the specific information sharing failures identified by the 9/11 Commission, and improve the U.S. government's ability to detect and disrupt terrorist plots in the homeland.

These initiatives have come in multiple forms, including new laws, executive orders, and directives; the establishment of new institutions and reforms of existing ones; the development of new systems and technical capabilities; and efforts to promote a culture of information sharing. They have been focused both within the federal government and with respect to the federal government's partnerships with state, local, and tribal governments, the private sector, and the general public. This section of the chapter will summarize in greater detail many of the key initiatives related to information sharing that have been made in the decade since the attacks of September 11, 2001.

Legislative Initiatives, Executive Orders and other Federal Policies

In the last decade there have been a number of laws passed that relate to information sharing, as well as a series of related Executive Orders, Presidential Directives, and other policies. This section briefly highlights a few of the most important of these laws and policies. Many of the relevant laws, orders, and policies established new institutions that are discussed in additional detail in the following section.

USA Patriot Act (2001)

The Patriot Act was passed into law only weeks after 9/11, and included a number of significant counterterrorism and law enforcement provisions. With respect to information sharing, it importantly removed the "wall" that had stifled the sharing of criminal investigative information (including wiretap and grand jury information) with intelligence agencies prior to the attacks of 9/11.

Homeland Security Act (2002)

The Homeland Security Act established the Department of Homeland Security (DHS) in order to bring together most of the key federal agencies with homeland security responsibilities into a single cabinet-level Department, and improve integration with respect to key missions such as border security and transportation security. The Act included several sections that were relevant to information sharing. The Act gave DHS the responsibility to share homeland security and terrorism-related information with other federal and non-federal entities. It also required the President to establish procedures for sharing homeland security information, and required that agencies implement those procedures.

Intelligence Reform and Terrorism Prevention Act (2004)

Congress passed the Intelligence Reform and Terrorism Prevention Act (IRTPA) following the release of the 9/11 Commission Report in an effort to implement many of its key recommendations. IRTPA included several very significant information sharing provisions. It vested the new Director of National Intelligence (DNI) with responsibilities related to intelligence information sharing, and tasked the new National Counterterrorism Center (NCTC) with "analyzing and integrating all intelligence possessed or acquired by the United States

Government pertaining to terrorism and counterterrorism." The Act also included a provision to require the President to establish an Information Sharing Environment that "provides and facilitates the means for sharing terrorism information among all appropriate Federal, state, local, and tribal entities, and the private sector through the use of policy guidelines and technologies."[6]

Implementing Recommendations of the 9/11 Commission Act (2007)

This legislation updated the provisions of IRTPA with respect to the Information Sharing Environment, established the Interagency Threat Assessment and Coordination Group (discussed later in the chapter), and updated DHS's intelligence and information sharing authorities.

Key Executive Orders

Several Executive Orders (EO 13311, EO 13356, EO 13388) were issued by President Bush between 2002 and 2004. These Orders were linked closely to the information sharing provisions of the Homeland Security Act and Intelligence Reform and Terrorism Prevention Act, describing how the Administration intended to implement policies in these areas consistent with relevant laws.

A second wave of notable Executive Orders (EOs) that relate to information sharing were issued by President Obama between 2009 and 2011. EO 13549 focused on improving the means by which state, local, tribal and private sector entities are able to receive security clearances and handle classified information. EO 13556 built on efforts over the previous six years to establish a clear framework for harmonizing disparate markings on unclassified but sensitive documents, now to be known as Controlled Unclassified Information (CUI). EO 13587 was issued in 2011 in response to a White House-led review of the large-scale disclosures of classified information by WikiLeaks in 2010, to better integrate information "safeguarding" with the broader set of information sharing systems and policies.

Other Policies and Directives

There are dozens of other directives, memoranda of agreement, and agency-level policies that relate to information sharing and which are important for understanding the broader information sharing framework. For example, Homeland Security Presidential Directives (HSPD) 6 and 11 from 2003 and 2004 address the management and use of watchlisting and screening information, and HSPD 24 (issued in 2008) builds on these directives by requiring agencies to use biometrics to support screening activities in a more integrated way. Another example of a key information sharing policy is the NCTC and Department of Justice agreement from 2008 (updated in 2012) that governs the terms of NCTC's access to information in datasets that broadly include non-terrorism information.[7]

Institutional Developments and Reforms at the Federal Level

A number of the laws referenced in the previous section established new institutions that have key information sharing responsibilities. This section discusses the roles that these institutions have played in promoting information sharing since their establishment. It also briefly discusses the reforms within the Federal Bureau of Investigation in the last decade.

Department of Homeland Security

As noted previously, the Homeland Security Act tasked DHS with sharing terrorism-related information with other federal agencies and with non-federal agencies, including state, local, and tribal entities, and the private sector. These responsibilities have been a priority of the Department since its inception, particularly with respect to outreach to non-federal entities, where DHS has played a critical role in supporting state and local fusion centers, and in sharing information with entities in the private sector that own or operate critical infrastructure.

DHS also contains nearly all of the key federal agencies that are responsible for managing the U.S. borders and ports of entry, including Customs and Border Protection, Immigration and Customs Enforcement, the Transportation Security Administration, U.S. Coast Guard, and Citizenship and Immigration Services. Efforts have been made within DHS to integrate and improve access to relevant databases maintained by each of these Departmental components with the objective of improving the ability of agencies to detect people who are attempting to enter the country illicitly and/or who could pose a threat to national security. A number of programs implemented by DHS in the past several years (e.g., Secure Flight, Western Hemisphere Travel Initiative) have been focused toward these objectives.

Director of National Intelligence (DNI)

In the IRTPA, the Director of National Intelligence is given the responsibility to "ensure maximum availability of and access to intelligence information within the intelligence community consistent with national security requirements"[8] and is also tasked with establishing policies, standards, and systems that facilitate intelligence information sharing.

Since 2005, the DNI and the staff within the Office of Director of National Intelligence have carried out these responsibilities by issuing a number of policies and directives for the IC, most notably Intelligence Community Directive (ICD) 501, released in 2009 and entitled "Discovery and Dissemination or Retrieval of Information within the Intelligence Community." ICD 501 directs intelligence agencies to shift from an ethos of "need to know" to one of "responsibility to provide," and sets forth mechanisms to improve the discoverability of information, outline how information can subsequently be used, and resolve disputes about access to information.

The DNI has also issued two unclassified strategy documents on intelligence information sharing: the Intelligence Community Information Sharing Strategy (released in 2008) and the Strategic Intent for Information Sharing (2011). These two documents outline key intelligence community principles and priorities for information sharing.

The DNI has also led the development of a set of projects intended to improve collaboration and information sharing across the intelligence community, including A-Space (a collaboration tool for analysts originally modeled after MySpace) and Intellipedia, the intelligence community's answer to Wikipedia.

National Counterterrorism Center (NCTC)

In recommending the establishment of NCTC, the 9/11 Commission noted that its essential mission would be to "pool all-source intelligence, foreign and domestic, about transnational terrorist organizations within global reach."[9] It thus contributes to information by bridging the traditional foreign-domestic divide, and ensuring that there is one place in the federal government that has access to all relevant information from the key federal agencies involved in counterterrorism including the CIA, FBI, NSA, and DHS.

The NCTC also plays a very significant role with respect to the terrorist watchlisting process via its management of the Terrorist Identities Datamart Environment (TIDE) database. TIDE serves as the all-source data repository for information known on watchlisted individuals, and thus facilitates a wide range of screening and investigative activities within the federal government.

Program Manager for the Information Sharing Environment

The Information Sharing Environment provision of the IRTPA established a Program Manager position (PM-ISE) to lead these efforts, consistent with law and with Presidential guidelines that were issued in 2005. Since the appointment of the first Program Manager in 2005, the PM-ISE has catalyzed and supported a number of key information sharing initiatives discussed elsewhere in this chapter, including (a) federal support for state and local fusion centers, (b) the Nationwide Suspicious Activity Reporting (SAR) initiative, (c) the Controlled Unclassified Information framework, and (d) the Interagency Threat Assessment and Coordination Group. The PM-ISE has also led efforts to promote government-wide standards and guidelines, including a set of privacy guidelines for information sharing. In 2011, the PM-ISE was given increased responsibilities for information safeguarding as part of EO 13587, which established a Classified Information Sharing and Safeguarding Office (CISSO) within the PM-ISE to implement many of the requirements of the executive order. (For more information, please see the chapter by Kshemendra Paul, PM-ISE, in this volume.)

Federal Bureau of Investigation (FBI)

The first four organizations highlighted in this section were all established after 9/11 as a result of legislation. However, many Departments and agencies have also taken steps to improve information sharing in the last decade, including the FBI. Immediately after the attacks of 9/11, the FBI quickly ramped up its counterterrorism efforts, primarily by increasing the number of investigative Joint Terrorism Task Forces (JTTFs). The FBI also now shares information on current investigations with federal partner agencies such as DHS and NCTC more readily, although it is naturally mindful of the need to protect the integrity of its ongoing investigations, and concerned about compromises to those investigations, as occurred in the case of Najibullah Zazi in 2009.[10]

The FBI also works closely with DHS on the dissemination of unclassified intelligence briefs to state, local, and tribal law entities, and leads the Infragard program, which focuses on sharing relevant information with the private sector. It is also responsible for operating the Terrorist Screening Center, which (along within NCTC) serves as the critical node within the terrorist watchlisting system.

Improved Mechanisms for Information Sharing

Effective information sharing requires a set of technical capabilities that facilitate the appropriate analysis and dissemination of information. In the last decade, federal government agencies have invested billions in improving capabilities that support information sharing. This section discusses several of the major types of investments that have been made.

Enhancements to Terrorist Watchlisting System

The 9/11 Commission report highlights weaknesses and gaps in the pre-9/11 watchlisting system, most notably related to how two of the hijackers (Khalid al-Mihdhar and Nawaf al-Hazmi) were able to enter the United States on legal visas even after they were identified as attending a meeting of al Qaeda members in Malaysia in 2000.[11] The federal government today has a consolidated watchlisting system that allows for individuals to be quickly nominated and vetted, with that information being used to inform screening activities by TSA, CBP, and the Department of State.

Analytic and Collaboration Systems and Capabilities

All major homeland security and counterterrorism agencies have made significant investments in the past decade to improve their ability to analyze information and identify what may be "signals" of terrorism against the broader "noise" of their collected data. In many instances these investments have been made within a particular Department or agency rather than IC-wide, although tools such as A-Space, Intellipedia, and the Library of National Intelligence are broadly available to analysts.[12]

Unclassified Federal Networks

Federal agencies have also invested heavily to improve their capabilities to share information and collaborate at the unclassified level (marked "For Official Use Only"). Networks such as the FBI-led Law Enforcement Online (LEO) and the state-run RISS networks have been joined since 9/11 by the DHS-led Homeland Security Information Network (HSIN). All three major systems provide mechanisms for federal agencies to disseminate unclassified threat reports and to facilitate collaboration among federal, state, local, tribal, and private sector entities, although the constituencies of each network contain some moderate distinctions.

**Cultural
Initiatives**

A fourth set of post-9/11 information sharing initiatives relate to addressing the cultural challenges associated with improved sharing of information. Even with optimal policies, organizational structures, and technologies, information would not be shared if there were cultural aversions to sharing information within and among key agencies. For this reason, there have been ongoing efforts to change the culture of "need to know" and break down the barriers and cultural divides between key agencies. These efforts are manifested in a number of ways, including senior officials' statements on the importance of information sharing, increased collocation of agencies' representatives, encouragement of the cross-agency "communities of interest," and increased incentives for joint duty assignments.

Perhaps most important on this issue has been the generational change within the intelligence community in the decade since 9/11, with around two-thirds of the IC workforce having been hired since 9/11. This younger generation of personnel within the intelligence community grew up using the Internet and online social networking platforms, and has an instinctive desire to collaborate across organizational boundaries. If these younger personnel retain these cultural attitudes as they are promoted within their organizations, it is likely that some of the remaining cultural barriers to information sharing will markedly diminish within the intelligence community.

**Information
Sharing
Initiatives
Focused on
State, Local, and
Tribal Entities**

Many of the activities discussed in the previous section are relevant to state, local, and tribal entities, but are primarily focused on information sharing within the federal government. This section briefly looks at several initiatives focused on information sharing with and among state, local, and tribal entities (primarily law enforcement agencies, but also inclusive of fire service and other first responder organizations).

State and Local Fusion Centers

States and major urban areas have established 72 fusion centers around the country in the last decade to serve as the focal point for analysis of threats and criminal activities in their area of operations, and to serve as a conduit for information sharing between federal agencies and the dozens or hundreds of local law enforcement agencies in each state or region. For example, many fusion centers run Terrorism Liaison Officer or Intelligence Liaison Officer programs that educate thousands of officials within their areas about terrorism tactics and targets. The majority of fusion centers are also connected to classified DHS and FBI systems, which enables them to have timely access to classified information on particular issues and threats. Fusion centers receive federal support from DHS, the FBI, and other agencies but are not run by the federal government.

Suspicious Activity Reporting (SAR)

In the planning for numerous terrorist plots within the United States, the would-be attackers have engaged in activities that warrant suspicion. In recent terrorism cases, such as the Fort Dix plot and that of Khalid Aldawsari, the reporting of suspicious activity has been the basis for FBI-led investigative activities and subsequent arrests.[13] However, the reporting of such activities will be ineffectual and potentially harmful to civil liberties if agencies are receiving reporting based primarily on religion or national origin.

To improve the SAR process and ensure that it is consistent with civil liberties concerns, several agencies (PM-ISE, DHS, DOJ, etc.) have worked in the last few years to develop the Nationwide Suspicious Activity Reporting Initiative (NSI). This initiative allows agencies to post suspicious activity reports on a local server, which is connected with servers in other states, urban areas, and federal agencies. The Initiative provides for training of individuals on the SAR processes and standards.

Interagency Threat Assessment and Coordination Group (ITACG)

The 2007 Implementing Recommendation of the 9/11 Commission Act (P.L. 110-53) established the ITACG detail at the National Counterterrorism Center, to be composed of law enforcement officers and first responders with a variety of backgrounds who would provide NCTC with input on the intelligence requirements and needs of frontline state and local officials.

Information Sharing with the Private Sector and the General Public

The federal government also shares terrorism-related information in certain circumstances with the private sector and the general public via a number of initiatives. For example, DHS and the FBI share information with key private sector partners via a number of programs and activities, including a set of sector-specific Information Sharing Analysis Centers and Sector Coordinating Councils, the FBI-led Infragard program, and the DHS and FBI co-led Domestic Security Advisory Council. A number of states and cities have their own local initiatives for sharing threat information with the private sector. And the general public is informed on threats via the National Threat Advisory System and other public messages on the threat, and has a vehicle to report suspicious activity via the DHS-led "See Something Say Something" campaign.

ASSESSMENT OF PROGRESS ON INFORMATION SHARING INITIATIVES

The previous section included a long list of informationsharing initiatives that have been carried out over the decade since 9/11. Collectively, they reflect a great deal of progress that has been made. Pieces of terrorism information that are potentially related to each other can now be shared across agency boundaries and without significant legal or policy impediments in a timely manner.

The key individuals and groups who influenced the post-9/11 informationsharing agenda have largely been positive in recent years about the progress that has been made. For example, Zoe Baird and Jeffrey Smith from the Markle Task Force assessed the progress that had been made as follows:

Over the last decade, our government has embarked on a "virtual reorganization" in how it answers the threat of terrorism. This shift in thinking has inspired reform in the way agencies and people collaborate and communicate. Top al-Qaeda leaders have been killed and new attacks on the homeland have been prevented because of this transformation in how agencies across government work together and share information in order to detect and preempt terrorist attacks. Substantial progress has been made in shifting the "need-to-know" culture toward a "need-to-share" paradigm, in which information flows more freely enabling greater collaboration between federal, state, and local agencies as well as the private sector.

Information is also increasingly decentralized and distributed. Informal and flexible groups of analysts from different parts of government and the private sector are able to work together and share expertise. Today, our government is able to function in hubs and spokes and distributed networks, empowering people at the edges of agencies instead of working in hierarchical pyramids.

> Information is shared, and teams from disparate parts of government go in and out of the National Counterterrorism Center and fusion centers nationwide. Ad hoc pursuit teams of experts or concerned officials form and disband as they see problems needing attention. The adoption of powerful social networking tools allows analysts to connect with colleagues throughout government. No longer must all information or requests for authority go up a chain of command or come down from on high.[14]

9/11 Commission co-chairs Tom Kean and Lee Hamilton reached a similar conclusion earlier in 2011, noting in Congressional testimony that "we believe that information sharing has improved considerably in recent years."[15]

In spite of the progress that has been made, there have been several terrorism cases in recent years that point to the need for further improvements with respect to information sharing. The 2009 attack at Fort Hood by Nidal Hasan highlighted the need for improved information sharing between the Department of Defense and the FBI.[16] In the case of David Headley, a U.S. citizen who was a key facilitator for the 2008 Lashkar-e Taiba attack in Mumbai, media reports indicate that federal government agencies had a number of reports on his terrorist connections but did not connect the reporting.[17] And in the case of Umar Farouk Abdulmutallab's failed attack on Northwest Flight 253 on Dec. 25, 2009, key agencies did not identify and correlate the relevant pieces of information, although the White House review of the attack noted that this was not a failure of information sharing, since all of the pieces of information were shared with other agencies.[18]

INFORMATION SHARING ISSUES AND CHALLENGES FOR THE NEXT DECADE

The progress that has been made in the decade since the attacks of September 11, 2001 to improve information sharing has been significant, but it is still incomplete and is challenged by a number of developments to the environment in which information sharing takes place. This final section of the chapter reviews key issues that are likely to have an impact on information sharing over the next several years.

Balancing Sharing with Safeguarding: The WikiLeaks Challenge

Perhaps the most significant informationsharing challenge at present follows from the disclosures of classified information by Wikileaks in late 2010, the Executive Branch's subsequent policy review, and the issuance of Executive Order 13587, entitled "Structural Reforms to Improve the Security of Classified Networks and the Responsible Sharing and Safeguarding of Classified Information."[19]

A number of federal agencies are currently engaged in technical efforts to improve the security and safeguarding of information on their classified networks, to prevent further large-scale breaches of information, including by trusted insiders. Agencies are working to deploy capabilities for role-based access on their networks and to improve real-time auditing of network activity to detect potential misuse by employees.[20] While senior officials have indicated that they are committed to ensuring that these technical changes will not impair information sharing, there are risks associated with the implementation of new security capabilities, to the extent that they make systems more cumbersome or go too far to reduce access to certain types of information.

Data Analytic Challenges

A second information sharing challenge for the next decade relates to the analysis and dissemination of information that has been collected by key agencies within the intelligence community. Russ Travers, then Deputy Director of the National Counterterrorism Center for Information Sharing and Knowledge Management, described this challenge at a Congressional hearing in 2010:[21]

> "The quantity and quality of information that comes in every day, literally terabytes, sometimes petabytes of information that come in, [are] sometimes described as vastly exceeding the holdings of the Library of Congress. It is an immense amount of information."

This information flow creates significant analytic challenges that have an impact on information sharing. If agencies decide to "share everything," the customers of such information will drown in data and be unable to make sense of what is truly significant. But if agencies withhold information, they run the risk of being called to account if there is a terrorism case where, in hindsight, information should have been shared. This conundrum creates the need for automated analytic capabilities that can match and correlate pieces of information and flag what appears to be significant pieces of information for analysts' attention.

Privacy and Civil Liberties—The U.S. Persons Challenge

Concern for privacy and civil liberties is a necessary component of an effective information sharing regime. Homeland security and counterterrorism activities in the U.S. cannot be developed and sustained without appropriate concern for these issues by government agencies and the integration of oversight into programmatic activities. This is especially true with respect to information sharing activities, where there are, in many areas, appropriate limits as to what can and should be shared, based on the source of information, to whom information is being distributed, and any legal or policy restrictions.

These issues may become more challenging with respect to the sharing of terrorism-related and homeland security information in the next several years. A further increase in "homegrown" terrorism plots and/or an increase in the participation of American citizens in overseas terrorist groups would complicate the efforts of agencies to share information on those individuals and their activities. As former Deputy CIA Director John McLaughlin testified before Congress in 2011[22]:

> First, I suspect there is still an inconsistent understanding of the laws and regulations that govern the acquisition and sharing of data that touches American citizens.
>
> Second, there is an understandable concern not to violate laws protecting our citizens' privacy. This can inspire a subtle kind of "risk aversion" in dealing with such data.

It is also possible that international privacy and civil liberties discussions will have an impact on the sharing of terrorism and homeland security information, as exemplified by the ongoing debates between the United States and the European Union about the sharing of Passenger Name Record (PNR) data.

Classification System and Security Clearances

Another ongoing challenge to information sharing relates to the system by which national security information is classified and the limitations that classification puts on the distribution of terrorism-related information. The system for classification within the federal government was designed during the Cold War to protect sensitive national security information from disclosure to foreign adversaries, and primarily involved interactions among federal agencies, although major research institutions and defense companies were also closely integrated into the classification system. The guiding principle of this system was "need-to-know"—limiting access to classified information to those who could articulate in advance their mission need for particular types of information.

This system for the classification of national security information has proven in many ways to be ill-suited for government activities related to homeland security and counterterrorism. There is still a strong need for a classification system, particularly with respect to the collection of terrorism information (other than open source information) and the sources and methods by which such information is collected. However, given the asymmetric and unpredictable nature of the terrorist threat, the potential audience for sensitive terrorism-related information is very broad, and includes not only key federal agencies, but also state, local, and tribal government entities, and the private sector. This creates a recurring conflict between the need to protect sensitive information and getting information to the broadest set of people who are in a position to act on it.

The federal government has addressed this challenge in several ways in the past decade. First, it has expanded the use of "tear-line" products that redact classified information and can be released to state and local law enforcement or the private sector with an unclassified "For Official Use Only" (FOUO) marking. The Department of Homeland Security and Federal Bureau of Investigation regularly issue joint bulletins that include unclassified tear-line information from otherwise classified reports.

Second, in 2009, the President signed Executive Order 13526 which updated security classification policies for the Executive Branch. One significant update in the new EO allows classified information from one agency to be "disseminated to another agency or U.S. entity by any agency to which it has been made available without the consent of the originating agency" as a general rule, unless marked to prohibit such dissemination.[23] This provision repealed the so-called "third agency rule," and in theory should enable a significant increase in information sharing, although in practice it has led to an increase in the use of markings such as originator control (ORCON) to restrict third-party dissemination.

Third, the federal government has greatly expanded the number of individuals in state and local government and in the private sector who have security clearances, typically at the Secret level, so that they can receive classified information appropriate to their responsibilities. While only a small fraction of state and local law enforcement personnel today have security clearances, there is now a critical mass of cleared individuals at the state and local levels who are able to brief senior local leaders (governors, mayors) and provide general guidance to their law enforcement colleagues on threats and how they should inform local policing or outreach activities.

Despite this progress, the classification system is still often cumbersome, and at times impedes effective information sharing between the federal, state, local, and tribal levels of government.

Sharing Information with the Private Sector

Progress has been made in sharing terrorism-related information with the private sector in the last decade through a variety of programs, as discussed earlier in the chapter. However, many in the private sector believe that significant improvements could be made in this area. In 2012, the National Infrastructure Advisory Council (NIAC) issued a report entitled "Intelligence Information Sharing: Final Report and Recommendations" that highlighted several deficiencies in terms of private sector information sharing.[24] The report argued that information sharing with the private sector was a low priority for federal agencies, and that DHS was not serving as an effective champion for information sharing with the private sector. The report also found misaligned incentives between the federal government and private sector with respect to information sharing. It recommended greater attention be paid to the information requirements of private sector stakeholders in the intelligence cycle and more streamlined mechanisms for disseminating information to the private sector be put in place.

Funding Challenges

Another potential challenge with respect to information sharing in the next several years relates to budgets and funding for key information sharing programs. If key federal programs are cut, many of the initiatives cited in this chapter are likely to stall. And if federal agencies are forced to cut interagency assignments and personnel rotations in order to maintain their core operational missions, then the growing cultural support for information sharing could be negatively impacted.

Measuring Progress on Information Sharing

One final information sharing challenge for the next decade relates to the means by which progress on information sharing can be measured and defining long-term goals for information sharing. The previous section of the report highlighted positive statements by notable policy leaders on the progress that has been made to improve information sharing in the last decade. These judgments were largely qualitative in nature, given the inherent challenges associated with coming up with meaningful quantitative metrics for information sharing. For example, a metric that looked at the number of reports that an agency shared with other agencies would not necessarily be meaningful in itself, without a clearer understanding of the value of information provided to other agencies.

The Program Manager for the Information Sharing Environment has made efforts to develop information sharing metrics, track them at the agency level, and hold agencies to account for them.[25] And various government-wide and agency strategies have articulated near-term and long-term objectives for information sharing. However, the Government Accountability Office found in 2010 that the PM-ISE had not yet articulated a comprehensive roadmap to implement the information sharing environment, and was critical of performance measures used by the PM-ISE, noting that many of them measured "outputs" rather than "outcomes."[26]

In the absence of clear and measurable objectives and reliable assessments of progress toward achieving them, it could become increasingly difficult to sustain support for key information sharing programs and activities in the next few years, especially in light of the challenging budget environment discussed in the previous section.

NOTES

1. This chapter was written by the author outside of his official capacity as a Congressional staff member, and the viewpoints expressed within do not necessarily reflect the official positions of the Senate Homeland Security and Governmental Affairs Committee.
2. 9/11 Commission Report, http://www.911-commission.gov/.
3. Markle Task Force Reports, http://www.markle.org/.
4. National Strategy for Homeland Security, 2002, http://www.ncs.gov/library/policy_docs/nat_strat_hls.pdf.
5. National Strategy for Information Sharing, 2007, http://nsi.ncirc.gov/documents/National_Strategy_for_Information_Sharing.pdf.
6. Intelligence Reform and Terrorism Prevention Act, 2004.
7. 2008 Memorandum of Agreement available at http://www.fas.org/sgp/othergov/intel/nctc-moa2008.pdf; 2012 update available at http://www.fas.org/sgp/othergov/intel/nctc_guidelines.pdf.

8. Intelligence Reform and Terrorism Prevention Act, 2004.

9. 9/11 Commission Report.

10. Discussion of the relevant facts of the case available at http://www.justice.gov/opa/pr/2009/September/09-nsd-1002.html.

11. 9/11 Commission Report.

12. For information on these and related analytic programs, see Director of National Intelligence report entitled "Analytic Transformation: Unleashing the Potential of a Community of Analysts," http://www.dni.gov/content/AT_Digital%2020080923.pdf.

13. For discussion of the role of suspicious activity reporting in the Fort Dix case, see *USA Today*, "Store Clerk's Tip Was Key to Foiling Fort Dix Terror Plot," May 9, 2007, http://www.usatoday.com/news/nation/2007-05-09-fort-dix-clerk_N.htm. With respect to the Aldawsari case, see *Lubbock Avalanche-Journal*, "Package 'Profile' Led Supplier, Shipper to Warn FBI of Aldawsari's Critical Chemical Buy; Intercepted Phenol Shipment Was the Key Ingredient," February 25, 2011, http://lubbockonline.com/local-news/2011-02-25/package-profile-led-supplier-shipper-warn-fbi-aldawsaris-critical-chemical-buy.

14. Markle Task Force testimony available at http://www.markle.org/sites/default/files/MTFSenateTestimony_10-12-11_2.pdf.

15. Testimony available at http://www.hsgac.senate.gov/download/2011–03–30-kean-and-hamilton-testimony-revised.

16. See "A Ticking Time Bomb: Counterterrorism Lessons from the U.S. Government's Failure to Prevent the Fort Hood Attack," Senate Homeland Security and Governmental Affairs Committee report, 2011, http://www.hsgac.senate.gov/download/fort-hood-report.

17. See "The American Behind India's 9/11—And How U.S. Botched Chances to Stop Him," http://www.propublica.org/article/david-headley-homegrown-terrorist.

18. See "White House Review Summary Regarding 12/25/2009 Attempted Terrorist Attack," http://www.whitehouse.gov/the-press-office/white-house-review-summary-regarding-12252009-attempted-terrorist-attack; and the Senate Select Committee on Intelligence's "Unclassified Executive Summary of the Committee Report on the Attempted Terrorist Attack on Northwest Airlines Flight 253," http://intelligence.senate.gov/100518/1225report.pdf.

19. Executive Order 13587, http://www.archives.gov/isoo/policy-documents/eo-13587.pdf.

20. See, for example, Congressional testimony by Teresa Takai and Thomas Ferguson, Department of Defense, March 2011, http://www.fas.org/irp/congress/2011_hr/031011takai.pdf.

21. From transcript of March 2010 Senate Homeland Security and Governmental Affairs Committee, http://www.gpo.gov/fdsys/pkg/CHRG-111shrg56838/pdf/CHRG-111shrg56838.pdf.

22. Testimony before Senate Homeland Security and Governmental Affairs Committee, http://www.hsgac.senate.gov/download/mclaughlin-testimony.

23. Executive Order 13526, http://www.gpo.gov/fdsys/pkg/FR-2010-01-05/pdf/E9-31418.pdf.

24. NIAC report, http://www.dhs.gov/xlibrary/assets/niac/niac-intelligence-information-sharing-final-report-01102012.pdf.

25. See Appendix A of the 2011 Annual Report to Congress by the Program Manager for the Information Sharing Environment, http://ise.gov/sites/default/files/ISE_Annual_Report_to_Congress_2011.pdf.

26. GAO report, "Information Sharing Environment: Better Road Map Needed to Guide Implementation and Investments," http://www.gao.gov/assets/330/321672.pdf.

10

DEVELOPING INFORMATION SHARING PROTOCOLS AND PLANNING POLICY TO SUPPORT HOMELAND SECURITY MISSIONS

David G. Kamien

CEO & Co-Founder, Mind-Alliance Systems

INTRODUCTION

U.S. military doctrine traditionally distinguishes "deliberate planning," which is done pre-crisis, from "crisis action planning," which is undertaken during an event that is unfolding. This chapter explains the need for a specialized form of pre-crisis planning called information sharing planning, designed to produce information sharing and communication protocols for homeland security missions. Effective disaster planning requires that organizations define the kinds of information that they send and receive in an emergency. Information sharing protocols support strategic and operational coordination with partners, collaborative risk management, and intelligence-informed decision-making.

The chapter provides a brief survey of a subset of the many policies, strategies, frameworks, plans, and standards that have already recognized the importance of information sharing. It argues that the technical initiatives to enhance the ability to enhance information discovery, access, and communication, must be supplemented with a planning effort—designing the interagency information and communication flows that are critical for shared situational awareness and operational coordination.

The chapter proposes changes in national homeland security policy that will be necessary to encourage stakeholders to engage in information sharing planning. Implementation of these changes will help integrate and harmonize fragmented homeland security efforts and capabilities into a "Whole of Nation" approach, and enhance information flow across all levels of governance, disciplines, sectors, and jurisdictions. The proposed approach will yield more effective integration and implementation of policies, processes, and technologies, and will promote responsible information sharing and safeguarding across the national security information enterprise.

INFORMATION SHARING IS A CENTRAL ASPECT OF HOMELAND SECURITY

The myriad organizations with a role in homeland security are linked politically, economically, operationally, and socially and depend on each other for the supply of information, human, financial, and physical resources. They operate in a dynamic and complex environment with multiple parallel, non-sequential, intersecting processes, and key capabilities, which are often ill-defined and lacking a single responsible process owner. During routine steady-state operations and minor emergencies, organizations interact and develop relationships of trust with a limited and known set of partners within their county, state, or region. However, a catastrophic disaster or terror plot that spans jurisdictions requires operational coordination with a vastly different set of organizations (e.g., neighboring states in the region, the federal government, foreign governments).

No organization, level of government, or nation can effectively manage the risk of catastrophic disasters—risk to its interests, people, operations, or reputation—in isolation from partner and stakeholder organizations that must be brought in to close gaps in capability.

Well-coordinated interorganizational networks can manage the risk caused by adverse events more effectively than organizations managing risk in isolation.[1] No single company or jurisdiction can succeed without intentionally leveraging and effectively integrating all the available assets (expertise, resources, and information), capability, and capacity available from partners in the organization, the region, and beyond. Collaborating, pooling, and sharing capacity makes organizations more effective and makes good business sense because it maximizes the effect of capabilities preventing duplication and wastage of efforts and resources.

INFORMATION SHARING IS ESSENTIAL FOR JOINT-PLANNING AND OPERATIONAL COORDINATION

Success in the collaborative risk management endeavor of homeland security requires the information management (e.g., acquisition, review, storage, and exchange of data, information, and knowledge) across boundaries by many different means. Sharing useful data or information between and within groups and organizations enables their participants to:

- Reduce uncertainty and inform risk management decision-making
- Gain better shared situational awareness—a common perception and understanding of the operational environment and its implications
- Decrease the complexity of the situation
- Coordinate and synchronize their operations
- Make situations more manageable

Information sharing leverages capabilities and enables agility on the part of the people and organizations that are included in a collaborative effort. It enhances the ability to successfully effect, cope with, and exploit changes in circumstances and the environment, in incremental, iterative, and adaptive ways. Information sharing is essential in every stage of a problem-solving process, including:

- Exploring a situation from multiple perspectives
- Identifying the problem
- Defining the problem
- Generating solutions
- Decision-making
- Implementing solutions
- Monitoring implementation
- Receiving feedback from others

Each of these stages is critical to determining whether or not interventions or actions will be effective. To accomplish their shared goals, coalitions of organizations must engage in joint planning and comprehensive preparedness efforts that combine the capabilities of government entities in disciplines such as emergency management, law enforcement, and public health, with voluntary agencies, faith-based organizations, the private sector, and advocacy groups.

THE IMPORTANCE OF INFORMATION SHARING RECOGNIZED IN POLICY

For many years, the policies, strategies, frameworks, plans, and standards governing homeland security, national intelligence, disaster preparedness, incident management, business continuity, and supply chain security have expressed, with varying degrees of clarity and explicitness, the vital importance of information sharing. The 2002 National Strategy for Homeland Security created in response to the Al Qaeda attacks of September 11, 2001 identified information sharing as a "foundation" of homeland security, and the 9/11 Commission Report highlighted numerous types of information sharing and communication failures.[2]

INFORMATION SHARING AND NATIONAL INTELLIGENCE REFORM

Information sharing has been a major theme of national intelligence reform over the last decade. The 2004 Intelligence Reform and Terrorism Prevention Act (IRTPA) established the position of a Program Manager to oversee the effort to create an Information Sharing Environment (the ISE-PM) in order to share terrorism information such as Suspicious Activity Reporting (SAR) between the myriad international, state, and local agencies, and even with private sector organizations (e.g., airlines) that have a role in prevention and protection missions.[3] This new paradigm significantly broadened the range of organizations deemed potentially capable of collecting, analyzing, and deriving value from intelligence information.

IRTPA redefined "national intelligence" and "intelligence related to national security" to include all intelligence—"whether gathered inside or outside of the United States, that involves threats to the United States, its people, property, or interests."[4] This imposed enormously more difficult requirements on the intelligence community (IC). Analysts in federal, state, and local level fusion centers, FBI Joint-Terrorism Task Forces (JTTF), and others are considered partners in the domestic counterterrorism effort. They must synthesize and analyze disparate occurrences, discover red-flags, and warn counterterrorism and law enforcement forces so they can react appropriately, whether by shadowing suspects to uncover more details and participants in a terror plot, or by immediately interdicting terrorists to prevent an imminent attack.

According to Thomas Fingar, the former Deputy Director of National Intelligence for Analysis, after the failed 2009 Christmas Day airline bombing, expectations and demands for the Intelligence Community escalated again. In his book *"Reducing Uncertainty: Intelligence Analysis and National Security,"*[5] Fingar rightly stresses that: "Now the criterion for success is detecting the plans and preparations of individual malefactors capable of killing hundreds of Americans by destroying a single airplane. Now the IC is expected to be able to pinpoint the location of individual terrorists, individual improvised explosive devices (IEDs), and individual shipping containers. The number of 'dots' to be collected and connected has expanded from a handful of big countries to literally billions of individuals located in almost 200 nation-states."

In contrast to the pre-9/11 environment characterized by agency-centric data repositories, analysts at the National Counterterrorism Center (NCTC) now have access to over 30 networks that contain terrorism information. However, collecting and providing access to information is a necessary but not sufficient condition for understanding. As Fingar points out: "Analysts are awash in data, and there are literally billions of times more 'dots' to be examined, evaluated, assessed, and integrated into analytical products. However, terabytes of data alone do not reveal event trajectories, what is driving them, where they are headed, what might derail or deflect them, or how they will interact with developments originating thousands of miles away." Many initiatives are underway to develop tools and techniques to enable information correlation and advanced analysis. However advanced these capabilities become, they will not obviate the need for agreements to make information available to appropriate partners, or for protocols governing the sharing and safeguarding of information, particularly when significant findings and red-flags are discovered and indicate an imminent attack. Naturally this must be accomplished subject to privacy and other civil liberties protections and guidelines.

The "analytic transformation" paradigm shift in the U.S. national intelligence community involved various aspects, including:

- Changing the culture of information sharing from disseminating information on a "need to know" basis to recognizing the "responsibility to provide"

- Utilizing online collaboration mechanisms such as A-Space and Intellipedia to support cross-IC analytic efforts
- Recognizing the importance of incorporating Open Source intelligence (OSINT) and engaging with subject matter experts from outside of government (see Intelligence Community Directive 205)

The National Strategy for Information Sharing (2007) provided a policy framework and directed many core initiatives critical to the Information Sharing Environment (ISE).[6] It aimed to improve the sharing of homeland security, terrorism, and law enforcement information related to terrorism within and among all levels of governments and the private sector. It also emphasized the need for a two-way flow of timely and actionable security information between public and private entities and highlights the importance of sharing with international partners.

The May 2010 National Security Strategy continued to emphasize the importance of information sharing, stating: "We are improving information sharing and cooperation by linking networks to facilitate Federal, state, and local capabilities to seamlessly exchange messages and information, conduct searches, and collaborate."[7] The October 2010 Wikileaks release of the Iraq War Logs and November 2010 release of U.S. State Department cables took some air out of the sails of advocates for greater information sharing. The ISE-PM and other federal government entities began to rebrand their efforts as "information sharing and safeguarding" initiatives. However, every responsible organization recognizes the basic need to share information.

CRITICAL INFRASTRUCTURE PROTECTION

The National Strategy for Maritime Security[8] emphasized the importance of information sharing in the context of achieving "maritime domain awareness" (MDA). So too, does the National Strategy to Secure Cyberspace (2003)[9] and President Obama's Comprehensive National Cybersecurity Initiative.[10]

The National Critical Infrastructure Protection Plan (2009) and associated Sector-Specific Plans recognized the importance of and have developed frameworks for public–private sector information sharing and coordination.[11] Numerous related mechanisms have been established to facilitate information sharing between private and public sector partners, including:

- Sector Coordinating Councils (SCCs)
- Sector Specific Agencies (SSAs) and Government Coordinating Councils (GCCs)
- State and Local, Tribal and Territorial–Government Coordinating Council (SLTT–GCC)
- Critical Infrastructure Partnership Advisory Council (CIPAC)
- Information Sharing and Analysis Centers (ISACs) and the Information Sharing and Analysis Center Council

In addition to these mechanisms, the following entities also play key roles in information sharing related to critical infrastructure protection:

- State and local Fusion Centers
- Joint Terrorism Task Forces (JTTFs)
- State and local Emergency Operations Centers (EOCs)
- DHS/ Intelligence & Analysis (I&A)
- DHS/ National Infrastructure Coordination Center (NICC)
- DHS/Regional Protective Security Advisors (PSAs) and Regional Mission Collaboration Staff
- DHS/Federal Emergency Management Agency (FEMA)
- The Classified Critical Infrastructure and Key Resources (CIKR) Engagement Working Group
- The Homeland Infrastructure Threat and Risk Analysis Center (HITRAC) Classified Information "Reading Room"

The National Infrastructure Advisory Council (NIAC) set out to determine whether the right people are receiving the right intelligence information at the right time to support robust protection and resilience of the Nation's critical infrastructure. According to the January 2012 NIAC "Final Report and Recommendations on Intelligence Information Sharing,"[12] there have been marked improvements in the sharing of intelligence information within the Federal Intelligence Community, and between the Federal Government and regions,

States, and municipalities. However, this level of improvement has not been matched in the sharing of intelligence information between the Federal Government and private sector owners and operators of critical infrastructure.

According to the report:

> Despite some notable successes, this bi-directional sharing is still relatively immature, leaving a large gap between current practices and an optimal system of effective public–private intelligence information sharing. We observe that trust is the essential glue to make this public–private system work. Trust results when partner capabilities are understood and valued, processes are tailored to leverage these capabilities, and these processes are tested and proven valuable to all partners. When breakdowns in information sharing occur, it erodes trust and is counterproductive to risk management.
>
> Information sharing is perhaps the most important factor in the protection and resilience of critical infrastructure. Information on threats to infrastructure and their likely impact underlies nearly every security decision made by owners and operators, including which assets to protect, how to make operations more resilient, how to plan for potential disasters, when to ramp up to higher levels of security, and how to respond in the immediate aftermath of a disaster.
>
> The Council believes that if properly managed, information sharing between the public and private sectors could be one of our most powerful tools to combat terrorism, natural disasters, and criminal activity.

The report goes on to say that nearly 10 years after 9/11, the DHS Office of Intelligence and Analysis is now developing a pilot program, the Sector Information Needs process, to engage the private sector in defining owner/operator requirements. The use of fusion centers for sharing intelligence information with the private sector varies dramatically across locations and sectors, but "overall seems comparatively modest." According to the report, "There are, however, several good models of success in this regard."

PRIVATE SECTOR BUSINESS CONTINUITY AND ENTERPRISE RESILIENCE

In corporate enterprises, the effort to manage risk and increase operational resilience is typically fragmented across business units, disciplines, and sub-organizations. This effort may involve functional areas including IT, accounting, legal, HR, and the security office, with each discipline having its own stakeholders, technical jargon, and regulatory compliance obligations (e.g., SOX, PCI, FISMA, HIPAA, FFRDC, NFPA 1600, ISO 28000). The corporate crisis management plan, business unit-specific business continuity plans, application-specific disaster recovery plans, and site-specific security and emergency response plans often have been authored by different people at different times, resulting in poor alignment of people, process, and technology. Private sector standards for business continuity, supply chain security, and resilience typically establish a desirable baseline for information sharing and developing notification and communication procedures, which are sometimes subject to audit. The 2011 flooding in Thailand, as well as the Fukushima Disaster, made companies with global supply chains aware that they needed to understand and mitigate risks associated not only with their direct suppliers, but also their second order dependencies on their suppliers' vendors. The leading global companies are now taking steps to establish information sharing and notification protocols supporting risk management across their supply chains.

EMERGENCY MANAGEMENT AND WHOLE COMMUNITY RESILIENCE

During Hurricane Katrina, many agencies and organizations were totally incapacitated, from the local level to the national. Consequently, there was a lack of communication and situational awareness which severely undermined the needed command, control, and coordination among DHS, the States, local governments, and other response organizations (voluntary, humanitarian, etc.). The outcome of Hurricane Katrina alerted policymakers to the inability of the State of Louisiana, federal, and local governments to share situational awareness and synchronize their emergency response efforts, particularly when communications infrastructure is destroyed and conflicting information is circulated. Naturally, when the fundamental capacity to communicate is missing, the ability to share information and coordinate the delivery of goods, services, and basic support will suffer.

At the March 30, 2006 hearing before the Committee on Government Reform, Chairman Tom Davis stated:

The 9/11 Commission found "the most important failure was one of imagination." Katrina was primarily a failure of initiative. But there is, of course, a nexus between the two.

Both imagination and initiative—in other words, leadership—require good information. And a coordinated process for sharing it. And a willingness to use information—however imperfect or incomplete—to fuel action.

With Katrina, the reasons reliable information did not reach more people more quickly were many, for example: the lack of communication and situational awareness paralyzed command and control; DHS and the States had difficulty coordinating with each other, which slowed the response; DOD lacked an information sharing protocol that would have enhanced joint situational awareness and communication between all military components.

Information sharing and situational awareness will always be predicated to an effective disaster response. With approximately 60 days remaining before the start of hurricane season on June 1st, this hearing will examine how the lessons learned regarding information sharing in the context of law enforcement, counterterrorism, and defense can be applied to disaster response.

Information sharing is the backbone of successful emergency preparation and response efforts. Historically, however, the Federal Government has been so compartmentalized, information sharing has been a pipe dream. The Federal Government is faced with the difficult task of transforming from a "need-to-know" information sharing environment to a "need-to-share." In addition, the bureaucratic stovepipe arrangement in Federal agencies restricts the Government's flexibility to analyze information quickly, assess the need for services, and respond effectively in emergency situations.

Government-wide information policy authority rests with the White House, in the Office of Management and Budget. I think the White House, through OMB, has a critical role in establishing and implementing policies and procedures for Federal information sharing. Whether we are discussing disaster management, counterterrorism, or law enforcement, overarching guidance and oversight to help Federal agencies establish a structure for partnering with one another and local and State organizations.(*sic*)

Given the lessons learned from Katrina, emergency managers and officials are obligated to the American people to produce a more nimble, effective, and robust response to predictable natural disasters. How can we avoid the inadequate information sharing and murky situational awareness that characterized the Government response to Katrina? Are impediments to more effective information sharing primarily technological, structural, cultural, or bureaucratic in nature?[13]

FEMA recognized the need for improvement and its *Comprehensive Preparedness Guide* (CPG-101)[14] emphasized the need to analyze information and intelligence needs in the context of engaging in preparedness planning with partners. FEMA's Regional Catastrophic Planning grant program raised the awareness of the need for joint-planning and information sharing at the regional level, which is the crucial interface between state and federal efforts and the nexus for mutual aid coordination in a catastrophic disaster. However, many of the regional planning efforts have stayed at the strategic or high-level operational planning levels. Some leading jurisdictions, such as those in the Regional Catastrophic Planning team in the greater New York area, have defined information needs associated with situational awareness for senior officials. However, most regional and state plans do not include protocols that specify precisely how operational information should flow between agencies and with the private sector. These information sharing protocols should not be limited to push notifications or information dissemination by other means. They need to address bidirectional communication by any means of transmission, including conference calls and face to face meetings. Many regions and states still lack shared doctrine, documented plans, standard operating procedures, and well-defined protocols needed to coordinate disaster preparedness and response. A particularly distressing factor is the lack of an operational coordination framework for prevention and protection of mission areas.

Many after-action reports and exercise reviews published in Lessons Learned Information Sharing (LLIS), U.S. DHS resource,[15] detail interagency communication and "information flow" problems. These issues unnecessarily impeded the mission (or exercises), and undermined situational awareness and operational coordination, endangering lives, and sometimes resulting in millions of dollars of preventable damages. Improving interagency information sharing and coordination procedures and capabilities remains a challenge for the emergency management community.

The new national preparedness frameworks under Presidential Policy Directive-8 (PPD-8) governing prevention and protection efforts provide strategic, rather than an operational–tactical level guidance. All of the five mission areas—Prevent, Protect, Mitigate, Respond, and Recover—include Planning, Operational Coordination, Public Information, and Warning as core capabilities. The Prevent and Protect mission areas both feature Intelligence and Information Sharing. PPD-8 constitutes a valuable effort to create a common language governing homeland security, but it does not provide a comprehensive framework for operational planning. Such a framework is lacking in the United States.

INFORMATION SHARING AND THE MILITARY'S COMPREHENSIVE APPROACH

Although this book's focus is on Homeland Security, it is important to point out that militaries from the United States, the North Atlantic Treaty Organization (NATO), and member nations who have a role in homeland defense and civilian crisis response, have recognized that they cannot succeed singlehandedly and that collaboration requires information sharing. The U.S. DOD's Strategy for Homeland Defense and Civil Support, which was published in June 2005, recognized the importance of information sharing and operational coordination with civilian authorities. The 2006 Quadrennial Defense Review also recognized the importance of shared situational awareness and called for an information sharing strategy to guide operations with federal, state, local, and coalition partners.

At the Bucharest Summit in April 2008, NATO leaders endorsed an Action Plan for the development and implementation of NATO's contribution to a "Comprehensive Approach." The Action Plan emphasizes that integrating military and civilian power is the key to increased efficiency and effectiveness in resource expenditures. Cooperative interaction facilitates the self-interests of organizations—the benefits of working with others (usually) exceed the costs.[16]

In reference to information sharing, NATO Allied Command Transformation has coined the slogan "Share to Win," and has established Network Enabled Capability (NNEC) initiatives such as NATO's Afghan Mission Network (AMN), which interconnects military and non-military partners. A basic tenet of NNEC is that effective communication of information will improve NATO missions and the decision-making capability of commanders and operators (see Figure 10-1).

In summary, military organizations have long been aware that they must harmonize and combine their efforts, capabilities, and resources with civilian governments and others into integrated, Whole of Nation, Whole of Government, and Whole Community approaches. Translating awareness of the importance of information sharing into action and transformed planning, management, and governance practices remains a challenge.

Figure 10-1

Mission success requires network enabled capability.

Source: "Information Sharing Planning & Management: A Key Capability for NATO" presented by the author at the 2012 NATO Network Enabled Capability Conference, March 27-30, 2012.

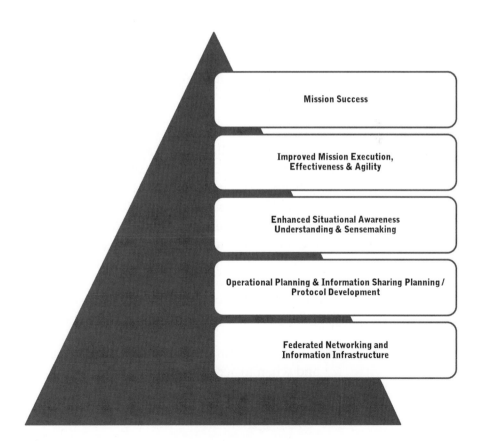

Mission Success

Improved Mission Execution, Effectiveness & Agility

Enhanced Situational Awareness Understanding & Sensemaking

Operational Planning & Information Sharing Planning / Protocol Development

Federated Networking and Information Infrastructure

INFORMATION SHARING AND COMMUNICATION
TECHNOLOGY CANNOT REPLACE PLANNING

The U.S. and other governments have spent billions of dollars on the technology infrastructure needed to support information sharing and communication in the context of homeland or "civil" security.[17] Technologists and system architects have focused on many kinds of projects, including:

- Wireless communication networks (land mobile radio, satellite, mesh networks) and radio system interoperability
- Establishing common information sharing network infrastructure between agencies
- Enabling (and controlling) "federated" access to databases (e.g., the National Suspicious Activity Reporting Initiative), "shared space" collaboration portals (e.g., the Homeland Security Information Network), and software technology applications for situational awareness and incident management
- Enabling machine-to-machine data exchanges using standards such as the National Information Exchange Model (NIEM)
- Utilizing new social web media and crowdsourcing systems to attain situational awareness and disseminate public alerts and warnings

The mere existence of network infrastructure, communication systems, or online collaboration applications does not guarantee successful information and communication flows. Information sharing is not simply about notification, or about ensuring the proper, appropriate, and timely dissemination of information "products" or reports. It includes sharing information during all kinds of routine or special operations and throughout all phases of the intelligence cycle (i.e., requirements, collection, storage, processing, analysis, production, dissemination, feedback, and update). Simply improving access to more data and information via sharing systems is not sufficient; people need training and exercises to know the following:

- Which information systems contain the data they need and how and when to access them
- What the mission-driven information needs, expectations, and commitments of their partners are

- Whom they are supposed to notify directly (person-to-person) or via a center (e.g., Dispatch, EOC, Communications) whether by radio, phone call, email, or face-to-face

Moreover, some information exchanges cannot be fully automated. People in the loop have to be guided. To be held accountable, they need to be guided by protocols provided during training and possibly during live events, which will be particularly important when circumstances require communication and coordination with non-routine partners.

Technology infrastructure is rapidly evolving and systems can almost always be made faster, more secure, resilient, and interoperable. In the future, artificial intelligence may, to a degree, automatically intuit people's changing and context-dependent needs for information and then filter and automatically route relevant information to the appropriate people in a timely manner. However, these systems will always require rules and protocols to serve as the basis for the intelligence that drives the automated system. These "business rules" will need to be continually updated in light of new threats, plans, sensors, and agreements between agencies. It will never be politically, legally, or technically feasible—or operationally useful—to centralize all the information (or rules for sharing) into one "secure" repository, or to route all the potentially useful data, information, and communication flows through a central hub.

The need for developing and refining information sharing protocols will always remain. This will require continuous input and participation from end users and subject matter experts who develop best-practice templates for various mission areas (aka "mission threads") and key capabilities for various threat scenarios. These templates will need to be adapted to fit the unique aspects of each region, state, and organization. There cannot be a one-size-fits-all solution, but some uniformity in expressing requests for information (RFI) and offering information (FYI) is valuable.

THE NEED TO DEVELOP INFORMATION SHARING PROTOCOLS

No matter how much technology is in place, optimal information sharing rarely happens spontaneously, even within a single organization. It will never occur between organizations with diverse cultures, values, goals, policies (e.g., governing security, privacy, and data protection), communication systems, and information resources which do not plan together. The complexity and magnitude of information networks and flow requires the systematic application of a deliberate planning process to operate effectively in the modern homeland security environment. The flow of information between mission partners and other stakeholders must be planned in order for decision-makers or operational personnel in the field to receive the essential elements of information they need in compliance with plans, procedures, and policies.

As part of the deliberate operational planning process, which ideally occurs well in advance of a crisis, organizations need to develop documented information sharing protocols, and incorporate them into training, exercises, and performance measurement and assessment. Partner organizations need to meet and develop an understanding of their shared responsibilities and interdependencies, and on the basis of this understanding, develop information sharing protocols to support the situational awareness and operational coordination requirements associated with their joint missions. Defining protocols for sharing and communication of operational information and intelligence enables organizations and communities to leverage their technical infrastructure and human resources, and reap the benefits of network-enabled capability investments.

Who precisely should be part of a working group that leads an information sharing-planning process and identifies subject matter experts, decision makers, and decision points? Clearly the composition of such a working group depends on the risk-causing events that are the focus of the initiative. For example, an effort to prepare for a nuclear reactor meltdown scenario may require identifying decisions that require input from an elected official (about when to evacuate a city), transportation and weather agencies, and a host of other specific federal, regional, state, and local agencies and roles. Those individuals need to be identified based on their statutory authorities and must be included in his process.

Organizations need to ensure that everyone with a role in their plans and operations have information sharing protocols and know what information to share and communicate. These individuals must have the skills and the technical capability to share, understand the rules for such sharing, and trust their counterparts enough to be willing to share. There should be a requirement for a specific individual, council, or task force to review and approve their final plan, identify who maintains the plan, and know who is responsible for cross-jurisdiction training, exercise, evaluation, and improvement.

LEADERSHIP AND MANAGEMENT ARE ACCOUNTABLE FOR DRIVING THE IMPROVEMENT OF INFORMATION SHARING

Ensuring that an organization communicates effectively is a key responsibility of its senior leaders and managerial staff. Individuals with past experience in real-world security and crisis situations understand the importance of information reaching decision makers in a timely manner. They know the value of working through the plans and procedures ahead of the crisis and troubleshooting issues proactively. Organizational leaders become aware of the importance of taking a proactive approach to defining information sharing and communication protocols, through experience with crisis situations, and by testing and rehearsing plans in training exercises in order to identify preventable communication issues and difficulties that undermine mission success.

Homeland security leaders need to build strong connectivity with their counterparts across the full spectrum of partners and constituencies. This is essential in order to establish the trust and relationships that will support effective information sharing, communication, and joint decision making. As discussed above, an absence of accurate information (or data overload) increases the level of uncertainty, amplifies complexity, impedes decision-making at all levels, and has a cascading adverse impact on the ability of others to manage risk, increasing the possibility of mission failure.

The goal of the leadership, therefore, should be "harmony of effort," which involves a spirit of cooperation, a method of negotiation, and management of interfaces between organizations to remove obstacles, facilitate cooperation, and allow organizations to do what they usually do in the most efficient and effective way possible. Leaders can overcome the feeling that "this is my turf" by focusing on their unique missions and tasks, as opposed to trying to monopolize information.

Anticipation and planning for a range of potential future scenarios is an essential part of preparedness. Deliberate planning and developing of information sharing protocols will decrease the level of uncertainty and the potential complexity of situations. Sharing emergency plans pre-event will enable coordination and transparency between agencies.

An organization and its leaders face the risk of public loss of trust if preventable information sharing and communication issues interfere with preparation, response, or recovery operations in a disaster situation. After a crisis, leaders will be expected to respond to three basic questions: what did you know, when did you know it, and what steps are you taking to ensure that this situation never happens again? Examination and revelations about the level of knowledge at various points in many crisis situations often reveals that warning signals of impending crisis were unrecognized or ignored. Weaknesses in preparedness that were unknown or ignored by leadership, as well as poor alignment between different parts of the organization, will become known. How leaders demonstrate their efforts to achieve situational awareness and understanding may determine whether or not the public confidence in the organization is increased, maintained, or lost.

Committees of inquiry investigating communication failures will ask the following two questions:

1. Did agency leaders allocate the requisite time, funding, and human resources to operational planning and to improving information sharing?
2. Did they assign responsibility and demand accountability for producing information sharing protocols defining how information is and is not to be shared in the context of organizational mandates, goals, outcomes, required interaction between organizations, regulations, and statutory requirements?

NATIONAL INFORMATION SHARING PLANNING POLICY

The fragmentation of responsibility for security and disaster preparedness among organizations with different objectives, which lack a shared culture and planning framework, makes it difficult to achieve coordination in homeland security. Clearly no single federal or state organization is solely responsible for improving all aspects of homeland security information sharing. No single entity is capable of defining (let alone imposing) operational information sharing protocols "top down" for other organizations and agencies. However, this is not an excuse for the lack of accountability for not creating information sharing protocols with partners.

National homeland security policy has recognized the importance of information sharing, joint-preparedness planning, and the need for coordination during a crisis. However, high-level policy and strategy documents emphasizing the importance of information sharing have not motivated key federal, state, and local agencies to produce effective field operating procedures governing information sharing in homeland security mission areas, even for those scenarios deemed highest risk (e.g., attacks on mass transit security, major hurricanes, and improvised explosives or nuclear devices that force evacuation). It is time for the White House, Congress, the Secretary of Homeland Security, and state offices of homeland security to develop a clear policy requirement that motivates constituent agencies to define and test information sharing protocols crucial for effective operational coordination.

Information sharing planning policies should:

- Require agencies to define the processes they use to develop and share interagency information sharing and communication protocols
- Require reporting on impediments to information sharing and assessment of the risk of information sharing gaps and communication breakdowns between agencies
- Establish mechanisms to review the effectiveness of developing and reviewing information sharing and communication protocols to determine if they are sufficient or deficient
- Establish a requirement to create a common standard for defining and specifying documented protocols governing interagency requests for information, information sharing, and communication, whether the required flow of information is between people, between people and computers, or between computers (i.e., the NIEM standard only covers programmatic system-to-system information flows)
- Require reporting of information sharing and communication issues to senior agency leadership, including identification of the statutory, regulatory, policy, technical, security, or other barriers that prevent such sharing
- Require assessments to identify and rank the severity of potential breakdowns, bottlenecks, delays, and single points of failure in communication that will impact partner agencies

White House policy should:

- Require DHS and other federal departments and agencies to demonstrate that they have developed information sharing plans and protocols for the scenarios deemed of the highest strategic risk to the nation
- Require federal, state, and local agencies to create and systematically review information sharing protocols with partners in exercises and to incorporate lessons learned
- Require DHS to author best-practice information sharing protocols for key roles, tasks, and decisions common to most states
- Require DHS to provide state and local agencies with training and technical assistance in the development of information sharing and communication protocols

CONCLUSION

Information sharing will remain the Achilles' heel of homeland security unless organizations foster a deeper understanding of their stakeholders' roles and information needs and develop information sharing protocols. Shared situational awareness cannot exist without information sharing. Through information sharing, coordination, and collaboration, disparate organizations can come to see themselves as members of a meta-organization or system-of-systems with common goals—a complex adaptive system that can adapt existing protocols to provide an appropriate response to a novel crisis situation based on (information) feedback from agents within the system or the environment.

Pioneering homeland security and emergency management directors have started to transition their agencies to a new paradigm of collaborative management of shared risk. They have begun to develop information sharing protocols because they recognize that this enables their agencies to leverage extensive investments in information and communication technology, better coordinate joint operations, and achieve greater unity of effort.

A recent court ruling in the case of the Virginia Tech shooting found the university guilty of negligence because it did not adequately notify and warn students of the shooting that had taken place on campus. This ruling indicates that the default presumption is that an organization responsible for the safety and security of its population must share information, issue notifications, and communicate effectively in order to accomplish their security and disaster risk- management objectives. In an era of smartphone coverage, crowdsourcing, and 24/7 news cycles, it will be impossible to hide an ineffective crisis response. In today's homeland security environment the organization's effectiveness, and even its reputation, will depend on its ability to share information in a timely, targeted, and consistent manner as part of a functional cross-agency team.

Leaders will eventually grasp the change-management potential of defining information sharing protocols for routine operations—change the flow of information and you change the performance of an organization.

ACKNOWLEDGEMENTS

The author would like to thank Howard Steinberg, Jan Ithier, Daniel Stevens, Mike Horsefield, and Andy Mazzeo for their reviews of this chapter.

NOTES

1. A crisis is a " … a major, (sometimes) unpredictable event that has potentially negative results. The event and its aftermath may significantly damage an organization and its employees, products, services, financial condition, and reputation."

2. See, for example, Chapters 3 and 8 of the 9/11 Commission Report, http://govinfo.library.unt.edu/911/report/index.htm.

3. See discussion of the Nationwide Suspicious Activity Reporting (SAR) Initiative (NSI) and the national network of State and Major Urban Area Fusion Centers in the chapter by Kshemendra Paul, the ISE Program Manage, in this volume.

4. Ibid.

5. Thomas Fingar, *Reducing Uncertainty: Intelligence Analysis and National Security*, Stanford University Press, 2011.

6. The White House, National Strategy for Information Sharing, October 2007, http://georgewbush-whitehouse.archives.gov/nsc/infosharing/index.html.

7. National Security Strategy, May 2010, www.whitehouse.gov/sites/default/files/rss_viewer/national_security_strategy.pdf.

8. The National Strategy for Maritime Security, September 20, 2005, http://georgewbush-whitehouse.archives.gov/homeland/maritime-security.html.

9. The National Strategy to Secure Cyberspace, February 2003, www.us-cert.gov/reading_room/cyberspace_strategy.pdf.

10. The Comprehensive National Cybersecurity Initiative, www.whitehouse.gov/cybersecurity/comprehensive-national-cybersecurity-initiative.

11. Nearly 10 years after 9/11, the DHS Office of Intelligence and Analysis is now developing a pilot program, the Sector Information Needs Process, to engage the private sector in defining owner/operator requirements.

12. Intelligence Information Sharing, January 10, 2012, http://www.dhs.gov/xlibrary/assets/niac/niac-intelligence-information-sharing-final-report-01102012.pdf.

13. "The Need to Know: Information Sharing Lessons Learned for Disaster Response," Hearing before the Committee on Government Reform, House of Representatives, 109th Congress, Second Session, March 30, 2006 Serial No. 109–143, http://www.fas.org/sgp/congress/2006/infoshare.html.

14. The Comprehensive Preparedness Guide can be accessed at http://www.fema.gov/pdf/about/divisions/npd/CPG_101_V2.pdf.

15. The Lessons Learned Information Sharing website address is https://www.llis.dhs.gov.

16. For an excellent treatment of this topic, see "Capability Development in Support of Comprehensive Approaches: Transforming International Civil-Military Interactions," Derrick J. Neal and Linton Wells II (eds.), Center for Technology and National Security Policy, Institute for National Strategic Studies, National Defense University, December 2011.

17. Sarah Laskow, "Homeland Security's Billion Dollar Bet on Better Communications," The Center for Public Integrity, February 16, 2010, http://www.publicintegrity.org/investigations/homeland_security/articles/entry/1925/.

3

INTRODUCTION TO PART III: INTEROPERABILITY, INFORMATION SHARING, AND COLLABORATION

William J. Bratton

Chairman, Kroll Advisory Solutions, Inc. and Former Chief of New York, Boston, and Los Angeles Police Departments. Co-author with Zach Tumin of Collaborate or Perish!: Reaching Across Boundaries in a Networked World

In today's increasingly networked world, organizations must collaborate across traditional boundaries or run the risk of irrelevance and failure. No one agency can do it alone. That is the most significant thing I learned in my 40 years in law enforcement and private security, and it remains one of the key lessons of 9/11. This section of the *McGraw-Hill Homeland Security Handbook* conveys valuable insights about holistic interoperability, information sharing, and collaborative homeland security.

As Zach Tumin and I reference in our book *Collaborate or Perish*, having a vision is the first, and most critical step in the process of achieving true collaborative partnerships and the interagency formation flows essential for joint mission success. Leaders at all levels must be passionate about the vision of a rigorous results-oriented approach to improving interagency information sharing, communication, and collaborative performance.

A significant issue impeding homeland security continues to be the lack of accountability and performance management regarding information sharing and collaboration. Homeland security leaders in major cities, states, and fusion centers and the US Department of Homeland Security need to adopt an approach to managing information-sharing improvement similar to the Compstat performance management approach developed in the NYPD in the 1990s. This approach is widely used by American police departments and federal agencies such as the FBI to curb crime and terrorism. Measuring and holding agencies accountable for improvement in information sharing can contribute significantly to ensuring success in fighting and preventing terrorist acts, just as it did in fighting crime in New York and Los Angeles. If your city, state, or region's managers have no way to quantitatively track whether or not the flow of information between agencies is improving over time, then you are failing to comprehensively manage performance, collaboration, and accountability.

To "right-size" performance improvement efforts, leaders and managers should focus their limited resources on identifying, managing, and improving information-sharing protocols for the highest-risk crime, terrorism, and hazard scenarios faced by their cities, states, and regions. For each threat, mission area, and activity, leaders need to define the "communities of interest" involved and ensure that members of these communities understand their respective roles and interdependencies. Each agency needs to identify and analyze the information needed by key responsibilities; design the ideal set of information flow and communication protocols for commanders, managers, officers, and responders in the field; secure commitments from partners they depend on; and constantly seek to increase the reliability of information and intelligence.

Similar to what was done when employing Compstat, the members of these communities should consider conducting weekly strategy discussions, planning meetings, and diagnostic exercises. They are then in a better position to report on the information-sharing problems identified, and prioritize those which may potentially impede mission success and create plans to address them. Gaining visibility into technical, legal, procedural, bureaucratic, and political impediments to information sharing is critical. Clear communication is also essential to collaboration efforts.

Agreeing and focusing on the most severe issues is essential, because agencies will not have enough manpower, funds, and political capital to fix every information-sharing issue. Progress reports are critical to enable governance, accountability, performance management, and oversight. Force multiplying collaborative initiatives will become increasingly important in the resource-reduced environment that we are now facing.

High performing fusion centers, state offices of homeland security and emergency management, regional catastrophic planning groups, and critical infrastructure operators that adopt this performance management approach will be able to demonstrate increased collaboration and mission effectiveness, measure efficiencies, gain status, and be better positioned to compete for increasingly scarce state and federal grant funding.

A greatly enhanced ability to forecast potential information-sharing performance problems in time to set up appropriate interventions will become the key to success in managing our response to homeland security challenges, crime, and other security-related issues in our increasingly complex society. As discussed in this section, computer technology will also likely be used to define information-sharing protocols, automatically indentify possible information flow issues in advance, and recommend and prioritize interventions based on intelligent decision support programs. The time for collaborative performance management in homeland security and counterterrorism information sharing has to now move from just a vision to a reality.

11

WHY WE FAIL—AND HOW TO SUCCEED

The 25 Pearl Harbor Deficiencies of Leadership and Planning: Their Pervasive Impact on Day-to-Day Operations, Emergency and Disaster Preparedness

Robert I. Desourdis, Jr.[1]

Science Applications International Corporation

AN HISTORICAL PERSPECTIVE

Each of the 25 critical documented deficiencies from the 1946 Congressional investigation of the 1941 Pearl Harbor attack[2] have been demonstrated in one or more examples from the 9/11[3] and Katrina[4] congressional reports.[5] Each of these deficiencies can also be found in reports from investigations of the Virginia Tech mass shootings[6] and Deepwater Horizon[7] (the Gulf oil "spill"). In addition to these examples, quotes from the Exxon Valdez report[8] and the Columbine report[9] further demonstrate lessons not learned from similar historic events. In this context, a *deficiency* in planning detailed day-to-day or contingency communications (and information sharing) causes a gap in situational awareness and command coordination at a critical time in the history of the incident or event, leading to *failure* in the optimal action-based response of the affected organizations and individuals. Arguably, these same 25 failures are evident in the recounting of the Titanic and Lusitania sinkings, the Challenger disaster, and many more, plus a multitude of daily incidents too small or too remote to achieve national or international awareness and detailed investigation. Of course, these are all *human failures of leadership and planning*, which lead to deficiencies in preparedness and failures in the ultimate response. As a result, our first responders, warfighters, and those facing these trials are arguably forced to display much greater initiative and self-sacrifice than necessary had those responsible for planning for these contingencies used best practices to share information and coordinate resulting action long before the incidents occurred. In each case, these planning deficiencies result in failure to achieve *holistic interoperability* among these individuals and organizations , defined as "a measure of *shared trusted understanding* that drives *predictable collaborative action* towards a common goal."[10]

The problem has nothing to do with technology; more accurately, it is the people who conceive, develop, manufacture, procure, deploy, and verify the technology that are responsible if the technology fails to meet the need. It is always the responsibility of people, those who plan day-to-day operations (e.g., coordinated activities) or response to major incidents, emergencies, or disasters. It was perhaps best stated in a quote from the 1946 Minority Report on Pearl Harbor by Senators Homer Ferguson and Owen Brewster.

> One cannot understand the defeat which the United States suffered on December 7, 1941, by attempting to analyze it in terms of economics, sociology, technology, or any other of history's neat pigeonholes. It arose from the nature of the men involved. In our opinion, the evidence before this committee indicates that the tragedy at Pearl Harbor was primarily a failure of men and not of laws or powers to do the necessary things, and carry out the vested responsibilities.[11]

All too often, large expenditures on the latest technology give the *perception* of improved security—but miss the core problem: the people who are to be linked by this technology. What will they (specifically) do with it, how and when, and why? These details are often ignored, *assumed* to be "someone else's job," believed to be already well understood, or a trivial matter best left to the users of the technology, if and when "the time comes." This sentiment was perhaps best expressed by Dorothy Thompson on December 8, 1941:

> Following the report of the tragedy that Secretary of the Navy Frank Knox made shortly after the event, the blunt-penned Dorothy Thompson poured an avalanche of scorn over her countrymen:
>> And I will tell you where the ultimate responsibilities lies [sic], for Hawaii and for everything else. It lies with us …
>>
>> For a whole generation the American idea has been to get as much as it could for as little effort. For a whole generation the American motto has been "I guess it's good enough."
>>
>> I accuse us. I accuse the twentieth-century American. I accuse me ….[12]

In all of the aforementioned disasters, there were people who warned of the impending incidents and alerted leaders and planners about the likely outcomes, but this insight and imagination were minimally considered or completely ignored. Even when investigations from well-known events similar to earlier incidents are documented and available, it appears that planners are not learning from prior incidents. This failure to learn from the past was evident in the handling of both the Virginia Tech mass shootings and the Deepwater Horizon disaster. Contingency planners arguably failed to take into account the lessons and recommendations available in detailed reports published following the Columbine shootings and the Exxon Valdez oil spill, respectively.

CONVENTIONS

Presentation of the Pearl Harbor deficiencies will be aided by a simple categorization of strategic versus tactical information, and the impact of scope and duration of incidents or emergencies on the individuals, entities (any organizational component), companies, or agencies involved.

Strategic Failures   The Pearl Harbor deficiencies have both *strategic* and *tactical* impacts on preparedness and response. Strategic failures generally involve the long-term preparation period before the incident or event, during which foreknowledge, or forecasting, could provide forewarning of a threat or event. In general, a strategic planning failure reduces the capability to properly collect, integrate, and understand the information needed to forecast events. The failure to properly interpret, or use the forecast (or *intelligence*) to improve *imagination* or *insight* into intent and potential impact, reduces situational awareness and increases the prevalence of additional deficiencies and the ultimate failures. For incidents like Pearl Harbor and 9/11, strategic failures reduced the effectiveness of the vast, collected intelligence to provide proper alert and warning, much less effective preparedness. This reduced effectiveness is most often due to decentralization (incomplete information), misinterpretation (failed understanding), paraphrasing (or restatement with built-in assumptions), or inadequate dissemination of the collected information.

The fundamental strategic failures are not made when the collected information is incomplete, misinterpreted, paraphrased, or inadequately disseminated; they are made long before by the leaders and planners who fail to insist on development of written, documented, understandable, vetted, and verified information-sharing plans. If the people, orchestrated processes, and automated tools are not in place and proven long before information of strategic importance is collected, the system or people, process and tools are already predisposed to the resulting (associated) operational failures. It is the planning of actionable information sharing and the correlated tasks and activities driven by vetted coordination plans that must become automatic (or automated) for those involved. All too often, these information flows and correlated planned actions are considered too unimportant, already done or "someone else's job," to address in detail using best information-sharing planning practices.[13] The consequences of this deficient planning are documented in the investigations of a repeated history of strategic and tactical failures. Anything can be made better—it is never "good enough."

Tactical Failures

Tactical failures prevent or minimize information sharing within the time span of incident detection, response, and immediate aftermath. By the time the incident occurs, it is too late to correct the deficiencies in leadership and planning—which took place days, weeks, months, perhaps even years before the incident—that caused these failures. If the deficiencies are mitigated or eliminated upon detection, during or following the incident or event, it is most often due to the valued initiative and self-sacrifice of the responders themselves—having had to reconfigure their information sharing "in real time" to meet critical needs. Usually, many individuals will have foreseen this eventuality,

Figure 11-1

Holistic
interoperability
continuum[14]

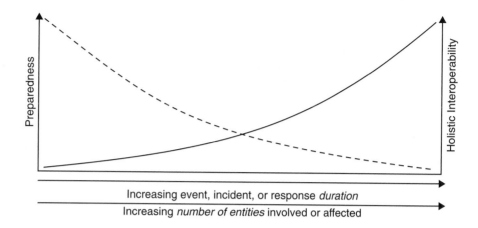

but other deficiencies (as has been shown[15]) prevented their recommendations from being heard, much less implemented.

**Holistic
Interoperability
Continuum**

Figure 11-1 shows the level of single-entity preparedness on the left vertical scale and the need for multi-agency (holistic) interoperability on the right vertical scale.[16] (In this context, an "entity" could be an individual, a unit, or small group of individuals, a bureaucracy, or a stand-alone organization, such as a police department.) The dashed curve descending to the right measures the preparedness of any single entity, which does well for lesser scale incidents of short duration operating alone. But as we move to the right, this single entity is far less prepared for the demand of a larger scale incident of a long-term duration in a multi-agency environment. However, as the solid curve represents, the level of preparedness (and information sharing) required to operate effectively in this long-term multi-organization environment increases as we move to the right in the figure. This multi-entity environment can be viewed as information islands or stovepipes, both strategic (what is the forecast or intent?) and tactical (what's happening now and what are we all doing about it?), as shown in Figure 11-2.

The information-sharing islands and stovepipes in the figure are the effect and not the cause of failed holistic interoperability, that is, shared trusted understanding that drives predictable collaborative action. Trying to use technology alone to link the stovepipes and fill the gaps between islands, which has been the tendency of government and industry for decades, is analogous to fighting a disease by attempting to mask the symptoms. The advantages of deploying technology

Figure 11-2

Information islands
and stovepipes
despite technology

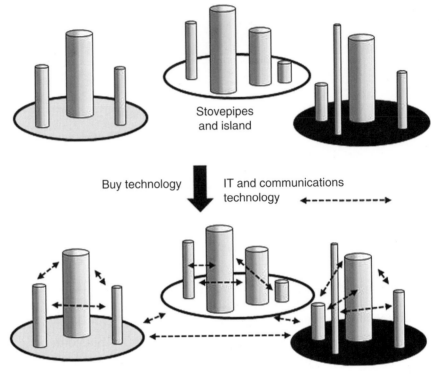

irrespective of its success are (1) it appears as if those responsible are taking definitive action and pushes the responsibility to those within each stovepipe who now "can" communicate; and (2) procuring and deploying equipment and software is far simpler than addressing the core human issues that are well-documented in the Pearl Harbor deficiencies. Technology only provides the "solution" to link information-sharing stovepipes and islands if it is designed to fill information-sharing gaps needed to achieve holistic interoperability, as determined and integrated into a multi-entity concept of operations (CONOPS) and integrated standard operating procedures (SOPs) by the "stovepiped" entities themselves.

In what follows, we will refer to a "specific information flow." By "specific information," we mean message content type (e.g., voice, data, video), filtering (content management and tailoring), length (time or bits), priority (from safety-of life highest to administrative lowest), need for acknowledgement, time to live, number of retires, security (encryption), number of hops (relay points), and other details.

The process of institutionalizing (not just discussing) these details, as well as the details themselves, has the following advantages:

- Forces all stakeholders to think carefully about who needs to know what, how, and when, particularly in fast-paced (tactical) safety-of-life situations
- Uncovers gaps between planning and expectations that are best found well before an incident occurs, illustrating how subtly and insidiously these deficiencies impact any operation
- Provides a *justifiable* information-sharing need to test for technology gaps, *then* use best practices (i.e., systems engineering[17]) to guide procurement of what's needed to fill this gap
- Establishes the basis for new or upgraded technology to automate this specific information exchange and remove responsibility to ensure the exchange from the workload of the stakeholders themselves—it just happens as planned to the extent practicable

This chapter includes many quotes from key investigations of the incidents recounted. Although some effort is taken to address the context in which these quotes were made, it is not possible to convey a complete understanding of the associated preparedness, response, and aftermath in each situation. Moreover, space limitations as well as the volume of investigation content preclude a detailed historical recounting of these events associated with each tragedy. In addition, there are many more examples of these deficiencies in each of the cited reports than could be recounted in this work—the reader is encouraged to refer to them for further examples and details. It is strongly recommended that anyone reading this chapter also read the books and reports cited in this work and draw their own conclusions regarding the relationship of the results of these investigations to the 1941 Pearl Harbor deficiencies.

Prologue and Dedication

This chapter will add the April 2007 Virginia Tech mass shootings (and a Columbine perspective) and the April 2010 Deepwater Horizon (and an Exxon Valdez perspective) to the incidents that further demonstrate the Pearl Harbor deficiencies found in the 9/11 and Katrina reports.[18] This addition emphasizes that it is the people and their leadership and planning deficiencies—not the technology—that are ultimately responsible for the strategic and tactical outcome.

Virginia Tech Mass Shootings

The deadliest mass-murder incident in American history occurred when on April 16, 2007, one student, senior Seung Hui Cho, murdered 32 and injured 17 students and faculty in two related incidents on the campus of Virginia Polytechnic Institute and State University ("Virginia Tech").[19]

A detailed review of the 2009 addendum to the full report on the events leading to the crime, details of the incident, and the subsequent response was reviewed to seek further examples of the 25 Pearl Harbor deficiencies. The Virginia Tech shootings have many similarities to an earlier incident, when "two disgruntled seniors at the school [Columbine High School], Dylan Klebold and Eric Harris, who were determined to kill as many teachers and fellow students as possible, first, by planting and detonating two 20-pound propane bombs in the school cafeteria and then by shooting survivors fleeing the inferno they hoped to create."[20] The lessons learned from Columbine—published in May 2001—were readily available to all with the same responsibilities nationwide.

On January 28, 2000, Governor Bill Owens created by executive order a Columbine Review Commission to inquire into the Columbine High School tragedy April 20, 1999, and to submit recommendations on several matters: (1) law enforcement handling of the crisis; (2) the sufficiency of safety protocols as used at Columbine High School; (3) an evaluation of emergency medical response and evacuation techniques employed at Columbine; (4) the appropriateness of victim assistance at the scene; (5) identification of key factors that might have contributed to the tragedy and of methods that might prevent similar future occurrences; and (6) an examination of other relevant issues related to the tragedy.[21]

The Columbine lessons learned will be compared to each of the 25 Pearl Harbor Failures in what follows, as well as similar failures leading up to the Virginia Tech shootings and response six years later. Again, we will see that the same deficiencies in planning and ultimate strategic and tactical failures are evident in spite of Columbine and the other intrinsically similar events discussed above.

Deepwater Horizon

The "Path to Tragedy," in Part I of the President's Commission Report, perhaps best summarizes the causes and effects that will be clearly reminiscent of the Pearl Harbor deficiencies and failures, yet again.

> On April 20, 2010, the 126 workers on the BP Deepwater Horizon were going about the routines of completing an exploratory oil well—unaware of impending disaster. What unfolded would have unknown impacts shaped by the Gulf region's distinctive cultures, institutions, and geography—and by economic forces resulting from the unique coexistence of energy resources, bountiful fisheries and wildlife, and coastal tourism. The oil and gas industry, long lured by Gulf reserves and public incentives, progressively developed and deployed new technologies, at ever-larger scales, in pursuit of valuable energy supplies in increasingly deeper waters farther from the coastline. Regulators, however, failed to keep pace with the industrial expansion and new technology—often because of industry's resistance to more effective oversight. The result was a serious, and ultimately inexcusable, shortfall in supervision of offshore drilling that played out in the Macondo well blowout and the catastrophic oil spill that followed.[22]

As will be shown, one of the Pearl Harbor deficiencies is to focus on what people think *might* happen, usually affected by their personal point of view (perhaps impacted by their best interests), and not what logically *could* happen. This might/could dichotomy was pervasive throughout deficient planning long before any of the disasters illuminated below had occurred. Two decades before the "impossible" happening on the Macondo, another "impossibility" occurred.

> On March 24, 1989, Alaskans awoke to the shock of disaster. Shortly after midnight, the 987-foot-long supertanker Exxon Valdez had run hard aground on Bligh Reef, spilling 10.8 million gallons of crude oil into the unspoiled waters of Prince William Sound. The worst case had occurred.[23]

Strangely similar to the "Path to Tragedy" summary of the Deepwater Horizon disaster,

> The historical record developed by the Alaska Oil Spill Commission is clear: The original rules were consistently violated, primarily to insure that tankers passing through Prince William Sound did not lose time by slowing down for ice or waiting for winds to abate. Concern for profits in the 1980s obliterated concern for safe operations that existed in 1977.[24]

The report states an epitaph directly correlated with our dedication below and oddly reminiscent of the conclusion of the Pearl Harbor Minority Report by Senators Homer Ferguson and Owen Brewster as well as Dorothy Thompson:

> This disaster could have been prevented—not by tanker captains and crews who are, in the end, only fallible human beings, but by an advanced oil transportation system designed to minimize human error. It could have been prevented if Alaskans, state and federal governments, the oil industry, and the American public had insisted on stringent safeguards. It could have been prevented if the vigilance that accompanied construction of the pipeline in the 1970s had been continued in the 1980s.[25]

It also shows that it is not the people at the scene, but strategic and tactical plans and conventions forced on those who are there when the impossible occurs. The leaders and planners whose planning replicates the Pearl Harbor deficiencies seem never to be present at the scene when their deficiencies turn to failure and then disaster and tragedy.

Dedication

The insidiousness nature of the Pearl Harbor deficiencies is such that the lack of coordinated and assured information sharing among individuals and organizations is a minimal requirement for the alert, preparedness, and response enterprise. These deficiencies are ingrained in how people work together and share information, as well as the threat and risk-based information-triggered actions within and among multiple individuals, entities, and organizations. In what follows, we will review quotes from the investigative reports for the Virginia Tech mass shootings and the Deepwater Horizon environmental disaster, and present earlier related recommendations from the Columbine and Exxon Valdez reports, respectively.

These lessons and realizations from Columbine and Exxon Valdez were available—perhaps even considered—years before the Virginia Tech and Deepwater Horizon incidents again clearly demonstrated the 25 Pearl Harbor deficiencies and failures. It will be shown that these failures still dominate any understanding of "why" these threats were not strategically mitigated or prevented with the resulting tragic consequences.

This chapter is meant to address the failures of leadership and best-practices planning that are the direct cause of ineffective and inefficient preparedness and response. The initiative and self-sacrifice of our day-to-day employees, public safety responders, our soldiers, and anyone on the frontline of any enterprise must be far greater than necessary in order to compensate for these failures in planning. There are several key reasons for this poor planning, but it is these frontline people and first responders who must live with, or suffer, the effects. It is in their honor that the points made in this chapter are dedicated.

Finally, the people involved in the assessment and subsequent warnings about the future murderer's behavior and potential threat at Virginia Tech; the people who underwent its wrath against the vulnerable and innocent students on that day; and the public safety community who saved lives that could be saved and dealt with the families and grief were all clearly intelligent, patriotic and caring people … and many were and are heroes. The author, whose daughter was in a building adjacent to where the first two victims were shot at Virginia Tech on the morning of April 16th and telephoned her dad that she was "OK," dedicates this work to them.

THE PEARL HARBOR DEFICIENCIES

Two excellent references describing preparation, execution, response, aftermath, and investigation of the attack on Pearl Harbor in 1941 were written by Gordon William Prange, Donald M. Goldstein, and Katherine V. Dillon, and entitled *At Dawn We Slept: The Untold Story of Pearl Harbor* and *Pearl Harbor: The Verdict of History.*[26] The *Verdict of History* ends with a recounting of the 25 Pearl Harbor failures in the Congressional Report.

... Assistant Counsel Morgan presented in his draft report twenty-five "supervisory, administrative and organizational deficiencies" apparent in the Army and Navy. These the majority accepted. High-level schools of both services studied them at the direction of Nimitz and Eisenhower, then respectively CNO [Chief of Naval Operations] and Chief of Staff. Moreover, at J. Edgar Hoover's direction, Morgan lectured to the FBI about these principles.

The final report explained that the committee posed these points "not for their novelty or profundity but for the reason that, by their very self-evident simplicity, it is difficult to believe they were ignored." Morgan confined himself strictly to factors illustrated by the attack, producing chapter and verse to back them up. The applicability of these points *far transcends Pearl Harbor* [*emphasis* added], so they deserve serious review ...[27]

A review of each of the Pearl Harbor deficiencies summarized in Figure 11-3 is fundamentally important to understanding how to plan for day-to-day as well as major operations and coordination among individuals and organizations to avoid the resulting failures. This work is therefore not directed at those who are in the frontline of public or private operations—it is intended for those in the background who plan operations and provide the necessary tools to implement those plans. In all of the well-documented tragedies, where it was apparent to many well before the incidents had occurred (and usually documented) that such deficiencies existed, it was the authorities and their planners who ultimately must carry the responsibility for their impact.

In what follows, a diagrammatic depiction of each Pearl Harbor deficiency is shown for illustrative purposes. The meanings of the symbols used in these diagrams are shown in the legend of Figure 11-4. In the diagrams that follow, it is assumed desirable to have all entities coordinating according to a common action plan X, Y, or Z—not following different operational plans. These diagrams are not intended to represent best practice in any domain. They are intended as graphics to help explain the deficiencies beyond the narrative alone. As explained in the parent reference relating these deficiencies to subsequent disaster investigations,

Figure 11-3a

Thirteen of the 25 Pearl Harbor deficiencies reported in the Congressional Investigation of the attack on Pearl Harbor. It is these "failures of men" that were largely independent of technology.

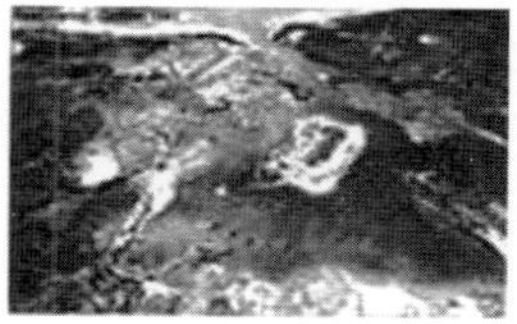

Pearl

"East Wind, Rain"

Sabotage?

Air raid, Pearl Harbor!
This is not a drill!
Image credit: US Navy

#	Deficiency	Description
1	Organization	Multiple parallel organizations with ambiguous authority
2	Assumption	Information sharing is taken for granted or assumed
3	Omission	Information distribution is incomplete, people and entities excluded
4	Verification	Commands/information sent, no follow-up to ensure understanding and action
5	Supervision	Close supervision to verify understanding and predictable action not provided
6	Alertness	Heightened alert is believed undermined by repeated training and exercises
7	Complacency	Vigilance relaxes from the day-to-day lull of "business as usual"
8	Intelligence	Distributed intelligence sources with limited dissemination
9	Attitude	Superiors do not engage in open dialogue with peers and subordinates
10	Imagination	Worst-case scenarios not included in preparedness and response planning
11	Communications	Information exchanged is ambiguous, convoluted, or contradictory
12	Paraphrase	Messages altered according to assumption with no verification
13	Adaptability	Conventions not altered despite unforeseen environment

Figure 11-3b

The remaining 12 Pearl Harbor failures, primarily leader shortsightedness and inter-organizational jealousy, letting their personal relationships impact their planning and decisions, while delegating responsibility with limited authority.

USS Show

USS Maryland and USS Oklahoma

USS Arizona then

...and now
Image credit: U.S. Navy

#	Deficiency	Description
14	Disclosure	Intelligence so protected that it is inaccessible to those who urgently need it
15	Insight	Inadequate understanding of the threat make risks poorly estimated
16	Dissemination	Information is not provided to subordinates who need to know
17	Inspection	Leaders do not know or understanding their personnel and critical systems
18	Preparedness	Prepare for consequences of what a threat might do, instead of what it can do
19	Consistency	Official direction is contradicted by unofficial speculation from authorities
20	Jealousy	Individual or organizational one-upmanship for real or perceived self-benefit
21	Relationship	Personal friendships inhibit identification and resolution of deficiencies or gaps
22	Priority	Failure to prioritize critical needs over day-to-day activities
23	Reporting	Supervisors and subordinates fail to share situational awareness
24	Improvement	Failure to identify gaps, particularly in worst-case scenarios, and correct them
25	Delegation	Responsibility is delegated with no authority to act

Figure 11-4

Graphics legend

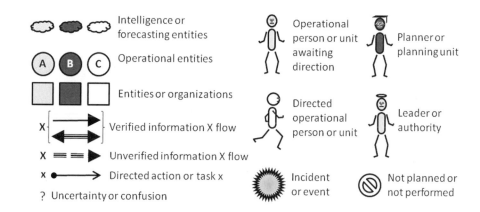

these named deficiencies have been generalized from the military-centric context of Pearl Harbor to planning and coordination for any human endeavor.

In what follows, it is important to distinguish a "deficiency" from a "failure" in operational planning and implementation. In this context, a *deficiency* is a condition or characteristic of inadequate planning that elevates the associated risk of ineffective situational awareness or command coordination (an information-sharing *failure*). Information-sharing implementation could involve either strategic or tactical preparations needed to prevent, detect, protect, alert, respond to, or recover from an incident or event. Historically, a deficiency of *complacency* exists that accepts these risks, perhaps through the deficiencies of *insight* or *imagination,* but nevertheless sets the stage for one or more holistic interoperability *failures* when the time comes. Methods to prevent, avoid, or minimize planning deficiencies that produced the classic Peal Harbor failures in historic disasters are also provided. These methods apply to all holistic interoperability planning by groups of organizations, entities within an organization, and the associated individuals.

Organization

Deficiency. Multiple chains of command with overlapping or ambiguous authority can lead to confusion in the execution of tasks and activities (Figure 11-5). Different information flows through these organizations produce unpredictable results, but certainly confusion on the part of those that are directly involved with the managing of or responding to an event. Such confusion is found in all the major documented tragedies and disasters, but it is also true in countless day-to-day situations for businesses and government.

Figure 11-5

Deficiency of organization. Convoluted organizational structures can lead to no one knowing what exactly needs to be done to respond to a crisis.

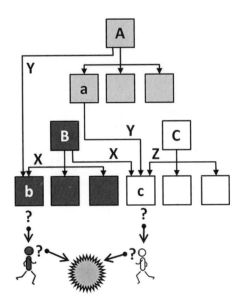

Morgan scored Bloch's [Rear Admiral Claude C. Bloch, Commander of Fourteenth Naval District, which included Pearl Harbor] admission that he did not know whom Kimmel [Admiral Husband E. Kimmel, Commander of the Pacific Fleet] would hold responsible for shortcomings in regard to aircraft readiness. He also criticized Bellinger's [Rear Admiral Patrick N. L. Bellinger, commander of Patrol Wing Two] "wholly anomalous" position whereby he was "responsible to everyone and to no one." Morgan warned, "The pyramiding of superstructures of organization cannot be inductive to efficiency and endangers the very function of our military and naval services." (Or, of any other organization, for that matter.)[28]

The 9/11 Commission directly references this organizational confusion.

"Surprise, when it happens to a government, is likely to be a complicated, diffuse, bureaucratic thing. It includes neglect of responsibility, but also responsibility so poorly defined or so ambiguously delegated that action gets lost." That comment was made more than 40 years ago, about Pearl Harbor. We hope

> another commission, writing in the future about another attack, does not again find this quote to be so apt.[29]

Prevention. In order to avoid this deficiency, specific responsibilities, authorities and chains of command must be *defined, documented, vetted, tested,* and *verified* repeatedly and regularly using a set of both possible (see the "Imagination" section later in the chapter) as well as probable incidents or emergencies spanning day-to-day and worst-case disaster scenarios. Each scenario would involve the sequence of strategic and tactical actions to prevent, detect, protect, alert, respond to, and recover from the incident, emergency, or disaster. There is often not one authority directing these individuals, entities, or organizations to bring them together to plan contingencies and ensure that unambiguous and unified direction is ensured. Even if such authority existed, the assumption is that such planning had already been done, or if not done, that the time, resources, or necessary techniques to correct this deficiency exist (i.e., best practices such as organizational development[30] and enterprise architecture[31]). As the old expression goes, "there's never time to do it right, but there's always time to do it over."

Assumption

Deficiency. A common deficiency in the planning and execution of many operations is the belief that other people or organizations are performing certain actions or sharing certain information (Figure 11-6). It is often *assumed* those other individuals or entities within one organization, much less across organizations, will receive or share certain information or act in some way given this information. This assumption is made in the absence of documented and vetted information-sharing plans and the concomitant action plans, for example, CONOPS and integrated unit SOPs, contingent upon specific information. It is often assumed that the terminology in a message, whether coded or in "natural language" will have a common meaning and that all who receive the message will have the full context (i.e., situational awareness) upon which to interpret the information and await events or act as expected. As will be shown below, the deficiency of assumption leads to many more insidious forms of information-sharing failures. In other words, these deficiencies are not independent of one another, but produce an overlapping effect that is more complicated and subtle.

Figure 11-6

Deficiency of
assumption

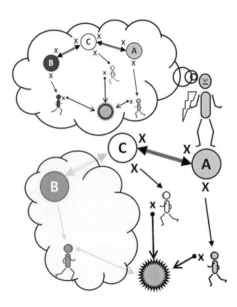

Morgan dealt briefly here with assumptions—those slippery
paving stones on the road to Pearl Harbor. "The testimony of
many crucial witnesses contains an identical note: 'I thought he
was alerted'; 'I took for granted he would understand'; 'I thought
he would be doing that.' " With those words Morgan's analysis
soared far beyond the lessons taught by a military operation,
however significant, and entered into a fundamental region of
the human condition. How often similar phrases signal tragedies
in every field of life![32]

One of those "fields of life" would be evident on 9/11, when a lack of
imagination, intelligence, insight, and perhaps *alertness* and *complacency*
had led to assumptions that guided the planning:

In sum, the protocols in place on 9/11 for the FAA [Federal Aviation Administration] and NORAD [North American Air Defense
Command] to respond to a hijacking presumed that

- The hijacked aircraft would be readily identifiable and
  would not attempt to disappear;

> - There would be time to address the problem through the appropriate FAA and NORAD chains of command; and
> - The hijacking would take the traditional form; that is, it would not be a suicide hijacking designed to convert the aircraft into a guided missile [like hundreds of Japanese Kamikaze pilots had done for spiritual beliefs in World War II]
>
> On the morning of 9/11, the existing protocol was unsuited in every respect for what was about to happen.[33]

Prevention. The deficiency of *assumption* is avoided by ensuring (through day-to-day use, training and exercise) that specific scenario-dependent information flows among all planned stakeholder entities and organizations occur as planned. Of course, this planning should include the scenario-dependent tasks and information flows between the stovepipes and islands that continue to characterize the holistic interoperability among many public-serving and public-facing as well as private entities.

Omission

Deficiency. Arguably the most common deficiency in the planning and execution of many operations is the exclusion of one or more relevant entities from the planning process, much less (and it is often too late by then) the exclusion of those entities from the execution of a plan as well (Figure 11-7). All of the tragedies listed at the beginning of this chapter suffered from this planning deficiency, resulting in both strategic and tactical failures of holistic interoperability. The deficiency of omission has a number of causes that are related to other Pearl Harbor deficiencies, particularly *imagination, insight, assumption, jealously,* and *relationships*. In every case, something is known by an entity that would have a major impact on the decisions and actions of one or more other entities, but it is not shared or not shared when most needed. The consequences of lost life and property, much less other economic and efficiency impacts, are often traced, in the subsequent investigations, directly to this planning deficiency.

Morgan addressed the deficiency of omission by addressing a single example of failing to warn Pearl Harbor of the infamous Japanese "one-o'clock deadline" on December 7th, but the authors of *The Verdict of History* added that

Figure 11-7

Deficiency of omission. While organizations A and C have a shared understanding to do X when responding to an event, the information was not shared with B, which responds to the event by doing Y.

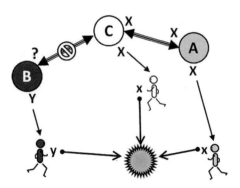

> ... Kimmel and Short should have been informed concerning the consular intercepts in regard to Pearl Harbor and the other military installations on Oahu. How much this grievous mistake contributed to the final disaster one cannot know. But the lesson is all too clear. If the United States conducts its high-level intelligence policy the same way in the nuclear age, it will not only court its own calamity but deserve its fate.[34]

The deficiency of omission persisted as 9/11 approached.

> The 1995 procedures [information-sharing procedures applied to the Federal Intelligence Surveillance Act (FISA)] dealt only with sharing between agents and criminal prosecutors, those working on intelligence matters and those working on criminal matters. But pressure from the Office of Intelligence Policy Review, FBI leadership, and the FISA Court built barriers between agents—even agents serving on the same squads. FBI Deputy Director Bryant reinforced the Office's caution by informing agents that too much information sharing could be a career stopper. Agents in the field began to believe—incorrectly—that no FISA information could be shared with agents working on criminal investigations.
>
> This perception evolved into the still more exaggerated belief that the FBI could not share any intelligence information with criminal investigators, even if no FISA procedures had been used. Thus, relevant information from the National Security Agency

> and the CIA often failed to make its way to criminal investiga-
> tors. Separate reviews in 1999, 2000, and 2001 concluded inde-
> pendently that information sharing was not occurring, and that
> the intent of the 1995 procedures was ignored routinely. ...[35]

Prevention. The deficiency of *omission* is avoided by vetting each
scenario with all stakeholder entities and letting them decide if they
have a role or not. This approach not only helps mitigate a leader's
or planner's deficiencies in *imagination* and *insight*, but it also helps
build the trust among all entities that is so critical in achieving holistic
interoperability. More specifically, if I trust what you'll do with the
information I provide you, and your subsequent actions support the
objective and don't hurt my efforts—perhaps even help them—then
I will provide that information to you (albeit possibly filtered). If this
goal is present in the detailed information-sharing planning with all
entities with a perceived role, then the resulting CONOPS and integrated SOPs will be valuable to all stakeholders.

Verification

Deficiency. The deficiency of *verification* (Figure 11-8) involves providing direction to subordinates or coordinating entities, but failing to verify that the actions they will subsequently take—including
information they intend to distribute—is specifically intended by that
direction. Of course, this deficiency is connected to the *assumption* that
the direction provided is understood in all its complexity, and this is
where the basic deficiency exists. This deficiency is made worse in its
effects when it launches activities prone to other deficiencies, such as
omission, because it has been assumed, but not verified, that the subsequent actions would alert or coordinate with certain entities.

Figure 11-8

Deficiency of
verification. The
leader believes he
has transmitted
information X to his
subordinate. However,
the subordinate
does not verify this
information and takes
action Y.

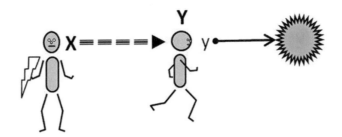

Prevention. *Verification* is a critical element of data communications to ensure that information received is correct between computers, but individuals often fail to communicate real information effectively. For this reason, if a supervisor provides direction, the supervisor needs to verify, perhaps by inspection of the subordinate's activities, that the specific desired action is being taken. This "supervisor–subordinate" relationship may be only a temporary necessity for the situation at hand. In one of the world's most critical safety-of-life-and-property, day-to-day activities, pilots are directed by air traffic control ground control stations to take specific actions to avoid aircraft or rough weather while optimizing the route to their destination. In every case, the pilot's SOP is to repeat exactly the directions heard. Anyone who has monitored air traffic control and pilot conversations hears this verification and becomes aware that retransmissions are sometimes required to ensure the pilots take the required action. This example is an excellent day-to-day best practice in *verification* to prevent the major emergency and potential ensuing disaster of air-to-air collisions. Air traffic control operators have an important automatic means to verify pilot's actions in the form of radar, which is the critical sensor technology providing ultimate verification. There are many situations in public safety, emergency management, and commercial operations of all types where consequences are great, but this simple verification is not done as a rule.

Supervision

Deficiency. The deficiencies of assumption and verification combine to define the deficiency of *supervision* (Figure 11-9), in which critical direction is not verified by those in authority to ensure the required actions are taking place. This deficiency is based on the failure of a supervisor, or someone in charge, to take steps to ensure the right information is being shared and the appropriate tasks or actions are being performed. Based on our air traffic control example, a deficiency of supervision would occur if our ground controller did not carefully listen for or to a pilot's response or monitor that aircraft's radar return to ensure compliance with direction. This failure has many manifestations in all other commercial, public-facing, and serving domains, but the bottom-line results are the same. The responsible authority in a situation fails to ensure that critical directions are being followed.

Prevention. Proper supervision is dependent upon the experience and skills of leaders and planners to ensure that those receiving

Figure 11-9

Deficiency of supervision. The leader of organization C fails to inspect effective communications with the planner, failing to verify the planner's understanding of the need for X. The planner subsequently transmits information Y to their subordinate, who acts on that information in response to the event.

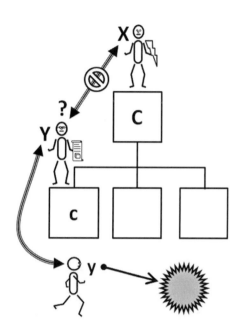

direction perform the intended information sharing or actions/tasks intended. However, this direction must be specific and communicated unambiguously, or failures of *communications* could minimize the impact of intended supervision. Supervisors "cannot check everything" personally—this was a commander's rejoinder to this identified issue in the Pearl Harbor investigation. The necessity therefore is to prioritize those "checks" that involve critical safety of life and property or organizational well-being and make sure they are verifiable. Perhaps technology would fill a gap in verification that would enable the supervisor to have the situational awareness—much like the radar for air traffic control or Global Positioning System (GPS) position tracks for mobile operations. In any event, those directing strategic and tactical operations must ensure that their directions are being executed to the detail or face the consequences—as has historically been the result.

Alertness

Deficiency. Although there had been claims that too many alerts at Pearl Harbor had dulled awareness of the impending attack (Figure 11-10)—that is, too many false alarms triggered natural *complacency*—the Assistant Council disagreed.

Figure 11-10

Deficiency of alertness. Despite the repeated exercises of how to respond to an event, when the actual event occurs, subordinates are confused as to how or whether to respond.

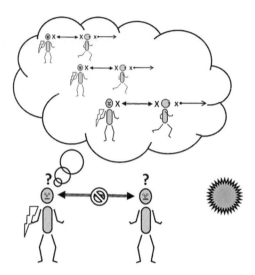

Morgan cited the "cry wolf" argument, which he considered invalid. He observed that repetition could not have relaxed the Hawaiian commands because they were never truly alert to begin with. Thus Morgan disagreed with the school of thought which holds that repeated warnings can blunt alertness by making the warnings commonplace. Morgan appeared to have the more cogent argument. Far better to send the fire engines on nine goose chases than hesitate the tenth time and allow a major conflagration to burn out of control.[36]

Apparently, the same deficiency of alertness prevailed before the Deepwater Horizon incident:

The Commission examined in great detail what went wrong on the rig itself. Our investigative staff uncovered a wealth of specific information that greatly enhances our understanding of the factors that led to the explosion. ... There are recurring themes of missed warning signals, *failure to share information* [emphasis added], and a general lack of appreciation for the risks involved. ...[37]

Prevention. In many situations, the cost of responding to a false alarm is much smaller than the potential consequences of ignoring it. Morgan's analogy regarding fire engines is oversimplified given that, once deployed, they may be further from the "real" fire, but without solid proof of a hoax call, a response will be made. It is for a similar reason that the U.S. Coast Guard responds to every "May Day" call, despite frequent hoax calls. Public safety answering point (PSAP) call-takers are trained to answer every call; police officers monitor their radios continuously when on patrol; and pilots are always monitoring air traffic control—the next call might be for them. Alertness must be built into the CONOPS of multiple entities and the integrated SOPs of the individual entities involved, while maximizing the technical and other means to ascertain the validity of the alert.

Complacency

Morgan found complacency (Figure 11-11) understandable but not acceptable in those whose job it is to be prepared for a wide range of operational scenarios, some with forewarning and many unforeseen. It is compounded by day after day of routine, perhaps boring and uneventful hours, days, weeks, and months. "But the American soldier, sailor, and airman … in maintaining his alertness to anything or nothing, he has to fight his own instincts. Yet that is his job."[38] There are many instances of such complacency in the tragedies of most note. Certainly, authorities responsible for situational awareness on December 7th, aircraft security on September 11th, aboard Deepwater

Figure 11-11

Deficiency of complacency. Day-to-day routine can lull all levels of an organization into believing "it will not happen today," reducing *alertness* and *preparedness*.

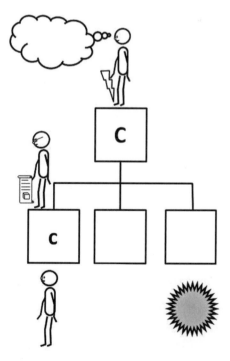

Horizon on April 20th, and on the Virginia Tech campus on April 16th had not imagined nor prepared for the scope of the events that were about to happen despite strategic and tactical information.

In the case of Hurricane Katrina, the failure of complete evacuations led to preventable deaths, great suffering, and further delays in relief.

- Evacuations of general populations went relatively well in all three states.
- Despite adequate warning 56 hours before landfall, Governor Blanco and Mayor Nagin delayed ordering a mandatory evacuation in New Orleans until 19 hours before landfall.
- The failure to order timely mandatory evacuations, Mayor Nagin's decision to shelter but not evacuate the remaining population, and decisions of individuals led to an incomplete evacuation.
- The incomplete pre-landfall evacuation led to deaths, thousands of dangerous rescues, and horrible conditions for those who remained.
- Federal, state, and local officials' failure to anticipate the post-landfall conditions delayed post-landfall evacuation and support.[39]

The deficiency of complacency was evident to the Deepwater Horizon investigators as well.

In the years before the Macondo blowout, neither industry nor government adequately addressed these risks. Investments in safety, containment, and response equipment and practices failed to keep pace with the rapid move into deepwater drilling. Absent major crises, and given the remarkable financial returns available from deepwater reserves, the business culture succumbed to a false sense of security. The Deepwater Horizon disaster exhibits the costs of a culture of complacency.[40]

Prevention. In addition to training and drills, the use of Red Team tactics to seek our "soft spots," and even review teams to assess one or more entities or organizations for the Pearl Harbor deficiencies described in this chapter, it would help to maintain a situational awareness that would challenge this deficiency. Such day-to-day or frequent challenges are necessary to maintain the *alertness* that is essentially the opposite of *complacency*.

Intelligence

The classic deficiency of *intelligence* (Figure 11-12) has been a concern for many years. Its critical importance directly impacts strategic warning and *alerting* as well as corresponding tactical *preparedness*. Its usual cause stems from different individuals and entities within organizations that have some of the information regarding intent of individuals or groups, or in the case of natural events, sensor data and corresponding forecasts. These entities do not share the information due to other deficiencies, such as *imagination, insight, jealously, relationships,* or *improvement*. This data is not centralized, that is, different humans or computers (or both) have awareness of only portions of the

Figure 11-12

Deficiency of intelligence. When leaders of organizations do not work together, they each only have part of the information required to respond in a collaborative manner to an event. If information is only shared within, rather than between organizations, the ultimate response may be at cross-purposes.

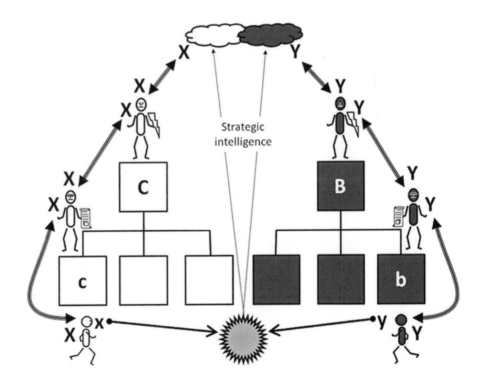

information available. They perhaps would judge the same information differently in timeliness, trustworthiness, variability, interpretability, feasibility, etc.

> Morgan expressed the logical opinion that no system could "compensate for lack of alertness and imagination. Nevertheless," he added, "there is substantial basis ... to conclude that the system of handling intelligence was seriously at fault and that the security of the Nation can be insured only through continuity of service and centralization of responsibility in those charged with handling intelligence." Thus Morgan and later the majority of the committee accepted the concept ... that intelligence must not be regarded "just as another tour of duty," but as a profession.
>
> The most agreed-upon of Pearl Harbor lessons—the need for a centralized pool of intelligence—has taken a beating in the course of time. The Central Intelligence Agency as revealed unto us over the past few years is not precisely what those who suffered at and from Pearl Harbor had in mind.
>
> As of September 1975, Representative Otis Pike of New York, chairman of the House Intelligence Committee, doubted that the United States would know of an attack about to be launched. The country has thousands of dedicated intelligence gatherers but, "above the gathering level, it just bogs down every single time. It is not absorbed, it is not delivered." In other words, if Pike was correct, not quite thirty-four years after Pearl Harbor the United States was back where it started in regard to intelligence—data available but lacking proper evaluation and dissemination. This gives one a depressing look at the Nation's capacity to learn from experience ...[41]

Although Morgan briefed his principles to the FBI,[42] they apparently had not made a lasting impression prior to 9/11:

> ... performance in the Bureau was generally measured against statistics such as numbers of arrests, indictments, prosecutions, and convictions. Counterterrorism and counterintelligence work,

> often involving lengthy intelligence investigations that might never have positive or quantifiable results, was not career-enhancing. Most agents who reached management ranks had little counterterrorism experience.[43]

Although the connotation of this deficiency is government intelligence, we expand this definition to include weather, its evolving impact (e.g., flooding), and other natural as well as military and terrorist intentions. We must also include an understanding of what cooperating (presumably) and other entities and organizations are doing in the current situation. Failure to have the full situational awareness assembled from all that is known by at least one appropriate (and competent) authority within the scope of the incident is a substantial deficiency. It impacts many other deficiencies, such as *imagination, insight, alertness, preparedness,* etc. The deficiency of intelligence not only had a major, disastrous impact on Pearl Harbor and 9/11, but also certainly on Virginia Tech and Columbine, in which individuals and some entities had expected and warned of the impending danger, but to no avail.

> During Cho's junior year at Virginia Tech, numerous incidents occurred that were clear warnings of mental instability. Although various individuals and departments within the university knew about each of these incidents, the university did not intervene effectively. No one knew all the information and no one connected all the dots.[44]

Even after a threat to commit suicide led Cho to protective custody and a commitment hearing, many of those with direct knowledge of all of the information about his behavior and statements were not consulted.

> A special justice designated by the Circuit Court of Montgomery County presided over the commitment hearing for Cho held shortly after 11:00 a.m. on December 14. Neither Cho's suitemate nor his roommate nor the detaining police

> officer nor the pre-screener nor the independent evaluator nor the attending psychiatrist attended the hearing. The pre-screening report was read into the record by Cho's attorney. The special justice reviewed the independent evaluation form completed by the independent evaluator and the treating psychiatrist's recommendation. He heard evidence from Cho. The special justice ruled that Cho "presents an imminent danger to himself as a result of mental illness" and ordered "O-P" (outpatient treatment) "—to follow all recommended treatments."[45]

There had been important lessons learned several years earlier when another strategic intelligence failure led to disaster.

> On several occasions while they were being dealt with by Jefferson County authorities, the two gave overt indications that they were dangerous; regrettably, a failure among authorities to share the information they had about the two allowed the pair to cloak their deadly intentions from law enforcement officials, prosecutors, and school teachers and officials. As an example of the data available to authorities, while Klebold and Harris were participating in the probationary diversion program for juvenile offenders because of the vehicle break-in, authorities became aware of, but did not act on threats made by Eric Harris against another Columbine student.[46]

Prevention. Planning for intelligence in its fullest context involves the appropriate (perhaps filtered) information-sharing planning among all stakeholders, and "all" is a key word. There may be information from unprotected sources, which when accumulated and properly understood with the other information (including sensors and other technical means), could produce *actionable* information. It was the failure to assemble all available information (whether for a massed attack of carrier-borne planes or a mass shooting on a Virginia college campus) and act much like the U.S. Coast Guard, PSAP, police responders, and pilots that arguably would have changed the course of major tragedies, perhaps for the better.

Attitude

The elitist or superior behavior of a supervisor or other authority can (and did) have the effect of deterring subordinates and others from questioning direction, pointing our potential deficiencies, and warning of imminent failures. Apparently, this phenomenon of attitude (Figure 11-13) was important enough in the Pearl Harbor investigation to make it an important one of the 25 deficiencies.

> ... But the investigation had revealed such a "persistent failure" in this regard that Morgan considered the lesson obvious: "... the military and naval forces failed to instill in their personnel the wholesome disposition to consult freely with their superiors for the mutual good and success of both superior and subordinate."[47]

Figure 11-13

Deficiency of attitude. When leaders have an attitude of superiority, subordinates are unwilling or unable to participate in decision-making, which often results in a serious disconnect within organizations.

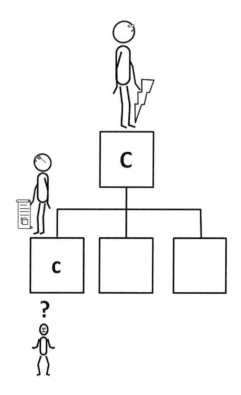

The behavior of those who have achieved a particular rank or position may be expected to produce some level of aloofness, but when this behavior prevents subordinates and others from a free exchange of concerns or recommendations, it reduces information sharing within and among entities. This reduction can heighten many other deficiencies, particularly *jealously* and *improvement*.

Prevention. Many well-known and professional techniques have long been available to cure an individual from a sense, or at least a displayed sense, of superiority. It is part of supervisor training (or should be) in many organizations. Independent of this training, however, it is possible that it can evolve over time despite earlier training and may be a natural trait of some people finding themselves in a leadership role. Perhaps if it were not for the deficiencies of *inspection, jealously* and *relationship*, a deficiency of attitude could be mitigated before the inherent failures of *alertness* and *preparedness* are degraded.

Imagination

Deficiency. The deficiency of *imagination* (Figure 11-14) results from a failure to infer from collected intelligence the intent of a potential adversary or the consequences of an emergency situation. Often, events are imagined in a report to superiors (such as the Pearl Harbor attack) and documented in exercise after-action reports (such as with Hurricane Pam just before Katrina), but it makes little or no difference in their subsequent actions. The 9/11 Report found that use of aircraft as suicide weapons had been imagined by some in the administration.

Figure 11-14

Deficiency of imagination. Planners who plan for only one possible eventuality and fail to take into account all possible scenarios, however unlikely, put their organizations at great risk.

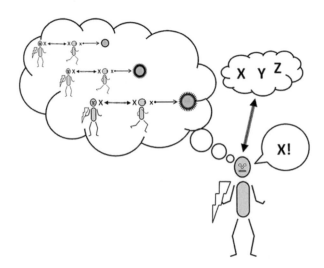

In his testimony, Clarke commented that he thought that warning about the possibility of a suicide hijacking would have been just one more speculative theory among many, hard to spot since the volume of warnings of "al Qaeda threats and other terrorist threats, was in the tens of thousands—probably hundreds of thousands." Yet the possibility was imaginable, and imagined. In early August 1999, the FAA's Civil Aviation Security intelligence office summarized the bin Ladin hijacking threat. After a solid recitation of all the information available on this topic, the paper identified a few principal scenarios, one of which was a "suicide hijacking operation." The FAA analysts judged such an operation unlikely, because "it does not offer an opportunity for dialogue to achieve the key goal of obtaining Rahman and other key captive extremists. ... A suicide hijacking is assessed to be an option of last resort."[48]

However, there were other key goals, but they had not been imagined. Imagination was not boosted by events at Columbine and the ensuing report in planning for similar emergencies at Virginia Tech.

The Emergency Response Plan of Virginia Tech was deficient in several respects. It did not include provisions for a shooting scenario and did not place police high enough in the emergency decision-making hierarchy. It also did not include a threat assessment team. And the plan was out of date on April 16; for example, it had the wrong name for the police chief and some other officials.[49]

Prevention. Minimizing the impact of this deficiency requires that intelligence analysts and other analysts, as well as those with access to information, consider the broadest possible import of the available information regarding intent or capability. This deficiency is not about selecting from among possibilities; it is about ensuring that the full range of conceivable outcomes from available information is at least the starting point for more refined analysis. It is essential to include a broad assessment of possibility in order to address the related deficiencies of *insight* and *preparedness.*

Communications

Deficiency. This deficiency is not involved with technical means of transmission, it is purely the clarity of information intended to be conveyed in a message, any message. Many examples of *communication* deficiencies (Figure 11-15) that lead to ambiguity and confusion can be found in each of the investigative reports of tragedy and disaster. It was first cited explicitly in the 1946 report.

Morgan pointed out that the evidence reflected "an unusual number of instances where military officers in high positions of responsibility interpreted orders, intelligence, and other information and arrived at opposite conclusions." ... "Dispatches must be unmistakably clear, forthright, and devoid of any conceivable ambiguity." He also considered that in these instances "brevity of messages was carried to the point of being a fetish rather than a virtue." Dispatches must be of "sufficient amplitude to be meaningful not only to the sender but, beyond reasonable doubt, to the addressee as well."[50]

Figure 11-15

Deficiency of communications. Unclear communication between parties responsible for planning and response can lead to ambiguous interpretations of direction and incorrect action.

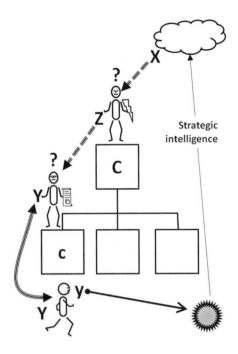

Prevention. The use of natural language and simple sentences with common vocabulary, agreed to by all stakeholders in planning specific information-sharing CONOPS and integrated SOPs, provides the best means of mitigating this deficiency and avoiding the otherwise eventual failures. The deficiency of communications is often avoided in practice when individuals and entities that have worked together for many years share information, but this evolved holistic interoperability can break down in less familiar environments (see Figure 11-1). Prevention requires care and consideration be applied to what might seem like the most insignificant details, but many times these details, if misinterpreted, lead to nonlinearly momentous failures in holistic interoperability. Specific, natural language-wording conventions, verbs, and descriptive phrases can be employed. In our air traffic control example, conventional units of altitude, speed, bearing, and radio frequency are used on each call, and all operators and pilots employ the same trained convention.

Paraphrase

This subtle deficiency is the addition of more information to a message or other data than was intended by the sender (Figure 11-16). It occurs when the receiver *assumes* that the sender had information available or was acting according to specific direction, and then uses this supplemental information when forwarding or relaying the sender's message to others. It also is found in the interpretation of regulatory language and other guidelines, particularly where the strictest—and

Figure 11-16

Deficiency of paraphrase. Interpretation of messages and transmittal of information based on a presumed meaning can result in potentially incorrect action being taken based on incomplete or incorrect information.

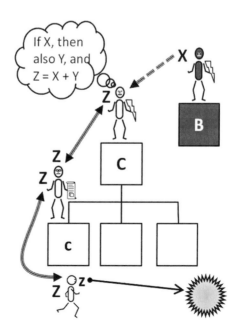

Disclosure

Deficiency. In our society, protection of health care and other information is critically important, but it is not worth risking others' lives, as in the Virginia Tech case. In that case, the deficiency of the *paraphrase* meant that critical intelligence was not shared because of an effective paraphrasing of the regulations.

> University officials in the office of Judicial Affairs, Cook Counseling Center, campus police, the Dean of Students, and others explained their failures to communicate with one another or with Cho's parents by noting their belief that such communications are prohibited by the federal laws governing the privacy of health and education records. In reality, federal laws and their state counterparts afford ample leeway to share information in potentially dangerous situations.[53]

In this way, the paraphrase prevented disclosure that may have changed events on April 16th in Blacksburg, Virginia. To ensure *alertness* after events such as Pearl Harbor, 9/11, and Columbine, all legal means for disclosure to the appropriate authorities should be understood, vetted, and not delayed through *complacency*. See Figure 11-18.

Prevention. The disclosure of information in critical situations should be built into the detailed planning for information sharing as part of multi-agency CONOPS and single entity, integrated SOP development.

> Three basic types of disclosures are permitted under these medical information privacy laws ...
>
> Situations where privacy is outweighed by certain other interests. For example, providers may sometimes disclose information about a person who presents an imminent threat to the health and safety of individuals and the public. Providers can also disclose information to law enforcement in order to locate a fugitive or suspect. Providers also are authorized to disclose information when state law requires it.[54]

Figure 11-18

Deficiency of disclosure. Leaders who are provided with information but fail to disclose it to planners (or others) for fear of revealing an information source, so planners are unaware of the need to prepare for events foreseen by others.

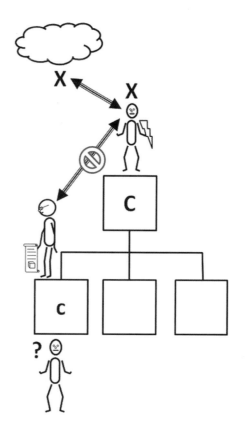

Thus, certainty over any security or heathcare regulations should be well understood and documented when developing information-sharing plans. What may or may not be shared, by whom, when, and how, should all be incorporated into these plans.

Insight

Deficiency. The deficiency of *insight* (Figure 11-19) stems from failing to *imagine* that a repetition of events seen elsewhere "could actually happen here." It is different than the deficiency of *imagination* in that the incident or event is well imagined, perhaps so thoroughly imagined that it strangely becomes unbelievable.

> ... For years the U.S. Army and Navy had conducted war games against a Japanese air attack on Pearl Harbor. But apparently this idea had been for so long a cliché of training exercises that the reality, when it came, surprised all concerned as much as if the idea had never crossed their minds.[55]

Figure 11-19

Deficiency of insight. In this case, alertness is diminished because the leader is lulled by repeated training and exercises for an incident into considering it as a routine scenario, and become "blinded by the self-evident."[56]

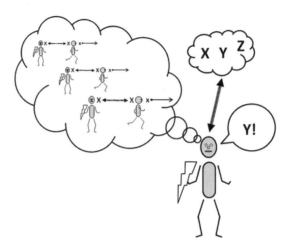

In each of the before-mentioned tragedies, individuals had the insight to see "it" coming. They wrote reports (e.g., Pearl Harbor, 9/11, and Katrina) or notified authorities (e.g., Deepwater Horizon, Virginia Tech) and then assumed that those responsible would take the strategic appropriate action. If the leaders and their planners suffer from the deficiency of *insight*, failing to have situational awareness through complacency (i.e., it's "good enough"), it further amplifies deficiencies such as *alertness, preparedness,* and *improvement,* among others.

Prevention. If deficiencies of *intelligence, alertness,* and *preparedness* undergo improvement through careful development of information-sharing CONOPS and agency-integrated SOPS, the positive impact on the *insight* deficiency could avoid the associated failure. In this regard, all of the Pearl Harbor deficiencies are interrelated and so need to be addressed collectively. *Insight* must transcend not only what is on the fringe of imagination, but as the Pearl Harbor example shows, permit leaders and planners to properly read the signs that it "could happen here" and not be "blinded by the self-evident."[57]

Dissemination

Although Washington had access to all Japanese diplomatic traffic, they not only didn't share this traffic with the commanders of the Army and Navy at Pearl Harbor, they didn't even tell them the capability existed. Many students and teachers as well as mental health care professionals knew of Cho's state of mind before the Virginia Tech killings, and several knew of suicide threats, but much of the information was not disseminated even to people who were allowed to receive it. There are many other examples of such blind protection of information, and the resulting deficiency of dissemination (Figure 11-20) means that our responders, operators, and the public are exposed to far greater risk than they know.

Figure 11-20

Deficiency of
dissemination.
While leaders and
planners may have
information important
to preventing or
responding to
an event, failure
to disseminate
that information
to individuals
or collaborating
agencies can
leave responders
unprepared for
eventualities.

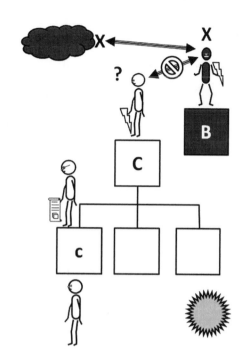

Morgan cited Turner's testimony "that he regarded an attack on Pearl Harbor as a 50-50 possibility. Assuming this to be correct," Morgan continued, "there can be little doubt … that he could have given the commander in chief of the Pacific Fleet the benefit of his conclusions had he been disposed to do so."[58]

Perhaps complacency or other deficiency prevented such a conclusion from reaching Hawaii, as the Navy in Washington thought they had prepared the commanders in the Pacific for the coming war. The dissemination deficiency differs from disclosure, in that the latter involves information protection, where the former does not—people and entities that could know are not told; it was not in the plan to do so proactively.

In the Virginia Tech case, even Cho's parents were not informed of his suicide threats or other behavior.

When Cho's parents were asked what they would have done if they had heard from the college about the professors', roommates', and female students' complaints, their response was,

> "We would have taken him home and made him miss a semester to get this looked at … but we just did not know … about anything being wrong." From their history during the high school years, we do know that they were dedicated to getting him to therapy consistently and also consented to psychopharmacology when the need arose.[59]

Prevention. As stated above, all stakeholders must collaboratively develop specific information-sharing plans (CONOPS and integrated SOPs) that address expected and unusual (but possible) scenarios, with built-in adaptability to address the diversity of reality. As with alertness, it is better to push potentially critical information to those who've been determined to have the (legal) need to know, alerting them if necessary to its presence, than to risk their not having it in time.

> The VTPD [Virginia Tech Police Department] erred in not requesting that the Policy Group issue a campus-wide notification that two persons had been killed and that all students and staff should be cautious and alert.[60]

The dissemination deficiency is driven by the deficiencies of *imagination, complacency, alertness, insight,* and *preparedness,* among others, as the resulting failures of situational awareness and information sharing cascade from the strategic to the tactical timeframe of an emergency, incident, or event.

Inspection

Deficiency. In the Pearl Harbor event, Morgan's draft report was particularly focused on the ultimate authorities on Oahu who manifested many of these deficiencies. He noted this as inspection deficiency number 17: "An official who neglects to familiarize himself in detail with his organization should forfeit his responsibility."[61] In other words, those with ultimate responsibility should know the people and capabilities under their authority, their needs, strength, and vulnerabilities for improvement. Since their leadership and support is critical to identifying and improving information sharing and other operational gaps, inspection of the facilities governing the well-being of the enterprise is essential. See Figure 11-21.

Figure 11-21

Deficiency of inspection. A leader who fails to engage with his organization and employees may be unaware of the resources, training needs, and knowledge base of the individuals and the enterprise.

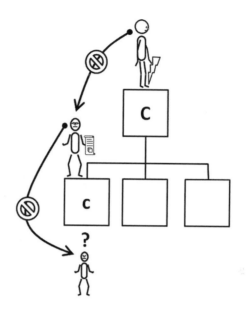

Prevention. The Pearl Harbor deficiency of *inspection* can be mitigated through the old adage "management by wandering around (MBWA)"[62] that enables leaders and their planners to better understand their enterprise, whatever its purpose. Progression through various critical scenarios in tabletop as well as walk-around modes would be key elements of an *improvement* plan to mitigate or eliminate many if not all of the Pearl Harbor deficiencies and risk-based failures. Clearly, development of detailed, scenario-based CONOPS and SOPs in this way would achieve holistic interoperability through mitigation of the inspection deficiency.

Preparedness

Deficiency. The heart of the deficiency of *preparedness* (Figure 11-22) is the contention over what's probable versus what's possible; that is, preparing for what you think (subjectively) is likely to happen instead of being prepared for what could happen.

> Here was the old problem of enemy intentions versus capabilities. U.S. military leaders in 1941 were far too concerned with what Japan might do, not with what it was able to do. Yet history has shown that if an enemy can launch a certain kind of attack, in all probability he will do exactly that. His intentions cannot hurt his opponent; his capabilities can, if properly utilized.[63]

Figure 11-22

Deficiency of
preparedness.
Planners who
fail to plan for
an adversary's
capabilities may find
themselves preparing
for less-impactful
scenarios than those
that can ultimately
occur.

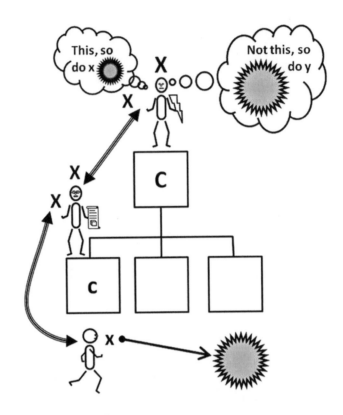

In this regard, the Virginia Tech Report Annex addressed the same issue occurring over 60 years later.

> The Virginia Tech police may have erred in prematurely concluding that their initial lead in the double homicide was a good one, or at least in conveying that impression to university officials while continuing their investigation. They did not take sufficient action to deal with what might happen if the initial lead proved erroneous. The police reported to the university emergency Policy Group that the "person of interest" probably was no longer on campus.[64]

The Pearl Harbor message passing through these events to the present continues to demonstrate that *preparedness* for what could happen is essential, not only what is believed likely to happen. In other words, "it's *not* good enough" until one is prepared for the worst case.

In reality, this is no different than removing subjective probability and considering what's possible, given all threat information, and being prepared as best as possible for that outcome.

Prevention. Assessing the risk of a given scenario is certainly valuable in supporting contingency plans for many scenarios to be included in CONOPS and SOP development for information sharing in support of coordinated action. This assessment, however, must not exclude the capabilities of real threats because of low orders of subjective probability estimates. The risk assessment must include the expected cost of the full range of possibilities given threat capabilities. In this way, perhaps selected video surveillance and lockable doors, as well as shared intelligence on proven threats to the public safety, or strengthened levees, or mandatory drilling shut-down rules, and the associated (perhaps automated) early alerting systems would be worth the cost, given the price paid for the alternative.

Consistency

This deficiency (illustrated in Figure 11-23) addresses authorities providing official direction throughout an organization, but then providing private comments to subordinates or others that tempers or reduces the impact of the official statement. This behavior may have reduced alertness on Oahu before the attack. In the broader context, it applies to the differing messages disseminated to officials and the

Figure 11-23

Deficiency of consistency. A leader who sends mixed messages to his/ her subordinates, will find that no one in the agency or organization has a clear idea of what is expected of them.

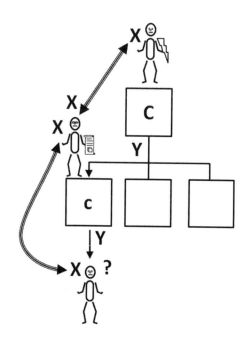

public driven by immediate reporting of evolving (and changing) situational awareness. For example, inconsistent direction given to those in the stricken South Tower on 9/11 shows the confusion created by the lack of information available to authorities.

> The 9/11 system remained plagued by the operators' lack of awareness of what was occurring. Just as in the North Tower, callers from below and above the impact zone were advised to remain where they were and wait for help. The operators were not given any information about the inability to conduct rooftop rescues and therefore could not advise callers that they had essentially been ruled out. This lack of information, combined with the general advice to remain where they were, may have caused civilians not to attempt to descend, although stairwell A may have been passable.[65]

Of course, this example also represents a deficiency of *dissemination* of critical information to dispatchers responding to the trapped and likely future victims of the South Tower collapse. Consistency in information sharing from official sources is closely guarded on a day-to-day basis, but large-scale crises (recall Figure 11-1)—crises that quickly go beyond someone's training and experience—lead to this deficiency.

Prevention. Prevention of inconsistent information requires careful and detailed planning of what data should be provided to whom (including the public), when, and how, and under different probable and possible scenarios. These information-sharing CONOPS and integrated SOPs would include checks and balances to ensure that the deficiencies of communications and paraphrase do not damage the trust required to achieve holistic interoperability.

Jealously

Deficiency. As Morgan states, "Personal or official jealousy will wreck any organization."[66] The deficiency of *jealousy* (Figure 11-24) is heightened by competing budget allocations, staffing allotments, and other mundane factors that impact the deficiencies of *relationships, dissemination, omission,* and other potential cross-organizational deficiencies. The Katrina Report also demonstrates friction between different medical units deployed to the disaster area:

Figure 11-24

Deficiency of
jealousy. When
individuals, entities,
or organizations
desire the
responsibility/
authority, resources,
or other attribute
of others, it can
establish an
uncooperative
environment and
amplify the impacts
of other deficiencies.

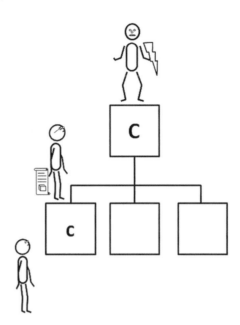

- Information was not being effectively communicated to the DMATs [Disaster Medical Assistance Teams] from either of the MSTs [Medical Support Teams].
- There was considerable friction between DMATs and the MSTs. An 'us and them' attitude was prevalent.[67]

Prevention. The identification and correction of jealously between and among individuals, entities, and organizations is not an information-sharing issue, but arguably can provide a major impediment to achieving holistic interoperability. One approach for building these relationships (see "Holistic Interoperability Continuum" earlier in the chapter) is to work in collaborative sessions to develop the specific, scenario-based information-sharing CONOPS and integrated SOPs critical to achieve holistic interoperability.

Relationships

Deficiency. The personal *relationships* (Figure 11-25) between key or other individuals impact their willingness to coordinate and share information and also impact the relationships of their subordinates. As Morgan stated, "Personal friendship … should never be accepted in lieu of liaison or confused therewith where the latter is necessary to the proper functioning of two or more agencies."[68] These relationships can have their benefits in official work:

Figure 11-25

Deficiency of
relationships.
Personal relationships
between leaders
in organizations or
organizational entities
can determine the
effectiveness with
which the involved
organizations will
cooperate in planning
for response.

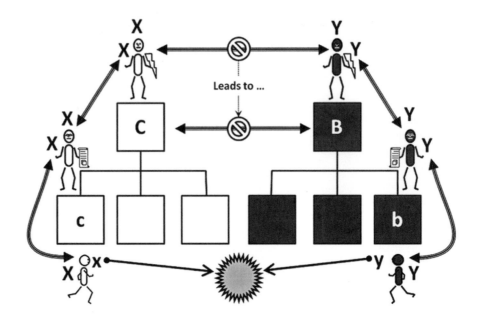

Moreover, analysts had difficulty getting access to the FBI and intelligence community information they were expected to analyze. The poor state of the FBI's information systems meant that such access depended in large part on an analyst's personal relationships with individuals in the operational units or squads where the information resided. …[69]

… but they can also restrict information flows.

Responsibility for domestic intelligence gathering on terrorism was vested solely in the FBI, yet during almost all of the Clinton Administration the relationship between the FBI Director and the President was nearly nonexistent. The FBI Director would not communicate directly with the President. His key personnel shared very little information with the National Security Council and the rest of the national security community. As a consequence, one of the critical working relationships in the counterterrorism effort was broken.[70]

Information and collaboration were impacted positively by relationships before April 16th at Virginia Tech.

> The VT campus police also have excellent working relationships with the regional offices of the state police, FBI, and ATF. The high level of cooperation was confirmed by each of the federal, state, and local law enforcement agencies that were involved in the events on April 16, and by the rapidity of coordination of their response to the incident and the investigation that followed. Training together, working cases together, and knowing each other on a first-name basis can be critical when an emergency occurs and a highly coordinated effort is needed.[71]

Prevention. Although it is obviously beneficial to have the close personal relationships described above during crises, therefore ensuring information sharing among key responders when needed, these relationships are dependent on specific individuals that will not always be in these organizations. What would happen if this comradery broke down for personal reasons? At best, these relationships—and many others—should become institutionalized among all stakeholder agencies through the process of developing detailed CONOPS and SOPs for information sharing and coordinated action. Once these relationships are institutionalized into permanence, specific information-sharing documentation can be developed and vetted.

Priority

Deficiency. This deficiency is the *prioritization* (Figure 11-26) of routine matters above those fundamentally important to the operation and safety of the enterprise and its activities. In the Pearl Harbor context, Morgan believed that the overall commanders had failed to properly prioritize defense considerations over day-to-day activities.

> What seemed to be involved here was a faulty sense of priorities. Granted that Kimmel and Short were exceedingly busy men—what commander on or near their level was not in that buildup year of 1941? But both suffered from overconcern with the routine aspects of their jobs at the expense of the truly important ones.[72]

Figure 11-26

Deficiency of priority. Leaders who "can't see the forest for the trees" will find themselves unprepared to respond to catastrophic events for which they are supposed to have been prepared.

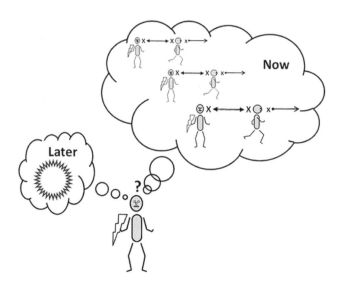

During the Katrina response, the breakdown in unified command at the state emergency operations center (EOC)

> ... hampered FEMA's [the Federal Emergency Management Agency's] ability to meet state and local requests for commodities. Without a unified command, some state and local officials began submitting commodity requests outside FEMA's normal logistics channels. FEMA, in turn, started fulfilling such requests on an "ad-hoc" basis before these requests were properly authorized or logged into its logistics system. When supply requests and subsequent supply distributions were not logged, FEMA could not accurately keep track of the resources it staged at regional facilities. As a result, supplies and equipment were delivered not according to specifications, delivered late, or not delivered at all, and priority needs were not met.[73]

Prevention. Risk/expected-cost ranking of priorities heuristically provides a defendable approach for prioritizing critical *improvement* and *preparedness* tasks and activities, such as improving critical information sharing to achieve holistic interoperability. Again, the development of multi-agency CONOPS and entity-integrated SOPs for information sharing with adaptability for both well-defined, day-to-day incidents and major disaster scenarios provide the best planning activities to avoid this deficiency.

Reporting

Deficiency. The reporting deficiency is closely related to deficiencies number 3, *omission*, and 16, *dissemination*. It focuses on the failure to inform superiors or subordinates about important information, perhaps because of the assumption that these individuals or entities already have this data or don't need it. There are many day-to-day as well as major incident examples of this deficiency. Most of all, this deficiency expresses the need for complete, shared situational awareness among the command and control or management component of any entity or organization (Figure 11-27). This need is particularly true when these individuals or entities each have an important function in the operation of the enterprise, where maintaining holistic interoperability is critical to successful operation.

Prevention. As with the *omission* and *dissemination* deficiencies, prevention of the *reporting* deficiency requires the maintenance of complete situational awareness among individuals and entities within the organization. This awareness can use a variety of technologies and systems, but ultimately must require a positive acknowledgement that information has been received and understood, much like it should be when information is shared among any critical stakeholders.

Improvement

Deficiency. Although motivated by failed administrative handling of the Magic (cryptologic) diplomatic intercepts on Oahu, we interpret the deficiency of *improvement* as what would today be called a failure of quality control and enhancement. A more general consideration of the

Figure 11-27

Deficiency
of reporting.
Information sharing
is bidirectional.
Information must
be shared both
up and down the
chain of command.
Subordinates may
choose not to report
issues or problems
across or "up the
chain," judging it
unnecessary or
doing so because of
other deficiencies,
e.g., jealousy or
relationships.

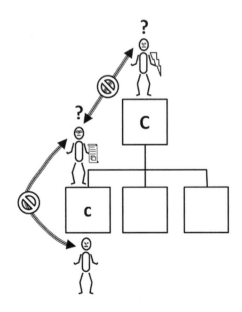

deficiency of improvement encompasses all aspects of the information sharing that drives holistic operability and interoperability to achieve enterprise goals. The *improvement* deficiency is arguably related to the accusation of Edith Thompson from December 8th of 1941, where she stated that the American motto was "I guess it's good enough." This motto reflects the American desire (she wrote) to get as much as possible for as little effort, perhaps the deficiency of real improvement is explained along these lines. See Figure 11-28.

Prevention. One approach to avoiding the failures associated with the deficiency of improvement is to use the table of Pearl Harbor deficiencies in Figure 11-3 as a holistic interoperability checklist. Review in detail all aspects of your organization's holistic internal operability and external interoperability. Verify that none of these classic Pearl Harbor deficiencies can be found. Once such deficiencies are found, and they will be found, consider the development of information-sharing CONOPS linking all stakeholders and integrated agency SOPs to mitigate or eliminate them.

Delegation

Deficiency. The last of the Pearl Harbor deficiencies is that of *delegation* (Figure 11-29), in which it was found that officers had responsibility but not the authority to execute the necessary actions. As Morgan stated, "In a well-balanced organization there is close correlation of responsibility and authority."[74]

Figure 11-28

Deficiency of improvement. When leaders and planners believe their capabilities are "good enough," they fall into the trap noted by Dorothy Thompson on December 8, 1941.

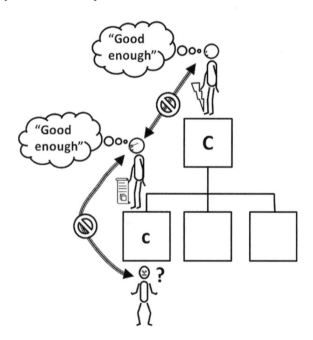

Figure 11-29

Deficiency of delegation. If leaders assign responsibility for action but do not also provide the authority to act, subordinates are put into a precarious position.

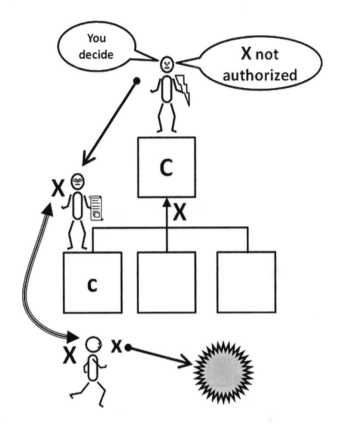

... But in Washington as well as Hawaii no one, "except the highest ranking officers, possessed any real authority to act in order decisively to discharge their responsibilities." He [Morgan] urged that in the future, "There should be a close correlation between responsibility and authority; to vest a man with responsibility and no corresponding authority is an unfair, ineffective, and unsatisfactory arrangement."[75]

Arguably, in a fast-moving tactical situation, such as a shooting on campus, the police are perhaps the first and best to determine the need to send an alert across the campus.

... However, while the Virginia Tech campus police had the authority to send a message, they did not have the technical means to do so. Only two people, the associate vice president for

University Relations and the director of News and Information, had the codes to send a message. The police could not access the alerting system to send a message. The police had to contact the university leadership on the need and proposed content of a message.[76]

Prevention. Use scenario-based CONOPS and integrated SOPs to establish close and immediate balance between responsibility and authority, aligning the criticality of the need and domain of expertise with the expertise of the selected authority.

SUMMARY

This chapter has explained the deficiencies in leadership and planning from the 1946 Congressional investigation of Pearl Harbor and presented examples of these same deficiencies found in the 9/11, Katrina, and Virginia Tech reports. The exercise performed here can be done using any thorough investigation of any disaster, which turned into tragedy when so much strategic awareness was available but not used.

Careful consideration of Morgan's points reveals that many of them are separate facets of a single problem—the failure to communicate. This aspect of the matter may well stand as one of the basic causes of the Pearl Harbor tragedy [and arguably all others], second only to the failure to believe in its possibility. One by one these failures pass in sorry review: failure to ensure understanding; failure of seniors to supply all available relevant information to juniors; failure to supervise and follow through; failure of juniors to be sure they understand their seniors; lack of clarity of expression.

The failure of 1941 to apply such principles as Morgan's cost the United States dearly at Pearl Harbor; hence they must be considered as lessons to be learned from the debacle. Any country, any organization, indeed any individual, can profit by pondering these points.[77]

Note that the Pearl Harbor failures had nothing to do with failures of technology. In all cases, including 9/11, Katrina, Virginia Tech, and so on, people were using the technologies and systems their leaders and planners had chosen for them. If some people were not in the technical communications loop, the configuration had been designed that way. In other words, people envisage, conceive, develop, engineer, manufacture, procure, test, deploy, train, and sustain the technology used. For this reason, it is always the people—and not the technology—that completely determine how we will face day-to-day and major incidents, emergencies, or disasters in the future. Knowing how these people and their organizations will *communicate* in the fullest sense of detail will be essential in determining whether the lessons from Pearl Harbor, Exxon Valdez, Columbine, 9/11, Katrina, Virginia Tech, and Deepwater Horizon, and many more, will ever be learned.

Finally, the people involved in the assessment and subsequent warnings about the future-murderer's behavior and potential threat at Virginia Tech; the people who underwent its wrath against the vulnerable and innocent students on that day; and the public safety community who saved lives that could be saved and dealt with the families and grief, were all clearly intelligent, patriotic and caring people ... and many were and are heroes. The author, whose daughter Danielle Marie Desourdis, was in a building adjacent to where the first two victims were shotat Virginia Tech on the morning of April 16th and telephoned her dad that she was "OK," dedicates this work to them.

ACKNOWLEDGEMENTS

The author wishes to thank Dr. Donald M. Goldstein, a coauthor of *At Dawn We Slept* and *The Verdict of History* for his suggestion to use the 25 Pearl Harbor deficiencies as a holistic interoperability checklist. He also thanks John M. Contestabile for the interoperability dichotomy depicted in Figure 11-1. The author also thanks Rozlyn A. Reece for her quality assurance review of the chapter and both Mary F. Cates and Charlotte A. Lee for their expert reviews. The author also wishes to thank Bev S. Weiler for her helpful copy editing as well as contribution of most figure captions—which we agreed would support understanding. The author also would like to thank his daughter Amanda Michelle Desourdis for her suggestion of the use of explanatory figures and editing recommendations. Mr. Desourdis also thanks Mr. Kamien for the opportunity to contribute to this important work by renown homeland security thinkers and doers.

NOTES

1. This chapter contains the analysis and opinions of the author and do not necessarily represent the opinions of any other individual or organization. The entire intent of the work is to raise awareness of the 25 Pearl Harbor deficiencies, their impact on our lives today and in future, and their importance in ensuring homeland security.

2. Gordon William Prange, Donald M. Goldstein, and Katherine V. Dillon, *At Dawn We Slept: The Untold Story of Pearl Harbor* (New York: McGraw-Hill, 1981).

3. National Commission on Terrorist Attacks Upon the United States, *The 9/11 Commission Report: Final Report of the National Commission on Terrorist Attacks Upon the United States*, July 2004, p. 7 (hereafter cited as *The 9/11 Report*).

4. Select Bipartisan Committee to Investigate the Preparation for and Response to Hurricane Katrina, Failure of Initiative, *Final Report of the Select Bipartisan Committee to Investigate the Preparation for and Response to Hurricane Katrina* (Washington, DC: U.S. Government Printing Office, 2006), http://www.gpoacess.gov/congress/index.html, (hereafter cited as *The Katrina Report*).

5. Robert I. Desourdis, Jr., Peter J. Rosamilia, Christopher P. Jacobson, James E. Sinclair, and James R. McClure, "Pearl Harbor, 9/11, and Katrina: Same Lessons Not Yet Learned," Chapter 2 of *Achieving Interoperability in Critical IT and Communication Systems* (Boston/London: Artech House, 2009) 21–87 (hereafter cited as *Achieving Interoperability*).

6. System Planning Corporation, *Mass Shootings at Virginia Tech Addendum to the Report of the Review Panel*, Governor Timothy M. Kaine, Commonwealth of Virginia, November 2009 (hereafter cited as *The VA Tech Report Addendum*).

7. National Commission on the BP Deepwater Horizon Oil Spill and Offshore Drilling, *Deep Water: The Gulf Oil Disaster and the Future of Offshore Drilling*, Report to the President, January 2011 (hereafter cited as *The Deepwater Horizon Report*).

8. Alaska Oil Spill Commission, *Spill: The Wreck of the Exxon Valdez*, Final Report, February 1990 (hereafter cited as *The Exxon Valdez Report*).

9. State of Colorado, *The Report of Governor Bill Owen's Columbine Review Commission*, Hon. William H. Erickson, Chairman, May 2001 (hereafter cited as *The Columbine Report*).

10. "Interoperability Defined," Chapter 1 of *Achieving Interoperability*, p. 11.

11. Prange, Gordon William, Donald M. Goldstein, and Katherine V. Dillon, P*earl Harbor: The Verdict of History* (New York: McGraw-Hill Companies, 1991), 267–68.

12. Ibid., 4.

13. "Best Practices for Achieving Interoperability," Chapter 4 of *Achieving Interoperability*, pp. 107–89.

14. John M. Contestabile, *Concepts on Information Sharing and Interoperability*, January 21, 2011, white paper funded under an Urban Area Security Grant to the national Capital Region from the U.S. Department of Homeland Security, Johns Hopkins University/Applied Physics Laboratory.

15. "Pearl Harbor, 9/11, and Katrina: Same Lessons Not Yet Learned," Chapter 2 of *Achieving Interoperability*, pp. 70–71.

16. The author credits John M. Contestabile for contributing this concept as an important factor in the cause of deficient planning.

17. "Best Practices for Achieving Interoperability," Chapter 4 of *Achieving Interoperability*, pp. 169–79.

18. "Pearl Harbor, 9/11, and Katrina: Same Lessons Not Yet Learned," Chapter 2 of *Achieving Interoperability*, pp. 21–87.

19. *The VA Tech Report Addendum*, 5.

20. *The Columbine Report*, i.

21. Ibid.

22. *The Deepwater Horizon Report*, xiii.

23. *The Exxon Valdez Report*, iii.

24. Ibid.

25. Ibid., iv.

26. Prange, Gordon William, Donald M. Goldstein, and Katherine V. Dillon, *At Dawn We Slept: The Untold Story of Pearl Harbor* (New York: McGraw-Hill Companies, 1981); and Gordon William Prange, Donald M. Goldstein, and Katherine V. Dillon, P*earl Harbor: The Verdict of History* (New York: McGraw-Hill Companies, 1991), 267–68 (hereafter cited as *The Verdict of History*).

27. *The Verdict of History*, 552.

28. Ibid.

29. *The 9/11 Report*, 406.

30. *Achieving Interoperability*, 117–25.

31. Ibid, 137–55.

32. *The Verdict of History*, 552.

33. *The 9/11 Report*, 18.

34. *The Verdict of History*, 553.

35. *The 9/11 Report*, 79.

36. *The Verdict of History*, 554.

37. *The Deepwater Horizon Report*, ix.

38. Ibid., 554–55.

39. *A Failure of Initiative*, 2.

40. *The Deepwater Horizon Report*, ix.

41. *The Verdict of History*, 555.

42. *The Verdict of History*, 552.

43. *The 9/11 Report*, 72.

44. The *VA Tech Report Addendum*, 2.

45. Ibid., 47.

46. *The Columbine Report*, 21.

47. *The Verdict of History*, 556.

48. *The 9/11 Report*, 345.

49. *The VA Tech Report Addendum*, 17.

50. *The Verdict of History*, 557.

51. Ibid., 557.

52. *The Katrina Report*, 326.

53. *The VA Tech Report Addendum*, 2.

54. Ibid., 65.

55. Ibid.

56. *The Verdict of History*, 558.

57. Ibid.

58. Ibid.

59. *The VA Tech Report Addendum*, 49.

60. Ibid., 3.

61. *The Verdict of History*, 559.

62. Tom Peters and Robert H. Waterman, *In Search of Excellence* (New York: HarperCollins/HarperBusiness, 1982/2004), 289.

63. *The Verdict of History*, 559.

64. *The VA Tech Report Addendum*, 2–3.

65. *The 9/11 Report*, 295.

66. *The Verdict of History*, 560.

67. *The Katrina Report*, 298.
68. *The Verdict of History*, 60.
69. *The 9/11 Report*, 77.
70. Ibid., 358.
71. *The VA Tech Report Addendum*, 13.
72. *The Verdict of History*, 561.
73. *The Katrina Report*, 325.
74. *The Verdict of History*, 561.
75. Ibid., 562.
76. *The VA Tech Report Addendum*, 16.
77. *The Verdict of History*, 562.

12

KEY REQUIREMENTS FOR ENABLING INFORMATION SHARING PLANNING AND POLICY AUDITS

Jean-François-Cloutier and David G. Kamien

Mind-Alliance Systems

INTRODUCTION

This chapter describes key requirements for implementing an Information Sharing Planning (ISP) and policy audit process supported by management software. The goal of ISP is to support collaborative risk management efforts by ensuring policies specify how people should share information effectively both during routine operations and potential or anticipated events. ISP provides a framework for improving the flow of information, internally and with partners, and reduces the likelihood of the infamous Pearl Harbor communication failures (see Desourdis, this volume), which would likely magnify the impact of adverse events.

This chapter illustrates an approach to ISP enabled by Mind-Alliance Systems' Channels tool, a software system used for systematically defining, managing, and continuously improving the policies governing the flows of information that are essential for strategic, operational, or tactical decisions and tasks in the homeland security arena. The chapter describes the development of a tool to enable these functions to be mapped in ways that support and catalyze organizational discussions about information sharing policy. The chapter shows how information sharing requirements are modeled as information flows between tasks that produce or use information, and tasks that need information to start, terminate, or succeed. Task definitions specify what is to be done, a profile of the agents assigned to it, the location (if relevant), the events caused, and the goals achieved, if any.

REQUIREMENTS FOR AN INFORMATION SHARING PLANNING PROCESS

Information sharing is essential for homeland security and requires deliberate pre-crisis planning.[1] As the saying goes: "Failing to plan is planning to fail." Homeland security professionals recognize that the flow of information across disciplines is still a work in progress. A small sampling of the many cross-discipline areas where information sharing can be improved includes:

- Event-specific information among public safety officials and other decision makers, who currently are over-reliant on the news media for situational awareness
- Information flow between public health entities and law enforcement during steady-state (routine) operations
- Information flow between law enforcement, fire, and emergency medical services during steady-state operations
- Information flow among law enforcement, public safety, and the private sector at all levels of the National Terrorism Advisory System ("Elevated" and "Imminent")
- Information exchange between law enforcement and the public during steady state operations (including the need to incorporate social media protocols and constraints)
- Information exchange between law enforcement agencies and the media to ensure unified messaging during crises

When homeland security and intelligence professionals are asked about the tenets of effective information sharing practices, a complex picture emerges.[2] Effective information sharing requires that the right data and information are shared with the right people and machines (i.e., data are relevant to the recipient's tasks or decisions in context of the situation). Key decision makers must be identified and targeted for specific decision-points throughout the process. It is essential to clearly define information needs and requirements for disparate activities, tasks, and decisions. All needed information should be provided in a fast, timely, and efficient manner. The essential elements of information that need to be sent and received for each decision or task to be executed by plan participants must be defined, along with the timeliness requirements for sharing and communication of that information. It is important for all parties to understand the time-frames for delivering information during "routine," "elevated," and "imminent" threat conditions. Effective information sharing planners specify reliable and resilient means of communication and transmission mechanisms (systems, tools, networks), and ensure that a robust backup infrastructure is in place. Experienced planners recognize the critical requirements regarding appropriate classification and protection of information. Classified information must be protected and shared securely with authorized users in a policy-compliant manner. In the end, an effective information sharing plan ensures that the right quantity of data or information is provided to the correct recipient(s); the content is clear and accurate; the source, data, and means of transmission of the information are trusted.

Of equal importance to the planning of when, what, and with whom information is to be shared is the question of how information is captured, collected, filtered, processed, stored, and disseminated (i.e., managed). The right (standard) format (meta-data, terminology) and semantics must be used for the information itself and for information exchange protocols. Data output from systems use a standard format, enabling programmatic integration so information can be shared and data consumed as a service.

Leveraging this integration, dynamic information can be readily accessed and shared with easy-to-use tools, and the management of this information is governed by clear processes and documented protocols that are easily understood by executing agents. Personnel are trained on information sharing protocols and perform practice exercises. These exercises allow agency management the opportunity to correct or enforce information sharing behavior and ensure that people use information responsibly. Information sharing issues (problems) are proactively sought, identified, analyzed, and mitigated based on impact severity. Information sharing improvement initiatives are planned strategically and associated with the identified issues.

IMPLICATIONS FOR THE ISP PROCESS

In light of these requirements and potential deficiencies, a systematic framework is essential for effective planning, managing, auditing, and continuously improving the policies and protocols governing information sharing and the associated intended communication.

An ISP process should enable mission partners to collaboratively define specific information flows between them in order to achieve greater unity of effort and thereby increase the likelihood of success in their joint undertaking. The process must help ensure that flows of information within and across organizations are defined in the ways needed to enable coordination of operations, collaboration, joint decision making, and compliance with policies.

An ISP framework needs to establish processes for:

- Securing leadership support for the planning effort
- Defining the participants in the planning effort and setting the scope and objectives for the development of the information sharing plan and protocols
- Evaluating existing internal and interagency communication protocols and associated policies
- Mapping and understanding the planned information network and flow between stakeholders
- Developing protocols by analyzing stakeholder information needs associated with tasks and decisions
- Expressing information sharing protocols precisely, ideally in a manner that can be interpreted and analyzed automatically by machines
- Assessing the planned flow of information for compliance with procedures, directives, and policies
- Analyzing the issues that already do or potentially will impede information sharing
- Evaluating potential consequences of failing to receive or share information and taking steps to remedy them via a variety of mitigation or remedial measures
- Evaluating, improving, and maintaining procedures based on lessons learned and best practices identified through training, exercises and real-world events.

To be effective in the homeland security and intelligence arena, a planning framework and process for developing information sharing protocols must be inclusive, collaborative, and flexible. It must be capable of uniting organizations with different missions, people, processes, technologies, organizational goals, cultures, values, interests, and approaches to planning and sharing information. See Figure 12-1.

Figure 12-1

Each mission's partners have different culture, people, technology, and processes.[3]

People	Technology	Process
• Personnel	• Physical Networks / Data Transport	• Interests & Priorities
• Leadership	• Standards-Based Interoperability of Networks, Systems and Devices	• Doctrine and Planning Frameworks (Strategic, Operational, Tactical)
• Communities of Interest		• Management Guidance/Direction
• Objectives/ Motives/Missions	• Data Exchange Formats	• Enterprise Architecture & BPM
• Resources	• Network Security	• CONOPS
• Decision-Making	• Cyber Defense	• Security Levels
• Trust Level	• Systems & Applications Integration	• Mission/Info Assurance
• Communication	• Meta-data Standards	• Information Management
• Trusted Partners	• Technical Interoperability Aspects	• Guidance & Procedures
• Culture (Values, Norms, Beliefs, Principles, Stories, Metaphors, Styles, Mental Models, Language Skills, Mindsets)		• Governance & Oversight
	Other	• Compliance Requirements
• Working Schemes and Habits		• Duty to Share and Protect
• Training & Education	• Material Assets	• Knowledge Retention Policies
• Lessons Learned	• Facilities	• Staff Processes and Procedures
• Best Practices	• Budgets	• Security Clearances
• Belief in Benefits of Info Sharing	• Terminology	• Degree of Integration with Other Organizations
• Past info Sharing Failures	• Information Needs and Assets (DIME, PMESII, HSCB)	
• Languages Spoken		

The framework should address the need for holistic interoperability necessary for efficient and effective multi-agency collaboration, which Desourdis defines as "a measure of shared trusted understanding that drives predictable collaborative action towards a common goal."[4]

ISP also needs to account for existing efforts to map information flows and enhance the discoverability and dissemination of information through standards and middleware; such as efforts already undertaken by enterprise architects in the Department of Defense, the intelligence community, and the U.S. Department of Homeland Security. Frequently, efforts to analyze information flow focus on requirements for system integration rather than policy compliance, protocols for field-use, accountability, or ongoing performance improvement.

An ISP framework must also acknowledge the variety of perspectives and roles inherent in the process. Senior leaders, operational planners, knowledge managers, operators (e.g., tactical leaders), lawyers, and others all have essential roles in information sharing planning (see Figure 12-2).

Figure 12-2

An information sharing planning framework must unify various perspectives.

Commanders / Leaders

- Ensure information flows support these types of missions!
- Who are our partners?
- Which missions require information sharing plans?

Operational Planners

- How can we efficiently analyze information requirements of people at all levels?
- Which information flows are mission-critical?
- Which info sharing/communication failures are preventable?

Enterprise Architects

- How can we best support requests for information?
- How can we define and refine best practices?

Knowledge Managers

- What should be the standard practice for this type of task or decision, in terms of accessing, sending, receiving, and sharing information?

Info Assurance

- Which information flows pose unacceptable risk?
- How can that risk be reduced?

End Users

- How can I define my info needs and confirm sharing commitments?
- How can I access current, easy-to-follow protocols for reporting and obtaining information?

Strategic and operational planners, for example, should concern themselves with:

- Defining the scenarios and missions for which the organization needs to plan, based on a comprehensive threat and risk analysis for the given jurisdiction, region, or discipline
- Specifying the key decisions and tasks that require information sharing in that mission context
- Identifying preventable information flow problems (e.g., identifying the earliest time when available information can be consumed, as well as any potential delays such as bottlenecks or single points of failure)
- Ensuring that people know how to use protocols to share information effectively during routine operations when anticipated events occur or are suspected to have occurred

TOWARDS AN ISP METHODOLOGY

Mind-Alliance Systems developed its ISP methodology for homeland security considering a wide variety of conceptual frameworks and methodologies, including (see Figure 12-3): Program/Project Management, Organizational Development, Strategic Planning, Scenario Planning, Capabilities-based Planning, Enterprise Architecture, Systems Engineering, Risk Management, and Performance Measurement & Assessment.[5]

Using this ISP process, planners check that their organizations have identified:

- The scenario events that create risk (or generate opportunities for gains)
- The tasks that need to be executed in order to mitigate that risk (or capture opportunities for gains), and assigned them to qualified members of their organization
- The roles and agents (humans or machines) these tasks are assigned to in a relevant jurisdiction

Information sharing procedures are then defined, specifying the essential elements of information people need to send and receive when they execute their assigned tasks. Information sharing needs

Figure 12-3

The information
sharing planning
process

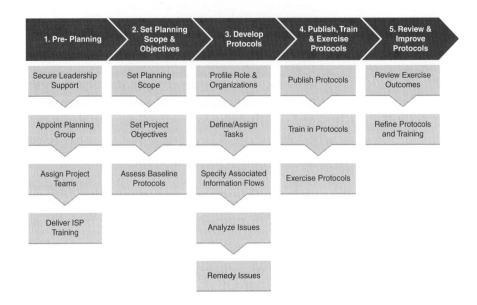

to take place via approved communication networks and channels (means of transmission and endpoints, such as telephone numbers, email addresses, etc.), and in a manner compliant with policies. Parties to information sharing protocols commit to sharing information according to plan, with the understanding that the information they provide is strictly to be used for executing the target task.

To plan the flow of information, planners from different organizations collaboratively map the required information flow. They determine what information needs to be shared; who will communicate it, as well as the means of transmission; how quickly information needs to be received; classification levels, and governing policies. Once potential information flow problems are detected, their impact needs to be assessed to determine which risk mitigation goals would not be achieved if the task were to fail utterly, or should some information not be shared as planned. Then planners can define improvements needed to optimize response effectiveness and coordination.

Information sharing protocols need to be incorporated into operational plans, training and exercise programs, and information systems. Planning partners should conduct exercises to assess their information sharing capability; to measure and assess the completeness, speed, resilience, and policy compliance of information sharing; and to mitigate the risks of preventable failures in communication.[6] Exercises should be designed to assess whether participants know who to contact, how to make contact, and what information needs to be communicated. The stakeholders should conduct an after-action review and report findings, as appropriate, to top organizational management of participating agencies. In assessing its information sharing and communication capability, the organization should consider new standards and best-practice models. If findings from the after-action review indicate shortcomings in the plan and the ability of the organization to execute it, the organization should revise its communication procedures, provide remedial training, and deploy relevant systems to support improvements in information sharing and communication. Building on the findings of each agency's action review and appropriate changes to their plan implementations, the team should update the plan to maintain its utility in light of new threats, new facilities, new regulations, and new systems.

Since the definition of ideal operational information flows constantly changes, information sharing protocols need to be updated regularly. Information needs change as adversaries adopt new strategies and tactics or natural events evolve over time, but these needs also change when evolving technology enables new types of data collection (e.g., when new sensors are deployed), and when the organization's policies, plans, and operational procedures are updated.

The ISP process yields insight into the needed improvements to information sharing plans and capabilities.[7] To solve information sharing problems and issues, organizations may need to deploy various strategies. They may also need to update their operational doctrine, policies, procedures, and training. And they may need to purchase or integrate technology systems and sensors. By ranking the severity of the information sharing issues encountered, organizations can better prioritize and allocate resources to remediating them.

ISP SOFTWARE REQUIREMENTS

Inputs and outputs of the ISP and model-building process include a variety of data about the environment and knowledge of information sharing (IS) practices as shown in Figure 12-4. Outputs of this process include analytics for planners and protocols (aka "job-aids") for field use.

Figure 12-4

Inputs and outputs
of the ISP and
model-building
process

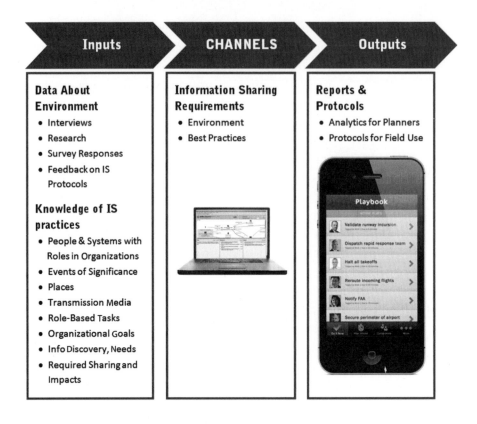

An effective ISP tool enables planning, testing and execution of efficient information sharing practices and protocols by expressing existing information sharing (IS) and communication procedures in a computer-based modeling and analysis environment, as shown in Figure 12-5. This environment allows users to visualize all the organizations and roles involved and the information flow for each day-to-day or emergency scenario.[8] The development of software to facilitate the ISP process was a significant challenge because of the extensive requirements on such a system. These requirements include:

• Expressivity requirements
• Diagnostics
• Analytics
• Usability in a data-rich, collaborative setting

Visualization is essential to the information flow modeling and planning effort (see Figure 12-6). Coordinating operations with other agencies

Figure 12-5

Information flow modeling interface (Copyright 2012 Mind-Alliance Systems, LLC).

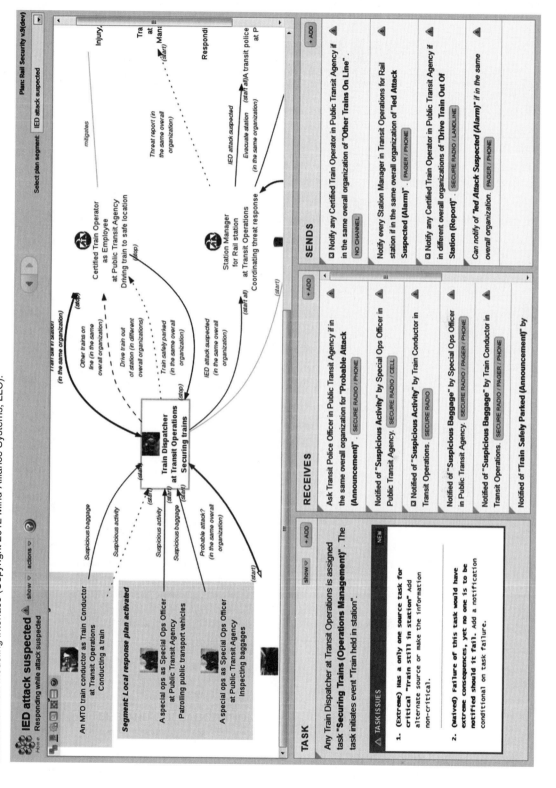

263

Figure 12-6

Network diagrams show the planned flows of information between agents, between roles, and between organizations.

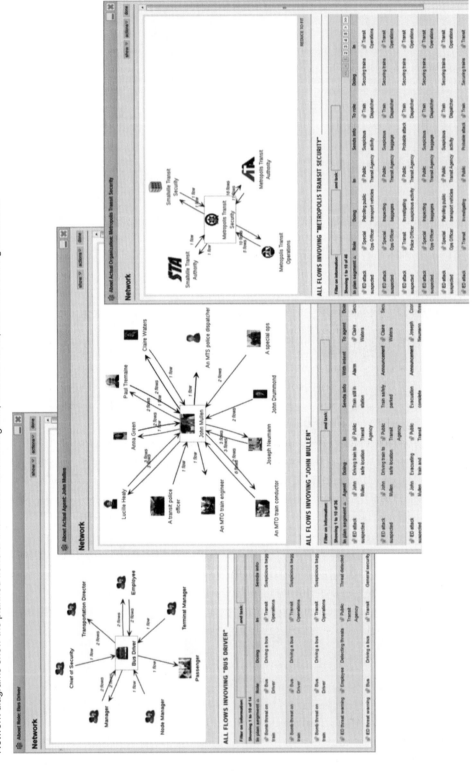

and partners is complex, involving many potentially dynamic factors that need to work in synchronization under changing circumstances. Most organizations do not yet employ an ISP system for mapping, analyzing, and optimizing the flow of information across their organization and with partners. The visual mapping of IS flows brings clarity and order to what otherwise is a complex collection of formal procedures and informal practices, often only inaccurately and incompletely stored in the minds of a few individuals. With so many dynamic elements involved in realistic information sharing environments, critical information flows can easily be forgotten, or become out-of-sync or out-of-date due to changes in organizations, personnel, systems, and procedures. Developing an information sharing plan is sufficiently complicated, even for simple scenarios, to require computer support. When dealing with multiple scenario-based plans for more than a handful of organizations, the complexity is such that systematically identifying and prioritizing deficiencies is impossible without the help of software.

Figure 12-7 shows one of the many types of diagnostic visualizations supported: failure impact analysis, which answers the "so-what" question ("What would be the cascading impact of a failed task or information flow?").

Figure 12-8 shows a different visualization: information dissemination analysis, which was designed to reveal answers to such high-level questions as: What is the source and destination of a specific shared element of information? Who uses it? How is it transformed along the path between source and destination? Can—and will—it arrive in time and where it is needed?

Other visualizations help organizations evaluate and rank the severity of information sharing issues and problems that could adversely impact the ability of specific functional roles to execute mission-critical decisions and tasks. For organizations with limited resources, visualizations ease the process of prioritizing the remediation of issues based on risks and the associated impacts on plan execution. This risk-based approach helps organizations demonstrate documented progress in reducing the number of potential communication failures and issues, whether this has been accomplished through training, planning, technology, exercises, memoranda of understanding, or by other means.

ISP software helps agencies with a role in homeland security validate that their plans and procedures define both the tasks to be performed and the associated information sharing protocols, at the organization,

Figure 12-7

Computer-based IS deficiency and failure impact analysis

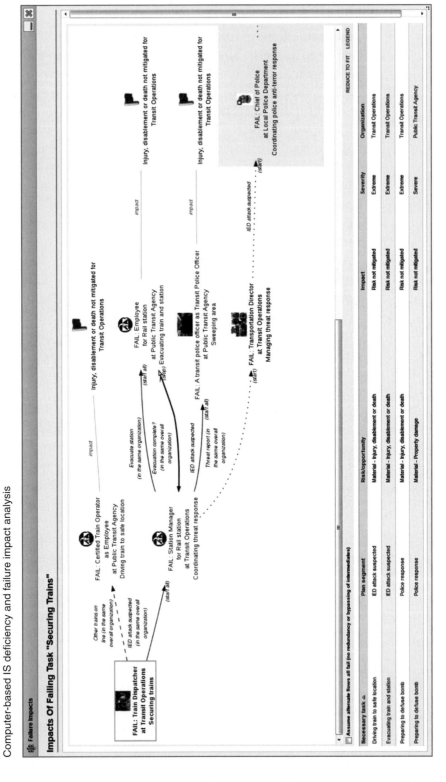

Figure 12-8

Analysis of the dissemination of an essential element of information

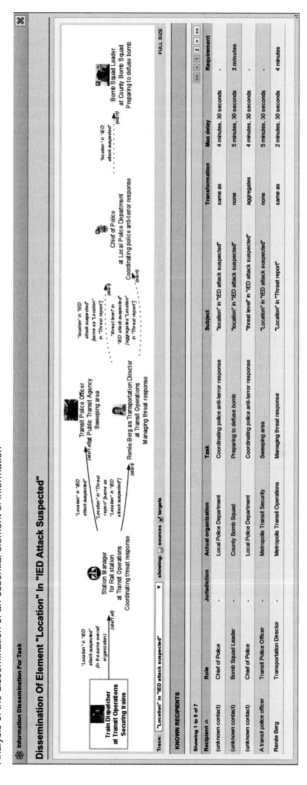

role and agent levels. Profiling the key stakeholders and participants that must execute tasks and share information in order to effectively execute missions supports mutual understanding between the many organizations and disciplines involved in homeland security.

CONCLUSION

In this chapter, we have introduced key requirements for a system for efficient and effective ISP, justified the necessity for use of a computer-based tool and showed samples of a defined best-practices tool for conducting ISP. A performance management approach to information sharing will contribute immensely to homeland security mission success, particularly in mitigating or eliminating the information-sharing deficiencies of Pearl Harbor, 9/11, Katrina, Virginia Tech, Columbine, Deepwater Horizon, and Exxon Valdez. In those events, flaws inherent in the communications planning and planners "set the stage" for these tragedies.

ACKNOWLEDGEMENTS

The authors would like to acknowledge the assistance of Stuart Friedman, Robert Desourdis, Ph.D., Roger Kamien, Ray Guidetti, Eileen Larence, Reed McMillan, and Felice Maranz.

NOTES

1. See David Kamien, "Developing Information Sharing Protocols and Planning Policy to Support Homeland Security Missions," in Chapter 10 of this book.

2. Well-known characteristics of ineffective (i.e., deficient or failure-prone) information sharing are described in the Chapter 11, "Why We Fail—and How to Succeed" by Robert Desourdis in this book.

3. All illustrations sourced from "Information Sharing Planning and Management: A Key Capability for NATO" Mind-Alliance Systems paper for the 2012 NATO Network Enabled Capability Conference, March 27–30, 2012.

4. Robert I. Desourdis, Peter J. Rosamilia, and Christopher P. Jacobson, eds., *Achieving Interoperability in Critical IT and Communication Systems* (Boston: Artech House, 2009).

5. For an example of performance management as applied in law enforcement, see W. J. Bratton and S. W. Malinowski, "Police Performance Management in Practice: Taking Compstat to the Next Level, *Policing: An International Journal of Policy and Practice* 2, no. 3 (2008): 259–265.

6. Organizations that intend to comply with the Homeland Security Exercise and Evaluation Program (HSEEP) should conduct evaluations to determine whether the implementation of After-Action Review (AAR) items either positively or negatively impacted operations.

7. DHS Science & Technology, FEMA, and the New York State Office of Emergency Management have provided funding for applying the ISP process in various projects.

8. For those interested in technology for developing information sharing plans, see J. Cloutier, D. Kamien, and R. I. Desourdis, "Channels: An Information Flow Modeling System to Support Planning and Interoperability" in Technologies for Homeland Security (HST), 2011 IEEE International Conference, November 15–17, 2011.

13

THE INFORMATION SHARING ENVIRONMENT (ISE)

Mr. Kshemendra Paul

Program Manager, Information Sharing Environment

INTRODUCTION

The threats against the American people and our institutions have compelled us to accelerate responsible information sharing across every level of government. The operators, analysts, and investigators who protect our nation need access to the right information at the right time, shared in a secure manner. Since Congress called for the creation of the Information Sharing Environment (ISE) in 2004, steady progress has been made to build a broad foundation for information sharing across the federal government, as well as with our state, local, and tribal partners, the private sector, and the international community. The ISE focuses on sharing terrorism, homeland security, and weapons of mass destruction information across five communities: law enforcement, defense, intelligence, homeland security, and foreign affairs.

BACKGROUND OF THE INFORMATION SHARING ENVIRONMENT (ISE)

In December 2004, Congress passed and President George W. Bush signed the Intelligence Reform and Terrorism Prevention Act of 2004 (IRTPA). Section 1016 of IRTPA called for creation of the Information Sharing Environment (ISE) and established the Program Manager for the Information Sharing Environment (PM-ISE) with government-wide authority to plan, oversee, and manage the ISE.

271

The law also established an Information Sharing Council (ISC) to advise the President and the PM-ISE on the development of ISE policies, procedures, guidelines, and standards, and to ensure proper coordination among Federal departments and agencies participating in the ISE.[1]

The attributes of the Information Sharing Environment as described in IRTPA[2] include the following:

- Ensure that the ISE provides and facilitates the means for sharing terrorism information among all appropriate federal, state, local, and tribal entities, and the private sector through the use of policy guidelines and technologies.
- The President shall, to the greatest extent practicable, ensure that the ISE provides the functional equivalent of, or otherwise supports, a decentralized, distributed, and coordinated environment that—
    - (A) connects existing systems, where appropriate, provides no single points of failure, and allows users to share information among agencies, between levels of government, and, as appropriate, with the private sector;
    - (B) ensures direct and continuous online electronic access to information;
    - (C) facilitates the availability of information in a form and manner that facilitates its use in analysis, investigations, and operations;
    - (D) builds upon existing systems capabilities currently in use across the government;
    - (E) employs an information access management approach that controls access to data rather than just systems and networks, without sacrificing security;
    - (F) facilitates the sharing of information at and across all levels of security;
    - (G) provides directory services, or the functional equivalent, for locating people and information;
    - (H) incorporates protections for individuals' privacy and civil liberties; and
    - (I) incorporates strong mechanisms to enhance accountability and facilitate oversight, including audits, authentication, and access controls.

IRTPA Section 1016 (f)(2) requires the Program Manager to assist in developing policies, as appropriate, to foster the maturity and proper operation of the ISE, and coordinate a complex set of factors: governance and engagement, strategy and policy alignment, business process harmonization, and guidelines, standards, and architecture. This leadership and coordination enables ISE mission partners to build to common specifications. Terrorism-related information can flow between partners, as can other classes of information, such as other intelligence and law enforcement information, while ensuring the protection of the American people's privacy, civil rights, and civil liberties.

To guide efforts to establish the ISE and implement the requirements of IRTPA, on December 16, 2005, President Bush issued a memorandum for the Information Sharing Environment.[3] This memorandum delineated two requirements and five guidelines that prioritize the efforts that the President believed were most critical to the development of the ISE, and assigned responsibility to relevant Cabinet officials for resolving some of the more complicated information sharing issues. Pursuant to the President's memorandum, recommendations were developed and submitted to the President on a variety of information sharing related issues, including: ensuring the information privacy and other rights of Americans are protected in the development and use of the ISE; improving information sharing with foreign partners and allies; and establishing a framework for information sharing between federal, state, local, and tribal governments, and the private sector. These recommendations were submitted to the President and approved for implementation on November 16, 2006.

PURPOSE AND SCOPE OF THE ISE

The Program Manager, Information Sharing Environment (PM-ISE) facilitates the development of the ISE by bringing together mission partners and aligning business processes, standards and architecture, security and access controls, privacy protections, and best practices. Consistent with the direction and policies issued by the President and the Office of Management and Budget, the PM-ISE issues government-wide procedures, guidelines, instructions, and standards, as appropriate, for the management, development, and proper operation of the ISE.

Figure 13-1

Scope of the ISE

As depicted in Figure 13-1, the ISE provides integrated terrorism-related information to support analysts, operators, and investigators as they carry out their responsibilities across the law enforcement, public safety, defense, intelligence, homeland security, and diplomacy communities.

The ISE comprises any mission process that is intended or is likely to have a material impact on detecting, preventing, disrupting, responding to, or mitigating terrorist activity. Examples include: terrorism watchlisting, person and cargo screening, suspicious activity reporting (SAR), and alerts, warnings, and notifications.

The PM-ISE serves as a change agent, and facilitator for innovation and discovery in providing ideas, tools, and resources to mission partners and assists them in removing barriers, facilitating change, and ensuring that ISE implementation proceeds efficiently and effectively. The PM-ISE ensures that the ISE is built to improve sharing and protection of terrorism, homeland security, and weapons of mass destruction (WMD) information.

To facilitate the development of this environment, the PM-ISE co-chairs, with the National Security Staff (NSS), the Information Sharing and Access Interagency Policy Committee (ISA IPC), which governs ISE's direction and progress; and also partners with the Office of Management and Budget (OMB). It is primarily through this partnership that program direction, funding, and performance measurement are effectively achieved. Departments and agencies are responsible for developing, deploying, modifying, and maintaining their respective investments; they play an active role in determining the policies and priorities of the ISE and are an integral part of the ISA IPC. In addition, the information they share and the tools used to share it are a part of the ISE.

ISA IPC members include the following:

- Central Intelligence Agency
- Department of Commerce
- Department of Defense
- Department of Energy
- Department of Health and Human Services
- Department of Homeland Security
- Department of the Interior
- Department of Justice
- Department of State
- Department of Transportation
- Department of Treasury
- Federal Bureau of Investigation
- General Services Administration
- Joint Chiefs of Staff
- National Counterterrorism Center
- Office of the Director of National Intelligence

To provide integrated, cross-government guidance, the PM-ISE and OMB/NSS established a framework for department and agency investments within the ISE. OMB/NSS programmatic guidance, the PM-ISE policy framework, and the ISE standards and guidelines provide the tools to effectively manage performance throughout the ISE and the ISA IPC. The tools in this effort are: governance and engagement, strategy and policy alignment, business process harmonization, and guidelines, standards, and architecture. These tools, along with ISA-IPC governance and the commitment of departments and agencies, support the strategic roadmap for achieving a more robust ISE. The PM-ISE enables its mission partners to better perform their operations by facilitating access to information and services that contribute toward a shared antiterrorism mission.

ISE MISSION PARTNERS

The ISE mission partners comprise the following five communities:

- defense
- intelligence

- homeland security
- foreign affairs
- law enforcement

The support of mission partners is critical to the success of the ISE. They have a vital leadership role for the delivery, operation, and use of the ISE, and are accountable for delivering value by aligning policy, processes, and information. While the law granted the PM-ISE government-wide authority—a unique capability allowing the office to work with existing programs to facilitate assured information sharing—the actual implementation is with mission partners.

It is the partners' agencies that conduct mission operations, develop and implement policy and procedures, and make investments to interconnect systems, networks, databases, and business processes. In the six years since the Congress directed the creation of the ISE, ISE mission partners have taken significant steps toward establishing a strong foundation.

For example, the Nationwide SAR Initiative, and core capabilities and enablers, such as the National Network of Fusion Centers, the Federal Bureau of Investigation's Field Intelligence Groups and Regional Intelligence Groups, and the National Information Exchange Model (NIEM), have produced results and show ongoing promise. The PM-ISE's role is to help mission partners find common mission equities, implement functional and technical standards, and resolve policy issues.

The ISE is realized by the investments of its mission partners—the bureaus and agencies of federal, state, local, and tribal governments, the private sector, and international governments—and it is made relevant through its use by frontline law enforcement, public safety, homeland security, intelligence, defense, and diplomatic personnel.

MATURING AND STRENGTHENING THE ISE

Balancing, Sharing, and Safeguarding

The PM-ISE and its mission partners commit to enhancing our national security through responsible sharing and safeguarding of classified information. On October 7, 2011, President Barack Obama signed Executive Order 13587, which was the culmination of a comprehensive review by federal government departments and agencies of the breach of classified information that was released by the WikiLeaks Organization starting in July 2010.[4] The Executive Order directed structural reforms aimed at strengthening oversight regarding the responsible sharing and safeguarding of classified information access and use. Numerous actions have been taken across the federal government to mitigate technical security and information access-related vulnerabilities since the WikiLeaks incident. In addition, new governance and oversight mechanisms in place are aimed at identifying new and emerging vulnerabilities.

Culture

Achieving a culture where responsible information sharing is the norm rather than the exception was a major goal of IRTPA. This goal was also reiterated in the 2005 Presidential Guidelines and Requirements in Support of the ISE. Changing the culture of an organization, particularly a large organization, is a formidable challenge. The breadth and complexity of the ISE compounds the task because the environment extends across all levels of government in the United States, into parts of the private sector, and includes foreign government partners as well.

In order to achieve a change in the culture, leaders at all levels of federal, state, local, and tribal government must set expectations and clearly demonstrate their commitment to responsible information sharing policies and goals. Use of appraisal system tools, commitment to quality training, and judicious, credible use of incentives by leaders at all levels of government can contribute to the imperative for cultural change.

Privacy

IRTPA prescribes the broadest possible sharing of information for counterterrorism purposes. It also explicitly recognized that such sharing must respect privacy, civil rights, and civil liberty (P/CR/CL) protections. A critical step in the safeguarding of P/CR/CL is the development and adoption of a written P/CR/CL policy that meets the standards of the White House ISE Privacy Guidelines. Several ISE departments and agencies have developed ISE Privacy Policies and have also made measurable progress in implementing the ISE Privacy Policies by modifying business processes and updating sharing agreements to align with the new policies. State, local, and tribal partners have worked to develop privacy policies that are "at least as comprehensive as" the ISE Privacy Guidelines, a standard prescribed as a prerequisite for receiving terrorism-related information from federal entities. All federal agencies also ensure that personnel receive training with a specialized privacy and civil liberties protection component at least annually.

CASE STUDY: NIEM

One of the core standard frameworks of the ISE is the National Information Exchange Model (NIEM). NIEM provides a commonly understood way to connect data that enables diverse communities of people to consistently "speak the same language" as they share, exchange, accept, and translate information efficiently. It was developed in partnership with federal, state, local, and tribal governments, the private sector, and academia, and is a key focal point for standards-based innovation. NIEM was launched in 2005 through a partnership agreement between the Departments of Justice and Homeland Security and signed by the agencies' Chief Information Officers. NIEM is not a software program, computer system, standard, or data repository, but a common vocabulary and mature framework for information exchanges among governmental entities, private sector, and international partners.

NIEM-based standards innovation is already yielding results, both for government mission partners and industry. DHS and DOJ now use NIEM as part of their IT strategic plans, Requests for Proposals (RFPs) to vendors, and grant language to state, local, and tribal governments. Both agencies believe that this has helped improve internal efficiency and interoperability. DOJ, working through the Bureau for Justice Assistance and DHS, has developed grant language for state, local, and tribal partners that supports the use of NIEM at all levels of government (i.e., federal, state, local, tribal, etc.). This guidance "requires all grantees to use the latest NIEM specifications and guidelines regarding the use of XML for all grant awards." In addition, industry is beginning to integrate NIEM and support for specific information exchanges into standard product and service offerings. For example, several commercial products support the NIEM-based Suspicious Activity Reporting (SAR) functional standard, and vendors are beginning to innovate on top of the current SAR standard. Standards-based innovation and adoption challenges the status quo and presents a way forward to significant improvements in mission effectiveness and efficiency.

LEVERAGING STANDARDS-BASED DATA EXCHANGES FOR SUSPICIOUS ACTIVITY REPORTING

Several key initiatives of the ISE continue to mature, providing a more effective operating capability. The Nationwide Suspicious Activity Reporting (SAR) Initiative (NSI) continues to implement standardized processes and policies that provide federal, state, local, and tribal law enforcement with the capability to share timely, relevant SAR information that has a potential nexus to terrorism, while ensuring that the privacy, civil rights, and civil liberties of Americans are protected. The NSI builds on what law enforcement and other agencies have been doing for years—gathering information regarding behaviors and incidents associated with criminal activity—and establishes a standardized process whereby SAR information can be shared among agencies to help detect and prevent terrorism-related criminal activity.

From 2008–2009, the PM-ISE evaluated the policies, procedures, and technology concepts needed to implement a unified SAR process across federal, state, local, and tribal governments. The results of the ISE-SAR Evaluation Environment, documented in a series of publically available reports, showed that the unified process not only enhanced counterterrorism efforts, but also strengthened privacy, civil rights, and civil liberties protections. Moreover, although the Evaluation Environment was focused on SARs that were indicative of terrorism-related crimes, both the steps in the NSI cycle and the data elements in the ISE-SAR functional standard are adaptable to other types of criminal behavior.

In March 2010, the Department of Justice established an NSI Office to facilitate the implementation of the NSI across all levels of government and assist participants in adopting compatible processes, policies, and standards that foster broader sharing of SARs, while ensuring that privacy, civil rights, and civil liberties are protected in accordance with federal, state, local, and tribal laws and regulations. Updated information on the NSI can be found on the National SAR Initiative website (http://nsi.ncirc.gov).

The NSI is one of the ISE's most significant accomplishments to date and the best example of the ISE in action: an interrelated set of harmonized policies, mission processes, and systems that leverage ISE core capabilities and enablers to empower the men and women on the frontline to access and share the information they need to keep the country safe.[5]

In some cases, such as the NSI, the PM-ISE helps sponsor promising mission partner initiatives by providing seed money, subject-matter expertise, or other resources to launch the activity. The aim is always to develop these initiatives in full partnership with mission owners. In addition, as improved business processes and supporting policies and technical solutions are developed and deployed, the PM-ISE helps identify, promote, and spread best practices and, where possible, influences resource allocation decisions to ensure the institutionalization and potential reuse of these mission partner capabilities.

FUSION CENTERS AND INFORMATION SHARING BETWEEN STATES AND REGIONAL STAKEHOLDERS

Fusion centers serve as focal points for the receipt, analysis, gathering, and sharing of threat-related information between the federal government and state, local, tribal, and private-sector partners. Located in states and major urban areas throughout the country, fusion centers are designed to empower frontline law enforcement, public safety, fire service, emergency response, public health, critical infrastructure and key resources (CIKR) protection, and private-sector security personnel to understand the local implications of national intelligence and help local officials better protect their communities. Fusion centers provide interdisciplinary expertise and increased situational awareness to inform decision-making at all levels of government. Fusion centers are owned and operated by state and local entities with support from federal partners in the form of personnel, training, technical assistance, exercise support, security clearances, grant funding, and connectivity to federal systems and technology.[6]

In September 2010, federal, state, and local officials completed a Baseline Capabilities Assessment—the first nationwide, in-depth assessment of fusion centers to evaluate fusion center capabilities and to establish strategic priorities for federal government support. Based on the results, fusion centers made progress in building their capabilities and addressing previously identified gaps. In 2010, all 56 FBI field offices conducted self-assessments regarding their relationships with fusion centers, which provided a comprehensive understanding of how the FBI is currently engaging with fusion centers. The FBI plans to continue close collaboration at both the field office and headquarters levels to standardize processes, clarify procedures, and facilitate more effective engagement with fusion centers.

One of the federal government's priorities for coordinating support to fusion centers was to clearly define the parameters for the allocation of federal resources to fusion centers. The Fusion Center Sub-Committee of the ISA IPC developed the Federal Resource Allocation Criteria policy, which defines objective criteria and a coordinated approach for prioritizing the allocation of federal resources to fusion centers.

Representatives from federal, state, local, and tribal agencies—including High Intensity Drug Trafficking Areas (HIDTAs), fusion centers, DHS, the White House Office of National Drug Control Policy, DOJ, FBI, the National Drug Intelligence Center, and the PM-ISE—met in February, 2011 to explore how best to leverage fusion centers and HIDTAs as uniquely valuable resources and partners. As a result of their discussions, these partners are continuing to build and formalize relationships within their states through business plans and concepts.

CONCLUSION AND FUTURE OF THE ISE

The 2007 National Strategy for Information Sharing (NSIS) provided the foundation for institutionalizing the requirements of IRTPA and the President's Guidelines and Requirements in Support of the ISE. A future National Strategy for Information Sharing and Safeguarding will build upon the NSIS.

Building the ISE is an ongoing effort. It is a process that must evolve and adapt to emerging technologies and threats. To remain relevant and effective, enhancements and extensions to the foundations of the ISE are critical. While we celebrate the achievements and progress made towards sharing information and disrupting terrorist attacks, we also recognize that improvement is always important.

The security of this nation depends upon our collective resolve to mature information sharing and safeguarding capabilities to ensure that anyone with the appropriate mission need can discover and access actionable information at the right time to successfully prevent harm to the American people and protect national security. Sharing must be done responsibly, seamlessly, and securely with safeguards in place to prevent unauthorized disclosure and protect the privacy, civil rights, and civil liberties of the American people. Ultimately, the purpose of sharing and safeguarding information is to inform and drive fact-based decisions by the analysts, investigators, and operators charged with ensuring the security of our nation.

For more information about the ISE, please visit the website at www.ise.gov.

NOTES

1. Intelligence Reform and Terrorism Prevention Act of 2004 (IRTPA), as amended, P.L. 108–458 (December 17, 2004), §1016.
2. Intelligence Reform and Terrorism Prevention Act of 2004 (IRTPA), as amended, P.L. 108–458 (December 17, 2004), §1016.

3. White House Memorandum for the Heads of Executive Departments and Agencies, SUBJECT: Guidelines and Requirements in Support of the Information Sharing Environment, December 16, 2005.

4. Executive Order 13587—Structural Reforms to Improve the Security of Classified Networks and the Responsible Sharing and Safeguarding of Classified Information, http://www.whitehouse.gov/the-press-office/2011/10/07/executive-order-structural-reforms-improve-security-classified-networks-.

5. Nationwide SAR Initiative, http://www.ise.gov/nationwide-sar-initiative.

6. 2011 ISE Annual Report to the Congress.

14

FUSION CENTERS: TOUCHPOINTS THAT PROMOTE NATIONAL PREPAREDNESS AND INTELLIGENCE-LED POLICING

W. Ross Ashley, III

Executive Director, National Fusion Center Association

Ray Guidetti

Captain, New Jersey Regional Operations Intelligence Center

INTRODUCTION

In the days leading up to September 11, 2001, one of the key individuals involved in the planning and execution of the attacks—Ziad Jarrah—was stopped by a Maryland State trooper for speeding on Interstate 95. While the trooper had no way of knowing that the person he had stopped was embarking on a mission to attack the United States from within its borders, the encounter validates that state and local authorities likely will be the ones to encounter and stop terrorists en route to commit a deadly attack. Moreover, this contact between terrorist and law enforcement officer also solidified the need for law enforcement and other public safety personnel to have better access to intelligence in order to determine if a suspicious individual is a criminal suspect or a known terrorist.

Today, ten years later, state and major urban area fusion centers have sprung up as intelligence nodes across the nation to facilitate information and intelligence sharing among local, state, tribal, territorial, and federal entities.[1] Through the establishment of protocols, training, relationships, and technology, the capacity to collect and analyze information and provide decision makers at the federal, state, and local levels of government with actionable information, the ability to use information to thwart a terrorist attack or interdict a criminal act is far greater than the days pre-9/11, when Ziad Jarrah seemed to be unfettered in his mission to hijack and crash United Airlines Flight 93.

While state and major urban areas own and operate fusion centers, the federal government has focused considerable effort and monies to support them as they have developed and matured into information and intelligence sharing nodes. Of course, a central policy consideration for the next decade is what steps the federal government should take to ensure counterterrorism, law enforcement, and other homeland security needs are met through the continued support, development, and sustainment of the National Network of Fusion Centers. Today, many ponder the importance of fusion centers, and the discussion continues as to whether these state and local entities add value toward advancing national preparedness and intelligence-led policing.

Information and intelligence sharing between federal, state, local, and tribal governments has improved dramatically since 9/11 and has transformed public safety. After 9/11, it quickly became clear that enhanced contributions by state and local law enforcement in support of counterterrorism efforts were essential, especially after the realization that state and local law enforcement had encountered some of the 9/11 hijackers. The 9/11 Commission cited improved information sharing among state, local, tribal, and federal authorities as one of the critical imperatives for building robust terrorism prevention, protection, and response capabilities. In response, state and local governments independently—*without the federal government pushing them*—began to establish fusion centers to connect the 18,000-plus disparate law enforcement agencies to better share information.

Today we have 77 fusion centers designated by Governors across the nation that integrate all aspects of public safety information to help secure this nation. The "National Network of Fusion Centers" has been embraced by the Departments of Homeland Security and Justice as a focal point of collaboration in support of federal counterterrorism efforts and other homeland security priorities. In fact, the 2010 National Security Strategy of the United States specifically cites fusion centers as a central element in preventing future acts of terrorism. Simply put, this decentralized and organically developed network is a national asset, and sustainment of that asset is a shared responsibility across all levels of government. In the absence of fusion centers, there is no other nationwide mechanism for leveraging the breadth and depth of more than two million public safety practitioners in every corner of the country for homeland security purposes. Notably, as seasoned intelligence experts and information analysts from all levels of government will concede, some of the most important information and actionable intelligence that we depend on to protect the country flows up, not down—the granular information is collected at a state or local level and then fused to permit all levels of government to act decisively in the protection of Americans. That is a central purpose for the fusion centers, and one that they have fulfilled well.

However, fusion centers are more than simply information sharing hubs. They embody a process—the *fusion process*—that has fundamentally changed how information is gathered, shared and transformed into useful intelligence at the federal, state, and local levels. It is about analyzing national threat information in a local context, passing critical state and local information up to the national intelligence community, and disseminating relevant and actionable information to state and local decision makers. It is about systematically changing the culture of public safety information sharing so that the cop on the beat knows exactly what to do when she observes suspicious behavior. It is also about protecting public safety while actively protecting the privacy, civil rights, and civil liberties of American citizens. In fact, all 77 designated fusion centers have an approved privacy policy that is at least as comprehensive as the Information Sharing Environment (ISE) Privacy Guidelines.

The National Network is what the 9/11 Commission and the Intelligence Reform and Terrorism Prevention Act of 2004 (IRTPA) envisioned: a decentralized, distributed network that involves all levels of government and collaborates routinely on information analysis and sharing with federal intelligence and law enforcement partners. If the federal government does not continue to take steps to ensure this network is strengthened and sustained, we will start moving away from the vision of the 9/11 Commission and IRTPA vision, leaving the nation more vulnerable to successive attacks on public safety—large and small—that could have been prevented through a well-supported National Network of Fusion Centers.

As the threat of homegrown violent extremism (HVE) has risen, the role of state and local law enforcement has become indispensable in detecting and preventing terror attacks. Efforts are underway—supported by the Department of Homeland Security and the Department of Justice—to train state, local, and tribal law enforcement officers to recognize and report behavior-based suspicious activity. The fusion centers are essential in this effort as both training hubs and receivers of suspicious activity reporting.[2]

This chapter seeks to continue the dialogue related to the concept of fusion centers, and stimulate discussion surrounding the importance that fusion centers have in enabling the nation's homeland security framework and intelligence-led policing at the state and local level.

Chapters by Beckner, Kamien, Kamien and Cloutier, and Paul discuss the need for information sharing planning protocols for governing operational communications among public safety stakeholders as an indispensable component of homeland security sustainment. This chapter asserts that fusion centers, as both individual entities and as a collective national network, are the strategic touchpoints necessary for the integration and harmonization of overall homeland security capabilities. This chapter will also provide an understanding of what fusion centers are as they relate to information sharing force multipliers, state and local intelligence production entities, and models for safeguarding privacy, civil rights, and civil liberties in an era where government, the public, and the private sector must increase collaboration and share information in order to defend a nation against terrorism and crime.

The chapter is divided into five sections. The first section provides a short historical evolution of fusion centers by reviewing national level policy guidance written on behalf of fusion centers. The second section provides an understanding of how fusion centers support national preparedness. The third section offers an appreciation of how fusion centers support intelligence-led policing. The fourth section provides the reader with an understanding of the key issues fusion centers practitioners face daily as they relate to information sharing, intelligence production, and the protection of privacy, civil rights, and civil liberties. The final section concludes with recommendations for continued strategic and operational development of the National Network of Fusion Centers.

FOUNDATIONAL CONCEPTS: THE EVOLUTION OF THE FUSION PROCESS

Not long after the tragic events of September 11, 2001, several states began to stand up early versions of fusion centers in an effort to share information related to counterterrorism efforts. Shortly thereafter, recognizing the value in collaboration among federal, state, and local public safety officials, the National Governor's Association (NGA) Center for Best Practices ranked the development of a state intelligence fusion center as its second-highest priority in January 2005.[3] The position of the NGA was a significant catalyst in the evolution of fusion centers, in that it indicated a need to quickly provide guidelines to assist in establishing and operating fusion centers. The *Fusion Center Guidelines*,[4] established in response to the NGA report,[5] has been considered the principal guiding document for the development of State and Major Urban Area fusion centers. The document provides clear direction on what is needed to ensure all fusion centers operate in a consistent and standardized manner. It focuses on the activities required to carry out the *fusion process*, which is defined in the *Guidelines* as:

> *The overarching process of managing the flow of information and intelligence across all levels and sectors of government and private industry. It goes beyond establishing an information/intelligence center or creating a computer network. The fusion process supports the implementation of risk-based, information-driven prevention, response, and consequence management programs. At the same time, it supports efforts to address immediate or emerging threat-related circumstances and events.*

While the document is expansive, its scope does not encompass the function of the analytical operation within a fusion center. The *National Criminal Intelligence Sharing Plan* (NCISP) is among the foundational documents upon which the *Fusion Center Guidelines* were developed.[6] The NCISP is a collection of 28 recommendations that detail the essential elements required to carry out "intelligence-led policing in a manner that provides public safety decision makers the information they need to protect the lives of our citizens." The NCISP defines analysis as the:

> *Portion of the intelligence process that transforms the raw data into products that are useful. This is also the function that separates "information" from "intelligence." It is this vital function that makes the collection effort beneficial. Without this portion of the process, we are left with disjointed pieces of information to which no meaning has been attached. The goal is to develop a report where the information has been connected in a logical and valid manner to produce an intelligence report that contains valid judgments based on information analyzed.*

Additionally, the NCISP called for all law enforcement agencies to adopt minimum standards for intelligence-led policing to support the development of professional analytic products. From the NCISP we learn that analysis turns "raw data into products" and helps to ensure that judgments are based on sound evidence and reasoning. This is an important foundation for our understanding of analysis, but it does not provide us with a definition of what "analytic excellence" is, or what a center performing analysis at a high level would be expected to achieve.

In response to the NCISP, the International Association of Law Enforcement Intelligence Analysts (IALEIA) developed the *Law Enforcement Analytic Standards.*[7] The standards are divided into two sections, one for analysts and one for analytic products and processes. The monograph emphasizes the need to use analyzed data to "direct and support law enforcement operations." The document is essential for guiding fusion center analytic operations as they relate to supporting criminal investigations, including terrorism, and planned revisions will address how the analytic standards can relate specifically to fusion centers. A companion document to the *Analytic Standards* is the

Analyst Toolbox,[8] which provides an overview of the tools that analysts can draw upon when conducting analysis. The standards and toolbox are helpful to understand the essential elements of analysis (and the skills required to be a successful analyst) but they are focused more on a foundational level of performance rather than an extraordinary level of analytic achievement.

In September 2008, the *Baseline Capabilities for State and Major Urban Area Fusion Centers* identified the core capabilities and standards necessary for fusion centers to perform basic functions.[9] The baseline capabilities were called for in the *National Strategy for Information Sharing,*[10] which outlined the role and responsibilities for federal, state, and local entities as they relate to fusion centers. Many consider the *Baseline Capabilities* document to be a central requirement of the establishment of a National Network of Fusion Centers. The document describes the need for fusion centers to develop, implement, and maintain a production plan detailing the types of analysis and products they intend to provide to their customers. Additionally, the document explains the importance of enhancing analytic skills within fusion centers, and the different types of analytic specialization that may be required within a fusion center environment. Despite the document encompassing, at a high level, the analytic function within a fusion center, it is written more narrowly toward describing activities as opposed to defining basic, intermediate, and advanced levels of analysis.

The *Critical Operational Capabilities for State and Major Urban Area Fusion Centers, Short-Term Gap Mitigation Guidebook* is a follow-on to the *Baseline Capabilities* document.[11] The guidebook was designed to assist all fusion centers to achieve maturity levels in the four critical operational capability areas (COCs). The four COCs are defined as: Receive, Analyze, Disseminate, and Gather.

- COC#1—Receive—is aimed at having the capacity to receive both classified and unclassified federal information.
- COC#2—Analyze—is aimed at assessing local implications of threat information through the use of a formal risk assessment process.
- COC#3—Disseminate—is aimed at having the capacity to deliver information and intelligence products to those state, local, and private sector constituencies that have the right and need to know.

- COC#4—Gather—is aimed at having the capacity to collect and share relevant information, to include suspicious activity reports that can assist the federal government with better understanding the national level threat picture.

The COC workbook begins to provide doctrinal guidance, to a limited degree, regarding how to process federal threat information in the fusion center environment. The guidance promoted by the COCs connotes a shift away from a law enforcement-centric analysis function that has characterized traditional law enforcement intelligence, to something more akin to a hybrid model that is mission-appropriate for fusion centers and sits between the Intelligence Community (IC) and law enforcement on a spectrum of analytic complexity.

NATIONAL PREPAREDNESS

The 9/11 Commission and the Intelligence Reform and Terrorism Prevention Act of 2004 (IRTPA) envisioned a decentralized, distributed network that involves all levels of government and collaborates routinely on information analysis and sharing with federal intelligence and law enforcement partners to detect and prevent terrorism. More recently, Presidential Policy Directive 8: National Preparedness (PPD-8) outlines a national preparedness system that includes a series of integrated frameworks, which include the mission areas of prevention, protection, mitigation, response, and recovery. When gauging fusion centers against both the overarching guidelines of the IRTPA and PPD-8, one can see precisely how these state and local information sharing and intelligence production hubs can fulfill precisely what has been requested by the both the legislative and executive branches of the United States government when it comes to safeguarding the nation.

Fusion centers, by their very nature, are expected to be the principal focal points for vertical and horizontal information sharing within their respective Area of Responsibility (AOR). This unique dynamic creates a level of responsibility that positions fusion centers as critical nodes in connecting state and local level entities to the federal government for the purpose of advancing homeland security. It also places them as "gateways to government" for state, local, tribal, and private sector communities. The information flow among federal, state, and local levels of government and a fusion center is bidirectional. This two-way exchange between the fusion center and the federal government is but-tressed by the assignment of federal personnel to the state- and urban area-owned centers.

The COCs, referred to earlier, outline a process flow whereby the federal government passes threat information directly to state and major urban area fusion centers with the expectation that it is deliv-ered to state and local constituencies, to include the private sector, in a timely and relevant manner. This requires that fusion centers have the capacity to receive classified information, assess against local implica-tions, disseminate the information and intelligence in a surgical man-ner to those that have the right and need to know it, and then follow up by providing back to the federal government information from the local environment that adds additional nuance and context to the original threat information. This process flow, detailed in Figure 14-1, ensures that, as outlined in IRTPA, all levels of government collabo-rate on intelligence needed to prevent and detect terrorism.

The National Threat Advisory System (NTAS) replaces the Homeland Security Advisory System (HSAS) and is designed to communicate ter-rorist threat information to government agencies, first responders, and the public. The federal government relies on fusion centers, through the COCs, to process federal threat information and provide a local overlay of threat and risk before passing it on further to its intended consumers.

Figure 14-1

Processing federal
threat information

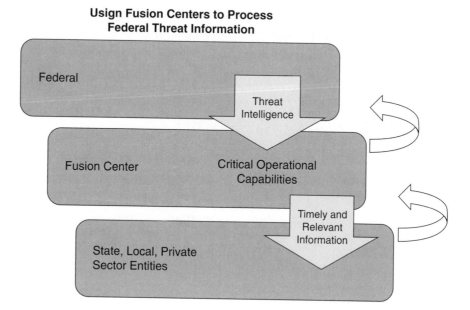

**Usign Fusion Centers to Process
Federal Threat Information**

Federal

Threat
Intelligence

Fusion Center   Critical Operational
Capabilities

Timely and
Relevant
Information

State, Local, Private
Sector Entities

PPD-8 delineates our nation's systematic approach for preparedness as it relates to those threats and hazards that pose the greatest risk to the safety and security of the United States. The directive is divided among five-core mission areas needed to achieve a level of national preparedness by:

- Preventing, avoiding, or stopping a threatened or an actual act of terrorism
- Protecting our citizens, residents, visitors, and assets, against the greatest threats and hazards in a manner that allows our interests, aspirations, and way of life to thrive
- Mitigating the loss of life and property by lessening the impact of future disasters
- Responding quickly to save lives, protect property and the environment, and meet basic human needs in the aftermath of a catastrophic incident
- Recovering through a focus on the timely restoration, strengthening, and revitalization of infrastructure, housing, and a sustainable economy, as well as the health, social, cultural, historic, and environmental fabric of communities affected by a catastrophic incident[12]

Figure 14-2 provides an illustrative assessment of how fusion centers can support national preparedness by exercising their own capabilities that center on collaboration, information sharing, and intelligence production.

The *Baseline Capabilities for State and Major Urban Area Fusion Centers: A Supplement to the Fusion Center Guidelines* articulates the fusion process capability areas as:

- Planning and Requirements Development
- Information Gathering/Collection and Recognition of Indicators and Warnings
- Processing and Collation of Information
- Intelligence Analysis and Production
- Intelligence/Information Dissemination
- Reevaluation

Figure 14-2

Assessing
fusion centers
against national
preparedness
mission areas

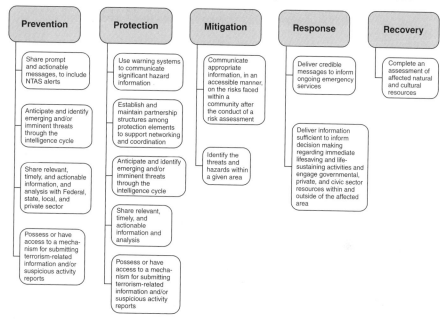

Fusion Centers Support of the National Preparedness Mission Areas

Prevention	Protection	Mitigation	Response	Recovery
Share prompt and actionable messages, to include NTAS alerts	Use warning systems to communicate significant hazard information	Communicate appropriate information, in an accessible manner, on the risks faced within a community after the conduct of a risk assessment	Deliver credible messages to inform ongoing emergency services	Complete an assessment of affected natural and cultural resources
Anticipate and identify emerging and/or imminent threats through the intelligence cycle	Establish and maintain partnership structures among protection elements to support networking and coordination	Identify the threats and hazards within a given area	Deliver information sufficient to inform decision making regarding immediate lifesaving and life-sustaining activities and engage governmental, private, and civic sector resources within and outside of the affected area	
Share relevant, timely, and actionable information, and analysis with Federal, state, local, and private sector	Anticipate and identify emerging and/or imminent threats through the intelligence cycle			
Possess or have access to a mechanism for submitting terrorism-related information and/or suspicious activity reports	Share relevant, timely, and actionable information and analysis			
	Possess or have access to a mechanism for submitting terrorism-related information and/or suspicious activity reports			

Those fusion centers that have demonstrated a maturity level in the Baseline Capabilities possess the capacity essential for sustaining the five core mission areas required for national preparedness. Beginning in 2011, DHS and DOJ implemented assessment processes to evaluate the maturity level of fusion centers, both individually and as a collective network. The annual assessment process is designed to gauge the overall capability of the National Network of Fusion Centers and to provide technical and resource assistance needed to close gaps identified in the assessment process.[13] The assessment process has been critical for three practical reasons:

- It has helped fusion centers clearly identify capability gaps that must be addressed.
- It has provided a clear purpose for federal grant assistance to ensure a fully functioning national network is maximally able to conduct vital operations.
- It has demonstrated to DHS and Congress that the national network is becoming stronger and more capable to support the homeland security mission and that the federal government is receiving a substantial return on investment.

INTELLIGENCE-LED POLICING

While intelligence-led policing was introduced to American law enforcement officially in 2003 with the publication of the NCISP, its meaning and application is still elusive for many of the 18,000 police agencies in the United States. The NCISP states, "The primary purpose of *Intelligence-Led Policing* is to provide public safety decision-makers [with] the information they need to protect the lives of our citizens."[14] Criminal justice professionals who advocate for the integration of intelligence-led policing as a means to combat both crime and terrorism have elaborated on this description. Below are two examples:

> The collection and analysis of information related to crime and conditions that contribute to crime, resulting in an actionable intelligence product intended to aid law enforcement in developing tactical responses to threats and/or strategic planning related to emerging or changing threats.[15]
>
> Intelligence-led policing is a business model and managerial philosophy where data analysis and crime intelligence are pivotal to an objective, decision-making framework that facilitates crime and problem reduction, disruption and prevention through both strategic management and effective enforcement strategies that target prolific and serious offenders.[16]

Similar themes are woven through these definitions. Analysis, intelligence, and strategy materialize as common elements between the two distinct descriptions. It is these same elements that begin to speak to why fusion centers are integral for advancing and sustaining intelligence-led policing in the United States. It is critical to understand that the fusion process is not just beneficial to the counterterrorism mission—it is clearly also beneficial to everyday efforts to prevent and investigate all types of crimes.

Nevertheless, it is Ratcliffe's conceptual representation, dubbed the 3i-Model, for illustrating intelligence-led policing (see Figure 14-3) that offers a framework within which fusion centers fit.

Figure 14-3

Ratcliffe's 3i-model
of intelligence-led
policing

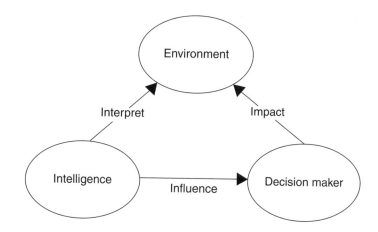

The 3i Model ... is an approach to policing and resource allocation that places a great deal of emphasis on interpreting the
criminal environment in order to influence decision-makers and
create desired impacts upon the criminal environment. Collecting and analyzing information to produce finished intelligence
products will provide decision makers with situational awareness and a common understanding of the operating environment. Once informed, decision-makers can impact their environment through strategic, operational, or tactical initiatives.[17]

Across law enforcement in the United States, the number of analysts
employed within police agencies is rather low relative to the perceived
need for them. In fact, it is common knowledge among the practitioner community that the average police department does not possess analytical personnel or the function itself. Without an analytical
function, who will carry out an essential element of intelligence-led
policing that requires interpreting the environment through analysis,
per the 3i model and definitions above?

While there are exceptions in major urban areas or with the Federal
Bureau of Investigation's Field Intelligence Groups located within
respective Field Divisions, for the most part, it is the regional fusion
center that possesses the largest contingent of analysts in a given area
who are focused on interpreting the environment for patterns, trends,
and anomalies. That is why fusion centers are well-suited to advance
intelligence-led policing. Even a fusion center with only a handful of

analysts fills a critical gap in the local law enforcement capability set, especially in states with a more suburban or rural population.

Law enforcement agencies nationwide have taken advantage of their respective fusion center's analytical capacity to employ intelligence-led policing that informs resource allocation. Below are two examples of where fusion centers have carried out intelligence-led policing for their constituents.

> At New Jersey's fusion center, the integration of geospatial statistical modeling into the analyst's toolbox is enabling individuals to graphically display high-probability violent crime areas. This has increased police officers' abilities to uncover crime trends in the Jersey City criminal environment. This technology, originally and operationally used by the military, can transfer easily to analyze terrorist threats and other domestic environmental hazards. Essentially, geospatial statistical modeling is strengthening the fusion center's ability to carry out intelligence-led policing.[18]
>
> Working cooperatively with the U.S. Attorney's Office, the Massachusetts State Police's firearms identification section and its crime laboratory, Boston Police Department, ATF, Massachusetts Criminal History Systems Board, and other local police agencies, the Commonwealth Fusion Center (Massachusetts' designated statewide fusion center) began collecting, processing, and analyzing crime and weapons-trace data to provide policymakers with data on firearms crime patterns, the types of weapons recovered at crime scenes or during arrests, and the source cities and states of these guns.[19]

Fusion centers offer law enforcement agencies opportunities to showcase the value and encourage the adoption of intelligence-led policing considered essential in the post 9/11 era. As fusion centers continue to develop their analytical and intelligence production processes, their respective state and local law enforcement agencies will naturally benefit. The byproduct of better fusion center analysis translates into more richly informed decision-making aimed at resource allocation for public safety leaders. This will no doubt facilitate better crime and problem reduction, as well as crime disruption and prevention initiatives, even as it facilitates greater collaboration with federal agencies on terrorism threats.

KEY CONSIDERATIONS FOR FUSION CENTER OPERATIONS

What follows are twelve key considerations in the form of questions that provide the reader with an intimate understanding of the challenges fusion centers across the nation face daily as they relate to fusion center customers, information sharing, intelligence production, resource sustainment, and safeguarding privacy, civil rights, and civil liberties.

Who are the Customers of Fusion Centers? What are the KEY Dynamics of the Relationships with those Customers?

Fusion center customers include the broad set of public safety practitioners, governmental executives, and critical private sector interests that reside within the jurisdiction a particular center serves. There is no cookiecutter makeup to a fusion center's "average customer." There is no single product set that works for every jurisdiction. There is no uniform time frame within which customers require certain information or intelligence. Fusion centers must juggle requirements from multiple customers and must tailor products and services in a way that is responsive to complex requirements.

Each fusion center is responsible for determining who within its [Area of Responsibility] AOR requires information and intelligence products that address threat and risk related to crime, counterterrorism, and homeland security. These constituencies include law enforcement, public safety, emergency management, governmental, and private sector personnel and organizations. While intelligence and information products created are based on the needs of the requestor, the decision maker that individual fusion centers aim to inform runs the gamut from line-level police, investigators, fire, and EMS personnel to Mayors and the Governor; from Attorneys General and State Homeland Security Advisors to State Police Superintendents to the municipal police chief; from private sector security managers to emergency management and risk mitigation planners.[20] Each of these decision makers requires a different type of product or service from the fusion center to inform them about threat, risk, and problems within the environment.[21]

While customer sets may differ among fusion centers, what is certain is the need for fusion center practitioners to manage the producer–consumer relationship with utmost attention toward "care

awareness to inform decision makers at all levels of government. The varied structure, mission scope and areas of the AOR of each individual fusion center, however, often make it difficult for their personnel and constituents to gauge exactly where these information sharing and analytical enterprises align within the larger National Security framework. As such, fusion centers find themselves caught between addressing state and local priorities and the expectation they will focus on national priority missions by serving as the primary focal points for the exchange of threat and vulnerability information with the Federal government.[27]

Balancing priorities for fusion center leaders is more about applying the skill of juggling than it is following a prescribed method or approach. While the federal government looks to fusion centers as primary information exchange nodes capable of processing federal threat information, fusion centers are owned, operated, and managed by state and local entities. This dynamic of state and major urban area ownership can lead to centers prioritizing host agencies' needs above federal initiatives that may require fusion center attention. Nonetheless, because federal priorities are often aligned to a national threat, which undoubtedly galvanizes state and local constituencies, the pressure for fusion center directors to prioritize local requirements over federal ones is usually effectively managed. Challenges arise when the federal government asks for fusion center participation in assessing national capabilities while the fusion center's attention and resource are engaged in addressing local initiatives.

What are the Challenges to Sustainable Funding for Fusion Centers?

There is no standard budget blueprint for fusion centers. Funding models and sources vary widely across the National Network. Since fusion centers are not standalone entities, but instead components of either law enforcement or homeland security organizations, funding for them often comes from the budgets of their parent organizations. According to an early 2012 survey by the National Fusion Center Association, the majority of funding for National Network of Fusion Centers comes from non-federal sources.[28] According to the survey, more than 60% of funding for fusion centers comes from state or local government sources. The remaining percentage comes primarily through DHS preparedness grants, specifically the State Homeland

Security Grant Program (SHSGP) and the Urban Areas Security Initiative (UASI). While some fusion centers utilize very limited or no federal funds there are fusion centers that are primarily or solely reliant on federal funds to be part of the National Network.[29]

Individual fusion centers will be sustained as long as they are providing value to their home agencies and their state and local customer base. This value comes in the form of either a product or a service. With shrinking or stagnating budgets at all levels of government, fusion centers that do not create value for their customers risk irrelevance. Of course, irrelevance translates into unsustainable operations. Federal funding sponsors (primarily DHS) have expectations that fusion centers are helping achieve the federal homeland security and counterterrorism missions. Meanwhile, state and local funding sponsors expect that state and local needs are being met. Centers that are primarily funded with federal grant resources are at risk when grant programs are cut by Congress.

Since there is no single dedicated federal source of funding for fusion centers, sustainable funding depends on the combination of a statutory requirement for states to allocate 25% of their SHSGP and UASI grants to "Law Enforcement Terrorism Prevention Activities" and strong grant guidance that requires investment justifications for fusion centers in every state grant application. Yet, even with a required investment justification, states that are subject to "state minimum" grant allocations through DHS grant programs may find that federal funding is inadequate—as the overall grant pie shrinks—to support fusion centers. In such cases, supplemental investment by state sources becomes critical for sustainment.

Is Involving the Private Sector in Fusion Centers a Good Idea? Does it Work?

Homeland and hometown security requires active participation of all parts of society. The private sector's capacity for contributing information to fusion centers in order to assist with understanding the threat and risk environment is critically important in building an information sharing environment needed to advance homeland security. A fusion center's capacity for contributing threat information to the private sector is equally as beneficial toward ensuring protective measures are in place to prevent, detect, and deter nefarious activity.

The Intelligence Reform and Terrorism Prevention Act of 2004 (IRTPA) called for "creating an information sharing environment for the sharing of terrorism information in a manner consistent with national security and with applicable legal standards relating to privacy and civil liberties."[30] From this act, the President created the Information Sharing Environment (ISE) and a project manager to establish, implement, and maintain the ISE. Involving the private sector with fusion centers is precisely what the Information Sharing Environment envisioned to help prevent terrorism.

> Fusion centers are uniquely situated to empower frontline law enforcement, public safety, fire service, emergency response, public health, Critical Infrastructure and Key Resources (CIKR) protection, and private-sector security personnel to understand local implications of national intelligence, enabling local officials to better protect their communities.[31]

The terrorist attacks of September 11, 2001, are a stark reminder of the importance that the private sector can play in thwarting terrorist attacks through the sharing of information. Philip Bobbitt, in *Terror and Consent*, graphically outlines how the division between the private sector and law enforcement contributed to the FBI being unable to provide the airlines with the names of two terrorists the CIA had warned about.[32] The reforms put in place through the IRTPA encourage a stronger relationship between the private sector and law enforcement.

Private sector security personnel are in unique positions to identify and provide suspicious activity reports (SARs), either directly to their respective fusion centers or to local law enforcement agencies that in turn forward this information to their fusion centers. The fusion center can provide a local overlay of known information to enhance the vetting of a SAR prior to sending it off to the Joint Terrorism Task Force and to the national Shared Space for further analysis. The fusion center role as the primary focal point of information sharing, either within a state or in an Urban Area Security Initiative, enables it to act as an efficient conduit for information provided by the private sector in local jurisdictions that should be forwarded up for a national, federal, or IC review.

Through the use of a Fusion Liaison Officer (FLO) program, the fusion center can develop and sustain information sharing relationships with the private sector. The intent is to leverage the "eyes and ears" of the public to maximize the quality and quantity of information on possible threats coming in for analysis. The FLOs from the private sector share information with the fusion center in a manner that safeguards privacy, civil liberties, and civil rights. Policies and training underpin the private sector FLO's relationship with their corresponding fusion center.

The relationship between the private sector and fusion centers is only now beginning to materialize, owing to the short evolution of fusion centers. The Faisal Shahzad case, where a Connecticut resident attempted to detonate an explosive in Times Square, and the Najibullah Zazi case, where a Colorado resident conspired to attack New York City transit lines, are examples of how relationships between the private sector and fusion centers can assist with interdicting or investigating terror plots. In both cases, the fusion centers in New York and Colorado were instrumental in processing information related to the independent conspiracies. In the New York case, an alert AAA employee filed a SAR with the New York State Intelligence Center regarding a call on May 2, 2010—when Shahzad called for assistance because he had locked his keys inside the vehicle. This was the same vehicle later recovered at the airport with a firearm inside on the day Shahzad was arrested.[33] This information was forwarded to the FBI to support investigation and corroboration. In the Colorado case, fusion liaison officers assisted the FBI JTTF with gathering the pertinent information related to Zazi's purchase of precursor chemicals needed to develop an improvised explosive device.[34]

How should Fusion Centers be Staffed? How should the Various Roles be Trained? Are there Missing Skill Sets that would be Helpful in Fusion Centers?

Responses to questions regarding fusion center staffing often center on analysts. However, this view can have the effect of downplaying the utility of different types of analytical tradecraft in a fusion center environment, and can also fail to appreciate the mission space within which many fusion centers operate. In order to meet the expectations of their customer bases, individual fusion centers ought to be staffed with people who are able to effectively and efficiently deliver high-quality products and services requested from their consumers—whether those people are analysts or not.

There are different types of analytical functions that offer state and local constituencies value. Crime analysts, criminal intelligence analysts, intelligence analysts, geospatial analysts, risk analysts, statistical analysts, and network analysts are some of the analytical roles found in fusion centers. Two important factors often drive the decision on what type of analytical staff a fusion center should employ: customer needs and hiring budgets.

As an example, in New Jersey, the fusion center has come to rely on geospatial predictive analysis as a capability for producing high quality products aimed at informing decision makers about future resource allocations. Geospatial predictive analysis relies on statistical modeling.

> Geospatial statistical modeling for law enforcement is a methodology based on identifying discernible geospatial preferences associated with a perpetrator's conscious and unconscious activities leading up to criminal behavior, a gang action, or a terrorist threat. By applying a structured geospatial model, hundreds or even thousands of geospatial factors can be fused together to produce geospatial patterns of statistical similarity among criminal location preferences. These patterns, once understood by analysts, can be mapped to a geographic area. Displayed visually as a density pattern, the analysis of these factors can aid in defining the probability that conditions exist for the specific activity of concern to emerge and, more importantly, its location. Further, the analysis of underlying factors permits the development of action plans to counter the event.[35]

In addition to analysts, many fusion centers employ commanders, supervisors, intelligence managers, detectives, investigators, liaison personnel, administrative support personnel, and interns from law enforcement, homeland security, counterterrorism, and other public safety agencies. The FBI and DHS also contribute personnel to fusion centers. Those personnel may include agents, intelligence officers, analysts, and reports officers.

While analytical skills are important for all personnel assigned to a fusion center regardless of their assignment, it is just as critical, oftentimes more so, for personnel to be able to synthesize information. The nature of a fusion center is to receive multiple feeds of information from disparate entities. The capacity to synthesize these information feeds results in investigative leads, the uncovering of new patterns and trends, and unique opportunities for interdicting nefarious activity or designing operational initiatives to suppress or control illegal activities.

The training of fusion center personnel does not follow a standardized national level model. While the *Law Enforcement Analytical*

Standards provide guidelines for analysts who work in fusion centers, the diverse nature of positions assigned to fusion centers make it difficult for one training regime to exist across the National Network of Fusion Centers. Fusion center personnel attend training delivered by their host agencies, their respective states, the federal government, professional organizations, and expert private vendors.

Fusion centers are more than just a director managing a group of analysts. The mission and customer needs of a particular fusion center will inevitably determine the types of positions a fusion center must staff. These positions run the gamut, but all have a strong nexus toward building the capabilities of analysis and synthesis of information.

Are Analytical Products, Situational Awareness Reporting, and Near-Real-Time Intelligence Support for Operations all Provided by Fusion Centers? Which one is of Greater Value to Customers?

Fusion centers conduct assessments and produce intelligence products related to state and local level threats and risks. This information is often shared nationally across the fusion center network; however, the aim of intelligence production is to inform state and local decision makers about their local threat environment in order to support planning, operations, resource allocation, and training.

In order to be effective, it is critical that fusion centers answer four important questions for their consumers:

1. What has happened?
2. What is happening?
3. What is about to happen?
4. What could happen?[36]

That said, fusion centers that posses a diverse set of capabilities are able to provide a mix of products and services that match customer needs. This is crucial for maintaining the customer's attention and sustaining the value of the fusion center. Intelligence products come in the form of situational awareness reports, analyses, and forecasts. Forecasting is the most complex of these three products and requires refined tradecraft that many novice analysts lack. Elevating the forecasting capabilities of fusion centers would help to meet underlying expectations of key fusion center customers, especially at the state, local, and tribal levels.

Although a diverse product line is important for fusion centers, the nature of their customers, primarily law enforcement and public safety entities, requires them to produce intelligence products that inform operational decision-making. The reference to "timely and actionable" products is a common request heard throughout the fusion center network. After all, it is the analyst who bears considerable responsibility for constructing an image of the threat environment and they must be able to convey that picture to operational decision-makers by providing sound recommendations.[37]

How much Crowdsourcing and Collaboration through Fusion Centers is Required by Communities of Interest that Include Non-Governmental Stakeholders?

Fusion centers, by their very nature, aspire to be focal points of information sharing and knowledge centers capable of actionable intelligence production within their given jurisdiction. Despite this well-intentioned ambition, constrained analytical resources, limited subject matter expertise, and constant turnover among analytical personnel sometimes prevent centers from achieving optimal proficiency in this area. Crowdsourcing can help fusion centers tackle problems that fall outside their comfort zone.

Philip Bobbit, in *Terror and Consent: The Wars for the Twenty-First Century*, relates how the national intelligence community (IC) in many ways faces a similar dilemma as fusion centers. The IC has historically grappled with balancing the mining of open source information versus acquiring secrets in their efforts to collect relevant information on a specific topic, issue, or problem. With a rapidly evolving threat landscape where IC analysts may not have the same subject matter expertise in a given area as an academic, journalist, or blogger, harnessing knowledge through crowdsourcing is essential. For this reason, in 2008 the Director of National Intelligence established overarching doctrine and policy that guides analytic outreach in an open, overt, and deliberate manner to those outside the IC.[38] By exploring the outside experts that possess new ideas and alternative perspectives, the IC as a whole can improve and enrich their analysis and intelligence products.

Fusion centers can be best served by following a similar model as Intelligence Community Directive-205. In many ways this does occur in informal exchanges at the local level, where, depending on the issue, local subject matter experts provide expertise in a given area to assist with research, analysis, and production efforts related to ad hoc issues. This is achieved mainly with academic institutions that offer subject matter experts in the form of an interested professor or doctoral student who assists in research, topical areas of study, and even analytical techniques such as mapping or network analysis.

While there is no formalized program within the National Network of Fusion Centers to engage in crowdsourcing with outside experts or the public, an emerging effort to recognize Centers of Analytical Excellence within the National Network of Fusion Centers has begun. The National Fusion Center Association, at the time of this writing, is spearheading an effort to identify those fusion centers that possess a specialized expertise that could greatly benefit the overall national network by increasing its capacity for analysis in specific areas.[39] As this concept continues to materialize, it is likely that other crowdsourcing efforts will follow to include developing communities of interest outside the fusion center community to assist with better understanding threat and risk in a given jurisdiction or for a specific issue.

What are the Best Practices and Challenges for Fusion Centers with Regard to their Interaction with State Agencies, Local Law Enforcement, and Other Public Safety Entities?

The very nature of fusion centers requires them to play a support function in their interaction with other state agencies or local law enforcement or public safety entities. To be a primary focal point within a jurisdiction, whether at the state level or within a UASI region, requires fusion centers to be at the center of communities of trust among these entities. This trust can be built over time by demonstrating open communication, transparency, accountability, and information security.

A key element toward building strong relationships between a fusion center and its stakeholders is to ensure that service and trust are hallmarks of the fusion center's interaction. Unlike most interagency task forces at the state and local level, where agencies supply personnel knowing fully that the executive agency is responsible for prioritizing operations, fusion centers often work in reverse: information sharing requirements of the contributing agency guide or direct fusion center operations.

The meritorious nature of policing, which invariably fuels a culture of pluralism among law enforcement agencies, will always create challenges for fusion centers to achieve a unity of effort among those it seeks to work with or within close proximity.[40] Another key element for building trust among fusion centers and its interagency partners is to develop a governance model that brings members from other agencies together to strategically influence fusion mission, roles, and responsibilities. A fusion center governance body and associated processes is a practical way to align diverse viewpoints around a unified, collaborative, and value-added purpose that is ultimately right for fusion center customers.[41]

What Planning Should Fusion Centers do and Lead?

Fusion centers can play an important role in prevention, operational, and resiliency planning in their respective jurisdictions. Threat information regarding crimes, threats, and hazards are funneled to most fusion centers for review and analysis, which gives them the opportunity to identify patterns, trends, and anomalies. The results of this analysis can offer enhanced opportunities for informing planning efforts by local and state government, emergency management, and public safety executives.

Critical Operational Capability #2—Analysis—requires that fusion centers have the capability to produce formalized risk assessments by analyzing federal threat information against an overlay of local information, which includes known offenders, terrorists' tactics, techniques, and procedures, and area critical infrastructure and key resources. While many fusion centers are still developing their ability to produce formalized risk assessments, fusion centers in general continue to work toward achieving high levels of proficiency in assessing threat and risk needed to inform planning and resource allocation decisions.[42]

Historically, the emergency or crisis planning function in states and UASI regions is relegated to the emergency management discipline. Response plans crafted by emergency management personnel are designed to encompass all hazards related to disaster planning and preparedness, emergency response, hazard identification, crisis mitigation, business continuity, continuity of operations, and resumption of critical services. Fusion center operations can be maximized with the help of professional planners that the emergency management community can offer. Planners can provide fusion center personnel with a comprehensive perspective needed to better understand the impact that analyst recommendations can have on the environment prior to informing operational decision-making.[43] Conversely, the more mature fusion centers become, the greater likelihood that their own analytical proficiency can support emergency management planning efforts. The exchange of information sharing requirements, coordinated operations, and trusted relationships will ensure that fusion centers and emergency management programs can mutually support and benefit from planning initiatives.

Most fusion centers are already engaged in planning efforts for law enforcement operations because they are components of a law enforcement agency. Because of their focus on threats and intelligence-led policing, fusion centers often lead planning efforts aimed at reducing and preventing crime. Intelligence analysis and mapping products form the foundation of intelligence needed to inform strategic and operational decision makers about the criminal environment.

The capability for receiving, analyzing, disseminating, and gathering information related to threats offers fusion centers unique opportunities to either lead or enhance planning efforts related to emergency preparedness, law enforcement, or homeland security. Fusion centers are also in a unique position to assist with resiliency planning efforts. For example, in New Jersey, a state with extensive critical infrastructure, the fusion center is working with the state's Homeland Security Office and the Office of Emergency Management on analysis and outreach efforts. The analysis is related to interdependencies that can be impacted during a catastrophic event and to providing intelligence needed to build resiliency plans.

How do Fusions Centers Address Civil Liberties, Civil Rights, and Privacy Issues Related to Criminal Intelligence?

Fusion centers have a well-defined program that addresses protecting privacy, civil liberties, and civil rights. Each recognized fusion center within the National Network of Fusion Centers is required to have an approved privacy policy that meets standards at least as stringent as the Information Sharing Environment privacy standard. Each center is also required to have a dedicated privacy officer that attends training provided by the Department of Homeland Security.

> Both fusion center directors and the federal government have identified the protection of privacy, civil rights, and civil liberties as a key priority and an important enabling capability to ensure fusion centers protect the legal rights of Americans while supporting homeland security efforts. It is critical that fusion center personnel not only receive training to understand the need to protect privacy, civil rights, and civil liberties, but also have a policy in place clearly outlining how this will be achieved.
>
> To help with these efforts, the DHS Privacy Office, working in collaboration with the DHS Office of Intelligence and Analysis (I&A) and the Program Manager of the Information Sharing Environment, began an independent review in November 2009 of fusion center privacy policies. Today, we are pleased to announce that all [77] officially designated fusion centers have successfully completed this important step and received letters from the DHS Chief Privacy Officer stating that these policies have been

> determined to be at least as comprehensive as the Information Sharing Environment (ISE) Privacy Guidelines.
>
> The completion of these privacy policies by all fusion centers is a milestone to support the sharing of terrorism and other homeland security information between the federal government and fusion centers during situations involving time-sensitive and emerging threats.[44]

Fusion center privacy policies provide avenues for addressing information sharing and intelligence-related issues that state and local entities may encounter. For instance, before a fusion center disseminates a finished intelligence product, it is reviewed against the standards articulated within that center's privacy policy to ensure that safeguards are in place. This practice helps ensure that information sharing between fusion centers and their "partners sufficiently protect Americans' privacy and civil liberties while sharing important terrorism and homeland security information."[45] The ability to continually provide value to trusted partners and protect the public ultimately depends on maintaining their trust. Federal, state, local, and tribal stakeholders in the National Network are keenly aware of this reality, and take extraordinary steps to ensure privacy, civil rights, and civil liberties are maintained even as timely and actionable intelligence is provided to decision makers.

ADVANCING FUSION CENTERS TO UNDERPIN HOMELAND SECURITY AND INTELLIGENCE-LED POLICING

When discussing fusion centers, there is often an interest in comparing them to Joint Terrorism Task Forces (JTTFs) or High Intensity Drug Trafficking Areas (HIDTAs). The question about their similarities is often asked in the interest of evaluating fusion centers' value proposition in times of budgetary cutbacks and constrained resources. Of course, there are many differences with fusion centers as they relate to JTTFs and HIDTAs (see Figure 14-4). The first, of course, is the time that all three have been in existence. In comparison to the others, fusion centers are newcomers. Their short history was begun in the aftermath of the tragic events of September 11, 2001, when the need to tear down silos to facilitate information sharing was universally recognized. The pressure of defending the nation

Figure 14-4

Comparison of
fusion centers
and JTTFs and
HIDTAs, adapted
from http:www.dhs.
gov/files/programs/
gc_1298911926746.
shtm

Fusion Centers	High Intensity Drug Trafficking Area Investigative Support Centers
Owned and operated by state and local authorities	Created by the National HIDTA Program and sponsored by the ONDCP
Deal with terrorism, criminal, and public safety matters across multiple disciplines, including law enforcement, public safety, fire service, emergency response, public health, and private sector security	Focus on narcotics-related matters and support investigative agencies in the identification, targeting, arrest, and prosecution of key members of criminal drug organizations
Receive, analyze, disseminate, and gather threat-related information	Provide for the collocation and communication between federal and SLTT law enforcement agencies in counterdrug investigations, eradication, and interdiction
Produce actionable intelligence for dissemination to appropriate law enforcement and homeland security agencies	Provide narcotics-related investigative case support, lead generation, and prepare threat assessment, strategic report, trend and pattern assessments, and organizational studies

Fusion Centers	Joint Terrorism Task Forces
Managed by state and local authorities, and include federal, SLTT, and private sector partners from multiple disciplines (including law enforcement, public safety, fire service, emergency response, public health, and critical infrastructure)	Managed by FBI, and include federal and SLTT law enforcement partners
Deal with criminal, public safety, and terrorism matters across multiple disciplines	Deal primarily with terrorism matters and other criminal matters related to various aspects of the counterterrorism mission
Share information across disparate disciplines on topics such as terrorism, criminal activity, and public safety	Work with SLTT partners to share critical infrastructure information with the federal government
Fusion centers add value to their jurisdictional customers by providing a state and local context to threat information and collaborate with the Federal Government to enhance the national threat picture	104 JTTFs investigate terrorism cases across the FBI's 56 field offices and coordinate their efforts via the National Joint Terrorism Task Force, a fusion of local, state, and federal agencies acting as an integrated force to combat terrorism on a national and international scale
Serve as centers of analytic excellence to assess local implications of threat information to (1) produce actionable intelligence for dissemination to law enforcement and homeland security agencies, and (2) perform services in response to customers' needs	Primarily conduct terrorism investigations; however JTTFs share intelligence with law enforcement and homeland security agencies, as appropriate

has not been lost on fusion centers. One of the primary dangers, as time passes without a major terror attack, is complacency. Fusion centers are the vanguard of the national terrorism prevention effort, and it is inside the evolving National Network of Fusion Centers where complacency in the face of evolving threats is directly confronted. While HIDTAs and JTTFs were able to mature during more peaceful times, fusion centers have had to learn to crawl and run at the same time.

Unlike JTTFs and HIDTAs, fusion centers are extensions of state and local law enforcement or homeland security agencies. Owned by state and local agencies, they often compete for funding and resources with internal constituencies within their parent agencies. While JTTFs and HIDTAs have a primary emphasis on terrorism or drugs respectively, most fusion centers instead have a focus on a myriad of issues that include "all crimes, all hazards, and all threats." Whereas JTTFs and HIDTAs have primarily investigative responsibilities, fusion centers are primarily analytical and facilitate information sharing within their states or regions. It is the multiplicity of functions within a respective fusion center that is the double-edged sword. Of course, the connotation of being all things to all people can be challenging in terms of maintaining a constant ability to meet customer expectations; however, fusion centers are increasingly able to provide value-added products and services to many customers.

Sustaining fusion centers is critical to our nation's homeland security efforts. Sustainability does not just come in the form of funding. The value, in terms of products and services, is what state and local customers remark upon when they discuss fusion centers and the need to support them. What follows are three overarching recommendations that can best serve fusion centers as they look to the future. These recommendations are drawn from the questions and answers addressed previously, and serve to bolster fusion centers as promoters of national preparedness and intelligence-led policing.

Recommendation #1

State and local government leaders should develop relevant policies and governance structures that ensure fusion centers can effectively and efficiently manage and sustain state or local level Information Sharing Environments to make sure that government, the private sector, and the public can share information and intelligence about terrorism, crime, and hazards in an effort to prevent terrorism, build preparedness, and enable intelligence-led policing.

Recommendation #2

The National Network of Fusion Centers, in cooperation with federal, state, and local level government leaders, should mirror the IC's ICD-205 to enable fusion centers to leverage crowdsourcing opportunities and initiatives that can bolster analytical capacities and resources needed to better understand threats related to terrorism, crime, and hazards in an effort to build preparedness and enable intelligence-led policing.

Recommendation #3

State and local government leaders should develop relevant policies and leverage governance structures that ensure fusion centers are properly resourced and safeguard privacy, civil rights, and civil liberties, as they advance information sharing and intelligence production initiatives designed to build preparedness and enable intelligence-led policing.

CONCLUSION

Fusion centers may be precisely what the *Final Report of the National Commission on Terrorist Attacks Upon the United States* called for as it detailed tearing down silos, sharing information, and connecting the dots. In fact, ten years later, Thomas Kean, the co-chairman of the 9/11 Commission, remarked that information sharing among federal, state, and local levels of government and the private sector has improved considerably, due in part, to the advance of fusion centers. Governor Kean made these remarks while visiting the New Jersey Regional Operations Intelligence Center during the ten-year anniversary of September 11, 2001.

While fusion centers have much to learn and a lot of room to grow, their very nature makes the National Network an indispensable asset for promoting national preparedness, preventing terrorism, and advancing intelligence-led policing. By carrying out structured and standardized information sharing processes, fusion centers have the capacity to process federal threat information and deliver to state, local, and private sector constituencies the information they need to prevent and better prepare for an attack or for the impact of a catastrophic event. These same processes offer fusion centers the opportunity to gather information locally, such as suspicious activity reports, which can assist federal entities to better understand the nation's threat picture. Equally as significant for fusion centers is their capacity to analyze local information related to crime and provide intelligence products necessary for police leadership to make better decisions regarding resource allocation and operational planning. As fusion centers balance national and local priorities, their aptitude for adding value to their full customer base continues to grow as the Network evolves.

Although fusion centers are relatively new to the public safety and intelligence scene, their inherent capacity for promoting national preparedness and intelligence-led policing makes them important structures that are essential to sustain both homeland and hometown security for years to come. Their sustainment and continued growth will undoubtedly rely upon well-informed policy and resource allocation decisions at the federal, state, and local levels of government.

Finally, looking to the future, the fusion center community as a whole must find a way to assess its value from a customer perspective. This chapter emphasizes customer expectations related to information sharing and intelligence production on many levels; however, there is no one agreed-upon standard governing the entire Network. Yes, there are customer surveys and feedback sheets attached to analytical products, but the culture of fusion center customers is such that providing this type of feedback is generally not emphasized. One could view fusion center evaluation as similar to assessing the success of non-profit organizations: Instead of focusing on the bottom line (profit), one must focus on evaluating success in attaining mission objectives. A measure of success for fusion centers might be a blended assessment of baseline and critical operational capabilities, customer satisfaction, and repeat customer feedback. Together, this amalgamation of attributes can demonstrate the effectiveness and value proposition of a functioning enterprise that is meeting the many objectives of a diverse customer set, regardless of the domain. Accomplishing this level of effectiveness will require centers to embrace innovation, merge technologies and analytic disciplines, and use creativity to meet the demands of its multifaceted customer set. In response to this challenge, the fusion center community will likely explore many variations of what it means to be a successful fusion center, until the market itself (customer demand) shapes what success looks like.

STUDY RESOURCES SECTION

U.S. Department of Justice's Global Justice Information Sharing Initiative. (2004) *National Criminal Intelligence Sharing Plan*

U.S. Department of Justice's Global Justice Information Sharing Initiative. (2004) *Law Enforcement Analytic Standards*

U.S. Department of Justice's Global Justice Information Sharing Initiative. (2004) *Minimum Criminal Intelligence Training Standards for United Stated Law Enforcement and other Criminal Justice Agencies*

U.S. Department of Justice's Global Justice Information Sharing Initiative. (2006) *Fusion Center Guidelines: Developing and Sharing Information and Intelligence in a New Era*

U.S. Department of Justice's Global Justice Information Sharing Initiative. (2006) *Analyst Toolbox*

U.S. Department of Justice's Global Justice Information Sharing Initiative. (2008) *Baseline Capabilities for State and Major Urban Area Fusion Centers: A Supplement to the Fusion Center Guidelines*

U.S. Department of Justice's Global Justice Information Sharing Initiative. (2009) Navigating Your Agency's Path to Intelligence-led Policing

U.S. Department of Justice's Global Justice Information Sharing Initiative. (2010) *Operational Capabilities for State and Major Urban Area Fusion Centers, Short-Term Gap Mitigation Strategy Guidebook*

U.S. Department of Justice's Global Justice Information Sharing Initiative. (2010) *Common Competencies for State, Local, and Tribal Intelligence Analysts*

NOTES

1. Note: The reference to fusion centers throughout this chapter refer to the state and major urban area fusion centers that the Department of Homeland Security and Department of Justice have recognized because of their focus on Fusion Center Baseline Capabilities and Critical Operations Capabilities. At the time of this writing, the Department of Homeland Security recognized 77 fusion centers.

2. Statement of W. Ross Ashley III, Executive Director, National Fusion Center Association, March 7, 2012, to the Subcommittee on Homeland Security, Committee on Homeland Security Appropriations, United States House of Representatives.

3. National Governor's Association Center for Best Practices (2005) Issue Brief: Homeland Security in the States: Much Progress, Much Work.

4. U.S. Department of Justice's Global Justice Information Sharing Initiative, *Fusion Center Guidelines: Developing and Sharing Information and Intelligence in a New Era*, 2006.

5. A number of other organizations also played an important role in identifying and advocating on behalf of a set of formal guidelines for fusion centers to include: the U.S. Department of Justice's (DOJ) Global Justice Information Sharing Initiative (Global); the Criminal Intelligence Coordinating Council (CICC) in support of the Bureau of Justice Assistance, Office of Justice Programs; and the Homeland Security Advisory Council, which advises the Department of Homeland Security.

6. U.S. Department of Justice's Global Justice Information Sharing Initiative, *National Criminal Intelligence Sharing Plan*, 2004.

7. U.S. Department of Justice's Global Justice Information Sharing Initiative, *Law Enforcement Analytic Standards*, 2004.

8. U.S. Department of Justice's Global Justice Information Sharing Initiative, *Analyst Toolbox*, 2006.

9. U.S. Department of Justice's Global Justice Information Sharing Initiative, *Baseline Capabilities for State and Major Urban Area Fusion Centers: A Supplement to the Fusion Center Guidelines*, 2008.

10. The White House National Strategy for Information Sharing, 2007, http://georgew bush-whitehouse.archives.gov/nsc/infosharing/index.html.

11. Department of Homeland Security & GLOBAL, *Critical Operational Capabilities for State and Major Urban Area Fusion Centers, Short-Term Gap Mitigation Guidebook*, 2010.

12. Department of Homeland Security National Preparedness Goal, 1st ed., September 2011, p. 1.

13. Department of Homeland Security homepage, 2011 Fusion Center Assessment and Gap Mitigation, http://www.dhs.gov/files/programs/fusion-center-assessment-gap-mitigation.shtm (accessed April 7, 2012).

14. Global Intelligence Working Group, *National Criminal Intelligence Sharing Plan* (Washington, DC: U.S. Office of Justice Programs, 2003).

15. David Carter, *Law Enforcement Intelligence: A Guide for State, Local, and Tribal Law Enforcement Agencies,* 2nd ed. (Washington, DC: U.S. Office of Justice Programs, 2009), 80.

16. J. H. Ratcliffe, *Intelligence-Led Policing* (Cullompton, UK: Willan Publishing. 2008), 89.

17. New Jersey State Police, New Jersey State Police: Practical Guide to Intelligence-led Policing, 2006, http://www.njsp.org/divorg/invest/pdf/njsp_ilpguide_010907.pdf.

18. Raymond Guidetti and James W. Morentz, "Geospatial Statistical Modeling for Intelligence-Led Policing," *The Police Chief* 77 (August 2010): 72–76.

19. David Lambert, Intelligence-Led Policing in a Fusion Center, *FBI Law Enforcement Bulletin,* 2010,http://www.fbi.gov/stats-services/publications/law-enforcement-bulletin/Dec2010/intelligence_feature (accessed April 7, 2012).

20. U.S. Department of Justice, Global Justice Information Sharing Initiative (2006) Fusion Center Guidelines: Developing and Sharing Information and Intelligence in a New Era: Guidelines for Establishing and Operating Fusion Centers at the Local, State, and Federal Levels, p. 14.

21. J. Abold, R. Guidetti, and D. Keyer, "Strengthening the Value of the National Network by Leveraging Specialization: Defining 'Centers of Analytical Excellence,'" *Homeland Security Affairs Journal* (in press, 2012), 5.

22. J. Nicholl, "Task Definition," in J. H. Ratcliffe (ed.), *Strategic Thinking in Criminal Intelligence,* 2nd ed. (Annandale, NSW: The Federation Press, 2009), 66.

23. Statement of W. Ross Ashley III, Executive Director, National Fusion Center Association, March 7, 2012, Subcommittee on Homeland Security, Committee on Homeland Security Appropriations, United States House of Representatives.

24. Bureau of Justice Assistance, Nationwide SAR Initiative, http://nsi.ncirc.gov/.

25. J. Nicholl, Task Definition.

26. GLOBAL (2008) Baseline Capabilities for State and Major Urban Area Fusion Centers, p. 2.

27. S. Hewitt, W. Carter, and R. Guidetti, "Fusion Center Doctrine: A Plan to Balance National and Local Priorities" (policy recommendation paper, National Fusion Center Association, 2011).

28. National Fusion Center Association Survey, 2012.

29. Note: As a analogy, this is very similar to the Assistance to Firefighter Program. There are communities that do not have the tax base to support a fire department or the purchases of expensive "apparatuses," as they term them. The AFG program ensures to the greatest possible extent that every American has equal access to lifesaving public safety. The AFG funds are distributed based on formulas that take into account rural/urban and full-time/volunteer and combined departments.

30. Intelligence Reform and Terrorism Prevention Act of 2004, Public Law 108-458 December 17, 2004.

31. Information Sharing Environment Annual Report to the Congress, Prepared by the Program Manager, *Information Sharing Environment,* June 30, 2011, p. xii.

32. Philip Bobbitt, *Terror and Consent: The Wars for the Twenty-First Century* (New York: Alfred Knopf).

33. Department of Homeland Security Fusion Center Success Stories, http://www.dhs.gov/files/programs/gc_1296488620700.shtm#3.

34. Ibid., http://www.dhs.gov/files/programs/gc_1296488620700.shtm#9.

35. Raymond Guidetti and James W. Morentz, "Geospatial Statistical Modeling for Intelligence-Led Policing," *The Police Chief* 77 (August 2010): 72–76.

36. Note: Neil Quarmby, in his chapter "Futures Work in Strategic Criminal Intelligence" in J. Ratcliffe (ed.,) *Strategic Thinking in Criminal Intelligence,* 1st ed. (Annandale, NSW: Federation

Press, 2004), provides a descriptive overview regarding futures work in the law enforcement domain. Quarmby's work underscores the value that specific categories of intelligence products have in answering decision makers' key questions about the threat environment.

37. J. Ratcliffe, ed., *Strategic Thinking in Criminal Intelligence,* 1st ed. (Annandale, NSW: Federation Press, 2004), 11.

38. Office of the Director of National Intelligence (2008) Intelligence Community Directive Number 205 Analytic Outreach.

39. J. Abold, R. Guidetti, and D. Keyer, Strengthening the Value of the National Network by Leveraging Specialization: Defining "Centers of Analytical Excellence."

40. R. Guidetti, "Collaborative Intelligence Production," in J. H. Ratcliffe (ed.), *Strategic Thinking in Criminal Intelligence,* 2nd ed. (Annandale, NSW: Federation Press, 2009), 222.

41. Ibid, 226.

42. Information Sharing Environment Annual Report to the Congress, Prepared by the Program Manager, Information Sharing Environment, June 30, 2011, p. 42.

43. Interview with Captain Christian Schulz, New Jersey State Police Office of Emergency Management (March 30, 2012).

44. See DHS website, http://blog.dhs.gov/2011/04/fusion-centers-meet-important-privacy.html.

45. Ibid.

15

THE NECESSITY OF INTERAGENCY COLLABORATION

Steven Pugh

Captain, United States Air Force

INTRODUCTION

One of the principal, and most accelerated, changes in recent U.S. history is the nation's reliance on information technology. Five decades ago, the impact of digital infrastructure on our way of life was essentially nonexistent. Today, the United States' digital infrastructure has become a strategic national asset. Pundits have warned of adversarial hackers who could infiltrate and shutdown critical Industrial Control Systems (ICS) such as water treatment facilities, power grids, or even nuclear power stations—their warnings are not without merit. A whole-of-government approach must be used to confront and thwart these new, advanced threats.

The domain of cyberspace is unique for the Department of Homeland Security (DHS) because it is the only main mission area that is man-made. It is also the newest of the mission areas. Additionally, cyberspace enables or supports all other mission areas with which DHS has been charged. Another unique aspect is that cyberspace literally permeates all facets of the government, not just DHS. Because of this unique characteristic, the success of DHS is intimately tied with its ability and capacity to work effectively with other departments and agencies—known as interagency collaboration.

In addition to the broad nature of cyberspace, the scope of knowledge required to secure and defend cyberspace, and the scale of the Internet, make developing a solution challenging. Some of the problems within cyberspace are simply too broad for one department to take on singlehandedly. Fortunately, as Mr. Stanton from Johns-Hopkins University writes, "Cyberspace lends itself to such collaboration between government and private actors" (Stanton, 2008). To avert digital disaster, a comprehensive solution must be achieved. An attacker needs only one vulnerability to gain access to a digital network and wreck havoc.

In a fiscally constrained environment, the nation needs to leverage as much efficiency as possible. Thomas Stanton writes, "Interagency collaboration, important before, has become essential for program managers. Agencies must begin to pool administrative resources to jointly enhance the quality of their programs" (Stanton, 2011).

The idea of interagency collaboration has a solid theoretical foundation, though its execution has a rather inconsistent record of accomplishment. The lessons of past failures can show us where an organization's inability to work outside itself has led to unimaginable consequences, and yet we can easily point to overwhelming success when agencies have utilized their individual strengths by working together. We can learn from these case studies and use them as models as we move forward as a successful nation.

Knowledge sharing should be among the top priorities for the government when it comes to securing our digital infrastructure. Many of our adversaries use the same tools, tactics, and techniques to silently move through our networks; agencies need to share this data so we can present a solid, unified front in the face of cyberspace adversaries.

Additionally, protecting our digital infrastructure plays into the larger strategy of cyberspace deterrence. The Department of Defense publicly declared, "Defending the homeland is an important part of deterrence" (*Department of Defense*, 2011). We can effectively deny, disrupt, and minimize adversarial activity by securing our critical assets. These behaviors present a solid foundation that our government leaders rely on when discussing response actions towards an adversary for cyberspace aggression.

The US commercial sector needs guidance on proper cyber-hygiene. Large companies can often afford to hire cyberspace security experts, but small businesses may not. Wars now target the will of a population in addition to military forces, and altering a person's livelihood is a quick way to erode support of military action.

CASE STUDIES

Success with respect to DHS defending digital infrastructure, information technologies, and Industrial Control Systems hinges on successful collaboration. The USG response to Hurricane Katrina, and findings detailed in the 9/11 Commission Report, punctuate the need for increased interaction between organizations overall. The intelligence community, in response to the 9/11 Commission Report, moved from a position of "need to know" to "need to share." FEMA was totally reorganized due to their post-Katrina performance. The failures experienced by government collaborations usually garner much attention—especially during campaign season—so this chapter will focus on successes to show that collaboration can, and does, work.

Below are three recent examples of our country, both governmentally and commercially, leveraging the idea of collaboration to positively respond to disastrous or difficult situations. These examples prove the efficacy of collaboration and will hopefully fuel your imagination for areas where collaboration can work. Information technology is a significant collaboration enabler and must be used to its fullest potential.

Haiti Disaster Response

On January 12, 2010, a 7.0 magnitude earthquake struck Haiti just outside the highly populated capital city of Port-au-Prince. There was a lot of destruction to the national infrastructure, and death in the city was tremendous during and after the incident. In fact, the earthquake aftermath was far more serious than the actual trembles. The international community recognized the country was in distress and banded together to bring much-needed aid to the Haitian people. The USG specifically created the Haiti Joint Information Center (JIC) led by the US Agency for International Development (USAID). The purpose of the JIC was to provide information to external agencies and partners. A common problem with international aid in disaster areas is poor coordination caused by a lack of information. The JIC became a nexus for all USG aid to the Haitian government and played a key role in the disaster relief effort.

USAID, under the US Department of State, led the collaboration, but many government and international organizations collaborated with them. Agencies such as the US Department of Defense, US Department of Homeland Security, US Department of Health and Human Services, World Health Organization, and many other Non-Governmental Organizations. The JIC is a prime example of the types of collaboration to expect in the future. The common thread of this collaboration that led to its success was helping the Haitian people. The scale of the disaster was so large, no one organization could have helped Haiti to the same degree that the international community together did.

Google Hack and Response

The collaboration in response to the Haiti Earthquake was deliberate and intentional on the part of the USG. In contrast, the response to a hacking spree of US companies that happened in the last half of 2009, code named Operation Aurora, was not so deliberate, yet the results were just as effective, relatively speaking.

To summarize the incident, Google first publicly disclosed the exploitation in a blog post titled "A New Approach to China," in January 2010—the same day as the Haiti Earthquake. In the post, Google asserted they were not the only targets of an advanced persistent attack. Further, a primary goal of the attackers was access to Chinese human rights activists' email accounts ("A new approach," 2010). The primary attack vector was an exploit written against the Microsoft Internet Explorer and triggered through highly successful spear-phishing campaigns.

The response, another collaboration involving international partners—though more commercial than governmental—was extremely effective. Google publicly announced they had been compromised and put the incident in the public domain. Several governments took the information and subsequently issued advisories against using the vulnerable application. Security researchers and information security specialists around the world began analyzing the code and developing countermeasures. Other companies discovered the intrusions and remediated them. Microsoft wrote and issued a patch for the vulnerability, shutting down the attack vector. In addition, other security researchers have continued analyzing the code, and even going so far as to fingerprint the code, which could lead to future attribution of the developers at some level.

Many of the organizations involved with Operation Aurora are highly technical, capable entities, but the amount of resources and time required to respond to the information technology breach was too large for any one company to address individually. The breadth of knowledge possessed by the security researchers, the initial announcement by Google sparking the efforts, the advisories by governments raising public awareness, and response by Microsoft to patch the vulnerability—only through collaboration was a broad, inclusive reaction possible.

Shared Responsibility, Pooled Resources

The Department of State has been charged with helping manage and distribute foreign aid, but due to recent wars in Iraq and Afghanistan, the Department of Defense has begun playing a larger role in assisting other countries. This role is officially outlined in Section 1206 Security Assistance Program of the National Defense Authorization Act of 2006 ("Section 1206", 2007). The Department of Defense is authorized to spend up to $200 million to help foreign countries become stable and counter terrorism.

Because of the overlapping roles between the Department of Defense and Department of State, Secretary Robert Gates penned a memo to Secretary Hilary Clinton outlining an idea called Shared Responsibility, Pooled Resources (Gates, 2009). In the memo, Secretary Gates recognized that the two departments have not always agreed on certain subjects and proposed a new idea that he believes will remove some of the obstacles to topics that have impeded progress in the past. Essentially, Secretary Gates advocated for collaboration between the Department of State and the Department of Defense for all of the right reasons. He even went so far as to specifically mention the financial resources would be in one pot and both parties would be required to agree on decisions, thus incentivizing the two departments to work. The effect of not working together would effectively freeze financial access for all involved—a strong motivator for results.

New initiatives are constantly being proposed in and around the Washington DC area for the betterment of our government. As of this writing, the State Department has yet to agree to the "Shared Responsibility, Pooled Resources" proposal, but that does not mean some form of this idea will not be instituted in the future. The memorandum gives us the inside-look at how our department secretaries are embracing the idea of collaboration to achieve new possibilities and extend their reach farther than ever before.

DHS AND COLLABORATION

There is a very strong likelihood an individual employee within DHS will need to collaborate at some level, between different offices or mission areas, or even as part of a joint task force at the highest levels of our government with other departments or nation states. Either way, collaboration and the principles of collaboration apply. DHS and the relationships within the organization are simply a microcosm of the larger relationships between departments. Each employee, no matter their position, must recognize the importance of collaboration within DHS.

In a US Government Accountability Office report titled "An Overview of Professional Development Activities Intended to Improve Interagency Collaboration," the office states, "gaps in national security staff knowledge and skills pose a barrier to the interagency collaboration" ("An Overview," 2011). The report goes on to point out that the Department of Homeland Security has one of the most comprehensive professional development training activities with respect to interagency collaboration, yet lacks professional rotational programs. The significance of the report is that knowledge and skill gaps, recognized at high-levels of government, can be prevented through adequate training and development.

DHS implemented structural and programmatic changes, based on a Homeland Security Review, to encourage and build a culture of collaboration. Not only were the organizational structures realigned with a new focus, but so were key projects. The DHS website states the department "leverages resources within federal, state, local, territorial, and tribal governments, coordinating multiple agencies and programs into a single, integrated effort focused on protecting the American people and their homeland." The department has acknowledged the need to collaborate and identify specific areas, like preventing terrorism and securing our borders and cyberspace.

DHS is on the right path towards building a successful, sustainable culture of collaboration. The ultimate success lies in the hands of those working for and with DHS. To enable individuals, they must be taught about collaboration and how to properly approach collaborative initiatives.

HOW TO COLLABORATE

Collaboration is ultimately about information flow. The information can be transmitted through many modes of communication, so having the ability to effectively communicate is a critical skill. This effective communication comes in many forms, such as drafting e-mail, verbal communication, nonverbal communication, and other components germane to emotional intelligence, especially in the domain of knowledge work.

The information flow within a collaborative team is built on trust. Ensuring congruence between interactions, perceived motivations, and the goal of the connection, can reinforce trust. Relationships are the single most important linkages to foster during collaborative efforts, because conflict will naturally arise. Transparency, common goals, and communication will only forge the relationships needed to successfully manage the conflict (Evans & Wolf, 2005).

The USG working environment today necessitates collaboration. No one factor has solely created the environment, but reduced resources contribute a major role in the necessity to collaborate—these include not only monetary resources, but also intellectual resources. Moreover, politically speaking, the allocation of resources is more about the top-line than it is about the bottom-line. Agencies are repeatedly told to "do more with less," which translates into, "Increase the top-line while lowering the bottom-line." The way to achieve this dichotomy is consolidating resources and leveraging strengths, where possible, thereby allaying organizational weaknesses.

Faster decision-making and response cycles are an additional, compelling reason for collaboration. Information technology has enabled ubiquitous, near real-time access to information—especially with the advances in mobile technology. In the chapter written by Don Adams in this volume, Adams highlights enterprise service buses, comprised of Service Oriented Architecture, Business Process Management, and Business Optimization, being used to make quick changes to end user applications, resulting in a better flexibility and adaptation to external business environments. Decisions, especially choices involving multiple components of government, must be made faster, and the ability to rapidly respond to changing conditions must evolve. The example of the Haiti Joint Information Center and the "Shared Responsibility, Pooled Resources" proposal are great examples of collaborations at the highest levels of government and show USG departments working to stay engaged in shaping the way our nation deals with decisions and challenges.

Intellectual capital is a large national asset that starts with individuals and has worldwide impact. The collaborative environment is a great facilitator of sharing information. Innovative projects in the commercial sector often rely on matrix teams to develop the next business venture. Matrix organizations refer to collaboration on a smaller scale within a company. The USG can accomplish the same goal. Therefore, it is important for individuals to continually develop themselves by learning, but the real value is in what they do with that knowledge. Do they keep it to themselves and become a linchpin, one man strong, or do they share their knowledge, teach others, and multiply the effect they have on those around them?

To allow successful, repeatable collaboration, organizations must have a culture that develops and rewards collaboration (Ibarra & Hansen, 2011). Ibarra and Hansen assert that collaborative leaders are needed to direct and mentor teams toward collaboration and ensure conflict is handled in a healthy manner. Collaborative leaders must work to build personal relationships outside of their comfort-zone and get to know people in strategic positions outside of their organization. Most importantly, a collaborative leader must demand results. The outcome of collaboration, what is actually produced, is directly proportional to the team's potential. However, the team's ability to meet that potential is directly proportional to the individuals involved. Leaders who demand results will provide the proper motivation for individuals to function as a cohesive team, navigating through healthy conflict, and producing something none of the disparate parts could have achieved on their own. Collaborations are not about individuals, but they cannot become successful without them. The common good must come first. Each individual must believe the group is more effective than the individuals are.

Healthy conflict within collaboration is "natural and necessary" (Weiss & Hughes, 2005). Collaborations are not immune to group dynamics. Healthy conflict is a positive interaction that can enhance teamwork. Typically, within teams or matrix organizations, conflict arises from competing interests, priorities, competencies, perspectives, and information. Again, trust can play a vital role in ensuring the conflict stays productive. Serious, high-performance collaborators learn how to deal with conflict in a wholesome manner. Conflict resolution is not the focus of this chapter, but there are many scholarly articles and case studies on the topic of collaboration conflict resolution. The reader is highly encouraged to spend some time developing an understanding of conflict management.

CONCLUSION

Collaboration is an effective way to enhance the way the USG operates. It is up to leaders to encourage collaboration, individuals to engage and develop key relationships, and everyone to acknowledge when collaborations succeed or learn from those that do not.

Operating in today's political, financial, and military environments compels our nation to find efficiencies whenever possible. While the US continues to rely on digital infrastructure, we must rely on collaborations, partnerships, and alliances to protect those vital interests. The scale is something never before seen, and the speeds at which events occur on the digital infrastructure require ever faster decision cycles. As a nation, we have the capacity to transcend and preempt catastrophes within our information technology, but to reach the level needed, we must capitalize on our intellectual capital while building the next generation of experts. Our nation is admittedly strained financially, and large monetary cuts have been projected for the foreseeable future. Collaboration and teaming are prime candidates to meeting mission needs while conserving resources.

Once we realize the synergy gained through collaborations, our nation will become even more efficient and effective at preserving the freedom of citizens within our borders, as well as our interests abroad. It is up to us to engage with each other, build relationships, and learn how to collaborate. It truly is a new way of doing our government's business.

REFERENCES

"A New Approach to China." 2010. January 12. http://googleblog.blogspot.com/2010/01/new-approach-to-china.html.

An Overview of Professional Development Activities Intended to Improve Interagency Collaboration, GAO-11-108. Washington, DC: General Accountability Office. 2011. http://www.gao.gov (accessed December 23, 2011).

Collaboration at the Department of Homeland Security. 2011. April 6. http://www.dhs.gov/xabout/gc_1301072402960.shtm.

Department of Defense Cyberspace Policy Report: A Report to Congress Pursuant to the National Defense Authorization Act for Fiscal Year 2011. Section 934. 2011. http://www.defense.gov/home/features/2011/0411_cyberstrategy/docs/NDAA%20Section%20934%20Report_For%20webpage.pdf.

Evans, P., and B. Wolf. 2005. "Collaboration Rules." (cover story). *Harvard Business Review* 83(7/8): 96–104.

Ibarra, H., and M. T. Hansen. 2011. "Are You a Collaborative Leader?" *Harvard Business Review* 89(7/8): 68–74.

Robert M. Gates, Memorandum for Secretary of State: Options for Remodeling Security Sector Assistance Authorities. OSD 13826-09. December 15, 2009. http://www.washingtonpost.com/wp-srv/nation/documents/Gates_to_Clinton_121509.pdf (accessed December 20, 2011).

Section 1206 Security Assistance Program—Findings on Criteria, Coordination, and Implementation, GAO-07-416R. Washington, DC: General Accountability Office, 2007. http://www.gao.gov (accessed December 23, 2011).

Stanton, T. H. 2008. *Defending Cyberspace: Protecting Individuals, Government Agencies, and Private Companies Against Persistent Evolving Threats*. Retrieved from http://advanced.jhu.edu/academic/government/publications/Defending_Cyberspace.pdf.

———. 2011. August 21. *Interagency Collaboration Can Maximize Tight Budgets*. http://www.federaltimes.com/article/20110821/ADOP06/108210305/1037/ADOP00.

Weiss, J., and J. Hughes. 2005. Want Collaboration? *Harvard Business Review*. 83(3): 93–101.

4

INTRODUCTION TO PART IV: RISK MANAGEMENT, DECISION MAKING, AND COMMUNICATION

In homeland security and counterterrorism, the total risk cannot be eliminated but it must be reduced and managed. In the first chapter of this section, Parnell, Dillon-Merrill, and Bresnick explain key risk management fundamentals and describe the importance of a systematic decision-making process for efficiently allocating antiterrorism resources. They offer strategies relevant to all organizations involved in homeland security that need to rationally allocate resources to protect critical infrastructure.

Vidali and Hutchens then outline significant lessons learned, best practices, and feasible approaches towards achieving a sustainable state of pervasive readiness, which is the concept of readiness as an integral part of the very fabric of a nation. The concept of readiness—the ability to prepare for, respond to, and recover from crises and natural disasters—is easy to grasp in principle, yet exceedingly difficult to implement. This is due to the fragmentation of processes within the public safety sector and a fundamental failure to understand the difference between capacity building and capability building to achieve readiness. A strategy is required that will enable heterogeneous public safety communities to achieve operational agility before, during, and after a crisis, while optimizing their allocation of funding to arrive at a balanced readiness posture. The authors offer a practical approach to establishing a framework for effectively measuring readiness against a government's prioritized Hazard/Threat Identification and Risk Assessment.

In order to have a credible message and communicate effectively about risk and risk management efforts, organizations must manage risks well. Prof. Baruch Fischoff's chapter offers key insights about the psychological perception of risk and offers guidelines for creating appropriate communication channels and relations with the public. This capability is key to delivering relevant information concisely and comprehensibly to the public during difficult times.

In times of crisis, effective risk communication can be vital, serving to guide how people react in response to a major incident. In this respect, risk communication is a fundamental part of managing the response to terrorism. To enhance its efforts at risk communication, in 2011 the Department of Homeland Security replaced the color-coded Homeland Security Advisory System (HSAS) with the National Terrorism Advisory System (NTAS). James Carafano examines the flaws of the HSAS and the framework laid out for the new NTAS system in terms of the principles of effective risk communication about terrorist threats.

16

INTEGRATING RISK MANAGEMENT WITH HOMELAND SECURITY AND COUNTERTERRORISM RESOURCE ALLOCATION DECISION MAKING

Dr. Gregory S. Parnell

Professor of System Engineering at the U.S. Military Academy at West Point; Senior Principal Analyst at Innovative Decisions, Inc.

Dr. Robin L. Dillon-Merrill

Associate Professor at McDonough School of Business, Georgetown University; Senior Principal Analyst at Innovative Decisions, Inc.

Terry A. Bresnick

Senior Principal Analyst at Innovative Decisions, Inc.

THE IMPACT OF TERRORISM ON NATIONAL, STATE, AND LOCAL COMMUNITY RESOURCE ALLOCATION

The attacks on New York City and Washington, DC, on September 11, 2001, and the human, physical, economic, and psychological devastation associated with the attacks have had a dramatic impact on decision making at the national, state, and local community levels. In response to the attacks, one of the largest government reorganizations resulted in the new Department of Homeland Security (DHS) with the goal to better focus the federal government to counter terrorism. Through DHS, the federal government has significantly increased spending on counterterrorism through federal programs and grants to states and cities. Also, significant changes have occurred in the Intelligence Community (IC) to provide better sharing of intelligence information. In addition, many organizational and resource allocation changes have been implemented by states and local communities.

As more counterterrorism resources have been made available at each level of government, cost-effective resource allocation has been a difficult challenge. Additionally, since 9/11 there has been an increasing recognition that models focusing on terrorism and resource allocation for counterterrorism measures need to consider that terrorists are intelligent adversaries who can adapt to our measures. Risk shifting is another important concern. If we spend money to reduce the risk in one city, we may not eliminate the risk, but rather just shift the risk to another city. For these reasons, more explicit decision frameworks are required to determine the best resource allocation strategies.

COUNTERTERRORISM (CT) DECISION-MAKING FRAMEWORK

The authors have developed a framework to describe the scope of counterterrorism (CT) decision making and to identify types of CT decisions. Table 16-1 identifies the decision-making level, the purpose of the decision, the type of decision, the timing of the decisions, and the decision implementation.

Resource allocation decisions include planning, programming, budgeting, and execution of the budget (i.e., the first four types of decisions). The fifth type of decision is real-time crisis management, and in these situations, the decision maker only has time to respond according to plans and programs that have been implemented. However, prior to the actual crisis, resource allocation decisions include all levels of decision makers, all purposes of actions, various periods for decision making, and various elements to evaluate project alternatives. In addition to including all levels, the resource allocation framework must

Table 16-1 Counterterrorism Decision-Making Framework	**Level of Decision (Who)**	**Purpose (Why)**	**Type of Decision (What)**	**Timing of Decisions (When)**	**Decision Elements (How)**
	International, National, Non-Governmental Organizations, Federal Department, State, County, Local Community, Companies, Individuals	Prevent Deter, Detect, Warn, Protect, Respond, Recover	Planning, Programming, Budgeting Executing Budget, Crisis Management	Multi-year, Annual, Monthly, Real-time	Law, Policy, Procedures People, Technology

look across columns in Table 16-1, because different levels will have different priorities. For example, the local communities and the county governments will primarily serve as first responders if an event occurs, so they may focus more on allocating resources to response and recovery activities, while the federal government may allocate more resources to detection and warning systems.

The initial budget increases following 9/11 brought about a transfusion of new funding that went primarily to the most obvious benefits including upgrading facilities (e.g., additional physical barriers), increasing the number of personnel (e.g., air marshals), changing procedures (e.g., increased screening), and enhancing knowledge through research studies (e.g., bioscreening), information sharing, and so on. As additional funds continue to be made available, national, state, and community leaders need to continually assess the appropriate focus for their level of decision making and how they can integrate CT budgetary decisions into their resource allocation processes.

THREE COUNTERTERRORISM RESOURCE ALLOCATION APPROACHES

CT projects are having, and will continue to have, a significant impact on the funding available for each organization's mission, and ultimately, the services that these government organizations are able to provide the public. Funding CT initiatives involves significant trade-offs and opportunity costs—that is, funds allocated to CT initiatives are not available for other services. We believe that three major CT resource allocation approaches exist:

1. *Develop a standalone CT resource allocation process.* In this approach an organization (public or private) establishes a funding level for all projects that will reduce the risk of terrorism. All CT projects compete for these funds. The allocation process involves identifying the current risks of terrorism and funding projects that reduce these risks. The key analytical tasks are risk assessment and risk management.

2. *Integrate CT into an organization's mission assurance resource allocation process.* In this approach, the organization establishes a funding level for all mission assurance activities that reduce the risks to achieving the organization's mission and make systems more resilient. Mission assurance projects would include all projects designed to deter, defend, protect, or respond to natural

disasters and man-made threats. This approach is consistent with the "All-Hazards" approach advocated by the Federal Emergency Management Agency (FEMA). Projects could reduce the likelihood of the occurrence of an event that impacts mission accomplishment, reduce the vulnerability of the system to an event, and/or reduce the consequences of the event, if it occurs. CT projects would compete with other mission assurance projects for the mission assurance funding. This process encourages synergies between these projects. Again, the key analytical tasks are risk assessment and risk management, but the scope is different. The scope is all mission assurance projects.

3. *Integrate CT funding into an organization's overall resource allocation process.* In this approach CT is considered an important requirement that the organization must meet. However, CT projects must compete for funding with all other organization projects. Funding decisions are based on the costs and benefits of each project. CT projects are assessed based on the "benefits" they provide in terms of risk reduction and resiliency. Again, risk assessment and risk management will be key considerations, but the scope is the entire project portfolio of the organization.

In all three resource allocation processes there will be significant trade-offs between mission, risk, and customer (stakeholder) impact. Risk management actions will impact customers and stakeholders. CT projects may have negative impacts such as inconveniencing customers (e.g., airport screening) and infringing on civil liberties. Since 9/11, American citizens have been more willing to tolerate inconveniences and some impacts on their civil liberties to be protected against terrorism. However, this may change if significant time passes without a successful major terrorist event.

Because of the trade-offs required, we believe that successful CT resource allocation will involve four key tasks: stakeholder analysis, risk assessment, evaluations of multiple (often conflicting) objectives, and risk management. Organizations facing CT decision making need objective clear, traceable analysis processes to support resource allocation decision making. This process should be based on decision and risk analysis techniques. Kirkwood (1997) offers a useful framework for resource allocation decision making that uses (1) multi-objective decision analysis to quantify the benefits and (2) optimization to determine the most benefit for the resources available. Furthermore, to be ultimately successful, organizations must develop a risk management culture that identifies, analyzes, and reduces life cycle risks.

LESSONS FROM OTHER IMPORTANT RISK APPLICATIONS

In the previous section, we recommended that risk analysis and risk management will be key techniques for CT resource allocation. Risk analysis has been successfully used in several important applications. In this section, we examine lessons learned from risk analysis research and resource allocation procedures that have been used in some of these applications.

Natural Disasters

Researchers interested in natural disasters have developed a deep knowledge base on many topics of importance to counterterrorism. This research includes, for example, studies on how to most effectively communicate warnings to the public (e.g., Mileti and O'Brien 1992), how people prepare, respond, and recover from disasters (e.g., Mileti 1999), and how to effectively plan mass evacuations (e.g., Mileti 1999). Wenger et al. (1975) empirically examined the myths associated with individual behaviors in response to a disaster and found, for example, that panic and looting rarely occur, while altruistic behaviors are the more common response. Also, they found that most of the initial search and rescue activity is accomplished by the victims themselves rather than organizations generally categorized as first responders.

In order to share learning among CT efforts and natural disasters, FEMA is advocating an "all-hazards" approach to emergency operations planning at the state and local levels. Because of the diversity of both risks and targets, an all-hazards approach that focuses on preparedness and encompasses terrorism, natural disasters, and other environmental challenges will likely present a more optimal use of resources. The full list of FEMA hazards includes dam safety, earthquakes, extreme heat, fires, floods, hazardous materials, hurricanes, landslides, multi-hazard, nuclear, terrorism, thunderstorms, tornadoes, tsunamis, volcanoes, wildfires, and winter storms (FEMA Hazards 2004). This approach is similar to the mission assurance resource allocation approach described previously. FEMA has developed special software to do Benefit-Cost Analysis for Hazard Reduction projects (FEMA/BCA 2004).

Commercial Nuclear Power

The nuclear power industry, more than any other risk application area, has integrated the use of probabilistic risk analysis (PRA) for risk analysis and risk management. The original probabilistic risk analysis process was developed in the commercial nuclear power industry in the 1970s (USNRC 1975). The U.S. Nuclear Regulatory Commission and the nuclear power industry jointly developed fundamental procedures and handbooks for PRA models (USNRC 1983; and Vesely 1981). Today, the nuclear power industry is moving toward risk-based regulations, specifically, using PRA to analyze and demonstrate lower cost regulations without compromising safety (Davison and Vantine 1998; Frank 1988). Research in the nuclear industry has also supported advances in human reliability analysis, external events analysis, and common cause failure analysis (USNRC 1991; Mosleh 1993; and USNRC 1996).

Space Systems
During the Apollo program, pessimistic risk estimates discouraged NASA's use of the probabilistic risk analysis (PRA) methodology. Furthermore, the notion of failure risks often clashes with the engineering culture that is primarily based on safety factors. The problem with safety factors is that they do not allow prioritization. Since the Challenger accident, NASA management has increasingly adopted the use of PRA for the identification and management of risks in the space shuttle program and for other development projects (e.g., Galileo and Cassini) (Paté-Cornell and Dillon 2001). These PRA models are currently implemented in a software tool called QRAS (Quantitative Risk Assessment System), which was specifically designed to address the risk modeling requirements of space missions (Groen et al. 2002). QRAS uses a combination of event sequence diagrams and fault trees where the event sequence diagrams are used to describe possible risk scenarios and fault trees model the details of each event in the scenario. We describe these tools and others in the next section.

Information Assurance (IA)
Information assurance is defined as activities that protect and defend information systems by ensuring their availability, integrity, authentication, confidentiality, and non-repudiation (JP 3-13 1998). Information assurance requires a risk assessment and risk management approach that will deal effectively with life cycle threats from adversaries to information systems and information. Cohen, in his information system classification scheme, lists 37 potential adversaries (Cohen 1997). In general, all references agree on a basic set of adversaries; they differ in how specific adversary subsets should be grouped. One

useful grouping of these adversaries is into nine major adversary classes (Buckshaw et al. 2004):

1. Foreign Intelligence Services (FIS)
2. Information Warriors
3. Cyber Terrorists/Activists
4. Hackers/Crackers/Script Kiddies
5. Malicious Insiders
6. The Press
7. Organized Crime/Lone Criminals
8. Law Enforcement
9. Industrial Competitors

The research that has been done in analyzing attack scenarios for information systems and networks is an important approach that can be applied to far broader types of adversarial attacks beyond IA.

COMPARISON OF CT WITH OTHER RISK APPLICATIONS

Table 16-2 compares counterterrorism with these other risk applications. CT has many similarities and some major differences to other risk applications. A shaded box in Table 16-2 indicates that the source of the risk applies to that application. The major difference among applications is the primary source of risk. CT and IA both have similar primary sources of risk: foreign governments, groups, and individuals.

Table 16-2

Sources of Risk in Important Risk Application Areas

Sources of Risk		Anti-Terrorism	Natural Disasters	Commercial Nuclear Power	Space Systems	Information Assurance
Primary source of risk	Foreign countries					
	Hostile groups					
	Hostile individuals					
	Environment (weather, earthquakes, etc.)					
	Technology					
Secondary sources of risk	Organizational issues					
	System design					
	Human error					

In both cases, the major risks are from malicious attacks propagated by intelligent and determined adversaries who can adapt their strategies to circumvent protective measures (Bier 2004). IA differs from CT in that technology is also included as a primary source of risk for IA because even without malicious behavior and intelligent adversaries, hardware fails and software has bugs. Technology is identified as a primary source of risk for commercial nuclear power—for example, valves and pumps fail in nuclear plants and require maintenance—and while nuclear power plants are designed to withstand severe natural disasters, in the worst case, environmental factors could pose risks to the plants. For natural disasters, the risks are from environmental factors. Hurricanes and earthquakes can be devastating, but they cannot become stronger in response to actions taken to fortify systems. For space systems, the hostile environmental conditions of space are primary risks as well as the technology. Systems can be damaged by orbital debris and parachutes can fail to open for space probes.

The secondary sources of risk are common to all application areas. Organizational factors refer to an institution's culture and management practices, and these factors can be sources of risk in all applications. In the Columbia Investigation Report, the board states that the organizational practices of NASA were as much to blame for the accident as the foam debris (CAIB 2003). For example, one factor common to all application areas considered here is organizational barriers that prevent effective communication of critical safety information and stifle professional differences of opinion. This problem is a risk for counterterrorism and was cited by the 9/11 Commission in discussing problems with the coordination of intelligence among the major agencies. System design errors occur in all applications; this is realized when there is a major event that the system should have been able to withstand but could not. Similarly, all the applications are subject to human errors.

DISCUSSION OF ANALYSIS TOOLS AND TECHNIQUES

Based on our review of the characteristics of CT resource allocation, we will focus our review on the tools of systems engineering, risk analysis (risk assessment and risk management), decision analysis, game theory, and benefit-cost analysis techniques. When applying any of these tools, one must remember that many personal judgments and biases influence people's future behavior in terms of decision making regarding risks and uncertainties. A separate chapter of this handbook, "The Psychological Perception of Risk," by Dr. Baruch Fischhoff, discusses some of these factors in more detail. What follows is a brief summary of some of the biases that are relevant to our discussion and that need to be considered when evaluating risk trade-off decisions:

- *Availability* (Tversky and Kahneman 1974). Events are judged as frequent or probable to the extent that they are readily "available" in memory. People tend to judge events as likely or frequent if the events are easy to imagine or recall—however, the memorial availability of objects and events depends on many factors besides the actual frequency.

- *Invincibility* (Weinstein 1987). Negative events are judged less likely to happen to the subject than to his or her peers (i.e., "It can't happen to me … "). Also, if risks are preventable, people believe they will be more effective than others at avoiding the risk.

- *Confirmatory Bias* (Doherty et al. 1996; Wason 1960 and 1968). Given information favoring a focal hypothesis, subjects rarely select diagnostic data relevant to an alternative hypothesis. In the case of the Shuttle Columbia, the one analytical resource available, Crater, predicted damage deeper than the actual tile thickness. Rather than become concerned, NASA engineers discounted the evidence because previous calibration tests with small projectiles showed that Crater predicted deeper penetrations than were actually observed (CAIB 2003). It was easier for the personnel involved to disregard the evidence than consider an alternative hypothesis.

- *Disregard for Event Independence.* People assume that since a disaster has recently occurred, it is less likely to recur soon—that is, "lightning doesn't strike twice in the same place" (Lindell and Perry 1992).

- *Near-Miss.* Events that are near-misses with no obvious sign of "near-failure" can decrease a decision maker's perception of the risk. Feeling the situation to be less risky, decision makers are more confident of a successful outcome and more likely to choose a risky alternative than those without near-miss information (Dillon and Tinsley 2008).

These and other biases contribute to the challenge of making decisions when risks and uncertainties are involved, and therefore decision makers need to rely on tools to support their planning, analysis, and resource allocation processes.

Systems Engineering Techniques

Terrorists are intelligent, adaptive adversaries. Successful terrorists will plan an attack from a systems perspective. They will seek the weakest link in the system that will help them achieve their objectives and attack at that point. The 9/11 attacks were the result of systems planning. The terrorists believed that the airline security systems could be defeated. They were successful in their attempts to simultaneously commandeer four airplanes. In doing so, they defeated policy, technology, procedures, and people. They took advantage of policy and procedural gaps between the FAA and the military. Only the bravery of passengers prevented the fourth airplane from potentially crashing in Washington, DC.

To be effective in deterring and preventing such threats, homeland security planners must also take a systems perspective. They must understand how the elements of the system operate including organizations, hardware systems, software systems, and human components of the system. Systems engineering offers many useful tools for understanding systems and system complexity (Buede 2009; Parnell, Driscoll, and Henderson 2011). These tools include stakeholder analysis, systems design, systems simulation, and systems analysis.

Alternative Generation Table

Alternative generation tables are common tools used in system engineering (and in decision analysis). The purpose of this tool is to identify the key dimensions of the alternatives, to compile lists of the different decisions that can be made for each dimension, and to generate an alternative by combining one decision from each key dimension.

As a simple example, Table 16-3 shows an alternative generation table for a large city's response to an elevated alert for a potential chemical release by a terrorist. There are four functions that each alternative must address: threat detection, warning, protection, and response. Each function can be performed by several means. Each alternative uses one or more of the means to perform each function.

Table 16-3

Illustrative Example of an Alternative Generation Table

Elevated Alert Alternatives	Detect	Warn	Protect	Respond
Manpower Intensive	Patrols	Sirens	Containment	Citizens
High Tech	Ground and Airborne Sensors	TV	Gas Masks	Emergency Medical Teams
Combined	Both	Multimedia	Both	National Guard

For example, the High Tech alternative uses ground and air sensors for detection, multimedia for warning, gas masks for protection, and the National Guard for response.

Advantages and Disadvantages. There are several advantages of the alternative generation table. First, the table explicitly identifies of the dimensions of the alternative. Second, the table can be used to focus creativity on the new ways of performing each function and the overall alternative. Third, the table helps define integrated alternatives. Fourth, the table generates a lot of alternatives ($3^4=81$ in the simple example above.) Finally, the table provides a useful tool to communicate with stakeholders and decision makers. Unfortunately, if all functions are not identified, the alternatives will not be complete.

Risk Analysis Techniques

Risk should be evaluated at the level of analysis that is sufficient for planning effective risk mitigation strategies. Often, a categorization or screening of risks based on a risk matrix may be sufficient. In some cases, the relative importance provided by risk ranking is more critical and a more sophisticated technique is required. Because many definitions have evolved for several key risk concepts, we provide a set of definitions in Table 16-4 for relevant terms before describing several

Table 16-4

Definitions of Risk Analysis Terminology

Different disciplines use different risk analysis terminology. We will use the following definitions [DHS, 2010, NIPC, 2002, and SEI, 1996].

- **Asset**—Person, structure, facility, information, material, or process that has value (DHS, 2010).
- **Event**—An occurrence that has the potential to impact an asset (e.g., loss of power).
- **Attack**—An action by an adversary or competitor aimed at degrading the operation of an asset, denying use of it, or destroying it.
- **Probability**—The likelihood the risk will occur (SEI, 1996). When one is assessing counterterrorism risks, the threat probability is determined by both the capability and the intent.
- **Threat**—Natural or man-made occurrence, individual, entity, or action that has or indicates the potential to harm life, information, operations, the environment, and/or property (DHS, 2010).
- **Vulnerability**—Physical feature or operational attribute that renders an entity, asset, system, network, or geographic area open to exploitation or susceptible to a given hazard (DHS, 2010).
- **Impact/consequence**—Effect of an event, incident, or occurrence (DHS, 2010).
- **Timeframe**—The period when action is required in order to mitigate the risk (SEI, 1996).
- **Thresholds for acceptable risks**—All the resources in the world cannot mitigate all possible risks; therefore, in most situations a level (i.e., threshold) must be determined where risks that fall below the that level in severity are simply accepted and no resources are expended mitigating those risks.
- **Risk**—Potential for an unwanted outcome resulting from an incident, event, or occurrence, as determined by its likelihood and the associated consequences (DHS, 2010).
- **Countermeasure**—Action, measure, or device intended to reduce an identified risk (DHS, 2010).
- **Risk assessment**—Product or process which collects information and assigns values to risks for the purpose of informing priorities, developing or comparing courses of action, and informing decision making (DHS, 2010).
- **Risk management**—Process of identifying, analyzing, assessing, and communicating risk and accepting, avoiding, transferring or controlling it to an acceptable level considering associated costs and benefits of any actions taken (DHS, 2010).

important risk analysis techniques including fault trees, threat/vulnerability/consequence tables, risk matrices, Failure Modes and Effects Analysis/Critical Items Lists, and probabilistic risk analysis.

Fault Trees (Attack Trees)

Fault trees have been in use in reliability analysis since the 1960s. They were originally developed by Bell Telephone Laboratories to evaluate the safety of the Minuteman Launch Control System (Henley and Kumamoto 1992). Special applications of fault trees have been referred to as threat trees, attack trees, and vulnerability trees (Buckshaw et al. 2004). In a fault tree, an undesirable event is postulated and the possible scenarios for this top event to occur are systematically identified (Modarres 1993). Through the analysis, all possible component failures are identified that can contribute to the occurrence of the top event. Figure 16-1 presents an example attack tree (Buckshaw et al. 2004). The analysis considered possible paths that an adversary could use to defeat the confidentiality of an e-mail transmission. In order to obtain access to the e-mail information, the adversary would need to both intercept the e-mail and decrypt it. In the branch for intercepting the e-mail, the adversary could obtain the e-mail one of two ways: he or she could have installed a sniffer that picked up the message or an insider could have forwarded the message to the adversary. Several options are shown in Figure 16-1 for how the adversary could decrypt the message.

Figure 16-1

Example fault/attack
tree

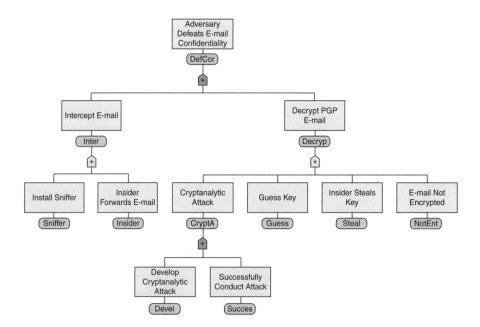

Advantages and Disadvantages. The primary advantages of fault trees are (1) a fault tree analysis is focused on identifying paths in the system that can lead to failure, (2) the analyst can concentrate on one particular system failure at a time, (3) the results provide a graphical aid to help managers visualize system weaknesses, and (4) the trees can serve as a basis for more sophisticated risk analysis techniques such as probabilistic risk analysis. Disadvantages include (1) only problems that contribute to the top event are modeled so the model may have limited applicability in a dynamic threat environment where threats and vulnerabilities are constantly changing and (2) in its traditional form, component outcomes are Boolean (i.e., failed state or not failed state), but real situations may have many partial failure states.

Threat, Vulnerability, Consequence Tables

An example of the asset vulnerability-consequence table is shown in Table 16-5. Such tables allow for a systematic consideration of each asset. The table can be used to identify and assess critical assets, analyze vulnerabilities, and assess risks based on consequences.

Advantages and Disadvantages. These tables are useful tools for screening or categorizing major assets, but because of the focus on consequences and the lack of any likelihood estimates, this method does not distinguish between the low- and the high-probability events. Also, the focus on consequences can cause a misallocation of resources to very low probability events rather than more likely events with less extreme consequences.

Risk Matrices

Risk matrices are constructed of ordinal scales used to "score" risks. A scale index associates specified levels with qualitative descriptions.

Table 16-5	Assets	Undesirable Events	Loss Assessment
	Key personnel	Loss of availability due to injury or death	High
Asset Vulnerability-Consequence Assessment Table (ARM 1996 and CIA 1996)	File server	Loss of availability due to power disruption	Critical
	Customer data	Loss of confidentiality due to unauthorized insider access	High
	Principal production facility	Loss of availability due to natural disaster	Critical
	Pipeline	Loss of availability due to sabotage	Medium

Figure 16-2

Example risk matrix

Source: Adapted
from Miltary
Standard 882C and
multinational oil
company.

Probability of Occurrence	I Catastrophic	II Critical	III Marginal	IV Negligible
A Frequent	I A	II A	III A	IV A
B Probable	I B	II B	III B	IV B
C Occasional	I C	II C	III C	IV C
D Remote	I D	II D	III D	IV D
E Improbable	I E	II E	III E	IV E

		Risk Level
IA, IB, IC, IIA, IIB, and IIIA	Unacceptable (reduce risk through countermeasures)	1
ID, IIC, IID, IIIB, and IIIC	Undesirable (management decision required)	2
IE, IIE, IIID , IIIE, IVE and IVB	Acceptable with review by management	3
IVC, IVD, IVE	Acceptable without Review	4

Matrices can be used individually or in conjunction with other more detailed methods. Figure 16-2 shows an example of this technique.

Advantages and Disadvantages. Risk matrices are useful tools for screening or categorizing major risks versus minor risks. But because of the lack of any likelihood estimates, this method does not distinguish between the low- and the high-probability problems. Because of a lack of knowledge concerning potential likelihoods, the results can cause excess resources and concern to be expended on very low probability issues rather than on more likely ones. With tightened budgets or more complex decisions (e.g., the need to rank risks or make design trade-offs), a more sophisticated risk analysis technique may be required. When using risk matrices as a screening tool for a more quantitative analysis, however, one should be careful of the overall magnitude of the risks that have been assumed to be negligible.

Failure Modes and Effects Analysis and Critical Items Lists (FMEA/CIL)

Failure Modes and Effects Analysis and Critical Items Lists (FMEA/ CIL) originated as a formal methodology in the 1960s when demands for improved safety and reliability extended studies of component failures to include the effects of the failures on the systems of which they were a part (Bowles 1998). FMEA is an inductive analysis that systematically details all possible failure modes and identifies their resulting effects on the entire system. Possible single failure modes in a system are identified and analyzed to determine the effect on surrounding components and the system. Most FMEAs have a criticality component, and one of the most common methods is the Risk Priority Number (RPN). The RPN for a failure mode is determined from an ordinal scoring and multiplication of three components: the likelihood of occurrence, the severity, and the likelihood of detection. For example, the likelihood of occurrence would score a 10 if there is considered to be a *very high* likelihood, the severity ranking may score a 4 for *minor effects,* and the likelihood of detection may be a 6 if the failure is *detectable with an instrument during regular operations.* For this example, the RPN is 240. RPNs for different system components are then compared to set risk priorities.

In general, the steps in the FMEA process are as follows (Onodera 1997):

1. Definition of system
2. Development of functional and reliability block diagram
3. Extraction of failure modes
4. Analysis on FMEA worksheet
5. Analysis of failure causes and failure effects
6. (Optional) Identification of failure detection and failure probability
7. (Optional) Evaluation of criticality level
8. Countermeasures and recommendations

Table 16-6 provides an example FMEA analysis for a component of a missile system (adapted from Henley and Kumamoto 1992).

Advantages and Disadvantages. The main advantage of the FMEA process is its simplicity. Because of the lack of statistical data in many situations, the validity of likelihood estimates are often challenged, and FMEA avoids this problem. The method is useful for analyzing risks that do not involve complex trade-offs, for example, in the development of inspection plans. Also, FMEA is useful early in the design process when little operational data is available to identify potential

Table 16-6

FMEA Example
(Henley and
Kumamoto 1992)

Item	Failure Modes	Cause of Failure	Possible Effects	Criticality	Possible Action to Reduce Failure Rate or Effects
Motor case	Rupture	a. Poor workmanship b. Defective materials c. Damage during transportation d. Damage during handling e. Overpressurization	Destruction of missile	Critical	Quality control of manufacturing process and materials; inspection and pressure testing of completed cases; suitable packaging during transportation and handling

functional failure modes and when the design is still easily changed. The primary shortcoming of the FMEA process is that the analysis generally does not include notions of failure probability. Also, it may not recognize the risks from a component that appears in several parts of the system and from external events that damage multiple components at once. CIL can be misleading because a criticality 1 component with a low probability of failure may represent a smaller risk than a criticality 3 item with a higher probability of failure. Also, numerical scales that are not based on the explicit assessment of the risk but rather on the subjective and implicit combinations of frequencies and consequences can be misleading.

Probabilistic Risk Analysis (PRA)

A PRA seeks to measure the risks inherent in a system's design and operation by quantifying both the likelihood of various possible low-probability accident sequences and their consequences. PRA is based on a functional analysis of the system, identification of the failure modes, and estimation of the probabilities of external events and component failures. The PRA process for a particular facility starts with an identification of the initiating events of accident sequences, computation of the probabilities of reaching different final systems states given the initiating events, and evaluation of the consequences of different degrees of system failure. A PRA model is usually based on event sequence diagrams and fault trees. The results of a PRA are often represented by a distribution of the probabilities of different potential system states (i.e., a risk curve) based on best estimates of the model and parameter values (Paté-Cornell 1996).

Figure 16-3 shows a high-level probabilistic risk analysis for the failure of one Mars Rover in 2003.

The data shown are for illustrative purposes only and are shown in Bayesian network format. Major events with significant risks were modeled and included: schedule failure, launch failure, failure in

Figure 16-3

Example high-level probabilistic analysis of failure risk of Mars Rover (Paté-Cornell, Dillon, and Guikema 2003)

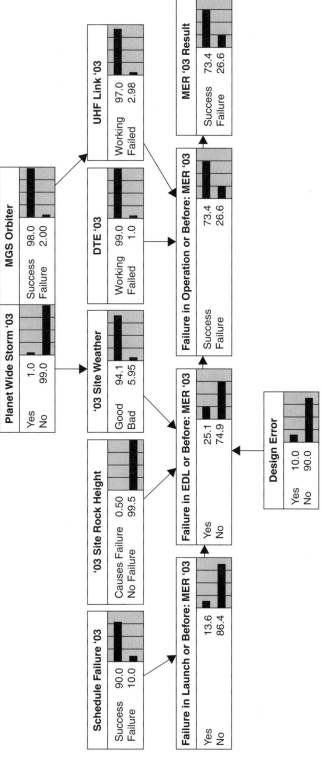

entry-descent-landing (EDL), and failure in operations. The success of these major events are influenced by other uncertain events including the rock height at the landing site, the weather, possible design errors, and the communications channels (direct-to-earth, or DTE, link; ultra high frequency or UHF link; and the Mars Global Surveyor, or MGS, link). Based on this illustrative data, the rover has about a 1 in 4 chance of failure.

Advantages and Disadvantages. PRA permits ranking problems based on their probabilities (mean future frequencies) and consequences. This ranking is useful for setting priorities when budgets are limited. PRA is most useful when little statistical data are available to assess the failure probability of a whole system. The PRA focuses on decomposing the system into subsystems and components for which more data are generally available. The major criticism is that, depending on the level of detail, PRAs may require large amounts of data and in most cases must rely on subjective estimates of probability. In addition, event tree models do not include the potential actions of adaptive adversaries.

Decision Analysis Techniques

The primary objective of decision analysis is to determine which alternative course of action will maximize the expected utility for the decision maker. Decision analysis is based on a set of logical axioms and is a systematic procedure to aggregate probabilities and preferences based upon those axioms (Bodily 1992). Decision analysis provides the framework for including values and preferences to determine if the potential benefits are worth the associated risks, but one of the tools of risk analysis previously discussed is needed to quantify the risk of potential alternatives. Risk analyses are often carried out as part of a decision analysis, for example, for decisions that affect the likelihood that accidents or exposures result in fatalities (Keeney 1982).

Unique to decision analysis is the creation of a preference model to evaluate the alternatives and possible consequences. This preference model includes information about value trade-offs, equity concerns, and risk attitudes (Keeney 1982). Figure 16-4 shows the values hierarchy that was developed as part of an information assurance multiple objective decision analysis model of how an adversary values an attack on an information system (Buckshaw et al. 2004). With decision analysis (Kirkwood 1997), a complete mathematical model can be developed to evaluate the adversary's attacks. As shown, the hierarchy includes an overall objective and four measures. The adversary wants to maximize his or her attack value based on four components: maximizing the

Figure 16-4

Adversary value
hierarchy

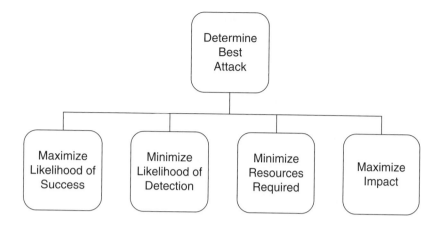

likelihood of success, minimizing the likelihood of detection, minimizing resources required, and maximizing the impact of the attack.

Advantages and Disadvantages. The advantage of decision analysis is the systematic treatment of preferences, alternatives, and uncertainty. The disadvantage of decision analysis is that it takes decision maker support and time to obtain preferences (from senior leaders and key stakeholders), alternatives (technical experts), and probabilities (technical experts).

Scenario Analysis

Scenarios are an "internally consistent story about how events relevant to your decision *might* develop over time" (Kirkwood 1997). Scenario analysis is an excellent technique for understanding the potential consequences of decisions due to uncertainties about the future. Scenarios have been used for over 20 years by decision analysts (Keeney and Raiffa 1976, p. 465) and risk analysts. Scenarios are often represented with tree structures. If the scenario trees include key decision points, then they are referred to as a decision tree. If the scenarios only include probabilistic events, then they are often called event sequence diagrams. Kirkwood (1997) provides a summary of the scenario literature relevant to decision analysis. Kirkwood recommends that scenarios be used for design of alternatives and assessment of alternatives. Scenario analyses have been used to avoid strategic surprise (Engelbrecht et al. 1995) and to evaluate system concepts (Jackson et al. 1999).

The following would be illustrative scenarios that could be used for Homeland Security risk analysis:

- A large truck bomb explodes in tunnel in a major city.
- A bioterrorism event occurs on a mass transit system.

- Coordinated information attacks on the telecommunications system.
- Destruction of multiple dams.
- Simultaneous attacks on the oil refineries and pipelines.

Advantages and Disadvantages. The major advantage of scenarios is that they help bound the decision space when we cannot reasonably identify all of the possible outcomes. The disadvantage of scenarios is that they take time to develop, and they may not be all inclusive of the possible terrorist attacks.

Game Theory Models

The tools described above are useful for assessing the probabilities of different scenarios while including the preferences of the decision maker. The challenge exists when we can no longer model the problem simply from the decision maker's perspective but need to consider two sides in competition. Game theory models can be constructed to include both an attacker and a defender (Bier 2004; Dresher 1961; Paté-Cornell and Guikema 2002). In a game theory model, one would consider how each side would respond to intelligence information about the other side's actions during the last time period, and would model each side's decisions regarding actions in the upcoming time period based on the information that each has accumulated so far.

Advantages and Disadvantages. The major advantage of game theory is that the models can include intelligent adversaries who would adopt different offensive strategies based on the defensive actions taken by the defender. The disadvantage is that they take time to develop, and at some point, an arbitrary starting and ending point need to be established.

Intelligent Adversary Models

The use of event tree models designed for natural hazard and engineering system risk analysis for homeland security risk analysis of intelligent, adaptive adversaries has been criticized by researchers (Parnell et al., 2010) and National Academy reviews (NRC 2008). One of the earliest efforts to combine decision analysis and game theory was Paté-Cornell and Guikema (2002). For a summary of the issues, the literature, and a comparison of events trees with intelligent adversary models, see Merrick and Parnell (2011). Figure 16-5 provides an example of an intelligent adversary model using decision trees where decisions by adversaries are treated as utility maximizing decisions rather than random chance nodes.

Figure 16-5

Intelligent adversary decision tree models (Merrick and Parnell 2011)

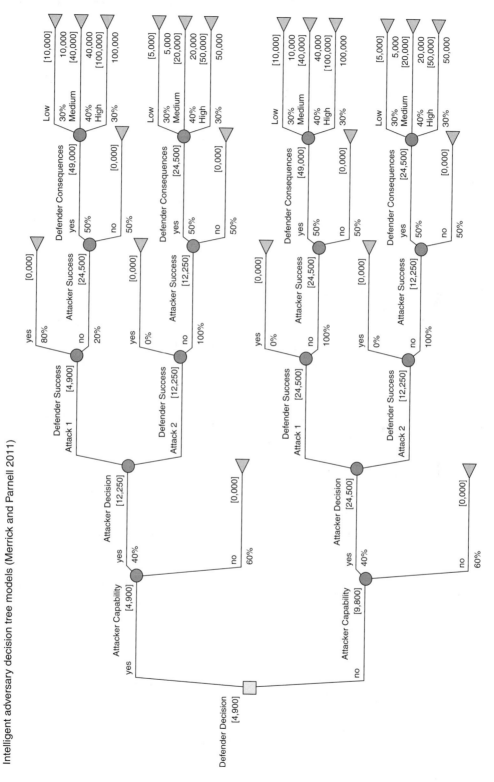

Advantages and Disadvantages. The major advantage of intelligent adversary models is that the models can include adaptive adversaries who would adopt different offensive strategies based on the defensive actions taken by the defender. The second advantage is that they show the risk-shifting behavior of attackers. The major disadvantage is that the modeler must make assumptions about the adversary's attack objectives/utility functions.

Benefit-Cost Analysis

Benefit-cost analyses are often used as the key criteria for deciding which CT projects to fund. In its simplest form, benefit-cost analysis uses a benefit-cost ratio to rank projects (Kirkwood 1997). This methodology is only appropriate if the project benefits and costs are both independent and we have only one budget constraint. More often the benefits from multiple projects are not independent. Projects can be substitutes or they can be complementary. Likewise costs may be dependent. In addition, we usually have many constraints. For example, it may be cheaper to perform multiple projects that are bundled into a program. Even if independence exists within benefits and costs, the key issues are how to measure these benefits and costs. In commercial projects, the benefits and costs may both be measured in dollars. In many public applications, including counterterrorism, it may be difficult to quantify the benefits and, perhaps, the costs (e.g., loss of privacy) in dollars.

In many public decision-making applications, benefits (and sometimes costs) can be captured using multiple objective decision analysis (Kirkwood 1997) and costs can be the life cycle costs or the acquisition costs. If we forgo the benefit-cost ratio and determine the highest benefit projects for our budget, we no longer have to worry about the benefit and cost independence assumptions. Using optimization techniques, we can develop a very flexible process (Kirkwood 1997; Parnell 2004).

Continuing our information system design example from Figure 16-4, the decision analyst works with the system engineers to identify potential countermeasures that will reduce the adversary's attack value. The decision analyst then determines the set of countermeasures that would have the best combination of cost and impact on operational users of the information system. Figure 16-6 (Buckshaw et al.) shows the impact of adding additional countermeasures. First the most effective countermeasures are used, and then the curve reflects diminishing returns and then negative returns. The flat part of the curve is the low-risk solution.

Figure 16-6

Cost–benefit
curve for
information system
countermeasures

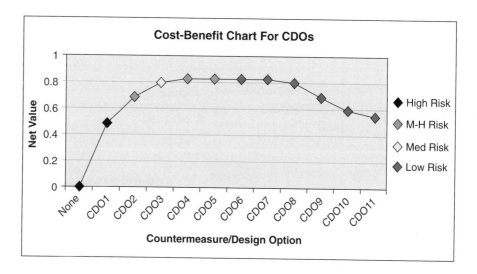

Advantages and Disadvantages. The advantage of benefit-cost analysis is that it provides a common framework for comparing homeland security projects. The use of multiple objective decision analysis can be a credible method as an objective and defensible basis for measuring the benefits. The time spent discussing the CT countermeasures will be more objective and more focused. The disadvantage of benefit-cost analysis is that it takes support and time to quantity the benefits (from senior leaders and key stakeholders) and to obtain credible cost data (key cost experts).

SELECTION OF RISK ANALYSIS TECHNIQUES

We have described several techniques to analyze the risk for the variety of risks faced by homeland security decision makers. Our experience is that the risk analyst should tailor the technique to the homeland security threat. For example, events trees may be appropriate for engineered systems and natural hazards, but threats due to intelligent, adaptive adversaries will require a more sophisticated model to capture the dynamics of the attacker and defender actions.

Key Tasks for a Methodology for Integrating Risk Management and Counterterrorism Resource Allocation

The Department of Homeland Security faces three daunting challenges. First, they must assess continuously what could go wrong (i.e., what are the risks) when assets, threats, vulnerabilities, and consequences are constantly changing. Second, they must prioritize the risks and determine which are the most important. Finally, they must implement cost-effective strategies to deal with those risks. To

Figure 16-7

Tasks for
methodology for
integrating risk
management and
counterterrorism
resource allocation

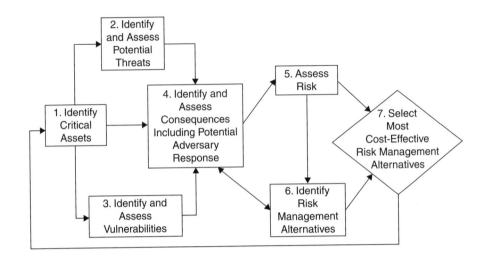

meet these challenges, we must identify the key risk assessment, risk management, and resource allocation tasks. Figure 16-7 shows the key tasks that we believe must be included in a methodology to integrate risk management for CT resource allocation. Next, we describe each of these tasks.

Identify Critical Assets

The methodology begins with the identification of the critical assets. Risk analysts should use a systematic process to evaluate the major system assets and determine the critical assets. Key stakeholders should be involved in the process. System architecture diagrams that identify the key assets, systems flows, and interdependencies can be very useful. If the system architecture does not exist, the development of the architecture should be the first step in the process. Once the major assets have been identified, a screening process is needed to determine the critical assets. A model or screening criteria can be used to identify the critical assets. The screening criteria may include potential for casualties, potential of economic disruption, and symbolic importance.

Identify and Assess Potential Threats

The second step in our process is to identify and assess the threats to homeland security. A threat assessment can be based on either type of threat or sources of threat. The ODP (Office of Domestic Preparedness) toolkit focuses on the type of weapon that terrorists might use and includes chemical, biological, radiological, nuclear, and explosive

(DHS, 2003). The alternative is to focus on sources of threat—in other words, any organization with capability and intent to launch an attack on the system. It is essential to develop a range of scenarios that represent the types of attack that might occur. A scenario is a plausible (not necessarily probable) sequence of events that define a potential threat. Each defined scenario should consist of target assets, weapons, and modes of delivery.

Identify and Assess Vulnerabilities

Once the attack scenarios have been selected, the next step in the overall process is to evaluate the vulnerability of the critical assets in these scenarios. For a given weapon and target scenario, the probability of an attack scenario being successful depends on the ability to detect the attack, the warning time, the system response to the attack, and the ability of the attacker to overcome the response. In answering the above questions, it is important to consider for each target, any current countermeasures, relevant physical layouts, geographical configurations, and so on that might prevent access to the target, that might aid in detecting the attack in progress, or that might assist in defeating the attack when detected.

Identify and Assess Consequences Including Potential Adversary Responses

The next step is to assess the potential consequences of successful attacks on critical assets. This step is critical because, with limited resources, we must concentrate on the vulnerabilities with the most significant consequences. Some of the potential consequences may be casualties, economic disruption, and loss of public confidence. In addition, if risk management actions are considered, we must include the potential adversary responses including attacking the next highest consequence targets (risk shifting).

Assess the Baseline Risk

Once we have completed the first four steps, we have the information to assess the baseline (i.e., current) risk. This risk assessment must consider the probability, the consequences, and the timeframe (i.e., the period when action is required in order to mitigate the risk). This assessment provides the foundation for risk management. It also provides a total system risk assessment that allows the decision makers and risk analysts to focus their risk management efforts.

Identify Risk Management Alternatives

If the baseline risk assessment is not acceptable, we need to consider risk management alternatives. We need to involve stakeholders and technical experts in a structured process to identify potential risk management actions. These actions can include all the aspects identified in the right-hand column of Table 16-1. Again, a useful decision analysis technique is the alternative generation table (Kirkwood 1997) shown previously in Table 16-3.

Select the Most Cost-Effective Risk Management Alternatives

Next, we assess the risk reduction of each of the risk management actions. This is not necessarily an easy task. Unlike natural disasters and engineered systems, the terrorist is an intelligent, adaptive adversary and can change behaviors based on the strategies that we implement. In addition, this assessment is a portfolio decision problem. We want to determine the most cost-effective portfolio of risk management actions. In addition to risk, other factors must be considered, including the impact of the risk reduction actions on stakeholders and customers.

Finally, once the resource allocation process is complete, the impacts need to be continually evaluated through a feedback loop. Because the adversary is adaptive and will continue to change strategies, we must continually evaluate our own strategies to keep focused on the most cost-effective allocations.

Toward a Methodology for Integrating Risk Management and Counterterrorism Resource Allocation

In order to develop a methodology to integrate risk management and counterterrorism resource allocation, we must identify the techniques that are most applicable for each of the tasks. Table 16-6 provides this mapping. The shaded boxes identify the *potential* to use each technique to perform one of the risk management tasks. For example, scenarios analysis helps to identify threats, vulnerabilities, and consequences.

Each organization's methodology should be tailored to its unique challenges and circumstances. To develop a methodology, each organization should select at least one technique for each task. Most importantly, the techniques must be linked to provide consistent analysis. For examples, probabilities obtained using probabilistic risk analysis and consequences obtained from scenario analysis can both be used in decision analysis.

Also, the technique selected may depend on the number of threats and the potential consequences. For example, if the number of threats is very large and the consequences are small, the Threat, Vulnerability,

Table 16-7

Technique Applicability to Risk Methodology Tasks

Techniques	Risk Assessment and Risk Management Tasks						
	1. Identify Critical Assets	2. Identify and Assess Potential Threats	3. Identify and Assess Vulnerabilities	4. Identify and Assess Consequences Including Potential Adversary Responses	5. Assess Baseline Risk	6. Identify Risk Management Alternatives	7. Select the Most Cost-Effective Risk Management Alternatives
Alternative Generation Table						Applicable	
Fault Trees (Attack Trees)		Applicable			Applicable		
Threat, Vulnerability, Consequence Tables			Applicable				
Risk Matrices				Applicable			
Failure Modes and Effects Analysis				Applicable			
Probabilistic Risk Analysis			Applicable				
Scenario Analysis		Applicable		Applicable		Applicable	
Decision Analysis		Applicable	Applicable	Applicable			
Game Theory Models						Applicable	
Intelligent Adversary Models			Applicable		Applicable		
Benefit-Cost Analysis							Applicable

Consequences Tables may be appropriate. If the threats are fewer and the consequences significant, a more detailed analysis, such as fault tress, may be appropriate.

CONCLUSIONS

Homeland security and counterterrorism are massive undertakings. The total risk cannot be eliminated, but it must be reduced and managed. Risk analysis requires an organizational culture change that takes time and expertise to succeed. The key is to use a systematic process to identify the critical system assets, assess the risks, and make smart risk management decisions. It is important to tailor the risk analysis techniques to the potential consequences and resources involved. Major terrorism consequences warrant more detailed risk analysis techniques. Based on experience in many decision and risk analysis applications, we recommend the following:

- **People.** People are the key to risk assessment and risk management. Businesses and organizations need to acquire and train personnel in systems engineering, decision analysis, and risk analysis disciplines. Senior leaders must ensure that risk analysts have access to the best subject matter experts to complete their analyses.
- **Synergies.** We believe that counterterrorism projects have many synergies with other mission assurance activities. For example, risk management actions to disperse operations to multiple locations may increase system resiliency and reduce the system vulnerabilities and potential consequences of terrorism and natural disasters.
- **Processes.** We have outlined a framework for a general, flexible methodology. More detailed procedures will be needed.
- **Timing.** The most cost-effective time to factor risk management into the decision process is in the system design. System countermeasures made after the system is fielded are always more costly and, typically, less effective.
- **Culture.** In this chapter we have focused on risk analysis. To be successful, the organization must develop a security culture that involves effective risk awareness, risk assessment, risk management, and risk communications. (Other chapters of this handbook offer excellent recommendations for these areas.)

We have focused in this chapter on quantitative techniques that represent the "technical" side of resource allocation decision making. It is important to recognize that CT is a problem that requires "sociotechnical" solutions. The best quantitative analyses may fall on deaf ears if the "social" and organizational aspects of the solution are not understood and considered as well. Through the use of a resource allocation process based on detailed and thorough risk assessment, as well as on social and organizational considerations, effective and efficient management of the risk of terrorism is possible.

ACKNOWLEDGEMENTS

The authors would like to acknowledge that several colleagues provided useful ideas and suggestions that influenced our thinking about the chapter. Specifically, we acknowledge Vicki Bier, Don Buckshaw, Michael Cassidy, Bob Reynolds, and Ralph Semmel.

REFERENCES

Bier, Vicki. 2004. "Should the Model for Security Be Game Theory Rather Than Reliability Theory?" *4th International Conference on Mathematical Methods in Reliability: Methodology and Practice.* June 21–25, Santa Fe, NM.

Bodily, Samuel. 1992. "Introduction: The Practice of Decision and Risk Analysis," *Interfaces* 22, no. 6 (November/December): 1–4.

Bowles, John B. "The New SAE FMECA Standard." *1998 Proceedings of the Annual Reliability and Maintainability Symposium*, pp. 48–53.

Buckshaw, D. L., G. S. Parnell, W. L. Unkenholz, D. L. Parks, J. M. Wallner, and O. S. Saydjari. 2004. "Mission Oriented Risk and Design Analysis of Critical Information Systems." Technical Report 2004–03. Innovative Decisions Inc. (August).

Buede, Dennis M. 2009. *The Engineering Design of Systems: Models and Methods.* 2nd ed. New York: John Wiley & Sons.

CAIB (Columbia Accident Investigation Board). NASA. Washington, DC, August 2003.

Cohen, Fred. 1997. "Information System Attacks: A Preliminary Classification Scheme." *Computer & Security* 16, no. 1: 29–46.

Davison, Mark, and William Vantine. 1998. "Understanding Risk Management: A Review of the Literature and Industry Practice." *European Space Agency Risk Management Workshop, ESTEC* (March 30–April 2): 253–256.

Department of Homeland Security (DHS). 2003. *Office of Domestic Preparedness: Special Needs Jurisdiction Toolkit.*

———. Department of Homeland Security (DHS). 2010. *DHS Risk Lexicon.*

Dillon, R. L, and C. H. Tinsley. 2008. "How Near-Misses Influence Decision Making Under Risk: A Missed Opportunity for Learning." *Management Science* 54, no. 8 (August): 1425–1440.

Doherty, M. E., R. Chadwick, H. Garavan, D. Barr, and C. R. Mynatt. 1996. "On People's Understanding of the Diagnostic Implications of Probabilistic Data." *Memory and Cognition* 24: 644–654.

Dresher, M. 1961. *Games of Strategy* (Englewood Cliffs, NJ: Prentice Hall).

Engelbrecht, J. A., Jr., R. L. Bivins, P. M. Condray, M. D. Fecteau,, J. P. Geiss II, and K. C. Smith. 1996. "Alternate Futures for 2025: Security Planning to Avoid Surprise." Air University Press, Maxwell Air Force Base, Alabama (April).

Federal Emergency Management Agency. 2004. *Benefit-Cost Analysis (BCA) of Hazard Mitigation Projects.* http://www.fema.gov/library/viewRecord.do;jsessionid=478492E5A481DAEA B42C04F9CF407434.WorkerLibrary?id=4185.

———. 2004. *Hazard List.*

http://www.ready.gov/be-informed.

Frank, Michael. 1998. *A Survey of Risk Assessment Methods from the Nuclear, Chemical, and Aerospace Industries for Applicability to the Privatized Vitrification of Hanford Tank Wastes.* Report to the Nuclear Regulatory Commission (August).

General Accounting Office (GAO). 2003. *Critical Infrastructure Protection, Challenges for Selected Agencies and Industry Sectors.* Washington, DC. GAO–03–233 (February).

Groen, F., C. Smidts, A. Mosleh, and S. Swaminathan. 2002. "QRAS: Quantitative Risk Assessment System." *Proceedings of RAMS 2002, Annual Reliability and Maintainability Symposium.*

Haimes, Y. Y. 1998. *Risk Modeling, Assessment, and Management.* New York: John Wiley & Sons.

Henley, E. J., and H. Kumamoto. 1992. *Probabilistic Risk Assessment: Reliability Engineering, Design, and Analysis.* New York: IEEE Press.

Homeland Security: Information Sharing Responsibilities, Challenges, and Key Management Issues. 2003. GAO–03–1165T. Government Accounting Office (September 17).

Jackson, J. A., G. S. Parnell, B. L. Jones,, L. J. Lehmkuhl, H. Conley, and J. Andrew. 1997. "Air Force 2025 Operational Analysis." *Military Operations Research* 3, no. 4: 5–21.

Joint Chiefs of Staff/Department of Defense. 1998. Joint Publication 3–13, Joint doctrine for Information Operations. Washington, DC: Pentagon.

Kaplan, S. 1997. "The Words of Risk Analysis." *Risk Analysis* 17, no. 4.

Kaplan, S., and B. J. Garrick. 1981. "On the Quantitative Definition of Risk." *Risk Analysis* 1, no. 1: 11– 27.

Keeney, Ralph. 1982. "Decision Analysis: An Overview." *Operations Research* 30, no. 5 (September/ October): 803–838.

Keeney, R. L. 1992. *Value-Focused Thinking: A Path to Creative Decisionmaking.* Cambridge, MA: Harvard University Press.

Keeney, R. L., and H. Raiffa. 1976. *Decision Making with Multiple Objectives: Preferences and Value Tradeoffs.* New York: John Wiley & Sons..

Kirkwood, Craig W. 1997. *Strategic Decision Making: Multiobjective Decision Analysis with Spreadsheets.* Belmont, CA: Duxbury Press.

Lindell, M. K., and R. W. Perry. 1992. *Behavioral Foundations of Community Emergency Planning.* Washington, DC: Hemisphere Publishing Corporation.

Merrick, J., and G. Parnell. 2011. "A Comparative Analysis of PRA and Intelligent Adversary Methods for Counterterrorism Risk Management." *Risk Analysis* 31, no. 9: 1488–1510.

Mileti, Dennis S., and Paul W. O'Brien. 1992. "Warnings During Disaster: Normalizing Communicated Risk." *Societal Problems* 39, no. 1 (February): 40–57.

Mileti, Dennis S. 1999. *Disasters by Design: A Reassessment of Natural Hazards in the United States.* Washington, DC: Joseph Henry Press.

Modarres, M. 1993. *What Every Engineer Should Know About Reliability and Risk Analysis.* New York: Marcel Dekker.

Mosleh, Ali. 1993. *Procedure for Analysis of Common-Cause Failures in Probabilistic Safety Analysis.* Washington, DC: Division of Safety Issue Resolution, Office of Nuclear Regulatory Research, Nuclear Regulatory Commission.

National Research Council. 2008. *Department of Homeland Security. Bioterrorism Risk Assessment: A Call for Change.* Washington, DC: National Academies Press.

Onodera, Katsushige. 1997. "Effective Techniques of FMEA at Each Life-Cycle Stage." In *1997 Proceedings of the Annual Reliability and Maintainability Symposium,* pp. 50–56.

Parnell G. S., C. M. Smith, F. I. Moxley. 2010. "Intelligent Adversary Risk Analysis: A Bioterrorism Risk Management Model." *Risk Analysis* 30, no. 1: 32–48.

Parnell, G., P. Driscoll, and D. Henderson, eds. 2011. *Decision-Making in System Engineering and Management*, 2nd ed. New York: John Wiley & Sons.

Paté-Cornell, M. E. 1996. "Uncertainties in Risk Analysis: Six Levels of Treatment,"*Reliability Engineering and System Safety* 54: 95–111.

Paté-Cornell, M. E., R. L. Dillon, and S. D. Guikema. 2004. "On the Limitations of Redundancies in the Improvement of System Reliability." *Risk Analysis* 24, no. 6: 1423–1436.

Paté-Cornell, M. E., and Robin L. Dillon. 2001. "Probabilistic Risk Analysis for the NASA Space Shuttle: A Brief History and Current Work." *Reliability Engineering and System Safety* 74, no. 3: 345–52.

Paté-Cornell, M. E., and P. S. Fischbeck. 1994. "Risk Management for the Tiles of the Space Shuttle." *Interfaces* 24: 64–86.

Paté-Cornell, M. E., and S. D. Guikema. 2002. "Probabilistic Modeling of Terrorist Threats: A Systems Analysis Approach to Setting Priorities Among Countermeasures." *Military Operations Research* 7, no. 4.

National Infrastructure Protection Center (NIPC). 2002. "Risk Management: An Essential Guide to Protecting Critical Infrastructure." Washington, DC (November).

Software Engineering Institute (SEI). 1996. *Continuous Risk Management Guidebook*. Pittsburgh: Carnegie Mellon University.

Tversky, A., and D. Kahneman. 1974. "Judgment Under Uncertainty: Heuristics and Biases." *Science* 185. no. 4157: 1124–1131.

U.S. Nuclear Regulatory Commission (USNRC). 1975. *Reactor Safety Study: Assessment of Accident Risk in U.S. Commercial Nuclear Plants.* WASH–1400 (NUREG–75/014). Washington, DC: U.S. Nuclear Regulatory Commission.

———. 1983. *PRA Procedures Guide*. NUREG/CR–2300. Washington, DC: U.S. Nuclear Regulatory Commission.

———. 1991. *Procedural and Submittal Guidance for the Individual Plant Examination of External Events (IPEEE) for Severe Accident Vulnerabilities.* Final Report. Washington, DC.

———. 1996. *A Technique for Human Error Analysis (Atheana)*. Washington, DC: Division of Systems Technology, Office of Nuclear Regulatory Research.

Vesely, W. E. 1981. *Fault Tree Handbook*. Washington, DC: Office of Nuclear Regulatory Research.

Wason, P. C. 1960. "On the Failure to Eliminate Hypotheses in a Conceptual Task." *Quarterly Journal of Experimental Psychology* 12: 129–140.

———. "Reasoning about a Rule." *Quarterly Journal of Experimental Psychology* 20: 273–281.

Weinstein, N. D. 1987. *Taking Care: Understanding and Encouraging Self-Protective Behavior.* Cambridge: Cambridge University Press.

Wenger, Dennis E., James D. Dykes, Thomas D. Sebok, and Joan L. Neff. 1975. "It's a Matter of Myths: An Empirical Examination of Individual Insight Into Disaster Response." *Mass Emergencies* 1: 33–46.

17

PERVASIVE READINESS:
PIPEDREAM OR POSSIBLE?

Ari Vidali

Chief Executive Officer
Envisage Technologies Corporation
Bloomington, Indiana – USA
ari.vidali@envisagenow.com

Jason D. Hutchens

Director, Planning and Assessment
Indiana Department of Homeland Security
Indianapolis, Indiana – USA
jhutchens@dhs.in.gov

OVERVIEW

> *The art of war teaches us to rely not on the likelihood of the enemy's not coming, but on our own readiness to receive him; not on the chance of his not attacking, but rather on the fact that we have made our position unassailable.* —Sun Tzu, The Art of War

Over the past decade, there has been a significant increase in catastrophic events worldwide. Since 2001, the United States has responded to a wide spectrum of critical incidents both natural and man-made.[1] The combined impact of these events has contributed to a growing sense of urgency, and with it a renewed call for our nation to increase its *resilience*: a term defined by the Obama Administration as "the ability to adapt to changing conditions and withstand, and rapidly recover from disruption due to emergencies."[2]

As the nation watches the aftermath of the triple calamities of earthquake, tsunami, and atomic reactor meltdowns which struck Japan; the flood waters rising along the Mississippi River; or the poignant images of citizens from Texas to Florida rummaging through the rubble of homes and businesses devastated by an historic tornado outbreak,[3] there is a growing concern that despite the rhetoric, studies, and billions invested, there is as yet little consensus on what constitutes resilience,[4] let alone how it can be achieved in actual practice. A few courageous and rational voices have been raised in a reasoned attempt to call on policymakers to craft "a shared-and *actionable—*vision for a resilient America…" and a well-defined path toward an operational approach to achieving it.[5]

While policymakers, academia, and the private sector agree that resilience is a highly desirable goal, it is also recognized that resilience itself needs to be defined, planned for, and developed in advance; that is, before communities, infrastructure or systems are compromised.[6] Thus, achieving resilience is largely a function of our ability to establish, maintain, and measure readiness[7] at all levels: individual, community, state, and national.

The inherently unpredictable nature of emergencies makes it difficult to determine a perfect response[8] to a particular incident or disaster in advance. In addition, because response organizations typically operate with constrained resources, it is rarely possible to achieve ideal preparedness. What is needed are practical ways to proactively assess our readiness, so that government leaders as well as the public know what they can and cannot expect during a crisis.

Efforts to address every shortfall that has been identified in advance will either create unsustainable demands for increased expenditures, or focus limited resources on shortfalls that may not in fact be the most vital readiness issues that we need to solve. Within the complex landscape of public safety, it remains very difficult to answer fundamental questions such as "Are we ready?" or "What do we need in order to become ready?" And yet, answers to questions like these are vital for making effective decisions about how to allocate our resources.

Capacity Versus Capability

There have been several attempts to gauge readiness. Some have focused on evaluating the resources and activities easiest to quantify, using them as predictors of what our response systems should be able to accomplish. For instance, we know that having the proper equipment is important, so if that equipment is not available, response operations are unlikely to go well. However, these simplistic approaches often do not differentiate between the purely quantitative measure of *capacity* (individual response assets such as vehicles, radios, or equipment), and qualitative measurement of response *capability* (which includes factors such as the personnel, skills, training, and the coordination required to respond).

As an example, if a jurisdiction has 10 fire engines (capacity), but only has qualified drivers for two of them (capability), then the actual deployable response resources for a disaster are two fire engines. This relationship between capacity and capability is represented as:

$$maxCapacity \cap maxCapability = Ready\ Resources$$

While an understanding of the capacity needed during a crisis or disaster is important, it is crucial to distinguish the capabilities required to support that capacity. The prevailing inability to differentiate and accurately measure *both* capacity and capability can have the effect of misleading decision makers into making poor investment decisions, and may cause still more harm by fostering a false sense of security regarding a given jurisdiction's overall readiness level.

The Readiness Gap and the State of Indiana's Approach

With towns, cities, and states across America facing severe budget deficits, an eroding tax base, higher demands for services, and escalating costs, funding for public safety has been drastically reduced.[9] First-responder personnel are being furloughed or laid off, and vital equipment upgrades are being delayed as most communities struggle just to maintain basic services. At the same time, both the cost of public safety and the public's expectations continue to rise. The long-term effect of these trends is to create a widening readiness gap (Figure 17-1), which is rapidly eroding the ability of many communities to prepare for, respond to, and recover from critical incidents.

The State of Indiana faces these same headwinds, and yet over the last few years it has succeeded in making significant strides towards the implementation of a pervasive readiness strategy, a strategy which not only evolved to address these trends, but also to galvanize people, processes, and technology to counteract them.

Before Governor Daniels took office in 2005, he called a meeting of the many disparate organizations which held a public safety function, including: the Department of Health, Indiana National Guard,

Figure 17-1

Readiness gap

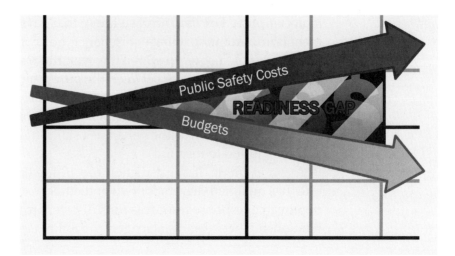

State Police, State Fire Marshal, and others. He asked the assembled participants, which of them had control over multi-disciplinary dispatch of response personnel and assets. The consensus was that they all had "a good working relationship" and would respond to requests for support as needed. The Governor concluded that this patchwork approach to command-and-control would severely limit operational agility by slowing down the decision cycle during a crisis, potentially causing higher casualties and increased economic damage, while perpetuating duplicative costs and inefficiencies.

This insight provided the impetus to centralize, and in 2005 Indiana consolidated all of its emergency management and homeland security efforts into a single department, creating the Indiana Department of Homeland Security (IDHS) with a central mission: To safeguard the lives and property of the citizens of Indiana.

This chapter outlines some of the key principles and practical applications which have been pioneered in the State of Indiana. This approach has led to a reduction of fragmentation by two means: first, by implementing a unified regional structure called the "District Model," and second, by the evolution of a practical, data-driven approach to public safety which creates a foundation for effective measurement of readiness against a state's prioritized Hazard/Threat Identification and Risk Assessment (HIRA). Finally, we will discuss some concepts essential to the future development of a measurable framework to support state- and nation-wide pervasive readiness.[10]

A FRAMEWORK FOR PERVASIVE READINESS

> *It's not the strongest of the species that survives, nor the most intelligent, but the one most responsive to change. —Charles Darwin, On the Origin of Species, 1859*

Disasters, having no geographical, economic, or social boundaries, frequently impact multiple jurisdictions. Over the last few years, Indiana has experienced five federally declared disasters or emergencies that spanned large regions of the state. During these disasters, many local communities were overwhelmed and required help from beyond their jurisdictional boundaries. Requests by the impacted communities often exceeded the state's ability to effectively provide the needed resources. As a result, Indiana relied on mutual aid agreements[11] with other states and the federal government to support the response efforts.[12]

Indiana learned many lessons during these disasters, including that readiness is a responsibility shared by all layers of society. In other words, to achieve resilience on any scale will require a culture of **pervasive readiness** that permeates our governments, local communities, organizations, and businesses, and includes individual citizens.[13]

The Federal Emergency Management Agency (FEMA) outlined this concept in its recent strategic plan, calling for innovation and collaboration to support community-wide disaster preparedness:

> *… it takes all aspects of a community (Volunteer, Faith, and Community-based organizations, the private sector, and the public including survivors themselves)—not just the government—to effectively prepare for, protect against, respond to, recover from, and mitigate against any disaster. It is therefore critical that we work together to enable communities to develop*

> *collective, mutually supporting local capabilities to withstand the poten-*
> *tial initial impacts of these events, respond quickly, and recover in a way*
> *that sustains or improves the community's overall well-being. How com-*
> *munities achieve this collective capacity calls for innovative approaches*
> *from across the full spectrum of community actors, including emergency*
> *management, to expand and enhance existing practices, institutions, and*
> *organizations that help make local communities successful every day,*
> *under normal conditions, and leverage this social infrastructure to help*
> *meet community needs when an incident occurs.*[14]

To further our nation's resilience, the Obama Administration has called for the establishment of a "national preparedness goal," which "will be informed by the risk of specific threats and vulnerabilities and include concrete, *measurable*, and *prioritized* objectives to mitigate that risk."[15] (emphasis added)

Achieving this goal will require a rethinking of the structure of public safety, and a standardized process for assessing risks and optimizing readiness. Without a disciplined approach, we are like a pilot with no instrumentation: unlikely to reach our destination, and unlikely to know it even if we do.

The Critical Importance of Structure

"You can't manage what you don't measure." This well-known adage from the business world applies equally to public safety. Without being able to measure something, we cannot tell if it is getting better or worse. Without this information, managers cannot systematically improve it. To measure, we must collect data (inputs and outputs), determine how those will be expressed as a standard (metric), and compare the measurement to a benchmark to evaluate progress (outcomes). In addition, it is important to ascertain the most practical level of granularity, i.e., level of detail, for each measurement. For example, a theoretical hierarchy used to measure the country's readiness level might be similar to the one shown in Figure 17-2.

The further one travels toward the base of the triangle, the more complex and fragmented the information sources become. Achieving optimal granularity for measurement will often entail a trade-off between accuracy and cost.

Beginning in 2005, Indiana began to seriously rethink both public safety policies and structure. Governor Daniels challenged the state

Figure 17-2

National hierarchy

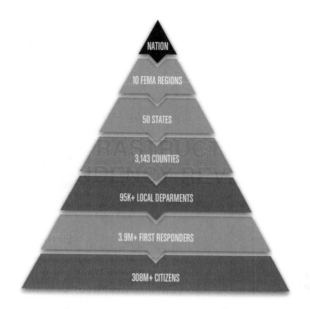

to seek increased efficiencies, consolidate duplicative services, and reduce waste. To measure progress, agencies were asked to develop key performance indicators (KPIs)[16] for core "citizen-facing" services.[17]

For public safety, the result was the creation of an Indiana Department of Homeland Security (IDHS), which was made responsible for administering State and Federal grant programs, setting standards, managing compliance, and coordinating activities across the entire continuum of readiness, response, and recovery.

For measurement, the IDHS quickly helped to alleviate the vexing problem of fragmentation. It did this, first, by creating a regionalized approach to capability aggregation and readiness measurement (*the District concept*); and second, by consolidating its disparate information sources into an automated enterprise system,[18] which serves as a focal point for capturing and harmonizing state-wide compliance and readiness data (see Figure 17-3).

One of the reasons current methods for measuring readiness have proven inadequate is that most jurisdictions lack reliable basic, qualitative information about their response assets,[19] the critical skills, training, and availability of personnel, and the status of emergency supplies.[20] This lack of data, which is the single largest impediment to measuring our readiness, is caused by the inherent *fragmentation of our public safety community.*

Fragmentation is a deeply embedded systemic problem affecting many levels of public safety. It permeates everything from policies,

Figure 17-3

Indiana state
hierarchy

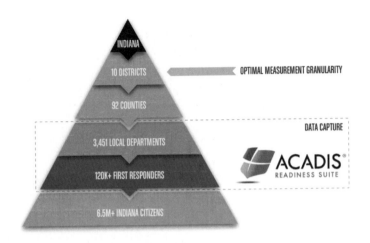

budgets, and jurisdictional authority to process, personnel, and critical resources. In many cases, even core operational support functions (such as situational awareness, communications, and vital information systems and data) remain fragmented, and are either redundant or unable to interoperate effectively.

Reducing Fragmentation: The IDHS District Model

IDHS established ten Homeland Security districts across the state of Indiana (Figure 17-4) with the primary purpose of enhancing mutual aid through a regional approach to preparedness planning. Together, these districts focus on common strategic goals and objectives to meet national, state, and local homeland security and public safety needs. This approach strengthens emergency preparedness and response operations, reduces overall public safety costs, and encourages regional cooperation and teamwork.

Each district is comprised of multiple counties with various different needs, resources, and capabilities. The makeup of each district is unique and can differ considerably from one area to another. Communities within a district can range from rural farmland and small towns to sprawling urban areas.

The district approach of IDHS reduces fragmentation and benefits all levels of government as well as the administration of vital services during disasters. According to a 2010 report by the IDHS,[21] the district approach encourages collaboration and cost saving, and it "streamlines the mutual aid process enabling the counties in each district to directly support one another, and in turn, the Districts to also support each other." The report also notes that regional planning can eliminate redundancies and increase emergency responders' capabilities

Figure 17-4

Indiana districts

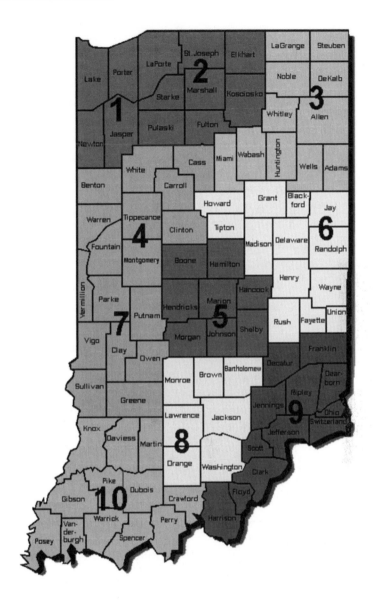

by allowing districts to leverage shared emergency response assets. In addition, the approach makes the most of federal grant funds which can be applied to district-wide needs, thus benefitting all counties within a district.

At the national level, FEMA implemented a similar concept through the establishment of ten regions (see Figure 17-5) designed to provide advice, training, and funding to sustain and improve capabilities and coordination for disaster preparedness, protection, response, recovery, and mitigation between states, tribal, and federal governments.

Figure 17-5

FEMA regions[22]

Regional offices act as the liaison and coordination hub between member states and the Department of Homeland Security on specific risks and matters relevant to their region.

QUANTIFYING RISK—BEYOND BASIC RISK ANALYSIS

> *Managing risk is fundamentally looking ahead to the possibility of a disaster that is yet to happen and then to make cost-benefit driven plans to prevent disaster or to reduce our vulnerability to the disaster or mitigate the effects of disaster.* —Michael Chertoff, former Secretary for Homeland Security, October, 2008.

A critical tool for public safety is a Hazard/Threat Identification and Risk Assessment which is the essential foundation for the readiness cycle, as well as any public planning process. A risk assessment is the process of measuring the potential loss of life, personal injury, economic injury, and property damage resulting from potential hazards and man-made threats. A simple formula for identifying and evaluating a hazard-specific risk (R_h) combines a hazard's probability of occurrence and its impact. For example, the equation below illustrates that the hazard (**H**) multiplied by a population's vulnerability to that hazard (V_h) produces a quantifiable hazard-specific risk.[23]

$$R_h = H \times V_h$$

Based on this analysis we should be able to conclude that the higher the risk the more urgent it is that the vulnerabilities to the hazard be reduced by mitigation and readiness efforts. If, however, no vulnerability exists, then there will be no risk. An example of this would be a flood occurring in an unpopulated area. While this formula does attempt to adjust for vulnerability, IDHS was dissatisfied with this and other basic risk assessment techniques available as they lacked sufficient granularity to assist policymakers and emergency mangers in making key decisions about asset allocation.

In order to gain a deeper understanding of the possible threats across the state, the Indiana Department of Homeland Security, in partnership with the Indiana Intelligence Fusion Center, developed a comprehensive, state-wide analysis of potential natural, technological, and human-caused hazards. This analysis is data driven and derived from information surrounding actual events and experiences over the past 50 years. The IDHS evaluated and ranked each hazard and threat based on a Calculated Priority Risk Index (CPRI) scoring mechanism.

The CPRI allowed a hazard, once identified, to be evaluated individually based on probability of occurrence, severity and impact, warning time, and duration. Each of the assessment criteria was assigned a weighted numerical value based on a modified version of the Calculated Priority Risk Index (CPRI). The Magnitude/Severity element of the CPRI was modified to capture not only the extent of damage, but also the degree to which the hazard could impact response operations. Each hazard was scored based on the criteria outlined in the modified CPRI (see Table 17-1 at the end of this chapter). The hazards were then assigned a **Risk Rating** based on the weighted CPRI Score (see Figure 17-6).[24]

Modified Calculated Priority Risk Index Categories and Definitions:

- **Probability:** The chance that a particular hazard/threat will occur, causing serious injuries and deaths, damage to property and critical infrastructure, disruption of essential systems and services, and degradation of emergency response capabilities.
- **Magnitude/Severity:** The relative size and overall impact a hazard/threat will have should it occur.

Figure 17-6

Risk rating table

Risk Rating	CPRI Score
4 – Severe Risk	4.0
3 – High Risk	3.0 – 3.99
2 – Moderate Risk	2.0 – 2.99
1 – Low Risk	1.0 – 1.99

- **Warning Time:** The amount of time between the initial warning and the onset of hazardous conditions.
- **Duration:** The length of time the direct effects of a particular hazard/threat will remain active.

It is important to note, that an effective risk assessment is possibly the most vital prerequisite for readiness, as it is the foundation for the entire readiness cycle. Risk analysis should be the basis of most aspects of public safety and influence everything from planning and budgeting to equipping, training, and exercising. Without it, policy-makers and emergency managers lack the necessary tools to make informed decisions.

Unfortunately, most state-wide public safety risk assessments are blunt instruments at best: unable to accurately contextualize risks within a granular geographic boundary or to take into account the fundamental interdependencies of critical infrastructure with the potential to cause cascading hazards.[25]

To achieve measurable readiness requires more precision than a basic statewide CPRI score is capable of delivering. As a result, in 2011 IDHS significantly expanded its approach in order to encompass a compre-hensive analysis of hazards facing each district, including the economic impact of hazards, and the inherent vul-nerabilities within a district (e.g., general populations, functional needs populations, and impoverished populations). Identifying individual hazards and juxtaposing them with district vulnerabilities provides quan-tifiable means of prioritizing risks within each district, thereby increasing the effec-tiveness and accuracy of comprehensive emergency planning, and ultimately foster-ing unity of purpose among all public safety stakeholders.[26]

Indiana's approach to risk measurement is more precise because it utilizes a mathematical foundation to increase the accuracy of risk scoring. The Priority Risk Index (PRI) is designed to contextualize risks within a district and can rank each risk by adjusting it via quantifiable factors such as:

1. **Population Index:** Measures the consequence based on the quantity and type of people residing within a District
2. **Economic Index:** Measures the value of a District's fiscal impact on the state
3. **Special Events Index:** Quantifies the increased vulnerability and consequences of those events which prompted the mass gathering of people within a District in the previous year
4. **National Security Index:** Scores the increased consequences from a hazard or terrorist attack which impacts a Defense Industrial Base (DIB)
5. **Critical Infrastructure Index:** Quantifies the vulnerability and consequence of a District with infrastructure identified as critical
6. **Preparedness Index:** Adjusts risks based on previous investments in response capabilities

A FOCUS ON ALL-HAZARDS READINESS

Readiness is a continuous cycle of planning, organizing, training, equipping, exercising, evaluation, and improvement activities designed to ensure effective coordination, cooperation, and the enhancement of capabilities to prevent, protect against, respond to, recover from, and mitigate the effects of natural disasters, acts of terrorism, and other man-made disasters (see Figure 17-7).[27]

The more prepared a state or region is for a *specific* disaster, the less impact that event is likely to have. Having ready assets pre-positioned before a crisis occurs enables a more agile and effective response, and can limit the potential damage that a threat or hazard is able to generate.[28] For example, in case of pandemic, having sufficient vaccine on hand, a well-planned distribution methodology (which has been exercised), and sufficient qualified personnel and volunteers to administer the vaccination program will increase the effectiveness of the response. The State of Indiana has refined the all-hazards[29] approach to public safety. This means that all hazards are considered

Figure 17-7

The readiness cycle

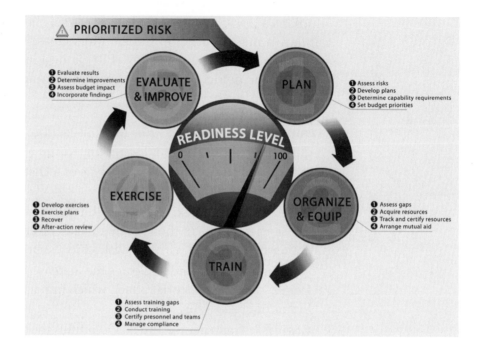

during risk assessment and prioritized on the basis of impact and likelihood of occurrence. Indiana focuses its efforts on managing the readiness cycle for the following key reasons:

1. All critical facets of public safety operations are represented, as optimal readiness implies that prevention, response, and recovery operations are balanced.

2. It focuses activities on emergency management functions for which IDHS has preeminent responsibility and encourages shared responsibility for outcomes.

3. It dovetails with federal initiatives such as the National Response Framework (NRF) or the National Incident Management System (NIMS), so commonalities can be leveraged for efficiency.

4. Measuring readiness provides the necessary information to enable the highest return on investment for the state across all types of investments.

5. Tracking readiness will enable near real-time visibility into district-specific needs, vulnerabilities, and help pinpoint mitigation strategies.

**Collecting
Readiness Data**

Measuring readiness requires the ongoing collection and consolidation of meaningful, accurate, and authoritative data[30] relative to existing response capabilities; and, therein lies the problem. The fragmented and complex nature of public safety makes this difficult, and without automation, expensive as well. Most fire, police, and EMS departments are understaffed and overworked. Few have the time, personnel, or inclination to enter data into a new information system solely for the purpose of measurement, yet without these data, they will not be able to accurately assess their readiness level for an identified risk. So how can emergency response departments overcome this resistance? One way is to collect the information needed while individual first responders and departments provide routine information to their certifying authority. Public safety organizations can implement technology that simplifies mandatory reporting requirements and captures much of the data required for readiness measures as first responders execute individual phases of the readiness cycle. This solution simultaneously lowers the cost of operations and of readiness measurement for all involved.

Indiana is working to solve this problem by implementing a centralized information management platform called the Acadis Readiness Suite (see Figure 17-8).[31] This technology provides the state with a centralized, web-based system for cataloging, managing, and sharing authoritative information regarding the location,

Figure 17-8

Acadis readiness
suite

credentials, and readiness level of its personnel and assets. This includes readiness capabilities across all public safety disciplines. The Acadis system certifies personnel as "ready" based on a variety of configurable criteria, and gives IDHS the ability to verify what each first responder is authorized to do during a crisis. Response assets such as vehicles can be assigned a NIMS type[32] and their readiness level for dispatch is likewise tracked.[33] Each "readiness certificate" has a pre-established timeframe for recertification, alerting personnel that it is time to check the status of that asset. This approach vastly simplifies the collection of readiness data for public safety personnel and assets.

For Indiana, the solution has helped replace many mandatory processes that required lengthy paper forms which had to be entered into a database manually. For example, ambulance service providers are required to be certified along with their vehicles in order to maintain their license to operate. For an ambulance to be certified, it must be in working order, have the appropriate equipment onboard, and the correct type of radio installed. Ambulance providers are audited periodically to ensure compliance. Likewise, every year police officers must report their in-service training (continuing education). By automating the compliance tracking of items such as these, IDHS has been able to simplify the aggregation of the data required to evaluate each district's readiness level.

MEASURING READINESS—PUTTING IT ALL TOGETHER

> *Greatness, it turns out, is largely a matter of conscious choice, and discipline.*—*Jim Collins*[34]

We began this chapter by arguing that a practical approach is required to establish a framework for pervasive readiness that can be effectively measured against a government's prioritized Hazard/Threat Identification and Risk Assessment (HIRA). All of the previously discussed elements are pre-requisites to an effective readiness measurement strategy. While each element may have independent value, public safety organizations will need to put all of the components into practice in order to measure their readiness with any accuracy.

There are five essential steps to measuring readiness, which are applicable at the local, regional, and national level:

1. Determine structure and measurement granularity.
2. Develop a Prioritized Risk Index (PRI).
3. Collect and consolidate readiness data.
4. Calculate Risk-Specific Readiness (RSR) scores.
5. Utilize an adjusted CPRI to measure optimal readiness.

Over the past few years, Indiana has excelled at implementing a disciplined approach to assessing its risks and collecting the requisite information to quantify existing capabilities. However, in order to make resource allocation decisions that have the highest probability of increasing a district's overall readiness, emergency managers need a more precise way to measure a district's readiness level relative to each specific risk. In addition, policymakers need ways to optimize risk-specific readiness in order to ensure that resources are not wasted by *over-preparing* for a specific hazard.

To accomplish this requires a Risk-Specific Readiness (RSR) scoring mechanism which assigns a readiness level to each of a district's individual risks. The Risk Specific Readiness (RSR) score is computed on an inverse scale to the CPRI, and acts as a meta-adjustment to it.

Each readiness assessment element is based upon a phase of the readiness cycle and is assigned a weighted numerical value. Readiness elements are then scored based on the criteria outlined in the Risk-Specific Readiness Matrix (see Table 17-2 at the end of this chapter). The RSR Scores can then be assigned a Readiness Rating based on the weighted RSR Score. In other words, the readiness rating for a prioritized risk within a district is a function of: (1) planning for that specific risk, (2) the district's level of organization and equipment, (3) training, and (4) risk-specific exercises conducted by a district.

District Risk-Specific Readiness

$$(D_r)RSR = fn(P_r, OE, T, E_r)$$

where:

D_r = A prioritized risk within a district
P_r = Risk-specific planning
OE = Organization and equipment
T = Training
E_r = Risk-specific exercise

Figure 17-9

Readiness rating
table

Readiness Rating	RSR Score
4 – Ready	4.0
3 – Mostly Ready	3.0 – 3.99
2 – Moderately Ready	2.0 – 2.99
1 – Not Ready	1.0 – 1.99

Once an RSR score has been calculated, the ratings, shown in Figure 17-9, can be assigned to enable emergency managers to interpret the numerical value.

Juxtaposing the CPRI score to the RSR score will enable emergency managers and policymakers to quickly gain a qualitative insight into a region's readiness posture for each specific threat, and will allow managers to make informed trade-off decisions when planning readiness activities or deciding how to allocate scarce resources (see Figure 17-10). By tracking these scores over time, a district can measure changes[35] to its overall risk-specific readiness. These data can be valuable to emergency managers when communicating to policymakers and leaders both the positive and adverse impacts of policies, changes in budget, or staffing. Finally, a similar approach could greatly assist the federal government in measuring the impact of grant funding allocated towards increasing preparedness.

**Optimizing
Readiness**

Policymakers need to know how to properly optimize readiness within resource constrained environments. The approach outlined here provides a solid framework for achieving a balance between

Figure 17-10

District readiness
summary table

2012 District X – Readiness Summary				
Prioritized Risks	**Risk Rating**	**CPRI Score**	**RSR Score**	**Readiness Rating**
1 – Severe Winter Storm	Severe	.20	3.20	Mostly Ready
2 – Major Flood	High	.45	2.85	Moderately Ready
3 – Hazmat Incident - Transportation	Moderate	−1.85	4.00	Ready
5 – Violent Tornado (≥ EF3)	Moderate	.45	2.20	Moderately Ready
6 – Cyber Attack - Grid	Low	.30	1.90	Not Ready

known risks and the public safety capabilities required to effectively respond to, and recover from them. Utilizing the data in hand, it is now possible for governments to easily calculate their *optimal readiness* for a given threat by simply subtracting the RSR score from the CPRI. The remainder provides an **Adjusted CPRI score** which represents how optimal a district's readiness posture is for each given threat.

Adjusted CPRI Calculation:

$$(D_r)CPRI - RSR - Adj\ CPRI$$

If the above calculation yields a *negative* score, the state or region is *overprepared* and has likely allocated too many resources towards that risk. If a *positive* score is obtained, they are *underprepared* and should consider additional measures to increase readiness for that particular risk. A score close to zero (0) indicates an optimal balance between risk and readiness. A score falling within ± .25 points could be considered within an acceptable optimization threshold (Figure 17-11).

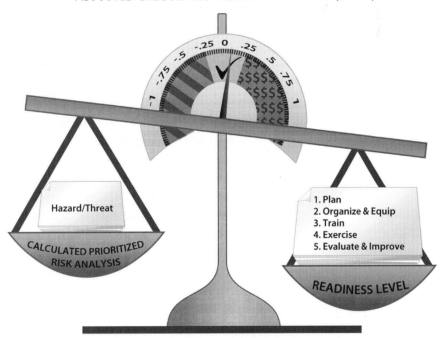

ADJUSTED CALCULATED PRIORITY RISK INDEX (ACPRI)

Figure 17-11

District adjusted
CPRI

2012 District X – Adjusted CPRI			
Prioritized Risks	**Risk Rating**	**Adj. CPRI**	**Conclusion**
1 – Severe Winter Storm	Severe	.20	Acceptable Readiness
2 – Major Flood	High	.45	Underprepared
3 – Hazmat Incident - Transportation	Moderate	−1.85	Overprepared
5 – Violent Tornado (≥ EF3)	Moderate	.45	Underprepared
6 – Cyber Attack - Grid	Low	.30	Underprepared

DRIVING CHANGE – BUDGETS AND PERFORMANCE MEASURES

To throw our hands up and say, 'but we cannot measure performance in the social sectors the way you can in a business,' is simply a lack of discipline. —Jim Collins[36]

Ensuring safety requires an understanding of risk and the implementation of a risk management strategy. The sector is reeling under the combined impacts of doing more with less and justifying their expenditures with demonstrable return on investment. In essence, the "new normal" for public safety will more closely mirror the private sector than at any time in the past.

However, the way leaders and public safety professionals act to manage risk is often limited by funding, staffing, bureaucracy, and competing priorities. Public safety domains[37] are fragmented and locked into programmatic and funding silos. Failure to strategically align these domains and focus them towards a common set of goals has often resulted in poor allocation of public funding.

Utilizing a disciplined Hazard/Threat Identification and Risk Analysis process and the corresponding Readiness Measurement provides policymakers with a clear roadmap for achieving readiness. However, policymakers must find ways to institutionalize the approach. There are two ways change is most likely to happen: reactive public policy to an adverse event or proactive leadership which aligns budgets and performance measures to increase return on investment for taxpayers.

Budgets— Resource Problem or Priority setting/ Planning Problem?

When setting priorities for 2012 and beyond, governments must accept the resource constrained environments they now operate within; status quo is no longer an option. Confronted with lower budgets, leaders have to be disciplined, prioritizing spending on the most essential facets of their public safety mission.

Further, the current economic climate is producing additional benefits such as broader cross-agency planning and a better understanding of the impacts of decisions on the entire public safety ecosystem. This realization is beginning to result in the sharing of resources, reduction of duplication, better and more routine information sharing, and most importantly, casting off the silo mentality of the past.

Government at all levels has seen many concepts familiar to the private sector make their way into daily practice, such as cost-benefit analysis, return on investment, and value add. Even agencies who provide essential services are now having to compete for priority among policymakers as well as demonstrate continued improvement and efficiency. This new culture of discipline within government has made those charged with oversight of governmental services look to *evidence based practices, data driven strategies,* and *technology* to innovate and reduce costs. As James Taylor put it: "The greatest ROI becomes possible when automating and improving operational decisions across the enterprise."[38]

Performance Measures—The Importance of Asking the Right Questions First

Performance measures are discussed more often than they are understood by those who require them and by those who will succeed or fail by them. Until recently, performance measures were not all that much of a concern to government service providers, as they were only required to measure pure inputs (budgets, staff, resources) and outputs (clients served, services rendered).

However, the measuring of outcomes based on performance measures creates a greater level of accountability. To understand performance measures, it is crucial to understand business processes and how to align them towards achieving an agency's vision and mission. Performance measures document continued improvement as well as progress towards the desired future for the organization. Failing to clearly articulate outcome-based performance measures reflects a lack of vision for an organization's future constituency needs, budget realities, and leadership objectives.

Performance measures typically align to either justify investment of taxpayer dollars or to measure progress towards stated goals. To support the business case for governmental entities, it is essential that agencies and domains across the entire ecosystem agree upon key performance indicator (KPI) measures that reflect the needs of the community. The challenge lies in overcoming fragmentation in state and federal guidance, policies, strategies, and funding, as well as disconnected performance measures.

This was most recently discussed in the report entitled "Perspective on Preparedness: Taking Stock Since 9/11."[39] The report concluded that we still have a long way to go:

> *We uniformly believe that our Nation is significantly better prepared than it was on September 11, 2001—each of us has significant anecdotal data, unique to our jurisdictions, to support this premise. Yet we acknowledge that while stakeholders across the Nation have been working to improve preparedness, specific, measureable outcomes for these efforts have yet to be defined and assessed. ... Federal policymakers have an admittedly mixed record in integrating local, State, Tribal, and Territorial perspectives into federally developed policy and guidance. There is no consistent, standardized way for local, State, Tribal, and Territorial governments to meaningfully influence the preparedness policy process.*[40]

The diagram shown in Figure 17-12 provides an example showing how key performance indicators shared between traditional law enforcement, homeland security, and emergency management domains would strengthen and unify public safety, while beginning to address the concerns raised by the cited report.

This example illustrates how key performance indicators can begin to align funding, guidance, strategies, vision, and unity of effort between all levels of government, while still respecting our federalist form of government. As shown in Figure 17-12, the process begins with state-level key performance indicators driving the funding decisions of state administrative agencies, and then aligning guidance, strategies, and vision with well-defined performance measures (output and outcome).

Clearly this is no small challenge. However, it is not only possible, but worthy of the efforts of well-informed policymakers to act boldly and effect positive change. Recently, President Obama's Homeland Security and Counterterrorism advisor, John Brennan, raised a call to action:

Figure 17-12

Key performance
indicators

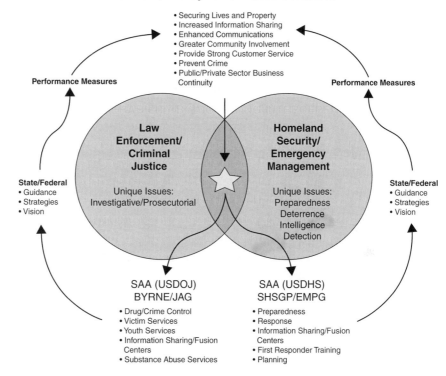

State Level Key Performance Indicators

• Securing Lives and Property
• Increased Information Sharing
• Enhanced Communications
• Greater Community Involvement
• Provide Strong Customer Service
• Prevent Crime
• Public/Private Sector Business
  Continuity

Performance Measures   **Performance Measures**

Law Enforcement/ Criminal Justice

Unique Issues:
Investigative/Prosecutorial

Homeland Security/ Emergency Management

Unique Issues:
Preparedness
Deterrence
Intelligence
Detection

State/Federal
• Guidance
• Strategies
• Vision

State/Federal
• Guidance
• Strategies
• Vision

SAA (USDOJ) BYRNE/JAG

• Drug/Crime Control
• Victim Services
• Youth Services
• Information Sharing/Fusion
  Centers
• Substance Abuse Services

SAA (USDHS) SHSGP/EMPG

• Preparedness
• Response
• Information Sharing/Fusion
  Centers
• First Responder Training
• Planning

> *But rather than a reason to fear, this must be a catalyst for action. Instead of simply resigning ourselves to what appears to some to be inevitable, we must improve our preparedness and plan for all contingencies. Instead of simply building defensive walls, we bolster our ability at all levels, federal, state, local, and the private sector to withstand disruptions, maintain operations, and recover quickly.*[41]

PUBLIC SAFETY ECOSYSTEMS

> *We need to move away from the mindset that Federal and State governments are always in the lead, and build upon the strengths of our local communities and, more importantly, our citizens. We must treat individuals and communities as key assets rather than liabilities. —W. Craig Fugate, FEMA Administrator*

It is clear that today the public, and those charged with its safety, live in a different and more complex world than existed a decade ago. Some threats have remained static, but much has changed, with new threats and risks emerging daily that continue to highlight the fragmentation of our public safety community. As long as fragmentation is the norm, public safety response structures will remain brittle and emergency response agencies will continually be forced to resort to heroic efforts to respond to and recover from disasters.

Achieving "resilience" will necessitate a rapid evolution, which will eventually lead to the extinction of fragmented legacy structures that create barriers between public safety organizations and the communities and citizens they serve. It is imperative that we begin viewing public safety as an ecosystem of interdependent organizations, communities, people, and processes. Like its namesake, a public safety ecosystem is a highly symbiotic community whose scope encompasses the entire "Ready–Respond–Recover" lifecycle. This collectivity is more than the sum of its parts, because it focuses individual behavior towards a common set of goals and achieves resilience through increased levels of individual self-sufficiency, collaboration, and resource sharing among all stakeholders.

The economic reality facing local, state, and federal governments[42] is also becoming a catalyst for the active involvement of both the private sector and citizens. As former Secretary of Homeland Security Michael Chertoff pointed out in 2008, readiness is too big a job for government alone:

> *The partnership model also acknowledges the reality that it is simply impossible and impossibly expensive for the government to handle 100 percent of the homeland security preparedness, prevention, response, and recovery responsibilities in the 21st century. There are too many places, too many things, and too many people for the government to take on the job of doing everything itself.*[43]

Public safety ecosystems will break down the traditional barriers that separate us because readiness concerns everyone. It is not the sole purview of governments, emergency managers, or first responders, but also is in the interest of communities, private organizations, and citizens who all have to work together as a unified team. Each has a vital role to play within the context of readiness, incident response, and recovery. Citizens are quite capable and willing to take responsibility for their own safety and security and that of their families. By quantifying risk and our readiness to meet that risk, we can more accurately set expectations and inform the public of the appropriate steps they should take to increase their readiness level. Developing a pervasive readiness framework and measuring our readiness provides all stakeholders with the information needed to assess the risks we face and make informed trade-off decisions.

CONCLUSION

Much work remains to be done to further evolve the concepts and refine the metrics for readiness measurement outlined here. However, a basic and practical framework for readiness measurement is a vast improvement over the *status quo* and has allowed Indiana to prioritize its investments, achieve significant cost savings, reduce redundancy, increase cross-jurisdictional coordination and materially reduce the overall fragmentation of the public safety system across the state. The authors continue to conduct basic research into readiness measurement, and, together with the Indiana Department of Homeland security, we are expanding upon the concepts we have outlined.[44]

Table 17-1 Modified Calculated Priority Risk Index	0.45	0.3	0.15	0.1
	Probability	**Magnitude / Severity**	**Warning Time**	**Duration**
	4 – Highly Likely	**4 – Catastrophic**	**4 – Minimal**	**4 – Prolonged**
	• Event is probable within the calendar year. • Event has up to 1 in 1 year chance of occurring (1/1 = 100%) • Chance of event is greater than 33% likely per year. • Event is "highly likely" to occur	• Local jurisdiction is overwhelmed and unable to effectively respond to the hazard. Local resources are inadequate or non-existent. Complete loss of communications. Massive regional, state, EMAC and federal response is required. Federal disaster declaration. • Local and regional medical services are unable to manage the volume of injuries and fatalities. Mass evacuation, sheltering, and care of displaced residents, medical patients, high risk and vulnerable populations are required.	• No-notice up to 6 Hours	• More Than 1 Week

(Continued)

Table 17-1

Modified Calculated
Priority Risk Index
(Continued)

	0.45	0.3	0.15	0.1
	Probability	**Magnitude / Severity**	**Warning Time**	**Duration**
	4 – Highly Likely	**4 – Catastrophic**	**4 – Minimal**	**4 – Prolonged**
		• Loss of public utilities, government and essential services for more than 1 month. Widespread destruction of critical infrastructure, public and private property. More than 50% of critical and non-critical facilities and infrastructure damaged or destroyed. Extended emergency response operations lasting more than 1 month may be required.		
	3 – Likely	**3 – Critical**	**3 – Marginal**	**3 – Extended**
	• Event is probable within the next three years. • Event has up to 1 in 3 years chance of occurring (1/3 = 33%) • Chance of event is greater than 20% but less than or equal to 33% per year. • Event is "likely" to occur.	• Local jurisdiction is unable to effectively respond without District-level mutual aid support and significant state assistance. Local resources have been expended and local agencies have reached the limits of their capabilities. Communications seriously degraded with significant impact on operations. State disaster declaration. • Local medical services are unable to manage number of injuries and fatalities. Patients require transportation to regional medical facilities outside of the affected areas. Local area evacuations, sheltering, and care of displaced residents, medical patients, high risk and vulnerable populations are required. • Loss of public utilities, government and essential services for up to 1 month. Significant damage to critical infrastructure, public and private property over a large area. Up to 50% of critical and non-critical facilities and infrastructure damaged. Emergency response operations lasting up to 1 month may be required.	• 6 to 12 Hours	• Up to 1 Week
	2 – Possible	**2 – Moderate**	**2 – Limited**	**2-Intermediate**
	• Event is probable within the next five years.	• Local jurisdiction is able to effectively respond with significant inter-local mutual aid support and limited state assistance. Local and mutual aid resources are adequate to support response. Communications systems operating near capacity. Local medical services are able to manage volume of injuries and fatalities but are near the limits of their capabilities. Only critically injured patients are diverted to facilities outside of the affected areas. Limited evacuations and sheltering required.	• 12-24 Hours	• Up to 1 Day
	• Event has up to 1 in 5 year chance of occurring (1/5 = 20%). • Chance of event is greater than 10% but less than or equal to 20% per year. • Event could "possibly" occur.	• Loss of public utilities, government and essential services for up to 1 week. Significant damage to critical infrastructure, public and private property over a localized area. Up to 25% of critical and non-critical facilities and infrastructure damaged. Response operations lasting up to 1 week may be required.		

1 – Unlikely	1 – Negligible	1 – Optimal	1 – Brief
• Event is probable within the next 10 years. • Event has an up to 1 to 10 years chance of occurring (1/10 = 10%). • Chance of event occurrence is less than or equal to 10% • Event is "unlikely" to occur.	• Local jurisdiction is able to manage incident with standard mutual aid and little or no state assistance. Local resources are adequate to support response. Communications system operating normally. Local emergency. • Local medical services are able to manage number of injuries and fatalities with on hand personnel and resources. • Loss of public utilities, government and essential services for up to 24 hours. Damage contained to a single incident scene and immediate area. Up to 5% of critical and non-critical facilities and infrastructure damaged. • Response operations lasting up to 72 hours may be required.	• 24+ Hours	• Up to 6 Hours

Table 17-2

Calculated Risk Specific Readiness

0.25 Plan	0.30 Organize/Equip	0.30 Train	0.15 Exercise
4 – Comprehensive • Plan is connected to real time resource and capability databases • Modeling allows leaders to simulate risks against actual capabilities and resources and see shortfalls • Trending • Changes to readiness levels are monitored and advanced planning occurs when possible	**4 – Capabilities based Organization** • Capability and Resource information is shared with other organizations easily through connected systems and interoperable equipment • Large scale emergency response coordination with private industry and other governmental agencies • Certifications for equipment and resources are monitored for readiness • Gap analysis is regularly updated	**4 – Constant** • Daily practices reinforce best practices • Mentoring and apprenticeship opportunities for complex skills • Job rotation and cross-functional teams used to spread knowledge • Adequate sustainment for current and future training needs	**4 – Comprehensive** • Feedback from simulations is incorporated into revised plans (AARs and CAPs) • Live simulations occur routinely on a variety of hazards • Simulation of recovery, not just the event • Community involvement • Participation in state and federal level full scale exercises
3 – Moderate • Historical situations are examined; needs for capabilities including training and equipment reflect best practices in incidence response • Plans are updated within one month as changes in resource availability occur • Plans demonstrate an all-hazards approach • Plans are vetted with stakeholders	**3 – Asset based Organization** • Existing equipment is certified as ready • Sufficient equipment to deal with occasional medium scale emergencies • Mutual aid plans in place to deal with large scale emergencies • Sustainment plan in place for current and future capacity and capabilities	**3 – Routine** • Knowledge/skills/abilities are being taught • New employee orientation prepares employees for expected disasters • Training environments are similar enough to hazard conditions to develop muscle memory • Current sustainment for training documented	**3 – Moderate** • Evaluation of simulations occurs (AARs and CAPSs) • Simulations of the highest probability risks occur at least annually • Actual resource counts are used in exercise • Interagency involvement (state and local) and future funding sustainment plan

(Continued)

Table 17-2

Calculated Risk
Specific Readiness
(Continued)

0.25	0.30	0.30	0.15
Plan	**Organize/Equip**	**Train**	**Exercise**
2 –Limited	**2 – Moderate**	**2 – Limited**	**2 – Limited**
• Hazards are prioritized based on probability • Plan exists but information is stale after years • Plans exist but do not follow the National Response Framework and/or FEMA's CPG 101 Guide Version 2.0 (2010)	• New equipment purchases support national interoperability standards (NIMS) • Sufficient personnel and equipment to deal with routine local emergencies • All hazard incident training for some first responders	• Annual classroom and simulation training for the highest probability risks • Annual classroom training for other hazards • Received local, state and federal training	• Table top simulation of the highest probability risk occurs annually • Limited functional exercises and local level exercises • Sustainment plan for exercises for immediate needs
1 – Minimal	**1 – Minimal**	**1 – Minimal**	**1 – Minimal**
• Lacks knowledge of the threats and risks • Required capacity and capabilities not understood • No documented plans exists	• Shortage in capacity exists to deal with local emergencies • Shortage in capability exists to deal with local emergencies • No continued funding mechanism for current sustainment	• Annual classroom training for the highest probability risks • Required basic level training completed • No identified sustainment plan for training for immediate future	• Response plans do not exist or are updated only after actual disasters based on lessons learned • No sustainment plan • Local jurisdiction exercise only

NOTES

1. These have ranged widely in severity and scope from acts of man such as terrorist attacks, the catastrophic BP oil spill, technological events including power grid crashes, the nuclear meltdown in Japan and cyber security breaches, to severe weather incidents with massive earthquakes, tsunamis, volcano eruptions, hurricanes, tornadoes, winter storms, and flooding, all occurring within short spans of time.

2. *Presidential Policy Directive-8 (PPD-8), National Preparedness* (Washington, DC: The White House, March 30, 2011), http://www.dhs.gov/xabout/laws/gc_1215444247124.shtm.

3. Among many severe weather events as of May 23, 2011, a total of 1,170 tornadoes were reported in the United States. To date, 2011 has produced the most tornado-related deaths in the United States since 1936, http://en.wikipedia.org/wiki/Tornadoes_of_2011.

4. Some say resilience is a function of resources and adaptability, while others argue that it can be engineered into systems. It is our view that, in practice, national resilience amounts to a sum of its parts and can only be achieved at a micro-level. National resilience stems directly from the ability of individuals, families, organizations, corporations, and communities to adapt to the new conditions a crisis imposes while minimizing casualties, securing basic quality of life and preserving their core values and identity.

5. *Interim Task Force Report on Resilience*, The George Washington University Homeland Security Policy Institute, May 16, 2011, http://www.gwumc.edu/hspi/policy/report_Resilience1.pdf.

6. *Concept Development: An Operational Framework for Resilience*, Homeland Security Studies and Analysis Institute, August 27th, 2009.

7. In this context, readiness implies the state of being fully prepared for something, including mitigation efforts (attempts to reduce the effects of disasters or to prevent hazards from developing into disasters altogether).

8. By this we mean the entire Ready → Respond → Recover continuum as our public safety community has a shared mission to (1) mitigate known risks where possible; (2) maintain a state of readiness to contain the effects of forecasted disastrous events to minimize loss of life, injury, and damage to property; (3) provide rescue, relief, rehabilitation, and other services as necessary in the aftermath of the disaster; and (4) maintain a capability and resources to continue to sustain essential functions.

9. Over the last seven years, Homeland Security Grant Program funding for the Indiana Department of Homeland Security has diminished over 89% from over $55 million to just over $5.6 million in 2011.

10. The term "pervasive" can be defined as existing in or spreading through every part of something. Thus, "pervasive readiness" is the idea of readiness as an integral part of the very fabric of our nation.

11. Many state, tribal, and local governments and private nonprofit organizations enter into mutual aid agreements to provide emergency assistance to each other in the event of disasters or emergencies. These agreements often are written but occasionally are arranged verbally after a disaster or emergency occurs. Federal Emergency Management Agency, Disaster Assistance Policy 9523.6.

12. Enabling Government Efficiency, Implementation of the State of Indiana Homeland Security District Concept, Indiana Department of Homeland Security, December 2010.

13. We can likewise take examples from other countries such as Switzerland or Israel which have endured, or continue to endure, significant and prolonged disruptions to their societies. During World War II, Switzerland (a small but industrialized country with virtually no raw materials and limited agricultural capacity due to the alpine nature of the topography) was completely surrounded by Germany and had to find innovative ways to increase food production. Every available green space was cultivated with bread grain, vegetables, or potatoes. This approach enabled the Swiss to achieve a remarkably high level of self-sufficiency (resilience) during a prolonged crisis.

14. FEMA Strategic Plan 2011–2014.

15. Presidential Policy Directive-8 (PPD-8), The White House, March 30, 2011, p. 2.

16. KPIs are performance measures commonly used by an organization to evaluate its success or the success of a particular activity in which it is engaged. For more, see http://en.wikipedia.org/wiki/Performance_indicator.

17. For example, at the Bureau of Motor Vehicles (BMV), Daniels said, time was money: "Cut wait times and Hoosiers [Indiana citizens] have more time to run their businesses or work at their jobs." As a result, the Indiana BMV won an international award for customer service for cutting wait times at license branches and they achieved this while at the same time instituting federal-required steps to ensure IDs were secure (Real ID).

18. IDHS uses the *Acadis Readiness Suite* software to manage real-time tracking of personnel, training, and response resources, http://www.envisagenow.com/acadis.

19. Such as their current number, location, and disposition.

20. Among many examples of this phenomenon, the authors had the opportunity to discuss these issues with a Colonel from the National Guard who indicated that while there was a general idea of the number of Humvees available across the state, the Guard did not know which armory they were located in nor which were operational.

21. Enabling Government Efficiency, Implementation of the State of Indiana Homeland Security District Concept, IDHS 2010.

22. Image source: http://www.fema.gov.

23. Another typical formulation is this: Risk = (T, V, C), where T = Threat, V = Vulnerability and C = Consequence).

24. Indiana State Hazard/Threat Identification and Risk Assessment, 2010.

25. Indiana's severe winter storm in February of 2011 created significant road hazards but also had the cascading effect of wide-area power outages in subzero conditions.

26. *State of Indiana Homeland Security District Risk Score and Comparative Analysis*, 2011.

27. This process evolved out of the Homeland Security Presidential Directive-8 (HSPD-8) and is being further refined under the previously referenced PPD-8, http://www.fema.gov/pdf/government/npg.pdf.

28. The need to affect a rapid response to an emergency is why we have trained police, firefighters, or emergency personnel on pre-positioned standby 24/7 and why our Nation maintains the Strategic National Stockpile (SNS), which is maintained by the Centers for Disease Control and Prevention. It consists of medicine and medical supplies that would be necessary to respond to a public health emergency. See Centers for Disease Control and Prevention, Office of Public Health Preparedness and Response: *Strategic National Stockpile*, http://www.cdc.gov/phpr/stockpile.htm.

29. While there can be similarities in how one reacts to disasters, event-specific actions form the basis for most emergency plans.

30. Prior to the establishment of the Department of Homeland Security, there were six separate database systems that contained information regarding the certifications/credentials of personnel. Many of the records were duplicates, or lacked detail. Essentially, it was impossible for the State to get an accurate tally of the force strength by discipline available to respond to specific emergencies.

31. Envisage Technologies, Public Safety: The Best Protection Is Your Homeland Security Workforce, http://www.envisagenow.com/acadis/public_safety.aspx.

32. The National Incident Management System (NIMS) provides a systematic, proactive approach to guide departments and agencies at all levels of government, nongovernmental organizations, and the private sector to work seamlessly to prevent, protect against, respond to, recover from, and mitigate the effects of incidents, regardless of cause, size, location, or complexity. NIMS Resource typing is the categorization and description of response resources that are commonly exchanged in disasters through mutual aid agreements. The National Integration Center (NIC) has developed and published over 120 resource typing definitions. See http://www.fema.gov/emergency/nims/FAQ.shtm#item1a.

33. This new capability is under development and expected to come online in 2011.

34. Good to Great and the Social Sectors, 2005, p. 31.

35. Tracking changes over time will ensure that *both* improvements and/or deterioration of a district's readiness posture can be effectively monitored.

36. Good to Great and the Social Sectors, p. 7.

37. Law Enforcement, Fire, Emergency Medical, Homeland Security, Emergency Management, and Public Health, to name a few.

38. Business Rule Revolution: Running Business the Right Way, October 2006.

39. See Conference Report accompanying Public Law 111-83, the Homeland Security Act of 2010.

40. Report to Congress of the Local, State, Tribal, and Federal Preparedness Task Force, September 2010, page x.

41. Remarks by John Brennan, Assistant to the President for Homeland Security and Counterterrorism, at the Center for Strategic and International Studies (CSIS), May 26, 2010.

42. The United States House of Representatives recently passed an appropriations bill for the Department of Homeland Security (DHS) in fiscal 2012 that cuts about $1 billion from the department's budget in 2011, largely by cutting grants for local first responders.

43. Remarks by Michael Chertoff, Secretary of the US Department of Homeland Security, *The Future of Homeland Security*, The Brookings Institution, September 5, 2008, http://www.hstoday.us/briefings/today-s-news-analysis/single-article/house-dhs-spending-bill-sets-up-fight-over-grants-funding-for–2012/1742de01e117309261d52aad155e52df.html.

44. The authors in collaboration with other scholars are working on a "Readiness Maturity Model" concept, which will provide a "meta-view" of readiness and resilience.

18

THE PSYCHOLOGICAL PERCEPTION OF RISK

Baruch Fischhoff

Howard Heinz University Professor, Carnegie Mellon University

"Risk communication": Provision of concise, comprehensible, credible information, as needed to make effective decisions regarding risks.

INTRODUCTION

The Challenge Terrorists seek to undermine public morale, to the point where societies collapse or lose their momentum, at home and abroad. The direct route to this goal involves instilling terror, undermining citizens' well-being, ability to function, and confidence in their way of life. One indirect route involves disrupting normal life, by interfering with economic activity, travel, education, leisure, elections, and the like. A second indirect route involves alienating people from their leaders, by throwing doubt on the two cornerstones of trust: competence and honesty. A successful attack (or even a false alarm) may leave citizens feeling that their authorities not only failed to protect them but also denied them the ability to protect themselves (e.g., by not providing needed material resources and candid situation assessments). A third indirect route involves turning citizens against one another, by creating the feeling that they are receiving differential treatment, perhaps even with some people profiting while others are suffering.

In these ways, terror is a continuous mind game, punctuated by events with horrific physical consequences. As a result, counterterrorism involves a battle of wits, for the hearts and minds of civilian populations. Communicating effectively about risks is one element of that battle.[1] It requires accomplishing three tasks.

Task 1: Manage risks well, so as to have a credible message to communicate. Unless they have made reasonable progress in managing terror, the authorities will find it difficult to inspire confidence in their messages. The very need to communicate can suggest that they have not done their job. If the authorities have inconsistent policies (e.g., in setting alert levels or requiring safety practices), then their messages may prompt further skepticism.

Task 2: Create appropriate communication channels. These channels not only deliver content but also are part of the message. Improvised, fragmentary, and uncoordinated channels should reduce public confidence by suggesting poor execution in other, less visible aspects of terror risk management. Effective, appropriate channels should increase public confidence by demonstrating that a common framework underlies the authorities' preparation, alert, crisis, and recovery plans. The accepted standard for risk communication has two-way channels in which recipients are treated like partners, invited to participate in shaping how risks are managed and entitled to share what is learned about them. In contrast, one-way channels send the message that the public is being managed, told no more than what the authorities choose to reveal. One-way communications have their place, in public relations, public affairs, and emergencies with no time for consultation. However, over the long run, it takes two-way communication for the public's needs to be heard and honored.

Task 3: Deliver decision-relevant information, concisely and comprehensibly. Developing effective content begins with rigorous analysis of the facts that citizens need to know in order to make the choices facing them. That analysis must be followed by empirical study of what audience members already know, and then the design of communications bridging the critical gaps. That design must balance the conflicting demands of brevity and completeness. On the one hand, it must use (and be seen as using) recipients' time efficiently. On the other hand, it must provide enough background for recipients to integrate its message with their evolving "mental models" of the situation.

These three tasks interact. In order to manage risks (task 1), the authorities must make assumptions about citizens' behavior. For example, when will people comprehend, trust, obey, and execute instructions to evacuate, shelter in place, get (or avoid) medical treatment, leave children in school (or collect them), surrender personal data, report on neighbors' actions (or suspicious packages), maintain emergency supplies, or install computer firewalls? The answers to these questions depend on the effectiveness of the communications channels that the authorities select (task 2) and the content put through them (task 3). That effectiveness shapes, in turn, citizens' faith in the authorities and the appropriate assumptions about their behavior (task 1).

Incompetent communications can further terrorists' short-term and long-term goals. For example, a common misconception is that people panic during a crisis, behaving irrationally as individuals and groups.[2] A large body of research contradicts that belief, finding that people typically respond reasonably, even bravely, to such challenges.[3] People may act ineffectively when forced to rely on poor information. However, the fault then lies with the inputs to their decisions, not with how they make them. In hindsight, citizens will be critical of officials who failed to collect the right information; they will be unforgiving of officials who failed to disseminate the information that they had or misrepresented it for unacceptable reasons (e.g., hiding their failings).

Behavioral research provides the scientific foundation for effective terror risk management. Those who ignore it needlessly put the public—and their own reputations—in peril by relying on hunches. For example, the myth of panic encourages the unwarranted use of coercive measures (e.g., hiding risks; sending soldiers, rather than first responders, to emergency scenes), treating the public as though it cannot be trusted to behave responsibly. Such policies incur the short-term risk that coercion will be less effective than mobilizing the self-organizing properties of a motivated, intelligent populace. They take the long-term risk of undermining public trust by violating the social contract between citizens and authorities. If so, then social resilience may be sacrificed, in a misguided attempt to protect physical well-being. Terror is a multiple-play game. Actions that undermine a society's cohesion will reduce its ability to defend itself, as well as forfeiting some of what it values.

The Resources

The confrontation with terrorism has revealed new risks and changed the shape of old ones (e.g., those faced by aviation and shipping). The new risks and the new wrinkles are often intellectually and emotionally challenging. They involve complex, novel phenomena. They require expertise distributed over multiple disciplines and cultures. They are dynamic and uncertain. They pose difficult trade-offs: your money or your life, your life or your liberty, my freedom or yours.

They require vigilance, from already weary people. They evoke social tension, in an already complex time.

Although the legacy of existing risks adds to the stress of managing the new ones, that experience also provides people with resources. One such resource is knowledge about related risks and control mechanisms (e.g., how to evacuate a building, how to reach loved ones quickly). A second resource is strategies for thinking about risks (e.g., where to get second opinions, how to contemplate difficult trade-offs). These strategies have been documented in behavioral decision research and behavioral economics, overlapping fields that study behavior in ways that allow comparing it with formal models defining optimal performance.[4] Those comparisons show how much specific imperfections matter, how they come about, and how they might be corrected (if improvement is needed). The basic research in these fields has been applied extensively with health, safety, and environmental risks.[5] Many of those risks are intellectually and emotionally challenging, in ways that prepare people for dealing with terrorism. Applying that research here constitutes a "defense dividend" from investments made in studying into such "peaceful" threats.

Given the urgency of terror risk communication, we can ill afford to reinvent this research—unless we have powerful evidence that the usual rules of behavior are repealed when people face terrorism. As a result, the remainder of this chapter begins with research into other risks, and then proceeds to guarded extrapolations to terror. The next three sections deal with the three tasks facing risk communication described earlier. The first deals with the second task, creating appropriate channels. These channels constrain the nature and reach of the communications. Within these constraints, decision-relevant facts must be communicated concisely and comprehensibly. The next section considers the science relevant to this task. It leads to treatment of what risk communication contributes to the first task, managing terror risks effectively.

CREATING APPROPRIATE COMMUNICATION CHANNELS

Other Risks

Health, safety, and environmental risk communications are a central social function, shaping relationships between citizens and authorities.[6] Experiences with them provide both lessons and expectations for terror risk communication. In the western democracies, the evolving standard calls for a high degree of shared responsibility. It reflects faith (and hope) that officials can create the facts that the public needs for effective decision making, and then deliver those facts in a comprehensible, credible form. The outcomes of this social experiment will depend on both institutional commitment and technical execution. By facilitating that execution, risk research may enhance institutions' commitment, by showing their leaders that effective public engagement is possible.

Figure 18-1 shows how the Canadian Standard Association has conceptualized this process. On the right appear a variant of the standard steps in risk management. It is unusual only in requiring managers to ask whether they have completed each step well enough to go on to the next one. The left-hand side shows two-way risk communication as essential to each stage. Thus, citizens must be heard and be informed from when risk analyses are formulated to when they are executed. That engagement asserts their right to know about and shape risk management. It is a striking departure from the one-way communication strategy sometimes known as "decide-announce-defend."

Figure 18-1

Steps in the Q850 risk management decision-making process—simple model

Source: CSA, July 1997. *Risk Management: Guideline for Decision-Makers* (CAN/CSA Q850-97) Canadian Standards Association.

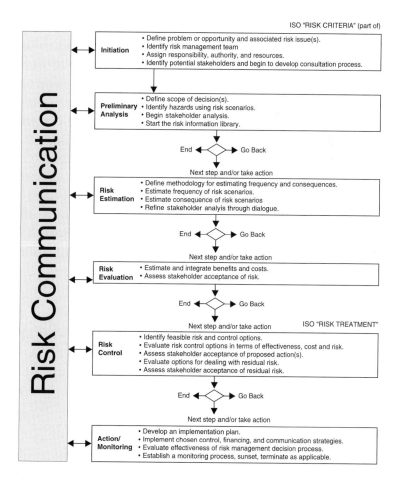

Many bodies have advanced similar policies. In the United States, they include the Presidential-Congressional Commission on Risk[7] and the Environmental Protection Agency.[8] In the United Kingdom, they include the Royal Commission on Environmental Pollution,[9] Health and Safety Executive,[10] Parliamentary Office of Science and Technology,[11] and Cabinet Office.[12] All endorse involving the relevant publics, understanding and addressing their needs, while taking advantage of their expertise. All recognize the importance of trust for risk management, and the centrality of open, competent communication in securing it.

The evolution of this philosophy is reflected in a series of reports from the U.S. National Academy of Sciences. The "red book"[13] recognized that risk analysis inevitably reflects both science and politics. Even if scientists manage to avoid the direct influence of vested interests, their choice of analytical topics and risk outcomes takes a position on which issues matter; so do decisions about whether to invest in creating data that could support or undermine particular interests (e.g., monitoring health or environmental effects of hydrofracking). The red book advocated recognizing these issues explicitly, so that stakeholders know whether their concerns are being addressed. Doing so requires hearing stakeholders describe those concerns—through direct consultation and basic research into what generally matters. Although this stance presaged the current (two-way) communication standard, the immediate response to the red book was a quest for full separation: scientists would assess the risks, while officials would decide what to do about them. That separation was designed to keep scientists from spinning their results and politicians from claiming unwarranted expertise. It was naturally appealing to scientists hoping to perform purely "objective" research—and ignore how political power shapes research agendas.

Improving Risk Communication[14] asserted the public's right to know the results of risk analyses. That commitment envisioned an active public, unwilling to wait for scientists and officials to manage risks and, thereby, decide the public's fate. It also reflected the view that the public can understand risks—contrary to many experts' belief in citizens' incompetence (captured in phrases like "real versus perceived risks," "hysterical public," or "panic"). The report concluded that citizens could fill a constructive role, if provided with diligently prepared communications.

One body of research evidence supporting this conclusion examined the sources of disagreements between laypeople and experts regarding risks. It found that, rather than just reflecting lay ignorance or stupidity (as experts often claimed), disagreements may also arise from experts (1) using terms differently than lay people (e.g., which outcomes they treat as the "risk" of a technology; how they weight catastrophic potential); (2) falling prey to self-serving biases, assuming the worst about the others' motivation and biases; and (3) being insufficiently critical of their own evidence. A common finding is that citizens are most skeptical when that evidence is weakest, such as assessments of low-probability, high-consequence events.[15]

Understanding Risk[16] revived the red book's intertwining of science and values by challenging the claim that scientists can simply do their work and leave the politics to others. Rather, it showed how the framing of any risk analysis expresses some values. They are seen in its choice of topics (why some outcomes are studied and not others) and definition of terms. For example, "risk" could mean just mortality or also include morbidity; its definition must assign weights to different consequences. Even weighting all deaths equally expresses values. It places no greater value on deaths to young people, mothers, or those exposed to a risk involuntarily.[17] The report argues that stakeholders should participate in choosing these definitions—and that risk analyses conducted without the public's involvement are unlikely to serve its interests.

Citizen involvement was further endorsed by the congressionally mandated Committee on Setting Priorities for the National Institutes of Health.[18] It led to creation of a Citizens Advisory Panel, chaired by the head of NIH. Another NRC report, *Toward Environmental Justice*, called for "participatory science," involving citizens in the design and conduct of studies affecting their communities.[19] That participation takes advantage of their expertise (e.g., in exposure processes), while ensuring that research results are shared with them. Such involvement should improve citizens' scientific and policy-making sophistication while increasing the chances of their accepting the results of risk analyses seen as collaboratively produced.

Terror Risks   Given the variety of terror risks and publics, potentially changing over time, this section will not attempt to summarize what people believe about terror. Rather, it will consider how to create a consultative process integrating risk analysis and communication, like that depicted in Figure 18-1, to meet the demands of several terror risks.

Smallpox vaccination. In 2002 to 2003, the United States sought to vaccinate first responders and healthcare workers against *vaccinia*, a virus closely related to familiar strains of smallpox. The campaign generated considerable acrimony, including controversy over the risks faced by healthcare workers and compensation for health problems that they suffered or "caused" by transmitting diseases to others. A fraction of the initial vaccination goal was achieved, accompanied by disagreement over whether that meant that the program had failed or that the need for it had been reassessed.

Whatever the lesson of this campaign, mass vaccination is a plausible prospect in the struggle against terror, not to mention pandemics of infectious diseases arising from natural causes.[20] The risks and benefits of such campaigns are sufficiently uncertain that responsible risk management must begin with a formal analysis of the anticipated impacts of alternative programs. A two-way risk communication process would begin by enlisting stakeholders to identify the consequences that matter to them. For healthcare workers, that list would have some obvious entries, including their personal health risks and health benefits for others. Nonetheless, having workers nominate those consequences directly conveys respect for their work and well-being. Involving them might also reveal less obvious consequences, such as the effects of vaccination on their insurability, legal liability for secondary infections, or ability to provide emergency services. Analyses that neglect vital outcomes are guilty of misplaced precision in analyzing the factors that they do consider.

As the analytical process continues, healthcare workers would follow its work, ensuring that the results are comprehensible and credible. They would contribute their knowledge about how healthcare works (e.g., needle stick rates, compliance with precautionary rules) and how it might be improved. Analogous consultations could shape the analysis to meet the informational needs of other stakeholders. For example, members of immunocompromised groups might want estimates of disease and side effect rates specific to their condition. First responders would have their own issues and concerns. Minority groups might have special suspicions and needs for assurance. In each case, the needed two-way communications could be conducted directly, through representatives, or with social research (e.g., surveys, in-depth interviews).

Domestic surveillance. Managing terror requires police work. That means placing some people under some degree of surveillance, reflecting some measure of suspicion. By design, the process reduces their privacy. Even when suspicions lead nowhere, they still impose costs. Those costs might be as small as having a note in one's file (indicating a suspicion that was raised and dismissed) or as large as a lingering shadow of doubt complicating one's job, health, and so on. These risks to innocent civilians must be justified by reductions in terror risks. "Cleared suspects," such as travelers who pass airport screening, receive benefit from that reduction in compensation for the costs. Suspect groups pay the price of surveillance, with possibly compensating benefits (e.g., demonstrating the innocence of most members, catching or deterring the few bent on trouble).

Explaining the risks and benefits of surveillance programs is a familiar chore for police officials. Controversies over profiling show the difficulties of getting it right, played out against the history of relations between specific police forces and communities, constrained by limits to the information that can be shared without compromising operations (and the community's security). Approached as a risk communication task, surveillance procedures would be accompanied by a dialogue with stakeholders. As elsewhere, creating channels for respectful, proactive communication carries a message in itself. The content of those communications should improve stakeholders' understanding of both specific policies and general principles (e.g., legal protections). Content would flow in both directions (e.g., informing authorities about community sensitivities, discussing problems that might be addressed without reducing effectiveness).

These communications must be grounded in formal analysis, no less than ones regarding hazardous technologies, with the special challenges of discussing programs without revealing details that compromise their efficacy. One critical topic is likely to be the acceptable rates of false positives and negatives with surveillance methods of varying intensity and targets of varying frequency. Other things being equal, there will be more innocent people with less discriminating procedures, rarer targets, and greater aversion to missing guilty ones. For example, if there are very few guilty individuals, they may only be found with very intrusive procedures and high arrest rates.

These relationships are well understood by decision scientists.[21] Applying them often produces unintuitive results. For example, people intuitively exaggerate how well many diagnostic procedures work and underestimate how difficult it is to detect rare phenomena.[22] As a result, institutions require a commitment to analysis, lest they be misled by intuition and create inappropriate expectations among those who depend on them. It's important to know when the best possible program is still very porous.

Decontamination standards. Chemical, radiological, and biological attacks impose both immediate costs and longer-term ones, arising from their ability to disrupt everyday life. Avoiding contaminated areas incurs economic costs from lost business, relocation, reduced property values, and so on. It may also incur health costs from the stresses of dislocation (e.g., lost income, family tension, difficulty maintaining healthcare regimens). A comprehensive analysis of decontamination standards would consider all these effects, and then determine acceptable trade-offs through a consultative process. The result might be accepting exposures different from those adopted elsewhere for the same threat—if there are different control options or distributions of risks and benefits. For example, tolerable radiation exposures may be different for patients, healthcare practitioners, nuclear power plants works, and residents of areas contaminated by "dirty bombs" (radioactive dispersion devices). Those inconsistencies will reflect the beliefs, values, and political power of the individuals involved. As a result, terror risk managers cannot simply adopt an existing standard.[23]

Creating cleanup standards for terrorist contaminations requires dedicated deliberations, informed by scientific research and social values. Such novel choices require participants to "construct" preferences from their relevant basic values.[24] They can often be aided by neutral presentation of alternative options. For example, it may help to consider the suite of exposure standards for a given contaminant, and then reflect on the politics and realities leading to it. Unless standards are set before they are needed, the process of creating them will add confusion to already stressful situations. The result may serve parochial interests, pushing people back into buildings more quickly than they want or keeping them out when they would gladly accept a small risk in return for resuming normal life and work.

Thus, establishing cleanup standards requires a socially credible process, informed by research into the effects of both radiation and the disruptions caused by reducing radiation risks. No stakeholder will be familiar with all the technical issues. Neither will any expert (e.g., health physicists will know about radiation, but not stress). As elsewhere, the act of consultation should lend credibility to the eventual risk management standard. Communication materials developed to inform standard setters could be adapted for broader distribution, informing the public about the contamination, the standard, and the standard-setting process. Good explanations and a credible process should reduce public anxiety.

DELIVERING DECISION-RELEVANT INFORMATION
CONCISELY AND COMPREHENSIBLY

Other Risks

The logic of creating the content of communications is straightforward: (1) Analytically, determine the facts most relevant to predicting the outcomes that matter most to citizens. (2) Empirically, determine what citizens know already. (3) Creatively, design messages to close the critical gaps, applying scientifically sound information-processing principles. (4) Empirically, evaluate the impact of the messages. (5) Iteratively, repeat the process, until acceptable understanding is achieved.[25]

The analytical process of prioritizing information is essential to making best use of a narrow communication channel. Citizens will have other things on their minds (e.g., suffering from a medical condition, anxious about relatives). Poorly chosen content can narrow the channel further: Why pay attention to messages saying things that are irrelevant or go without saying? Why trust ones that omit vital facts or treat recipients like idiots, needing explanations for obvious things?

When people face well-formulated personal or policy decisions, they need *quantitative* estimates of the probability and magnitude of the risks and benefits affected by their choices. They may also need *qualitative* information about the processes determining those outcomes, so that they have an intuitive feel for them, along with the feeling of competence needed to "follow the action" about them. Qualitative information is essential to people who are formulating decision options or monitoring their environment for changes.[26]

As an example of formal analysis of quantitative information needs, consider patients facing carotid endarterectomy, which involves scraping out the carotid artery, for patients with atherosclerosis. Although successful surgery can reduce the risk of stroke, many things can go wrong, so many that it is hard to bear them all in mind. However, analysis finds that only a few risks are severe enough and likely enough to matter to many surgery candidates.[27] Thus, while no risks should be hidden, communication should focus on these critical ones (death, stroke, and facial paralysis).

As an example of formal analysis of quantitative information needs, consider what teens need to know about HIV-AIDS in order to reduce their risks, without unduly constraining their lives, ostracizing others who may be ill, and so on. Teens need quantitative information about prevalence, transmissibility, and the like. They also need qualitative information about the key processes determining those outcomes, both to give the estimates credibility and to allow teens to create better options (e.g., prevention strategies, partner screening). Teens' general knowledge of infectious disease, partly acquired through intensive HIV-AIDS education, means that many facts go without saying. However, there are often gaps in their knowledge that undermine the value of what they know. For example, they may not have been taught or learned on their own what determines the risks of different sexual practices. Like most people in most situations, they may not realize how small risks mount up through repeated exposure. Closing these gaps in ways that reinforce feelings of self-efficacy can help teens manage these risks while achieving their other goals (e.g., friendship, intimacy, enjoyment).[28]

Although the details of communications vary by context, they can draw on design principles, identified in behavioral research.[29] For example, individuals' ability to process risk communications depends on basic competencies. They need numeracy in order to understand the impacts of risks and risk reduction measures. They need language literacy in order to process written messages. They need scientific literacy in order to grasp the content of messages that, with terror, can span many domains. The research shows how to assess these competencies and address their gaps.[30]

People's responses are also constrained by their cognitive capacity. Given its limits, they must either acquire domain-specific knowledge or rely on robust but imperfect *heuristics*. Such rules of thumb simplify problems and provide approximate answers, at the price of somewhat predictable biases. For example, people seem to count, almost automatically, how frequently they see events. As a result, they can estimate frequencies well, except when some events are disproportionately visible. Unless people stop to think about whether appearances are deceiving and then can correct for the bias, relying on experience may mislead them.[31]

Researchers relying on behavioral theories and methods have found ways to increase lay understanding of many risks. For example, one challenge is giving a feeling for very low probabilities. There are about 310 million people in the United States. Because it is hard to bear that denominator in mind, when thinking about risks with a few salient casualties in the numerator, communicators need to compute the actual risk. As mentioned, people often struggle to see how risks accumulate through repeated exposure, hence neglect small recurrent risks (e.g., driving without a seat belt). Here, too, it can help to do the calculations so that people do not have to do that for themselves. Verbal quantifiers (e.g., "likely," "rare") can imply different quantitative equivalents to different people (and even to the same person in different situations). As a result, people need numbers, lest they be misled.[32]

Even when people understand the facts of a decision, they may have difficulty making decisions if the events are unfamiliar. In effect, people may not know what it would mean to experience those outcomes. Conventional survey research is ill-suited to eliciting preferences among such unfamiliar prospects; not knowing what they want, respondents may look for clues for what to say or answer arbitrarily. Constructive valuation methods seek to help people understand the options and themselves by suggesting alternative perspectives, trying to deepen respondents' understanding without biasing it.[33]

One aspect of that challenge is predicting personal emotions. A simple example is anticipating how one will feel if an investment goes bad or one becomes sick. Current emotions can color those predictions. For example, anger increases optimism, as well as the tendency to blame other people, rather than complex situations, for problems.[34] Those shifts might be useful in mobilizing for an immediate fight. They might undermine policy-making by amplifying a natural tendency toward undue optimism.

Terror Risks

Applying the reservoir of behavioral research required overcoming several institutional barriers. One is that many risks have yet to be analyzed from the perspective of citizens' decision-making needs. A second is that many officials are empty-handed when they must communicate about terror events because no one has done the needed communication research. A third is that there is little or no systematic tracking of public perceptions, meaning that officials often must fly blind regarding the needs of their public. When officials must improvise, they risk losing trust that is hard to restore.[35]

Unfortunately, many experts' first response is, in effect, to tell citizens to "go away while we figure things out." When they do speak, experts may be tempted to spin the facts for their audience's "own good." That may mean magnifying risks in order to motivate citizens or understate them for calming effect—rather than leveling with people so that they can make informed choices. A common form of ineffective communication involves rhetorical comparisons of the form "why get so exercised about terror when you're still smoking" or "only five people have died from anthrax [so far], compared with 40,000 annually from motor vehicle accidents." Such comparisons not only put many people off by their tone but have no logical foundation when the situations differ in other ways (e.g., benefits, control options).

One common institutional response is training experts in communication skills, emphasizing principles like those in the appendix to this chapter. Although such training might reduce misconceptions about the public (e.g., the myth of panic), it is difficult to change behavioral patterns, especially when people tend to "regress" to old behaviors in stressful situations. Moreover, better communication skills can go only so far without good answers to the audience's questions: "What is happening?" and "What should I do?" The best communicator has little chance, without staff support, of creating concise, comprehensible messages.

The remainder of this section sketches conclusions about content that might emerge from systematic treatment of the three examples. These speculations are, of course, no substitute for systematic analysis, design, and evaluation.

Smallpox vaccination. Communications here might be needed to inform choices such as whether to create a national stockpile, participate in a national vaccination campaign, evaluate a past one, or help someone who has been exposed. Each choice will demand different quantitative information, suited to its potential outcomes. Each requires elements of the same qualitative information about what smallpox is, how it can be controlled (or spread), and which people and institutions are involved. The more complete individuals' core of related beliefs, or mental models, the less needs to be said, meaning that communication should become easier if the content is right.

Unless they receive directly relevant information, people will draw on seemingly related beliefs. With smallpox, these might relate to other infectious diseases and vaccines. Communicators should be particularly alert to cases where such reasonable inferences are misleading. For example, during the run-up to the 2003 smallpox vaccination campaign, a survey found that few Americans confidently believed that vaccination could be effective after exposure. Somehow, U.S. communicators had failed to make that easily understandable fact salient. Nor had they conveyed the vital fact that anthrax is not easily transmissible.[36] These communicators may have failed in their analysis (not identifying these facts as vital), their empirical research (not assessing lay beliefs), or their messages (not getting the content through clearly).

Individuals' mental models for health decisions naturally include the other people involved, including healthcare providers. As a result, smallpox vaccines will be perceived against the backdrop of controversies over other vaccines, in both civilian populations (e.g., MMR) and military (e.g., anthrax).[37] Despite that mistrust, a 2002 survey found that most people agreed that "If smallpox breaks out somewhere, we should quarantine the area."[38] Thus, at that time, there was the trust needed to support such a draconian program. This valuable resource could be imperiled in many ways, including a tendency to disparage the public for failing to know facts that experts had communicated poorly. Scientifically sound communications provide our best hope at protecting the commons of public goodwill needed to manage terror risks.

Domestic surveillance. Citizens evaluating these policies need quantitative information about the magnitude of the threat, the chance of identifying legitimate suspects, and the damage done by "false positives." They need qualitative information about how the policies work, such as what is known about the effect of arresting a group (e.g., male students from a given country) on radicalizing those individuals or their community. They need to know how the effects vary by policy. For example, to what extent does protecting civil liberties issues reduce the yield from questioning, by restraining interrogators, or increase it, by encouraging cooperation?

How much officials know about these processes is important information, revealing how confidently policies can be adopted. Also important is information about which facts cannot be shared without compromising the program, revealing how far the public is being asked to accept policies on faith. When facts are scarce, people will make their own inferences based on the possibly unrepresentative cases that draw their attention. Securing fair judgment of policies requires careful analysis of what can be said about it. Given the natural tendency for initial beliefs to shape later ones, proactive communication is essential, both for its content and its demonstration of respect.

Decontamination standards. At the time of a dirty bomb attack, citizens will want to know how to protect themselves. They will want to know whether to shelter in place or try to evacuate, what to eat and drink, what to do with their clothing, and so on. Their inferences will shape their approach to the decontamination that follows, as will their previous encounters with radiation issues and those managing them (e.g., nuclear weapons, power, and medicine).

Research into perceptions of these risks finds misunderstandings that should be manageable with proper communications.[39] For example, people confuse radioactivity (the potential to do damage) and radiation (the release of energy, doing damage). Treating the former eliminates the latter and is often possible (e.g., removing clothes and showering after exposure), especially if steps are taken to make cleanup easier (e.g., not inhaling particles, closing external air ducts). Although people can easily understand such messages, they may not think of them spontaneously. Without clear messages, they cannot know whether the dose is like medical x-rays, domestic radon, nuclear weapon fallout, or high-level radioactive waste.

As elsewhere, the messengers will be part of the messages. Here, the institutional legacy is a difficult one. Managing nuclear materials has been among society's most contentious issues. The authorities involved with decontamination will have to distinguish themselves from those associated with Hiroshima, the Nevada Test Site, Three Mile Island, Chernobyl, Yucca Mountain, Fukushima, and the like. That will be hard without a deliberative process involving stakeholders' representatives. In the United States, a recent Blue Ribbon Commission recommended just such consultation.[40]

MANAGING RISKS WELL, SO AS TO HAVE A CREDIBLE MESSAGE TO COMMUNICATE

Other Risks

Decision makers need the best science available, including an assessment of how good it is. The trust that analyses deserves depends on (1) how completely it covers the relevant topics, (2) how well those pieces are integrated, and (3) how candidly they are qualified. To this end, experts need to have and convey a realistic assessment of their own competence, bounding their domain of expertise and coordinating with experts from other domains. That requires overcoming the territorial and commercial imperatives that can lead disciplines and consultants to exaggerate their capabilities.

One way of disciplining expert judgment is through formal risk analyses. The managers of such analyses identify valued outcomes and the processes affecting them, and then recruit relevant experts.

Risk analysts then elicit these experts' beliefs, uncertainties, and controversies, after which they integrate that knowledge, sensitive to its omissions. Although the basic formalisms of risk analysis are well established (and under constant refinement), their implementation is a human process, which requires attention to how groups are assembled and their judgments elicited.[41]

Another National Research Council report in the red book series characterized these issues. Examining the central role of judgment in risk analysis, *Science and Judgment in Risk Assessment*[42] noted the great uncertainty surrounding many risks, which arise from complex conjunctions of environmental, industrial, social, psychological, and physiological processes. It offered standards for diagnosing and disclosing the role of expert judgment and for eliciting it in a disciplined way.

One potential problem with risk analysis, or any other formal procedure (e.g., cost-benefit analysis) is that it can stifle creativity by focusing attention on evaluating existing proposals rather than generating new ones. A second is that it can emphasize readily quantified factors (e.g., monetary costs) over more qualitative ones (e.g., public morale, minority group feelings). A third is that it can disenfranchise those unfamiliar with the analytical formalisms, even if they have substantive knowledge of risk topics.

Figure 18-2 shows a risk analysis combining social, biological, and engineering knowledge in predicting the performance of public water systems after contamination.[43] It has the form of an *influence diagram*.[44] Each node represents a variable. An arrow connects two nodes, if knowing the value of the variable at the tail facilitates predicting the value of the variable at the head. For example, the greater the water utility's awareness of outbreak potential, the greater is the chance that it will conduct special studies or creating a multi-agency task force. Estimating risks with the model requires inputs from multiple disciplines, including microbiology (dose-response relationships), engineering (filtration and testing), ecology (land use), communications (message penetration), and psychology (perceived risk, actual response). Applications specify values for each variable and dependency, and then predict the risks and uncertainties.

One application arises when *Cryptosporidium*, a protozoan parasite, enters the system through sewage effluent discharges or fecally contaminated storm runoff (e.g., from feedlots, deer). Although

Figure 18-2

Influence diagram for
predicting risks from
Cryptosporidium
intrusion in domestic
water supplies

Source: Casman et. al
(2000).

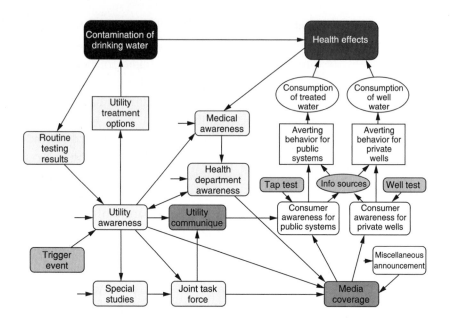

many infected individuals are asymptomatic or recover within two weeks, the disease can be fatal to immunocompromised individuals (especially those with AIDS). The model was created as the integrating core of a project designed to reduce risks by communicating with consumers. However, running the model found that even perfect communications would have no effect because tests for *Cryptosporidium* were so ineffective that vulnerable consumers will have been exposed before a warning could reach them. Thus, even if every consumer received a perfect message and followed its instructions precisely, an emergency system relying on "boil water" notices would not protect the most vulnerable. Indeed, such a system could increase risks by reducing the perceived need for better controls.

The same system might, however, work for readily detected pollutants, like many strains of *E. coli*. Moreover, information about the limits to *Cryptosporidium* testing is essential to decisions about land use (affecting the risk of intrusions) and water system engineering (e.g., investment in filtration systems). That knowledge can also provide the qualitative information needed to satisfy citizens who want to know why "boil water" notices are needed and who issues them. Where timely communication is possible, it might need to convey (1) what happened, (2) which uses pose danger (brushing one's teeth?), and (3) what "boiling water" entails.

Terror Risks

Behavioral research can improve terror risk management both by creating better communication processes and by clarifying their limits. An indirect contribution is that communication researchers are sometimes the sole social scientists on risk management teams dominated by engineers, lawyers, and natural scientists. In that role, they can both show where social science research is needed to replace intuitive theories and recruit social scientists with needed expertise. Treating the three examples in greater depth might raise issues like the following.

Smallpox vaccination. Effective vaccination programs must convey clear, trustworthy information that recipients can integrate with their existing mental models. One barrier that communication research should examine is the exaggerated sense of personal invulnerability found in many situations where people imagine some sense of control (e.g., being able to tell who is a carrier).[45] A second, and contrary, barrier is underestimating the value of vaccines, not knowing when they can be effective after exposure. Any vaccination plan must make some assumptions about the prevalence of these beliefs. If those assumptions are wrong, then the programs may not provide needed communications, thereby undermining citizens' decision making and trust. The anecdotal reports of runs on ciprofloxacin during the anthrax attacks of 2001 were partially attributed to distrust associated with poor communication.[46]

Domestic surveillance. Individuals' ability to judge others is one of the most heavily studied topics in psychology. One clear result is that the ability to make complex judgments (e.g., personality, dangerousness, propensity for taking risks) is acquired slowly, even under favorable conditions for learning (concentrated trials with prompt, unambiguous feedback). A second clear result is that people do not recognize these limits, exaggerating how well they (and others) can make such judgments. Thus, convincing stories can have unwarranted impact. Even experts' judgments are sufficiently inconsistent that simple statistical models can outperform them.[47] Appropriate surveillance policies require knowing how good even the best evidence is, so that the best gambles can be taken.

Decontamination standards. Expert panels are a natural way to set cleanup standards, drawing on members' knowledge of the science and intuitions about what constitute appropriate reasonable trade-offs. Threats to their success include (1) adopting standards from other domains with qualitatively different risks or benefits; (2) adopting standards that reflect political compromises, rather than trade-offs focused on public well-being; (3) misreading citizens' feelings about their own well-being; and (4) and failing to communicate their conclusions in a clear, trustworthy way. A consultative process, supported by behavioral research, can reduce these risks by improving the standards, educating citizens, and demonstrating respect.

CONCLUSIONS

Terror risk communication requires analyses that draw on diverse specialists in order to identify the information worth communicating. It requires empirical research assessing citizens' beliefs and desires. It requires procedures that demonstrate officials' competence and honesty. Although the details of these challenges are unique, the same issues arise with many complex, uncertain threats. There, too, officials must (1) manage risks well, so as to have a credible message; (2) create appropriate communication channels, and relations, with the public; and (3) deliver relevant information clearly and concisely.

Given those experiences with other risks, implementing these practices is a known craft. Many similar guidelines suggest how to set the tone when interacting with the public during difficult times. In effect, these guidelines interpret normal human relations for risk situations. The one in the appendix of this chapter was written for and disseminated by the American Psychological Association during the 2002 Washington, DC, sniper attacks. However, proper two-way communication requires a consultative process, like that in Figure 18-1.

Selecting the content of risk communications requires situation-specific research. One must (1) determine the facts central to the decisions that recipients face, (2) determine what they know already, (3) design messages closing the critical gaps, and (4) evaluate one's success, repeating the process until acceptable levels of mutual understanding have been achieved. The design of these communications can (and should) draw on the extensive basic and applied research into judgment and decision making, identifying common communication challenges and ways to overcome them. Applying that knowledge requires a management structure with clear divisions of responsibility for ensuring (1) the scientific accuracy of the content, (2) the relevance of that content to the audience's decision-making needs, (3) its comprehensibility in the messages, (4) the quality of the material and communication channel, and (5) the satisfaction of political and legal institutional constraints. Without such discipline, communications will operate on the basis of intuitions, rather than science.

Communication is a primary point of contact between authorities and citizens. It success affects citizens' ability to make effective choices. It shapes their faith in the authorities. As a result, it can strengthen or weaken a society's ability not only to weather its struggle with terror but to emerge stronger from it.

BIBLIOGRAPHY

Ariely, D. 2008. *Predictably Irrational*. New York: HarperCollins.

Blue Ribbon Commission on American's Nuclear Future. 2012. Final Report. Washington, DC: Department of Energy.

Cabinet Office. 2002. *Risk and Uncertainty*. London.

Canadian Standards Association. 1997. *Risk Management Guidelines for Decision Makers* (Q850). Ottawa.

Casman, E., B. Fischhoff, C. Palmgren, M. Small, and F. Wu. 2000. "Integrated Risk Model of a Drinking Water-Borne *Cryptosporidiosis* Outbreak." *Risk Analysis* 20: 493–509.

Clemen, R. 1996. *Making Hard Decisions*. Belmont, CA: Duxbury.

Cvetkovich, G., and R. Löfstedt, eds. 1999. *Social Trust and the Management of Risk*. London: Earthscan.

Downs, J. S., W. Bruine de Bruin, and B. Fischhoff. 2008. "Patients' Vaccination Comprehension and Decisions," *Vaccine* 26: 1595–1607.

Downs, J. S., P. J. Murray, W. Bruine de Bruin, J. P. White, C. Palmgren, and B. Fischhoff. 2004. "An Interactive Video Program to Reduce Adolescent Females' STD Risk: A Randomized Controlled Trial." *Social Science and Medicine* 59, no. 8: 1561–1572.

Environmental Protection Agency. 2000. *Toward Integrated Environmental Decision Making* (SAB-EC-00-011). Washington, DC.

Fischhoff, B. 1992. "Giving Advice: Decision Theory Perspectives on Sexual Assault." *American Psychologist* 47: 577–88.

———. 1995. "Risk Perception and Communication Unplugged: Twenty Years of Process." *Risk Analysis* 15: 137–145.

———. 2005. "Cognitive Processes in Stated Preference Methods." In K-G. Mäler and J. Vincent, eds., *Handbook of Environmental Economics*. Amsterdam: Elsevier.

———. 2009. "Risk Perception and Communication." In R. Detels, R. Beaglehole, M. A. Lansang, and M. Gulliford, eds., *Oxford Textbook of Public Health*. 5th ed. Oxford: Oxford University Press.

———. 2011. "Communicating the Risks of Terrorism (and Anything Else)." *American Psychologist* 66, 520–531.

Fischhoff, B., N. Brewer, and J. S. Downs, eds. 2011. *Communicating Risks and Benefits: An Evidence-Based User's Guide*. Washington, DC: Food and Drug Administration.

Fischhoff, B., R. Gonzalez, D. Small, and J. Lerner. 2003. "Evaluating the Success of Terror Risk Communication." *Biosecurity and Bioterrorism* 1, no. 4: 255–258.

Fischhoff, B., and J. Kadvany. 2011. *Risk: A Very Short Introduction*. Oxford: Oxford University Press.

Fischhoff, B., S. Lichtenstein, P. Slovic, S. L. Derby, and R. L. Keeney. 1981. *Acceptable Risk*. New York: Cambridge University Press.

Fischhoff, B., P. Slovic, and S. Lichtenstein. 1983. "Lay Foibles and Expert Fables in Judgments About Risk." *American Statistician* 36: 240–55.

Fischhoff, B., S. Watson, and C. Hope. 1984. "Defining Risk." *Policy Sciences* 17: 123–39.

Gilovich, T., D. Griffin, and D. Kahneman, eds. 2002. *The Psychology of Judgment: Heuristics and Biases*. New York: Cambridge University Press.

Glass, T. A. 2001. "Understanding Public Response to Disasters." *Public Health Reports*, 116 (Supplement 2): 69–73.

Hastie, R., and R. M. Dawes. 2001. *Rational Choice in an Uncertain World*. Thousand Oaks, CA: Sage.

Health Canada. 2004. *Canadian Pandemic Influenza Plan*. Ottawa: Public Health Agency of Canada.

Health and Safety Executive. 1999. *Reducing Risks, Protecting People*. London.

Kahneman, D. 2011. *Thinking Fast and Slow*. New York: Farrar Straus & Giroux.

Kahneman, D., P. Slovic, and A. Tversky, eds. 2002. *Judgment Under Uncertainty: Heuristics and Biases*. New York: Cambridge University Press.

Institute of Medicine. 1998a. *Scientific Opportunities and Public Needs*. Washington, DC: National Academy Press.

———. 1998b. *Toward Environmental Justice*. Washington, DC: National Academy Press.

Lerner, J. S., R. M. Gonzalez, D. A. Small, and B. Fischhoff. 2003. "Effects of Fear and Anger on Perceived Risks of Terrorism: A National Field Experiment." *Psychological Science* 14: 144–150.

Krimsky, S., and A. Plough, eds. 1988. *Environmental Hazards: Risk Communication as a Social Process*. Dover, MA: Auburn House.

Leiss, W., and C. Chociolko. 1994. *Risk and Responsibility*. Kingston and Montreal: Queens and McGill University Press.

Lichtenstein, S., and P. Slovic. eds. 2006. *Construction of Preferences*. New York: Cambridge University Press.

Merz, J., B. Fischhoff, D. J. Mazur, and P. S. Fischbeck. 1993. "Decision-Analytic Approach to Developing Standards of Disclosure for Medical Informed Consent." *Journal of Toxics and Liability* 15: 191–215.

Morgan, M. G., B. Fischhoff, A. Bostrom, and C. Atman. 2001. *Risk Communication: The Mental Models Approach*. New York: Cambridge University Press.

Morgan, M. G., and M. Henrion. 1990. *Uncertainty*. New York. Cambridge University Press.

National Research Council. 1983. *Risk Management in the Federal Government*. Washington, DC: National Academy Press.

———. 1989. *Improving Risk Communication*. Washington, DC: National Academy Press.

———. 1994. *Science and Judgment in Risk Assessment*. Washington, DC: National Academy Press.

O' Hagan, A., C. E. Buck, A. Daneshkhah, J. R. Eiser, P. H. Garthwaite, D. J. Jenkinson, J. E. Oakley, and T. Rakow. 2006. *Uncertain Judgements: Eliciting Expert Probabilities*. Chichester, UK: John Wiley & Sons.

———. 1996. *Understanding Risk*. Washington, DC: National Academy Press.

Parliamentary Office of Science and Technology. 2001. *Open Channels: Public Dialogues in Science and Technology*. London: House of Commons.

Presidential/Congressional Commission on Risk. 1998. *Risk Management*. Washington, DC.

Royal Commission on Environmental Protection. 1998. *Setting Environmental Standards*. London.

Slovic, P., ed. 2001. *The Perception of Risk*. London: Earthscan.

Tengs, T. O., and A. Wallace. 2000. "One Thousand Health-Related Quality-of-Life Estimates." *Medical Care* 38, no. 6: 583–637.

Thomas, P. 2003. *The Anthrax Attacks*. New York: Century Foundation.

Treasury Board. 2002. *Communications Policy of the Government of Canada*. Ottawa.

APPENDIX: A STRATEGY FOR THE CONTENT OF RISK COMMUNICATIONS

Note: Explanations are italicized.

1. Acknowledge the gravity of the events and the tragedy of those who have suffered.

2. Recognize the public's concerns, emotions, and efforts to manage the risk.

   Everyone is needed to keep society functioning in a time of stress, and all should be rewarded for doing the best they can. Emotions are an important and legitimate part of responding to extreme events. Recognizing their existence creates a human bond with the audience. Recognizing the legitimacy of emotions can help people take the steps needed to manage them. Individuals needing special attention should be afforded ready access. However, the tenor of the communication should be adult to adult, assuming the ability to cope.

3. Assure the audience that the relevant officials are doing all that they can.

   The communicator cannot vouch for the competence of all officials or for the adequacy of the resources at their disposal. However, it should be possible to attest to their commitment.

4. Express a coherent, consistent communication philosophy (for all risks):

   • We will do all we can to help you to make responsible decisions for yourself and your loved ones.

   • To that end, we will provide you the best relevant information that we can, along with an idea of how good that information is.

   • We will not engage in speculation.

   • We may need to withhold information that may aid or comfort the enemy. Recognizing our duty to inform, we are following a socially acceptable procedure for deciding what to withhold.

   The commitment is to a partnership, with officials attempting to empower citizens to master difficult and potentially protracted challenges. The communicator will leave speculation to others (e.g., news media, ordinary citizens), knowing that many ideas will be discussed in a democratic society, preserving the role of being the definitive source for vetted information.

   We currently lack mechanisms for withholding information in a socially acceptable way. Although the social acceptability of mechanisms is an empirical question, I anticipate that it will include the involvement of ordinary citizens, serving in an advisory role.

I did not include withholding information that might cause panic. The disaster literature predicts little mass panic, unless officials behave in ways that erode trust in them. Withholding vital information might be construed as such behavior. People do not want to learn that they have exposed themselves and their loved ones to risks because they were not trusted to act like adults.

5. Provide quantitative risk estimates, including the attendant uncertainties.

   People need to know how big risks are, in order to decide what to do about them. Often those numbers are missing, because the experts have not produced them or have not disseminated them. Sometimes the numbers are incomplete, as when people see the death toll but not the total number of people exposed. An intuitively appealing message is, "The risk of X is smaller than being struck by lightning." However, it often offends people by trivializing their concerns, and misrepresents the risk by ignoring the many ways in which X differs from lightning (e.g., the associated uncertainty). It often appears manipulative, undermining the credibility of the source. Just giving the numbers, and uncertainties, is safer. Doing so requires the staff work needed to produce those estimates.

6. Provide summary analyses of possible protective actions, considering all the expected effects.

   People may ignore the fact that actions reducing one risk may increase other risks. They may not recognize the psychological costs and benefits of actions that reduce risk. They may not see the things they are losing (i.e., "opportunity costs") when they forgo activities in order to reduce risks. They may not be able to estimate the effects of their actions, exaggerating some, underestimating others. Presenting the best available understanding of these issues, in a standard format, should help people to develop coherent decision-making strategies. It respects individuals' right to make different choices, reflecting their personal values.

7. Lead by example, showing possible models for responsible bravery.

   People expect leaders to conduct themselves professionally, including their own exposure to risk. Such behavior can have a calming effect and model the sort of quiet "soldiering on" that many people want to show, in their own way, appropriate to their own circumstances.

8. Commit to earning and keeping the public trust.

We want to achieve market share as the source of unbiased information. Having such a source is essential for social coordination, in both the long and the short run. Communication processes should be evaluated to ensure their continued success. They should solicit continuing input from the public to ensure their relevance.

NOTES

1. B. Fischhoff, "Communicating the Risks of Terrorism (and Anything Else)," *American Psychologist* 66 (2011): 520–31.

2. B . Fischhoff, R. Gonzalez, D. Small, and J. Lerner, 2003, "Evaluating the Success of Terror Risk Communication," *Biosecurity and Bioterrorism* 1, no. 4: 255–58.

3. T. A. Glass, "Understanding Public Response to Disasters," *Public Health Reports* 116 (Supplement 2, 2001), 69–73.

4. D. Ariely, *Predictably Irrational* (New York: HarperCollins, 2008). D. Kahneman, *Thinking Fast and Slow,* (New York: Farrar Straus & Giroux, 2011.)

5. B. Fischhoff and J. Kadvany, *Risk: A Very Short Introduction* (Oxford: Oxford University Press, 2011).

6. G. Cvetkovich and R. Löfstedt, eds., *Social Trust and the Management of Risk* (London: Earthscan, 1999). B. Fischhoff, S. Lichtenstein, P. Slovic, S. L. Derby, and R. L. Keeney, *Acceptable Risk* (New York: Cambridge University Press, 1981). S. Krimsky and A. Plough, eds., *Environmental Hazards: Risk Communication as a Social Process* (Dover, MA: Auburn House, 1988). W. Leiss and C. Chociolko, *Risk and Responsibility* (Kingston and Montreal: Queens and McGill University Press, 1994).

7. Presidential/Congressional Commission on Risk, *Risk Management*, Washington, DC, 1998.

8. Environmental Protection Agency, *Toward Integrated Environmental Decision Making* (SAB-EC-00-011), Washington, DC, 2000.

9. Royal Commission on Environmental Protection, *Setting Environmental Standards,* London, 1998.

10. Health and Safety Executive, *Reducing Risks, Protecting People,* London: 1999.

11. Parliamentary Office of Science and Technology, *Open Channels: Public Dialogues in Science and Technology* (London: House of Commons, 2001).

12. Cabinet Office, *Risk and Uncertainty,* London, 2002.

13. National Research Council, *Risk Management in the Federal Government* (Washington, DC: National Academy Press, 1983).

14. National Research Council, *Improving Risk Communication* (Washington, D.C.: National Academy Press, 1989).

15. B. Fischhoff, S. Lichtenstein, P. Slovic, S. L. Derby, and R. L. Keeney, *Acceptable Risk* (New York: Cambridge University Press, 1981). B. Fischhoff, P. Slovic, and S. Lichtenstein "Lay Foibles and Expert Fables in Judgments about Risk," *American Statistician* 36 (1983): 240–55,

16. National Research Council, *Understanding Risk* (Washington, DC: National Academy Press, 1996.)

17. B. Fischhoff, S. Watson, and C. Hope, "Defining Risk," *Policy Sciences* 17 (1984): 123–39.

18. Institute of Medicine, *Scientific Opportunities and Public Needs* (Washington, DC: National Academy Press, 1998a).

19. Institute of Medicine, *Toward Environmental Justice* (Washington, DC: National Academy Press, 1998b).

20. Health Canada, *Canadian Pandemic Influenza Plan* (Ottawa: Public Health Agency of Canada, 2004).

21. R. Clemen, *Making Hard Decisions* (Belmont, CA: Duxbury, 1996). R. Hastie and R. M. Dawes, *Rational Choice in an Uncertain World* (Thousand Oaks, CA: Sage, 2001).

22. T. Gilovich, D. Griffin, and D. Kahneman, eds., *The Psychology of Judgment: Heuristics and Biases* (New York: Cambridge University Press, 2002).

23. T. O. Tengs and A. Wallace, "One Thousand Health-Related Quality-of-Life Estimates," *Medical Care* 38, no. 6 (2000): 583–637.

24. B. Fischhoff, "Cognitive Processes in Stated Preference Methods," in K-G. Mäler and J. Vincent, eds., *Handbook of Environmental Economics* (Amsterdam: Elsevier, 2005).

25. M. G. Morgan, B. Fischhoff, A. Bostrom, and C. Atman, *Risk Communication: The Mental Models Approach* (New York: Cambridge University Press, 2001).

26. B. Fischhoff, "Giving Advice: Decision Theory Perspectives on Sexual Assault," *American Psychologist* 47 (1992): 577–588. B. Fischhoff, "Decision Research Strategies," *Health Psychology* 21, no. 4 (2005): S9–16.

27. J. Merz, B. Fischhoff, D. J. Mazur, and P. S. Fischbeck, "Decision-Analytic Approach to Developing Standards of Disclosure for Medical Informed Consent," *Journal of Toxics and Liability* 15 (1993): 191–215.

28. J. S. Downs, P. J. Murray, W. Bruine de Bruin, J. P. White, C. Palmgren, and B. Fischhoff, "An Interactive Video Program to Reduce Adolescent Females' STD Risk: A Randomized Controlled Trial," *Social Science and Medicine* 59, no. 8: (2004): 1561–1572.

29. B. Fischhoff, "Risk Perception and Communication," in R. Detels, R. Beaglehole, M.A. Lansang, and M. Guilliford, eds., *Oxford Textbook of Public Health*, 5th ed. (London: Oxford University Press, 2009). P. Slovic, ed., *The Perception of Risk* (London: Earthscan, 2001).

30. B. Fischhoff, N. Brewer, and J. S. Downs, eds., *Communicating Risks and Benefits: An Evidence-Based User's Guide* (Washington, DC: Food and Drug Administration, 2011).

31. T. Gilovich, D. Griffin, and D. Kahneman, eds., *The Psychology of Judgment: Heuristics and Biases* (New York: Cambridge University Press, 2002). D. Kahneman, P. Slovic, and A. Tversky, eds., *Judgment Under Uncertainty: Heuristics and Biases* (New York: Cambridge University Press, 2002).

32. B. Fischhoff, "Judgment and Decision Making," *Wiley Interdisciplinary Reviews: Cognitive Science* 1, no. 5 (September/October 2010), http://wires.wiley.com/WileyCDA/WiresArticle/wisId-WCS65.html. M. G. Morgan, B. Fischhoff, A. Bostrom, and C. Atman, *Risk Communication: The Mental Models Approach* (New York: Cambridge University Press, 2001).

33. S. Lichtenstein and P. Slovic, eds. *Construction of Preferences* (New York: Cambridge University Press, 2006).

34. J. S. Lerner, R. M. Gonzalez, D. A. Small, and B. Fischhoff, "Effects of Fear and Anger on Perceived Risks of Terrorism: A National Field Experiment," *Psychological Science* 14 (2003): 144–50.

35. B. Fischhoff, "Risk Perception and Communication Unplugged: Twenty Years of Process," *Risk Analysis* 15 (1995): 137–145.

36. B. Fischhoff, R. Gonzalez, D. Small, and J. Lerner, "Evaluating the Success of Terror Risk Communication," *Biosecurity and Bioterrorism* 1, no. 4 (2003): 255–258.

37. J. S. Downs, W. Bruine de Bruin, and B. Fischhoff, "Patients' Vaccination Comprehension and Decisions," *Vaccine* 26 (2008). 1595–1607.

38. See note 39.

39. M. G. Morgan, B. Fischhoff, A. Bostrom, and C. Atman, *Risk Communication: The Mental Models Approach* (New York: Cambridge University Press, 2001).

40. Blue Ribbon Commission on American's Nuclear Future, *Final Report* (Washington, DC: Department of Energy, 2012).

41. M. G. Morgan and M. Henrion, *Uncertainty* (New York: Cambridge University Press, 1990). A. O' Hagan, C. E. Buck, A. Daneshkhah, J. R. Eiser, P. H. Garthwaite, D. J. Jenkinson, J. E. Oakley, and T. Rakow, *Uncertain Judgements: Eliciting Expert Probabilities* (Chichester, UK: John Wiley & Sons, 2006).

42. National Research Council, *Science and Judgment in Risk Assessment* (Washington, DC: National Academy Press), 1994.

43. E. Casman, B. Fischhoff, C. Palmgren, M. Small, and F. Wu, "Integrated Risk Model of a Drinking Water-Borne Cryptosporidiosis Outbreak," *Risk Analysis* 20 (2000): 493–509.

44. R. Clemen, *Making Hard Decisions* (Belmont, CA: Duxbury, 1996).

45. T. Gilovich, D. Griffin, and D. Kahneman, eds., *The Psychology of Judgment: Heuristics and Biases* (New York: Cambridge University Press, 2002).

46. P. Thomas, *The Anthrax Attacks* (New York: Century Foundation, 2003).

47. R. Hastie and R. M. Dawes, "Rational Choice in an Uncertain World," (Thousand Oaks, CA: Sage, 2001).

19

NATIONAL TERRORISM ADVISORY SYSTEM

James Carafano

Deputy Director, The Kathryn and Shelby Cullom Davis Institute for International Studies and Director, Douglas and Sarah Allison Center for Foreign Policy Studies, The Heritage Foundation

Jessica Zuckerman

Research Associate, Homeland Security and Latin America; Douglas and Sarah Allison Center for Foreign Policy Studies, The Heritage Foundation

EFFECTIVE RISK COMMUNICATION AND RESPONDING TO TERRORISM

In May 2011, the Department of Homeland Security launched the National Terrorism Advisory System (NTAS), doing away with the oft-criticized Homeland Security Advisory System (HSAS). The new system has sought to more effectively communicate clear, timely, and specific information about the nature of the terrorist threat to the American public, the private sector, government actors, and first responders, as well as to airports and other transportation hubs.

The creation of NTAS marks an important effort by DHS to enhance the Department's efforts at risk communication. In times of crisis, effective risk communication can be vital, serving to guide how people react in response to a major incident. In this respect, risk communication is a fundamental part of managing the response to terrorism.

This chapter examines the basics of the HSAS and its fundamental flaws. Similarly, it seeks to examine the framework laid out for the new NTAS system in terms of the principles of effective risk communication.

PRINCIPLES OF EFFECTIVE RISK COMMUNICATION

More than 10 years after 9/11, one of the key challenges in communicating risk with regard to the threat of terrorism in the United States is combatting complacency. Research has suggested that individuals are more likely to act on warnings when they perceive the risk being communicated to be certain or imminent.[1] Thankfully, due to the concerted efforts of the U.S. law enforcement and intelligence communities, there has been a low incidence of successful terrorist attacks since 9/11. However as few individuals have experienced the threat of terrorism firsthand, members of the American public may be more likely to discount the perceived risk.

Nevertheless, despite this challenge, several key principles can help guide leaders in fostering effective risk communication. Public alerts should be:

- *Credible.* Information should come from a trusted source in a timely, accurate, and consistent manner. Often a government is prone to withhold from making announcements or decisions until it has all the facts, but delivering timely information is often much more important. Likewise, credibility depends not only on the content of the message but also on the manner in which it is communicated.
- *Specific.* Audiences tend to simplify messages and also have limited intake of new information. Public alerts must therefore be simple and precise.
- *Understandable.* Alerts should be in clear and straightforward language.
- *Actionable.* Public alerts should seek to empower decision making and provide positive actionable steps for citizens, in order to inform behavior, calm anxiety, and restore order.[2]

FAILURES OF THE HOMELAND SECURITY ADVISORY SYSTEM

The Homeland Security Advisory System (HSAS) was established by Presidential Homeland Security Directive 3 in March 2002. The system was designed to designate various levels of national preparedness in anticipation of a terrorist attacks, providing alerts to government agencies, the private sector, and American citizens. By establishing common terms for these levels and providing for homeland security intelligence to be communicated, HSAS sought to enable DHS to integrate and disseminate information effectively.

Among the American public, the HSAS system may have been known best for its color-coded system of threat warnings, ranging from low risk of attack signified by the color green to high risk of attack signified by red. Yet despite the range of threat which HSAS was intended to convey, over the life of the system, the nation spent the vast majority of time at the elevated and high threat levels (yellow and orange). In fact, until the systems abolishment in May 2011, the threat level had remained high for the aviation section and elevated for the rest of the United States since August 2006.

Over the entire course of the program's existence, the threat level changed 17 times, yet the threat level was never lowered to low or guarded (green and blue).[3] Similarly, the threat level was only once raised to red. This was on August 10, 2006, in response to the UK arrest of 24 individuals allegedly plotting to blow up U.S.-bound commercial airliners with liquid explosives.[4] Ultimately when elevated and high threat levels became the norm, HSAS lost credibility and the public seemingly began to fail to take the alert system seriously.

Not only did the consistently elevated threat level serve to create apathy and complacency, but the system was flawed in that the American public did not understand the distinction between the threat levels. For most, the difference between elevated and high were distinctions without a meaningful contrast or actionable steps for citizens to follow. Further, the alerts were nearly always generic and nonspecific, such that citizens had no way to understand how the alerts related to their local communities and families.[5]

THE NATIONAL TERRORISM ADVISORY SYSTEM

After a little more than eight years of operating the HSAS, the Department abolished the system. In May 2011, DHS then created the National Terrorism Advisory System (NTAS), which sought to more effectively communicate the risk of terrorist attacks by providing timely and detailed information to the American public, government agencies, first responders, the private sector, and airport and other transportation hubs.[6]

Rather than reemploying the previous five-tiered, color-coded system, the National Terrorism Advisory System was streamlined to offer only two alerts:

- *Imminent Threat Alert.* Warns of a credible, specific, and impending threat against the United States.
- *Elevated Threat Alert.* Warns of a credible threat against the United States.

NTAS alerts also provide a brief summary of the threat, the alerts duration, affected areas, steps for public preparedness, instructions on how to stay informed, as well as further details related to sectors affected, the nature of the threat, actions being taken by authorities, and/or information as to the credibility of the threat.[7]

In addition to providing clear, specific, and actionable information, NTAS alerts may also be directed specifically to law enforcement and the private sector, rather than the general public where appropriate. Further, NTAS alerts also contain sunset provisions, indicating exactly when an increase in threat level will expire. Alerts may be extended beyond the initial period if additional information indicates the need for such an extension.

Initial threat information may originate from the intelligence community, federal, state, or local law enforcement; the private sector; or critical infrastructure and key resource sectors. Once obtained, the Department of Homeland Security may decide to bring together senior leaders in a meeting of the Counterterrorism Advisory Board (CTAB). Recommendations of the CTAB are forwarded to the Secretary of Homeland Security, who decides whether to issue a NTAS alert. Once decided, alerts are disseminated through state and local partners, the media, DHS's NTAS webpage, and e-mail alerts, as well as through Facebook and Twitter.[8]

AN EVOLVING SYSTEM: FROM HSAS TO NTAS

NTAS seeks to better adhere to the principles of effective risk communication, providing credible, specific, understandable, and actionable information. In doing so, it also helps to reduce the psychological impacts of terror alerts and the cost of response, while also working to enhance cross-governmental information sharing and avenues of public threat communication.

Psychological Impact

Research has shown that the public is more apt to prepare for disasters when:

- Risk is seen as high and the threat immediate.
- Warnings are issued from a credible source.
- Alerts are repeated through multiple avenues, with the information provided being easily understandable and utilized.[9]

Changes in color codes, which dominated the public perception of what HSAS represented, meet none of these criteria. The lack of specific advisories and the absence of clear guidance on what actions individual citizens ought to take under each threat level ultimately detracted from the positive role of HSAS. By failing to provide actionable steps, HSAS created a kind of cognitive dissonance in which there was a disconnect between warnings of critical vulnerability and the instruction to the public to continue with business as usual.

Further, while little research exists on the effects on individuals mental health of long periods of heightened alert, anecdotal evidence seems to show that in the case of the HSAS system, prolonged periods of alert seemingly logically served to desensitize citizens to continued alerts. Ultimately, some experts believe that HSAS became marginalized as a result of "a lack of understanding of its intended use as well as the absence of a well-orchestrated plan to guide its implementation at all levels of government."[10]

In crisis, citizen trauma and anxiety often stems from a sense of helplessness. Likewise, the more control individuals perceive over a situation, the smaller they perceive the associated risk. This is why ensuring alerts are actionable is a central principle of effective risk communication.

The National Terrorism Advisory System, unlike its predecessor, thus seeks to provide steps for the public to follow during a state of heightened alert. By providing information on how the public can help authorities, increase personal and community preparedness, and stay informed, NTAS empowers citizens and reduces anxiety.

Of course, any effort to persuade a significant number of Americans to take commonsense precautions during threat periods that may span several years between major attacks requires carefully tailored, consistently reinforced, pre-alert education. Thus, in addition to NTAS, public engagement efforts such as DHS's "See Something, Say Something" and Ready.gov continue to be important.

**Information
Sharing**

Despite the perception that NTAS is primarily a warning system for the general public, it has a wide range of purposes. NTAS also provides a tool for information sharing between federal, state, local, and private sector responders and is essential to an effective national preparedness and response strategy. Through the establishment of common terms and national performance and preparedness standards, NTAS enables DHS to more effectively integrate and disseminate information.

Under HSAS, obstacles to effective information sharing and cross-governmental risk communication were created by the all-inclusive nature of the alert system. Lacking in specificity, HSAS generally failed to communicate significant details about the nature and location of the terrorist threat. As such, when the HSAS alert level was raised, the whole nation had to ratchet up security—even where no credible threat existed or where a region may not have been directly at risk. Such a response did little or nothing to inform state and local governments or the public of specific threats.[11]

With a program that communicates the nature of the threat in greater detail, including specific locations and sectors that may be targeted, the hope is that the new NTAS system will alleviate many of these issues, serving to better allow states and localities to make informed decisions on when to ratchet up capabilities and lowering unnecessary security spending.

**Cost of
Response**

Of course, any national system of this magnitude will have significant fiscal implications. Increased security resulting from changing the alert status in its first two years of the Homeland Security Advisory System required an estimated $1 billion per week at the federal level. The additional costs incurred by state and local governments and the private sector, as well as the impact on the economy overall, such as reducing consumers' confidence or affecting business travel and tourism, were more difficult to estimate but nevertheless present.[12]

According to a report from GAO in June 2004, federal agencies reported average daily costs between $190 and $3.7 million for the three code-orange alert periods covered in the study. For the first two code-orange alert periods, states reported additional costs ranging from approximately $7,900 to $8 million; localities reported additional costs of $2,800 to $28 million. Costs for the third period ranged from $2,000 to about $7 million for states, and from $3,000 to about $4 million for localities.[13]

At this writing, an alert under the new National Terrorism Advisory System had not yet been issued. The precise associated costs of response therefore remain largely unknown. Nevertheless, the specific nature of NTAS alerts, sunset provisions, and information on affected areas will help to aid federal agencies, state and private sector leaders, and local communities in determining if and to what degree increased preparedness activities are needed. The enhanced ability to make these needs assessments will allow for the reduction of unnecessary blanket spending, permitting DHS and its partners to spend on those measures that best protect the nation.

Modes of Communication

A 2009 assessment of the Homeland Security Advisory System by a task force of the Homeland Security Advisory Council called for HSAS to "stay current with the communications revolution and adopt an 'all tools' approach in reaching the general public," incorporating blogging alerts, social media (i.e., Twitter, Facebook, Wikis, etc.), e-mail alerts, and delivery of alerts to smart phones and PDAs.[14]

In Japan, following the Great Eastern Earthquake, the government employed an extensive warning system that included mediums ranging from traditional warning sirens to social media tools.[15] The Japanese government used social networking fairly effectively, as did its citizens. According to reports, within an hour after the quake, tweets from Tokyo topped 1,200 per minute.[16] In the United States, DHS has committed to take similar efforts with the new National Terrorism Advisory System, promising to transmit alerts via Twitter, Facebook, and e-mail.

The use of social media for risk communications offers several benefits, the greatest of which is the ability to reach a greater number of people at a greater speed by connecting to modes of communication that citizens are plugged into throughout their daily lives. Nevertheless, key challenges to using social media during a crisis exist, first and foremost being the issue of information assurance—knowing whether data is precise and reliable.

During a large-scale crisis in particular, information can be spotty, as communication systems are down and officials have difficulty collecting information and providing situational awareness. In addition, in a swiftly changing environment, first reports can later prove erroneous. Social media can compound this issue, as rumors, perfidy, and faulty information can be widely dispersed with great speed. Here crowdsourcing, in a similar manner to how high levels of accuracy are maintained on Wikipedia by allowing individuals to edit the work of others, can help sort good information from the bad. Of course, unlike in the world of online encyclopedias, in a crisis, accuracy could mean the difference between life and death.[17]

Similarly, governments not only need to ensure that their own actions in the use of social media are legitimate but also that malicious actors are not undermining government efforts through social engineering or by mimicking government activities to spread false information. In 2010, for instance, the Twitter account of the Indonesian president's disaster advisor was hacked, causing fake tsunami warnings to be sent out and spreading panic among the public in light of the devastating tsunami just six years earlier.[18] These risks must be guarded against in the use of social media as a component of NTAS.

RISK COMMUNICATION: THE NEXT DECADE AND BEYOND

Building on the lessons learned from the failures of the Homeland Security Advisory System, the new National Terrorism Advisory System offers a great improvement in DHS's efforts at risk communication. In particular, unlike HSAS, NTAS offers more detailed information on the nature of the terrorist threat, seeking to communicate specific information on the potential location and targets of any credible terrorist threat. NTAS alerts also provide actionable steps for citizens to follow, helping to create an empowered public and reduce anxiety caused by feelings of helplessness. Further improving on the legacy HSAS system, NTAS has streamlined the number of alert levels, and offers a sunset provision to make the duration of an elevated threat level clear.

Yet while NTAS is a vast improvement over past risk communication efforts, more can be done to improve the current system. DHS should look to continue to develop the National Terrorism Advisory System and expand the procedures and methods to create risk communication frameworks for other homeland-security-related activities, particularly for use in responding to unanticipated dangers. Ultimately, DHS should look to merge terrorist alerts into an "all hazards" alert system with common formats and methods of dissemination.

With the systems use of social media, efforts must also be taken to ensure the continued legitimacy and credibility of system alerts. The costs and benefits of integrating HSAS with other alert systems such as the AMBER alerts used by various states and the National Weather Service advisory system might also be considered.

Finally, and perhaps most important, more attention must be given to how the emerging national preparedness system can best exploit the warnings that may be provided by an effective NTAS. Particular emphasis should be given to human capital and leadership programs that will train the next generation of homeland security professionals, public safety leaders, and government officials.[19] Effective risk communication ultimately means nothing without people to lead the nation through the crisis and ensure the security of the United States in the years to come.

NOTES

1. James Carafano and Mark Sauter, *Homeland Security: A Complete Guide to Understanding, Preventing, and Surviving Terrorism* (New York: McGraw-Hill, 2005).

2. Ibid.; Barbara Reynolds and Matthew W. Seeger, "Crisis and Emergency Risk Communication as an Integrative Model, " *Journal of Health Communication*, 10:43–55, 2005.

3. Department of Homeland Security, *Chronology of Changes to the Homeland Security Advisory System,* May 13, 2011, http://www.dhs.gov/xabout/history/editorial_0844.shtm (accessed April 5, 2012).

4. James Jay Carafano, Ph.D., and Jessica Zuckerman, "The Current Threat Level: Ending Color-Coded Terror Alerts," Heritage Foundation *Webmemo* No. 3068, November 30, 2010, http://thf_media.s3.amazonaws.com/2010/pdf/wm3068.pdf (accessed April 5, 2012).

5. Editorial, "Stopping the Next Terror Plot," *Daily Caller*, April 2, 2011, http://dailycaller.com/2011/05/02/stopping-the-next-terror-plot/ (accessed April 5, 2012).

6. Department of Homeland Security, *National Terrorism Advisory System Public Guide*, April 2011, http://www.dhs.gov/xlibrary/assets/ntas/ntas-public-guide.pdf (accessed April 5, 2012).

7. Ibid.

8. Department of Homeland Security, *National Terrorism Advisory System Interim Stakeholder Information Handbook*, http://www.co.monterey.ca.us/oes/pdf/NTAS-Interim-Stakeholder-Handbook.pdf (accessed April 5, 2012).

9. Kathleen J. Turner et al., *Facing the Unexpected: Disaster Preparedness and Response in the United States* (Washington, DC: Joseph Henry Press, 2001), 30.

10. Advisory Panel to Assess Domestic Response Capabilities for Terrorism Involving Weapons of Mass Destruction, *Forging America's New Normalcy: Securing Our Homeland, Preserving Our Liberty*, p. 27.

11. James Jay Carafano and Ha Nguyen, "Warning: We Need a Better Warning System," Heritage Foundation *Commentary*, January 8, 2004, www.heritage.org/Press/Commentary/ed010804a.cfm (accessed April 5, 2012).

12. For example, the U.S. Conference of Mayors estimates the cost at approximately $70 million per week. New York City spends about $5 million per week when the alert level is raised. Boston estimated its costs at about $100,000 per day.

13. GAO Report, "Homeland Security: Communication Protocols and Risk Communication Principles Can Assist in Refining the Advisory System," 36–37.

14. Department of Homeland Security, *Homeland Security Advisory Council Task Force Report and Recommendations,* September 2009, http://www.dhs.gov/xlibrary/assets/hsac_task_force_report_09.pdf (accessed April 5, 2012).

15. James Jay Carafano, Ph.D., "The Great Eastern Japan Earthquake: Assessing Disaster Response and Lessons for the U.S.," Heritage Foundation *Special Report* No. 94, May 25, 2011,

http://www.heritage.org/research/reports/2011/05/the-great-eastern-japan-earthquake-assessing-disaster-response-and-lessons-for-the-us#_ftn24 (accessed April 5, 2012).

16. "Tweets from Tokyo Top 1,200 Per Minute," *Silicon Republic*, March 12, 2011, http://www.siliconrepublic.com/new-media/item/20872-tweets-from-tokyo-top-1-200 (accessed May 17, 2011).

17. Carafano, "The Great Eastern Japan Earthquake."

18. Carafano, *Wiki at War: Conflict in a Socially Networked World* (College Station, TX: Texas A&M University Press, 2011).

19. For an overview of homeland security training and education programs, see James Jay Carafano, Ph.D., "Missing Pieces in Homeland Security Education, Assignment, and Professional Education," Heritage Foundation *Executive Memorandum No. 1013*, October 16, 2006, http://www.heritage.org/research/reports/2006/10/missing-pieces-in-homeland-security-interagency-education-assignments-and-professional-accreditation?query=Missing+Pieces+in+Homeland+Security:+Interagency+EducationAssignments+and+Professional+Accreditation (accessed April 5, 2012); and Jena Baker McNeill and James Jay Carafano, Ph.D., "Building Leaders: Improving National Security Professional Development," Heritage Foundation *Webmemo* No. 3082, December 14, 2010, http://www.heritage.org/research/reports/2010/12/building-leaders-improving-national-security-professional-development (accessed April 5, 2012).

5

INTRODUCTION TO PART V: PROTECTING CRITICAL INFRASTRUCTURE

Joseph Nimmich

Retired Admiral U.S. Coast Guard, Raytheon Homeland Security

This section describes challenges and approaches to protecting critical infrastructure, including airports, airplanes, water facilities, and information systems and assets. It also presents a guide for organizing a regional infrastructure protection effort.

As a collection of activities and facilities, infrastructure that supports the economy, public health and welfare, and security is complex, pervasive, and thus particularly open to terrorism. Rae Zimmerman explains that to make infrastructure secure, we need to understand its interdependencies and their relationship to infrastructure vulnerabilities. Interdependencies among infrastructures and other activities magnify their contribution both positively and negatively, and are of growing concern in the infrastructure security arena. The challenge for line agencies that typically specialize in one type of infrastructure is to organize themselves so as to address interdependence specifically across a wide range of functions, including management and finance.

Water utilities, both drinking water and wastewater, provide essential services to the public on a 24/7/365 basis. The chapter by Stanley

States reviews some of the natural, accidental, and man-made threats that drinking water and wastewater systems are vulnerable to. It also discusses some of the steps that utilities take to mitigate these vulnerabilities, and some of the actions that they take to respond to events.

Rafi Ron and Robert Faber explain why governments devote a disproportionate share of their resources to protect airplanes and airports. They then analyze how a small handful of terrorists could successfully carry out 9/11, and provide a critical examination of the technology-centric aviation security response to that attack. A shift to risk-based assessments that combine intelligence assets and passenger risk analysis to target the individuals who pose the greatest threat seems to be underway. Achieving a reasonable balance between a secure aviation system and a passenger screening approach that preserves the value of travel will save money and lives. The most effective system will build on the strengths of an open society and exploit the weaknesses of the terrorists who seek to destroy a way of life they oppose.

The chapter by Paula Scalingi, based on the *TISP Regional Infrastructure Protection Guide,* offers a framework for developing a regional disaster resilience action plan. It outlines, in practical detail, how to organize and implement an effort to engage regional stakeholders in the protection effort. An action plan developed using this framework will cover a wide array of strategic, operational, and financial planning dimensions of regional preparedness.

20

CRITICAL INFRASTRUCTURE AND INTERDEPENDENCY REVISITED

Rae Zimmerman

Professor of Planning and Public Administration
Director, Institute for Civil Infrastructure Systems (ICIS)
Wagner Graduate School of Public Service, New York University

Note: This work was originally supported by several grants, including the National Science Foundation (NSF) Cooperative Agreement No. CMS–9728805 for the Institute for Civil Infrastructure Systems (ICIS) at New York University (in partnership with Cornell University, Polytechnic University of New York, and the University of Southern California); Urban Infrastructure in a Time of Crisis (grant number 0204660) and Bringing Information Technology to Infrastructure (grant number 0091482); and a grant from the U.S. Department of Homeland Security (DHS) through a subaward from the University of Southern California for the first Homeland Security Center of Excellence. The author's opinions, findings, and conclusions or recommendations are not necessarily those of NSF or DHS.

CRITICAL INFRASTRUCTURE AND ITS SECURITY

Infrastructure supports the economy, public health and welfare, and security in ways that are often difficult to ascertain. Interdependencies among infrastructures and other activities magnify their contribution to these sectors both positively and negatively, and are of growing concern in the infrastructure security arena. The importance of infrastructure is portrayed in a number of ways. One is the contribution of infrastructure to the gross domestic product (GDP). An estimate by the World Bank is that the GDP increases 15 percent as infrastructure capital doubles.[1] Given the difficulty of estimating specific social and economic contributions of infrastructure, another overall way of assessing its contribution has been in terms of the value of infrastructure assets. U.S. assets in 2009 were valued at several trillions of dollars directly for the utilities and transportation sectors alone and a larger amount if other related sectors are included.[2] These estimates of asset value or financial impacts may not take into account dependencies and interdependencies among infrastructure sectors and between these sectors and other parts of the economy, or at least do not make those relationships explicit.

The security of infrastructure has become a major objective of national policy. Since the mid-1990s or earlier these policies have been reflected in regulations, guidelines, executive orders, reports, legislation, plans, and strategies. Infrastructure security in general evolved out of earlier concerns over protecting communications. That theme continues to dominate infrastructure security policy, attaining more prominence as cybersecurity has had increasing attention along with its increasing interconnections with other infrastructures.

As a collection of activities and facilities, infrastructure is complex, pervasive, and thus particularly open to terrorism. To make infrastructure secure, we need to understand its interdependencies and their relationship to infrastructure vulnerabilities.

Definitions: Infrastructure, Critical Infrastructure, and Interdependent Infrastructure

The current term *infrastructure* is relatively new, dating from about the 1980s, and earlier, and the concept had to do mainly with military installations and public works.[3] In 1997, the President's Commission on Critical Infrastructure Protection (PCCIP) adopted a definition that refers to networks, processes, synergy, and continuity "to produce and distribute a continuous flow of essential goods and services."[4]

The concept of *critical infrastructure* and its interdependencies with other sectors is even more recent than the concept of infrastructure, and links infrastructure and security. Both ideas followed a national emphasis on the performance of infrastructure to promote health, safety, and welfare. For example, Presidential Decision Directive (PDD) 63 defined critical infrastructure as "those physical and cyber-based systems essential to the minimum operations of the economy and government."[5] PDD 63 clearly acknowledged interdependence in the critical infrastructure sectors, emphasizing information technology and cybersecurity, and called for "a particular focus on interdependencies" in the development of sector plans. Section 1016(e) of the Patriot Act of 2001 defined critical infrastructure as "systems and assets, whether physical or virtual, so vital to the nation that the incapacity or destruction of such systems would have a debilitating impact on security, national economic security, [or] national public health and safety or any combination of these matters."[6] As policies regarding critical infrastructure evolved, the scope of the concept evolved as well. The National Infrastructure Protection Plan (NIPP) of 2009 identified critical infrastructures together with a broader set of sectors called critical infrastructure and key resources (CIKR) comprising 18 sectors that include "agriculture and food, defense industrial base, energy, healthcare and public health, national monuments and icons, banking and finance, water, chemical, commercial facilities, critical manufacturing, dams, emergency services, nuclear reactors, materials, and waste, information technology, communications, postal and shipping, transportation systems, and government facilities."[7] HSPD–7 provides the foundation for critical infrastructure protection, and the U.S. DHS authority to protect critical infrastructure originates in the Homeland Protection Act of 2002.[8] The categories are similar to those used in lifeline engineering, for example, which focuses on transmission and distribution systems.[9] The continuing significance of critical infrastructure is reflected in the annual designation by the President of the United States, since 2009, of December as Critical Infrastructure Month.

This chapter emphasizes the transportation, energy, water, environmental services (wastewater disposal), and telecommunication sectors, which like infrastructure in general share certain features, such as their customers, the nature and configuration of the services they provide, the type and location of their facilities, and the prevalence of interconnections among them.

Policies Regarding Vulnerability

Several types of policies are directly related to infrastructure vulnerability and the capacity to affect its resilience to overcome it. Three policies are discussed briefly in this section, namely policies regarding the condition and performance of infrastructure, natural hazards, and security.

Condition and performance. Condition potentially affects the ability of infrastructure to withstand a wide range of threats, and is often a function of design, operation, and maintenance. Prieto, for example, discussed the relationship between safety and the "core capacity" of infrastructure, specifically with regard to the transit infrastructure in

New York City, which, he found, was in good condition and thus was able to respond to, and recover from, the September 11, 2001 attacks on the World Trade Center (abbreviated 9/11).[10] O'Rourke, Wang, and Shi discussed how the performance of lifelines (distribution and transmission lines) after an earthquake is related to their performance beforehand.[11] Engineering design and construction practices as well as operation and maintenance affect condition and performance and can be indicative of the ability to withstand impacts. For example, the Schoharie Bridge in New York State was vulnerable to flood waters because its piers were embedded in sand, and the collapse of the Nimitz freeway during an earthquake was attributed in part to differences in the reinforcement of the piers on the two sides of the roadway.[12] The Minneapolis bridge collapse in 2007 was attributed to the interaction between the structural capacity of the bridge relative to the stresses to which it was exposed from excess loads during a construction operation.[13]

Improving the condition of the nation's infrastructure was emphasized in the book *America in Ruins*.[14] Earlier, several failures of transportation infrastructure had prompted the creation of the National Transportation Safety Board as an independent entity in 1967;[15] and failures of dams, such as the collapse of the Grand Teton Dam in 1976, reinforced the need for the National Dam Inspection Program that already had been provided for in 1972. Also, the electric power outages of 1965 and 1977 affected millions of customers,[16] as did the extensive 2003 northeast U.S. and Canada blackout. In fact, Some analyses show increasing trends in number of outages from the early 1990s to mid-2000s and increasing duration from the mid-1990s to mid-2000s."[17] Such problems led to changes in national policy and legislation, and are often the foundation for receiving federal funding.

Some studies focused on the investment in infrastructure as a factor in condition and performance, and hence vulnerability, arguing that budget allocations often fell short of needs. In the 1980s and 1990s, estimates of shortfalls were issued by government agencies such as the Joint Economic Committee in Congress and the Congressional Budget Office. The American Society of Civil Engineers (ASCE) has been assessing the condition of the nation's infrastructure along with investment shortfalls since 1988.[18] In fact, ASCE gave an overall rating of D to infrastructure in its 2005 and 2009 report cards, and in 2009 did not give any infrastructure sector a grade higher than C+.[19] These ratings generally do not explicitly take into account the effect of interconnectivity among infrastructures on condition and performance.

Natural hazards. Concerns about natural hazards have created increasing pressure for proactive, protective rather than reactive infrastructure public policy. In the twentieth century and early twenty-first century, for instance, earthquakes and hurricanes revealed the fragility of much infrastructure. This has been compounded by what the U.S. National Oceanic and Atmospheric Administration and the Federal Emergency Management Agency have pointed out as continuing record-setting years during the first decade of the twenty-first century with respect to extreme natural hazards with record levels of damages, and climate change is expected to add to this problem. The serious damage to infrastructure during earthquakes—for example, the 1989 Loma Prieta (California) and 1995 Kobe (Japan) earthquakes—and the sequence of hurricanes that struck the Gulf Coast states in 2005 reinforced the need for the National Incident Management System (NIMS) that first began in the early 2000s and was updated in 2008 that adopted an "all-hazards" approach that includes natural disasters as well as terrorism.[20] Experience with natural hazards provides important lessons for designing infrastructure security.

The "security age." Since 9/11, infrastructure policy has focused more extensively on security. A year after the attacks, the National Research Council analyzed each infrastructure sector as a basis for assessing its vulnerability to intentional attacks.[21]

The 1990s saw a series of terrorist attacks worldwide, including the attack on the World Trade Center in New York City in 1993. From the mid-1990s on, protecting critical infrastructure from intentional attacks has had a central place in federal policy, regulation, and fact-finding. Examples include Executive Order (EO) 13010 in 1996 and the report of the President's Commission on Critical Infrastructure Protection (PCCIP) in 1997. An initiative of the Critical Infrastructure Assurance Office (CIAO) increased awareness of infrastructure as a target of terrorism and began to develop a management structure for its security. Presidential Decision Directive (PDD) 63 also emphasized infrastructure. Examples since 2000 include EO 13231 in 2001; the Patriot Act of 2001; Homeland Security Presidential Directives (HSPDs) 7 and 8; the National Strategy for Homeland Security (2002), developed from the Patriot Act; the National Strategy for the

Physical Protection of Critical Infrastructures (2003), and others in the late 2000s already mentioned above. The report of the 9/11 Commission (2004) proposed reshaping security policy and management, and many elements of this report were related to infrastructure.

Organizationally, infrastructure security management was reflected in the increased interest in infrastructure, especially in the 2008 National Response Framework[22] and the 2009 National Infrastructure Protection Plan, and coordinating entities emerged at high levels of the federal government and in the U.S. DHS. Specific federal offices have been opened to be responsible for homeland security, focusing on critical infrastructure and overlaying a complex existing organizational structure within traditional line agencies for managing various types of infrastructure.

Terrorism and Infrastructure Policy

Incidents of terrorism, sabotage, and vandalism throughout the world before and after 9/11 have been factors in shaping government policy with regard to the protection of infrastructure.

Examples. Transit systems outside the United States were targets of several hundred incidents during the twentieth century.[23] Notably, sarin gas was released in three subway lines in Tokyo in 1995, a subway car was bombed as it entered a station in Paris in 1995 (7 people were killed and 80 injured in that attack); and these attacks continued through the first decade of the twenty-first century, with bombings in Moscow, Angola, Manila, Madrid, London, and Mumbai.[24] In the United States, the most symbolic attack on transit was the direct and indirect damage to the subway system in New York City on 9/11. Vandalism has also affected rail systems in the United States; for instance, Amtrak's Sunset Limited was derailed in Arizona in 1995.

Electric power has been a target of terrorism at several stages of production and consumption. Oil and gas pipelines have been particularly hard hit in Iraq and elsewhere.[25] In particular, the dependency of the energy sector on information technology has created some potential vulnerabilities to cyber attacks. The U.S. General Accounting Office (GAO) (now the Government Accountability Office), citing a private survey, noted that 70 percent of over a thousand cyber attacks in the first half of 2002 on the energy and power sectors included at least one attack that was considered severe.[26] Various components of transmission and distribution are vulnerable to attack. For example, vandalism caused a power outage in October 2004, when two bolts were removed from a transmission tower in Milwaukee, Wisconsin; a rail line was also disrupted, because the tower fell onto the tracks.[27]

Water systems worldwide have been affected by simple damage inflicted on small components, by break-ins, and by contamination. In 2003, break-ins were reported in Carpentersville, Illinois; Volusia, Florida; Willcox, Arizona; Grand Rapids, Michigan; Shelton, Washington; and Montreal, Canada.[28] In 1992, Kurdish rebels threatened to use potassium cyanide to poison the water system of a military base in Turkey; much earlier, in 1973, a German biologist had threatened to contaminate water supplies with biological toxins.[29] An actual incident was the sabotage of the Ta' Kandja water galleries in Malta: a pipe supplying chlorine was intentionally replaced by one containing fuel.[30] There have been fewer accounts of breaches of wastewater treatment, but one noted by the U.S. GAO involved a disgruntled employee of an Australian company who used a radio transmitter to hack the controls of a sewage treatment system and released about 264,000 gallons of raw sewage into parks and rivers in 2000.[31]

The U.S. GAO also notes an example of an attack on telecommunications: in 1997 a teenager in Worcester, Massachusetts, disabled switching stations, "disrupting telephone service for 600 residents and the fire department and causing a malfunction at the local airport."[32] Unintentional physical disruptions of communication systems provide insights into the consequences of communication disruptions from any source. For example, unintentional ruptures in fiber-optic cables during construction have caused not only small local outages but also very disruptive widespread outages in airport systems.

Trends. START has indicated that terrorist incidents have been increasing at least worldwide in the first decade of the twenty-first century.[33] For transit, a database for 1920–1997 indicated a rise in terrorism.[34] Regarding energy fuels, attacks against oil and gas pipes are noteworthy in countries outside of the United States.[35] Cyber attacks have also escalated, for example, according to annual reports by Symantec.[36]

INTERDEPENDENCIES AMONG INFRASTRUCTURES

Interdependence is a significant attribute of today's infrastructure, and this concept has been part of the relevant federal law on infrastructure since the 1990s. Before 9/11, PDD 63 had provisions for identifying and analyzing interdependence, and CIAO was expected to identify interdependence among key infrastructure sectors. Immediately after 9/11, EO 13231 contained a section (8 c viii) establishing a standing committee on infrastructure interdependencies.

"Interdependency" refers to a wide range of connections among physical facilities, services, and customers. Thus a related concept is interconnectedness:

> Interconnectedness refers to a formal linkage between two different systems. A related term, interdependence, connotes a stronger relationship in which two systems not only are connected, but depend upon one another in some way, such as functionally. Not all interconnected systems are interdependent, but all interdependent systems are interconnected.[37]

Another related term is "interoperability." Many forms of interdependency exist at various scales, ranging from small components within a single infrastructure sector or facility to multiple infrastructure systems that can work sequentially or simultaneously.

Categories   Interdependence of infrastructure has been categorized in several ways. How it is categorized is important, because different categories imply different behaviors and analyses. Rinaldi, Peerenboom, and Kelly's categories are physical, cyber, geographic, and logical.[38] This chapter emphasizes interdependence as functional and spatial.[39] EO 13010 implicitly categorizes interdependency in terms of threats, as physical and cyber threats. The basic concepts of dependence and interdependency are consistent and others can be distilled as follows:

- Geographic, spatial, or physical interdependence typically refers to the co-location of two kinds of infrastructure that may or may not function together.
- Functional interdependence (including cyber and logical interdependence) refers to two facilities or services that rely on each other in order to operate that may or may not be located near each other.
- Economic and financial interdependence refers to the dependence of sectors on one another as sources or recipients of goods

and services and other resources; these relationships are often captured by input-output methods or other techniques intended to compensate for the limitations of input-output.

Interdependence can be sequential, parallel, or a combination of both. Also, it can be unidirectional (usually called dependence) or multidirectional.

Mechanisms Interdependence can affect the operations of infrastructure in many ways. On the one hand, connectivity is often intentional, having been designed for economic and technological reasons. On the other hand, ignoring unintentional consequences of interdependence can have catastrophic effects.

Rinaldi, Peerenboom, and Kelly[40] describe failures associated with interdependence as cascading, escalating, and common-cause. In rare instances, there may be dampening effects. According to Rinaldi, Peerenboom, and Kelly, in a cascading failure, a disruption in one infrastructure causes a disruption in another; in an escalating failure, the effect on the next infrastructure increases in severity or recovery time; in a common-cause failure, two independent infrastructures are disrupted by the same cause, often at the same time. Time is important in assessing vulnerability; this factor includes response time, the duration of a disruption or outage, and the time required for repair and restoration.

Zimmerman identified a number of interdependencies that led to system failures.[41] O'Rourke noted some dramatic cascading failures as a consequence of earthquakes.[42] Other interdependencies were revealed—or first appreciated—on 9/11.[43] Because of interconnections among various telecommunication and computing systems within the World Trade Center, for example, Internet outages had local effects as far away as South Africa.[44]

FACTORS CONTRIBUTING TO INTERDEPENDENCE

Interdependence typically develops in connection with patterns and rates of population growth that influence not only the use of infrastructure services but also the consumption of resources, such as land,[45] in ways that can increase vulnerability. That infrastructure has grown rapidly is apparent from general trends in consumption or usage of infrastructure services. Despite efficiencies, the consumption of energy tripled, and the use of water doubled, from 1950 to 2000;[46] there have also been significant increases in travel by automobile and mass transit,[47] and in telecommunications (exemplified by the growth in the use of cell phones).[48]

Also, growth in infrastructure is mainly characterized by a combination of fewer, centralized production facilities, and by very long networks in which services are delivered far from where they are produced or travelers' destinations are far from their points of departure. To cite two dramatic examples of long networks, there are an estimated 2 million miles of pipeline and 2 billion miles of cable for information technology and telecommunications.[49]

Sites of production and consumption are critical nodes that vary by type of infrastructure. There are many such nodes: for instance, there are some 500 airports providing commercial service and 14,000 smaller ones and oil wells are estimated at 600,000.[50] The number of discrete sites (for production, processing, storage, transmission or transfer of goods, people and services, etc.) is even more impressive as cited by the National Research Council: for example, the U.S. Department of Transportation bridge inventory indicated that there are nearly 600,000 highway bridges.

Despite the large number of nodes, the following United States examples, convey the intensity of infrastructure centralization that potentially contributes to interdependence. As a broader context, the U.S. Bureau of the Census data indicates that population is concentrated: just nine states account for about half of the U.S. population.

- 6.8 percent of all community water supply systems serve 45 percent of the population, and the proportions are similar for wastewater treatment systems: In 1950, the average publicly owned treatment works (POTWs) served 7,790 people; in 1996, this figure had risen to 11,838.[51]

- In the energy area, of 225 petroleum refineries, 54 percent are located in only four states—Texas, California, Louisiana, and Pennsylvania—and of 2,776 electric power plants, 51.4 percent are located in 11 states.[52] Three states—Texas, Wyoming and Louisiana—accounted for about 40 percent of the U.S. energy production in 2009.[53]

- In transportation, in 2010, 4.8 billion hours of delay occurred in 439 areas, and almost 60 percent of the hours were in 15 "very large" urban areas (defined as having populations exceeding

3 million)[54] given that much of the population is concentrated in those areas.

- Annual public transportation trips including bus and rail transit were 10.4 billion in 2009, with transit systems in New York, Chicago, and Los Angeles accounting for about 40 percent of the total (APTA 2011, p. 7, 8);[55] moreover, generally half of the rail transit infrastructure such as stations and track was concentrated in just a few systems.[56]

ANALYZING INTERDEPENDENCE

Direct and indirect attacks on infrastructure seem to involve very simple means even if tactics and strategies are complex. For example, according to NTSB the derailment of Amtrak's Sunset Limited in Arizona in 1995 (an incident in which 1 person died and 65 were injured) was accomplished simply by removing some nuts and bolts from a piece of track at a crucial point—a trestle—and disabling a signal so that the train engineer was unaware of the damage.

More complex incidents involving interdependencies are not easily quantified. Analyses generally concentrate on assessing threats to infrastructure, vulnerability and risk of attack, or consequences of an incident. Although approaches differ in their use of engineering or economics, they are generally based on scenarios: scripts created to reflect the components, relationships, and behavior of interdependent systems. Methods currently in use or being developed for creating scenarios often begin with a set (or "suite") of indicators and conceptual models such as influence diagrams, followed by fault and event trees that provide a basis for quantitative analyses, risk analysis, and decision analysis. Influence diagrams show linkages at a single point in time, not necessarily implying sequences of events or decisions.[57] Decision trees or trees adapted to events, such as fault and event trees, show sequences of occurrences and are a basis for assigning probabilities to the phases.

Scenarios usually make implicit assumptions about outcomes, assumptions that are only as accurate as the scenario itself and can be very difficult to scrutinize or test. An alternative is to base the scenario and the probability of outcomes on actual data. Attack scenarios for infrastructure are different from those for other situations, and this fact also complicates analysis. For example, the impact of an incident can be deepened, and recovery can be slowed, if different kinds of attacks take place simultaneously—say, a cyber attack along with a physical attack or the release of a chemical used in infrastructure operations (e.g., chlorine, which is used in wastewater treatment plants) or conveyed by infrastructure. The U.S. GAO calls such an incident a "swarming attack."[58]

Models

Economic and engineering models for interdependent infrastructure take various approaches. They often combine techniques such as risk analysis, event and fault tree analysis, game theory, and geographic information systems (GIS). Although economic and engineering models can be applied within a single infrastructure sector, they are usually applicable across sectors as well.

Economic models can also be applied to interdependence between infrastructure and the rest of the economy. Such models have been developed by Haimes and Jiang,[59] with U.S. Department of Commerce, Bureau of Economic Analysis data; by Henry and Dumagen,[60] who used the same databases to identify linkages between information technology, other infrastructure, and the economy at large; and by Rose et al.,[61] who used "computational general equilibrium" analyses to estimate economic and business impacts.

Engineering models use various techniques. Martz and Johnston[62] used event tree analysis as the basis for a risk analysis of military installations involving munitions storage and the transport of a missile. Pate-Cornell[63] used an overall systems approach. GIS have been combined with lifeline engineering to estimate the reliability of infrastructure lifelines exposed to natural hazards, and with spatial overlays to analyze interdependencies statistically.[64] Risk analysis has been applied to the safety of infrastructure.[65] The risk ranking technique developed by Haimes[66] has been applied to individual infrastructure systems, such as water distribution[67] and transportation;[68] it can be extended to multiple interactions. Mili, Qui, and Phadke[69] apply risk assessment to scenarios associated with the failure of large-scale electrical systems; this analysis could be extended to interactions between electrical and nonelectrical systems. Economic and engineering frameworks can often be combined, particularly in the work being done at the national laboratories. Network theory is another approach used to portray and model attack scenarios for infrastructure.[70]

Another type of analytical approach encompasses social-psychological dimensions of terrorism and the communication of risk. For example, some techniques apply the social-psychological behavior of decision makers and the general public to infrastructures such as electric power and railroads in situations that do not involve terrorism.[71] Other methods have focused on risk communication associated with terrorism.[72]

Indicators

Indicators are inputs to or outputs of a model. They are often expressed as ratios or rates derived externally—from other models or empirical research. (The examples of centralization listed previously are simple indicators.) Indicators are easy to use and are a component of various models, but many are not designed, in themselves, to capture the complexity of interdependence.

Ratios of actual cases of failure and of recovery after failure are an important approach to the development of infrastructure interdependency and dependency indicators. One indicator derived in this way is a ratio of two frequencies: how often one infrastructure causes failure in another, and how often it is affected by failure in another. When this indicator was applied to about 100 cases across the United States, water mains appeared to have the highest ratio of damage caused to damage incurred.[73] This result is supported by common sense: when a water main breaks, the consequences can literally spill over into other sectors. Another approach to indicator construction, focusing on infrastructure recovery after the 2003 U.S. and Canada blackout based on dependency on electric power, found considerable variation in the time it took transportation and water infrastructure to recover after electric power was restored.[74]

INSTITUTIONAL INTERDEPENDENCE

How can interdependence be managed? Traditionally, each type of infrastructure is dealt with separately and interconnectivity is considered as separate add-ons to that infrastructure. But if dispersed systems are to be effective buffers against terrorist attacks, interdependence must be integrated at the outset.

Government

The U.S. GAO has summarized the proliferation of governmental organizations at the federal level to manage infrastructure security, identifying:

at least 50 organizations involved in national or multilayer cyber CIP (civil infrastructure protection) efforts. These entities include 5 advisory committees; 6 Executive Office of the President organizations; 38 executive branch organizations associated with departments, agencies, or intelligence organizations; and 3 other organizations. These organizations are primarily located within 13 major departments and agencies mentioned in PDD 63. Other departments and agencies, in addition to the 13 mentioned in PDD 63, are also involved in CIP activities.[75]

The U.S. Congress, also, has many committees and subcommittees addressing infrastructure security. In addition, under PDD 63, Information Sharing and Analysis Centers (ISACs) were created to bridge the gap between public and private sector infrastructures; this linkage was considered essential because 80 percent of the U.S. infrastructure is said to be under the control of the private sector.[76] Furthermore, NIMS formally incorporates many levels of government into "incident responses," regardless of what caused an incident or what its impact is.

Concern for infrastructure security had caused changes in the organization of government even before 9/11. The responsibility for security began within councils and coordinating entities and gradually became part of line agencies. Following are some highlights.[77]

PDD 63 (1998) generally relied on existing line agencies for the security of specific types of infrastructure, added several coordinating and cross-cutting layers to integrate them, and located them close to the executive office through agencies such as the National Coordinator for Security, Infrastructure Protection, and Counterterrorism, who chaired a Critical Infrastructure Coordination Group (CICG); a National Infrastructure Assurance Council; and a chief information officer. Communications were a pervasive element in programs intended to protect critical infrastructure; in this regard the National Infrastructure Protection Center (NIPC) and the ISACs—especially the warning system—are significant. PDD 63 also contains a planning function in the form of the National Infrastructure Assurance Plan; and research capabilities were provided, for example, by CIAO, within the Department of Commerce.

After 9/11 a Critical Infrastructure Protection Board cutting across many governmental functions was established by EO 13231. It was abolished in 2003 after the formation of the Office of Homeland Security and DHS (the latter was created under the Homeland Security Act of 2002). Critical infrastructure remained a focus, through two U.S. DHS directorates: Information Analysis and Infrastructure Protection (IAIP) and Science and Technology. IAIP assumed many functions regarding protection and security.[78] The considerable reliance on the line agencies for infrastructure protection continued. The strong focus on information technology, distinct from other forms of critical infrastructure, is evident throughout the organizational history of homeland security. Infrastructure continues to be a focus of congressional legislation. In the 108th Congress alone more than one-fifth of the bills reported pertained to critical infrastructure, typically involving transportation.[79] Still, GAO noted in 2002 that many goals were not being met on schedule.[80]

The most dramatic structural changes in homeland security are likely to result from the 9/11 Commission Report,[81] which emphasized communication and information transfer practices. Traditional agency controls over communication and infrastructure are part of the centralized intelligence structure proposed by the commission.

The Public

Policy, including organizational policy, is often driven by public concern, and surveys have found increasing public concern over the vulnerability of infrastructure to terrorism. In 2001, Herron and Jenkins-Smith[82] conducted a nationwide telephone survey of 935 people; in 2002, they did a panel survey of 474 of these respondents; a survey had also been done in 1997, and a follow-up to this included critical infrastructures. The results, some of which were statistically significant, were as follows:

- Threats to infrastructure were perceived as being greater from foreign sources than domestic sources.
- The level of perceived threats from both foreign and domestic sources increased between 1997 and 2001 but decreased between 2001 and 2002 (though the decrease in the mean score was relatively small and only significant for water supplies at the $p < 0.01$ significance level).
- When respondents ranked the threat to eight types of critical infrastructure (including banking and finance and emergency services) in 2002, they placed water supply systems and oil and gas supplies and services first and second; that is, respondents rated these two infrastructures as potentially being threatened more.

Surveys and polls are typically conducted annually and have found continuing public interest in security,[83] but they typically do not disaggregate responses for infrastructure or type of infrastructure sector or the trade-offs and comparisons among them and their relationships.

TECHNOLOGY AND INTERDEPENDENCE

Information Technology

The information technology (IT) revolution has pervaded almost every sector of the economy, including infrastructure; and the interdependence of IT and other infrastructures was underscored by the widespread anxiety over Y2K. In infrastructure, IT generally encompasses computing and communications, and the means to operate, control, monitor, and analyze other systems.[84] The connection between IT and other infrastructures has been enhanced on the supply side by the tremendous growth in the availability of IT in the form of wireless phones, cell phones, cell phone sites, the Internet, and broadband. On the demand side, infrastructure sectors have become important consumers of IT; nationwide, infrastructure is estimated to account for one-third of investment in IT.[85]

The use of IT to "enable" infrastructure provides enormous opportunities but can also increase vulnerability when IT does not perform as expected and infrastructure management is unprepared for that contingency. The extent to which other infrastructures rely on IT and the implications of that reliance has been the subject of studies and various specialized reports.[86] Interest in the vulnerability of critical infrastructures to cyber attack has motivated federal policy in this area. The CERT Coordination Center (CERT/CC) at Carnegie Mellon University in Pittsburgh, Pennsylvania, monitors such intrusions, and between 1999 and 2003 it reported an increase from 9,859 to 137,529 incidents. At least 70 percent of electric utilities have reported cyber intrusions.[87]

Energy

Energy drives other infrastructure and other sectors of the economy. Large-scale outages seem to be increasing in frequency, extent, and duration,[88] but not all of them affect customers. Large outages, such as those of January 1998 and August 2003 (in the northeastern United States and Canada), have underscored the interdependence between electric power and the overall economy, as well as IT. In the outage of August 2003 (which is estimated to have cost $4.2 billion to $10 billion),[89] an initiating factor may have been a cyber failure in critical operating areas, including software and emergency backup. The cyber failure soon combined with weaknesses inherent in the network in Ohio, causing a rapidly spreading series of outages.[90] These outages then disrupted many other systems, including transportation and water supplies.[91]

REDUCING VULNERABILITY BY MODIFYING INTERDEPENDENCY

Securing infrastructure to reduce the consequences of incidents often emphasizes "hardening" through design and operation and providing short-term backup systems. Another way to provide security involves alternative infrastructure technologies, such as "green technologies." Proponents of sustainability and environmental protection have advocated such technologies, which are already influencing the design of energy, transportation, water, and communication systems. Concepts that were once tangential or marginal have entered the mainstream with regard to the planning and development of infrastructure. Renewable energy is an important part of public energy policy that has implications for other infrastructure that depends on energy.

These technologies offer opportunities to combine security with environmental protection and the conservation of energy, but certain limitations need to be recognized. The criteria for secure infrastructure generally include the ability to separate from heavily networked, centralized systems; locating services close to the users; flexibility in changing deployment patterns through mobility or other means; and the use of raw materials and other resources that are ubiquitous and not easily destroyed.[92] Green technologies meet many of these criteria; however, these technologies, especially those for producing energy, are built to operate intermittently, and when they are not operating, they rely on networked systems for infrastructure.

Renewable Energy Sources That Can Be Decoupled

Energy is often the first link in a critical infrastructure network. Therefore, renewable sources of energy are a critical factor in reducing the vulnerability of such a network. Renewable energy sources are those that can be regenerated or are not used up, and thus are not greatly threatened or disrupted by an attack, though they are vulnerable as regards their delivery to users. Renewable forms of energy include solar (photovoltaics), wind, geothermal, sea heat-gradient, and tidal. Usually, these energy sources are local or specific to a particular production process or cycle. According to DOE's Energy Information Administration,[93] the consumption of renewable energy resources accounted for 8.2 percent of the United States' 98 quadrillion BTUs of energy consumed in 2010 (preliminary), and about 54 percent was accounted for by biomass and hydroelectric combined. Electric power generation has used by far the largest amount of renewable energy, accounting for 60 percent of renewables, primarily from hydropower, and the industrial sector ranks second, which draws most of its renewables from biomass.[94]

Although renewable energy is still a small share of total energy consumed, solar and wind energy are being increasingly used in local settings. For example, in New York City the redevelopment of the World Trade Center area includes "green energy," and Battery Park City in downtown Manhattan already relies on photovoltaic energy. A serious obstacle to local use of fuel cells has been constraints on space for energy storage, but new nanotechnology may overcome this problem.[95] Use of renewables in transportation has been less impressive; this sector accounts for only about one-third of the consumption of renewable energy, primarily alcohol fuels (ethanol).[96] Also, there is debate over the net effect of environmentally friendly sources of power such as electric and hydrogen vehicles.

It should be noted, with respect to security, that many of these technologies ultimately connect back to centralized production facilities. Some systems that appear to be decoupled, such as backup units for electric power and the other systems to which it connects, may not in fact be independent of centralized energy production. For example, generators that run on diesel fuel are decentralized and decoupled from the grid when in use but are not renewable resources and are produced at centralized sites. However, storage mechanisms enhance the ability of infrastructure to decouple from large networks and reduce dependence on centralized energy sources at least for a short time.

Renewables and other energy technologies are promising, and a thorough systems approach is needed to evaluate them fully.

Technologies for Rapid Recovery

The technology needed to repair infrastructure after destruction from any cause has been growing rapidly. Bridges are a notable example of where temporary bridges as well as permanent sections can be swung into place after a collapse. When a segment of the San Francisco Bay bridge was destroyed in an earthquake, it was repaired in less time than building a new bridge would have taken. Rapid construction techniques can also be used for other bridge structures such as long spans and overpasses, at least for temporary repairs.[97] The rapid (though temporary) repair of infrastructure at the World Trade Center showed that managers were able to adapt their services very quickly.

CONCLUSION

The interdependencies and dependencies among infrastructures seem to be increasing, potentially contributing to infrastructure vulnerability, but these vulnerabilities are being more broadly acknowledged.[98] The increasing use of information technology across infrastructure sectors is a factor in increasing interdependence. New approaches to designing, using, and managing infrastructure show promise, at least in reducing the consequences of terrorism; but security still represents a challenge to management. The challenge for line agencies that typically specialize in one type of infrastructure is to organize themselves so as to address interdependence specifically across a wide range of functions including management and finance and across infrastructure sectors.

The lessons learned so far include the ubiquity, diffuseness, and complexity of infrastructure services that are important factors for technology and building institutions. The public has shown its concern about threats to infrastructure, and these concerns also need to be incorporated into institution building.

Incidents that threaten infrastructure have included terrorism but also other events and incidents. The history of the role of dependencies and interdependencies in magnifying vulnerability needs to be recorded and analyzed—particularly in terms of the operational issues associated with infrastructure and with human responses—to produce a comprehensive picture of how various elements interact during an event.

NOTES

1. The World Bank, "How Much Does Infrastructure Contribute to GDP Growth?" *World Bank Research Digest* 5, no. 4 (Summer 2011) p. 7, http://siteresources.worldbank.org/DEC/Resources/84797–1154354760266/2807421–1288872844438/7530108–1313070714827/GDP_Growth.pdf.

2. U.S. Census Bureau, *Statistical Abstracts of the United States: 2012*, Table 781, "Net Stock of Private Fixed Assets by Industry: 2000 to 2009" (2012), http://www.census.gov/compendia/statab/2012/tables/12s0781.pdf, citing U.S. Bureau of Economic Analysis (2010), Table 3.1ES, Current-Cost Net Stock of Private Fixed Assets by Industry, http://www.bea.gov. Earlier estimates were provide by J. P. Gould and A. C. Lemer, eds., *Toward Infrastructure Improvement: An Agenda for Research* (Washington, DC: National Academy Press, 1994) 18.

3. A. Altshuler, "Infrastructure Investment" (book review), *Journal of Policy Analysis and Management* 8 (1989): 506. See also D. C. Perry, "Building the Public City: An Introduction," in D. C. Perry, ed., *Building the Public City: The Politics, Governance, and Finance of Public Infrastructure* (Thousand Oaks, CA: Sage, 1995), 1–20.

4. S. M. Rinaldi, J. P. Peerenboom, and T. K. Kelly, "Identifying, Understanding, and Analyzing Critical Infrastructure Interdependencies," *IEEE Control Systems* (December 2001): 12, citing the President's Commission on Critical Infrastructure Protection, Critical Foundations: Protecting America's Infrastructures (1997), http://www.ciao.gov.

5. U.S. Executive Office of the President, "The Clinton Administration's Policy on Critical Infrastructure Protection: Presidential Decision Directive 63" (May 22, 1998).

6. The U.S. Patriot Act of 2001.

7. U.S. Department of Homeland Security, *National Infrastructure Protection Plan* (Washington, DC: DHS, 2009), 3. Nuclear reactors, materials, and waste are counted as one sector.

8. Ibid., 2.

9. T. D. O'Rourke, Y. Wang, and P. Shi, "Advances in Lifeline Earthquake Engineering," Proceedings of the Thirteenth World Conference on Earthquake Engineering (Vancouver, CA, August 1–6, 2004).

10. R. Prieto, "The 3Rs: Lessons Learned from September 11," presented at the Royal Academy of Engineering, 2002.

11. O'Rourke, Wang, and Shi, 2004.

12. R. Zimmerman, "Planning and Administration: Frameworks and Case Studies," in John Ingleton, ed., *Natural Disaster Management* (Leicester, UK: Tudor Rose, 1999), 225–7. This is also cited in R. Zimmerman, *Transport, the Environment and Security* (Cheltenham, UK, and Northampton, MA: Edward Elgar Publishing, 2012), p. 189.

13. National Transportation Safety Board (NTSB) "Highway Accident Report: Collapse of the I–35W Highway Bridge, Minneapolis, MN, August 1, 2007" (2008), http://www.ntsb.gov/doclib/reports/2008/HAR0803.pdf.

14. P. Choate and S. Walter, *America in Ruins* (Durham, NC: Duke University Press, 1983).

15. NTSB, "History of the NTSB," http://www.ntsb.gov/about/history.html.

16. North American Electric Reliability Council (NERC), "Examples of Major Bulk Electric System Power Outages," n.d., http://www.nerc.com/docs/docs/blackout/Blackout Table.pdf.

17. J. S. Simonoff, C. E. Restrepo, and R. Zimmerman, "Risk Management and Risk Analysis-Based Decision Tools for Attacks on Electric Power," *Risk Analysis* 27, no. 3 (2007): 547–70.

18. American Society of Civil Engineers, *Report Card for America's Infrastructure* (Washington, DC: ASCE). https://apps.asce.org/reportcard/2005/index.cfm; http://www.infrastructurereportcard.org/.

19. American Society of Civil Engineers report cards for 2005 and 2009 are respectively available at https://apps.asce.org/reportcard/2005/page.cfm?id=103 and http://www.infrastructurereportcard.org/.

20. U.S. DHS, National Incident Management System (NIMS) (Washington, DC: U.S. DHS, December 2008), http://www.fema.gov/emergency/nims/.

21. National Research Council (NRC), *Making the Nation Safer: The Role of Science and Technology in Countering Terrorism* (Washington, DC: National Academy Press, 2002).

22. U.S. DHS, National Response Framework (2008), http://www.fema.gov/pdf/emergency/nrf/nrf-core.pdf.

23. Mineta International Institute for Surface Transportation Policy Studies, "Protecting Surface Transportation Systems and Patrons from Terrorist Activities," (Washington, DC: Mineta Institute, 1997), 23.

24. START, "Background Report: On the Fifth Anniversary of the 7/7 London Transit Attack" University of Maryland/START (2010), p. 6, http://www.start.umd.edu/start/announcements/July07_LondonMetroBombing_2010.pdf. For more detailed accounts, see R. Zimmerman,

Transport, the Environment and Security (Cheltenham, UK, and Northampton, MA: Edward Elgar Publishing, 2012), Chapter 7.

25. J. S. Simonoff, C. E. Restrepo, and R. Zimmerman with the assistance of W. E. Remington, "Trends for Oil and Gas Terrorist Attacks," I3P Report no. 2, The Institute for Information Infrastructure Protection (November 2005), http://www.thei3p.org/docs/publications/ResearchReport2.pdf.

26. U.S. General Accounting Office, "Critical Infrastructure Protection: Significant Challenges Need to be Addressed," GAO–02–961T, 2002, pp. 13–14, http://www.gao.gov/new.items/d02961t.pdf.

27. "Tampering blamed in power outage," *Chicago Tribune*, October 12, 2004, http://articles.chicagotribune.com/2004–10–12/news/0410120157_1_tower-passenger-and-freight-trains-bolts.

28. R. Zimmerman, "Water," in R. Zimmerman and T. Horan, eds., *Digital Infrastructures: Enabling Civil and Environmental Systems through Information Technology* (London: Routledge, 2004a), 80.

29. A. S. Khan, D. L. Swerdlow, and D. D. Juranek, "Precautions Against Biological and Chemical Terrorism Directed at Food and Water Supplies," *Public Health Reports* 116 (2001), p. 7. See also Zimmerman (2004a).

30. P. Cachia, "Saboteur Contaminates Water Supply at Ta' Kandja," *di-ve news* 10 (November 2003). See also Zimmerman, 2004a.

31. U.S. General Accounting Office, "Critical Infrastructure Protection: Challenges and Efforts to Secure Control Systems," GAO–04–354 (March 2004), 17. See also Zimmerman (2012).

32. U.S. GAO, ibid., 17.

33. START, "Background Report: 9/11, Ten Years Later," University of Maryland/ START (2011), p. 4, http://www.start.umd.edu/start/announcements/BackgroundReport_10YearsSince9_11.pdf.

34. Mineta Institute, (1997).

35. Simonoff, Restrepo, and Zimmerman, (2005).

36. Symantec Corporation, "Internet Security Threat Report Trends for 2010," 16 (2011), https://www4.symantec.com/mktginfo/downloads/21182883_GA_REPORT_ISTR_Main-Report_04–11_HI-RES.pdf. See also Zimmerman (2012), Chapter 6.

37. R. Zimmerman, "Social Implications of Infrastructure Network Interactions," in *Sustaining Urban Networks: The Social Diffusion of Large Technical Systems* (London: Routledge, 2005), 69.

38. Rinaldi, Peerenboom, and Kelly.

39. R. Zimmerman, "Decision-Making and the Vulnerability of Critical Infrastructure," *Proceedings of IEEE International on Systems, Man, and Cybernetics* (2004b).

40. Rinaldi, Peerenboom, and Kelly, (2001) 22.

41. Zimmerman, (2005).

42. T. D. O'Rourke, "Prospectus for Lifelines and Infrastructure Research," in B. Stenquist, ed., *The Art and Science of Structural Engineering: Proceedings of the Symposium Honoring William J. Hal* (Upper Saddle River, NJ: Prentice Hall, 1993), 37–58.

43. R. Zimmerman, "Public Infrastructure Service Flexibility for Response and Recovery in the September 11th, 2001, Attacks at the World Trade Center," in Natural Hazards Research and Applications Information Center, Public Entity Risk Institute, and Institute for Civil Infrastructure Systems, *Beyond September 11th: An Account of Post-Disaster Research*, Special Publication 39 (Boulder, CO: University of Colorado, 2003a), 241–268.

44. National Research Council, "The Internet under Crisis Conditions: Learning from September 11" (Washington, DC: National Academy Press, 2003).

45. U.S. Environmental Protection Agency (EPA), "Development, Community, and Environment: Our Built and Natural Environments" (Washington, DC: EPA, November 2000).

46. R. Zimmerman and T. Horan, eds., *Digital Infrastructures: Enabling Civil and Environmental Systems Through Information Technology* (London: Routledge, 2004); see the editors' article "What Are Digital Infrastructures?" 71.

47. U.S. Department of Transportation, Federal Highway Administration, Highway Statistics (Washington, DC: U.S. DOT); U.S. Department of Transportation, Federal Transit Administration, National Transit database. These trends are covered extensively in R. Zimmerman, Chapter 2, *Transport, the Environment, and Security: Making the Connection* (Cheltenham, UK, and Northampton, MA: Edward Elgar Publishing, 2012).

48. Cellular Telecommunications and Internet Association, "Semiannual Wireless Industry Survey" (Washington, DC: CTIA, 2010). See also Zimmerman, 2005, p. 71.

49. D. Bart, Presentation for the Defense Standardization Program Conference: An Update on ANSI Homeland Security Standards Panel (HSSP), ANSI-HSSP, Private Sector Cochair, March 17, 2004.

50. NRC, *Making the Nation Safer*, 212 and 201.

51. R. Zimmerman, "Water," in *Digital Infrastructures*, eds. R. Zimmerman and T. Horan (London, UK: Routledge 2005), p. 81, citing U.S. EPA "The Clean Water and Drinking Water Infrastructure Gap Analysis," September 2002, http://www.epa.gov/ogwdw/gapreport.pdf.

52. U.S. Bureau of the Census, 1997, http://www.census.gov/prod/www/abs/manu-geo. html (accessed October 29, 2004); The number of power plants by state can be aggregated by year from the data in http://www.eia.gov/electricity/data.cfmencapacity.

53. Computed from U.S. Department of Energy, Energy Information Administration, "State Ranking 1. Total Energy Production, 2009 (Trillion Btu)," 2009, http://205.254.135.7/state/state-energy-rankings.cfm?keyid=89&orderid=1.

54. D. Schrank, T. Lomax, and B. Eisele, "2011 Urban Mobility Report," College Station, TX, Texas A&M University System, Texas Transportation Institute, 2011, p. 5 and computed from p. 24, http://tti.tamu.edu/documents/mobility-report–2011-wappx.pdf.

55. *American Public Transportation Association, Public Transportation Fact Book 2011* (Washington, DC: APTA, 2011) 7–8.

56. R. Zimmerman, (2012), Chapter 2.

57. R. Clemen and T. Reilly, *Making Hard Decisions with Decision Tools* (Pacific Grove, CA: Duxbury, 2001), 67–68.

58. U.S. GAO, "Critical Infrastructure Protection: Significant Challenges Need to Be Addressed," GAO–02–961T, (July 24, 2002), p. 14.

59. Y. Haimes and P. Jiang, "Leontief-Model of Risk in Complex Interconnected Infrastructures," *Journal of Infrastructure Systems* 7, no. 1 (2001): 1–12.

60. D. Henry and J. Dumagen, "Economics," in R. Zimmerman and T.A. Horan, eds., *Digital Infrastructures: Enabling Civil and Environmental Systems Through Information Technology* (London: Routledge, 2004), 155.

61. A. Rose, J. Benavides, S. Chang, P. Szczesniak, and D. Lim, "The Regional Economic Impact of an Earthquake: Direct and Indirect Effects of Electricity Lifeline Disruptions," *Journal of Regional Science* 37, no. 3 (1997): 437–58.

62. H. Martz and M. Johnston, "Risk Analysis of Terrorist Attack," *Risk Analysis* 7 (1987): 35–47.

63. E. Pate-Cornell, "Probabilistic Modeling of Terrorist Threats: A System Analysis Approach to Setting Priorities Counter Measures," *Military Operations Research* 7, no. 4 (December 2002): 5–20.

64. O'Rourke, Wang, and Shi, (2004).

65. G. Apostolakis, "The Concept of Probability in Safety Assessments of Technological Systems," *Science* 250, no. 7 (December 7, 1990).

66. Y. Haimes, *Risk Modeling, Assessment and Management* (New York: John Wiley & Sons, 2004), and earlier editions.

67. B. Ezell, J. V. Farr, and I. Wiese, "Infrastructure Risk Analysis Model" and "Infrastructure Risk Analysis of Municipal Water Distribution System," *Journal of Infrastructure Systems* 6, no. 3 (2000): 114–17, 118–122.

68. M. Leung, J. H. Lambert, and A. Mosenthal, "A Risk-Based Approach to Setting Priorities in Protecting Bridges against Terrorist Attacks," *Risk Analysis* 24, no. 2 (2004): 963–984.

69. L. Mili, Q. Qiu, and A. G. Phadke, "Risk Assessment of Catastrophic Failures in Electric Power Systems," *International Journal of Critical Infrastructures* 1, no. 1 (2004): 38–63.

70. See R. Zimmerman (2012), *Transport, the Environment, and* Security (Chapter 1, for applications to transportation systems), Cheltenham, UK, and Northhampton, MA: Edward Elgar Publishing.

71. B. Fischhoff, P. Slovic, S, Lichtenstein, S. Read, and B. Combs, "How Safe Is Safe Enough: A Psychometric Study of Attitudes Toward Technological Risks and Benefits," in P. Slovic, ed., *The Perception of Risk* (London and Sterling, VA.: Earthscan, 2000), 80–103.

72. B. Fischhoff, "Assessing and Communicating the Risks of Terrorism," in A. H. Teich, S. D. Nelson, and S. J. Lita, eds., *Science and Technology in a Vulnerable World* (Washington, DC: AAAS, 2002), 51–64. See also B. Fischhoff, R. M. Gonzalez, D. A. Small, and J. S. Lerner, "Evaluating the Success of Terror Risk Communications," *Biosecurity and Bioterrorism: Biodefense Strategy, Practice, and Science* 1 (2003): 255–58.

73. R. Zimmerman, Decision-making and the Vulnerability of Critical Infrastructure," *Proceedings of the IEEE International Conference on Systems, Man, and Cybernetics* (2004).

74. R. Zimmerman and C. E. Restrepo, "The Next Step: Quantifying Infrastructure Interdependencies to Improve Security," *International Journal of Critical Infrastructures* 2, no. 2/3 (2006): 215–230. See also Zimmerman (2012), p. 220.

75. GAO, (2002), p. 17.

76. Ibid., 26.

77. Ibid. For more detail, see also National Academy of Engineering, Computer Science, and Telecommunications Board, "Critical Information Infrastructure Protection and the Law: An Overview of Key Issues" (Washington, DC: National Academy Press, 2003).

78. GAO, (2004), p. 27.

79. TheOrator.com, "Bills Concerning U.S. Homeland Security, Introduced in the 108th Congress," http://www.theorator.com/bills108/issues/homeland_security.html (accessed July 25, 2012).

80. GAO (2002), p. 10.

81. National Commission on Terrorist Attacks upon the United States, "The 9/11 Commission Report" (New York: W. W. Norton & Company, 2004).

82. K. G. Herron and H. C. Jenkins-Smith, "U.S. Public Response to Terrorism: (Panel Study 2001–2002)," College Station, Texas A&M University, August 2003, pp. 3, 22–28; Table 2.5.

83. These are summarized by R. Zimmerman (2012), Chapter 7.

84. Zimmerman and Horan, (2004), p. 6

85. Henry and Dumagan.

86. Zimmerman and Horan, (2004); NRC, (2002, 2003).

87. GAO, (2004), pp. 6, 12.

88. Simonoff, Restrepo, and Zimmerman, (2007).

89. Electricity Consumers Resource Council, "The Economic Impacts of the August 2003 Blackout" (February 2, 2004).

90. U.S.-Canada Power System Outage Task Force, "Final Report on the August 14th, 2003 Blackout in the United States and Canada: Causes and Recommendations," April 2004. See also Zimmerman (2012), p. 226.

91. R. Zimmerman, "NYC Needs Systems to Blunt New Blackouts," *Newsday*, (August 27, 2003b), p. A31. See also Zimmerman and Restrepo, (2006).

92. R. Truly, "New Energy Systems Enhance National Security," DOE, National Renewable Energy Laboratory, (March 14, 2002), http://www.nrel.gov/news/press/2002/0902_security.html.

93. U.S. Energy Information Administration, *Annual Energy Review 2010* (October 2011), p. 290, http://205.254.135.7/totalenergy/data/annual/pdf/aer.pdf.

94. Ibid., 297 and 295. The transportation context for renewables is covered by Zimmerman, (2012), Chapters 1 and 4.

95. C. Lenatti, "Nanotech's First Block-busters," *Technology Review* (March 2004): 46–52.

96. U.S. Energy Information Administration, (2010), p. 295. The transportation context for renewables is covered by Zimmerman, (2012), Chapters 1 and 4.

97. For a more detailed discussion of these rapid recovery strategies and others, see Zimmerman, (2012), Chapters 1 and 6.

98. U.S. DHS, NIPP, (2009).

This chapter is an updated version of and includes portions of the author's chapter in the first edition of the handbook: Rae Zimmerman, "Critical Infrastructure and Interdependency," Chapter 35 in The McGraw-Hill Homeland Security Handbook, edited by D. G. Kamien. New York, NY: The McGraw-Hill Companies, Inc., 2006, pp. 523-545.

21

HOMELAND SECURITY FOR DRINKING WATER AND WASTEWATER UTILITIES

Stanley States, Ph.D.

Director of Water Quality and Production
Pittsburgh Water and Sewer Authority

Water utilities, both drinking water and wastewater, provide essential services to the public on a 24/7/365 basis. They are designed with a great deal of redundancy to help ensure uninterrupted service. Despite these efforts, utilities are potentially subject to interruptions resulting from a variety of emergencies. Natural disasters (e.g., hurricanes, blizzards, earthquakes, tornadoes, flooding) and major accidents (fires, explosions, electrical power grid failures, equipment failures, accidental contamination) have impacted utilities for years. While water systems have always been susceptible to emergencies caused by human activities, ranging from simple vandalism to thefts and incidents perpetrated by disgruntled insiders (e.g., employees, contractors), the attacks of September 11, 2001, increased awareness of the possibility of a public utility being targeted by terrorists.

As with most industries, drinking water and wastewater companies typically have limited money, staff, and time to prepare for emergencies. Utilities also have a number of other requirements that compete for limited resources. These include dealing with aging infrastructure and responding to ever more stringent federal, state, and local regulations intended to protect the health and safety of the communities served. For drinking water systems the overarching regulation is the federal Safe Drinking Water Act and its continually evolving amendments governing the chemical, microbiological, and radiological quality of drinking water. For wastewater systems the primary regulation is the federal Water Pollution Control Act (Clean Water Act), which limits the public health and environmental impacts of the treated liquid effluent ultimately discharged to receiving streams and the waste biosolids disposed of in landfills. Drinking water and wastewater utilities must also respond to newly discovered public health and environmental contaminants such as the trace concentrations of pharmaceuticals, personal care products, and endocrine disruptors that have been detected in wastewater plant effluents, surface and ground waters, and even drinking water supplies in recent years. Security and emergency preparedness needs are just one of a number of concerns for the water industry.

Prior to the attacks of September 11, 2011, most emergency planning at utilities focused on accidents, equipment failures, and the specific natural disasters that are most likely to occur in a given water system's location. In the several year period immediately following 9/11, the emphasis on emergency planning for utilities shifted to incidents initiated by humans. In fact, the federal Bioterrorism Act of 2002 mandated that all U.S. drinking water utilities serving more than 3,300 persons conduct a formal vulnerability assessment to identify intentional acts to which a specific water system might be vulnerable. This regulation also required drinking water utilities to update their emergency response plans to include man-made events identified in the vulnerability assessment.

The major hurricanes of 2005 (Katrina and Rita) redirected attention to vulnerabilities associated with natural disasters and refocused water utility emergency preparedness efforts to an "all hazards" approach.

Several factors contribute to the difficulty experienced by water utilities in devoting money, staff, and time to security and emergency preparedness. First of all, there are relatively few regulations actually mandating that utilities devote significant resources to this area. In most states, the primary regulatory agency responsible for overseeing the activities of drinking water and wastewater utilities is usually the state department of environmental protection, environmental resources, or public health. These agencies typically require utilities to develop and maintain emergency response plans (ERPs) and associated operations and maintenance plans (O&M plans). As mentioned, the federal government, under the Bioterrorism Act of 2002, required drinking water systems (but not wastewater systems) to conduct formal vulnerability assessments and then to develop ERPs to include man-made events. Other than these requirements, there are few regulations across the United States requiring specific actions by utilities in the areas of security and emergency planning.

Secondly, government grant money to underwrite improvements to security has been sparse for utilities. Most grant funding has been directed to state and county emergency response agencies and public safety entities such as police, fire, and Hazmat.

Finally, while there have been a number of terrorist attacks in the United States over the past two decades (e.g., the 1995 Oklahoma Federal Building bombing, the initial truck bombing of the World Trade Center in 1993, the attacks on New York and Washington on September 11, 2001, the 2001 mail-borne anthrax attacks, and the Fort Hood shootings in 2009) as well as a series of unsuccessful incidents (e.g., the Christmas 2009 attempt to blow up a commercial airliner over Detroit and the failed Times Square car bombing in 2010).

Few threats or attacks have been directed toward water utilities. While this is, of course, the most desirable situation for utilities and the people that they serve, it makes it difficult for utilities to justify allocating significant resources to protect against terrorism and other man-made events.

In spite of the difficulties experienced by water utilities in maintaining an emphasis on emergency planning and security, it is still important that utilities devote attention to these issues. The primary mission of drinking water and wastewater utilities is protection of public health and public safety (e.g., providing potable water for consumption and sanitary needs, guaranteeing adequate water for fire protection, providing effective removal and treatment of sanitary and industrial wastes). Ensuring that utilities maintain adequate ERPs and improving protection against natural disasters, accidents, and human-initiated events is consistent with this health and safety mission. Additionally, the public expects that utilities are placing proper emphasis on these activities. Should a community be significantly impacted by a disaster involving a water utility, the public would justifiably be very critical if the impact were exacerbated by a lack of due diligence on the part of the utility. This chapter reviews some of the natural, accidental, and man-made threats that drinking water and wastewater systems are vulnerable to. It also discusses some of the steps that utilities take to mitigate these vulnerabilities, and some of the actions that they take to respond to these events.

THREATS TO DRINKING WATER AND WASTEWATER UTILITIES

There are approximately 53,000 community drinking water systems in the United States. Another 106,000 non-community systems serve schools, rest stops, fairgrounds, campgrounds, and so on. The size of these drinking water systems varies greatly, ranging from some 30,000 groundwater systems that serve fewer than 500 consumers to more than 400 community water systems that serve more than 1 million people each. There are also 16,000 public wastewater systems in the United States serving communities ranging from housing developments to the largest cities.

To what extent are these drinking water and wastewater utilities vulnerable to natural disasters, major accidents, and intentional acts?

Natural Disasters   All utilities are at risk for damage from natural disasters. The types of disasters that a particular utility is susceptible to varies in different parts of the country but may include drought, extreme heat, extreme cold, ice storms, blizzards, flooding, landslides, hurricanes, tornadoes, and even volcanic activity. Natural disasters can also include disease outbreaks ranging from seasonal flu epidemics to influenza pandemics. In the case of certain disasters, such as hurricanes, major winter storms, or flooding, there may be a warning period, extending from hours to several days, during which the utility can prepare for the event. In the case of other disasters, such as tornadoes and earthquakes, there is typically no advanced warning.

Des Moines, Iowa, 1993—Record-breaking rains hit the Midwest in July 1993 resulting in a 500-year flood in Des Moines. The flood inundated the drinking water treatment plant, forcing officials to shut down the plant and the city's water system for seven days. Municipal drinking water for 250,000 customers was not available for drinking, cooking, bathing, or sanitary purposes. Once the treatment plant was dewatered, equipment dried, and pump motors reconditioned, the treatment plant resumed operation and finished water was again pumped into the distribution network. After extensive bacteriological testing, the "Boil Water" order was lifted five days later (AWWA 1995).

Los Angeles, California, 1994—The Northridge Earthquake struck Los Angeles on January 17, 1994. While it lasted only 15 seconds, it measured 6.6 on the Richter scale and left 3 million people without electrical power. The earthquake shifted the ground and caused

2,000 water main ruptures, resulting in a loss of water service for 600,000 customers of the Metropolitan Water District of Southern California. Agencies from all over California assisted the water utility in repairing the damage, and within four days service had been restored to 90 percent of the customers (AWWA 1995).

New Orleans, Louisiana, 2005—Arguably, the greatest natural disaster ever to strike the United States was Hurricane Katrina, which hit the Gulf Coast in August 2005. The City of New Orleans was devastated, with 1,400 people killed, thousands more injured, 200,000 homes and businesses destroyed, and 300,000 residents displaced. Most of the damage in the city occurred when Katrina's storm surge in Lake Pontchartrain collapsed several sections of protective levees and flood waters filled in low-lying neighborhoods to the north and east of the central business district and the French Quarter.

The Sewerage and Water Board of New Orleans (SWBNO) is in charge of drinking water, wastewater, and continuously pumping storm water drainage out of New Orleans and into Lake Pontchartrain. Winds and floodwaters wiped out electrical power throughout the city and destroyed much of SWBNO's drinking water, wastewater, and drainage removal infrastructure. Floodwaters submerged pump motors and control systems and completely swamped the city's main wastewater treatment plant. Toppled trees ripped open hundreds of water mains. While the Carrolton Drinking Water Treatment Plant escaped major flooding, it suffered damages significant enough to halt the pumping of river source water for a period of days. Also submerged were hundreds of SWBNO's service vehicles parked at the central maintenance garage. This significantly interfered with efforts to manage water breaks and maintain drinking water pressure for fire protection and other needs.

New Orleans lost its supply of drinking water, its wastewater system. and its mechanical drainage system for weeks. A "Boil Water" advisory, issued by Louisiana state officials, remained in effect until early October. SWBNO's rebuilding costs were estimated to reach $2.3 billion (Scharfenaker 2006).

Accidents

Milwaukee, Wisconsin, 1993—The largest waterborne disease ever to occur in the United States struck Milwaukee in April 1993. The gastroenteric ailment Cryptosporidiosis is caused by the parasite *Cryptosporidium spp.* A large number of *Cryptosporidium* oocysts were believed to have washed into the Milwaukee River, the source water for the city's drinking water, from area dairy farms and/or sewage plants. The unusually high number of oocysts, coupled with some treatment failures at the drinking water plant, led to this accidental epidemic. A total of 400,000 people, out of a customer base of 1 million people, became ill and as many as 100 already immunocompromised victims died. A "Boil Water" advisory was issued to protect the population until the system could be thoroughly flushed and disinfected. The costs of the event totaled $31.7 million in medical expenses and $64.6 million in productivity losses (Proctor et al. 1998).

Spencer, Massachusetts, 2007—An accidental overfeed of a treatment chemical, sodium hydroxide, occurred overnight at the small drinking water treatment plant. While there were no fatalities, a total of 93 people, from a population of 12,000, were treated at area hospitals for minor skin or esophageal irritations (Abel and Naughton 2007).

Pittsburgh, Pennsylvania, 2008—While battling a warehouse fire, firefighters accidentally pumped approximately 50 gallons of fire suppression foam in the reverse direction, through a fire hydrant, and into the Pittsburgh drinking water distribution system. The foam was quite visible to customers and impacted a significant portion of the downtown business district. While the foam was not highly toxic, the product's Material Safety Data Sheet (MSDS) indicated that it did pose a potential threat to people if it came into contact with eye tissue. The water company had to valve off and isolate the affected portion of the distribution network, and extensively flush and test the water in those neighborhoods to remove the contaminant before a "Do Not Consume or Shower" advisory could be lifted the next morning (States et al. 2008).

Boston, Massachusetts, 2010—Treated drinking water flows to the City of Boston through a 17-mile-long, 10-foot-diameter underground main. A 1-ton steel coupling on this main failed, releasing eight million gallons of water per hour into the Charles River, and leaving thousands of people without any water for more than 24 hours. The Massachusetts Water Resources Authority rerouted water around the leak and supplemented flow with untreated water through an old aqueduct not used in decades. While this water was deemed safe for showering, toilet flushing, and fire protection, a "Boil Water" advisory was issued for drinking and cooking for 750,000 households (2 million people) in Boston and 29 surrounding communities. The state governor declared a State of Emergency. The "Boil Water" advisory was lifted three days later after repairs were completed and several rounds of extensive bacteriological testing of water were completed throughout the drinking water distribution system.

Accidents that significantly impact drinking water and wastewater utilities do not necessarily have to originate in the water system:

Northeastern United States, 2003—There was a major failure of the electrical grid in the Northeastern United States and parts of Canada. Computer glitches in Ohio caused inaccurate readings along First Energy's electrical power lines. Cascading effects among Northeastern utilities resulted in the shutdown of more than 500 electrical generating units in the United States and Canada. The loss of electrical power interfered with the ability of several major cities, including Cleveland, Ohio, and Detroit, to pump finished drinking water to their customers for more than a day. The Cleveland blackout disabled the water authority's four main pumping stations, which provide water to 1.5 million customers. The subsequent depressurization of the water system in these cities required "Boil Water" advisories for several additional days following restoration of service (Keefe 2006). Wastewater treatment plants in blacked-out cities, which lacked adequate backup electrical generation systems, discharged million of gallons of untreated sewage to receiving waters (Congressional Research Service 2005).

China, 2005. An explosion occurred at a petrochemical plant in Jilin City in Northern China, releasing 10 tons of benzene and nitrobenzene into the Songhua River. The 50-mile-long slick of contaminants had a significant effect on water supplies and became an international incident when it eventually flowed into Russia. Drinking water service was shut off for four days to 4 million consumers in Harbin, the capital City of China's Heilongjiang Province located 200 miles downstream from where the explosion and chemical release had occurred. The spill also denied water service to many consumers in smaller towns along the river. Fortunately, the spill did not result in reported injuries or deaths, but it did cause a panic, resulting in and the hoarding of food and water (Yardley 2005).

Malevolent Acts   *Sources of Attacks*

Drinking water and wastewater utilities have experienced damage over the years from intentional events. Most of this has been in the form of simple vandalism and theft, but it has also included sabotage by insiders (e.g., disgruntled employees, contractors) who are responding to perceived injustices. Since 2001, concern has also been expressed in the water industry over the possibility of attacks from domestic or international terrorists.

Vandalism has always been a common occurrence affecting the multiple, geographically spread out facilities of utilities, some of which are situated in remote locations. A particular concern with simple vandalism is the possibility that it could go too far and cause more serious problems. For example, if the teenager who is painting his girlfriend's name on the side of drinking water storage tank decides to dump the remainder of the paint into the tank, the simple act of vandalism may now affect the safety of the public water supply. Another concern with vandalism has arisen since 9/11. Incidents such as kids cutting through a cyclone fence surrounding a drinking water reservoir used to be considered a nuisance that necessitated additional maintenance efforts to repair the fence. With the increased security concerns following the attacks of 2001, utilities must now investigate such an event to ensure that the trespasser didn't also tamper with the stored water. Vandalism isn't what it used to be prior to 9/11. Following is an example of simple vandalism that significantly impacted a community in Blackstone, Massachusetts:

> *Blackstone, Massachusetts, 2006.* Three teenagers scaled a 10-foot cyclone fence topped with barbwire, climbed to the top of a 1-million gallon finished water storage tank, and broke open the hatch in the small town of Blackstone, Massachusetts. When the breach was discovered by utility workers the morning after the break-in, utility officials, the media, and the public became concerned because it could not be immediately determined whether or not the intruders had tampered with the drinking water stored in the tank. A "Do Not Use" advisory was issued by the state regulatory agency until tests could be completed to verify the safety of the water. For a several-day period, water consumption was limited to bottled water, restaurants were closed, and the distribution system had to be extensively flushed as a precaution. When water quality tests were completed and

the teenagers were arrested, it was determined that the breach did not involve contamination of the water supply. However, this simple act of vandalism significantly impacted residents, businesses, and schools in the region due to concerns over possible contamination (WHDH-TV, Boston, Massachusetts).

Insider attacks are of particular concern not only in the water industry but in most businesses and activities. Insiders, who may include disgruntled employees, former employees, and contractors, pose a special threat because they often have detailed insider knowledge of the workings of a utility and its vulnerabilities. Their motivation may include labor disputes, revenge, or anger over real or imagined problems. Insiders also have special access to facilities not afforded others. It's a common situation for a drinking water or wastewater plant operator to be working alone on a night shift with complete access to the treatment plant and other facilities. A couple of documented incidents illustrate this threat:

Duquesne, Pennsylvania, (1986)—Two drinking water treatment plant operators were arrested for intentionally dumping 100 pounds of a treatment chemical, potassium permanganate, into the clearwell of a small town's water plant. While no one was injured, the town's drinking water turned purple in color, causing a great deal of consternation among residents. The motivation for the disgruntled employees' actions was the desire to underscore potential water utility vulnerabilities that could result from recent staff downsizing actions (Owenbey et al. 1988).

Canton, Ohio, 2002—A former water department employee was charged with poisoning a pair of municipal wells with the organic compound trichloroethylene. During a six-day crisis, thousands of homeowners with private wells were advised not to drink or bathe in their water pending testing of wells and streams by the Ohio Environmental Protection Agency (WaterTech Online.com 2002).

Gilbert, Arizona, 2011—A wastewater treatment plant operator was the sole employee working a midnight shift. The operator, armed with a handgun, walked through the facility, methodically turning off major operating systems at the plant. Left untreated and unvented, the sewage in the treatment plant would cause a buildup of methane gas, which could cause an explosion. The operator called 911 and notified officials about his actions approximately three hours after he had begun to sabotage the utility. SWAT officers negotiated with him for two hours before they arrested him. The officers escorted wastewater employees through the plant during the standoff so that they could restart the systems. While the perpetrator's neighbors reported being unaware of any mental instability, the operator had reportedly lost his home to foreclosure two years earlier (*Homeland Security News Wire*).

Terrorist attacks on drinking water or wastewater utilities have generally been believed to be unlikely because they would not provide the same sensational media video footage as is generated by an attack on an airplane, train, subway, or some iconic building. This may or may not be true. Another piece of conventional wisdom holds that one of the most feared attacks on a water utility, intentional contamination of a public drinking water supply, is too sophisticated and would require too much contaminant to be successful. Unfortunately, this is not true.

Because the provision of drinking water and sanitary services are basic necessities, a terrorist attack on these systems, either via a physical attack on a critical facility or intentional contamination, would likely have a profound impact on the confidence of the public in the safety of these services. The negative effect on public confidence would include not only the attacked utility, but other utilities throughout the country. The impact would be magnified with greater numbers of injuries, illnesses, or deaths. Such an attack would be successful terrorism because it could create widespread fear as well as significant social and economic disruption.

The notion that drinking water utilities could be the target of sabotage or terrorism has been acknowledged by the U.S. Justice Department over the years. Just prior to World War II, FBI Director J. Edgar Hoover (1941) wrote the following statement in an article published in the *Journal of the American Water Works Association*:

> It has long been recognized that among public utilities, water supply facilities offer a particularly vulnerable point of attack to the foreign agent, due to the strategic position they occupy in keeping the wheels of industry turning and in preserving the health and morale of the American populace. Obviously, it is essential that our water supply facilities be afforded the utmost protection.

Years later, following the 2001 terrorist attacks, FBI Director Robert Mueller made a similar statement:

Poisoning food and water supplies may be an attractive tactic in the future. Although technologically challenging, a successful attempt might cause thousands of casualties, sow fear among the U.S. population, and undermine public confidence in the food and water supply.

Factors that make drinking water and wastewater systems potential targets for domestic or international terrorists include the fact that these are essential services. The public must have uninterrupted access to safe drinking water for consumption, sanitary purposes, industrial uses, and fire protection. The public also requires continuous provision of wastewater services for public health and environmental protection. Wastewater systems collect, treat, and safely dispose of sanitary waste, industrial waste, and storm water runoff. Additionally, the perception that water systems are government entities, even if in reality some of them are private or investor-owned businesses, makes them potential political targets. Furthermore, the fact that water utilities are spread over large geographic areas and include many facilities that are relatively easy to access (e.g., treatment plants, pumping stations, reservoirs, storage tanks) makes them difficult to physically protect.

There have been terrorist attacks planned against water systems. Some of the attacks were thwarted. However, others were actually carried out with fatal results:

Chicago, 1972—Members of the Order of the Rising Sun, an American fascist organization dedicated to creating a master race, were found to be in possession of 30 to 40 kg of a *Salmonella typhi* bacteria culture (which causes typhoid fever). The group allegedly planned to introduce the pathogen into the water supplies of Chicago, St. Louis, and other cities (Purver 1995; Falkenrath et al. 1998). One of the two individuals charged with conspiracy to commit murder was a college student who had developed the bacterial culture in a school laboratory.

Arkansas (1985)—The FBI discovered that a white supremacist group in the Ozark Mountains known as "The Covenant, The Sword, and The Arm of the Lord" had acquired a drum containing 30 gallons of potassium cyanide. They confessed that their intent was to poison water supplies in New York, Chicago, and Washington, DC (Tucker 2000).

Philippines, 1987—A pesticide was used to intentionally contaminate drinking water provided in plastic containers to police recruits in Mindanao. The media reported 19 fatalities and 140 illnesses.

Istanbul, 1992—Kurdish terrorists attempted to poison the water supply of a Turkish Air Force compound with potassium cyanide. A cyanide concentration of 50 mg per liter was discovered in the water stored in the tanks serving the military base. The plot was discovered before anyone was poisoned. The PKK claimed responsibility for the attack (Chelyshev 1992).

Paris, 2002—Al-Qaida operatives were arrested with plans to attack the drinking water network in the Eiffel Tower neighborhood of Paris (Kroll 2006).

Afghanistan, 2002—U.S. military personnel recovered documents from caves in Afghanistan indicating that al-Qaida had assessed American drinking water distribution networks, pump stations, and other assets as possible targets for sabotage.

Saudi Arabia, 2003—Al-Qaida threatened U.S. water systems in a call to a Saudi Arabian magazine. The threat included the statement that Al-Qaida does not "rule out … the poisoning of drinking water in American and Western cities" (Associated Press 2003a, Waterman 2003).

Michigan, 2003—Four incendiary devices were found inside a water bottling plant's pumping station. The plastic bottles, containing a flammable liquid, were safely removed without injury to personnel or damage to the facility. The Earth Liberation Front (ELF), an American domestic terrorist group, claimed responsibility for the attempted arson while accusing the water company of stealing well water for profit. ELF's written acknowledgment of responsibility read: "Clean water is one of the most fundamental necessities and no one can be allowed to privatize it, commodify it, and try and sell it back to us" (Associated Press 2003b).

Pakistan, 2008—Pakistani police arrested five Sunni militants who planned to use cyanide powder to poison water in Karachi during the Shiite Muslim festival of Ashura. Police reported that "the aim was to cause widespread human losses." Police recovered 500 grams of cyanide that the extremists planned to mix with water distributed at kiosks established for the festival (*Wall Street Journal* 2008).

Pakistan, 2009—The Water and Sanitation Agency of Pakistan was directed to stop supplying water to the city of Multan from storage tanks after receiving information that the Pakistani Tehreek-e-Taliban had obtained large quantities of poison to contaminate the city's water supply. The water authority was instructed to pump water directly through tube wells (*Daily Times* 2009).

In reality, the probability of a specific water system becoming the target of a terrorist attack is miniscule. However, the possibility of a water system somewhere becoming the target of a terrorist attack is real and the consequences could be significant. Furthermore, the probability that a particular drinking water or wastewater utility will become the target of a disgruntled employee or vandal that must be investigated to ensure that the event isn't a terrorist attack is very high. For these reasons, water utilities in the current environment must pay some attention to defense against and response to malevolent acts from all sources.

Types of Attacks

Intentional, malevolent attacks on drinking water or wastewater systems, whether they involve vandalism, insider scenarios, or actual terrorism can take a number of forms (e.g., physical assaults, release of hazardous treatment chemicals, cyber attacks, or potentially the most onerous, intentional contamination). Case studies illustrating each of these are presented below.

Physical assault on one or more components of a drinking water or wastewater system is a concern for the water industry. Such an attack could involve the use of an improvised explosive device (IED), a vehicle-borne improvised explosive device (VBIED), or an improvised incendiary device (IID). These devices are considered to be likely weapons in a water system attack because the materials to make them are easier to acquire and require less technical expertise to assemble than sophisticated chemical agents or biological pathogens. Physical destruction of water facilities could deny service to individuals, medical care, industrial production, and other activities. A disruption in water service if coordinated with arson would compound the impact. Furthermore, because much of the equipment in drinking water and wastewater systems, such as pumps and power sources, are custom designed, it could require months to replace them (President's Commission on Critical Infrastructure 1996).

A number of physical attacks on water systems have been reported:

Zambia, 1999—A bomb blast in Lusaka, destroyed the main water pipeline, cutting off water for the city of 3 million (*Financial Times Global Water Report* 1999).

Iraq, 2003—Insurgents destroyed a major water pipeline in Bagdad. The attack occurred around 7 a.m. when a Volkswagen stopped on an overpass near the Nidaa Mosque and an explosive was fired at the 72-inch-diameter water main in the northern section of Bagdad (Tierney and Worth 2003).

Nepal, 2006—Maoist insurgents detonated explosives in two water reservoir tanks and damaged distribution lines, disrupting the drinking water supply for 20,000 people.

Sri Lanka, 2006—Powerful explosives in Colombo were used to destroy the main water distribution pipeline to the capital. Parts of the city were left without drinking water. The explosions occurred hours after the government imposed laws to deal with Tamil Tiger separatists who were fighting to create a separate homeland for Sri Lanka's ethnic Tamil minority (Associated Press 2006).

Release of hazardous treatment chemicals could occur at both drinking water and wastewater plants. Intentional or accidental release of chlorine gas from pressurized 150-pound bottles, 1-ton cylinders, 55-ton railroad tank cars, or 90-ton railroad tank cars at a drinking water or wastewater facility, or en route to a facility, could be lethal for utility employees and residents in the surrounding community. Other dangerous treatment chemicals present at many water plants include ammonia and sulfur dioxide.

Washington DC (2001)—At the time of the Pentagon attack on 9/11, a string of railroad cars filled with gaseous chlorine intended for the Blue Plains Wastewater Treatment Works sat idle on a rail spur across the Potomac River from the Pentagon. Had these cars been struck by the hijacked plane, it is conceivable that the number of casualties in downtown Washington may have been even greater than those that occurred among Pentagon workers (NRC 2002).

Cyber attack has become an increasing concern for most government agencies, businesses and utilities in this country and overseas. Many of the cyber attacks have involved industrial espionage in which billions of dollars worth of proprietary information has been stolen online from major corporations. In many cases these thefts have been initiated in foreign countries.

Throughout the world, supervisory control and data acquisition systems (SCADA) control a variety of critical facilities and infrastructures including nuclear power plants, chemical plants, electric utilities, natural gas utilities, and drinking water and wastewater utilities. SCADA systems automatically turn pump switches on and off, and control equipment in geographically dispersed facilities. These SCADA systems are vulnerable to attacks ranging from those perpetuated by individual computer hackers seeking attention and bragging rights, to disgruntled employees and former employees, to domestic and international terrorists attempting to damage facilities and injure or kill people. An example of a cyber attack executed by an insider occurred in 2000.

> *Queensland, Australia, 2000*—An intentional cyber attack occurred at a wastewater utility soon after a contractor completed a major upgrade of a plant SCADA system. A former employee of the contractor was upset over not being hired directly by the utility following completion of the job. With his insider knowledge of the computer system, and using a wireless connection and a stolen computer, the frustrated former employee hacked into the utility's SCADA system 46 times during a 10-week period. On some of the occasions the hacker shut down pumps. During one incident the perpetrator caused the overflow of thousands of gallons of raw sewage into a river, into a park, and onto the grounds of a hotel. The attack resulted in a cleanup costing USD $26,000. The hacker was arrested, sent to prison for two years, and ordered to reimburse the expense associated with the cleanup (Kroll 2006).

Intentional or accidental contamination of a wastewater system could cause severe damage to property and possible injury or death to people. Flammable or explosive substances could be introduced into the collection system through a manhole or even a building drain. The level of sophistication for this scenario could be as simple as the theft of a gasoline tanker truck and injection of its contents into a sewer catch basin. Such an incident would not only damage wastewater infrastructure but also other underground utilities, such as gas, electric, and drinking water. Incendiary or explosive materials could be placed in the sewage system essentially turning the system into a pipe bomb to attack high-profile buildings, stadiums, streets, or public events. Toxic substances could be added to the wastewater collection system or treatment plant. The safety of utility employees or individuals in the surrounding community may be jeopardized if harmful vapors or aerosol are released. Toxins could also damage microorganisms used in the treatment process shutting down treatment.

Akron, Ohio, 1977—An intentional, malevolent injection of a flammable substance into the collection system resulted in a series of sewer explosions in this city. At least 3,000 gallons of petroleum naptha and isopropyl alcohol had been dumped into the sewer during the night by perpetrators at a strikebound rubber plant. Officials theorized that when the material entered the sewer it was too rich to ignite. However, as it flowed downstream, it became diluted to explosive range and finally ignited 3.5 miles from the point of injection. Although fortunately no one was injured, one mile of sewer line was destroyed. Damage costs exceeded $10 million.

Mexico, 1992—An accidental contamination of the municipal sewage collection system in Guadalajara, Mexico's second largest city, resulted in a particularly tragic chain of events. A series of nine separate explosions occurred over a four-hour period in the sanitary sewer network. The cause of the explosions was gasoline leaking from the state-run Pemex underground pipeline into the sanitary sewer collection lines. Residents of the Reforma district of the city had complained for three days about a strong gasoline-like odor wafting up from the sewer drains. Officials could not find the leak, did not order an evacuation, and called off their investigation several hours before the explosions began. The explosions killed 206 people and injured 1,460; damaged 1,148 buildings; destroyed 250 businesses and 500 vehicles; left 15,000 people homeless; and forced the evacuation of 25,000 people. Seven miles of sewer pipe exploded, some of which was 18 feet in diameter. The event gouged a 20-foot-deep trench along sewer mains in a 20-block area. A number of people were apparently buried alive. Damage costs were estimated at $75 million in U.S. currency. Investigators eventually concluded that the ultimate cause of the sewer explosion was the faulty installation of a water main several years earlier, which leaked onto a gasoline line lying underneath. The subsequent corrosion of the gasoline pipeline, in turn, caused leakage of gasoline into the sewers (*Time Magazine* 1992, Dugal 1999).

Intentional or accidental contamination of drinking water supplies is probably a more significant concern because the contaminant would be directly ingested and such an event could potentially affect a large number of people in a relatively short amount of time. A contamination incident could remain undetected until people become ill and show up in hospital emergency rooms. In the case of waterborne pathogens with a long incubation period, illnesses may not occur until several days following the introduction of the contaminant.

The President's Critical Infrastructure Assurance Office (1998) addressed the possibility of intentional contamination of drinking water systems:

> The water supplied to U.S. communities is potentially vulnerable to terrorist attacks by insertion of biological agents, chemical agents, or toxins. ... The possibility of attack is of considerable concern. ... [T]hese agents could be a threat if they were inserted at critical points in the system; theoretically, they could cause a large number of casualties.

Khan et al. (2001), from the U.S. Centers for Disease Control and Prevention (CDC), concluded that while the general focus of those involved with antiterrorism has been on intentional aerosol delivery of contaminants, there is no easier way for a terrorist to disseminate a chemical or biological agent than through the intentional contamination of food or water supplies. They wrote:

> A review of naturally occurring food and waterborne outbreaks exposes this vulnerability and reaffirms that, depending on the site of contamination, a significant number of people could be infected or injured over a wide geographic area.

With or without significant numbers of injuries or deaths, an intentional contamination of a public water supply could produce fear and diminish public confidence in the ability of government to protect its citizens.

There are a number of locations within a water system that could potentially be exploited by a perpetrator to introduce a foreign substance into a public water supply. There are a number of types of substances that could potentially be used to contaminate drinking water. Some of these would be more dangerous than others, but the categories that have been suggested in the open literature include pathogens (bacteria, viruses, protozoans), biotoxins (poisons that are naturally synthesized by some microorganisms and higher organisms), industrial chemicals, radioactive substances, and even weaponized chemicals (chemical warfare agents).

A number of intentional contamination events have occurred in drinking water systems, and many more have been threatened and were either unsuccessful or were thwarted:

Edinburgh, Scotland, 1990—Nine people living in the same apartment complex were diagnosed with giardiasis, an infectious gastrointestinal disease caused by the parasite *Giardia lamblia*. The complex was provided drinking water from two roof-top tanks. The investigation conducted following the clinical diagnosis revealed that the one of the tanks contained high coliform bacterial counts and fecal deposits below the tank's inspection hatch. The tank had apparently been intentionally contaminated with fecal material containing Giardia (Ramsay and Marsh 1990).

China, 2003—In an effort to promote sales, a home water purification device salesman dumped approximately 500 mL of an unnamed pesticide into a drinking water reservoir in Henan Province. The reservoir supplies 9,000 homes. No deaths were reported but 64 people were sickened and 42 of these individuals were hospitalized (BBC 2003).

Italy, 2003—An unknown assailant, and possibly one or more copycats, injected detergent, bleach, and acetone into plastic-bottled water on store shelves. Using a syringe, the perpetrators injected the contaminants just below the cap where the puncture hole would be difficult to detect. Twelve people were hospitalized (CNN).

Pittsburgh, Pennsylvania (1980)—The most significant intentional contamination of drinking water ever to occur in the United States occurred in the Beechview neighborhood of Pittsburgh in 1980. A perpetrator injected between 1 and 10 gallons of a solution of the pesticide chlordane, dissolved in a kerosene carrier, into an 18-inch transmission main in the distribution system. While nobody was ever arrested for this crime, it is suspected that the perpetrator(s) were employees of the suburban water company serving that portion of the city and were involved in an ongoing labor strike occurring at that time at the utility. 150 people were reported to have become ill (Moser 2005).

VULNERABILITY ASSESSMENT

As discussed, drinking water and wastewater utilities are subject to a variety of threats from natural disasters, accidents, and intentional acts. Ideally, a water utility should formally evaluate its susceptibility to various threats by conducting a vulnerability assessment. This information is particularly useful when a utility subsequently determines what steps it should take to mitigate or reduce these risks, and what contingencies need to be addressed in the utility's ERP.

The Public Health Security and Bioterrorism Preparedness and Response Act (Bioterrorism Act) was signed into law (PL 107-188) in June 2002. The federal Bioterrorism Act required every community drinking water system serving more than 3,300 persons to conduct a vulnerability assessment (VA), and to submit a copy of the VA to the U.S. Environmental Protection Agency. The primary objective of this requirement, which was put into place one year following the terrorist attacks of 2001, was to produce a VA that addressed vulnerabilities associated with malevolent acts. It is interesting to note that this mandate only applied to drinking water utilities and not wastewater systems. Furthermore, this was only a one-time mandate in that drinking water utilities have never since been required by the federal government to update their vulnerability assessments. However, despite the limited regulatory requirement, regulatory agencies at all levels of government, and drinking water and wastewater industry organizations, continue to urge all drinking water and wastewater utilities, regardless of size, to maintain a current vulnerability assessment.

Regulatory and industry organizations worked together to develop a number of tools that water utilities could use to facilitate their preparation of vulnerability assessments. Some of these tools were computerized, some were paper based, some were geared toward larger utilities, while others were intended for use by small systems. Various tools include the Risk Assessment Methodology for Water (RAM-W), the Vulnerability Self-Assessment Tool (VSAT), the Security Self Assessment Tool for Small and Very Small Systems, and the Security and Emergency Management System (SEMS), among others.

Most of the original emphasis on conducting vulnerability assessments, and most of the tools developed to assist this endeavor, focused on man-made events. With the national shift in emergency preparedness focus to an "all hazards" approach following the major hurricane season of 2005, there has been an increasing emphasis on utilities maintaining up-to-date vulnerability assessments that deal with natural disasters and major accidents as well as malevolent acts. To help compare risks among various critical infrastructures (including the water industry as well as the power industry, transportation, telecommunications, etc.), the U.S. Department of Homeland Security several years ago asked each critical infrastructure to voluntarily implement the Risk Analysis Management for Critical Asset Protection (RAMCAP) methodology. RAMCAP is a framework that can be used to modify existing VA tools so that they provide comparable output allowing comparison of risks among all of the critical infrastructure sectors. For the water sector, RAMCAP is not limited to terrorism but addresses risks from all hazards.

MITIGATION OF RISK

Once a water utility has determined the risks it faces from natural disasters, accidents and man-made events, and especially after a formal vulnerability assessment has been conducted, the next step is to determine which safeguards or mitigation measures should be put into place to protect assets and reduce vulnerability. Mitigation measures can include physical facility improvements, operational modifications, and changes in utility policies and procedures. Ideally, the mitigation measures should address deficiencies identified in the VA.

Realistically, it is impossible to completely eliminate risk. Each utility must decide the amount of risk that it is willing to live with and then determine what it will take to bring the utility to that level of protection. All proposed mitigation measures (physical, operational, procedural) must be considered in light of the constraints under which the organization operates. These include financial capabilities, staff resources, political restrictions, social and cultural considerations, and legal and regulatory limitations. All of these must be evaluated in a complex assessment that asks the question: "Does the degree of risk reduction justify the cumulative costs, financial and otherwise, of the mitigation steps?"

In selecting mitigation measures, utilities should utilize the principal of "protection in depth," or "defense in depth." This approach entails using several layer of defense against a natural disaster, accident, of malevolent act. The approach helps ensure that the utility is protected even if one or more of the protective barriers fail. In terms of physical protection against trespassing, a defense in depth approach may involve erecting a fence around a critical facility, utilizing closed circuit camera surveillance, and securely locking windows and doors on individual buildings.

Another general recommendation for mitigation of risk is that utilities strive to obtain multiple benefits from the mitigation steps that they implement. Ideally, a specific mitigation step not only helps to protect against malevolent acts, but it also helps protect against unintentional emergencies such as accidents and natural disasters, and even enhances day-to-day operations. An example would be a drinking water utility modifying its distribution system to improve system redundancy in the form of backup water transmission mains feeding a particular service zone. This mitigation step not only facilitates isolation of portions of the distribution system in the case of an accidental or intentional contamination event, but also ensures continuity of service in the event of a water main break.

Mitigation of Risk Through Physical Facility Improvements and Physical Protection Systems

Physical protection of water facilities against natural disasters and major accidents involves commonsense hardening of physical structures. Initial construction and subsequent upgrades to utility facilities in regions of the country that are periodically exposed to extreme weather events such as tornadoes or hurricanes require greater investments in material and design than areas not affected by such challenges. Similarly, utilities located in areas susceptible to flooding should have their critical facilities built, to the extent possible, out of the flood plane.

Concerning protection against intentional acts, a number of approaches can be employed. The operational philosophy of this type of physical protection involves denying or delaying access, detection of an incident, validation of the detection, and response. This can involve the following measures:

- *Lighting.* An often underestimated, inexpensive security measure that deters intruders, makes trespassers more visible, and enhances coverage by surveillance cameras.
- *Barriers (perimeter security).* Obstacles such as fences, walls, gates, Jersey barriers, and bollards that increase an intruder's entry and withdrawal time, and may even act as a deterrent for vandals and other less determined adversaries.

- *Access control.* Locks (mechanical or electronic) that secure buildings and other facilities and may be activated by simple keys or more sophisticated swipe cards, PIN numbers, or even biometric identification devices.
- *Visual surveillance.* Typically involves closed-circuit TV and consideration of details including field of vision, resolution, required lighting, and archiving of video images.
- *Intrusion detection.* Includes both interior and exterior intrusion detection devices that alert utility or security personnel of individuals crossing a protected zone. Technologies are varied, and in some cases quite sophisticated, and may include microwave, ultrasonic, infrared, sonic, vibration, fiber optic, and video motion sensors.
- *Security guards and patrols.* Typically the most expensive approach for improving physical security.

Mitigation of Risk Through Operational Measures:

A variety of operational measures can be employed to decrease the vulnerability of water utilities against natural, accidental, and human initiated risks.

- *System redundancy and backups.* Can be installed for both equipment and processes to increase the resiliency of a water system. For example, a pressure zone in a drinking water distribution network should be served from two storage tanks or reservoirs, or directly from the treatment plant, rather than from just one source. This permits continuity of service in the event of a major transmission main break and permits isolation of storage facilities if they become damaged or contaminated. Similarly, since both drinking water and wastewater utilities are critically dependent on electrical power, pump stations should be fed from more than one main power supply or be augmented with backup electrical generating capability.
- *Chemical treatment countermeasures.* A particular safety concern for both wastewater and drinking water utilities that use gaseous chlorine is the accidental or intentional release of this dangerous treatment chemical into the environment. Chlorine cylinders should be stored in a secure location and separate from other chemicals to avoid potential chemical reactions. Continuous gas leak detectors should be installed to monitor for leaks along with containment structures and chemical scrubbers to protect against physical damage inflicted on chlorine storage vessels.

- *Backflow prevention program.* Installation and maintenance of backflow prevention devices in private residences as well as industrial sites is an effective protection against accidental backflow of contaminants into the drinking water distribution system.

- *System plans and modeling.* Should an accidental or intentional contamination event occur in either the drinking water distribution network or the wastewater collection system, it is useful to be able to predict where the contaminant slug is travelling. With this information, portions of the distribution or collection systems can be isolated to prevent the spread of contaminants. A knowledge of the hydraulics of the distribution or collection system and accurate information on the locations of critical valves is essential for accomplishing this task.

Mitigation of Risk Through Policies, Procedures, and Training

The least expensive approach to reducing vulnerability to damaging accidents, natural events and intentional acts is typically through changes in company policies and procedures, and provision of additional training to personnel.

- *Emergency preparedness training for employees.* Every employee should be made aware that security and emergency preparedness is an important aspect of their job. The goal is to establish an "all hazards" approach to risk management that is integrated into the culture of the utility. This can be accomplished through security and emergency preparedness training.

- *Emergency notifications.* Employees should understand emergency notification procedures. Updated emergency 24-hour phone numbers should be accessible to appropriate personnel. Key personnel should have access to these numbers at all times.

- *Emergency contracts.* To expedite acquisition of outside assistance during any type of disaster, emergency contracts should be set in place ahead of time. These can include contractor services for large main breaks, water hauling contracts for occasions when public water use has been restricted, and emergency laboratory services for contamination analysis, among others.

- *Mutual aid agreements.* In addition to emergency contracts with vendors and commercial contractors, utilities are strongly encouraged to establish mutual aid agreements with other water companies for assistance in critical situations. The Water and

Wastewater Agency Response Network (WARN) is a formal network of voluntary, intrastate, mutual aid agreements that have been initiated in all 50 states. The network is based on the concept of utilities helping utilities and is intended to provide distressed water systems with emergency staffing, equipment, and supplies on short notice.

- *Crisis management human resources programs.* Establishment of these types of programs can help decrease the risk of malevolent acts being committed by disgruntled or troubled employees (Work Place Violence). These programs typically involve training for supervisors on how to recognize behaviors that might signal problems.
- *Controlled access to key facilities.* An important step in securing utilities is accounting for all individuals entering and exiting utility property, especially key facilities. This includes employees and nonemployees. All utility personnel should be encouraged to be aware of strangers in critical areas such as the treatment plant.

EMERGENCY RESPONSE

Virtually every utility will at some point be affected by a natural disaster or major accident. Financial, cultural, and political considerations place practical limitations on the extent to which physical facility improvements and physical protection systems can be employed to safeguard utilities against such events. And it is impossible to prevent certain malevolent acts, especially vandalism, from occurring. For all of these reasons, utility managers need to emphasize effective planning of their responses to natural disasters, accidents, and man-made events to reduce the impact on drinking water and wastewater systems and the public. The importance of response planning is underscored by the inclusion of public works staff as official first responders, in the early stages of an incident, under Homeland Security Presidential Directive 8 (HSPD 8). Utility personnel are described in HSPD 8 as being responsible for the protection and preservation of life, property, evidence, and the environment. Under the directive, public works personnel include drinking water and wastewater system employees.

An ERP is one of the most effective tools that a utility can develop to improve their emergency response.

Emergency Response Plans

Most states have required water utilities to maintain emergency response plans for years to deal with unexpected contingencies. The Public Health and Bioterrorism Preparedness and Response Act of 2002 (Bioterrorism Act) required all drinking water utilities serving more than 3,300 people to prepare or upgrade their existing ERPs to incorporate the findings of their vulnerability assessments and address intentional acts.

An ERP is a guidance document that water and wastewater utilities follow to direct their response to emergencies. The plan should be comprehensive enough to cover natural disasters, accidents, and major equipment failures as well as terrorism and other intentional acts. ERPs should specify notification procedures, identify resources available, and assign roles and responsibilities to specific individuals and groups within the organization. Most importantly, the emergency response plan must specify response actions that will control the impact of a critical incident, prevent the incident from escalating, and enhance the recovery process.

An ERP is a working document that should be reviewed and revised on a regular basis. Ideally, an ERP should be coordinated with local emergency response organizations, regulatory agencies, and elected officials prior to an emergency. All utility personnel must know their individual roles as specified by the plan. Key personnel should be familiar with the entire plan. The plan should be kept as simple as possible to ensure understanding and effective execution by everyone assigned a role, and should be periodically exercised.

Emergency Operational Responses

While specific responses should be described for a wide variety of situations in an emergency response plan, the following list of responses to an accidental or intentional contamination event in a drinking water system serves as an example of specific steps that a utility might take to deal with such an emergency.

- *Emergency notification.* Notification of the state regulatory agency that oversees the utility is mandatory in most states for any situation in which the safety of the public water supply may be in question. If there is a possibility that a contamination event may be intentional, the police must also be notified as soon as possible.
- *Increase chlorine residuals,* A step that can be quickly taken by a drinking water utility if they suspect a contamination event

(Brosnan 1999). This could be effective for inactivating pathogens or oxidizing readily oxidizable chemical contaminants. This step would be most effective for water companies that utilize booster chlorination within the distribution network itself.

- *Isolate storage reservoirs or tanks.* This response should be taken for any that are suspected of being contaminated. This is especially practical if a water system has built-in redundancy that ensures that a particular service area can be supplied with water from more than one finished water source.

- *Isolate portions of the distribution system.* This step should be taken for any that are suspected of being contaminated. This will help to prevent the spread of contaminants throughout the entire distribution network.

- *Collect and analyze samples.* This measure should be taken to determine if the suspected contamination event is real and to identify the contaminant(s).

- *Notify the public of the situation and issue an advisory for steps that they should take to protect themselves.* Advisories may range from Boil Water notices to Do Not Use notices depending on the nature of the contaminant. Public notifications should generally be issued by the utility after consultation with state regulatory authorities and public health officials.

Emergency Management

Over the years, a recurring set of problems has been encountered in the management of large-scale emergencies in the United States. A single incident may affect multiple infrastructures and community services. The scale of an incident may exceed the capacity of local, state, and federal responders. Response agencies may have different organizational structures. And incompatible communications and terminology differences may exist between various agencies.

The National Incident Management System (NIMS) is a standardized management plan that provides a core set of concepts for incident command and multi-agency coordination during emergency response. The goal is to establish common principals, terminology, organizational structures, and procedures that all responders can follow during an emergency to better coordinate response actions. This approach is applicable to all types of emergencies including those affecting public utilities. Water utilities are strongly encouraged to ensure that their personnel receive basic training in NIMS. In fact, adoption of NIMS is a precondition for receipt of federal preparedness grants for public utilities just as it is for other organizations in this country.

The Incident Command System (ICS), a basic component of NIMS, has been used to coordinate the activities of multiple response agencies in emergency situations in the United States for the past 40 years. The purpose of ICS is to ensure effective incident management. While police, fire, and other emergency responders are well versed in the use of ICS, this is a relatively new concept for water and wastewater utilities. However, should an emergency situation occur that significantly affects a water system, ICS will be employed by agencies responding to the event. Therefore, utility personnel are strongly encouraged by regulatory agencies and industry organizations to become familiar with this approach and utilize it in their emergency response.

REFERENCES

Abel, D., and M. Naughton. 2007. "Spencer Water Supply Contaminated: 93 Treated at Hospitals after Plant Malfunction." *The Boston Globe,* April 26.

American Water Works Association. 1995. *Emergency Planning for Water Utilities.* Video catalog #64068.

Associated Press. 2003a. "Water Targeted, Magazine Reports." Associated Press, May 29. New York.

———. 2003b. "Incendiary Devices Placed at Michigan Water Plant." Associated Press, September 25. New York.

———. 2006. "Explosion at Water Line Affects Potable Water Supply to Sri Lankan Capital." Associated Press, December 7. New York.

British Broadcasting Company (BBC). China Salesman "Poisoned Water." BBC News, October 6.

Brosnan, T., ed. 1999. *Early Warning Monitoring to Detect Hazardous Events in Water Supplies.* Risk Science Institute Workshop Report. Washington, DC: International Life Sciences Institute.

Chelyshev, A. 1992. "Terrorists Poison Water in Turkish Army Cantonment." Telegraph Agency of the Soviet Union (TASS), March 29. Moscow.

CNN. "Italy on Alert for Water Poisoner." December 9, 2003. http://www.cnn.com/2003/WORLD/europe/12/09/italy.water.reut/.

Congressional Research Service (CRS). 2005. *Terrorism and Security Issues Facing the Water Infrastructure Sector.* CRS Report for Congress. The Library of Congress, April 25. Washington, DC.

Daily Times. 2009. "Multan Suspends Water Supply from Tanks Amid Poisoning Fears." *Daily Times* (Pakistan), November 12.

Dugal, J. 1999. Guadalajara Gas Explosion Disaster. *Disaster Recovery Jour.* 5 (3).

Falkenrath, R. A., R. D. Newman, and B. A. Thayer. 1998. *America's Achilles' Heel: Biological and Chemical Terrorism and Covert Attack.* Cambridge, MA: MIT Press.

Financial Times Global Water Report (FTGWR). 1999. Zambia: Water Cutoff. FTGWR, March 19.

Homeland Security News Wire. 7 April 2011. "Wastewater Employee Charged with Terrorism After Idling Plant." http://www.homelandsecuritynewswire.com/wastewater-employee-charged-terrorism-after-idling-plant.

Hoover, J. E. 1941. "Water Supply Facilities and National Defense." *Jour. AWWA* 33(11):1861.

Keefe, R. 2006. "Security Lacking in Networks Controlling Critical Infrastructures." *Austin American Statesman,* October 2.

Khan, A., D. Swerdlow, and D. Juranek. 2001. "Precautions Against Biological and Chemical Terrorism Directed at Food and Water Supplies." *Public Health Rep.* 116:3.

Kroll, D. J. 2005. *Securing Our Water Supply: Protecting a Vulnerable Resource.* Tulsa, OK: PennWell.

Moser, R. 2005. "Purposeful Contamination of a Distribution System with Chlordane Affecting 10,000 People." *Proc. 2005 AWWA Water Security Congress.* Oklahoma City/Denver: AWWA.

Mueller, R. 2003. Testimony Before the Senate Select Committee on Intelligence Hearing on Worldwide Threats to the Intelligence Community, February 11. Washington, DC.

National Research Council (NRC). 2002. *Making the Nation Safer: The Role of Science and Technology in Countering Terrorism.* Washington, DC: National Academies Press.

Ownbey, P. J., F. D. Schaumburg, and P. C. Klingeman. 1988. Ensuring the Security of Public Water Supplies. *Jour. AWWA* 80(2):30. Denver, CO.

President's Commission on Critical Infrastructure Protection. 1996.

President's Critical Infrastructure Assurance Office. 1998. *Preliminary Research and Development Roadmap for Protecting and Assuring Critical National Infrastructures.* Washington, DC. http://ciao.gov/roadmap-e.pdf.

Proctor, M., K. Blair, and J. Davis. 1998. "Surveillance Data for Waterborne Illness Detection: An Assessment Following a Massive Waterborne Outbreak of *Cryptosporidium* Infection." *Epidemiol. Infect.*, 120, 43.

Purver, R. 1995. *Chemical and Biological Terrorism: The Threat According to the Open Literature.* Canadian Security Intelligence Service (unclassified). Toronto, Ont., Canada.

Ramsay, C. N., and J. Marsh. 1990. "Giardiasis due to Deliberate Contamination of Water Supply." *Lancet* 336:880.

Scharfenaker, M. 2006. "Battered New Orleans." *Jour. AWWA* 98(1):18.

States, S., J. Carroll, G. Cyprych, K. Hayes, J. Kuchta, M. Little, A. Pyle, M. Stoner, C. Westbrook, and L. Casson. 2008. "An Accidental Contamination Event in the Pittsburgh Drinking Water Distribution System." *Proc. 2008 AWWA Water Security Congress.* Denver: AWWA.

Tierney, J., and R. F. Worth. 2003. "Attacks in Iraq may be Signals of New Tactics." *New York Times.* August 18.

Time Magazine. May 4 and May 11, 1992.

Tucker, J. B. 2000. *Toxic Terror: Assessing Terrorist Use of Chemical and Biological Weapons.* Cambridge, MA: MIT Press.

Wall Street Journal. 2008. "Pakistan Arrests 5 Suspected of Planning Cyanide Attack." *Wall Street Journal*, January 19.

WaterTech Online.com. 10/30/2002. "Former Water Department Worker Accused of Poisoning Wells." http://secure.gvmg.com/watertechonline/newsprint.asp?print=1&mode=4&N_ID=35673

Waterman, S. 2003. "Al-Qaida Threat to U.S. Water Supply." *United Press International*, May 28.

Yardley, J. 2005. "Rural Water Worries Persist After Chinese Chemical Spill." *New York Times*, November 27.

22

CIVIL AVIATION SECURITY: ON THE GROUND AND IN THE AIR

Rafi Ron

CEO, New Age Security Solutions (NASS)

Robert Faber

Former Senior Oversight Counsel, House Transportation Committee

THE PSYCHOLOGICAL BATTLE OF AVIATION SECURITY

Terrorism can be thought of as the use of violence, or the threat of violence to exert influence over large segments of the civilian population to bring about change or create fear.

Why do governments devote a disproportionate share of their resources to protect aviation as a potential target? With vulnerabilities in other transportation modes as well as stationary venues, what accounts for the persistent interest in airplanes and airports? The answer is likely found in the nature of the aviation experience itself and the value terrorists place on elevating their "status" in the eyes of their peers and rivals.

Airplane travel by definition is the transportation mode of choice to meet the time-sensitive needs of an increasingly fast-paced, just-in-time culture. It therefore enjoys greater prestige as a mode of travel and delivery and consequently as a target. Passengers who travel by air, for both business and leisure, are more likely to be opinion leaders and frequently have higher incomes than the populace at large— a status itself not lost on terrorist organizations.

To be sure, terrorists are also busy targeting trains (Madrid 2004), buses (London 2005), ships (Yemen 2000), and public gatherings (repeatedly). But destroying a plane is the gold standard by which terrorists are measured. This is in part because of the effort that has been undertaken to make air travel secure. Terrorists who can penetrate the aviation security system feel they have accomplished more than less secure targets.

But perhaps more fundamentally, air travel adds extra emotional potential. It embodies an additional element of "drama," so compelling in a media-driven culture. A certain percentage of passengers on all flights are afraid of flying in the first place; therefore, tensions begin at an elevated level. People are well aware they uniquely lack control of their environment on an airplane. Quite independent of terrorist intentions, air passengers depend on the expertise and judgment of hundreds of people to ensure a safe flight: pilots, mechanics, air traffic controllers, etc.

Terrorists have the potential to enhance the drama and attract attention to their cause when they target aircraft. They can easily draw out a threat to aviation over a period of hours, preying on the inherent fear of an aviation passenger's sense of vulnerability. If the terrorists choose, they have time to force travelers, media, governments, and the public to watch and agonize over the pending disaster.

All of these factors feed the fundamental goals of the terrorists: to raise their status among their peers and rivals by grabbing the world's attention and forcing decision makers to consider their policies and positions. In the terrorists' world, enhancing the respect for their family, tribe, or organization is the highest aspiration in this life and many believe "self-sacrifice" will bring their ultimate reward in the hereafter. Such goals are more attractive than wealth or convenience or integrity. They have succeeded if others respect them. It makes no difference whether it is brought about by admiration or fear; either one enhances their status. Their only fear is failure and the resulting dishonor.

PRE–9/11 HISTORY

Aviation hijackings began as early as the 1930s, remaining a rare occurrence through the 1950s. For the most part, they were not carried out by terrorists. They were the activities of criminals or people seeking political asylum. In the United States, little attention was given to the threat until the 1960s when an international trend of hijacking airplanes to Cuba developed, including a couple of flights from U.S. airspace. Few of these flights resulted in personal injuries.

The hijacking of an Israeli El Al aircraft in 1968 was the start of a darker chapter in aviation attacks. A campaign was initiated that ultimately included U.S. flights overseas a well as Israeli and European aircraft, on the ground and in flight. The transition was from largely isolated incidents, to a sustained effort by certain Palestinian factions and others to use aviation hostages and casualties to leverage change in the national policies of their adversaries.

The face of international terrorism underwent one of its most radical changes in 1972 with the Munich massacre. Members of the Black September group killed 11 Olympic athletes and a West German police officer for reasons unrelated to the Olympic Games. The terrorists no longer sought to gain sympathy for their political cause. They put the world on notice that no setting was exempt in their quest to use civilian casualties to gain deference in their wider conflict.

Non-lethal aviation attacks continued in the United States, with a number of well-publicized hijackings through the 1970s and '80s. Domestic hijackings were still driven by individuals or small groups seeking money, asylum, or personal goals. Outside the United States two developments characterized the attacks on civil targets, including aviation venues. First, funding for terrorism expanded into the domain of state-supported paramilitary organizations. And second, the cost counted in human victims continued to climb.

For a brief time, U.S. citizens were spared as primary targets, but in the mid-1980s, American civilians began to die in terrorist attacks. Deadly aviation attacks were finally focused on the United States in December 1988, when the majority of victims who died on Pan Am Flight 103 were Americans. The period from 1968 to 1988 established aviation as a prime terrorist target and prompted several revisions to U.S. and international flight procedures.

During the 1990s, many terrorist elements transitioned from secular objectives to religious commitments. Explosives were increasingly smuggled onto aircraft in the luggage of suicide bombers or by terrorists who could plant a bomb and escape before it was set to explode. At home, Americans suffered from extreme right- and left-wing domestic terrorist violence in the 1990s as well as foreign attacks, but there were no more aviation incidents until 2001. Consequently, public attention and therefore political commitment to aviation security waned.

The U.S. Federal Air Marshal Service (FAMS), established in the 1960s, grew to more than 1,700 members in the early 1970s. But after the Federal Aviation Administration (FAA) adopted mandatory passenger screening in 1973, the FAMS program was merged with U.S. Customs Service and few sky marshals remained. Because of the expanded terrorism of the 1980s, the program saw a brief revival, but its emphasis switched from domestic to international flights. In time, their numbers again diminished. On September 11, 2001, there were less than three dozen U.S. air marshals worldwide.

Private companies under contract to the airlines began conducting passenger screening in 1973. FAA regulated the responsibility, while local airports often exercised supervision as well. Prior to 9/11 passenger screening at the airport primarily consisted of answering questions like, "Did you pack your own bags?" and "Has your luggage been in your possession at all times?" followed by a walk through a metal detector and an x-ray of carry-on bags. At the time, a broad variety of common items used in daily life were permitted in carry-on luggage that have since been banned.

Less obvious to most air travelers was a computer screening system run by the airlines in coordination with the Federal Bureau of Investigation (FBI) and FAA. It was in response to the increased use of explosives throughout the 1990s. The Computer Assisted Passenger Prescreening System, or CAPPS, as it was known, was instituted in 1998 to review passenger identification (e.g., a driver's license), purchasing patterns, and baggage profiles. Travelers who triggered the criteria of CAPPS were "selected" for additional screening. That typically involved having their checked baggage held until they boarded or screened using explosives detection equipment.

THE RESPONSE OF GOVERNMENT, INDUSTRY, AND THE TRAVELING PUBLIC TO 9/11

On the morning of September 11, 2001, CAPPS identified half of the 9/11 terrorists as "selectees," but the only consequences were holding their checked bags until they boarded the flights or, in one case, subjecting the checked bag to explosives detection. None of the security measures taken under the prevailing rules impeded the terrorist's plans. In fact, although an assumption is often made that private screeners failed to do their job, even the presence of box cutters in the terrorists' carry-on luggage was not considered a threat. Consequently, the 19 hijackers succeeded in commandeering 4 long-range airplanes, using them to kill nearly 3,000 people and causing billions of dollars in damage that day. The financial, societal, and psychological costs that have ensued since then are incalculable.

How could such a small handful of terrorists be able to carry out such a hugely successful strategy? In a word, "globalization"—in the hands of their terrorist mentors. Al-Qaeda had been a multinational paramilitary organization for a decade. It had access to hundreds of millions of dollars a year. Al-Qaeda used global resources to raise money, distribute its philosophy, and recruit the 9/11 terrorists. Not only did such global tools provide the resources to craft the terrorist action, globalization was used as never before to carry out the plan. Internet information provided an avenue for terrorist cells to book flights, monitor events, and find flight training schools. Real-time global communication channels facilitated last-minute coordination that an army general would have envied just a few short years before.

Perhaps more than any other factor, al-Qaeda studied globalization to determine what terrorist act would cause the greatest impact to its victims, both individually and nationally. They exploited the dependencies on globalization to maximize the effect of their actions. Their choices changed the aviation security paradigm. Instead of using explosives to kill people and destroy planes, they were determined to use fully loaded airplanes to serve as guided missiles to destroy iconic institutions of the United States. They failed only in their predatory desire to destroy the White House or the U.S. Capitol.

Effects

The immediate consequences of the 9/11 attack were the grounding of all commercial and general aviation flights over the United States within hours as well as diverting international flights bound for the United States at the time of the attacks. Although commercial aviation was allowed to generally resume within a couple of days, general aviation didn't fully return to U.S. airports for more than four years. In the days following 9/11, the United States adopted a security posture, already seen in some international airports but shocking to American citizens. Armed National Guard troops patrolled selected airport terminals, while military aircraft flew protective missions over and near several major U.S. cities.

Congress immediately swung into action, passing the Aviation and Transportation Security Act (ATSA) in November 2001, forming the Transportation Security Administration (TSA) within the Department of Transportation (DOT). TSA was essentially tasked with taking over the responsibility for passenger and baggage screening by the end of 2002. Such an effort resulted in the hiring and training of 60,000 new employees in a single year. Hundreds of explosive detection systems (EDS) and explosives trace detector (ETD) machines were purchased and put into service by TSA, even as local airports scrambled to reconfigure terminals so they could accommodate the equipment and TSA agents that would be screening passengers and baggage.

A Screening Partnership Program (SPP) initially allowed five airports to continue conducting private contract screening under TSA regulations. That program has undergone limited expansion in several states, although TSA does not favor increasing the number of airports that can participate.

The President also took direct action in the wake of 9/11, forming the Office of Homeland Security (OHS) to facilitate interagency coordination and ensure full federal cooperation in meeting the new threat. By November 2002, the Homeland Security Act passed, replacing the OHS with the Department of Homeland Security (DHS) and combining an array of existing federal law enforcement, intelligence, disaster management, border protection, and transportation agencies. The FAMS was also rebuilt into a force numbering in the thousands, new training facilities were dedicated for their use, and marshals were deployed to cover hundreds of high-priority domestic and international flights.

After early resistance, TSA eventually implemented a Federal Flight Deck Officers (FFDO) program in mid-2003, arming airline pilots as a force multiplier for the FAMS. In addition, airlines took steps to harden airplane cockpits against guns and explosives. As of the 2013 budget year, however, the government is proposing to reduce the FFDO budget by 50 percent.

Shortly after it began regular operation, TSA also proposed the development of a new Computer Assisted Passenger Prescreening System, dubbed CAPPS II. It was designed to access background information held in commercial and government databases that would be correlated to the data provided by a potential passenger when a reservation was initiated. It would check the authenticity of information such as birthday, phone number, address, credit card, and passenger travel patterns. The program never materialized because privacy, supervision, and budget management issues caused it to be terminated in 2004. Various programs are being instituted in its place including TSA's Secure Flight, TSA PreCheck, and Trusted Traveler programs through the Customs and Border Protection agency.

Integral to the CAPPS programs were the maintenance of "No Fly" and "Terrorist Watch" lists. The former being individuals deemed inappropriate to board an airplane because their past behavior warranted exclusion (use of counterfeit tickets, disruptive behavior, or individuals specifically known or suspected of being a threat to aviation). On 9/11 there were less than two dozen people on the list. By November 2001 there were more than 400. In 2008, DHS indicated there were 2,500 on the no-fly list, but claims vary widely. The Terrorist Watch list, in contrast, contains the names of people known or reasonably suspected of having possible links to terrorism.

The United States Government Accountability Office (GAO) stated that as of 2007 there were 755,000 people on the consolidated watch list. GAO also stated, "Within the federal community, there is general agreement that the watch list has helped to combat terrorism." At the same time, a number of people have claimed they were erroneously placed on the list and have had difficulty getting their name removed. Among the people claiming to have been incorrectly put on the list are several entertainers and members of Congress. DHS now maintains a Traveler Redress Inquiry Program (DHS TRIP) to provide a point of contact for individuals who believe they have been adversely and inappropriately impacted by such programs.

From the inception of TSA and DHS, there were concerns about effectiveness and cost overruns in these agencies. Early on, congressional oversight investigations, reports from the DHS Office of Inspector General (DHS OIG), and the GAO documented (1) "cost-plus-a-percentage" contracts prohibited in the federal government, (2) contracts without periodic performance evaluations, and in some cases (3) contracts where 30 to 50 percent of costs were attributed to wasteful and abusive spending practices.

The U.S. government also took a retrospective look at the issues giving rise to 9/11 and the steps needed to address the gaps in aviation security. Most notably, Congress and the President formed the National Commission on Terrorist Attacks Upon the United States in the fall of 2002, better known as the 9/11 Commission. It was a bipartisan working group that produced a final report (*The 9/11 Commission Report*) in July of 2004, with more than 40 recommendations. In September 2011, a private, nonprofit group chaired by the two individuals who chaired the 9/11 Commission released an assessment of the government's implementation of the *9/11 Report*. In it they recognized the progress that has been made and highlighted a number of the areas where goals identified by the Commission remain unrealized.

INNOCENCE LOST: A NEW PARADIGM

In recent transnational conflicts involving armed combat, the United States has relied on its technological prowess to maintain an advantage over its opponents. It stood to reason then that the smaller the opponent the greater the advantage. The response to 9/11 was centered on the "bigger technology is better" solution. Rather than focus government resources on a human factor analysis to identify those who presented the greatest risk, the consensus was that it was better to scale up the technology to process all travelers identically. The presumption was that such treatment is more equitable and avoids the racial and ethnic profiling concerns raised in the context of law enforcement and cultural discrimination. The challenge, however, is that while criminal activity covers a tiny fraction of the population and it is addressed by hundreds of thousands of law enforcement officers nationwide, screening for air travel requires processing hundreds of millions of travelers annually at roughly 450 airports. Each year there are severe budget challenges to maintain the existing equipment, compounded by financial pressure to install new technology each time the terrorists present a novel threat. Indeed, the question has been raised whether we have reached the limit of technological screening, as suicide bombers have begun to internalize explosives within their bodies.

Consequently, the tide has started to shift in recent years to risk-based assessments that combine intelligence assets and passenger risk analysis to target the individuals who pose the greatest threat. Here it is critical to distinguish between effective aviation security and law enforcement responsibilities. Specifically, local police departments seek to deter unlawful activity by their presence and to apprehend criminals when a crime is committed. In contrast, the objective of aviation security is to anticipate malicious behavior and deny terrorists the opportunity to wreak havoc.

In balancing human behavior analysis against a one-size-fits-all technological strategy, the issue that is often raised is ethnic profiling. However, the choice is not whether to adopt or avoid ethnic profiling. On the contrary, racial and ethnic profiling are not only illegal uses of government power; they are ineffective tools in identifying terrorists. Rather, effective human factor analysis considers things such as a traveler's point of origin, behavior inconsistent with the circumstances, unusual travel arrangements, and inability to give consistent answers about destinations and objectives. This flows from the fact that a person who is about to carry out a major terrorist attack, likely ending in his or her death, is rarely able to successfully mimic the behavior of the average business or leisure traveler. In the section on "Technology and Human Factors," we will explore this in more detail.

In analyzing the threats facing aviation today, professionals also have recognized that air safety must now be viewed as one piece in an international three-dimensional chess game. Where hijackings were once the work of specific radical groups largely focused on single issues and affecting discrete passenger groups, the game has changed. Now state-sponsored paramilitary organizations with global access to schedules, plans, diagrams, satellite photos, and weapons may use an airplane bombing to protest antinuclear sanctions. Or they may attempt a cyber attack on the aviation navigation system in one country to affect trade policies in another. Consequently, the intelligence precursors that elevate aviation security threats must be broader than previously considered.

Similarly, efficient aviation security can no longer look at passenger carry-on and checked baggage as the principal source of threats to air travel. Not only are there expanded threat vectors from inside and outside the airport, but effective protection requires a comprehensive strategy that ensures that increased security in one aspect of air travel does not reduce security in another. Such an approach must manage not only a variety of physical threats, but it must also integrate diverse local and federal authorities with competing budgets, responsibilities, and training. We will start with an analysis of the threat vectors facing modern aviation, followed by a discussion of the organizational challenges.

AN EXPLOSION OF THREAT VECTORS: CHASING YESTERDAY

Generic Threat Changes

Events since September 11, 2001 have demonstrated a dramatic change in the threat environment. Until 9/11 terrorist threats were characterized by attacks calculated to result in a limited U.S. response. The objective was to push the envelope as far as possible without breaking it. Hence, certain threats and methods were to be avoided.

On the morning of 9/11 we witnessed the new type of terrorism characterized not by a fear of aggressive U.S. reaction but, rather, seeking to foster immediate celebrations in their own streets while provoking a U.S. reaction that would increase the anti-American feelings in the terrorists' own society. Under the new terrorist threat, there is no room for any limiting factors; the success of the attack is defined by the largest number of casualties, the triggering of extreme political (and military) U.S. reaction, and the applause it receives in the terrorists' own society. Consequently, any threat is acceptable if it succeeds.

Studying the attacks or attempted attacks against U.S. aviation since 9/11, we conclude that they were aimed at the destruction of the aircraft and its passengers during the flight. This is a natural consequence of the steps to reinforced cockpit doors and keep them locked, coupled with terrorists' new expectation of passenger's reaction, and the potential presence of federal air marshals. The probability of successfully hijacking a jet has dropped low enough that terrorist commanders have at least temporarily abandoned hijacking as a modus operandi.

Unfortunately, the corollary conclusion we can draw from continuing attacks and attempts to destroy American aircraft during that same period by mid-air explosions is an indication that current aviation security measures do not serve as a deterrent. Unless new mitigation measures are effective, it would be safe to assume that simultaneous attacks, similar to those planned in the mid-1990s to bring down a dozen U.S. bound flights over the Pacific Ocean and the "liquid bomber" plot in 2006 aimed at killing thousands of passengers over the Atlantic, will likely be planned for the future.

The international efforts to fight terrorists in their caves and camps have severely disrupted their command, coordination, and communications structures. The result has shifted the initiative to local small groups that have more limited contact with their inspirational and professional leadership. Consequently the skill level of their operatives has suffered, as seen by the failures of both Richard Reid[1] (the "shoe bomber") and Abdulmutallab[2] (the "underwear bomber") to actually activate their devices. On the other hand, the small size of the resulting terrorist cells, a high level of compartmentalization, and few members with documented terrorist connections make it more difficult to learn about their existence.

Specific New Threat Vectors

The threats can be grouped into four categories: hijacking, destruction of the airplane in flight, a proximity attack against the aircraft on the ground or during takeoff and landing, and attacks against the public side of the airport. Although it is neither possible nor advisable to fully discuss the expanding number of threat vectors, it is useful for professionals and policymakers to be aware of emerging trends and vulnerabilities. The following list demonstrates in part the asymmetry of the aviation security net. Some are discussed in more detail in this chapter.

Hijacking

Once the terrorist's threat of choice, all attempted hijackings since 9/11 have failed either by passengers overpowering the hijacker(s) or with the hijacker(s) ultimately surrendering. All were isolated incidents, apparently not sponsored by the major terrorist cartels.

Aircraft Destruction

This alternative has been attempted since 9/11 by terrorists who sought to pose as passengers while carrying bombs (shoe bomb, underwear bomb, liquid bombs[3]) that would be detonated once the aircraft was in flight. It was also the objective of the "printer bombs"[4] (cargo packages; see "Cargo Security in the International Distribution Stream" later in the chapter) used in October 2010. Although the vast majority of aviation security funding has focused on passenger and baggage screening, neither methodology was useful in stopping these threats.

To circumvent passenger screening procedures, local terror cells have turned to recruiting people that already have access to airports' secured areas, such as the 2007 attack planned against JFK airport. Individuals can be used to ferry contraband weapons material between the public and "sterile" zone of airports. On occasion such transfer can even take place without the knowledge of the person carrying the weaponizable material. Then the material can be used directly or passed along to a passenger or other accomplice who entered the sterile zone through standard screening procedures. More attention will be given to this in the "Insider Threat" section.

A third concern is the porous nature of many airport perimeters. Some U.S. airports are open on one or more sides to an unguarded body of water. Others have miles of fence that are not patrolled. Some have electronic monitoring systems that are inadequate for various reasons. And finally there are many commercial airports that have facilities on the far side of the airport enclosure (within the sterile zone) that are managed under completely different rules than the main terminal and tarmac, yet are directly accessible to the commercial side.

Even when airports have presumably secure borders, amateur penetrations occur. In 2010, a 16-year-old young man stowed away in the landing gear housing of an aircraft after breaching the perimeter security undetected at the Charlotte, NC, airport. A disoriented driver found his way onto an active taxiway of the Philadelphia International Airport in February 2012. While not terrorist attacks, they indicate a certain porosity in what are considered secure perimeters.

Proximity Attack

Penetrating the perimeter not only raises issues in terms of getting explosives and personnel onboard aircraft without passing through security screening, but it also highlights direct vulnerability of planes to car/truck bombs driven alongside the aircraft. In 2009, the driver of a stolen truck accessed the tarmac at Phoenix, Arizona's Sky Harbor International Airport by crashing through two chain-link perimeter fences. The vehicle managed to drive next to loaded commercial jets taxiing and preparing for takeoff. When the driver was captured, it was discovered he was a criminal, but not a terrorist.

Perhaps more chilling is the availability of shoulder-launched surface-to-air missiles from arms dealers. These man-portable air-defense systems (MANPADS or MPADS) can be purchased on the black market at prices ranging from several hundred dollars for older models to over a hundred thousand dollars for newer ones. There are reports of three MANPADS having been fired at commercial aircraft operating outside the United States since 9/11. Congress has held hearings on the issue and allocated millions of dollars to find solutions. The cost of installing adequate defensive equipment on commercial aircraft, however, is very high. Other options being pursued include U.S. State Department efforts to engage foreign governments to secure and destroy surplus MANPADS stockpiles. Greater awareness of the issue and observations in and around airports can further reduce the threat.

Airport Attacks

With the emphasis on protecting aircraft during flight from passenger or cargo bombs, terrorists continue to focus on the airport facility itself as a point of attack. Terrorist attacks against airport facilities and personnel date back to the 1960s. In 1972, a Japanese Red Army attack at Ben Gurion Airport in Tel Aviv killed 26 people and injured

80 others. In the United States after 9/11 a gunman opened fire at Los Angeles International Airport while standing in line at the ticket counter of Israel's El Al Airlines, killing three and wounding four others before an airline security officer killed him. Terrorist airport bombings since then have included Glasgow (Scotland), Hat Yai (Thailand), Madrid (Spain), and Davao (Philippines). Most recently they struck Moscow's Domodedovo International Airport in early 2011, killing 37 and wounding nearly 200 people.

Many airports have public roadways near airport runways and taxiways. Parking lots, regularly free from any inspection, are often close to terminals. And large numbers of passengers congregate in airport lobbies for check-in. All can serve as detonation locations where bombs can be placed in close proximity to the traveling public. Design features can be built into terminals and airports to minimize these risks. In addition, greater steps can be undertaken to educate passengers, employees, and even security personnel to become more aware of their surroundings and potential threat vectors.

The threat environment is increasingly dynamic. Terrorists have the advantage when they need only learn the weaknesses of the new security technology. We gain the advantage when we have a flexible airport security strategy that reduces traveler waiting lines while creating unexpected obstacles that are hard for terrorists to assess.

BAG SCREENING, PASSENGER SEARCHES, FAMS, AND PUBLIC SAFETY

Since 9/11, TSA has made multiple changes to their travel rules impacting both carry-on and checked luggage as well as personal screening techniques. To avoid unpleasant surprises at the airport, travelers must maintain a constant vigil to ensure they know the current status of TSA's prohibited items list and personal search protocols. Even then, TSA's current search protocols are highly offensive to many travelers.

The prohibited items list has evolved over time. Scissors, lighters, small hand tools, beverages, and personal gels have all taken turns on and off the list. TSA has confiscated 10,000 guns and millions of knives and lighters. In some cases, passengers can remedy their lapse in judgment if there is a postal kiosk at their screening point or if they choose to leave the security line and return a prohibited item to their car. So far there have been no reported cases of TSA thwarting a potential hijacking by confiscating such items.

The prohibited items list also applies to checked baggage. There are items prohibited in the airplane cabin but permitted in checked baggage and vice versa. Some items are prohibited from both locations. In either case, TSA has the authority to open checked baggage and does so about 15 percent of the time. If passengers use TSA-approved locks, screeners have keys to open the bag. If passengers don't use TSA-approved locks, screeners can and will get into the bag any way necessary, including destroying the zippers and locks. In some cases TSA will compensate travelers for damaged luggage or contents, but it is not automatic. Thousands of travelers a year file such claims. If TSA opens a bag for inspection, they are supposed to leave a notice to that effect.

Personal screening has received the broadest attention by the traveling public in recent years. In 2002, random gate re-screening became a common secondary process. Although it was subsequently dropped, it has seen a comeback in the TSA repertoire of passenger screening techniques. Secondary screening has evolved from spread-eagle wanding just beyond the screening line to inspections while seated in nearby chairs, individual spaces, and cubicles. More recently, random and secondary screenings have involved detached inspections of prosthetics, the use of full-body backscatter x-rays, and "close inspection" pat downs that have angered many travelers and policymakers.

Following the 9/11 attacks the FAMS was incorporated into TSA. After the formation of DHS, it resided for a time in the Bureau of Immigration and Customs Enforcement (ICE). FAMS has since been returned to TSA. The FAMS was one of the first active units within TSA—by late 2001—long before the screener force was deployed. In addition to their standard federal law enforcement training, air marshals are qualified as expert marksmen and proficient in close hand-to-hand combat, and trained to respond in the unique confines of a plane at 30,000 feet.

Since the 9/11 attacks, the FAMS has asked airlines to provide first-class seats for air marshals, providing them with a tactical advantage against terrorists charging the cockpit. To maintain their covert status, marshals typically fly dressed as "average" travelers. Occasionally marshals have been called on to take action in the airplane's coach cabin. In 2010, the airline industry petitioned the government to place air marshals outside the first-class cabin. They argue that terrorists can no longer successfully storm the cockpit because the doors and bulkheads have been reinforced. The attacks since 9/11 have focused on explosives carried by passengers in the coach cabin. The airlines believe undercover air marshals patrolling the main body of the aircraft can achieve greater value.

Although TSA is known for employing the vast majority of the screeners at the nation's airports, it also performs regulatory functions over (1) the private screeners in the SPP, (2) selected security planning and operations by local airport authorities, and (3) certain aspects of the airline industry. Prior to the federal government taking over screening in 2002, FAA regulations were used to govern the security protocols of private companies and local governments.

Many of the TSA's regulations have covered their own behavior and that of the traveling public passing through the security checkpoints. In contrast, the European Union continues to move in the direction of separating the regulatory function from the implementation and auditing function in the area of aviation security. In the United States, both the DHS OIG and GAO have issued reports indicating shortfalls in the implementation of 9/11 Commission recommendations or legislative requirements; however, neither has direct authority to enforce their audit findings. As a secondary issue, TSA's implementation is limited by the competing budget requirements within the agency, between itself and other DHS programs, and among national budget priorities. Separating the regulatory programs designed to carry out congressional authorizations from budget and management limitations may allow a more objective focus on balancing the priorities based on risk analysis.

Another aspect of comprehensive airport security is the adoption of Airport Security Plans (ASPs). The purpose of an ASP is to overlay all airline, airport, and federal operations with a single, consistent security plan. Such plans are supposed to be designed to clarify responsibilities, open lines of communications, provide for adequate training, anticipate airport-specific threat vectors, and provide for adequate resources/responses in the event of an attack. Because many airports and their legal counsel see greater liability associated with more specific plans, ASPs are often vague. Nevertheless some airports such as Boston's Logan International have gone beyond the minimum requirements to improve existing security and improve the response if terrorists attempt to use Logan as a staging point for future violence.

TECHNOLOGICAL SOLUTIONS VS. RISK MANAGEMENT—
APPROACHES TO PASSENGER SCREENING

Fighting terrorism in a civilian environment has always presented a challenge in democratic societies. Fundamental to western democracy is the idea that all people are equal and therefore should be treated equally by their government. Terrorists, on the other hand, view openness and the principal of equality as vulnerabilities to be exploited. Later in the chapter we will look at the privacy and civil liberty implications. In this section, we are concerned with the effectiveness and practicality of technology based versus risk management based approaches to aviation security.

In the "equality" model, focused primarily on technology, a single security process applies to all air travelers. Everyone is assumed to be equally likely to commit a terrorist act if he or she has the tools available. The objective is to make sure they do not possess the tools to carry out a terrorist plan. All travelers are processed through the same technology to ensure impartial disarmament.

Under the "risk management" approach, the assumption is that each passenger represents a different level of risk and therefore requires a different level of security processing. Potential passengers undergo a multiphase process that starts with the concept that all travelers are free to board with little delay, unless something triggers further consideration. As the individual risk factor of each traveler is found to increase, the security process is adjusted to match the risk.

The risk management strategy also assumes that the depth of search that would be required to effectively detect all concealed weapons, if everyone is subjected to the same technology or physical examination, is not feasible due to cost, time, and space. And ultimately most people would find it unacceptable because of the required level of privacy intrusion.

Furthermore, since 2001 we have seen that the aviation attacks attempted under the equality model have ended with the terrorists successfully bringing their devices on board or being stopped by good intelligence work before they arrived at the airport. Prior to 9/11 there were many other cases where terrorists were able to overcome the equality screening process.

Immediately following a terrorist attack or other major breach of aviation security, the suggestion is often made to implement the "Israeli model" of risk assessment to screen air travelers. This is motivated in part by the fact that the last successful aircraft-related terrorist attempt against El Al, the Israeli national airline, was in 1986.

Israeli Model

What then is the Israeli model? It is a multilayer system that begins outside Israel's Ben Gurion International Airport or at gates where El Al processes passengers flying to Israel. Vehicles approaching the Ben Gurion terminal are stopped by guards and asked a couple of questions about where they are coming from or the purpose of their visit. If an individual reveals a nervous response, further questioning or inspection may be pursued before the vehicle is allowed to enter the airport.

Security agents with special training circulate throughout the terminal, looking for suspicious behavior. Before passengers approach the check-in counter, they are required to show their travel documents and answer a series of questions by trained security personnel such as why they are traveling to or from Israel, followed by a few general questions about the trip in order to identify consistencies or inconsistencies in their story. Depending on the tone, body language, and content of the passengers' replies, additional screening may be required. Passengers also go through a metal detector, and their bags are x-rayed.

Arab passengers and critics of the system have commented that many individuals are discriminated against in what amounts to "racial profiling." Israeli officials indicate that the risk profile is not based solely on ethnic, religious, or national affiliation, but rather on a combination of factors that also include behavior, travel information, and prior intelligence.

Transferring the Israeli experience as-is to the U.S. faces several barriers including a different cultural setting, legal and ethical challenges, and a much larger number of passengers. However, creating an "American model" that incorporates lessons learned from Israel's risk based approach has been in the works for several years.

The Massachusetts State Police implemented the first U.S. version of the program in 2002 at Boston Logan International Airport. Based on the success of the Massachusetts program and despite initial federal opposition, TSA subsequently adopted a form of the concept and started its Screening of Passengers by Observation Techniques (SPOT) program in 2004. Integral to the SPOT program are TSA's Behavior Detection Officers (BDOs). Behavior detection currently is a significant component in TSA's security strategy. The TSA program is undergoing a major upgrade in 2012 through the increase of actual contact and verbal interaction with passengers. However, there are still no efforts to include airport police and frontline personnel.

TSA has come under criticism for the SPOT program by commentators skeptical that behavioral observations alone can detect potential terrorist behavior. TSA has reported that BDOs have identified illegal activities resulting in nearly 2,000 arrests across the country, with the most significant case being an individual who was discovered to have explosive components at the Orlando airport in 2008.

TSA conducted a pilot program in 2011 where BDOs conducted passenger interviews and assessed the result. To date the process has not been adopted nationwide. The SPOT program and general passenger screening remains largely a one-size-fits-all system that relies on a technology and pat-downs for all passengers. The trusted traveler programs are discussed in the section on civil liberties.

Technology and Human Factors

The reliance on advanced technology in combination with the "treat everyone alike" policy to secure our domestic security has had the advantage of avoiding sensitive political issues like assessing what constitutes impermissible discrimination or how to correct for human errors in judgment. Unfortunately, it has led to the use of technologies and procedures that have left many Americans with the belief that the cure is worse than the disease, or at least that there have to be alternatives that are legally and morally more acceptable.

Two technical problems have surfaced with this high-tech approach. First, the technology always follows the attacks, or in other words, the initiative has been in the hands of the terrorists. This approach favors the terrorists' success, as they have a virtually infinite number of alternative methods to bring an attack. Developing a technological mitigation after an attack allows them to study and develop a workaround for one static defense after the other in their march to bring devastation.

The other shortfall is a reliance on the assumption that knowledge of a risk will lead to the development of a technological method that is able to deliver a good or excellent defense. This assumption has proven to be incorrect. For instance, when the "liquid bombers" were discovered in 2006, no technology or regulations were in effect to limit liquids in carry-on luggage, despite the fact that a Korean Airways jet was the subject of an attack using liquid explosives in the 1980s. In the absence of a technological solution TSA turned to the only alternative available within the equality model: ban liquids in quantities that could be lethal and screen everyone for compliance.

Up to this point the terrorists have been using their strongest tool, suicide bombers, while in one sense we have been defending with one of the weakest alternatives in a large advanced society, that of trying to use technology to process hundreds of millions of people each year as if they posed an equal risk, thereby creating a security environment disliked or abhorred by most of the people it is designed to protect. The good news is that we have the opportunity to use one of the greatest strengths of an open and free society, the ubiquitous awareness of day-to-day realities, against their weakest point, the use of ill-informed novices, trained in isolated indoctrination camps.

The human factor has proven in many cases to be the Achilles' heel of the terrorist movement. Unlike the general belief that terrorists are well trained and have all the necessary personality and character elements to make them successful, in reality most of them are poorly prepared with little, if any, life experience.

In fact, suicide bombers are vulnerable for the very reasons that lead them to become suicide bombers. Since healthy people in Western societies have an irresistibly strong sense of self-preservation, individuals who have had that driven from their mind often behave "just a little different" than the average person one would encounter at a mall or an airport. How do terrorist provocateurs achieve such devotion to a cause? They create indoctrination settings where they can substitute a compelling promise in the mind of their followers such as promising to rescue their family from poverty (the families of suicide bombers are often compensated), earn eternal bliss for their sacrifice, or save their society from unspeakable horrors.

It is rare for rational people to seek suicide. Rarer still are individuals who are willing to commit suicide in public. Even less likely are those who will commit suicide in public with the objective of murdering as many of the people around them as possible. At each stage the person becomes less grounded in the daily realities that govern normal behavior and more likely to be identified by aberrant behavior and less likely to be able to provide cogent responses to everyday questions. Ferreting out suicide bombers is not the challenge of trying to determine the demeanor of a businessman by observing what watch he is wearing. A terrorist is trying to maintain a cover story with minimal experience and a poor understanding of the culture he or she is trying to mimic. At the same time they are struggling to suppress the adrenaline rush that comes with summoning the willpower needed to destroy their own life.

The mindset and reactions of a suicide bomber are really quite different than a criminal or a spy because spies and criminals seek self-preservation and long-term covert success. Even at the height of the Cold War, the ability to successfully maintain a cover was a challenge for seasoned agents. The problem for those who control suicide bombers is that its difficult to find people with experience. Certainly the shoe bomber and the underwear bomber bear out the hypothesis.

On the other hand, what can be borrowed from the Israeli experience is the potential to develop highly professional skills within security personnel and security programs that can discretely and relatively innocuously challenge the terrorist on the personal level in an environment that can be modulated to create unexpected difficulties for them while being of little consequence for the average traveler. The human interaction environment can often provide much of what is needed to proactively search for assailants in a domain where the defenders have the advantage. The "challenge interviews" are an example of this approach. Increasing the pressure on the terrorists' weakness in the human domain can be a key to future success.

INSIDER THREAT

Of the threats to aviation listed previously, the insider threat is perhaps the most insidious because it represents a risk posed by people who are already trusted. Hundreds of thousands of transportation workers and ancillary providers support the U.S. aviation industry. They include not only the mechanics, pilots, and flight attendants but also the food service personnel, fuel suppliers, and information technology specialists. Their access to the planes, airports, and mission-critical systems pose serious security questions. While the vast majority of such personnel are not risks, a host of examples make it clear that the few who are intent on clandestine activity must be identified.

The risk, however, goes far beyond those who seek to do harm. Because of their access, insiders make perfect conduits as carriers for threat-inducing activity without their knowledge. People may carry something from someone they trust without closely inspecting it, or individuals who move bulk items may not inspect all of the components. Consequently, not only must insiders be cleared, but they should also be thoroughly trained and motivated to function as another layer of security in their own right.

To manage the first part of the problem, TSA in coordination with U.S. Coast Guard (for maritime workers) conducts background checks concerning transportation workers who have unescorted access to the secure areas of airports and shipping docks. The goal is to develop uniform security threat assessments (STA) across all modes of transportation so that the same standards apply and workers active in multiple areas only need acquire a single security badge.

The process of establishing an effective set of credentialing protocols for transportation workers has been long in the making. Soon after 9/11 there was a move to develop a Transportation Worker Identification Credential (TWIC) Program. Under the program, workers would be issued a single TWIC card containing tamper-resistant biometric credentials. The cards are issued pursuant to thorough background checks, and corresponding data is checked in real time to ensure appropriate access. GAO has said the TWIC program has suffered from lack of oversight and poor coordination. It is currently limited to the maritime sector, and thousands of people who have been issued the cards cannot use them. Steps are underway to correct the problems.

There are also issues associated with assessing trustworthiness, including consistent standards, effectiveness, and frequency of evaluation. For instance, in the TWIC program (maritime), felony convictions within seven years can disqualify a worker, whereas in the aviation sector, the disqualifying time may be 10 years. Similarly, the DHS OIG found in 2011 that 10 percent of the badges issues to aviation workers were based on omissions or inaccuracies in key applicant data fields.

Unfortunately, while we have been fortunate that U.S. airports and airlines have not been subject to a successful insider attack, there is clear evidence of transportation workers engaging in illegal activity. In 2007, an airline employee used his security privileges to smuggle a duffel bag containing 13 handguns, an assault rifle, and 8 pounds of marijuana aboard a flight from Orlando to San Juan. Puerto Rico police subsequently arrested him. In 2006, two air marshals were arrested for using their credentials to engage in a cocaine smuggling conspiracy. While these are isolated incidents that do not reflect on the broader aviation community, they illustrate the vulnerabilities that remain of concern to security specialists.

CARGO SECURITY IN THE INTERNATIONAL DISTRIBUTION STREAM

Threats to the aviation system from explosive laden cargo parcels have also been a reality since the beginning of passenger service. In 1933, an on-board explosive device took down a United Airlines flight from Cleveland to Chicago. It remains a highly vulnerable avenue for terrorist action.

According to the DOT, of the 11 billion tons of air cargo entering the United States each year, a third of it is shipped on passenger jets. The remainder arrives on cargo-only aircraft. Within the United States, TSA mandates that 100 percent of the cargo is subject to screening. However, as terrorists become more sophisticated, some dangerous packages are missed.

Two packages containing personal printers were shipped from Yemen in 2010 and addressed to synagogues in Chicago. Each contained enough explosive to level a large home and easily bring down a plane if detonated in mid-air. One package was discovered and disabled in Dubai and the other in England. However, neither was detected through screening. Both were only discovered when authorities were alerted by intelligence agencies. Indeed, after the package in England was detained, it was subjected to explosives detection equipment, sniffer dogs, and x-rays—none of which identified the package as a bomb. The TSA administrator was subsequently asked if the U.S. screening system would have likely detected the bombs. He said, "In my professional opinion, no."

Since 9/11 the United States has relied heavily on a program called the "Known Shipper Program." It is premised on the concept that all businesses or individuals that ship packages on U.S. flights are cleared by a procedure approved by TSA and are, therefore, "known shippers." To the extent that it allows manufacturers and others with end-to-end control of their products to move items in commerce, it operates fairly smoothly. The DHS OIG has stated that current methods do not provide assurances that only known shipper cargo is transported on passenger aircraft.

TSA also employs a procedure for screening 100 percent of the cargo on passenger airplanes originating in the United States. But significant portions of cargo originating overseas are not screened. In addition, some domestic shipments are palletized prior to arriving at the shipping facility and are not broken down prior to screening, raising questions of adequacy. In light of the printer bomb attempt, it has been argued that all air cargo be thoroughly screened. The International Air Cargo Association has indicated that TSA should structure regulations based on the differences among the various sectors of the air cargo supply chain and take into consideration the commercial implications of the regulations. TSA has chosen to push back the 2011 deadline for foreign carriers to screen all incoming cargo.

To address outstanding cargo shipping risks, TSA continues to build relationships with foreign shipping sources to increase security and reliability. If tamper-proof manifests can be placed on sealed cargo that has been reliably screened at the point of origin, risks will be greatly reduced. In addition, the Hardened Unit Load Devices (HULDs) that hold air cargo are being improved to contain more significant blasts. TSA is also increasing its enforcement profile on cargo shipping. In early 2012, the agency fined a cargo company $1 million for failure to properly screen cargo that was destined for passenger aircraft.

PUBLIC EDUCATION, AVIATION SECURITY, AND CIVIL LIBERTIES

With the breakdown of the U.S. aviation security system on 9/11, the one bright spot was the passenger effort on United Flight 93. They are regarded as heroes who stopped the terrorists from destroying the U.S. Capitol or White House. Since 9/11 there have been two attempted terrorist attacks on flights to the United States—Richard Reid's shoe bomb attempt in 2001 and Abdulmutallab's 2009 underwear bomb attack. Both were curtailed by passenger action. In addition, numerous flights have been stopped, delayed, or ended early because of passenger or airline reaction to suspicious behavior. Unfortunately, while some have apparently curtailed questionable behavior, others proved to be unwarranted concerns.

Official government reaction to citizen self-help has been mixed. A number of programs have been instituted asking passengers on all modes of travel to watch for and report suspicious behavior or packages. They are typically known by catchy phrases like "See Something, Say Something" or "Excuse me, is that your bag?" On the other hand, the official advice is, "If you see suspicious behavior, do not confront the individuals involved." And the FAMS is very clear: they do not encourage passenger self-help—when an air marshal is present. The problem is, air marshals aren't on most flights and they travel undercover when they are present. So depending on one passenger's behavior, another's personality, and the presence or location of an air marshal, a variety of awkward and dangerous scenarios have occurred. Marshals have drawn their weapons on innocent passengers. In addition, passengers have inadvertently struck air marshals. For the most part, marshals have been called upon to quell bad passenger behavior, less because of terrorism and more to manage pompous personalities or the excessive use of alcohol.

While ideally passengers could be given the type of information and training that would assist government in identifying terrorists, a great deal of the interaction has led passengers to dread their interaction with TSA rather than seek ways to be helpful. When Congress transferred the screening from the private sector to the public sector, the reasons stated included more professional qualifications, better training, greater security, and a more consistent experience from one airport to another. While the realization of those goals has been the subject of intense debate and numerous oversight reports since 9/11, one conclusion has achieved an almost universal agreement: passengers are unhappy with the travel experience and particularly the security screening.

In an effort to create a more secure aviation environment, TSA adopted a screening model that treats everyone virtually identically. The operating assumption is that every person who presents himself or herself at the gate could be a terrorist. Therefore, an impartial, technologically driven process is used to determine if a passenger is attempting to bring weapons onboard the aircraft. The premise is that all people, no matter their age, physical condition, or ingenuity, are equally hampered from being a threat if they are denied access to specific (prohibited) items onboard the plane. Whether that is accurate of not, every time a new terrorist threat is activated (or an older one is deemed less dangerous), the technological sieve is adjusted to scan passengers and their luggage.

As weapons are redesigned to circumvent the scanning, the scanning process and equipment become more comprehensive in virtually separating the passengers from their clothing and belongings. The object is to create a system where the ability to inspect the passenger is greater than the terrorists ability to conceal the weapon. As a result, in the last few years, travelers have been asked to remove more clothing prior to passing through the checkpoint as well as subject themselves to either pat-downs or revealing x-ray machines. A growing number of people regard such processes and equipment as an illegal form of search in the hands of the government. The problem is compounded by a recent move on the part of terrorists to internalize the weapons. Their willingness to put their life at risk is not matched by passenger's willingness to put their health or privacy at risk to find such items.

The government's move toward a risk-based assessment lies in developing the concept of identifying "trusted travelers" through a pre-evaluation process. Under this approach, passengers can link their frequent flier account to a government background check by providing additional personally identifying data. The government uses the background information to assess the risk posed by the traveler. In cases where potential passengers do not have frequent flier accounts, a separate application can be filed with the agency. The trusted traveler programs are operated by TSA and CBP.

Reaction to these pilot programs is mixed. Some feel such information is not secure in the hands of the government and fear the data will be used for other government programs, unrelated to passenger safety. Others believe it is simply too great an invasion of personal privacy. And a third group feel that trusted traveler programs provide inappropriate perks to people who have the financial resources to travel frequently and can therefore avoid waiting in the lines that frustrate most travelers.

One implication of these programs is the impact on passengers traveling under "false" names. Aside from the obvious issues associated with name changes based on a change in marital status, many Americans do not travel under their legal name. Some people have assumed their middle name as their standard identification, but it may not match official databases. Others use nicknames or initials. And there are those who have historically traveled under a false name because they don't want their true location to be known for personal or business reasons.

Irrespective of the concerns people have with the government's access to personal information in such a program, it will only be as effective as the process used to verify that the person attempting to board the plane is the same person identified in the background check. In other words, how easy will it be to prohibit security ID theft? Elements of the program are continuously refined, but to ensure authenticity, some form of biometric (fingerprint, retinal scan, face recognition, etc.) verification is needed. That in turn will require that the government maintain some form of a national identity database. Such programs have been historically opposed by a broad section of the public based on concerns about privacy, government intrusiveness, discrimination, and cyber theft of government databases. Nevertheless, support for the use of verifiable biometric IDs is growing both domestically and internationally.

Between the two alternatives of subjecting all travelers to increasingly intense scanning on the one hand or allowing certain passengers to reduce their physical scrutiny and delay by disclosing biometrically verified personal information on the other hand lies the option of "challenge interviews" and "analytical risk assessment." This latter program of individual risk assessment in real time avoids the intense technological and physical scrutiny of the one-size-fits-all approach for most travelers as well as the need to use biometrics and a national identity database. Ultimately it will be up to the public which of these programs or combination of programs is used to maintain a reasonably safe travel environment.

Until new programs are adopted, passengers are learning to adapt their routines to reduce the hurdles posed by air travel. Frequent travelers recommendations include the following:

- Check the TSA website before a flight to ensure knowledge of the current prohibitions.
- Think through what should be in carry-on versus checked baggage before leaving for the airport.
- Wear easily removed shoes and jackets.
- Be prepared before reaching the checkpoint to show identification.
- Determine in advance what items must go into the x-ray bins.
- Develop a mental checklist of what must be retrieved on the far side of screening.
- Consider whether to pack non-liquid snacks or food items (or buy consumables for use on the aircraft after passing through the security scanners).

SHARED RESPONSIBILITY FOR SECURITY

To be effective, aviation security must cover not only passenger and cargo aircraft but also the airport and systems that support the aviation system at large. Terrorists have the luxury of selecting the weakest link as the target for their attack, while government agencies, airlines, airport authorities, aviation employees, and passengers are each challenged to foster a balanced security standard throughout the system.

The comprehensive nature of the threat places a premium on developing a unified security solution at the airport level. Steps have been taken through the ASPs, federal funding, and local initiatives to bolster scarce resources in the effort to reduce the terrorist threat. The increasing challenge at the local level is the relatively large number of independent parties that dictate the final security result without a clear structure of authority and responsibility. The inevitable lack of consistency within a given airport or between airports leads to security gaps and vulnerabilities that may be avoided by greater attention to a unified and coordinated responsibility structure.

An example of this issue is the division between passengers screening (TSA) and airport facility security (local). The safety and security of passengers, crew, and citizens on the ground are joint goals of both agencies. True flight security is the sum of their collective effort. If both have effective deterrents, are complementary, and are properly coordinated, the risk of a threat succeeding is low. However, if either, or both, are ineffective or mismatched, the security chain is weak. Whether shortfalls are the result of inadequate funding, lack of coordination, or poor execution, the advantages to be realized in the "layered" approach to U.S. aviation security are only effective if the layers overlap and there is no clear path for the terrorists to exploit.

Local airport security includes not only perimeter management but also standard access control and first response to breaches or attacks. In some cases, municipal first responders are facing misguided citizens or petty thieves. But given the nature of aviation security, they could just as well be the first ones on the scene of a chemical, biological, or radiation (CBR) attack or responding to explosive and other proximity attacks. Consequently, at any moment the first agency to take control of a scene may be airport security personnel, local police, or a municipal fire department. Because a host of federal agencies could equally be called upon for immediate response, authority may be exercised by TSA, CBP, FBI, or ATF. Effective mitigation of an attack may depend on making a timely determination of which agency should be in control and how resources are to be deployed.

A coordinated response to such an event may be the only chance for agencies to connect the intelligence dots and consequently avoid a terrorist "bait-and-switch" plot—that is, a serial attack where the first stage is designed to lure responding emergency personnel or to position civilian populations so that a more devastating attack is possible because of building evacuation plans or bystander curiosity. While an actual terrorist attack will force all agencies to collaborate at some level, the height of an attack is not the time sort out responsibility and authority. Confusion can lead to missed opportunities or underperformance.

In September 2011 and again in March 2012, GAO reported on actions needed to reduce duplication, achieve cost savings, and strengthen DHS mission functions. Airport authorities face an even greater challenge because they lack the authority to compel preplanning and coordination among other local jurisdictions and federal authorities. Several are making headway, but few hold weekly meetings with all the relevant local, state, and federal agencies to review intelligence and establish protocols for dealing with electronic information exchange, establishing real-time jurisdictional authority in a crises, or managing an emergency with the diverging languages in the airport workforce.

At the local level, two planning issues dominate aviation security. The first is responsibility for standards and their implementation on and off the airport premises. Factors such as building codes (explosion resistance), public roadway offsets from runways, and traffic management are not standardized and often not considered. In a given case, aesthetics, budget, and outdated land use patterns may receive greater consideration—prior to an attack.

The budget issue is a second, separate consideration itself. While the direct screening operation is budgeted by the federal government, the local impacts and airport facility security financing is the responsibility of the authority that runs the airport, a decision that is necessarily influenced by commercial considerations. In that context, security is regarded as a "non-productive" factor when budget items are prioritized. Such items must be balanced against environmental obligations, maintenance costs, expansion plans, and other security considerations. At the same time, costs are weighed against income factors like raising concession fees, increasing landing/parking fees, and local tax revenues.

The TSA and FAA can exercise regulatory authorities that impact local safety and security programs. Additional regulations could be put in place to create greater uniformity at the municipal level. However, agencies at all levels have the option of taking proactive steps to foster greater voluntary cooperation. If federal regulatory steps are undertaken to ensure great local consistency, issues will arise concerning the implications of the Unfunded Mandates Reform Act of 1995 (UMRA), which focuses federal decision making on the compliance costs incurred by government entities and private sector parties affected by such regulations.

Currently federal funding flows to local jurisdictions with commensurate impacts on airport budgets through various grant and loan programs, including the FAA Airport Improvement Program, DHS Transportation Security Grants, and congressional appropriations. Although much of the money flows outside direct airport grants, its presence in the local budgets is a factor in balancing priorities. This is a double-edged sword because while the government may choose to develop and fund a new grant program to increase funding for security, it may reduce other sources that are relied on by local governments to offset security expenditures. All this is in light of ongoing pressures to lower federal spending. As a consequence, questions arise as to whether greater system efficiency and savings can be achieved by steps such as:

1. Allowing more local airports to take advantage of the SPP.
2. Transferring the BDO function to local jurisdictions.
3. Undertaking a revised screening system that focuses on responding to risk analysis rather than processing virtually all travelers under a maximum risk category.

Independent of action by the federal government, local airports have the opportunity to identify their security needs and implement a program, in coordination with other agencies, that will develop clear lines of responsibility and authority in preparation for an attack. Streamlined command rules will enhance preparedness, expedite first response, and improve incident management. Integration of federal agencies into the planning can move the process one step closer to creating a comprehensive program that will make it much more difficult for the terrorists to succeed.

Finally, frontline airport police units are a critical part of airport security. They are often called on to respond to perimeter breaches and to help manage passenger conflicts at TSA screening stations. They are also available to provide terrorist surveillance and would be logical to play a central role in counterterrorism response. However, unlike other specialized local police teams such as SWAT teams, the airport positions often do not enjoy the prestige, training, equipment, and staffing of their central office colleagues.

BETTER INTELLIGENCE AND LAYERS OF SECURITY

Because of the primary goal of aviation security is deterrence against terrorist attacks rather than investigations after the fact, a significant premium is placed on actionable intelligence—that is, information that is specific enough to provide a basis for setting policy or taking action. Sometimes that information comes from the laptop computer of a terrorist leader in a distant country. Other times it comes from domestic surveillance or monitoring terrorist related Web traffic. But often it is the product of last-minute observations in the mind of a flight attendant, air marshal, or airport security officer who views it in light of other valuable intelligence.

If the flight attendant doesn't have the training or the air marshal isn't in a position to make the observation or the airport security officer hasn't been briefed, opportunities to prevent harm are lost. As valuable as the proverbial "smoking gun" may be, better intelligence is much more than searching for conclusive information in distant lands, so that it can be used to alert authorities to the threat of a pending attack, of a specific type, in a specific location. Actionable intelligence is the product of diverse collection, tedious analysis, and most importantly, delivery to the right people in a timely and useful form.

Different players in the aviation security matrix play different roles. Federal agencies may need to serve as aggregators of local data points. On the other hand, local authorities are sometimes in a better position to aggregate information from federal sources so they can be alert to potential behaviors or actions at the airport.

At programs in the Miami and Boston airports, janitors are trained to notice unusual items as they make their regular rounds. Service personnel are often in locations where security personnel never frequent and where terrorists are likely to engage in last-minute preparation without fear of discovery. For instance, the cleaning personnel may be alerted to look for cut wires, pieces of electronic equipment, and unusual-smelling liquids or powders. Frequently, such personnel have little initial interest in dealing with the law enforcement system, but with proper arrangements, training, and incentives, they have served as key players in the intelligence-gathering field.

The lesson applies to individuals throughout the system that are in a position to add value to terrorist deterrence programs. As terrorist threats evolve and aviation security managers seek to be one step ahead instead of one step behind the threats, new approaches can be instituted to change the security paradigm. These steps may even be able to reduce costs, increase deterrence, and ease travel restrictions.

At the same time, vigilance is needed to avoid steps that weaken security. For instance, in 2009, TSA inadvertently uploaded its airport-screening manual, which included several closely guarded secrets about the screening process, to a public Internet site. At a House Subcommittee on National Security, Homeland Defense and Foreign Operations hearing in 2011, a GAO report was released indicating that there were 25,000 TSA security breaches since 2001.

PROTECTING THE TRAVEL EXPERIENCE

In the end, the objective of these programs and the enormous financial commitments they represent is a reasonable balance between a secure aviation system and one that preserves the value of travel. The impacts from failing to strike that balance may be more than just financial losses to the airline industry and humiliation and inconvenience to the traveling public. Studies from Cornell University suggest that hundreds of automobile deaths can be attributed to the people specifically seeking to avoid air travel security protocols and thousands may be attributable to people who avoid flying because of their fear of terrorist attacks.

So what will air travel and aviation security look like in the future? The International Air Transport Association (IATA), representing the international airline industry, envisions "security tunnels" one day that passengers can walk through. Under this scenario, travelers who have submitted security applications, passed government background checks, and have biometric identification use a tunnel for "known travelers." People whose background has created an elevated risk would walk through a tunnel with additional equipment such as full-body scanners and explosive sniffers. The remainder would be processed through the normal channels. Their luggage would be scanned, but they would not have to remove clothing, be patted down, or asked to unpack—unless the process raises an alarm or they were selected for random, enhanced screening. So far the technology does not exist to make such a plan a reality.

Others envision the development of an "American model" of screening based on the personal information currently being provided to the airline, short challenge interviews during the check-in process to clear the majority of travelers, detailed screening for those who pose a greater risk, and finally denial of boarding for those who are found to have generated unacceptable risks based on their known terrorist background or attempts to carry on dangerous materials.

Ultimately some form of screening protocol is required to move average passengers quickly through the process and on to their desired destinations. To date the focus has been on treating everyone as a potential terrorist and processing each traveler through a virtually identical technology or pat-down system. The currently proposed risk-based approaches are focusing on travelers providing detailed information to the government so that it can conduct background checks, eventually coupled with biometrically verified identification systems in order to participate in trusted traveler programs. The latter do not guarantee quick processing but significantly improve the odds in the absence of random testing. A third alternative (the American model) would allow passengers to travel without revealing much personal information but would require engaging in short conversations with trained personnel to verify that the passenger does not pose a risk to fellow travelers.

Experience demonstrates that different people respond differently to the same restrictions in a given set of circumstances. Some people prefer to travel more anonymously. Others have more time to go through longer screening procedures. And there are many regular travelers that would prefer to participate in background checks to speed their passage through the terminal and onto the plane. It may be that a system can be developed that allows passengers to choose the path that most closely fits their needs. Each alternative would provide the same level of protection but would meet the variable needs of travelers. At the same time it could cut the cost of the current system that uses uniform technology to screen virtually all travelers.

In any case, passenger screening is only one of many tools that must be employed to ensure aviation security. The most effective system will build on the strengths of an open society and exploit the weaknesses of the terrorists who seek to destroy a way of life they oppose.

NOTES

1. Richard Reid, under directions from al Qaeda, attempted to board a flight from Paris to Miami on December 21, 2001, but was detained for questioning because he was disheveled, paid for his ticket with cash, had no luggage, and failed to answer questions. Although the process caused him to miss his flight, French authorities took no further action and he returned home.

    The following day, he again attracted attention, but no further investigation was undertaken and he was allowed to board the flight. During the flight, passengers complained about smelling smoke. A flight attendant caught him lighting matches and admonished him to stop. Subsequently, when passing by, she attempted to get his attention but was met with physical confrontation. She then noticed a shoe with a fuse and Reid holding a lit match. She, another attendant, and fellow passengers subdued Reid and secured the fuse before the shoe bomb could be detonated. It contained enough explosives to take down the plane.

2. On December 25, 2009, Abdulmutallab, operating under al Qaeda direction, boarded a flight from Amsterdam to Detroit intent on bringing down the aircraft with explosive materials sewn into his underwear. Shortly before reaching Detroit, Abdulmutallab spent 20 minutes in the aircraft lavatory, presumably assembling the components. Once back at his seat, passengers smelled an unusual odor, heard a sound like firecrackers, and saw the wall of the plane and his pants on fire. One of the passengers tackled him while the crew used a fire extinguisher to put out the flames. Again the plot was foiled by operator error and passenger/crew action.

3. In the summer of 2006, terrorists plotted to detonate liquid explosives on at least 10 transatlantic airlines. The scheme was uncovered and the perpetrators were arrested before any of them could board the flights.

4. See Cargo Security section.

23

CREATING DISASTER RESILIENT REGIONS THROUGH *WHOLE COMMUNITY* ENGAGEMENT

The Regional Disaster Resilience: A Guide to Developing an Action Plan, 2011 Edition is reprinted in this chapter with permission from The Infrastructure Security Partnership and includes an introduction by Guide Lead Project Author

Paula L. Scalingi, Ph.D.

Executive Director, BayArea Center for Regional Disaster Resilience

The *Regional Disaster Resilience Guide* has its genesis in the immediate aftermath of the September 11, 2001 terrorist attacks with a small group of security and emergency management practitioners and experts, who recognized that protection and prevention was not enough in an interdependent and uncertain world. They saw regions and communities increasingly challenged by all-hazards threats and events that could affect public health and safety, the economy, environment, and way of life. For these experts, a major concern was the complex interconnections from asset to global level among infrastructures and other essential service providers, and that there was limited knowledge of these interdependencies, associated vulnerabilities, and the potential for cascading impacts that could devastate a region. An additional challenge was that understanding interdependencies and all-hazards consequences required unprecedented, information sharing, cooperation and collaboration among many diverse stakeholder organizations. It became clear there was a need for a simple, low-cost "doable" and sustainable process to bring together regional stakeholders in collaboration with federal and state partners to improve disaster resilience.

The Infrastructure Security Partnership (TISP), created in late 2001 to represent individuals and organizations involved in the design, construction, and operation of infrastructure, took on the mission of facilitating a national dialogue on security and resilience related to the nation's built environment. Spurred by Hurricane Katrina in the late summer of 2005, a TISP national Task Force of representatives from federal, state, and local government agencies, private sector, and non-profit organizations produced in 2006 the first Regional Disaster Resilience Guide. The Guide was designed for use by any individual with interest in improving the capacity of their organization or community to withstand major incidents or disasters. In the last five years, the Guide has been used by many organizations and has provided a tool for developing regional resilience initiatives in several regions of the U.S. and in Canada.

In 2010, TISP convened a second Task Force to produce an updated an expanded Guide that incorporated new information and insights gleaned from several years of lessons learned from disasters and disruptions, exercises, workshops, studies, assessments, and regional resilience initiatives. The 2011 Edition describes a tested and stakeholder-validated process that can be customized to develop a cross-sector, multi-jurisdiction resilience improvement roadmap. Like the original 2006 version, the updated Guide contains basic information—key definitions and fundamental principles underlying the need for, and how to achieve regional resilience; background on infrastructure interdependencies and potential impacts; a comprehensive list of focus areas and priority issues that should be considered, and a checklist of typical preparedness gaps with recommended activities to address them. Most importantly, the Guide outlines a multi-step approach to develop a regional resilience Action Plan through identifying and bringing together in partnership and trust the necessary broad stakeholder base of public, private, and non-profit organizations; conducting workshops, a baseline assessment of capabilities and needs; a regional interdependencies exercise, and other activities to develop a stakeholder-driven resilience strategy of recommended short, medium, and longer-term activities to address the shortfalls. Lastly, the Guide addresses the challenges facing Action Plan implementation and offers practical ways to organize, maintain, and sustain continued stakeholder collaboration and interest and obtain necessary funding and expertise to move towards regional resilience.

REGIONAL DISASTER RESILIENCE: A GUIDE TO DEVELOP AN ACTION PLAN, 2011 EDITION

Purpose and Scope

The *RDR Guide* is intended to provide practitioners and experts from government, the private sector and other interested organizations with a tested holistic approach, framework, and guidance to develop and implement a flexible and dynamic Action Plan to improve the resilience of their organization, community or region for all-hazards incidents and disasters. Toward this end, the *RDR Guide* provides recommendations that can be incorporated into an Action Plan for short-, medium-, and long-term activities that build upon existing capabilities to address resilience needs.

The *RDR Guide* also provides a tool to design and operationalize an ongoing regional resilience strategy through a year-long collaborative, stakeholder-driven process. This Action Planning process:

- Encompasses all elements of the disaster lifecycle—preparedness, mitigation, response, recovery/long-term restoration—and prevention and protection;
- Addresses communications and information sharing, business and operational continuity, logistics, supply chains, resource issues, human factors, public education and training, and exercises;
- Highlights infrastructure interdependencies, a fundamental determinant of disaster resilience that factors into all its aspects;
- Covers all natural and manmade hazards, including cyber threats, aging and deteriorating infrastructures, agricultural, technological, and environmental incidents and disasters, weapons of mass destruction, and pandemics and other major health events; and
- Incentivizes cross-sector, multi-jurisdiction, and cross-discipline collaboration and cooperation and lays the foundation for lasting public-private partnerships to enhance regional resilience.

Key Definitions

The following are definitions for key terms that are used throughout the *2011 Regional Disaster Resilience Guide for Developing an Action Plan*. These terms currently do not have universally agreed definitions and have different meanings for organizations, sectors, and disciplines. The policy foundation for disaster resilience is only now evolving; thus, consistent with the goal to have the *RDR Guide* meet the needs of the broad stakeholder constituency, these definitions are crafted in simple language using common terminology to accommodate diverse perspectives.

In the context of the *RDR Guide*:

- *Disaster resilience*, for regions and communities, refers to the capability to prepare for, prevent, protect against, respond to or mitigate any anticipated or unexpected significant threat or event, including terrorist attacks, to adapt to changing conditions and rapidly recover to normal or a "new normal," and reconstitute critical assets, operations, and services with minimum damage and disruption to public health and safety, the economy, environment, and national security.

- *A region* is an area that is recognized as such by its stakeholder organizations. A region can be a single- or multi-jurisdiction area, portion of a state (or province), or may span national borders. Regions have accepted cultural characteristics and geographic boundaries and tend to coincide with the service areas of the infrastructures that serve them. A region may be comprised of multiple communities.

- *A community* is defined as a group of stakeholders with some form of commonality, whether that be background, interest, performance of a particular function, geographical region (including and not limited to a village, municipality, state or province, or nation), or where shared institutions and culture exist. Communities may cross physical and political borders at local, state, regional, or national levels.

- *The private sector* is comprised of diverse for-profit and non-profit organizations and resources not under government ownership.

- *Key stakeholders* include individuals, private and public sector organizations, community groups and institutions, and other organizations that:
  - Face challenges in an event or disaster;
  - Have responsibilities in emergency preparedness, operations, and management; and
  - Play major roles in providing the essential services and products that underpin the economic vitality of a community or region, the health and safety of its citizens, and support national security.

- *Critical infrastructures* include assets, systems, and networks, both physical and virtual, that support communities and regions, and which are so vital that if destroyed or incapacitated would disrupt the security, economy, health, safety, or welfare of the public. Critical infrastructure may cross political boundaries and may be manmade (such as structures, energy, water, transportation, and communication systems), natural (such as surface or ground water resources), or virtual (such as cyber, electronic data, and information systems).

- *Infrastructure interdependencies* refers to the physical and virtual linkages and connectivity among critical infrastructures and other essential service providers, including supply chains. Interdependencies have the potential to cause disruptions under certain conditions that can impact multiple infrastructures, affecting essential government services, businesses, and individuals in an entire region with far-reaching health and human safety, economic, societal, environmental, and national security consequences. Interdependencies can exist at multiple levels of increasing complexity and extend beyond a community, a state, and nations.

- *All hazards* refers to any significant threat or event—natural or manmade. This includes natural disasters, system failures, accidents, technological disasters, infrastructure deterioration, and malevolent acts.

- *Risk management* is the process of identifying, analyzing, assessing, and then selecting and evaluating, and implementing strategies and actions for maximizing resilience within limited resources.

- *Mitigation* involves implementing measures prior to, during, or after an incident to reduce the likelihood of its occurrence or its consequences.

Fundamental Principles Underlying the RDR Guide

The *RDR Guide* and the regional disaster resilience planning process it outlines are based on the following fundamental principles that are grouped below in five broad resilience requirement categories:

1. *Holistic Approach that Addresses Infrastructure Interdependencies*

    - *A holistic, regional, disaster lifecycle approach that addresses prevention, protection, preparedness, mitigation, response and recovery/long-term restoration is essential to ensure that organizations, communities, regions, states/provinces and nations can withstand disasters of all types, particularly extreme events.*

    - *From the grassroots to global levels, infrastructures are increasingly complex and interconnected, resulting in physical and cyber vulnerabilities that are only just beginning to be understood.* Public and private sector organizations are becoming increasingly aware of infrastructure interdependencies. However, there is a great need to broaden the understanding of the extent and effects of these interdependencies on organizations' responsibilities, operations, and business practices, particularly regarding large-scale or long-term disruptions.

- *Disaster resilience requires a holistic, all-hazards regional approach* that covers natural disasters of all types: human error, systems failures, pandemics, and malevolent acts, including those involving cyber systems and chemical, biological, radiological, nuclear, and high yield explosive weapons.

- *Infrastructure assets, systems, and networks, and the interdependent supply chains and resources that enable their operation, are only as resilient as the region in which they are located* because of infrastructure dependencies and interdependencies.

2. *Cross-Sector, Multi-Jurisdiction Collaboration through Public-Private Partnerships*

- *Regional resilience rests at the grassroots level* with local government and key stakeholder organizations in partnership with state and federal government. The federal role is primarily to provide resources and assistance to localities and states consistent with policy and legal mandates.

- *Creation of regional public-private partnerships is necessary to bring key stakeholders together to build trust, foster information sharing and coordination; identify and assess vulnerabilities and other resilience needs;* and to develop and implement improvements. Such partnerships should include all levels of government; utilities and other service providers; businesses essential to localities for goods, services and jobs, including manufacturers, producers, processors, and distributors of important commodities and products); non-profits, including social service organizations; community institutions (e.g., schools, faith-based and ethnic organizations); and academic institutions.

3. *Assessment, Planning, & Mitigation for Regional Resilience*

- *There has been extensive work already accomplished by local governments, state agencies, and many businesses and other organizations that should be leveraged* to work toward regional resilience. At the same time, *local, regional, state, and federal disaster management plans need improvement to deal with today's major events and disasters.*

- *Proactive and innovative approaches, tools, technologies, training, and exercises, as well as unprecedented cross-jurisdiction collaboration and planning are required.* This is particularly important for local jurisdiction in those states that function through "home rule." This all must be accomplished in cooperation with private sector and other key stakeholders.

- *Development and maintenance of Mutual Assistance Agreements, User Agreements, Memorandums of Understanding, and other types of cooperative arrangements are essential to sound preparedness planning and disaster management.* Such mechanisms enable jurisdictions (localities, states/provinces, and nations), private sector organizations, and other stakeholders to work out in advance of emergency resource requirements and allocations, security and legal issues, sharing of proprietary information, and cost-reimbursement.

- *Where useful, codes, standards and guidelines should be applied within and across organizations and jurisdictions* to enhance security and preparedness.

- *Ensuring that supply chains can continue delivery of critical products, materials, and components is essential* to disaster resilience and the vitality of the industrial base, which has a direct and profound impact on regional/national economies and national security.

- *The ability of regions to recover expeditiously from disasters is contingent on the resilience of critical services and systems,* both public and private, which may be jeopardized by absence of essential personnel.

- *Security and damage resilience should be built into cyber and physical systems in the development phase* based on assessed risk under multiple high and low probability scenarios.

- *Government and key stakeholders should collaborate to develop consistent, practical, flexible approaches and methods to measuring organizational, community, and regional resilience.*

4. *Regional Coordinated Incident Management & Decision-Making*

- *Determining and effectively coordinating organizational and jurisdictional roles and responsibilities in major events and disasters are essential for regional resilience.* Along these lines, integration of defense assets into regional preparedness in an appropriate manner is necessary to address incidents and disasters that require resources above and beyond those available at the state and local level.

- *An integrated and complementary virtual and physical approach is required to help determine how best to secure and make resilient interdependent infrastructures, ensure expeditious response and recovery and improve regional resiliency* to address all-hazards events and disasters. Consequently, there needs to be increased interaction among physical and cyber security personnel, emergency managers and operators to raise awareness of threats and vulnerabilities.

- *The anthrax attacks of October 2001, followed by the 2003 SARS epidemic and the 2009 H1N1 pandemic, demonstrate the need to incorporate public health with emergency management and practitioners in other functional areas in an holistic approach covering all aspects of resilience*—preparedness, medical and other response and recovery needs to address any all-hazard event or disaster that has significant impacts on health and safety. Such an event will challenge healthcare organizations with dramatic increases in patient load and reductions in available health and medical capacity, while at the same time disrupting critical infrastructures and other essential service providers on which healthcare organizations depend.

- *Managing environmental hazards is integral to regional disaster resilience.* Waste products and toxic holding sites should be considered security risks as well as environmental risks, and taken into account in response and particularly in recovery.

- *The private sector has a wealth of available resources and capabilities for resilience* that must be incorporated into regional disaster response and restoration planning and activities. Likewise, non-profit organizations have resources that can provide substantial benefits.

5. *Risk Communications, Information Sharing, & Situational Awareness*
   - *Securing and managing necessary data on infrastructure interdependencies and potential consequences pre-event, during, and after an incident or disaster are essential.* This requires cross-sector cooperation and establishing ways for two-way information sharing to identify, collect, securely store, integrate, analyze, and appropriately exchange information.

- *Clearly expressed, coordinated information and communications, tailored to different constituencies and needs and conveyed through a variety of mechanisms to reach target populations are essential* to expedite response and recovery for significant events and disasters. Such mechanisms need to be assessed for stakeholder utility and tested frequently to ensure that they meet their objectives, and are both redundant and resilient.

- *Community institutions, ethnic and faith-based groups, at-risk populations, and the general public must be involved in planning and exercises*, with particular focus on education and awareness of threats, impacts, and local emergency response procedures.

- *Promoting and actively developing a "culture of resilience" and raising awareness of steps individuals can take to improve personal and family preparedness* should be a priority focus.

- *The media has a unique and integral role in disaster management*, performing crucial information dissemination and education functions, on occasion as first responders, and as essential stakeholders with operational and business continuity needs. For these reasons, the media needs training, including participation in preparedness planning and exercises, to help it fulfill these highly important roles and responsibilities.

- *A comprehensive regional risk communication strategy should be developed* that encompasses all of the above.

Building the Action Plan Framework

Focus Areas & Priority Issues

The organizing framework for the Action Plan outlined in this chapter is a set of 14 focus areas with corresponding priority issues that cover the disaster lifecycle. The focus areas, which were identified by the broad stakeholder community and validated by the original TISP *RDR Guide* Task Force in 2006, have been updated, re-evaluated and expanded by the current RIDR Task Force.

- *In developing a regional Action Plan, stakeholders should examine and customize this list to develop their own set of focus areas and priority issues based on their organizational and broader regional concerns and needs.*

This will be accomplished through targeted workshops, surveys and stakeholder focus groups, as described in the next section, which focuses on the Multi-Step Resilience Process.

Focus Areas

I.   Characterization of the Regional All-Hazards Threat Environment

II.   Infrastructure Dependencies and Interdependencies Identification and Associated Significant Vulnerabilities and Consequences for Regional Resilience

III.   Regional Resilience Roles, Responsibilities, Authorities, and Decision-Making

IV.   Risk Assessment and Management

V.   Alert and Warning, Two-Way Information Sharing, and Situational Awareness.

VI.   Regional Response Challenges

VII.   Recovery and Long-Term Restoration Challenges

VIII.   Continuity of Operations and Business

IX.   Specialized Sector-Specific Regional Disaster Resilience Needs—Cyber Security Process Control, IT Systems, Transportation, Energy, Water and Wastewater Systems, Dams and Levees, Hospitals and Healthcare, and Air and Seaport Resilience

X.   Human Factors, Community Issues and Education

XI.   Legal and Liability Issues

XII.   Public Information and Risk Communications, including Media

XIII.   Exercises and Training

XIV.   Determining Regional Resilience Financial and Other Resource Needs

Multi-Step Regional Resilience Process

Developing an Action Plan and sustaining a continual regional resilience improvement process are accomplished through a systematic, incremental approach based on a multi-step process (see Figure 23-1). This process has been utilized by regional organizations, states, and localities in different regions of the United States and in Canada over the past decade.

The process is designed to bring together key regional stakeholders to collectively raise awareness of infrastructure interdependencies and disaster preparedness gaps, and to develop a roadmap of activities to address these needs. A facilitating organization is necessary to

Figure 23-1

Developing
an action plan

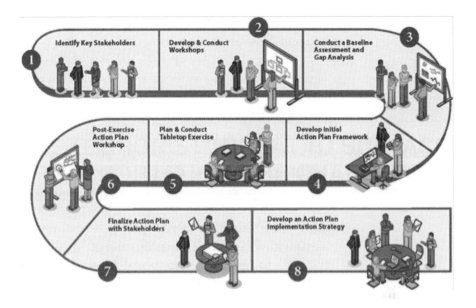

assist in this process. This entity will provide the small support team that will actually do the work for busy stakeholders. This team may be no more than two or three individuals skilled at working with large groups of diverse individuals and who have good organizational and drafting skills and understanding of disaster resilience issues.

The process entails:

• Setting up and convening a cross-sector, multi-disciplinary work group of key stakeholder organizations; holding a kick-off meeting, an educational workshop, and a tabletop exercise; and conducting a survey, focus groups, and interviews, as well as open source research to develop a baseline understanding of capabilities, findings, and needs.

• Integrating this information into a stakeholder-coordinated Action Plan to identify short-term, medium-term, and long-term improvement activities.

Following is the process outlined in eight steps. However, it can be tailored to fit regional stakeholder needs with additional or less steps as required. It is designed to enable regions to utilize existing collaborative mechanisms and initiatives, "piggy-back" on local and state exercise programs, and leverage already existing best practices and solutions. Once completed, the process, including the public-private partnership it builds through developing the Action Plan, provides a regional test-bed to undertake activities with support from federal agencies, private sector, and other sources.

Step 1: Key Stakeholder Engagement '

Identify and convene a broad representative range of experts, emergency management, public health, and other government agencies and private and non-profit stakeholders to join in an initiative to develop a disaster resilient region. Within this broad stakeholder community, invite the "core" organizations that have the most significant roles or functions in assuring disaster resilience be part of a work group to provide oversight and direction for the Action Plan development through meetings and conference calls.

Multi-member organizations, such as Chambers of Commerce, Councils of Government, and non-profit associations should be recruited to assist with this effort. This core group of 30-50 organizations will become the de facto steering group that will lead the resilience initiative.

The workgroup should represent major utilities; key local, state, and regional federal government organizations (including defense installations); businesses; non-profits; and academic and community institutions. Associations that represent broad organizational memberships should be invited. (For those regions that already have existing collaborative mechanisms, it is important to ensure all key stakeholders are represented. (See the TISP *RDR GuideToolkit* on the TISP website for a Key Stakeholder Identification Template.)

Step 2: Workshops

Develop and conduct one to two educational/training workshops to allow stakeholders to explore significant issues and provide guidance and insights from experts on priority issues for incorporation into the Action Plan.

The workshop(s) also should enable participants to share and identify mutual goals and priority concerns and examine current emergency plans, roles, and responsibilities; and ideas for solutions to identified shortfalls. Infrastructure interdependencies should be a major focus. The number of attendees may range from 100-250 representatives of regional public-private sector organizations. A primary goal of the workshops is to develop an understanding of regional interdependencies and establish a trusted collaborative network to advance organizational, community, and regional resilience.

Step 3: Baseline Assessment & Gap Analysis

Conduct a baseline assessment (gap analysis) assessing existing resilience and response capabilities and recovery needs.

This can be accomplished using open source information, a stakeholder survey, focus groups, and interviews. The Gap Analysis should cover the focus areas and priority issues identified by the participating stakeholders. (This step should be kept simple, as it can be labor and time intensive, depending on the size of the region and the extent of preparedness capabilities.)

Step 4: Initial Action Plan

Develop the initial draft Action Plan framework from results of the preceding activities using the stakeholder-validated focus areas and priority issues.

The Support Team will develop, from the information collected up to this point from the workshops, survey, interviews and other stakeholder interactions, a detailed draft outline, or framework for the Action Plan. The Action Plan framework will be coordinated with the work group of core stakeholders and updated. This framework will be fleshed out with new information and insights from Step 5: Tabletop Exercise–both the development process for the exercise and the lessons learned during the exercise itself.

You will find that all the sections are important to different organizations. The stakeholders will pretty much select what they think are the priority areas.

Step 5: Tabletop Exercise

Plan and conduct a tabletop exercise with a scenario selected and designed by the stakeholder work group members to illuminate gaps or areas for improvement in the Action Plan.

This is an essential requirement for the Action Plan. The tabletop is not a conventional exercise and does not test a plan, rather it enables stakeholders to explore and discuss vulnerabilities and consequences in a trusted environment using a scenario they themselves develop through a process facilitated by the support team of conference calls and a few face-to-face meetings. The exercise also helps generate interest and enthusiasm to make necessary resilience improvements.

The exercise should focus on the threats the stakeholder see as highest priority and focus particularly on infrastructure interdependencies and cascading impacts to maximize information sharing and uncover areas affecting mitigation, response, and recovery that need attention. The findings and recommendations will provide significant information for incorporation into the Action Plan. A listing of sample exercise scenarios can be found on the *RDR GuideToolkit* on the TISP website. These can help the work group customize a scenario that reflects real and potential threats the region may have to confront.

Step 6: Post-Exercise Action Plan Workshop

Hold a post-exercise Action Plan Development Workshop to enable stakeholders to examine and prioritize findings and recommendations in the exercise report and information from other relevant activities for incorporation into the Action Plan.

The workshop enables stakeholders to review the draft After Action report prepared by the support team and make corrections and additions that will be in the final exercise report. The exercise results then can be incorporated into the Action Plan.

Step 7: Final Action Plan

Coordinate and finalize the Action Plan with the core stakeholder group.

The process for finalizing the Action Plan is similar to that used to draft the framework. The support team coordinates the draft Action Plan with the stakeholder work group to ensure it meets their needs and reflects their recommendations on activities to be undertaken. The final Action Plan, which includes the comments and changes provided by the work group, should be considered an initial and dynamic regional resilience strategy that will be updated with new information and lessons learned as part of a continuous improvement process.

Step 8: Action Plan Strategy

Develop an Action Plan Implementation Strategy of prioritized activities that includes lead and participating organizations for respective projects, creation of work groups to define project requirements, determine milestones, funding requirements, and sources of technical and other assistance. (See the TISP RDR GuideToolkit for an Action Plan Implementation Template that can be used for this purpose.)

The Multi-Step Regional Resilience Process can take one to two years, depending on availability of resources and whether a region already has an organized public-private partnership and/or well-developed disaster preparedness capabilities.

The process benefits significantly from having a dedicated facilitating entity that can perform the outreach, organizing and administrative functions necessary to convene the stakeholders and assist them to undertake the Action Planning activities. This entity can be a chamber of commerce, council of governments, a non-profit organization or some other regional entity that can convene cross-sector and multi-jurisdiction stakeholders.

Important Considerations in Developing Action Plans

The language used in producing the Action Plan and in documents supporting other activities in the multi-step process (e.g., workshop invitations and agendas, tabletop exercise scenario, educational backgrounders, etc.) should be in common, non-technical language and without acronyms. Because the majority of the stakeholders will be private sector or representatives or community groups of different functional areas and cultures, terminology and procedural documents typically used by government for training and exercises should be avoided or made "stakeholder friendly."

- Coordination of successive drafts of support documents for the Multi-Step Process and the evolving Action Plan is crucial to a successful outcome, as is ensuring the process, including the events, meets the perceived needs of the key stakeholders. Stakeholders must feel they have a "stake" in, and ownership of the process and the Action Plan or they will not invest staff time and continue to actively participate.

- In some cases, the activities recommended in the Action Plan may have already been undertaken by localities and states or provinces, or stakeholder organizations in other regions or nations, including international organizations. These "best practices" should be identified and leveraged where possible to help avoid "recreating the wheel" and to expedite progress in implementing the Action Plan.

- Most of the activities in the Action Plan will require involvement by multiple organizations and many longer-term projects may require federal collaboration with regional stakeholders to provide technical expertise and funding.

- Potential lead and contributing organizations for each of the recommended activities likely will not be immediately specified upon completion of the Action Plan. Also, Action Plan activities may not be initially prioritized. Project leads and "partner" organizations, determination of priority activities, and detailed requirements for each activity will be determined by local jurisdictions with the key stakeholders according to their own timetable and available resources.

- Implementation of Action Plan activities will depend on availability of resources and stakeholder goals and interests, which may change for a variety of reasons over time.

Developing the Action Plan

I. Characterization of the Regional All-Hazards Threat Environment

Priority Issues: *Defining the magnitude of threats in an interdependent age (economic and environmental impacts, major loss of life, and impacts to public* *health, security and well-being); priority all-hazards threats (high probability/ high impact events, low probability/high impact events); unanticipated signifi- cant events; level of key stakeholder understanding of pandemics and chemical, radiological and nuclear threats.*

Needs: Better understanding of, and ability to rank in terms of sig- nificance, all-hazards threats while taking into account infrastructure interdependencies.

Recommended Actions

Short-Term: Identify potential physical, cyber, economic, health-related and/or environmental threats, either directly to the region or indi- rectly through interdependencies, taking into account, where possible, unexpected events.

Medium-Term: Undertake a regional threat assessment to prioritize all- hazards threats and then factor them into regional and organizational continuity and mitigation plans.

Long-Term: Develop a comprehensive "Regional Continuity Plan" centered on interdependencies that includes all jurisdictions and cov- ers all hazards. This Regional Continuity Plan will incorporate, be synchronized, and be compatible with existing local and state disaster preparedness, public health and management plans.

II. Infrastructure Dependencies & Interdependencies Identification and Associated Significant Vulnerabilities & Consequences

Priority Issues: *Identification and prioritization of critical assets, vulner- abilities and preparedness gaps—sector-specific and threat-specific; assess- ments of potential and cascading impacts, including impediments to response and recovery; development of the assessment tools and expertise necessary; ensuring confidentially of proprietary and sensitive data.*

Needs:

- Greater awareness of dependencies and interdependencies-related vulnerabilities and consequences—economic, health and safety, environmental, societal, and security; additionally, what it means for creating resilient regions, communities, organizations, and individuals in a major incident or disaster.
- Refined and proven tools and methodological approaches for use at the local level that can assess impacts, including restoration

costs, of interdependencies and associated vulnerabilities under steady-state conditions and under all-hazards scenarios.

- Regional infrastructure risk assessments focusing on high-risk areas and interdependencies impacts assessments of evacuations and sheltering in place plans under different scenarios.

- Interdependencies assessment tools to better analyze the impacts of pandemics and other significant health-related events.

- Understanding of interdependencies–related restoration needs in a regional disruption, e.g., mitigation strategies, priorities, sequencing, work-arounds, and time lines.

- Ways to raise awareness within organizations of their dependency upon supply chains and IT-related resources to maintain critical operations.

- Incorporation of logistical interdependencies into risk assessments, emergency management, and business continuity plans.

- Information for key stakeholders on the impacts of prolonged electric power disruptions and rolling blackouts.

- Integration of emergency management, public health, physical security and cyber security interests and functions in interdependencies analysis.

- Increased understanding of cross-national border interdependencies for critical infrastructure services, supply chains, and trade.

- Increased understanding of worldwide commerce and communication dependencies and vulnerabilities associated with the use of the Internet.

- Training related to interdependency-focused regional exercises.

- Development of improved modeling and simulation capabilities at universities and research institutions to enable quantitative and qualitative assessments to make informed decisions.

Recommended Actions

Short-Term

- Create or strengthen public-private partnerships focused on regional preparedness with the goal of sharing information, gaining greater understanding of regional interdependencies, building trust, and mutual preparedness planning and project implementation.

- Develop a series of regional tabletop exercises to enable stakeholders to further drill down on priority challenges posed by infrastructure interdependencies.
- Hold workshops focusing on target areas where further understanding of interdependencies is required (e.g., energy, transportation, water and wastewater systems, evacuations, public health and healthcare communications, and IT systems, etc.).
- Provide stakeholders with an infrastructure interdependencies inventory template that can be used by organizations in-house to enable mapping of physical and virtual interdependencies.
- Establish a regional cross-sector interdependencies work group to develop requirements for sharing high-level interdependencies-related information, utilizing information fusion centers.
- Develop a web-based, lessons-learned database for key stakeholders to capture and share knowledge from regional exercises and training.

Medium-Term
- Undertake a regional resilience economic impact study focusing on priority scenarios and incorporating interdependencies considerations.
- Revise and improve existing preparedness and disaster management plans to address interdependencies.
- Examine evacuation and sheltering or shelter-in-place plans to ensure they are realistic, taking regional interdependencies into account.
- For scenarios that would require lengthy recovery, develop a strategy for long-term sheltering needs that identifies potential sites and how to provide basic services to these sites for extended periods.
- Leverage existing transportation modeling and interdependencies analysis capabilities to develop an evacuation assessment system to assist in evacuation decision-making.
- Identify interdependencies-related economic, health, and safety impacts of security measures that may be put in place during a disruption or attack (e.g., closing ports, interstates, tunnels, airports, bridges or borders) to assess how these activities could complicate response and recovery activities.

- Create incentives for academic studies of cross-national border and global interdependencies, vulnerabilities, and consequences that affect business continuity and the broader regional economy.

Long-Term

- Identify and build on existing interdependencies assessment tools to evaluate health/safety, environmental, societal, and economic impacts from high-priority scenarios, and identify preparedness gaps and potential cost-effective mitigation options.
- Develop modeling capabilities to better understand the impact of pandemics, other biological, chemical and radiological events on critical infrastructure interdependencies, accounting for physical, virtual (cyber), and human dimensions.
- Develop, using available capabilities, an interdependencies analysis system—for mapping, visualizing and analyzing interdependencies that includes procedures for organizations to provide agreed high-level information.
- Develop a means to provide a secure, virtual, database to "house" contributing organizations' information with agreed security safeguards and legal provisions regarding unauthorized disclosure of information.
- Develop and evaluate through a pilot project an integrated analysis capability (a "toolset" of models and systems) that can be used at the local level to assess and provide cost-effective protection and mitigation decisions regarding interdependent infrastructures and organizations for use during preparedness planning, response and restoration.
- Provide incentives for private and public sector and non-profit stakeholders to undertake interdependency-focused vulnerability assessments and share information, as appropriate.
- Utilize (H1N1 pandemic, NLEs, and regional disasters) lessons learned, and other findings from events with high health impacts to upgrade local/state plans and undertake mitigation activities to improve regional heath resilience.

III. Regional Resilience Roles, Responsibilities, Authorities, & Decision-Making

Priority Issues: *Organizational structures for effective preparedness, response and recovery/restoration; decision-making—cross-jurisdiction, cross-sector,* *cross-discipline; home rule, cultural, and other challenges; authorities, legal, and regulatory, issues.*

Needs:

- An effective regional multi-jurisdictional organizational incident command/area management structure with a well-defined decision-making process for response and for recovery. Such an organizational structure should extend across two or more states or across national borders to accommodate large-scale disasters that affect extensive geographic regions.
- Improved coordination of command and control-related issues in a regional disaster that includes federal (civilian and defense), state, local agencies, private sector, and non-profits.
- Clarity of roles and responsibilities of government (civilian and defense), private sector, and other key stakeholders in a regional disaster.
- Integration of defense facilities and assets in regional preparedness planning (pre-event as well as post-event).
- Information on where, when, and how defense assets will support and interact with civilian government and private sector organizations.
- Better understanding of lines of authority among federal and local government law enforcement entities.

Recommended Actions

Short-Term

- Hold regional workshops on incident management (physical and cyber) and on the National Incident Management System (NIMS).
- Create a work group of key stakeholder representatives to discuss and delineate roles and responsibilities of government authorities at all levels, including private sector and various other stakeholders.

Medium-Term

- Incorporate into public health and hospital contingency planning procedures to deal with incidences in which the number of casualties may exceed the surge capacity of emergency response medical facilities.
- Develop as necessary memorandums of understanding, mutual assistance pacts and other cooperative agreements, including across-state and national borders.

- Incorporate into a regional exercise program drills to explore roles and responsibilities and include key public and private sector stakeholders, including relevant federal agencies, components of those agencies, and defense entities. Incorporate lessons learned into preparedness plans.

Long-Term: Build upon existing emergency and public health plans and activities to improve regional incident management and broader regional response and recovery, taking into account federal, state, and local government roles and responsibilities and incorporating key private sector, non-profit, and community stakeholders.

IV. Risk Assessment & Management

Priority Issues: *Cost-effective preparedness, prevention, protection, and mitigation; guidelines and standards; backup/redundant systems, remote operations; reconstruction and rebuilding to achieve "new normal"; determining financial and personnel resources required to ensure critical functions and operations; availability of IT technical expertise and other personnel shortages.*

Needs:

- A regional risk assessment capability to:
  - Predict accurate and comprehensive consequences to a full spectrum of threats over a wide range of time scales;
  - Address infrastructure dependencies and interdependencies;
  - Cover health, safety, environmental, societal, and economic impacts, including destabilizing various markets and re-establishing new forms of business; and
  - Enable informed decision-making on resilience alternatives.
- Identification of other public and private risk assessment capabilities that can be customized for communities and regions. Detailed methods for making these capabilities available to local users.
- Inventory of current protection and mitigation capabilities in use or in development, including their costs, benefits, and risks.
- Improved ways to identify and prioritize critical assets and facilities.
- Access to low or no-cost technical, risk assessment expertise for small businesses and non-profit organizations.

- Detection, monitoring and sensor systems, along with mitigation technologies.
- Improved ways to communicate risk information to multiple audiences (e.g., policy and decision makers, private sector stakeholders, and the general public).
- A regional risk management strategy identifying prioritized actions that should be undertaken.

Recommended Actions

Short-Term

- Determine risk and resilience-based criteria to use to identify critical assets and facilities within the context of regional needs.
- Identify existing capabilities, expertise, and other support that can be utilized to undertake a regional risk assessment.
- Conduct a series of targeted scenario-based regional workshops to gain greater information to support a regional risk assessment and enlist stakeholder participation.

Medium-Term: Undertake a regional threat assessment that quantitatively and qualitatively ranks critical infrastructure and other essential community assets in terms of risk to public health and safety, societal well-being, the environment, and economy, taking interdependencies into account.

Long-Term

- Develop a regional all-hazards risk assessment.
- Develop or adapt existing analysis tools to examine the impacts of risk management decisions on regional resilience.

V. Alert & Warning, Two-Way Information Sharing, & Situational Awareness

Priority Issues: *Focus on local to federal and cross-sector levels; potential mechanisms, including traditional and social media; process issues—collection, storage, integration, analysis, dissemination and related security and proprietary data concerns; utilization of state and municipal information fusion centers in all-hazards resilience; alert and warning/notifications; systems interoperability; messaging to schools and other institutions with significant populations, data collection capabilities availability, including international information; collection, coordination, dissemination; IT Systems reliability, resilience, and security; telecommuting, including "last mile issue" and teleconferencing issues; HIPAA* *restrictions on individual health information; utilization of advances in communications technology for tailoring messages to target populations.*

Needs:

- Well-defined "triggers" for emergency alerts and activities for various scenarios.
- Assessment of the effectiveness of alert procedures and systems, including what information needs to be conveyed, how to convey it, and to which organizations and individuals, and how it will be coordinated and disseminated, ideally from a central focal point and through multiple messaging mechanisms appropriate to target audiences.
- Proven protocols, interoperable technolgies, and communication mechanisms to facilitate alerts and information sharing on resilience-related issues with the business community, non-profits, social service groups and other stakeholder constituencies, including individuals, organizations, and utilities that may be in remote areas.
- An operational, integrated regional all-hazards two-way information-sharing capability among government agencies with the broader stakeholder community.
- An understanding of the role of regional and state fusion centers in information sharing, along with the roles of other key contributors to an information sharing system.
- Protocols for engaging the media in training and exercises for all-hazards incidents in providing situational awareness during emergency preparedness and response phase.

Recommended Actions

Short-Term: Create or utilize an existing work group of appropriate local government and key stakeholders to discuss and determine realistic triggers for emergency alerts and activities for different scenarios.

Medium-Term

- Evaluate regional alert capabilities and identify ways to improve alert information coordination and dissemination.
- Leverage available capabilities and work to date and additional capabilities to develop an operational regional all-hazards two-way

information-sharing capability among government agencies and the broader stakeholder community that utilizes the regional or state fusion centers, or both. As part of this effort, delineate the role of the fusion center in information sharing, along with the roles of other key contributors.

- Create or leverage an existing work group of appropriate local government and key stakeholder representatives to develop a media outreach and engagement strategy focused on disaster resilience.

- Incorporate communications and critical IT resilience into public and private stakeholder continuity plans, including testing of telecommuting capabilities by staff and investigation into telecommuting alternatives.

Long-Term: Create and implement an information exchange system to provide better monitoring, collection, assessment, and reporting of a the range of data necessary during a disaster or major event and a situational awareness capability to facilitate incident/disaster response.

VI. Regional Response Challenges

Priority Issues: *Evacuations; providing sheltering short-term, including nontraditional sheltering alternatives; infrastructure interdependencies impacts that can complicate response; ensuring essential disaster lifeline resources—food, water, fuel, medical supplies, etc.; identifying and certifying response and other essential workers for site access; ensuring hospital and healthcare surge capacity; at-risk populations—assisted living residents, non-English speaking groups, the homeless, prisons, economically stressed individuals and families, and other "at-risk" populations; animals and livestock; mortuary issues; communicating with responders, key stakeholders, business community and general public; access to personal protective equipment; prioritized distribution of vaccinations/anti-virals, other medical/hygiene supplies, and related needs; determination of essential personnel for anti-virals; lab analysis capabilities; disaster sheltering during a pandemic or other unconventional bio-event; school closure/daycare issues; business closures; event cancellations; social distancing; travel restrictions—local, domestic, and international; quarantines; insurance issues; national border-crossing issues; disinfection/decontamination and related issues; individual and family resilience needs; pet care issues; security for vaccine distribution, hospitals, grocery stores, and pharmacies; mutual aid agreements; resource requirements and management; logistics and supplies availability; cooperation, coordination, including cross-state and cross-national border, on plans, activities.*

Needs:

- A regional evacuation plan that could move large numbers of individuals from homes and businesses in a chaotic situation of transportation gridlock, power outages, damaged buildings and structures, and limited communications.
- Provisions for sheltering large numbers of individuals, including long-term sheltering, and a strategy to support the needs of displaced families and individuals.
- Strategy for enhanced outreach, education, and awareness on response procedures, including on evacuations and sheltering under certain scenarios and provisions for "special populations," including tribal nations and individuals in nursing homes and assisted care facilities and prisons.
- Procedures for certification/credentialing of emergency, medical/healthcare, utility, and other essential personnel to enable them to assist in medical response or regain access to their place of work.
- Review and further expansion of mutual assistance agreements among hospitals, localities, private sector organizations, and non-profits, including with organizations outside the potential disaster impact region, in other jurisdictions or cross-national borders.
- Improved cross-jurisdiction coordination to address home rule issues.
- Improved plans and procedures to ensure vaccine availability and distribution, availability of staff, and access to laboratory health data.
- More focus on preparedness for biological, chemical or radiological attacks or technological disasters, including assessments of the impacts from these types of events on infrastructures and other essential services, associated interdependencies and economic and societal consequences.
- A strategy to incorporate local media into response activities.
- Incorporation of regional and national defense assets in preparedness planning and disaster management.
- A strategy for identifying volunteers available to assist in response and a mechanism and procedures for training, certifying, and incorporating them into emergency planning, including exercises and drills.
- Inclusion of private sector resources along with government assets in a regional disaster response resource inventory system.

- Coordination of local emergency response and business continuity plans of key stakeholders, including non-profits and community institutions.
- Virtual integration of local Emergency Operations Centers (EOCs) in a region and/or creation of a physical regional EOC that includes private sector and other stakeholder representatives.
- Updating and testing existing formal and informal cooperative agreements or mutual understandings for response and recovery activities.
- Interoperable communications systems for first responders and key stakeholder personnel responsible for restoring essential services.
- Dedicated channels for stakeholders to report to government agencies during regional emergencies to prevent inundation by requests for status reports.
- Up-to-date "yellow pages"—a regularly updated resource directory of disaster response/recovery points-of-contact, including "who does what." Should include logistics and supply components for crucial items such as fuel supply and distribution.
- Protocols for secure response information exchange and nondisclosure agreements.
- Communications disruption contingency plans and exercises and targeted drills to test communications systems under emergency conditions.
- Tabletop and field exercises to test evacuation and sheltering procedures.
- A common terminology to bridge the gap among security, defense, emergency management, and IT communities.
- Routine inclusion of private sector and community organizations with government in preparedness planning.
- Training for private sector organizations in the National Incident Management System (NIMS), that is tailored to business continuity plans.
- Procedures to expedite clearances for appropriate private sector responders and healthcare workers and to credential essential personnel who need to travel and have access to sites during emergencies.
- Emergency response contracts for key activities that state/local governments can pre-negotiate and set in place in advance of an event.

- Inclusion in preparedness plans of community institutions and organizations that serve at-risk populations.

Recommended Actions

Short-Term

- Determine optimal criteria for an effective regional multi-jurisdictional organizational incident command/area management structure for response that integrates public health with emergency management and other necessary expertise; assess the current incident command structure against these criteria, and identify areas of improvement.

- Develop and conduct evacuation planning workshops with scenarios to assess current evacuation plans for realistic timelines and effective procedures.

- Determine long-term sheltering needs (e.g., location options, housing, provision of essential services, costs, etc.) and incorporate into regional preparedness planning.

- Determine procedures for certification/credentialing of emergency, medical/healthcare, utility, and other essential personnel to enable them to assist in response or regain access to their place of work.

- Undertake a survey of current mutual assistance agreements with organizations outside the potential disaster impact region, including cross-national borders.

- Develop a strategy to incorporate local media in response activities under certain scenarios.

Medium-Term

- Harmonize cross-jurisdiction emergency management and public heath plans to mitigate policy differences that can result in conflicting procedures and public information.

- Assess pandemic influenza vaccine distribution challenges and public information impacts and develop/improve procedures to ensure effective and coordinated distribution and administering of vaccines across local jurisdictions.

- Create and conduct targeted workshops and exercises that focus on communication, information sharing, and on roles and responsibilities.

- Examine state laws related to social distancing and other preventative measures during a pandemic.

- Develop procedures for incorporating volunteers into emergency planning, including exercises and drills.
- Develop additional alternate care facilities throughout the region to reduce the hospital surge burden.
- Develop a region-wide outreach, education, and awareness strategy on response procedures, including evacuations and sheltering, for "special populations," including tribal nations and individuals in nursing homes and assisted care facilities and prisons.
- Work with regional and national defense assets to identify what capabilities would be available and in what timeframe during response and recovery, and how to incorporate these assets into preparedness planning and exercises.
- Identify, assess, catalogue, and incorporate potentially necessary private sector assets into a regional disaster resource inventory system.
- Develop an emergency backup communications systems inventory and assessment with recommendations for mitigation measures using extreme disaster needs as the baseline.
- Establish a regional emergency operations center linking regional government, utilities, and other key stakeholder EOCs and the state EOC.
- Create a forum to enable emergency management and security personnel to meet with their counterparts in customer and service provider organizations to share information on disaster management plans in a secure environment.
- Review and where needed create mutual assistance agreements among jurisdictions, private and public sector organizations or among civilian and regional defense facilities.
- Include key private sector stakeholders, non-profits and community organizations in exercises and other preparedness planning activities.
- Assess the needs of community institutions and facilities, (e.g., schools, nursing homes) and of disabled and other at-risk populations during a large-scale disaster.
- Identify changes to, or creation of, "Good Samaritan Laws" to facilitate private-public sector coordination/cooperation.

Long-Term
- Develop a multi-year exercise strategy of tabletops and field exercises to test government and private sector response

procedures and cooperation and identify gaps and potential corrective actions.

- Establish an alternate regional EOC that would be able to replace a regional EOC displaced in an emergency.
- Develop a coordinated response resource management strategy for regional emergencies that involves federal agencies (including defense) and key stakeholders and centralizes planning for relief supplies, food, water, clothing and shelter, including temporary housing; such a strategy would also include transportation to evacuate threatened areas and to transport relief workers, law enforcement and first responders, and utility repair crews.

VII. Recovery & Long-Term Restoration Challenges

Priority Issues: *Planning for recovery and restoration; restoration management structure; roles and missions—federal, state, local, private sector, and community; decision-making cross-jurisdiction, cross-sector, cross-discipline; prioritization of service restoration; resource requirements and management; debris removal/hazardous materials handling; damage assessment, inspection and certification, resources, and processes; effects of environmental degradation; long-term housing needs; support for displaced individuals; ensuring regional economic resilience—restoring housing, businesses, schools, faith-based facilities; pre- and post-event mitigation challenges for design, construction, reconstruction, detection, monitoring, and decontamination; and regulatory and legal constraints.*

Needs:

- An effective regional organizational structure for recovery and long-term restoration after a major event or disaster with a well-defined process that involves the stakeholder organizations necessary to make informed decisions on priority issues, taking into account health and safety, economic, environmental, social, and political considerations.
- An integrated regional resource management plan for recovery and restoration in large-scale disasters that includes how government (civilian and defense) and private sector and non-profit personnel, equipment, and other resources could be accessed and secured quickly.
- Ways to circumvent procedural, bureaucratic, and political issues to acquire critical resources, e.g., mobile communications and

emergency power generators, emergency back-up equipment, and critical components; temporary housing, food, water, and medicines.

- Procedures for long-term economic restoration, including which agencies will have lead roles in recovery activities, how to involve the private sector and what mechanism would be set-up to oversee these activities. (Activities will involve priorities such as debris cleanup and removal, pipeline safety issues, hazardous materials clean up, and availability of dumpsters for waste material, debris, and spoiled food.)

- An inventory of the types of post-disaster recovery assistance that could be made available to localities, the private sector and other stakeholders, including federal help (civilian and defense) for recovery.

- Assurance of adequate stockpiles of fuel, generators, waste management, and medical supplies and sustenance for hospitals, elder care, schools, etc., to meet needs in an unexpected regional disruption lasting more than 72 hours.

- Plans for temporary and longer-term housing and other provisions for "displaced persons," including prison inmates, addicts, mentally handicapped people, illiterate and homeless individuals, the impoverished, and alcoholics. These plans should take into account the impact on cities and localities that must accommodate a large influx of displaced individuals.

- Regional consequence assessments of impacts to critical infrastructures and essential services based on likely scenarios to more accurately gauge potential recovery and restoration needs.

- An operational capability for recovery/long-term restoration that includes:
  - A mechanism and process for sharing information on potential resources and determining their availability, including the amount and location available from different jurisdictions, the private sector, and non-profits.
  - Procedures for acquisition of expertise needed for inspections and certification of food, agriculture, utilities, and other service providers before these facilities can return to operation.

- MOUs and MOAs among regional stakeholders, jurisdictions, and states on resources to be supplied and under what conditions and how reimbursement will be handled.

- Study of psychological, social, and economic factors that can affect post-event business retention and sustainability.
- Incentives and rewards to keep small businesses operating and encourage them to return to the region if they have left.
- Education for private sector organizations about how federal and state disaster response resources and/or reimbursements are requested and allocated.
- Coordinating plans of charitable and other non-profit institutions in providing essential services and supplies.
- Strategies and procedures to deal with volunteers and unsolicited donations.

Recommended Actions

Short-Term

- Build upon existing local jurisdiction recovery plans to develop an effective regional organizational structure for recovery and long-term restoration with a well-defined decision-making process that involves key stakeholder organizations.
- Identify and develop a database of the types of post-disaster recovery assistance that can be made available to localities, the private sector and other stakeholders, including federal help (civilian and defense) for recovery.

Medium-Term

- Create a process for information sharing about potential resources that might be available from the private sector and non-profits and include procedures that address compensation and liability issues.
- Develop and incorporate into a regional continuity plan procedures for resource acquisition and management that include expertise needed for inspections and certification of food, agriculture, utilities, and other essential services.
- Undertake an assessment of regional psychological, social, and economic factors that can affect post-event business retention and sustainability.
- Identify incentives to keep small businesses operating after a regional incident or disaster, and to return to the region if they have left; determine what legal or policy provisions may need to be developed or changed.

- Creation and implementation of a plan to stockpile, or provide access to electric power generators and other emergency back-up equipment and supplies.
- Assess inventories of supplies in schools, hospitals, nursing homes, other community facilities, and prisons to ascertain what additional resources would be needed for major events or disasters.
- Inventory federal resources that are accessible to public and private sector organizations for recovery, and incorporate into a brochure and post on local jurisdiction websites.
- Develop a volunteer management system that addresses contributions of non-profits and other groups and pre-certifies and credentials experts (healthcare, damage assessment, builders and other contractors) to assist in a disaster recovery.
- Develop a template for a regional disaster restoration plan for use by businesses, non-profit and public sector organizations to supplement continuity plans.
- Undertake a survey of local government agencies, utilities, and other key service providers and commercial enterprises to determine expected equipment and personnel availability and needs in a prolonged regional disruption.

Long-Term
- Leverage work already accomplished on restoration to assess long-term physical, economic, environmental, and societal impacts, with focus on biological, chemical, and radiological attacks or incidents.
- Develop a disaster management resource inventory with analytic capabilities on public, private sector, and non-profit resources available for restoration, including subject matter and technical experts, manpower, vehicles, food, water/ice, pharmaceutical supplies, temporary housing, equipment, and services, with point of contact information.

VIII. *Continuity of Operations and Business*

Priority Issues: *Pre-event preparedness, mitigation—remote siting, back-up systems and building in redundancies, preservation of vital records, etc.; operational challenges associated with loss of services/damage to assets; ensuring essential staff; providing access to information and situational awareness; addressing challenges for small and medium businesses; identification of* *essential operations and business activities; assessment of potential disruptions to operational and business services, including logistics, suppliers, customers, availability of truck drivers, warehouses, etc.; business liaison with Emergency Operations Center; involvement of the broad range of businesses in unconventional threat preparedness activities; notification and provision of employee information, training of employees, and other human resource issues; and testing of continuity plans and procedures.*

Needs:

- Accelerated and expanded local government outreach to and training for area utilities, businesses and other organizations on how to improve continuity to take into account regional resilience challenges.
- Assistance to small and medium enterprises and other organizations lacking resources and expertise to understand requirements for self-sufficiency for 72 hours or more in a major regional emergency.
- A template or process for businesses, hospitals, academic, and community institutions to assess their critical operations, essential needs and availability of critical assets to ensure continuity of operations and business.
- Means to better understand and analyze supply chain vulnerabilities and disruption impacts associated with interdependencies.
- Cost-effective security and mitigation measures to ensure supply chains and just-in-time deliveries.
- Exercises and drills to test organizational continuity plans that involve key service providers and suppliers.
- Involvement of businesses, such as retail, manufacturing, distribution, and service organizations in regional preparedness planning and exercises.
- Information and best practices for businesses and other organizations on dealing with workforce policy issues in an event or disaster.
- Cost-effective backup and redundant systems, remote data storage, and other mitigation measures.

Recommended Actions
Short-Term

- Develop a strategy for expanded outreach and awareness for area businesses on regional resilience that covers the issues of particular concern to small and medium-sized enterprises, including on how to upgrade operational and business continuity plans and where to obtain information for this purpose.

- Assess and improve current continuity plan templates for businesses, healthcare facilities and other organizations, taking interdependencies into account.
- Create an on-line "All-Hazards Regional Resilience Lessons Learned" resource that provides information for businesses and other interested organizations on planning, tools, and other best practices that can be used to improve operational and business continuity.
- Develop with business stakeholders an economic resilience risk mitigation strategy as part of a broader regional continuity plan that includes actions to address business continuity challenges and identify ways to make and incentivize improvements.
- Create templates for in-house interdependencies workshops and exercises that can be utilized by businesses to test plans and procedures.
- Develop cooperative arrangements with key suppliers and customers that address security and resiliency needs for supply chains.

Medium-Term
- Improve methodologies and approaches for organizational vulnerabilities and risk assessments that take interdependencies into account.
- Adopt management strategies to ensure availably of and access to critical equipment, materials, components, and products, including from offshore sources.
- Identify challenges regarding confidentiality and legal constraints to collaboration with supply chain organizations and ways to address these issues.
- Undertake outreach and education of key suppliers on interdependencies and conduct onsite "total system" assessments.

Long-Term
- Develop processes and tools to identify and assess supply chain vulnerabilities/interdependencies and disruption impacts; also risk assessment and decision support systems to determine optimal mitigation measures.

- Develop a model process to establish continuous resilience improvement through benchmarking and metrics.

IX. Specialized Sector-Specific & Other Regional Disaster Resilience Needs

(Covers unique sector needs and recommended actions not referenced in other focus areas)

A. Ensuring Regional Cyber Security and IT System Resilience—
phone, cellular, Internet-based systems

Needs:

- Educational tools and approaches to:
  - Increase the knowledge of key stakeholder organizations about new and emerging cyber threats and vulnerabilities to operational and business systems, including supervisory control and data acquisition (SCADA) and process control systems;
  - Address misconceptions about the technical capabilities of computer networks to withstand attacks and recover quickly, and the challenges of resorting to manual operations;
  - Enhance incident response and mitigation.
- Ways to exchange information on cyber threats and incidents for regional cyber disruption management.
- Development of criteria on when to stand up an Emergency Operations Center for a cyber attack.
- Technologies for intrusion detection and protection.
- Mobile backup and alternative computer and communications capabilities (local, long distance and wireless) in significant disasters.
- Development of plans to restore electronic and communications systems expeditiously among critical communications systems/ providers.
- Ongoing information security and resilience training for all stakeholders.

Recommended Actions
Short-Term

- Assessment of communications and critical IT vulnerability to prolonged disruptions under certain scenarios and improvement of plans and capabilities to ensure these essential functions continue or can be expeditiously restored.

- Undertake testing of mass telecommuting by staff to enable remote working after a major incident or disaster.
- Identify alternatives to telecommuting that can be utilized by businesses and organizations to continue operations post-disaster.
- Determine cyber incident threshold criteria for stand up of Emergency Operations Centers.
- Develop and conduct cyber security and incident response awareness workshops customized for stakeholder personnel, media, and the general public.
- Provide cyber security and resilience guidelines for government, businesses and other organizations.
- Incorporate cyber security and resilience challenges into regional and targeted exercises.
- Create a regional cyber security and resilience all-hazards coordination group of key stakeholders to raise awareness of threats, incidents and challenges, share information and focus on resilience activities.
- Develop a list of IT security experts that can offer their time and expertise to help small organizations increase their information security operations and awareness.
- Establish data backup and off-site storage procedures to minimize impacts from cyber attacks or other events and assist in rapid reconstitution.

Medium-Term: Create a cyber security and regional resilience incident management system that enables key stakeholders to communicate on threats and to address significant disruptions.

Long-Term

- Develop or improve existing assessment tools for impacts on communications and IT systems from events and disasters, including weapons of mass destruction attacks and electromagnetic pulse (EMP).
- Improve methods and technologies to harden IT systems to better withstand catastrophic events, as well as to better prevent and thwart cyber attacks.

B. Transportation Regional Resilience—*road, including freight, shipping, and mass transit); rail; maritime and air transport systems; bridges and tunnels*

Needs:

- Increased local government and broader stakeholder awareness of transportation-related vulnerabilities, associated interdependencies, and regional public safety and economic consequences for all hazards, including aging and deteriorating infrastructure.
- Regional all-hazards transportation mitigation strategies.
- Greater coordination on response and recovery from transportation-related incidents among transportation, emergency management, public works, and other local officials within and across jurisdictions.
- Regional transportation emergency response and recovery planning for all-hazards events that would significantly disrupt transportation.
- Regional public information strategy addressing the needs of businesses, utilities, healthcare facilities and the general public for prolonged transportation disruptions.
- Information on what federal resources (waivers, technical assistance, funding) is available to assist with major damage or loss of critical transportation assets, such as a bridge.
- Transportation emergency exercises that bring together transportation public and private sector representatives with emergency managers, public health officials, key stakeholders, and community groups.
- Transportation disruption management assessment tools that can demonstrate the impacts on traffic congestion and neighborhood arterial roads of alternative routing.

Recommended Actions

Short-Term

- Identify available federal, state, and local, and private sector resources available to assist with recovery from an event or disaster involving damage or destruction of critical transportation assets; determine the process and time it would take to access these resources.

- Inclusion of public and private sector transportation representatives in federal, state, and local Emergency Operation Centers and in fusion centers as essential partners in cross-sector information sharing.
- Development of a transportation disruption exercise program that enables transportation, public works, emergency management, public health, and key stakeholders to raise awareness and test and upgrade jurisdictional and regional transportation emergency plans and procedures.

Medium-Term

- Establish a web-based system to provide information to shippers, delivery services, and drivers on closures and alternate routes.
- Undertake an assessment of transportation-related vulnerabilities, associated interdependencies and regional public safety and economic consequences for all hazards, including aging and deteriorating infrastructure across all modes and upgrade jurisdictional and organizational emergency and continuity plans and capabilities.
- Develop transportation emergency public information procedures as part of a regional disaster resilience outreach and education strategy that identifies target community businesses, groups, and the media, and utilizes town hall meetings and surveys to understand transportation needs and expectations.
- Identification of risk-based transportation resilience mitigation measures, including research into hardening techniques for transportation assets to withstand catastrophic events.

Long-Term

- Creation of a regional transportation emergency response and recovery plan as part of a broader all-hazards regional continuity plan that includes:
  - Procedures for coordination and sharing of transportation emergency and continuity plans among jurisdictions and transportation operators;
  - An incident command structure and rescue and recovery procedures for bridge or tunnel structural damage or failures;
  - Transportation emergency response procedures to ensure fire and emergency vehicles can reach those in need and transport the injured to hospitals;

- Pre-event designation of a command post or posts for bridge or tunnel failures and for emergency response boats and helicopters that can make water rescues;
- A single point for transportation disruption-related alert and warning and ongoing information to the public using communications mechanisms that provide information on road, bridge or tunnel closures and detours and alternate routing in languages reflecting the ethnic makeup of the region;
- Provisions for ensuring emergency back-up power for traffic management signs and cameras, posting rerouting signage, debris removal, and securing adequate personnel for directing traffic (e.g., law enforcement, trained volunteers, and in major disasters, National Guard);
- Backup plans for loss of mass transit routes and assets that take into account public needs, shortage of drivers, transit-related union issues, etc.;
- Transportation management plans to deal with the loss of a bridge or tunnel that could require in some cases years to rebuild;
- Resilience measures for dispersed, isolated transportation infrastructure and contingency plans (back-up systems or system redundancy, and other mitigation measures) to address damage or destruction; and
- Supply chain mitigation measures to work around transportation disruptions (for example, a central two-way communication resource for freight carriers, movement limits on certain types of freight to off-peak hours, use of media to distribute information and notifications to truckers, creation of a travel time MapQuest function on the Internet, suspending local jurisdiction noise ordinances to enable trucks to use certain roadways or undertake deliveries at night, creating legislation to permit lifting of weight restrictions for trucks temporarily, creating additional HOV lanes or having HOV only in all lanes within a certain time of day, putting in a special use lane for transit and freight, and banning parking on streets).

• Develop and enhance existing transportation management models to enable decision-making on alternative routing to deal with all-hazards transportation emergencies.

C. Energy Regional Resilience—*electric power, natural gas, fuels availability, distribution, and storage; data collection, information sharing, response, recovery challenges, and energy risk mitigation.*

Needs:

- Raising awareness and understanding of the regional energy infrastructure and energy related all-hazards threats, needs, priorities, and challenges.
- A regional approach to energy investment (in infrastructure upgrades, renewable energy, and smart grid and other advanced technologies) that strengthens energy resilience.
- Increased knowledge of regional energy-related interdependencies (production, supply and distribution/delivery).
- Determining information sharing and situational awareness needs for regional energy disruptions.
- Effective planning to ensure effective regional energy emergency response and recovery.
- Enhanced cooperation and coordination among key energy resilience stakeholders—local and state officials, energy providers and related organizations, critical infrastructures and essential service providers and other significant customers (including community and academic institutions and commercial enterprises).

Recommended Activities

Short-Term

- Study of the regional energy profile examining characteristics of energy usage, major utilities and related service territories; sources of electricity; location of the transmission and distribution infrastructure (e.g., major electric lines/substations, major gas pipelines/storage facilities); primary suppliers of petroleum fuels, storage facilities, refineries, and/or major pipelines.
- Assessment of significant all-hazards threats to the energy infrastructure/provision of services that could result in prolonged outages and range of consequences.

Medium-Term

- Identification and assessment of energy and broader infrastructure interdependencies, associated vulnerabilities and consequences of prolonged outages and disruptions.

- Develop or implement a regional energy ensurance/resilience plan as part of a regional continuity plan in partnership with relevant agencies, energy service providers, key infrastructure and major business owners and operators, state energy assurance office and other relevant state agencies, the U.S. Department of Energy and other federal agencies.

Long-Term: Development of a regional mitigation/energy resilience strategy that includes pre- and post-event prevention, protection, and mitigation resource needs to determine investments for:

- Mitigation, smart grid, energy efficiency, renewable energy sources, and green technologies;
- Resources needed for energy exercises and training, backup/redundant systems, remote operations, and feasibility and security studies;
- Reconstruction and rebuilding energy infrastructure; and
- Financial and personnel resources required for resilient regional energy functions and operations.

D. Water and Wastewater Systems Regional Resilience—*threats, vulnerabilities/interdependencies and potential impacts, prevention and mitigation, and risk communications.*

Needs:

- Improved understanding of potential all-hazards disasters and events on water and wastewater assets, systems, and operations that take infrastructure interdependencies into account.
- Enhanced contaminant detection, vulnerability and consequence assessment tools for water/wastewater systems.
- Regional all-hazards risk assessment and mitigation strategy focusing on water and wastewater systems that address realistic timelines to reconstitute services under different scenarios and optimal mitigation measures.
- Local government and key stakeholder awareness and access to tools, technologies, and approaches that can assess infrastructure, community, and regional water and wastewater systems resilience.
- Incorporation into business and operational continuity, local jurisdiction and regional planning of procedures and measures to improve all-hazards water and wastewater resilience.

- Public outreach and awareness strategy on water and wastewater resilience challenges that addresses the needs of the broad stakeholder community and includes alert and warning procedures and education on potential water contamination and service disruptions issues.

- Mutual assistance agreements among water utilities and local jurisdictions to deal with prolonged water services disruptions.

- Pilot projects and regional exercises to build on existing water/wastewater systems regional resilience.

- Improved assessment capabilities and better coordination of federal, state, and local water quality protection activities.

- Improved communication and coordination among utilities and federal, state, and local officials and agencies to provide needed information about threats, including on chemical, biological, and radiological contaminants that could impact water and wastewater systems.

Recommended Actions

Short-Term

- A regional risk assessment initiative that examines the range of threats to water and wastewater systems, vulnerabilities, health and safety, environmental, and economic consequences with focus on interdependencies. The study should include a baseline assessment of available capabilities, including detection, monitoring, decision-support systems, policies, plans and procedures and utilize workshops and tabletop exercises that enable utility and local government personnel, private sector and other community stakeholders to examine preparedness, response and particularly recovery needs.

- Identification of ways to strengthen communication and coordination among utilities and federal, state, and local officials on water system-related resilience issues.

Medium-Term

- Upgrading of emergency response and continuity plans by water utilities, businesses, and other regional stakeholders using lessons learned from the regional risk assessment.

- Creation or expansion of existing mutual assistance agreements among water utilities and local jurisdictions to deal with prolonged water services disruptions.

- Development of a public outreach and awareness campaign that addresses water systems prolonged disruptions that is customized to target groups—commercial facilities, utilities, healthcare facilities, at-need populations and residents. The strategy should include alert and warning procedures and effective guidance for "Do Not Drink and Do Not Use" orders and on decontamination and disposal of contaminated materials.

Long-Term

- Develop and conduct an ongoing program of regional workshops and pilot projects focusing on improving water and wastewater systems resilience.
- Continued enhancement of vulnerability and consequence assessment tools, protective measures for SCADA systems and administrative networks, increased information for chemical, biological, and radiological contaminants that could affect water systems, and real time, on line monitoring for dangerous contaminants.
- Continued expansion and increased coordination of activities by federal, state, local government, and commercial laboratories to improve capabilities to analyze for chemical, biological, and radiological contaminants in drinking water through standardized protocols and procedures.
- Identification of existing government-developed, private sector and non-profit tools, technologies and best practices that local stakeholders can utilize to assess infrastructure, community, and regional water and wastewater systems resilience.
- Development of a collaborative stakeholder-based approach to design metrics for water and wastewater resilience.

E. Dam & Levee Regional Resilience—*dam and levee-related flood threat, consequence assessment, and mitigation; alert and warning, multi-agency information-sharing, and related public information issues.*

Needs:

- Inventory and characterization of regional dams and levees.
- Vulnerability assessments of these dams and levees.
- Assessment of potential flood threats associated with dam/levees and impacts—health, safety, economic, environmental, and societal.

- Holistic regional risk assessment and mitigation strategy focused on dam and levee associated all hazards scenarios.
- Improved regional inundation maps.
- Greater understanding of potential earthquake impacts to regional dams and levees.
- Development or enhancement of existing dam and levee emergency action plans.
- Improved coordination among local dam and levee owners and operators, local government and key stakeholder organizations on emergency plans and procedures.
- Risk communication strategy to inform public on dam and levee flood risks.
- Improved situational awareness of dam and levee-related flood events.
- Effective and expeditious alert and warning for dam-related flood evacuation.
- Standardized criteria for assessing dam and levee-related risk levels.
- Improved interagency (federal, state, local) communication and coordination on potential dam-related flooding challenges.
- Tools and mitigation techniques and technologies that dam and levee owners and operators and localities can use to improve regional dam and levee resilience (detecting, monitoring, assessing structural integrity issues, and preventing or mitigating damage or failure).
- Methodology for measuring dam and levee-associated regional resilience.

Recommended Actions

Short-Term

- Assess existing alert and warning protocols, procedures, processes, including federal, state, and local coordination, for dam and levee-related flood threats and identify necessary improvements.
- Undertake a public information capabilities gap analysis for flood threats.

Medium-Term

- Undertake an inventory and study of the regional dam and levee system to assess potential all-hazards flood scenarios, to include information on seepage, detection and monitoring methods, potential breaching scenarios, protection projects, code enforcement, and a prioritized list of potential consequences and mitigation options.

- Develop an initial regional flood risk mitigation strategy that would be part of a regional contingency plan focusing on scenarios and that identifies options and resources to secure, harden, and/or relocate critical assets; remove hazardous materials from potential inundation areas; and identify necessary legal and regulatory waivers.

- Develop or upgrade of existing flood inundation maps.

- Develop a regional risk communication strategy that identifies information needs of target audiences, and procedures, mechanisms and tools for outreach and communication.

Long-Term

- Develop a comprehensive regional flood emergency management plan that includes information on flooding impacts and associated infrastructure interdependencies, details trigger events, describes state and federal agency authorities and required actions for local jurisdictions and regional stakeholders at different flow conditions during the course of a flood.

- Develop a dam and levee threat/response regional situational awareness capability.

- Identify federal and other tools, technologies and best practices that dam and levee owners and operators and localities can use to improve regional dam and levee resilience, to include detection, monitoring and assessing structural integrity issues and preventing or mitigating damage or failure.

- Develop standardized criteria for assessing risk and measuring dam and levee-associated regional resilience.

F. Hospitals & Healthcare Resilience—*hospital capacity issues; staff availability; availability of pharmaceuticals, medical and other materials; hospital-related public safety and security issues; alternative care facilities; availability of essential services, power, and fuel, including for backup generators, ambulances, etc.; critical vendor availability (elevator and equipment maintenance, technical assistance, food service, janitorial services, emergency medical services, power generators).*

Needs:

- Improved healthcare plans for access to staff and technical expertise to ensure adequate surge/patient resourcing capacity to deal with a major event or a disaster.
- Improved vaccine distribution and effective public information on vaccine availability and access.
- Identification, recruitment, training and credentialing of volunteer health experts to augment healthcare workers in a significant emergency.
- Ensuring part-time and full-time surge personnel and volunteers to augment regular response staff and relieve pressure on healthcare providers.
- Outreach to healthcare managers regarding cooperative agreements to share staff in emergencies.
- Inclusion by healthcare organizations in continuity plans in collaboration with vendors on their expected needs for supplies of specialized equipment, technical assistance, and other resources, and how these resources would be prioritized and allocated to specific hospitals and other healthcare facilities.
- Greater understanding of direct and indirect infrastructure interdependencies that affect hospitals and other healthcare providers in different disaster scenarios with focus on disruptions that could curtail operations or require healthcare facility evacuation and closure.
- Assessment of hospital security needs and availability of security assets during major events and particularly those that may produce prolonged disruptions or cause public panic.
- An agreed approach for identification and certification of healthcare staff and medical emergency personnel to move across local jurisdictions in a regional emergency.
- MOUs or agreements with partnering regions and states, as well as cross-border to share healthcare resources.
- Capabilities to provide better monitoring, information collection, assessment and reporting on:
  - Laboratory-confirmed significant illness and disease hospitalizations and deaths to fulfill local, state, and federal reporting requirements, as well as information on suspected deaths and intensive care unit admissions; and

- o Emergency department and outpatient facility visits for influenza-like illness and tracking trends in disease activity by age group.
- Information on the status of staff, equipment, supplies and other resources needed by hospitals and medical facilities to meet surge requirements.
- Information on absenteeism levels at schools and producing school absenteeism reports for public health and school district authorities.
- An ongoing surveillance reporting capability for healthcare, public health, and key stakeholders during periods of disease outbreaks.
- Awareness for healthcare providers and the public on clinical signs and symptoms, diagnosis, treatment, and infection control measures.
- A regional health information exchange capability that includes an electronic case reporting system for healthcare institutions.

Recommended Actions

Short-Term

- Develop or leverage an existing template for hospitals and other medical facilities to inventory pre-event/monitor post-event essential assets and resources that are necessary for surge capacity under specific scenarios.
- Develop and conduct a workshop bringing together local public health officials and regional healthcare facility managers to discuss barriers to sharing staff in regional emergencies, and what strategies, including pre-event agreements could be put in place to facilitate this.
- Develop an assessment that inventories existing emergency healthcare-related memorandums of understanding and agreements and includes recommendations to expand them, and identifies other areas for new agreements to enhance regional health resilience.

Medium-Term

- Create a regional volunteer health worker program of volunteers categorized by expertise, focus and projected assigned responsibilities during an event or disaster. Provide necessary levels of training and certification for providing certain types of emergency services.

- Undertake a study that assesses estimated numbers and types of trauma cases in different scenarios, triage strategies, projected necessary healthcare capabilities, gaps and potential solutions.
- Creation of a work group of local public health, healthcare organization representatives and key stakeholders involved in the supply of essential healthcare resources to develop a decision-making process to prioritize allocations of critical equipment and resources to healthcare facilities during a regional incident or disaster.
- Survey hospitals and other large medical facilities on their security needs under various scenarios and make or improve existing arrangements with local law enforcement and security firms to provide resources if necessary.
- Build on state and local activities on certification procedures for first responders and other essential personnel to cover heath-related personnel.

Long-Term

- Develop a risk assessment system that assesses hospital and healthcare facility vulnerabilities and associated interdependencies and consequences for different disaster scenarios.
- Examine and if necessary develop policies to ensure that hospitals collaborate with other healthcare providers and supply chain organizations to develop and exercise business continuity plans.
- Determine alternative medical standard of care strategies and decision-making procedures.
- Create a program to develop:
  - An electronic health resilience information exchange system to provide better monitoring, information collection, assessment and reporting of a wide range of health-related information necessary during a pandemic or other major health-related event; and
  - A regional health resilience situational awareness capability to facilitate incident/disaster response and recovery.

G. Air & Seaport Resilience—*all hazards threats, vulnerabilities, and associated consequences and risk-based prevention and interdependencies, mitigation measures, metrics for sector regional resilience.*

Needs:

- Identification of airport and seaport critical operational and support assets to include facilities, infrastructure, equipment and other goods and services, including organizations involved in transportation services (freight, people, and mail).
- Assessment of all hazards threats that could impact air and seaports, potential vulnerabilities and associated interdependencies, and health and safety, environmental, and economic consequences on port operations and services, customers and supply chains, and the overall regional economy.
- Incorporation of airport and seaport officials into regional emergency planning and incident management.
- Airport and seaport stakeholder collaborative groups focusing on resilience and security that include local, state, and federal agencies, utilities, and commercial organizations (hotels, restaurants, retailers etc.) that support port operations.
- Outreach and education strategy for airport and seaport key stakeholders on all-hazards threats that could disrupt port operations.
- Port emergency and continuity of operations plans that are coordinated with and incorporated into plans of local jurisdictions and major port stakeholders and customer organizations.
- Identification of potential prevention and mitigation approaches, tools, and technologies to improve port resilience.
- Port communications that are integrated with local law enforcement, security, emergency management, public health, state and major municipal fusion centers and relevant federal agencies (e.g., Coast Guard, military facilities).
- Workshops, exercises, and drills that bring together port, local, state, and federal officials, port stakeholder community, regional utilities and other relevant stakeholders.

Recommended Activities

Short-Term

- Creation or expansion of existing airport and seaport stakeholder collaborative groups focusing on resilience and security to include key public and private organizations involved in port operations and services.

- Incorporate airport and seaport emergency and continuity of operations plans into local government and major port stakeholder planning.
- Develop an all-hazards risk communication strategy for the airport and seaport key stakeholder communities and broader regional stakeholders.
- Develop and conduct regional port-focused exercises that bring together relevant government agencies and the port stakeholder community.

Medium-Term

- Develop airport and seaport regional resilience risk management strategies as part of a comprehensive regional continuity plan that:
  ○ Identify critical operational and support assets;
  ○ Cover all-hazards threats, vulnerabilities and infrastructure dependencies and interdependencies; impacts on port operations and services and the overall regional economy; and
  ○ Provides for optimal prevention and mitigation approaches, tools, and technologies.
- Enhance coordination and integration of port communications and information sharing with local government, state, and federal civilian and defense agencies and fusion centers.
- Conduct joint training and exercises for airport and seaport officials and local, state, and federal officials to facilitate regional emergency planning, incident management, and response and recovery decision-making.

Long-Term: Undertake airport and seaport prevention and mitigation activities identified in the regional risk management strategy.

X. Human Factors, Community & Family Issues, & Education

Priority Issues: *Types of societal challenges and needs pre- and post-disaster; understanding and dealing with psychological impacts; identifying and addressing family assistance needs, at-risk populations and ethnic and cultural groups, academic institutions—daycare centers, schools, colleges and universities, and community centers; ensuring people return to a region post-disaster—creating the incentives and an acceptance of the need for a "new normal" and willingness to invest in creating it; and developing the necessary outreach and education initiatives.*

Needs:

- Identify and include at-risk individuals and groups in all-hazards preparedness planning and exercises of service organizations that provide assistance to these individuals and groups, including families, children, and ethnic and cultural groups.
- Outreach, education, and ways to improve assistance to families, groups, and at-risk individuals that are unable to access information on preparedness or to afford preventative health measures, medical and psychological care, and long-term sheltering and support associated with incidents or disasters.
- Examine resilience needs of schools, colleges and universities, community centers, faith-based institutions and other institutions that serve large populations and how they can be utilized to educate on disaster impacts and help communities adapt to a "new normal."

Recommended Actions

Short-Term

- Identification of at-risk populations and the non-profit organizations that serve them (families, children, and the elderly; ethnic, faith-based, cultural, or special groups).
- An inventory of regional capabilities and resources that assist agencies and organizations representing at-risk populations.
- An assessment of the needs of these groups.

Medium-Term: Develop a societal resilience strategy that builds on current public health and non-profit activities, engages these target populations and the non-profit organizations that serve them, and identifies ways to further improve assistance to them.

The strategy will include:

- Identification of points of contact within these groups;
- Activities to address identified needs;
- An outreach and education program of optimal ways to disseminate information on all-hazards threats, potential consequences, and preparedness actions based on what types of communications and communication channels are most effective for particular groups; and
- Integration of these groups into preparedness activities and exercises.

Long-Term

- Incorporation of the societal resilience strategy into jurisdiction preparedness and disaster management plans and broader regional continuity plan.
- Ongoing implementation of the comprehensive approach to incorporate a wide range of activities focused on at-risk populations, identifying improvements where gaps exist, and incorporate into emergency preparedness, response, and recovery planning.

XI. Legal & Liability Issues

Priority Issues: *For government agencies, businesses—workforce policy issues, e.g., compensation, prolonged absences, social isolation and removal of potentially contagious employees, safe workplace rules, flexible payroll issues, contractual issues, information from/coordination with regulators; privacy issues; ethical issues; union-related issues; liability associated with vaccine distribution and administering.*

Needs:

- A compendium of legal and liability issues associated with disaster preparedness, response, recovery or mitigation for private sector, non-profit, and government organizations.
- Identification of best practices and solutions to workplace issues utilized by stakeholders in other regions.
- Incorporation of procedures to address legal and liability issues into emergency management and continuity of operations/business plans.
- Identification of necessary amendments to existing laws and regulations that would address challenges from significant incidents and disasters.

Recommended Actions

Short-Term

- Develop and conduct a regional workshop to discuss legal/liability issues and policy gaps that impact preparedness.
- Develop recommendations for legislations, standards, or other actions taken to lessen these constraints.

Medium-Term: Develop a hardcopy and on-line brochure of examples of legal and liability issues associated with disaster preparedness, response, recovery, or mitigation for private sector and government organizations. The brochure should also identify best practices to deal with work place-related policy and liability issues.

Long-Term: Evaluate, revise, and develop existing or new policies and procedures to address legal and liability constraints that adversely affect regional disaster resilience.

XII. Public Information/Risk Communications, Including Media

Priority Issues: *Requirements for developing and implementing a coordinated regional approach with focus on different constituency needs: private sector (business and service communities), general public, cultural and other groups; needs and recommended activities related to the media pre- and post-disaster.*

Needs:

- A comprehensive regional public information plan for incidents and disasters that covers health, safety, and associated preparedness, response, and recovery issues addressing different scenarios.
- A single Internet website for regional emergency preparedness/management and related public health information that provides detailed, clear, consistent, coordinated information.
- A process to ensure timely information is provided to the public on vaccine availability and distribution and priority groups for vaccination that takes into account that private sector organizations and the general public have different information needs.
- Recognition of the local media as a "first responder" in significant incidents or disasters and a means to communicate critical information and educate the public.
- Ways to use the Internet and social networks for outreach during pre- and post-disaster preparedness response and recovery phases.
- Identification and access to disaster-related open source information that the media can use to gain awareness and better communicate to the public.
- Inclusion of local media in regional and targeted workshops and exercises.
- A vulnerability assessment of the Emergency Broadcast System and other regional warning systems to ensure they are fully reliable.

- A strategy to maintain civil order if critical infrastructure services are disrupted and the opportunity for civil unrest escalates.
- Education at K-12 levels on resilience-related issues.

Recommended Actions

Short-Term

- A disaster public information and communication plan that identifies:
  - The types of information provided;
  - Target audiences, including at-risk and other groups;
  - Types of media used;
  - What messages should be conveyed;
  - Designated communicators;
  - What vulnerabilities exist regarding communications systems that could impede information dissemination; and
  - Types of educational tools required.
- Development, with selected media, of guidelines on how to utilize the media in large-scale disasters.
- *RDR Guides* for media on critical infrastructure interdependencies to help them understand the issues, weapons of mass destruction events (nuclear, radiological, biological and chemical), and cyber attacks.
- Refine procedures to provide public service announcements, including developing alternate and redundant ways to inform the public during a regional disaster.
- Creation of a short list of trusted subject matter experts to provide expertise to media under the director of designated public information points-of-contact.
- Conduct a training course on interacting with the media for essential employees in the event of an emergency.
- Undertake a training course for law enforcement personnel on how to deal with civil unrest and panic situations during a disaster.

Medium-Term

- Develop a risk communications tool-box (guidelines, procedures, and information to facilitate effective communication of pertinent, all hazards disaster-related information to the public and media; should include a glossary of common terms).

- Develop a comprehensive regional public information strategy for incidents and disasters that covers health and safety and associated preparedness, response and recovery issues addressing different scenarios, identifies target audiences, what information to convey, and how it would be coordinated and disseminated.
- Designate and develop a single regional Internet website for regional emergency preparedness/management and related public health information that provides detailed, clear, consistent, coordinated information with links to local jurisdiction and other relevant websites.
- Creation of a regional Joint Information Center that includes public affairs officers of key public, private sector, and non-profit stakeholder organizations.

Long-Term: Development of a dynamic web-based system to enable key stakeholder personnel to get answers from experts on all-hazards disaster resilience issues.

XIII. Exercises, Education, & Training

Priority Issues: *Target audiences; Incident Command System training for private sector organizations; focus on training from "business" perspective; inclusion of key stakeholder organizations in full-scale exercises; development and documentation of lessons learned from regional and targeted regional exercises, workshops, and other training events; training tools and activities (course curriculum webinars, workshops, train the trainers, etc.), that can be incorporated into regional disaster resilience activities.*

Needs:

- A regional strategy for resilience training and education.
- Educational forums for local media to enable them to better understand the challenges of regional disasters, what to expect from government, utilities and other key stakeholders, and to provide knowledge of local, state and federal disaster plans.
- A multi-year program of tabletop and field exercises that has a regional focus, involves all key stakeholders and selected media, and does not overburden or "exercise to death" local organizations.
- Education for stakeholders, media, and legislators on the following:
  - Regional infrastructure interdependencies and their impacts on regional disasters;

> ○ Impacts of long-term power outages and rolling blackouts;
>
> ○ Cyber threats and disruptions;
>
> ○ Pandemic flu and other significant health-related threats; and

- Weapon of mass destruction (radiological, nuclear devices, chemical) impacts, response, and recovery issues.

Recommended Actions

Short-Term

- Incorporate in a regional five-year exercise plan at least one tabletop exercise per year that includes the broad key stakeholder community.
- Develop and conduct an educational seminar for local media that includes local government officials to address priority all-hazards disaster scenarios and public communication challenges, including how the media and local government can effectively cooperate to convey information to the public.
- Develop a strategy as part of a broader regional resilience continuity plan for training and education for businesses, community institutions and the general public.
- Develop and conduct targeted workshops to discuss response and restoration for challenging scenarios that will require specialized scientific and technical expertise, for example a chemical, radiological or nuclear incident or bio-attack.

Medium-Term

- Develop tools for educating public officials and citizens on local disaster preparedness and management plans and challenges, e.g., specialized publications, a "trade show" type booth set-up outside public meetings to disseminate public information, etc.
- Create a public-private exercise planning work group to develop a coordinated multi-year plan of tabletop and field exercises that avoids duplication of effort.
- Develop training courses for the public and media and interested staff of key stakeholders on the impacts of long-term power outages and rolling blackouts; regional infrastructure interdependencies and their impacts; cyber threats and disruptions; and weapons of mass destruction impacts, response, and restoration issues.
- Develop a web-based calendar of homeland security-related events to provide a heads-up to stakeholders on training opportunities and to de-conflict event schedules.

Long-Term: Continue regular regional exercises to further broaden interdependencies knowledge at deeper levels and to evaluate new and upgraded plans, procedures, and prevention/mitigation measures.

XIV. Determining Regional Resilience Financial & Other Resource Needs

Priority Issues: *Determining resources needed for pre- and post-event protection and mitigation and training and exercises; post disaster funding/reimbursement: federal, state, and local governments; private sector; criteria for assistance, assistance availability, and challenges for the private sector; non-profit and community organizations; loans and incentives to small and medium size businesses for disaster preparedness.*

Needs:

- Information on disaster assistance available from various federal and state sources with criteria and guidelines for applying.
- Avenues for local jurisdictions to secure funds for pre-event mitigation activities for high-probability, high-consequence threats.
- A disaster assistance mechanism with procedures to enable the collection of funds from non-government sources, including private donations that can provide vetted, appropriate distribution to businesses that suffer either direct or indirect harm.
- Ways in which government assistance programs for the private sector could be expanded.
- Innovative collaborative arrangements among financial institutions to provide loans and other investment funds to restore and rebuild communities.
- Access to disaster assistance best practices that states, localities, private sector, and non-profit organizations have developed.

Recommended Actions

Short-Term

- Create or utilize an existing work group to explore ways in which government assistance programs can be expanded for the private sector.
- Develop and conduct a targeted workshop that includes relevant federal officials and local government agency and political officials to discuss ways to secure resources (e.g., types of grants, programmatic funds, in-kind, volunteer and other available support) for resilience activities.

Medium-Term

- Develop a brochure (hardcopy and electronic) outlining disaster assistance available from federal and state sources with criteria and guidelines for applying.
- Encourage and promote collaboration among regional financial institutions to devise procedures, including mutual agreements, to facilitate investment for post-disaster recovery and restoration.

Long-Term: Develop options for a regional assistance non-profit mechanism that can enable the collection of funds from non-government sources, including private donations and that can provide vetted, appropriate distribution to businesses that suffer either direct or indirect harm from incidents or disasters.

Establishing the Regional Disaster Resilience System

The Action Plan is an initial effort to identify activities that can be undertaken individually and collectively by regional stakeholders to improve disaster resilience. At the same time, the Action Plan provides a checklist and avenue for systematically assessing and upgrading plans, procedures, policies, expertise, protection, mitigation tools, and technologies to assist this effort.

Action Plan Implementation

Once the Action Plan is finalized and validated by the stakeholders, the next steps are to reconvene them to prioritize the activities in the Action Plan to develop a "doable number" of actions that stakeholders wish to undertake and for which funding and/or expertise are available. At the Action Planning Workshop, the stakeholders will also begin to determine which agencies and organizations will be the lead for each of the activities and other organizations that wish to participate in the respective projects. The final step will be to create or utilize existing work groups, committees, or other mechanisms to develop requirements for the respective activities, including a work plan and schedule for project completion.

The coordination and finalization of the Action Plan marks the end of what is the first phase to develop the Regional Disaster Resilience System. The Action Plan, as previously noted, is a dynamic roadmap leading towards enhanced resilience and should be considered an integral element in a continuous improvement process in which lessons learned from events and disasters, as well as results from additional regional tabletops and conventional exercises, workshops and other events are incorporated as new needs with corresponding activities to address them.

The Importance of a Resilience-Focused Public-Private Partnership & Facilitating Entity

As noted previously, there should be an existing collaborative arrangement or a public-private partnership created to undertake implementation of the Action Plan. This partnership may well be informal, with membership open to interested key stakeholder organizations and no defined organizational structure. Many government and business organizations for legal or ethical reasons are not able to join in formal agreements with governance systems.

Even more essential to Action Plan implementation is the availability of a facilitating organization or mechanism to reconvene stakeholders, assist in establishing the work groups to develop requirements for Action Plan activities, and provide basic administrative and logistics support services. This facilitating organization will also help in identifying potential implementation resources—grants and other financial resources, expertise, and tools and technologies that can be leveraged.

Stakeholders may elect to set-up this mechanism themselves or a community or regional group or association may take on this role. This mechanism optimally should be an established non-profitable to take in funds from different sources, public and private, for cooperative activities. There are a growing number of diverse resilience-focused public-private partnerships and various models for this type of mechanism across the United States and in other nations. In the United States alone, there are dozens of these at the multi-state, state, county and local levels. Some large metropolitan areas and states may have multiple collaborations centering on the needs of different communities and groups.

All of these collaborations have unique characteristics based on the regions they serve and the interests of the member organizations. Some examples of regional resilience partnerships in the United States at the state and city level include the following:

- Pacific NorthWest Economic Region's Puget Sound Partnership and broader Pacific Northwest Partnership for Regional Infrastructure Security and Resilience (five states and five Canadian provinces and territories)
- All-Hazards Consortium (nine Mid-Atlantic states)
- Southeast Emergency Response Network (11 Southern states)

- Southeast Wisconsin Homeland Security Partnership
- Safeguard Iowa Partnership
- New Jersey Business Force
- State Partnership—Utah
- Alaska Partnership for Infrastructure Protection
- ReadySanDiego Business Alliance

Maintaining Momentum & Sustainability

There are broad and inter-related challenges to forward progress towards regional resilience once the initial foundation is laid with the stakeholder-validated Action Plan. These challenges center around two big issues:

1. Continuing and sustaining stakeholder enthusiasm and momentum generated by the Multi-Step Process, as well as gaining the necessary support and encouragement from government, private sector, and political leaders; and
2. Obtaining resources to undertake implementation of initial Action Plan activities.

These fortunately are surmountable. What is most important is establishing and sustaining a working regional public-private partnership to assist in identifying preparedness shortfalls, validating and prioritizing the Action Plan activities selected for implementation and undertaking individual and collaborative solutions to address these gaps.

Also essential is the need to create, within this regional partnership, ways to enable the secure sharing of information, engage multiple organizations in project development, and pool resources from various organizations while avoiding conflict of interest. This will require on the part of local and state governments a flexibility and willingness to give partnership members a say in regional planning, implementation, and funding decisions.

Creating or enhancing an existing public-private partnership with a dedicated part-time facilitator—ideally a community or regional organization in this role—is sufficient. Support from a few key leaders may be all that is necessary, particularly if these include county and municipal emergency management, public health and other key agency officials with disaster resilience missions, and major businesses in the community. Universities and colleges in the region can provide valuable support through providing expertise or venues for meetings and events.

Securing the Necessary Resources

Critical to the success of regional efforts to achieve disaster resilience is the federal government, both civilian and defense, which will need to provide the technical expertise, seed money, and in certain cases, substantial investment for many of the activities in the Action Plan. A key challenge will be determining how to best develop the organizational structure and programs to do this that can supplement traditional state and local funding mechanisms. Few models exist that enable federal dollars to be provided to regional entities. Consequently it is important that facilitating organizations supporting regional partnerships have non-profit status to allow provision of grants and other government funds for resilience enhancements.

Regarding resources, there are an increasing number of avenues—public program funds and grants, foundation and non-profit resources, and private sector investment. Particularly promising is the new priority focus at the federal level on resilience in the United States and by an increasing number of other national governments. (See the TISP *RDR GuideToolkit* website for information and links to additional useful sources of assistance.). With access to public seed money for resilience projects, increasingly local industry and business interests are also contributing to these efforts.

At the same time, impediments to providing public funds directly to regional mechanisms need to be overcome through policy changes where necessary. This is significant, because most community resilience improvement activities will have no single lead organization but multiple stakeholders participating. Traditional funding through state and local government may not be available or appropriate where funds and support from multiple sources are involved. Also, state and local governments express concern about not being able to meet "unfunded mandates" from resilience action planning activities.

Measuring Progress Made

There is currently considerable focus and discussion among national policymakers, academicians, and others in the research community on metrics for all hazards resilience. A number of disparate efforts are underway to develop resilience measurement capabilities and metrics, some that focus on infrastructures or based on still evolving regional risk assessment approaches. There also has been much work accomplished over the past decade that can be leveraged—physical and cyber security standards, guidelines, and assessment tools and technologies for infrastructure sectors and facilities.

There are various rationales commonly cited on the need for qualitative and particularly quantitative methodologies and tools for measuring resilience. Measuring resilience would:

- Enable prudent allocation by government and the private sector of scarce resources for research and development of prevention and mitigation solutions;
- Provide facility owners with leverage to obtain lower insurance rates; and
- Inspire communities to improve their resilience "level" in order to be "certified resilient" to enable them to attract business investment and new residents.

While these rationales have appeal, as the *RDR Guide* demonstrates, developing an initial baseline understanding of a region's resilience to all-hazard disasters is a complex undertaking requiring a holistic, systematic approach by a broad number of stakeholder organizations. Compounding the problem is that there as yet no general consensus or policy foundation for disaster resilience, nor accepted criteria to determine resilience, or what would constitute an optimal "resilience level."

An additional significant complicating factor is that infrastructure interdependencies are only at best understood at superficial levels, as are human behavioral issues during emergencies. Also, there is the dilemma of defining what needs to be measured, for what purpose, how to accomplish this and to do so on a cost-effective basis; also, how disparate, sensitive, and proprietary data necessary will be collected, stored, assessed, aggregated, and weighted; who will be responsible for assessing it, what tools will be used (or need to be developed) and what resources will be available to support these activities.

Beyond these challenges, measuring disaster resilience requires addressing resilience from the component, asset, and system levels to organizational, community, regional, national, and in some cases global levels. Many organizations may choose not to be involved in developing regional resilience metrics on the basis they are already subject to federal, state, and local regulatory requirements and other standards and guidelines that obligate them to provide safety, reliability and security data. Private sector organizations will not be required to provide proprietary or sensitive information to the government or other stakeholders.

Looking at these hurdles, some experts have suggested that simple criteria could be used to assess resilience levels, for example, the existence of local jurisdiction emergency plans that reference resilience, or conduct of a regional risk assessment, the number of exercises held, existence of a public-private partnership, etc. While these actions indicate that stakeholders have developed a level of awareness and are working together to become more resilient, the actions do not in themselves demonstrate resilience.

In sum, determining realistic, practical and meaningful ways to measure all-hazards disaster resilience is a challenging undertaking that will involve many "players" and will take years to evolve. Subsequent updates of the *RDR Guide* will provide information on measuring regional resilience and metrics as they are developed.

What is Doable in the Near-Term

While it is premature to devise ways to measure resilience in quantitative terms, there is a simple, practical, flexible, stakeholder-focused approach to determining progress made—the Action Plan developed through the Multi-Step Process. The Action Plan framework of focus areas and priority issues provides stakeholders with a self-developed broad set of criteria—essentially a resilience checklist—for what they themselves have determined needs to be accomplished. Thus, progress towards resilience can be measured in terms of Action Plan activities initiated, in progress or completed. As the Action Plan is augmented with additional needs and remedial activities over the years, it provides a running inventory and status report on the increasing disaster resilience level of a region or community.

Building a Culture of Resilience

Developing disaster resilience is a complex and continuous undertaking. It is made all the more difficult by still-evolving understanding of infrastructure interdependencies and limited analytic capabilities to assess potential threats, associated vulnerabilities and disruption consequences, determine cost-effective protection and mitigation options, and measure progress made.

The fact that so many stakeholder organizations have roles and responsibilities or vested interests in disaster resilience adds additional complications and makes multi-jurisdiction, cross-sector and discipline cooperation and coordination essential. An additional, impediment, as has been noted, is the lack of regional mechanisms that can secure funds and support from multiple sources for resilience projects that have no single responsible or "lead" entity. These issues, however, should not impede localities, states, private enterprises, and other organizations from undertaking the activities in the Action Plan, many of which will fall into the "low-hanging fruit" category.

The greatest challenge will be maintaining forward movement on the Action Plan towards regional disaster resilience. Local governments and other organizations will need to take leadership roles for Action Plan activities and a proactive approach to retain and expand stakeholder interest and involvement. In-kind support from stakeholder organizations in the form of personnel involvement in regional resilience activities will be a crucial resource. Most key stakeholders are already involved in many volunteer initiatives and activities in addition to their normal professional duties. This means that progress on implementing Action Plan activities will depend on the willingness of people to provide the necessary leadership, enthusiasm, and expertise to move forward.

The Biggest Benefit: Stakeholder Collaboration & Empowerment

The regional resilience system process outlined in the *RDR Guide* has many benefits—bridging cultural differences among community groups and professional disciplines, building relationships and trust, and exploring and uncovering interdependencies-associated and other resilience gaps. The greatest value, however, is that many stakeholders will emerge out of the experience with a sense of ownership of the Action Plan and a willingness to work together in a partnership to address the shortfalls and the improvement activities they have identified.

Moreover, some individuals will "self-select" themselves for leadership roles and one or more organizations may step into a facilitating role for a regional partnership. This collaborative arrangement, whether formally constituted or informal, will generate and maintain forward movement and momentum on the Action Plan. It is this partnership that we will need to build, maintain, and sustain the continuous process of improvement that increases regional resilience in the years ahead.

Further information, please see: www.tisp.org

6

INTRODUCTION TO PART VI: DISASTER PREPAREDNESS AND EMERGENCY MANAGEMENT

Gregory T. Brunelle

Deputy Director of Operations of the New York State Office of Emergency Management

The illiterate of the 21st century will not be those who cannot read and write, but those who cannot learn, unlearn, and relearn.

—*Alvin Toffler*

Most, if not all, of the students contemplating entering the field of emergency management, as well as those joining the ranks of local, state, or federal emergency management organizations, are drawn to their positions by a desire to help their fellow citizens during the most calamitous of times. Frequently these individuals cite the terrorist attacks of September 11, 2001, or other major disasters such as Hurricane Katrina, as motivation for their interest. Many express a particular interest, perhaps energized by the adrenaline that accompanies emergency work, in responding to disasters.

The genuine work of emergency management is far less exciting than the sliver of time that is devoted to response operations. Even major, complex disasters quickly become long-term recovery efforts. The day-to-day activities of the emergency manager, and generally the majority of their work projects, are focused on the other phases (as described within this section) of preparedness, recovery, and mitigation; work accomplished in office suites by professionals in business attire who attend meetings, type reports, and engage in project management. The purpose of pointing this out is not to deter anyone from pursuing study or work in the field of emergency management. There is room, and a genuine need, for anyone who wishes to contribute, regardless of the root of their altruistic motivations.

Contemporary practitioners of most disciplines know well that their chosen fields of study have advanced to their current depths and maturity through centuries of research, study, and practice undertaken by generations of men and women who labored before them. They often have centuries of data and theories upon which to build their research and execute their practices. The bodies of literature, which lay the foundation of their training and education, provide them with guidance and direction as to what works in their field and, often more importantly, what doesn't work. This literature is "established": recognized by the public and academia as definable, having clear boundaries, predicated upon quantifiable research, and providing the entering student with a clear course of study, from novice to master practitioner.

It is often stated that the discipline of emergency management is "emerging." The intent of this statement is to convey that emergency management is relatively new, and not as fully formed as other, more traditional academically-grounded disciplines. Is this a true assumption? And, if it is, what does that mean for the current student and practitioner?

Certainly the title of "emergency manager" has only recently entered widely used lexicon, perhaps just in the past 30 years. As detailed in this section, "civil defense" was the name given to the practice of coordinating governmental and public response to disasters (primarily nuclear attacks) prior to the last quarter of the twentieth century. With the establishment of the Federal Emergency Management Agency (FEMA), Americans were exposed to the term "emergency management" for the first time. Since then, it can be argued that the public's awareness of emergency management has increased with the advent of the 24-hour news cycle, which allows for more in-depth coverage of emergencies and disasters. By the start of the twenty-first century, it was common for local, state, and federal emergency managers to be quoted by the media, cited as the public safety member or organization responsible for coordinating the wider response. But public awareness of a job title and adoption of terminology does not make a discipline.

It is assumed that practitioners of the emergency management discipline have a much shallower pool of literature and knowledge from which to draw. But is this actually true? For more than a century researchers from a variety of fields of study have been examining disasters that have affected populations. As a result of that research, government entities have passed legislation and enacted codes and ordinances, as well as reorganizing portions of operational structures. For example, major fires that killed dozens and sometimes even hundreds of citizens have directly led to contemporary building codes, including fire escapes, sprinkler systems, audible and visual alarms, and occupancy levels. Breakwaters have been built along harbors and coastlines following disasters resulting from hurricanes and tsunamis. While the research has not been conducted under the banner of emergency management, it exists and should be considered relevant to our discipline. There does remain much left to be examined.

As stated, emergency management is an emerging field. Over the course of the past several decades, practitioners and scholars (many of whom are former practitioners-turned-scholar), have begun to build an impressive library of emergency management-specific literature. Their efforts have begun to give shape not just to the field of study, but also to the scope of responsibility and work that current practitioners undertake. There is a tremendous amount of research waiting to be undertaken which will not just inform current emergency managers; it will advise and guide other disciplines as well. As emergency management scholars examine societal behavior during disasters, engineers will be better informed to design new bridges, buildings, and roads; psychologists will be better suited to treat those exposed to traumatic experiences; community planners and engineers will be able to design cities and critical infrastructures that better protect the citizens who rely on these services. The chapter in this section devoted to the lessons learned from the efforts to evacuate New Orleans during Hurricane Katrina will inform many disciplines besides emergency managers.

The chapters within this section represent some of the latest research in the field of emergency management. Collectively they provide the student with a review of how our field has rapidly evolved over the past many years. The concepts contained within are important for not just the student new to the field, but also to current emergency managers, regardless of their level of experience. The chapter entitled "Emergency Response: An Overview" deftly leverages the concepts of complexity to explain the processes behind a "routine" day-to-day emergency response and the interconnectivity of various disciplines during large, complex disasters. It is essential for emergency managers to understand the psychological consequences of terrorism, and the chapter by Tanielian and Stein provides a solid foundation for this understanding.

Governor Martin O'Malley of Maryland provides an outstanding contribution by demonstrating the pragmatic approach to investing limited resources in definable projects whose positive impacts are achieved not just during disasters but every day, thereby immediately improving the safety of Maryland's citizens.

The exploration of meta-leadership as it relates to disaster response represents the latest niche of emergency management study, and perhaps one of the most important. Nearly every report compiled to examine a major disaster in the past 30 years identifies the effect the quality and capabilities of key leaders have had on the outcome of the emergency response. It is critical that not only research on disaster leadership continue, but that new and seasoned emergency managers become intimately familiar with these concepts and identify ways in which they can grow to become effective in the manner described.

The "Advice in Crisis" chapter explores vital forms of collaboration between crisis management leaders and lawyers in disasters. The authors provide examples of real-time dilemmas confronting emergency managers—each case fraught with uncertainty, time constraints, and the gravest of consequences for the public.

No field of study reaches an end. There will always be more questions to ask and new ways of approaching old and new challenges.

Just as we expect our doctors to stay current with the latest medical practices, our citizens expect us to be effective and astute emergency management practitioners. This requires that we continue to explore our chosen field, ask questions (even difficult ones), and learn from one another.

24

LEARNING FROM HISTORY: THE EVOLUTION OF EMERGENCY MANAGEMENT IN THE UNITED STATES

Jude Colle

Principal at JZ Colle & Associates

Claire B. Rubin

President, Claire B. Rubin & Associates, LLC

This chapter provides a brief account of emergency management in the United States, how it evolved over the past century, and where it intersects with homeland security. The United States has experienced disasters since the nation was founded, yet many people are of the impression that 9/11 was the formative force behind the U.S. emergency response and homeland security systems.

The chapter covers events and outcomes starting with the twentieth century; it includes a brief review of several key concepts and terms critical to understanding the emergency management field, a discussion of some of the political forces and the organizational context in which emergency management activities are conducted, and finally some thoughts about the future of this critical public service. The authors draw heavily on research done for the new book *Emergency Management: The American Experience, 1900–2010*, in which they were both involved.

IMPORTANCE OF KNOWING THE HISTORY OF EMERGENCY MANAGEMENT

Why study history—especially the history of emergency management? The history of emergency management in the United States is more than a litany of devastating disaster events during the past century. The full context of such events is needed in order to interpret events, problems, and issues. We need to document and learn not only from our own experiences but also from others to avoid fatal mistakes. Additionally, if we don't know what worked in the past, we won't be able to repeat it. And if we are unaware of what didn't work, we are more than likely to repeat it! Santayana said it best:

> Those who cannot remember the past are condemned to repeat it.[1]

The U.S. emergency management system developed for the most part in reaction to events rather than through thoughtful, proactive, and deliberate use of science, research, and an understanding of what works and doesn't work. Nationally, an emergency management system featuring public sector responsibility evolved over the past century. During that time, the expectation of citizens and state and local governments has risen substantially with regard to the government's role in disasters. As has been seen in some recent major disasters, such as Hurricane Katrina and the BP Oil Spill, those expectations may be somewhat unrealistic given the complex nature of our federalist system of government. As specified in enabling legislation, the federal government has distinct powers and responsibilities that may be used only to supplement state and local capabilities, and must await a request from state and local governments before it can step in. Therefore, the federal response system may not always be able to move in quickly to assist states. In addition, "our Constitution makes some powers of government discrete, e.g., local governments determine land use and building standards, but other responsibilities of state and local governments are shared or may even overlap."[2]

Another reason that emergency management is a difficult field of public management is that "disasters are rare, attention-grabbing, tragic, and even catastrophic events, and so by nature, they catch people by surprise even when there is a history, statistically predictable pattern, and likelihood of their occurrence."[3]

KEY CONCEPTS IN DISASTER AND EMERGENCY MANAGEMENT

Before going further into our discussion of emergency management, it may be useful to review a few concepts (and their associated terms) critical to understanding this field. These concepts include the phases of emergency management, the hazards and associated categories of disasters, and disaster declarations.

Phases in Emergency Management

Traditionally there are four phases in the emergency management cycle. While each is distinct and can stand alone, these phases often overlap:

- *Mitigation.* Steps to prevent future disasters or minimize the effects of unavoidable events. The homeland security field has added a fifth phase, prevention; however, the emergency management field considers prevention a form of mitigation. We cannot prevent a natural hazard from occurring, but we can take steps (mitigation) to minimize its effects on people and property.
- *Preparedness.* Steps taken to prepare for disasters; this includes developing plans, stockpiling supplies, and conducting simulations.
- *Response.* Putting the preparedness plans into action by taking steps to deal safely with an ongoing disaster. Includes actions to save lives and protect property, and to evacuate and shelter people and animals.
- *Recovery.* Steps taken to return to normal or a safer situation following a disaster. Includes restoration of buildings and properties and financial assistance to victims.

This chapter focuses mainly on the response phase.

Hazards and Categories of Disasters

Hazards have always existed. They can be natural phenomena, such as hurricanes and earthquakes, or man-made, such as oil spills and releases of chemical products. Hazards become disasters when they affect humans and the built environment, causing injuries and deaths as well as damage and destruction. Disasters in the United States are traditionally grouped into three categories according to the underlying hazard:

- *Natural hazard.* Examples include storms, floods, hurricanes, tornados, earthquakes, volcanoes, viruses, and so on.
- *Man-made accidental hazard.* Examples are chemical spills or a train derailment resulting in a release of toxic material.

- *Man-made deliberate hazard.* Examples include sabotage of an industrial plant or transportation venue, or acts of terrorism.

Presidential Disaster Declarations

Since 1950, presidents have had the authority to officially declare disasters and commit federal resources to assist states and locals. This authority was granted in the Disaster Relief Act of 1950 (as amended by the Stafford Disaster Relief and Emergency Assistance Act).

A presidential disaster declaration must first be requested by the governor, who specifies the disaster is of such severity and magnitude that responding to it effectively is beyond the capacity of the state and local government. The governor's request includes a damage assessment and an estimate of the amount and type of damage. The request is submitted through FEMA to the President. If the President declares a disaster, the state is expected to assume 25 percent of the response costs; in rare cases, such as Hurricane Katrina, this cost-share is waived.

From 1951 through the end of 2011, there have been 2,049 Presidential Disaster Declarations (see Figure 24-1); virtually all for disasters caused by natural hazards except:

- Five declarations for chemical/biological disasters—all between 1962 to 1992 (water contamination, methane gas seepage, chemical waste (Love Canal), and a chlorine barge accident)[4]
- Four declarations for terrorism (World Trade Center explosion in 1993; Oklahoma City bombing in 1995; and the 9/11 attacks in New York and Virginia in 2001)

The remaining 99.6 percent of disaster declarations were for natural hazards. Of those, flooding and severe storms account for over half

Figure 24-1

Declared disasters by year

Data source: Federal Emergency Management Agency; www.fema.gov.

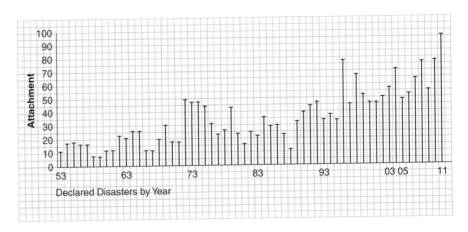

Declared Disasters by Year

of the declarations, followed by tornadoes and fires. Statistically, Americans are far more likely to experience a natural disaster than an act of terrorism.

EVOLUTION OF DISASTER RESPONSE IN THE UNITED STATES OVER THE PAST CENTURY

As noted earlier, a frequent misperception regarding emergency management (especially disaster response) is that 9/11 was the guiding force behind the system. Other beliefs are that there was no emergency management in the United States until the 1950s, or that the current system grew out of the old civil defense program. None of these are true.[5]

At the beginning of the twentieth century, disaster response generally was handled by the victims with help from their neighbors, religious organizations, or the surrounding community. Natural disasters were considered "Acts of God" and beyond the power of government to prevent or mediate. A few national humanitarian organizations, such as the American Red Cross, became involved in response, especially in aiding victims. Occasionally the federal government stepped in and provided military support or a one-time infusion of money. Typically, federal assistance was made available for major structural projects, such as dams, dikes, and levees, but usually not until years after the disaster event.

As time went on, perceptions of the role of government in disaster response gradually changed. For example, in 1927 after the Great Mississippi Flood, at the federal level, a "flood czar" was appointed.[6] In 1933, the State of California began addressing earthquake hazards in at-risk areas in a variety of ways. The Dust Bowl calamity in the 1930s led to a growing federal involvement in land management issues.

By mid-century, government at all levels had gradually become more involved in various aspects of emergency management. The evolution continued, driven in part by the nation's security concerns for the homeland during World War II and the subsequent Cold War.

One measure of the gradual increase in federal involvement is the legislative change in the definition of a disaster from "events caused by natural hazards" to include "man-made events and intentional acts of harm." In turn, this led to the development of a civil defense system to prevent and handle the consequences of such acts.

The passage of the Federal Disaster Assistance Act and the Civil Defense Act (both in 1950) led to the development of two interlocking systems for handling disasters—one focused on natural hazards and the other on civil defense. Increasing tensions with the Soviet Union in the 1960s, as well as the nuclear arms race, led to cyclical changes in funding and to programs that favored civil defense at the expense of natural disasters. However, following a series of natural hazards in the 1960s and '70s, states clamored for a single organization to deal with disasters. In response, President Carter created the Federal Emergency Management Agency (FEMA) in 1979. FEMA instituted a "dual use" system to address natural disasters and civil defense. In addition, FEMA was given the responsibility to develop and manage a "continuity of government" program to ensure federal government operations would continue in the event of a nuclear attack.

The emphasis on civil defense and nuclear attack during FEMA's first decade (1980s) again drained attention and resources from the natural disaster arena. The federal government was widely criticized for its slow response to natural events during this period. This criticism was not lost on Governor Bill Clinton, and after he was elected President, he chose James Lee Witt, an experienced state emergency manager, to head FEMA. Witt quickly shifted the focus to natural disasters and scrapped the dual-use policy in order to create the concept of "all hazards" for disaster response and management. "Both disaster relief funding and the types of disasters considered eligible for (federal) relief increased. ... Together, growth in political support for relief efforts and increased professionalism in emergency management created an environment where the federal government's role expanded. ..."[7] As the twentieth century concluded, emergency management was beginning to be regarded as the "quintessential" public service at all levels of government.[8]

In the first decade of the twenty-first century, the United States experienced three major catastrophic disasters, one in each of the three disaster categories:

- *Man-made deliberate.* The attacks on the World Trade Center in New York and the Pentagon in Virginia were the worst acts of terrorism in U.S. history (September 2001).
- *Natural.* Hurricanes Katrina/Rita across the Gulf Coast resulted in the largest impact and most costly natural disasters to date (September 2005).
- *Man-made accidental.* The BP Oil Well Explosion and Spill in the Gulf of Mexico was the largest and most costly domestic hazmat incident (April 2010).

Each of these disasters demonstrated unusually destructive characteristics, attracted significant national and international attention, and laid bare deficiencies in the plans, systems, and processes used for all phases of emergency management at all levels of government. Collectively they may be a harbinger of what is to come. As can be seen from the accompanying chart on declared major disasters (from *Congressional Quarterly*), the trend line for numbers of declared disasters has gone up relatively steadily since 1988. In fact, at the end of 2011 it was clear that the record has been broken—2011 had the most declarations in one year (99), of which 14 cost over $1 billion each![9]

POLICY, POLITICAL, AND ORGANIZATIONAL CONTEXT IN WHICH EMERGENCY MANAGEMENT EXISTS

This section focuses on some of the salient observations by Roberts, Ward, and Wamsley to highlight some of their astute observations about critical deficiencies and issues that persist in our national emergency management system. In the United States, emergency management exists within a policy and political framework that is in constant flux. "The field contains a wide variety of people and organizations with vastly diverse backgrounds and perspectives."[10] And in the inherently unstable environment of disaster response, change is continuous. In *Rediscovering Institutions: The Organizational Basis of Politics*, the authors provide a solid discussion on the problems that occur with attempts to reform government organizations that exist in highly unstable environments.[11]

In emergency management there is often a perceived distinction between political agendas and the need for an efficient and well-run response operation. According to Roberts, Ward, and Wamsley, this distinction is false because:

> [P]olitics is an integral part of policy making and implementation whether we acknowledge it or not. Nonetheless, this false dichotomy continues to shape perceptions and behavior within both the political and administrative systems. The result is that government decision makers often pursue political agendas in accordance with the assumption that government agencies can and will be able to use rational methods of management, thereby

> maximizing efficiency and economy in implementing policies. But [agencies] cannot always do so and "blame games" inevitably ensue among the participants.[12]

The authors go on to note that "fulfilling the aims of political agendas while maintaining the stability and efficiency that rational (management) methods require is inherently problematic."[13] Further, the authors discuss what they feel is the origin of this problem:

> The root of the problem is political, not scientific. In a complex system in which there is an overlapping of political authorities, the failure to achieve an effective response to a disaster leads to a political blame game. This process is fueled by the ever-present myth of "can do" rationality in administration in general and emergency management in particular. In emergency management, rising expectations of politicians and citizens … exacerbate the problem. As public expectations rise, the likelihood of a failure to live up to them increases as well. Thus, when a disaster leaves victims and the public at large demanding an explanation for the loss of their loved ones and their property, it should come as no surprise that no one is willing to accept blame.[14]

Another downside of the "can do" myth is the entrenched belief that "government should be run like a business—a belief that ignores the fact that government in general and emergency management in particular, is far more complicated than business."[15]

Any effort to conduct objective analysis of disaster responses and emergency management systems is complicated by the "blame game." The difficulty of "objectively analyzing complex and changing systems in a political environment contributes to the seeming inability of the U.S. to develop a stable system of response."[16] We ignore the complexity of the emergency management system and the role that this complexity has played at our own peril. This ignorance also has led to what Roberts, Ward, and Wamsley call "a chronically failing system."[17]

Further complicating the situation, the expectations of the many publics affected by a disaster of what the federal government will do are often unrealistic or unreasonable. For example, the cry of a local public official in the Miami/Dade County area of "where's the cavalry?" after Hurricane Andrew (1992) or of Governor Blanco's request to "send everything" after Hurricane Katrina (2005) indicates that local and state expectations are that the federal government will quickly come in and make things whole (while paying the bill for local response and recovery).

In addition to rising expectations by citizens and state and local officials, the expanding role of the federal government in disaster response has increased the complexity of the emergency management system. Federal involvement has led to a growth in the amount of coordination and the complexity of interactions among all levels of government.

DEVELOPING AN EFFECTIVE EMERGENCY MANAGEMENT SYSTEM

As discussed, effective and sustainable emergency management continues to elude all levels of government. Various organizational structures have been developed, tweaked, and/or discarded over the past century.

Roberts, Ward, and Wamsley state that "developing an effective system of emergency management requires understanding how networks function."[18] Researchers Laurence O'Toole and Kenneth Meier define networks as "structures of interdependence involving multiple organizations or parts thereof, where one unit is not merely the formal subordinate of the others in some larger hierarchical arrangement."[19] Networks form over a common mission; develop trust among participants; pool their resources and capacities, thereby achieving a synergy not available otherwise; and are usually effective where quick, decentralized decision making is required.

The emergency management system of the 1990s was similar to a network approach in which all levels of government were on equal footing. The federal government, rather than being in a "top dog" position, was viewed as a 'catalyst' for leadership.

The changes that took place in the emergency management system in the 1990s positioned the system neither at one centralized point with the federal government nor with state and

> local governments. Rather, the system resided in some middle ground between these levels of government. After the concerns of all the entities involved in the disaster response system were considered, the resulting perspective reflected a "multifactor" environment that was based on an understanding of the capacities of the various entities and the context in which each of the principal response organizations operated.[20]

As the authors noted, the key to success of this network approach was extensive communication between the 1990s FEMA (as a central leader and catalyst) and the numerous state and local governments and private and non-profit sector participants that made up the network.

> Ultimately, the office of the president was charged with developing an effective emergency management system to serve the national public interest, but state and local governments and private entities were considered equal partners with specific constraints that need to be addressed realistically and pragmatically.
>
> FEMA's role in the 1990s was to uncover potential barriers to collective action and collaboration and to develop incentives to overcome them. *To accomplish this, the agency … relied extensively on personal relationships and discussions with governmental and nongovernmental organizations throughout the U.S.* The goal was to establish solid relationships among all potential responders prior to an actual disaster.[21]

A return to the collaborative network that characterized emergency management in the 1990s and a commitment to building strong relationships and trust among and between all levels of government, the private sector, and citizens would go far to improve our emergency management system.

THE LIKELY FUTURE OF EMERGENCY MANAGEMENT IN THE UNITED STATES

The intent of this section is to consider the future of emergency management at the *national* level in the United States. An analysis of the today's headlines may provide a glimpse into tomorrow:

- As our population increases and more people move to disaster-prone areas such as the coasts, disasters are likely to be bigger, more complex, and costlier.

- Climate change and weather will likely become increasingly erratic, causing an upswing in the severity of natural hazards such as hurricanes, storms, floods, and tornados.

- Increasing geological stresses will cause earthquakes and volcanoes in unexpected places, outside the reach of most people's lifetime memories.

- Evolving terrorist threats, new diseases, and industrial accidents will test existing plans, programs, and processes, as well as our ability to cope with these events.

- All levels of government will be operating with economic and fiscal constraints and will be expected to do more with less.

- The growing global economy means more interdependence and secondary effects for the United States from international disasters, including disruptions in supply chains and economic losses.

What Is Needed to Meet the Demands of the Future?

The sheer scale and complexity of the issues facing emergency management in the future are daunting. Addressing those issues and meeting the myriad of needs for an effective system requires a firm and continuous commitment on the part of government, the private sector, and citizens. Numerous steps are worth taking, but the most critical include the following:

- A macro-level vision coupled with far-sighted, comprehensive, and strategic thinking about emergency management. The "Strategic Foresight Initiative" launched by FEMA, and its first report, "Crisis Response and Disaster Resilience 2030," is an excellent step in this direction.[22]

- Strong leaders and knowledgeable managers with the ability to galvanize, motivate, and inspire.

- An informed and responsible citizenry that takes appropriate steps to protect themselves and their families.

- A return to the collaborative network that characterized emergency management in the 1990s and a commitment to building strong relationships and trust among all levels of government, the private sectors, and citizens.

- More training and education in risk management, decision science, and management of complex systems.
- A strong and unwavering commitment to pre-disaster mitigation, which James Lee Witt called the "ultimate form of emergency management." The National Institute of Building Sciences has done research that shows for every $1 invested in mitigation, $4 can be saved post disaster.
- A restructuring of the National Flood Insurance Program and similar ventures that have sought to reduce risk for people in disaster-prone areas. These programs inadvertently encourage risk taking by property owners who continue to build in risky areas, confident that federal tax monies will bail them out.
- Require state and local governments to consider the consequences of building in disaster-prone areas and engage in proper mitigation and/or force property owners to assume 100 percent of the risk and not expect taxpayers from across the nation to pay for their losses.
- Fund more research in all phases of emergency management and encourage widespread use of existing research coupled with better science and technology—both basic and applied.

CONCLUSION

Although the 9/11 disasters were a major milestone, they were not the first or only formative force behind the United States emergency response and homeland security systems. Emergency management systems have been around for decades, with ever expanding roles by governments at all levels. Concurrently, citizens and politicians often have rising, and unrealistic, expectations of what government—especially the federal level—can deliver. Emergency management has become the quintessential public service, but without the level of funding and political support to conduct the job properly. The can-do attitude will only work if basic knowledge of disasters and needed leadership and management capabilities are developed for the complex, continuously changing, unpredictable, unstable, and chronically underfunded field of disaster response. As we go forward into an uncertain but likely more complicated future, we need a strong commitment from our citizens and political institutions to meet the emergency management challenges of tomorrow.

NOTES

1. George Santayana, *Life of Reason,* vol. 1, 1905.

2. Patrick Roberts, Robert Ward, and Gary Wamsley, "The Evolving Federal Role in Emergency Management," in *Emergency Management: The American Experience 1900–2010,* 2nd ed., Claire Rubin, ed. (Boca Raton, FL: CRC Press, 2012), 247.

3. Ibid.

4. http://www.fema.gov/news/disasters.

5. For a complete discussion of the history of emergency management in the United States, see *Emergency Management: The American Experience 1900–2010,* Claire Rubin, ed. (Boca Raton, FL: CRC Press, 2012).

6. Herbert Hoover was appointed by President Coolidge to coordinate relief efforts after the Great Mississippi Flood of 1927.

7. Roberts et al., "The Evolving Federal Role in Emergency Management: Policies and Processes," 241.

8. As noted by Prof. William Waugh in Living with Hazards, Dealing with Disasters; 2000; M. E. Sharp.

9. Claire B. Rubin and Jessica Hubbard, "Year of the Billion-Dollar Disaster," *Emergency Management Magazine,* January/February 2012, 26–30.

10. Roberts et al. "The Evolving Federal Role in Emergency Management." 252.

11. James March and Johan Olsen. *Rediscovering Institutions: The Organizational Basis of Politics* (New York: Free Press; 1989).

12. Roberts et al. "The Evolving Federal Role in Emergency Management," 252.

13. Ibid.

14. Ibid., 253.

15. Ibid., 254.

16. Ibid., 253.

17. Ibid., 254.

18. Ibid., 263.

19. Laurence O'Toole Jr. and Kenneth Meier, "Modeling the Impact of Public Management: Implications of Structural Context," *Journal of Public Administration Research and Theory* 9 (October 1999): 507.

20. Roberts et al., 264.

21. Ibid.

22. Federal Emergency Management Agency, "Crisis Response and Disaster Resilience 2030: Forging Strategic Action in an Age of Uncertainty," Progress Report Highlighting the 2010–2011 Insights of the Strategic Foresight Initiative, January 2012, http://www.fema.gov/about/programs/oppa/strategic_foresight_initiative.shtm.

25

A CITY ONCE UNDERWATER: LESSONS LEARNED AND THE STORY OF THE NEW ORLEANS EVACUATION PLAN

J. W. Sneed

LtCol USMC (Retired); Deputy Mayor of Public Safety, Director of the Office of Homeland Security and Emergency Preparedness, City of New Orleans

Stephen A. Murphy

Former Planning Section Chief, New Orleans Homeland Security and Emergency Preparedness; Current Director of Emergency Management, Loyola University

Matthew A. Kallmyer

Former Deputy Director of New Orleans Homeland Security and Emergency Preparedness; Current Director of the Atlanta–Fulton County Emergency Management Agency

INTRODUCTION

On August 29, 2005, the City of New Orleans was impacted by one of the most devastating hurricanes ever recorded. Hurricane Katrina's impact to the city was unparalleled and was one of the single worst natural disasters in United States history.[1] Nearly 80 percent of the city was under water at levels averaging approximately 7 to 9 feet, with a few locations experiencing levels upwards of 15 to 20 feet. These flood water levels remained across the vast majority of the city for weeks and in some cases over a month, as illustrated in Figure 25-1. To the east, the

Figure 25-1
Flood Inundation

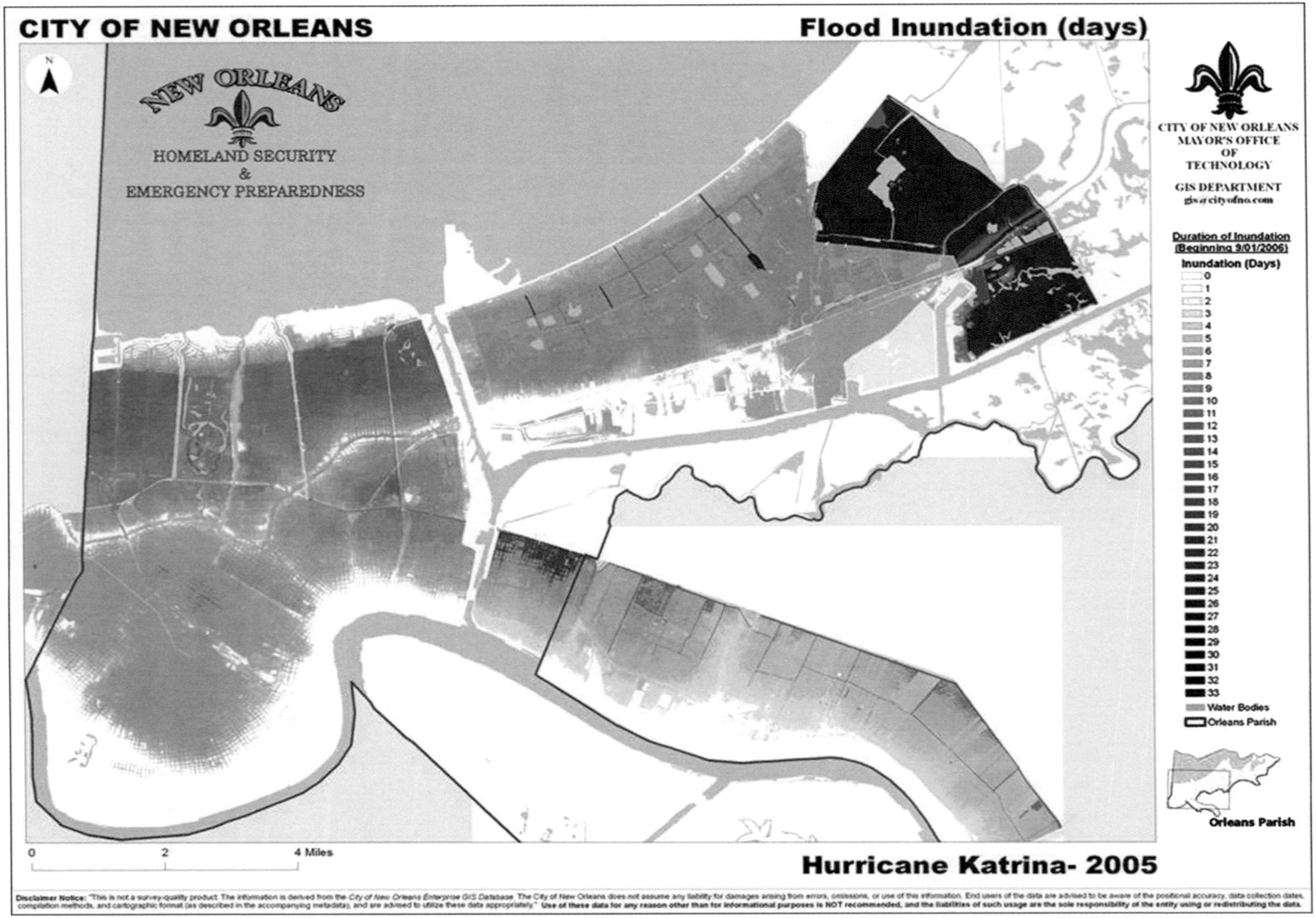

map clearly indicates excessive flooding and extended inundation. The rebuilding process, even for the homes which remained intact following the initial force of the levee breach, would be monumental, needing complete renovations, as the homes would be completely infested with mold and uninhabitable.

Katrina produced nearly 22 million tons of debris, flooded approximately 16,000 businesses, and destroyed 40 schools.[2, 3] The exact total economic impact may never be known, but estimates suggest the storm itself caused nearly $135 billion in damages, far surpassing any other disaster in history.[4]

The preceding portrayal clearly illustrates the desperate need for a pre-incident evacuation plan and education concerning the response delivered to the population. The following chapter conveys some of the challenges the City of New Orleans faced in meeting this need following Hurricane Katrina. While most textbooks have offered a look at the various actions taken during the response phase of Hurricane Katrina, this chapter uncovers the complexities of the ultimate emergency preparedness hurdle: *A complete, citywide evacuation before the threat even impacts the city.* It will further detail the steps taken to develop a plan to achieve this Herculean task. The planning assumptions, considerations, and strategies facing the City are discussed and explained as the story of the City Assisted Evacuation Plan is described.

The United States government, international humanitarian experts, and academic scholars have all delivered great contributions to the field of emergency management and the current twenty-first-century threats facing society and our environment. Many of these contributions and advancements are referenced constantly across the preparedness sector in attempts to create a culture of preparedness and resilient community. This chapter illustrates strategies created locally combined with those existing best practices to further enhance the culture of preparedness in New Orleans and attempt to build stronger community resiliency. Please reference other chapters of this book and outside materials, such as the Federal Emergency Management Agency's (FEMA) website, for more complete understanding of the planning process and the planning cycle.

The authors of this chapter would like to recognize the heroic efforts and contributions of those involved in the creation, implementation, and maintenance of the City Assisted Evacuation Plan. While there were several key players that had a significant role and deserve recognition, special thanks goes to the core team members: Col. Terry Ebbert, former Director of the New Orleans Office of Homeland Security; Jerry Tate, former planner of the New Orleans Office of Homeland Security; Dr. Jullette Saussy, former Director of New Orleans EMS; Tom Ignelzi, former Planning Section Chief of the New Orleans Office of Homeland Security; Collins Simoneaux, former Deputy Planning Section Chief of the New Orleans Office of Homeland Security; Kristen Sparacello, former GIS Specialist with the New Orleans Office of Homeland Security; and Major John DiMartini, Louisiana National Guard Liaison Officer and Operations Section Chief at the Union Passenger Terminal.

THE 2005 NEW ORLEANS MINDSET

Before the plan is described, we must understand the mindset of the City of New Orleans at that time. By understanding this mindset, a greater appreciation can be made of the difficulties confronting emergency planners during the creation of the City Assisted Evacuation Plan. In many ways, Hurricane Katrina was the wake-up call for the nation, especially New Orleans, regarding natural disasters in much the same way 9/11 was regarding man-made disasters.

The summer of 2005 brought with it the typical excitement of outdoor summertime fun as well as the associated dreaded, intense heat in the Crescent City. Despite being inundated annually with weather-related events, the mindset of the typical New Orleanian had grown to be more complacent than those in the current field of emergency management would appreciate. For decades, the annual beginning to the Atlantic Hurricane Season, June 1, came and went without much impact to the Crescent City and the attention paid to that date became minimal. Why should it be a concern? It had been, after all, 40 years since the last major tropical cyclone impacted the New Orleans area. Despite reminders of the symbolic and seemingly arbitrary date of June 1, the general public was unfazed regarding the fact that New Orleans sits below sea level and also rests in the crosshairs of "hurricane alley."

The overwhelming majority of the residents were more concerned with wondering how bad the summer heat and humidity would be and how that would affect the Saints training camp than updating their hurricane plans for evacuation or sheltering. Everyone was lulled into thinking they were being protected. Year after year, storms threatened to impact the New Orleans Metro area, but some voodoo magic always prevailed and forced these systems to either veer away from New Orleans or lose their intensity at the last possible minute. The greatest impact was woody debris, minor power outages, and localized street flooding. These less than dramatic incidents are what led to the creation of hurricane parties or an unscheduled day off from work or school. Many New Orleanians would rent a hotel room for the duration of the storm and conduct what some call "vertical evacuation." By remaining high and dry in the hotels across the city, many citizens began to believe this was all that was necessary to avoid disaster. Was this good practice? Would the hotels be capable of supporting their guests for the first few days after a catastrophic incident? If the water treatment facilities and the sewerage system were compromised, wouldn't the hotels be compromised as well?

Year after year, an ever-increasing number of New Orleanians opted to remain behind to "weather a storm" in some fashion and not evacuate the area. Many of them believed that since they survived Hurricane Betsy, or were not adversely affected, why should another storm force them out? Forty years had passed since Hurricane Betsy targeted New Orleans in the summer of 1965, which marked the last major storm prior to 2005 that significantly impacted the City. Hurricane Betsy[5] was a colossal Category 4 storm that caused severe damage across the Gulf Coast of Louisiana as well as levee failures that resulted in widespread flooding across New Orleans. But the fact remained that a growing number of people, despite the threat, felt safe remaining in the City, adopting an "out of sight, out of mind" mentality.

This mindset coupled with the newer term coined "preparedness fatigue" has further complicated the job of emergency managers. However, Katrina changed the mindset of many across the New Orleans area for the foreseeable future, as it presented a "perfect storm" of sorts.

It is no secret that New Orleans is considered a major tourist destination. The combination of southern hospitality, rich culture, world-renowned cuisine, and old-time jazz provides an intoxicating elixir that is sure to charm and captivate even the toughest critic. Another large tourist draw for the City of New Orleans is the Ernest N. Morial Convention Center. The 1.1 million square feet of contiguous exhibit space has easily allowed this property to be one of the largest convention facilities in the nation, and it consistently ranks in the top 10 in popularity for convention and trade show destinations. During this particular weekend, the City was playing host to the annual EMS Expo, which is arguably the largest annual gathering of emergency medical personnel in North America. The lulled mindset and tourism draw was in full effect as Katrina approached.

Planning Process Begins

The aftermath of Hurricane Katrina was devastating. The content of this chapter is not designed to cover what happened, but to uncover the reasons for and complexities of building an evacuation plan. For specifics regarding Hurricane Katrina, please reference the Greater New Orleans Data Center and other reputable resources.

Immediately upon reconstitution of the city, just weeks after the storm's flood waters began to recede, the focus of the New Orleans Office of Homeland Security became clear and monumental at the same time. Former Director, Col. Terry Ebbert, USMC (Ret), delivered objectives for immediate action: (1) Determine why people did not evacuate prior to the storm; (2) develop a functional evacuation plan before the start of the 2006 Hurricane season (June 1, 2006); (3) create and maintain an environment where the decision to evacuate becomes more desirable than remaining behind; (4) provide greater support to citizens who need special assistance; and (5) implement measures to greatly enhance the security of city resources. These objectives became the berthing concept of the City Assisted Evacuation Plan (CAEP).

Emergency management practitioners know that identifying the risk and conducting a Hazard Vulnerability Assessment, or HVA, initiates the planning process. The risk assessment is the beginning of the entire preparedness cycle and should be updated at least annually for every community. As communities evolve, so do the risks, rendering former risk assessments obsolete over time. The risk to New Orleans, which is a tropical cyclone in this case, was clear and easy to identify. The question still remained, though; what level of tropical cyclone intensity would trigger an evacuation? That was the more detailed portion of this risk assessment and analysis that needed addressing.

To understand the intensity of hurricanes, emergency management practitioners must become familiar with the Saffir-Simpson Hurricane Wind Scale. Named for its developers Herb Saffir, a wind engineer, and Bob Simpson, a meteorologist, Atlantic hurricanes are categorized into five levels of intensity by the Saffir-Simpson Scale (see Table 25-1).[6] The scale provides wind speed intensity associated with each category of storm ranging from the lower level of a Category 1 up to the highest level of a Category 5.

Table 25-1

2012 Saffir-Simpson
Hurricane Wind Scale

Category of Storm	2012 Expected Wind Speeds
Category 1	74–95 mph
Category 2	96–110 mph
Category 3	11–129 mph
Category 4	130–156 mph
Category 5	>157 mph

Hurricane Katrina was, like a select few others, tangled across the parameters of the Saffir-Simpson Scale categorizations. As it made landfall, Hurricane Katrina was a Category 3 storm but produced a storm surge associated with a Category 5 storm according to the 2005 Saffir-Simpson Scale. During the creation of the CAEP, the Saffir-Simpson Scale still associated wind speed and expected storm surge with each other inside its categorical rankings. However, it is important to remember that, as of the 2010 Hurricane Season, the Saffir-Simpson Hurricane Wind Scale (SSHWS) no longer provides estimates for storm surge and inland flooding from rainfall[7] because the two are not consistently correlated as originally categorized within the scale. The 2012 modifications to the SSHWS are meant to resolve any potential for confusion associated with conversions among the various units used for wind speed in advisory products and are reflected in Table 25-1. The National Hurricane Center advises that the 2012 change broadens the Category 4 wind speed range by 1 mile per hour (mph) at each end of the range, yielding a new range of 130 to 156 mph. It is also important to note that this change will not alter the category assignments of any storms in the historical record, nor will it change the category assignments for any future storms.[8]

After consulting with the planning team, which included federal partners, local stakeholders, and local subject matter experts, the HVA stratified the risk by strength of storm, and a trigger for evacuation was determined to be if the City was in the "cone of error" of a Category 3 or stronger storm. However, the HVA also determined that depending on the magnitude of a specific storm system, a strong, slow-moving Category 2 storm tracking in a perfect line with New Orleans might trigger an evacuation as well. In similar fashion, with the flexible and scalable initiatives common throughout emergency management, the plan had to remain flexible and alive, ready to become operational at a moment's notice.

Table 25-2

Reasons for not
Evacuating[10]

Primary Reason for Not Evacuating	Percentage of Post-storm Evacuees
Did not have a car or way to leave	34%
Thought the storm would pass and not be as bad	28%
Physically unable to leave	5%
Had to care for someone physically unable to leave	7%
Waited too long	7%
Just did not want to leave	10%
Worried about possessions being stolen	4%

**The Question
Remains:
Why Didn't
the Residents
Leave?**

Leaning on academic theory, studies, and critical analysis of the situation, the reasoning and compilation of supporting data behind the formulation of the CAEP began. During an interview of 680 randomly selected New Orleans Hurricane Katrina evacuees in Houston, TX, performed by The Washington Post, The Henry J. Kaiser Family Foundation, and Harvard School of Public Health, it was noted that people did not evacuate for a litany of reasons (see Table 25-2).[9] Of those interviewed, there were several glaring overall problems that needed to be addressed inside the new CAEP concept if an effective or plausible plan were to be devised.

The findings presented in the table provided the planning group with significant challenges, but nonetheless, this study highlighted some of the planning concerns and provided an excellent reference source to support the planning process. Two glaring problems were identified for the post-Katrina population of the City should an evacuation become necessary: (1) New Orleans has a population that would be in clear need of assistance (regardless the reason) and (2) an informative process would need to coincide with an evacuation plan to convince citizens of the urgency to evacuate.

To help alleviate some of the noted challenges embedded in the findings and provide transportation to the ones in need, the planning group needed to realize and understand how many people were actually in need of assistance during an evacuation and how many transportation resources would be required to accomplish the entire evacuation process. Academic research in psychology, behavioral analysis, and social aspects of crises suggests that at least 10 percent, maybe up to 15 percent, of the population will be incapable of self-rescue, enduring paralyzing anxiety, when facing an emergency situation and will remain incapable of self-rescue while the stressor itself is prevalent.[11] Paralyzing anxiety, the inability to quickly adapt and have rapid, effective decision making, and being overwhelmed with the care and compassion of a loved one—all presented planning pieces had to address and incorporate methods to reach this portion of the population. Based on the survey findings and the literature on psychosocial aspects of disasters, the planning team estimated that approximately 10 to 15 percent of the population would be in need of assistance during an evacuation.

Despite these findings and planning estimates, a few unanswered concerns remained. Were all of these residents healthy enough to ride in an over-the-road coach bus, or were there residents within the population needing additional assistance during transport? During an evacuation, proper transportation should be addressed in much the same way as shelter operations. Individuals whose fragility, mobility, and functional and/or medical disability makes them particularly vulnerable and at-risk in disaster situations will not likely be sheltered with the general population for obvious reasons. Without any documentation to cross-reference for a litany of reasons, this complex issue was difficult to overcome. Based on feedback from subject matter experts within the City's Emergency Medical Service division (New Orleans EMS, or NO EMS) and the healthcare community, a determination was made that of the residents requiring evacuation assistance (10 to 15 percent of the post-Katrina population), 20 percent would require medical resources during an evacuation. During the planning process, this portion of the population came to be known as "Needs Medical Resources."

In the post-Katrina environment, it proved to be very difficult to ascertain the true re-population figures. External partners such as the Greater New Orleans Data Center and the Centers for Disease Control and Prevention, who conducted door-to-door surveys, were able to gather this important information and projected that the population was approximately 250,000 to 300,000 by 2007 to 2008.[12] Based on previously discussed analyses, emergency planners were finally able to create a planning figure of 25,000 to 30,000 individuals that would require transportation assistance, and 5,000 of those individuals would fall under the category of Needs Medical Resources.

Logic Model

To complete the foundation of the planning cycle, a logic model was created to help illustrate the overall flow of decisions and resources needed to fulfill those decisions. A logic model describes the sequence of events for bringing about change by synthesizing the main program elements into a picture of how the program is supposed to work. Often, this model is displayed in a flow chart, map, or table to portray the sequence of steps leading to program results (see Figure 25-2). One of the virtues of a logic model is its ability to summarize the program's overall mechanism of change by linking processes to eventual effects. The logic model can also display the infrastructure needed to support program operations. Elements that are connected within a logic model might vary but generally include inputs (e.g., staff, resources, essential functions), activities, outputs (e.g., who is being reached), and results ranging from short-term or immediate (e.g., awareness of CAEP and education of it) to mid-term or intermediate (e.g., build confidence or increase overall all-hazard preparedness) to long-term effects (e.g., create overall culture of preparedness and resilient community). Creating a logic model allows stakeholders to clarify the program's strategies; therefore, the logic model improves and focuses program direction. It also reveals assumptions concerning conditions for program effectiveness and provides a frame of reference for one or more evaluations of the program.[13]

Specifically, a program planning logic model allows managers to sequence a course of actions that describe how investments link to results.[14] Factors included in such a model include:

- *Inputs.* Resources, contributions, investments that go into the program
- *Outputs.* Activities, services, events, and products that reach people who participate or who are targeted
- *Outcomes.* Results or changes for individuals, groups, communities, organizations, communities, or systems
- *Assumptions.* The beliefs we have about the program, the people involved, and the context and the way we think the program will work
- *External factors.* The environment in which the program exists, including a variety of external factors that interact with and influence the program action[15]

As shown in Figure 25-2, the CAEP Logic Model identified desired outcomes and assets needed to fulfill them in similar fashion as the Nation Response Framework suggests within the Emergency Support Function (ESF) matrix. By leaning on those most frequently active in preparedness and response, engaging nontraditional partners capable of assisting, or completely tasking an agency, department, or stakeholder with an element of this puzzle is common sense across the multifaceted

Figure 25-2
CAEP Logic Model

City Assisted Evacuation Plan (CAEP) LOGIC MODEL

INPUTS	OUTPUTS		OUTCOMES - IMPACT		
	Activities	Participation	Short	Medium	Longer term
What we invest	What we do	Who is reached	Short-term changes we expect	Medium term changes we expect	Long-term Changes we Expect
1. People a. Staff b. Contractors c. Volunteers 2. Materials 3. Time 4. Planning Processes 5. Financial Resources a. Money 6. Equipment 7. Knowledge a. Lessons Learned b. Best Practices c. Research d. New Ideas 8. External Technical Assistance	1. Conduct After Action Reviews Lessons Learned 2. Research a. Best Practices b. Congressional Reports & Investigations c. Interviews d. Literature Searches e. Conduct Surveys 3. Meetings a. Stakeholders b. Partners(Fed, State, Regional, Local) 4. Build Partnerships & Network 5. Indentify Resources Needed 6. Develop a Plan 7. Conduct Drill to Test the Plan	1. People with Critical Transportation Needs (CTN) 2. People that Need Medical Resources (NMR) 3. Civic Groups 4. Church Groups 5. Elderly 6. Homeless 7. Illegal Immigrants 8. Voluntary Organizations Active in Disasters (VOAD) 9. Non-Governmental Organization (NGO) 10. Local Partners 11. Regional Partners 12. State Partners 13. Federal Partners 14. Private partners	1. Awareness a. Informing People that a Plan Exists 2. Increased Knowledge a. Importance of Preparedness 3. Attitudes a. Resistance to New Ideas & Concepts 4. Skills a. How to Develop an Emergency plan b. How to Develop an Emergency Kit 5. Opinions a. Doubts that the Plan can be Accomplished. 6. Motivation a. Self Reliance	1. Change Policy a. Create New Laws 2. Increased Public Confidence a. In the CAEP b. In the Office 3. Increased State of Preparedness a. Personal b. Community c. Government 4. Training	1. Greater Support for Citizens who Need Special Assistance. 2. Create and Maintain an Environment Where the Decision to Evacuate Becomes more Desirable than Remaining Behind. 3. Implement Measures to Greatly Enhance the Security of City Resource.

ASSUMPTIONS

1) Levee's cannot withstand a Category 3 Hurricane
2) 25,000 people will require evacuation assistance
3) 5,000 people will Need Medical Resources
4) Evacuees with have pets that need to be evacuated
5) People that need assistance will register and self identify
6) There would be enough resources to accomplish the mission

EXTERNAL FACTORS

1) National Weather Service's limitations regarding prediction of storms path of intensity
2) Majority of the resources needed to accomplish the mission are contracted.

©MAK

discipline of emergency preparedness and management. These engagements are also reflected throughout federal guidance such as the NRF,[16] PPD 8,[17] and current "Whole Community Approach"[18] to disaster preparedness. The logic model simply orients the planning concepts in a business fashion to create streamlined and necessary steps to achieve the desired outcome, assisting in efficiencies.

Transportation Assistance

The next consideration was how the city would provide transportation assistance. Historical mass movement of individuals relied on bus caravans, carrying maximum capacity of 40 to 50 passengers each, driving out of an area or city. Given the projected number of population needing assistance, that would equate to nearly 500 to 800 over-the-road buses through confirmed contracts and agreements. This possible, single-mode solution carried an immediate planning obstacle, as the impact of 800 or more buses on the road would certainly be a chokepoint for the roadways and hinder the contraflow mechanism, where all lanes of an interstate are opened in a single direction beginning at a specific point. An alternative complement had to be used in conjunction with buses. Regardless, the reliance solely on buses would exhaust local capacity and large, possibly out-of-state, pre-event contracts would be needed to fulfill this resource delta. This would further complicate the mission, since many of these bus vendors would be entering the dangerous, soon-to-be evacuated city with operators unfamiliar with the local terrain. These outside bus operators, despite the fact that these resources would be providing evacuation support, became a major concern, potentially complicating the system due to their lack of familiarity of the City's unique roadway system as well as the location of the various predetermined shelters throughout Louisiana and other states. It was determined that this, as a single resource option, was not viable.

Tri-modal Evacuation

The New Orleans local bus station is co-located with an Amtrak Station, called the Union Passenger Terminal, or UPT, and is home to not only massive queuing lines but also train access. You may ask: Why trains? We answered: Why not? And our answer did not stop there. Decisions were made to rely on an innovative, but extremely complex, tri-modal evacuation model that would use existing infrastructure and resources for a portion of the operations and require additional support for outbound evacuation ops. The tri-modal model relied on planes, trains, and over-the-road buses to evacuate the city.

With the use of trains, projected evacuation efficiencies ramped up dramatically while simultaneously providing an extremely quick and safe system. A single train pulling 10 passenger cars filled with 65 residents per car could move a large amount of people on a track system that would not be crowded and slowed by other vehicles using the roads. This was a perfect scenario because not only did it alleviate extremely heavy road traffic due to self-evacuees and the over-the-road buses, but it allowed for large portions of the population to evacuate safely and efficiently together. A mandatory evacuation carries with it a level of stress unknown to anyone never before experiencing it. Roadways and interstate systems become impassable, and eliminating congestion becomes a priority. Exits will be closed and the standstill traffic can lead to gas outages on the roadway in addition to becoming a chokepoint for mission accomplishment. Trains can easily alleviate that congestion and reduce the burden on the state law enforcement agents directing contraflow and controlling access points on and off the interstate roadways. The ultimate goal was to remove people from the threat, but also to reduce as much stress and anxiety as possible. The decision, at the time, was easy, and agreements were made with the Federal Emergency Management Agency (FEMA) to allocate the resources to the city.

To complete the tri-modal evacuation model, planes entered the equation due to similar reasons—quick evacuation and ability to move large numbers. With assistance from various federal and state entities, decisions and agreements were made to transport residents from the UPT to the International Airport on local transit buses. From there, these evacuees would be flown to another city and sheltered. With FEMA providing assistance and coordination, major agreements were confirmed with the airlines as well as the Louis Armstrong International Airport and the coordination toward mission accomplishment resonated throughout the partnership. Coordination of these moving pieces would be critical, and detailed planning elements are deeply embedded in this model.

The Pick-Up Points

The major launching pad out of the city was determined, but how would the residents get there? As already discussed, many residents did not have vehicles or proper transportation and a vast majority of them relied on public transportation. New Orleans, like every major metropolitan Statistical Area (MSA), has one (if not multiple) public transit systems, and many center around buses.

A Memorandum of Understanding (MOU) was immediately made with the New Orleans local transit authority, the Regional Transit Authority (RTA). The question was then raised: would every bus stop be needed, or would using every bus stop even be feasible? The resource was only half the battle.

By cross-referencing re-population numbers and re-population density with RTA's ridership statistics, the footprint of the local transportation aspect took its initial shape. Based on these elements, 17 RTA bus stops were identified as evacuation pickup points across the New Orleans area and became the primary collection points of the CAEP (see Figure 25-3). Multilingual directional flyers, detailed maps, public service announcements, and close partnerships with the Red Cross, community-based organizations (CBOs), and faith-based organizations (FBOs) for community outreach provided the necessary public engagement to inform residents of the concept and properly identify these stops as being the CAEP pickup points. Individuals were tasked with familiarizing themselves with these points (normal bus stops that were in high use following the storm and four specific sites at senior centers for the elderly) and, in theory, would go to them should an evacuation order be given. From these points, buses would transport the residents to the UPT for complete evacuation. Further, addressing family cohesion at the time of disasters is important. By allowing for triage and family cohesion in the queuing lines at the UPT, the residents could be evacuated with family members.

The resources used to complete this portion of the plan were local transit buses and therefore could not be considered for over-the-road travel covering great distances, reemphasizing the importance UPT triage and outbound portion of the planned system.

Triage

At this point, the system had confirmed (a) how to provide transportation for the population to the UPT and (b) how to provide complete evacuation transportation modes from that point. The schematic shown in Figure 25-4 describes the process flow of the CAEP and the general population pick-up points, as well as the hospital and the tourism industry evacuations.

However, a complex, underlying layer of operations and detailed preplanning protocols was still needed. Once at the UPT, the planning process became extremely complex. How could a quick decision be made to determine if someone could ride on a bus or a train for

Figure 25-3
Evacuation Pick-up Points

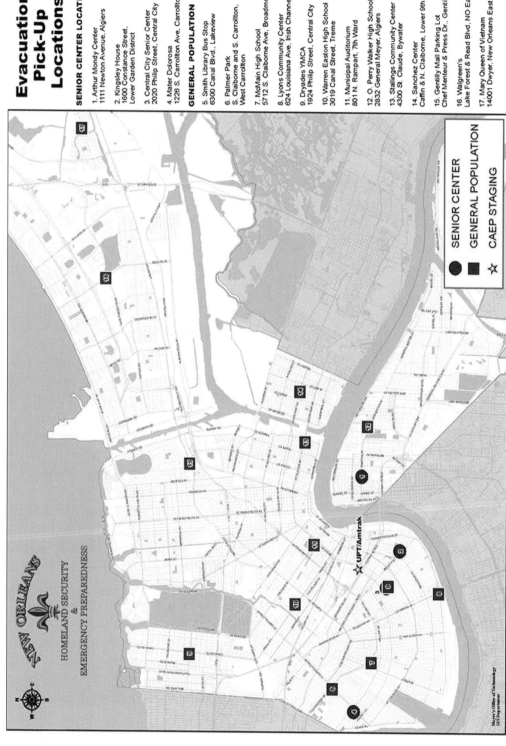

Evacuation Pick-Up Locations

SENIOR CENTER LOCATIONS

1. Arthur Mondy Center
1111 Newton Avenue, Algiers

2. Kingsley House
1600 Constance Street,
Lower Garden District

3. Central City Senior Center
2020 Philip Street, Central City

4. Mater Dolorosa
1226 S. Carrollton Ave. Carrollton

GENERAL POPULATION

5. Smith Library Bus Stop
6300 Canal Blvd., Lakeview

6. Palmer Park
S. Claiborne and S. Carrollton,
West Carrollton

7. McMain High School
5712 S. Claiborne Ave. Broadmoor

8. Lyons Community Center
624 Louisiana Ave. Irish Channel

9. Dryades YMCA
1924 Philip Street, Central City

10. Warren Easton High School
3019 Canal Street. Treme

11. Municipal Auditorium
801 N. Rampart, 7th Ward

12. O. Perry Walker High School
2832 General Meyer, Algiers

13. Stallings Community Center
4300 St. Claude, Bywater

14. Sanchez Center
Caffin & N. Claiborne, Lower 9th Ward

15. Gentilly Mall Parking Lot
Chef Menteur & Press Dr., Gentilly

16. Walgreen's
Lake Forest & Read Blvd. NO East

17. Mary Queen of Vietnam
14001 Dwyer, New Orleans East

SENIOR CENTER ●
GENERAL POPULATION ■
CAEP STAGING ☆

CITY OF NEW ORLEANS   **City Assisted Evacuation Plan**

Figure 25-4

Process Flow

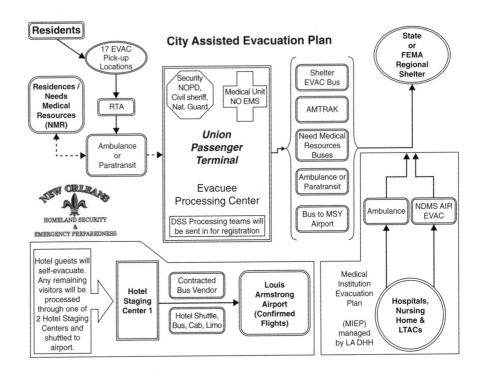

a lengthy period of time without decompensating medically? Were these individuals, referred to at the time as Needs Medical Resources, or NMRs, capable of riding on a train or sitting upright in an over-the-road coach bus seat? Was there an underlying pulmonary issue that would prevent them from flying? Led by the Director of New Orleans EMS at the time, Dr. Jullette Saussy, and New Orleans EMS Liaison Officer to the New Orleans Office of Homeland Security and Emergency Preparedness at the time, Matthew Kallmyer, the planning team developed a triage model to properly place individuals on one of the three modes of transportation. A color-coded triage marking scheme was developed to clearly identify which category of transportation assistance for which an evacuee was triaged. Any underlying condition that was identified as having the potential to lead someone to decompensate would be effectively triaged to a transportation mode that properly addressed the needs of that individual. Figure 25-5 shows the complexities of the triage system onsite at the UPT.

To further complicate the triage system, many of the population members would likely be evacuating with extended family members, so emphasis also had to be placed on keeping families together despite the aforementioned transportation triage. For example, if a member of an evacuating family could not fly, then no one in that family together

Figure 25-5

Transportation Triage

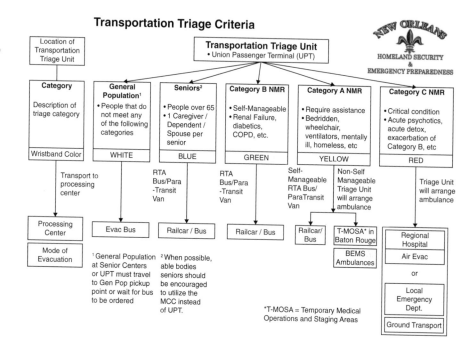

Transportation Triage Criteria

at the UPT would be sent to the airport and a different transportation method would be determined.

The transportation triage required to deliver a successful full-scale evacuation seemed to intensify as discussions and strategies progressed, much like peeling an onion. The more it was addressed, the more complex it became. By placing so much focus on the triage importance at the UPT, the planning team soon realized the need for efficiency and precision.

In an attempt to assist in the efficiency of this portion of the plan, a telephone system dedicated to the preregistration for assistance was established. The general public was encouraged to call 311 from any local phone to register for the CAEP. It is also important to note that during the course of a normal business day, the 311 call center operated much like an assistance number for the citizens of New Orleans. Operators fielded questions regarding property taxes and parking tickets, and also accepted requests for service such as street light outages, potholes, and clogged drains.

In developing a telephone preregistration process, the CAEP began to take shape into a community-based and needs-driven process. When a citizen contacted the 311 call center and requested evacuation assistance, the 311 operator walked the caller through a telephone triage system while gathering pertinent information such as home address, the number of people in the immediate family needing assistance, age, whether or not they had pets, and whether or not anyone at that residence had a medical or mobility issue. If the caller's answers to these questions indicated that medical assistance may be needed, the case file was transferred to the Health Department and New Orleans EMS to verify the true medical need and determine the proper mode of transportation for that particular individual. The Health Department, along with the state Department of Health and Hospitals, and the New Orleans EMS, along with the New Orleans Office of Homeland Security and Emergency Preparedness, conducted CAEP client call-back campaigns to determine the true need. If it was concluded that the individual needing additional care required a para-transit vehicle, then the file reflected such and, during an evacuation, a para-transit unit would be sent to that individual's home for evacuation assistance. If the healthcare experts managing these case files concluded that an individual was limited by conditions that prevented mobility (i.e., was homebound and/or bedridden), the case information became priority within New Orleans EMS team, who conducted a home visit and determined the final mode of transportation needed. Many cases uncovered vague answers surrounding the condition of an individual, which prompted more detailed triage notes and questions within the NO EMS outreach. For example, a person may claim to be bedridden, but in actuality the person sits upright in a chair and watches television for 5 hours a day. In this example, this individual in not truly bedridden and the transportation triage for this individual changes drastically. This potential oversight in triage can become critical, as ambulances are among the scarcest resource within the entire evacuation process. Having an ambulance retrieve an individual that could have been transported via a para-transit could prove detrimental to the resource pool and process altogether. Properly identifying the transportation needs is crucial, and in many cases it may require multiple home visits through the year to capture real-time condition factors. While extremely time-consuming and requiring multi-agency coordination, preregistration from the triage perspective alone is a worthwhile, critically valuable component.

Pets

Medical conditions and moving massive amounts of residents were not the only challenge facing the creation of the CAEP. Although the previous discussed survey indicated that pets were a not necessarily major reason people did not evacuate, many pet owners needed to feel secure that the plan addressed their pets and provided pet and animal safety. If there was any uncertainty surrounding this, the individuals might not heed the warning and choose to remain in the city to care for their pet. The complexity of this issue was not as superficial and easily addressed as it may sound, so agreements were made with the local Society for the Prevention of Cruelty to Animals (SPCA) to ensure proper coordination was occurring with the animal experts.

During the planning process, it was determined that pets would also need to undergo transportation triage and be tagged to indicate their family and ownership. However, pets were not allowed on trains or planes, and the State required that pet owners needed to be sheltered in close proximity to pet shelters to assist in the ongoing care of their companion animal. By default, the buses, which are typically not in the business of transporting pets with owners, became the mode of transportation to take residents out of the city if the pet could in fact remain on the lap of the owner. Further, for those pets that exceeded lap size, special climate-controlled pet transports were contracted to transfer them to a specialized pet shelter within close proximity of the owners' shelter.

Emergency management practitioners are always planning for contingencies, and the pet transport plan was no exception. When a pet owner could not be sheltered near the shelter of larger pet companions, an alternative care program was established. The Louisiana Department of Corrections in concert with the Department of Agriculture and Forestry developed a plan where these animals could go to "pet prison," where they were provided shelter, interaction, and affection by the inmates until the hurricane passed. This truly became a tremendous partnership and one that received many accolades.

The state of Louisiana Department of Wildlife and Fisheries, who is the lead agency charged with the evacuation and sheltering of household pets during a declared disaster in Louisiana was ultimately tasked with the oversight of ESF 11: Agriculture and Natural Resources.[19] In 2006, the Louisiana Legislature passed Legislative Act 615, which stated that local governments and animal/pet facilities must file an emergency plan with the local office of emergency preparedness as well as the Louisiana Department of Agriculture and Forestry by March 1 on an annual basis. This plan had to provide specifics for the humane evacuation, transport, and temporary sheltering of service animals and household pets in times of emergency or disaster.[20] The logistical challenge of locating specialized vehicles to accomplish the mission of a humane evacuation was immense, further supporting the concept that all aspects must be addressed within the planning phase for a truly successful plan.

Don't Wait Until It's Too Late

Another challenge associated with the reasons residents did not evacuate, as discussed earlier, was addressing the informative aspect of the overall plan and convincing the public to indeed evacuate. There is an evacuation window of opportunity that needs to be engrained into the City. In discussing this, it was determined that a timeline of the entire potential threat was needed to provide a common operating picture for both internal and external partners. Emergency Operation Centers across the country understand and perform a significant portion of the traditional common operating picture. However, the traditional common operating picture was often broken down at the jurisdictional boundaries. Eliminating the traditional silos of information sharing and operational planning, not only across agencies or departments but also across jurisdictions, was prudent then and remains a focal point today.

Focusing on this planning aspect, a timeline was conceptualized, in collaboration with the entire New Orleans Metro Region. This guide was provided to all stakeholders, including public safety and healthcare facilities, to ensure everyone worked off of the same sheet of music, so to speak, and ultimately from the same triggers.

There are many moving parts to a hurricane evacuation, and none may move as much as the storm itself. The creation and adoption of a complete timeline was critical. The various key milestones of the CAEP are captured on the timeline shown in Figure 25-6 and highlight how operations initiate from the inevitable H-Hour, which indicates the time at which the outer bands of the hurricane (speeds at that distance from the eye are tropical storm force winds) reach the Gulf Coast of Louisiana (H minus zero, or H–0).

From H-0, all operations are backed out for mission-driven actions. Close inspection of the State of Louisiana specific milestones, located across the bottom portion of the timeline, reveals where a major planning hurdle presented itself at the point where Phase 3 of the State of Louisiana contraflow plan was scheduled to initiate.

The Louisiana State Police developed a tiered evacuation process associated with the contraflow mechanism, as illustrated in the timeline in Figure 25-6. As you can see on the timeline, the southernmost parishes evacuate first at H-50, followed by the middle at H-40, then northern parishes of the southern corridor at H-30, which is when contraflow itself is implemented. During evacuations of large populations due to adverse weather (e.g., hurricanes and tropical storms), contraflow traffic operations are often implemented. This procedure

Figure 25-6

H-Hour Timeline

2012 New Orleans City Assisted Evacuation Plan Timeline

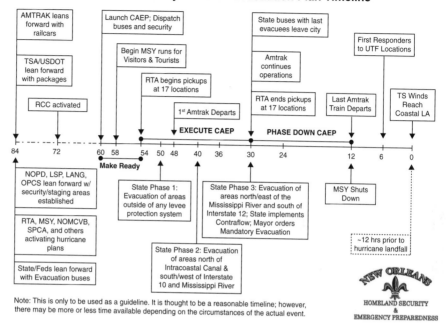

Note: This is only to be used as a guideline. It is thought to be a reasonable timeline; however, there may be more or less time available depending on the circumstances of the actual event.

opens up the opposite lanes of traffic on highways to allow travelers to exit the threatened areas quickly and ease traffic congestion.[21]

As the local planning deepened, New Orleans had to ensure contraflow for those self-evacuating was being addressed and that the CAEP itself interfaced with the Louisiana State Police's plans surrounding the contraflow mechanism.

Other than theoretically improving traffic flow, contraflow also means no additional resources can enter the city from that point forward because all Interstate lanes at that time are traveling out of the City. Further, it indicates a time when the entire operations for evacuation must be complete because of severe road congestion. For this reason, our timeline had to expand outward to ensure better evacuation traffic flow. The entire pick-up effort is massively labor-intensive and time-sensitive. Coordination is critical and the timeline is an aid to ensure success.

Once the Governor's Office of Homeland Security and Emergency Preparedness and the Slidell Office of the National Weather Service agree on the H-Hour, the CAEP can begin leaning forward to prepare for the operation of picking up the population at the 17 pick-up points at H-54 (or 54 hours from the expected tropical storm forced winds in the hurricane's outer bands striking the coast of Louisiana).

Given that the areas surrounding New Orleans are also going to be evacuating, a regional approach was adopted and the timeline itself became uniform for the entire state of Louisiana. The only differences are localized operations at particular times across the H-Hour timeline, but all of these stem from the same H-0 timeframe and maintain the same contraflow process.

At H-30, marking the timeline's end of the CAEP evacuation operations, the city is nearly 30 to 40 hours away from impact. Remember, the winds striking the coast are another 10 to 12 hours away from New Orleans, thus adding an additional amount of time before the winds reached the city. Because of this, the messaging to the public is crucial and the public's willingness to comply with the warning cannot be overstated. The plan was locked in place, but this communication piece was an unknown variable at this time. Having lived through Hurricane Katrina, was the New Orleans population willing to evacuate an entire 30 hours prior to a storm impacting the city? After all the years of "weathering a storm" at home, were these individuals and families truly going to comply with this order and evacuate?

2008: Ready or Not

By the time June 1, 2008, rolled around, the risk was clear and the CAEP was thick with detailed planning elements, job responsibilities, site safety plans, and Memorandums of Understanding. However, as all emergency management practitioners know, the planning cycle is never complete. Following the necessary steps of the traditional planning cycle (see Figure 25-7), a full-scale exercise of the CAEP was conducted in the early summer of 2008. This exercise actually uncovered critical points of improvement in the flow of evacuees at the UPT as well as the transportation triage process. Depending on the frequency of the RTA transit bus arrivals and the number of individuals on those buses, the volume of the evacuee staging in the queue inside the UPT could become extensive. By allowing for triage to occur along the exterior of the UPT as well as the interior (as the lines were queuing), the outbound boarding and flow could rapidly increase. As buses arrived, a triage and registration staffer, much like a maître d' at one of the many culinary establishments in New Orleans, would greet the passengers and begin the triage process immediately rather than trying to absorb everyone in the interior UPT lines. Being aware of this potential point of improvement was important and it had an easy solution, but it nonetheless emphasizes the importance of exercises. No one could have anticipated the volume reaching the limits so

Figure 25-7

The Planning Cycle

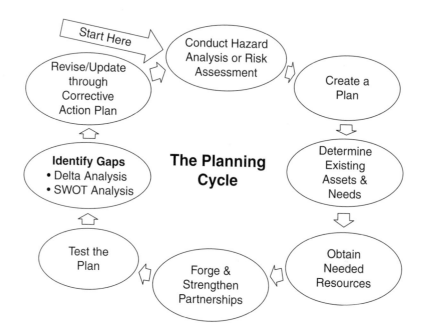

quickly at such a venue made for mass transport. Regardless, the lesson was learned; a Delta Analysis and Corrective Action Plans (CAP) were drafted and formally adopted into the CAEP. This proved vital in the coming months as hurricane season intensified. Shortly after the CAP was fully integrated into the CAEP, the CAEP would be activated in a real-life, mission-driven evacuation operation.

In August of 2008, Hurricane Gustav battered the Gulf as a powerful Category 3 storm and had a trajectory directly toward the City of New Orleans. The CAEP was becoming operational and New Orleans was gearing up to accomplish, to our knowledge, the largest pre-storm evacuation of a major metropolitan area in the history of the United States.

As Gustav tracked toward New Orleans and messages were released that the CAEP would be activated, the 311 preregistration calls began inundating phone lines in relentless fashion. Five days prior to the decision to activate the CAEP, less than 5,000 people had preregistered for evacuation assistance, leaving little true knowledge of the logistical needs outside the planning assumptions. Whether this was due to procrastination or the "denial that anything will happen" mentality of old, no one will ever know. The residents simply had adopted this preregistration component as completely as they had adopted the CAEP pick-up points and plan itself. Fortunately, thorough planning already projected the resources needed based on the academic literature and research questionnaires. Beginning at

H-84 (refer to the timeline in Figure 25-6 for an operational picture), nearly 18,000 phone calls were made to 311 over the following 2-day period. Although such calls were cutting it close, the citizen adoption of this portion of the plan indicated that this was acceptable to the residents as well as being a critical piece of future planning needs.

Within the 24-hour operational period of the CAEP, New Orleans was able to successfully evacuate approximately 20,000 people using the detailed plan, proving that the plan worked. New Orleanians truly accepted the concept of evacuating despite the aforementioned concerns including the potential unwillingness to adopt the CAEP and heeded the warning. The success of such a plan hinges not only on the thoroughness of the planning but also the willingness of the society to comply. New Orleanians certainly rose to the occasion, and the success has been a benchmark across the emergency management discipline. Hurricane Gustav was a successful citywide evacuation of nearly 97 percent of the city. While the entire area was indeed evacuated successfully, the planning did not stop there. The planning cycle of the CAEP still needed to undergo and absorb after-action reviews, critical analysis, and external scrutiny from individuals with varying levels of emergency management experience.

Gustav and Katrina: Lessons Learned

A major focal point following the success of Hurricane Gustav centered on the labor-intensive operation. Because our first responders are busy performing other critical operations before the storm, the plan was structured to depend heavily on volunteer support and had to incorporate a volunteer management section. While the local success of Gustav was clear, the operation could not have been done without community involvement and volunteer agencies such as the Southeast Louisiana Chapter of the American Red Cross and other Volunteer Agencies Active in Disasters (VOADs) and individual volunteers wanting to help fellow New Orleanians. For Hurricane Gustav, the volunteer force was nothing shy of incredible. However, because VOADs typically have a preexisting niche in the grand scheme of response, a gap presented itself. Why isn't there a group designed to specifically assist with the evacuation process and whose members could be educated about potential roles and responsibilities during an evacuation? This concept gave birth to a new volunteer agency called Evacuteer.org, a perfect blend of volunteerism and the desire to help one's neighbor. All emergency management practitioners understand that volunteer management can often be more labor-intensive than the mission itself, especially if an agreement is not in place. Further, assistance can become problematic if the volunteer personnel are not qualified for the mission and there are no existing means of pre-credentialing. Evacuteer.org sought to bridge that gap, creating qualified volunteers to fill a specific niche much like an ESF agency fills a specific role. Evacuteer.org originated as an idea from its founder, Robert Fogarty, and through extensive collaboration with the New Orleans Office of Homeland Security and Emergency Preparedness, the organization began to make an impact and recruit its volunteer pool. To ensure that effective contributions could be made by evacuteers in future activations, a program was created in conjunction with the New Orleans Office of Homeland Security and Emergency Preparedness as well as the Southeast Louisiana Chapter of the American Red Cross to provide evacuteers with a global understanding of the entire evacuation operation and specific response skills. This training regimen would allow for seamless integration into vital staffing roles during a mandatory evacuation. This relationship was instrumental in accomplishing such an operation, and the coordination has allowed for other cooperative staffing in various emergency situations outside of the evacuation process.

Another major lesson can be found in the hospitality industry. New Orleans thrives on tourism, and thousands of tourists visit the City weekly regardless of the season. Early concerns for the CAEP planning team revolved around the hotel and lodging in the City. The concerns stemmed from the fact that the plan called for an early evacuation, ultimately impacting the operations of the hotel, because many of their support staff required evacuation assistance. However, after coordinating with the local leaders of the industry and the hotel general managers, collective decisions and agreements were made to incorporate the tourism industry into the CAEP process, as illustrated in Figure 25-4. This relationship and partnership has thrived over the years since, and the industry is a major partner for various preparedness initiatives across the entire region.

Another major lesson learned can be found in coordination that occurred with the healthcare industry. While the scope of this chapter focuses on the City Assisted Evacuation Plan creation, another level of intense and detailed planning occurred between the New Orleans Office of Homeland Security and Emergency Preparedness and the healthcare community. The ultimate result of this strong coordination was the creation of the Medical Institution Evacuation Plan (MIEP). Since the MIEP utilized the preestablished timeline and triggers, these two plans easily interfaced in a seamless fashion. This coordination led to full-scale exercises conducted at the New Orleans Lakefront Airport by the National Disaster Medical System (NDMS) and the Louisiana State Department of Health and Hospitals, where Department of Defense C-130 medically configured transport planes landed and retrieved litter-bound patients (manikins) from staging areas as a way to test the functionality of the revised medical piece of the plan. Many iterations of the MIEP have existed since Hurricane Gustav due to funding and initiatives out of the local's control, placing prudence on the necessity of the coordination. Without this collaboration and coordination, silo planning may have existed and the common operating picture would have been jeopardized. The healthcare industry and entire the ESF 8 community are constantly involved in the local emergency management planning cycles. One cannot overemphasize the importance of this interface.

Along those lines, a major piece of the learning process lies within the Emergency Support Function (ESF) structure. All emergency management practitioners are well aware of the ESFs within the National Response Framework. The lessons learned from the 2005 and 2008 hurricane seasons have been pivotal in creating an extensive build-out of the local ESF coordination. Outreach to nontraditional partners has increased and participation has been welcomed with potential partners. Exercises and real-world mass gathering events have provided opportunity for their physical involvement in the Emergency Operations Center.

As indicated across the entire chapter, the importance of public/private engagements and partnerships cannot be overlooked. This chapter explains the planning process to evacuate a large population facing disaster in a very short timeframe. While the story of the CEAP clearly shows evacuation strategies, a critical piece to Continuity of Operations for a local municipality facing such an evacuation is the reconstitution of critical infrastructure and the return of the citizens. On top of being concerned about the health and well-being of the residents, the evacuees represent the tax base for the City. With that said, the reentry portion of the CAEP is arguably more complex than the evacuation itself. Because of the focus of this chapter, the reentry process will not be provided in detail. However, a major consideration and lesson learned from the process can be seen in the reentry portion. The entire reentry process is based on such partnerships and provides an opportunity to address business continuity for various local businesses. Every business in the City is urged to apply to the New Orleans Office of Homeland Security and Emergency Preparedness for a business reentry placard bearing the name of the local business. Each applicant will create a profile describing the type of business sector in which they operate, allowing the New Orleans Office of Homeland Security and Emergency Preparedness to understand the level of critical infrastructure performed at the business. Because safety is a major factor upon reentry, every business cannot simply return when they choose. Potable water, electricity, damaged roadways, and so on are reasons to control the reentry process. In doing so, the New Orleans Office of Homeland Security and Emergency Preparedness formulated a tiered reentry process in which businesses received a placard reflecting the level of critical functions performed within the City. Tier 1 placards are the immediate critical infrastructure, Tier 2 businesses/infrastructure are in support of Tier 1s, and Tier 3s are supporting the remaining portion of infrastructure. Annual updates to these profiles and physical retrieval of the placard allows for further fostering of relationships and potential partnerships across all areas of concern beyond hurricanes. While the reentry process is specific to a mandatory citywide evacuation order, it has long served New Orleans well and provided an opportunity to foster relationships and partnerships for other planning initiatives and strategies across the community. Business continuity planners and risk managers from all sectors want to plug into city preparedness as much as possible, and this platform provides a stepping stone for greater possibilities. Current cross-pollination of this concept can be seen in partnerships stemming from the culture of preparedness developed before and after Gustav, none more obvious than the private sector relationships in bioterrorism response and countermeasure distribution (in the Cities Readiness Initiative) and annual community stakeholder educational summits. These valuable partnerships have been instrumental in developing our community outreach efforts especially as we strive to create a more resilient New Orleans.

There were several major lessons to be learned from the experiences following Hurricanes Katrina and Gustav and their impacts to New Orleans. Table 25-3 elaborates the discussion points previously covered and alludes to a few additional ones:

Table 25-3

Additional Lessons Learned

Lesson	Details
Community buy-in and stakeholder adoption (emergency planning)	Critical piece to the overall success was community buy-in. Without the stakeholders across the area, the plan would have failed. Bringing these pieces together, much like the ESFs, is vital.
Community buy-in and adoption	The citizens listened. The successful evacuation prior to Hurricane Gustav can only be attributed to the population heeding the warning.
Preregistration of evacuation assistance worked	Updating the New Orleans 311 database is critical and allows for proper resource allocation and transportation for individuals needing additional care. Annual call-back campaigns and PSAs are delivered to encourage updates to files.
Proper trigger identified and followed	Following the Category 3 storm identified by the risk analysis is critical. The safety of citizens and property cannot be successful with mixed messages over a mandatory evacuation. Evacuation is not just a local mission. Contracts need to be activated and local delivery of resources cannot be done overnight. The longer one waits, the more dangerous and challenging the mission becomes.
Identification and enforcement of essential employees	Consideration should be made as to how civil code is written for payment to various levels of essential employees. An evacuation of this magnitude is very labor-intensive and needs an "all-hands-on-deck" approach. Also, consideration must be made to public safety, where the typical shifts of 1/3 on − 2/3 off no longer can be allowed during these times.
Emergency Operations Center	Cannot overstate the importance of annual training for all EOC reps, not just public safety. This should include any ESF expected to report during any given emergency, such as public works, utilities, VOADS, etc
Emergency Operations Center	Redundant power and redundant/interoperable communications are critical. Establishing protocols for running a Multi-agency Coordination System (MAC) within the EOC was a tremendous part of our success and allowed for extensive Public Safety coordination.
Nursing Home Coordination	Evacuations are expensive and triggers are established at private agencies indicating when to evacuate. Following an established trigger is critical, as contracted transportation is likely going to be taxed. Many transportation providers have multiple contracts, so if a facility delays its evacuation beyond a pre-identified trigger as written into contract, the potential exists for local responders to absorb additional evacuation needs into already stretched capacity.
Considerations needed in the federal transportation and sheltering plans	Cities are in fact responsible for evacuation plans to protect their residents and likewise the states are responsible for similar missions when it becomes more than a local impact. Our experience has illustrated that a regional federal sheltering plan should be seriously considered and the need for multi-use facilities closer to potential threat areas is a must. This would assist in alleviating the overall evacuee transport time and assist in the local management of establishing out-of-state sheltering contracts, which have become cumbersome and extremely difficult to finalize. Consideration for federal evacuation plans and transportation plans could prove instrumental in securing rapid evacuation of threatened areas.

CONCLUSION

The mantra "All disasters are local" is heard coast to coast across the preparedness field, and with the economy remaining in a state of flux, emergency managers charged with the mission of preparedness must get creative while remaining thorough, effective, and, of course, efficient. To aid in the adaption of this new environment, cross-jurisdictional partnerships and collaborative efforts are becoming a necessity. Among others, the removal of traditional silos and vertical planning will reduce redundancy, bridge informational and resource gaps, and allow for effective best practices. Further, it enhances regional resiliency and encourages participation in educational endeavors to properly inform residents of personal planning strategies, local protocols, and regional threats. Establishing extensive ESF networks as well as local public/private sector partnerships are reshaping traditional emergency planning and response, as well as resource management. Flexibility is going to remain an operational constant, but the preexisting relationships and agreements within the local community and surrounding area are becoming more prevalent and necessary than ever before. This further extends into business continuity and continuity of operations, which ultimately assists in the down line logistics of reconstitution and recovery from a disaster. All disasters are local, and this real-life disaster planning experience hopefully elaborates on ways to refine local plans across the country to ensure readiness and coordination.

NOTES

1. Richard D. Knabb, Jamie R. Rhome, and Daniel P. Brown, Tropical Cyclone Report: Hurricane Katrina, August 23–30, 2005, http://www.nhc.noaa.gov/pdf/TCR-AL122005_Katrina.pdf.

2. Louisiana Recovery Authority, Hurricane Katrina Anniversary Data for Louisiana, August 2006.

3. Greater New Orleans Data Community Data Center, *The New Orleans Index*, January 2008.

4. Melissa Schigoda, News Release: Facts for Features, Hurricane Katrina Impact, August 19, 2011, http://www.gnocdc.org/Factsforfeatures/HurricaneKatrinaImpact/index.html.

5. UPS, Weather Bureau, *Hurricane Betsy, August 27–Sept . 12, 1965: Preliminary Report with Advisories and Bulletins Issued,* September 15, 1965, http://docs.lib.noaa.gov/rescue/hurricanes/QC9452B48H81965.pdf.

6. National Hurricane Center, "Minor Modification to Saffir-Simpson Hurricane Wind Scale for the 2012 Hurricane Season, " n.d., http://www.nhc.noaa.gov/pdf/sshws_2012rev.pdf.

7. National Hurricane Center, "The Saffir-Simpson Hurricane Wind Scale," February 1, 2012 (update), http://www.nhc.noaa.gov/pdf/sshws.pdf.

8. National Hurricane Center, "Saffir-Simpson Hurricane Wind Scale," (n.d.) http://www.nhc.noaa.gov/aboutsshws.php.

9. The Washington Post/Kaiser Family Foundation/Harvard University, Survey of Hurricane Katrina Evacuees, September 2005, http://www.kff.org/newsmedia/upload/7401.pdf.

10. J. S. Tyhurst, "Psychological and Social Aspects of Civilian Disaster, " *Canadian Medical Association Journal* 76 (1957), 385–93.

11. John Leach, "Why People 'Freeze' in an Emergency: Temporal and Cognitive Constraints on Survival Responses," *Aviation, Space, and Environmental Medicine* 75, no. 6 (2004): 539–542.

12. GCR, "GCR Releases Population Estimate for December 2007," http://www.gcrconsulting.com/downloads/gcr_population_december2007.pdf.

13. CDC, Framework for Program Evaluation in Public Health, *MMWR* 48 (RR11; September 17, 1999): 1–40, http://www.cdc.gov/mmwr/preview/mmwrhtml/rr4811a1.htm.

14. Division of Cooperative Extension, "Logic Model," University of Wisconsin-Extension, http://www.uwex.edu/ces/pdande/evaluation/evallogicmodel.html.

15. Ibid.

16. FEMA, "National Response Framework," January 2008, http://www.fema.gov/emergency/nrf/.

17. FEMA, Presidential Policy Directive 8: National Preparedness, http://www.fema.gov/prepared/ppd8.shtm.

18. FEMA, "A Whole Community Approach to Emergency Management: Principles, Themes, and Pathways for Action," FDOC 104–008–1, December 2011, http://www.fema.gov/library/viewRecord.do?id=4941.

19. FEMA, National Response Framework, http://www.fema.gov/emergency/nrf/.

20. Louisiana Department of Agriculture and Forestry, State Regular Session, Senate Bill No. 607, 2006, http://www.ldaf.state.la.us/portal/Portals/0/AHS/State%20Vet/Act615.pdf.

21. NOAA, "AWOC Winter Weather Track FY09," http://wdtb.noaa.gov/courses/winter-awoc/documents/color_PDFs/IC323.pdf.

26

FROM RESPONSE TO RESILIENCE: STATE EMERGENCY PREPAREDNESS PRIORITIES

Martin O'Malley

Governor, Maryland

THE EVOLUTION OF HOMELAND SECURITY

Perhaps the most lasting and lifesaving tribute we can give to those who died on September 11, 2011, is to better prepare our nation for the likelihood of the next attack, and the inevitability of the next hurricane or tornado.

On 9/11 it became all too clear that the United States' cities are the second front in a new kind of war. As major population centers, hubs of cultural and economic activity, focal points for the nation's critical infrastructure, and home to symbolic national institutions, cities are, and continue to be, the most likely targets of foreign terrorism on American soil.

9/11 proved that local law enforcement, firefighters, and emergency medical technicians are the new soldiers in this new war on the home front. The federal government and state governments do not have fire departments or medical units, and there is no time to bring personnel and equipment in from elsewhere when terror strikes. 9-1-1 is a local call.

A decade after the events of that tragic day, much has changed, and much has remained the same. As the 9/11 Commission concluded:

Today, our country is undoubtedly safer and more secure than it was a decade ago. We have damaged our enemy, but the ideology of violent Islamist extremism is alive and attracting new adherents, including right here in our own country, ... the terrorist threat will be with us far into the future, demanding that we be ever vigilant, ... Our terrorist adversaries and the tactics and techniques they employ are evolving rapidly. We will see new attempts, and likely successful attacks.

The federal government has made a host of organizational changes, and governments at every level have invested to "provide for the common defense." The nation has lived through a decade of new and evolving threats, including the troubling rise of violent, home-grown "lone wolf" terrorists and groups, and a looming cybersecurity threat.

In addition to the man-made threat of terrorism, the past decade has also been marked by extreme weather events—hurricanes, severe winter weather, and tornados—occurring with what seems to be increasing frequency and intensity, and touching every part of the nation, including areas that had previously thought to be at low risk.

Because 9-1-1 remains a local call, the challenge to elected leaders is to determine how best to equip, train, and prepare our frontline forces for the inevitable natural and man-made hazards they will face. Increasingly, it has also become clear that we must leverage the skills, resources, and expertise in every part of our community.

Maryland, with its proximity to the nation's capitol, major air and water ports, a heavily used regional transit system, and expansive public and private critical infrastructure assets, has confronted a microcosm of the issues that face our nation. This chapter provides some lessons learned that we can glean from Maryland's experiences.

LESSON 1: YOU WILL BE GOOD AT WHAT YOU DO EVERY DAY

By definition, emergencies are stressful, chaotic, and unpredictable, and they happen when they are least expected or wanted. A routine afternoon can be unexpectedly shattered by the howling winds of a tornado or rattled by the blast of a homemade improvised explosive device (IED). When the alarm bell rings, there will not be time to rehearse. First responders must be prepared in these situations to execute well-known plans and functions.

We've learned over this past decade that the key factors that may make the most critical difference in preserving life and public safety are the most basic. Can we communicate? Do we have power?

In Baltimore, our philosophy when purchasing security equipment was "dual use, daily use." Only in rare cases would we purchase equipment that would, in a manner of speaking, be sealed behind a window that read, "BREAK GLASS IN CASE OF TERRORISM." This rule had an important foundation: The day the glass was broken, more than likely the batteries would be dead, the adaptors would not fit, and the person who had bought it and best knew how to use it might be retired.

That's why for the last 10 years, Marylanders have been pursuing—first in Baltimore, then in the state as a whole—a set of 12 basic, core capacities to improve homeland security. An immune system is strong not because it outnumbers the bad bugs, but because it's better connected than the bad bugs. Some of the core capacities overlap, because each is connected in some way to the other, as in the body's immune system. Here is the list Maryland developed:

1. **Interoperable communications—every day.** First responders should have modern, interoperable radios and robust, computer-aided dispatch and records management systems (CAD/RMS). Police officers, firefighters, and emergency medical technicians should be able to use the same radios that they carry to work every day to communicate with fellow officers and firefighters in other jurisdictions, and in other departments. CAD/RMS allows first responders to share data, so that dispatchers can provide potentially lifesaving information before a response begins, whether it is background information on a location, such as an indication it contains hazardous materials, or law enforcement data about a resident's criminal history. Shockingly, these critical tools are not universally available, at the state, or sometimes even the local level. Interoperable radios were not available on 9/11, and in too many cases still are not today.

   Interoperability must not stop at jurisdictional lines. In Maryland, local jurisdictions first banded together to create regional cross-county interoperable networks. However, true, statewide interoperability requires a major, and costly, state-led effort in conjunction with local jurisdictions. Maryland's first-ever statewide radio and CAD/RMS systems are under construction, with the first components coming on line in 2012. The result will be an environment in which a cross-county pursuit involving multiple state and local police and sheriff's departments, traffic departments, and public works can all be managed without anyone involved needing to pick up a second radio. The same will be true at a multiagency, multi-jurisdiction response to a 9/11 event.

2. **Robust, integrated closed-circuit television (CCTV) networks to secure critical infrastructure such as power and water treatment plants and provide vital information during emergency response.** CCTV is a force multiplier and a response aid. Baltimore City began the last decade with very few cameras, and as recently as five years ago, the State of Maryland did not even know how many CCTV cameras it had, or where they were exactly. Within two years of 9/11, the City had built up a network of cameras, which has grown to more than 500 today, and the state government has documented the location and technical specifications of more than 8,400 state-owned and operated CCTV cameras. First responders need the ability to monitor highway cameras to aid in evacuation control, and direct access to cameras placed in patrol cars, helicopters, and marine vessels to aid in incident response. Cameras need to be able to transmit images via the Internet so that video feeds can be shared among key facilities, such as Emergency Operation Centers and mobile command posts.

    However, building CCTV systems is not enough. CCTV systems must be integrated and shared to fully leverage their capabilities. CCTV systems will, quite naturally, be constructed by all levels of government and even by the private sector to protect critical facilities. Maryland's State Highway Administration (SHA) vastly improved its ability to monitor roadways not only by purchasing and installing new CCTV cameras but by integrating state and locally owned CCTV systems into a single network. This in turn improved local jurisdictions' response capabilities, increased the number of individuals monitoring the camera system for trouble, and created shared situational awareness between state and local responders.

Providing information to the public is important as well. In the last few years alone, Maryland more than tripled the number of cameras available online to the public. Technological advances have also made cameras more effective, with software available to alert operators to suspicious packages on a subway or light-rail platform or at the fence line of a port or other secure facility. Today, video can be sent to police officers and other first responders on their laptops and handheld devices such as smartphones. This is in contrast to 9/11, when a New York Police helicopter could not send video images of the disintegrating building to allied responders.

3. **Rapid, robust intelligence and information sharing at every level.** Fusion centers and improved local and state police intelligence operations have been a major area of focus over the past 10 years. In Maryland, five years ago the state's new fusion center was only focused on terrorism. Yet the same assets—the same personnel, data, skills, and expertise—are needed to unravel a violent terrorist plot as are needed to combat the more domestic threats of gang violence. Practically speaking, terrorism cases often start out looking like something much different. Money laundering, illegal guns, and other "traditional" law enforcement issues may prove to be terrorism-related, but the connections will not be made if crime fighting and counterterrorism occur in silos.

There is a reason the term "fusion" is used. Fusion centers also depend on local buy-in and relevance to remain vital. Accordingly, Maryland developed a hub-and-spoke system, opening three regional fusion centers throughout the state to collect and analyze information at the local level on cross-county issues, which could be combined with statewide data. This recognized the practical reality that terrorist planning and preparation could occur in any corner of the state, but the only way to develop a talented, vital statewide intelligence community is to develop one that is relevant daily. The tools have improved as well. License plate reader data (LPR) are gathered from throughout the state and networked into the fusion center, allowing analysis relative to critical infrastructure sites, but also speeding the reaction to an Amber Alert for an endangered child. Maryland's fusion center today brings together personnel from 30 state, local, and federal agencies ranging from the Coast Guard to the Gang Unit, and in a typical year, now handles nearly 12,000 requests of all kinds from local law enforcement, more than twice as many as five years ago.

4. **Focus on securing transportation systems.** When U.S. Navy Seals seized intelligence from al-Qaeda leader Osama bin Laden's compound, they found materials focusing on attacking the rail system. Water ports, airports, highways, train stations, subways, and rail lines all must be fully hardened against attack with permanent physical and electronic countermeasures such as CCTV, lighting, and fencing. Terrorist networks have demonstrated a repeated preference for attacking transportation systems. Some systems, such as rail and the nation's highways, are inherently open and, as a result, even more difficult to secure than other critical infrastructure.

   Therefore, many transportation targets are difficult to harden. In the case of ports and railroads, many traditional physical countermeasures are impossible. To take an oversimplified example, rail generally cannot be fenced in at two ends. Targets that can never be secured completely can still be hardened enough to deter an attack; this is done through multiple layers of defense, particularly through surveillance and awareness. In Baltimore, we invested substantially in strategically placed CCTV technology and lighting for large open areas such as the Inner Harbor and facilities that are difficult to secure, such as rail lines.

   Surveillance technology must be paired with real monitoring—for example, there must be rapid and reliable consequences to trespassing. Awareness must be fostered among the general public, such as transit riders, and key partners, such as workers at ports and airports, to increase the likelihood that suspicious activity will be noticed and reported.

5. **State and local government must know where their critical infrastructure is and whether it is publically or privately owned, and they must take steps to harden and protect it.** In 2001, very few counties or cities had conducted a vulnerability assessment of their critical infrastructure—tunnels, hospitals, and Emergency Operations Centers (EOCs), but also privately owned chemical plants and other facilities that are either vital to the community's daily operation or contain potentially harmful materials that could be weaponized.

Terrorists may also target communities and populations of interest. These same communities, in turn, can serve as vital partners and resources for law enforcement to detect and prevent events such as attacks by individual lone-wolf actors, including U.S. citizens inspired toward violence by terrorist rhetoric.

Vulnerability assessments must also increasingly focus on information infrastructure and security. The cyber infrastructure, a vital element of national commerce, finance, and daily life, has become a target of sophisticated attacks from both domestic and international groups which many government and private sector entities are unable to defend.

One of the most vital tools for understanding—and managing—critical infrastructure is a map. Maryland created a smart map entitled OSPREY, which stands for One Situational Picture Real-Time EmergencY system. OPSREY is an interactive Geographic Information System (GIS) mapping system that includes Maryland's critical infrastructure sites, sorted into categories, such as public health facilities, shelters, and government facilities. OSPREY overlays both static information, such as flood plains, and real-time data, such as road closures, to provide first responders with vital big-picture information to put events into context.

For example, a road closure during a hurricane that impacts a nursing home in a flood plain may be significantly more critical than a road closure in a downtown area or on a major highway. Maryland also offers a publicly available version of OSPREY that redacts some sensitive information for security reasons, but provides a wealth of data and tools to the public, including CCTV camera feeds showing real-time road conditions.

6. **Effective hazmat and bomb squad response are core homeland security capabilities.** Every metropolitan region should have a hazmat team and a bomb response team, and there should be sufficient units statewide to provide a mutual aid response to any jurisdiction within a minimal amount of time.

Prior to 9/11, Maryland had bomb squads and hazmat teams, but viewed them as separate units, and probably not as core counterterrorism assets. However, response to a WMD is likely to involve both types of teams, often working together.

A widespread event could quickly tax local units, making it essential to have a flexible regional response network of units that can provide mutual aid and are familiar with one another's equipment and personnel and train and exercise together. These units require specialized equipment and training, but form a core part of our domestic defense against the most dangerous materials that could be used against us.

7. **First responders need personal protective equipment.** Prior to 9/11, personal protective equipment (PPE), such as a face mask, chemical suit, or breathing apparatus, was widely viewed as being only for firefighters. As a nation, we learned on 9/11 that police officers and other responders need the same sort of protective equipment because all first responders may be called upon to protect the lives of the public in extremely dangerous environments.

   This equipment should be interoperable across agencies, as in a real-world event, equipment is likely to become contaminated and need to be rapidly shared and replaced. Fortunately, PPE has been used widely by law enforcement for response, so smart policies to store caches of equipment may make sense where it is not practical to purchase equipment for every officer. However, training and fit-testing are not optional, and there is no reason to believe the threat from biological, chemical, and radiological hazards will diminish as the technology to utilize them as weapons improves.

8. **Planning is critical.** Our country would never send troops to fight in a foreign country without extensive planning. Likewise, governments need plans that are keyed to their local hazards and "likely worst case" scenarios. This should include plans for no-notice and advance-notice evacuation, including special needs populations and those reliant on public transportation as well as residents of hospitals, nursing homes, and assisted living centers. There should also be plans to shelter those evacuees. Other critical plans include continuity of operations (COOP) or continuity of government (COG) plans. Although these plans were often developed with an eye toward losing specific buildings and facilities as the result of a terrorist event, several years ago the H1N1 threat showed that governments could lose large portions of their workforce through naturally occurring events as well. The need for COOP plans has evolved

since 9/11 to include responding to a diffuse, decentralized threat or incident like a pandemic that impacts the availability of personnel as much or more than loss of buildings or power.

9. **Drills and exercises are the glue to make sure plans and equipment will work when they are needed.** Plans do not mean a lot unless they are rigorously exercised. A robust exercise program can be expensive, not just in financial terms but also in terms of time. In Maryland, the governor and cabinet participate in an annual cycle of four homeland security exercises—a terrorism drill, a continuity of operations drill, a hurricane drill, and a severe winter weather drill. This is not always an easy commitment, but the result is that new and old personnel are well versed in emergency plans and systems. This also ensures there is a continuous effort to improve emergency response plans. A robust after-action program is also needed for both exercises and real-world events. There is no better starting point for improving preparedness than the areas that did not work well during a real-world incident or a drill.

10. **Backup power and communications are essential in any— and every—emergency.** Ten years ago, backup power and communications were not widely viewed as a matter of public safety and a power or communications outage was something to be tolerated. However, facilities like EOCs must have access to mobile backup power generators or, even better, have their own permanent generators or be pre-wired to accept power from mobile generators. There should be layers of redundant communications. For example, Maryland connected 911 centers, local EOCs, and other key facilities to the state's "voice over Internet" backup system, in addition to deploying satellite phones and maintaining ham radio networks. Any system, no matter what it is, can fail. The only way to prevent losing the ability to communicate is to have multiple systems that will only fail under different circumstances. An expensive facility or specialized piece of hardware or equipment is useless if it is not possible to power it.

11. **A robust, real-time biosurvelliance system should be deployed for early detection and tracking of outbreaks.** Maryland has connected every acute-care hospital in the state to a single, electronic biosurveillance system, named ESSENCE. Every day, ESSENCE collects the symptoms of patients reporting to

emergency rooms and to paramedics, the sale of over-the-counter medicines like cough syrup, and the use of prescription drugs, and even school absenteeism.

Prior to 9/11, this information was available, and often already in the health department's hands or within other parts of government, but it was not all pulled together into one system for situational awareness and analysis. The best line of defense was that an astute doctor might notice something was out of the ordinary. However, by 2009 during the H1N1 outbreak, ESSENCE was able to track the emergence and spread of the virus, leading to better decisions about positioning scarce resources like antiviral medications.

12. **The ability to deal with mass casualty incidents and surge in the health system.** Although your favorite medical drama on television may show the local emergency room dealing with an influx of dozens of critical patients, in real life the system does not—or should not—work that way. If possible, patients from a single large event will be transported to various hospitals throughout a region to avoid overtaxing any one facility, and in truly massive events it will be necessary to consider alternatives, such as setting up treatment facilities in the field at the site of the event.

Mass casualty events are not restricted to terrorist attacks, however, and the number of patients that defines a large event is smaller than many may think. The capsizing of a water taxi in Baltimore, a nightclub fire in Rhode Island, or a bus crash can all result in numbers of critical patients that could quickly overwhelm nearby healthcare facilities.

Ten years ago, in Maryland we did not have the tools to deal with a mass casualty incident or hospital surge. When hospitals needed to update their status and had to divert patients to other hospitals, or share information across hospitals about critical medicines and supplies, it was done by fax and phone, in separate systems.

Today, we have created an integrated health and medical dashboard that automates what used to be separate critical systems, and ambulances in metropolitan areas are being equipped with handheld patient-tracking devices so that vital statistics and photos can be electronically transmitted from the field to receiving hospitals, improving not only patient care but the ability to reunite families.

LESSON 2: USE CLEAR, PLAIN LANGUAGE, SET GOALS, AND UNDERSTAND THAT WHAT GETS MEASURED GETS DONE

One of the key elements of Maryland's core capabilities for homeland security was to establish clear, plain language and specific goals. For example, the first part of Maryland's goal for interoperable communications states: "First responders in every region in Maryland should have access to a fully digital, trunked radio system which all response partners can access in order to transmit and receive voice and data." This language is fairly precise—it is not a general, philosophical statement suggesting that all first responders should be able to talk to one another. The goal purposefully lays out some very specific details (e.g., the system should be digital, not analog). This was done intentionally. It is important that goals are clear and understandable by all, and that they establish specific milestones.

In Maryland we chose to set a relatively limited number of goals. There are 12 core goals, not 50. There are many critical things that must be done—and are in fact under way—which are not included in the 12 core goals. However, establishing a limited set of goals was essential to ensuring that they would be widely understood, institutionalized, and focused upon. This keeps in mind the saying that if everything is a priority, nothing is a priority.

While our goals have evolved somewhat over time to reflect lessons learned, technological changes, and the emergence of new threats, we've generally kept them consistent. Why? Two reasons. First, if an objective is constantly being changed, how can it ever be achieved? Second, the goals represent critically important capabilities that we seek not only to attain but to sustain.

Our hazardous materials and bomb squad goal states that "Every metropolitan region should have a Type 1 Haz Mat team and a Type 1 bomb response team, either as one unit, or separate units, and there should be sufficient units statewide to provide a mutual aid response in any jurisdiction within a minimal amount of time." Clearly, this does not represent a one-time effort. It is not enough to reach the mark once. Although Maryland currently has sufficient Type 1 Haz Mat and bomb response teams to meet this goal, we have chosen not to remove it from the core capabilities.

This leads to a final, critical point. Things that get measured are things that get done. Baltimore City built upon the lessons of the CompStat process pioneered by the New York City Police Department to manage operations through the use of data, extending the process to all City services. The homeland security mission is equally amendable to these efforts. As noted, Maryland's bomb squad goal indicates that there should be sufficient bomb squads to provide "mutual aid response in any jurisdiction within a minimal amount of time." But what does that mean? The Federal Bureau of Investigation has a national standard of four hours for a bomb squad response. Maryland's state and local bomb teams joined together to establish a regional response network to achieve the core goal, and set their own standard of a one-hour response, and regularly collect and report data. As a result, the squads know that they achieve a one-hour response—anywhere in Maryland—more than 90 percent of the time. Data collection allows them to track and rapidly diagnose and respond to any changes in their real-world response capabilities.

LESSON 3: HOMELAND SECURITY IS AN ALL HAZARDS, ALL THE TIME JOB

In the immediate aftermath of the September 11, 2001 attacks there was not a U.S. Department of Homeland Security, nor had we even agreed what to call the new discipline. Homeland defense? Would it involve only prevention and response to terrorism, or something else? Over time, it has become clear that the same personnel, skills, and equipment that are needed to respond to an event like the 9/11 attacks are the same ones that are needed to respond to naturally occurring or accidental events. After all, there is not a separate homeland security fire department.

These beliefs were borne out in Maryland in 2005 when Hurricane Katrina struck the Gulf Coast. Baltimore City, relying largely on federal homeland security funding, had developed an independent, City-owned urban search and rescue (USAR) team outside of the existing federal emergency management agency (FEMA) system. Although the team had been developed with an eye toward responding to a massive building collapse from a terrorist attack, it was perfectly suited for the mission of searching flooded houses door to door in St. Bernard Parish in Louisiana. Once a clear mission had been assigned, the 60-person USAR team from the fire department, a 40-person SWAT team from the police department, and a 50-person department of public works team were rushed down to Louisiana to assist. A new fire department mass decontamination truck the City had purchased to assist in response to a radiological or chemical incident was rushed off the factory floor to assist in decontaminating Maryland National Guardsmen that were serving alongside Baltimore's personnel conducting search and rescue in contaminated waters. The fact that Baltimore's personnel and equipment were able to be used so effectively was not an accident.

The federal government, in the form of new Presidential Policy Directive 8 (PPD–8) and recent guidance from the U.S. Department of Homeland Security, has clearly begun to embrace this reality. The federal government has begun to talk about state and local equipment, supplies, and specialized teams as a national network of critical assets that one community can deploy to help another in times of extreme need. Indeed, from Katrina to Joplin, this has proven to be the case.

LESSON 4: IT IS NOT A MATTER OF IF, BUT WHEN— THE QUESTION IS HOW WE RESPOND AND RECOVER

Another lesson the past 10 years have taught is that we can never completely prevent an emergency from occurring. A lone individual who does not care whether he or she lives or dies can commit a violent act using readily available materials, and it is not possible to hold back the winds of a hurricane or know precisely when and where a tornado will strike. Responsible government—and citizens—need to plan not just to prevent the event, but to plan for the day after the event. Our goal, in all cases, should be to return our daily lives back to normal as rapidly as possible.

This way of thinking is increasingly gaining traction throughout the country as the result of the work of leaders such as Dr. Stephen Flynn, and is often referred to as "resilience." A resilient community is one that plans ahead. A resilient community hopes for the best, but it plans for the worst so that the worst times will be short-lived and their impact will be limited. Restoring basic services, like power and communications, or better yet ensuring they are not lost, reopening schools, transit system, and other public facilities as soon as possible, and helping ensure that goods and commerce begin flowing again as soon as possible are core elements of resilience. This leads to a final lesson—although government has a major role to play, it should not—and cannot—build a resilient community alone.

LESSON 5: WE ARE ALL IN THIS TOGETHER, AND NO ONE HAS A MONOPOLY ON EXPERTISE

In 2003, Hurricane Isabel struck the East Coast, surprisingly flooding large swaths of downtown Baltimore and other sections of Maryland that were typically immune from flood waters. However, in truth not everyone was surprised. Maryland's "watermen," the men and women that live and work on the Chesapeake Bay harvesting crab, oysters, and other delicacies (with many families spanning across several generations), were not all surprised by the historic "surge" the Bay experienced during Isabel. The years of real-world experience and hard-fought expertise of the men and women who know the Bay best exceed even the best forecast models. That is why during hurricane season, government officials in Maryland now consult with the watermen and groups like Masters, Mates and Pilots (MM&P), which are responsible for guiding, or "piloting," large ships in the Port of Baltimore.

The lesson here is that no one can do it alone. There are legions of examples of private sector businesses providing not only much needed supplies but also supply chains and logistical support and expertise to bring much needed relief to disaster sites in our country. One of the first jobs of any citizen should be to take the simple but critical steps to have a plan for their own family in an emergency, and to give aid to their neighbors when possible. Although help will be on the way, it may not be immediate, and it may be needed more elsewhere, so anything that can be done to avoid becoming a victim is actually also assisting someone else who has been less fortunate.

FEMA has embraced these ideas as well, referring to a "whole community" approach to emergency management that relies on all levels of government, the private sector, and the general public, working together to get a community back on its feet as soon as possible. This is not an admission of defeat by government but instead a reality—there will always be something unexpected in any emergency, but there may be someone already there in the community, closest at hand, who has the expertise or specialized equipment to deal with it. Partnerships are effective and provide a strategic advantage that cannot be ignored.

CONCLUSION: HOMELAND SECURITY IS HOMETOWN SECURITY

The threat to the home front, and the need to work together is not without precedent. During the War of 1812 America's cities were also the frontlines of a war with a foreign adversary, as the nation's capital itself fell before British invaders. Now, 200 years later, the second front is here at home once again, and the War of 1812 holds powerful lessons for today's leaders.

Baltimore's defenders in the War of 1812 had the wisdom to understand a reality local officials would be wise to take to heart today: When the enemy is at the gates, the usual recourses of waiting for help or hoping that someone else will get the job done are not options. If the unusual coalition of local government, citizens (including large numbers of immigrants and freed slaves), and owners of private businesses had not risen up to form a united defense, Baltimore might have burned, just as Washington, DC, burned 40 miles to the south. During the War of 1812, Congress was scattered throughout the woods around Washington, but the British forces were turned back from Baltimore by local militias and a fort built with private funds. That fort was Fort McHenry, the inspiration behind the "The Star-Spangled Banner."

Today, we can do no less. State and local elected officials must confront the challenging reality that the next terrorist attack could occur tomorrow; the next natural disaster could occur in your community. They must rally every available resource and make the decision to invest their time, personnel, and financial resources. Doing so is not easy—resources are scarce, the challenge is immense, and overcoming institutional barriers represents a major organizational and leadership challenge. However, it can be done, and it must be done.

Like Baltimore's defenders almost 200 years ago, we must dig our own trenches and equip our own frontline defenders—police officers, firefighters, and paramedics—with the tools they need for the war on the home front, and look to the resources already in place in our home towns.

27

EMERGENCY RESPONSE: AN OVERVIEW

Ray Lehr

Statewide Interoperability Director, State of Maryland

Americans have grown to expect that when disaster strikes, the government will dispatch appropriate help. Depending on the size and nature of the emergency, that help could come from a firehouse down the block or a specially trained unit several states away. Firefighters, the police, and emergency medical technicians are generally called "first responders." They are responsible for evaluating an incident at the outset, and the decisions they make at the scene can save lives and lessen the impact of the event. On the basis of their observations, analysis, skill, training, and instincts, they will either handle the incident or call for additional support from local, state, or federal resources.

WHO DOES WHAT?

Usually, the first notification of an incident is a call to 9-1-1. The call is received in a public safety answering point (PSAP) that is responsible for sending the right personnel—typically the local fire department, emergency medical services, police, or sheriff—to the scene to begin controlling the event. First responders apply incident command (IC) procedures standardized in the National Incident Management System (NIMS) so that their efforts are coordinated and information and decisions follow a predetermined protocol.

The need for standardized IC procedures derived from the difficulty of controlling wildfires in the western United States. Fast-moving fires that might consume forests, homes, and businesses require vast resources. Thousands of people with widely varying skills, from dozens of agencies and jurisdictions, must be organized on short notice and deployed to areas—often remote places—where they must maintain that structure for days or weeks. After some disastrous fires in southern California in 1970, several of the agencies involved formed Firefighting Resources of California Organized for Potential Emergencies (Firescope) to develop coordination and a decision process. Firescope developed a structured incident command system (ICS), which has since been accepted by major emergency response organizations and supported by the federal government through the release of the National Incident Management System (NIMS) that FEMA manages and trains potential responders, public and private. As various agencies respond and provide support, the system expands and establishes a unified command structure that designates a single agency to lead the efforts, assigning specific responsibilities to supporting groups that have the appropriate skills. The federal government has taken the process one step further in creating the National Response Framework (NRF) that provides coordination in support of local responders based on 15 Emergency Support Functions (ESFs). Figure 27-1 shows the basic organization of the incident command system (ICS).

Under ICS, most jurisdictions establish a command post, usually a vehicle (e.g., a chief's car, command van, or communications bus). The incident commander assigns a staff member to record or log in support agencies and personnel when they arrive and give them a

Figure 27-1

Basic structure of incident command system

Source: FEMA.

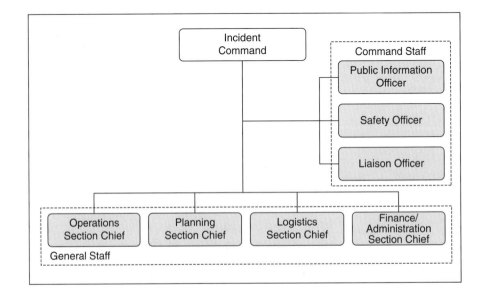

radio or assign a frequency. Some supporting units will be put to work immediately. Others will be assigned to a staging area nearby or will take a position in the command vehicle to coordinate their activities in support of the lead agency. These standard procedures are documented in the jurisdiction's general emergency plans.

Civil defense (CD) agencies first developed emergency plans in the 1950s when a nuclear attack was thought to be inevitable. CD, the precursor to emergency management agencies, created and maintained such plans with input from local first responders. Today, emergency management officials are expected to develop operational plans for various natural disasters. Since 9/11, many local branches of the Emergency Management Agency (EMA) or Office of Emergency Management (OEM) have increased their staff to plan for terrorism, in addition to natural disasters. This new focus is considered "all-hazards" planning, response, and mitigation.

In addition to an operational plan for disaster management, plans are used for scheduled events such as marathons, large public gatherings, sporting events, and so on. Each agency needs a communications plan covering what information needs to be exchanged, who will talk to whom, and how updates and briefings will be conducted. NIMS requires a Form 205 be completed by the designated Communications Unit Leader (COM-L), a person trained and certified for this responsibility. Figure 27-2 shows a page from the Form 205 used for the Grand Prix Auto Race held in Baltimore in August 2011.

Operational and communications plans also provide a methodology for training exercises that can be modified to fit each region's unique needs. When the plans are applied frequently during exercises and routine events, they will become second nature to the responders and will help the various response agencies to develop interrelationships. Decision makers and emergency managers should not be meeting for the first time when a crisis occurs; if they have already developed trust and an understanding of each other's roles and capabilities, their coordination in an emergency will be much smoother.

Many people who testified before the 9/11 Commission described the attacks as "unimaginable." That may have been true of the specifics, but emergency planners had, long before, addressed high-rise fires, mass evacuations, collapsing buildings, and rescue and recovery operations. Nobody can predict the next major catastrophe, but thoughtful planning will provide the foundation for any possible scenario.

Figure 27-2
Sample incident radio communications plan

Baltimore City Incident Management Team

| Incident Radio Communications Plan | | | Incident Name GP Race 2011 | Date/Time Prepared 8/29/11 0800 | Operational Period Date/Time 8/30/11 07:00-21:00 |

Basic Radio Channel Utilization

Function	Radio Type/Cache	Group/Channel	Frequency/Tone	Assignment	Remarks
Unified Command	BC 800 MHz	BC CITY - B10	B10	Unified Command	Communications Between and to All Unified Command Personnel
Operations	BC 800 MHz	BCFD Support 1	B2	Fire & EMS Groups	FD Units Dispatch & Main OPS - All FD Units Monitor
Tactical	BC 800 MHz	BCFD Support 2	B3	Fire & EMS Groups	Expansion For Tactical If Needed - Will Be Assigned By MCU
Tactical	BC 800 MHz	BCFD Trn1	B4	Fire & EMS Groups	Expansion Tactical If Needed - Will Be Assigned By MCU
Consult/Lateral EMS	BC 800 MHz	BCFD Trn 2	B5	EMS Group Support	EMS Consult and Lateral
Tactical	BC 800 MHz	BCFD Event 1	B6	SOC Group/ UC Logistics	SOC Group/Logistics Lateral
Tactical	BC 800 MHz	BCFD Event 2	B7	PIT Crew	PIT Crew Logistics and Tactical
Lateral	BC 800 MHz	BCFD Event 3	B8	Branch 2 Director	Lateral with Branch 2 Director
Lateral	BC 800 MHz	BCFD Admin	B9	Admin/FCB/MCU	Administrative/Lateral For FCB/MCU
Lateral	BC 800 MHz	BCFD FG 3-2	B14	Fire Marshall Group	Lateral For Fire Marshall Group
Lateral	BC 800 MHz	BCFD FG 3-1	B15	UC Safety/Risk Management	Lateral For Safety and Risk Management
Lateral	BC 800 MHz	BCFD FG 3	B16		
Lateral	BC 800 MHz	BCFD/PD TG B11	B11	Branch 1 Director	Lateral with Branch 1 Director
	BC 800 MHz				

Prepared by (Communications Unit)
BC Patrick Walsh

NORMAL OPERATIONS

An estimated 240 million calls are placed to 9-1-1 in the United States each year. For all kinds of calls— fires, plane crashes, hazardous materials, mass casualty events, and terrorism—the common thread is a predetermined response and a unified command system designed to coordinate those activities.

When call-takers or dispatchers at the local 9-1-1 center answer a call, they ask a series of prescribed questions; the resulting data determines which agencies and units are dispatched. Most PSAPs have a computer-aided dispatch (CAD) system, which automatically assigns units based on location and call type. Once the units are under way, they maintain radio contact with a dispatcher from their agency and report status, request additional resources, and maintain communications until the situation is stabilized. PSAPs and dispatch centers are the command-and-control point for public safety activities, providing coordination with support agencies and an awareness of all activity within the jurisdiction. If the event is prolonged, an emergency operations center (EOC, usually run by the Emergency Management Agency) may be activated to support the on-scene forces. Personnel from the police, fire, transportation, health, utilities, and so on will gather at the EOC, exchange information, monitor activities, and make decisions necessary to support the on-scene incident commander. Routine events usually require the coordination of only one to three agencies. More complex events can involve dozens of agencies across local, state, and federal jurisdictions.

Table 27-1 shows basic responses for first-responder agencies, and Table 27-2 shows standard emergency operations.

Table 27-1 Basic Response for Three First Responders Note: There is some reserve capacity for additional incidents; for instance, large departments have off-duty personnel on call.	**First Responder Agency**	**Basic Unit/ Staffing**	**Normal Response Small Incident**	**Escalation Level 1**	**Maximum Response**
	Fire Department	Engine/pumper or truck/ladder, 3–7 fire fighters per unit	1 or 2 engines and 1 truck for small events, 1st alarm generally consists of 4 engines, 2 trucks, and a battalion chief	Additional alarm (2nd, 3rd, etc.) usually brings a like amount of units: 4 engines, 2 trucks, and a battalion chief. Specialized units as required (Hazmat, etc.)	85–90% of total resources,[1] Mutual aid from surrounding jurisdictions.
	Emergency Medical Service	Medic unit or ambulance, 2 paramedics, EMTs, or combination	1 medic unit	1–4 additional medic units 1 supervisor	50–60% of resources, Mutual aid from surrounding jurisdictions.

(Continued)

Table 27-1

Basic Response
for Three First
Responders

(*Continued*)

First Responder Agency	Basic Unit/ Staffing	Normal Response Small Incident	Escalation Level 1	Maximum Response
Police/ Sheriff	Patrol car 1–2 officers or deputies	1 car with backup	5–10 cars with supervisors, detectives, specialized units such as crime lab, bomb squad, etc. as needed	10–20% of resources. Mutual aid, State Police for additional support.

[1] Some reserve capacity is kept in service to handle additional incidents. Large departments have "callback" plans to bring in off-duty shifts to staff reserve apparatus.

Table 27-2

Standard Emergency
operations

Type of Emergency	Lead Agency Incident Command (IC)	Supporting Agencies/Role	Total Number of Personnel
Auto Accident	Fire if persons trapped or fire danger, EMS if injuries only. Police if no fire or injuries	Fire: Rescue, extrication, fire control/extinguishment, spill control/containment EMS: Victim treatment, transport Police: Traffic control, accident investigation Transportation: Traffic diversion	Fire: 4–10 EMS: 2–5 Police: 2–8 Transportation: 2–6
House Fire	Fire: Incident Command	EMS: Standby for treatment of victims Police: Control access to area and investigate if crime	Fire: 10–25 EMS: 2–5 Police: 2–8
Hazmat Incident	Fire: Incident Command	EMS: Standby for treatment of victims Police: Control access to area and investigate if crime Specialized Units: As needed	Fire: 10–25 EMS: 2–5 Police: 2–8 Specialized Units: 2–10
Bank Robbery	Police: Incident Command	EMS: Treats injured	Police: 4–10 EMS: 2–5
Hostage Situation	Police: Incident Command	Fire: Standby for tear gas, fire mitigation EMS: Standby for treatment of victims	Police: 5–20 Fire: 4–10 EMS: 2–5

Members of the general public, unless they themselves are affected, are usually unaware of most routine calls handled by first responders. However, the news media monitor incidents through radio scanners and will send reporters if an event involves injuries or deaths or disrupts traffic or other services

COORDINATION OF ACTIVITIES

When disaster strikes, first responders respond. This sounds simple, but sorting out responsibilities and activities to ensure that the response will make the situation better, not worse, is actually a complex matter.

Without clear, predetermined lines of authority and responsibility, the response may be confused and haphazard, escalating the emergency and putting more people in danger. For example, a fire department is clearly the lead agency when a building is on fire, but if evidence points to a set fire (flammable liquids or explosive devices present), the fire fighters should exercise caution in dousing the scene with water where police need to preserve evidence. As another example, police should not begin an evacuation of a building when the hazardous materials team recommends "sheltering in place." Similarly, an incident commander should not order the evacuation of an urban area without notifying the transportation department, or else gridlock and panic may ensue.

To avoid such problems, there must be frequent and reliable communication between agencies before, during, and after an emergency. Ideally, the incident commander should already have a relationship with the response agencies. As noted, a crisis is not the time to meet new people and bicker over who is in charge or what actions to take. Planning for disasters must be a top priority for all jurisdictions. Emergency planners should strive for as much participation as practical. Responsible leaders must ensure that emergency plans are practiced as frequently as possible.

Those managing prolonged events will need to hold a public information briefing to enlist the help of the media. If the media is shut out of the information flow, they may end up reporting rumors; the officials will then find it difficult to correct the record, and the media and the public will continue to wonder what is really happening. By scheduling press briefings at a safe distance from the scene, public safety officials can convey the facts to the public, give advice on how to remain safe until the incident is mitigated, and ensure that the media is relaying accurate details.

LARGE-SCALE EVENTS

Historically, in planning for large-scale events, the emergency management community has focused its training on perceived threats. (For instance, in the 1960s, it focused on the nuclear threat, and first responders became familiar with Geiger counters, dosimeters, and potassium iodide tablets.) An unanticipated event can leave first responders inadequately prepared.

On 9/11, the New York City police and fire departments—although they are among the world's largest and best-equipped public safety agencies—were not equipped to handle a disaster of such magnitude. Even though the Towers had been attacked less then a decade before, the first responders never planned for airplanes to be used as weapons of mass destruction. The burning fuel created a much more devastating effect on the buildings' structure than the previous attack using explosives. If the structural vulnerability of the World Trade Center had been known, it might have led to different tactics. However, it should be noted that a decade earlier, in 1991, the Philadelphia fire department was criticized for withdrawing its forces from a high-rise building believed erroneously to be near collapse.[1] In theory, engineers who are familiar with the structures involved should be contacted to provide expert guidance; but in reality that is usually impossible. Future advances in technology and computer modeling may be the best way to provide technical expertise to incident commanders.

Another problem in New York City on 9/11 was that the convergence of many firefighters on the scene, and the loss of the senior commanders when the first tower collapsed, left a void in the ICS for more than an hour.[2] Consequently, many off-duty firefighters, driven by admirable dedication and a desire to help, went into action with no clear orders and no radios, so that it became difficult to verify their presence and activities. Planning for future events must consider the desire of public safety workers to do something in a disaster, and such planning must include a preordained methodology for assigning them in a way that will maximize their effectiveness without placing them in danger and ensure that everyone is accounted for.

At large-scale events, incident commanders have a complex, taxing role. They may need to make split-second life-or-death decisions; mistakes on their part might cause the situation to spiral out of control; and they must direct an influx of well-meaning agencies.

As with military operations, the key is planning, practice, and an excellent staff. Incident commanders need a support staff capable of acting as a buffer: only the most necessary people and information should get to the incident commander. The commander's directions must be followed quickly and accurately. As an emergency escalates, routine radio transmissions should be minimized to make way for critical information. Incident commanders are frustrated when mundane reports ("We're ascending the stairs"; "We're arriving in the staging area") interfere with more important transmissions. Seasoned emergency workers know that reporting expected results wastes time and radio airtime; they should report only unexpected occurrences that need immediate follow-up. The newest generation of radios allows for emergency over-rides; personnel need to practice using such technology.

Modern radio systems also use computer technology to segment communications into "talkgroups"—computer-defined groups of radios linked together for a specific incident. Well-designed talkgroups can allow work units to coordinate their activities without blocking the flow of information to commanders or to, say, medical groups.

Figure 27-3 is an example of talkgroups. In this case, in Baltimore, the incident was a derailment and fire in a two-mile tunnel under a downtown business district. The fire burned for three days as firefighters uncoupled and removed the smoldering cars. At the time of the fire, a baseball game was beginning at Camden Yards, one-quarter mile from the south tunnel entrance, and the incident commander ordered an evacuation of the stadium. The situation was mitigated by the ability to coordinate numerous agencies, and that ability in turn was due to talkgroup design. The fire, police, and public works departments had considered their operational needs and had created talkgroups accordingly. Shared talkgroups such as B-11, FD-PD (fire department to police department) and B-12, FD-DPW (fire department to public works) allowed the agencies to exchange information. The

Figure 27-3

Talkgroups developed for the Baltimore fire department as part of the city's consolidated 800-MHz radio system; these groups were used in July 2001 at a tunnel fire involving a CSX freight train.

Source: The National Wildlife Coordinating Group, www.nwcg. gov.

Incident Radio Communications Plan			1. Incident name	2. Date/time prepared	3. Operational period date/time
4. Base radio channel utilization					
System/cache	Channel	Function	Frequency/tone	Assignment	Remarks
5. Prepared by [Communications Unit]					

system included an "all call" talkgroup that would have allowed the incident commander to communicate with all the assembled forces if a full evacuation became necessary.

WEAPONS OF MASS DESTRUCTION

Weapons of mass destruction are a serious potential challenge to the emergency response community. First responders would need to begin control and recovery operations while evaluating the nature of the weapon and determining the best course of action. Hot zones would need to be identified. The incident commander might have to stop rescue operations if the victims have received a lethal dose of the agent. Emergency services are not accustomed to abandoning victims, and this decision would be even more difficult if there were schools, nursing homes, hospitals, and fire stations in the hot zone. Training and exercises have been conducted to prepare commanders for WMD events, but the psychological effects of making such decisions could hamper the control of an incident in the critical early stages.

Also, military units would probably be among the early responders: the Department of Defense (DOD) has given considerable attention to supporting local agencies in a WMD event. But most local governments have not trained or even met with the military units that would be deployed. Local public safety officials need to consider the worst-case scenario for their community, learn what military units are likely to be deployed, and meet with the appropriate commanders to discuss capabilities and equipment and to plan joint training exercises. Another consideration for local officials is that some full-time police officers, firefighters, and EMS personnel are also members of the National Guard. First-responder agencies must know how many of their employees are members of the National Guard and are likely to be called up in an emergency, and how such a call-up would affect the local response. If the effect is likely to leave the local community short of trained personnel, a plan for additional recruiting, supplemental staffing, or cross-training must be developed.

TECHNOLOGY: INTEROPERABLE COMMUNICATIONS

A basic need of first responders is communication with each other during emergency operations. Most first responders use land mobile radio (LMR) systems. Portable radios for first responders must be operable in extreme weather and high humidity, and powerful enough to penetrate the concrete walls of structures they could be called to operate in.

Since 9/11, interoperable communications (Table 27-3) have received much attention. However, many groups were concerned much earlier about the problems of providing such communication: the Association of Public Safety Communications Officials International (APCO), Public Safety Wireless Network (PSWN), and Project SAFECOM have for some time been urging the removal of barriers to interoperability. The technical challenges include the multiple bands and frequencies assigned by the FCC to public safety, incompatible technologies, resistance from vendors, and a lack of funding.

The McKinsey Report and the report of the 9/11 Commission emphasized the need to improve communications in public safety agencies, and first-responder organizations such as the International Association of Chiefs of Police (IACP) and International Association of Fire Chiefs (IAFC) have made efforts to obtain the necessary funding.

The Department of Homeland Security, created after 9/11, has a division, the Office of Emergency Communications (OEC), which is the federal driver for interoperability. It provides guidance in developing governance, starting with a State Interoperability Executive Committee (SIEC), a single point of contact (Statewide Interoperability Coordinator (SWIC), and region structures to guide the interoperability effort. Guidance and templates, as well as lessons learned across the country, provide much needed guidance in assessing a state's interoperability and taking the necessary steps to allow all responders to communicate when the incident demands it.

Many states have used federal grants to obtain gap solutions such as patching devices, the connection of different frequencies through Voice or Radio over IP (Internet Protocol). Many jurisdictions have deployed the National Public Safety Advisory Council (NPSPAC)

Table 27-3

Levels of interoperability (simplified version)

Method of Interoperability	Degree of Complexity	Number of Agencies	Bands, Frequencies	Cost
Swap radios	Low	2–3	2–3	Low
Talkaround	Low	2–4	Same band	Moderate
Mutual aid channels	Low	2–6	Shared frequency	Moderate
Patch	Moderate	2–8	2–6	Moderate to expensive
System roaming	High	2–12	2–6	Expensive
Standards-based sharing of systems	High	2–20	Unlimited	Very expensive

interoperability frequencies assigned by the FCC. This allows any user from an assisting jurisdiction to use a common set of nationwide frequencies, provided they are deployed in the area of the event. The work of the DHS OEC has greatly advanced the goal of national interoperability for first responders, but much remains to be accomplished before a firefighter or law enforcement member from one state can travel across the country and operate as a supporting resource in a different state.

Many leaders believe the recent (February 22, 2012) passage of legislation assigning additional broadband spectrum (the D Block) to public safety and the creation of a Nationwide Public Safety Broadband Network will finally make national interoperability a reality. Congress has designated $7 billion for this network's creation, and the plan is to build it though a national governance body (FirstNet). At this time, many questions remain about the operation and maintenance of this mission-critical network, but the vast majority of public safety officials agree this is a major milestone for first responders. The same communications applications that people use to text, watch movies, and videos on small handheld smartphones will now be designed for police to have instant viewing of crimes in progress through CCTV or for firefighters to view building plans en route to a high-rise fire or for paramedics to send patient images to a specialist several states away to bring the correct diagnosis to emergency victims.

Many in the public safety community, governors, and members of Congress put aside partisan politics to make this network a priority. Only time and the continued hard work of public safety and telecommunications experts will guarantee its success.

In 1997, Baltimore began to tackle its problems regarding public safety communications: old radio systems that could not penetrate high-rise buildings, high maintenance costs, and a lack of interoperability. Then mayor, Kurt L. Schmoke, spent the money necessary to give first responders a system that solved those problems. The city's consolidated 800-MHz radio system (described previously) was completed in 1999 at a cost of nearly $70 million. It provides communications between police, fire, EMS, and other city agencies through software-defined talkgroups. Each agency has up to 50 groupings available.

The city also had to reach agreements with the surrounding counties to give response partners seamless communications. For disparate systems to interoperate, it is necessary to share information that could compromise the total system if misused. Responsible parties are naturally reluctant to open their systems for the sake of events that might seldom or never occur. Thus, safeguards, both technical and operational, must be institutionalized among the sharing agencies.

Before 9/11, most jurisdictions had trouble convincing political and budget officials that interoperable communications would be cost-effective. Now, interoperability has become part of the lexicon of even civilians in federal, state, and local governments.

Interoperability technology exists today. The challenge is deciding what technology to choose and who will pay for it.

A PRACTICAL GUIDE TO PREPARING FOR INCIDENTS

First responders must focus on rescue, containment, and control. In the future, new tools and equipment will be developed to help make communications and information more readily available; but during a crisis, what makes the biggest difference is not technology or equipment, but people. Although senior officials should provide first responders with the best tools available, future events might make even the latest equipment useless. For example, a nuclear or radiological event could affect such a wide area that the communications infrastructure would be lost. A device placed in an urban environment could kill or injure not only civilians but a large proportion of the police, fire, and EMS forces.

How would your city recover from such an event? The only way to know is to conduct training and exercises that stretch your resources and—more importantly—stretch the minds of senior officials. Every community should conduct a thorough self-examination that includes the following questions:

What are the total resources available for a major event?

How would off-duty emergency workers be mobilized if the communications infrastructure failed?

Where would additional (outside) support come from?

How would additional support be requested?

What are the chokepoints in the transportation network?

Where would mass casualties be taken for treatment?

Where could shelters and morgues be located?

How would a mass evacuation be conducted?

What critical networks would be affected by a large-scale power interruption for over a week?

How would government continue if the senior leadership was eliminated?

This list is not exhaustive, but it can form a basis for evaluation and for planning to deal with disasters. Once the plans are completed, officials should practice them frequently and invite participation from surrounding jurisdictions. The administrative staff should periodically review and update the plans, taking experience and new threats into account. Even if no disaster occurs, the interaction of many jurisdictions and agencies will improve the working relationships that are critical to everyday life.

NOTES

1. FEMA, United States Fire Administration, Technical Report Series, "High-rise Office Building Fire, One Meridian Plaza, Philadelphia, Pennsylvania," report by J. Gordon Routley, Charles Jennings, Mark Chubb, February 23, 1991 http://www.interfire.com/res_file/pdf/Tr-049.pdf.

2. See http://www.nyc.gov/html/fdny/pdf/mck_report/fire_operations_response.pdf.

28

UNDERSTANDING AND PREPARING FOR THE PSYCHOLOGICAL CONSEQUENCES OF TERRORISM[1]

Terri L. Tanielian, M.A.

Senior Research Analyst, Associate Director for Mental and Behavioral Health, Center for Domestic and International Health Security, The RAND Corporation

Bradley D. Stein, M.D., Ph.D., M.P.H.

Natural Scientist, Associate Director for Mental and Behavioral Health, Center for Domestic and International Health Security, The RAND Corporation

INTRODUCTION

Two of the various definitions of *terrorism* that have been offered are as follows:

> The illegal use or threatened use of force or violence; an intent to coerce societies or governments by inducing fear in their populations; typically with ideological and political motives and justifications; an "extrasocietal" element, either "outside" society in the case of domestic terrorism or "foreign" in the case of international terrorism.[2]
>
> The purpose of terrorism is not the single act of wanton destruction, it is the reaction it seeks to provoke: economic collapse, the backlash, the hatred, the division, the elimination of tolerance, until societies cease to reconcile their differences and become defined by them.[3]

What these definitions have in common is recognition that, beyond the physical damage caused by the event itself, terrorism is intended to have a psychological effect. It targets the social capital of a nation—cohesion, values, and ability to function. Therefore, successful counterterrorism and national continuity depend on effective interventions to sustain the psychological, behavioral, and social functioning of the nation and its citizens. From the impact of an attack (e.g., destruction and death) and the consequences associated with the response (e.g., economic loss and disruption) to the impact of preparedness and counterterrorism themselves (e.g., behavioral and social ramifications of new security procedures), there is an urgent need for an understanding of the development of effective intervention and tools for assessing and predicting psychological, behavioral, and social responses and counterresponses.

The attacks of 9/11 and the persistent threat of future terrorism demonstrate the importance of preparing the nation to respond more effectively. The emotional consequences of terrorism (which can include acute and long-term distress, anxiety, grief, depression, anger, etc.) pose unique challenges for government officials charged with planning prevention and response, and they raise important questions regarding the ability of the public health system to understand and prepare for such events.

The federal government has undertaken unprecedented efforts to increase the nation's ability to respond to terrorism, including the establishment of the Department of Homeland Security (DHS), the passing of the PATRIOT Act, and (to address bioterrorism specifically) the investment of over $4 billion in the public health infrastructure. However, little national or local policy has focused on the importance of addressing psychology or mental health as part of these efforts.

This chapter describes the psychological consequences of terrorism and outlines strategies for dealing with them. This information should prove useful for policymakers attempting to develop state and local response strategies.

WHAT ARE WE WORRIED ABOUT?

Much has been written about the emotional, cognitive, somatic (biological), and behavioral responses that can be expected in the immediate aftermath of terrorism. Many of these studies have focused on the incidence and prevalence of posttraumatic stress disorder (PTSD) and acute stress disorder, the impact on the use of health care services, and the impact on substance use (e.g., smoking and drinking). Many of the reactions that were identified after 9/11 (including increases in PTSD and the use of alcohol) have also been found, communitywide, after other large-scale traumas such as earthquakes, wildfires, and hurricanes. However, incidents of mass violence, such as shootings and terrorism, are intentional and are therefore the most psychologically disturbing type of disaster; thus their psychological consequences are frequently more severe.[4]

Beaton and Murphy's review of responses to terrorist events suggested that up to two-thirds of those directly affected (either as a victim or as a relative) are psychologically impaired to some degree.[5] They may experience a wide range of emotional and behavioral consequences that include PTSD, a psychiatric disorder characterized by persistent flashbacks or nightmares, extreme irritability or jumpiness, and emotional numbing or avoidance of reminders of the trauma. Others may develop other anxiety disorders, depression, and problems with substance use, as well as symptoms that do not meet the criteria for PTSD.[6]

The documented prevalence of such problems after specific events varies widely, perhaps because of differences in the populations involved, the nature of the events, and the methodologies used in the studies. Typically, the researchers have screened victims to identify symptoms of posttraumatic stress and to determine whether these symptoms meet the criteria for a clinical diagnosis of PTSD. For some victims, however, these symptoms may not initially meet the criteria; but if left untreated for some months after the first screening, they may become more severe.

WHO WILL MOST PROBABLY BE AFFECTED?

Individuals most likely to be affected, psychologically and behaviorally, by a terrorist event include those who were injured, those who were present or nearby, those (such as first responders) who were exposed to trauma as a result of their attempts to help victims, and those (such as vulnerable populations) who were already at risk of developing psychological symptoms. Also, terrorism may be more likely than other traumatic events to cause a psychological reaction in individuals who were far from the attack but are nevertheless concerned about being in danger.

Direct and Indirect Victims

Studies conducted immediately after 9/11 found a range of emotional and behavioral reactions, both in the cities where the attacks occurred and across the country. For example, three to five days after 9/11, 44 percent of a national sample of Americans reported experiencing substantial emotional stress.[7] One to two months after 9/11, 8 percent of residents sampled in Manhattan reported symptoms consistent with PTSD, and 10 percent reported symptoms consistent with depression.[8] During this time frame, estimates of probable PTSD in areas close to the attack ranged from 3 percent in Washington, D.C., to 11 percent in the New York metropolitan area.[9] Subsequent surveys of the general public found a decrease in the prevalence of severe emotional distress,[10] but—at least in New York City—such surveys also found changes in health-related behaviors, such as a persistent increase in the use of cigarettes, alcohol, and marijuana[11] and an increase in missed doses and suboptimal doses of antiretroviral therapies among HIV-positive men.[12] Such behavioral changes can have a wide public health impact and as such need to be considered as well.

First Responders

First responders—traditionally thought of as the police, firefighters, and emergency medical technicians (EMTs)—care for both survivors and the dead and also face the possibility of having to enter a dangerous environment. Thus they may witness mass carnage and destruction, and their own health and well-being may be imperiled. Considerable attention has been given to emotional repercussions among first responders, particularly those who responded to the bombing of the Murrah Federal Building in Oklahoma City in 1995 or to the attack on the World Trade Center (WTC) on 9/11. Studies by North and Herman and their colleagues[13] suggest that the experience of responding to such events significantly increases the risk of symptoms of PTSD and other psychiatric sequelae.

Vulnerable Populations

Terrorism can have an especially profound effect on vulnerable populations such as children, racial and ethnic minorities, and those with an existing psychiatric illness. Individuals in a community who are exposed to a terrorist act experience a range of psychological reactions that affect how the incident is managed. At one end of the range are behaviors of normal people under abnormal circumstances, such as wanting to return to their families immediately, regardless of official advice or orders to stay in place. These normal reactions may either help or hinder efforts to contain a threatening agent; deliver medical care; and reduce the morbidity, mortality, and costs associated with the disaster. At the other end of the range are new behaviors or exacerbated habitual behaviors that are disruptive to the community, such as refusing to be evacuated.[14]

Children are a vulnerable population of particular interest. One study found that when children were more distressed, their parents spent more time talking with them.[15] It seems likely that these parents were trying to reassure the children, but in a situation where parents as well as children may feel threatened, we cannot draw a conclusion about the implications of this finding without more information about the actual conversations. Possibly, another factor, such as the parents' own distress, causes longer parent-child conversations about terrorism and also intensifies the psychological effect of terrorism on children. Another possibility is that the correlation is not between parent-child conversations and symptoms, but rather between conversations and reported symptoms. That is, perhaps parents who spend more time in such conversations become more aware of their children's mental state and therefore report more symptoms; in other words, the conversations serve as a means for parents to find out about the psychological impact of terrorism on their children. Still another possibility is that in some cases the conversations may heighten children's worries and psychological reactions, particularly if the parents warn the children to avoid public places, take precautions against anthrax, or the like.

In studies in Israel of children repeatedly exposed to terrorism, many children evidently felt insecure, were worried about safety, and were ready to expect the worst.[16] In research in the United States several months after 9/11, children commonly remained worried about being victims of terrorism.[17] Further research is needed to determine whether such feelings might result from repeated warnings or threats of terrorism even when no actual events occur. Parents are likely to influence how children respond to terrorism, and there are few other types of traumatic events where the potential threat to both parent and child is comparable. Additional studies will contribute to an evidence base allowing better-informed recommendations to parents about how to help children cope with terrorism.

Several studies have investigated whether ethnicity and culture are predictive of psychological and behavioral reactions. Studies of residents of New York City after 9/11 found differences among populations in outcomes and in the utilization of services. In a large-scale epidemiologic study, one predictor of PTSD was Hispanic ethnicity.[18]

Also, African-American and Hispanic respondents were less likely than white respondents to use services or take medications. The researchers attributed this disparity to various cultural factors, including valuing self-reliance, expressing emotions in certain ways, and having reservations about sharing emotions with others.

Individuals with preexisting psychological illnesses or mental health problems also appear to be at greater risk of experiencing psychological consequences of terrorism.[19] For example, in one study, prior depression or anxiety was associated with higher levels of posttraumatic stress symptoms after 9/11.[20]

Understanding—and mitigating—the likely consequences for vulnerable populations will be a critical component of counterterrorist preparedness, planning, and response.

STRATEGIES FOR PREPAREDNESS AND RESPONSE

Although additional research on preparedness and response is still needed, the studies conducted so far have found that after terrorist events, community-oriented responses (such as those aimed at and based on existing community relationships) have been instrumental in managing psychological consequences. These studies examined responses in Oklahoma City in 1995[21] and in and around New York City and Washington, D.C., after 9/11.

Overall strategies for preparing the public and the appropriate resources to respond to large-scale traumatic events can be organized according to specific populations (e.g., victims, responders, vulnerable groups) and according to phases of the event (pre-event, acute, post-event, long-term post+event). The strategies can be divided into two categories with distinct but overlapping goals: (1) to provide immediate psychological management to allow for effective public health and emergency response strategies (e.g., by mitigating or preventing psychological distress and fear, and by minimizing potential, unnecessary demands on the health care system); and (2) to reduce both short-term and long-term psychological morbidity.

Traditional responses to an emergency such as a disaster typically include deploying trained mental health specialists to the place or places directly affected; this deployment can include groups such as the American Red Cross and other mental health organizations. These responders then become available to offer crisis counseling and management, screen for mental health problems, provide psychological first aid, and provide supportive counseling to those in need who ask for help. There may also be funding from the Federal Emergency Management Agency (FEMA) to provide psychoeducational materials to the community and to ensure that counseling services are available throughout the recovery process. To repeat, these traditional strategies have usually been implemented by trained mental health professionals who are available to those requesting them. However, the strategies need to be adapted and applied to other populations that may not be included in the traditional emergency response system, particularly those that, during screening, are not identified as needing such services and those that may not feel comfortable about coming forward for help. In addition, more training regarding the types of consequences, and effective strategies for mitigating them, may be needed for the special provider groups who will play a critical role in responding to the various psychological needs that are likely to arise: mental health specialists, informal care providers, and other existing social support systems within the community.

WHAT WORKS? DEVELOPING AND EVALUATING INTERVENTIONS

The nation's ability to respond to the psychological consequences of terrorism depends in part on the availability of effective interventions. We need reliable tools and strategies for assessing symptoms in different affected populations, and for distinguishing between individuals who are likely to recover and those who will require more intense interventions.[22] Once a population is identified as needing treatment, the efficacy of the available interventions needs to be understood. The needs of those who have been directly affected by an event may differ from the needs of those who were not directly affected. There is currently no universally applicable strategy. Experts in mental health following a disaster should design and evaluate clinical interventions such as psychotherapy, medication, and counseling to ensure the delivery of effective care at the right time and by the right persons.

In recent years, attention has been given to the effectiveness of psychological debriefings and "critical incident stress" debriefings. These techniques were developed to allow guided processing of a stressful event within a group of individuals having the same level of exposure to the event (such as a group of emergency responders after a fatal fire).[23] However, empirical research is inconclusive regarding the effectiveness of these interventions, and more work is needed to understand if, when, and for whom these models are appropriate and helpful. Early intervention strategies for individuals exposed to mass violence must be culturally relevant, sensitive to individual differences, and sensitive to the context in which members of specific groups (e.g., people with special needs, first responders, and minorities) have experienced the traumatic event. Based on evidence and application of best practice guidelines available, Ritchie, Friedman, Watson et al. (2004) outlined several key components for early mental health interventions following chemical, bacteriological, radiological (CBR) attacks.[24] These strategies involve prior planning and involve several key stakeholders.

WHO CAN RESPOND?

Mental Health Specialists

After communitywide disasters, including terrorism, individuals with training in mental health (e.g., licensed social workers, psychologists, and psychiatrists) have often played an important role in the immediate response. These specialists can provide psychoeducation and emotional support (such as the techniques grouped under the term "psychological firstaid") and crisis counseling to people who have been directly affected by the event. People who have actually participated in such activities and in coordinating the broader response to the disaster have identified at least three areas for improvement.

First, in some cases, many local specialists in mental health and specialists from outside the area may descend on the scene of a disaster, potentially putting themselves at risk and hampering the activities of other responders. Second, many mental health specialists are not trained in, or are not even familiar with, psychological first aid or currently agreed-on best practices for working with victims in the immediate aftermath of a disaster. Third, experts in mental health in the context of disasters generally agree that many traditional interventions (e.g., psychoanalysis) are inappropriate following a terrorist event or a large-scale disaster.[25]

Accordingly, efforts are now under way in many communities (such as some in Connecticut and Massachusetts), and in the mental health field more broadly, to train individuals to respond to a disaster. One example is the American Red Cross Disaster Mental Health training program. Efforts are also being made to develop plans to restrict access to a disaster site to those individuals, identified in advance, who have expertise in "disaster mental health response."

Informal Care Providers and Community Organizations

In a terrorist attack, informal care providers (such as teachers, supervisors, and faith-based organizations) can be instrumental in providing information and support to victims and their families, and in helping to manage the psychological consequences of the event.

Schools will be in a unique position to provide grief counseling, reassure students about their safety, and monitor students with severe stress reactions.[26]

Work sites also provide an opportunity for individuals to express their concerns and receive information following an incident.[27] If response strategies include isolating employees or quarantining buildings, employers will need to understand their role in implementing a public health response, as well as in managing the psychological consequences of the event and the response.

The clergy were cited as one of the most frequently sought sources of help in surveys conducted after 9/11. They represent another important source of informal care and support. Response planners should consider how churches and other religious organizations can work together to manage the psychological consequences of terrorism.

HOW CAN WE ENSURE THAT THE RESPONDERS ARE READY?

More work is needed to prepare community-level care providers to respond to the psychological consequences of terrorism. For instance, little is known about what education and training the providers will need for responding to psychological consequences, and little is known about the skills involved.

The participation of those familiar with psychological and psychiatric issues will be critical to all phases of planning for preparedness at the local and state level. In the planning phases, such individuals can help devise appropriate strategies for communicating about risk; can help develop educational materials that are sensitive to risk perception and to emotional and cognitive responses and processing; and can help train and educate emergency response personnel with regard to detecting and treating traumatic reactions.

During the acute management phase of a terrorist event, trained mental health professionals can be part of the response team to help diagnose neuropsychiatric complications associated with some biological or chemical agents, and to distinguish between psychosomatic symptoms and organic symptoms. Over the longer term, they can provide appropriate and effective interventions for victims who have been directly affected and for others who are experiencing psychological distress, including members of the general population.

A few specific issues having to do with mental health specialists require further consideration by federal, state, and local preparedness planners: workforce size and training requirements for disaster response and terrorism specifically; the "surge capacity" of the mental health treatment system for handling psychological casualties; and effective interventions to address the needs of diverse affected populations.

CONCLUSION

Uncertainty and lack of information about the specific or unique psychological effects of terrorism may complicate the task of state officials who must develop mental health plans as part of overall preparedness. Also, the way response plans are implemented and communicated might generate or mitigate fear and anxiety in a particular population. Clearly, understanding how to manage the psychological consequences of terrorism is critical to developing and implementing realistic, appropriate response strategies.

The emergency response system, including the public health system, must be prepared for a terrorist attack and have strategies in place to minimize its psychological consequences. Initial preparation should include collaborating and coordinating with a variety of agencies involved in homeland security (emergency responders, hospitals, public health officials, etc.) to ensure the inclusion of individuals who understand and can respond to the psychological aspects of terrorism: emergency responders, health care providers, including mental health professionals, and other health care personnel. An effective communication system will be essential in order to apply recommendations for responding to and mitigating public uncertainty and distress. State and local health departments should consider developing a three-prong approach to planning, similar to that used by FEMA: education, preparedness, and action. Finally, strategies for preparedness need to address the mental health consequences of a terrorist attack as well as the issues of physical health.

NOTES

1. The article is based on a related work in *Milbank Quarterly*, September 2004. See also B. D. Stein, T. L. Tanielian, D. P. Eisenman, D. Keyser, M. A. Burnam, and H. A. Pincus, "Emotional and Behavioral Consequences of Bioterrorism: Planning a Public Health Response," *Milbank Quarterly* 82:3 (2004): 413–55.

2. National Research Council, *Terrorism: Perspectives from the Behavioral and Social Sciences,* N. J. Smelser and F. Mitchell (eds.), (Washington, D. C.: National Academies Press, 2002).

3. Tony Blair, speech to joint session, U.S. Congress, 17 July 2003; http:news.bbc.co.uk/2/hi/uk_news/politics/3076253.stm.

4. F. H. Norris, *Fifty Thousand Disaster Victims Speak: An Empirical Review of the Empirical Literature, 1981–2001* (Rockville, Md.: Substance Abuse and Mental Health Services Administration, 2001).

5. R. Beaton and S. Murphy, "Psychosocial Responses to Biological and Chemical Terrorist Threats and Events: Implications for the Workplace," *Journal of the American Association of Occupational Health Nurses* 50:4 (2002): 182–9.

6. See the following: L. Abenhaim, W. Dab, and L. R. Salmi, "Study of Civilian Victims of Terrorist Attacks (France 1982–1987)," *Journal of Clinical Epidemiology* 45:2 (1992): 103–9; H. S. Desivilya, R. Gal, and O. Ayalon, "Extent of Victimization, Traumatic Stress Symptoms, and Adjustment of Terrorist Assault Survivors: A Long-Term Follow-Up," *Journal of Trauma and Stress* 9:4 (1996): 881–9; T. A. Grieger, C. S. Fullerton, and R. J. Ursano, "Posttraumatic Stress Disorder, Alcohol Use, and Perceived Safety after the Terrorist Attack on the Pentagon," *Psychiatric Services* 54:10 (2003): 1380–2; C. S. North, "The Course of Posttraumatic Stress Disorder after the Oklahoma City Bombing," *Military Medicine* 166:12 (Supp.) (2001): 51–2; C. S. North, S. J. Nixon, S. Shariat, et al., "Psychiatric Disorders among Survivors of the Oklahoma City Bombing," *Journal of the American Medical Association* 282:8 (1999): 755–62; and D. Reissman, E. Whitney, T. Taylor, et al., "One-Year Health Assessment of Adult Survivors of *Bacillus anthracis* Infection," *Journal of the American Medical Association* 291:16 (2004): 1994–8.

7. M. A. Schuster, B. D. Stein, L. Jaycox, et al., "A National Survey of Stress Reactions after the September 11, 2001, Terrorist Attacks," *New England Journal of Medicine* 345:20 (2001): 1507–12.

8. S. Galea, J. Ahern, H. Resnick, et al., "Psychological Sequelae of the September 11 Terrorist Attacks in New York City," *New England Journal of Medicine* 346:13 (2002): 982–7.

9. W. E. Schlenger, J. M. Caddell, L. Ebert, et al., "Psychological Reactions to Terrorist Attacks: Findings from the National Study of Americans' Reactions to September 11," *Journal of the American Medical Association* 288:5 (2002): 581–58.

10. R. C. Silver, E. A. Holman, D. N. McIntosh, et al., "Nationwide Longitudinal Study of Psychological Responses to September 11," *Journal of the American Medical Association* 288:10 (2002): 1235–44. See also B. D. Stein, L. H. Jaycox, M. N. Elliott, et al., "Emotional and Behavioral Impact of Terrorism on Children: Results from a National Survey," *Applied Developmental Science.*

11. D. Vlahov, S. Galea, J. Ahern, et al., "Consumption of Cigarettes, Alcohol, and Marijuana among New York City Residents Six Months after the September 11 Terrorist Attacks," *American Journal of Drug and Alcohol Dependence.*

12. P. N. Halkitis, A. H. Kutnick, E. Rosof, et al., "Adherence to HIV Medications in a Cohort of Men Who Have Sex with Men: Impact of September 11th," *Journal of Urban Health* 80:1 (2003): 161–6.

13. C. S. North, L. Tivis, J. C. McMillen, et al., "Psychiatric Disorders in Rescue Workers after the Oklahoma City Bombing," *American Journal of Psychiatry* 159:5 (2002): 857–9. D. Herman, C. Felton, and E. Susser, "Mental Health Needs in New York State Following the September 11th Attacks," *Journal of Urban Health* 79:3 (2002a): 322–31.

14. C. DiGiovanni, Jr., "The Spectrum of Human Reactions to Terrorist Attacks with Weapons of Mass Destruction: Early Management Considerations," *Prehospital and Disaster Medicine: The Official Journal of the National Association of EMS Physicians and the World Association for Emergency Physicians in Association with the Acute Care Foundation* 18:3 (2003): 253–7.

15. Stein et al. (forthcoming).

16. J. A. Shaw, "Children Exposed to War/Terrorism," *Clinical Child and Family Psychology Review* 6:4 (2003): 237–46.

17. Stein et al. (forthcoming).

18. Galea et al. (2002).

19. Norris (2001).

20. Silver et al. (2002).

21. B. Pfefferbaum, J. A. Call, and G. M. Sconzo, "Mental Health Services for Children in the First Two Years after the 1995 Oklahoma City Terrorist Bombing," *Psychiatric Services* 50:7 (1999): 956–8.

22. National Institute of Mental Health (NIMH), *Mental Health and Mass Violence: Evidence-Based Early Psychological Intervention for Victims/Survivors of Mass Violence—A Workshop to Reach Consensus on Best Practices* (NIMH Publication No. 02-5138) (Washington, D.C.: U.S. Government Printing Office, 2002).

23. Ritchie E. C., M. Friedman, P. Watson, R. Ursano, S. Wessely, and B. Flynn (2004) Mass Violence and Early Mental Health Intervention: A Proposed Application of Best Practice Guidelines to Chemical, Biological, and Radiological Attacks.

24. J. T. Mitchell, "When Disaster Strikes: The Critical Incident Stress Debriefing Process," *Journal of Medical Emergency Services* 8 (1983): 36–9. See also J. T. Mitchell and G. S. Everly, "Critical Incident Stress Management and Critical Incident Stress Debriefings: Evolutions, Effects, and Outcomes," in B. Raphael and J. P. Wilson (eds.), *Psychological Debriefings: Theory, Practice, and Evidence* (New York: Cambridge University Press, 2000), pp. 71–90.

25. NIMH (2002).

26. B. D. Stein, T. L. Tanielian, M. E. Vaiana, et al., "The Role of Schools in Meeting Community Needs during Bioterrorism," *Biosecurity and Bioterrorism: Biodefense Strategy, Practice, and Science* 4:1 (2003), pp. 273–81. See also M. D. Weist, M. A. Sander, N. A. Lever, et al., "School Mental Health's Response to Terrorism and Disaster," *Journal of School Violence* 1:4 (2002): 5–31.

27. W. Goldman, "Terrorism and Mental Health: Private-Sector Responses and Issues for Policy Makers," *Psychiatric Services* 53:8 (2002): 941–3.

29

CRISIS PREPAREDNESS AND CRISIS RESPONSE: THE META-LEADERSHIP MODEL AND METHOD

National Preparedness Leadership Initiative A Joint Program of the Harvard School of Public Health and the Harvard Kennedy School of Government

Dr. Leonard J. Marcus, Dr. Barry C. Dorn, Dr. Isaac Ashkenazi, Joseph M. Henderson, and Eric J. McNulty

Dr. Leonard Marcus is the founding Co-director of the National Preparedness Leadership Initiative (NPLI), a joint program of the Harvard School of Public Health and Harvard's Kennedy School of Government. Dr. Barry Dorn is the Associate Director of the NPLI. Dr. Isaac Ashkenazi is the Director of Urban Terrorism Preparedness at the NPLI and the former Surgeon General of the Home Front Command of the Israel Defense Forces. Joseph M. Henderson, M.A. is a senior executive with the Centers for Disease Control and Prevention. Eric J. McNulty is the Senior Associate at the NPLI. For more information on the NPLI, visit http://www.hsph. harvard.edu/npli February 2012

"Meta-leadership teaches you how to manage large, complex, anomalous events. It's about how you work across government and large complex organizations to create unity of effort."

Thad Allen, Commandant (ret.), U.S. Coast Guard[1]

Leadership challenges are never greater than in the face of mass scale, complex, catastrophic disasters. The exact contours and content of the situation tend to be blurred. Secondary disasters are in process. Misery is growing quickly. Many agencies and organizations activate in response. Multiple options for action are available. Politicians demand answers. The public is agitated. The media goes into overdrive, ready with its own pundits to diagnose what you should and should not be doing. In such chaotic, demanding circumstances there are leaders whose scope of thinking, capacity for unifying influence, and quality of timely performance make a meaningful difference. We call these people "Meta-leaders."

During crises, these meta-leaders are able to marshal and engage action that is both comprehensive and cohesive—often far beyond their formal or expected bounds of authority or scope of command. They integrate and thereby leverage an extensive range of agencies, organizations, and people into formally and informally coordinated deliberate and decisive activity. This unity of effort may require integrating the efforts of federal, state, local, and tribal officials. It may involve civilian and military entities. International organizations may be providing assistance. Activities are not limited to designated government agencies within the official chain of command. They also encompass businesses, faith-based organizations, community agencies, and members of the general public mobilized into purposeful action. During a major incident—be it a terrorist attack such as those that occurred on 9/11 or a natural disaster such as the May 2011 tornado strike that hit Joplin, Missouri—just such a wide breath of activity is necessary to meet the catastrophe head-on and to mitigate its impact on the population.

Derived through field observation and analysis of leaders in high-stakes, high-pressure crisis situations, the five dimensions of meta-leadership framework and practice guide these people and serve as an organizing structure for understanding the performance necessary to effectively lead through multifaceted disaster responses. Meta-leadership is to preparedness and response leadership what ICS (Incident Command System) is to preparedness and response management. These two are complementary, as success requires both effective leadership and management.

THE DEMANDS OF CRISIS LEADERSHIP

The Deepwater Horizon oil spill in the Gulf of Mexico in spring 2010 is an example of a complex, catastrophic event. It affected five states—from Texas to Florida—as almost 5 million barrels of oil disgorged into the Gulf from a ruptured underwater well. According to the U.S. Coast Guard, there were more than 48,000 personnel involved in the response at its peak. More than 9,000 vessels were deployed (one-third of which were private "vessels of opportunity"). Thirty-four federal agencies were involved, along with many state and local entities. Offers of assistance from 16 foreign governments were accepted.[2] This data only begins to outline the complexities of this event.

During circumstances when rapid problem solving is at a premium, authority and accountability structures become more reciprocal and relational, since there are so many sources of authority, most of which are not ordered within the same hierarchical structures or legal frameworks.[3] The situation on the ground is often complex, networked, emotional, and chaotic.[4] Organizational boundaries function as semi-permeable membranes rather than hard walls with the involvement of multiple internal and external entities in the response.

The intricacies and demands of leadership in such an environment are often obscured by the focus of policies, protocols, and embedded theories that view leadership as a top-down leader-subordinate construct, typical of hierarchical organizations.[5] Ancona and Backman found that approximately 85 percent of the existing leadership literature assumed a hierarchical leadership structure.[6] Yukl argued that many leadership theories dealt with a single level of processes because it is difficult to develop multi-level theory.[7] Multi-level reality, we argue, is exactly what homeland security leaders face and thus is the impetus for our work. The traditional boss-to-employee relationship, for one, has been formalized in clear roles, authority structure, rules, job descriptions, and responsibilities that prescribed performance and productivity expectations.[8] Many relationships critical to leadership success are not so structured.[9] Theories of matrix organizations look at cross-functional relationships, though generally within a single organization.[10] All of these are valuable, but none are sufficient on their own for the multiplicity of challenges that a crisis leader faces in the midst of a disaster.

These theories also do not fully capture what occurs when leaders must catalyze action well above and beyond their formal lines of decision making and control. We argue that the best evidence of effective leadership in these situations is unity of action among all stakeholders toward a common goal. To achieve this, we argue that crisis leaders must simultaneously lead "down" in the traditional sense, "up" to influence the people or organizations to which they are accountable, and "across" to activate peer groups and others with whom there is no

Figure 29-1

The five dimensions meta-leadership model, showing up, down, and across roles and their connection to the person and the situation.

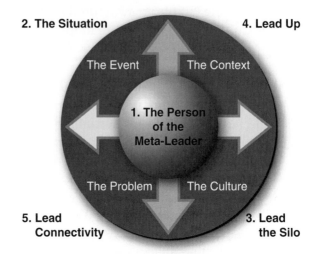

formal subordinate relationship (see Figure 29-1). As was seen during the April 2009 advent of H1N1 in North America, the response to an emerging threat that affects so many states, countries, businesses, and so broad a swath of the population ultimately must be viewed as an integrated whole. We describe such broadly envisioned, overarching leadership as "meta-leadership."[11] Meta-leadership addresses leadership challenges that cross inter- as well as intra-organizational boundaries. We explore here how meta-leadership encompasses a wide range of leadership scholarship and maps the critical interdependencies that apply during crisis preparedness and response.

THE MODEL OF META-LEADERSHIP: ORIGINS AND EXTENSIONS

Our group has been working since shortly after 9/11 to better understand the intricacies of starting up a preparedness and response system in this country that would be resilient in the face of terrorism and other novel threats. We surveyed extensive international leadership experience of both failures and successes and incorporated an academic understanding for conflict and the complexities of negotiating connectivity among stakeholders with differing interests drawn from earlier work in this area.

We opted from the start to engage in an inductive process, wherever possible investigating crisis leadership successes and failures as they occurred in the field. Through that we set out to develop a generalizable model, along with methods to teach and practice what was learned. We reasoned that leadership for extreme and novel events demanded a unique set of competencies and proficiencies that could best be studied in the moments they occurred. It turns out that these were less unique to response than were they essential to the full range of homeland security activities; the heightened demands of crisis response merely brings them into high relief. It was out of this process that we coined the word meta-leadership and developed its five dimensions of practice.

Individually and collectively we have been on-scene interviewing and observing leaders during and in the aftermath of a range of domestic and international events. A partial listing includes in the United States the 9/11 and anthrax scare (2001), the SARS outbreak (2003), Hurricane Katrina response (2005), advent of H1N1 (2009), Deep Water Horizon Gulf Oil crisis (2010), and internationally, the Rwanda Humanitarian crisis (1994), the Sarin attack on the Tokyo subway (1995), the Great Hanshin Earthquake in Japan (1995), the United States Embassy bombings in Nairobi, Kenya (1998), the Mumbai terror attack (2008), the devastating earthquake in Turkey (1999), the Indonesian-Thai tsunami (2004), the Second Lebanon War in Israel (2006), the Chinese Sichuan earthquake (2008), the Gaza War in Israel (2009), the Haiti earthquake (2010), and the Japanese triple disaster—earthquake, tsunami, and radioactive release (2011).

In these investigations, we have identified a range of leadership successes and failures. Perhaps the most significant failures have been in the leaders' difficulty in reaching critical perceptions and, through those, to understand, make decisions, and clearly and confidently communicate direction to followers. Conversely, the most significant successes among these leaders has been their capacity to accurately discern the situation, comprehend how the crisis differently affects distinct constituencies, and lead themselves and others—up, down, and across—in a balanced, flexible manner.

We have instructed more than 400 senior leaders in meta-leadership through the National Preparedness Leadership Initiative at Harvard University—many of whom held senior leadership position in post-9/11 incidents—and have presented local, regional, and international seminars to well over 10,000 people. The principles and practices of meta-leadership have subsequently been applied in a variety of situations.

The prefix "meta" is likened to its use in "meta-research," which systematically identifies cross-cutting themes found in many different studies, or "meta-analysis," which likewise combines and synthesizes findings about a range of questions in search of overarching themes and conclusions. Meta-leadership connects what have otherwise been disparate areas of inquiry about leadership into a cohesive, interdependent framework. It is also likened to its use in "metamorphosis." Not only must the leader catalyze change, viewing evolution as an active rather than a passive process, but the leader must build and maintain a capacity for intentional leadership—able to remain proactive in the midst of circumstances that can otherwise be overwhelming. Indeed, when one examines the criticism of the U.S. government after the attacks of 9/11, the attention is largely focused on the inability of the various intelligence and law enforcement agencies to coordinate their efforts.[12] When one looks at the response to Hurricane Katrina, the failure of federal, state, and local agencies to act cooperatively and collaboratively has a prominent role in the tragedy.[13]

Meta-leadership has its greatest impact in situations with high stakes and a high number of stakeholders. Scale, scope, and complexity are perspectives not generally addressed in theories primarily examining mission, motivation, or power structure such as transactional versus transformational leaders (Burns 1978; Bass 1990).[14,15] By intentionally linking the efforts of these many actors and many otherwise disconnected organizational units, the meta-leader—often operating without direct authority—is able to leverage and integrate activities to accomplish something that would not otherwise be achievable.[16] All meta-leaders are leaders first, but not all leaders are meta-leaders.

THE FIVE DIMENSIONS OF META-LEADERSHIP: DESIGN, CONCEPT, AND PRACTICE

The five-dimension meta-leadership model integrates an immense volume of leadership analysis, practice, and scholarship. As we have observed adoption of meta-leadership across complex public and private organizational systems and networks, we note three critical benefits during times of crisis: (1) A shared conceptual framework, mission, and vocabulary that facilitates intentional networking and cohesion beyond formal organizational boundaries to unify different stakeholders and sets a higher standard and expectation for performance and impact; (2) A purposeful strategy of action designed to advance coordinated planning and activity; and (3) A pragmatic, shared set of practice tools that guides and directs those leading together through a complex event. Meta-leadership enables significant positive and powerful outcomes to become more achievable.

By design, meta-leadership addresses the complexities of generating a unity of action when many different people, organizational units, and competing priorities must be focused into a strategy, plan, or mission for broad adoption.[17] In concept, it is a question of best aligning the plan of action with the problem or crisis at hand: What personal and contextual factors affect what meta-leaders see, perceive, decide, and ultimately act upon?[18] In practice, it is a puzzle of optimally engaging three facets of organizational connectivity—up, down, and across—and asking questions such as: Who are the many stakeholders that must be influenced and how can they best be leveraged to catalyze meaningful action? What other entities could or should be engaged to create a greater probability of success? This is particularly important during a large, complex event that involves organizations that are not part of a clear command-and-control structure.

These broad themes translate into the five dimensions of meta-leadership practice. The first two, the leader's self-awareness and an accurate perception of the situation, are foundational conditions: optimal action is not possible without them. The other three are the dimensions of organizational or interpersonal action: "down," or leading in one's designated purview of authority; "up," or leading those to whom one is accountable; and "across," or leading connectivity across the various entities. The meta-leader utilizes all five interdependent dimensions, variably leveraging each dimension of thinking and practice as called for by circumstances, and always having these different yet complementary perspectives at hand.

What is distinctive about meta-leadership concept and practice is the intent to draw these many elements into a unified framework. The description of the dimensions that follow does not intend to describe or reference all that has been said or could be said on each topic, but rather to describe key aspects and their fit into the overall framework.

DIMENSION ONE: THE PERSON OF THE META-LEADER

Meta-leaders begin with knowing themselves and the impact they have on others (see Figure 29–2). A high degree of emotional intelligence[19] is one critical characteristic of the person of the meta-leader.

Figure 29-2

Dimension One

1. The Person

Hold a mirror
to yourself
as a leader

People who direct the response to large scale emergencies must convey these attributes: self-awareness, self-regulation, motivation, empathy, and social skills. Self-awareness, in particular, has been shown to correlate with leadership effectiveness.[20] They have an understanding of the impact that personality, experience, culture, emotional expression, and character have on others: this is the "who" of the construct.[21, 22] The self-discipline, drive, understanding, and capacity to form meaningful and satisfying relationships are critical in the effort to cross the usual divides and boundaries of organizational, professional, and cultural association.[23]

Whenever one operates outside of one's formal purview or across clearly drawn boundaries, personal and organizational risk is increased. Thus meta-leaders must also understand how to build, manage, and keep trust, especially in situations where decisions and actions must be taken without complete information or certainty such as when operating in a volatile crisis situation. Organizational cohesion in high stress situations has been found to be lacking where trust-based relationships are absent.[24] When people are evaluating whether or not to trust, they weigh factors related to the decision maker and the situation.[25] The meta-leader understands this dynamic and the appropriate actions to take to achieve the greatest commitment from a wide scope of stakeholders. Trust is often built over time. When action must be more immediate, the meta-leader may utilize confidence as an interim goal: what can one do to build the confidence of others that one will perform as promised and what can they do to provide that same assurance to you?

The second critical component is that meta-leaders are willing to take a large, complex problem and entertain a wide range of possible solutions.[26] They have abundant curiosity to imagine that which has not otherwise been discovered.[27, 28] That the meta-leader has an aptitude for seeing the bigger picture is particularly important in a fast-changing, emotionally charged crisis.

These characteristics are important not simply because of organizational constructs but also the hard-wiring of the human brain. In a stressful situation, the brain's response is activated by the amygdalae,[29,30] a section of the brain triggered by fear and anger. It is where the primal responses of "freeze, flight, or fight" originate (the triple F). These responses derive from primal survival instincts that work to suppress all other thinking in favor of a narrow range of "fight, flight, or freeze" behaviors.[31] One cannot lead effectively when the amygdala response is dominant because it acts to overtake higher level thinking and strategic behavior in favor of panicked reaction.

Our term for this amygdala-controlled state is the emotional "basement." The characteristics above enable the meta-leader to understand that he or she is in the emotional "basement" and to consciously move up to the middle level of the brain (the "tool box") and help lead others up as well—generally through ingrained routines and responses, that is, the practiced procedures, protocols, or patterns of past experiences that trigger constructive activity and an aura of relative calm[32]—and then up to strategic thinking in the "new brain" or cortex. For example, imagine a patient in a hospital suffering a cardiac arrest. After a brief moment of recognition when the amygdala is activated and adrenaline is pumping for clinicians, they go into a rote set of actions. These are routine and well rehearsed. These actions help them climb out of the basement. If those "tool box" actions do not resolve the problem, the most expert or innovative members of the team will consider other options to save the patient—using the highest level of thinking.

The lesson in Dimension One is that a leader must first lead him- or herself: if one can't lead oneself, one will not be able to lead others. However, one will not be able to lead oneself without sufficient self-knowledge. The meta-leader is in constant pursuit of greater self-understanding.

It takes great self-awareness, stamina, and discipline to manage one's gut-level responses in a stressful situation and intentionally elevate one's mental activity. The meta-leader with self-knowledge and self-control becomes a role model for others. Emotional intelligence and a wide outlook provide the perspective to chart the possibilities and help prompt this vital climb.[33] It has been achieved when followers mimic the focus and direction that is being modeled.

DIMENSION TWO: DIAGNOSING THE CHALLENGE, CHANGE, OR CRISIS

The task of diagnosing and communicating the operational context—what is actually happening—is among the most difficult yet most critical in any crisis scenario. Finding the most appropriate course of action to respond to an emergency scenario depends first on precisely determining what is occurring.[34, 35] This involves not simply observing surface phenomena, but "tuning in to the organizational frequency to understand what is going on beneath the surface."[36] (See Figure 29-3.)

Situations can be grouped into two general categories: relatively static and dynamic. In relatively static situations, which you experience in your day-to-day work, problems are routine, knowledge is monotonic with few contradictions, and activity is moving in predictable directions at predictable rates. Changes are minor, there is time for information gathering and analysis, and adaptation, where required, is generally easy.

Figure 29-3

Dimension Two

2. The Situation

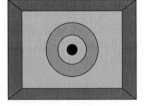

Your picture of
the event must
constantly adjust

Dynamic situations, as found in crises, have distinctly different characteristics: Problems are complex and the common operating picture is blurred. Change can be dramatic, sudden, and traumatic. Knowledge is anti-monotonic and characterized by contradictions and information overload. Order is distorted and space indistinct. Timing, both of the unfolding events and the leader's deployment of resources, is less predictable. Time becomes an enemy as the need for decision and action is immediate. These decisions and actions have a domino effect—positive or negative—throughout the response system.

Maintaining self-discipline and instilling a sense of order in the midst of seeming chaos is the challenge of crisis leadership. The difficulty of leading in a dynamic situation is compounded because there is often a gap between objective reality and subjective assessment or perception.[37] This is why Dimension One, self-knowledge, is so important to Dimension Two. This gap is further magnified when many different stakeholders are involved, a great deal of information is required to diagnose the problem, the stakes and emotions are high, or the analysis and action are time-constrained—the very characteristics of a crisis. The greater the complexity, the more difficult it is to develop an evidence-based, clear, and actionable description of what is occurring and with that, to develop the most appropriate response. This objective reality, and the ability to convey it to others, is at the heart of Dimension Two.

In practice, the meta-leader must grasp, work with, and narrow the likely reality-belief gap—the discrepancy between what is actually happening and what the leader perceives is happening. The leader does this aided by the collection and analysis of further information, the passage of time, and the perspective of hindsight. Such complex circumstances demand the capacities and skills for strategic "situational awareness,"[38] the connectivity between the personal capacities and understandings embedded in meta-leadership Dimension One and the realities of the situation that are addressed in Dimension Two.

Especially in times of stress, there can be difficulties in information flow between organizational units, competition among hierarchies, restrictions based on security clearances, and priorities that are in conflict. The meta-leader can be caught in the cross fire. In a complex catastrophe, the many stakeholders involved naturally each have their own analysis and interpretation of the "objective problem" in accord with their distinct interests, concerns, and mission space.[39]

The meta-leader also understands that each stakeholder uses a distinct "frame" built of values, experience, objectives, and priorities that filters what is seen and how risk is perceived. These frames, or guiding operational assumptions themselves tend to be hard to see, appear complete but rarely are, and are hard to adjust.[40] For example, the aftermath of a mass casualty event may bring the FBI into the same operational sphere as FEMA. One approaches the situation with an enforcement mindset; the other with a population relief and support perspective. This may spur conflict as each pursues its mission. The meta-leader looks for ways in which these differences can complement rather than contradict one another in order to integrate the divergent perspectives into a cohesive, new, value-added picture of the event.

The meta-leader closes the gaps by building connectivity and identifying leverage points that can transform potential discord into opportunity. Rather than focusing on who is "right," the meta-leader looks for how what each stakeholder brings can foster a greater understanding of the situation and development of a mutually agreed positive outcome. The meta-leader draws upon a basic premise of systems thinking: that no one has all of the answer and that everyone involved has some of the answer. Thus collaboration, not competition, is the logical pursuit for assembling as many pieces of the response puzzle as possible. Additionally, with a cohesive image of the problem, it is more likely that a wider variety of stakeholders will be motivated to contribute to the achievement of the solution. This analysis at times requires identification of confusing cross-cutting themes, priorities, and considerations in order to derive the most accurate assessment of what is unfolding. The meta-leader recognizes that the size of the gap between perception and reality will shift, and hopes diminish, over time.

In practice, the anticipation of additional and more accurate information and the expectation that the situation will remain fluid for some time does not relieve the meta-leader of responsibility; it puts even more pressure to assess when there is enough information and when there has been enough debate to move to action. It is an iterative process of divergence and convergence with concrete intermittent points of agreement.[41] Herein one finds both the tension and the paradox of Dimension Two: In a complex crisis, a quick assessment that is close to the mark and moves the process forward is better than a slow though more accurate one that comes too late to make a difference.

The meta-leader understands that success and failure may be measured differently by different stakeholders[42] yet the leader must make decisions and take action. For example, the Deep Water Gulf oil crisis was in fact many events, including (1) an environmental impact event; (2) a large global corporate event; (3) a small-business event; (4) a legal event; (5) a political event; (6) an engineering event; (7) a media event; (8) a public relations event; (9) a federal event; (10) a state event; (11) a local or "parish" event; and (12) a policy event.[43] Each of these events involves different combinations of stakeholders, each with their own perceptions and priorities. The National Incident Commander in that event, Admiral (ret) Thad Allen, when asked in an April 19, 2011, *Washington Post* interview how to focus people when resolving a problem when there are emotions involved responded:

> I'm a strong believer in a concept ... called "meta-leadership." There are five attributes of a meta-leader that make you successful in a large, complex problem or crisis: how you lead down, how you lead up, how you lead across organizations, your understanding of the event itself and managing yourself and emotions as a leader. They use a metaphor "going to the emotional basement." When you're in a position of responsibility, you cannot spend a lot of time going to the emotional basement. You've got to figure out a way to pull yourself out of it, not only for what you need to do as a leader, but as an example to the folks that are working for you. I've found that in a crisis, the higher up you are, the more you're going to be the one that has to pull yourself and everyone else out of the emotional basement, stabilize what you're doing and focus on what needs to be done. If you can't do that, you're going to get consumed in pathos and everything that's going on and not serve yourself or the country well. You could look to your subordinates or your superior, but there are going to be times where you walk alone, and you need to learn to do that.

The meta-leader draws upon the capacities outlined in Dimension One to distinguish which priorities are most important to the overall endeavor and calculates both the potential upsides and downsides of each option for each of the different stakeholders. These calculations are then applied to advance a cohesive framework and a cohesive set of actions.

The meta-leader has the perspective and measured patience to work with ambiguity. If the situation was clear and every action had a certain and predictable cause and effect, the skills of the meta-leader likely would not be called into action. However, complex, multi-tiered relationships, high-consequence organizational predicaments, and difficult interpersonal conflict each by their nature do not come with clearly obvious computations for what is right and what is wrong.[44] Not everyone faced with these ordeals is equally able to establish a calculated assessment and then rise to the challenge: these are among the strategic and analytic capacities uniquely associated with the meta-leader.

DIMENSION THREE: LEADING THE BASE

While the bulk of literature focuses on leading within one's immediate base of operations, the meta-leadership model emphasizes aspects of that practice that complement other dimensions. Individuals who rise to be meta-leaders generally have their own organizational base of operations within which followers see them in charge.[45] In that entity, the leader carries formal authority, has resources at his or her disposal, and functions within a set of rules and roles that define expectations and requirements. Those subordinates expect adherence to allegiances and loyalties, trusting that the leader will advocate on behalf of their best interests.[46] In bureaucratic terms, these accomplishments are often measured in expanding resources, authority, or autonomy for the entity and its members. In many bureaucratic settings, departments and divisions compete amongst one another, and followers expect their leaders to triumph on their behalf.[47] See Figure 29-3.

For the would-be meta-leader, the support of his or her constituents is essential to achieving influence within the larger system. Understanding how one is perceived (see Dimension One), demonstrating an ability to diagnose and explain the context in which the group is operating (see Dimension Two), and having a productive relationship with his or her boss (see Dimension Four) are all critical to garnering that support. The support of the meta-leader's follower base as well as the regard in which the followers hold the meta-leader are clear signals that can be read by other constituencies.

Figure 29-4

Dimension Three

3. They Lead the Silo

Commitment

Support your
staff so they will
support you

The meta-leader is a leader of leaders and fosters leadership development throughout the system, though first at home among his or her constituents. Leadership, after all, does not reside with one person. In robust organizations, it is embedded among many people and at multiple levels of the hierarchy.[48] This requires a sense of leadership confidence and security: strong, smart, capable followers are not seen as a threat but rather as a vital asset.[49] They seek followers strong enough to challenge them on occasion.[50] It is the meta-leader's devotion and commitment *to* his or her followers that generates the same *from* those followers. Subordinates do not follow the meta-leader because of a pay-based transactional relationship but rather because they believe in what the meta-leader stands for and is striving to accomplish.

What if the would-be meta-leader has not effectively engaged the commitment of his or her direct followers? It would be awkward and difficult for the leader to establish credibility in the wider system if that quality is not established in the home base of operations.[51] Followers, in fact, serve as ambassadors for the meta-leader, amplifying the efforts and attitudes of the meta-leader by creating their own linkages among counterparts in other organizations. Without their support, it would be difficult to leverage influence and activity beyond the scope of immediate authority. And, of course, much of leadership is modeling—thinking, behavior, and action that others not only follow, but imitate. Both strengths and weaknesses are copied.[52] Close colleagues and constituents best know their leader and often are the arbiters of their leader's ascent to meta-leader. This was certainly in play during the early days of the H1N1 outbreak when CDC Acting Director Dr. Rich Besser, who was well schooled in meta-leadership, had lead responsibility for guiding the response to the event. He effectively rallied the CDC workforce to quickly assess the virulence and transmissibility of the threat so that appropriate actions could be taken to address health concerns and develop a vaccine against the disease.

The unity of purpose and reliability of achievement that the meta-leader inspires throughout his or her direct domain of responsibility is the foundation for work beyond the direct confines of official authority and power. The confidence, direction, and dependability fostered within serve as the exemplar for what is communicated to the larger system of influence and action. That same momentum could serve to impress or intimidate his or her boss, a critical factor for the fourth dimension of meta-leadership.

DIMENSION FOUR: LEADING UP

The vast majority of people who work in organizations have a boss. The head of a government agency often works at the behest of an elected official. Below that director are a series of senior managers who report to him or her and who, in turn, serve as bosses to their staffs. Non-profits are headed by Executive Directors who report to a board of directors. Corporate CEOs likewise report to stockholders who are represented by a board with oversight authority.

Dimension Four, being able to effectively work with and influence those to whom one is accountable, is an important element of wider leadership within the system (see Figure 29-5). Followership, like leadership, is a matter of rank and behavior.[53] Meta-leaders do not let rank be a limiting factor but are careful not to upstage their bosses except in the most extreme of circumstances. By carefully cultivating and managing the most productive relationship with the boss, the meta-leader/subordinate may end up with as much or more power and influence than his or her superior.[54] This is particularly important during a crisis when a subject matter expert is leading up to an elected or appointed official who has limited expertise in the particulars of the crisis at hand.

The meta-leader is a great subordinate. What does this mean? The meta-leader/subordinate brings to the boss a valuable perspective

Figure 29-5

Dimension Four

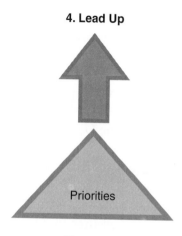

4. Lead Up

Priorities

Know your
boss's priorities
and deliver

when he or she has closer proximity to the work, has greater subject matter expertise, and can better perceive the problems on the ground as well as solutions to address them. Strategic decision making entails simultaneous activity at multiple levels of an organization; the meta-leader as follower can help ensure that the boss is connected and informed of both formal developments as well as the "offline" work that happens in small groups or in one-on-one conversations.[55] Among the other distinguishing characteristics of the meta-leader is the willingness and commitment to speak truth to power.[56] This is a quality critical to responsible followership, and the meta-leaders should expect the same from his or her subordinates.

In leading up, the meta-leader helps the boss recognize situational priorities and advances a crisis response that prioritizes mission success over personal costs or benefits.[57] In so doing, the meta-leader crafts vertical connectivity and bidirectional feedback. Influence is shaped by informing and educating the boss. The meta-leader also recognizes that there are many people simultaneously leading up during an emergency. In addition to subject matter experts, there are political advisors who bring a very different set of considerations to the counsel provided to the boss. While the crisis leader is focused on operational matters in the field, the political advisor is focused on public attitudes, perceptions of the media, considerations regarding political rivals, and the implications for the reelection of his or her boss. The crisis meta-leader rather than being surprised by these seeming contradictions must anticipate them, even before the crisis, developing relationships and alliances that can be leveraged when they could matter the most. In the moment, seniormost homeland security leaders may find themselves spending relatively little time on the technical response and much more leading up to mayors, governors, agency heads, Cabinet secretaries, and even the President as we witnessed in both the H1N1 pandemic and the Deepwater Horizon oil spill.

Bosses, of course, vary in style and temperament, and the meta-leader appreciates that as with any relationship, this is one that must be carefully and strategically managed.[58] The great meta-leader/subordinate manages assumptions, does not promise what cannot be delivered, and assures that the boss is never surprised. This last point is a sensitive matter. While bad news and valid criticism are hard to deliver, followers who tell the truth and leaders who listen to it are an unbeatable combination.[59] Meta-leaders also remember that the boss has a boss and work to ensure that they are providing the information and support necessary for his or her boss to lead up as well.

There is another aspect of leading up: your accountability and that of your boss to the general public. Any crisis whether terror attack, natural disaster, or other incident brings with it uncertainty, confusion, and fear. The goal of terrorists is to delegitimize the government in the eyes of its citizens. Average citizens have not drilled for response. They are not privy to assessments other than those provided through the media. They are dependent upon leaders for information, direction, and a model for how to behave (see Dimension One on behavior modeling). Effectively leading up to the public, and helping elected officials to do so, requires a vision beyond that of functional responder. It includes empathy, authenticity, and an ability to communicate in a way that ordinary people can understand. These were qualities displayed by New York Mayor Giuliani in the immediate aftermath of the World Trade Center attacks on 9/11. It is among the most important undertakings of a meta-leader.

DIMENSION FIVE: LEADING ACROSS THE SYSTEM

In building a wide sphere of influence, the meta-leader grasps that just as vertical, "up-down" linkages are important, so too are horizontal linkages. By leveraging adjacent centers of expertise and capacity, including resources and assets outside of his or her own organization, the meta-leader is able to engage the full spectrum of needed agencies and resources to create an extended network sufficient for effectively responding to a crisis.[60] Generating connectivity could be limited to proximate organizations, or could be more broadly defined to incorporate constituencies, such as the private and nonprofit sectors, that may not have been traditionally considered. Dimension Five is the ability to generate a common, multidimensional thread of interests and involvement among entities that look at an emergency from significantly different yet complementary vantage points. By combining their assets and efforts, the meta-leader envisions and activates more than what individual stakeholders could see or do on their own. (See Figure 29-6.)

Why is this both important and difficult? While a solution or opportunity may be apparent to all, it may be less obvious that only by collaborating can each of the entities optimize the response—especially if that collaboration requires sharing proprietary knowledge or technologies, opening systems or processes, or contributing some other asset that is viewed as a source of competitive advantage or jurisdictional prerogative. These different stakeholders may not, on their own, recognize the greater impact that they could generate together. In fact, they might very well see themselves in competition with one another. The first challenge for the meta-leader is defining what working together looks like along with its benefits—and why it is urgent to act now.[61] To be effective, the meta-leader must influence, engage, and unify these many different entities. The people representing each entity must be moved by the powerful advantages of acting in concert and by the

Figure 29-6

Dimension Five

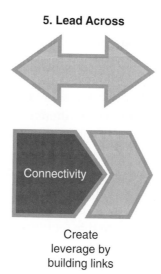

5. **Lead Across**

Connectivity

Create
leverage by
building links

enlarged possibilities generated by working together. And they likewise must be assured that individual units will "stay in their lanes," avoiding the tendency to wade into one another's areas of responsibility or authority, a move that would raise the competitive ire of others and ruin opportunities for collaboration, especially if one entity wants to grab credit for the work of others. According to Admiral (ret) Thad Allen, "Meta-leadership teaches you how to manage large, complex, anomalous events. It's about how you work across government and large complex organizations to create unity of effort."[62]

There are many hurdles to overcome. Chief among them is egocentric opposition from potential collaborators: the "silo mentality" of people and organizations as well as turf battles among those involved.[63] Within the comfortable and familiar confines of distinct organizational units, success is measured, rewards are achieved, careers are advanced, and objectives are sought attuned to the interests and well-being of the silo and its constituents. There is a natural tendency for people to ask "what's in it for me?" The potential for creating cross-cutting benefit is curtailed when silos that could be working together see themselves merely as competitors.[64] This destructive competition can be particularly intense when budgets are shrinking. The meta-leader is able to focus attention on the shared opportunity while at the same time tempering those forces of suspicion and jealousy that constrain their achievement.[65]

To do this, the meta-leader must identify and understand the individual intrinsic motives of these different stakeholders with the understanding that it is possible to create linkages in thinking and action, aligning these disparate yet complementary spheres into a unified plan of action. He or she must also clearly articulate ways in which each entity can contribute to the overall mission of the response. Entities must be recognized for their unique profile of interests, experiences, and contributions to the shared enterprise. While it is common for people to focus upon the differences and conflicts among them, the meta-leader turns the attention to points of agreement: shared values, aspirations, objectives, and circumstances. With a new appreciation for their points of commonality, stakeholders are able to creatively envisage what they could accomplish together—an end state that this desirable and compelling for all, building new equations of common ground and achievement. Often this requires strange bedfellows to work together, enemies to be invited to a common table, and people to appreciate a new or different set of values, objectives, and incentives. The intrinsic motives of each individual are thereby harnessed to achieve what is accepted as the greater good.[66] The meta-leader knows action and early triumphs are a critical factor in demonstrating the value added of working together.[67]

Push-back and resistance are to be expected in fashioning this new alignment of strategy and action.[68] Bureaucratic entities characteristically reward internally focused leadership that simply builds the budget, authority, and autonomy of their own endeavors.[69] The introduction of collaboration may require some traditionally competitive constituencies to turn away from well-entrenched attitudes about and behaviors toward one another.[70] If such push-back and resistance are anticipated and planned for, they are far less likely to undermine the shared purposes.[71] Expecting it, meta-leaders craft an alternate reward structure, through which stakeholders are acknowledged and encouraged for their work in building shared solutions.

Cohesion of action cannot begin in the moment of a crisis; it must be embedded into the strategy and activity of preparedness, a purpose and mission upheld by the meta-leader.[72] It is akin to carefully crafting interlocking gears. When it is time to move, the cogs link in a way that ensures movement and not stasis. For this reason, designing cross-system linkages of action is a visionary and methodical building endeavor, by which both the process and outcome of the effort attest to the value and benefits of working toward common purposes. This can be done through formal agreements, semiformal activities such as an interagency task force, and informal activities such as a peer discussion group that meets over lunch. Each of these can contribute to establishing collaboration and coordination among otherwise distinct organizations.

As stakeholders experience the demonstrable advantages of leveraging the expertise and capacity of others, and as they recognize the added influence gained when their contributions are likewise leveraged by others, impact and collaborative value both rise. Even so, the meta-leader recognizes that to keep the shared endeavor on track, these linkages must be carefully monitored and adjusted so that they survive the expected bumps of both preparedness and response and remain current with new developments, demands, and challenges.

UNITY OF EFFORT: THE OUTCOME AND EFFECT OF META-LEADERSHIP

What is the distinct meta-leadership mindset? What is its value during times of crisis? It is the intentional drive to forge both analytic and pragmatic linkages: how one thinks and acts. These deliberate linkages leverage deductive insights building from the interdependencies between the five dimensions of practice. Meta-leadership is a holistic, systems-based approach to leadership; competence with the components is not sufficient. Meta-leadership mastery requires deft, agile, and simultaneous activity across and among all five dimensions.

For example, what results from the link between Dimension One, *the person*, and Dimension Two, *the situation*? During a crisis, the sensation of panic, the biases, and the personal distortions among some in leadership positions can distract and misdirect the perceptions of the situation. A chasm forms between what is actually happening and what leaders perceive to be happening, a phenomenon the can take the response astray. The discipline and balance that comprise Dimension One of meta-leadership practice encourage the leader toward accurate analysis of the circumstances surrounding the event, a purposeful link intended to drive optimal situational awareness. Similarly, Dimension Three, *leading down*, linked with Dimension Four, *leading up*, when combined enhance the vertical connectivity of an organization, increasing the likelihood that strategies from higher levels translate effectively into operations and tactics at the lower levels and that information, problems, and successes at the frontlines are communicated up to the top. This ensures that situational awareness at all levels of the organization then translates into effective refinement of strategies and operations. And when these four dimensions are linked with Dimension Five, *leading across*, then other organizations, agencies, and individuals are included into a wider scope of awareness and functioning. Deliberately paying attention and then intentionally linking these five dimensions of practice is what drives the practice of meta-leadership.

The work of the meta-leader is in forging strategic, coordinated, and collaborative effort among stakeholders in pursuit of a common goal. To paraphrase General (ret) Michael Hayden: Autonomy of action for the parts, unity of purpose for the whole.[73] In such a connected system, each individual and organizational unit is aware that it has a role in a larger mission and that there are others up and down the organizational chart as well as various entities not in the hierarchy that compose the allied enterprise.

For leaders, achieving this unity of purpose requires synchronized, balanced activity across and between all five dimensions of meta-leadership. One cannot proceed sequentially leading down, then up, and then across; direction given to subordinates may affect the boss and other stakeholders. The meta-leader must calibrate for the multidimensional impact and implications of decisions and actions as they are taken. The meta-leader thus reaches past the usual bounds of isolated, linear organizational thinking and functioning. By understanding interdependencies and how the action in one sphere will influence the others, the meta-leader can leverage connections established in preparedness to remain proactive rather than becoming reactive in a crisis. There are a number of critical questions for the meta-leader: How do we define success and encourage it across the organizational spectrum? What are the critical dependencies? How will information, resources, and assets flow? How will interests and incentives be optimally aligned? How will rewards be distributed? It is up to the meta-leader to compose a compelling, integrated picture and message, engage each actor, and chart the impact they together will accomplish.[74]

Creating a unity of purpose and harmony in operations does not require "tearing down the silos." In fact, silos have important functions: Training, practice, professional advancement, and new knowledge and skills occur in the concentrated environment of the silo. Silos, however, must be able to work in concert when circumstances dictate.

Of course, there are distinct differences between building connectivity before the incident and exercising it effectively after the incident. Once an incident occurs, the situation moves quickly from static to dynamic. It will not conform exactly to the scenario on which plans and drills were based, people go to the basement, and unexpected elements burst forth. Thus, many aspects of the situation appear out of focus. The meta-leader uses the framework of the five interdependent dimensions as he or she strives to establish and maintain as much clarity as possible—both for him- or herself and for those being led. Meta-leaders do not simply create connections; they leverage them as a strategic network to produce results.

When clarity and connectivity are achieved, individuals and the entities in which they work are better able to leverage one another. They can do more in the midst of a crisis because they have a wider scope of resources at their disposal. Information is more readily available, expertise is more widely accessible, and tangible assets are more generously shared. Inter-entity competition as a primary motivator is reduced because success is less about prevailing in a turf battle and more about achieving the overriding goals of the crisis response. [75]

ON BEING A META-LEADER

What does it take to be a leader and what further is required to assume the added challenges of being a meta-leader? To be sure, there are many who occupy positions of formal authority who may think themselves leaders when in fact their influence is marginal or their position even resented.[76] These people beg the question of just what is leadership and how it differs from management or raw power.[77] Similarly, it is tempting to anoint oneself a meta-leader, a distinction that personifies an analytic perspective and broad scope of influence.

The word "leadership" is often used as if it were attached to a rank or role. Think of the designations "leadership role" or "senior leadership team," for example. One of the reasons that we coined a distinct term—meta-leadership—is that it is not used in this way. Our belief is that one is a leader if one has followers. It is behavior-based and not dependent on either rank or role. Every organization has "go to" people who are not necessarily high in the hierarchy. These are people to whom others look for direction and inspiration. They garner enthusiasm and support without needing an official sanction. People follow them. They understand that when one has followers, one must understand why and what those followers need and expect if they are to be expected to contribute their ideas, energy, and skills to the job at hand. So, too, are these leaders good followers of those to whom they are accountable. They are meta-leaders, and the meta-leadership framework is designed as a tool and technique for more broadly developing this capacity and capability.

The "science" of meta-leadership lies in understanding the five dimensions and how each contributes to a larger whole. The "art" is in achieving proficiency using all five dimensions simultaneously and knowing, for example, when to command and when to seek consensus, when to step up aggressively, and when to let others move to the fore. Mastery is not the pursuit of perfection but rather a commitment to achieving ever-greater aptitude, comfort, and confidence being the leader that is needed at any given moment. This does not mean being artificial; it means being so authentic that one can sense what followers need of a leader in order to accomplish the mission and then delivering it. It means being as dynamic as the situation and nimble enough to deliver those parts of one's self that will bring out the best in others.

Meta-leaders galvanize others through their capacity to appeal to more than just personal gain or parochial organizational welfare.

They are relentlessly curious and thus continually discover more about their own interests, motivations, and capabilities, as well as of those around them. Meta-leaders convincingly define a higher purpose—making the case that by acting above, beyond, and across the confines of their own organizational entities, the component members will accomplish more and function with less friction, and therefore the work each is involved in will be more rewarding. When effectively presented, the meta-leader's vision and the process charted are so compelling that others follow.[78] In doing this they utilize some of what has been described as transformational leadership. They must also, however, demonstrate effectiveness with constituencies beyond those who would traditionally be described as their "followers." Additionally, they must be able to work with (and sometimes within) organizations that are traditionally bureaucratic, such as regulatory and government agencies, or structures such as collective bargaining agreements that prescribe a transactional relationship.

Transformational leadership alone does not capture the capacity and capability needed to exert such leadership. Able to identify the gaps between what could or must be done and the will and capacity to do it, meta-leaders coalesce the knowledge, organizational workings, and context to achieve an otherwise unachievable cohesion of effort.[79] They navigate multiple environments and constraints in order to achieve the overarching objective.

Meta-leaders combine two aspects of the leadership equation to create a broad expanse of influence. The first is traditional hierarchical leadership, their primary source of recognition and authority. The second aspect of this equation is akin to social movement leadership,[80] what religious leaders, political figures, and humanitarian advocates exercise to inspire and engage people when they do not have the power of a paycheck, promotion, or sanction to persuade followership. It is that blend of commitment to a purpose, charisma, the talent to motivate, and appreciation for the fine art of timing that is at the heart of the informal side of leadership performance. While the exercise of formal leadership incorporates a measure of these qualities, meta-leaders must do both as they influence and rally others—without direct authority to command participation—to a shared, broader purpose.

There is another aspect of the meta-leadership model that is not often discussed in leader development: the permission to fail. Missteps and mistakes will be made. That is not only inevitable; it must be acceptable. No one thought of as a "great leader" has achieved that status only through success. Lessons, sometimes the most valuable, have been learned through failure. Innovation cannot happen without failure. This is exemplified by the Institute of Brilliant Failures in the Netherlands that chronicles how "mistakes" actually led to great gains.[81] The difference between those for whom failure is a stepping stone and those for whom it is career ending is knowing how to fail without jeopardizing the larger mission: fail *early* so that you have sufficient resources to correct course; fail *fast* so that you have time to recover; fail *smart* so that you gain knowledge and insight into how to improve outcomes in the future. We must learn to fail or we will fail to learn.[82]

CONCLUSION

Leadership of a complex, catastrophic crisis arguably is among the most challenging of leadership tasks imaginable. What is generally known or expected suddenly evaporates. Leaders must quickly take hold of their own emotional equilibrium, assess what is happening, predict what will happen next, and then activate an appropriate response—all with no time to spare.

Just as organizational forms evolve to better meet the needs of the times, so too must leadership styles and methods. For the first three-quarters of the twentieth century, command-and-control dominated both management and leadership in Western countries, in part because much of the managerial class shared the experience of military service. It was a familiar model with centuries-old roots, and there are still times when command-and-control can be effective. The emergence of large-scale and novel threats has, however, challenged the capacity of any one organization or limited set of organizations—such as the government agencies working in isolation—to rise to the task. Agility, adaptability, and learning-while-doing are essential characteristics of an extended homeland security enterprise that incorporates multiple levels of public sector players along with the private and nonprofit sectors as well as the general public. Meta-leadership is a framework and practice method designed for the challenges of leading in complex situations where one does not control all of the necessary resources or personnel, where fast-moving, multiple events distort clarity, or where jurisdictional restraints complicate action. Meta-leadership is a model and framework well-suited to situations in which the currencies of trust and influence are more important than formal authority. In particular, during times of fiscal austerity when government agencies are finding budgets slashed and personnel reduced, leaders must find ways to leverage capacity together so that they can accomplish more with fewer resources. In an emergency, the public will expect that everything will be done to save lives and restore their sense of safety and security. We do not present meta-leadership as a script that is simply to be followed; success is not achieved by flawlessly reciting one's lines. The framework must be imbued with the leader's humanity, and the leader must allow others to do the same. It is constructed to unify one's internal *capacity* to lead with one's external *capability* to exercise leadership down, up, and across a full range of stakeholders. It provides tools and techniques for building both.

The meta-leadership model described here emerged out of observation and analysis of leaders in crisis situations involving tense emotions and highly fluid circumstances. In such instances, collaboration across networks and leading by influence beyond authority are critical to survival. It also emerged out of the triumphs and failures of leadership at the time: the difficulties in getting organizations and people to work together when unity of effort was the best hope for mounting an effective response, and the inspiration and results when communities, businesses, and public agencies joined forces to accomplish what otherwise would have been inconceivable. Finally, it draws on the expanding understanding of neuroscience and brain function to both diagnose the root cause of behaviors under stressful conditions and suggest pragmatic countermeasures leaders can take to rise to the demands of the situation.

While the application of the meta-leadership model in more routine situations may not be so dramatic, it is no less important. The correlations between the two situations—the need for fast action, collaboration across organizational boundaries and among divergent stakeholders, and the focus on achieving positive outcomes, to name just three—speak to the value of the meta-leadership model for guiding daily leadership, preparedness leadership, and crisis leadership.

In this complex web, extraordinary crisis leaders emerge, able to generate greater value by balancing the expectations, needs, and contributions of all of the players in the extended enterprise. For those meta-leaders who excel in their strength of character, keen analytic skills, the ability to lead, follow, and engage a wide range of people extends their influence well beyond their formal authority. They forge both impact and collaboration that would not have otherwise been achieved. These meta-leaders—who certainly predate this model that seeks to describe them—deserve continued study so that their important work and contributions can be better appreciated and understood, better supported, and taught to others.

NOTES

1. D. Verton, Adm. Thad Allen: Changing Government Requires Flexible, Learning Leaders, 2011.

2. RADM Peter Neffenger, U.S.C.G., Personal communication, March 9, 2011.

3. T. Wagner, *The Global Achievement Gap* (New York: Basic Books, 2008), 28.

4. Green (2007). "Leading a postmodern workforce." *Academy of Strategic Management Journal* 6: 15–26.

5. For example, see M. Weber, *The Protestant Ethic and the Spirit of Capitalism: And Other Writings* (New York: Penguin Group, 905); R. Likert, R., *The Human Organization: Its Management and Value* (New York: McGraw-Hill, 1967); A. S.Tannenbaum and W.H. Schmidt, "How to Choose a Leadership Pattern," *Harvard Business Review* (1973, May/June); J. M. Burns, *Leadership* (New York: Perennial, 1979); B. M. Bass, *Leadership and Performance Beyond Expectation* (New York: Free Press, 1985).

6. D. Ancona and E. Backman, "It's Not All About You," *Harvard Business Review* (online), April 26, 2010, http://blogs.hbr.org/imagining-the-future-of-leadership/2010/04/its-not-all-about-me-its-all-a.html (accessed May 5, 2010).

7. G. Yukl, *Leadership in Organizations* (Upper Saddle River, NJ: Prentice Hall, 2002).

8. R. M. Fernandez, "Structural Bases of Leadership in Intraorganizational Networks," *Social Psychology Quarterly* 54, no.1 (1991): 36–53.

9. M. Hackman and C. Johnson, *Leadership: A Communication Perspective* (Long Grove, IL: Waveland Press, 2000).

10. S.Thomas and L.S. D'Annunzio "Challenges and Strategies of Matrix Organizations: Top-level and Mid-level Managers' Perspectives," *Human Resource Planning* (March 2005), http://www.allbusiness.com/public-administration/administration-human/394122–1.html.

11. L. J. Marcus, B. C. Dorn, and J. M. Henderson, Meta-Leadership and National Emergency Preparedness: A Model to Build Government Connectivity, *Biosecurity and Bioterrorism: Biodefense Strategy, Practice, and Science* 4 no. 2 (2006): 128–134.

12. T. Kean, L. Hamilton, R. Ben-Veniste, B. Kerrey, F.F. Fielding, J. F. Lehman, J. S. Gorelick, T. J Roemer, S. Gorton, and J. R. Thompson, *The 9/11 Commission Report* (New York: W.W. Norton & Company, 2004).

13. T. Davis, H. Rogers, C. Shays, H. Bonilla, S. Buyer, S. Myrick, M. Thornberry, K. Granger, C. Pickering, B. Shuster, and J. Miller, A Failure of Initiative: Final Report of the Select Bipartisan Committee to Investigate the Preparation for and Response to Hurricane Katrina, 2006, http://www.gpoaccess.gov/katrinareport/fullreport.pdf (accessed May 26, 2009).

14. Burns, 1978.

15. B. M. Bass, "From Transactional to Transformational Leadership: Learning to Share the Vision," *Organizational Dynamics* (Winter 1990): 19–31.

16. E. H. Schein, *Organizational Culture and Leadership* (San Francisco: Jossey-Bass, 2004).

17. Marcus et al.

18. P. G. Northouse, *Leadership: Theory and Practice* (Thousand Oaks, CA): Sage, 2004.

19. D. Goleman, *Emotional Intelligence: Why It Can Matter More Than IQ* (London: Bloomsbury, 1996).

20. A. G. Tekleab, H. P Sims, Jr., S. Yun, P. E. Teluk, and J. Cox, "Are We on the Same Page? Effects of Self-Awareness of Empowering and Transformational Leadership," *Journal of Leadership & Organizational Studies* 14, no. 3 (February): 185–202.

21. S. A. Kirkpatrick and E. A. Locke, "Leadership: Do Traits Matter?" *The Executive* 5 (1991): 48–60.

22. F. Trompenaars, *Riding the Waves of Culture* (New York: Irwin, 1994).

23. D. Goleman, *The Emotionally Intelligent Workplace: How to Select for, Measure, and Improve Emotional Intelligence in Individuals, Groups, and Organizations* (San Francisco: Jossey-Bass, 2001).

24. T. A. Kolditz, *In Extremis Leadership: Leading as If Your Life Depended on It* (San Francisco: John Wiley & Sons, 2007).

25. R. F. Hurley, "The Decision to Trust," *Harvard Business Review* (September 2006): 55–62.

26. R. Giuliani, *Leadership* (New York: Hyperion, 2002).

27. R. J. Sternberg, "The Nature of Creativity," *Creativity Research Journal* 18, no. 1, (2006): 87–98.

28. R. J. Sternberg, "A Systems Model of Leadership: WICS," *American Psychologist* 62, no. 1 (2007): 34–42.

29. W. B. Cannon, *Bodily Changes in Pain, Hunger, Fear, and Rage: An Account of Recent Research into the Functions of Emotional Excitement*, 2nd ed. (New York: Appleton-Century-Crofts, 1929).

30. H. S. Bracha, T. C. Ralston, J. M. Matsukawa, A. E. Williams, and A. S. Bracha, "Does 'Fight or Flight' Need Updating?" *Psychosomatics* 45 (2004): 448–449.

31. Society for Neuroscience, "Fear and the Amygdala," *Brain Briefings*, 1998, http://www.sfn.org/index.cfm?pagename=brainBriefings_fearAndTheAmygdala (accessed November 2, 2007).

32. R. S. Zander and B. Zander, *The Art of Possibility* (Boston: Harvard Business School Press, 2000).

33. R. Heifetz and M. Linsky, *Leadership on the Line: Staying Alive Through the Danger of Leading* (Boston: Harvard Business School Press, 2002).

34. J. D. Bransford and B. S. Stein, *The Ideal Problem Solver: A Guide for Improving Thinking, Learning, and Creativity* (New York: W. H. Freeman, 1993).

35. J. E. Pretz, A. J. Naples, and R. J. Sternberg, "Recognizing, Defining, and Representing Problems, in J. E. Davidson and R. J. Sternberg, eds., *The Psychology of Problem Solving* (New York: Cambridge University Press, 2003), 3–30.

36. R. Goffee and G. Jones, *Why Should Anyone Be Led by You: What It Takes to Be an Authentic Leader* (Boston: Harvard Business School Press, 2006).

37. V. Hazleton, W. R. Cupach, and D. J. Canary, "Situation Perception: Interaction Between Competence and Messages," *Journal of Language and Social Psychology* 6, no. 1 (1987): 57–63.

38. See, for example, K. S. O'Brien and D. O'Hare, "Situational Awareness Ability and Cognitive Skills Training in a Complex Real-World Task," *Ergonomics* 50, no. 7, (2007): 1064–1091.

39. Australian Public Service Commission, "Tackling Wicked Problems: A Public Policy Perspective, 2007, http://www.apsc.gov.au/publications07/wickedproblems8.htm (accessed November 5, 2008).

40. D. Clyman, "Decision Traps," presentation, 2003, http://www.darden.edu/varoom/documents/DecisionTrapsTalk-NOVA-v1–200304-Handout–3.pdf (accessed December 2, 2008).

41. M. Roberto, *Why Great Leaders Don't Take Yes for an Answer* (New York: Pearson, 2005).

42. P. H. Daly and M. Watkins, *Advice and Dissent: Viewpoint into the Fishbowl*, 2006, http://www.govexec.com/features/0806–01/0806–01advp1.htm (accessed April 1 2009).

43. B. C. Dorn and E. J. McNulty, "Improving Situational Awareness: A Meta-Leadership Approach," *Disaster Recovery Journal* 25, no. 1 (2012), http://www.drj.com/2012-articles/winter–2012-volume–25-number–1/improving-situational-awareness-a-meta-leadership-approach.html.

44. K. A. Slaikeu and R. H. Hasson, *Controlling the Costs of Conflict: How to Design a System for Your Organization* (San Francisco: Jossey-Bass, 1998).

45. D. T. Phillips and J. M. Loy, *Character in Action: The U.S. Coast Guard on Leadership* (Annapolis: The Naval Press, 2003).

46. R. Heifetz, *Leadership without Easy Answers* (Cambridge, MA: Belknap, 1999).

47. R. G. Lee and B. G. Dale, "Business Process Management: A Review and Evaluation," *Business Process Management Journal* 4, no.3 (1998): 214–25.

48. P. G. Northouse, *Leadership: Theory and Practice* (Thousand Oaks, CA: Sage, 2004).

49. R. J. Sternberg, "A Systems Model of Leadership: WICS," *American Psychologist,* 62, no. 1 (2007): 34–42.

50. Goffee and Jones, 2006.

51. B. S. Romzek, "Employee Investment and Commitment: The Ties That Bind," *Public Administration Review* 50, no. 3 (1990): 374–82.

52. Ibid.

53. B. Kellerman, *Followership: How Followers Are Creating Change and Changing Leaders* (Boston: Harvard Business Press, 2008).

54. Ibid.

55. Roberto, 2005.

56. W. Bennis, "The Dilemma at the Top: Followers Make Good Leaders Good," *New York Times*, December 31, 1989.

57. M. Useem, "Leading Your Boss," *The Economic Times,* November 13, 2003, http://leadership.wharton.upenn.edu/l_change/up_lead/ET_Nov_13_03.shtml.

58. Marcus et al., 2006.

59. Bennis.

60. R. Ashkenas, D. Ulrich D, T. Jick, and S. Kerr, *The Boundaryless Organization: Breaking the Chains of Organizational Structure* (San Francisco: Jossey-Bass, 2002).

61. J. Kotter. 1996. *Leading Change* (Boston: Harvard Business School Press).

62. D. Verton, "Adm. Thad Allen: Changing Government Requires Flexible, Learning Leaders," *AOL Government,* December 1, 2011, http://gov.aol.com/2011/12/01/adm-thad-allen-changing-government-requires-flexible-learning/.

63. R. L. Hughes, R. C. Ginnett, and G. J. Curphy, *Leadership: Enhancing the Lessons of Experience* (New York: McGraw-Hill, 2006).

64. S. Schuman, *Creating a Culture of Collaboration: The International Association of Facilitators Handbook* (San Francisco: Jossey-Bass, 2006).

65. Marcus et al., 2006.

66. L. J. Marcus, B. C. Dorn, and E.J. McNulty, *Renegotiating Health Care* (San Francisco: Jossey-Bass, 2011).

67. Kotter, 1996.

68. D. Bornstein, *How to Change the World* (New York: Oxford University Press, 2007).

69. V. A. Thompson, "Bureaucracy and Innovation," *Administrative Science Quarterly* 10, no. 1 (1965): 1–20.

70. S. Goldsmith and W. D. Eggers, *Governing by Network: The New Shape of the Public Sector* (Washington, DC: Brookings Institution Press, 2004).

71. Yukl, 2002.

72. R. L. Daft, *The Leadership Experience* (Mason, OH: South-Western, 2005).

73. PBS, "Interview with Michael Hayden," *Frontline*, August 19, 2010, http://www.pbs.org/wgbh/pages/frontline/are-we-safer/interviews/michael-hayden.html.

74. B. C. Dorn, E. Savoia, M. A. Testa, M. A. Stoto, and L. J. Marcus, "Development of a Survey Instrument to Measure Connectivity to Evaluate National Public Health Preparedness and Response Performance," *Public Health Reports* 122, no. 3: 329–338.

75. Dorn et al., 2007.

76. Bennis, 2003

77. A. Zaleznik, "Managers and Leaders: Are They Different?" *Harvard Business Review* (January 2004, originally published in May 1977).

78. B. Nanus, *Visionary Leadership: Creating a Compelling Sense of Direction for Your Organization* (San Francisco: Jossey-Bass, 1992).

79. Kotter, 1996.

80. C. Barker, A. Johnson, and M. Lavalette, *Leadership and Social Movements* (Manchester, UK: Manchester University Press, 2001).

81. Institute of Brilliant Failure, http://www.briljantemislukkingen.nl/EN.

82. M. D. Cannon and A. C. Edmondson, "Failing to Learn and Learning to Fail (Intelligently): How Great Organizations Put Failure to Work to Improve and Innovate," 2004, http://www.hbs.edu/research/facpubs/workingpapers/papers2/0304/04–053.pdf (accessed February 22, 2012).

30

ADVICE IN CRISIS: LEADERS, LAWYERS AND THE ART OF DISASTER MANAGEMENT[1]

Eric Stern

Co-Chairman of the Critical Incident Analysis Group at the University of Virginia and Professor of Political Science/Crisis Management at the Swedish National Defense College.

Gregory Saathoff, MD

Executive Director of the Critical Incident Analysis Group, Conflict Resolution Specialist for the FBI's Critical Incident Response Group and Associate Professor of Research in Public Health Sciences and Emergency Medicine at the University of Virginia School of Medicine.

Brad Kieserman

Chief Counsel of Federal Emergency Management Agency. The views expressed in this article are his own and do not necessarily reflect the view of the Federal Emergency Management Agency, the Department of Homeland Security, or the United States government.

INTRODUCTION

Crises, such as Stafford Act Disasters, place inhumanly difficult demands on all affected human beings. Leaders are forced to make some of the most critical choices of their careers—often with lives and livelihoods hanging in the balance—under the most difficult imaginable circumstances. Many of these decisions raise profound legal (and ethical) questions. Do leaders have the authority to intervene force-fully in the course of events? What are the legal implications of a given action if things go as planned, and even more importantly, if they go wrong?

Consider the controversy that arose during Hurricane Katrina in 2005 concerning whether state and local officials in Louisiana issued mandatory evacuation orders soon enough and provided residents necessary information and assistance to flee from the path of the storm. How do decision makers and their lawyers deal with the fact that those who fail to leave their homes endanger primarily them-selves, not other people? Should government officials use force to compel compliance with an order to evacuate? Do public officials have a duty to rescue those who resist mandatory evacuation orders or to provide effective means for residents to leave safely? In another example of the intersection of legal dilemma and disasters, the U.S. Army Corps of Engineers faced the dilemma of whether to "operate a spillway"—in other words breach a levee—and intentionally flood 200 square miles of prime Missouri farmland during the 2011 flood season, sparing the city of Cairo, Illinois, but placing scores of rural homes and agricultural livelihoods at risk. These are examples of real-time dilemmas confronting emergency managers—each case fraught with uncertainty, time constraints, and the gravest of consequences for the public.

Traditionally, journalists and scholars alike have placed leaders in the spotlight and examined the extent to which they rise to the challenge—or crash and burn—in the decisive moment. In this equa-tion, the role of advisors is obscured.

In recent years, however, there has been an increasing realization that a key determinant of success or failure in crisis stems from the interdependent relationship between leaders *and* their advisors. Wise leaders choose their advisors well and know when (and when not) to listen to them.[2] Unwise leaders choose their advisors poorly and act without the benefit of good advice—often with devastating con-sequences. While there have been a substantial number of studies of leader–advisor dynamics (particularly in the realm of foreign policy-making), the relationship between leaders and lawyers in disasters has thus far received relatively little attention.

In a collaborative research effort launched in September of 2010, a multi-disciplinary team of researchers from the University of Virginia worked closely with senior leaders and lawyers from the Federal

Emergency Management Agency (FEMA) to explore effective—and less effective—forms of collaboration between leaders and lawyers in crises. We called this initiative, "Advice in Crisis" (AIC). Following more than 60 AIC interviews with senior leaders and lawyers as well as numerous group discussions, a number of key findings emerged.[3] In the remainder of this chapter, we will examine the context of disaster management (with emphasis on the response and early recovery stages) and pose three central questions:

- What do leaders need from their lawyers in disasters?
- How can lawyers most effectively advise their leaders in disasters?
- How can leaders get the most out of their lawyers in such situations?

DISASTERS ARE DIFFERENT

Disaster operations require advice and decision-making processes to function at a high level under very difficult circumstances. It is useful to conceptualize disasters like other crises in terms of three subjective criteria: threat, uncertainty, and urgency.[4] Let us consider these in turn, as they are not only helpful in distinguishing crises from other types of situations but also provide a means for probing and preparing to act in them.

First, crises are associated with threats to (and often potential opportunities to promote) core values cherished by decision-makers and/or their constituencies. These include human life, security, public health and welfare, democracy, civil liberties and the rule of law, economic viability, and public confidence in leaders and institutions. Emergency managers and their lawyers must also be prepared to cope with different ways of thinking about (and conflicts among) these values.[5] For example, one way to approach disaster decisions "involves looking back at a disaster after it has occurred and deciding what to do about it or how to clean it up"[6]—this perspective is called *ex post*. Another approach "involves looking forward and asking what effects the decision we make during this disaster will have in the future—on parties who are entering similar situations and [have not] yet decided what to do, and whose choices may be influenced by the consequences" of our decisions[7]—this perspective is called *ex ante*.

Second, crises exhibit high degrees of uncertainty regarding the nature of the threat, the contours of an appropriate response, and/or the possible ramifications of various courses of action. One can imagine the effects of uncertainty in the aftermath of the 2011 Japan earthquake, tsunami, and nuclear disaster as decision-makers attempted to account for possible aftershocks and the probability of radiological releases. Another type of uncertainty has to do with media and public reactions to potential interventions or policy choices.

Third, crises are associated with a sense of urgency. Those in crisis perceive events as moving quickly and there are fleeting windows of opportunity to influence their course. Additional time pressure stems from the relentless pace of the 24-hour news cycle. Decision-makers and their organizations must cultivate the capacity to diagnose situations and formulate responses under severe time pressure. Thus, crises force decision-makers to make some of the most consequential decisions in public life under extremely trying circumstances.

These circumstances not only complicate decision-making, but also greatly increase the difficulty of developing legal advice in crises. A special task force created under the direction of Vice President Gore, known as the National Performance Review, generally found that " … government lawyers were insufficiently innovative and operated in a 'culture laden with red tape.'"[8] The rapidly moving milieu of disaster operations can further exacerbate the perception of lawyers as impediments and perpetuate such negative stereotypes. As one Incident Commander put it, "You lawyers never want to let us get on with things. I'm trying to save lives and protect property, and all you want to do is tie us up with legalisms. I don't have time for the law when lives and property are at stake."[9]

In fact, "normal" modes of developing, providing, communicating, and receiving advice may be inappropriate or even counterproductive under disaster conditions. Indeed, even under everyday conditions, many of the government managers and officials that we interviewed reported seeing "agency lawyers as essentially 'nay-sayers,' who were quick to point out the legal risks in various courses of action but less quick to array the legal risks or recommend feasible options."[10] Taken together, the characteristics of crises (core values at stake, uncertainty, and time compression), coupled with traditional perceptions of government lawyers as obstacles even under optimal conditions, can result in severe role conflict within and across professions.[11] As one experienced practitioner observed:

> Emergency responders and managers attempting to save lives and protect property must be action-oriented as they deal with fluid, very dangerous situations. Due to the extreme danger posed by hazardous substances that may well be weaponized, terrorism HAZMAT events in particular require prompt, correct action. In such a situation, professionals often perceive the lawyer who gets in the way of timely action as an obstacle to dealing with the event. Attorneys may find themselves literally locked out of emergency operations centers unless they have taken the pains to become a part of the team during the early stages of emergency management.[12]

WHAT DO LEADERS NEED FROM THEIR LAWYERS?

FEMA leaders need lawyers who will be loyal (and trustworthy) members of their teams, working effectively with other team members towards mission fulfillment. They need lawyers who can keep up with the rapid pace associated with the response phase of a disaster and who have the endurance to keep up that pace for weeks or months at a time, if necessary. They need lawyers who have a can-do attitude and who are willing to work creatively with the available legal authorities (such as those stemming from the Stafford Act, among others) to enable rapid development and deployment of solutions to urgent problems. Crisis leaders do not need lawyers who are risk averse and whose knee-jerk reaction is to say "no" in a climate of fast-paced crisis decision making where adaptation and innovation are essential to success. When identifying obstacles to a potential crisis action, leaders need their lawyers to distinguish clearly between matters of habit ("The agency never does that"), guidelines, policy, and statutory prohibitions. Leaders and their lawyers can overcome some types of apparent obstacles more easily than others. Habits may be easier to change than policies, and policies are easier to change (or circumvent) than laws. However, leaders also value integrity and judgment. They need a lawyer who is willing and able to pull the 'emergency-brake' if the team is on a collision course with the law. As one seasoned Federal Coordinating Officer (FCO) put it, "I don't want my lawyer to keep me out of court; I want my lawyer to keep me out of jail."

A key finding of the AIC leader interviews was that FEMA decision-makers preferences coincided with the SALT performance standard recently developed by FEMA's Chief Counsel. (See the appendix, What is "SALT"? at the end of this chapter.) The acronym SALT describes the criteria to assess the individual performance of FEMA legal professionals: **S**olution oriented, **A**rticulate, **L**egally sufficient, and **T**imely. SALT provides a tool for FEMA attorneys and their client-partners to assess their performance on a particular matter, particularly during crisis operations. These criteria are also a means for attorney self-evaluation and reflection, as well as a benchmark for review by supervisors and peers.

HOW CAN LAWYERS MOST EFFECTIVELY ADVISE THEIR LEADERS IN DISASTERS?

Based on the AIC project interviews, the researchers were able to distill three best practice models drawn from the skills repertoire of a number of the best performing and most experienced FEMA lawyers. The interview responses converged around three key secrets of success consistently employed by high performing lawyers. The first model, **PREP** focuses on mission preparation and outlines measures lawyers could take to be better prepared for field deployments, enabling them to orient themselves rapidly in a disaster, its socio-political context, and the crisis team (e.g., the leadership of a FEMA Joint Field Office). The second model, **GAIN** explores the group context and the complex negotiation of role demands necessary to gain trust and influence and strike an appropriate balance between team cooperation and the unique responsibilities of the lawyer in a crisis organization. The final model, **SOAP**, outlines a systematic procedure for producing and delivering substantive legal advice and managing risk (informed by a holistic analysis of practical, legal, and ethical considerations) to leaders. Each of these models will be briefly explicated below.

Mission Preparation and Readiness (PREP)

Leaders and top lawyers at FEMA agree that a key prerequisite for success is being prepared for the rigors of practicing law in crisis or disaster environments. The pace is fast and disaster lawyers must hit the ground running. The following section outlines four key categories of preparation that may be helpful in improving the likelihood of a successful performance. While they do not guarantee success, they clearly improve the odds. Furthermore, failure to prepare will stack the deck towards failure.

The following bullet points summarize some ways to prepare oneself for deployment and pave the way for good collaborative relationships with colleagues (see the GAIN model in the next section):

- *Prepare for availability and extended absence:* Two of the factors most emphasized by FEMA leaders and top-performing lawyers interviewed by Advice in Crisis researchers are availability and commitment. Clients want lawyers to be readily available and prepared to commit to longer deployments.
- *Establish predeparture communication* by phone and/or e-mail with key team members and collaborators inside and outside of the organization.

  Doing so enables lawyers to connect with their clients, other team members, and partners at an early stage, by establishing relationships and providing communication links that can help to improve the lawyer's situational awareness going into a situation.
- *Meet and greet leaders (e.g., the FCO) and team broadly on arrival.* Lawyers should follow up with predeployment contacts, and complement these contacts with additional personnel introductions, once on site. By doing so, lawyers not only signal sociability, but also approachability and willingness to be a part of the team.
- *Know your redlines.* In engineering, "redline" refers to the maximum engine speed at which an engine or motor and its components are designed to operate without causing damage to the components themselves or other parts of the engine. For emergency management lawyers, "knowing your redlines" means having a clear understanding of ethical duties and the limits of the law and how these bounding factors might present themselves in a disaster setting before providing advice in crisis.

Furthermore, the prospects for providing successful advice improve if lawyers do not wait for field deployment or first meetings of dedicated crisis/disaster teams at HQ to begin mission reconnaissance. Once assigned, lawyers should immediately begin informing themselves about the situation, context, and role they will be assuming.

Similarly, it is critical to gather/secure access to general and specialized legal resources on paper and/or in electronic form. This is particularly relevant for field deployments, but also can facilitate the development of timely and legally sufficient advice at Headquarters or in interagency environments. Effective crisis attorneys search and compile resources for anticipated issues involving, among others: authorities (for FEMA and collaborating agencies), regulations, guidelines, policy, opinions, precedents, new or recent initiatives or changes in policy or guidance, as well as particularly relevant points of local law. The PREP module concludes with suggestions regarding practical packing lists, which we will not discuss in this chapter for reasons of space.

Social-Behavioral Elements Required for Effective Advice in Crisis (GAIN)

From a social-behavioral perspective, the FEMA attorney faces challenges that are unusual, if not unique, within the legal profession. The first challenge is linked to the very identity of the agency. Simply put, to be effective, FEMA attorneys must embrace the fact that "emergency" is their middle name. The second challenge is that within these emergencies, whether they involve response or recovery, the FEMA attorney is like a traffic cop at a busy intersection at rush hour, facing people who must share the crisis road on their way to specific agency-specified destinations. The competition for the road reveals tensions: between field units and headquarters, FEMA and DHS (including the Inspector General), FEMA and the interagency process, state and federal government, and not least between OCC and clients. The FEMA attorney must know the law and be fair, but must also expect to face myriad stakeholders coming from various directions.

One cannot read this discussion about best practices without being struck by the abrupt nature of crises in general and disasters in particular, and the active engagement required by FEMA attorneys from the moment that they "parachute into the team." The vernacular of crisis can easily become "win–lose" or "succeed–fail." Expressions like "team player," "responsiveness," "integration into the team," "avoidance," and "isolation" speak to just a few of the behavioral caveats specific to the very tricky business of providing advice in crisis.

In the process of interviewing crisis leaders, FCOs, and attorneys for this Advice in Crisis project, it became clear that the process of advice—how it is developed and delivered—was as important to effectiveness as the content of the advice. Although knowing the law well is necessary, it is clearly not sufficient when dealing with crisis advice during the response and recovery phases. FEMA attorneys must attend to the dynamics of communication as they stand with

Regional Administrators, FCOs, or other leaders under the difficult conditions associated with disaster response and recovery.

Based upon the collective experience of crisis leaders and some of their finest and most effective attorneys, we developed the GAIN model of the social-behavioral elements of advice in crisis. The elements of GAIN include: *Group Dynamics; Active Engagement; Individual Requirements;* and *Negotiation.*

Group Dynamics

Because FEMA attorneys work within a crisis team, they must not only be aware of the group dynamics of the team, but also must be prepared to adapt to and try to *shape* them. Large-scale disaster response and recovery requires a rapid deployment of professionals from federal, state, and local arenas. These players meet in group constellations within and outside of FEMA that can initially be daunting, particularly for the inexperienced crisis attorney. It is within these group settings that the attorney's ability to connect and function effectively with others is tested in a quite public arena.

The Crisis Team: In order to appreciate the power of group dynamics in the days and months following the onset of a disaster (or other form of crisis), it is important to be aware of the critical role of group development as a factor impacting group performance. Often, groups may be rapidly constituted at the outset with many players that do not know one another well. In such situations, an effective group leader—such as an FCO—can provide form, structure, and constructive accountability to group members, minimizing individual uncertainty that might otherwise inhibit engagement and performance.[13] Leaders can clarify the rules of the game, coordinate, motivate and support members, and thus leverage their energy and commitment. As groups develop over time and stronger bonds emerge among the members, they are more prone to other conformity-based group dynamics such as 'groupthink,' especially in highly stressful circumstances.[14]

An effective crisis team is greater than the sum of its parts and requires that the crisis attorney become an integral member of that group. If the attorney has successfully joined, real engagement and meaningful communicative interaction will occur. If not, the attorney may become irrelevant and isolated. How does an attorney become an effective member of the crisis team? First, the attorney must value the team identity and seek a role as an integral member. But that is only the first step, as one must also understand two of the most important elements of successful group integration: Time and Timing.

Time and Timing: Shared experience of dramatic, traumatic effects is a powerful connective force: Bonding within crisis groups occurs rapidly. The initial response phase can have a searing effect on a crisis team. When led by an effective FCO, the charged atmosphere of the first few days can lead to a sealing or a bonding of a group that quickly becomes not only cohesive, but also potentially exclusive. Therefore, it is advantageous for the attorney to get in early and stay for as long as possible. Hours and days matter, and once that bonding has occurred, it is more difficult for a latecomer to bond with others in the crisis team.

Group dynamics evolve over time and this is not always to the advantage of an attorney who parachutes in and is then called away to another disaster. The group may actually feel offended if it experiences the attorney's departure as elective in nature. While *timing* is important, the correlate to effective crisis team integration is *time* itself. Much of the positive effect of early bonding will be lost if an attorney announces "in two weeks I will be taking annual leave, so please get your questions to me while I am still here." Groups mature, and as time passes the bonds become stronger. Although the initial phase is important, the attorney who arrives early and departs early has abandoned an opportunity to develop within an integrated team. If the attorney's actions suggest the calendar is more important than membership within the crisis team, then that attorney's membership will quickly lapse.

The attorney must not be perceived of as "high maintenance." This includes being overly demanding or being unreasonable about the workspace assigned to the attorney. The AIC leaders described an attorney who was almost sent home from a major disaster for being rude and demanding on prioritizing the set up of the cubicles for the attorney's staff. This was a very large operation with many top-level staff taking operational roles. Everyone had to make do. In another case, an attorney complained bitterly about being in an office in the basement level of a building and created unnecessary bad will. (The FCO had decided to place the attorneys in this more private office—instead of in an open space on the main floor as an interim measure—until the operations stabilized.)

By contrast, a very successful disaster attorney with a particularly can-do attitude described having to make do with a picnic table her first day on the scene because there was no space in the Emergency Operations Vehicle. She had a laptop but no Internet access, cell phone, or printing capabilities. She did have, however, a legal pad, her Stafford Act and regulations, and her computer files, and was able to set up shop and get to work. Another trio of attorneys had to share a data cable for email access for the first week or so after Hurricane Katrina. Each attorney had 20 minutes each hour for email and Internet access. They were seated at lunch tables with all the other FEMA staff in the cafeteria of the National Guard. This type of "close-quarters collaboration" can understandably result in the type of bonding that yields a resilient and effective team. *Attorneys need to be flexible on workspace issues in the field.* If an enclosed office is not feasible, then is there an office or private area for consultations or phone conversations available when needed? If a dedicated fax machine cannot be arranged, can the attorney use the FCO's fax machine? Is the attorney's space near the FCO and other command staff and sufficiently apart from the State staff and more open areas as a safeguard? Attorneys should adhere to the office hours of the field office and not their normal routines. If the command staff is in by 7:00 am, the attorney should also follow that schedule. This is particularly important for the lead attorney. Being unavailable or having a subordinate attend early morning command staff meetings will be duly noted by the command staff and will undercut the lead attorney's authority. In fact, the lead attorney may be considered the lead in name only, as team members gravitate to the attorney staff that is there for them outside of "banker's hours."

The attorney must continue to foster the relationships made as part of the crisis team after the crisis has ended and the team has disbanded until the next event. When crisis team members reach out to the attorney from their home base or from another disaster with an issue or question, the attorney needs to prioritize this inquiry whenever possible. As fellow team members, they are not just clients, but colleagues who have faced adversity together.

Challenges to the Group: Not all crisis teams are created equal. Depending upon the leadership and chemistry, some groups can evolve in unhealthy and even destructive ways. A skilled crisis attorney should be aware of the dangers of the unhealthy group, which can devolve quickly into a destructive process character-ized by either excessive conformity (i.e., groupthink) or excessive conflict.[15] Effective disaster attorneys maintain an understanding of the importance of ethics, consistency, and adherence to pro-fessional boundaries. When a group is allowed or encouraged to breach boundaries, behave in an unethical manner, or when inad-equate leadership is shown, members as well as the agency and other stakeholders will suffer. The attorney who maintains pro-fessional boundaries and behaves in an ethical manner not only safeguards his/her own reputation, but also serves as a model for others in the group which can help serve as a course correction for the group. With skilled leadership from FCOs, unhealthy groups are the exception and not the rule. But even unhealthy groups can be well served by attorneys who consistently adhere to profes-sional boundaries and ethics—this is why one of the PREP activi-ties is "know your redlines." In fact, in crisis as in other settings, lawyers have an opportunity—even a duty—to exercise this form of leadership.[16]

Attorney's Role within the Team: Certainly, the attorney's role within the team is to provide legal advice to clients during the response and recovery phases. That is not as simple as it sounds, and in fact requires a thoughtful situational awareness. What are the needs of the moment? What will the team require next week? Is there a legal issue that has not been addressed that will be certain to unravel unless identified by the attorney and addressed by the FCO and the team? It is not enough to bond early and integrate well into the team. Contin-ued integration into the team requires situational awareness in order to address present legal needs *while at the same time* identifying future legal landmines.

Within the group, the crisis attorney must maintain a balance between outsider and insider status—a team *player* who must at times shift gears and serve as a kind of *referee*. This is a challenge, because the two roles must often be played more or less simultaneously. Ide-ally, the crisis attorney maintains the trust of individual crisis team members, but also relates to the group as a whole. At the same time, the crisis attorney's role is distinct from any other. While unlike the FCO, the crisis attorney does not maintain a leadership role within the group the attorney's distinctive skill sets are unique within the group.

Active Engagement

In order to bond with the team, experienced crisis attorneys must also be actively engaged in the process. That activity provides opportunities to demonstrate commitment, purpose, and competence—potentially enhancing the status of the attorney in the group. In fact, many leaders would like their crisis attorneys not only to serve as technical experts on matters of the law, but also as wise counselors supporting not only the leader but also the decision-making process in a broader sense. A leader, such as a FCO, can benefit greatly from a partnership with an effective attorney. Through active listening, attorneys can acquire knowledge of the event, and the concerns of the leader and other team members—thus achieving better, more productive, and seamless integration into the fabric of the team.

Active engagement is a process that necessitates all of the intellectual and interpersonal skills required of a fine attorney. Active engagement is antithetical to a passive or static approach. If crisis is similar to a contact sport played on a field, the attorney should be with the action on the field as a player/referee and not in the stands watching or in the press box opining. Obviously, while some discussions (and the attorney's contribution to them) in the disaster arena will be very public, other discussions with leaders and team members are best kept private (see also the section on Producing Substantive Advice in Crisis).

A crisis presents a pressure-filled environment that demands attention and focus throughout the response and recovery phases when legal counsel is required. Active engagement is therefore a process that:

- *Begins* with accessing relevant documents even before arrival at the crisis site;
- *Continues* through phone, Internet, and face-to-face access of the attorney's collegial network both on-site and off; and
- *Leads to* team interactions that are sensitive to the needs of both individual team members and the group as a whole.

Individual Requirements

The attorney's role within the crisis team represents a paradox of sorts: To be a great team member, one must remain distinct. Because most FCO-led response and recovery teams in FEMA contain only one attorney, attorneys must resist the potential to become submerged into the larger group process if it would risk diluting the attorney's professional identity and integrity in the process. This speaks to the conundrum of being both a player on the team as well as referee. In such a scenario, the FCO may take the role of coach—not always readily embracing the calls of the referee, but always appreciating the need for an experienced interpreter of the rules of the game. The one major difference is that in the game of FEMA crisis (in the JFO setting, for example), the FCO coach can ultimately overrule the attorney referee. Whether one is a player–referee or traffic cop at a busy intersection, these important roles require knowledge of the rules and sensitivity to the situation at hand. Without an appreciation for the group process, active engagement, and individual requirements, a crisis attorney is not in a position to provide the most effective counsel.

There is, therefore, a need for the attorney to absorb and deal with the natural tensions that exist within any crisis team. Even when the attorney has bonded with the group and been embraced by the team, there will be conflicts among those who are dedicated to the mission. When these current or budding conflicts are legal in nature, the crisis attorney will experience the singular brunt of these tensions, which require counsel rather than judgment. How does the crisis attorney approach these situations? The best approach is through a process that attorneys are uniquely experienced and trained to deploy— negotiation.

Negotiation

Negotiation is the final element of the GAIN model, It represents a crucial challenge of providing advice in crisis. Speaking literally, various forms of negotiations take place in both intra- and inter-agency contexts associated with disasters. Lawyers often play a key role in guiding and facilitating these negotiations in order to support fulfillment of mission and other obligations within the context of the law. However, the notion of negotiation also provides insights into the lawyer's predicament in another sense. As we have already pointed out, the social, political, psychological, ethical, and legal terrain of a major disaster is complex and fraught with tensions and pitfalls that must be successfully *negotiated* by lawyers and leaders alike.

Our emphasis on a negotiation mindset may at first surprise new FEMA attorneys who approach advice in crisis with an FCO-led team. After all, doesn't advice in crisis involve interpretation of the Stafford Act? The Stafford Act is settled law and requires interpretation, not negotiation. So, if interpretation is the necessary skill, why is negotiation relevant?

While the Stafford Act is the critical piece of legislation that serves as the legal foundation for FEMA's response and recovery-related actions, it is written in such a way that it can be applied to disparate and often unforeseen disaster events—and the client is typically well aware of the potential for flexibility in interpretation. The crisis attorney must therefore be adept at both interpreting and translating the Stafford Act in a wide variety of situations. The attorney who wants to be persuasive and effective must also recognize that successful delivery of a legal interpretation may require a negotiation with the client who has preconceived expectations, contrary views on the scope of his or her authority, or misplaced perceptions that the legal interpretation will thwart an operational need.

Crises generate questions and the most important of the five senses for crisis attorneys is *auditory*. Hearing alone, however, is not sufficient. *Listening* is the real key. Crisis negotiators who deal with life and death issues are adamant about the obligation to listen prior to beginning a negotiation. In the life and death of disaster, crisis attorneys maintain that same obligation. Before rushing to an answer, one must first appreciate not only the content but also the nature of the question. The temptation to speak too quickly, whether it is due to hubris, anxiety, or naiveté, must be resisted. This is particularly difficult since the time frame for listening *and* processing is severely compressed in the crisis scenario. A dearth of time, however, does not mean that these crucial steps are skipped but rather that they occur in rapid fashion. Before responding, the successful crisis attorney runs the issue through an almost instantaneous mental checklist of broad statutory authorities and bright line prohibitions.

In order to listen, the crisis attorney who is actively engaged realizes that the negotiation is in part a translation of the crisis into words that the client can understand. Lastly, negotiation provides a useful mindset for the crisis attorney strategically placed in multiple agency, interagency, intergovernmental (federal, state, local, tribal), and public/private/non-profit cross-sectoral processes. The delivery of a legal interpretation, even for attorneys, often requires consensus building, especially in a crisis environment.

Negotiation during crisis requires both the content of knowledge and the process of interpersonal engagement under extreme time and resource constraints and competing interests. Negotiation between the needs of the group versus individual stakeholders can fulfill a critical role in serving and supporting the FCO's leadership of the crisis team. Whether that translation process occurs between individuals or within a crisis team or an agency, the effective crisis attorney is in a position to shed light during the heat of crisis.

Producing Substantive Advice in Crisis (SOAP)

Sense-making

The first step toward effective substantive advising in a disaster is to make sense of the situation (see leadership tasks). This may seem obvious, but it is a nontrivial and ongoing task as the disaster and post-disaster contexts tend to be complex and dynamic. Just as one feels as if one is getting one's bearings and has a good understanding of the situation and problems to be faced by the lawyer, the client, and the broader team in which the lawyer is embedded, new developments will necessitate updating and rethinking. It is an iterative process and one which may require abandoning previously held views and priorities[17] as the operating picture evolves.

While sense-making is in part an intuitive activity,[18] it can be improved and facilitated by using a set of core questions to challenge the "environment" and improve contextual and situational awareness. This is not only a way of combatting the phenomenon of stress-induced tunnel vision noted above, but also a good practice for lawyering and decision-making under more normal situations.

Asking the following questions can help lawyers (and leaders) better **make sense** of the situations facing them and improve performance in disasters and crises.

- Which **values** are at stake in this situation and for whom?[19]
- What are the key **uncertainties** in this situation (and how might information gathering, analysis, consultation, etc. reduce them)?
- What is the **time frame** for developing and delivering advice (which is in turn related to the client or team's time frame for action)? Are there ways of buying time without compromising the mission, public affairs messaging, or otherwise delaying the workflow in the team?

Effective sense-making, a key part of problem solving, is facilitated by contextual awareness. A very common source of failure in disaster management (not to mention public policy writ large, business, and personal life) is building solutions around underdeveloped or inappropriate specifications of the problem.[20]

Options

In providing advice to leaders and other clients in disaster operations, lawyers will engage at different stages of the problem solving process. In some cases, a decision maker will have a preferred option. For example, in one disaster in a remote Alaskan village, the FCO strongly preferred partnering with voluntary agencies to leverage assistance resources to provide replacement housing. Accordingly, FEMA attorneys developed a transactional framework allowing the Agency to provide funds for log house kits for displaced households, which were constructed under the supervision of the Mennonite Disaster Service and furnished by Samaritan's Purse.

The attorney is likely to face questions of the following nature:

- Are we authorized (or can you find me the authority) to do X?
- Are we prohibited from doing X?
- What are the legal (and possibly ethical, practical, political, or other) risks associated with doing X?
- How can we manage the legal and other risks associated with doing X?
- Is there a better (e.g., faster, cheaper, more effective, and/or less risky) way than X to achieve the goal?
- What were the lessons learned the last time we did X?

Clients may also identify a short list of two or more options under serious consideration and ask for a relative analysis of the costs, risks, and/or benefits associated with them. If there is a single or limited number of favored options on the table, the attorney should follow the assessment process described in the next section.

In other situations, and especially if the lawyer is brought into the process at an early stage, lawyers may be asked to be a part of the process of identifying or developing options. This may involve drawing upon historical/organizational memory or the current set of procedures to help generate options, or it may entail a creative process of coming up with a novel approach. Obviously, the latter is more likely to be necessary when FEMA is facing a situation which is qualitatively or quantitatively different significantly from those faced in the past and which have shaped the frame of reference and established action repertoire.[21] It is crucial in such circumstances for the attorney to understand the delicate interface of law and policy and the need to work in partnership with program staff in developing novel approaches. Failure to involve and integrate the subject matter program experts can lead to perfectly legal plans on paper that are not executable on the ground. Program staff must have buy-in on the suggested solution, as they will actually have to execute the plan and deal with the consequences.

Again, once an option or limited set of options has been produced, the lawyer should shift to *assessment*.

Assessment

The assessment process is critical to producing high quality advice in crisis. While assessment should be seen as a broad process drawing upon multiple perspectives on the option or options under examination, many lawyers focus explicitly on only one or two of these perspectives (and perhaps treat some of them in a more intuitive or explicit fashion). The best disaster lawyers, however, analyze options in a systematic and comprehensive fashion. This process draws upon four dimensions and gives attorneys the ability to weigh and integrate the results of this process in the advice they give to their clients and teams. The key dimensions of assessment are: *authorization, prohibition, risk,* and *judgment.* Let us begin with authorization.

Does the option appear to be *authorized* by the Stafford Act or supplementary authority? Disaster lawyers should keep in mind that Stafford was deliberately formulated to be a broad and flexible instrument and is subject to alternative and evolving opinions. The authorities available under Stafford may be interpreted broadly or narrowly, in part according to the policies and priorities set by FEMA's leadership (and the White House), as well as the zeitgeist of the times.

While the Stafford Act tends to loom large in the assortment of authorities at the disposal of FEMA, it is critical to keep in mind that other supplementary authorities may be available and provide authorization for actions which clients deem necessary or useful in addressing the needs of responding organizations, survivors, and other parties. Should these authorities not be directly available to FEMA, at times they may be borrowed from other agencies through cooperative agreements.

For example, FEMA assisted the United States Agency for International Development (USAID) after the 2010 Haiti Earthquake with assets and personnel to support the response efforts. These assets included Mobile Emergency Response Support (MERS) personnel and equipment, the Incident Management Assistance Team (IMAT) West, and an Incident Response Vehicle (IRV), to help establish communications for relief efforts on the ground and provide subject matter expertise and technical support. These activities were undertaken pursuant to an Inter-Agency Agreement with USAID under the authorities of the Foreign Assistance Act of 1961.[22]

Part of being solution-oriented (and getting to yes) is about being creative in developing (and arguing) defensible rationales for authorizing practically necessary action under extreme circumstances. The next dimension of assessment is prohibition.

Is there a specific legal or policy-based prohibition and from what does it derive? When examining prohibitions and other forms of potentially prohibitive constraints, it is critical to distinguish between prohibitions and whether they stem from the Constitution, statutes (including appropriations law), regulations, executive orders, policies, tactical guidelines (e.g., FEMA letter from the Administrator), and/or past agency policy and/or practice. Note that lesser order prohibitions (especially those stemming from past agency policy) may well be amenable to change or dispensation in consultation with leaders within or outside of FEMA, especially if in tune with broader trends and shifts in policy and or political/operational imperatives. Situational and contextual factors will determine the viability and appropriateness of such courses of action.

Note: *When communicating to clients that certain prohibitions appear to be insurmountable obstacles to a particular course of action, lawyers should be specific about the source and nature of those prohibitions! It is important to work with the clients on formulating a Plan B or C if the favored course of action appears impossible to implement. It is also important to store these non-starter options for future reference in case there are calls for post-crisis legislative proposals.*

The third dimension of assessment is *risk*. What are the legal (and other) risks associated with this option in relation to other alternative courses of action or inaction. Disaster management is fraught with risk, and disaster managers are aware and often willing to accept a degree of (and in extreme situations more than a little) risk. Many of the leaders interviewed strongly emphasized their desire "to do the right thing," despite potential legal exposure. Lawyers who seek to avoid legal risk completely will be perceived as obstacles to effective disaster management and are likely to be marginalized within their teams. Furthermore, legal risks must be weighed against other forms of risk (to life, property, FEMA reputation, political viability, ethics in the broader sense of the word, etc.), when giving advice. The old adage "desperate times call for desperate measures" captures the balancing act that FEMA leaders are called upon to undertake when making crucial decisions during and in the aftermath of disasters.

When it is, or may be, necessary to embark upon a course of action fraught with legal risk, part of the lawyer's task is to look for ways of managing or minimizing these risks. For example, contemporaneous documentation (not only of the legal opinion but also of the situational imperatives and deliberative process behind the measure in question) may help to protect the leaders and lawyers involved. Formulating a viable exit strategy should also be part of the implementation plan. What are the metrics? Are there objective standards in place? How will this be conveyed to the State, applicants, the public, and Congress?

Last, but not least, is the imperative to exercise and apply *judgment* to the matter in question.[23] Leaders (and other clients) told the Advice in Crisis investigators of their strong motivations "to do the right thing" during and after disasters. Leaders of good character, judgment, and intention often have an intuitive sense of what needs to be done in critical situations like disasters. Bases for such normative determinations may have to do with meeting urgent needs of survivors, preventing disproportionate direct or collateral damage, or living up to fundamental norms of fairness. As stated succinctly by one veteran disaster lawyer interviewed by the Advice in Crisis team: "Is this for the greater good?"

As in other areas of the law, it is necessary to address that question in two ways:

- Is this for the greater good *in this situation*?
- Is this for the greater good in terms of the precedent it would set and/or the incentive structure it would create?[24]

One aspect of exercising judgment is knowing when to seek different perspectives, consult more experienced attorneys, or elevate a decision. Further complicating this exercise in judgment is the sense of urgency and attendant time compression associated with crises. Hence, one important and recurring role decision-makers will ask lawyers to play is helping to decide when "to ask permission" and when "to seek forgiveness." It is unlikely that the lawyer will have the time and information necessary to consider thoroughly all of the potential options and consequences associated with a particular decision in crisis operations. Emergency management lawyers must come to the table knowledgeable, and with a strong ethical compass and readily accessible network for technical reach back (for example to FEMA OCC)—without these capabilities, the lawyer will not be prepared to exercise and apply judgment effectively in crises.

Finally, one of the most important dimensions of judgment is determining whether a particular solution is practically viable and can be implemented. While the lawyer may not be the only one around the table who can weigh in on the practicality or mechanics of implementation, lawyers may have highly relevant input to contribute on this point because of their legal expertise and general knowledge and experience. Disaster management, like politics, is the art of the possible.

Provision of Advice

Once the previous steps have been completed, lawyers will need to communicate the advice produced to clients and/or to the disaster management teams in which they are embedded. Doing so effectively requires adapting and packaging the advice in ways that are appropriate to the situation and the context in which the advice is being delivered as noted in the discussion of the socio-behavioral (GAIN) dimension. Consider the following factors:

- *Situation:* Is the work taking place under crisis-like conditions and what is the time frame involved? How much pressure is on the disaster management team and its leaders?
- *Organizational context*: What is the nature of the organizational context (headquarters, regional office, JFO, etc.) and the local culture?
- *Venue and form*: Is it most appropriate to convey this advice to a leader or other client in a one-on-one situation, at a senior staff meeting, at an all-hands meeting (generally not!), at a meeting with state and local officials, etc.? Should one deliver an oral or a written opinion? If written, will an informal email suffice, or is a more formal written document necessary?

- *Risk picture*: Generally speaking it is better to package advice in terms of alternative levels of risk associated with the option or options in question, rather than binary black and white (i.e., you can or cannot go forward with a particular course of action). However, in cases characterized by unacceptably high levels of legal risk (and not least when other compensating humanitarian imperatives are not part of the picture); leaders want their lawyers to be prepared to "pull the emergency brake" and express their objections in the strongest possible terms.

- *Leader/collaborator personalities*: Clients vary greatly in their approach to processing information, open-versus closed-mindedness, big picture versus detail orientation, familiarity / expertise with the relevant legal issues and modes of legal reasoning, ability to function in stressful environments, etc. The most effective disaster lawyers cultivate the ability to adapt to the personalities and (leadership) styles of their clients. Given the same problem and assessment of options, a lawyer might choose to do a three-minute nutshell brief to a big-picture and action-oriented leader, while presenting the same material and results in a fifteen-minute briefing to another more detail oriented, reflective, and legally interested leader.[25] In this sense, being articulate in the SALT sense, is partly in relation to the person or persons to whom the advice is being delivered.

As noted, provision of advice should be consistent with the SALT performance standard and be: **Solution-Oriented, Articulate, Legally Sufficient**, and **Timely**. In addition, as noted above, it is advisable to prepare to mitigate risk and defend potentially controversial measures through the production of contemporaneous documentation.

Finally, lawyers can and often should play a role in developing or reviewing messaging/external affairs guidance pre- and post-decision. For example, in response to the devastating April 2011 tornados that struck Alabama and Mississippi, FEMA OCC worked in conjunction with the White House, FEMA leadership at Headquarters and in the field, and with program staff on developing a streamlined private property debris removal plan called "Operation Clean Sweep." OCC also assisted the External Affairs and Program staff on press releases and fact sheets. OCC is also engaged in gathering data for lessons learned from the project.

HOW CAN LEADERS GET THE MOST FROM THEIR LAWYERS?

The AIC research also points to a number of best practices, which skilled leaders use to get better service from their lawyers. Note that some of these points really derive from good management practices in a broader sense, and are not necessarily specific to the leader–lawyer relationship. These are:

- *Bring the lawyer in early.* The top performing lawyers interviewed in the study emphasize that a good understanding of the unfolding event, the key personalities, and the emergent dynamics within the team provides the lawyer with a contextualized perspective conducive to good problem solving.

- *Include the lawyer in the response phase.* Though some leaders prefer to count on forgiveness for potentially controversial actions taken in the most acute phases of a disaster—fearing that lawyers will delay and unnecessarily constrain a rapidly moving disaster response—most of our interviewees found that a properly trained and prepared lawyer with the right stuff can be a major asset in disaster response. Such lawyers can help to find creative ways around obstacles and enable rather than needlessly constrain action.

- *Help the lawyer understand the big picture and the commander's intent.* Leaders and lawyers alike emphasized the importance of leaders taking the time to explain to the lawyers (and other core team members) what they are trying to achieve and why. Such knowledge is essential for promoting heedful inter-relating, good judgment, and effective teamwork.

- *Clarify expectations* regarding the lawyers' role and the workflow. Some leaders wish the lawyer to play a broad problem-solving and analytical role as "wise counselor"; others are primarily interested in the lawyer's technical expertise. In either case, it is important for leaders to be explicit regarding what they desire and expect. Similarly, it is essential to be clear about timelines, deadlines, and reporting formats so that both parties are on the same page about what needs to be done and by when.

- *Dialogue the advice and provide feedback*: Wise leaders engage in an ongoing dialogue with their lawyers. For example, if given a "no" from the lawyer, they probe to determine the nature of the obstacle. Is the problem an absolute legal prohibition or a previous agency policy or guideline that could be changed (or an exception authorized) by a phone call to the agency leadership? Similarly, they provide *feedback* to the lawyer about the substantive advice and the way the lawyer delivered it—this feedback gives the lawyer a chance to adapt and better serve the leader and the team as time goes on. Several of our interviewees emphasized that, in extreme cases, lawyers who are not performing well and who have proved unable to make use of constructive feedback from their leaders should be replaced.

CONCLUDING THOUGHTS

We have labeled the interaction between lawyers and decision-makers in the context of disaster operations "Advice in Crisis." The double entendre is intentional. In the first and straightforward meaning, advice in crisis connotes the provision of legal advice during unstable and dangerous situations. In the second and ironic meaning, advice in crisis describes what happens when lawyers attempting to advise emergency managers and other crisis leaders are *not* prepared to deliver legal services in conditions where core values are threatened, uncertainty is pervasive, and time is of the essence. These lawyers, who may be very capable in steady-state transactional or litigation settings, find themselves in a crisis within a crisis as they fumble or muddle through their interactions with decision-makers. In this chapter, we have developed a framework designed to facilitate achieving the former connotation, while helping to avoid the latter. We based that framework on systematic analysis of data culled from specialized literature, case studies, and interviews/focus groups with FEMA veterans, and government and non-government stakeholders.

Let us conclude by observing that in a pioneering study published in 1991, leading crisis researchers Uriel Rosenthal (who went on to become Foreign Minister of the Netherlands) and Paul 't Hart pointed out that the roles of decision-maker and expert tended to blur in many of the crisis cases they had studied.[26] The AIC research revealed that many FEMA leaders are quite familiar with the law pertaining to their domains (a fact that their lawyers should remember when formulating and communicating advice). Furthermore, FEMA lawyers have many opportunities to exercise leadership in guiding their clients to good choices, guiding and mentoring subordinates in their work, and interacting with peers in the agency and the interagency process. Still on the whole, leaders and lawyers have distinct, vital, and interdependent roles to play in disaster management. It is our hope that the best practice models formulated in the *Advice in Crisis Project* will contribute to better collaboration between leaders and lawyers in disaster management, not only at FEMA, but potentially in other contexts as well.

APPENDIX: WHAT IS "SALT"?

SALT is a set of individual performance criteria linked to the FEMA Office of Chief Counsel (OCC) Mission Statement. OCC employees apply SALT to assess their legal advice, counsel, risk analysis, dispute resolution services, and other assignments. Consistent application of SALT supports OCC's mission accomplishment and reinforces the trust relationships necessary for our senior leaders and client-partners to feel confident in seeking and using OCC services as an integral part of their business processes. In every action and encounter, and in all the advice we provide, we are –

Solution-Oriented – Where others see obstacles, we focus on legally viable solutions and outcomes. We are open to ideas of others and provide options, constructive alternatives, and creative solutions to legal problems. We support continuous learning and collaborative environments that foster new ideas, understanding, and better ways to execute FEMA's mission. We help resolve conflicts, and eliminate needless barriers that interfere with the Agency's efforts to achieve its mission. We assess what is valuable from current and past activity in our practice, document it, and share with those who need to know.

Articulate – We express our positions and explain law and policy in an organized, well-reasoned, and persuasive manner, both orally and in writing. We use language that is appropriate to the client-partner, without use of undue "legalese" that might confuse or distort the message.

Legally Sufficient – To the extent operational conditions permit, we apply the aphorism "Salt away the facts, the law will keep." This means we aggressively develop the facts before applying the law to arrive at legal conclusions and options. When we render a legal opinion, in any form, we cite to legal authorities (using the *Bluebook* for all written work) to demonstrate that our opinion substantially satisfies applicable statutory, regulatory, and Federal executive branch requirements so that our client-partners and those who may later review our opinions understand our reasoning. We are professionally responsible and uphold our duties to our clients, courts, and the legal profession.

Timely – We deliver advice and counsel on demand, where and when our client–partners need it, and aggressively anticipate issues and obstacles to mission accomplishment. By being proactive, responsive, and accessible, we prevent problems. We meet the timelines required to support critical or urgent Agency operations, and communicate with our clients to establish appropriately prioritized timelines for routine matters. To the extent operations permit, we provide our colleagues with sufficient time in which to review, consult, and coordinate on complex issues.

NOTES

1. This chapter draws heavily upon a longer report published as Appendix A to the FEMA *Disaster Operations Legal Resource* (November, 2011; see note 2 below for full citation). The authors would like to acknowledge very important contributions to this chapter by Mary Ellen Martinet, Patrick Walsh, Adrian Sevier, Rachael Bralliar, Elisabeth Renieris, and Dr. Christopher Holstege. Thanks also for valuable feedback on a preliminary draft from numerous colleagues at the Swedish National Center for Crisis Management Research and Training (CRISMART).

2. Thomas Preston, *The President and His Inner Circle: Leadership and the Advisory Process in Foreign Affairs* (New York: Columbia University Press, 2001).

3. For a complete list of project interviews, see Eric Stern, Gregory Saathoff, Mary-Ellen Martinet, and Brad Kieserman, "Advice in Crisis: Towards Best Practices for Providing Legal Advice Under Disaster Conditions," *FEMA Disaster Operations Legal Resource* (2011), A53–A56.

4. Arjen Boin et al., *The Politics of Crisis Management: Public Leadership Under Pressure* (Cambridge: Cambridge University Press, 2005).

5. Barbara Farnham, *Roosevelt and the Munich Crisis: A Study of Political Decision-Making* (Princeton, NJ: Princeton University Press, 1997).

6. Ward Farnsworth, *The Legal Analyst: A Toolkit for Thinking about the Law* (Chicago: University of Chicago Press, 2007).

7. Ibid.

8. Ibid.

9. William C. Nicholson, "Building Community Legal Capabilities for Post 9-11 Terrorism Preparedness" (paper presented before the FEMA Higher Education Conference, May 30–31, 2002).

10. Gary J. Edles, "Assessing 'Who is the Client' in the Government Context," *Administrative and Regulatory Law News* 31, no. 1 (Fall 2005): 10–13.

11. George, *supra* n. 12; Irving L. Janis, *Crucial Decisions: Leadership in Policymaking and Crisis Management* (New York: Free Press, 1989).

12. Nicholson, "Building Community Legal Capabilities for Post 9-11 Terrorism Preparedness."

13. Arjen Boin et al., *The Politics of Crisis Management*; Stephen Worchel, Wendy Wood, and Jeffry A. Simpson, *Group Process and Productivity* (London: Sage, 1992).

14. Irving L. Janis, *Crucial Decisions*; Paul Hart, Eric K. Stern, and Bengt Sundelius, *Beyond Groupthink: Political Group Dynamics and Foreign Policy-Making* (Ann Arbor: University of Michigan Press, 1997).

15. Hart, Stern, and Sundelius, *Beyond Groupthink.*

16. *Cf.* Ben W. Heineman, Jr., *Lawyers as Leaders*, 116 Yale L.J. Pocket part 266, 266–71 (2007).

17. *Cf.* John R. Boyd, *Destruction and Creation* (unpublished, 1976), available at http://www.goalsys.com/books/documents/DESTRUCTION_AND_CREATION.pdf (last visited July 24, 2012).

18. Malcolm Gladwell, *Blink: The Power of Thinking Without Thinking* (New York: Little, Brown, 2005).

19. Ralph L. Keeney, *Value-Focused Thinking: A Path to Creative Decisionmaking* (Cambridge, MA: Harvard University Press, 1992); Ian I. Mitroff and J.R. Emshoff, "On Strategic Assumption-Making: A Dialectical Approach to Policy and Planning," *Academy of Management Review* 4, no. 1 (1979): 1–12.

20. Ian I. Mitroff and Abraham Silvers, *Dirty Rotten Strategies: How We Trick Ourselves and Others into Solving the Wrong Problems Precisely* (Stanford, CA: Stanford Business Books, 2010).

21. Henry Mintzberg, Duru Raisinghani, and Andre Theoret, "The Structure of 'Unstructured' Decision Processes," *Administrative Science Quarterly* 21, no. 2 (1976): 246–75.

22. Pub. L. 87-195, 74 Stat. 424 (1961), as amended (current version at 22 U.S.C. §§ 2151- 2431k [2011]).

23. Stanley A. Renshon and Deborah W. Larson, *Good Judgment in Foreign Policy: Theory and Application* (Lanham, MD: Rowman & Littlefield, 2003).

24. Farnsworth, *The Legal Analyst.*

25. George, *supra* n. 12; Preston. *The President and His Inner Circle*; Paul Kowart, *Groupthink or Deadlock: When Do Leaders Learn From Their Advisors?* (Albany: State University of New York Press, 2002).

26. Uriel Rosenthal and Paul 't Hart, "Experts and Decision Makers in Crisis Situations," *Knowledge: Creation, Diffusion, Utilization* 12, no. 4 (1991): 350–72.

7

INTRODUCTION TO PART VII: PRIVATE SECTOR SECURITY AND RESILIENCE

Ira Tannenbaum

Director of Public/Private Initiatives, New York City Office of Emergency Management

It is almost impossible to have a conversation about public–private partnerships without hearing the often-quoted fact that 85 percent of the critical infrastructure in the United States is operated by the private sector. However, this actually understates the importance of the private sector because every aspect of a community's ability to function depends on the private sector in some way. Restoring infrastructure such as power and water to a neighborhood does not automatically create resiliency. Businesses need employees and those individuals need private sector organizations of all kinds and sizes—food service, child care, pharmacies, medical offices etc.—for a community to be considered truly resilient.

Increasingly, public sector emergency managers realize that building trusted relationships with the private sector is essential. Certainly, the private sector can donate material, resources, and supplies. For example, a sports franchise with a stadium and large parking area might allow it to be used as an emergency staging area, or a major retailer can provide commodities. However, the private sector can also serve as a force multiplier for emergency management communication. This works in two directions—delivering messages from the public sector, and serving as a source of information that informs situational awareness.

For example, a highly effective way to credibly and quickly communicate to hundreds of thousands of employees in the private sector is to partner with an umbrella group (e.g., Building Owners and Managers Association, Chambers of Commerce, or local trade organizations) that can rapidly and credibly disseminate messages to hundreds of member organizations (building management companies). Each of these member organizations can in turn further disseminate the information to thousands of companies (their tenants). This efficiency is why some emergency management agencies have included private sector association representatives in their Emergency Operations Centers during a crisis as the Private Sector Emergency Support Function (ESF) under the National Incident Management System (NIMS).

Additionally, and perhaps most fundamentally, the very resilience of local businesses and organizations is probably the best resource they bring to the table. The public sector does not want to find itself replacing the work that the private sector does so well on a day-to-day basis—we would much rather find ways to work together to get those businesses back up and running. This requires effort on both sides: The private sector needs to see the benefit in investing in continuity planning and be committed to their role in the community, even if the short-term financial prospects are challenging. At the same time, the public sector must commit to making sure that the efforts of the private sector are not in vain. We must be committed to providing the basic services needed by businesses, while at the same time not competing with them once they reopen (by handing out commodities for free across the street).

Public sector emergency management agencies need to approach information sharing and communication with the private sector thoughtfully. The private sector has an insatiable thirst for information, and needs to know about events and circumstances that impact their business:

- Will public sector plans disrupt transportation or other services?
- Will the stock market be open tomorrow?
- Will there be alternate side parking tomorrow?
- What does mandatory evacuation mean? Will you go door to door and force us out?

It is also important for public sector managers to recognize that every organization's need for information is different. Very often, the absence of a relationship leads to skepticism about the requests being made. Why do they need this information? Is this really relevant to their operation or is it just feeding the desire to "get the scoop"? In part, this requires the understanding that the complex nature of businesses may include dependencies or locations (buildings with back-office operations won't always be emblazoned with corporate logos) that we may not be familiar with. The public sector must get away from the stewardship mentality of telling the private sector what we think they need to know and accept the idea that we don't always know—we need to trust in this dialogue—and talk *with* the private sector not *at* them!

In the same vein the private sector must understand that the public sector does not exist to provide them with protection from having to plan or make decisions.

Managing expectations is crucial: emergency managers must explain to the private sector what may or may not happen during an emergency. Even the best relationships are guided by and exist within legal and political limitations. Whether it is the inability to share protected personal information, such as the identities or locations of aviation incident survivors, with employers (despite their best intentions), or simply not being able to preempt a mayoral announcement and notify a business about an impending evacuation order, there are going to be times when we can't share information. Although the public sector can issue emergency notifications to the general public via mechanisms like Notify NYC, it usually cannot direct private sector businesses to take specific action. Often, a city's position most typically will be: "You have already taken responsibility for caring for them. If there is a storm coming, this is business decision you need to make yourself."

The key is to involve the private sector in the entire emergency management cycle, from preparedness through response, so that no effort exists in a vacuum. The private sector's participation in the planning effort can help the public sector better understand where the private sector is coming from, and together we can identify ways to achieve our goals. For example, in the aviation incident scenario, while information release might not be an option, public sector organizations are able to develop notification protocols to let survivors know that their company is looking to help them.

come together if those recommendations had been in place before the attack.

There are many things that, as members of the public, we do not know and may not know for several years: whether the U.S. government departments reorganized under DHS are functioning better than they were beforehand; whether the country would have been better protected by a smaller, more selective reorganization; whether we should change, weaken, or strengthen the PATRIOT Act; whether the reorganization of the intelligence community will make us safer. Also, many high-profile critics tell us that the steps the government has taken to protect the national infrastructure are not enough, that the infrastructure is still vulnerable. (They are right, but why should we want to give that information to our enemies?)

Anyone who thinks seriously about this threat must conclude that there could be another terrorist attack at any time, with no warning, no chatter, no raising of the alert level, no government announcement, and none of the commentary we normally receive from experts in the media.

The effort to carry the war to certain terrorists abroad was necessary and has been helpful; the arrests of many al-Qaida operatives worldwide may have delayed a follow-up attack on the United States. The work of the Joint Terrorism Task Forces (JTTF) has made it much more difficult for terrorists to recruit, organize, and put together an operation in the United States without fear of detection and further arrests.

However, there is nothing to suggest that terrorists have given up. On the contrary, there is an ongoing barrage of threats against the West, and innumerable individuals are willing to sacrifice their lives in an attack on the United States. Preventing such an attack may be beyond the resources of federal, state, or local governments. There is a saying: "The government has to get it right 100 percent of the time; the enemy has to get it right just once." Therefore, the government needs help.

The private sector owns or operates more than 85 percent of the nation's critical infrastructure and thus should be in the forefront of governmental efforts to protect the country. Corporations must play a significant role in reducing the risk of an attack against the business infrastructure and in preparing for the consequences of an attack if one occurs. Corporate America has to help turn soft targets into tough targets and increase its own survivability.

Major corporations need to take the responsibility for developing and implementing fundamental security practices, including risk assessment, baseline security, emergency planning, crisis management, screening of employees, and protecting critical infrastructure. Corporations also need to examine their vulnerabilities, dependencies, and logistic needs and determine how they will function if they are temporarily denied the use of certain assets. Most important, DHS needs to form an interactive partnership with the private sector.

Corporations must consider how they would function during and after a catastrophic attack on the United States. How would they move people and products if air traffic was grounded for a long time? How would they handle a serious power outage? What would they do if sea cargo was delayed because of a threat against a seaport, if a truck bomb exploded in a tunnel or on a bridge, if there was a bomb or chemical attack against rail transportation, if a suicide bomber attacked the lobby of a corporate building, if the financial markets were forced to close for several days, if the supply chain was interrupted, or if manufacturing facilities were attacked and seriously damaged? Any of these situations could occur with little or no warning.

Corporations should assess how they would respond if there was a dirty bomb attack in a major American city, if their employees were too frightened to go to work or too anxious to stay on the job, if there was a rumor of an imminent nuclear threat to a large city like New York. (I refer the reader to Graham Allison's book *Nuclear Terrorism*, published in 2004.[1])

For some corporations, 9/11 changed the explicit responsibilities of their security functions; and for all corporations, it should have changed the implicit responsibilities. Corporate security has a new challenge; it must look to the future, help plan for what may be unimaginable, try to shine a light into the dark corners of extremism and see what is there to fear, what the threat is, and what actions must be taken to mitigate the threat.

I will suggest steps to improve security across the business infrastructure, starting with risk assessment.

SECURITY RISK ASSESSMENTS

Every business site should have a risk assessment. Risks to employees, facilities, and physical and intellectual assets vary from country to country and from location to location within a country. Risks can be human-made or natural; they include hurricanes, floods, earthquakes, chemical spills, and violence in the workplace as well as terrorism; but the focus here will be on terrorism.

Each site must be reviewed so that the security organization has a realistic understanding of the threat there. The risk assessment should look at the number of employees, the business mission at the site, the location, and the environment. For instance, a site near a major government building, a chemical facility, or a building that is part of the financial infrastructure may have substantially greater risk than a site in or near a residential area. Each site must be surveyed and evaluated according to comprehensive security criteria because each site is unique in some way. A risk assessment should always include input from the person or persons ultimately responsible for running the business at that location. Risk assessments often require information from noncompany sources, including consultants, media reports, security professionals, local law enforcement agencies, and the government and its intelligence organizations. When analyzing all this information, be aware that many sources have their own agenda. Consequently it is important to have access to skilled analysts and operations personnel who are not part of official policy making. Fortunately, several organizations provide straight up-and-down reporting.

One excellent source of information concerning locations outside the United States is the Overseas Security Advisory Council (OSAC), a partnership between the U.S. Department of State and the business community. OSAC has existed since 1985 and has analysts and country councils in some 60 nations. (Its Web site, administered by the Department of State's Bureau of Diplomatic Security, is www.ds-osac.org/constituents/login/login.cfm.)

Security consultants offer various services that can aid risk assessment: bulletins, newsletters, Web sites, monthly and quarterly reports, and in-depth country reports covering political, economic, and security issues. Such consultants range from one person trying to cover the globe to large well-staffed companies with impressive country or regional expertise. Many consultants provide an excellent product— timely, accurate, and well-balanced. Others are little more than news clipping services offering no analysis. Thus it is important to choose wisely when information from a consultant is to be used in risk assessment. Know what type of information is needed, what the consultant can reasonably be expected to contribute, and where the consultant is situated regarding a particular issue. Consultants can often note patterns and trends and can do research for specific information, but they may have little or no ability to predict terrorist operations or targets.

Even experienced government intelligence analysts, using highly sensitive human and signal intelligence and with unrestricted access to reports of interrogations of terrorists, have not been able to consistently identify specific targets before the fact; instead, they tend to take the past as an indicator of the future.

BASELINE SECURITY

To repeat, the business community may have no warning of an attack and thus no ability to *surge*—to quickly put together a response to a threat. Therefore it is important to build and maintain a strong baseline security program, which can be enhanced if there is a significant unforeseen change in the threat. The following baseline program is a modified, abridged abstract of IBM's security manual.

Baseline security can be understood as the processes that must be in place to deal with known general threats, not specific threats. It can be conceptualized somewhat like security at an airport, where certain fundamental processes must operate day in and day out, regardless of any specific threat, to prevent aircraft from being taken over by attackers or blown up by suicide bombers, and to prevent anyone from stashing explosives on an aircraft, carrying explosives on board, or storing explosives in luggage. Similarly, a corporate baseline security program is a blueprint for protecting human, physical, and intellectual assets. It should meet the corporation's fundamental, daily security needs. It should address today's concerns. It should inspire confidence in the employees and senior management. Security at a business location must be seen not as a stand-alone process but as a fully integrated part of the business.

The corporation must develop a baseline security program that need not ride a roller coaster whenever the government or the media report a possible terrorist threat. Senior management and employees need to feel confident that the company's security program is focused, on target, comprehensive, and responsive.

Specific changes in risks can justify enhancing the baseline program. Additions can be made if there are specific threats or significant new terrorist tactics. For instance, if there were a series of truck or car bombs against a particular corporation anywhere in the world, the corporation could increase baseline security by including vehicle barriers, security fences, hydraulic wedges, fixed or retractable bollards, antiram foundation walls, heavy-duty drop bars, etc.

Some corporations have already added such measures to their baseline security. Some firms are including more stringent processing for loading dock operations; some are vetting limousine drivers and drivers of delivery trucks who have access to their facilities; some have increased the offset from vehicle parking areas to buildings; some use protective film on windows facing courtyards, parking areas, and the street. Actually, these steps are part of baseline security at certain firms, but for many corporations they would represent an addition to baseline security. Baseline security has to be tailored to each company and will depend on the nature and location of the business. The following categories (again, from an abridged version of IBM's security manual) indicate some areas that should be covered in the baseline requirements.

Perimeter Lighting

Good perimeter lighting helps reduce crime, protects employees, gives employees a greater sense of safety and security, reduces accidents, allows for better surveillance by security personnel, and allows closed-circuit television (CCTV) cameras to operate at night or in darkness or semidarkness. The lighting should meet the requirements specified in the Illuminating Engineering Society (IES) Standards, or the local equivalent.

Primary Vehicular Access Controls

Physical security at the primary vehicular entrance will depend on the nature and location of the business. Entrances to plants, laboratories, and headquarters on a campus-style site should have an installed gatehouse that is staffed during regular business hours and can be operated remotely during nonbusiness hours. Driveways should be designed and constructed to hinder or prevent a high-speed vehicle approach to lobbies or buildings, particularly where some floors of a building overhang the basic structure. Bollards, landscaping, speed bumps, and other techniques should be used to impede or prevent vehicle access to areas with high concentrations of people.

Secondary Vehicle Access Entrances

These entrances should be capable of being closed, so that access to the location is via the primary entrance only.

Possible Concealment Areas

A clear line of sight along the building perimeter should be maintained; and any containers, such as trash receptacles and recycling containers that could be used to conceal an explosive device should be removed from close proximity to the building. Also, detection devices should be installed to provide an early warning of any unauthorized entry.

Other Access Points

Less obvious entrances to a building such as grills, gratings, manhole covers, utility tunnels, skylights, and roof vents should be designed to prevent entry into the building, or to any critical utilities. Access to the roof from the ground via exterior stairs or ladders should be prevented.

Building Perimeters and Interior Security

All perimeter doors designated as emergency exits should be constructed of heavy-duty material and equipped with a locking device. The door jambs, hinges, and locks should be designed to resist forced entry. A controlled access system should be used that expedites employees' entrance but denies unauthorized entrance. There are many such systems on the market.

Tailgating is a problem that requires constant vigilance and employee education. Employees should understand that there can be business risks as well as security risks in allowing anyone to follow them through a controlled access system without proper authorization. Every employee should be vigilant in enforcing this requirement.

Lobbies

All lobbies should have a system to control access from the lobby into the company's interior space, including elevators. A security control center or a receptionist in the lobby should have an inconspicuous panic alarm, monitored by a control center that can respond to an emergency. If the alarm is activated, all doors providing entry into the building interior space should lock automatically. Doors should allow for emergency exit, and doors from the exterior to the lobby should remain unlocked to allow law enforcement or emergency response personnel to enter the lobby.

Where elevator access is from the lobby, activation of the panic alarm should cause all elevators to stop at a floor other than the lobby, and not return to the lobby until the situation has been stabilized. Facility entrances that are opened remotely or manually (or both) should have audio and visual devices for identifying individuals before allowing access to the facility. Restrooms in lobbies should be locked, and people with packages should be prohibited from taking the packages into a restroom.

Windows and Exterior Glass

Operable windows on the ground floor should be constructed to prevent unauthorized or undetected entry. Shatter-resistant glazing should be used on windows in exterior walls adjacent to the areas where there are normally large concentrations of people, and on ground-, first-, second-, and third-floor windows facing streets or in direct proximity to parking areas.

Loading Docks

The access to loading docks should be carefully controlled. Delivery trucks should be vetted in advance when possible; otherwise, they should be checked when they come on-site. Given the threat of car and truck bombs, it is poor security policy to allow any delivery vehicle onto a site and up to a loading dock without first identifying it and what it is transporting. Loading docks should have written emergency response procedures with adequate guidance for dock and security personnel. Staffed loading docks should be equipped with panic alarms that are monitored on-site or off-site by a control center. Unstaffed loading docks should have audio and visual devices to permit the identification of an individual before allowing access to the building's interior.

Mail Rooms

Access to mail rooms should be restricted to authorized individuals. Doors and windows leading into mail rooms should be constructed so as to protect against forced entry. Entry points should be monitored by intrusion detection sensors during unstaffed hours. Procedures should be in place for identifying and responding to a "suspicious mail" incident. Mail room personnel should receive semiannual training and updates as necessary. Security personnel should closely examine mail-handling procedures, including procedures for special deliveries and for after-hours deliveries that might not normally go through the normal mail room screening process. It is especially important to ensure that appropriate baseline security is observed when mail room services are contracted out.

Underground Parking Garages

Underground parking garages present a significant risk. A car, van, or truck loaded with explosives can be parked under the building, where an explosion will do the most damage to structural integrity. Consequently, a garage parking area immediately below the company's location must be carefully controlled and limited to authorized vehicles. Badge access should be required. This can be challenging in a building with several tenants, but it should be a no-compromise requirement.

Critical Utilities and Chemicals

A utility is "critical" if its destruction, or damage to it, could cause significant revenue loss or present a danger to the community. Critical utilities include electrical substations, tank farms, water chillers, utility tunnels, satellite ground stations, microwave parabolic reflectors, communications towers, waste treatment centers, water wells, and chemical storage areas, to name just a few. Such utilities must receive special attention in a risk assessment and must be adequately protected as part of baseline security.

The storage of large amounts of toxic or explosive chemicals also requires special attention. Some companies have highly trained, armed security personnel to protect chemical facilities or storage. If that is not practical, barriers, fences, and other access controls should be used to prevent or delay entry. Two layers of fencing are advisable, so that an object cannot be placed against a chemical tank or thrown over a fence in close proximity to the tank. At least one fence should be strong enough to stop a vehicle, and the second fence should be high enough to prevent anyone from climbing into the restricted area. Fences should be topped with concertina wire and alarms. CCTV should be part of the defensive perimeter; it will provide an early warning of any attempted penetration of the protected area. Local law enforcement should be informed of the chemical storage, and a plan should be worked out to ensure its prompt response in an emergency. Movement of chemicals on-site should be tracked and recorded manually or by computer.

Access to chemical storage areas by employees or contractors should be closely controlled. Trucks delivering toxic or explosive chemicals should be vetted by prenotification at least several hours beforehand. If possible, anyone delivering hazardous chemicals to the site should undergo a criminal background check. Employees or contractors with access to areas where hazardous chemicals are stored should also have a background check and should be given appropriate training.

EMERGENCY PLANNING

After risk assessment and baseline security, the next area to consider is emergency planning. Good emergency planning will save lives; poor emergency planning may cost lives.

Elements of Emergency Planning

Emergency planning is site-specific: many aspects of the plan will depend on local conditions. An emergency plan for corporate headquarters in a 40-story office building in Manhattan will be different from that of a small branch office in a rural area. Still, the basics of emergency planning are much the same everywhere. The objective is to minimize the risk of injury or death and protect intellectual and physical property. The emergency plan should include procedures for incidents such as natural and human-made disasters, threats and acts of violence against people and property, political or civil unrest, demonstrations, and catastrophic events in close proximity to the business location.

The emergency plan should include designation of a crisis management team (CMT) with alternative members, a crisis management center, and an alternative center. The CMT should normally include people from senior line management, human resources, the legal department, security, facilities management, communications, finance, the medical department (if any), and others as necessary.

The plan should also include telephone numbers for contacting the following persons: all major company business leaders at other sites in the area, the landlord if the building is rented or leased, and employee listings: home addresses; home, office, and cell phone numbers; and pager numbers. Employee listings should be sorted alphabetically, or by zip code, or—for many overseas locations—by neighborhood code. Additional listings should include all local medical personnel, ambulance services, hospitals, and other medical facilities; all local police and fire departments units; all state and county law enforcement units in the area; the local National Guard unit; the Red Cross and Salvation Army; the local office of DHS; the local and state DHS representative; the Environmental Protection Agency; the Federal Office of Emergency Management; the local FBI office; security managers from other businesses in the area; the Weather Bureau; all major local media stations, including radio and television; and the company's consultants and other contacts as necessary.

The emergency plan should provide a means to contact and account for employees who work at the site, work at home, work at other businesses, or are visiting the site from other locations. If a catastrophic event occurs outside normal business hours, employees should know where to turn for information and guidance. Also, all employees should plan how to contact family members in an emergency and should know what arrangements have been made for their children in school. If employees are worried about their families, it will be much more difficult to apply a cohesive emergency plan during business hours.

The corporation must have a security emergency plan, every site should have an emergency plan, and individual employees and their families should have an emergency plan. All employees should be aware of Web sites where they can obtain advice and guidance on preparing for and dealing with an emergency. Two outstanding Web sites are those of DHS at www.ready.gov and the Federal Emergency Management Agency (FEMA) at www.fema.gov/areyouready.

There is a need for considerable redundancy in contacts because the people or offices you normally call or deal with may not be available during a serious incident—they may be preoccupied with the emergency, or it might occur after business hours or on a weekend or holiday.

Every corporation and security organization should understand the importance of evacuation drills, particularly in high-rise buildings. Such drills must be more than just planning exercises and more than just mentally stimulating; they must include stress factors, challenging scenarios, and unanticipated complications. In a crisis, employees will respond well to situations they have been trained to deal with, but less well to situations that are totally unexpected. There should be semiannual testing of facility evacuation in at least one of the following situations: an unspecified threat, a fire, an incident involving hazardous materials, a bomb threat, and an explosion.

Education

Education of employees, particularly first-line managers, is crucial to the success of an emergency plan. Well-trained, educated employees are the company's first line of defense in a life-threatening incident.

Education should include some appreciation of potential threats and possible consequences. Selected employees with key roles, such as wardens in a building evacuation, must be trained and retrained. All employees should know how to respond to a fire, a bomb threat, an evacuation, a suspicious letter or package, a power outage, and other emergencies. They should understand their site or location procedures. This information should be provided the first day they report to work at a specific location. Security personnel and all employees—including secretaries, assistants, receptionists, and mail room workers—who are responsible for receiving packages and parcels should be trained to recognize and deal with suspicious articles. (The need for such training became apparent during the anthrax threat.) Also, telephone operators, secretaries, receptionists, and security personnel should be trained in dealing with threatening calls.

CRISIS MANAGEMENT

Much of the planning for site-specific incidents is also applicable to a catastrophic attack. Corporate security experts must elevate site-specific planning to develop means for dealing with local or regional catastrophic events such as the attacks on the transportation system in Madrid and the attacks against commercial air transportation in Russia in 2004—or attacks against targets such as chemical storage areas and nuclear facilities. Is the corporation prepared to act in such an emergency? Is it prepared to respond so as to protect its employees, help its customers, protect its property, keep itself functioning, and be a good corporate citizen?

The Crisis Management Team

Every major business location should have a CMT with members as appropriate from line management, communications, human resources, facility management, finance, and security. Other executives may be called on to support the CMT as necessary. At the pinnacle of the corporation there should be a corporate crisis management team (CCMT).

CMTs work simultaneously at several levels: at the site or city level where an incident occurred, at the country or geographic level where support may be provided, and at the corporate level where policy must be made. The crisis management chain of command should be fully understood and adhered to throughout the company.

Although local and state governments and the federal government have the primary responsibility in dealing with an incident, the private sector would be involved in many ways. A city government can hardly evacuate people if the evacuation process has not already been worked out with local companies that have a large number of employees. Chaos can result if public planning and private-sector planning are not integrated.

One main responsibility of the local CMT is to account for employees in the affected areas and find ways to help employees and local customers, issue instructions to local managers and employees, warn employees of areas to avoid, instruct employees to work from home or report to other work locations, and help keep the business running.

Employees might be advised to remain at work because streets, trains, subways, or roads are dangerous. In a chemical or dirty bomb attack, it may be prudent for employees to remain at certain locations rather than be evacuated into the street. Crisis management should include steps to take during a local chemical or radiological attack. The plan should answer such questions as how the building can be secured, whether employees are safer inside a building or outside, whether (and how) heating, ventilation, and air-conditioning systems (HVACs) should be shut down, what is the safest area of the building, how to deal with people coming from an outside contaminated area into the company's secured area, how employees who have been exposed to chemicals or radiation can be decontaminated, how (and under what circumstances and authority) employees can be evacuated from a contaminated area to a clean area, and how the CMT can communicate with employees who were not at the site at the time of the incident. (Some of these issues are addressed in *Survival Handbook for Chemical, Biological, and Radiological Terrorism* by Elizabeth Terry and J. Paul Oxer, P.E., published in 2003—a book that deserves to be better-known.[2])

All members of the CMT should keep a copy of the emergency plan in their offices and at home (since an emergency may occur after business hours). All the important names, numbers, contacts, and directions should be stored on a disk or on the hard drive of a laptop, ready for instant use. At the site or business location there should be a crisis management room equipped with an AM-FM radio that can operate on batteries and several televisions connected to cable and network news. The room should have thinkpads with dial-up connection; several telephones that bypass the PBX equipment; telephone service that will leave a message simultaneously on the business telephones, cell telephones, and home telephones of key members of the CMT; a good-quality VCR with recording capability; video conferencing capability (at large locations); and a means of quickly obtaining the names of all employees and their managers working in the area.

The crisis management team leader (CMTL) at every level should be a senior line management executive with the authority to make and implement decisions. CMTLs must be able to operate across functional lines, not just represent their own line of business. There should be an alternative CMTL who can take over if the leader is not available. Local CMTs should be empowered to make immediate decisions that affect the security and safety of local employees. They should not act merely as communicators of problems to the next level of management, or as a conduit from senior management to employees. They must be empowered to act.

Communication and the CMT

In its area of direct responsibility, the local CMT should be the public face of the company to employees, customers, clients, and business partners.

Its most important immediate responsibility is to get information out to local employees. The difficulty it confronts is that the situation may be unclear and the facts uncertain, with too many unknowns. CMTs may be tempted to postpone communications until they have most or all of the facts. Wrong! Communication is the glue that keeps the employees together.

Local CMTs may never have all the information they want, but employees are waiting for something—for some sign that management is aware of the incident and taking action. In a catastrophic incident, local CMTs will be racing against the rumor mill; they must take control of the situation, and they do this through communications. The local CMT should move quickly to get out a brief message to employees indicating what facts it has and reassuring employees that it is responding to the crisis and will provide frequent updates. Some immediate dialogue between the CMT and the employees, and between managers and employees, is necessary to maintain control of the situation.

However, local CMTs should not become the voice of the company. That role is usually reserved for corporate headquarters or for the CCMT. The local CMT should avoid communications that are not specific to the immediate situation, or communication that could be considered as enunciating corporate policy. It should not communicate directly with the media unless the content is approved by or coordinated with corporate communications or the CCMT.

Human Resources and the CMT

The role of human resources on the local CMT is to account for employees and ensure their well-being. In a serious attack, this can become a Herculean task. First, there must be a good method for identifying people who normally work in the affected area; this may be partially accomplished through the regular line management chain. The representative of human resources on the local CMT should set up a subgroup to help account for employees and to handle the calls that will come in to the CMT from up-line management and from the families and friends of employees. This information should be provided periodically to the local CMT and the CCMT.

The local CMT should be prepared to provide humanitarian aid to employees and in some cases to their families. This should be handled by the representative of human resources on the CMT. At the local and the corporate level, human resources should be prepared to provide guidance for employees' welfare. The CMT should have available employees, or experts on retainer, with extensive experience in dealing with people in need. The CMT must be prepared to provide medical or psychological assistance to employees or their families. Human resources should have available a database that can provide the names and locations of employees with skills that might be needed in a catastrophic incident.

One lesson of 9/11 is that accounting for and communicating with employees can be difficult. Employees should be provided with at least three contact numbers to be used in an emergency: their manager's telephone number, the security contact for the location, and an 800 number in the area. For instance, there could be one 800 number for all the employees of a company working in one city; in an emergency they could call that number and receive a message providing general instructions.

Security and the CMT

Security will have many staff roles on the CMT or CCMT. One important role is to help the CMT prepare for a major incident: good preparation is the key to responding successfully. The security organization should act as the corporation's "over-the-horizon radar," reviewing the past, looking at the present, and considering the future. Fundamental risk assessments should have been conducted for every major location in the company, and security should ensure that CMT training and emergency planning encompass these risks.

During an actual crisis, security should be the CMT's principal contact with federal, state, and local law enforcement agencies and other agencies as necessary. If the incident occurs at or near a leased facility or rented facility, security or facilities management should be in contact with the landlord. Security should act as the eyes and ears of the CMT, providing updates on significant developments and participating in any decisions. If the site does not have an in-house medical team, security should maintain contact with local medical facilities and ambulance services. Some incidents may require coordination with DHS or the Federal Office of Emergency Management. Security should have the appropriate contacts with these agencies. Once again, I stress the importance of redundancy in contacts.

One area of contacts that is often overlooked by security professionals is medicine. If the United States suffers a significant chemical, biological, or radiological attack, contacts in the medical community will be very important. If security does not already have good sources and contacts in this area, it should start developing them now. Many hospitals are at 85 percent capacity or more; they do not have much capacity to surge. In an attack involving weapons that inflict mass casualties, a great deal of the initial response may have to be organized by private companies, at least to the extent of advising their employees what immediate steps to take. This too requires good contacts within the medical community, at the local hospitals, with local medical services, at the Red Cross, with public health officials, and with specialists in chemical or biological hazards. Some companies have a medical staff that is responsible for this liaison; such a company should make sure that the medical staff has a role on the CMT. In other companies, human resources should be responsible for developing and maintaining these contacts.

During a major incident, security should be able to get a quick reading on how other local organizations are responding. A check with security representatives from these other companies will be helpful. Is everyone else responding in the same way as your company? If not, why not? This information may or may not change the CMT's response, but in any case it will help them understand how others are dealing with similar issues. In this role security is both a purveyor and an adjudicator of information to the CMT. Security should be able to judge and comment on the merits of the actions being taken by other companies.

SOURCES AND CONTACTS

In some situations a good source may be impossible to find. A primary responsibility for security is to evaluate threats as they relate to a particular business, not necessarily to the population in general. In that sense, threat assessment is company-specific. Security may start with a general threat, but at some point it must ask how, if at all, the information affects a particular business.

Corporate security organizations should consider their information requirements for at least the next 10 years. If the corporation is mostly domestic-based, its information requirements are probably narrower than those of an international corporation. Still, domestic corporations as well as international corporations need good information, from good sources. But what is a good source? Every politician, every political commentator, every media figure, every academic expert on terrorism seems able to tell us what happened yesterday and what will happen tomorrow, but never what will happen today. The best anyone may be able to say is that what has happened before will probably happen again.

Since 9/11, much attention has been focused on the likelihood of a follow-up attack. Many people wonder why there has been no such attack yet. Was the government's response after 9/11 so formidable that al-Qaida was temporarily thrown off balance, or is al-Qaida planning an attack that will not take place for several years? We do not know, of course, although the government has made the next attack much more difficult than 9/11.

As a result of this uncertainty, security directors and their staffs are continually seeking information that might provide some warning of an attack. Unfortunately, the likelihood that any contact or source will have such specific information is close to zero. The warnings provided by the U.S. government since 9/11 have been very general, and all over the map. This is not necessarily a fault. If the government has specific information concerning an attack, it will probably be shared initially with a very limited number of people, because the first objective will be to prevent the attack.

A more likely situation is that the government will have a piece or a few pieces of information suggesting a terrorist attack but not indicating the time, place, or target. Often government agencies will provide a list of possible sector targets because they do not have more specific information. Security directors must penetrate this haze to determine if their companies should take any special security measures. To do this effectively, they need more specific information, in at least three categories: (1) information concerning the terrorist group that may be planning an attack; (2) some idea of the city, location, or target of the attack; (3) most importantly, some sense of the veracity and quality of the information that led to the warning.

In addressing the first two categories, security directors need to know the name or identifying characteristics of the group, its history of targets, its recent attacks, statements it may have made on its Web sites concerning future attacks, where it has attacked before, and where it says it will attack in the future. Much of this background information is provided by the government or can be obtained from consultants. Such information can help security professionals make judgments as to whether their company fits the targeting patterns of a particular group, or if there is a perceived threat to their company. As with politics, all threats are local.

32

CORPORATE EMERGENCY MANAGEMENT

Donald L. Schmidt

Emergency Response Planning Practice Leader, Marsh Risk Consulting

INTRODUCTION

What Is Emergency Management? Many terms are used for emergency management in the private sector: emergency response planning, contingency planning, crisis management, disaster planning, etc. However, *emergency management*, the term used in the public sector, is more inclusive and is becoming increasingly popular in the private sector. Emergency management has four phases: mitigation, preparedness, response, and recovery. Since September 11, 2001 one more phase has emerged from mitigation: prevention or deterrence.

Emergency management begins with mitigation—identifying a threat; assessing its potential impact on people, facilities, operations, and the environment; and taking steps to reduce the probability of occurrence or the severity of consequences. Preparedness involves organizing and training people, providing facilities and equipment, and developing policies and procedures for responding. The response phase includes actions taken to safeguard people and stabilize the incident. In the private sector, recovery includes continuity of critical business functions, addressed in business continuity plans, and disaster recovery. Crisis management is an overarching executive-level plan that includes making strategic decisions; communicating with stakeholders such as employees, stockholders, customers, and suppliers; and addressing the emotional needs and health care of affected employees and their families, i.e., the human impact.

National Preparedness Standard: NFPA 1600

The National Commission on Terrorist Attacks upon the United States (9/11 Commission) reviewed the need for preparedness in the private sector and noted in Chapter 12 of its report:[1] "the private sector controls 85 percent of the critical infrastructure in the nation [and] the 'first' first responders will almost certainly be civilians."

The commission acknowledged that lack of a standard contributed to lack of preparedness. It asked the American National Standards Institute (ANSI) to develop a standard for the private sector. After a series of workshops that included representatives from many private-sector industries and associations as well as public officials, ANSI's Homeland Security Standards Panel endorsed *NFPA 1600, Standard on Disaster/Emergency Management and Business Continuity Programs.*[2] NFPA 1600—on which this chapter is based—was promulgated by the National Fire Protection Association (NFPA) under the consensus-based process of standards development accredited by ANSI and established common criteria for emergency management and business continuity.

Congress then acted on the recommendation of the 9/11 Commission and incorporated Section 7305, Private Sector Preparedness, into the National Intelligence Reform Act of 2004, Title VII—Implementation of 9/11 Commission Recommendations. The Act, signed into Law by President Bush on December 17, 2004, recognizes NFPA 1600, Disaster/Emergency Management and Business Continuity Programs, as our national preparedness standard.

(a) FINDINGS.—Consistent with the report of the National Commission on Terrorist Attacks Upon the United States, Congress makes the following findings:

(1) Private sector organizations own 85 percent of the Nation's critical infrastructure and employ the vast majority of the Nation's workers.

(2) Preparedness in the private sector and public sector for rescue, restart and recovery of operations should include, as appropriate—

(A) a plan for evacuation;

(B) adequate communications capabilities; and

(C) a plan for continuity of operations.

(3) The American National Standards Institute recommends a voluntary national preparedness standard for the private sector based on the existing American National Standard on Disaster/Emergency Management and Business Continuity Programs (NFPA 1600), with appropriate modifications. This standard establishes a common set of criteria and terminology for preparedness, disaster management, emergency management, and business continuity programs.

(4) The mandate of the Department of Homeland Security extends to working with the private sector, as well as government entities.

(b) SENSE OF CONGRESS ON PRIVATE SECTOR PREPAREDNESS.— It is the sense of Congress that the Secretary of Homeland Security should promote, where appropriate, the adoption of voluntary national preparedness standards such as the private sector preparedness standard developed by the American National Standards Institute and based on the National Fire Protection Association 1600 Standard on Disaster/Emergency Management and Business Continuity Programs.

Coordinating Emergency Management, Business Continuity, and Crisis Management

In the private sector, the four phases of emergency management may be assigned to various individuals or groups. Many groups or individuals may share responsibility for emergency response, depending on the specific threat or scenario. For example, security is often responsible for dealing with bomb threats and a medical staff for dealing with medical emergencies. Business continuity, including the recovery of information technology, may be assigned to another group, on-or off-site. Crisis management, including communication, may be handled by the corporate staff, with only limited responsibilities assigned to local managers who would interact with local news media.

The resources needed for effective emergency response, business continuity, and crisis management can be significant, depending on the size and nature of the business. Each function also requires specialized skills and expertise. Therefore, responsibilities for these three functional areas are typically split among several persons or groups. But the plans must be connected and well coordinated to ensure the most effective response.

**Program
Development**

An emergency management program is developed stepwise, but with flexibility, allowing individual entities to do what best meets their needs. A summary of the nine steps follows:

Step 1. Develop an executive or managerial policy statement that defines the organization's vision, goals, and objectives. This statement should vest authority in those charged with responsibility for development, implementation, and execution of the emergency management program. This is important during program development and is essential for critical, time-sensitive decisions such as an evacuation—which should not be delayed because of lack of authority.

Step 2. Assign a knowledgeable, capable manager to oversee the program. Organize a planning committee that includes people familiar with the facility, employees, operations, hazards, and resources. The committee may include representatives from areas such as facilities management, engineering, environmental health and safety, security, medical, risk management, human resources, finance, public relations, government or regulatory affairs, and legal.

Connectivity and coordination between the emergency planning committee on the one hand and business continuity and corporate crisis management plans on the other are essential. There are significant opportunities for sharing information or jointly assessing a terrorist threat to quantify its potential impact on facilities and business operations. Emergency response and business continuity teams can jointly determine the location and specifications of the emergency operations center. They can also jointly develop an incident command structure to facilitate effective flow of information and coordinated planning, damage assessment, and logistics. The committee should seek beyond the organization for those who can provide input, who have a role in the plan, or who must review or approve the plan. Outside resources can include public fire departments, hazardous-materials response teams, law enforcement, emergency medical services, the local emergency planning committee (LEPC), contractors, and vendors. Outreach should address prompt notification and warning of threats that may affect the organization's facilities, coordination of response procedures, and establishment of a unified command structure.

Step 3. Identify terrorist threats; assess the vulnerability of people, property, and business operations; and quantify potential severity.

Develop planning scenarios to determine the necessary organization, resources, policies, and procedures.

Step 4. Identify statutory requirements that must be addressed in the program. Next, determine the capabilities needed to respond effectively to identified scenarios. Assess the availability and capability of resources including communication and notification systems, facilities, equipment, trained personnel, and utility systems (such as ventilation). Evaluate the response time and capabilities of public emergency services for each scenario, especially for large-scale or widespread incidents.

Step 5. Compare available resources and capabilities with the resources and capabilities needed. Any gaps should be addressed in the facility's program.

Step 6. Organize a team to execute protective actions such as evacuation, shelter-in-place, and first aid as well as more advanced actions such as bomb searches, firefighting, dealing with hazardous materials, or conducting a search and rescue. Structure the organization using the incident command system to enable effective supervision of personnel and coordination with external public emergency services and other internal and external resources.

Step 7. Write threat- and facility-specific response procedures for detection, notification, and warnings and for basic protective actions such as evacuation, shelter-in-place, and lockdown. More advanced capabilities and procedures—including search and rescue, firefighting, and dealing with hazardous materials—may be warranted if public capability is lacking and the facility must therefore be more self-sufficient. Management must support advanced capabilities, and programs must comply with regulations.

Step 8. Train personnel and exercise the plan. Weaknesses in the program that have been identified during exercises or during post-incident critiques should be addressed through corrective action that strengthens the overall program.

Step 9. Audit the program periodically and add or revise components to ensure that it meets current needs.

PROGRAM MANAGEMENT

Management Commitment and Policy

An emergency management program should be supported by senior management, whose direction will enable wide participation by experts within the organization and increase the probability that planning will be completed on schedule. Management must be briefed on mandatory elements of the program (e.g., evacuation plans) as well as options for enhanced response such as medical aid, firefighting, rescue, and handling hazardous materials. Development of the plan, procurement of equipment, training, drills, and exercises require initial and long-term funding. Management must therefore be informed of options and costs.

Senior management should document the organization's vision, mission statement, goals, and objectives. Management should vest authority in those assigned responsibility for the program, and this should be clearly documented. The document should be widely distributed, so all employees know who is in command during an emergency and who is responsible for updating the plan. Management must also hold those persons assigned responsibility for emergency management accountable, to ensure adequate preparedness.

Regulations and Standards

Many laws, rules, or regulations require emergency planning (e.g., planning for evacuation), and certain standards specify the scope of emergency plans (e.g., staffing, equipment, and training of those involved in firefighting, hazardous materials response, or medical care). Regulations have been promulgated at the federal, state, and local levels. Voluntary standards are prepared by organizations such as NFPA and can be adopted and enforced by political jurisdictions. The U.S. Department of Homeland Security (DHS) is working with ANSI to build a comprehensive, online database of standards for homeland security.

Federal requirements include Occupational Safety and Health Administration (OSHA) standards (29 CFR 1910) applicable to firms with 10 or more employees. Notable examples are 1910 Subpart E, Exit Routes, Emergency Action Plans, and Fire Prevention Plans; 1910.120, Hazardous Waste Operations and Emergency Response; and 1910 Subpart L, Fire Protection (which includes requirements for detection, alarms, fire protection equipment, and firefighting).

Numerous environmental regulations require, or specify requirements for, emergency planning. They pertain to hazardous waste, prevention of oil pollution and chemical accidents, response to spills, the community's right to know, and transportation of hazardous materials.

Since the private sector controls about 85 percent of the critical national infrastructure, federal regulations promulgated since 9/11 require assessment of terrorist risk, mitigation of threats to critical facilities, implementation of emergency response plans, and business continuity or recovery. Many industry associations—in the chemical industry, financial services, healthcare, telecommunications, transportation, the energy sector, maritime operations, etc.—have prepared their own guidelines to meet the federal regulations.

Approximately half of the states in the nation have adopted NFPA 1, Uniform Fire Code® (UFC); most of the remaining states have adopted the International Fire Code (IFC) developed by the International Code Council; and several states have a different code or no code. UFC and IFC require basic emergency planning for most types of facilities. They require additional protection and planning for high-hazard facilities such as those that manufacture, use, or store hazardous materials; those that have many occupants, such as high-rise buildings; and those that are public venues, such as theaters and concert halls. Numerous cities and counties have also adopted their own fire codes or have ordinances addressing local requirements.

The Life Safety Code® developed by NFPA has been adopted by 38 states. It specifies minimum standards for exits, emergency planning, etc., for new and existing structures. OSHA recognizes compliance with the 2000 edition as meeting the requirements of 29 CFR 1910.35.

Other standards and recommended practices published by NFPA address various aspects of emergency planning. Examples applicable to planning for terrorism include NFPA 1620, Recommended Practice for Pre-Incident Planning; NFPA 471, Recommended Practice for Responding to Hazardous Materials Incidents; NFPA 600, Standard on Industrial Fire Brigades; and NFPA 1670 Standard on Operations and Training for Technical Search and Rescue Incidents.

THREAT ASSESSMENT

The emergency management program should be designed to protect people and facilities against site-specific scenarios. Understanding of site-specific scenarios requires identification of the type of threat; point of origin (where the bomb explodes or the chemical is released); impact area (area affected by the initial event and its subsequent development and spread); and the vulnerability of the facility, personnel, and operations.

Terrorist threats include chemical, biological, radiological, nuclear, or explosive (CBRNE) attacks; cyberattacks; firebombs; and attacks by armed intruders. The point of origin of an explosion could be a basement parking garage (World Trade Center, 1993) or a truck bomb outside a building (Murrah Federal Building, 1995). The attack could destroy the building and heavily damage adjacent buildings, or it could be limited to a portion of the building. A hazardous chemical or biological agent released outside can spread, depending on meteorological conditions (wind speed, direction, cloud cover, temperature, and humidity). Anthrax spores released from an opened package could be spread by a ventilation system to contaminate an entire building, or be contained within a separate package-reception facility.

The impact of each threat also depends on the vulnerability of people, buildings, and building systems. A vulnerability assessment will identify weaknesses in site layout; perimeter and building security; building construction; and the arrangement of utility systems that can compromise the ability to deter, detect, or respond to a terrorist threat or attack. The vulnerability assessment should identify opportunities to mitigate, prevent, or deter an attack or reduce its scope and consequences.

The program manager must assess all credible threats and visualize possible scenarios. Plans must then address the personnel, organization, facilities, equipment, training, and other resources needed to respond to each scenario.

MITIGATION

Mitigation is reduction of the probability of occurrence or the severity of an attack. It involves physical and operational measures to prevent or delay an attack or lessen the effects of an attack that does occur. Mitigation of exposure to terrorist threats should address site selection, building design, building utilities, space planning, physical security, operational security, security policies and procedures, and computer security.

Site selection and placement of the building on the site are important decisions. Ideally, maintain at least 100 feet of separation between buildings, public streets, and parking areas. Place buildings so they are not parallel to the street or parking area. Angling a building can help deflect the blast wave of an explosion.

Buildings can be constructed to better withstand an explosion or to maintain structural stability, allowing occupants to evacuate. Laminated glass or inside curtains can contain flying glass. Critical utility systems such as emergency power supplies, potable water and water for fire protection, communications systems, and ventilation systems (including smoke exhaust and stairwell pressurization) should be protected. Redundancy should be built in if the threat of terrorism is significant.

Space planning can also protect people and critical operations within a building. Locate people away from exterior glass facing nearby streets or publicly accessible parking areas. Locate critical operations such as computer rooms in the central part of the building behind security barriers to restrict unauthorized access. Segregate potential target areas such as lobbies for visitors, package reception areas, loading docks, and areas accessible to unauthorized persons. Ideally, high-volume package reception areas should be located in a separate building or at a remote, segregated part of the building equipped with a separate ventilation system to contain any explosion or release of hazardous material.

Provide increasing levels of security from the property line to the heart of the building where critical operations are located. Consider fencing, gates, high-visibility lighting, and surveillance or security guards at the property line. Prohibit unauthorized vehicular and pedestrian access to the property. Review grounds to identify areas where people can hide or where packages can be hidden. Lock mechanical equipment rooms to prohibit unauthorized access to air controls and fan rooms. Protect external air intakes accessible to outsiders—especially any located within reach of ground level.

Provide a combination of qualified personnel, physical barriers, intrusion detection devices, and alarm systems to prevent unauthorized access to the site, the building, and critical areas within the building. Physical barriers such as walls, locks, and electronic access control help keep people out of unauthorized areas. Intrusion detection systems include surveillance cameras (closed-circuit television with or without recording capability) and detectors that sound an alarm. A sufficient complement of qualified security personnel is critical because physical security measures can be compromised if an experienced terrorist has enough time.

RESOURCES

Many resources are essential to effective response: personnel, facilities, systems, equipment, supplies, funding, etc. Personnel include trained employees, contractors, and public emergency services (fire, law enforcement, emergency medical services, hazardous-materials cleanup, etc.). Facilities, systems, and equipment include emergency operations centers, first aid equipment, medical supplies, detection systems, fire suppression systems, occupant notification or other warning systems, communication capabilities (e.g., two-way radios, pagers, telephone systems, call centers), ventilation systems, smoke exhaust systems, and exits.

Critical resources include a system to warn occupants to take protective action, an adequate complement of properly arranged exits to facilitate evacuation, communications systems and equipment to alert public officials and members of the emergency organization, and a communication system for use by members of the emergency organization.

As a part of program development, all resources—their availability and capabilities—must be assessed. Which personnel are available to respond during normal business hours and after hours? How quickly can they be notified, and when would they arrive on-site? What are their capabilities? What is the response time of public-sector emergency personnel? What is their knowledge of the facility and are they able to deal with the scenarios identified during the threat assessment? If public emergency services are overwhelmed by a large-scale incident, what resources must the private organization have to safeguard employees?

Identify all resources available for emergency response including facilities, personnel, or equipment owned or available under a "mutual aid" agreement. Inventory these resources and document them in the plan. Identify any gaps between required resources and available resources, and adjust the plan to address these.

EMERGENCY ORGANIZATION

Every facility should organize a team to respond to emergencies. The organization may be limited to basic protective actions such as evacuation and shelter-in-place, or its response can be more extensive if the management supports and staffs a larger and more capable team.

Emergency Manager

A knowledgeable, capable emergency manager should be appointed to develop the emergency organization and threat- and site-specific response procedures. This manager should have the authority to make critical decisions during an emergency, such as when to evacuate and when to shelter in place. The emergency manager should be familiar with all facilities, building construction, utility systems, occupancy hazards, communications and warning systems, fire detection and suppression systems, exit systems, and the location of occupants within all buildings. The emergency manager should be well-trained, knowledgeable about terrorist threats and scenarios, and capable of leading the emergency organization.

Emergency Response Teams

The emergency organization must at least assign responsibility for notifying public emergency services (e.g., law enforcement, fire, and emergency medical services) and warning building occupants to take protective actions. Primary and backup notification should be addressed in the plan.

The emergency organization may be limited in size and staffed only to evacuate personnel or shelter personnel in place. Larger facilities may warrant organizing teams for evacuation, shelter-in-place, first aid, firefighting, hazardous-materials response, search and rescue, and bomb searches. The role and responsibilities of each team—its structure, staffing, required equipment, and training requirements—should be written out in an organizational statement. The statement should meet OSHA requirements and specify precautions to ensure the safety and health of first responders.

Evacuation Team

A team should be organized to facilitate prompt evacuation. An emergency manager who is able to quickly assess a potential threat should have the authority to order evacuation. The following are suggested roles for the evacuation team:

- The evacuation team leader has responsibility for the evacuation plan under the command of the emergency manager.
- Floor wardens facilitate the evacuation of every floor. Wardens must ensure that all areas have been evacuated, including restrooms, storage rooms, and any areas whose occupants might not hear the evacuation order or alarm system.
- Monitors should supervise the descent down stairwells. They direct occupants to the correct stairwell and ensure that doors are

open and the pathway is unobstructed. They inform evacuees to stay to the right and where to move—to the level of exit discharge (ground floor) or to a predetermined intermediate floor.

- Elevator monitors prohibit evacuees from using elevators and direct them to the nearest stairwell. Lobbies for passenger and service elevators should be monitored.
- Aides ("buddies") should be assigned to assist evacuees with special needs. Pairing a capable individual with each evacuee needing special assistance will speed evacuation. The aides should assist their charges to a safe area where they will await rescue. Obviously, buddies should be located near those they will assist, and alternative buddies should be considered.
- Monitors should be assigned to the assembly point to record the names of people who arrive there and to confirm that everyone who was in the building has been evacuated. These assembly monitors should have access to the employee roster and visitor logs, which they should use as checklists.

Shelter-in-Place Team

A team should be organized to move occupants to the interior of the building and to close off the building from outside air. Assign building facilities or engineering personnel to shut down the ventilation system. Close all air intakes and exhaust dampers, either from a central command center or manually, unit by unit.

Instruct the evacuation team to move people to the interior of the building, away from windows and doors. Assign security staff members to close the exterior doors and advise occupants to remain in the building until it is safe to move outside.

Bomb Search Team

A bomb search team includes people who are familiar with the building and its contents. They are best able to detect suspicious packages or objects that are out of place and therefore suspect. Train the bomb search team to conduct a search and to recognize suspicious objects. This includes knowing how to section a room from floor to ceiling and search each section. The search team also needs to understand precautions such as prohibiting the use of potential triggering devices (radios, cellular telephones, etc.).

Search-and-Rescue Team

The emergency organization may need to provide rescue services until the public fire department arrives on-site, or if the fire department is unable to provide required services because it is unable to reach the site or because the magnitude of the incident overtaxes its resources.

Other teams can include firefighting, medical response, property conservation, and decontamination.

INCIDENT COMMAND SYSTEM

A terrorist incident will probably require substantial resources from the private sector and the public sector, and the two must work well together. Successful control of the incident requires an incident management system that assigns roles and responsibilities and allows for effective and efficient use of all resources.

The incident command system (ICS) is a management system designed to integrate facilities, equipment, personnel, procedures, and communications within a common organizational structure. ICS is used for all types of emergencies, small or complex, by federal, state, local, and tribal government and by many private-sector and nongovernmental organizations. It normally has five major functional areas as shown in Figure 32-1: (1) command, (2) operations, (3) planning, (4) logistics, and (5) finance and administration. ICS has been designated by the National Incident Management System[3] for use in the U.S. public sector.

The roles and responsibilities of the emergency manager and emergency response teams should be defined in accordance with the five sections of ICS. Assign the emergency manager to be the facility's incident commander (IC), and assign subordinates to the three sections of the command staff: government liaison, safety, and public information. The IC (emergency manager) can handle planning for smaller incidents, but large-scale incidents will probably require another person to head the planning section. Organize evacuation, shelter-in-place, firefighting, first aid and medical aid, hazardous-materials handling, search and rescue, and other teams under the operations

FIGURE 32-1

The five sections of ICS and the three command staff positions

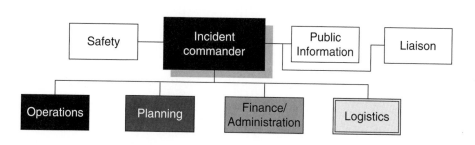

section. Professionals from the finance, accounting, insurance, and risk management departments can staff the finance-and-administration section. Appoint staff members familiar with resource needs and methods of acquisition to handle logistics.

Incident Commander

Decisions made by the IC during the initial minutes after detection are key to safeguarding people. Recognizing critical needs and prioritizing limited resources require knowledge of the various hazards posed by terrorists' weapons. Specific responsibilities of the IC include the following:

- Activate the emergency response plan and elements of ICS
- Ensure that public emergency services and members of the emergency organization are notified and informed where to report (or not to report, if conditions are unsafe)
- Assess the situation—identify the nature of the threat and its potential impact on people, buildings, and the environment
- Determine incident goals, objectives, and immediate priorities
- Consider the threat of secondary devices
- Order building evacuation, sheltering in place, or a combination of both to move people out of danger
- Establish a perimeter around the "hot zone" where the hazard exists or could spread (e.g., the area around a suspected bomb or an area contaminated by a chemical weapon)
- Establish a command post at a safe location upwind and upgrade away from direct involvement with victims, responders, or emergency response vehicles
- Ensure that adequate safety measures are in place
- Provide a detailed situation report to management and government officials when they arrive on-site
- Manage incident operations

Operations Section

The chief of the operations section is responsible for managing all operations to protect personnel and stabilize the incident.

For small organizations, the emergency manager acting as IC will probably assume responsibility for operations. Operations include:

- Evacuation
- Shelter-in-place

- Search and rescue
- Decontamination, first aid and medical treatment
- Firefighting
- Site security
- Fire suppression, ventilation, and elevator systems control in the building

Planning Section

The chief of the planning section reports directly to the IC and is responsible for collecting, evaluating, disseminating, and using information about the development of the incident and the status of resources. Planning is essential to an understanding of the current situation and how it could develop so that alternative strategies can be formed. This includes assessment of the nature of the incident; its immediate impact; its actual or potential spread, risks, and hazards; the implementation of control strategies; and the availability and capabilities of resources.

Logistics Section

The logistics section, which also reports to the IC, provides facilities, services, and materials. It must identify the service and support requirements for planned and expected operations and then procure resources.

Finance and Administration

The finance-and-administration section manages the financial aspects of the incident within the constraints of the organization's policies, procedures, and governance rules. This includes compiling time records for personnel working to stabilize the incident or cleanup; compiling a record of expenditures; communicating with all departments to compile estimates of damage and interrupted business for any insurance claims; notifying and coordinating with insurance brokers and underwriters' claims staffs to prepare and settle claims resulting from the incident; and providing a financial summary. Units under the finance-administration section include documentation, time and costs, and claims.

Command Staff

Three staff positions support the IC: liaison, safety, and public information.

The liaison officer is responsible for interacting on-site with governmental agencies, including law enforcement, firefighters, emergency medical services, environmental agencies, and public health workers. When agencies assign representatives to the incident, the liaison officer will coordinate with them. The liaison officer's goal is to provide information to the public agencies on-site or provide access to the persons who have the information that will enable these agencies to control the incident.

The safety officer is responsible for monitoring and assessing hazardous and unsafe situations and developing measures for personnel safety. The safety officer will correct unsafe acts or conditions and should be authorized to stop or prevent unsafe acts when immediate action is required. The safety officer should also investigate accidents, recommend corrective action, and prepare an accident report to submit to the compensation-claims unit.

Someone from public relations or public affairs acts as the public information officer responsible for collecting and releasing information about the incident to the news media and other agencies and organizations. The public information officer should be a competent spokesperson, familiar with the organization's media relations policies and procedures—especially policies for approving the release of information. The public information officer establishes a media briefing area and acts as the single contact person for release of information to the media and others, schedules regular press briefings, controls the release of information, and coordinates with government officials to refer specific questions that should be answered by public authorities.

Incident Command Post

An incident command post (ICP) is a place at a safe distance from the incident where the IC can observe and direct operations at the scene of the incident. It can be a place outside a building, a motor vehicle, or a convenient location within a building. It should not be confused with the emergency operations center (EOC), which is an on-site, off-site, or virtual meeting place for incident management. The IC's responsibilities include the following:

- Establish the ICP at the time of the emergency
- Communicate emergency organization and responding public agencies

When public emergency services arrive on-site, they will establish their own command post. If possible, relocate the private-sector command post adjacent to it. This will enable easier communications and allow the organization to contribute to the unified command of the incident.

Emergency Operations Center

The EOC is a command and communications center with personnel who gather, retrieve, analyze, process, and display information to coordinate response to an emergency. Staff the EOC with members of the emergency organization, executive management, department managers, and support staff to receive and distribute messages, post the incident status, and track resources. Equip the EOC with the following:

- Sufficient telephone lines—direct (i.e., not switched through a PBX) and independently powered (so service will not be disrupted if primary and emergency electrical power is lost). In a severe incident, telephone service and telecommunications may be impaired, so plan for alternative communications.
- Access to electronic mail and the Internet.
- AM-FM radio, television, and emergency alert system radio.
- Dry-erase board, flip charts, or poster board with markers and erasers.
- Copies of drawings of all building utilities including ventilation (e.g., air intake locations, air-handling unit controls, and exhaust dampers), electrical equipment (locations and areas served by transformers, substations, generators, and disconnects), natural or propane gas, water, and sewage.
- Site plans showing the location of buildings, parking areas, roadways, and other surrounding properties.
- Building plans showing the layout of each floor, the location of any command center for control of building utilities, the location of stairwells and their levels of exit discharge, the location of areas of refuge, and elevator lobbies.
- Video and 35-millimeter still cameras with spare videotape, film, and batteries for documenting damage and cleanup activities.

EMERGENCY RESPONSE PLAN

Each facility should have documented, site-specific policies and procedures for response to terrorism scenarios, including events inside or outside the building, events that affect a region or the nation, and attacks that can affect the availability of required infrastructure (e.g., electricity, natural gas, steam, and potable water). Specific scenarios should include an explosion, a suspect package, a bomb threat (received by telephone, mail, e-mail, web site, or orally), release of chemicals (industrial and warfare), a biological agent, pandemic infection, and a cyberattack.

ALERTING, WARNING, AND COMMUNICATIONS

A prompt, effective means of alerting public agencies and internal response teams to respond to a threat is critical. Establish a primary means of notification and ensure that there is reliable backup communication in case the primary system fails or is overtaxed.

Warning systems such as emergency voice communication systems or simple public address systems are important. They should have backup power, and speakers must be located so that all occupants of the building can hear important announcements. Document operating instructions in the plan, and be sure that competent persons are able to activate the system. Scripts should be prepared in advance for scenarios identified in the threat assessment, and personnel must be capable, if necessary, of speaking clearly in several languages to communicate with all occupants. Provide a means of warning occupants with impaired hearing or sight. Training should ensure that all building occupants are familiar with the sound of the evacuation signal, so they will respond immediately.

Other communications capabilities such as two-way radio systems should be interoperable between all responders who must work together. Establish a command channel for the leaders of the tactical response teams to talk with the incident commander. Assign radio channels and program radios to ensure that the teams handling evacuation, sheltering-in-place, medical aid, rescue, hazardous-materials response, security, etc., can talk as needed. Assess the reliability of the radio communications systems and prepare plans to deal with a loss of communications capabilities.

To alert public agencies, provide complete information about the emergency including specific location (site, building, and area within the building), number and location of any victims (their symptoms or injuries), the nature and spread of the hazard, and actions taken to stabilize the situation or protect life and property.

Establish notification and escalation procedures to ensure prompt notification of managers involved with business continuity, corporate crisis management, etc., as the scope of the incident grows or its impact increases.

Periodically, inspect and test all systems and equipment used for alerting, warning, and communications to be sure they are reliable. Fire alarm systems or emergency voice communication systems should be tested in accordance with applicable codes and standards such as NFPA 72, National Fire Alarm Code®. Maintenance specified by the manufacturer and by applicable codes and standards should be done.

PROTECTIVE ACTIONS

Evacuation

Every building should have an evacuation plan based on an assessment of factors such as the following:

- Construction and layout of the building
- Potential terrorist targets within the building (e.g., mailroom, lobby, loading dock, parking garage)
- Number and concentrations of occupants, including number and location of those with special needs
- Occupant notification systems
- Building utility systems (especially ventilation)
- Fire protection systems (e.g., sprinklers and smoke control systems)
- Exits and exit routes

Plan development should include preparation of building floor plans with clearly marked paths to primary and secondary exits.

Hazards within the building such as the mailroom or a lobby where a bomb might explode should be identified, and alternative evacuation routes should be designed to avoid them.

Concentrations of occupants in auditoriums, cafeterias, and conference rooms require extra attention to ensure that exits are adequate for the maximum number of occupants. These areas are also potential targets because of the concentration of people in them.

Occupants with special needs should be identified in advance, usually voluntarily, to protect their privacy. Anyone with an obvious disability will require assistance, and plans should address this. The plans should also anticipate that there will be others who will not identify themselves as having special needs but will nevertheless need assistance. These could include people with arthritis or temporary conditions such as a sprained ankle or a broken leg. Heart disease, emphysema, asthma, or pregnancy can reduce a person's stamina to the point where assistance will be needed to descend stairs. This is especially true if there are any airborne contaminants.

A high-rise building presents two challenges: the number of occupants and the time necessary to evacuate them all safely. Evacuation plans for high-rise buildings require an assessment of the building and its exits as well as close coordination with the building's management team and the local fire department. Full evacuation of a high-rise building is not typically ordered when a fire alarm system is activated. Initially, the floor where the alarm sounds and two floors above that floor are evacuated down below the floor where the fire alarm has activated. The next zone to be evacuated would include the two floors below the fire floor because these floors would be used as staging areas by firefighters. The number and location of floors to be evacuated could change, depending on the location and spread of fire and smoke, arrangement of the ventilation system, and any vertical penetrations in the floors. The evacuation plan may call for all floors within the air-handling zone to be evacuated. Severe incidents would require full evacuation. Occupants should not be directed to the roof.

Evacuation plans should identify areas of refuge. These include oversized landings of a stairwell or fire and smoke compartments within a floor. The refuge areas should have a means of communicating with the evacuation team leader or firefighters. The number of people who can safely occupy the refuge area and the circumstances when the area would be used should be addressed in the evacuation plan.

Elevators should not be used for evacuation when there is a fire, smoke, or an airborne hazard. During a fire, elevators may be recalled automatically to the first floor. Older elevators may stop at the fire floor, putting their occupants in danger. Use of elevators during a terrorist attack that is spreading an airborne hazard into or within a building could worsen the spread.

The evacuation plan should be designed to overcome any limitations in the building's exits: limited audibility of the building's fire alarm or occupant notification systems, inadequate exits, poor marking of exits, obstructions or impediments, long travel distances, and dead ends. Once the limitations have been identified, the evacuation plan can emphasize alerting in noisy areas (or areas where the alarm system is not loud enough) and the use of extra floor marshals to move occupants along or to redirect them around bottlenecks.

A building with several tenants requires close coordination with the building's manager to ensure that building plans and the tenant plan work seamlessly. Close coordination and effective real-time communication during an evacuation are essential.

Evacuation plans must also address the shutdown of processes or equipment that would create a hazard if they were left running after their operators were evacuated. The time necessary to shut down this equipment should be determined, and the safety of operators while they are shutting down the process or equipment should be addressed.

Evacuation Scenarios

The decision to evacuate part or all of a facility depends on the nature of the emergency and the area affected. The release of a chemical or biological agent or a bombing inside the building would call for evacuation. However, an incident that occurs outside the building and does not threaten the building or its occupants would not require evacuation. In fact, evacuation of the building could put people in harm's way—for example, if a chemical, biological, or radiological hazard was overspreading the path of evacuees.

Bomb threats are another special case. There are various options for handling such threats. If a suspected device is found or there is credible information that an explosive device is in a building, the building should be evacuated. However, a telephoned bomb threat that includes no specific information may not require evacuation. Evacuation scenarios should be discussed with law enforcement authorities, who should approve all procedures.

No evacuation plan is perfect, and no plan can anticipate every possibility. Therefore, the IC has to assess the threat to the building occupants and make the best decision possible. Occupants will tend to make their own decisions if they have had prior experience in an emergency or if leadership is lacking. A thoughtful evacuation plan that is communicated clearly and practiced should work well.

Evacuation Routes and Assembly Areas

Evacuation routes should be established for every floor of each building. Each map should also indicate the location of the primary and secondary assembly areas.

Primary and secondary assembly areas should be separated from each other by direction (e.g., north and south) so that both are not subject to the same event. They should be located away from the staging

FIGURE 32-2

Matrix of possibilities: chemical or biological, indoors or outdoors

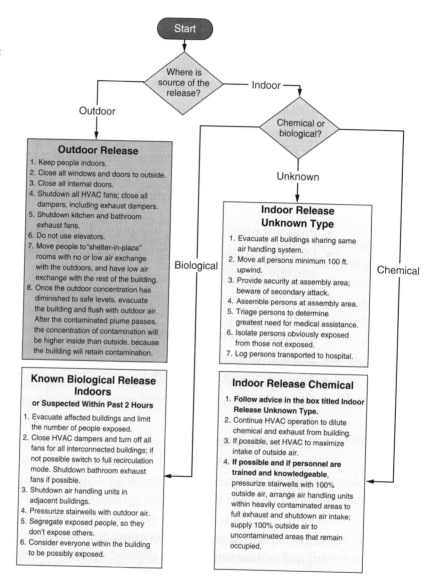

If these signs are not present, the source is probably indoors or in (or near) one of the building's air intakes. To cause immediate symptoms indoors, a very large or very toxic outdoor release near a building's air intake would be required.

Determination of Protective Actions

The location of the terrorist incident, known and potential hazards, and obvious property damage and casualties determine protective actions. The response must also anticipate the possibility of further terrorist attacks.

The location of an attack may be within the building, immediately outside, a few blocks away, or miles away. An attack that occurs miles away could still pose a threat to the site from airborne hazards such as chemical or biological agents or radioactivity.

The scope of any hazards may not be known for hours or much longer, so the initial assessment of the threat should anticipate potential hazards. Any explosion could release airborne chemical, biological, or radioactive hazards. If there are any symptoms or signs of chemical or biological agents, declare an emergency, assess what is known, and implement protective actions.

Protective actions must address all the potential hazards posed by the terrorist act including fire, structural collapse, airborne hazards, and the threat of similar or different additional attacks. A major explosion could cause significant property damage, inflict casualties, and spread airborne hazards. The target building could collapse onto adjacent buildings or onto people in the street. Airborne hazards within a building could spread throughout the building, affecting other occupants. An airborne hazard released outside could infiltrate a building.

Emergency procedures should stress protection of people first. This could include evacuation from an unsafe building or environment or sheltering in place to protect people from airborne hazards outside the building. Any sick or injured people should be given first aid by a qualified emergency response team or triaged for treatment by public emergency medical services. If the safety of building occupants is properly addressed and there are sufficient trained and equipped personnel, other efforts could be undertaken. These could include firefighting, containment of hazardous materials that may have been released, salvage, and property conservation. A large-scale incident that overtaxes public emergency services may require extraordinary efforts by the emergency response team and others to assist victims.

The initial assessment of an incident requires determining the type of hazard, its source, and the extent of any spread.

Airborne Hazards   If the initial assessment reveals an actual, suspected, or potential airborne hazard, its source should be determined. If an explosion or vapor cloud is reported or observed outside the building, protective actions should be appropriate for an outside hazard. If an airborne hazard could have occurred within the building, possibly from a malicious act or the opening of a package, or if an outside airborne hazard may have infiltrated the building, protective actions should be appropriate for an inside hazard.

Outdoor Release, Biological or Chemical

Minimize exposure by taking as many of the following actions as possible:

- Indoors—move anyone who is within a 500-foot radius of the release site.
- Notify police and firefighters to evacuate areas a minimum of one mile downwind in accordance with the Emergency Response Guidebook.
- Follow shelter-in-place procedures—close all windows and doors to the outside; close all internal doors; shut off all HVAC fans and close all HVAC dampers, including exhaust dampers; do not use elevators, since they create a piston effect and can pump air into or out of the building.
- Once the outdoor concentration has diminished to a safe level (as determined by the IC), evacuate the building and flush it with outdoor air. After the contaminated plume passes, the concentration of contamination will actually be higher inside the building than outside, because the building will tend to retain contamination that managed to enter.

Indoor Release, Biological or Chemical

Follow these procedures:
- Evacuate the building
- Gather all evacuees at assembly areas, but no closer than 100 feet from the evacuated building
- Provide security at the assembly areas to prevent a secondary attack

Have evacuees congregate at assembly points upwind of and at least 100 feet from the building (preferably much farther). As soon as possible, separate people known to be exposed from those who may not have been exposed. Account for all evacuees and provide first aid as required.

Indoor Release, Biological

A biological agent will probably not cause immediate symptoms, and the type of biological agent (or even whether it is real or a hoax) may not be known for hours or possibly days. In fact, a biological agent can be introduced into a building without the occupants even knowing about it.

Take the following protective actions if a release is known or suspected to have occurred within the past hour or two:

- Close HVAC dampers and turn off all fans. Operation of any HVAC system will exhaust air (and the biological agent) to the outdoors, possibly infecting people who do not know they are at risk.
- Pressurize stairwells with outdoor air, if possible.
- Limit the number of people exposed.
- Segregate those with symptoms, those potentially exposed, and those who have had close contact with others who have been exposed—unless the biological agent is determined not to be contagious (e.g., anthrax).
- Log the names, addresses, and contact information of those who have been exposed.

Radiological Incident

A conventional explosion may scatter radioactive material, or an aerosol containing radioactive material could be spread over a wide area. Some people may be injured and many may be contaminated or exposed. A radiological hazard will not be known for sure until government officials assess the scene. Therefore, take the following precautions.

- Remove seriously injured people from the source of radiation, stabilize the injuries, and arrange transportation to hospitals.
- Establish a perimeter around the source, and restrict entry to rescue personnel only.
- Check everyone near the scene for radioactive contamination. Establish a decontamination area and decontaminate people whose injuries are not life-threatening (broken arms, etc.) before sending them to hospitals.
- Detain uninjured people who were near the event or who are inside the control zone until they can be checked for radioactive contamination, but do not delay treatment of injured people or transport to a hospital for this purpose.
- Inform nearby hospitals to expect the arrival of radioactively contaminated and injured people.

Fires and Explosions

When a fire or explosion is detected, notify the fire department and describe the nature of the fire, its location, and any fire alarm zones that have been activated. Advise the fire department of the building entrance closest to the scene.

If an explosion occurs, attempt to determine its cause. If an explosion is not known to be accidental, assume that it could have dispersed a chemical, biological, or radioactive hazard. Follow instructions for indoor or outdoor release of chemical or biological agents.

The IC should order evacuation of the building or portions of the building to protect the occupants. The IC should also set up a command post near the building or adjacent to the location of the fire. Direct the emergency response team to their assigned areas, as necessitated by the conditions reported. When the public fire department arrives, inform its IC of the nature of the emergency and action being taken. Building plans, a two-way radio, master keys, and other information should be provided as requested.

Supervise fire protection systems (e.g., sprinklers, fire pump, and water supply control valves) and utility systems (generators, electrical disconnects, HVAC, gas, etc.). Ensure that all sprinkler systems and fire pumps are operating properly. If there is a power outage or potential outage, monitor any generators to ensure that they have started and are running smoothly. Disconnect power to part or all of the building at the direction of the fire department's IC. Activate any building smoke exhaust system and manipulate the HVAC system at the direction of the fire department's IC. If there is no directive from the fire department's IC, shut down the air-handling system to prevent the spread of smoke.

Keep the building entrance and driveway areas free for access by the fire department. Occupants should be directed to emergency exits and assembly areas away from the building. Unauthorized persons should be kept off the property.

Suspicious Package or Letter

Terrorists might package an explosive device or a biological agent such as anthrax and send it through the mail or by courier. Everyone should be aware of the indicators of packages that may contain a terrorist weapon and of the procedures for emergency response.

General Characteristics

Following are some characteristics of suspicious incoming letters or parcels. Any one characteristic may not be reason for concern,

FIGURE 32-3

Indicators of a
suspicious package

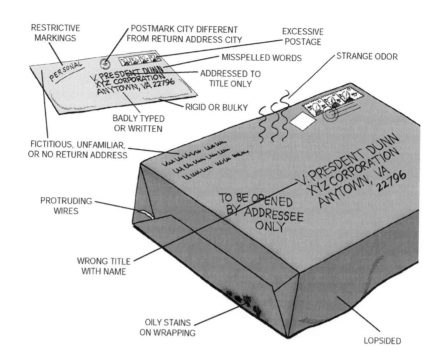

but multiple characteristics should arouse suspicions and be a reason for taking precautions and conducting further evaluation. See Figure 32-3.

- Hand delivery.
- No postage or excessive postage.
- Package is unexpected or from someone unfamiliar to the addressee.
- Receipt is followed by an anonymous call asking if the item was received.
- Package is addressed to someone no longer with the organization or is otherwise outdated.
- Address is handwritten or poorly typed; title is incorrect or appears with no name; common words are misspelled.
- There is no return address or an unverifiable return address.
- Package is marked "Personal," "Confidential," "Fragile—Handle with Care," "Rush—Do Not Delay," "To Be Opened in Privacy," "Your Lucky Day Is Here," or "Prize Enclosed."
- Package is of unusual weight relative to its size or is lopsided or oddly shaped.

- There are soft spots or bulges.
- There is a strange odor or a stain.
- There is a powdery substance on the outside.
- There is a "sloshing" sound. (Mail bombs typically do not "tick.")
- There is pressure or resistance when the package is opened; this may indicate a mail bomb.
- There is an unusual amount of tape.

Package Marked "Anthrax" or Is Powdery

If a letter or package is marked "anthrax," has a powdery substance on the outside, is leaking a powder, or contains a powdery substance when opened, the following actions should be taken:

- Notify the emergency response team immediately. Describe the location of the package and the reasons why you are suspicious. The emergency manager or another authorized person will determine if law enforcement or the fire department should be notified.
- If any contents have spilled, shut down the building's ventilation system to prevent the spread of the powder.
- Do not shake, open, or empty the contents of any suspicious envelope or package.
- Do not sniff, touch, taste, or look closely at the package or at any contents that may have spilled.
- Do not carry the package or envelope; do not show it to others; do not allow others to examine it.
- Put the envelope or package in a plastic bag or some other container to prevent leakage of the contents. Within the mail center, the package should be placed in a holding-transport container.
- If there is no container, cover the envelope or package with anything (e.g., clothing, paper, or an upside-down trash can) and do not remove this cover.
- Leave the area and section it off to prevent others from entering (i.e., keep others away).
- Wash hands with soap and water to prevent spreading any powder to the face.

When a Suspicious Item Is Found

If a suspect item is found, take the following actions:

- Notify the emergency manager.
- If the package is believed to contain a powdery substance, if a vapor or gas (e.g., aerosol) is released, or if any contents have spilled, shut down the building's ventilation system to prevent the spread of any powder or vapor and evacuate all occupants of the air-handling zone or zones that could be cross-contaminated.
- The emergency manager should direct notification of police and fire departments, which will notify additional agencies as needed.
- Alert employees in the immediate area and others located in adjacent areas that a suspicious letter or package has been found.
- If the suspicious item is believed to be a bomb, evacuate the surrounding area for 150 feet in all directions, including the floors above and below. If the package is found outside, evacuate 1,850 feet in all directions.
- Put the suspicious item in a sealed container and move it to an isolated area. If the package is believed to be a bomb, place it in a bomb-holding container. If there is no container available, leave it alone.
- From a safe distance, the person who finds the suspected package should write down any reasons for suspicion (e.g., excessive postage, no return address, rigid envelope).
- Without making direct contact with the suspicious item, record all available information from all sides: name and address of addressee, name and return address of sender, postmark cancellation date, post office codes, types of stamps, other markings or labels, other peculiarities (such as oil stains, tears, a flap sealed with tape, or a flap not glued down).
- Record all information about the suspected letter or package. If possible, photograph the package from all sides without moving it. The photographs may be used to verify the package as legitimate or to show responding emergency personnel.
- Contact the addressee to ask for identification or verification of the letter or package.

Before calling for outside assistance, attempt to find out if the sender or addressee has any knowledge of the item or its contents. If the addressee can positively identify the suspected item, it may be opened with relative safety. If the addressee cannot verify the letter or package and only the sender can be contacted, determine whether the letter or package still represents a threat.

Bomb Threats

Bombs have historically been the weapon of choice for terrorists. People carrying explosive devices are aware of the danger of a premature explosion and have a natural desire to set the explosive and leave the area. However, suicide attacks have proved that assumptions about quick entry and exit are no longer necessarily valid.

Easily accessible locations such as lobbies and unlocked doors can hide an explosive device. Other possible areas are stairwells, restrooms, janitors' closets, unused offices, and display areas.

When a bomb threat is received, the predetermined chain of command must be activated. Record all details and communicate with the emergency manager to determine whether to evacuate. The credibility of the threat must be assessed, given the available information, and the emergency manager must decide the following:

- Whether or not the building should be evacuated
- The scope of any evacuation—full or partial
- The duration of any evacuation

Bomb Threats by Telephone

Give all personnel, especially telephone operators and receptionists, a checklist to record information about bomb threats, such as the characteristics of the voice and any background noises heard during the call. Do the following:

- Keep the caller on the line as long as possible. Ask the caller to repeat the message. Record every word spoken.
- If the caller does not indicate the location of the bomb or the time of detonation, ask.
- Inform the caller that the building is occupied and detonation of a bomb could result in death or serious injury to many innocent people.
- Pay particular attention to background noises, such as motors running or music playing, that may give a clue to the caller's location.
- Listen closely to the voice (male, female), voice quality (calm, excited), accent, and any speech impediment.

- Immediately after the caller hangs up, notify the emergency manager and fill out the bomb threat form. See Figure 32-4.

Bomb Threats by Letter

When a written threat is received, save all materials, including any envelope or container. Once the message is recognized as a bomb threat, further unnecessary handling should be avoided. Every possible effort must be made to retain evidence such as fingerprints, handwriting or typewriting, paper, and postal marks. These will prove essential in tracing the threat and identifying the writer.

FIGURE 32-4

Bomb threat form

Source: Department of Treasury; Bureau of Alcohol, Tobacco, and Firearms

Department of the Treasury
Bureau of Alcohol, Tobacco and Firearms
BOMB THREAT CHECKLIST

1. When is the bomb going to explode?
2. Where is the bomb right now?
3. What does the bomb look like?
4. What kind of bomb is it?
5. What will cause the bomb to explode?
6. Did you place the bomb?
7. Why?
8. What is address?
9. What is your name?

EXACT WORDING OF THE BOMB THREAT:

_____
_____
_____
_____
_____

Sex of caller: _____   Race _____

Age: _____   Length of call: _____

Telephone number at which call is received: _____

Time call received: _____

Date call received: _____

CALLER'S VOICE

☐ Calm   ☐ Nasal
☐ Soft   ☐ Angry
☐ Stutter   ☐ Loud
☐ Excited   ☐ Lisp
☐ Laughter   ☐ Slow
☐ Rasp   ☐ Crying
☐ Rapid   ☐ Deep
☐ Normal   ☐ Distinct

☐ Slurred   ☐ Whispered
☐ Ragged   ☐ Clearing Throat
☐ Deep Breathing   ☐ Cracking Voice
☐ Disguised   ☐ Accent
☐ Familiar *(If voice is familiar, who did it sound like?)* _____

BACKGROUND SOUNDS:

☐ Street noises ☐ Factory machinery
☐ Voices   ☐ Crockery
☐ Animal noises ☐ Clear
☐ PA System   ☐ Static
☐ Music   ☐ House noises
☐ Long distance ☐ Local
☐ Motor   ☐ Office machinery
☐ Booth   ☐ Other *(Please specify)*

BOMB THREAT LANGUAGE:

☐ Well spoken (education)   ☐ Incoherent
☐ Foul   ☐ Message read by threat maker
☐ Taped   ☐ Irrational

REMARKS: _____

Your name: _____

Your position: _____

Your telephone number: _____

Date checklist completed _____

ATF F 1613.1 (formerly ATF F 1730.1, which may still be used) (6-97)

Although written messages are usually associated with generalized threats and extortion attempts, a written warning of a specific device may occasionally be received.

TRAINING, DRILLS, AND EXERCISES

The emergency plan is only as good as the knowledge and ability of the emergency organization and the IC. Terrorist incidents are extremely challenging and will place great demands on the emergency organization. Therefore, a high level of training is required for all members of the organization, its leaders, and all employees.

Training and drills should cover the location, controls, supervision, shutdown, and use of systems and equipment as defined in emergency procedures. This includes notification, communication, ventilation systems, smoke exhaust, stairwell pressurization, and fire suppression systems.

Knowledge of all emergency procedures, including evacuation and sheltering in place, is essential. Procedures for response to CBRNE scenarios should be covered, so all personnel understand their role and responsibilities. The roles, responsibilities, procedures, and activation of the ICS should be covered.

Conduct tabletop, functional, or full-scale exercises using realistic scenarios to challenge members of the emergency organization and evaluate the adequacy of response procedures. Carefully scripted and facilitated exercises offer good training and give people an opportunity to work together to manage challenging incidents. These exercises can identify weaknesses or deficiencies in the plan or in the ability to execute the plan.

All facilities must prepare an emergency action plan (EAP) as defined by OSHA. The OSHA standard requires training of designated employees to assist in the safe and orderly emergency evacuation of employees. Train all employees in the EAP when it is first developed, whenever employees' duties under the plan change, and whenever the plan itself is changed.

Training for fire brigades, rescue teams, and hazardous-materials teams must be commensurate with their duties and functions. Training requirements are spelled out in the OSHA and NFPA standards.

Train medical response teams in the protocols for treatment of chemical, biological, and radiological exposure. They should at least be able to recognize the signs of exposure and be familiar with immediate triage, treatment, segregation, and decontamination requirements.

Considerable training is available from public sources, through distance learning on the Internet, and from colleges and universities. Private contractors provide training in first aid, CPR, use of automated external defibrillators, firefighting, rescue, and dealing with hazardous materials.

Outline the scope and frequency of training in the emergency plan and the regulatory requirements (e.g., OSHA standards, fire prevention, and life safety codes). Document all training in a master file, including dates, subject material, instructor, and duration. Maintain records for review by regulatory authorities.

CRITIQUES, AUDITS, AND EVALUATIONS

At the conclusion of any incident, prepare a report documenting chronology, the use of personnel and resources, and what procedures did and did not work well. Conduct an incident debriefing with all personnel involved. Include representatives from the external agencies that were involved.

Periodically audit the facility's capability to respond to terrorist incidents. Review policies, procedures, staffing of the emergency organization, use of the incident command system, scope of training, and the results of drills and exercises. Look at record keeping. The audit should compare current capabilities with required capabilities and regulatory requirements. Review the "threat environment," changes in the facility, and vulnerabilities. Does the capability to respond to terrorist threats meet the current needs of the facility? Document any discrepancies between needed capability and actual performance.

Compile a list of actions to be taken to improve response, assign these to a responsible person, and establish due dates. Also, establish a process with management oversight to ensure that the corrective actions are completed on schedule.

NOTES

1. National Commission on Terrorist Attacks upon the United States, *The 9/11 Commission Report* (New York: Norton, 2004).

2. National Fire Protection Association, *NFPA 1600, Standard on Disaster/Emergency Management and Business Continuity Programs* (Quincy, Mass: National Fire Protection Association).

3. On 28 February 2003 the President issued Homeland Security Presidential Directive (HSPD) 5, "Management of Domestic Incidents," directing the secretary of Homeland Security to develop and administer a National Incident Management System (NIMS). On 1 March 2004 NIMS was published by DHS; it includes ICS for use in the public sector.

33

OPERATIONAL RESILIENCE FOR PRIVATE AND PUBLIC SECTOR ORGANIZATIONS

William A. Gouveia, Jr.

Managing Director, Consulting SunGard Availability Services

"Inside of a ring or out, ain't nothing wrong with going down. It's staying down that's wrong."

Muhammad Ali

Homeland security professionals are familiar with the range of capabilities designed to help critical infrastructure organizations manage operational risks such as business continuity plans, crisis management plans, information technology recovery plans, pandemic plans, incident response plans, and so on. However, in designing these capabilities to address potential disruptions, large, complex, interconnected, and ever-changing private and public sector organizations have struggled to develop adequate models to effectively assess, manage, and mitigate operational risks that cut across and between functional areas.

This chapter begins with a brief overview of operational risk management within homeland security, then discusses a series of related challenges that public and private sector organizations face, and finally offers homeland security professionals with an agile and integrated approach to managing operational risk.[1] Rather than approach the topic from the perspective of how to respond to and recover from a disruptive event, the concepts discussed here will center on building operational resilience into and across organizations.

OPERATIONAL RISK IN HOMELAND SECURITY: CURRENT CONCEPTS, CAPABILITIES, AND CHALLENGES

The United States Department of Homeland Security's *Risk Management Fundamentals* offers the following discussion of resilience and risk management: "One of the foundational concepts of homeland security is the need to build resilient systems, communities, and institutions that are robust, adaptable and have the capacity for rapid recovery. Resilience and risk management are mutually reinforcing concepts."[2] While these concepts are indeed mutually reinforcing, translating that into practice has been a struggle for large enterprises because of the complexity involved in aligning a range of risk management capabilities—with a range of stakeholders, equities, and perspectives—into a model that builds resilience. To inform this discussion, it is worthwhile to walk through several of the various risk management capabilities involved in operational resilience:

- *Business Continuity Management (BCM), Continuity of Operations (COOP), or Continuity of Government (COG).* Focused on ensuring the organization is able to respond to an incident and recover the processes deemed critical to continuity of operations.
- *Disaster Recovery (DR).* Responsible for recovering the IT infrastructure, applications, networks, and data critical to ensuring organizational processes can be executed.
- *Enterprise Risk Management (ERM).* Responsible for coordinating risk management across the organization by managing the risk management life cycle that includes assessing, validating, controlling, and monitoring risk mitigation activities.[3]
- *Security.* Responsible for protecting the people and critical infrastructure of the organization, generally from a physical ("gates, guard, and guns") as well as a cyber (data, applications, networks) perspective.

Most critical infrastructure organizations have some form of these capabilities and many have made significant investments in these areas. Nevertheless, the challenge facing large organizations is how to integrate the value of these functions and surmount the management, funding, standards, and compliance issues discussed below.

Management of a critical infrastructure organization is a complex, multifaceted challenge that is often approached in stovepipes.

For example, most private and public sector organizations treat business continuity and disaster recovery as unrelated to cybersecurity. Although there has long been recognition of this, few organizations have embraced an integrated approach to building operational resilience. The current reality is that most large organizations contend with management silos that place barriers around transparency, efficiencies, and dependencies that preclude full understanding of organizational risks and complicate efforts to evaluate operational resilience. Many ERM leaders apply frameworks (such as that of the Committee of Sponsoring Organizations of the Treadway Commission, or COSO) to assess and validate risk but continually face challenges in seeing across management silos to analyze all enterprise risks as well as gain buy-in from across departments on how to best monitor, manage, and control operational risks.

Funding plays a key role in defining the level of risk appetite and establishing who manages which risks. Funding for risk management activities is often distributed between various functions such as finance, compliance, operations, and IT with no clear idea on how these funds are allocated and how effectively the spending is combined to manage cross-cutting risks.[4] In addition, many organizations find themselves with overlapping or competing approaches to risk, often driven by different policies and procedures.

Standards related to operational risk and resilience have proliferated over the past decade and now offer homeland security professionals a dizzying array of frameworks, guidance, and best practices. These standards can provide a solid foundation, but the challenges are often how to select the most appropriate standard and how to adopt a generic standard for a specific organization. For example, this uncertainty regarding which guidance is most relevant for the needs of their organization is often seen in the area of Business Continuity Management (BCM). To emphasize the point, the following standards and regulations pertain to business continuity:

- ASIS International Business Continuity Guidelines (International)
- ANSI ASIS SPC.1–2009: Organizational Resilience: Security, Preparedness, and Continuity Management Systems— Requirements with Guidance for Use American National Standard
- Basel Capital Accord
- Business Continuity Institute (BCI)—The BCI Good Practice Guidelines (International)

- BSI Group—Business Continuity Management. Specification (BS 25999–2:2007; UK)
- BSI Group—Information and Communications Technology Continuity Management. Code of Practice (BS 25777:2008; UK)
- BSI Group—IT Service Continuity Management. Code of Practice (Publicly Available Specification [PAS] 77:2006; UK)
- Canadian Standards Association—Z1600 Emergency Management and Business Continuity Programs
- DRI International—Generally Accepted Practices for Business Continuity Practitioners (International)
- U.S. Federal Financial Institutions Examinations Council (FFIEC)—Business Continuity Planning IT Examination Handbook, March 2008
- HB 221:2004—Business Continuity Management Handbook (Australia)
- HB 292:2006—A Practitioner's Guide to Business Continuity Management (Australia)
- ISO/PAS 22399:2007: Societal Security—Guideline for Incident Preparedness and Operational Continuity Management
- ISO 22301: Societal Security—Preparedness and Continuity Management Systems—Requirements
- ISO/IEC 27001:2005—Information Technology—Security Techniques—Information Security Management Systems—Requirements
- IT Infrastructure Library (ITIL) v. 3 (International)
- Monetary Authority of Singapore—Business Continuity Management Guidelines
- U.S. National Fire Protection Association (NFPA) 1600—Standard on Disaster/Emergency Management and Business Continuity Programs (2007 Edition)
- U.S. National Institute of Standards and Technology (NIST)—Special Publication 800–34
- North American Electric Reliability Corporation (NERC)—Critical Infrastructure Protection Cyber Security Requirement 009
- Prudential Standard APS 232—Business Continuity Management (Australia)
- Singapore Standard SS 507:2004—Business Continuity/Disaster Recovery Service Providers

- SPRING Singapore Technical Reference (TR) 19:2005—Business Continuity Management
- U.S. Public Law 110–53—Implementing Recommendations of the 9/11 Commission Act of 2007, Title IX, Private Sector Preparedness

In addition, the U.S. Department of Homeland Security (DHS) has launched the Voluntary Private Sector Preparedness Accreditation and Certification Program (PS-Prep). PS-Prep asks businesses to voluntarily certify that their program meets certain preparedness standards and "to enhance nationwide resilience in an all-hazards environment by encouraging private sector preparedness."[5]

This profusion of standards and regulations serves as a double-edged sword for practitioners. Although they give credence and significance to the work they do by gaining the attention of examiners and auditors, professionals are often at a loss in determining with which standards they should comply. It is therefore the responsibility of the practitioner to use the intent of these standards to create a culture of resilience, and not just a culture of standards compliance.

The homeland security community can benefit from the work of these national and international standards organizations and draw from the past decade's evolution from best practices (e.g., BCI's Good Practice Guidelines) to national and international standards (e.g., BS-25999 and ISO-22301) to the overarching framework discussed in the next section.[6] As homeland security professionals work through the challenge of determining how many and which of the many relevant standards they should consider for adoption, it is often helpful to first evaluate overarching frameworks to determine operational resilience needs and then explore which of the relevant standards might best meet these needs.

Compliance is another key driver for operational resilience. Business leaders are increasingly required to focus their attention on investing in operational resilience—not only to better prepare for and recover from disruptive events and protect and sustain services, but also to satisfy various categories of compliance requirements:

- *Regulatory and legal compliance* with laws from state, local, and federal governments that require organization policies, practices and procedures be followed
- *Contractual compliance* with business agreements between partners, customers, and other organizations that are committed through

contracts and service-level agreements (SLAs) with penalties for noncompliance or nonperformance

- *Organizational compliance* with external auditors and internal controls, often related to the frameworks or standards discussed above

Viewed from an operational perspective, organizational compliance is often the foundation for the management engagement and commitment required for homeland security leaders to define the day-to-day operational tasks that are developed, refined, and followed by the organization.

OPERATIONAL RESILIENCE: A FRAMEWORK FOR INTEGRATING CAPABILITIES TO MANAGE RISK

What is a homeland security professional to do with all of the challenges around implementation and the different guidance, standards, and regulations available for assistance? How can one move beyond these challenges to a model that evolves an organization from simply managing its known risks to being truly resilient? Can the critical infrastructure organizations that have had business continuity and disaster recovery plans for many years verify that these plans are fully functional and actionable?

As mentioned, this uncertainty is often the result of approaching risk management activities in a top-down, fragmented way that focuses on addressing defined disruption scenarios. In increasingly complex operational environments, there is often the following:

- A lack of convergence between operational risk activities
- A lack of common language to communicate about risk
- An overreliance on governance, risk, and compliance (GRC) software and other technologies
- No means to measure managerial competency in these areas
- An inability to confidently predict outcomes during times of stress or disruption.

Although risk should be evaluated and understood strategically, organizations can only gain the ability to recover from or adjust easily to change by embracing resilience at the enterprise level and embedding it operationally.

Homeland security leaders should consider Carnegie Mellon's CERT Resilience Management Model (CERT-RMM) as a formal approach to operational resilience that moves beyond traditional barriers to implementation and control. The CERT-RMM model describes the essential processes for managing operational resilience, and provides a structure from which an organization can begin process improvement of its Business Continuity/Disaster Recovery (BCM/DR), IT Security, and other organizational efforts. By improving these processes, critical infrastructure organizations can more easily predict the performance of services under uncertain conditions, manage unknown risks, meet their mission under adverse circumstances, and return to normal when the adversity is eliminated.

Moreover, the CERT Resilience Management Model is the first known model in the security and continuity domain that includes a capability dimension. This provides an organization a means by which to measure its ability to control operational resilience and to consistently and predictably determine how it will perform under times of stress, disruption, and changing risk environments.

Highlights of Carnegie Mellon's CERT Resilience Management Model (CERT-RMM)

- Provides a deep process definition across four categories: enterprise management, engineering, operations management, and process management
- Focuses on four essential operational assets: people, information, technology, and facilities
- Includes processes and practices that define four capability levels for each process area: Incomplete, Performed, Managed, and Defined
- Serves as a meta-model that includes references to common codes of practice such as ISO27000, ITIL, CobiT, and others such as BS25999 and ISO24762
- Includes process metrics and measurements that can be used to ensure that operational resilience processes are performing as intended
- Facilitates an objective measurement of capability levels via a structured and repeatable appraisal method

In plain English, the model creates a formal method in which to execute tasks in ways that build resilience. So how do we ensure that investments in operational resilience will increase our confidence that services will continue to meet their mission, even during times of stress and disruption? And by so doing, how are we able to justify such investments to senior managers?

Positioning operational resilience to build a stronger organization is accomplished by articulating the business need and showing how to meet it—in a tangible and measurable way at an affordable cost with a positive return. In the context of operational risk, it is often the answer to the questions of "Where does it hurt the most?" and "What high-impact, high-loss events would put us out of business?" A key step in this process is to identify the senior manager who most cares about the answer to these questions and to make sure that he or she is on board as the visible champion and sponsor of operational resilience investments.

As a first step, by posing the following questions to relevant stakeholders (including operational leaders, security officials, technology and finance specialists, etc.), organizations can begin the conversation about operational resilience:

1. Does your organization bring all key operational stakeholders (such as security, BCM, and ERM) together in an integrated resilience program?
2. Do you understand your operational resilience requirements? What standards and regulations inform these requirements? How resilient do you want to be?
3. How resilient are you? Where are your best targets for improvement? Does your organization focus recovery resources on the key business functions that need to be resilient and recoverable?
4. How do you address processes across your enterprise? How does technology enable resilience?

In addition, those making the case for operational resilience must be able to demonstrate that investments are subject to the same decision criteria as other business investment such as alignment to business mission, strategic objectives, and critical success factors, which are the basis for determining the high-value services that support the accomplishment of strategic objectives. In short, presenting the following benefits can facilitate understanding, engagement, and investment by senior leaders in operational resilience:

- Lowered or eliminated redundancy and cost by optimizing between protection and sustainability strategies
- Greater compliance as well as improved metrics to demonstrate that compliance
- Lowered operational risks with an enterprise focus
- Improved processes that are measurable and manageable—and thus, more effective.

In conclusion, building operational resilience is a difficult task for homeland security leaders and one with a defined set of challenges and a proven set of obstacles. Fortunately, a comprehensive model exists to guide the process of embedding resilience into private and public sector organizations. By using the framework provided by CERT-RMM, organizations can develop a roadmap to achieve their resilience goals, better prevent and respond to change, and safeguard critical infrastructure.

NOTES

1. The scope of this chapter will focus on the vast majority of operational risk activities that are performed from an organizational perspective rather than a systemic one; that is, it will primarily address how to make private and public sector organizations more resilient.

2. *Risk Management Fundamentals,* Homeland Security Risk Management Doctrine, April 2011.

3. The *U.S. DHS Risk Lexicon,* 2010 Edition, provides the following definition of risk management: "Risk management is the process for identifying, analyzing, and communicating risk and accepting, avoiding, transferring, or controlling it to an acceptable level considering associated costs and benefits of any actions taken." Risk management can mean many things in the context of homeland security; for example, government agencies generally leverage a risk model focused on probability and impact to guide policy, design regulation, and inform operational decisions. Private sector critical infrastructure managers such as financial services institutions develop sophisticated operational risk controls to address fraud, insider trading, and money laundering. To facilitate a meaningful dialogue on operational risk, tone must consider proven models for helping stakeholders develop a clear grasp of how to manage risk across functional areas. A widely accepted definition can be found in ISO 31000, Enterprise Risk Management, in which risk is the "effect of uncertainty on objectives" on "any public, private or community enterprise, association, group or individual." However, to narrow this down to a homeland security context, the real challenge is to ensure that organizations can continue to carry out their mission in the presence of operational stress and disruption—noting that this stress and disruption comes from risk.

4. In terms of responsibilities, Finance will focus on matters related to interest rates and return, while traditional Risk Management departments focus their attention on transferring risk through insurance and other third-party solutions. Within Operations, risk management can vary from being focused at a strategic level within leadership down to the individual

business units or departments charged with executing processes for the organization. Risk within IT can fall into any number of focus areas around project management, control, systems review, architecture, and information security.

6. FEMA, Voluntary Private Sector Preparedness Accreditation and Certification Program, http://www.fema.gov/media/fact_sheets/vpsp.shtm.

7. For more on standards, see Dr. Nader Mehravari's presentation on *BCM Frameworks: From Best Practices to Standards to Overarching Models*, March 22, 2012, http://www.brighttalk.com/webcast/188/4087.

34

BUILDING A RESILIENT NATION

Stephen Flynn

Co-Director of the Kostas Research Institute for Homeland Security; and Professor of Political Science at Northeastern University

Sean Burke

Associate Director of the Kostas Research Institute

Assuring security, safety, and prosperity in the twenty-first century requires building and maintaining resilience in the face of chronic and catastrophic risks. Americans must brace themselves in the years ahead for large-scale disruptions, fueled by unconventional conflict around the globe, changes in climate, and the sheer complexity and interdependencies of transnational modern systems and networks. Ensuring that individuals, communities, and critical infrastructure have the capacity to withstand, respond to, rapidly recover from, and adapt to man-made and natural disturbances will prove indispensible to sustaining our way of life and quality of life. Alternatively, a lack of resilience will be a competitive disadvantage, with individuals and investors avoiding places and companies that cannot provide continuity of essential services in the face of stress. Moreover, resilience provides deterrence value to adversaries whose aim is mass disruption or destruction, as attempts to target resilient societies or systems will gain little return for their nefarious efforts.

Building resilience requires a strategy for harnessing America's greatest assets: civil society and the private sector. To accomplish this, Washington must revisit the approach it adopted after the attacks of September 11 that has increasingly mired federal law enforcement, border, and transportation agencies in a Cold War-era legacy system of classified documents and security clearances. Security officials blocked from sharing information on threats and vulnerabilities with the public will only grow increasingly isolated from those to which they are responsible. Barriers to adequately informing and empowering civil society must be removed. In the end, only a well-informed citizenry can effectively defend the nation from the diverse range of risks to the homeland.

Building resilience also requires that the government not promise more protection and assistance than it can deliver. The indisputable fact is that there never will be enough professionals at the right place at the right time when terrorists or disasters strike. Intelligence and technologies are fallible, and the forces of nature cannot be deterred. Experience has shown time and again that when it comes to detecting and intercepting terrorist activities or dealing with a catastrophic natural event, the first preventers and first responders will almost always be civilians and system operators who by circumstance find themselves unwitting targets of terrorists or in the path of a disaster when it strikes.

Importantly, in order to better develop the nation's capacity to manage danger and disasters, the government must be careful to not end up alienating the people they are working to protect. Advancing security measures without spelling out the vulnerability they were designed to address can lead to a resentful and uncooperative public. This anger and skepticism will in turn impede future government efforts to improve security. Forcing the public to accept a safety or security measure without fully explaining why it is necessary and what it is supposed to accomplish is exactly the wrong way to build the trust necessary for long-term success. The public sector needs to look at the private sector and everyday people not as potential victims to be protected, but as essential allies whose active collaboration is indispensable to building a more resilient society.

If there is one lesson to take away from the twentieth century it is that it is both futile and counterproductive to pursue safety and security efforts with the avowed aim to eliminate risks. While risks can and should be mitigated, it gets exponentially more expensive and difficult to try and reduce those risks to zero. Not only will those efforts face the law of diminishing returns, they will also invariably generate unintended consequences. Instead, the goal must be to develop policies and incentives that encourage resilience at the community level, and within and across networks and infrastructure sectors locally, regionally, and nationally.

A focus on resilience translates into the need for strategies and tactics that encourage neighbors to work with their neighbors. For assuring the continuity of operations of essential systems and networks, the users, designers, operators, managers, and regulators all have a shared interest in infrastructure resilience, and each has an important role. Engaging and integrating the multiplicity of parties into a common effort to build a more resilient nation should be civil society's first priority if our country is to thrive in the turbulent century ahead of us.

RESILIENCE AS A COUNTERTERRORISM IMPERATIVE

The value of resilience as a counterterrorism imperative was detailed in the National Security Preparedness Group report, "Assessing the Terrorist Threat," published in September 2010. As the report notes, the changing nature of the terrorist threat comes as a result, in part, of the growing recognition within terrorist organizations that attacks on the West and especially the United States can still be effective without being catastrophic. As an example, the attempted bombing of Northwest Airlines Flight Number 563 on Christmas Day 2009 demonstrated that even near-miss attacks can generate disproportional political fallout and scrambling to implement expensive and economically disruptive new protective measures.

When America's adversaries see evidence that relatively small and unsophisticated attacks can cause outsized mayhem for a minimal investment, they have an incentive to lower the bar for recruiting terrorist operatives, to include identifying and training individuals who belong to the society targeted for attack. Recent cases within the United States and elsewhere in the West indicate that this recruitment is growing. Radicalization and training is being facilitated by an increasingly diverse array of global bases from which terrorist groups operate. The profile of a terrorist has become increasingly blurred as the Internet has become a tool for radicalization, allowing the ranks to be filled by those who are drawn to radical causes from the privacy of their own homes. Among the newest operatives drawn from Western nations, the only common denominator appears to be a new-found hatred for their native or adopted country; a degree of dangerous malleability; and a religious fervor justifying or legitimizing violence that impels these very impressionable and perhaps easily influenced individuals toward potentially highly lethal acts of violence.

The diversity of recent terrorist recruits presents a formidable challenge for intelligence and law enforcement agencies. Sophisticated attacks such as those carried out on New York and Washington, DC, on September 11, 2001, turn out to be more susceptible to being detected and intercepted than smaller scale attacks that are planned and executed locally. This is because they require a group of operatives working as a team that is supported by ongoing communications with those overseeing the planning. To boost the prospect of a successful attack, operatives must conduct surveillance and rehearsals. Money, identification documents, safe houses for operatives, and other logistical needs have to be supported. All this focused effort and activity, along with the time it takes to organize a major attack, creates opportunities for detection and interception by intelligence and law enforcement officials.

Less sophisticated attacks, on the other hand, particularly those being conducted by homegrown operatives and lone wolves, are almost impossible to prevent. In the May 2010 bombing attempt on Times Square, it was a sidewalk T-shirt vendor, not the NYPD patrolman sitting in a squad car directly across the street, who sounded the alarm about Faisal Shahzad's explosive-laden SUV. Shahzad was not in any federal or NYPD database that identified him as a suspected terrorist.

The October 2010 air cargo incident involving explosives hidden in ink cartridges shipped from Yemen is consistent with this trend toward smaller attacks, but with the added element of aspiring to create significant economic disruption. The would-be bombers could not know if the cartridges would be shipped on a commercial airliner with hundreds of passengers or on a dedicated air cargo carrier with a small flight crew. That was not important, since they understood that destroying any plane in midair would trigger U.S. officials and others to undertake an extremely costly and profoundly disruptive response that would undermine the movement of global air cargo.

Given that smaller-scale terrorist attacks are being motivated because they are more difficult to stop and that they can still yield a response by the targeted society that is extremely harmful to that society, it follows that there is tactical and strategic value associated with investing in the means to sustain critical functions and better respond to and rapidly recover from attacks when they occur. If attacks have limited potential to disrupt a society in any meaningful way, undertaking those attacks becomes less attractive to a potential adversary.

Alternatively, a lack of resilience that results in unnecessary loss of life, destruction of property, and disruption of key networks and functions is reckless. It is also a strategic vulnerability in an era when non-state actors will continue to elect to wage their battles in the civil and economic space rather than the conventional military space.

RESILIENCE AS DISASTER MITIGATION

Individuals, community, and corporate leaders often convince themselves that disasters reside in the realm of chance and fate. But the reality is that such risks are more routine than people are willing to acknowledge and many naturally occurring events have some degree of predictability. In addition, the overwhelming costs associated with disasters are almost always associated with failures to prepare for them up front. Losses and damages rise exponentially when risk mitigation measures that ensure adequate robustness are not in place, when responses to disasters are poorly planned and executed, and when efforts to speed recovery and implement changes based on lessons learned receive too little attention. In most cases, a more prudent and realistic investment is to manage risks by building the skills and capabilities to do three things: (1) maintain continuity of function in the face of chronic disturbances, (2) develop the means for graceful degradation of function when placed under severe stress, and (3) sustain the ability to quickly recover to a desired level of functionality when extreme events overwhelm mitigation measures.

Accordingly, while the danger that disasters will occur is inescapable, enhancing resilience will always provide a positive return on investment. On a micro scale, it is far more cost-effective to make an upfront investment in safeguards that mitigate risk and consequences than to pay the price for response and recovery after a foreseeable hazard manifests itself. Examples are legion. The Deepwater Horizon disaster in the Gulf of Mexico in 2010 where inadequate attention to preventative measures and lack of planning for dealing with the aftermath of what was widely viewed as a low-probability event ended up leading to a massive ecological disaster and a significant disruption of the offshore drilling industry. The failure of the crucial emergency vents at the Fukushima Daiichi nuclear facility following the March 2011 earthquake and tsunami provides another compelling example. The hydrogen explosions that occurred after the loss of power rendered the vents inoperable triggered not just a local nuclear disaster.

It also caused cascading consequences to international transportation networks, global supply chains, and the worldwide investment into new nuclear power plants.

From a macro standpoint, a society's level of resilience will increasingly be a source of its global competitiveness. This century will be marked by major disruptions arising from man-made and natural threats. There is the risk of pandemics, earthquakes, and volcanoes, and more frequent and destructive storms associated with climate change. With increasingly complex and interdependent networks supporting modern global economic activity, problems in one part of the system can quickly have cascading consequences across the entire system. The countries, communities, and systems that are most able to manage these risks and recover quickly will be the places where people will want to live, work, and invest. Those that are so brittle that they break instead of bend in the face of familiar and emerging risks will become the national and global backwaters.

BUILDING INFRASTRUCTURE RESILIENCE

Like recognizing the inevitability of earthquakes, hurricanes, and tornadoes, Americans have also begun to make an uneasy accommodation to the ongoing threat of terrorism as well. The May 1, 2011, killing of Osama bin Laden did not put an end to attacks on innocent civilians and critical infrastructure on U.S. soil. However, even with the risk of terrorism now a permanent fixture of twenty-first-century life, U.S. policymakers and elected officials have generally not grasped the extent to which decisions about infrastructure investment, design, and regulation can play a role in decreasing, or increasing, that risk. As a consequence, they miss the opportunity to provide a compelling rationale for investing in infrastructure and ensuring that any new investments incorporate measures that will mitigate the risk and consequence of attempted and successful attacks.

The need for, and benefits of, building more resilient infrastructure is clear and compelling even in the absence of terrorism and natural disasters. Regularly, the media reports the consequences of deferred maintenance and repair of old and overstressed infrastructure. Collapsing bridges, congested highways and airports, inefficient seaports, and an antiquated passenger rail system provide the evidence that the United States is neglecting a national transportation system once the envy of the world. Consider the power grid that cannot handle seasonal temperature fluctuations and old pipelines that fail under residential homes and the picture is one of reckless neglect of the essential underpinnings of an advanced society. Modern Americans are acting like grandchildren who are heirs to a mansion that they refuse to maintain. From the street it still looks like a nice house. But as the wiring and plumbing start to fail, the house becomes increasingly unlivable.

Taking infrastructure for granted is not something the United States can afford to do. A new emphasis on building resilience can help change the public's lack of enthusiasm for stepped-up investments in the foundation of an advanced society. That resilience can provide safety and security as well as bolster competitiveness translates into a ripe opportunity for broadening the political base of support for the effort. There is historical precedence for successfully making this kind of case. In creating the interstate highway system, President Dwight Eisenhower made sure to highlight the national defense value that the system could provide by supporting rapid mobilization and urban evacuation.

While emphasizing the role that infrastructure plays in ensuring the nation's resilience can strengthen the case for investing in infrastructure, the process of embedding resilience into infrastructure requires specific measures and actions. For the most part, the expertise for developing and the capacity for carrying out those measures and actions does not lie within the federal government. It is the owners and operators of the nation's infrastructure who are best able to identify and mitigate vulnerabilities to the systems they run. Yet the information and intelligence about threats to infrastructure lie almost exclusively within a federal government that is reluctant to share what it knows out of a concern that this knowledge will end up in the wrong hands. The result is that important information and perspectives are not shared, compromising the goal of advancing infrastructure resilience. Intelligence and law enforcement agencies do too much homeland security work behind closed doors, with the private sector and the general public relegated to the sidelines. Ostensibly, preventing the release of information about vulnerabilities or protective measures in order to keep such information out of the hands of potential adversaries seems to make sense. The problem is that such restrictions can also undermine devising defenses for seaports, dams, waterworks, and other critical infrastructure. It will be a bridge's chief engineer who will know the best means to protect a suspension bridge—in ways that would often not occur to law enforcement or military professionals within a federal security agency. But still today, government officials too often fail to ask the engineer.

The federal government is aware that it needs to greatly improve cooperation with the private sector. In 2010, the Department of Homeland Security's Office of Infrastructure Protection announced a project called the Engagement Working Group (EWG). The purpose of the EWG is to share classified information with representatives of the private sector in order to better develop strategies to counter threats to infrastructure. While this is a commendable effort, arguably there is a serious flaw with the program. Federal officials will provide security information only to vetted company security officers, who in turn are typically barred from relaying such information to executives and managers who do not hold active security clearances. As a result, investment and operational decisions are often made with little if any attention paid to the potential security stakes—especially for companies wherein security officers are not a part of the C-suite or where their recommendations are automatically assumed to pose added cost with little or no return on investment. Furthermore, without well-tended relationships with decision makers beyond the corporate security office, federal officials will continue to miss out on critically needed insight and perspective of much of the financial and operational expertise of corporate America.

The federal agencies responsible for protecting this country, and their state and local counterparts, still need to do much more work to integrate fully the expertise of owners and operators of critical infrastructure and systems. Effectively and efficiently countering both natural and man-made threats requires both a more open dialogue between federal officials and infrastructure experts and the implementation of truly cooperative, public–private, practitioner-guided programs that build infrastructure resilience.

One promising model for advancing a cooperative, practitioner-guided infrastructure resilience process is the Port Authority of New York and New Jersey's Applied Center of Excellence for Infrastructure Resilience (ACEIR). When the Department of Homeland Security was formed in 2003, it chartered 12 academic Centers of Excellence with the goal of fostering multidisciplinary research in security technologies and processes and providing thought leadership on security policy. This was a good start, but an important next step is to properly test and validate solutions that can function in a demanding operational environment. The White House National Security Strategy released in 2010 recognizes this imperative and calls for employing innovative technology and processes through new, strong, and flexible public–private partnerships in order to create next-generation resilient infrastructure. ACEIR provides a model for forging that kind of partnership to better bridge theory with practical application.

Metropolitan New York offers the ideal environment for developing and testing infrastructure resilience measures. The Port Authority's facilities support the movement of people and goods for one of the world's most densely populated and commercially active regions. The diversity of facilities that include the World Trade Center site and multi-modal transportation systems (tunnels, bridges, bus terminals, airports, maritime facilities, mass transit rail) and that cross state borders can test concepts in the environment where they need to be most effective: at the intersection of critical infrastructure interdependencies. And, without addressing the vulnerabilities of critical infrastructure interdependencies, the end game of a more secure society will never be achieved.

As a test bed, the Port Authority can subject promising technologies and processes to very demanding operational volume and velocity challenges. Those that hold up under the kind of enormous operational stress to which systems in New York are subjected are likely to fare quite well if adopted nationwide. Infrastructure operators would know that there is little risk that these tools and practices would fail in their urban areas.

The Port Authority stood up ACEIR to facilitate the provision of a real-world test platform for technological applications and processes. Its purpose is to ensure that research projects are vetted at the outset by frontline operators, engineers, and managers, and that results are evaluated by an advisory board of internationally respected practitioners and academics. Over time, ACEIR can also provide a venue for industry input into federal research and development projects. Rather than simply evaluating projects developed by federal agencies, the ACEIR board of advisors could be an excellent source for identifying research needs. As it continues to develop, ACEIR can and should be replicated in other regions and for other infrastructure sectors.

Efforts to advance infrastructure resilience must have as a strategic priority ensuring that any new investments made in extending the life span of current infrastructure systems take in account the need to integrate measures that will ensure their continuity in the face of disruptive risk. The time for doing so is now. The latest evaluation of the nations inventory of infrastructure by the American Society of Civil Engineers resulted in a grade of "D." They identified an investment gap of more than $2 trillion to repair U.S. roads, bridges, ports, and other critical facilities and systems. That tab cannot be put off indefinitely. When the nation finally begins to attend to its ailing foundations, it will have a historic opportunity to incorporate measures that ensure its resilience in the face of man-made and natural disturbances.

BUILDING COMMUNITY RESILIENCE

The United States is still in the formative stages of crafting the means to secure infrastructure and build resilient infrastructure systems. The most serious challenge to address is the interdependencies among infrastructure sectors. The inescapable reality is that no system operates in isolation. Because these interdependencies are so vast and complicated, the best place to try and understand them is not at the national level but within regions and communities. This means that developing resilient infrastructure systems must necessarily be from the bottom up as opposed to the top down.

Building resilience from the bottom up necessitates greater transparency about threats and vulnerabilities and the tools to deal with them. The U.S. government needs to be more transparent with the public. Too many policymakers think that honest discussion regarding dangers creates excessive public fear. However, secrecy actually exacerbates public anxiety. A feeling of vulnerability to threats persists with the feeling of powerlessness to mitigate such threats. For more than a decade now, Americans have been regularly reminded of the danger of terrorism but government officials have not provided all the information necessary to handle the hazard. If a process of providing the public with all available information to withstand, recover from, and adapt to man-made or natural disruption or disaster is prioritized and fully executed, citizens will be able to make decisions that will allow them to assert some control over their fate, take some stress out of the event, and dramatically increase the likelihood of a better outcome.

A bottom-up approach also means advancing resilience at the community level by ensuring that the individuals and the civic and business leaders of those communities have the tools to do so, that they have a way to measure their progress, and, very importantly, that there will be clear benefits for reaching a recognized standard. One way to tangibly reward communities is to provide them with better bond ratings and lower insurance premiums if they are able to demonstrate that they have adopted measures that both drive down the risk of damages and improve the speed of recovery. But making insurance an ally in dealing with the risk of catastrophic events is challenging for three reasons. First, insurers tend to steer away from things that may involve ruinous losses and insolvency. Second, insurers want to have as broad a pool of policyholders as they can to diversify the risk. Therefore, they need to be confident that enough people will elect to buy their insurance product to allow for this diversification. Third, private insurance companies need to be confident that the measures they would be subsidizing by way of reduced premiums do in fact mitigate risk and that their clients are actually adopting these measures.

Federal and state governments can help lower or eliminate each of these barriers for insurers. For instance, government could cap the risk that insurance companies face by effectively becoming a reinsurer. That is, the government can establish a ceiling on the amount of losses a private insurance company would have to pay, and agree to make up the difference to the policyholder if the losses exceed the cap. The government can also help ensure an adequate pool of customers for the insurance companies by providing a tax break to the insurers who write new policies or by providing grants to communities to subsidize the initial premiums. Finally, the government can establish and reinforce the standards against which the insurance incentive is set.

A very promising model for deepening private–public cooperation and aligning financial incentives for building and maintaining preparedness at the local level is the Community Resilience System Initiative that has been developed by the Community and Regional Resilience Institute (CARRI) at Oakridge National Laboratory. CARRI has led an effort to define the parameters of resilience, modeled on the creation of the fire and building codes over a century ago. Drawing on a two-year prototype effort undertaken in Charleston, South Carolina, Gulfport, Mississippi, and Memphis, Tennessee, the initiative set out to identify the policies, practices and capabilities that can increase the ability of communities to maintain essential functions with little disruption or, when disrupted, to recover those functions rapidly and with minimal loss of economic and social value. To accomplish this, the initiative sought to help community stakeholders (1) understand what characterizes resilience, (2) how to assess resilience, (3) how to prioritize options for improving their resilience, (4) how to objectively measure the impact of the improvements, and (5) how they can be rewarded for their investments.

After two years of field research, CARRI spent an additional 18 months convening a network of former governors and former and current mayors, emergency planners, finance and insurance executives, representatives from various government agencies, and academics to develop detailed guidelines and comprehensive supporting resources that will allow communities to devise resilience plans. These insights have been embedded into a Web-enabled tool that can be quickly modified and upgraded as new lessons are learned. Presently, the tool is being tested by several communities across the United States.

The community resilience system has been designed to provide community leaders the ability to assess their resilience, plan how to make their communities more resilient, implement and sustain those plans, and evaluate and revise planning as needed. The system includes an emphasis on infrastructure, thereby infusing it with the kind of local knowledge and expertise that will improve the prospects for it to be replicated and quickly adopted by other communities nationwide.

Working to build national resilience reinforces what unites a society as opposed to what divides it. Quite simply, it is not possible to build resilience without substantial cooperation and collaboration at all levels within a society. Individuals must develop the means to withstand, rapidly recover from, and adapt to the risks they face at a personal and family level. Companies and communities must look within and beyond themselves to ensure that they are prepared to handle what may come their way as a result of internally and externally generated risks. Finally, at the national, level, the emphasis on resilience highlights the necessity for forging relationships and developing protocols for dealing with shared risks.

In short, a determination to confront ongoing exposure to catastrophic man-made and natural disasters is not an act of pessimism or paranoia. Nor is it something that is inherently a cost center. It is a mature recognition that things go wrong from time to time, and that in preparing for such times, one is reminded not to take important and critical things for granted.

CONCLUSION

In early June 2010, the authors had the opportunity to see a dramatic symbol of resilience just outside of Gulfport, Mississippi, and a few hundred yards from the shore of the Gulf of Mexico. In an area devastated by Hurricane Katrina in August 2005, there stands a live oak tree known locally as the Friendship Oak. The tree is approximate 50 feet tall with a trunk that measures about 18 feet in circumference, deep and sprawling roots, and boughs that stretch 150 feet. The Friendship Oak has stood sentinel on that spot for more than 500 years.

Live oaks are nature's own models of resilience. They have adapted to their environment by developing the capacity to withstand what periodically comes their way. When sailing ships were built of wood, it was lumber from live oak trees that was the most sought after material for building the curved portions of a vessel's hull where the most strength was needed. As communities and as a country, Americans should think of the live oak as a guide for how to manage the risk of terrorism and disaster. Like these magnificent trees, the American people need to adapt and grow—to be able to cope with what will inevitably come their way, but also, importantly, to be able to stand tall, confident, and true to the individual and national potential in the process.

Portions of this text were originally published in *TR News*, July-August 2011, pp. 4–11, and are used with permission of the Transportation Research Board, on behalf of the National Academy of Sciences. None of this material may be presented to imply endorsement by TRB of a product, method, practice, or policy.

35

THE COMMUNITY RESILIENCE SYSTEM: OPERATIONALIZING A WHOLE COMMUNITY APPROACH

M. J. Plodinec

Community and Regional Resilience Institute

INTRODUCTION

The Federal Emergency Management Agency (FEMA) has promulgated a new doctrine—*A Whole Community Approach to Emergency Management*—to serve as a

> foundation for increasing individual preparedness and engaging with members of the community as vital partners in enhancing the resiliency and security of our Nation.[1]

When successfully implemented, such an approach has tremendous potential for leveraging resources and energy in the private and nonprofit sectors to enhance the resilience of communities.

However, while emergency managers are being encouraged to use this new approach, there is little practical experience in this country to guide them. Further, a Whole Community approach calls on emergency managers to employ skills that may have been seldom needed in the past. Most importantly, they are required to establish relationships and forge partnerships with others in the community—to move from command-and-control to collaboration. Even if equipped with the proper skills, the emergency manager simply may not know who appropriate partners are.

In late 2011, the Community and Regional Resilience Institute (CARRI) initiated pilot testing of its Community Resilience System and process. This is one of the first (and certainly the most ambitious) effort to implement a Whole Community approach in the United States. This marks the culmination of a four-year-long effort involving over 200 community leaders; federal, state, local, and tribal representatives; researchers; and members of the financial and insurance communities. It is already offering some important "lessons learned" to emergency managers in terms of how to implement a Whole Community approach.

In this chapter, we first describe what a Whole Community approach entails. We then introduce the Community Resilience System (CRS) and process. The CRS process has been based both on lessons learned from previous disasters (e.g., Hurricane Katrina) and on advice from community leaders. We describe in detail the first two steps, forming the leadership team and assessing the community. We then describe the initial pilot testing of the CRS. We close with some general guidance for emergency managers looking to implement a Whole Community approach in their own communities, including some observations based on initial pilot testing.

WHOLE COMMUNITY APPROACHES

Whole Community approaches to emergency management are already in use in the United Kingdom, the Netherlands, and elsewhere.[2] The basic premise behind any Whole Community approach is relatively simple. If the whole community is going to be impacted by a disaster, then the whole community should be involved in planning to respond to and recover from disruptive events. As the United States has moved toward an "all-hazards"/"maximum of maximums" approach to emergency management planning, it has become increasingly clear that most local governments do not have the resources needed to both respond to and recover from disaster.[3] By involving all sectors of the community in planning, all of the resources that would be used for response and recovery in the community—whether belonging to the local government, nonprofit organizations, private business, or even individuals and neighborhoods—can be used more efficiently and effectively.

It has also become clear that Whole Community approaches can offer a significant opportunity to "build back better." Many communities, especially urban areas, are held in thrall by a "tyranny of the present." Neighborhoods and their supporting infrastructure were built decades ago based on the patterns of residence and commerce that existed at the time they were built. In the meantime, the neighborhood may have gone through several waves of change, transforming the character and purpose of the neighborhood. For example, Harlem, in New York, was successively primarily Dutch (the Roosevelts lived there), Irish, Jewish, Italian, and African American within the span of 100 years. Its character has changed from the upper class to the impoverished, and it now is experiencing a renaissance due to gentrification. Amidst the human tragedies, the devastation of disaster can sweep away irrelevant remnants of the past and offer opportunities to rebuild to facilitate a desired future.

A key part of implementing a Whole Community approach is determining what constitutes the "whole community." This can be done several ways. A simple approach might be to simply break down the community into economic, infrastructural, and social components. A more complex approach might employ the "Seven Capitals" concept.[4,5,6] As we will describe in a later section of this chapter, CARRI has chosen to parse the community in terms of community service areas.

However the parts of the community are delineated, they should include all of the important stakeholders within the community. For smaller communities, this might include representatives of local government, economic organizations (e.g., local businesses and financial institutions, the local chamber of commerce), civic organizations (e.g., local charities and providers of human services), those responsible for the community's infrastructure (e.g., local utilities), those responsible for the natural environment (possibly local government), and individuals and families (e.g., leaders of neighborhood associations, influential members of the clergy). For larger, more diverse communities, each of these categories needs to be subdivided to reflect both their diversity and the degree of specialization within the community.

COMMUNITY RESILIENCE

"Community" can be defined several ways. From an emergency management standpoint, it is probably most useful to think in terms of a community as

A group of individuals and organizations bound together by geography and perceived self-interest to efficiently carry out common functions.

This definition emphasizes that a community has a geographic character. From an emergency management perspective, geography can play a key role both in terms of shaping the natural risks the community faces as well as imposing constraints on the actions that can be taken in either response or recovery.

The definition also emphasizes the importance of self-interest as the glue that holds the community together. The members of the community belong to the community because they believe they benefit from being a part of it. The benefits may be financial, or social, or simply an emotional sense of well-being. But individuals—and organizations—must see benefits or else they are unlikely to contribute to the community. As we will discuss later, recognizing this aspect of community is an essential part of successfully implementing a Whole Community approach.

Resilience (derived from the Latin *resalire*, "to spring back") has become an important term in the language of many disciplines ranging from psychology to ecology. Unfortunately, there is no commonly accepted definition of resilience that is used across all disciplines. CARRI has adopted the following definition for community resilience:

The capability to anticipate risk, limit impact, and bounce back rapidly through adaptation, evolution, and growth in the face of turbulent change.

More simply, community resilience is managing change. This means anticipating what may happen, and limiting negative consequences while trying to seize the opportunities afforded by change.

In the emergency management context, this means that the community must first know its risks, especially those extreme events that may threaten the community's continuity (e.g., hurricanes, pandemics, recessions). Insofar as the community can, it must mitigate those risks, limiting potential consequences. For those risks the community cannot mitigate, the community must prepare to respond to and recover from those risks if indeed they become reality in its starkest form. The emergency manager is centrally involved in each of these activities.

DEVELOPMENT OF THE COMMUNITY RESILIENCE SYSTEM[7]

Beginning in 2009, CARRI spearheaded an initiative to develop a Community Resilience System—a consistent and systematic approach that any community could follow to become more resilient. This Community Resilience System Initiative (CRSI) was a two-year collaborative effort that determined what American communities needed in order to become more resilient to the variety of threats they face and recommended a concrete course of action to support communities in their resilience-building efforts. The process resulted in the development of the Community Resilience System (CRS), a practical, Web-enabled process that helps communities to assess, measure, and improve their resilience to threats and disruptions of all kinds.

The CRS is based on the work of three groups. The Subject Matter Working Group was made up of 60 "thought leaders" in resilience, disaster management, and other aspects of community change management. The Community Leaders Working Group was made up of leaders from each aspect of community life, reflecting the belief that achieving a more resilient community requires involvement of the whole community. The Resilience Benefits Working Group had representatives from the financial and insurance industries, as well as from federal funding agencies (e.g., Small Business Administration, Economic Development Administration, FEMA, Housing and Urban Development, and others) with an eye toward ways to incentivize communities to become more resilient.

The work of the three working groups was overseen by a steering committee, a diverse group of senior leaders who have served in the public and private sectors with expertise in banking and finance, economic development, emergency management, government (both as elected officials and city/county managers), humanitarian assistance, hazard research, marketing, and public policy. The CARRI staff was responsible for coordinating the efforts of the working groups, reporting back to the steering committee, and ultimately for developing the CRS in accord with the recommendations of the steering committee.

THE COMMUNITY RESILIENCE SYSTEM

Overview

Briefly, the CRS embodies a six-step process aimed at community action in software provided through the Internet (see Figure 35-1). In a very real sense, the CRS is a "decision support system," helping communities to decide what actions they need to take to become more resilient, and then supporting them in taking action.

In the first step, the community organizes for decision and action. This entails defining the community, developing a leadership team representative of the whole community, and putting together a communications and engagement plan to ensure that the entire community is engaged in decision and action. While the public does not need all of the data that the leadership team may collect, it is important that the public has ready access to the information used to decide on courses of action.

In the second step, the leadership team—and the entire community—carries out an assessment of the community and its resilience. This is structured as a "whole of community" assessment, but communities are encouraged to take selective bites based on the resources they have available. Coming out of this are detailed answers to questions such as "What is our community? What is our current capacity?

Figure 35-1

The community resilience system and process

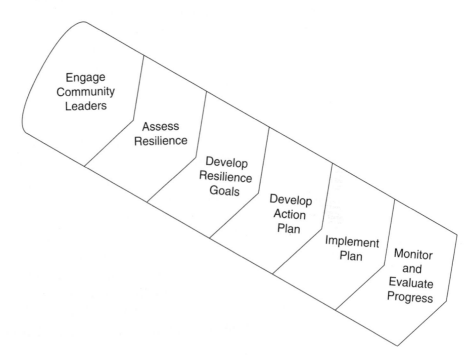

What are the significant threats facing us? What assets are at risk from those threats? What resources do we have available for recovery?" These answers also provide potential actions that a community can take to become more resilient. Clearly, this is primarily a data-gathering and interpretation process. The CRS provides confidential storage of the data for the community's leadership team, as well as templates to help them transform that data into the information needed to decide on actions.

The third and fourth steps are traditional visioning, goal setting, and action planning. Support is provided to the leadership team every step of the way as they ultimately decide on the actions they will take to make the community more resilient.

The last two steps revolve around implementation of the action plan and resilience program monitoring. The CRS is aimed not only at developing a good action plan but also (and especially) at taking action. As a result of those actions, a well-developed program must be in place to monitor progress and to determine whether adequate progress is being made toward reaching the community's goals. If not, then the action plan must be adjusted to more rapidly reach the goals.

The most important parts of the CRS are the first two steps in Figure 35-1: engaging the community and its leadership and assessing the community's resilience. Failure to engage either the community's leaders or the public often results in failure of community initiatives. An action plan that is not based on an objective assessment of the state of the community may waste community resources trying to achieve goals that the community cannot realistically reach. A lack of positive action is the key indicator of failure of a Whole Community initiative.

The CRS provides not only a process but also resources to help the community take the steps indicated. It currently contains over 250 individual resources—guidance documents from a variety of sources, templates, and a Community Snapshot based on demographic data. In addition, success stories are provided; the CRS does not simply provide the community with a checklist but with assistance keyed to each step, and examples of how other communities have had success.

Forming the Leadership Team

Formation of the team that will lead the community's effort may be the most important step in the entire CRS process. Certainly, it is the root cause of failure for many (if not most) unsuccessful community initiatives. For example, the recovery of New Orleans after Katrina was delayed because city government initially tried to dictate to the neighborhoods the manner of recovery for each. The city was quickly pulled up short by often fierce opposition. Recovery began in earnest only when the city began engaging with the leaders and residents of individual neighborhoods and allowed them to formulate their own plans, reflecting the desires and aspirations of their residents.[8]

This also represents one of the major challenges for any Whole Community effort: achieving goals developed horizontally across the community by using existing vertical command/action structures.

Horizontal goals

Achieving greater resilience is a classic wicked problem[9]—hard to define, no easy solutions, crosses stovepipes. The community team leading the effort needs to develop goals and decide on actions that reflect a consensus across the entire community.

Vertical command/action structures

In general, communities generally take action through hierarchical chains of command. These chains of command may be prodded into action by the public, but the actual work is almost always accomplished through vertical stovepipes, either acting alone or, more rarely, in concert.

In developing the CRS, this suggested that the leadership team ought to have the following qualities:

- It should represent the full fabric of the community.
- Its members should be committed to achieving greater community resilience.
- It should be able to mobilize the resources necessary to achieve greater community resilience, both within and outside the community.
- It should function as a team working for the good of the community, and not be driven by individual agendas.

Based on these desired qualities, the leadership team should include the following to be successful:

- Voices trusted by individuals and families. This might be the heads of neighborhood associations, media leaders, or respected clergy. These should be recognized as being able to accurately portray the views and concerns of "their people," and to speak on their behalf. Collectively, the leadership team should be perceived by the public as inclusive—reflecting the views of the diverse demographic and institutional groups that make up the community.

- Local government(s). Local government might be represented by a mayor, a city or county administrator, or the head of the city or county council. Local government should be a part of the team because it can command a variety of resources. It can also provide continuity to the effort and act as a "Great Convenor."

- Economic institutions. These might be local businesses, or a chamber of commerce or a trade association. While the private sector's concerns may differ from those of the public sector, the private sector has both resources and external connections that the public sector does not have. It is wise to make use of these.

- Community institutions including organizations that provide social services, education, or cultural opportunities, most often on a not-for-profit basis. Often, these groups are the best reflections of a community's identity, or at least its aspirations. In that sense, they collectively become the embodiment of a community's values.

- Representatives speaking for the built environment or infrastructure sector (e.g., transportation, utilities) and the natural environment. Often, the service providers are not part of the community (e.g., a regional utility, a statewide environmental organization). If they do not wish to participate, it signals an often-overlooked vulnerability to the community.

Community Engagement

Once a solid leadership team is formed, it is imperative to engage the rest of the community as soon as possible and keep them informed of progress in a timely manner. The basic assumption behind the CRS approach is that we are living in an age of influence—every stakeholder has at least some veto power, which means that there has to be a community consensus for action to be taken (and action is the ultimate goal). The CRS helps the community to achieve this consensus in three ways:

- As described, formation of a leadership team that is representative of the entire community, with trusted voices that will be heeded by the community, is a crucial factor in achieving the needed consensus. The key word is "trust." It is tremendously more difficult to reach a consensus within a community without trust.

- Once the leadership team is formed, the CRS guides the team through development of a community awareness and engagement strategy. This includes identifying stakeholder audiences and selecting methods for communicating with each audience as well as responsibilities for communications. For each step of the CRS, desired outcomes for community awareness and engagement are identified, and appropriate communications processes explained. All of this is embedded in an *Awareness and Engagement Planning Matrix*. This is a living document that grows as the leadership team proceeds through each step of the CRS.

- The CRS contains communication materials (e.g., presentations, draft press releases) and examples of communications successes for the leadership team to use. At each step, the team is provided with suggested awareness and engagement processes appropriate to that step. For example, the goal of communications for the first step is primarily community awareness. Thus, messaging is primarily about what community resilience is, and that a team representative of the community has been formed to take action to enhance the community's resilience. For the second step, the goal shifts to reaching a consensus about the state of the community, the significant threats facing it, and its resilience to those threats. Thus, the community as a whole has to be engaged in a variety of ways to ensure that the assessment is an appropriate basis for developing an action plan.

Assessment

Most of the existing methods for assessing community resilience[10, 11, 12] rely on the expert judgment of outside experts. However, the community, collectively, knows itself better than any outside expert. Many of these methods use nationally available statistical data to "measure" the resilience of the community and are focused on finding weaknesses and vulnerabilities. While identifying weaknesses is useful, a community also needs to identify its strengths, since these provide the springboard for overcoming its weaknesses.

Further, most often existing assessment instruments provide only a single value, or index, to the community. Thus, a community with a weak economy but a strong social structure may be ranked as equivalent to one with the opposite character even though the actions each needs to take to improve themselves are quite different. In this sense, trying to represent the whole community with a single number is not the most effective way to drive action.

Another problem with existing assessment methods is that there is virtually no data reflecting the status of a community's infrastructure available at the national level. Thus, this important aspect of the community is ignored by existing approaches.

The assessment method developed for the CRS is designed to overcome these flaws of existing methods. It rests on a foundation of both research and practice—most particularly the guidance given by the Community Leaders Working Group. The basic foundations are detailed in the following.

The CRS must be action-oriented

This means that the CRS assessment step must be structured to lead to action. It is not enough to provide a number and then leave it to the community to figure out what it means. In the CRS, the assessment is carried out by the leadership team with the involvement of the entire community. In general, the leadership team is directed to provide answers to each of the following (shown graphically in Figure 35-2):

- What is our community now?
- What threatens us?
- If a risk becomes a reality, how severe will the consequences be?
- If disaster strikes, how resilient will we be?

Based on the information the community provides, potential actions are suggested based on successes achieved by other communities.

A community is made up of many different parts, each of which has its own resilience

This is the essence of any Whole Community approach, and it played a crucial role in shaping the assessment step. First, it means that the

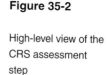

Figure 35-2

High-level view of the CRS assessment step

community needs to be able to look at its constituents in a consistent manner that minimizes the chance of missing any important segment. While there are a variety of ways to do this—the Seven Capitals,[4,5,6] a simple breakdown à la the Triple Bottom Line,[13] and Bruneau et al.'s T-O-S-E framework[14] are examples. We chose instead to break down the community into 18 "community services." We did this because they mapped well onto the National Disaster Recovery Framework[15] and other disaster-related ways of looking at a community, and because they are more intuitive than the others cited above. The Appendix at the end of this chapter provides more detail on each of the service areas.

Second, because each service area has its own resilience, each service area should be individually assessed, with potential actions identified through the assessment.

Third, this clearly renders single-valued resilience indices irrelevant, especially because if the purpose of the assessment is to drive action. However, in developing the CRS assessment method, several approaches were investigated to determine what their individual components might tell community leaders about the resilience of each service area.

These included SoVI (and the excellent follow-on work by Susan Cutter and co-workers),[10,16] and the outstanding work by Fran Norris and Kathy Sherrieb.[11] (The Resilience Capacity Index developed by Kate Foster and co-workers at the University of Buffalo is a more recent example of a single valued index.[12]), Not surprisingly, there were important pieces of information that were not included in these "statistical" approaches. As a result, nonstatistical means of assessing various aspects of resilience are included in the CRS, in the form of qualitative questions, and detailed "yes-no" queries.

Resilience is not merely a number, but rather a function of the particularly peril faced

In other words, it is not simply resilience, but resilience to what. This meant that, as part of the assessment, the community leaders needed to identify the significant threats facing the community. As a result, the community assesses service areas only in terms of the threats the community actually faces.

For a given threat, the resilience of a service area can be evaluated in terms of a general loss-recovery curve

For an actual disaster, a tremendous amount of work has tended to show that, in general, the loss-recovery curve is a good approximation of what happens for a given part of a community, for example, for each service area. See Figure 35-3. (The work of Wallace and Wallace on low-income housing in New York provides a very interesting example in terms of measures of crime and sexually transmitted disease.[17])

In the figure, three possible outcomes of a disaster are depicted. After a disaster, an overwhelming majority of the community will want to get back to the "Old Normal"—the way things were. In general, several years may be required to get back to that level of service. On the other hand, some communities will not be able to get back to a New Normal equivalent to the Old Normal—either the devastation is too great or there may simply not be enough resources available to restore service to the same level as before. Healthcare for the Lower Ninth Ward of New Orleans is a telling example of this, particularly with the closure of Charity Hospital, the major source of healthcare to the area for which a substitute has yet to be found. Some communities, however, will find ways to actually improve themselves after a disaster. Some of the other neighborhoods in New Orleans (e.g., Broadmoor) have actually increased the level of services available to their residents and have arguably become more vital and vibrant communities.[18]

Figure 35-3

Loss-recovery curve depicting recovery of services after a disruptive event

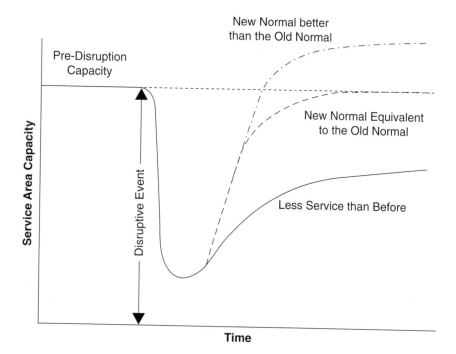

This curve is also useful because it leads to useful questions about community recovery for each service area: the baseline capacity in the community; the loss that would occur if the community experienced a disruptive event; the resources available to the community for response and recovery; and the community's ability to use the resources for recovery. Thus, it leads naturally to four strategies a community can use to limit impacts from a disruptive event and to speed its recovery:

- Increase baseline capacity, including building in redundancy. Resilient communities often have reserve capacity that can dampen the impacts of disruptive events.
- Reduce potential losses, through prevention or mitigation.
- Increase the resources available for response and recovery, both internal and external to the community.
- Increase the community's ability to access and use available resources. An important part of this is community connectedness.

While the first two are the types of actions that might be taken in a normal emergency approach, the last two most likely are not. However, the response to and recovery from Hurricane Katrina provide examples of the importance of each.

Prior to Hurricane Katrina, the Village L'Est community had already developed plans for community improvement and, in fact, had developed a Community Development Corporation (CDC) to provide financial resources for implementation. One of the plans in the works was to build a retirement home, surrounded by a communal farm and a farmers' market. While Katrina interrupted those plans, it did not stop them. The community found ways to leverage the resources in the CDC to ultimately improve the community. For example, at the community's urging, FEMA built a temporary trailer park on the site of the retirement home, in such a way that the utility infrastructure for the trailer park could be used for the intended retirement home.[8]

Often the ability to use the resources at hand is more important than garnering more resources. The sad spectacle of the flooded school buses in New Orleans that could have been used to evacuate those who could not readily flee the rising waters was grim testimony that this factor cannot be ignored. Conversely, the rapid recovery of African Americans who belonged to the New Orleans' Social Aid and Pleasure Clubs in spite of their relative lack of resources is a testament to their ability to use what they had effectively to recover more rapidly.[8]

Figure 35-4

Assessment of
community resilience
in the community
resilience system

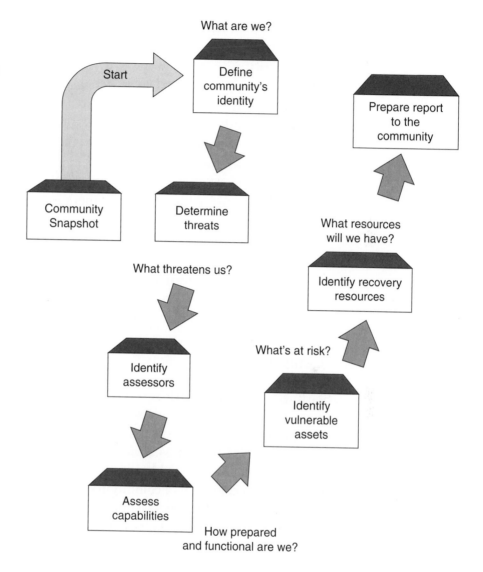

The CRS assessment module thus has the following parts, depicted
in Figure 35-4:

- A *Community Snapshot* containing statistical data about various
  aspects of the community. For each parameter, we compare the
  community's value to a state and national average.
- A *Community Identity* worksheet containing subjective data about
  the community. For example, where do people gather or shop.
  The worksheet also is used to determine the public's satisfaction
  with the level of service provided.

- A *Community Profile* template community leaders can use to integrate the Snapshot and the Identity into a report to the community.

- A *Community Threat Assessment.* In this, the community considers a wide spectrum of possible threats (natural and technological disasters, pandemics, economic shocks, and terrorist activities) to determine which are relevant to them.

- *For each of the 18 service areas,* there is a detailed assessment focusing on baseline capacity, critical (to the community) assets at risk, and recovery and redevelopment resources. Coming from these are lists of potential actions that could be taken, and shortfalls identified.

- A *Whole Community Resilience Analysis* template for combining all of the assessment information into a report to the community. This is intended to help community leaders focus the public's attention on those areas needing action.

PILOTING THE CRS

Starting in the fall of 2011, seven communities began to use the CRS to assess and enhance their resilience: Anaheim, CA; Anne Arundel County, MD; the Charleston, SC, tri-county region; Gadsden, AL; Greenwich, CT; Gulfport, MS; and Mt. Juliet, TN. In early 2012, a group from St. Louis, MO, was added as a pilot community at their request. In each case, a core team of community "champions" was formed that took responsibility for shepherding the community through the process. Each is proceeding at their own pace using those parts of the CRS that they feel are best suited to their community. Although the rates of progress have been uneven, each of the communities is making progress.

IMPLEMENTING A WHOLE COMMUNITY APPROACH

CARRI's experiences in developing and now piloting the Community Resilience System and process can provide useful lessons for an emergency manager seeking to implement any whole community approach:

- "Whole Community" means all of the stakeholders who can either support or impede progress. It is clear from CARRI's initial experience with the CRS that those communities who have most successfully engaged the entire community have been the ones who have made the greatest progress.

- However, it is difficult for an emergency manager to bring all of the relevant constituencies together by him- or herself. Emergency managers are heroes by nature; forming partnerships and collaborating with (not commanding and controlling) the rest of the community are skills that some may not possess. Thus, it is best if the emergency manager has other "co-champions" to help engage the rest of the community.

- Most communities have limited resources at the local government level. Thus, there is a real temptation to view a whole community initiative as a way to use resources outside government to achieve the emergency manager's goals. This is a path to frustration and potential failure. In order for a whole community approach to succeed, it must be based on "win-wins." The private sector, in particular, cannot be counted on to participate if they do not perceive that they are benefiting from a partnership.

- In spite of the potential pitfalls, Whole Community approaches should be considered as a way to strengthen any large community undertaking. For example, PandemicPrep in St. Louis (a partnership of local government, business, and healthcare providers) convinced local businesses to become closed points of dispensing vaccines and medication to their employees and their families in the event of a pandemic. It removed a huge potential burden (~700,000 people) from the public health system, while businesses found a big jump in employee morale.[19]

CONCLUSION

Many communities are finding that engaging the whole community is a highly effective way to achieve important community goals. Employing a Whole Community approach can help an emergency manager achieve a more prepared community, even in times of strained economic conditions. The Community and Regional Resilience Institute's Community Resilience System and process is one of the first Whole Community approaches in the United States. It offers a structured and consistent process for communities to organize, assess, plan, and implement actions to reduce the impacts of the threats they face, and to be ready to respond and recover more rapidly and effectively. It also can offer some important lessons to emergency managers as they operationalize their own whole community approaches.

APPENDIX: DESCRIPTION OF COMMUNITY SERVICES

Arts, Entertainment, and Recreation

Arts, Entertainment, and Recreation services involve providing venues and opportunities for community members to develop and share nonacademic skills such as artistic or athletic ability. Important assets for this service include theatres, cultural centers, places of worship, and parks, as well as events (performances, games, gatherings) where members of the community with nonacademic skills can share their talents. Such venues and events help create meaningful and enduring memories that foster a sense of place among community members. Providers may include local government, nonprofit groups (such as arts councils, community theatre groups, youth sports organizations), faith-based organizations, private foundations, and educational institutions.

Communications

Communications services involve the media and messaging that provide accurate and persuasive information to a community's members so that all other community services can be carried out as effectively as possible, especially when the community is in crisis. Communication media include television, radio, print media, telephone, cell phone (including satellite), and the Internet. Providers include telephone and Internet service companies, print media, and local television and radio stations. Local government usually plays a key role in times of crisis by ensuring that messages delivered to the community are timely, accurate, and consistent. Those responsible for other community services such as energy or water are also responsible for delivering timely and accurate messages.

Community Records

Community Records services involve maintaining the resources and facilities to house, store, and protect important community records. Ideally, important institutions in a community will maintain duplicate copies (paper or electronic) of critical community records in remote locations unlikely to be affected by a community crisis. Providers include local government, hospitals and local healthcare providers, businesses, and facilities where backup records are maintained.

Economy

Economic services involve the creation of conditions in a community that allow economic institutions to thrive and ensure a stable or improving quality of life for community members. The business sector is the primary provider of this service, with the public sector, school system, technical colleges, institutions of higher education, and support organizations such as Chambers of Commerce and Business Development Councils also playing important roles.

Education

Educational services include providing the academic opportunities and experiences that prepare community members to enter the workforce or to adapt to changes in the economy through retraining. Providers include public and private K–12 school systems, colleges and universities, and institutions that provide job training or adult retraining and/or other professional development services.

Energy

Energy services involve ensuring all community members have access to consistent and reliable energy supplies needed to live comfortably in their homes, commute to and from work, and carry out the economic and civic activities of the community. Providers include electric utilities; gasoline distributors and gas station owners; and natural gas, propane, and other fuel facility owners.

Financial

Financial services involve institutions and mechanisms that maintain vital ties to a community's financial resources. This service ensures that the community has access to a variety of sources of funding when needed, especially when trying to rebuild after a crisis. Providers include local government, economic institutions, insurance companies, and public and private sources of funds external to the community, as well as the savings of individuals and families.

Food Supply and Distribution

Food Supply and Distribution services involve ensuring an adequate food supply and distribution system (transportation and infrastructure) for the community so that food is readily available to community members. Providers include food retailers and their supply chains.

Housing

Housing services involve ensuring there is adequate and affordable housing for all community members, especially the local workforce. Providers include local government departments, private and public employers, private developers, and housing-focused nonprofit organizations.

Individuals and Families

Individuals and Families constitute a unique community service. It involves all systems, activities, and information that help all community members—including those with special needs and at-risk populations—prepare for disasters and become as self-reliant as possible, especially in times of crisis. This service encompasses the work of organizations and citizens' groups, formal and informal, that actively help ensure the well-being of community members. Providers include local government, social workers and counselors, nonprofit and faith-based organizations, employers (private and public), foundations, and other civic institutions.

Local Government

Local Government services encompass the range of administrative authorities provided to a community. Providers include a community's elected and appointed officials, personnel working for local-level public departments and agencies, and the local court system.

Natural Environment

Natural Environment services involve ensuring the natural environment is healthy, protected where necessary, expanded where possible, and accessible to community members. This service includes meeting air and water quality standards and maintaining outdoor recreation areas for activities such as fishing, boating, and hiking. Providers include local government environmental and planning departments, water utilities, local nonprofit environmental organizations, and citizens' groups.

Public Health

Public Health services involve actions and systems designed to protect and promote the physical and mental health of community members, including pets and livestock. Providers include public health departments, healthcare facilities (hospitals, clinics, clinical laboratories), trained health professionals (physicians, nurses, veterinarians, psychologists, psychiatrists) and organizations with which they are affiliated, medical supply chains, pharmacies, hospices, nursing homes and emergency medical transportation services.

Public Safety and Security

Public Safety and Security services include protecting the lives and property of community members through routine surveillance, training and deploying first responders for emergencies that put lives or property at risk, and planning for future crises. Providers include law enforcement, firefighters, emergency management personnel, emergency medical technicians, private security firms, and neighborhood associations.

Solid Waste Management

Solid Waste Management services involve maintaining the necessary infrastructure and systems to make sure the solid waste generated within the community is disposed of appropriately. This service protects community members from disease and helps ensure a safe, clean, and healthy living environment. Generally, local government is the provider of solid waste disposal, but the service is often subcontracted to private waste removal and recycling companies.

Transportation

Transportation services involve providing means for community members to travel to various destinations and for the movement of goods. Transportation services include systems and assets that facilitate travel by air, rail, road, or water. Providers include public and private transit companies, seaport and airport authorities, and local and state departments of transportation.

Water Services

Water Services involve providing all community members access to ample and healthy potable water and treating wastewater so it is suitable for free release. The community's water infrastructure includes a range of assets necessary to provide these services, including storage tanks, pipelines, drinking water and wastewater treatment systems, reservoirs, canals, and other water sources. Providers include local water utilities and state and local authorities that regulate water supply and wastewater discharges.

Workforce

Workforce services involve ensuring there is a match between the capacity and skills of a community's workforce capacity and the available employment opportunities. Providers include local government, local businesses and business associations, educational institutions, and unions.

NOTES

1. Federal Emergency Management Agency, "A Whole Community Approach to Emergency Management: Principles, Themes, and Pathways for Action," FDOC 104–008–1, December, 2011, Government Printing Office, Washington, DC.

2. Sharon L.Caudle and S. de Spiegelaure, "A New Generation of National Security Strategies: Early Findings from the Netherlands and the United Kingdom," *Journal of Homeland Security and Emergency Management* 7, no. 1 (2010): Article 35.

3. Federal Emergency Management Agency, "FEMA Strategic Plan: Fiscal Years 2011–2014," FDOC P–806, February, 2011, Government Printing Office, Washington, DC.

4. T. Hancock, "People, Partnerships, and Human Progress: Building Community Capital," *Health Promotion International* 16, no. 3 (2001): 275–80.

5. C. Jacobs, "Measuring Success in Communities: Understanding the Capitals Framework," South Dakota State University Cooperative Extension Services, 2007.

6. M. Roseland, *Towards Sustainable Communities: Resources for Citizens and their Governments* (Gabriola Island, British Columbia: New Society Publishers, 2005).

7. Community and Regional Resilience Institute, *Community Resilience System Initiative (CRSI) Steering Committee Final Report,* August 2011, http://www.resilientus.org/publications/crsi_final_report.html (accessed April 12, 2012).

8. Frederick Weil, "Rise of Community Organizations, Citizen Engagement, and New Institutions," in *Resilience and Opportunity: Lessons from the U.S. Gulf Coast after Katrina and Rita,* A. Liu, R. Anglin, R. Mizelle, and A. Plyer, eds., (Washington DC: Brookings Institution Press, 2011): 201–19.

9. C. West Churchman, "Wicked Problems," *Management Science* 14 no. 4: B141–42.

10. Susan L. Cutter, Christopher G. Burton, and Christopher T. Emrich, "Disaster Resilience Indicators for Benchmarking Baseline Conditions," *Journal of Homeland Security and Emergency Management* 7, no. 1 (2010): Article 51.

11. Kathleen Sherrieb, Fran H. Norris, and Sandro Galea, "Measuring Capacities for Community Resilience," *Social Indicators Research* 99 (2010): 227–47.

12. Kathryn Foster, et al. *Resilience Capacity Index,* http://brr.berkeley.edu/rci/ (accessed April 12, 2012).

13. John, Elkington, "Partnerships from Cannibals with Forks: The Triple Bottom Line of 21st Century Business," *Environmental Quality Management* 8, no. 1 (1998): 37–51.

14. M. Bruneau, et al. "A Framework to Quantitatively Assess and Enhance the Seismic Resilience of Communities," *Earthquake Spectra* 19, no. 4 (2003): 733–52.

15. Federal Emergency Management Agency, "National Disaster Recovery Framework," September 2011, Government Printing Office, Washington, DC.

16. S. L. Cutter, B. J. Boruff, and W. L. Shirley, "Social Vulnerability to Environmental Hazards," *Social Science Quarterly* 84 (2003): 242–61, doi: 10.1111/1540–6237.8402002.

17. D. Wallace and R. Wallace, "Urban Systems During Disasters: Factors for Resilience," *Ecology and Society* 13, no. 1 (2008): Article 18, http://www.ecologyandsociety.org/vol13/iss1/art18/.

18. Allison Plyer and E. Otiz, *The New Orleans Index at Six: Measuring Greater New Orleans' Progress Toward Prosperity* (New Orleans: Greater New Orleans Community Data Center, August 2011).

19. PandemicPrep.org, *Biodefense Network: Protect Your People;* http://www.pandemicprep.org/bio-defense-program/white-paper/ (accessed April 12, 2012).

36

COLLABORATION NOT ISOLATION: A JOINT APPROACH TO BUSINESS CONTINUITY AND RESILIENCE

Richard Stones

CSyp FSyI

High-profile terrorist events, dramatic disasters, and major industrial accidents all focus the mind into thinking that this is what all threats look like. The reality for the majority of businesses in the UK, however, is very different; it is the most mundane of events, the accidents that happened because somebody forgot to do what their procedure told them to do, or because they thought they could bypass a policy and do something another way, that presents a more realistic risk. The one thing you can be sure of when operating in this manner is that when it goes wrong, and it does, it costs money if you're lucky and life if you're not.

The UK business population comprises 95 percent subject matter experts, a group for whom the luxury of the corporate security advisor, the dedicated risk manager, or the occupational health and safety manager are a mere aspiration. More often this is a function performed by some other member of the workforce, who probably pulls in this extra work at home as an addition to their day job. These are the people that owners trust and depend upon to protect their businesses, and it is down to the goodwill of the workers that this usually is the case. Is this good? Is it best practice and could it be done better? Yes and no. Yes, because these people are generally the more trusted members of your workforce; they care about the business and take pride in the importance of their additional role But no, because it is

their presence in many cases did nothing more than result in an influx of calls from businesses to my team expressing concern over being approached by their CTSA. "Are we a target? Should we be worried?" were frequent questions. The answer was that the emphasis should not have been just on that one threat.

If 95 percent of the UK's businesses are based outside of our cities and their awareness of business continuity is minimal, then should we be approaching a conversation about good resilience by discussing terrorism or should we perhaps focus on something more tangible and something that is more relevant: crime? My wife's great at pulling teeth, but she doesn't have a clue about what lock, window frame, door frame, or alarm to fit. So why would we expect her to understand anything about resilience. We wouldn't. What does appeal, however, is if I can show her a saving on the expenditure necessary to reduce her vulnerability to crime. Once I have succeeded in this, I can then begin to discuss the other threats and the implications of those threats on her business. We aren't talking about her being subject of a targeted terrorist attack. We are talking about her resilience if the terrorist decided to target the power infrastructure or the banking network. Suddenly it begins to be put into a context she can relate to. With the addition of a few more basic business continuity practices in addition to basic crime prevention, we begin to develop a more informed business resilience process.

So if crime reduction is the catalyst for better business engagement, why should this be so? Security companies in the UK in many cases are much like unregulated financial advisors. They will sell the products that suit them, and these are not necessarily appropriate to address the issue that they have been asked to resolve. Is there a better solution? Well, Nottinghamshire Police thought there was.

In establishing a Business Crime Reduction Unit, we didn't just bring together a team of Home Office-trained crime reduction experts. We went further and trained them in the wider risk mitigations issues that our partners in policing, the fire and rescue service, our emergency planning teams, local authority community safety officers, and finally our trading standards teams thought may be relevant to better business risk mitigation. As a result, we now have a team of multifaceted staff that use crime as the catalyst for engagement with a business.

Businesses lack a coherent strategy for communication locally, regionally, or nationally, and as a service provider to potential crime victims, we, the police, needed to understand better the communication networks between neighbouring businesses, and we then needed to work with them to implement this strategy for the good of all the businesses in that locality. To encourage this mechanism, we began to monitor our overnight crime and task one of the team to engage with the latest crime victim as soon after the crime as was possible. In most cases this was less than 48 hours after the crime. We would then offer to provide short-term preventative advice to reestablish production. Our longer term objective, however, was to try to win the confidence of the business quickly in order that we could begin to work with them on the wider business risk, making the business owner and all the relevant business staff aware of those risks and threats, and then starting to work through an all-encompassing risk mitigation plan. We would then use this plan and try to encourage the business owner to champion wider business engagement on the estate. Adopting the principle that a business's responsibilities don't stay just on the premises and risk does not stop at the boundary of the business, their neighbouring businesses are a potential risk, as are suppliers and other bodies engaging with that business. The team then uses this opportunity to pull together neighbouring businesses with the intention of networking them to "collaborate and not isolate" in order that collectively they can begin to consider their combined risk to crime initially and to wider threats in the long term.

The team developed a template they would apply to each business crime victim with the following objectives:

- **Identify high-profile victims.**
  - Provide short-term preventative security advice through site security evaluation.
  - Identify longer term vulnerabilities including other partnership risks, e.g., fire or health and safety issues.
  - Demonstrate potential cost savings through better security and resilience planning.
- **Engage wider business community with statutory partners to design out crime.**
  - Form a business watch to protect collective interests.
  - Establish stronger partnership links to local authority, fire service, planning department, trading standards, etc.
- **Educate the business community in that area.**
  - Undertake premises risk assessments.
  - Network events with reputable security providers.

- o Form connections to other business support bodies, such as the chambers of commerce.
- o Provide role-specific training to staff, for example, a crime prevention training day for all staff from the various neighbouring businesses.
- **Communicate with businesses.**
  - o Recruit and register them with the Business Alert system to provide early warning of criminal activity in the locality.
  - o Hold quarterly estate management meetings, with security forming one aspect of the agenda.
  - o Distribute a business-written newsletter for neighbouring businesses within a geographic community.
  - o Conduct wider business networking events, including county, regional, and national events.
- **Provide a triage service.**
  - o Provide mobile guarding response—but with shared costs
  - o Negotiate reduced insurance because of implementation of good security advice.
  - o Set up temporary alarms.
  - o Offer lone worker support.

As a result of this approach, businesses have begun to collaborate to reduce risk. In doing so, they have combined resources to achieve more cost-effective solutions for crime reduction. Subliminally, we have introduced better resilience planning for wider risk mitigation. Prior to this point it was clear from local engagement that politics, parochialism, and egos masked effective engagement. The long-held perception that crime against business was not taken seriously by the public sector was used to mask the fact that behind the scenes, various independent business membership bodies did not trust each other to effectively represent each other, believing that because their agendas were not necessarily the same, the methods they applied to try to reduce crime could not be the same either. In addition, businesses perceived that cost of engagement outweighed the potential cost savings through participation and the assumed time commitment to engage in the model outweighed the time spent recovering post crime.

In 2006 the chambers of commerce and the Federation of Small Businesses locally took an interest in this approach and collaborated to form a wider business representative group: the East Midlands

Business crime forum. This body, representing the business sectors for the region of the East Midlands, Nottinghamshire, Derbyshire, Leicestershire, Lincolnshire, and Northamptonshire, began to adopt these principles to better target-harden their respective business communities.

In 2007 the UK Home Office agreed to fund and evaluate the business crime team and its success, and they corroborated the fact that businesses adopting the advice and recommendations of the business crime team were, irrespective of location, on average 64 percent less vulnerable to crime than those businesses that had not undergone the business crime survey process.

In 2011 the National Business Crime Forum was formed. I was asked to become a Director of the forum, and in doing so, I was asked to work with the nation's business membership organisations to look at wider risk and to apply crime reduction methodology to subtly influence better and more collaborative business continuity planning.

The forum now sees senior business leaders from bodies as diverse as the National Farmers Union through to the National Fraud Agency working together to raise awareness of risk and then use crime prevention as the premise for engaging with business to collaborate on all risk reduction.

I still never cease to be amazed that I meet with very successful businesspeople who have clearly committed a significant amount of time, money, and energy, burning the midnight oil on developing elaborate businesses that result in all the rewards you could wish for but who at the same time fail to consider applying the same methodology to protecting their businesses. If I or my team see this, if we get a "WIF" of something wrong in any of our businesses, we are now quick to try to engage and work with them, providing everything from basic crime prevention to comprehensive risk and security assessments to reduce risk. In doing so, we identify the potential local ambassador for our approach, target-harden their processes, and then work with them to roll out the response to the wider business community.

Can any of you reading this chapter honestly say that you have taken vendor–vendor resilience to this level? My findings so far have discovered that some businesses consider their immediate suppliers as a potential vulnerability and in some cases they do collaborate to address their combined risks. To be truly effective, however, the risk mitigation process needs to extend to the extremities of the supply chain. Like threats and risks facing businesses universally, the global business community no longer knows any boundaries, and as such, our business continuity and resilience plans need to expand to reflect this.

There are a few simple lessons learnt from this process. By using crime prevention as the primary method of engagement with businesses, police forces can have a significant influence on improving their resilience. Effective crime reduction and security advice is usually a quick win for the experienced crime reduction or security advisor. The effective application of the recommendations builds confidence between both the business and the police, and in the process, this stronger relationship allows for the application of wider business continuity and resilience methodology. This in turn serves to reduce the businesses risk further.

In addition, it has been necessary to overcome a few fundamental obstacles to collaboration:

- **Culture.** The long-held public sector belief that the private sector is affluent enough to resolve its own problems is a myth, made more apparent by the current economic climate. Many business are struggling and not only in the financial sense.
- **Procedure.** They are also struggling to cope with increased legislation and regulation, both of which come with attributed costs. The added distraction of crime prevention with the subtle long-term purpose of influencing resilience needs to demonstrate a quick cost saving to retain interest and participation.
- **Financial.** The spiral of decline that starts with crime serves to make it more difficult for businesses to invest even in the most basic security and crime reduction packages. Being a victim of crime affects future insurance premiums; preventing the crime occurring again requires investment. Do insurance companies listen when my team suggests that the recommendations they have made actually make a premise more resistant to crime than they would be if they adopted the insurance companies suggested solution? No. Should they? I'd like to think so. What we do assists the insurance company; we have reputations at stake also. Because we recommend a higher specification lock or door set than that perhaps specified on the insurance policy is done for a reason. We're not just ticking the box!
- **Political.** The conflicting agendas at local level between businesses, their membership organisations, and their

intermediary bodies makes the Suez Crisis and Watergate look like a bun fight. Competing egos and agendas have severely served to undermine the progress that could be made with business and business crime partnerships. Fortunately for businesses in Nottinghamshire and those participating in the UK regional and national business crime forum, these issues have been overcome and it is for the greater good that these bodies now work impartially with government and ACPO Association of Chief Police Officers to collaboratively address crime.

- **Motivational.** Ultimately businesses have got to want this solution and the question I frequently ask is based on my own personal experiences of seeing how hard my wife has had to work to establish her business. It's simple, really. We are here to help. I know how hard you've worked to get to this point. Let's collaborate and protect your effort, and in doing so, let's make your business more attractive to the big boys. Your knowledge and application of good continuity planning and resilience is a marketable commodity. Make the investment and it *will* pay you back.

The unique position that police forces hold in being involved in the early engagement with business post crime allows for them to quickly identify where a crime trend may be developing and then to use the concern that soon follows a crime to quickly network and work with those businesses in the affected area to encourage collaboration. In Nottinghamshire the business crime victims have been encouraged to act as the local champion for their business or estate community, using their personal experience to encourage wider business participation in networking their neighbouring colleagues. This has then usually entailed an open meeting where the police have presented their vision for more effective collaboration and then offered to provide security surveys to those premises whilst at the same time encouraging a greater collaboration.

Successful application of this approach has seen the formation of industrial estate business watch schemes being formed. These schemes have then worked together to introduce combined security schemes where the outlay for security hardware has been shared, and this has allowed for the installation of better, more cost-effective solutions for crime. As the momentum of these schemes has picked up, the issues and risks addressed have become more diverse, and in the process, wider risk and resilience issues have been incorporated.

A significant aspect of this work has seen the introduction of a messaging system that allows the police to communicate via e-mail, voice mail, or text to cell phone, with businesses by either geographic location or by sector. Simply, if a business can place itself in Yellow Pages, it can place itself on the messaging system to receive information from various public sector bodies. This process, relying on one system to message business, avoids the necessity for businesses to sign up to a multitude of different systems to receive messages from various public sector partners.

A further aspect of the system allows a business to nominate people with specific responsibilities to register on the system to receive role-specific information from bodies including the fire and rescue service, the emergency planning department, the police, and other contributors as necessary. In practice, the fire safety lead within business receives alerts regarding fire risk, the security lead receives information from the police, and so on. The reliance on one system rather than several allows for a very simplified engagement mechanism with the business community, and as a result, this trusted source serves to raise awareness in a consistent manner with the business community.

In 2010 the domestic version of the system was awarded a five-year contract to support Neighbourhood Watch nationally. In effect, businesses now registering on the business version of the system can then register their employees to receive similar crime- and risk-related messages at home in addition to work. The rationale behind this process being that best practice crime reduction applied at home may also be applied at work, and again the resilience chain extends further and begins to consider the extremities of resilience. This work is for another day, but has anyone considered how employee resilience can be influenced in support of the main businesses resilience?

8

INTRODUCTION TO PART VIII: THINKING, EDUCATION, AND TRAINING

Daniel Stevens

Training Coordinator and National Planning Cadre Manager, Department of Homeland Security, Federal Emergency Management Agency, Response Directorate

Many professions find it challenging to align training and education programs with the realities, lessons learned, and needs faced by the practitioner. A curriculum that includes hands-on experience, as well as continuous training and education is uncommon outside of the field of education itself. Lifelong careers in academia can result in being out of touch and a perception of being removed from the realities faced by the profession. Additionally, educational programs that don't include routine engagement with practitioners in the field often produce research which is not directly applicable or is not a priority need for that field. Similarly, a career that relies solely on experience and life lessons may eventually plateau, as colleagues become more knowledgeable on new and emerging trends learned through formal training programs. This impacts not just the individual but the profession as well, and has serious ramifications in the fields of Homeland Security, Domestic Preparedness, and Emergency Management. This section provides several emerging methodologies, thoughts, and suggestions in hopes of continuing the evolution in these emerging fields with respect to preparedness through training, education, and exercise.

Historically, training programs in emergency management and homeland security were often partitioned by discipline, jurisdiction, and/or level of government. The *X-Y County Fire Department* would rarely co-train with their law enforcement counterpart, or even with other firefighters from neighboring jurisdictions. Even less common were programs whose target audience included both federal and state personnel. This divide has gradually improved as a reaction to recent disasters and changes in policy. However, a more progressive and proactive approach is required in order to better *Prepare, Protect, Prevent, Mitigate, Respond, and/or Recover* from the next catastrophic disaster.

While the attack on September 11, 2001 was not the first major terrorist incident on our homeland, it did trigger a massive redirection in the culture and understanding of the need for change. In support of this, billions of dollars were poured into our economy in the name of *Domestic Preparedness.* In the earlier years of these grant programs, currently known as the Homeland Security Grant Program, state and local governments received an influx of money, usually through their state emergency management agency, to better train, exercise, and equip their first responders. Early on, these programs were tied to funding, which mandated that states adopt and implement the National Incident Management System (NIMS) and the Incident Command System (ICS). The change in culture, coupled with enormous financial assistance and standardized national policy, quickly pushed the community in the direction of increased coordination. First responders began taking ICS and WMD training with other disciplines and jurisdictions, and joint federal–state exercise programs like the Top Officials (TOPOFF) series became congressionally mandated. But it wasn't until 2005, after one of the worst hurricane seasons ever recorded in North America, did we fully begin to realize the need for a truly coordinated approach to all-hazards capability building. The Post Katrina Emergency Management Reform Act forced the entire homeland security and emergency management community into its current era of preparedness through deliberate catastrophic and regional planning, and increased collaboration between federal, state, tribal, local, and territorial entities. With these advances, new degree programs in homeland security and emergency management began to emerge, and so began the need to align training and education with the rapidly evolving field and practice. Despite these great strides in ICS, preparedness, and planning, there are several key changes that still must occur to further support the field through effective training and education.

One critical issue, supported by Dr. Renda-Tanali's article in this chapter, is that the field of homeland security and emergency management education requires an institution willing and able to perform the accrediting function of academic degree programs. Without this key element, we will continue to see inconsistency and a lack of understanding of what defines the field. Furthermore, it becomes increasingly difficult to evaluate programs and quantify the value or increased capability as a result of the training. Training and education must also be supported by a comprehensive framework of foundational policy and doctrine, not just at the national level, but aligned down to the tactical and field levels of operation. Doctrine allows the autonomy of each discipline, department, and jurisdiction to formalize and document how they apply policy through a foundation of deeply held core beliefs based on specific experiences. For example, FEMA's Incident Management and Support Keystone doctrine, released January 2011, is the foundational guide for FEMA's conduct during disaster operations. This process establishes a connection between the practitioner and the academic community through thorough research and analysis of real world capability requirements. In addition to accreditation and doctrine, one key element that has kept exercise, training, and education programs from reaching their potential is the lack of ingenuity. One of the most powerful lessons learned from recent catastrophic disasters was perfectly articulated in the *Final Report of the Select Bipartisan Committee to Investigate the Preparation for and Response to Hurricane Katrina:*

> If 9/11 was a failure of imagination, then Katrina was a failure of initiative. It was a failure of leadership.

Training programs have been and continue to be very slow and reactionary, lacking the creativity and insightful genius often found in more advanced academic fields. Programs need a charge of creativity to find better ways to weave together the first-responder community with formal academic programs. This might include structured cross-jurisdiction or cross-discipline rotations, mentorships, required reading, formalized information sharing practices, and a variety of ideas waiting to be institutionalized—ideas that can directly and immediately apply lessons learned into improved capability through research and analysis.

Lastly, and perhaps of most importance, is acknowledging that different funding streams will continue to result in different priorities. The emerging concept of *Whole Community*, to bring public, private, non-profit, and volunteer agencies together, will only nominally be supported unless there are coordinated national priorities supported by flexible grant programs. The Homeland Security Grant Programs are congressionally mandated for state and local governments, while other federal agencies provide similar financial assistance in the name of [health, environmental, etc.] preparedness. If 9/11 taught us the importance of training together, now the urgency is to start planning together. The entire federal community of emergency managers needs to align priorities, policies, and programs, to enhance our ability to collectively maximize the use of ever-dwindling resources. This must be done through a collaborative approach, which involves the whole community, but is guided by national policy.

These ideas, supported by the chapters contained in this section, will further evolve the field of preparedness through training, education, and exercises. We are at an exciting time in the evolution of homeland security and emergency management, but we must continue to proactively work together. All of us are part of the whole community and we are all responsible to set a culture that fosters training and education as a priority.

37

A SYSTEMS PERSPECTIVE ON HOMELAND SECURITY[1]

Sibel McGee, Ph.D.

Principal Analyst, Applied Systems Thinking Institute/Analytic Services, Inc, Adjunct Assistant Professor, University of Maryland University College

David Kamien

Chief Executive Officer, Mind Alliance Systems, LLC

… all of us are trapped in structures, structures embedded both in our ways of thinking and in the interpersonal and social milieus in which we live … Often, the structures are our own creation. But this has little meaning until those structures are seen … We are neither victims not culprits but human beings controlled by forces we have not yet learned how to perceive.[2]

INTRODUCTION

It is widely accepted that how we look at things determines what we see. Cognitive scientists have been the front-runners of this idea for a long time. The lenses through which we see things inform the assumptions we make, the ways we organize and process information, make sense of our observations, determine what/who is to blame for failures, and finally cure the problems we note. In other words, our approach to an issue preconditions the limits of our understanding.

Perhaps today more than ever, *complex* is the word most appropriate to describe the world around us. Everything we see is connected to everything else. These connections exist in ways that we see and appreciate, as well as in ways that are less obvious to the untrained eye and, in some cases, hidden entirely from our view. Our families, neighborhoods, communities, societies, organizations, and governments do not exist in a vacuum; they are part of broader systems, which reside in even larger systems. Social, political, and organizational outcomes and behaviors are results of a dynamic interplay of many forces interacting within and across these systems. We can identify, assess, and respond to these forces only if we adopt the appropriate lenses that enable us to perceive those forces. We need approaches and tools that enable us to see "wholes" as well as constitutive components, recognize the way components interact to form the whole, and understand how the whole in turn changes those components. In other words, we need to resist traditional thinking, which seeks to deconstruct something into its smaller pieces under the illusion that the aggregate knowledge of isolated parts will be same as the knowledge of the whole. We need to think holistically, appreciating systems for what they are: wholes composed of interlocking parts in constant interaction. Systems thinking is what we need to address the complexity of our world.[3]

The complexities that characterize the twenty-first century seem particularly present in and relevant to the homeland security domain, making adoption of systemic approaches by its practitioners and students a necessity. Even though we may have an intuitive understanding of individual elements of homeland security, we need to also understand and identify how these elements relate to one another—a task that is a lot more challenging. Appreciation of these relationships and linkages is integral both to an accurate understanding of the homeland security mission and objectives and to successful operations to serve them.

Despite the growing appreciation and application of systems thinking in a wide range of fields, it appears that its application to the field of homeland security has been to date rather limited.[4] However, the field of homeland security can immensely benefit from a systems perspective. The limited nature of systemic studies in homeland security may be due to the current state of the field as an emerging discipline. As a young field, homeland security is still in the process of constructing its own identity, debating basic questions such as what issues and areas it needs to tackle and where it fits within the broader social/political sciences. Eager to prove its value, students and practitioners of the homeland security domain may prioritize accumulation of knowledge on different homeland security issues over decisions on the utility of different approaches and methodological choices. Nonetheless, this may be the very time to construct our mental frameworks such that they can present and understand homeland security as a system that is characterized by inherent and complex relationships between its components. It is all too easy for researchers and professionals to be preoccupied with questions specific to their own specialty areas. The risk is that when sight of homeland security as a "whole" is lost, we are likely to neglect strategic thinking that cuts across the entire enterprise and blind ourselves to hidden drivers, novel angles, and much needed collaboration opportunities for effective resolution of issues.

In this chapter, we present a systems approach to homeland security. First, we present the homeland security domain and associated enterprise as a complex system. Second, we provide a brief introduction to the essential qualities of a systems assessment. Then we discuss a brief homeland security example to illustrate why systems thinking is important and relevant to tackling this and similar cases. We end the chapter by concluding that systems thinking can propel both the study and practice of homeland security.

HOMELAND SECURITY AS A COMPLEX SYSTEM

Few would disagree that homeland security is one of the most complex research and policy domains of our times.[5] However, we must understand the kind of complexity that makes homeland security a particularly challenging domain to study and manage.

The homeland security domain with its vast mission space and the ensuing multiplicity of stakeholders forms a complex sociotechnical enterprise that is composed of many parts or components. According to the Quadrennial Homeland Security Review (QHSR) Report (2010), the homeland security field consists of five broad mission areas: preventing terrorism and enhancing security, securing and managing our borders, enforcing and administering our immigration laws, safeguarding and securing cyberspace, and ensuring resilience to disasters.[6] The sheer number of conceptual issues, variables, stakeholders, agencies, and organizations to take into account in each of these mission areas may be overwhelming. This is, however, only *detail* complexity—that is, "the number of components (or variables) in a system or the number of combinations one must consider in making a decision."[7]

The homeland security field is also characterized by a far more challenging type of complexity: *dynamic* complexity. Dynamic complexity refers to the web of interrelations and "arises from the interactions among the agents over time."[8] It is seen in "situations where cause and effect are subtle, and where the effects over time of interventions are not obvious."[9] For example, a new strategy by the U.S. military may cause many immediate and delayed consequences in Iraq and elsewhere. A new screening technology introduced by the Department of Homeland Security (DHS) may require significant coordination among various DHS components with different missions, cultures, and procedures and may receive different reactions from different stakeholders influencing its implementation. International events may have homeland security implications. DHS agencies' missions may be impacted by these events, but they may also influence developments overseas by the way they engage local counterparts.

A critical quality of dynamically complex systems is their adaptive nature.[10] Far from being static, such system's agents change their thinking and actions as their interests, objectives, perceptions, and experiences change. This adaptive behavior causes, in turn, changes in dynamics of the system.[11] The homeland security mission may be considered an enabler of national security. In fact, threats to national security must be identified and stopped before they reach the U.S. homeland. When securing the southwest border, DHS component agencies need to assess the changing nature of the threat to include illegal immigration patterns, smuggling routes, nature of contraband, organized crime groups, and their operational parameters. For example, DHS agencies with a stake in border security and management need to pay close attention to Mexican cartels, as they represent key organized crime groups in the region that are capable of jeopardizing the security and management of the southwest border. If cartels show signs of practical collaboration with terrorist groups, then the same DHS agencies would need to adjust their objectives and operations accordingly. In addition to illegal immigration and contraband trafficking, terrorist infiltration and imminent attacks on U.S. soil would become leading concerns. The changing nature of the threat and the expanded scope of operations would require addressing additional risks and involving more stakeholders; as a result, far from being a static system, homeland security enterprise evolves through policy and practice, adapting to changing circumstances and novel requirements.

With its wide range of issues, extensive enterprise, and dynamic operation, homeland security is clearly a domain that presents both significant detail and dynamic complexity. We cannot depict and understand this domain accurately just by examining its components in isolation. Such reductionist approaches provide us only with incomplete and static snap shots of homeland security. We need to approach this domain from a systemic perspective so that we can step back to see the broader relationships and dependencies across its parts; identify interactions and feedbacks between its agents; understand their implications for policy, operations, and social outcomes; and exploit them to our advantage.

Specifically, the homeland security field can benefit from a systems perspective in defining and mapping its conceptual and operational design. Conceptual boundaries of the field need to accurately recognize and relate issues and areas that form the broader homeland security mission in order to recognize inherent relationships and dependencies between them and address their implications for policy and operations. For example, failures in border security can increase terrorism risk; creating a safe, secure, and resilient cyberspace is one way to control radicalization and fight terrorism; counterterrorism has to be aligned with law enforcement and intelligence; bioterrorism, in addition to public health and safety risks, has implications for emergency management.

A holistic review of homeland security field and its conceptual elements will help inform an effective operational strategy and roadmap. For effectively managing this extensive sociotechnical enterprise, it is critical that we correctly identify key stakeholders whose understanding, cooperation, and commitment is required for successful resolution of key homeland security problems. Many coordination and implementation complications experienced in homeland security among different levels of government, the private sector, and the public are likely an indication of inadequate systems perspective. Information sharing in implementation of suspicious activity programs and terrorism planning and exercises are just two examples of operational difficulty areas where there is discrepancy between conceptual boundaries and stakeholder boundaries.[12]

In sum, constitutive mission areas and the associated agencies of the homeland security enterprise cannot think and operate independently. Facilitating a shared understanding of the broader homeland security mission across its stakeholders and integrating their operations, planning, and exercises is critical for the practice of homeland security to move forward. Systems thinking offers concepts and tools to enable this task.

FUNDAMENTALS OF A SYSTEMS PERSPECTIVE

As a discipline and a mental framework, systems thinking offers a number of powerful concepts, principles, tools, and methods along with an underlying philosophy to assess complex systems and situations. In other words, "systems thinking is both a world view and a process; it can be used for both the development and understanding of a system and for the approach used to solve a problem."[13] There are a number of elements of any systems assessment. In our view, those highlighted in the sections that follow constitute some of the most critical (but not the least) of those elements.

IDENTIFYING COMPONENTS, RELATIONSHIPS, AND WHOLES

Systems thinking relies on the conviction that systems are composed of components (parts) that are connected.[14] Unlike the traditional analytic approaches, systems thinking advocates understanding not just components but also the way they fit together to form wholes. In a system, everything is related to everything else. Those elements without meaningful relationship to other parts of the system often serve as an indication of an underlying problem. Therefore, identifying accurately and completely the constitutive elements and their interrelationships is critical to understanding both the nature of the resulting system (that is, the whole) and its problems.[15]

IDENTIFYING AND LEVERAGING SYSTEM STRUCTURE AND PATTERNS

The way components/variables of a system are configured together through causal relations condition a system's structure and in turn system's behavior.[16] The systems thinker hopes to unlock the complexity of a system by understanding its underlying structures and identifying its associated behavior patterns.[17] The way different variables relate to each other is critical to identifying the type of feedback processes at work within the system. Once we establish an understanding of the causal relationships between different components—variables within a system—we can identify potential areas of policy interventions and predict how change in one of those variables will impact the behavior of the system. Depending on the nature of the relationships, such change can reinforce or balance the type of behavior observed in the system.

UNDERSTANDING EMERGENCE AND UNINTENDED CONSEQUENCES

Systems thinking promotes the idea that when otherwise disparate components are put together to form a whole, something distinct emerges out of their interactions. Gharajedaghi (2006) calls this "emergent properties" and defines them as "the property of the whole not the property of the parts, and cannot be deduced from properties of the parts."[18] Similarly, emergent properties "are a product of the interactions, not a sum of the actions of the parts, and therefore have to be understood on their own terms."[19] This is precisely why in dynamically complex systems, reducing a whole to its constitutive parts and investigating their individual qualities cannot generate adequate knowledge of the whole.

In sociotechnical systems, we do not always know what will emerge out of interactions of agents (stakeholders) and issues. We may anticipate some consequences, but then others may be surprising and rather puzzling to us. These are unanticipated consequences that may be either good or bad for a system. A systems thinker will work to facilitate those consequences that are beneficial to the system and remedy those that affect the system adversely.

LEVERAGING STAKEHOLDER PARTICIPATION

Taking stakeholder viewpoints into account may be the most indispensable element of a systems thinking-based assessment. Systems thinking promotes use of particularly participatory approaches that value and process different stakeholder perspectives. This is perhaps why systems thinking is best suited to assess sociotechnical systems where a significant human element is present and serves as a critical driving force for system performance/behavior. Parts of a sociotechnical system cannot be understood with approaches that are appropriate to assess detail complexity; stakeholders introduce a considerable level of unpredictability, as some of the processes and activities are driven by stakeholder relationships and interactions. These relationships and interactions are shaped to a great degree by different stakeholder interests, perceptions, experiences, and even feelings. As such, understanding distinct stakeholder perspectives on their role within the system as well as the mission and objectives of the system provide significant insights into stakeholder behavior and, in turn, a system's performance.[20] Incompatible perceptions are often the very reason behind stakeholder disagreements on problems and solutions within a system. Understanding and reconciling stakeholder perceptions within a system helps a systems thinker uncover root causes of problems, identify leverage points for policy interventions, and preempt potential complications during the implementation of solutions.

SYSTEMS THINKING APPLIED TO MASS TRANSIT SECURITY

Now that we have presented homeland security as a complex system of interrelated components and covered some very basic qualities of systems assessment, let us consider a specific homeland security issue where a systems-thinking informed perspective could be applicable and helpful: the challenge of preventing a terror attack on the mass transit rail system. Mass transit rail system has indeed been the target of numerous terrorist attacks during the past decade, such as bombings in Moscow, London, and Madrid, and plots to attack the New York City subway system. The mass transit system is vulnerable to high-casualty terrorist attacks because of the following:

- Limited capability to screen huge volumes of riders, luggage, and carry-on bags
- Open architecture, with access through multiple entry points
- Imperative to rapidly move large numbers of people quickly, particularly during peak work hours
- Publicly available schedules and predictable patterns of movement
- Underground and enclosed stations that maximize blast impact
- Close proximity to symbolic targets and critical infrastructure

Preventing attacks from reaching their final operational phase is essential because terrorists are rarely stopped during the execution phase of an operation, other than instances in which their equipment or weapons fail.[21] According to a 2007 Homeland Security Institute report:

> The important lesson learned is that it is highly effective to concentrate on the pre-execution phases of attempted terrorist attacks. Last-line fail-safe measures are critical to thwart undetected plots, as well as induce uncertainty into the terrorist planning process. However, the best way to influence the success or failure of an attack—at the tactical, operational, or strategic level—is to interdict the plot before the terrorists deploy to execute their plan.[22]

Because plots are most often foiled during the planning and pre-execution phases, it is essential to create an environment that can aid in the detection of indicators of terrorist activities that stem from lapses in terrorist operational security and the rapid reporting of potential attack planning and operational surveillance/rehearsal by vigilant regional agencies and an observant public.

Now consider just a few of the potential measures and procedures that can be adopted to cope with this threat:

- Instructing passengers to notify the authorities if they see suspicious behavior or objects (e.g., the "if you see something, say something" campaign)
- Use of information technology systems for collecting, correlating, and analyzing reports of suspicious activity; sharing suspicious activity reports and other information and intelligence with rail operators, local police, and fusion center analysts
- Use of video surveillance cameras with software for facial recognition and left-bag detection
- Use of sensors that can detect chemicals and radiation, and bomb-related materials
- Consideration of how road traffic and weather may impact the ability for security personnel to respond to the scene
- Consideration of how security operations would function if the communication systems were disabled

Following are some of the human and technical stakeholders and activities involved in this scenario:

- National, state, and local intelligence analysts, who have the ability to access a shared database of suspicious activity reports

- Passengers (the traveling public), who may notice their surroundings and any of the above information "signatures" and hopefully notifying the authorities about suspicious activity
- CCTV cameras recording activity and potentially detecting left bags and recognizing faces of known suspects
- Train conductors and operators, central dispatchers, and customer service personnel who answer the phone when people call to report suspicious activities
- Police, who patrol the station, platforms, and some of the trains, sometimes with canines trained in explosives detection
- Police dispatchers, who monitor CCTV displays, as they fulfill other duties simultaneously
- Local law enforcement at and near train stations along the route of the train taken by the terrorist

Consider some of the factors that make this challenge so complex:

- Al Qaeda-inspired terrorists continually study and adapt to our defenses; our recipes for prevention and protection must change as well.
- Rail systems cross states, counties, and municipalities jurisdictions.
- Many kinds of organizations have a role to play in mass transit security. Numerous federal, state, and local coordinating structures and processes are in place, as are physical (and virtual) facilities, such as multi-agency intelligence fusion and emergency operations designed to support vertical and horizontal integration.
- The organizations and roles that are expected to perform homeland security tasks and make decisions are subject to numerous policies (laws, regulations, directives, strategies, frameworks, and management systems), such as the National Incident Management System. Legal questions abound in every area, such electronic surveillance, and screening travelers.
- Many technologies (hardware, software, sensors), mechanical devices, and materials are utilized. The human-machine interface is key—a sensor may excel at detecting potential threats, with low false-positives, but unless response forces can react in a timely and effective manner, it may be for naught.

- Funding for security and disaster preparedness initiatives depends on various often unpredictable sources and complex bureaucratic mechanisms.
- The variety and volume of data and information relevant to security efforts is overwhelming.

A systems thinking approach will help the various stakeholders design a joint security concept, which interrelates their roles and responsibilities into an integrated system of systems taking the overarching mission into consideration. By understanding the interconnectedness of the missions, activities, and information needs of all the involved stakeholders, security managers can develop and implement an overarching security concept of operations. They can define field procedures with protocols for sharing information about potential threats (i.e., suspicious activities) during routine operations, and elevated and imminent threat conditions. This will enhance situational awareness so stakeholders will be able to coordinate their collective terrorism protection and prevention efforts and avoid delay in the flow of information. The alternative—each system owner working in isolation—is a recipe for failure. Even if each stakeholder organization optimizes the activities that it controls, the diffusion of responsibilities, the fragmentation of information analysis and sharing functions across multiple organizations, and the lack information sharing protocols will impede security, information sharing, and operational coordination.

A systems thinking perspective would raise, for example, the following types of questions during the formulation of the security concept and plans:

- What kind of problem are we dealing with?
  - Is it a "tame" problem with a clearly definable situation and need, and a solution can be clearly understood?
  - Is it a regular problem with a defined need and a difficult solution that is not obvious but can be understood?
  - Is it a "wicked problem" or "mess" that cannot be definitively described, responses cannot be meaningfully correct or false, and there is no definitive and objective solution?
- Where are the boundaries of the mass transit rail system both in space and time and organizationally? Are park-and-ride stations or airports with rail stations inside or outside of the scope of the mass transit rail system? Setting the boundary too broadly can

make the problem space so large and ill-defined that the task of assessing and solving the problem may be impossible.

- How do we define the system (or system of systems) being studied, and how can we understand its relationship to the external context and environment to see both the forest and the trees? Can we really secure the mass transit rail station in isolation from other systems, such as those dealing with immigration and border security (where suspects may enter the country and be photographed), from cybersecurity (which may detect probes to gain knowledge of security measures), and from legal system concerns about what kind of surveillance or bag searches are acceptable?

- How can law enforcement personnel be forewarned with intelligence data and suspect photos to prevent terrorists from entering the stations and trains in the first place? When a person believed to be a terrorist is known to be in the areas, are local police provided with an image to aid in apprehending him or her?

- How will counterterrorism measures impact crime patterns and law enforcement activities?

- When a passenger reports suspicious activity, is it possible to quickly utilize the surveillance cameras in place to get "eyes on" fast enough to assess the situation in real time?

- Should response always come in the same form—say a uniformed police officer or team—or should undercover cops be deployed in certain circumstances?

- When a passenger reports suspicious activity, are potentially related suspicious activity reports retrieved from a shared database? If video cameras capture the facial image of a person engaged in suspicious behavior (e.g., someone who has intentionally abandoned a bag or other object), is that image subject to matching against terrorist databases or the images of people reported in other suspicious activity reports?

- When a sensor detects, for example, a chemical weapon, are local responders notified to wear protective gear when they deploy to the area?

- Do rail operators and security personnel know how to balance the interest of keeping the trains running on schedule, with the need to stop trains carrying suspected terrorists from entering crowded stations?

- Are the computer systems involved protected adequately from cyber attack?
- Can we model and simulate the cascading impact of stopping a train with a suspicious passenger on the rest of the system? How will travelers react when they become aware of a potential bomb?
- How will weather impact the ability to detect suspicious behavior?
- What could be the political and economic implications of security measures?
- Are there circumstances—such as an increased threat level—when more stringent security measures should be employed? How will they impact the functioning of the overall system?
- If advanced standoff detection technologies are deployed, how will they be perceived by civil liberties groups and the traveling public and their behavior as they move through the station?
- How will defense of the mass transit system impact the targeting considerations of terrorists? Will they shift to softer targets?
- If a train or a station needs to be evacuated, how will we cope with people with special needs or people who do not speak the local language?

Systems thinking also will apply to the process of formulating security policies, plans, procedures, and information sharing protocols for mass transit security stakeholders. How can we engage the various stakeholders in a systematic process of hearing multiple viewpoints and perspectives related to answering questions such as those above? By synthesizing and analyzing the numerous aspects of the mass transit security challenge, and by developing an increasingly deep understanding of context, underlying structures, and interrelationships that underlay complex security situations, security planners and solution designers can make more reliable inferences about behavior and discern opportunities for change.

In an analytical and specialized world, each consultant is normally concerned with only one area of specialty. They assume that the other parts are working correctly or, if not, somebody else is taking care of them. They conveniently assume that they are the only game in town. However, the ultimate effectiveness of the homeland security system is defined more by the interactions among the parts rather than the sum of the actions of the parts taken separately.

A systems methodology of defining problems and designing solutions requires stakeholders engaging together in identifying the context, defining the right problem, and designing the right solution specific to their own context.

CONCLUSION

Systems thinking is a powerful discipline to approach complex systems and resolve challenging problems of our age. It relies on some very basic concepts and ideas that are present in many simple and complex systems around us:

- We can get a more accurate and complete picture of reality by focusing on both components and relationships between components rather than components alone.
- By mapping the relationships between components/variables, we can understand the internal structure of a system, as well as how systemic behavior emerges as a result of that structure.
- The way different variables relate to each other is critical to identifying the type of feedback processes at work within the system.
- In dynamically complex systems, components'/agents' interactions are likely to change and evolve. What will emerge out of their interactions cannot always be known in advance
- Viewing elements/issues as parts of a broader system allows us to have a deeper understanding of problems.
- Understanding and engaging different stakeholder in a system is critical both to define problems and to identify and implement solution strategies

Homeland Security is a young field of study and practice. The mental framework its students and practitioners adopt will guide how this system and its issues are viewed and what kinds of attempts are made to resolve its problems. It is crucial to recognize that such choices will have long lasting implications not only for the future of homeland security as a discipline but also for U.S. homeland and public safety. As such, students and practitioners of homeland security field carry significant responsibility to identify and adopt appropriate approaches to ensure rigorous research and effective policy decisions and operations. Systems thinking is a powerful approach that can move homeland security forward both as a discipline and as a domain of practical operations.

NOTES

1. We would like to thank Jamie Frittman who reviewed earlier drafts of this chapter and made valuable suggestions.

2. Peter M. Senge, *The Fifth Discipline* (New York: Currency, 2006), 160.

3. Senge (2006) defines systems thinking as "a discipline for seeing the structures that underlie complex situations, and for discerning points of high and low leverage change." The word "structures" denotes the web of relations between parts within a whole. For the definition and a general discussion of systems thinking, see Peter M. Senge, *The Fifth Discipline* (New York: Currency, 2006), 69.

4. Systems thinking has widely been applied to a wide variety of fields ranging from management and information science to environment and epidemiology.

5. Some other similarly complex domains include healthcare, economy, and education.

6. U.S. Department of Homeland Security, *Quadrennial Homeland Security Review Report: A Strategic Framework for a Secure Homeland (QHSR)* (N.P.: U.S. Department of Homeland, February 2010).

7. John D. Sterman, *Business Dynamics: Systems Thinking and Modeling for a Complex World* (New York: Irwin/McGraw-Hill, 2000), 21.

8. Ibid., 21.

9. Peter M. Senge, *The Fifth Discipline* (New York: Currency, 2006), 71.

10. Sterman (2000) argues that dynamic complexity arises when systems are "dynamic, tightly coupled, governed by feedbacks, nonlinear, history dependent, self-organizing, adaptive, counterintuitive, policy resistant and characterized by trade-offs." See John D. Sterman, *Business Dynamics: Systems Thinking and Modeling for a Complex World,* (New York: Irwin/McGraw-Hill, 2000), 22.

11. Ibid., 22.

12. Information sharing difficulties between federal, state, and local law enforcement agencies are well publicized. Terrorism planning and exercises that incorporate all required homeland security stakeholders are rare. Most notably, such activities rarely involve the private sector and public even though conceptual boundaries would clearly involve issues that are directly related to them. See Sibel McGee, Catherine Bott, Vikram Gupta, Kimberly Jones, and Alex Karr, *Public Role and Engagement in Counterterrorism Efforts: Implications of Israeli Practices for the U.S.* (Final report, Arlington, VA: Homeland Security Institute, April 2009).

13. Robert Edson, *Systems Thinking. Applied: A Primer* (Arlington, VA: Analytic Services Inc, 2008), 5.

14. For more information about systems thinking and its approach to understanding wholes and constitutive elements, see John Boardman and Brian Sauser, *Systems Thinking: Coping with the 21st Century* (Boca Raton, FL: CRC Press, 2008); Peter Senge, *The Fifth Discipline: The Art and Practice of the Learning Organization* (New York: Currency, 2006); and Peter Checkland, *Systems Thinking, Systems Practice* (New York: John Wiley & Sons, 1999).

15. Failing to identify the components of a system and their relationships completely results in a partial view of a system, often resulting in inadequate conceptualization of the associated problems. Known as the "error of the third kind," such inadequate understanding may be a result of misconceptualization of the system or capturing only part of the system. For a detailed discussion on this, see Ian I. Mitroff and Abraham Silvers, *Dirty Rotten Strategies: How We Trick Ourselves and Others into Solving the Wrong Problems Precisely* (Stanford, CA: Stanford Business Books, 2010).

16. Understanding the causal relationships between different components/variables, issues, and activities within a system is the first step towards identifying structures in a system.

17. John D. Sterman, *Business Dynamics: Systems Thinking and Modeling for a Complex World* (New York: Irwin/McGraw-Hill, 2000), 107. Sterman defines a system's structure as "consist[ing] of the feedback loops, stocks and flows, and nonlinearities created by the interaction of the physical and institutional structure of the system with the decision-making processes of the agents acting within."

18. Jamshid Gharajedaghi, *Systems Thinking: Managing Chaos and Complexity* (Boston: Elsevier, 2006), 46.

19. Ibid., 46.

20. For more information on why understanding and reconciling different stakeholder perspective is a systems thinking requirement, see Peter Checkland, *Systems Thinking, Systems Practice* (New York: John Wiley & Sons, 1999).

21. Edward McCleskey and Diana McCord, *Underlying Reasons for Success or Failure of Terrorist Attacks: Selected Case Studies*.

22. Ibid. 3.

38

PERCEPTUAL FRAMING OF HOMELAND SECURITY

Linda Kiltz, Ph.D.

Assistant Professor of Public Administration

This chapter analyzes the phenomenon of homeland security through the development of three conceptual lenses that were created out of the existing literatures in criminal justice, public administration, organization behavior and international relations. These conceptual lenses include (I) Homeland Security as a Criminal Justice Problem/ Terrorism as a Crime, (II) Homeland Security as an International Relations Problem/Terrorism as War, and (III) Homeland Security as an Organization Design Problem/Terrorism as a Network. Each conceptual lens consists of theories, practices, values, beliefs, and assumptions that serve to shape how the threat of terrorism is perceived as a problem, and how the problem is resolved in the form of homeland security policy and programs. These conceptual lenses highlight how perceptual filters can significantly alter how individuals and organizations understand and explain phenomena or events.

"We see the world, not as it is, but as we are—or, as we are conditioned to see it."

Steven R. Covey in *The 7 Habits of Highly Effective People.*

"Surprise occurs the moment we realize our view of the world no longer matches reality."

Wayne Burkan in *Wide Angle Vision.*

a Crime, (II) Homeland Security as an International Relations Problem/Terrorism as War, and (III) Homeland Security as an Organization Design Problem/Terrorism as a Network. This chapter explains the characteristics and assumptions of each of these conceptual lenses based on a comprehensive literature review.

The first part describes the characteristics of Lens (I) Homeland Security as a Criminal Justice Problem/Terrorism as a Crime, the second part focuses on Lens (II) Homeland Security as an International Relations Problem/Terrorism as War, and third describes Lens (III) Homeland Security as an Organization Design Problem/Terrorism as a Network. The characteristics of each lens are based on those items most frequently represented in the literature. However, there is no one paradigm or clear consensus in the academic disciplines on how homeland security is understood, and therefore what homeland security policies might be most effective against the threat of terrorism.

Scholars and practitioners in criminal justice, international relations, and public administration bring different educational backgrounds, experiences, values, and beliefs to their study of historical events and new phenomena. Thus, these individuals may see completely different things when they look at the same events.[22] (See Figure 38-1.) Joel Barker wrote, "What may be perfectly clear and visible to one person is invisible to another because of differing paradigms."[23] Viewing

Figure 38-1

Multiple frame analysis

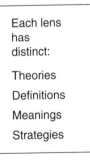

Each lens has distinct:

Theories

Definitions

Meanings

Strategies

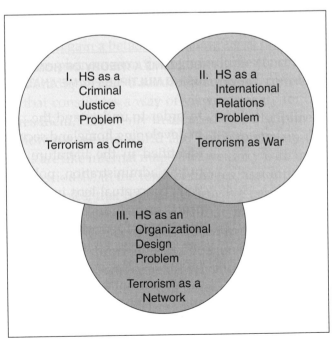

I. HS as a Criminal Justice Problem

Terrorism as Crime

II. HS as a International Relations Problem

Terrorism as War

III. HS as an Organizational Design Problem

Terrorism as a Network

the world through conceptual lenses is like looking at a distant object through a straw—it allows a person to be focused on one specific item but blocks the larger view or the ability to look at the event from an alternative viewpoint. If we are to understand homeland security, then we must look at it from multiple perspectives and be able to put our own perspective aside so we can see that of others. Thus, we begin by analyzing each conceptual lens with their distinct theories, definitions, meanings, and strategies in a process called multiple frame analysis.

LENS I: HOMELAND SECURITY AS A CRIMINAL JUSTICE PROBLEM/TERRORISM AS A CRIME

Key Elements of the Criminal Justice Lens

By looking at terrorism as crime and from a criminal justice lens, key characteristics of homeland security and terrorism are highlighted. First, the criminal justice lens defines terrorism as a crime that is politically motivated. Theodore Honderich defines political violence as the "use of force against persons or things; a use of force prohibited by law, directed to a change in the policies, system, territory of jurisdiction, or personnel of a government or governments, and hence also directed to changes in the lives of individuals within societies."[24] Unlike other offenders investigated by the FBI, those identified as terrorists have committed or are suspected of having committed crimes for political reasons. However, despite the motivation, acts of terrorism can include crimes such as murder, kidnapping, arson, and destruction of property, which are acts designated to be illegal by state and national criminal codes.

Second, terrorism is defined as an act of violence whose purpose is to coerce or intimidate a government or population to obtain political or social benefits. For example, the federal statutes on terrorism define international and domestic terrorism as "activities that involve violent acts or acts dangerous to human life that are a violation of the criminal laws of the U.S. or of any state, and appear intended to intimidate or coerce a civilian population; to influence the policy of a government by intimidation or coercion; or attempt to affect the conduct of government by mass destruction, assassination, or kidnapping."[25] What distinguishes terrorism from common crimes is that the conduct is motivated by political, ideological, and religious ends.

Third, terrorism is distinct from ordinary domestic crime in a number of ways. Criminals are characterized as opportunistic, impulsive, self-centered, and undisciplined.[26] For most criminals, crime is a way for obtaining goods and violence is employed as a means to obtain money or material goods for the criminal's own self-interest. Terrorists, by contrast, normally plan their operations and their violent acts are intended to have consequences (political or social), and to make a symbolic statement about a political cause.[27] In addition, terrorists are motivated by ideology, while criminals are generally not committed to any specific ideology. Finally, most criminals avoid committing crimes in public and are oriented toward escape. Terrorists, however, use political violence to gain public attention to their cause, they train and prepare for their missions, and are attack oriented.[28]

Fourth, counterterrorism strategies to prevent and deter terrorism can be found in part in crime prevention and deterrence theories. A primary purpose of criminal law is to deter or to dissuade a person from committing a crime because he or she fears being punished through fines or incarceration. Deterrence theory from the perspective of criminologists assumes that individuals are rational actors who choose to obey or violate the law by a rational calculation of the risk of pain from incarceration, social stigma, or death penalty versus the potential pleasure and economic gain derived from a criminal act.[29] Homeland security policy since 9/11 has included activities focused on deterring terrorism by passing legislation (e.g., the PATRIOT Act) that created new terrorism-related crimes, such as acts of violence against mass transportation systems, and made penalties more severe for those convicted of such crimes.[30] The primary weakness of using legal sanctions as a deterrent of terrorism is that the actual or perceived threat of formally applied punishment by the state has not been proven to provide a significant marginal deterrent effect as it does with criminals.[31]

To complement deterrence strategies, law enforcement agencies often employ crime prevention strategies. Among the most visible crime prevention measures are those that include various forms of target hardening and increasing the physical security of potential targets of crime. Target hardening includes the installation of locks, bars for windows, intruder alarms, fences, and other devices that make crime more difficult to carry out. Other situational crime prevention strategies include physical, electronic, and procedural measures that serve to deter criminals from attacking, detecting them if they do attack, delaying them so they can be apprehended, and denying them access to certain targets.[32] These types of measures were clearly seen after 9/11 at airports, government buildings, and port facilities where new fences, barricades, scanners, and surveillance systems were adopted.

Lastly, the criminal justice lens identifies homeland security as a criminal justice problem that should be handled by local, state, national, and international law enforcement agencies. Law enforcement agencies are concerned with preventing and deterring crime, gathering evidence, determining the guilt of the individuals responsible for a particular act, and apprehending and bringing the perpetrators to trial. The criminal justice approach offers a broad range of counterterrorist strategies to deter, prevent, and respond to terrorism that is quite different from an international relations and organizational design perspective.

The contemporary criminal justice system in the United States has played a key role in homeland security when terrorism has been perceived as a crime, because all parts of the criminal justice system are activated when an individual or group commits an act of terrorism within the United States and they are caught, prosecuted, and found guilty of the crimes. The criminal justice system consists of three main components: law enforcement agencies charged with investigating crimes and apprehending suspects; the court system where a determination is made whether a suspect is guilty as charged; and the correctional system charged with treating and rehabilitating offenders and with incapacitating them.

In the criminal justice lens, local, state, and federal law enforcement agencies play a critical role in homeland security. At the national level, the Federal Bureau of Investigation has been designated the lead federal agency in investigating terrorist groups in the United States and acts of terrorism directed at Americans overseas. The FBI received this authority through a series of presidential directives and legislation including President Reagan's national security decision directive #30,[33] the Omnibus Diplomatic Security and Antiterrorism Act of 1986,[34] and President Bill Clinton's Presidential Decision Directive 39.[35] Although the FBI has had this role for over 20 years, throughout most of the 1990s, counterterrorism was not seen as the priority in this organization. Before 9/11, the highest priority goal for the FBI was the reduction of violent crime, including organized crime and drug and gang related violence.[36] However, since the terrorist attacks on 9/11, the highest priority for the department has been to protect Americans by preventing acts of terrorism.[37]

The International Association of Chiefs of Police (IACP) argued that all "terrorism is local" and that regardless of the global and international connections, any actual terrorism attack is going to occur at the local level, and it will be local first responders that will initially deal with the attack.[38] As first responders to a terrorist attack, local police officers will be responsible for assessing the crime scene for hazards, calling for and providing medical assistance, identifying victims and witnesses, securing the crime scene and physical evidence, and notifying supervisors and investigators who will be handling the case.[39] In addition to responding and investigating terrorist attacks after they occur, local police are required to be more proactive in preventing and detecting acts of terrorism by intelligence gathering and analysis and by completing threat and vulnerability assessments in their jurisdictions.[40] From the criminal justice perspective, terrorism is considered a criminal matter to be handled by local, state, and national law enforcement agencies. Law enforcement is concerned with gathering evidence, determining the guilt of the individuals responsible for a particular act, and apprehending and bringing the perpetrators to trial.

Criminal justice is not only viewed in the United States as a system, but also as a process that takes offenders through a series of decision points beginning with the investigation of a crime and arrest of suspects, continuing to adjudication where guilt or innocence is determined in a trial, and concluding with correctional treatment and release.[41] While this process is more complex than this and can vary based on if the crimes are classified as misdemeanors or felonies, what is critical about this process is that it is bound by specific constitutional procedures and protections. The formal justice process implies that criminal defendants charged with a serious crime are entitled to a full range of rights under the law, including the right to refuse to answer questions when placed in police custody, the right to a speedy and public trial by an impartial jury, and the right to have trial procedures subject to review by a higher authority, to name a few. This lens identifies homeland security as a criminal justice problem that is best resolved by utilizing the institutions and processes of the criminal justice system (see Table 38-1 for a summary). The criminal justice approach offers a broad range of counterterrorist strategies to deter, prevent, and respond to terrorism that is quite different from an international relations perspective.

Table 38-1	**Analysis**	**Criminal Justice**
Characteristics of Lens I	Definition of Terrorism: Key characteristics	– Terrorism defined as a crime that is politically motivated and is an illegal activity – Act of violence whose purpose is to coerce or intimidate a government or population – Many types of crimes can be committed in a terrorist act
	Key Theories explaining violent behavior from the following levels: • Individual • Organization/group • Nation state • International/world system	– Terrorists can be distinguished from ordinary criminals – Theories from criminology and criminal justice help to explain terrorist behavior by groups and individuals and include: deterrence, general strain, routine activity, rational choice, and crime prevention theories
	Primary Homeland Security Strategy: • Primary organizations responsible • Goal/purpose	– Law enforcement agencies, especially the FBI, and those organizations that make up the criminal justice system. – Often reactive to crimes versus proactive – Focus on investigating crimes, gathering evidence, apprehending suspects, and successfully prosecuting suspects for crimes. – Homeland security efforts focus on crime prevention strategies, intelligence gathering, enhancing law enforcement powers, and increasing penalties for crimes related to terrorism

LENS II: HOMELAND SECURITY AS AN INTERNATIONAL RELATIONS PROBLEM/TERRORISM AS WAR

Key Elements of the International Relations Lens

This lens conceptualizes terrorism as a form of warfare and is grounded in an international relations foundation, thus presenting key characteristics that are distinct from the other lenses. First, homeland security is linked to national security in protecting the United States and its interests at home and abroad. In the wake of the terrorist attacks on September 11, 2001, the United States required a guiding vision to outline national strategy to combat the terrorist threat at home and abroad. Under President Bush five new strategies were published[42] that related to specific aspects of homeland security and combating terrorism, in addition to an updated National Security Strategy. Although there are many definitions of national security, the U.S. Armed forces defines national security as a "collective term encompassing both national defense and foreign relations of the United States. Specifically, the condition provided by: (a) a military or defense advantage over any foreign nation or group of nations; (b) a favorable foreign relations position; or (c) a defense posture capable of successfully resisting hostile or destructive action from within or without, overt or covert."[43] While national security refers to the aggregate of security issues, both foreign and domestic, facing America, homeland security refers to the

acts of aggression with military operations in Afghanistan in response to 9/11/01 as well as in Libya after the Berlin Disco bombing in 1986.

Nonmilitary, repressive options include nonviolent covert operations such as disinformation campaigns, intelligence gathering and analysis, economic sanctions, and enhanced physical security of possible targets or target hardening. Conciliatory counterterrorism options do not involve the use of force or other repressive methods and can include diplomacy to negotiate acceptable resolutions to a conflict, and social reforms to address the root causes of terrorism.[67] Legal responses to terrorism include actions by international organizations such as the United Nations and World Court.

Each of these options has been used by various administrations to prevent, deter, and respond to terrorism, but some of these options can pose significant ethical and legal dilemmas for policymakers.[68] Central to the development of these responses in the international relations lens is the importance of preemption and deterrence in preventing terrorist attacks by transnational terrorist organizations and nation-states.[69] Finally, this lens identifies homeland security as an international relations problem that is best resolved by utilizing the institutions and processes of the U.S. national security apparatus (see Table 38-2 for a summary).

Table 38-2	Analysis	Internationl Relations Frame *Post Cold War*
Characteristics of Lens II	Definition of Terrorism: Key Characteristics	– Rise of transnational actors with no state sponsors – Increase in sectarian terrorist groups – Terrorism is a strategy of asymmetrical warfare that is directed at civilians or noncombatants in violation of the laws of war – Is a rational strategy whose purpose is to coerce or intimidate a government or population in order to obtain political, social, or religious goals – Is a form of psychological warfare as a means of instilling fear in a population
	Key Theories explaining violent behavior.	– Terrorists can be distinguished from insurgents though there is overlap between the two – Theories from international relations help to explain terrorist behavior by non-state actors include: globalization theories
	Primary Homeland Security Strategy: • Goal/Purpose	– Overlap between U.S. National Security Strategy and homeland security Str. – Focus is on creating and implementing long-term grand strategies related to GWOT – Serves to promote U.S. national interests at home and abroad. – Homeland security is linked to counterterrorism efforts that include diplomacy, military force, intelligence gathering and analysis, covert actions, targeted and untargeted prevention, financial controls, and economic sanctions
	• Organizations	DoD, State, NSC, Intelligence

LENS III: HOMELAND SECURITY AS AN ORGANIZATIONAL DESIGN PROBLEM/TERRORISM AS A NETWORK

Key Elements of Homeland Security as an Organizational Design Problem/ Terrorism as a Network Lens

In Lens III, a number of characteristics are highlighted. This lens analyzes homeland security from an organizational design and public administration perspective. First, this lens focuses on the importance of the design and structure of the government organizations tasked with homeland security. It argues that rational, hierarchical, bureaucratic designs and practices are likely to face significant challenges in deterring, preventing, and responding to terrorism attacks in the future because they are not well-suited for operating in complex, unstable environments. Yet in the wake of 9/11, one of the largest bureaucratic organizations was created—the Department of Homeland Security (DHS) was created with passage of the Homeland Security Act of 2002. DHS was created to centralize the resources and expertise of 22 diverse federal agencies into a supra-bureaucracy in order to achieve greater coordination in homeland security within federal agencies and with state and local government and the private sector.

The issue of homeland security is one of many complex problems that must be addressed by our elected leaders and government organizations at the local, state, and federal level. The coordinated execution of agreed upon programs and policies in homeland security is fundamentally the responsibility not only for the Department of Homeland Security but also for a vast network of government agencies, nonprofit organizations, and private enterprises working in a concerted effort to prevent, deter, and respond to terrorist attacks within the United States. Though a network of organizations are involved in these homeland security efforts, the primary structure of government organizations is a hierarchical model with bureaucratic organizational structures.[70] Bureaucratic structure are often described as having a clear hierarchy in which there is supervision of lower offices by higher ones, a clear chain of command and authority, established rules, policies and procedures (red tape), a division of work, and clear lines of communication, which is best suited for stable and predictable work environments.[71] However, organizations dedicated to homeland security often operate in environments that are dynamic, complex, and uncertain, thus requiring an organic network structure that is highly decentralized, flexible, and adaptable.[72] The large-scale failure of the federal government in responding to Hurricane Katrina in 2005 clearly highlighted the coordination challenges faced by traditionally bureaucratic organizations.

A number of public administration scholars argue that network governance structures are the most effective in responding to increasingly complex social and political problems that span across organizations and levels of government.[73] Network models of organizations and governance are significantly different than hierarchical models.[74] First, while hierarchies have a single authority structure created under a chain of command, networks have a divided authority structure. Second, in a hierarchical structure, activities are guided by clear goals and well-defined problems, while in a network, there are various and changing definitions of problems and goals. Third, a network is a highly organic structure that is decentralized and may integrate multiple levels of government and a variety of private and nonprofit organizations in order to deliver a service or meet policy goals. One of the greatest strengths of the network is its ability to bring together a group of experts and resources to solve problems in a rapidly changing and shifting environment. These capabilities are critical in preventing, deterring, and responding to a broad range of threats to the homeland. Homeland security is a shared responsibility with Congress, state and local governments, the private sector, nonprofit organizations, and the American people. To effectively integrate and coordinate these diverse stakeholders into our homeland security efforts, network governance structures will need to be created and maintained at multiple levels.

The next element of this lens focuses on the organizational culture, mission, and strategies of the agencies involved in homeland security. How terrorism, as well as other threats, are defined and conceptualized is determined largely by the lead agencies involved in homeland security, particularly the Department of Homeland Security, Department of Justice, Department of Defense, and the organizations associated with national intelligence and national security. As a result, counterterrorism policies and programs will take on the character of these organizations. For example, the FBI has historically taken a traditional law enforcement approach to counterterrorism whereby agents respond to crimes after they have occurred to gather evidence and build a case for prosecution. This approach can be clearly seen in their handling of the 1993 World Trade Center bombing.

The starting point for defining organizational structures is strategy. Chandler defines strategy as "the determination of the basic goals and objectives of an enterprise, and adoption of the courses of action and the allocation of resources necessary for carrying out these goals."[75] In the public sector, an agency's strategy can be articulated in its enabling legislation that defines its purposes and by its strategic plans, mission statements, policies, and adopted goals. For example, the Homeland Security Act of 2002 states the mission of the Department of Homeland Security is to "prevent terrorist attacks within the United States; reduce the vulnerability of the United States to terrorism; minimize the damage, and assist in the recovery, from terrorist attacks that do occur within the United States; and carry out all functions of entities transferred to the Department, including acting as a focal point regarding natural and man-made crises and emergency planning."[76] After 9/11, the FBI also changed its mission priorities and placed prevention of terrorist attacks as its number one priority. Some have argued that this focus on terrorism by DHS left the agency unprepared for large-scale natural disasters such as Hurricane Katrina.[77] The growing number of natural disasters combined with the increasing number of murders and drug-related violence on the U.S.-Mexican border and the increasing threats to our cyber infrastructure led to a significant change in the mission of the Department of Homeland Security. Under President Obama DHS has five homeland security missions: preventing terrorism and enhancing security; securing and managing our borders; enforcing and administering our immigration laws; safeguarding securing cyberspace; and ensuring resilience to disasters.[78] Strategy formulation and changes typically begin with an assessment of the opportunities and threats in the external environment and is an ongoing process for government organizations such as DHS.

Organizational culture is very important to organizations, and culture change is a critical component of organization transformation. Organizational culture is defined as "the set of values, guiding beliefs, understandings and ways of thinking that is shared by members of an organization and taught to new members as correct."[79] Edgar Schein argued that "culture matters because it is a powerful, latent, and often unconscious set of forces that determine both our individual and collective behavior, ways of perceiving, thought patterns, and values."[80] In turn, cultural elements determine strategy, goals, and modes of operating. For example, law enforcement agencies, such as the FBI perceive terrorism as a crime, thus their counterterrorism strategies must be underpinned by the guiding principle of the rule of law and implemented through the criminal justice approach.

Understanding organizational cultures helps to explain some of the interorganizational and intraorganizational conflicts that occur in implementing policies and programs in homeland security. A conflict highlighted in the 9/11 Commission Report was that between the FBI and CIA in sharing intelligence information on suspected terrorists. This conflict can be explained in part by the drastically different organizational cultures and strategies of these organizations.

The culture of intelligence driven organizations differs from those of pure law enforcement organizations.[81] While (foreign) intelligence[82] organizations are interested in long-term infiltration, active and passive monitoring, and deterrence, the law enforcement bias is to arrest and prosecute. Also, the primary goal of an intelligence organization is to (1) determine what intelligence should be collected to advance national interests; (2) systematically collect that raw intelligence; (3) apply analytical tools to the raw information in the development of informed judgments; and (4) share that finished intelligence with national-level policymakers and other officials with a demonstrated need to know. "Tradecraft," or the how, where, and why intelligence gathering takes place, is of utmost importance.[83] Recruitment of sources and penetration of groups operating in United States is highly valued by intelligence organizations. Finally, there are fewer legal restrictions on overseas CIA operations than FBI investigations at home or abroad.

By contrast, the primary goal of a law enforcement agency, such as the FBI, is to respond to criminal activities and to deter future crimes. In general, this goal is achieved by rigorous investigation of criminal activities and close cooperation with prosecutors. Discrete, individual criminal cases are the driving factor in law enforcement organizations, while broader trends and relationships among social variables, such as political, economic, and military factors, drive intelligence organizations.[84] When law enforcement entities operate within the United States, civil liberties and the rights of U.S. citizens are of paramount concern. As a result, the FBI is governed by a complex range of investigative guidelines and polices, and statutes and constitutional limits when intelligence is being gathered in the United States against foreign agents or U.S. citizens.[85] This lens not only focuses on the organizations involved in homeland security but also on the organizational structure of terrorist groups.

Threats to homeland security come from terrorist organizations or movements often in the form of loosely linked networks of varied groups. These groups can range from highly organized and trained operatives to groups of potential actors who lack training or stable organizational structures. Today's terrorist networks are different than past terrorist organizations in their design, technology, and tactics and pose unique challenges.[86]

Terrorism research often includes studies on how terrorist organizations are structured and how these structures have changed and adapted to their environment. In the past, the tendency was to assume that terrorists belonged to identifiable organizations with relatively clear command and control structures (pyramid organization) with a defined set of political, social, and economic objectives.[87] Terrorist organizational structures have evolved into more loosely linked network structures to survive in a constantly changing threat environment. As law enforcement, intelligence, and military operations have successfully found and captured operatives in terrorist organizations, these groups have had to find new ways to evade authority, to become more adaptable and resilient, and to ensure their organization would survive if the main leaders were captured or killed.[88]

Arquilla and Ronfeldt, in their study of terrorist organizations, define a network as "a set of diverse, dispersed nodes that share a set of ideas and interests and are arrayed to act in a fully intermitted networked manner."[89] Arquilla and Ronfeldt argue that these networks have little or no hierarchy or official authority.[90] Also, decision making and operations are decentralized thus tactical operations can be initiated and carried locally without central leadership.[91] The network organization often has a decentralized cell structure consisting of a small group of people and a team leader. The leader is usually the person with the most experience, and he or she is responsible for ensuring the tasks of the cell are carried out and for communicating and coordinating with other cells. Since 9/11, Al-Qaeda has made numerous transformations and has morphed into a multidimensional network of networks. The challenge in homeland security is in designing governance structures and networks that are effective and efficient at preventing, deterring, and responding to terrorist attacks and other natural and man-made hazards. (See Table 38-3 for a summary of this lens.)

Table 38-3

Characteristics of
Lens III

Analysis	Organization
Definition of Terrorism: Key Characteristics	- Terrorism is seen as a network of autonomous groups and individuals that are motivated by a common ideology but may have diverse goals and tactics - Terrorists are rational actors who organize according to their mission, tasks, and threat environment - Terrorist organizations have many structures including hierarchical, umbrella and network structures

Primary Homeland Security Strategy:
  • Structure, Mission, Strategy and Culture of Primary Organizations Responsible
  • Importance of Network Structures
	- Literature from PA and organizational theory used to explain how U.S. government agencies organize to prevent, deter, and respond to terrorism
	- Pre 9/11, FBI, FEMA, and State Dept. were designated as lead agencies; these agencies were organized like traditional government bureaucracies with hierarchical structures
	- First responders using ICS will form the first networks in responding to attacks
	- Given the complex nature of homeland security, network structures are needed but at time of 9/11 attack the network governance literature was in its infancy
	- Network structures are different than hierarchies but networks are needed to deal with the wicked problem of terrorism
	- Design, develop, and coordinate a network governance structure including all levels of government, business and non-profits in a collaborative effort to deter, prevent and respond to terrorism.
	- Need to align organizational structures to mission, strategy, tasks, technology, and operating environment
	- Organizational culture is important to change efforts and framing how homeland security and terrorism are perceived

CONCLUSION

The purpose of this chapter was to begin the effort to build a theoretical foundation for homeland security by creating a framework based on three distinct conceptual lenses developed from the academic literature in the fields of criminology, international relations, organization studies, and public administration. These conceptual lenses included (I) Homeland Security as a Criminal Justice Problem/Terrorism as Crime, (II) Homeland Security as an International Relations Problem/Terrorism as War, and (III) Homeland Security as an Organization Design Problem/Terrorism as a Network. Each conceptual lens consists of theories, practices, values, beliefs, and assumptions that can serve to shape how critical events are perceived, and as such, how these events are understood and the problems addressed in the form of homeland security programs and policies. Criminology, organization theory, public administration, and international relations each bring unique theoretical perspectives that contribute significantly to our understanding of homeland security, but none individually provides an adequate picture of the challenges of homeland security theory or policies needed to address modern threats and hazards.

Homeland security is a complex problem that spans many academic disciplines, professions, and organizational boundaries. It encompasses both foreign and domestic policy issues, and involves government organizations at all levels, as well as businesses, nonprofit organizations, and citizens. In fact, homeland security is so complex that multiple perspectives are needed to analyze the phenomenon because one perspective simply misses too much or fails to see critical pieces of the problem that need to be addressed. Thus, further research should be encouraged that is interdisciplinary and seeks to break down some of the disciplinary barriers within the field of homeland security. This requires a focus on processes and incentives that will bring scholars and policymakers with these different perspectives together.

It is clear that conceptual lenses heavily influence whether we will be aware of new problems, how we give meaning to what we observe, and how we perceive or understand new phenomenon. Unexpected changes are often difficult to perceive, let alone address because they simply are not captured within our mental maps or conceptual lenses that we use to make sense of the world. To ensure we are not surprised by another 9/11, it is critical that we continue to broaden our conceptual lenses as it relates to homeland security.

In the rapidly changing environment of the information age, problems are constantly morphing into new forms, thus the life cycle of any particular solution is likely to be very short. Therefore, an important challenge for scholars and government leaders is to lead the process of continuing to analyze our existing conceptual lenses as they relate to homeland security, as well as to lead the process of constructing new conceptual lenses. A useful next step would be to apply the lenses to a number of terrorist attacks and conduct a multiple case study. Multiple frame analysis can be used to analyze critical cases such as the attacks on the World Trade Center in 1993 and 2001. A comparative analysis of these two events can be conducted to see how our conceptual lenses and perceptions have changed over time. In addition, further research is needed on the lenses used in multiple frame analysis in order to more clearly define the theories, concepts, definitions, and principles in each. Also, additional lenses can be added to the framework such as those that look at homeland security from an emergency management, public health, or risk management perspective and applied to other cases. Also, further research is needed to understand how these conceptual lenses are formed and shared, and changed within government organizations, as well as among elected officials. The use of multiple lenses in analyzing complex phenomenon such as homeland security is important because when used alone, one perspective or lens can miss key elements and capture only a small part of the phenomenon we are observing. Using multiple perspectives allows us to develop explanations that help us understand specific aspects of homeland security as well as to identify alternative paradigms that serve to help transform our theories, traditions, rules, and standards of practice.

NOTES

1. Numerous initial newscasts of Fox, CBS, ABC, and CNN newscasts the morning of 9/11 can be viewed on YouTube at http://www.youtube.com/watch?v=1wXwcAzRa_Q&feature=relmfu.

2. Ibid.

3. CNN.com Transcripts. (September 11, 20001, 08:48ET). At http://transcripts.cnn.com/TRANSCRIPTS/0109/11/bn.01.html

4. Ibid.

5. Ibid.

6. CNN.com Transcripts (December 4, 2001, 15:18 ET), http://transcripts.cnn.com/TRANSCRIPTS/0112/04/se.04.html.

7. Peter Lance, *Triple Cross* (New York: Regan, 2006), 243.

8. Simon Reeve, *The New Jackals: Ramzi Yousef, Osama bin Laden and the Future of Terrorism* (Boston: Northeastern University Press, 2002), 4.

9. Numerous initial newscasts of Fox, CBS, ABC, and CNN the morning of 9/11 can be viewed on YouTube at http://www.youtube.com/watch?v=1wXwcAzRa_Q&feature=relmfu.

10. CNN News coverage of WTC attacks from 8:50 am to 11:30 am, http://www.youtube.com/watch?v=uT9jkBGFlr0&feature=related.

11. CNN.com Transcripts (December 4, 2001, 15:18 ET) http://transcripts.cnn.com/TRANSCRIPTS/0112/04/se.04.html.

12. National Commission on Terrorist Attacks upon the United States, *The 9/11 Commission Report* (New York: W.W. Norton, 2004).

13. William C. Nicholson, *Homeland Security Law and Policy* (Springfield, IL: Charles C Thomas, 2005), 120.

14. Office of Homeland Security, *National Strategy for Homeland Security* (Washington, DC: White House, July 2002).

15. U.S. Department of Homeland Security, *Quadrennial Homeland Security Review* (Washington DC: White House, 2010), 13.

16. Nicholson, *Homeland Security Law and Policy*, 121.

17. Defined in *The American Heritage Dictionary* at http://www.yourdictionary.com/paradigm.

18. Joel Barker, *Paradigms: The Business of Discovering the Future* (New York: HarperBusiness, 1993).

19. George W. Bush, "Securing the Homeland: Strengthening the Nation" (Washington DC: White House, 2002), p. 27, http://www.whitehouse.gov/homeland/homeland_security_book.pdf.

20. There are many theories of deterrence in criminology. See, for example, Raymond Paternoster and Ronet Bachman, *Explaining Criminals and Crime* (Los Angeles: Roxbury Publishing Company, 2001); also see Deryck Beyleved, *A Bibliography on General Deterrence* (Farnborough, UK: Saxon House, 1980).

21. There are a multitude of theories on deterrence. See Herman Kahn, "Three Types of Deterrence," in *Classics of International Relations*, edited by John Vasquez (Englewood, New Jersey: Prentice Hall, 1986), 303–307; and Paul Huth, *Extended Deterrence and the Prevention of War* (New Haven, CT: Yale University Press, 1988).

22. The influence of paradigms on researchers and scholars is described in Thomas Kuhn, *The Structure of Scientific Revolutions* (Chicago: University of Chicago Press, 1970). Also see Samuel P. Huntington, "Paradigms of American Politics: Beyond the One, the Two and the Many," *Political Science Quarterly* 89 (1974): 1–26.

23. Joel Barker, *Paradigms: The Business of Discovering the Future* (New York: HarperBusiness, 1993), 43.

24. Peter Merkl, *Political Violence and Terror* (Los Angeles: University of California Press, 1986), 20.

25. 18 U.S. 2331 (2009).

26. Douglas Bodrero, *State Roles, Community Assessment, and Personality Profiles* (Tallahassee, FL: Institute for Intergovernmental Research, 2000).

27. Bruce Hoffman, *Inside Terrorism* (New York: Columbia University Press, 2006), 41.

28. Ibid., 174.

29. Ronald Ackers, *Criminological Theories* (Chicago, IL: Fitzroy Dearborn, 1999), 77.

30. P.L. 107–56; 115 U.S. 272 (2001).

31. Ronald Ackers, *Criminological Theories* (Chicago, IL: Fitzroy Dearborn, 1999), 80.

32. National Crime Prevention Institute, *Understanding Crime Prevention* (Boston: Butterworth, 1986).

33. Ronald Reagan, *NSDD 30*, April 10, 1982, http://www.fas.org/irp/offdocs/nsdd/nsdd–030.htm.

34. P. L. 99–399 expanded the FBI's jurisdiction to include investigating acts of terrorism directed against Americans overseas.

35. William Clinton, *PDD 39*, 1995, http://www.fas.org/irp/offdocs/pdd39.htm. PDD 39 was signed in 1995 as the U.S. Policy on Counterterrorism, which further defined the roles of the FBI.

36. See Department of Justice, *FY 1999–2001 Annual Accountability Reports*, http://www.usdoj.gov.ag.annual reports. Some documents list counterterrorism as a top priority from 1998 to 2001, such as The DOJ Budget goals memo from Attorney General Janet Reno (April 6, 2000), which lists counterterrorism as a priority in FY 2002, http://www.americanprogress.org/kf/renomemo.pdf. Also, the FBI strategic plan from May 8, 1998 has listed counterterrorism as a Tier One priority. Available at www.americanprogress.org/kf/fbi98.pdf.

37. Department of Justice, *Fact Sheet: Department of Justice Anti-Terrorism Efforts Since Sept. 11, 2001*, September 5, 2006, http://www.usdoj.gov/opa/pr/2006/September/06_opa_590.html.

38. International Association Chiefs of Police, *From Hometown Security to Homeland Security* (Washington DC: IACP, 2005), 3. Also see Douglas Bodero, "Law Enforcement's New Challenge to Investigate, Interdict and Prevent Terrorism," *Police Chief*, February 2005, 41–48.

39. Paul Maniscalco, *Terrorism Response: Field Guide for Law Enforcement* (Boston, MA: Pearson, 2002).

40. For information on the role of local police in gathering domestic intelligence for homeland security, see Jonathan White, *Defending the Homeland* (Belmont, CA: Wadsworth, 2004). For information on threat and vulnerability assessments, see J. Leson, *Assessing and Managing the Terrorism Threat* (Washington DC: Bureau of Justice Assistance, 2005).

41. For a detailed explanation of the criminal justice process, see Joseph Senna and Larry Siegel, *Essentials of Criminal Justice* (Belmont, CA: Wadsworth, 2001), 11–17. Also see Bureau of Justice Statistics, "The Criminal Justice System Flowchart," 1997, http://www.ojp.usdoj.gov/bjs/flowchart.htm#efiles.

42. Testimony of Randall A. Kim, managing director, homeland security and justice issues, General Accounting Office, before the subcommittee on national security, emerging threats, and international relations, House Committee on Government Reform, February 3, 2004, http://connection.ebscohost.com/c/articles/18173863/combating-terrorism-evaluation-selected-characteristics-national-strategies-related-terrorism-gao-04-408t.

43. "National security" in US NATO Military Terminology Group (2010). JP 1 (02) Dictionary of Military and Associated Terms, 2001 (as amended through 31 July 2010). (Washington DC: Joint Chiefs of Staff, U.S. Department of Defense, 2010), p. 361.

44. *National Security Strategy of the United* States, September 2002, http://georgewbush-white-house.archives.gov/nsc/nss/2002/,19.

45. *National Security Strategy of the United States,* May 2010, http://www.whitehouse.gov/sites/default/files/rss_viewer/national_security_strategy.pdf, 2.

46. Ibid., 18.

47. Though there are multiple definitions of terrorism, when all of these definitions are synthesized, the most common elements are that the acts are conducted by subnational groups, target noncombatants, intended to create fear among a larger population, intended to obtain publicity, are in violation of international and domestic laws, and are motivated by political, religious, or ideological beliefs.

48. *National Security Strategy of the United* States (September 2002), p. 5, http://georgewbush-whitehouse.archives.gov/nsc/nss/2002/.

49. Everett Wheeler, "Terrorism and Military Theory," in *Terrorism Research and Public Policy,* ed. Clark McCauley (Portland, OR: Frank Cass, 1991), 131.

50. Anthony Cordesman, *Terrorism, Asymmetric Warfare, and Weapons of Mass Destruction* (Westport, CT: Praeger, 2002), 8.

51. Everett Wheeler, "Terrorism and Military Theory," in *Terrorism Research and Public Policy,* ed. Clark McCauley (Portland, OR: Frank Cass, 1991), 21.

52. Thomas Schelling, *Arms and Influence* (Lanham, MD: Rowman & Littlefield, 2002).

53. Daniel Byman, *Deadly Connections* (Cambridge, MA: Cambridge University Press), 2005; Anthony Cordesman, *Terrorism, Asymmetric Warfare, and Weapons of Mass Destruction* (Westport, CT: Praeger, 2002); Grant Wardlaw, *Political Terrorism* (New York: Cambridge University Press, 1989).

54. Michael Stohl, *The State as Terrorist* (Westport, CT: Greenwood Press, 1984).

55. Christopher Layne, "The War on Terror and the Balance of Power: The Paradoxes of American Hegemony," in *Balance of Power: Theory and Practice in the 21st Century,* ed. James Wirtz and Michel Fortmann (Stanford, CA: 2004), 116.

56. *National Security Strategy of the United* States (September 2002), http://georgewbush-whitehouse.archives.gov/nsc/nss/2002/,6.

57. James Dougherty and Robert Pfaltzgraff, *Contending Theories of International Relations* (New York: Harper & Row, 1981), 368.

58. Glenn Snyder, *Deterrence and Defense* (Princeton, NJ: Princeton University Press, 1961), 148.

59. See Carol Winkler, *In the Name of Terrorism* (New York: State University of New York Press, 2006); Timothy Naftali, *Blind Spot* (New York: Basic Books, 2005).

60. Thomas Friedman, *The Lexus and the Olive Tree* (New York: Farrar, Straus & Giroux, 1999).

61. Samuel Huntington, *The Clash of Civilizations and the Remaking of the World Order* (New York: Simon & Schuster, 1996).

62. Benjamin Barber, *Jihad vs. McWorld* (New York: Bantam Books, 1995), 249.

63. Joseph Stiglitz, *Globalization and its Discontents* (New York: W. W. Norton & Co.), 7.

64. Bernard Lewis, *The Crisis of Islam* (New York: Random House, 2004), 113–19.

65. See Bernard Lewis, *The Crisis of Islam* (New York, Random House, 2004), 113–19; Jessica Stern, *Terror in the Name of God: Why Religious Militants Kill* (New York: Ecco, 2003).

66. See Paul Pillar, *Terrorism and U.S. Foreign Policy* (Washington DC: Brookings Institution, 2001); Philip Heymann, *Terrorism and America: A Commonsense Strategy for a Democratic*

Society (Cambridge, MA: MIT Press, 1998); James Corum, *Fighting the War on Terror* (St. Paul, MN: Zenith, 2007); Gus Martin, *Understanding Terrorism,* 2nd ed. (Thousand Oaks, CA: Sage, 2006).

67. Gus Martin, *Understanding Terrorism,* 2nd ed. (Thousand Oaks, CA: Sage, 2006).

68. A comprehensive analysis of counterterrorism options is found in Boaz Ganor, *The Counterterrorism Puzzle* (New Brunswick, NJ: Transaction Publishers, 2005).

69. Ibid.

70. Stephen Goldsmith and William Eggers, *Governing by Network* (Washington, DC: Brookings Institution Press, 2004).

71. Ibid. Also see Henry Mintzberg, *Structures in Fives: Designing Effective Organizations* (Englewood Cliffs, NJ: Prentice Hall, 1983).

72. Stephen Goldsmith and William Eggers, *Governing by Network* (Washington, DC: Brookings Institution Press, 2004).

73. See Robert Agranoff, *Managing Within Networks* (Washington DC: Georgetown University Press, 2007); David Monihan, *Leveraging Collaborative Netwroks in Infrequent Emergency Situations* (Washington DC: IBM Center for the Business of Government, 2005); Stephen Goldsmith and William Eggers, *Governing by Network* (Washington, DC: Brookings Institution Press, 2004).

74. Ibid.

75. Alfred Chandler, *Strategy and Structure* (Cambridge, MA: MIT Press, 1962), 13.

76. P.L. 107–296.

77. William Waugh and Richard Sylves, "Organizing the War on Terrorism," *Public Administration Review* 62 (September 2002): 145–153; William Waugh, "Terrorism, Homeland Security, and the National Emergency Management Network," *Public Organization Review* 3 (December 2003): 373–85.

78. See *Quadrennial Homeland Security Review* (2010), http://www.dhs.gov/xabout/our-mission.shtm.

79. Edgar Schein, *The Corporate Culture Survival Guide* (San Francisco, CA: Jossey-Bass, 1999), 13.

80. Ibid., 14.

81. For a brief assessment of the cultural differences between intelligence and law enforcement, see Gorman Siobhan, "FBI, CIA Remain Worlds Apart," *Government Executive,* August 1, 2003. See also Richard Best, *Intelligence and Law Enforcement: Countering Transnational Threats to the U.S.,* CRS Report RL30252, December 3, 2001. See also Mark Riebling, *Wedge: The Secret War Between the FBI and the CIA* (New York: Knopf, 1994).

82. Foreign intelligence is defined as information relating to the capabilities, intentions, or activities of foreign governments or elements thereof, foreign organizations, or foreign persons. See the National Security Act of 1947 (50 U.S. Code, Chapter 15, §401a).

83. For a brief discussion of how foreign intelligence tradecraft differs from Homeland Security tradecraft, see Bruce Berkowitz, "A Fresh Start Against Terror," *New York Times,* August 4, 2003, p. A17.

84. Ibid.

85. Richard Best, *Intelligence and Law Enforcement: Countering Transnational Threats to the U.S.,* CRS Report RL30252, December 3, 2001.

86. Bruce Hoffman and Ian Lesser, *Countering the New Terrorism* (Santa Monica, CA: Rand., 1999); Marc Sageman, *Understanding Terror Networks* (Philadelphia, PA: University of Pennsylvania Press, 2004).

87. Jonathan White, *Terrorism and Homeland Security* (Belmont, CA: Wadsworth, 2006).

88. Chris Dishman, "The Leaderless Nexus: When Crime and Terror Converge," *Studies in Conflict and Terrorism* 28 (2005): 237–252.

89. John Arquilla and David Ronfeldt, *Networks and Netwar: The Future of Terror, Crime and Militancy,* RAND Report, 2001.

90. Ibid., 7.

91. Ibid.

39

EMERGENCY EXERCISE DESIGN PRINCIPLES AND OBJECTIVES

Robert McCreight

George Washington University

Emergency exercise design and evaluation is a fundamental part of any organization's overall strategy for displaying readiness and preparedness for major crises and complex emergencies. Emergency exercises are vital to the effective performance of emergency teams, staff and support personnel for at least five primary reasons:

- Measuring the overall readiness of a state or local emergency management components
- Determining how effectively these response elements perform their critical roles
- Assessing utilization of appropriate technology to aid in managing the crisis
- Validating the accuracy of emergency plans and standby procedures
- Observing how the overall operational tasks of crisis management are implemented

These five areas deserve periodic review and affirmation, as they often underpin the workings of ordinary emergency management staff, leadership, and resources. Often it is assumed that if a robust and detailed emergency plan is in place, adequate measures have been taken to prepare for most emergency events. Contingency planning only takes one so far, and then the issue of actual performance looms as a daunting challenge. Without periodic exercises it is the proverbial unanswered question. Without knowing how decisions will be made under stress, how unforeseen problems are tackled, how unexpected personnel and equipment snafus are overcome, and how the entire enterprise of crisis management is implemented, there is a significant zone of unacceptable risk. Untested assumptions, false estimates, unreliable data, and similar errors will undermine the emergency teams, which do not set aside time and effort to determine how differential situations will be handled.

Designing, coordinating, and conducting realistic and challenging emergency exercises is not easy and not cheap. Regrettably, many towns and cities may have money enough for emergency plans, resources sufficient to acquire new equipment and train staff, and enough time to discuss response strategies in advance of a real crisis. However, it is often that few have the time and money to annually conduct readiness exercises and truly validate the operational performance of their teams and their equipment in a realistic and challenging scenario event. State emergency agencies and the federal government have helped alleviate this problem through targeted grants and other funding mechanisms, but frequent, well-designed, and taxing exercises seldom occur as often as needed.

For most governments, the requirements and guidance developed by the U.S. Department of Homeland Security (DHS) for the National Incident Management System (NIMS) and the Incident Command System (ICS) provides adequate material to train and develop their teams. For those jurisdictions granted access to the system, there is also the special guidance and technical materials provided by the DHS-sponsored HSEEP (Homeland Security Exercise Evaluation Program) program. The HSEEP program is composed of seven types of exercises. The first four are "discussion based," and the last three are "operations based." Operations-based exercises are more progressive than discussion-based exercises. Additionally, within the operations-based exercises and the discussion-based exercises, each exercise type builds upon the last. The four discussion-based exercises are the Seminar, Workshop, Tabletop Exercise, and Games. The three operations-based exercises are the Drill, Functional Exercise, and Full-Scale Exercise. In addition, the IS-139 course is available from FEMA for those wishing to further enhance their training on this subject.

Often, however, many state and local governments along with commercial manufacturing and business operations may wish to develop and construct exercises on their own to test and evaluate how their respective organizations function under the extended stress of a disaster or crisis. Examining emergencies that can be completed within 8 hours or less are quite different from extended stress emergencies, which may continue for days. With limited budgets and soaring operational costs, it makes sense to develop and refine emergency readiness, sharpen response, and build resilience where possible to offset the devastating effects of a major disaster.

Well-designed emergency exercises cover the array of routine response tasks, including some novel and unexpected events, while establishing realistic metrics to gauge the extent to which emergency response staff and local communities can display readiness for all-hazard crisis situations. Untested assumptions are usually dangerous when it comes to knowing how your own emergency personnel will respond. Exercises can help overcome that problem.

> The goal in exercise design is to establish a comprehensive and regularly scheduled exercise program built on one another to meet specific operational goals, challenge leadership teams, stress emergency responders, test critical equipment, and enable response staff the opportunity to demonstrate their competence in all emergency functions. The range of progression for exercises is very flexible to meet local community needs and can be conceptualized as simple to complex, from one day to several days, and from tabletop to deployed field events, where realism and genuine challenges can be tackled without risk of harm to life or property.

EXERCISE DESIGN OBJECTIVES

- *Confirm individual/team training (Knowledge—skills—task performance).*
- *Demonstrate key emergency response performance functions.*
- *Verify human—technology interface/operations.*
- *Assess problem solving.*
- *Examine response readiness metrics.*
- *Observe reaction to extended or novel stress incidents.*
- *Evaluate target capabilities.*
- *Determine issues and areas for further tests.*

Exercise value is determined by certain design principles. Following are some of these:

- Exercises ought to enable managers and leaders to confirm that all personnel expected to perform critical tasks have been adequately trained to perform essential functions under both normal and crisis conditions. It is vital to verify that emergency responders have the knowledge, skills, and abilities (KSAs) to tackle a variety of emergency situations.
- Emergency personnel must demonstrate a capability to perform essential emergency tasks and functions at a level of performance competence and quality that is the best possible under the circumstances.
- Exercises enable a fault-free environment to examine how responders can utilize special equipment essential to their jobs and identify issues regarding equipment performance safety issues and fit with the user.
- Exercises aim to simulate realistic crisis situations and examine how individuals and responder teams, along with management, solve problems and tackle unexpected events.
- Exercises can create a simulated environment where extended stress or unexpected and novel pressures can be examined in terms of their effects on responders.
- Exercises provide a glimpse of responder capabilities to handle divergent situations and enable a more realistic assessment of functional performance under different crisis situations.
- Exercises enable identification of persistent operational or technical problems and specify areas where response functions may be less than optimal, which can be further examined and tested in future exercises.

EXERCISE DESIGN PRINCIPLES

One approach advocates emergency exercise progression through a structured series of learning events, from the known to the unknown and from the simple to the complex. Walter Green's (Green's) Exercise Alternatives for Training Emergency Management Command Center Staffs exercise approach models are all built upon the fundamental educational principle that progressively difficult emergency exercise training leads to the most effective learning and comprehension, which ultimately increases emergency preparedness. He asserts "gradual progression," allows for increased flexibility, such as greater ability to vary exercise characteristics based on the participants' experience levels, and a more extensive range of exercise training program participant involvement options (e.g., individual/self-directed learning, individual/classroom training, team).

Green also favors the periodic use of "just-in-time" training, which tests emergency staff readiness immediately prior to an unannounced mini-exercise to observe quick reaction and strategy development. He states that the emergency management progression training can be tailored to emergency mitigation, preparedness, and response training and their specialized needs.

Following are another set of key considerations that emergency exercise designers must contemplate:

- Selection of the design team (based on expertise and skills)
- Scenario exercise focus (simple versus complex emergency situation)
- Exercise location (physical layout of exercise area)
- Schedule of exercise (less than 4 hours—full day—two days?)
- Type of exercise (tabletop—drill—deployed—full scale)
- Exercise focus (team performance—problem solving—developing response strategies, etc.)
- Key exercises incidents to evaluate (major event versus several linked major events)
- Exercise evaluation team (should be drawn from design team)

See Figure 39-1.

Figure 39-1

Exercise design layout

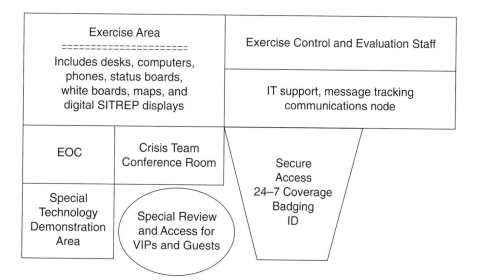

Keeping these work areas distinct inside a facility to house the exercise is important, as the spatial boundary between VIPs, evaluators, and IT support staff helps create a more realistic environment for players. This configuration also allows for a separate area to test and evaluate emerging technologies.

The overarching goal of emergency exercise training is improved preparedness (Gebbie and Valas, 2006). Emergency preparedness refers to a readiness to react constructively to a threat or hazard in a way that minimizes the negative impact on people, physical structures, and systems. Emergency exercise training is a critical component of emergency preparedness. The achievement of emergency preparedness includes in addition, but not limited to, the personnel and equipment to support appropriate emergency management and actions.

RAND corporation research suggests exercises should be part of a regularized quality improvement cycle and embedded inside organizational development programs as a natural progression in raising the collective expertise of staff and management. We can understand the values suggested here by looking at a typical progression in exercise development that incorporates RAND suggestions, Green's perspective, and the combined insights of other exercise theorists.

Generally speaking, the combined wisdom of experienced exercise designers reflects the series of deliberate steps shown in Figure 39-2 as fundamental to effective exercise design. Following

Figure 39-2

Exercise design steps

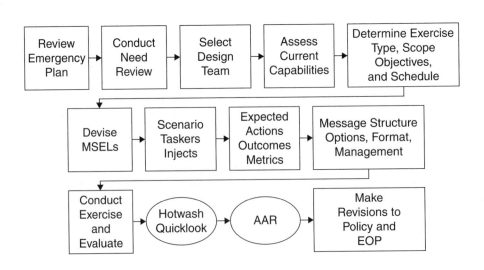

the major steps depicted will help steer a balanced development pattern for exercises.

LOOKING AT TABLETOP EXERCISES

In this case we will look at the simple steps involved in tabletop exercises, which is typically four hours or less in duration and requires the cooperative participation of a team that would normally work together to resolve an emergency. The tabletop problem is often stated simply in a paragraph or less, along with a brief scenario, a map, key facts in the emergency environment, and guidelines for discussion regarding how best to end the crisis. Suggestions for tactical and strategic issues and approaches are discussed.

Tabletop-Exercise Goal

✓ To exercise the relationships between state and local public health agencies and their healthcare delivery partners by responding to a pandemic influenza emergency.

Slide 4

Specific Objectives

✓ Exercise the joint-response capabilities between public health agencies and their healthcare partners in key response categories:
  – Surveillance & Epidemiology
  – Command, Control, & Communications
  – Risk Communication
  – Surge Capacity
  – Disease Prevention & Control

✓ Identify strengths and areas needing improvement with regard to the response.

Slide 5

Expectations

✓ No health department is fully prepared for this type of public health emergency.

✓ Open and honest dialogue and feedback are encouraged throughout the exercise

✓ Participants should feel free to ask questions of one another and challenge each other's assumptions.

✓ No one will be singled out or punished for what they say during the exercise.

✓ You will act on what you learn.

Slide 6

Scenario Situation

Disease samples and isolates extracted from Mexico and Peru are assessed at CDC, which has tentatively identified the suspect virus as H5N1 but not conclusively pending further tests. From serotypes and samples, it appears that young adults aged 10–30 are most susceptible and the attack rate is near 20% with a nearly 40% fatality rate within 3 weeks of onset of symptoms. CDC suspects direct person-to-person transmission is the culprit, and it appears the virus outbreak is in Canada, Europe, and Asia as well. WHO has declared a transition to Pandemic Alert Level 5. At least 22 reported cases within 20 miles of your town have been reported during the last 48 hours, and you are 30 miles from a major city.

Tabletop teams reflect the major players in a real health emergency and are divided into two teams. One team involves hospital leaders and health workers; the other team involves wider emergency management leaders and planners. Exercise runs for three hours with break and wrap-up discussion.

Tabletop Focus: Team Decisions

Decision 1 (1-hour discussion)

For public health agency partners:

- What actions should be taken to engage partners in stepped-up surveillance efforts?
- How will any prior planning for surveillance be utilized in this situation?

- What guidance should be provided to healthcare partners regarding their surveillance efforts?
- How will the local public health agency coordinate surveillance and reporting with partners?

For healthcare partners:

- What responsibilities related to surveillance do hospitals and frontline physicians have?
- What expectations do healthcare providers have for public health agencies?
- What type of surveillance should be established in emergency rooms?
- What is the role of hospitals and laboratories during stepped-up surveillance efforts?

For all participants: (Since two separate task groups are working simultaneously during the first hour—public health and healthcare partners—when initial discussion is complete, both groups meet in plenary and discuss the following four questions for 30 minutes.)

- How would stepped-up surveillance be different from normal influenza-surveillance activities?
- How is information on cases systematically collected and aggregated?
- Who will communicate what information to labs?
- Should anything be done to ensure that existing response systems are working correctly?

Fifteen minute guided plenary discussion summarizing answers both groups gave in their discussion sessions.

Decision 2 (1 hour discussion)
If a formal ICS is activated:

- Who is responsible for activating ICS protocols?
- Who is in charge of the ICS?
- What partner agencies will be involved in the ICS?
- How will the ICS be used to manage the response across partner agencies?

If a formal ICS is not activated:

- Is there a defined trigger for when it is appropriate to establish a formal ICS?
- How will all healthcare partners be involved in coordinated decision-making pre-ICS?
- What communication channels will be used across partner agencies?
- What partner agency is in charge of coordinating and leading stepped-up surveillance efforts?
- What partner agency is responsible for reviewing global, national, regional, and local influenza-activity trends to identify emerging problems?

A general discussion tying together the ideas generated from Decision 1 and Decision 2 follows, isolating ideas about the best surveillance, emergency response, and epidemiology investigations can be pursued. Lines of inquiry will extend to precautionary public measures designed to curtail or confine the spread of the virus and direct protective public actions and options. General emergency managers and planners should assess the degree to which key operational decisions, command and control issues, and options have been discussed and evaluated.

This is just a sample schematic to illustrate how basic and straightforward a tabletop design can be. Design must always be tailored to the experience level, technical challenges, and special demands reflected in the group undergoing the exercise.

Another key issue in exercise design and evaluation is to test and stress ordinary and complex liaison relationships between local government, state government, and other emergency assistance providers. This would include exercises to test the overall operations, functions, and decision-making behaviors of the Emergency Operations Center (EOC). Tabletop exercises can help pinpoint communication, coordination, and information sharing issues and possible problems, along with areas where staffing, employee training, and procedural guidance may be an issue.

In full-scale and functional exercises, the EOC is activated. That is, the officials and support staff assemble at a central location for the activity. The EOC provides a place where local government officials can do together what they cannot do separately and serves as a central coordinating point for major decisions about resolving the crisis. It is a place where all official problems, actions, and requirements can be voiced, displayed, and acted upon, and where decisions can be made to guide actions in the future. If an exercise is designed to test the functional performance of an EOC, the following tasks and functions can be assessed:

- Alert notification
- Account for response/recovery personnel
- Communications
- Telephone, radio, amateur radio connectivity/reliability
- Resource coordination and control
- EOC operations procedures, incident command guidance, mutual aid agreement
- Emergency public information
- Information generated from public prior to, during, and after emergency
- Damage assessment (infrastructural damage, private property, key transit zones)

Exercise evaluators need specific events and behaviors to monitor and assess, which is normally reflected in a comprehensive exercise design plan. Evaluators are looking at task performance, quality of response, teamwork, and innovation in problem solving. Here are some additional areas of focus:

- Completion of assigned tasks
- Identification of unfinished tasks
- Coordination of strengths/weaknesses
- Communication of strengths/weaknesses
- ICS issues and problems
- Individual, team, and leader performance
- Novel approaches/problem solving

Most often, emergency exercises have as their overall aim the examination of specific Emergency Support Functions (ESFs) and the performance of crucial tasks, which often are the responsibility of local emergency staff. Determining exactly what local versus state emergency personnel are expected to do and plan for is the best starting point for most exercises. These include the following:

a. Evacuation/sheltering
b. Mutual aid
c. Resource management
d. Emergency public information
e. Mass casualty care
f. Post-emergency recovery strategies

In sum, what matters most in emergency exercise design is having a firm grasp of your purposes and goals in conducting the exercise itself. Reinforcing staff performance of critical tasks, testing to see if staff can handle unexpected developments, and ascertaining whether existing plans and technologies actually work as intended are all essential foundations for a robust exercise program. This also requires the development of metrics that reflect the standard of emergency response expected by the public and that match the overall status of emergency management standard practices and procedures nationally for handling a wide variety of emergency situations.

REFERENCES AND RESOURCES

Alexander, D. 2003. "Towards the Development of Standards in Emergency Management Training and Education." *Disaster Prevention and Management* 12: 113–23.

Federal Emergency Management Agency. 2003. *IS–139 Exercise Design.* http://training.fema.gov/EMIWeb/IS/is139lst.asp (accessed January 17, 2009).

Gebbie, K., and J. Valas. 2006. *Planning, Designing, Conducting, and Evaluating Local Public Health Emergency Exercises* (New York: Columbia University Press).

Green, W., III. 2000. *Exercise Alternatives for Training Emergency Management Command Center Staffs* (Boca Raton, FL: Universal).

Homeland Security Exercise and Evaluation Program. (n.d.). *Mission and exercise types.* https://hseep.dhs.gov (accessed January 17, 2009).

Lurie, N., C. Nelson, and J. Wasserman. 2007. "Assessing Public Health Emergency Preparedness: Concepts, Tools, and Challenges." *Annual Review of Public Health* 28: 1–18.

40

HIGHER EDUCATION IN HOMELAND SECURITY: CURRENT STATE AND FUTURE TRENDS

Irmak Renda-Tanali, D.Sc.

Collegiate Associate Professor, Director of Homeland Security and Emergency Management Master's Programs, University of Maryland, University College

INTRODUCTION

The terror attacks of September 11, 2001 validated the necessity of developing a cadre of professionals in the federal, state, and local government sectors as well as the private and nonprofit sectors in order to prevent and prepare for new attacks on U.S. soil. Since then there has been a significant growth in the number of graduate and undergraduate degree programs in emergency management and homeland security. The existing programs dealing with emergency preparedness against natural and accidental hazards quickly added new curriculum to cover terrorism preparedness as well. Today there are over 300 academic degree programs claiming to offer homeland security education; in the form of an associate's, a bachelor's, a master's degree, or a certificate.[1]

This chapter covers some of the most important issues about homeland security education. Because of space limitations, only those that are key to understanding the current issues and key challenges are highlighted. Using current resources, I will attempt to find answers to the following questions:

- What constitutes homeland security education?
- What key competencies should the students gain?
- Who are the key players in homeland security education provision?
- What are the future challenges, and how can they be addressed?

To this date, there is no organization that has been recognized or certified by the U.S. Department of Education or the Council for Higher Education to perform the accrediting function for homeland security academic degree programs.[2] However, since its inception, Homeland Security/Defense Education Consortium (HSDEC) has acted as a coordinating body by engaging academia and other interested agencies through holding conferences, issuing a newsletter, and offering internship opportunities. HSDEC was established in December 2004 by U.S. Northern Command (USNORTHCOM) and North American Aerospace Defense Command (NORAD), in collaboration with the University of Colorado, Colorado Springs; the University of Denver; and the U.S. Naval Postgraduate School. Its initial purpose was to provide the required knowledge and skill sets to support the national homeland security/homeland defense (HS/HD) mission that were not readily available in either the military or civilian communities for the command personnel and its allies.[3] The USNORTHCOM partners include first responders, Title 32 National Guard forces, federal agencies, and various other partners from government and private communities.[4] However, the CHDS higher-education program—a graduate program designed around policy, practice, and program needs identified through empirical research—is available only to government officials at the federal, state, or local level and is not open to private sector workers.[5] Because the nation's critical infrastructures (including oil, natural gas, electricity, food, and agriculture) are largely owned and operated by the private industry, and their vulnerability to deliberate attacks or unintentional acts could pose a serious threat to the nation's security, there was an obvious need to educate a cadre of private sector representatives in matters of homeland security. Thus, many academic institutions quickly jumped into the bandwagon of filling this critical need—albeit without much guidance nor any guidance as to what should constitute their curricula.[6]

Later HSDEC took the lead role of building and maintaining a community of higher education by instituting a network among these teaching and research institutions focused on promoting education, research, and cooperation related to and supporting the homeland security and defense missions,[7] and it expanded its affiliation into more than 250 universities, colleges, and other interested agencies.[8] However, because of the expanding size of the affiliated organizations, in 2008, HSDEC leadership decided to convert HSDEC into a member-run professional society, such as the International Association of Emergency Managers (IAEM), and named it Homeland Security and Defense Education Consortium Association (HSDECA).[9]

Since then, HSDECA planted the seeds for the accreditation process by forming a committee to examine other major academic accreditation bodies, such as Accrediting Board for Engineering and Technology (ABET). However, to date, with respect to undergraduate and graduate degree programs in homeland security, a consensus on what should constitute a common body of knowledge does not exist.[10] No professional association has took charge to offer a vetted set of or a published set of program-level learning outcomes—that is, a curriculum in terms of knowledge, skills, and abilities that students acquire at the program level.[11] One reason for the lack of consensus is that homeland security is inherently complex, multidisciplinary and interdisciplinary, and extremely dynamic, reacting to current events and politics surrounding the nation and world affairs in general.

There has been an ongoing debate on whether the sister fields of Emergency Management and Homeland Security should be combined or exist as separate academic disciplines. The Federal Emergency Management's (FEMA) training arm Emergency Management Institute (EMI) has spearheaded the efforts in emergency management higher education for curriculum development and program accreditation. The National Fire Prevention Administration (NFPA) 1600,[12] EMI Higher Ed Principles,[13] EMI recommended undergraduate outcomes, and the Foundation for Higher Education Accreditation would all be a part of the efforts in terms of reconciliation of the both fields. We will elaborate further on this debate, keeping in mind that the jury is still out.

EXISTING FRAMEWORKS FOR HS CURRICULA OFFERINGS

Despite a lack of consensus on what should be the core curriculum requirements, there are currently several existing approaches that differentiate the various graduate or undergraduate degree programs that offer homeland security education. Jeremy Plant and colleagues classified the existing HS programs according to the following founding principles:[14]

- Programs that were built on existing theory and coursework in such fields as Emergency Management, Criminal Justice, Intelligence, International Relations, Public Administration, or other social science fields
- Programs that modeled their curriculum after that of the Naval Postgraduate School's (NPS) Center for Homeland Defense and Security (CHDS), the designated national leader in HS education by the Department of Homeland Security (DHS)
- Programs that consider HS as a new field and built their curriculum through a rich dialogue between practitioners and academicians.

Despite the variations in approaches, several researchers agree that the primary focus of HS education must be to produce public servants with a public service ethos, and citizens who embody civic virtues, and these principles should constitute the basis for a HS curriculum.[15] In the sections that follow, we discuss the details of existing approaches to offering undergraduate and graduate degrees in HS.

Undergraduate Studies

In 2008, Jim Ramsay and colleagues gathered a panel of experts from around the country using a Delphi technique where they iteratively developed a consensus on what should constitute a set of educational objectives, a set of core academic areas, and definitions for those areas that represent broad practices in HS and program-level outcomes for a baccalaureate level HS degree. The panel consisted of eight homeland security professionals with extensive educational and professional credentials across a wide range of topic areas including emergency management, homeland security law and policy, terrorism studies, critical infrastructure and risk analysis, state and federal law enforcement, strategic planning and operations, and homeland defense.[16] According to the study, the following eight core academic areas were identified that make up the core of an undergraduate degree in HS:[17]

1. Intelligence
2. Law and Policy
3. Emergency Management

4. Risk Analysis
5. Critical Infrastructure
6. Strategic Planning
7. Terrorism, and
8. Environmental Security

The same team identified the following program outcomes for students who possess an undergraduate degree in HS:[18]

1. *Real-world experience.* Ability to apply HS concepts in nonacademic settings through an internship, cooperative, or supervised experience to include real-world experiences, strategies, and objectives.
2. *Professional ethics.* Possess an understanding of professional ethics and how they apply in the field of HS.
3. *Analytical skills.* Capability to utilize and evaluate analytical data applicable to HS.
4. *Research skills.* Demonstrate the ability to conduct research, compose a research paper, and deliver professional presentations and briefings in order to develop and refine analytical abilities.
5. *Technology fluency.* Identify, describe, and critically evaluate applicable HS technologies.
6. *Effective communication.* Demonstrate effective communication, especially in ways applicable to HS (e.g., policy analysis, briefings, strategic or risk communications)
7. *Teamwork.* Ability to work in teams
8. *Vision.* Knowledge of contemporary or emergency threats, challenges, or issues.

As for the mode of delivery, several experts agree that an undergraduate degree requires mainly a face-to-face learning mode with a traditional campus setting but can be supported with online components.[19]

In another consensus-seeking gathering, in June 2009, through what is called CHDS Model Curriculum Conference, selected members of the CHDS University and Agency Partnership Initiative made a concentrated effort to establish a baseline for what all programs should include to prepare new and current homeland security practitioners for the complex and overlapping components of the homeland security profession. The 11 main focus areas determined in the Model Curriculum Conference with focus areas are given in Box 40-1.[20]

Box 40-1

The 11 Areas
of Focus for
Undergraduate
Homeland Security
Education

Source: Persyn and
Polson, 2012

1. **Administering Homeland Security**
   a. Leadership and management: definitions, differences, and application (case studies)
   b. Homeland security financial aspects: budgets, planning, and grants
   c. Homeland security logistics
   d. Human resources and personnel management
   e. Organizational behavior
   f. Public administration in homeland security
   g. Current homeland security mechanisms

2. **Intelligence**
   a. Intelligence Community history and evolution
   b. Intelligence Community current structure and capabilities
   c. State and local intelligence capabilities
   d. The intelligence cycle
   e. Counterintelligence
   f. Covert or clandestine activities

3. **Public and Private Sector Partnerships**
   a. Private sector role in homeland security
   b. Public–private partnerships
   c. Private sector motivations
   d. Business continuity and resilience
   e. Public relations and public education
   f. Private sector role in planning
   g. Public versus private sector organizational functions

4. **Research and Analysis**
   a. Information literacy, collection, and management
   b. Theory awareness and application
   c. Inductive and deductive reasoning
   d. Applied statistics
   e. Spatial analysis and geographic information systems
   f. Evaluation research
   g. Quantitative and qualitative analyses

5. Emergency Management

a. All-hazards approach: natural and unintentional human caused

b. Definitions of important terms: emergency, catastrophe, disaster, hazards, threats, prevention, mitigation, preparedness, response, recovery, continuity of operations and government, delegation, accountability, and communications

c. Types and history of hazards (natural and human caused)

d. Land-use planning and resilient community design

e. Developing preparedness and instilling residence

f. Risk and its components: hazards, threats, vulnerabilities, consequences, and probability

   a) Conduct risk assessments using a variety of methods

   b) Apply risk-management perspectives in the context of federal, state, local, and private sector applications

g. Special and vulnerable population needs (homeless, disabled, pets, and others)

h. Exercise and evaluation programs

i. Employing technology (e.g., geographic information systems, communications, remote sensing, other)

j. Budgeting, grants, and management

6. Critical infrastructure (and Its Protection)

a. Critical infrastructure (CI) and key resources (KR) and interdependencies

b. Strategies, policies, programs, and agencies involved in CI/KR

c. Critical components in CI/KR within a context (local, state, federal, national, or business sector)

d. Global security threats and hazards impacting CI components

e. Required performance or level of protection of CI/KR in prevention, mitigation, response, and recovery to security threats and natural or human-caused hazards

f. Organizational, engineering, procedural, security, and response methods to achieve levels of protection

    g. Scalable assessment methodologies for micro- and macro-level risk at all levels

    h. Financial and operational relationships between critical infrastructure protection and business

7. **Strategic Planning**

    a. Integrated planning systems

    b. Disaster planning models for local, state, international, and private sectors

       a) Risk-based and scenario-based planning

       b) Deliberate and crisis-action planning

       c) Interagency and interorganizational coordination and planning

       d) Ties to the grant process (leveraging resources)

       e) National Incident Management System, Incident Command System, National Infrastructure Protection Plan, and National Response Framework

8. **Strategic Planning**

    a. Risk communication

    b. Cultural awareness and audience identification

    c. Communication planning and synchronization of messages

    d. Interoperability of messaging and strategies

    e. Role of the media

    f. Agencies and organizations (local, tribal, state, federal, and international)

    g. Public affairs, education, emergency communication

    h. Means and technology issues and challenges

    i. Community outreach

9. **Law and Policy**

    a. Society and civics

    b. Constitutional law, principles, and federalism

    c. Current government agencies, private agencies, and organizational structures

    d. Major statutes, executive directives, and orders

    e. National strategies

f. Regional, state, and local policies and strategies

g. International treaties, obligations, and cooperative efforts

h. Sector-specific laws and authorities

i. Civil–military relations

j. Policymaking process and analysis

k. Administrative law and regulatory processes

10. **Technology and Systems**

a. Role of technology in homeland security

b. Types of technology used in homeland security

c. Approaches to framing technology

d. Ethical and privacy considerations

e. Technology and development cycle

f. Network and cyber infrastructure protection

g. Consequences (unintended and intended)

h. Limitations and interoperability

11. **Terrorism: Causes and Consequences**

e. Definitions and distinctions

f. History, root causes, motivations, grievances

g. Theories of who joins or supports terror groups (radicalization and extremism)

h. How terror groups operate (tactics, organization, support)

i. Role of the media and Internet

j. Effects of terrorism

k. Counterterrorism (resources, application, policies), including military roles in counterterrorism

Graduate Studies   Christopher Bellavita and Ellen Gordon reviewed the principal themes presented by leading universities, agencies, and textbook publishers in an effort to conceptualize the core areas that graduate HS students should know. They identified 50 core subjects that come under the rubric of HS that they thought did not converge on any dominant paradigm. Bellavita and Gordon's perspective was of the NPS, and their student body consisted of mid- and senior-level government officials that hold positions related to HS (e.g., law enforcement, fire services, public health, emergency management, and other disciplines including HS). The overwhelming majority of their students are civilians who are oriented more toward practice than to theory, to applied knowledge rather than analysis. They assumed that the students were participants in the course rather than an audience for what they have to deliver.[21] Thus, in order to effectively teach the core concepts of HS to this group, Bellavita and Gordon came up with six *lines of inquiry* that allow students to explore the multiple dimensions that make up homeland security. The Lines of Inquiry they use are as follows:[22]

1. *Homeland security basics.* Consists of the minimum knowledge an educated homeland security professional should know. This includes:
   a. Events, incidents, and forces that shaped homeland security (e.g., National Strategy for Homeland Security and other strategies that support and complement homeland security)
   b. The relationship between state and local homeland security strategies and the National Strategy, as well as the structure of homeland security in the United States from the perspective of federalism
   c. The basic statutes that shape homeland security's legal terrain
   d. The contents of homeland security Presidential Decision Directives (HSPDDs)
   e. The national guidelines and procedures that structure how homeland security strategy and policy are implemented
   f. The reports and other documents that have significantly influenced the homeland security debate about policy and strategy
   g. How homeland security resources are allocated
   h. Terms used in the "discipline" of homeland security
2. *The mission.* Preventing terrorism, why and how?
3. *Strategies.* Options for accomplishing the mission
4. *Frameworks.* How things actually happen in the world, including information about the environmental variables such as personal, techno/rational, economic, legal, organizational, political, cultural, information, decision making, change, network, and leadership

5. *Leadership.* Especially in a networked, nonhierarchical, multiagency, multisector, multiprofessional environment where command and control does not operate very effectively.

6. *Learning.* How experiences can continuously be transformed into homeland security knowledge. This element underscores the need for lifelong learning in homeland security.

In graduate programs, there are three primary focus areas: teaching, research, and service.[23] One crucial role for graduate education is the preparation and training of new teachers and educators; however, since there are currently not many doctoral degree programs offered in homeland security, schools rely upon borrowing key faculty from related areas like International Relations, Security Studies, Geography, Political Science, Engineering, Criminal Justice, Public Health, and other fields.[24]

Students in graduate homeland security programs should study basic and applied research where they should become familiarized with qualitative and quantitative research methods, statistical analysis, and scientific writing courses. Advanced seminar coursework, theses, and dissertations provide the ability to conduct research.[25]

In summary, the following should constitute the roles and objectives for a graduate homeland security education:[26]

1. Scholarly development of a cumulative body of knowledge (including methods, techniques and theories) and advancement of homeland security as an academic discipline and professional field

2. Supporting of the professional development of specialists, technicians, analysts, and first responders (fire, law enforcement, and medical)

3. Preparation of students for additional advanced degree programs, workforce entry, or job promotion

4. Preparation and training of new educators and instructors

An overarching key competence that students of homeland security should acquire is critical thinking skills where students learn through problem solving, discussions, and critical inquiries. Students should not only think through the problems but also gather and analyze data for possible solutions.[27] Collins and Peerbolte stress the importance of integrating critical thinking skills into the homeland security curricula. They suggest that the following five critical thinking skills areas should be applicable to professionals who would be employed in homeland security and related fields:[28]

1. *Making inferences.* Being able to make decisions based on what one already knows

2. *Recognition of assumptions.* Differentiating between facts and assumptions

3. *Deductive reasoning.* Being able to make decisions based on the information given within specific statements or premises

4. *Interpretation.* Being able to weigh evidence of given data and determine appropriate generalizations

5. *Evaluation of arguments.* Being able to recognize faulty assumptions and weak arguments usually based on a number of assertive statements.

Research Needs

The advancement of the field requires the creation of new knowledge through basic and applied research and through the dissemination of the knowledge generated. Homeland security education should emphasize research skills, thus research opportunities should be provided to students and faculty. Today, the federal government is the leading provider of research funds concerning homeland security research. The major departments that act as funding sources are the Department of Defense, Homeland Security, Health and Human Services, Justice, and Agriculture. Major agencies that provide research funding include Environmental Protection and Central Intelligence. These federal departments and agencies usually leverage the existing Federally Funded Research and Development Centers (FFRDCs) and national laboratories for the advancement of research.[29]

One FFRDC is the Homeland Security Systems Engineering and Development Institute (HS SEDITM), which is operated by the MITRE Corporation. HS SEDI provides systems engineering, acquisition, and program management expertise in support of the overall homeland security mission.[30] Another one is the Homeland Security Studies and Analysis Institute (HSSAI), operated by Analytic Services, Inc., providing independent analysis of homeland security issues such as cross-cutting mission analyses, strategic studies and assessments, development of simulations and technical evaluations to evaluate mission trade-offs, and operational analysis across the homeland security enterprise, to name a few.[31]

The national laboratories include the DHS laboratories, which are Chemical Security Analysis Center,[32] National Biodefense Analysis and Countermeasures Center,[33] National Urban Security Technology Laboratory,[34] Plum Island Animal Disease Center,[35] and the Transportation Security Laboratory;[36] laboratories that are operated under the Department of Energy's National Nuclear Security Administration, which include Lawrence Livermore National Laboratory,[37] Los Alamos National Laboratory,[38] and Sandia National Laboratory;[39] and those under the Department of Energy Office of Science, such as Argonne National Laboratory,[40] Brookhaven National Laboratory,[41] Oak Ridge National Laboratory,[42] Pacific Northwest National Laboratory,[43] Idaho National Laboratory,[44] and others.

Additionally, the University Centers of Excellence established through the Homeland Security Act of 2002 under the Department of Homeland Security's Office of Science and Technology Directorate serve the provision of critical research needs. The purpose of these centers is to establish a coordinated, university-based system to enhance the nation's homeland security.[45] Managed through the Department of Homeland Security's Office of Science and Technology Directorate Office of University Programs, the Centers of Excellence are lead by one main university but consist of participating other universities and academic institutions, agencies, national laboratories, think tanks, and the private sector. Each Center of Excellence conducts multidisciplinary homeland security research and education with differing focus areas.[46] All Centers of Excellence work closely with academia, private sector, agencies affiliated with the Department of Homeland Security, and first-responders to develop solutions to specific problems as well as to provide training to the next generation of homeland security specialists.[47] The types of research conducted by the Centers of Excellence are a "mix of basic and applied research addressing both short- and long-term needs, and applicable to rapid response efforts."[48] Every year these Centers of Excellence showcase their research findings at an annual summit held in Washington, DC, demonstrate their prototype products, and share the results of their research for feedback and debate, as well as to find avenues for further collaboration. Although these centers compose the most concrete platform for integrating academia, the private sector, and the federal government in support of homeland security, there are two fundamental questions raised by the critics: (1) in the long term will the strong motivation continue for these synergistic relationships to survive and continue to help overcome (the sectors') administrative and functional differences, or will the motivation cease to exist? and (2) will real integration occur given the challenges of having so many different types of players whose cooperation, successes, or failures can put the success of the entire Centers of Excellence at risk?[49]

See Box 40-2 for a listing of the Centers of Excellence.

Box 40-2

Centers of
Excellence

*Source: Department
of Homeland
Security* http://
www.dhs.gov/
files/programs/
editorial_0498.shtm

There are currently 12 Centers of Excellence across the country.

- The **Center for Risk and Economic Analysis of Terrorism Events (CREATE),** led by the University of Southern California, develops advanced tools to evaluate the risks, costs, and consequences of terrorism.
- The **Center for Advancing Microbial Risk Assessment (CAMRA),** led by Michigan State University and Drexel University established jointly with the U.S. Environmental Protection Agency, fills critical gaps in risk assessments for mitigating microbial hazards.
- The **Center of Excellence for Zoonotic and Animal Disease Defense (ZADD),** led by Texas A&M University and Kansas State University, protects the nation's agricultural and public health sectors against high-consequence foreign animal, emerging, and zoonotic disease threats.
- The **National Center for Food Protection and Defense (NCFPD),** led by the University of Minnesota, defends the safety and security of the food system by conducting research to protect vulnerabilities in the nation's food supply chain.
- The **National Consortium for the Study of Terrorism and Responses to Terrorism (START),** led by the University of Maryland, informs decisions on how to disrupt terrorists and terrorist groups through empirically grounded findings on the human element of the terrorist threat.
- The **National Center for the Study of Preparedness and Catastrophic Event Response (PACER),** led by Johns Hopkins University, optimizes our nation's preparedness in the event of a high-consequence natural or man-made disaster.

- The **Center of Excellence for Awareness & Location of Explosives-Related Threats (ALERT),** led by Northeastern University and the University of Rhode Island, will develop new means and methods to protect the nation from explosives-related threats.

- The **National Center for Border Security and Immigration (NCBSI)**, led by the University of Arizona in Tucson (research co-lead) and the University of Texas at El Paso (education co-lead), are developing technologies, tools, and advanced methods to balance immigration and commerce with effective border security.

- The **Center for Maritime, Island and Remotes and Extreme Environment Security (MIREES)**, led by the University of Hawaii and Stevens Institute of Technology, focuses on developing robust research and education programs addressing maritime domain awareness to safeguard populations and properties in geographical areas that present significant security challenges.

- The **Coastal Hazards Center of Excellence (CHC)**, led by the University of North Carolina at Chapel Hill and Jackson State University in Jackson, Mississippi, performs research and develops education programs to enhance the nation's ability to safeguard populations, properties, and economies from catastrophic natural disaster.

- The **National Transportation Security Center of Excellence (NTSCOE)** was established in accordance with HR1, Implementing the Recommendations of the 9/11 Commission Act of 2007, in August 2007. The NTSCOE will develop new technologies, tools, and advanced methods to defend, protect, and increase the resilience of the nation's multimodal transportation. It comprises seven institutions:
  - Connecticut Transportation Institute at the University of Connecticut
  - Tougaloo College
  - Texas Southern University
  - National Transit Institute at Rutgers – the State University of New Jersey

> - o Homeland Security Management Institute at Long Island University
> - o Mack Blackwell National Rural Transportation Study Center at the University of Arkansas
> - o Mineta Transportation Institute at San José State University
> - • The **Center of Excellence in Command, Control and Inter-operability (C2I),** led by Purdue University (visualization sciences co-lead) and Rutgers University (data sciences co-lead), will create the scientific basis and enduring technologies needed to analyze massive amounts of information to detect security threats.

Future Challenges and Opportunities

Robert McCreight raised the following questions concerning the future of homeland security and emergency management education:[50]

- • How do we adequately prepare future generations for these fields?
- • What is the touchstone for ensuring competency in both fields?
- • How do we rectify and reconcile curriculum variation in both fields?
- • What constitutes bona fide professional education for both fields?

There is a common desire to balance a pragmatic "all-hazards" education with an educational program that targets enhancing terrorism prevention, preparedness, and response. Many urban cities face emergency management and homeland security issues on an everyday basis, and given the limited public funds, the preparedness efforts should not be geared toward specific types of threats and incidences but should consider the duality of the nuanced risks such as plane crashes, mass casualty events, subway accidents, and related crises regardless of whether intentionally or unintentionally induced.[51] This "double indemnity" should be at the core of education programs concerning homeland security.

Additionally, while the federal government has the responsibility to rein in the necessary resources for catastrophic events and/or crises that have national significance such as terrorist attacks aiming at our homeland, our allies, and our citizens overseas, the states and cities must be capable of managing the incidents at the waterfront.

This requires that local governments have the requisite skills, training, equipment, technology, and all the other resources for at least the first three days of a major incident before federal resources are fully deployed.[52] The dualism in the U.S. public administration system gives unique powers and authority to governors and state leaders under Article 10 of our Constitution in determining their own strategic options for strategies for survival. And each state has its unique sets of hazards and risks that require different approaches and differing sets of resources for solutions. That is one of the challenges for the homeland security education as well. The lack of a common core curriculum across the various homeland security degree programs spread across different geographical regions of the nation stems from the vast variations in the hazards and legal frameworks.

McCreight outlines the following four major unanswered issues that may challenge the fields for years to come:[53]

1. Under what circumstances, and for what mutually reinforcing benefits, should the fields of HS and EM be eventually merged academically to enrich the educational perspectives of both camps and help professionalize both fields?

2. Given our unique constitutional requirements under Article X, which authorizes state governors to act with powerful autonomy in terms of protecting their populations in nationally catastrophic situations, how significant is it that each state should pursue a robust, redundant, all-hazards response and recovery system totally independent of any requirements from Washington or the federal government?

3. How important is it that the fields of HS and EM attain professional recognition as an interdisciplinary career in both the public and private sectors by the year 2020? What steps must be taken to bring the business/industrial/commercial community into the fold?

4. What specific obligations and responsibilities does the United States have to coordinate and lead a truly global effort to construct a reliable and robust international system of common education and interoperable technologies in order to foster professional development and create a deployable cadre of all-hazards experts and teams to respond to any disaster or crisis anywhere in the globe?

There is a seeming movement for the fields of homeland security and emergency management eventually to come together. This highly debatable issue is reflected in the fact that the senior management of the HSDECA is taking a homeland security track to the Emergency Management Institute (EMI) Higher Education Conference in 2012 the first time, and that FEMA is implementing NPGS/CHS curriculum in its executive development curriculum points to a potential for possible merging at least in higher education (as of April 2012).

ACKNOWLEDGEMENTS

The author would like to thank Mr. Stephen S. Carter for his review and valuable feedback on this chapter.

BIBLIOGRAPHY

Bellavita, Christopher, and Ellen M. Gordon. "Changing Homeland Security: Teaching the Core." *Homeland Security Affairs* II, no. 1 (2006): Article 1.

Bullock, Jane, Goerge Haddow, Damon Coppola, and Sarp Yeletaysi. *Introduction to Homeland Security.* 3rd ed. Burlington: Elsevier, 2009.

Clement, Keith E. "The Essentials of Emergency Management and Homeland Security Graduate Education Programs: Design, Development, and Future." *Journal of Homeland Security and Emergency Management* (Degruyter) 8, no. 2 (2011): Article 12.

Collins, Matthew L., and Stacy L. Peerbolte. "An Exploratory Research Design Further Demonstrating the Need for the Integration of Critical Thinking Skill Curricula in Homeland Security and Emergency Management Higher Education Academic Programs." *Journal of Homeland Security and Emergency Management* (DeGruyter) 8, no. 2 (2011): Article 4.

Donahue Jr., Donald, Stephen O. Cunnion, Carey D. Balaban, and Ken Sochats. "Meeting Educational Challenges in Homeland Security and Emergency Management." *Journal of Homeland Security and Emergency Management* (DeGruyter) 7, no. 1 (2010): Article 19.

FEMA. *FEMA Higher Education Emergency Management Principles.* 2008. http://training.fema.gov/EMIWeb/edu/emprinciples.asp (accessed April 2, 2012).

Henkey, Thomas. "Sociology and the National Incident Management System (NIMS): Oil and Water?" *Journal of Homeland Security and Emergency Management* (DeGruyter) 8, no. 2 (2011): Article 15.

Jackson, Brian. "A Table-Top Game to Teach Technological and Tactical Planning in a Graduate Terrorism and Counterterrorism Course." *Journal of Homeland Security and Emergency Management* (DeGruyter) 8, no. 2 (2011): Article 3.

Kiltz, Linda. "Civic Mission of HS Education: A Response to McCreight." *Journal of Homeland Security and Emergency Management* (DeGruyter) 6, no. 1 (2009): Article 57.

Kiltz, Linda. "Developing Critical Thinking Skills in Homeland Security and Emergency Management Courses." *Journal of Homeland Security and Emergency Management* (DeGruyter) 6, no. 1 (2009): Article 36.

Kiltz, Linda. "The Challenges of Developing a Homeland Security Discipline to Meet Future Threats to the Homeland." *Journal of Homeland Security and Emergency Management* (DeGruyter) 8, no. 2 (2011): Article 1.

McCreight, Robert. "Educational Challenges in Homeland Security and Emergency Management." *Journal of Homeland Security and Emergency Management* (DeGruyter) 6, no. 1 (2009): Article 34.

McCreight, Robert. "Introduction to Journal of Homeland Security and Emergency Management Special Issue." *Journal of Homeland Security and Emergency Management* (DeGruyter), 2011: Article 5.

Persyn, John, and Cheryl Polson. "Foundations of Homeland Security Education." In *Introduction to Homeland Security*, Keith Gregory Logan and James D. Ramsay, 365–377. Boulder, CO: Westview Press, 2012.

Plant, Jeremy, Thomas Arminio, and Paul Thompson. "A Matrix Approach to Homeland Security Professional Education." *Journal of Homeland Security and Emergency Management* (DeGruyter), 2011: Article 8.

Ramsay, Jim, Daniel Cutrer, and Robert Raffel. "Development of an Outcomes-Based Undergraduate Curriculum in Homeland Security." *Homeland Security Affairs* VI, no. 2 (May 2010): 1–20.

Stewart, Todd. "Academe and Homeland Security." Chapter 55 in *The McGraw-Hill Homeland Security Handbook: The Definitive Guide for Law Enforcement, EMT, and All Other Security Professionals*, edited by David G. Kamien, 865–897. New York: McGraw-Hill, 2005.

Technical Committee on Emergency Management and Business Continuity. *NFPA 1600 – Standard of Disaster/Emergency Management and Business Continuity Programs.* Standards, NFPA, 2007.

USNORTHCOM. *United States Northern Command.* n.d. http://www.northcom.mil/about/history_education/history.html (accessed March 10, 2012).

Wallace, Donald, Craig McLean, William H Parrish, Sarah Soppitt, and Daniel Silander. "Transnational and Comparative Curricular Offerings in U.S. Post-Baccalaurate Programs: Benchmarking a Link from the US to the EU in Homeland Security Education." *Journal of Homeland Security and Emergency Management* (DeGruyter) 8, no. 2 (2011): Article 13.

NOTES

1. Donald Donahue Jr., Stephen O. Cunnion, Carey D. Balaban, and Ken Sochats, "Meeting Educational Challenges in Homeland Security and Emergency Management," *Journal of Homeland Security and Emergency Management* (DeGruyter) 7, no. 1 (2010): Article 19.

2. Jim Ramsay, Daniel Cutrer, and Robert Raffel, "Development of an Outcomes-Based Undergraduate Curriculum in Homeland Security," *Homeland Security Affairs* VI, no. 2 (May 2010): 1–20.

3. Ramsey et al., "Development of an Outcomes-Based Undergraduate Curriculum in Homeland Security"; USNORTHCOM, n.d.

4. Ramsey et al., "Development of Outcomes-Based Undergraduate Curriculum."

5. John Persyn and Cheryl Polson, "Foundations of Homeland Security Education," in *Introduction to Homeland Security*, Keith Gregory Logan and James D. Ramsay (Boulder, CO: Westview Press, 2012), 365–77.

6. Ibid.

7. USNORTHCOM, n.d.

8. Ramsey et al., "Outcomes-Based Undergraduate Curriculum."

9. Ibid.

10. Todd Stewart, "Academe and Homeland Security." Chapter 55 in *The McGraw-Hill Homeland Security Handbook: The Definitive Guide for Law Enforcement, EMT, and All Other Security Professionals*, David G. Kamien, ed. (New York: McGraw-Hill, 2005), 865–97; Robert McCreight, "Educational Challenges in Homeland Security and Emergency Management," *Journal of Homeland Security and Emergency Management* (DeGruyter) 6, no. 1 (2009): Article 34; Christopher Bellavita and Ellen M. Gordon, "Changing Homeland Security: Teaching the Core," *Homeland Security Affairs* II, no. 1 (2006): Article 1; Ramsay, Cutrer, and Raffel, "Development of an Outcomes-Based Undergraduate Curriculum in Homeland Security," *Homeland Security Affairs* VI, no. 2 (May 2010): 1–20.

11. Ramsay et al., "Outcomes-Based Undergraduate Curriculum."

12. Technical Committee on Emergency Management and Business Continuity, NFPA 1600-Standard of Disaster/Emergency Management and Business Continuity Programs, Standards, NFPA, 2007 (Technical Committee on Emergency Management and Business Continuity).

13. FEMA, *FEMA Higher Education Emergency Management Principles*, 2008, http://training.fema.gov/EMIWeb/edu/emprinciples.asp (accessed 4 2, 2012).

14. Jeremy Plant, Thomas Arminio, and Paul Thompson, "A Matrix Approach to Homeland Security Professional Education," *Journal of Homeland Security and Emergency Management* (DeGruyter), 2011: Article 8.

15. Linda Kiltz, "Civic Mission of HS Education: A Response to McCreight," *Journal of Homeland Security and Emergency Management* (DeGruyter) 6, no. 1 (2009): Article 57; Keith E. Clement, "The Essentials of Emergency Management and Homeland Security Graduate Education Programs: Design, Development, and Future," *Journal of Homeland Security and Emergency Management* (Degruyter) 8, no. 2 (2011): Article 12.

16. Ramsey et al., *Outcomes-Based Undergraduate Curriculum,* 7.

17. Ibid.

18. Ibid.

19. Donahue Jr. et al., 2010; Bellavita and Gordon, 2006; Ramsay et al., 2010.

20. Persyn and Polson, "Foundations of Homeland Security Education," 2.

21. Bellavita and Gordon, 2006, p. 3

22. Ibid.

23. Clement, 2011.

24. Ibid.

25. Ibid.

26. Ibid., 3

27. Linda Kiltz, "Developing Critical Thinking Skills in Homeland Security and Emergency Management Courses," *Journal of Homeland Security and Emergency Management* (DeGruyter) 6, no. 1 (2009): Article 36.

28. Matthew L. Collins and Stacy L. Peerbolte, "An Exploratory Research Design Further Demonstrating the Need for the Integration of Critical Thinking Skill Curricula in Homeland Security and Emergency Management Higher Education Academic Programs," *Journal of Homeland Security and Emergency Management* (DeGruyter) 8, no. 2 (2011): Article 4.

29. Todd Stewart, "Academe and Homeland Security," Chapter 55 in *The McGraw-Hill Homeland Security Handbook: The Definitive Guide for Law Enforcement, EMT, and All Other Security Professionals*, David G. Kamien, ed. (New York: McGraw-Hill, 2005), 65–897.

30. Homeland Security Systems Engineering and Development Institute, http://www.dhs.gov/xabout/structure/gc_1257350352029.shtm.

31. Homeland Security Studies and Analysis Institute, http://www.dhs.gov/xabout/structure/gc_1264778964330.shtm.

32. Chemical Security Analysis Center, http://www.dhs.gov/files/labs/gc_1225399127004.shtm.

33. National Biodefense Analysis and Countermeasures Center, http://www.dhs.gov/files/labs/gc_1166211221830.shtm.

34. National Urban Security Technology Laboratory, http://www.dhs.gov/files/labs/gc_1223664506703.shtm.

35. Plum Island Animal Disease Center, http://www.dhs.gov/files/labs/editorial_0901.shtm.

36. Transportation Security Laboratory, http://www.dhs.gov/files/labs/editorial_0903.shtm.

37. Lawrence Livermore National Laboratory, https://www.llnl.gov/.

38. Los Alamos National Laboratory, http://www.lanl.gov/.

39. Sandia National Laboratory, http://www.sandia.gov/.

40. Argonne National Laboratory, http://www.anl.gov/.

41. Brookhaven National Laboratory, http://www.bnl.gov/world/.

42. Oak Ridge National Laboratory, http://www.ornl.gov/.

43. Pacific Northwest National Laboratory, http://www.pnl.gov/.

44. Idaho National Laboratory, https://inlportal.inl.gov/portal/server.pt/community/home / 255.

45. Homeland Security Centers of Excellence, http://www.dhs.gov/files/programs/editorial_0498.shtm.

46. Ibid.

47. Ibid.

48. Ibid.

49. Jane Bullock, Goerge Haddow, Damon Coppola, and Sarp Yeletaysi, *Introduction to Homeland Security*, 3rd ed. (Burlington: Elsevier, 2009).

50. Robert McCreight, "Introduction to Journal of Homeland Security and Emergency Management Special Issue," *Journal of Homeland Security and Emergency Management* (DeGruyter), 2011: Article 5.

51. Ibid.

52. Ibid.

53. Ibid.

9

INTRODUCTION TO PART IX: SCIENCE AND TECHNOLOGY

John G. Voeller

Senior VP, Black & Veatch

Since the publication of the first edition of the *Handbook,* a vast array of changes have occurred in everything from the definition of homeland security, to the areas of emphasis and investment to the knowledge of our adversaries (human and natural), to the attitude of the public and stakeholders about all things related to the concept of security.

For some, homeland security began with 9/11, but for those better informed, the entire realm of dealing with events that could damage the people, property, stability, and structure of this nation began decades before the planes hit. What did start after 9/11 was the collaborative education of different portions of our expert and novice populations to understand how we needed to change to deal with tomorrow. That education is continuing 24×7, not from a static knowledge set but from a very dynamic collection of events, observations, interpretations, politics, and interactions that all feed a massive knowledge base we must use well to develop and execute value-added actions with one simple goal: *to ensure that we do not expend any more human, social, or financial resources on dealing with significant events or their aftermaths than necessary.*

This goal may not sound anything like the "get bin Laden and al Qaida" or "protect everything critical" or any of the other chants heard soon after 9/11 but it captures a massive evolution the nation, its people, and those tasked with "homeland security" have undergone.

Predictably, this evolution started with security as the primary if not sole focus. We listed all the sectors, decided what was critical and set about demanding that everyone do everything to secure things and people. This quickly illuminated how difficult it was to secure many things, how impossible it was to secure everything and how difficult it was to select what was "critical." Thus, the evolution moved to assume an attack and focus on protection. But again, the adversary could not attack everything so the probability of any one asset or group being damaged was so small that protection choices led many with major assets to feel it was not worth overt protection beyond good business practice. The evolution of response and recovery was largely one of over-emphasizing investment in these areas to the level where one small town took their new $280,000 rescue truck and placed it on a stand with flowers around it for all to admire as they were sure it would never be used. Much of this was not a response to homeland security as it was a political response to the opportunity to distribute Federal money widely in a benevolent form. Reconstruction/reconstitution did not evolve as it sounded like what the average post-disaster relief did so assumed already handled.

No one doubted these areas were each important and no one doubted that the state of the art of the time was not as good as could be done so investment in science and technology made imminent sense. Such investment ranged from detecting explosives to surveillance film recognition and situation interpretation, to terahertz-based through-the-wall vision to first-responder gear to save their lives and allow them to save others better. However, as the interpretation of homeland security and its points of emphasis shifted, the race to keep up with the internal changes in focus was completely asynchronous with a coherent long-term research plan and it is impossible to get task, mount a team, research what is needed and deliver a commercial product in the year or less than some of these changes in emphasis lasted. Much of this was not foreseeable when the 1st Edition was written. However, the next stages of the evolution of homeland security from the public to the federal agencies showed the first stages and their learning was being used to focus on more valuable efforts.

In the last two years, the understanding of the prior evolution stages and their limitations moved homeland security stakeholders to focus on resilience. Resilience is another one of those easy to misinterpret multi-syllable words we wrestle with but it is a very good word because its companion word is realism. That realism recognizes you cannot find every actor before they act, you cannot protect everything, you cannot respond until damage has happened, you cannot recover everything and the more effort expended to do the prior acts, the less you will have to reconstruct/reconstitute what you have lost. The realism of resilience is that you can expend effort in a controlled manner to improve the chances of a person escaping a collapsing building regardless of what caused the collapse. You can improve the chances that a bridge will still "bridge" after a catastrophic event. And you can inform and coordinate those trying to help those impacted by a major event in modern ways if you can enable the communications systems to be available during or soon after an upset condition.

Because the addition of resilience to existing assets and systems is often agnostic about the perpetrating event, it has a much higher likelihood of use and therefore much higher probability of return on investment on several levels. Resilience does not care if a hurricane or a bomb or an overload condition is stressing a building's beams but rather attempts to provide reasonable and cost-effective ways to deal with upset conditions without catastrophic failure or loss of life.

And because of this agnostic view, the adoption of measures to address resilience may be much more acceptable as investments in a way the prior evolutions of homeland security emphasis had trouble achieving except in special sectors like cyber. It is with this perspective that science and technology related to homeland security becomes a more interesting area for companies to invest in providing solutions and where the finding of those solutions will likely be undertaken by much larger audiences so that the skills of "foraging" described in this section will be critical.

Homeland security is not easy to understand, is nearly impossible to execute well or fully, and is difficult to get many to discuss because it includes images of terrible events and palpable disappointment that others could commit acts that repel positive members of society. The science and technology for homeland security was critical from day one, however you choose that day. But it is even more critical today and in the future because of two key elements not present at 9/11.

First, with the rise of the developing nations to full economic and governance partners, we see much more vividly how interconnected and interdependent we are as a world and therefore how much greater the map of our vulnerability is than we saw between 9/11 and the 2008 economic collapse. The latter event opened a whole new realm of threats and risks that are now clearly planted in most persons' minds around the world and makes learning about other risks from human misbehavior or governmental protection failures more tangible than ever before. We as a planet now feel or sense more risks or threats from climate and weather impact to identity theft to supply chain interruption and so much more than ever and (Science & Technology) can play a part of helping us find solutions or mitigation measures if supported.

The second reason S&T is important to the newest evolution of our understanding of homeland security is our lack of capacity to deal with major disruptive events. The 2008 financial collapse around the world and the ongoing illumination of consequences and their aftermaths has limited the resources we have to address catastrophic events. Who would have ever believed that a thing called a CDO could collapse much of the world's finances in a way that no natural or human action could have come close to causing. Who would have ever believed Wall Street housed such a WMD. But this "WMD" and others like it removed our collective ability to deal with any more than a limited number of major catastrophic events in any region and a different but equally limited number of such events at the nation-state level.

Science and Technology writ large from little devices to major socio-economic analysis results holds promise to minimize the demands that overt human, unpredictable but certain to occur natural and purely accidental events will visit on society. This section discusses the history of the HS-evolution and what S&T has done and could do and provides explicit examples of the diversity of expertise S&T can bring to us.

The one question we may want to ask as readers is where do I find a map of all these old and new threats and how many of these has our collective national and international bodies of S&T addressed or have plans to do so. No such shared body of knowledge that all relevant organizations can utilize exists—but it might be good to start one soon.

41

INFORMATION TECHNOLOGY AND INFORMATION SHARING

Donald S. Adams

Vice President, Chief Security Officer, and
Chief Technology Officer, Worldwide Government
TIBCO Software Inc.

EXECUTIVE OVERVIEW

In the five years since the first edition of this book, much has transpired in both information technology and in homeland security. While homeland security has been rapidly adopting many of the topics that were covered in the previous edition, technology has also been advancing on a very rapid curve. No longer are the technologies of the twentieth century adequate to the challenges of the twenty-first century.

In this section, we will first review some of the homeland security successes of the past five years. We also cover one homeland security failure that hopefully can lead us to the appropriate adoption of the twenty-first-century technologies and approaches that will ensure mistakes aren't repeated.

The Department of Homeland Security (DHS) has shown a great appetite and aptitude for adoption of mature, yet still leading-edge approaches to solving critical national security challenges. Examples include the following:

- The highly successful U.S. Citizenship and Immigration Service Person Centric Query (PCQ) solution, which has revolutionized the processing, identification, entitlement, and even potential fraud identification within the immigration and citizenship environment.

- The E-Verify system derived from PCQ, which determines an individual's right and entitlement to work in the United States, now in use nationwide
- The highly visible US-VISIT program, which captures, processes, identifies, and validates biometric, photographic, and historical information for all visitors to the United States
- The increase in the viability of border protection from ongoing and future planned research using complex event processing (CEP) to detect patterns of incursion and modern enterprise service buses to share information in real time

These are just a few of the initiatives undertaken by DHS to integrate the extended organization and then develop increasingly capable and intuitive new services for the citizens of the United States.

Advances in information technology are predicated on these initiatives. In particular, the adoption of modern technologies including service-oriented architectures (SOA), event-driven architectures (EDA), and predictive solutions have created agile "event-enabled agencies" capable of powerful new citizen solutions.

We shall review these new technologies—and also review some of the original IT and information sharing information from the first edition—in order to provide some continuity for what has evolved over the past years. Then we will explore what we believe will be possible in the years to come, as well as some conjecture as to what technologies might possibly mature and be utilized.

HOMELAND SECURITY IS A SUCCESS

As indicated in the executive summary, the Department of Homeland Security has aggressively and successfully adopted many of the recommendations highlighted in the first edition of this book. Several of the success stories were alluded to in the Executive Summary; details will be provided in this section.

USCIS

The first and most impactful project was the U.S. Citizenship and Immigration Service (USCIS) to revolutionize their interaction with future immigrants and citizens. For many new citizens, this is the first and often the lasting impression they have of the United States, their desired future home. The following provides insight into this initiative.

USCIS Program Overview

The Bureau of U.S. Citizenship and Immigration Services (USCIS) was created by the Homeland Security Act of 2002 to handle some of the functions of the Immigration and Naturalization Service, which was disbanded as a part of the governmental shake-up in the post 9/11 world. The USCIS is a component of the U.S. Department of Homeland Security (DHS).

The function of USCIS is to establish immigration services, policies, and priorities to preserve America's legacy as a nation of immigrants while ensuring that no one is admitted who is a threat to public safety. Included among the services provided by USCIS are immigration status and employment eligibility verifications that are supported by the Systematic Alien Verification for Entitlements (SAVE) and E-Verify programs, respectively.

The Challenges

USCIS inherited a major problem from its predecessor, the Immigration and Naturalization Service. USCIS needed a new solution to help resolve a two-and-a-half-year backlog of over 3,500,000 applicants. Their caseworkers were frustrated by their inability to resolve citizenship and residency applications and the constant calls from irritated applicants.

Imagine a typical USCIS caseworker who we'll call John. John just received a call from Solis Natura, an applicant for permanent residency. Solis is originally from an at-risk former Soviet republic, thus requiring a more thorough State Department vetting, including a background check in his native country. Solis has been waiting two years on a waiver because the background check has not come back. He is still unable to sponsor his wife into the country, and he won't be able to until a resolution occurs and is communicated to him.

John connects to the State Department IT server. He finds a flag on Solis' request and calls the State processor, Frank, who informs John that the process has been on hold for seven months awaiting additional information. On checking, Frank asserts that apparently his boss had failed to inform USCIS about the needed information. John returns to the phone, gets the needed address information from Solis, and provides it to Frank. Frank responds that he can now submit the updated background request and that they should have an answer in 45 days.

Figure 41-1

Prospective
Architecture

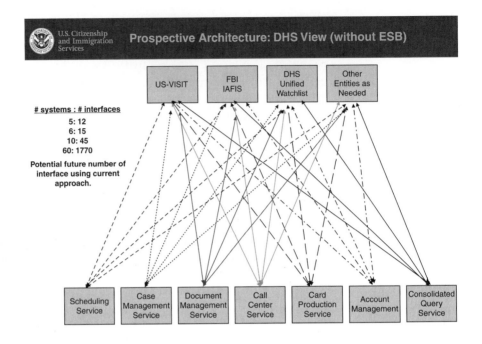

This problem was common across the millions of cases in the backlogs. Information is needed, a case is flagged in one of the 60 USCIS source systems, Figure 41-1, and the issue is not spotted until a frustrated person calls a caseworker prompting him or her to look for the person's status. This problem is also common among many other government agencies and unfortunately in large commercial business enterprises.

Solution

Person Centric Query (PCQ), Figure 41-2, service is able to tie together 60 sources of information into a single, cohesive view of the applicant connected by an enterprise service bus (ESB). With this modern solution, as any data relevant to Solis' application changes, John immediately receives just the right updated information, so he can rapidly respond to missing information and expedite the processing of Solis' application. Getting a little bit of critical information to the right caseworker reduced the two-and-a-half-year backlog of cases to less than three months.

This resulted in a lot of happy government workers, new residents, and citizens. With the more modern solution, Figure 41-3, Solis doesn't even have to call his caseworker. On the USCIS website (www.uscis. gov) he or his representative (with appropriate credentials) can see the status of his petition in real time, incorporating data from across the 60 source systems. He can also register for e-mail or SMS message

Figure 41-2

Proposed person
centric query
approach

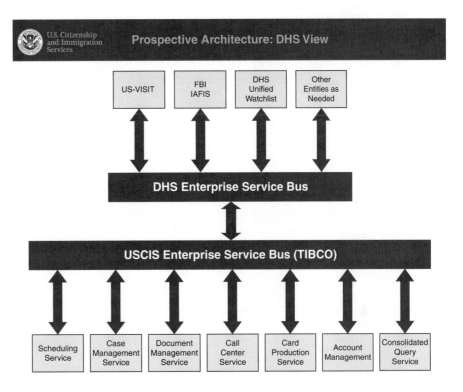

notification of any change in status, so there's no longer any need for him to call the caseworker. When Solis' wife arrives and gets her first job, E-Verify will allow her to immediately start work. This is an excellent example of the modern, automated systems that are being enabled by real-time, event-enabled technologies.

Results

Completing applications quicker leads to better customer satisfaction, and USCIS can now also respond more promptly to new mandates from the Congress. Caseworkers look forward to coming to work because their customers no longer hate working with them. As well, USCIS can now identify and prevent fraudulent or criminal immigration claims, enabling USCIS to be more agile, effective, and efficient on hot-button immigration issues—and it helped resolve a $460 million annual budget deficit.

USCIS extended its new system to implement E-Verify that compares the information of newly hired employees taken from Form I-9 (employment eligibility form) against their records. With E-Verify, work eligibility is automatically verified in 96.1 percent of cases with less than a 1 percent error rate. This allows employers to immediately

Figure 41-3
Consolidated person centric query display

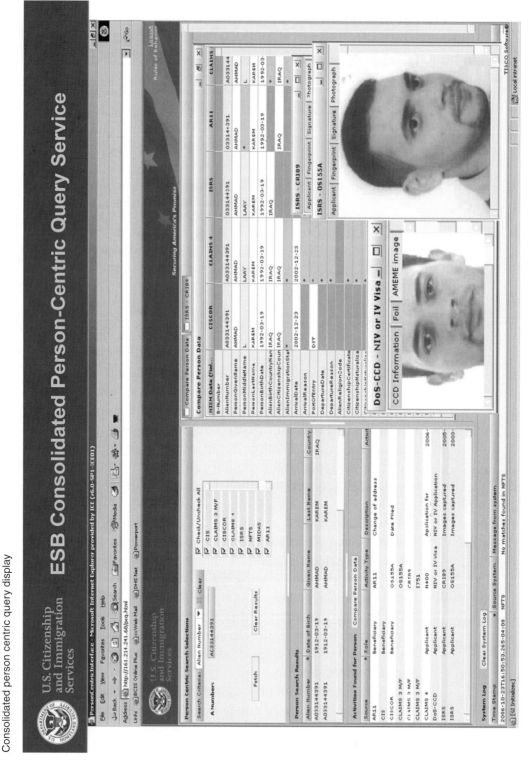

10/19/11 13:06

9

clear new workers, instead of waiting days to weeks. E-Verify has become highly successful for USCIS with more than 200,000 employers of all sizes across the United States using it to check the employment eligibility of their employees. In fact, it has proven so successful that about 1,000 new businesses signing up each week.

US-VISIT

The United States Visitor Immigration Status Indicator Technology (commonly referred to as US-VISIT) is a United States Department of Homeland Security immigration and border management system. The system involves the collection and analysis of identity documents and biometric data (such as fingerprints and photographs), which are checked against a set of databases to track individuals deemed by the United States to be terrorists, criminals, and illegal immigrants.

US-VISIT Program Overview

- The US-VISIT program is the centerpiece of the United States government's efforts to transform our nation's border management and immigration systems in a way that meets the needs and challenges of the twenty-first century.

- US-VISIT is part of a continuum of biometrically enhanced security measures that begins outside U.S. borders and continues through a visitor's arrival to and departure from the United States. It incorporates eligibility determinations made by both the DHS and the Department of State.

- US-VISIT currently applies to all visitors (with limited exemptions) entering the United States, regardless of country of origin or whether they are traveling on a visa or by air, sea, or land. Most visitors experience US-VISIT's biometric procedures—digital, inkless finger scans, and digital photographs—upon entry to the United States.

- In cases where a visitor requires a visa, the Department of State collects the visitor's biometric and biographic information through the BioVisa program. This data is then checked against watch lists, thereby improving the Department of State's ability to make a visa determination. When the visitor arrives in the country, US-VISIT procedures allow the DHS to determine whether the person applying for entry is the same person who was issued the visa by the Department of State, and then to perform additional watch list checks. This improves the DHS's ability to make admissibility decisions.

- US-VISIT entry procedures are currently in place at airports and seaports with international arrivals and in the secondary inspection areas of U.S. land border ports of entry.

- In August 2005, US-VISIT began a test of radio-frequency identification (RFID) technology at five land border ports of entry with Canada and Mexico to record the entry and exit of visitors who are required to carry a Form I–94 and enroll in the US-VISIT program.

- As the US-VISIT program moves toward fulfilling its vision for an automated entry-exit system at the border ports of entry into the United States, the border management system is continuing to improve through the innovative use of new technology.

The Challenge

The DHS faces incredible challenges. One of the most critical is processing an annual total of 46,298,869 entries that occur at just international air and seaports. Of those visitors, the previous manual vetting system led to only 273 U.S. Immigration and Customs enforcement arrests.

Starting in 2004, the U.S. Congress provided over $300 million per year to enable DHS to get a handle on this massive problem. The government knew that we were not identifying and resolving criminal, judicial, or scofflaw issues with the millions of people entering the United States. Seemingly simple issues like system delays in database access and network bandwidth prevent DHS from gaining enough insight into a visitor and his or her credentials in the average 30-second entry timeframe—especially when the visitor is standing in front of an immigration agent with 500 other people in line behind him or her.

Tom Freed, the program manager at DHS for US-VISIT, knew that modern messaging and information technologies could resolve even the toughest challenges that DHS faced in securing our borders. His five-year program has achieved results even beyond his initial vision and expectations.

Solution

The resulting US-VISIT program took a different approach to resolving the challenge than any previous effort. Tying all of the authoritative sources together on an enterprise service bus, they succeeded in making fast entry decisions with current information at their fingertips, stopping flagged travelers in unanticipated numbers. The new solution has increased the number of identified violators from hundreds to hundreds of thousands per year and has led to tens of thousands of arrests for criminal and potential terrorism issues.

Results

In its first year of operation the US-VISIT program resulted in 25,552 hits for consular officers overseas adjudicating these applications, and 236,857 as having overstayed their visas. There were 11,685 biometric watch list hits at ports of entry, which included many people with criminal histories or known terrorist associations. United States Citizenship and Immigration Services used the system to screen those who apply for immigration benefits, finding 31,324 situations that indicated violations of immigration policy and, in some cases, criminal activities.

Today, over 30,000 users at federal, state, and local law enforcement agencies take advantage of the shared, real-time information in US-VISIT to make critical decisions that impact the lives and safety of U.S. citizens and residents.

These examples show the effectiveness of the recommended service-oriented approach to architecture (SOA) built with an enterprise service bus (ESB) and standard data patterns, and using XML that was recommended in the first edition of this book. These are just a few examples that are public and can be expanded upon in detail. Other initiatives following the patterns recommended include Einstein at the DHS US-CERT, U.S. Customs and Border Protection, U.S. Counter-Terrorism Center, among others.

Border Security Advances

With over 100,000 miles of land and seashore borders to protect and with increasing scrutiny over how taxpayer dollars are spent in protecting our borders, the new reality is that more guards, guns, and fences will not be enough to ensure our security in the coming years. It is clear that new and innovative technologies will have to play a major role in cost effectively protecting our country and our freedoms.

A variety of new technologies will need to be incorporated into the U.S. Homeland Security arsenal to provide the millions of "eyes and ears" needed to more effectively counter terrorism. Focus areas include the following:

- Land-based observation and detection—sensor and video
- Aerial-based observation and detection, including UAV and satellite
- Sea, shoreline, and port security—sensors, cargo manifest correlations

- Biometric detection—facial recognition and thermal
- Cargo detection
- Radiation detection

To enhance the existing security arsenal, new technology must meet the following requirements:

- Adaptability, to change rules or tactics on the fly
- Interoperability with legacy defense, DHS, and agency systems in particular
- Situational awareness and instant response
- Ability to work with a wide variety of sensor data

The last bullet point is important for defense applications and is based, in part, on some established defense IT architectures, particularly the Joint Directors of Laboratories (JDL) sensor data fusion concepts combined with innovative complex event processing software from TIBCO Software.

JDL Data Fusion Model

The JDL data fusion model is directly applicable to detection theory, where patterns and signatures discovered by abductive and inductive reasoning processing (for example, data mining) is "fused" with real-time events. The JDL processing model, Figure 41-4, has survived the test of time as the dominant functional data fusion model for decades. The vast majority of the most complex real-time event processing architectures are based on the JDL model. It is worth noting that the JDL data fusion model is a communications infrastructure that looks remarkably similar to TIBCO's patented "information bus" and is based on the concept of a service-oriented architecture.

In fact, the art and science of multi-sensor data fusion has emerged as the underlying foundation for the state of the art in enterprise software, including TIBCO's rapidly growing Predictive Business® solutions, which have produced innovative deployments and applications in telecommunications, finance, transportation, and, of course, defense. All of these sectors require complex inference processing and the management of real-time events from distributed sensors, agents, and other processing components, including historical data-at-rest repositories.

There are three main meta-architectural components of the JDL model reflected in the following Figure 41-1. Perhaps the most important of these are events. Events can be local or external, and can originate from myriad sources in many formats. There is also the core complex event

Figure 41-4

Joint Directors of
laboratories data
fusion model

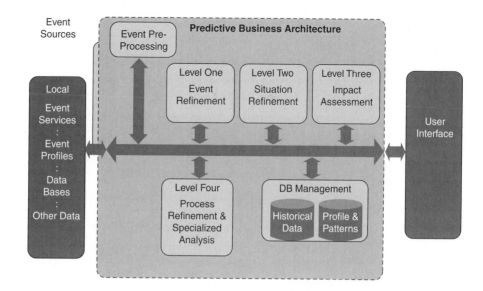

and/or the so-called event stream processing architecture, which the JDL model depicts as the "data fusion domain." We will use the terms *data fusion domain, data fusion, multi-sensor data fusion, complex event processing,* and *event stream processing* somewhat interchangeably in this chapter, as the concepts are independent of vendor implementation and have similar technical objectives and outcomes. Finally, there is the user interface, providing operational visibility into every technical and business process depicted in the model.

The objectives of homeland security organizations may differ in context, but the overarching technical goal is the same:

> *Correlate information gained from abductive and inductive reasoning processes with real-time events to infer current situational knowledge and predict both opportunities for, and threats to, security personnel to maximize assets and minimize liabilities.*

As America undergoes comprehensive updating of its infrastructure, it's a good time to review how advances in computer hardware and software can be employed to develop anew the IT platforms that will help the federal government overall and specifically the Department of Homeland Security provide advanced new services to citizens.

Recent efforts around software standards have resulted in more portable and manageable ways to create and share application modules; many of these standards for the first time enjoy broad support even among competing vendors. In the area of hardware, the performance capacity of RAM and network bandwidth enable near-real-time—and in many cases actual real-time—business intelligence based on the propagation, analysis, and visualization of real-time events and messages.

Federal agencies that have been tasked with updating critical services for the public—such as transportation, safety, law enforcement, and many others—are encouraged to consider a prominent role for new web service standards efforts, such as Service Component Architecture (SCA) and Open Services Gateway (OSG) architecture. Agencies should also consider the advantages that modern high performance message grid and CEP technologies can offer.

Now let's review these three technology areas in some detail.

First, for maximum performance and throughput, recent advances in hardware and software allow you to deploy applications that are highly memory resident. This means that applications are able to send information faster without having to make round trips to relational databases in order to perform transactions and to fault tolerance and reliability. How is this achieved? Here are observations and recommended strategies.

PERFORMANCE THROUGHPUT: CONSIDERATIONS

A message bus should be the core of the entire system. The message bus needs to be easily ramped up to support both business transactions and system management traffic, and also needs to have the interfaces so that probes and management hooks can be added as needed. The message bus needs to support different protocols in different areas of the platform. Examples include multicast in those areas needing high throughput to multiple receivers, but also include the ability to serially combine message bus servers so that you can do federated routing, store and forward across different application domains (a firewall is frequently employed), and publish and subscribe.

Message bus products have evolved to the point that they can handle thousands of transactions per second by leveraging large numbers of memory-resident servers, and can be easily deployed in a parallel fashion to increase availability and throughput. But they also require the out-of-the-box management facilities to become operational—for example, TIBCO messaging products are often employed in large numbers and therefore include the tools to manage a large number of message servers. Message layer products are also starting to include

Figure 41-5

Enterprise-scale
messaging

Messaging Workloads by **Industry**

Transportation
800 million messages/day

Wireless carrier
1 billion messages/day

Consumer website
2.6 billion messages/day

Auction site
250 thousand messages/sec

Financial institution
4.3 billion messages/day

Trading floor
43 billion messages/day

Airline
3.4 billion messages/day

Government organization
50 thousand messages/day

data grid capabilities, which is a way for messages to remain in replicated memory so that they can be "stored," queried, and correlated to other messages before they are actually read and consumed by the receiving application. Used in combination, the message bus and the data grid give you the best mix of reliable message propagation and the ability to understand how the messages relate to each other before they are sent to the receivers for processing. Figure 41-5 depicts real-world messaging experiences of large organizations.

An enterprise service bus (ESB) needs to be integrated with the message bus to achieve the best value from your next-generation platform. The ESB is the key component of a service-oriented architecture approach to designing, deploying, and operating shared services between applications and the data they require. The ESB needs to easily support edge protocols (like HTTP) for external communication, but also make use of the message layer (usually JMS) to reliably store the SOAP XML traffic when integrating applications that operate at different speeds, and also when many applications need to receive the same data message simultaneously.

The ESB also has very stringent throughput and uptime requirements; it needs to very quickly translate and stage the SOAP XML message traffic, performing translation between different application formats, and also handles agent-based integration with back-office data sources and applications (by agent-based we mean that the ESB is able to get real-time updates in changes to back-office systems). Whereas the message bus handles transport of messages, the ESB coordinates the different data flows, so therefore needs to excel at performing complex transactions, data staging, and routing of control between the different applications. In many cases the largest hurdle to achieving a large-scale shared services and consolidation strategy is the time and expense of on-ramping existing and legacy applications. Companies like TIBCO have therefore made it a company priority to offer as many off-the-shelf adapters (not API tool kits) to existing applications as possible, and in fact is the only company that has made this kind of investment. Other ESB vendors largely exist to provide a sales vehicle either for their COTS applications or as a sales vehicle to sell huge services engagements. TIBCO's approach, on the other hand, is to productize our integrations to a wide variety of back-office data sources, ranging from complex files to mainframes to a wide variety of COTS applications.

MAXIMIZE AVAILABILITY: CONSIDERATIONS

Earlier we mentioned new standards such as Service Component Architecture and Open Services Gateway Initiative (OSGI). Why are these standards so critical? The support for OSGI allows services platforms to support different versions of a service in parallel, meaning that you can update consumers for different versions much more incrementally and do away with "big bang" disruptive system changes. OSGI was created over a period of time by large-scale network operators (such as telecommunications and embedded device management platforms) and excels at providing large-scale operational change management (deploy, start, stop, update, etc.) for an enormous network with potentially thousands of services. OSGI is widely viewed as the successor to the e-commerce-centric Java 2 Platform, Enterprise Edition (J2EE) model that has been used widely but is now seen as inadequate in a distributed, network-centric world.

PREDICTIVE ANALYTICS (SITUATION AWARENESS) SOLUTIONS

In addition to awareness of potential efforts to intentionally disrupt your IT operations, it is imperative to be able to predict when other business activities might either be leading to problems or opportunities. CEP products add state modeling, rules processing, and event pattern matching capabilities to enable predictive analytics for trends and metrics. For example, in the area of uptime/availability management, by embedding CEP into your ESB framework rules base, the systems are then able to auto-correct when it detects service-level agreement (SLA) metrics are about to be violated by starting additional services or taking other anticipatory actions.

Staff Collaboration and Coordination

We view the areas of service-oriented architecture, business process management, and business optimization (by this we mean CEP and data visualization capabilities) as offering tremendous synergies when used together. Increasingly, the worlds of SOA and BPM are seen as two sides of the same coin: the applications used by end users must make use of shared services provided by the ESB to maintain security and also to increase the ability to make quick changes to end user applications due to changing external business environment. External and internal events can be used to drive staff workflows, which in turn can be used to better leverage service orchestrations. This can work in a closed loop in order to provide a more responsive organization.

Business Optimization

To thrive in today's increasingly fast-moving transportation environment, you must get ahead of the bottlenecks. You need the ability to identify developing situations and understand their potential impact, to alert the appropriate personnel and enable them to make a decision or take action, and to initiate necessary adaptation and effective responses as automatically and immediately as possible. That's the essence of business optimization. Most organizations are awash in data and events, processes and procedures, strategies and tactics. When you add agency and partner relationships, critical mission requirements, and management policies to the mix, it can be truly overwhelming.

Compounding the problem, many organizations do their jobs looking in a rear view mirror, relying on periodic reports and crunching historical data to link results with causes, develop new strategies, tactics, and resolve inefficiencies after the fact.

THE IMPORTANCE OF EVENTS

What most people think of as SOA doesn't inherently address all the capabilities needed to respond to the dynamics of real-time organizations. By analyzing their performance and operations in real time, they can more effectively capitalize on opportunities. To do this they need to gather individual events and sequences of events from multiple diverse sources at different layers in the organization and across the value chain.

Complex event processing aggregates information from distributed systems in real time and applies rules to discern patterns and trends that would otherwise go unnoticed. These patterns or trends can be correlated and fused into actionable knowledge. This gives organizations the ability to identify, anticipate, and act on opportunities represented by seemingly unrelated events. With CEP, organizations can map discrete events to expected outcomes, and relate series of events to key performance indicators (KPIs). CEP gives organizations insight into which events will have the greatest operational impact so they can focus their resources to seize opportunities and mitigate risks. One of the most interesting and powerful CEP capabilities is its ability to tell you about and act on events that should have happened already but in fact have not.

ARCHITECTURAL INSIGHTS—SUMMARIZED

This architecture insights section provides an informative baseline and some next steps as DHS considers new IT projects in the years ahead. Based on a review of several ongoing programs—including Person Centric Query, US-VISIT, and upcoming procurements—we group system architectural requirements into three broad areas:

The system architecture must provide maximum throughput with high visibility, insight, responsiveness, and the following requirements:

- The absolutely highest throughput and scalability to meet DHS's "high consequence" command and control environment
- Predictive business intelligence (BI) capabilities that are processed quickly and provide needed insight in a timely fashion
- Built-in reliability and guaranteed delivery with fault tolerance around CPU and network conditions
- Administrative tools and consoles with the ability to centrally monitor and manage many distributed services

Software vendors must provide demonstrated expertise at standing up large-scale systems; for example, providing a documented track record for deploying large-scale systems, support for the implementation effort with extensive knowledge of capacity planning (and necessary benchmarking case studies), plus experience in similar high-consequence environments (for example, the intelligence community, DHS, satellite control, the airlines, and the financial community).

The approach must provide maximum availability. In other words, the system should come out of the box with all the management and control interfaces needed to maintain the system in operational status:

- A software platform that provides out-of-the-box configuration and user interface settings to maintain uptime and SLA contracts.
- Availability should be manageable at very granular level, allowing control over individual services—for example, load balancing, fault tolerance, hot deployment, multiple simultaneous versions, and auto-restoration of an application exceeding SLA back to contracted levels, providing highly elastic capacity and provisioning.
- The software platform must be data center ready with an out-of-the-box, integrated management platform, so that technologies from various sources can still be deployed and managed effectively using local "best tools for job."

The architectural approach must provide maximum agility. In other words, the environment must be able to evolve easily for new challenges and changing requirements:

- Uses flexible and widely available skill sets; therefore, users can pick the best tool for a job and it will fit into the platform.
- Offers adherence to standards and is able to interoperate with and leverage open source as needed; this implies strong support for these key modern standards: SOAP, XML, Service Component Architecture (SCA), Open Services Gateway (OSGI), Java, JEE, and many more.
- Offers commonality of deployment and operations processes. In other words, artifact formats that are created in Java, .NET, Ruby, and C++ ecosystems should allow operators to use common workflow processes to create, manage, and update services. This frees development and security teams to focus on new functions, ability, and capability versus IT overhead.
- Incremental change is supported, so you do not have to rely on big-bang changes to services.
- Operators are provided out of the box with noninvasive and nondisruptive ways to add, change, or retire services; to hot deploy new services; and to support multiple versions of services, so service changes do not come at the cost of more downtime.

- Employs service virtualization, so that new services are easy to add without impacting clients and so that policies for security, reliable message contracts, and SLAs can be applied at deployment or at run time without hard-coding these contracts into service business logic.

THE FUTURE OF HOMELAND SECURITY TECHNOLOGY

Now that we've talked about successes of the past five years and the present state of critical standards, let's review the technologies that will drive the future for homeland security.

Four critical technological advances were not foreseen when the first edition of this book was written. While I had thought about some of them pending evolution of the technical underpinnings, they were not yet fully viable. They were like what I have put at the end of this edition as a perspective on the future. After adopting the four technologies covered here, you might want to imagine a future vision of what might be possible when the third edition of this *Homeland Security Handbook* is written in another five or six years.

The first of these technological advances is the transformation from the twentieth-century artifact of a database-centric, rotating mass media, transactional, query-response approach to architecture to Event-Enabled Architecture, a new environment where information and data are always in memory, rotating mass media exist primarily for archival and backup, and inquiries to databases have been transformed into rules-based, event-driven architectures with the capabilities to meet twenty-first-century challenges.

When the first edition of this book was released, memory was still too expensive to for businesses to consider running everything in memory. Inference rules engines were still in their infancy, content was king, and the king lived in a database. If you wanted to get at the information, you used an SQL query into the database and then waited for a response in its own time, driven by limitations in retrieval speed of a disk drive. Increasingly in the twenty-first century, in large-scale distributed memory grids, and rules-based inference engines are becoming real-time contextualized, actionable information from that data. Where content was king in the twentieth century, context is the important element in the twenty-first.

This transformation is closely linked with a vision for the Event-Enabled Infrastructure, in which events rather than transactions, an enterprise service bus, and large-scale distributed memory driven by rules replace the previous database-centric Enterprise 2.0. With the sevenfold drop in the cost of solid-state memory over the past few years, a massively distributed shared memory environment became both technically and fiscally feasible. Hundreds to thousands of computer systems sharing a singular shared memory environment brings an entirely new performance paradigm to the world of mission-critical information and more important event processing. Events have always existed in physical and information worlds, but technical and cost issues have limited event processing, correlation, and fusion to only the most critical environments like the space program and defense Command, Control, Computer, Communications, Intelligence, Surveillance and Reconnaissance (C4ISR) systems. Bespoke solutions for these challenges costing billions of dollars saved lives and allowed man to travel into space. Other enterprises could not afford billions

Critical national and global government systems—including fraudulent and stolen passport tracking for INTERPOL, the United Kingdom's e-Borders, and others—bogged down and failed because in many cases answers could not be retrieved fast enough to match the real-time interaction limitations with travelers who were aggravated by having to wait around. When this happened, officials either quit asking, as was the case in border clearance with invalid or stolen passports, or shut down (as was the case in the first summer of e-Borders deployment), because the tourists were in revolt from missing flights and connections waiting for e-Borders clearance.

When we look at some of the major security breaches over the last two decades—the first World Trade Center terrorist bombing in 1993; the 9/11 attacks in the United States; subsequent bombings in Bali, Indonesia, London, and Madrid; and, most recently, the failed attempt by an Al Qaeda recruit in 2009 to bring down an airliner bound for Detroit at Christmas—a common element is travel document fraud.

More often than not, the perpetrators were already on the radar of intelligence or law enforcement when they committed these acts, but no single agency or system was keeping track of their movements. Given the current systems in place in most of the world, how could they?

Right now, more than 500 million international arrivals cross borders every year without having their passports screened against INTERPOL's global database of almost 11 million stolen and lost passports reported by its member countries. It would just take too long given the limitations of the twentieth-century, database-driven technologies and approaches described above. Border control officers have minutes or even just seconds to decide their next course of action when they look at and process passports presented by travelers. These officers represent the last line of defense to prevent the entry of terrorists, fugitives, and other dangerous criminals into our countries.

The key to any effective anti-crime or counterterrorism response is providing just the right information to the right people at the right time with the appropriate context. But the law enforcement community has not been able to address the problem adequately because of fundamental limitations in the information technology available to them. INTERPOL has a wealth of high-value police information stored in its global databases, yet we need a way to rapidly share this extremely valuable information, hidden away in these resources.

In this critical adjacent challenge to homeland security, an approach that follows the new model described above will leverage advanced technology architecture to solve these problems. It could take the form of a real-time trustworthy communications platform, an enterprise equivalent to an addressable radio broadcast of information. This platform could enable a global-scale, distributed memory system to make risks and opportunities immediately available to officers. And CEP engine could help officers correlate past patterns with real-time events to better predict what needs to happen next. A major police force already uses this approach with CEP engines warning officers of unusual risks when they execute traffic stops.

These approaches could form part of a modern predictive law enforcement solution to assist with countering the threat of terrorist attacks. It would resolve the challenges where INTERPOL and national agencies experience unacceptable delays in their current search-query approach to using INTERPOL's database of stolen and lost passports.

These revolutionary approaches have information moving as *events in memory* instead of as *records in a database*. Events and data are processed in real time by CEP engines to identify, correlate, and predict levels of risk. Predictive law enforcement answers the delays inherent in existing approaches. By 2020, we will need to process the anticipated 1.2 billion travelers who will cross international borders—50 percent more than what we have now—and instantly alert the first-line officers that an individual presenting a travel document is wanted or dangerous, all without breaking the bank or adding unnecessary delays.

Figure 41-6

Sensors are
everywhere

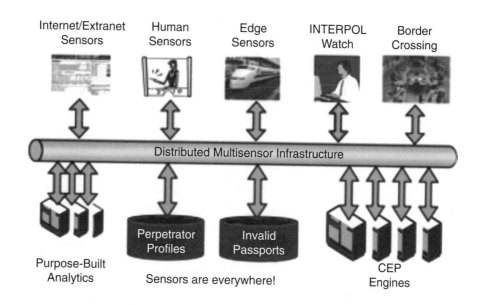

Predictive law enforcement will provide a widely distributed, trustworthy environment and massively distributed memory-based data and messaging grid products capable of supporting millions of interactions per second (see Figure 41-6). With this approach, every inquiry is simply an event handled by a system referencing a CEP-derived scorecard that reflects the level of risk of that specific passport and identity.

These scorecards would directly reflect INTERPOL-developed threat classifications for persons of interest based on factors like criminal record or past travel. If in the history of interactions with that passport, its asserted source or the individual carrying it has picked up an orange or red value, it is worth whatever level of further scrutiny border officers deem appropriate (see Figure 41-7). This is just one example of a critical global and national security challenge answered by our first architectural and technological approach for the future and represents unique and critical capability for the future of homeland security solutions.

The second revolutionary technical pattern is the use of private, public, and blended clouds for a number of good reasons, and a number of reasons that have not been thought through fully yet. I don't need to go into the aspects of cloud types, values, and perceived risks because everyone has been beating on your door to tell you what they think you should know, do, and buy/lease in the cloud.

Many in the business and academic communities have been up at arms, concerned that security risks are too high in cloud

Figure 41-7

Score cards are passed between levels

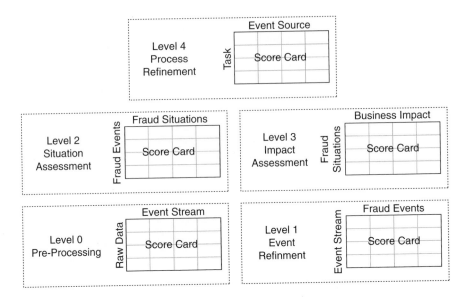

implementations, and therefore the status quo is better for sensitive government activities like homeland security. Many of those same individuals and organizations need research grants that would not be forthcoming if the issues were viewed clearly, and others have significant investment and long-term contracts to exploit and continue to profit from the status quo. Instead, I will delve into the fundamentals that we have known and the fundamental technical solutions we often ignore or forget in our rush to judgment.

Sensitive parts of the U.S. federal government used to send officers to the factory of manufacturers of computer servers that would process sensitive government information. They would then travel with the computers until they were turned over to government-controlled and protected storage. Other trusted individuals would sign for, deliver, and install them under multi-person controls and accountability. Interestingly, I just saw an article where these protections are being afforded the National Christmas Tree this year. This was a topic of discussion at a recent DISA/AFCEA Cloud event and not too many people appeared concerned about the fact that we don't seem to do that anymore. We were talking about best practices for the development and deployment of Multi-Tenant Cloud Centers at DISA, for a diverse group of defense agencies and services. The point was made by a few of the long-term security folks from the community, like me, that if you build, lease, or contract for one of these and there is no assurance that the hardware was not altered before or during installation, there would be few aspects of the center that would be trustworthy. Modified chips could theoretically help foster the exfiltration of sensitive information and help cover up the events. Worse, cyber-terrorists could watch for and slightly alter mathematical algorithms or steps in combat-related processes just enough at just the wrong time to marginalize our ability to properly or accurately execute missions.

After a hacking attack that had persisted undetected for days, a defense official was more concerned that they didn't know what they could trust in their networks and servers anymore than at the prospect that sensitive information was exfiltrated. They intonated that they would have to spend thousands of hours and untold other resources to review and validate all information that they would count on for critical decisions before they could be fully combat-capable again.

On top of trustworthy (or even untrustworthy) hardware, a multi-tenancy cloud center should use trusted operating systems like SE-Linux or Solaris with Trusted Features to mitigate and isolate the multiple tenants information from unintended blending or even internal exfiltration between competing organizations and trusted internal administrators, who may likely (as was the case in WikiLeaks) be the largest threat. The government, academia, and software vendors spent enormous amounts of money building, testing, and certifying trusted operating systems only to see them wither for lack of utilization. Every excuse from cost to complexity, difficulty in training users, and limitations in applications were used to take mandates for trusted operating system use off of the mandatory requirements for procurement and implementation of even sensitive government systems, and the developers never got their investments back. In reality, it was largely an issue of lack of understanding, motivation, or knowledge that drove these decisions on the government side, and fear of the costs to hire knowledgeable developers on the part of contractors.

If you start a multi-tenancy cloud center by paying attention to the two preceding best practices, you are three quarters of the way to being able to have faith in the services you will depend on for critical missions, or even sensitive but unclassified operations. Once you have taken care of the hardware exposures and properly installed a trusted operating system, then you have choices of Infrastructure as a Service (IAAS) software packages to provide the flexibility of dynamic allocation of servers, storage, and other resources as demands and missions change across the multi-tenant environment. You could in fact trust Amazon Web Services (AWS) to manage your clouds if you started from this baseline. To top off this environment, you need a mature cloud platform-as-a-service (PAAS) like the TIBCO Silver® product line to host your applications and services. Cloud PAAS provides all of the mission-critical management elements plus predictive allocation, de-allocation, provisioning, life cycle management, and performance guarantees against SLAs. The TIBCO Silver product line, for example, includes a CEP event-enhanced rules engine that can ensure that the system is dynamically adjusting deployments and loads as roles and missions change around the clock. It can do that with minimal human oversight and prevent SLAs from being compromised. Regardless of the type of cloud you need, the previously described event-enabled infrastructure should reside on the top level. A memory-resident, event-enabled, rules-driven infrastructure will ensure that just the right people can get information and context wherever and whenever they need it. Context-enhanced cloud environments providing information on time will redefine the Command, Control, Communications, Computer Intelligence (C4I) world. A friendly foreign intelligence organization indicated it could completely redefine how they would/could selectively share information in context.

When you begin to move past either a public cloud that has minimal privacy and trust issues or a private cloud that has significant privacy and trustworthiness issues, you arrive at a blended cloud supported by appropriate infrastructure. This is the real challenge, and there are many other elements of trust required. These elements are usually best provided by a highly trustworthy gateway appliance certified under Common Criteria at EAL-4+, like Layer 7's SecureSpan or IBM's DataPower. These highly trustworthy appliances provide robust Identification and Entitlements enforcement, Federation and mapping, secure token creation, and arbitration to meet the real challenges of blended cloud environments. In Layer 7's case, it includes an OASIS WS-Trust standard Secure-Token Server (STS) and Security Assertion Markup Language (SAML2) as well as Extensible Access Control Markup Language (XACML) for precise controls over access to sensitive information. With these capabilities in place and properly configured, it is entirely feasible to provide gated access to specific levels of information in secure private clouds from a generally more loosely controlled public cloud or any client vetted as entitled to the information. The control point and decisions thus become the association of an individual with a specific piece of information regardless of either's location. This well-managed environment will ensure that a senior leader who currently only has network access from his or her wireless mobility device to the public Internet can connect securely to the public cloud access arbitrator, properly authenticate him- or herself directly or through a token service, and if in addition to his or her identity the device is identified as capable of protecting sensitive information, can have that information securely delivered to his or her device.

The third technology approach is Enterprise Social Media for critical information sharing for the decision maker. In a model and approach like TIBCO's tibbr®, enterprises can ensure that decision makers receive all critical information when they need it and in an appropriate context for their rapid understanding. A leader can have his or her Enterprise Social Media app on a secure mobility device deliver all levels of sensitive information and context as it becomes available, without the leader having to go look for it. The leader can follow his or her fellow decision makers, support staff as well as direct output from appropriate sensor platforms, Command and Control (C2) platforms, Complex Event Processors, correlated and fused actionable knowledge, or any other appropriate information source. Imagine a scenario where BDA shows incomplete destruction of a target. An appropriate authority would have tracked planning, execution, and assessment regardless of their location and can re-task the target in seconds because they have the entire picture of information and context in their hands without having to go look for it.

In the Executive Overview, I promised you insight into a failure to use our recommended technologies and a philosophy for information sharing. Information sharing, or the lack of it, can make or break critical decision loops. A prime example of this is the intelligence failures that allowed the "Christmas Bomber"' to nearly succeed in his mission to inflict terror and embarrass the United States government. An analysis of this highly visible failure to appropriately share information follows.

The failed bombing of Northwest Flight 253 was a clarion call to action to resolve problems that have festered in the United States intelligence community for decades. Since the fall of the former Soviet Union, the intelligence community has been unable to adapt and adjust from the patterns that they were taught to the new, highly mobile, unpredictable environment they find themselves in today. The old patterns that had proven to be successful for the previous four generations while intelligence research and analysis against the Soviet Union was conducted were largely stationary and actually quite predictable. At a press briefing following the analysis of the failure, President Obama had the following to say:

The bottom line is this: The U.S. government had sufficient information to have uncovered this plot and potentially disrupt the Christmas Day attack, but our intelligence community failed to connect those dots, which would have placed the suspect on the no-fly list, In other words, this was not a failure to collect intelligence; it was a failure to integrate and understand the intelligence that we already had.

American intelligence analysts had the information but did not fully analyze or leverage that knowledge, the president said. "That's not acceptable, and I will not tolerate it."

There's enough blame to go around for everyone. But blame is not going to resolve the problem. The old ways of gathering and harvesting information for intelligence purposes and storing away in shoe boxes in case someone asks you a question is just not effective in today's world. First off, there's far too much information and far too many sources for even the best analysts to pull a needle out of a haystack, and that is what so many of today's potential attacks resemble. That said, what they need is the ability to capture the right information, at the right time, and act on it preemptively for a competitive advantage—what TIBCO refers to as the two-second advantage™—which is already enjoyed by modern industry leaders in other highly valuable, high through-put, higher risk, and highly profitable markets. In a Wall Street trading pit, a new offer in platform for a major telco, or any of the high-tech manufacturers, even a failed bombing or its corollary would have caused millions if not billions of dollars in direct and indirect financial cost and, as President Obama stated above, would not be tolerated. So where do we go from here to help the intelligence community to gain the advantages of an event-enabled, memory-based, and rules-driven infrastructure?

As the President stated, and as all of his leaders from the intelligence, homeland security, and the Counter-Terrorism Center reiterated, they have all the information—or did in this case—but do not have a way to make sense from it. Resolving this problem, then, must focus on ways to get those billions of seemingly unrelated bits of intelligence from thousands of sources into an environment where modern technology can assist those highly trained and skilled analysts in building and seeing the complex relationships that could have told them there was a high likelihood that this set of relationships looks like a potential attack scenario. An advanced information-sharing environment driven by modern sensors and a memory-based infrastructure around CEP engines with natural-language filtering, providing correlated fused decisions and recommendations and following rules and distributed to decision makers like those proposed in this chapter, would help them gain enough insight to prevent the event.

WHAT DID WHO KNOW AND WHEN?

Public information sources reveal the following:

1. NSA had an indicator that Al Qaeda was planning to use a "Nigerian" bomber for an attack against the United States.

2. CIA had an indicator that Umar Farouk Abdulmutallab had become a radicalized Islamist and potential terrorist following a meeting with his father, one of the richest and most influential people in Nigeria. CIA and the U.S. State Department both forwarded reports on this meeting to their headquarters.

3. CIA had an indicator that Umar Farouk Abdulmutallab was associated with Anwar al-Awlaki, a known Al Qaeda terrorist and recruiter of suicide bombers going back to his school days in London starting in 2006. They had further indicators of this relationship in Yemen, in November 2009, where Umar Farouk Abdulmutallab had overstayed his student visa to undertake training from Al Qaeda.

4. The State Department attempted to revoke Umar Farouk Abdulmutallab's student visa following the report from the interview with his father. The intelligence community requested that they not revoke his visa because of ongoing operations.

5. The UK intelligence community had indicators of Umar Farouk Abdulmutallab attending sermons and lectures by Anwar al-Awlaki, who they suspected of recruiting the suicide bombers for the London Subway attack. They identified Umar Farouk Abdulmutallab as an extremist and potential terrorist recruit as far back as 2006.

6. The UK government denied Umar Farouk Abdulmutallab's application to renew his student visa in 2009 based on their intelligence service's indicators and questions about the legitimacy of the educational institution he indicated he was accepted to.

7. CIA and NCTC had indicators that Al Qaeda was using pentaerythritol tetranitrate (PETN) based triacetone triperoxide (TATP) high explosives sewn into the underwear of a suicide bomber. The U.S. authorities had collaborated with Saudi Arabia after Al Qaeda failed in executing the head of Saudi Counter Terrorism using this approach.

So, clearly the U.S. government had enough indicators that a *Nigerian* student, *radicalized* by *Al Qaeda terrorist recruiter al-Awlaki* over *several years*, who had *overstayed his Yemeni visa* in order to attend *Al Qaeda indoctrination*, whose *father warned U.S. officials* about his son's radicalization, who paid *$2,831.00 in cash* for his airline ticket in Accra, Ghana, who used a U.S. visa that the *State Department had unsuccessfully tried to revoke*, and who had *no known relatives or connections in Detroit*, was a potential threat who should have at least been more closely screened, if allowed at all.

In twenty-first-century homeland security, the analysts at the Counter Terrorism Center (CTC) receive 8,000 new indicators about terrorists, warnings of potential attacks, and other threats every day. How can humans, even the brilliant and dedicated analysts at the CTC, absorb, process, and make logical recommendations on validity and levels of threats related to the event (or many seeming unrelated events) that generated the incoming indicators? The CTC, according to public sources, has been relegated to largely filtering and clearing-house functions to stage information from different agencies so that others can analyze and make decisions from it. For example, they clear multisource intelligence information and forward it to the FBI Terrorist Screening Center, where decisions like who goes on the no-fly list are made. This does not bode well for the community gaining an advantage over our new enemies. For example, the isolation and separation of roles does not lead to efficient multi-sensor data fusion and analysis or rapidly evolving threats like the underwear bomber.

PREDICTIVE ANALYSIS AND STAGING SYSTEM

The Predictive Analysis and Staging System (PASS) is not a current or currently planned solution. It is instead a thought piece on how to manage the flood of multi-sensor data inundating homeland security every hour of the day and night.

At the heart of PASS is a massive-scale solid-state distributed memory system, shared equally by all entitled players in the counterterrorism community. PASS is driven by events rather than transactions and database queries. All indicators and sensor input from all sources are passed into the memory environment, where it is processed by rules engines, matching engines, and USG bespoke engines for specialized analysis or fusion, and replaced in the memory system for any further processing or analyst access. Analysts can adapt the rules structures to an evolving environment. All iterative or final results may also be input to advanced rules processing as if they were another event. All results are available or may be tasked to a pool of analysts through a service-oriented business process solution. This is the third generation of enterprise architecture.

Using PASS, the NCTC, and its sources and downstream like the TSC, would have real-time access to correlated information and would likely have spotted Umar Farouk Abdulmutallab with even the simplest of rule-sets:

1. Process all subjects sourced from or input to TIDE.
   a. Raise priority for all Nigerians.
   b. Raise priority for all flying to the United States during Christmas holidays.
   c. Raise priority for all paying for airline tickets with cash.
   d. Raise priority for all who State department attempted to revoke visa.
   e. Raise priority for all with connections to Anwar al-Awlaki.
   f. Raise priority for all with current Al Qaeda connections or training.

Like the INTERPOL example before, this should introduce you to Umar Farouk Abdulmutallab and a very short list of others who deserve very close scrutiny. Thanks to the CTC and an event-driven infrastructure.

A little information sharing would have gone a long way.

The fourth quantum leap in information technology and sharing is the rapid adoption of enhanced mobility within the enterprise. This revolution presumes the dreams of futurist George Gilder in his seminal treatise *Telecosm* are reality. The precepts included the ubiquitous, unlimited bandwidth from fiber optics and wireless communication infrastructure and the existence of Gilder's previous treatise *Microcosm*, which predicted the future availability of microprocessor and microelectronics technology to process anything, anywhere, at any price point, making processing effectively free or trivial relative to its value to humankind. Most of us today have already transitioned to the early stages of this paradigm.

Our iPhones, iPads, Android phones, and tablets are the manifestation of the earliest stages of Gilder's two visions of Telecosm. Like the second edition of this book, the industry and technology changed so much that he published a second edition of *Telecosm*. The ubiquity of 3G, and 4G cellular, Mesh, Wi-Fi, and other wireless communications media are revolutionizing not just how we live but most importantly how we work, play, and interact with our fellow humans. Social media followed by trustworthy enterprise social media has redefined relationships, commerce, and soon even the most sensitive information sharing. This latter with enhanced mobility will replace or at least augment our entire vision of providing for homeland security as well as C4ISR for defense.

As I write and research this section on my MacBook Pro, I am connected on one of three secure Wi-Fi networks in my home and on ubiquitous 3G cellular from my iPad2, yet while I am in the rapidly disappearing time, in which I am not in range of some public or private Wi-Fi router. With 3G cellular and data, you can almost never get away these days. This was never so obvious to me than receiving an email on my iPhone 4, 50 miles from civilization in the middle of Kruger National Park in South Africa. Unfortunately, the ding of my phone spooked the leopard we were tracking. Fortunately it was a picture of my newborn granddaughter. I told the park ranger I was "photo hunting." This proved that I could never truly get away any longer.

This connectivity, this Telecosm, is defining the boundary and the "edge" of our physical world as well as the reciprocal "edge" of our virtual world.

Now, that is all well and good for the average wireless subscriber, but how about homeland security and other sensitive parts of the U.S. federal government? Where is the "secure Telecosm"? In actuality, there are a number of activities under way to provide comparable, trustworthy capabilities for those departments and agencies. There are no technical challenges that appear insurmountable. The activities at and around the National Security Agency (NSA) are the most interesting. One of these activities dealing with mobile technologies is discussed in the adjacent sidebar, provided by USAF Capt. Steven Pugh, who has been actively engaged in the creation of a top secret smartphone. Basically, the objective of the mobile team is to create

Figure 41-8

Mobility looks remarkably like telecosm; connected everywhere.

infrastructure and appropriate devices to provide top secret smartphones for decision makers and warfighters, while using only commercial products. Their efforts, depicted in Figure 41-8, fit directly into my descriptions in this section about Telecosm, in this case, the Secure Telecosm. Things that we in industry have taken for granted and our latest hires from the Millennial Generation, who are rapidly replacing us, cannot live without are like an obscure foreign language to the key decision makers conducting intelligence collection and analysis, managing deployment of assets, and conducting wars. They have been relegated to highly expensive but literally ineffective primitive tools that bind them to a desk, or worse yet, to a hardened vehicle or facility, tent, or forward deployed element because they need immediate access to what is happening. When command and control is personal and local, all aspects of the big picture and the effectiveness of the Observe Orient Decide Act (OODA) loop responses are severely impacted.

Sidebar 1 SNIP

System and Network Interdisciplinary Program
The System and Network Interdisciplinary Program (SNIP) is a three-year program at the National Security Agency for people with a bachelor's degree in some technical field such as computer science, electrical engineering, or mathematics. The program

is extremely competitive and only the nation's best and brightest candidates are accepted. The program's goal is to develop the next generation of experts in various technological fields—breadth and depth—with respect to computer network operations (CNO).

The program is composed of three main components, each lasting different lengths of time. The first part of the program lasts three months and is called core training. The most cutting-edge material, respect to CNO development, is taught during core training. The classes serve to fill knowledge gaps as well as expand on undergraduate experience by exposing the interns to different subjects within CNO. The next 24 months are spent touring in approximately five different offices within the NSA, which align with a predefined goal relevant to CNO development. The final component to the program is a three-month project that works toward some difficult problem.

In the case of the 2011 SNIP class, the final project was vulnerability analysis on commercial products used for secure mobile communications. The SNIP class broke the problem down into three focus groups: endpoints or handsets, enterprise servers, and the communications between the endpoints and servers. For more details, see the sidebar on "Emerging Secure Technologies."

Those living in ivory towers are a primary aspect of homeland security failures like the Christmas Bomber. Each tower knew part of the story but could (or would) not share with others. Of course, if all of those decision makers had tools for information sharing even equivalent to my corporate-connected iPhone and secure enterprise social media infrastructure, the linkages become hard to ignore. With a secure Telecosm serving homeland security, all categories of information sharing and decision execution can be collaborated, correlated, and fused into actionable knowledge and, either independently or by recommendation, executed upon. What is needed is a organization-wide event-enabled infrastructure as described earlier in the section securely linked to top secret protected global mobility devices with display and interface capabilities equivalent to the combination of an iPad and an iPhone 4s with a next-generation Siri. Not to say that device and capability are adequate to purpose, but they point the way for an advanced technology solution.

So, what is missing in the Telecosm and technology story above? As I told a group of Government System Integrators at the annual Intellect reception in London last year, applications tailored and optimized for Telecosm and mobility are still sorely missing. After our presentations, they had approached the head of the United Kingdom G-Cloud Initiative and me and asked that if in fact smaller, shared, and cloud-based (like Telecosm) were the future, what would they do to make a living. My initial answer was a question: Have you looked at *Telecosm* and the future it promised? None indicated that they had read it, but all committed that they were going to. There is enough missing from that vision to keep all of them busy for the next decade. What is that vision and promise? I will posit a possible scenario at the end of this section as a primer.

Sidebar 2
Evolving Security

Emerging Secure Technologies

Every day another event leads to another headline in the techno-blogosphere about a compromise of private data, or hackers breaching a sensitive system, or some nation-state pilfering another nation's intellectual property. There are thousands of other cybersecurity incidents that never get reported each year. The DHS needs information technology experts, and more specifically information security experts, to shape and protect the way America does business now and in the future. DHS needs to set the standard on how systems are configured and maintained. Our nation's cyberspace defenses must be improved, cyberspace awareness must increase, and secure technologies must be leveraged. As President Obama has said in the past about cyberspace attacks, "[the attacks are] one of the most serious economic and national security threats our nation faces."

Fortunately for the United States government, security has become increasingly more prevalent in the daily operations of many organizations. The importance on Internet security is directly proportional to the amount of reliance we have on information technology systems. One cornerstone of securing information is known as encryption, which can protect data while at rest or in transit—both important to address. When encryption first became part of mainstream vernacular, only spies and governments really executed it well. Pioneers in public sector, like Witfield Diffie,

Martin Hellman, Ralph Merkle, Ronald Rivest, Adi Shamir, and Leonard Adelman, were ahead of their time and laid the foundations with which we securely engineer information technology systems today. The biggest gift these men gave us was pushing cryptography outside of national-level expertise and letting the world use its creativity to contribute new and exciting ways of securing information.

In a speech given at the 2010 RSA Corporation Security Conference in San Francisco, California, General Keith Alexander, Commander, United States Cyber Command, stated, "Securing our nation's network is a team sport. We all have to work together to make this happen." His statement is profound because, as a military leader, he is speaking about more than just military networks. Further, he recognizes the importance of the civilian sector in securing the nation's networks. A major goal of the DHS is wading through the multitude of options available for securing the very networks on which our nation depends.

As a high-tech society, we are in a situation where we have the expertise and mature technology to provide the capability to secure any manner of data, whether in transit or at rest. Many entities within the world would like nothing better than to access the very data DHS has been charged to protect.

The SNIP final project tackled the challenge of using smartphones to protect data in transit by utilizing Voice over Internet Protocol (VoIP), wireless connectivity/bandwidth, high-functioning mobile devices, and virtual private networks. The major lesson learned in this project was that creating secure systems with commercial products is not only achievable, but on the verge of becoming ubiquitous.

Without going into the history of mobile telephony, suffice it to say, we've come a long way. Current technology is able to meet the needs of secure mobile communications. The remaining question is, "How?"

The SNIP project utilized a layered approach for the communications security. The first layer of security is known as DTLS-SRTP, implemented within the VoIP family of technologies, and encrypts both the control channel and data channel. The second layer of security was an Elliptic Curve Cryptography (ECC) virtual private network tunnel. The ECC tunnel is part of the cryptography suite known simply as "Suite B." The handsets were configured to push all traffic through the VPN tunnel and only used packet-switched networking.

This project is just one example where security is brought together, layered at different levels, to achieve a top secret level of security as accredited by the United States government. Not bad for only commercially available products. And this is just the beginning. In your future information technology endeavors: Be creative, be fearless, and most of all, be secure.

THE VISION: ASSERTIONS

In a foreseeable future all DHS information and hosted applications will reside on a blended cloud.

The globally accessible cloud environments will be protected, isolated, and blended by a combination of readily available off-the-shelf componentry.

All sensitive information will be encrypted.

A mature platform as a service (PAAS) will ensure that all requested information and services are delivered within SLAs to only those with an appropriate, current, and immediate need to know within security guidelines, levels of assurance for identity, and entitlements.

An evaluated, certified and accredited, trusted operating system will arbitrate, control, constrain, and transparently deliver information, execute both trusted and single-level applications, and provide global encrypted access to distributed resources within trusted criteria.

An evaluated, distributed cloud of trustworthy computer hardware will provide an event-enabled physical cloud of highly scaled distributed memory and archival or storage services. All disk storage will be on hardware where the controller or disks themselves will transparently encrypt and decrypt stored information. Information will be either flow encrypted and/or personally encrypted under policy, privacy, and personal controls. It may also be simultaneously encrypted for all of those categories.

A trustworthy computer and its interfaces and surrounding devices will have been reviewed against all design documents, specifications, and component part numbers. This may sound out of reach, but once signatures of a vendor-provided platform are completed, few changes will need to be updated for all subsequent procurements.

A trustworthy rules-based event-enabled monitoring and control infrastructure will further provide a "neighborhood watch" function reacting to all potential exfiltration attempts outside of specific policies.

At the edge, a trusted EAL4+ certified gateway will control all external requests and responses. Since all higher sensitivity information is encrypted, the task becomes manageable by an off-the-shelf set of devices. Depending on the sensitivity, either AES-256 or Block-B Elliptic Curve encryption of content and context information provides high assurance that even a nation-state attacker cannot achieve access without appropriate policy authorization and the decryption key. This means that the gateway has to perform far fewer assurance steps on outbound traffic. Strongly encrypted content delivered over a strongly encrypted TLS connection is not a high threat exposure. The neighborhood watch further ensures matches of content and encryption methods and strengths.

The endpoint is a top secret approved fixed or mobility device. There is little difference in the endpoint assurance for either category of connection. The TS mobility device will likely be an iPad or Android handheld with a hardened version of IOS or Android OS vetted by the NSA. Voice communications will be via a NSA/DHS-controlled Skype-like VoIP service environment. Devices, keys, access points, and provisioning will require government control. The earlier sidebar by Capt. Pugh describes one possible path to appropriate assurance for this device. A government-controlled Siri-like voice query and command service will allow these devices highly intelligent and intuitive human interface. A built-in Micro CAC card, or more likely a next-generation NFC interface and device, will bond the individual and the device. Access decisions will be made based on device, location, connectivity, an NFC device, and possibly a living presence biometric device, depending on the needed level of assurance. NFC technology is rapidly maturing and gaining adoption. Many of the NFC systems are currently Common Criteria Evaluated and Validated at EAL4+ by an accredited lab and a national cryptographic authority. Living presence biometrics can determine a match, normal blood flow, and electrical signal indications from contact with the skin and determine whether the item matched is in fact still connected and living as part of the trust model. Encryption and privacy will both be supported. Encryption to network node or distant device will be augmented by a key exchange model for face-to-face encryption and privacy. (I invented a system for the face-to-face encryption and privacy with legal information recovery over a decade ago.)

VISION: SCENARIO

Colonel Jack Rocker is forward-deployed in a frenemy country for military exercises. While having a cup of tea in a local establishment, he believes he recognizes a wanted terrorist. He surreptitiously takes a high-resolution photo of the person. Using his Micro CAC and the NFC in a stitched pocket in his jacket, the colonel sends the image and a flag to the cloud for immediate analysis and response. The secure TLS connection using his credentials connects to the nearest least-loaded trusted gateway.

Recognizing his credentials and the flag on the embedded encrypted image, the gateway sends it directly to the cloud services layer, where a waiting image analysis services decrypts the image and confirms the colonel's concern. The service passes the vetted image to a CEP engine, along with location and other context from the colonel's device. It also passes confirm and await instructions message to the colonel.

The CEP engines use all available geographical, political indicators, HUMINT, known associates, and past tactics and raise an indicator across DHS, ODNI, DoD, and CTC watch centers and provide rules and rationales for the indicator. Wherever the watch center staff members are, their TS secure mobility devices begin to buzz and flash warnings. Those in proximity bring their devices into adjacency and dynamically link displays into a extreme-high-definition display akin to a battle-cab display wall. They then begin interacting by voice with Ranger, their response advisor, and all of the information available to their clearance level. Ranger is trained to the voice of their device owner, so each battle director has a personal interface to the grid of mobility devices in the virtual display system. Ranger is a TS outgrowth of the initial voice-response solutions like Siri.

Based on the recommendations from the Predictive Battle space modules in the event-enabled infrastructure, all available intelligence, and political indicators, the senior battle staff approves a plan to deploy unmanned assets to track the target and await indications of his intent. The unmanned assets deploy and track the target. Colonel Rocker was able to have a waiter rub up against the target, inconspicuously placing smart-dust on his clothing that enhances the ability of the assets to track their new target. Using micro-HD infrared and visible light sensors, they are able to easily follow the target to another meeting place.

CMSgt Knight, a special operator, and his team follow out of sight and hearing until the target enters another meeting site. The chief has a local asset casually take a secure mobility device and associated sensors to the location. Glass detectors give full audio, and micro-cameras also tethered to the TS mobile provides a clear, almost three-dimensional view into the meeting going on inside. A Flash request includes images of all of the people attending the meeting in a Super High Frequency squirt to an overhead asset, which relays it through a secure gateway up to the event-enabled cloud for CEP analysis and facial recognition. The resulting alert raises indicators to their highest possible level of imminent threat.

Traveling on the other side of the world, the counterterrorism task-force commander, General Reed, is awakened. Seven of the targets known associates; each high-level terrorists in their own right are also in the meeting. The audio feed, auto-translated by Ranger and a latest generation of translation software pioneered by Google and enhanced by the NSA, indicates that they are about to assassinate the leader of this frenemy country and his cabinet in a swift attack involving a dozen suicide bombers. Also discussed are the code words that will launch the attackers and their individual targets.

General Reed immediately calls his counterpart General Gar in the frenemy country, using the alliance clearance mode on his TS mobility device, keys, and his NFC chip to have a secure and personal conversa-tion. The generals agree that all actions are authorized to interdict this national and potential global impacting attack. General Reed author-izes and releases a scenario plan provided by the event-enabled cloud infrastructure to all battle staff members worldwide and the command-ers of tasked assets. He then calls the President, since another nation's leader is the target. An unmanned General Atomics Predator C Avenger (Figure 41-9) overhead is given a FRAG tasking for time and target to deliver a pair of Hellfire missiles on the meeting in six minutes.

The chief's special operators and their local partners get in positions to meet the suicide bombers. They also launch a pair of AeroVironment Shrike silent observation platforms (Figure 41-10). The pair will pro-vide a "God's Eye" view of the interdiction that is about to take place. The Shrike is a highly stable quad-copter capable of flying at 30 knots and hovering for 40 minutes while delivering high-definition video and high-resolution images to the chief's team and from there to all of the battle elements around the world via their TS mobility devices.

General Gar has a stand-in with body armor walk in front of a win-dow in the cabinet office so that no one suspects a change. A native local speaker calls the suicide bombers team leaders with a burn phone and provides the intercepted code words to begin their simultaneous

Figure 41-9

General Atomics
Avenger

Figure 41-10

AeroVironment
Shrike

attacks. Using tranquilizer shells in silent rail weapons, the chief and his team disables and captures all but one of the suicide bombers.

The final bomber is spotted by a special operator who deploys and launches an AeroVironment Switchblade (Figure 41-10), which blows up the terrorist before he can get within 100 feet of the President look-alike.

Figure 41-11

AeroVironment
Switchblade

All of the command and battle staff watch all of the engagements in HD from the Shrike cameras over their TS mobility devices, and a permanent record is stored in encrypted holographic storage. All of this takes place in the span of six minutes.

On time and on target the Avenger delivers its Hellfires, leveling the meeting place. From initial contact to threat resolution in less than 40 minutes. This is the new average for critical responses made possible by an event-enabled secure and trustworthy cloud platform powered by remote sensors, CEP, and an infrastructure for TS mobility devices and services. In this scenario 30 senior leaders collaborated, planned, and executed an urgent operation in a remote country from 15 separate locations around the world. This is what the DHS can have in time for the third edition, if they start now.

42

GIS TECHNOLOGY FOR PUBLIC SAFETY, EMERGENCY MANAGEMENT, AND HOMELAND SECURITY

Russ Johnson

Director, Public Safety Industry Solutions, Esri

INTRODUCTION

Emergency Management and Homeland Security encompass a wide range of topics and mean many different things to different people. Government at all levels (federal, state, and local) is viewed as having primary responsibility for emergency management and public safety. Traditionally, the military has responsibility for public safety as it applies to threats from foreign governments. The constant threat of terrorism has expanded the role of emergency management, adding additional levels of complexity. This expanded mission necessitates greater coordination among law enforcement, homeland security, and other first responder organizations at all levels of government. This chapter will describe how geographic information system (GIS) technology plays a critically important unifying role for all aspects of emergency management, homeland security, and public safety

GEOGRAPHIC INFORMATION SYSTEM TECHNOLOGY

A geographic information system (GIS) integrates hardware, software, and data for capturing, managing, analyzing, and displaying all forms of geographically referenced information. GIS is used to capture, store, check, integrate, manipulate, analyze, and display data related to positions on the Earth's surface. Typically, a Geographical

Figure 42-1

Map layers can be selected and displayed (overlaid). These layers are linked to data tables that contain detailed information about the geographic features being displayed. The most powerful aspect of GIS is its comprehensive analysis capabilities. GIS analyzes and displays patterns, relationships, and trends through the geographic data layers to help users understand how the world works, make the best choice from among options, or develop plans through what-if scenarios.

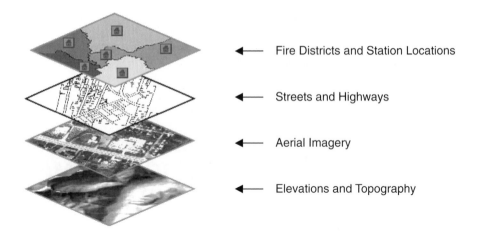

← Fire Districts and Station Locations

← Streets and Highways

← Aerial Imagery

← Elevations and Topography

Information System is used for handling maps of one kind or another. These might be represented as several different layers, where each layer holds data about a particular kind of feature (see Figure 42-1). Each feature is linked to a position on the graphical image on a map and a record in an attribute table. GIS can relate otherwise disparate data and information on the basis of common geography, revealing hidden patterns, relationships, and trends that are not readily apparent in spreadsheets or statistical packages, and often creating new information from existing data resources. GIS enables us to view, understand, question, interpret, and visualize data in ways that are easy to understand and act upon (see Figure 42-2).

Data stored in databases or in documents often have a geographical component such as an address, postal code, census block, city, county, or latitude/longitude coordinate. GIS enables the user to explore the spatial element of data such as critical infrastructure, or to assess crime patterns, analyze traffic use, and track the movement of vehicles, people, etc. In addition, GIS can model events, such as earthquakes, storm paths, bomb blasts, etc., and provide estimated consequences to the population, infrastructure, and natural resources. GIS helps in the analysis of and required decisions for all types of complicated problems.

THE EVOLUTION OF GIS TECHNOLOGY

GIS technology was initially used for complex analysis by trained GIS professionals. It has also been used extensively for printing static maps and continues to be used in those capacities today. The first GIS applications were developed for work stations, later becoming

Figure 42-2

Features on the map, when clicked, reveal detailed data stored in an attribute table.

desktop applications as personal computers became more powerful. GIS was somewhat "stove-piped" for several years. With the advent of the Internet, computer software advances, and cloud computing, GIS has evolved. It has become integrated into the overall information technology platform, it is easier to use, is more accessible, and can be configured to meet very specific work flow requirements without extensive training or technical skills required. GIS is now used in many industries routinely by operations personnel. There is greater access to geospatial data and dynamic data feeds (cameras, weather, tracking, sensors, etc.) from multiple sources, providing users with a more current view of events as they are occurring. Within the homeland security, public safety, and emergency management domains, GIS is increasingly being deployed and expanded.

Government agencies are typically responsible for rapid response to emergency calls within a geographic area, 24 hours a day. The first priority is getting to the emergency location quickly in order to take the appropriate action. GIS is used to assist first responders in meeting this fundamental objective. From the moment a call comes in to a 911 call center, to the time call-takers dispatch the appropriate public safety resources, GIS is at work providing the call location, routing assets to the scene, and providing access to premise information (preplans, previous call history, known hazards, etc.). Following are specific examples of how GIS is helping organizations meet complex public safety, emergency management, and homeland security missions.

EMERGENCY CALL HANDLING/DISPATCH

Dispatchers have an important responsibility to process emergency calls and send the appropriate public safety resources to the emergency location based on the type and urgency of the incident. GIS is an important component of the dispatch system. Dispatch systems or computer-aided dispatch (CAD) systems typically contain a file called the Master Street Address Guide, or MSAG. This file contains street address information and service areas for the jurisdiction that the dispatch center services. As emergency calls are received, they may be accompanied with address information from the telephone company's emergency phone record database. This address is entered or electronically transferred to the CAD system, which compares it (seeks to match) to the MSAG file. When the address is matched, the specific service area is also identified with the specific units that should be dispatched to the emergency. A computer-aided dispatch system integrates GIS and automatically geocodes the incident and displays it on a map. There are several benefits of having the incident displayed on the map. New calls reporting the emergency may have different addresses but are reporting the same incident that was previously recorded. The GIS map display visually displays that all of these calls with different addresses are in the same proximity as the original call. This enables the dispatcher to quickly understand they are all related to the same incident. Other benefits include:

- Global positioning system (GPS)—many public safety agencies response units are equipped with GPS devices. This provides the dispatcher (and perhaps other appropriate public safety managers) the ability to see locations of units through a GIS display and track them to the incident when dispatched. This is important during heavy call volume or for mobile vehicles such as police units and emergency medical units. This provides dispatchers a virtual or near real-time view of incident locations and emergency response units to activate an appropriate dispatch based on emergency unit availability.

- Routing—GIS can quickly analyze and display a route from a station or GPS location to the emergency call. This route (depending on the sophistication of the street file) may be the shortest path (distance) or the quickest path (depending on time of day and traffic patterns). This information can be displayed to the dispatcher and on a mobile computer screen in the response vehicle. Vehicles equipped with mobile computers and GIS can also benefit by providing first responders access to preplans, hazardous material locations, photographs, and other location-based documents linked to actual specific locations through the GIS map display.

- Move up and cover—during periods of high volume and simultaneous calls or a complex emergency, GIS can display areas of high risk that are left substantially uncovered. GIS can provide recommendations for reallocating available resources for better response coverage.

- Emergency wireless calls—Wireless technology and cellular telephone technology have added to the necessity of GIS. Wireless phone-reported emergencies are not associated with an address, and the caller may not know his or her address or street location. GPS-enabled cell phones can provide latitude and longitude coordinates during an emergency call. Other technologies are available that triangulate the call location between cell towers or measure strength of signal to provide approximate location information. These coordinates are relatively meaningless to a dispatcher, but GIS can quickly consume and display a latitude/longitude or other coordinate location. This enables the dispatcher to see the incident location or general area and the closest or quickest response units on the GIS display.

First Responders

Upon arrival at the incident, first responders depend heavily upon the concept of "size-up" to determine appropriate deployment actions. Size-up requires assessing the existing situation, probabilities, possibilities, and required actions, to save lives and protect property. Whether it is a fire, emergency, or law enforcement incident, first responders must evaluate the situation and determine a course of action. Firefighters, police, and rescue workers are well aware that the first few minutes of a call can be critical in determining its outcome.

Fire Rescue

During a fire emergency, firefighters respond, size up the situation, and deploy. A typical "room and contents fire" can reach flashover (rapid fire ignition and spread) within four to ten minutes of ignition, and occupants who have not already escaped are not likely to survive. Fire departments often inspect and develop pre-fire plans for many of the structures and facilities within their area of responsibility. Having access to pre-fire plans as they respond enables them to deploy faster and more safely (cuts down on size-up time with accurate data). Pre-plan information can be delivered through a GIS application (perhaps the same application that provides the location of the incident and the most efficient route). Some of the information that may be provided by a pre-fire plan includes:

- Floor plan
- Hydrant locations
- Occupancy type
- Utility control points
- Hazardous material locations
- Number of floors and basement
- Other

This information, along with other map data concerning the overall area is invaluable in performing rapid, accurate size up for effective deployment.

Law Enforcement

Geospatial intelligence is an important aspect of police response to calls for service. There is no such thing as a "routine" call, and GIS can quickly get information to responding officers that otherwise would not be available. This information can be critical in determining initial actions and the potential for the incident escalation. Every piece of information associated with a location may be of tactical importance, including:

- The history and types of calls to the address
- The occupants
- Nearby habitual offenders
- Current crime trends in the area
- Gang territories

Other tactical considerations, such as the locations of possible approaches/escape routes and cover and concealment locations are also important to police response and can quickly be revealed using GIS. By using geography in conjunction with all of the historic information associated with a location, dispatchers and officers can easily see what has occurred at that location or near that location within the past week, month, or year.

When the officer or incident commander arrives at the incident, he or she is responsible to manage the event rather than become part of the tactical deployment. The officer requires additional, different information to perform the command mission. Depending on the complexity and size of the incident, the information and data requirements may include the following:

- What other exposures or other facilities are threatened by this incident?
- Where should the incoming units be positioned to effectively support the units already on scene?
- If an equipment staging area or incident command post is required, where are parking lots, schools, churches, malls, or other suitable facilities located?
- If evacuation is necessary, where should people be directed?
- If helicopter evacuation of victims is required, where are suitable landing sites?
- If medical triage or decontamination is required, where can it be implemented?
- If hazardous materials are involved or a chemical plume is being generated, where is it going, what does it threaten, and what actions are required to protect and evacuate the public?
- If an explosion is possible, who needs to be evacuated and where is an immediate evacuation facility?
- In a larger scale incident (hostage, school attack, terrorist attack, etc.), law enforcement commanders would benefit from access to floor plans, imagery, utility networks and services, line of sight analysis, etc., to support command-and-control and incident management decisions.
- Touch screen technology coupled with mobile computers allows first responders to access information quickly to reduce size-up time, and results in quicker, safer deployment.

GIS provides first responders and incident commanders the right information, at the right time and place, which is easy to access and use. Much of the information first responders require has already been collected but resides in a variety of formats and in a variety of locations. GIS integrates the information and provides it graphically to first responders through maps. Beyond initial response, GIS can model explosions, plumes, and other potential emergencies. Instead of guessing or estimating evacuation requirements, transportation network problems, and other infrastructure threats, GIS will provide a more accurate prediction of the event and display the potential consequences.

Today, ruggedized computers with touch screen technology coupled with mobile computers enable first responders and officers to access accurate information quickly to reduce size-up time (see Figure 42-3). These types of capabilities are rapidly moving toward computer pad and smart phone devices.

SITUATIONAL AWARENESS

Situational awareness is best defined as:

- Knowing and understanding what is happening, when it is happening
- Predicting how situations could or will change over time and their potential impacts
- Acquiring the big picture and environment of situations

The traditional approach for obtaining situational awareness, beyond personnel observations in the field, would be to identify the information required by using databases, paper maps, plans bound in three-ring binders, web links, news, and voice communication. This process is extremely time-consuming and does not produce timely results.

The ability to have the required information for mission driven situational awareness when and where needed, can be achieved through geographic information system (GIS) technology. GIS integrates other technologies to provide users with the right types of information based on their specific requirements. GIS is foundational in providing personnel with enhanced situational awareness. For example, GIS can provide

Figure 42-3

Mobile screen. GIS mobile applications provide the tactical map interface to information and data important to first responders. Information such as preplans, floor plans, and other documents are linked to building facility addresses and are easily displayed by clicking or touching the map.

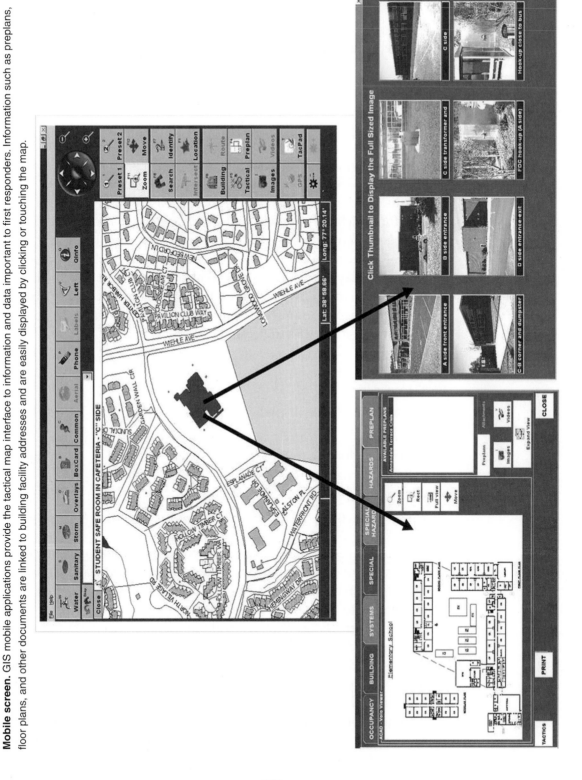

the user with the appropriate base map layers for their jurisdictional requirements. These base layers could include:

- Imagery
- Streets
- Critical infrastructure
- Elevations
- Combination of base layers

Additional data layers may be desirable based upon the specific mission for which the situational awareness viewer is being used. If GIS has been used to assess vulnerabilities, a layer depicting hazard, or critical values could also be part of the operational layers to "turn on" or display as needed. This can also include data such as historic incidents, planned events, etc. Dynamic sensor data can also be captured and displayed onto the map. These layers, depending upon the specific mission, could include:

- Hydrants
- Hazards
- Fire
- Crimes
- Flood plains
- Wildfire hazard areas
- Police beats
- Fire districts

The base layers combined with operational mission layers serve as a "canvas" for dynamic data which displays a real or near real-time picture of the area and specific circumstances. As dynamic data feeds are imported into the view, their significance or priority for action is much more apparent. For example, if real time incidents from the 911 system are imported into the situational awareness viewer and "fused" with the base and operational layers, their potential impact or importance can be easily understood. As traffic incidents occur, access to traffic cams from the viewer can provide a quick view into the impacts, traffic congestion, etc. Whether it is a chemical spill in a highly populated area or critical infrastructure important to the continuity of government operations, or a wildfire ignition in a highly flammable area near residential structures, the consequences of events and priority for action becomes clear. Examples of dynamic data can include:

- Traffic cameras
- Stream gauges
- Sensors
- Weather
- GPS tracking
- Work status
- Hospital bed status

Dynamic data enhances the user's ability to understand, react, and make accurate decisions.

Geospatial tools that support mission requirements add capabilities for operational decision support. These tools could include plume or explosion models, demographic reporting, road block requirements for emergency events, and others. Today, these tools are easy to initiate and run, with quick results. Running a plume model or drawing an impact area on the map can quickly return a report of population affected, critical infrastructure impacts, intersections that should be closed, and more (see Figure 42-4). This combination of base maps, operational layers, and dynamic data can provide a virtual picture of circumstances and potential impacts for a specific area. When other data such as plans, policy documents, checklists, floor plans, etc., are linked to geographical features on the map, a very powerful GIS-driven situational awareness platform is enabled (see Figure 42-5). In addition, this situational awareness picture can be shared with others who have the appropriate security credentials from remote locations and on mobile devices. As mobile devices continue to become more capable, field personnel can not only obtain situational awareness in the field, but can also update and make changes to the situational awareness viewer, which are immediately visible to everyone, from their mobile devices.

CRIME ANALYSIS

Geography has a major influence on crime. The features and characteristics of cityscapes and rural landscapes can make it easier or more difficult for crime to occur. The placement of alleys, buildings, and

Figure 42-4

Situational awareness is provided through an easy to use Common Operating Picture. This web-based application typically requires little training, and produces relevant geographic and dynamic data to provide a virtual, near real-time picture of existing conditions. This screen shot shows a traffic accident and access to live traffic cameras near the event.

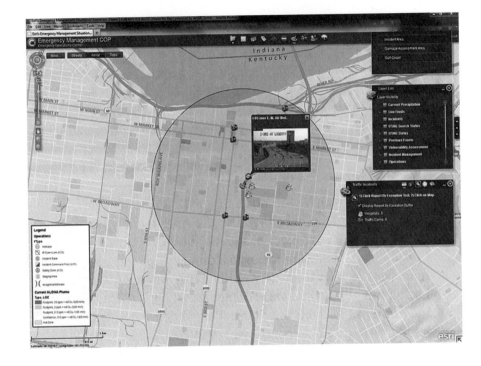

open spaces, for example, affects the likelihood that a criminal will strike. Combining geographic data with police report data and then displaying the information on a map is an effective way to analyze where, how, and why crime occurs.

Figure 42-5

Executive-level dashboards powered by GIS provide access to multiple live maps, real-time incidents, response performance history, charts, and other departmental information.

Figure 42-6

Crime analysis.
Individual crimes
or crime density
can be mapped
and displayed
based on types of
crimes by hour, day,
week, month, or
whatever the crime
analyst requires.
This enables law
enforcement officials
to easily see and
understand crime
trends and patterns
and determine
prescriptive staffing
requirements.

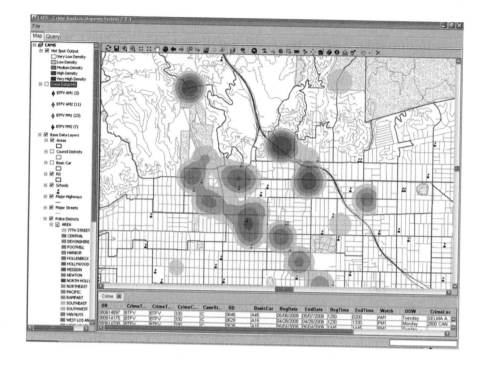

Using GIS, crime analysts map where crime occurs, combine the resulting visual display with other geographic data (such as location of schools, parks, and industrial complexes), and analyze and investigate the causes of criminal activity (see Figure 42-6). Recent advances in statistical analysis make it possible to add more geographic and social dimensions to the analysis. GIS enables crime analysis by:

- Identifying and highlighting suspicious incidents and events that may require further investigation
- Supporting pattern and trend analysis across multiple jurisdictions
- Enhancing the implementation of various policing methodologies to reduce overall crime and disorder
- Integrating traditional and nontraditional law enforcement data to improve overall analysis
- Educating the public with visual information to clarify crime concerns and enlist community action
- Providing tools and techniques to capture crime series and forecast future crime occurrences

The ability to access and process information quickly while displaying it in a spatial and visual medium allows agencies to allocate resources quickly and more effectively. In the mission-critical nature of law enforcement, information about the location of a crime, incident, suspect, or victim is often crucial to determine the manner and size of the response.

FIRE & RESCUE STATION LOCATION ANALYSIS

Locating the best sites to place fire stations is essential, particularly when budgets are tight and resources are limited. The factors to consider when locating stations are diverse and complicated:

- Response time performance goals
- Critical infrastructure at risk
- Historic incidents
- Water delivery systems
- Future development and growth, etc.

GIS is used to model and identify potential station locations by analyzing all of the desired and relevant data. GIS simulates the real road network for areas being analyzed, using actual travel distances, vehicle speeds, and time delays for roadway conditions (e.g., congestion, turning radius, weather, hills, etc.), accounting for one-way or unusable roadways, and implementing user-defined risk factors (see Figure 42-7).

Additional data used to ensure accuracy are historical incident patterns, incident concentrations, time of day, time of year, zoning, land use, values at risk, hazards, and other data based on local conditions. In some instances, an alternate fire company may arrive quicker, due to heavy traffic during peak travel hours.

The results of GIS computer studies are a series of color-coded maps of the street/roadway network that are easy to comprehend. These maps display a variety of information, such as the street segments that can be reached from all stations for a specified target travel time, the overlap between stations, the response area for each station, and other information as determined by local officials (see Figure 42-8).

GIS analysis can effectively illustrate problem areas, as well as proposed solutions. GIS can show various data for simulated responses to

Figure 42-7

Fire/EMS response
analysis. GIS can
very accurately
model drive times
based on the road
network, traffic
patterns by time
of day, and other
local variables.
This screen shot
illustrates four-, six-,
and eight-minute
predicted drive times
from a designated
fire station.

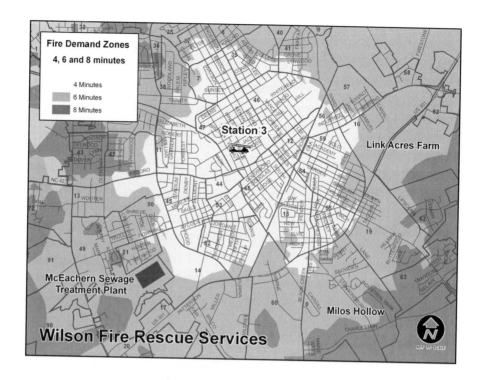

Figure 42-8

Fire/EMS response
analysis. This screen
shot illustrates
an eight-minute
time model with a
proposed new state
(station 6P). This
enables fire officials
to select and model
new station location
sites for optimum
response coverage.

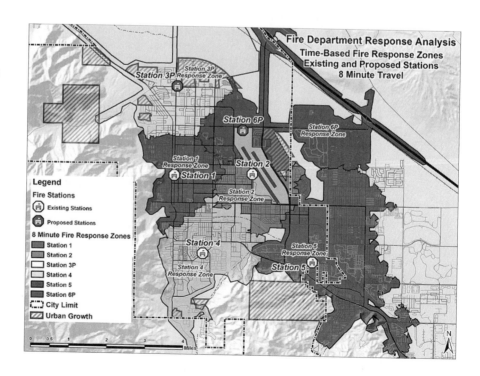

specific locations, including apparatus and personnel on a time-arrival sequence, multiple alarms, and travel time to each street segment in the system.

GIS analysis produces color maps that show the overlap between stations for a specified travel time. The color maps show the areas where there are two or more stations whose first-due response areas overlap, with the overlap colors being different from the station response area colors. These maps can be used to determine multiple-company response to an area or to show where stations are placed ineffectively. Areas that receive no coverage or deficient coverage are also displayed.

The response from mutual-aid stations can also be analyzed as part of the overall study to show the arrival of additional resources. This is particularly useful to show the response of special apparatus and teams, such as hazardous materials teams, advanced rescue teams, or other special teams. Given limited resources, an entire region can be analyzed using the total resources of the region.

Alternative and future station locations can be examined through the use of "what-if...?" scenarios using various fire station locations and travel times. The information from these programs can be integrated with the data from local and regional planning groups to show where new stations and/or roadways may be needed to best serve existing and growing communities.

EMERGENCY/DISASTER MANAGEMENT

A major responsibility of government is to protect life and property. To best handle that responsibility it is necessary to understand a community's vulnerabilities and risks to populations, infrastructure vital to sustaining the community, and natural resources. In addition, having awareness into emergency situations as they unfold, having the ability to collect and analyze intelligence, and maintaining a state of readiness through drills and response exercises increases a community's preparedness and ability to effectively respond and recover. GIS enables emergency management planners to conduct comprehensive community hazard and risk assessment.

HAZARD AND RISK ANALYSIS

Using GIS, vulnerability analysis starts by identifying natural and technological or man-made hazards. GIS enables planners to import or map hazards which may include the following:

Natural Hazards

- Earthquake faults
- Storm surge exposure
- Tsunami exposure
- Flammable vegetation
- Areas prone to severe weather events
- Landslides
- Floods

Technological Hazards

- Hazardous materials locations
- Transportation corridors where hazardous materials are routinely transported (rail, highway, etc.)
- Nuclear power plants
- Petroleum processing and storage facilities

Hazards, by themselves, may not be cause for alarm or necessitate mitigation actions. When hazards present potential danger to populations, infrastructure, or natural resources, planners have to decide what actions might be necessary. The next step in conducting a GIS-based vulnerability assessment is the identification and mapping of values that maybe at risk. These can include:

- Population centers
- Critical infrastructure, including: government facilities, hospitals, utilities, public assemblies, etc.
- Natural resources, including plant and animal habitats, commercial farming, etc.

As values are mapped and identified, those at risk will reside within the impact areas of natural hazards and or technological hazard areas. To further understand the potential consequence of an event on particular values or infrastructure, GIS can model plumes, explosions, floods, earthquakes, etc., and display projected areas of extreme, moderate, or light damage and estimated casualties (see Figures 42-9 to 42-11). This enables planners to prioritize mitigation requirements and determine response needs with a more accurate understanding of the consequences of a potential emergency.

1000   PART 9 • INTRODUCTION TO PART IX: SCIENCE AND TECHNOLOGY

Figure 42-9

This screen shot
illustrates mapping
and modeling natural
hazards in Louisville,
Kentucky. The river,
with a history of
flooding, is mapped
and a hundred-
year flood model is
displayed. This is
one of the primary
natural hazards in
the area.

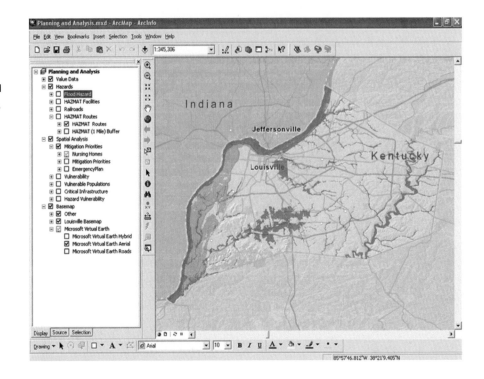

Figure 42-10

This screen shot
illustrates mapping
and buffering
technological
(man-made)
hazards (such
as hazardous
materials). The
buffer provides a
general estimate
of the impact area,
if an accident
occurred.

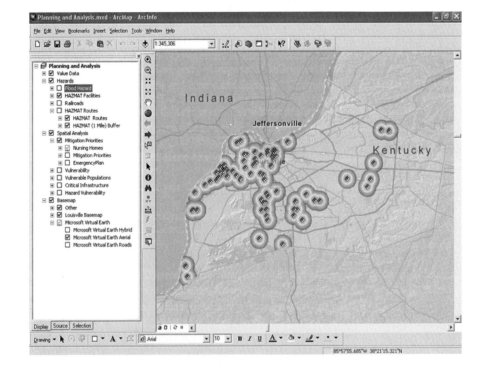

Figure 42-11

This screen shot combines all of the hazards and the values (critical infrastructure, population density, etc.) at risk into a weighted grid. The darker colored areas represent a combination of hazards and values. This enables emergency planners to identify high risk areas that may require some time of mitigation to reduce potential consequences.

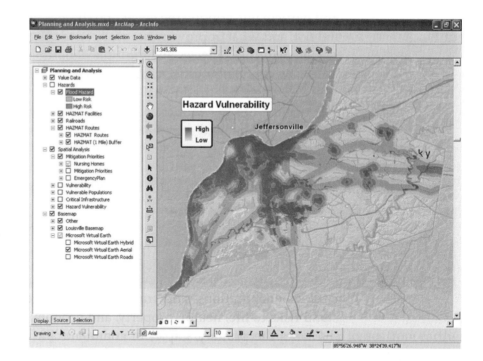

A GIS-based vulnerability analysis enables planners to develop a comprehensive and accurate understanding of a community's exposures. This analysis provides the foundation for the development of plans, mitigation, response, and training needs. From this analysis, new map layers and data are produced, which can be leveraged for ongoing situational awareness. Planning data becomes immediately accessible through a GIS-powered common operating picture for operational use on a daily basis.

RESPONSE EXERCISES

In order to stay current on skills, public safety agencies commonly run exercises known as response drills, which are an essential part of preparedness and are valuable in identifying strengths and weaknesses in any response plan. Exercises can be effectively targeted toward likely events. The GIS-based vulnerability analysis described earlier identifies hazards that could result in emergencies that impact the community's infrastructure and populations. Realistic drills and exercises can be developed based upon events identified through the analysis. Exercises are often followed by a debrief session whereby observers

Figure 42-13

This screen shot illustrates a HAZUS earthquake model run in southern California. One of the many reports GIS can provide and visually represent is a potential damage assessment. This map provides a view and report of potential freeway bridge damage. The model projects that most of the major transportation routes in southern California will be unusable. Emergency planners need to consider alternative methods of transporting supplies, moving people, and overall logistical support.

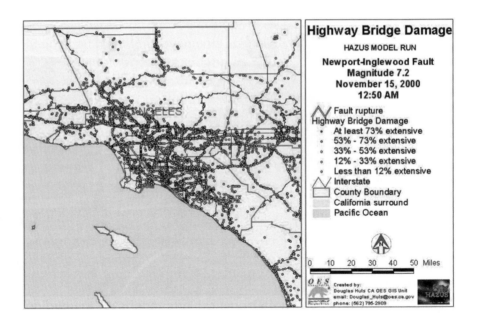

- Economic loss, including lost jobs, business interruptions, repair and reconstruction costs; and
- Social impacts, including estimates of shelter requirements, displaced households, and population exposed to scenario floods, earthquakes, and hurricanes.

When actual emergencies occur, HAZUS can be used to model the emergency that just occurred to give emergency management personnel a better idea of exactly what the consequences may be, as well as search and rescue priorities and recovery needs.

INTELLIGENCE ANALYSIS

For purposes of homeland security, surveillance and detection become critically important. Geographic information systems are central in the detection and prevention process. When analyzing intelligence data in a national or local situation, time and space relationships play a key role and GIS is ideal for consuming and analyzing complex problems involving dynamic time-sensitive events in confined or disparate locations.

Terrorism and criminal activities require funding, people, materials, and logistics. The connections between these patterns are time and space. GIS techniques can be used to correlate apparently disconnected events to see the big picture emerge from huge volumes of data. For example, geographic analysis can assist in the following:

- Understanding movements of people and resources across the world, a country, or a city in space and time. When and where do people come together in a critical mass with the potential to cause harm?
- Tracking proximity relationships: What critical resources are in proximity to possible suspects?
- Where resources should be deployed to prevent or minimize damage?
- Analysis of telephone usage (source and destination) can be used to place suspects in space and time.
- What groups of people are most vulnerable to infectious disease caused by terrorist activities?
- Tracking the locations of financial transactions.

The key is the fusion of data from disparate sources into a common spatial framework. As a growing range of sensors are deployed to gather information concerning suspicious activities, GIS can be used to integrate their information into a meaningful common picture. Thus, surveillance and detection activity are coordinated through the medium of a map. GIS provides powerful analysis tools that can help detect pending events, which allows government officials to implement actions that will prevent acts of destruction from occurring.

GIS provides analysts with a vital tool to study space and time phenomena during the detection and prevention phase. The threat of chemical, biochemical, and nuclear exposure is now a real possibility. Detecting potential attacks and tracking exposures is difficult and complex. The anthrax exposures in New York and Washington D.C. provided some experience into the difficulties associated with these types of attacks. GIS can geographically display and analyze where exposures have occurred and when. Trends and patterns can be determined, and persons requiring examination, inoculation, and possibly quarantine can be identified.

Chemical and biological attacks can be modeled, evacuation requirements can be determined, decontamination areas can be selected, and roadblocks can be identified, displayed, and rapidly provided to responders. This type of information can be time sensitive and data can now be delivered to those who need it, when they need it, in a medium that is easy to understand and act upon. The number of potential exposures can be predicted and the appropriate quantity of vaccines and medical supplies ordered.

Fusion Centers

Fusion centers were created under a joint project between the Department of Homeland Security and the U.S. Department of Justice's Office of Justice Programs between 2003 and 2007 to promote information gathering and sharing at the federal level between agencies such as the Central Intelligence Agency (CIA), Federal Bureau of Investigation (FBI), Department of Justice, U.S. Military, and state and local level government. Fusion centers bring multiple agencies together in one location to collect suspicious activity reports and share that information for coordination between intelligence agencies, law enforcement, and others involved in counterterrorism and law enforcement. Post-event reviews often discover that many different people and organizations had pieces of data, which, when all brought together, identifies valuable information and evidence of information that, if acted upon, could have prevented an incident. Fusion centers were established to bring people from various agencies together to share and "fuse" information to improve the ability to overcome threats to national security.

The purpose of a fusion center is to facilitate the collection, analysis, and dissemination of crime- and terrorism-related information. A fusion center is often defined as a collaborative effort of two or more agencies providing resources, expertise, and information. The goal is to optimize the ability to detect, prevent, investigate, and respond to criminal and terrorist activity.

Fusion center workflows are complex. The primary focus of a fusion center is to bring together and analyze suspicious activity reports and crime to identify pre-operational terrorist activity. The following are key workflow steps for a fusion center:

- Intelligence collection
- Data integration and fusion
- Information analysis
- Report production
- Knowledge dissemination

Figure 42-14

Data fusion. This map represents an intelligence gathering and analysis solution for Fusion Centers. Data of all types (crime incidents, suspicious activity reports, fire reports, and others, are collected within a common collaboration data repository. These reports are then rapidly mapped. Patterns, trends, or connected suspicious activities can be viewed and appropriate actions can be taken and coordinated.

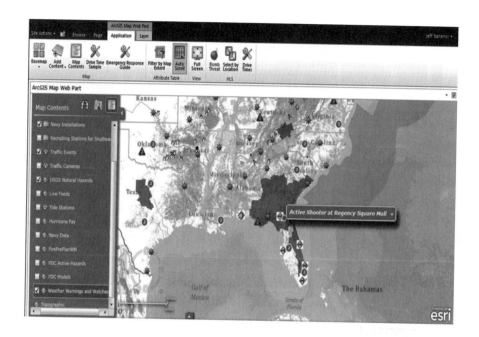

Many fusion centers today are using GIS to help meet this very challenging mission (see Figure 42-14). GIS supports the fusion centers through:

- Link analysis: Associations between people and places
- Threat identification: Confirmed Suspicious Activity Reports and their locations
- Risk assessments: Areas vulnerable to threats, such as critical infrastructure
- Critical infrastructure protection mitigation planning
- Crime analysis reports: Areas where crimes are occurring

GIS is playing an important role in fusion center workflows and is providing collaboration and communication throughout the intelligence cycle.

CRITICAL INFRASTRUCTURE PROTECTION

As described previously, critical infrastructure can be identified as part of a vulnerability assessment. When assessing critical infrastructure, vulnerability to attacks require a different approach. Critical infrastructure must be prioritized based upon its importance and overall routing, safe zones if rapid fire ignition and spread occurred, staging areas for fire equipment, and early warning systems to notify potentially affected communities if a wildfire occurred. In all, over 40 agencies and organizations collaborated and conducted multi-stakeholder planning and priority action plan development using GIS as the primary planning, visualization, and collaboration tool. In the summer of 2003, southern California began to experience very severe hot dry winds. A series of wildfires erupted and began to spread and consume thousands of acres, threatening communities, natural resources, and infrastructure. All of the GIS-driven plans came immediately into effect and orderly evacuations occurred. Firefighters from throughout the West mobilized to support the incident. Firefighters were given hard-copy maps developed during the GIS planning phase that guided them to safe areas, staging areas, and identified critical infrastructure protection priorities. As Incident Management Teams deployed to several different fires, GIS was used to prepare fire perimeter maps, model wildfire prediction, and provide operational tactical maps, public information briefing maps, and eventually damage assessment and rehabilitation maps. GIS was instrumental in the planning, mitigation, response, recovery, and overall collaboration for the management of a very serious situation. As a result, critical infrastructure and key facilities were protected, thousands of people were safely evacuated, fire suppression operations and priorities were safely followed and implemented, and recovery and rehabilitation was carried out quickly and efficiently

Tuscaloosa Tornadoes

When deadly tornadoes and other weather-related disasters hammered the South and Midwest in 2011, many cities and counties used geographic information system (GIS) technology to accelerate emergency search and rescue and storm damage recovery. Using GIS to create specialized maps, emergency responders were better able to make sense of the ruins left behind by the storms.

In Tuscaloosa, Alabama, a tornado cut a 5.9 mile path of destruction, killing 43 people, and damaging thousands of homes, businesses, and properties in its wake. The city's GIS Manager helped firefighters and engineers use handheld, mobile GIS devices with GPS for search and rescue and damage assessment. Using the data they collected along with address grids, GIS analysts created digital maps that rescuers and others used to identify heavily damaged buildings. The maps helped determine the type of structure that was there, and whether it

Figure 42-22

This map illustrates "damage triage" that occurred in the field by various damage assessment teams following the Tuscaloosa tornadoes. Because the area was devastated, street signs and reference points that would orient them to their specific locations were gone. Using handheld GIS and GPS devices, they were able to determine the specific property and report back instantly on the degree of damage or loss. These data were all gathered and were posted on the Situational Awareness Viewer.

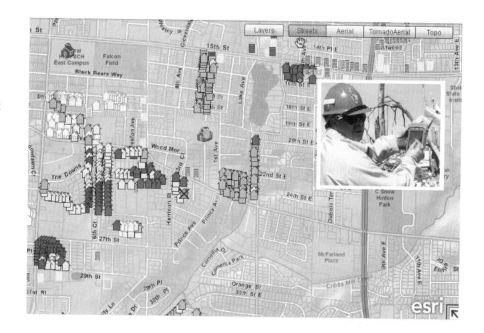

was residential or other, in a devastated area with no street signs left. GIS was instrumental in determining search and rescue priorities, establishing shelters, identifying critical short-term recovery priorities, and overall incident management (see Figure 42-22).

SUMMARY

Whether modeling disaster consequences, assessing critical infrastructure, or alerting residents to an impending tsunami, GIS-driven maps and applications help emergency personnel save lives, mitigate property damage, and speed recovery.

Situational awareness is the key to effective emergency management. GIS-driven situational awareness has evolved over the past decade to furnish current information to support missions across workflows. Situational awareness is enhanced by GIS technology, not by the implementation of a single application. GIS is a platform for delivering mission-specific applications that incorporate the abundance of GIS-ready data with operational data continually updated from the field to support analysis, decision making, and collaboration.

Before GIS was applied to emergency management, information for decisions was often limited to the experience and intuition of individual emergency personnel. GIS tremendously expanded the resources that can be used when evaluating a situation. Initially, GIS use focused on response efforts, especially the production of paper maps for briefings and personnel in the field. Static maps produced by the first Internet mapping websites also improved situational awareness for managers and incident commanders and kept the public informed. However, paper maps and static images both suffered from latency and the absence of interactivity. The timeliness of these maps was dependent on the update cycle and could not provide the most current information. Maps generated to answer one set of questions could not be queried to answer new questions spawned by response situations in constant flux, or address additional scenarios when working on planning, mitigation, or preparedness efforts.

New patterns of GIS have emerged that answer needs for timeliness, interactivity, accessibility, and collaboration. Extending GIS using cloud computing platforms has made web maps and applications almost instantly accessible for response to disasters. The implementation of GIS platforms in the cloud enables responders to rapidly obtain map services without procuring hardware, installing software, or impacting existing on-premises infrastructures.

The value of GIS in the cloud was demonstrated in 2010 when extensive flooding covered three-quarters of the state of Queensland, Australia. Responding agencies needed quick access to information on this rapidly changing situation. A Situational Awareness Viewer was implemented in just 12 hours that gave access to the latest, most accurate information on the situation in Brisbane.

Live incident response apps have become an increasingly popular method for sharing information about a disaster or capturing additional data from the public via posts to Facebook, Twitter, Flickr, and YouTube.

Mobile devices let responders enjoy bidirectional situational awareness in near real time. The Alabama Marine Police demonstrated how bidirectional capability could be applied to a large-scale disaster event. Responding to the massive oil spill in the Gulf of Mexico caused by the Deepwater Horizon incident in 2010, crews documented the location of booms and other apparatus using mobile devices. Maps, data, images, and video were immediately transmitted to incident command via a Broadband Global Area Network (BGAN). A GIS viewer displayed current maps at daily briefings. The result: Everyone in a five-state area could see the same information at the same time— a tremendous leap forward in situational awareness.

43

TECHNOLOGY FORAGING: A NOVEL APPROACH TO TECHNOLOGY PROBLEM SOLVING WITHIN THE DHS SCIENCE AND TECHNOLOGY DIRECTORATE

Michael Hopmeier

President, Unconventional Concepts, Inc.

Technology Foraging (TF) is a means of actively seeking out rather mature technology solutions to address defined capability needs or problems. It uses a proactive method of identifying existing sources of technology that engages them directly, with perhaps minimal modifications, to solve problems, as opposed to advertising needs and allowing potential providers to self-identify solutions.

This chapter discusses the philosophy behind this TF approach, describes its implementation with DHS Science & Technology (S&T), and provides insight and recommendations based on its initial phase of operation.

EXECUTIVE SUMMARY

Traditional approaches within the government to address capability needs via technology entail the following:

- Generating and validating a need through a sometimes complex and arcane process
- Advertising the need to a community that has potential solutions or approaches

- Choosing, through a competitive contracting process, the performers, who then follow through within the scope and direction of a defined contract

This process depends largely on the ability of the government to articulate a need effectively with little to no iteration, and the ability of a performer to accurately identify and satisfy the need, based almost exclusively on this single description.

Technology Foraging (TF) is a new and novel approach to satisfying capability needs for government applications and operations, by following a three-pronged process of identifying requirements, providing technology solutions, and presenting effective business plans. While still early in implementation, TF has proven extraordinarily effective.

First applied in 2011 in a large-scale, organized manner by the Science & Technology (S&T) Directorate of the Department of Homeland Security under the direction of Undersecretary Tara O'Toole, TF has proven to be an unusually effective means of rapidly identifying technology applications for addressing key mission needs areas across the breadth of the government's operating space and presenting effective business plans for application. The key problem, however, still remains in the implementation of this innovative process through the more conventional acquisition process.

While conventional government S&T programs are based on a reactive approach (the government publicizes a need and then potential performers react to it), TF takes a more proactive and aggressive approach. TF self-defines requirements based on input from credible and highly respected members of a user community and then seeks out and evaluates available technologies to fulfill this need, concluding with the development of a business plan for product development and market introduction. The streamlined approach allows for rapid development and transition of technologies, thereby resulting in significant cost and time savings. It is also draconian in its assessment of success, in that all "less than fully successful" efforts are terminated.

The hallmark of the TF process is actively seeking potential solutions rather than awaiting them to be self-identified by responders to government solicitations. Through a combination of experience, skill, and serendipity, potential providers of solutions are identified. This results in more rapid, cost-effective, and functional solutions than those that are often provided through the more conventional, cumbersome, and reactive approaches in the development and transition of technology.

This approach, however, works most effectively on well-defined, technologically mature problems where solutions can be effectively applied in short timeframes (six months) with minimal modifications or maturation. The focus is on rapid transition and application of mature products and technologies to new mission areas.

To date, the TF effort may be considered a significant success. Numerous specific opportunities have been identified and are currently under development, in transition, or in validation. The success of the project can perhaps best be summarized by a statement from the director of one of the laboratories visited by a foraging team. When asked at the end of the meeting about his impression, he said:

> This is a great concept. We never would have thought to look at an RFP for this idea, and if we had, we never would have connected the dots to understand how our work could apply. This has been a wonderful interaction and is now resulting in a wholly new concept that never would have come about without this discussion.

This, in essence, is why the TF program was initiated by DHS, and what will keep it alive in the future.

BACKGROUND

Current S&T strategy throughout the government generally is (1) find a need/requirement that is not currently met, (2) solicit S&T approaches to meet it, and (3) utilize source selection committees to assess the potential technical performance, cost, and schedule risks to determine which approaches should be pursued. Key factors in the success of this process are the identification of a "need/requirement" and understanding how well the anticipated technology may address the need/requirement. This strategy is commonly referred to as "technology push," where the technology owner sees a public solicitation and "pushes" the technology to fit the advertised need (Broad Agency Announcements (BAAs) and Request for Proposals (RFPs) are the most typical solicitation vehicles). For many different reasons, it is highly probable that numerous technologies are not submitted in response to each BAA or RFP. Frequently this occurs as a result of failure of technology developers/owners to be aware of a new or innovative application of their technology, or simply lack of interest in dealing with the government. Often, a disconnect occurs as a result of poor communication between the developer and technology holder.

The different Technology Foraging approach includes both an "active requirements pull" as well as an "active technology push." The requirements pull process is considered to be "active" because, unlike the current S&T strategy, technology solutions are aggressively sought on behalf of government users, especially those with capability needs to combat terrorism and support other homeland security missions. The technology push occurs when technologies are identified, through foraging, that exhibit potential for capabilities not yet considered by the user community. To support the foraging effort, teams are assembled to identify new and innovative technologies *at their source* (government and private labs, industry, academia, etc.) and to propose a development process that exploits those technologies that would not normally surface through a more conventional and less effective means of acquisition and problem solving.

In addition to focusing just on capability needs and technologies, TF also focuses on an equally important third criterion of "business plan/model to rapidly transition the technology." Additionally, TF is not constrained to following the three tasks in serial order. For example, in the push mode, technology may be discovered and pursued that may support a unique and important capability not "directly" identified in a documented need/requirement. However, with some manipulation of the technology, it can be brought in line with a particular need/requirement. Similarly, the TF process may also identify previously unknown or unimagined gaps and opportunities that may, after analysis, "create" a requirement/need.

All three criteria must exist and be able to be met in six months to meet the goals of the TF methodology. The TF aspect will be shaped by the requirements generated here, with business issues addressed by the team. There will be an iterative process among technology, transition, and requirement (i.e., we can meet 60 percent of the requirement in 120 days if we use this technology, but a company will have to combine it with another system to make it cost-effective).

TF creates and utilizes a panel process (subject matter expert team, or SMET) that will identify an array of opportunities that loosely (or tightly) fit within them. The TF process will down-select to projects that are needed, can be solved, and have business plans, and then pursue the best. If at any time one of the three criteria moves out of acceptable limits, that particular project will be terminated and, if appropriate, transitioned to another program.

The focus of TF is on identifying problems and *solving* them in six months or less per project and in being very draconian in terminating efforts that don't pay off, at least under this program. Definition of "success" will be product availability for general acquisition, coupled with broad-based community support and recognition of the solution.

The general intent of TF is to provide revolutionary or significant capabilities that have major impact on operations and mission capabilities. Minor, evolutionary changes, while important, are usually addressed through other approaches or efforts. Refer to Table 43-1 for a summary of the comparison of TF to a traditional acquisitions strategy.

Table 43-1

Technology Foraging vs. Traditional Acquisitions Strategy Overview

		Technology Foraging "Active Technology Pull"	Traditional Acquisitions Approach "Technology Push"
	What is the focus of this approach?	The focus is on rapid transition and application of established products to new mission areas.	The focus is to find a need that is not currently met and spend whatever money it takes to develop the S&T to fulfill that need. (The single metric is "requirement.")
	When is this approach applicable?	Works most effectively on well-defined technologically mature problems where solutions can be applied in short timeframes.	Conventional technology programs developed through "normal" requirements processes where there is little to no urgency.
	How is the need/ requirement identified?	Through consultations with experienced, community-recognized SMEs who possess a comprehensive understanding of capability gaps within their effected communities.	Self-generated by requesting government agency.
	How is the technology need made known to potential providers?	Teams are assembled to identify new and innovative technologies at their source (government and private labs, industry, academia, etc.) and to propose a development process that exploits these technologies in accordance with self-generated requirements from a strategic panel.	A technology owner sees a broad agency announcement (BAA) or requests for proposals (RFPs) and "pushes" the technology to fit that need. It is inherently reactive and the "best solution" is not community-wide, but only from those proposals submitted.
	Dependencies and weaknesses	Ability to rapidly exploit technology when identified.	Ability of the government to articulate the need effectively with little to no iteration, and the ability of a performer to accurately identify and fulfill that need, based almost exclusively on a single description.
	How are unsuccessful technologies treated?	Approach is draconian in terminating less than fully successful efforts if they fall outside primary focus.	Frequently program requirements evolve to be able to justify continuation of effort, even after it has clearly failed to meet its initial goals.

(*Continued*)

Table 43-1		Technology Foraging "Active Technology Pull"	Traditional Acquisitions Approach "Technology Push"
Technology Foraging vs. Traditional Acquisitions Strategy Overview (*Continued*)	Business plan/ model for transition	Essential aspect of tech foraging team is the development of a business plan and strategy for market introduction.	Usually evolves during hand off from program element to program element amongst many different offices. Sometimes never defined.
	Speed and effectiveness	Only engaging technologies that can be transitioned and applied in a short timeframe (six months).	Lengthy contract approval process prevents quick product introduction.
	Problems	Implementation of solutions through the conventional acquisition process.	• Curtails innovation through narrow focus. • Does not engage wider community by reactive approach. • Rapid deployment not available.

TECHNICAL APPROACH

The primary hurdle to overcome in the implementation of TF is reducing the bureaucratic overhead and minimizing the time normally needed to achieve a tedious acquisition policy. It is important to note that it is *acquisition policy* and NOT regulation that is being evaluated and circumvented where required. Policy has a tendency to evolve toward reducing or avoiding risk, independent of impact on mission accomplishment. The approach to be taken in TF, however, is one of risk management as opposed to risk avoidance or aversion.

The goal of this effort, as noted earlier, is the aggressive solution of problems, not merely the management of programs, which hopefully will lead, eventually, to solutions. Key to this effort is recognition that risk aversion may doom it to failure while a process of risk management may have a much higher chance of success. To quote FAR 1.102 (2) (c) (2): "To achieve efficient operations, the System must shift its focus from 'risk avoidance' to one of 'risk management.' The cost to the taxpayer of attempting to eliminate all risk is prohibitive." Accepting that risk is inherent to the goal of major success. This effort will move forward pursuing high-risk yet high-payoff processes and opportunities.

The basis of this effort will be one of technology pull, focusing on key problem solution opportunities, as opposed to technology push from technology developers. As a means for identifying new and innovative technologies for combatting terrorism and supporting homeland security, Technology Foraging Teams (TFTs) representing a variety of disciplines will visit various research organizations (labs, academia, and industry) to conduct on-site technology reviews. Each

TFT will consist of specially chosen principals who exhibit the following traits: broad-based ubiquitous knowledge; creativity, rapid collection, assessment, and conclusion capability; demonstrated ability to synthesize widely diverse information into systemic problem-solving approaches; and good, dynamic interaction with the other team members. In addition, a data recorder/staff support person will support the TFT. The key and preeminent factor in the creation and operation of the TFTs will be their ability to identify, develop, and exploit new and innovative concepts and approaches for solving high-priority problems.

METHODOLOGY

As the TF process was initially demonstrated, a methodology evolved that included several tasks for properly accomplishing a TF effort. These tasks will most likely evolve further as the TF process matures. The tasks, at this point, include the following:

- Identification and recruitment of senior advisory panel (SAP)
- Development of initial concepts
- Identification of highest priority capability requirements/needs
- Review by SAP

Figure 43-1

Technology foraging process. (Reprinted with permission from Unconventional Concepts, Inc.)

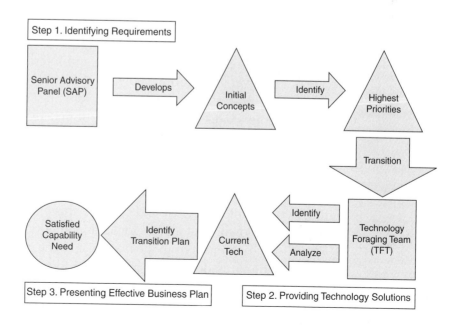

- Identification and recruitment of TFTs
- Identification and analysis of technologies
- Down-select to projects
- Initiate and pursue transition process

During the execution and application of each of these tasks, a reassessment and evolution of the process occurred. In the sections that follow, each task is discussed in further detail, along with some of the lessons learned.

Senior Advisory Panel (SAP)

As a first step, a panel of universally recognized and accepted experts from a variety of homeland security related fields was recruited. The goal was to ensure that they had the respect of their various career milieus (such as firefighting, emergency medicine, security, etc.), which would lend an instant air of credibility to the process, and would have real, as opposed to vicarious, knowledge and experience enabling them to identify opportunities for technology application. Members included a former FEMA Administrator and U.S. Fire Administrator, a former U.S. Coast Guard Commandant, a former U.S. Surgeon General and Sherriff, and several others. All the members combined extensive and unquestioned operation experience with the imprimatur of respect and instant recognition. The role of the SAP was to identify operational needs as well as to provide assistance in transitioning them through the business process.

Development of Initial Concepts

The original plan was to present the SAP with a small number of initial concepts and rely on their experience and interaction to provide more ideas. However, the process evolved into more of a red team/concepts assessment process wherein concepts were presented to the SAP, singly and in groups, and they provided input and recommendations. These concepts were based on a series of studies, proposals, and other resources that offered the potential for significant and revolutionary changes to current homeland security capabilities. The initial source of the proposals was a body of past concepts acquired by various organizations, including the Department of Defense and DHS. As this initial cohort of concepts is winnowed down, new sources for ideas and opportunities will be developed, including input from the frontlines of the operational community. In the end, an assortment of roughly 15 ideas were down-selected as being of value and operational relevance to the homeland security community, and from these the basis of the TFTs were formed.

Identification of Highest Priority Capability Requirements/ Needs

Working closely with the DHS, the initial concepts and 15 ideas were translated into capability requirements/needs for use by the TFTs. These high-priority requirements/needs became the basis for continuing the TF process.

Review by SAP

The SAP was used to review the initial concepts, 15 ideas, and resulting requirements/needs to ensure there was a consistency in the thread of development. This proved to be of great value, though a real challenge came in attempting to coordinate the schedule of numerous senior executive and operational personnel. This proved to be too complex and time-consuming, so a series of meetings with members of the SAP occurred in groups of two and three, both in person and via phone-con. While lacking the anticipated synergy of all the members together and exchanging ideas, it did provide an effective middle ground that allowed input from the members, the review of various concepts, and extensive discussions. In addition, on several occasions, members of the SAP attended field reviews of technologies, thereby offering the opportunity to meld both operational input and technical capability. This latter process proved particularly valuable in refining and transitioning concepts to operational venues.

Identification and Recruitment of TFTs

Central to the TF process is the ability to actively identify, pursue, and exploit technologies in support of the various self-identified needs. This is done, in large part, as a result of the interactions of the TFT. While a generally hard scientific, technical, or engineering background is desired, more important is the ability to work together as a team and synthesize new, novel, and unconventional ideas or applications in support of the concepts reviewed and passed by the SAP. In effect, the TFT acts as a brainstorming team, identifying, evaluating, and synthesizing technologies into needs that have been identified. The TFT draws on the creativity of the individual members and uses their breadth and depth of experience to bring together multiple points of view and experiences in a way that allows for the synthesis of new ideas and approaches to problems. Furthermore, it allows for a much broader array of technological opportunities and building blocks to be applied to a problem, as the various members of the TFT each have his or her own technology experience base to draw upon and bring to the discussion. The interaction, however, is not limited to just the TFT but includes the technology source/ supplier we are visiting. The TFT involves them in the process and develops a synergy with the supplier that allows for an increase in ideas and potential application of technologies products for vice applications.

The true value of the TFT process is the synergy and interaction that is developed among the members, allowing for new concepts to be developed as a result of "the whole is greater than the sum of the parts" approach. This approach allows for a freer exchange of ideas and more creativity in the process than the traditionally narrow-focused approach based on isolation and protection of ideas. While at first blush this may appear to be unworkable due to concerns over protection of intellectual property, so far it has proven to be remarkably successful, in large part because the TFT itself brings to the table a wealth of experience and creativity and it is willing and able to share it with the company or organization it is meeting.

Identification and Analysis of Technologies

Frequently companies, laboratories, and other organizations get focused on their end "product" or program. They often lose sight of the value of the technologies and infrastructure that enable their end goal. As an example, the DOD develops many weapon systems, and frequently as part of these programs, special-purpose telemetry and other measurement technologies and systems are developed in parallel to the primary systems. These measurement technologies and systems are needed to support the eventual test and evaluation of the primary system. If you ask many of these program offices about the technologies they are developing, they will freely discuss their "programs," such as the final weapon system, but miss the value of the telemetry they have developed, and frequently don't even mention it, as it is not the "program" but rather an ancillary support technology.

Often the most fruitful sources of technology have been the instrumentation branches or groups within an organization. In any event, the goal of the TFTs is to find *technologies*, NOT end products or systems, and determine new, novel, and valuable ways of integrating these technologies into functional capabilities.

Based on the knowledge, skills, and abilities of the TFT, in conjunction with the SAP, a hybrid concept/design evolves that incorporates the need, the available technologies, and the potential for transition/completion (the business plan). A trade-off design process, usually in real time, is done based on what is desired and what is possible. Only in the event that a reasonable accommodation can be achieved is the effort then pursued. It is expected and anticipated up front that an

"80 percent solution" (or whatever is an acceptable percentage to the user) will be achieved, but this is considered an acceptable trade-off to actually achieve a capability in a reasonable time (six months) as opposed to a "perfect" (which is never achieved) solution in several years and for many times the cost of a rapid effort.

DOWN-SELECT TO PROJECTS

The needs are developed through the use of the SAP process, the TFT identifies technologies and goes through an iterative process of balancing required/desired capabilities with realistic expectations, and the "last" step is the development of the business plan that pervades every step of the TF process.

Down-select is actually an ongoing and continuous process whereby any project that fails to continue to progress toward a completion goal within the defined timeline and cost will be cut at the point of this failure. All efforts are continuously reviewed and assessed for applicability and, where appropriate, either modified or terminated.

Initiate and Pursue a Transition Process

The source of most process problems resides where a discontinuity in operations or process is introduced. Within the current acquisition process, the transition process is a separate, more formal, acquisition and implementation effort, which is observed but not directed by the acquisition manger. The interface between these two processes has, as was predicted, resulted in some discontinuities and inefficiencies. Unlike this disjointed approach, the TF process includes the transition procedure as a core effort that identifies opportunities, fully characterizes them, and defines a path forward. In the ideal situation, a single program and management/operational chain will be responsible for all aspects of the TF process from beginning through final deployment.

In this initial implementation of the TF process, a separation was identified between concept development and analysis stage and actual fielding stage, which resulted in delays inherent in the handoff from one stage to another. This aspect of the operation is currently under review and should be improved over time and with sufficient experience.

In general, this phase should entail the definition of a specific acquisition strategy, identification of resources, and implementation of the strategy. In support of the DHS mission, this will entail the identification of specific resources (i.e., funding source) and contract vehicle and methodology for engaging performers to achieve the end goal.

RECENT IMPLEMENTATION

Recently, the effort was initiated by assembling a team of subject matter experts. The methodology was based upon DOD's CJCSI 3010.02B, whereby "reviews are independent assessments conducted by subject matter experts who provide informative concept critiques."

The initial step, a gap analysis, was performed by a TFT of SMEs. The analysis was performed based, in part, upon the results of the Project Responder follow-on study currently being completed within DHS S&T. In addition, the panel reviewed selected proposals and concepts from a variety of sources ranging from DOD to the intelligence community (IC)—in particular, the Office of the Director of National Intelligence (ODNI)—as well as gaps identified by the TFT members themselves.

Based on this initial gap analysis, the TFT then created a search strategy designed to identify potential technologies as well as possible business partners. The search methodology or "foraging" consisted of using creativity and initiative, on the part of the TFT members, to determine where the highest probability of successful technology locations might occur. This foraging consisted of collection and analysis of data, extensive discussions with researchers and technology developers (as opposed to just program managers and acquisition personnel), and aggressive pursuit of opportunities inside, as well as outside, the government. This was, in large part, an effort designed to optimize and expand the probability of serendipitous events. Technologies discovered as a result of this process were assessed not only in terms of filling gaps identified by the TFT but also as a means to stimulate discussion and assist in identifying heretofore unknown or unimagined gaps and opportunities.

The final stage, the business plan process, was designed to synthesize strategies based upon identified gaps and potential technologies to fill them. Key to this stage was a combination of background/experience in a wide array of business spaces as well as the ability to synthesize a strategy based upon gaps, available technologies, and perceived business drivers. Potential business strategies were discussed with both the TFT as well as other skilled experts in a variety of fields to increase the probability of the acceptance of any given strategy and approach. The goal was to develop plans to field technologies rapidly, including protection/use of intellectual property and related issues, to support this effort. While all relevant laws and regulations were followed, traditions and past methods of operation were not considered to be constraints; they were only contributed to the overall process.

As noted earlier, the overall process seeks to find the intersection of a gap, a technology to fulfill it, and a means of deploying the technology so it is usable in the field. If all three of these criteria are not met, a project will be terminated as rapidly as possible.

LESSONS LEARNED

For the most part, the process has been quite effective and functioned as predicted. Two areas have required modification to the original concept, however:

- Development of concepts and interaction with the SAP
- Transition from TF to the actual acquisition/implementation phase

As noted earlier, due to complex scheduling issues, the interaction with the SAP as an integrated whole has not been possible. That being said, the individual interaction involving assessment and input in small groups has turned out to be quite effective and satisfactory.

The transition aspect has been somewhat more problematic and is currently under evaluation to determine better and/or more effective approaches. Ideally, the entire process should be handled through a single, seamless methodology in which the need identification flows through the concept development, technology assessment, and ultimately, fields through a continuous process with no phase transitions. We are not quite there yet, but it is currently under assessment and evaluation.

SUMMARY

The TF process has shown to be an effective means of actively seeking out rather mature technology solutions to address defined capability needs or problems. Its proactive method to first identify existing sources of technology then engage them directly, with perhaps minimal modifications, to solve problems exhibits a beneficial efficiency over advertising needs and allowing potential providers to self-identify solutions.

44

SOCIAL MEDIA AND CROWDSOURCING TO HELP DISASTER MANAGEMENT

Jeannie Stamberger, Ph.D.

Researcher, Peace Innovation Lab, Stanford University, Stanford, CA
Adjunct Faculty, Disaster Resilience Leadership Academy, Tulane
University, New Orleans, LA
Former Adjunct Faculty, Disaster Management Initiative, Carnegie Mellon
Silicon Valley, Moffett Field, CA

Ahmed Nagy

Doctoral Candidate, IMT Institute for Advanced Studies, Lucca, Italy
Former Scholar, Disaster Management Initiative, Carnegie Mellon Silicon
Valley, Moffett Field, CA
Associate Researcher, Italian National Research Council (CNR-ISTI),
Pisa, Italy
Associate Researcher, Belgian Nuclear Research Center (SCK-CEN), Mole,
Belgium

INTRODUCTION

This chapter provides an overview of social media and crowdsourcing in disaster management with practical advice for the practitioner. We created this chapter imagining we had one hour to brief professional emergency managers curious about the practical use of social media and crowdsourcing to aid disaster management. We envisioned providing practical insights bolstered with case studies on the best practices, challenges, and risks of using these technologies in disaster management, and presenting a view on what may come next as the technology rapidly changes. We start with brief definitions and process descriptions of social media, crowdsourcing, and crowdsensing, and then discuss using these tools for the following purposes: obtaining situational awareness (of the disaster and the mood of the public), making sense of data (e.g., creating a map-based common operations picture), informing the public, soliciting donations, creating positive public relations (PR) (e.g., about your actions in the response), and efficiently organizing physical volunteers on the ground. We then discuss some common concerns, such as whether or not social media really is free, information accuracy, security concerns, and potential risks. Finally, we wrap up by highlighting research in future tools that will provide greater benefits and ameliorate some of the current issues.

For those unfamiliar with the buzz around these platforms in disaster response, the excitement stems from virtually free assistance in collecting accurate situational awareness, novel compilation and visualization of accurate complex digital information, extremely rapid coordination of private resources for disaster assistance organized by the public, and rapid dissemination of information during disasters. In essence, these tools are empowering a citizenry to participate and impact disaster management in a way it never has been able to before including: aiding emergency managers in the San Bruno fire by mapping incident information on site, and using crowdsourcing to translate emergency messages in the aftermath of the 2010 Haiti earthquake and help categorize and geo-locate messages from the ground during flooding in Pakistan so decisions makers could make sense of the data in a map format. The question addressed here is how can and how should professional emergency responders interact with these tools that provide a novel situation of lack of control by government agencies—that is, how do you take the good and toss out the bad?

DEFINITIONS

Social media, in the disaster response context, increasingly includes a vast number of types of software with the common feature that social interactions can occur. Beyond commonly recognized social media platforms such as Facebook which encourages social interactions and

Twitter which promotes sharing of information, additional platforms fall under this title that have other objectives, such as real-time collaboration on texts (e.g., Google Docs, Wikipedia, Salesforce Chatter) and sharing images (e.g., Flickr, Picasa). Rapidly, features enabling social interactions are being incorporated into software with diverse objectives including platforms that may originally be designed for social interactions, streamlining workflow (e.g., Salesforce.com), development of professional networks (e.g., LinkedIn), rapid information dissemination (e.g., Twitter to do-it-yourself instructables), and other uses. For example, Salesforce Chatter is a hybrid incorporating Twitter-like hashtag functionality, Facebook wall posts and user profiles, file sharing, chat features, and email, while adding workflow rules and approvals to create a tool for real-time collaboration with your team inside a corporation. These sorts of boundary crossings will occur as more platforms incorporate "social" features.

In a disaster response context, these platforms help enable access to the crowd through "crowdsourcing." Crowdsourcing is the process of providing small tasks for virtual workers to complete for pay, or for free in the disaster response context. However, as profiled in CrowdConf 2012, an industry conference sponsored by CrowdFlower, crowdsourcing has been taken to extremes from small tasks taking seconds to complete to large projects that look like outsourcing, where crowd workers compete to win a prize or business for design of a logo (e.g., 99Designs) or a hotel room of the future (e.g., jovato). Similarly, in disaster response, we are seeing crowdsourcing tasks range from the small (e.g., geo-referencing a county-like area in Pakistan to place a message received from Pakistan on a digital map), to complex tasks such as project and volunteer management (e.g., the CrisisCommons wiki compiling local information on Sendai at the request of UN OCHA) and managing an army of thousands of students providing work on the ground (e.g., Student Volunteer Army in Christchurch, New Zealand).

Finally, we distinguish *crowdsourcing*, which is a task that can be done from anywhere with an Internet connection, from *crowdsensing*, which requires being physically located on the disaster site, such as taking images of the disaster site. This distinction is particularly important to discuss the use of the crowd in obtaining situational awareness of the disaster and managing volunteers on the ground.

HOW DO SOCIAL MEDIA, CROWDSOURCING, AND CROWDSENSING WORK?

While there is much buzz about use of social media, fewer case studies are available documenting what worked and didn't work on the ground. In particular, there is often a lack of information documenting how crowdsourced information was used by professional responders, if at all.

Most of the success stories were led and driven primarily based on the effort of a small trusted and dedicated team of volunteers that used social media and crowdsourcing to harness a tremendous amount of manpower, filter through a tremendous amount of information, or provide real-time assistance to professionals. Often these small teams were previously unknown to professional responders, and composed of members were geographically distributed, and provided full-time assistance, as well as members that contributed periodically or joined late. The small team can develop *ad hoc* needed software to enable the crowd to do their work, merge software platforms or operate across them, and are savvy about social media use. Often these groups operate without sanction by a government agency, and once success has been demonstrated, they attempt to align their project with professional responders but many times have difficulty aligning needs. Sometimes a large effort is made by a single person within a professional response agency, but many times there are restrictions on platform use that prevent the full application of social and crowdsourcing tools by government agencies.

A key skill that these teams provide is merging platforms, an expensive service that this crowd provides for free. For example, the well-known crowd mapping of Haiti post-disaster, which received commendations from FEMA Director Fugate for being "the most comprehensive and up-to-date map available to the humanitarian community," required a crowdsourcing platform (CrowdFlower), and SMS texting tool (Frontline SMS), a map digitizing platform (OpenStreetMap), a Web-based mapping software (Ushahidi), among other platforms (e.g., Twitter). For example, text messages that came in during the Pakistan floods were sent to crowd workers via the CrowdFlower crowdsourcing platform, which were then geo-referenced, and the information was then sent into the Ushahidi-based map. Turnkey solutions, which obviate the need for manpower to merge platforms, such as the Ushahidi Crowdmap are in various levels of development, and we hope to see more of them in the future. Skilled teams have also augmented information streams with various data types including police scanner information, webcams of the disaster area, images and maps.

Another extremely valuable skill these groups can provide is disseminating a consistent information across different platforms in their respective vernacular or format (blogs, Tweets, Facebook pages, etc.). Most importantly the crowd tends to be savvy about using each platform and can customize messages so they are in an appropriate vernacular for each medium to make them more palatable—this is otherwise a nightmare and a long learning curve (in technology that is constantly changing) for an emergency responder or Public Information Officer (PIO) who is busy with other tasks.

WHAT CAN THE CROWD DO?

In this section we discuss examples of tasks that social media and crowdsourcing are extremely effective at doing on large scales.

Obtain Situational Awareness

The crowd has gathered situational awareness in a variety of data formats, from text messages to videos. Most simply, short tweets or short messaging service messages reporting a situation on the ground were used in Haiti and many other disasters to report a variety of types of situational awareness including structural damage, indicators of a spread of a disaster (e.g., smoke), levels of aid needed, and so on. Reliability of this information can be checked with direct communication with the person sending the message. This can be accomplished in Twitter by sending out a tweet with the Twitter handle in the message, and gets around whether or not that person is following you (e.g., "@tbliver can you send a picture of the structure damage?"). Requesting an image may be a method to get around false reports. Information is also rapidly reported in the form of images. CNN iReport capitalizes on this by harnessing the crowd through "assignments" to record images in disasters and other situations, which are posted on CNN's website. Videos were used in the March 2011 Japan tsunami when volunteers recorded and uploaded videos of lists of persons at shelters, and the crowd then transcribed this information and entered this information into Google Person Finder to facilitate reuniting people.

We are currently involved in a research project with the HITLabNZ to enable the crowd to collect higher quality on-the-ground assessments of structural damage using mobile phones and low-bandwidth collaboration with remote experts. Such tools will enable the crowd to collect increasingly accurate information on the ground and will facilitate the rapid digitization of information. "Tweak the Tweet" was a disaster syntax proposed by an author (Stamberger) and a collaborator Kate Starbird at EPIC in the University of Colorado, Boulder to help those on the ground understand how to provide high-quality information to responders, so that a Tweet "OMG house on fire!" could be re-sent as "#fire #loc 123 Church St # injured 3" which provides additional information about the location and severity of the fire in a manner that can be automatically extracted.

Make Sense of Data

The crowd is extremely valuable in making sense of data by mapping, filtering, translating, and digitizing information so it is searchable. Putting information from the ground into maps is a great example of how the crowd helps make sense of the data. In Haiti, virtual volunteers created a digital map of Haiti through tracing satellite imagery, and updated the base map with reports from the ground translated by volunteers with local knowledge. In the March 2011 Japan earthquake and tsunami, CrisisCommons was activated to compile Web-based information about the affected area (data sets and maps, official press releases and situational reports, and crowdsourced data sets and maps) at the behest of the United Nations Office of the Coordination of Humanitarian Affairs (UN OCHA) (see Further Reading at the end of the chapter for website information) to provide a single point of background information for those preparing to deploy. In the 2011 Shadow Lake Fire, a Virtual Operations Support Team (VOST) helped a PIO by filtering through the vast amount of information on the Web to find key pieces of information such as a blog of a citizen upset by potential property damage being caused by responders fighting the fire, a potential community conflict, which the PIO was then able to address.

The crowd is also an extremely efficient way to translate large volumes of messages in near real time, as exemplified in the Haiti 2010 earthquake. When emergency response systems failed, a text message emergency reporting system was quickly established in Haiti, since text messages were one of the few forms of communication still working. However, the U.S. military could not respond because many of the messages were in Haitian Creole. A quickly generated Web interface allowed Haitians, the diaspora, and French-speaking communities to collaborate online and employ local knowledge of areas and slang to translate the messages in near real time and use local knowledge to geo-locate messages. They processed 40,000 messages in the first six weeks alone, with an average turnaround time of a message of 10 minutes to get back to responders. According to the responders, this saved hundreds of lives and helped direct the first food and aid to tens of thousands. Collaboration among translators was crucial for data quality, motivation, and community contacts, enabling richer value-adding in the translation than would have been possible from any one person. A recent detailed account of this effort can be found in Further Reading.

The crowd is also very good at digitizing information to make it searchable. The crowd successfully transcribed videos of paper lists of persons at shelters in the March 2011 Japan tsunami and enter this information into Google Person Finder to facilitate reuniting families and loved ones, and relevant information from police scanners into Tweets. In the 2010 San Bruno, CA, fire, the California police scanner information was transcribed into Twitter messages by a volunteer in Texas. The crowd also had extremely high accuracy in identifying and tagging severity of damaged buildings from satellite imagery with high accuracy (Tomnod.com during the Christchurch, NZ, earthquakes). Once information is digitized, automated or semi-supervised tools can make sense of the data in digital maps, disseminate information across channels, and compile the information in searchable databases.

Solicit Donations

Social media has been effective at getting the word out for needed donations. Texting financial donations generated impressive rapid donations in the 2010 earthquake in Haiti, raising over $10 million to the Red Cross (with promotion by the U.S. State Department) from over a million donors in over three days. The $10 donations were enabled by the mGive platform, which allowed a donation to be added to the donor's cell phone bill when he or she sent a text to a specific number. (The Haitian event was unusual and fees were waived by cell phone carriers and mGive; however, for small-scale disasters, setup fees, annual fees, and per-donation flat and percentage transaction fees are charged.) The mayor of a town in Japan was extremely successful at publicizing the needs of his municipality through a YouTube video plea that went 'viral' and was seen by over 400,000 people. Social media was extremely active at getting the word out that Type O Negative blood donations were needed during the 2010 San Bruno Fire, with messages sent and forwarded about where donations could be provided as well as pledges to donate to encourage others. The Blood Centers of the Pacific who released the request for blood found the response to be rapid and the shortage was rapidly recovered.

Inform the Public/Create Positive Public Relations

The PIO in the San Bruno EOC used TweetDeck to monitor Twitter for information about the event (TweetDeck allows you to set up searches for various key words; finding the right key words to find the information you are looking for is an art of using the system). The greatest benefit was to identify the types of information that the public wanted to better craft information releases; they found that it did not provide additional situational awareness in comparison with watching local media stations, but that may have been because local media had a presence on Twitter and was likely using Twitter as an information source.

As reported by the EPIC group in University of Colorado, Boulder, a small team of volunteers was instrumental in assisting the PIO of the Shadow Lake Fire in Oregon in 2011. A team of eight virtual volunteers were used by the PIO of the 2011 Shadow Lake Fire in Oregon over several weeks to help the PIO monitor social media looking for negative coverage and irritated citizen groups, and to send out the latest information across a range of portals (its blog, its Facebook page, InciWeb, Twitter) to provide a consistent message. The team was coined a "Virtual Operations Support Team" (VOST) (see Further Reading for details).

Efficiently Organize Physical Volunteers on the Ground

The Student Volunteer Army (SVA) in Christchurch, New Zealand, is an extremely interesting example of social media and a small group of students who coordinated a large-scale volunteer effort to remove tons of liquefaction expelled in the 2010 and 2011 earthquakes in Christchurch. The September 2010 earthquake created tons of liquefied sediment (liquefaction) covering citizens' property to depths of several feet. A small group of students created a Facebook page to help students figure out how to help; the page went 'viral' and resulted in an extremely organized effort coordinated by a small group of students to provide safe organized volunteer placement, transportation, and food for 2,500 student volunteers, who cleared 65,000 tons of liquefaction over 2 weeks. In the subsequent 6.3 magnitude earthquake, 10,000 people joined the Facebook group Student Volunteer Army in 24 hours, and thousands of students were coordinated in a call center-like office that would collect requests for assistance by citizens, and teams of buses of students would go out in response to remove liquefaction. Out of necessity, the group created a platform allowing citizens to report needs via the Web, a free text message, or phone call, which was tied into a platform called GeoOp that coordinated geographically dispersed jobs. A student would review each need and delegate it to team leaders who would meet with their small team in the morning, write their group number on their hands and team members' hands, and head off on buses to work. Students also supported the morale of devastated residents, and provided hot meals, fresh water, and guidance to professional help. This student-led group eventually obtained sanction by Christchurch's local council, and ultimately assisted managing supply operations for government departments, and the city council. They provided 75,000 volunteer working hours that cleared 360,000 tons of liquefaction as well as offering other services (e.g., manning data entry positions). Social media tools such as Facebook were used to attract the crowd, but it was used in combination with other software platforms (e.g., the citizen request platform), manual processes (e.g., each request by a citizen was reviewed by a human and prioritized), and basic volunteer management techniques (e.g., T-shirts, writing team numbers on hands, having teams work together on subsequent days, delegating to team leaders). The SVA did not rely on social media platforms alone, but the incorporation of social media tools enabled a small group of students to manage an entire "army" of assistance. A key take-away message for professional emergency response organizations is to be prepared (from a leadership and policy position) to embrace such efforts, which help stretch the resources of the professional response and allow professional responders to focus their efforts on areas that need their assistance most.

HOW TO HARNESS SOCIAL MEDIA AND THE CROWD

This section briefly discusses basic steps that can be taken to harness social media and the crowd without requiring professional responders to become experts in these fast-moving technologies.

• Generally, the best advice is to harness the crowd, by finding a small trusted group of techie volunteers to work with you or support you. Find out what your social media policies are and push for making them flexible enough to allow you to harness social media and the crowd, or work with a trusted group of volunteers (e.g., a VOST) to help you out. Check out the Further Reading section for the full report on the VOST system used in the Shadow Lake Fire. That paper describes key components of the working relationship, such as a chat channel being the primary form of communication between the VOST and the professional responders, allowing various personnel to review and keep up with activities as well as providing real-time communication and a critical record of communications.

- If you need assistance and haven't done the grunt work to get a Twitter account, develop a following, update your website, put up a Facebook page, and so on, then the simplest thing to do is to use an official Twitter account (e.g., the city Twitter account) to send a message requesting assistance from the crowd. Send out several messages and include hashtags that may alert those that follow the evolution of the use of social media in disasters to find and put you in touch with trusted volunteers (e.g., #crisiscommons, #SMEM). Explain what you need, and likely (hopefully) the crowd will respond. This "beaconing" technique was effectively used in Haiti to respond to changing needs for medical personnel, which evolved from orthopedic surgeons to post-operative recovery specialists to infectious disease doctors over the course of the disaster recovery.

- If you have the time now, here are some tips for being better prepared to make use of these technologies when the time comes. Set up an official Twitter handle and establish a social media policy by giving several trustworthy employees the password and informing them about the hows and whys of posting Twitter messages. Make sure that everyone is familiar with how to update the account via an SMS message, which will be critical if Internet communications are temporarily compromised in your area. It is also helpful to be able to receive messages on your cell phone from an agency, so you see what your colleagues are posting ("Fast Follow" on Twitter).

- Put a widget in your public-facing website that allows your Twitter feed to be shown. This gets around the issue of having the public wonder when the website was last updated, and if the information is current. Instead of trying to find your web developer in the middle of a crisis to update the page, the public can now see updates changing by the minute in your Twitter stream.

- Remember that each medium (blog, Facebook, Twitter, press releases, etc.) requires a different format, jargon, and feel when phrasing the same message. This can make it extremely complex to post messages across multiple media in a way that is palatable and expected by the user. Keep this in mind, and rather than trying to keep up, remember that this is where your trusted volunteer group comes in.

- Expect tools to get both easier and harder. Social media sites are gaining more and more features that provide functionality (e.g., integrating Twitter streams into Facebook pages), making once-hard tasks easy by automating them or making them simple to implement. However, some problems will likely remain, such as page fractioning, volunteer burnout, more platforms being "required" to be used, lack of integration among new platforms, and so on. Currently, the human touch is critical for successfully harnessing social media and crowdsourcing; be wary of the benefits of entirely automated systems.

- Expect that time will be required to manage and respond to the crowd once they are activated. This is often the role of the trusted volunteer group and can often be a full-time round-the-clock job.

- Small disasters will likely have a smaller crowd to draw from.

- Start putting time and effort deciding which skills can be requested of volunteers and which services should be paid. Right now many valuable services are being offered for free, but as volunteers become more heavily relied upon to conduct critical and valuable labor, at some point, such work should be rewarded. See the article by Munro in the Further Reading section for a case in point when that occurred in the 4636 project among Haitians providing assistance in the Haiti 2010 earthquake. Similarly, platforms such as mGive.com provided its services for free during a major international disaster (Haiti 2010 earthquake), but business models for such products may rely on being a paid service during small disasters.

These are several examples of steps to take to start using social media and crowdsourcing effectively without having to become an expert in the field yourself. However, the platforms are constantly changing, so for the best advice, contact your trusted volunteer or join a number of social media and disaster discussion groups, including #SMEM on Twitter, CrisisCommons.org e-mail list, and the Department of

Homeland Security Virtual Social Media Working Group. These groups are excellent places to get the latest information on concerns regarding harnessing social media and the crowd, some of which we highlight in the section that follows.

CONCERNS

Social media is not free. While the platforms are free, there is significant time and effort required to monitor social media channels (24/7 in real time) and provide a response on a timeline that meets the public's expectations. The Australian-based airline Qantas experienced a PR nightmare when rumors and images on Twitter led the public to believe an A380 plane had crashed, and Qantas Twitter accounts were not active and provided an anemic response that did not quell rumors, creating panic among relatives of those on the flight (see Further Readings for details). Quantas now has dedicated resources to work with these "free" platforms, to prevent further such PR catastrophes.

Policies can't keep up with the technology. There are often challenges in adoption and creation of social media policies, particularly because new use cases are occurring and implications of policies are unclear as the technology continues to change. The Further Reading section includes an extremely complete article on the Roanoke Virginia police department's staged embrace of social media, including policy challenges. We have highlighted a case study from a police department because their experience is particularly illustrative due to the extreme "career-altering" situations in which social media can frequently place officers.

Crowd workers. There is concern among public safety and professional response communities that information from the crowd is wrong. However, we suggest that the reality is a more nuanced view. We found data errors by first responders, so being a professional responder doesn't make the information you generate necessarily accurate, and information generated by the crowd is not necessarily inaccurate. This perspective encourages a view of information accuracy no matter who is generating the information, and encourages the use of tools to increase accuracy of information no matter who generates it, and prevent misinformation/rumor/sabotage. The question is which tool yields the best response. Right now the best answer that we can give is to rely on virtual crisis responders with excellent reputations that have worked together before in this burgeoning field (e.g., a VOST). Other proposed solutions (e.g., pre-recruiting, pre-training volunteers, background checks, which is essentially the "old" way of doing things, which contrasts directly with the crowdsourcing model) require a large amount of initial effort investment for the return and are unrealistic or lack viral adoption. Instead, we encourage a much cheaper and faster approach of using your reliable network of virtual volunteers for certain tasks where information accuracy is critical, and using the rest of the crowd for other purposes (e.g., identifying rumor propagation that may result in PR issues or an influx of physical volunteers to show up in a certain place, detecting the emotional response of the crowd, identifying and correcting donation portals that are being promoted, and using the crowd as a canary in the coal mine for key activities that are verified before acting).

Terrorism. Information that was shared with the media and Twitter was monitored in real time by terrorists to kill more citizens in the hotels during the July 2011 Mumbai bombings by a Pakistani terrorist group. Twitpics by the crowd and real-time coverage by the media allowed terrorists to foil an Indian counterassault attack, killing soldiers. In these cases, social media by itself was not the culprit, but the release of information by journalists and amplification and misunderstanding of information spread by citizens contributed to this unfortunate perfect storm. See in the Further Reading section the presentation by Marc Goodman at Strata NYC 2011 on the terrorist use of technology in the Mumbai bombings.

These are just some of the concerns with the use of social media and crowdsourcing in disasters. In the next section, we discuss tools in research stages to help resolve some of these issues.

FUTURE TOOLS

Our research has been exploring the automation of key tools to simplify several stages in the information detection, sensing the mood of the crowd, and disseminating correct information. Here we describe three tools we have recently worked on: Salesforce Chatter for disasters, social media credibility assessment tool, and a social media listening tool.

Salesforce Chatter for Collaborating in Disasters

We are working with Salesforce Chatter developers to enhance Chatter so it scales for disaster coordination and collaboration across public and private organizations. Salesforce Chatter is an internal corporate communications platform that recently is allowing expansion to invited members that don't have a Salesforce.com account, allowing spontaneous groups to form. We are working with developers to ensure that Chatter has various features that enable people who have never worked together (such as businesses that use Chatter for internal purposes and NGOs that require aid) to gather virtually and coordinate in real time. Contact the authors if you would like to participate in requirements gathering and testing prototypes.

Social Media Credibility Assessment Tool

Credibility of information on social media is tricky to assess, and potential for low-credibility or false information to spread on social media is a key concern of practitioners. Credibility is tricky, because there are few metrics that evaluate the quality of a post; for example, the number of Twitter followers may be a poor indicator of message accuracy, because posting information first may attract followers but preclude evaluation of the accuracy of the information before posting—in other words, being first is more popular than being accurate. We therefore developed a semi-supervised framework called the Poster-Reporter-Message (PRM) algorithm, modeled on the PageRank algorithm, the original idea behind the Google search engine. The PRM algorithm calculates the credibility of a poster using the links among both messages and posters, and the credibility of a message is calculated based on reporter rating of the message credibility and poster credibility. Message credibility is ranked by reporters (either manual reporters or automated reporters trained on a training dataset) into three categories: rumor, low credibility, and credible. The initial credibility score for a given message is the sum of all the reporter scores. Pilot experiments support the approach.

CROWD SENTIMENT DETECTION DURING DISASTERS AND CRISES: A CASE STUDY OF THE SAN BRUNO FIRE

A key need for a PIO is to understand the emotions of concerned stakeholders and citizen groups, particularly to avoid conflict between the community and the response efforts. Here we summarize our work on automated detection of sentiment expressed on platforms that produce short messages such as Tweets and SMS texts. We used a case study of a gas pipeline explosion that occurred at 6:11 p.m. PDT on September 9, 2010, in San Bruno, California, a suburb of San Francisco, when a 30-inch-diameter steel natural gas pipeline owned by Pacific Gas & Electric exploded into flames 2 miles west of San Francisco International Airport. Immediately afterward, social media platforms including Twitter started exchanging messages regarding the event, with immediate concerns that this was another 9/11-like attack. An archive was set up on "Twapperkeeper" (www.twapperkeeper.com), a web-based archiving system, to collect Tweets with the hashtag "#sanbrunofire" or the words "sanbrunofire," and 3,698 Tweets were collected during the first 24 hours. We used this message stream to develop and test our sentiment detection tool, comparing our results with sentiment assessments made by crowd workers. Complex sentiment detection is nontrivial, and our work compares methods for evaluating sentiment in disaster microblogs and using the optimized system, which used techniques for emoticons, sentimental ontology, frequent lists of sentiment words, and Bayesian network to flexibly categorize tweets. The sentiment detection methods were derived from those used for documents; however, the unique characteristics of Twitter microblogs (e.g., short messages, emoticons, slang) required heavy modifications of the techniques. In future work, we aim at optimizing our system perhaps with other classification techniques, and as a service to be hosted in the cloud, to enable high load and throughput in near real time. The system can readily be used for other events such as man-made disasters (e.g., biological or chemical terrorist attacks), where the tool can assist in detecting early signals buried in massive amounts of data. Furthermore, we plan to test and extend our system to other domains, such as politics and sports.

FURTHER READING

In this YouTube video, the use of social media by terrorists in Mumbai bombings is described by Marc Goodman at Strata 2011 NYC, http://www.youtube.com/watch?v=6ueKilyThQg.

In the following YouTube video, the plea for supplies and transport by Mayor of Minami Soma City during the radiation leaks following Japan 2011 tsunami can be seen with English subtitles, http://www.youtube.com/watch?v=70ZHQ–cK40&feature=player_embedded.

To learn more about the sentiment detection platform, see "Crowd Sentiment Detection During Disasters and Crises: San Bruno Fire a Case Study" by Ahmed Nagy and Jeannie Stamberger, *Proceedings of the 9th International ISCRAM Conference*, Vancouver, Canada, April 2012.

To learn more about the role of CrisisCommons during the March 2011 Japan earthquake and tsunami, see http://wiki.crisiscommons.org/wiki/Honshu_Quake.

To learn more about augmented reality tools for citizenry to improve disaster response and recovery, check out the website of The Human Interface Technology Laboratory New Zealand (HIT Lab NZ) run by Director Mark Billinghurst at http://www.hitlabnz.org/.

To learn more about the Christchurch Student Volunteer Army, search for them on Facebook, or check out their website at http://www.sva.org.nz/.

To learn more about the use of social media to coordinate medical teams/supplies in Haiti, see Aleksandra Sarcevic, Leysia Palen, Joanne White, Kate Starbird, Mossaab Bagdouri, and Kenneth Anderson. "'Beacons of Hope' in Decentralized Coordination: Learning from On-the-Ground Medical Twitterers During the 2010 Haiti Earthquake." In *Proceedings of the ACM 2012 Conference on Computer Supported Cooperative Work (CSCW 2012).* (New York: ACM, 2012), 47–56, http://doi.acm.org/10.1145/2145204.2145217.

To learn more about the Mission 4636 crowdsourcing of translation by Haitians, see *Crowdsourcing and the Crisis-Affected Community: Lessons Learned and Looking Forward from Mission 4636* by Robert Munro (in manuscript form at the time of this publication).

For a description of the Qantas Singapore airline crash Twitter PR disaster, see http://www.tnooz.com/2010/11/04/news/qantas-a380-incident-a-lesson-in-social-media-and-web-pr/.

To learn more about the policy and institutional challenges faced by a police department embracing social media, see http://www.policechiefmagazine.org/magazine/index.cfm?fuseaction=display&article_id=2424&issue_id=72011. In addition, visit the Roanoke Police Department's Facebook page at http://www.facebook.com/rpdsafercity and the agency on Twitter at http://www.twitter.com/rpdsafercity.

45

EIS: GOALS, PROGRESS, AND CHALLENGES FOR THE UNIFIED INCIDENT COMMAND AND DECISION SUPPORT NATIONAL MIDDLEWARE

James W. Morentz, Ph.D.

JWMorentz, LLC
jim@jwmorentz.com

OVERVIEW

The Unified Incident Command and Decision Support (UICDS) national middleware[1] addresses the problem of emergency information sharing (EIS) among disparate organizations that are part of the complex and varying emergency management stakeholder community drawn from the local, tribal, state, and federal governments, critical infrastructure owner/operators, and volunteer organizations. UICDS is an open architecture and a set of middleware web services that allow commercial, government, academic, and volunteer technologies important to managing an incident to share information. As middleware, UICDS operates in the background, allowing existing applications to function for their end users unimpeded. There is no new user interface, no cost for the middleware, and no training needed for the end user. UICDS supports the doctrine of the National Incident Management System by creating EIS to answer key operational questions that are common to the disparate concepts of operations (ConOps) used across the many stakeholders. Supporting those different ConOps are different applications and technologies well suited and carefully chosen to meet the needs of different missions and organizations. UICDS enables trusted applications serving organizations to interoperate by creating sets of incident-related standardized data, called Common Operational Data (COD). COD is transparently transferred among UICDS nodes and then on to the UICDS-connected end user applications based on two-way sharing rules, content agreements, and secure authentication. UICDS also integrates with other EIS programs or data aggregators, becoming the gateway for sharing among sharing programs. The end result is the availability of COD through UICDS on any authorized application, allowing it to compose the exact right content for its end users, visualize the data, analyze it, improve it, and further share it back to the originators and other trusted partners to ensure collaborative decision making. This results in everyone in an incident having the same information from which their applications select and view in display formats that are ideal for their specific mission, decisions, and collaboration within the responding community.

BACKGROUND

Responding to an emergency has never been easy. It has always been characterized by uncertainty, lots of chaotic-appearing action, many government and civilian responders with different uniforms and equipment, and rapidly made decisions based on inadequate information. Better information, we have long thought, would reduce uncertainty, focus the action of the right responders, improve coordination, and result in better decisions. Toward this quest, many software applications and other technology innovations have charged to the rescue for more than three decades. These have improved operations of many of the parts of the emergency response community, but a significant gap remains in the ability of information technology to lead to better overall coordination and management of emergency incidents. This chapter describes an evolving generation of technology that focuses on EIS across all the different emergency technologies in order to fully provide effective response in all types of hazardous incidents, from daily small ones to the catastrophic.

From the early days of computing, military systems were held up as the prototype for civilian technology applications to improving emergency decision making. Those systems uniformly consisted of four elements: maps, data, models, and communication. What the military did not have to do with their hierarchically defined systems was share information across the many different types of organizations that make up the emergency management community.

In the early 1980s, with the advent of microcomputers, software applications emerged, notably the first commercial software for emergency management, the Emergency Information System in 1981. In the succeeding decade, software specifically designed for civilian emergency response organizations at the local, state, and federal government levels successively integrated Geographic Information Systems, sensors, satellite communication, packet radio communication, and intelligence analysis into the tools available, making them a comprehensive command, control, and communication system.

By the mid-1990s there were multiple vendors offering several different applications to support the complex emergency management stakeholder community in its efforts to prepare for, respond to, and recover from natural, technological, and terrorist incidents. It seemed that advances in technologies should be advancing emergency decision making.

THE PROBLEM

The attacks on 9/11 made it abundantly clear that the information technologies that were in place did not adequately bridge the gaps created by inadequate information and uncertainty. In fact, the information technologies seemed to exacerbate the problem when they became a reflection of the specific and diverse end user community (police, fire, emergency medical, emergency management, public works, health, environment, natural resources, and more) rather than a reflection of the *common mission* of the entire community. The reason for this is straightforward and understandable: People self-select into jobs; jobs are performed in organizations; and organizations constitute our disaster management system. Individuals choose to join the police rather than become emergency medical technicians or join the fire service or become emergency planners or join the National Guard or go into politics. Once an individual joins an organization, training and acculturation take place in order to help the individual fit the job so that he or she can meet the needs of the organization. All of these things breed distinctiveness, which is good because distinctiveness yields expertise.

But where distinctiveness creates risk and diminishes capabilities is when those experts are not part of a smoothly functioning team.

Where emergency disciplines were competitive in the past, they now engaged in competition through their information management—which they universally achieved by refusing to share information.

In an emergency operation today—whether responding to an actual event or to indications and warnings coming from an intelligence agency—each person, team, and organization knows about their own information. Police know police, fire knows fire, counterterrorism knows counterterrorism. But these response forces operate virtually in isolated information silos … until each shares their information *as they are able and enabled*. This results in gaps, overlaps, and inconsistencies in who knows what, when, which yields isolated information and clouded decision making.

Extend this problem from a single town or city to a large-scale disaster with many cities, a couple of states, a dozen federal agencies, numerous volunteer organizations, and hundreds of private sector, critical infrastructure owners and you begin to see the scope of the problem created by technologies that do not effectively share information and the scale of the needed solution.

DHS STEPS FORWARD TO SEEK A SOLUTION

A Broad Agency Announcement from the Department of Homeland Security, Directorate of Science and Technology (2004) launched Unified Incident Command and Decision Support (UICDS) with the following set of objectives: "The full capabilities of information management technologies should be brought to bear on behalf of the first responder community in the form of a system that allows first responders to manage the flow of data, voice, and video information in addition to other forms of information." More specifically, UICDS should enable "the capabilities that allow emergency responders to capture important incident-related information, analyze captured information, more effectively disseminate mission-critical information to emergency responders, present decision guidance options for the emergency response community, efficiently coordinate efforts of emergency responders, and store incident-related information for analysis."

In short, the goal of UICDS from the start has been cross-domain, cross-role, cross-function, cross-echelon, cross-hazard, and cross-application EIS and decision support for all individuals, teams, and organizations in the National Response Framework (NRF), National

Incident Management System (NIMS), and Incident Command System (ICS) to enable the complete life cycle of risk management: prevention, protection, response, and recovery.

A CONCEPT OF INFORMATION SHARING

EIS is achieved through a conceptual interoperability framework[2] introduced by John Contestabile of the Johns Hopkins Applied Physics Laboratory that includes three "layers" of interoperability—data, integration, and presentation. These layers can be considered to form an interoperability framework in which there are three levels that can be applied to most settings where interoperability is desired, and can be achieved with minimal impact to existing systems. The three layers composing the framework include the following:

- *Data layer.* Where all the various data sets and applications spread across various jurisdictions/agencies/disciplines reside.
- *Integration layer.* Publish the data out of the typically proprietary, customized, legacy/mainframe environment from which it came (in the data layer) into a web-enabled, Internet Protocol (IP) and standards-based open environment (in the integration layer). With data having been published into the integration layer, *interoperability can then be achieved by connecting the various tools found in that layer.*
- *Presentation layer.* Now that the data has been published into a handful of integration tools and those tools have been connected to achieve interoperability, the fused data needs to be "served up" to allow visibility across agencies/jurisdictions and disciplines by publishing into the presentation layer using a variety of channels.

Achieving interoperability requires understanding of, and use of, these three layers, as shown in Figure 45-1. Data comes from many different sources. One could try to achieve sharing at the data level, but it would require a multitude of interfaces among proprietary, legacy, and firewalled systems. A more achievable approach is to enable data to "publish" to the integration layer once. Many types of presentation tools could then touch the copy of the data held at the integration layer and visualize the data in special ways for the end user.

Why do this when each individual mission organization has its own source of information that satisfies its needs?

Figure 45-1

The three layers required for effective interoperability and information sharing are the presentation layer, integration layer, and data layer.

Source: Concepts on Information Sharing and Interoperability

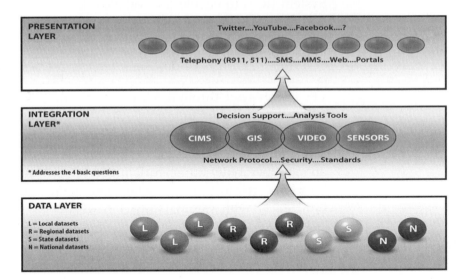

Conceptual Interoperability Model

Contestabile answers in two ways. The first is an operational value: The conceptual framework "describes a concept of operations whereby Integration layer applications can form the core of a 'Common Operating Picture' which can provide information to field personnel at the scene of an incident as well as the public." The second is a business value: "An inducement for jurisdictions to participate in such an information sharing framework is that they can gain access to a wide array of information to which they would otherwise not be entitled and they can reduce the overall cost of such systems by sharing the infrastructure and system expenses across the regional partners."[3]

To operationalize this vision, according to Contestabile, "Interoperability is achieved at the 'integration layer' by connecting the various tools at that layer to one another. This would result in only a few interfaces between a handful of key integration tools."[4]

One EIS architecture has taken on this challenge. It is the Department of Homeland Security, Directorate of Science and Technology, Unified Incident Command and Decision Support (UICDS™) middleware. UICDS alone is not the sole answer but used in combination with other pieces of the EIS puzzle creates effective, two-way, standards-based EIS for local, state, and federal governments and private sector critical infrastructure.

UICDS INTEGRATION ACROSS THE INTEGRATION LAYER

The Unified Incident Command and Decision Support is a national middleware supported by the Department of Homeland Security, Directorate of Science and Technology, Infrastructure Protection and Disaster Management. UICDS was architected to support the National Incident Management System, the national framework for incident management. Just as NIMS is a framework that permits distinctiveness within the framework, UICDS enables distinctiveness, and thus expertise, by cross-discipline EIS.

The hallmark of such EIS is UICDS middleware and its data exchange standards. These data exchange standards empower the end user application selected by the organization to support its concept of operation to share the essential information needed, no matter what data visualization tools are selected by the receiving organization, as seen in Figure 45-2.

This approach is in contrast to most information sharing designs, which fall into two categories. The first is a message router and the second is an aggregator.

The message router, at its most basic level, takes a packet of content and wraps an envelope around it with the address of the recipient, thus producing the message. The router receives a message packet and sends it to the receiver. An advantage of the message router is that a single message can be addressed to many recipients and the

Figure 45-2

The conceptual framework sees an interoperability middleware to integrate across disparate sources of data at the integration layer, a service provided by UICDS.

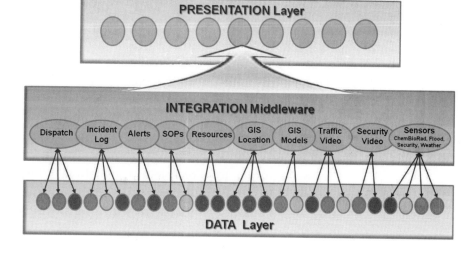

UICDS Integrates at the Integration Layer

router does the duplication of the message to send to all the recipients. Alerting systems are an example of message routers in their ability to take a single message sent to the router and provide it to many recipients (sometimes a huge number). Message routers are very effective means to share information from a source to recipients.

Aggregators generally consume data from many sources and consolidate it in a single location. A video console or dashboard, or a Common Operating Picture (COP), are examples of aggregators. Data, in the form of video camera feeds or geospatial information, is collected from cameras or multiple Geographic Information Systems (GIS) and made available in a consolidated format for use. Many people may access the dashboard or COP, but they are all doing it by sharing access to the same aggregated data and often the same presentation layer application.

Aggregators most often produce the aggregation of one type of information rather than the integration of all types of information. Aggregation is extremely effective and valuable for the end users of the aggregated data. However, aggregators can be guilty of creating a silo of aggregated information that is inaccessible to sharing among other end users. There are video aggregators and sensor aggregators and GIS aggregators, and so on. This still leaves the end user going to one screen for maps, another for alerts, another for sensors, and so forth.[5]

Both message routers and aggregators are important parts of information sharing. They are, however, not the most effective designs for one of the most critical features for EIS: two-way sharing among applications. True EIS requires two-way exchange of information in order to deliver to all applications in the presentation layer the appropriate operational data.

An aggregator is entirely one-way. Aggregators consume data sources and present the consolidated data to the presentation layer. Aggregators are not architected to enable data sources to share information with each other. The message router is different, but is essentially a one-way transfer of information. To achieve two-way exchange is possible with message routers through a set of sequential one-way exchanges. Data originates and then is sent through the message router to a recipient application, which then responds to the sender with another, independent message. Any correspondence between the two sequential message receivers is dependent on the content carried with the message. The second message must reference the first message in order for the originator to know that the message is a response to the original message. Thus, two-way exchange is possible through message routers if the applications on either end of the transaction do all the record keeping about the messages. This is manageable with a single sender and a receiver, but it gets problematic when a single message is sent to many recipients, each of whom responds to the originator and, perhaps, wants to originate a message to some of the other recipients. Managing the message record keeping is achievable but complex.

UICDS was designed to manage the content of its data. Having aspects of both aggregators and message routers in its design, UICDS distinguishes itself from other information sharing designs by this content management.

Indeed, in its fundamental architecture, UICDS routes messages. However, internal to UICDS, those messages are managed as content. They are tracked, related to those in sequence, and associated with other messages of similar or disparate types (e.g., incidents associated with maps associated with the resources sent to the incident). In some ways, UICDS is also an aggregator, allowing many sources of data to deposit data on the UICDS Core for subsequent sharing. But because UICDS manages content, when UICDS aggregates data, that data has a relationship to all other data about the incident and thus all the other types of data about the incident.

It is this design of UICDS that also enables it to operate at the integration layer to achieve several objectives in delivering comprehensive EIS:

- Provides two-way EIS among commercial and government incident management technologies to achieve collaborative decision making.
- Integrates other national message sharing programs.
- Integrates commercial and government data aggregator applications.
- Correlates information from all these sources into incident associations, meaning that every type of data about an incident can be available from one source.
- Provides content management for information associated with incidents so that connected applications know that they are getting the latest, authoritative source data available.

- Delivers standardized data into the existing applications used by incident-related organizations so no new applications or training are required.

The two-way nature of UICDS makes it ideal for delivering data for a common operating picture by bringing disparate data into the application layer and exposing it in a standard exchange format. But UICDS extends beyond situational awareness. It does not provide a new application everyone must use. It is true EIS among existing applications that enables each individual application—selected for its intrinsic value by an end user organization—to acquire common data and compose that data into a visualization that is appropriate for the end user. The application then can further process that data and resubmit it for sharing with the originating—and other interested—applications. Thus, UICDS builds many-to-many relationships among applications to meet the unique needs of very diverse end user communities created by the varied ConOps they construct.

In the following sections, the functioning of UICDS is explained from the macro to the micro, from UICDS deployment architecture at multiple agencies to the actual Web services that drive the data exchange.

THE UICDS ARCHITECTURE

The UICDS architecture is a partial mesh network of UICDS servers (known as UICDS Cores) that allow clients to collaboratively assemble and share emergency management information about an incident using Web services provided by their local UICDS server. Collaboration occurs transparently between client applications connected to one UICDS Core server and between client applications connected to different UICDS Core servers based on information sharing agreements. The UICDS Core itself is a suite of Web services that, in order to meet the many ConOps among the emergency management stakeholders, are configured in two interacting topologies: hub-and-spoke and peer-to-peer.

A single core uses a hub-and-spoke topology in which all client applications (one or many) connect to the core in a trusted partner relationship. See Figure 45-3. While trusted partner applications are notified only of items to which they have subscribed, any application can view all data on the core. Being an organization's client

Figure 45-3

Applications provide and consume fractional data in standard formats and shared to a UICDS Core in a hub-and-spoke topology. UICDS Cores exchange information in a peer-to-peer relationship according to rules established by the end user data owners. This allows the "right content" to scale to multiple jurisdictions and large-scale emergencies.

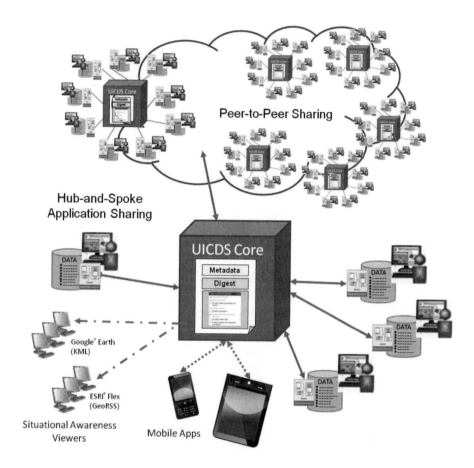

application means sharing only with the applications connected to that core. The core owner controls what other applications are connected to the organization's core. The only data an application receives is that which goes through the organization's core and is shared. The application is a client of the host organization's core for all sharing purposes, reducing control and independence of choice for the application. Thus, these are "trusted partners" who are sharing the same core that reflects a common mission.

The UICDS Web services peer-to-peer typology establishes a core-to-core sharing relationship in which data shared among cores is defined by bilateral sharing agreements between cores. Agreements are made to share between one core (and the applications connected) and other UICDS Cores and their applications. These agreements enable a robust ability to selectively share data to individual cores and thus to the applications connected to those cores, whether one or many. Installing a core gives an organization much greater capability to define sharing agreements with any other cores. Connecting any application to a core allows selective sharing of that application's data with the other core by established rules. Sharing easily can be turned off if a decision is made to exclude applications connected to a neighboring core from sharing data with an organization's core.

Multi-core, peer-to-peer relationships permit sharing among UICDS Cores in, for example, other states, or counties, or the private sector critical infrastructure. In turn, all of those cores' applications become sources for incident-related data to be put into every other organization's applications through UICDS. Having a UICDS Core lets the connected applications consume a wider range of information and control what is shared and with whom far better than the client relationship using another organization's core.

Those are the practical and policy reasons for installing either the hub-and-spoke topology of a single UICDS Core or establishing peer-to-peer connectivity through multiple UICDS Cores. The UICDS architecture combines both typologies in order to meet the expectations of all different types of end users for control of their data sharing with whom they desire, for the purposes they establish, and during the specific types of incidents they intend.

UICDS REAL-WORLD DEPLOYMENT

The UICDS network is a federated system of UICDS Cores, with each core representing an organization, an agency, or suborganization of an agency. This concept is illustrated in Figure 45-4 and shows deployments at the federal, state, county, and local levels. The peer-to-peer federation is defined by information sharing agreements contained in the core. These agreements are designed to follow local Memorandum of Understanding or Mutual Aid Agreements that define the terms and conditions under which agencies operate daily and in an incident. The guiding UICDS concept on information sharing agreements is that if an agency is willing to share its fire engine in an incident, it should be willing to share information about the fire engine. Thus, existing written operating agreements are the place to begin in determining a real-world deployment design.

UICDS deployment is achieved by distributing a decentralized, peer-to-peer network, as shown in the figure, of as many UICDS Core

Figure 45-4

UICDS deployments
connect diverse
agencies in a
peer-to-peer
relationships and
support applications
that deliver UICDS
information across
a wide range of
devices from a
responder's PDA
to vehicles to
mobile command,
small agencies,
cities, counties,
and statewide
implementations.

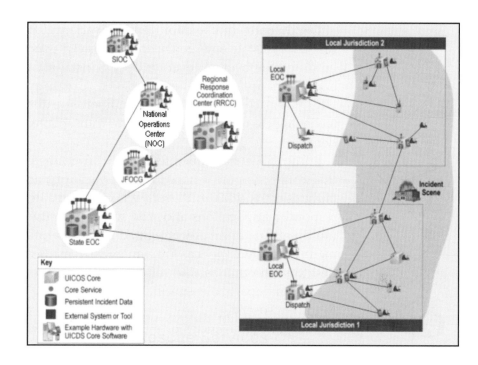

servers as will meet end user ConOps. For example, a large city, state, or multijurisdictional region's UICDS installation may be a federated network of UICDS Core servers fully integrated with computer-aided dispatch (CAD), traffic sensors, hospital admissions systems, public works equipment maintenance records, arrest and warrant management systems, weather sensors, and more. Scale down deployment of UICDS to a single computer, lower communication bandwidth, and fewer integrated external systems and UICDS serves any type or size of community—urban or rural, coastal or desert, ski resort or football stadium, multiagency and multijurisdictional, government or private sector critical infrastructure.

UICDS Cores can be installed on virtually any computer and network depending on the governance and policies of the participating organizations. Cores can be hosted by a government agency for several other agencies, or even a state for many of its jurisdictions. Core hosting can even be outsourced for those pilot sites that do not have the information technology infrastructure locally. Cloud-based hosting of UICDS Cores has been proven to be effective and cost-effective. This flexible design is intended to satisfy the most varied ConOps for emergency management required of the broad and diverse stakeholder community.

UICDS cores can be deployed in a variety of peer-to-peer configurations. The state emergency operations center or regional EOCs may be supported by a multiserver UICDS installation that could support dozens of applications that have 1,000 or more application end users. UICDS services would connect to numerous external applications and technologies, recording and storing transactions from multiple incidents.

Local EOCs may operate UICDS on a single lightweight server that could support a handful of applications and technologies and perhaps 500 to 1,000 end users, who would be interconnected to local responder applications and who would also use UICDS services for multiple smaller emergencies and daily operations. A local department or station (police, fire, emergency medical, etc.) could run a desktop computer as a server, a few interconnected external applications, and department-specific incident handling for 300 to 500 application end users.

Finally, local agencies or mobile command vehicles would have a UICDS Core on a notebook computer with a couple of interconnections to local applications perhaps supporting 50 to 100 application end users, many on wireless devices.

The key to understanding UICDS deployment is to understand that UICDS architecture can match virtually any operational ConOps and information sharing design that follows NIMS.

MAKING IT WORK: UICDS CORE WEB SERVICES

The UICDS architecture is built on service-oriented principles using open standards. Web service components have the function of authenticating external applications and technologies, exchanging standardized data, relating appropriate content, executing rules for sharing, and communicating the content payload to other UICDS Core Web services. The UICDS Core (hardware, software, and connectivity) is at the heart of the dual architectures of hub-and-spoke and peer-to-peer described earlier as allowing the interconnection existing responder systems both in local trusted partner environments and in widespread multi-agency and multi-jurisdictional networks. See Figure 45-5.

Each UICDS Core is a computer server that is a local point of integration for technology providers and agency services. UICDS Cores support three varieties of services: infrastructure, domain, and external.

Figure 45-5

The UICDS middleware design is a UICDS Core service set linked to external applications and technologies that operate independently but feed and receive information through UICDS. Each UICDS Core is linked to other UICDS Cores, allowing information to be shared between UICDS-connected applications and, ultimately, to application end users.

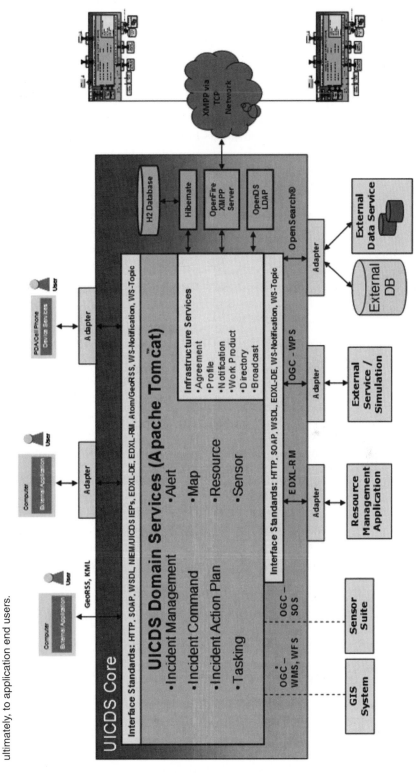

Infrastructure services enable the sharing of information between cores and are based on existing, established industry standards. Domain services provide for the management of information specific to emergency management, such as incidents, command hierarchies, tasking, and the common operating picture. These services rely on existing and developing standards in the emergency management domain.

Finally, each core provides external services, including the ability to register external applications using existing, developing, and future standards. It is through these external services that commercial and government technologies and software applications connect to UICDS. This connection is frequently called an "adapter." An adapter may be a component that is independent of but interacting with the application, or it can be incorporated into application code. The role of the adapter is to authenticate the application to the core and to translate application data into the UICDS standard data exchange formats. Adapters can connect to client applications (e.g., emergency management software), hardware (e.g., sensors), or other EIS tools, such as a data aggregator or message router.

Data is shared between UICDS-enabled clients that are connected to a UICDS Core using a SOAP framework (HTTP or HTTPS) over TCP/IP. Prior to accessing a UICDS core, UICDS clients are authenticated against a local Lightweight Directory Access Protocol (LDAP) database that is either supplied with a UICDS deployment or is part of the local IT infrastructure. Because UICDS is middleware, information to be shared is controlled at the source—the application. Applications control what information is shared via UICDS by only including selected information in the UICDS data exchanges.

Creation or modification of data is communicated to application clients via a role-based notification service. Applications connected to a core can be directly addressed for targeted notification delivery by combining the unique client registration and core names. This is important for core-to-core sharing of information.

Core-to-core sharing is based on agreements mutually established prior to data sharing. This does not mean a static, defined network; rather, agreements can be established within minutes during an emergency, allowing for dynamic construction of the UICDS network. The design of these agreements (technical agreements completed inside UICDS, not to be confused with Mutual Aid Agreements or other agreements by organizations to share) enables dynamic, incident-based data sharing topologies. Accompanying these agreements is the ability for user authentication, integration of external systems, and participation in information sharing agreements to be managed locally at each core, enabling agencies to retain control of local policies and support for their users and systems.

This core-to-core sharing allows applications connected to each core to share information. This information is exchanged using an eXtensible Messaging and Presence Protocol (XMPP) protocol using TLS over TCP/IP. This UICDS core-to-core EIS is automatic, but is governed by information sharing agreements that are controlled locally. UICDS core-to-core information sharing can be fully enabled, fully disabled, or limited by incident type.

TRANSPORTING CONTENT: FRACTIONAL DATA, STANDARDS, UCORE DIGESTS, AND UICDS WORK PRODUCTS

Because UICDS is designed to manage the content of EIS and content "ownership" is always a sensitive issue, UICDS adopted the concept of "fractional data." Detailed data is that whole complex of data needed to manage a single agency's response. Some "fraction" of that detailed data is needed to manage the relationship among agencies.

Fractional data was defined throughout Phase I of UICDS development (2005–2006), during which numerous end user outreach activities were held to determine what key data is needed to perform the overall NIMS-based management of an incident. In addition to this end user input, the UICDS team also examined existing data exchange standards. This was done because standards are the result of many previous end user interactions to achieve a consensus on some element of information exchange. When a standard existed, there was no need to examine anything more than its appropriateness for inclusion in UICDS.

Among the standards currently incorporated in UICDS as a means to define or exchange this "fraction" of the detail data shared through UICDS to manage the relationship among response organizations are the following:

- National Information Exchange Model (NIEM)
- Common Alerting Protocol (CAP)
- Emergency Data Exchange Language–Distribution Element (EDXL-DE)
- Emergency Data Exchange Language–Resource Messaging (EDXL-RM)

- EIS is achieved through middleware, providing data to existing applications requiring no new purchases or training through open interfaces readily employed by future technologies.
- EIS is secure, authenticated, and controlled by the data owner.
- EIS is scalable from small, everyday incidents to major, multi-jurisdictional catastrophic events.

The vision is expansive and evolving. Five million—and perhaps more than 10 million—Homeland Security Presidential Directive 12-compliant biometric identity cards provide access to UICDS-connected applications for emergency management personnel across the United States at all levels of the federal, state, local, and tribal governments, and the private sector. These millions of UICDS-connected application end users come from thousands of organizations that are joined in 24×7×365 situational awareness and decision support for each individual and the teams and organizations within which they operate.

Each UICDS-connected application end user is interconnected through open-standard interfaces on commercially available devices that are familiar to them—their existing phones, personal digital assistants (PDAs), tablets, mobile data terminals, computers, radios, and whatever digital device may emerge in the future. These end user devices have the primary function of exchanging normal, every day information, but when those existing applications are UICDS-enabled, information sharing begins and silos are broken down.

What UICDS provides on these existing communication devices through existing applications is an overlay of shared information provided by securely linking together authenticated applications and selecting information that is appropriate to each ongoing incident for display. UICDS rules can be established to detect the difference between a house fire and an industrial fire when entered in a dispatch system being monitored. When notified of the house fire, one UICDS Core and its connected applications might follow the sharing rules to ignore it, but those same rules can result in notifications of an industrial fire to other cores and applications.

One of the objectives of the UICDS initiative is to create the sharing infrastructure that can be seamlessly augmented by commercial and government applications that continually develop specialized capabilities for display or analysis in the future. As more advanced algorithms and implementations of agents, decision-support tools, location based mobile applications, and so on become available, the new technical capabilities can be added with straightforward Web service interfaces to UICDS. Thus, UICDS evolves with the technical capabilities of the profession.

LOCAL CONOPS DRIVE INFORMATION SHARING REQUIREMENTS

While the architecture of UICDS was driven by national doctrine established by DHS and other federal government organizations, the actual use of UICDS is designed to allow flexibility in implementation to accommodate all the various ConOps found in the host of different agencies at the federal, state, and local governments and private sector critical infrastructure and voluntary agencies engaged as part of the emergency management community.

The complex stakeholder community called upon to prepare for, respond to, and recover from attacks and disasters never will be served by a single ConOps and thus never by a single situational awareness tool or a single decision support system. That is what makes EIS so important. No matter what investment might be envisioned, what training programs might be developed, what policy guidance would be enunciated, or what grant programs might incentivize actions, there will always be differences among response organizations in ConOps, in methodology of disaster management, and in their selected software applications.

The challenge UICDS faced, then, was to architect to doctrine and implement to a common denominator that permitted flexibility in selection modes of incident operations. To that end, UICDS focuses on the interactions of stakeholders (public and private; federal, state, and local) to lead to the common goal (managing an incident). Implicit in such interaction is communication and information sharing around certain specific questions:

- **What is it?**
  - Incident management means keeping multiple agencies informed
- **Where is it?**
  - The geospatial view of the incident and the organizational response intended
- **Who's in charge?**
  - Organizing incident command or emergency support function as intended by the ConOps

example, the traffic speed sensor at 4th and Main, 10th and Broadway, 15th and I-66, and so on. Thus, the number of items for relevant feeds related to safety and security could number in the hundreds.

How to Make Sense of What Is Important?

UICDS allows applications to make sense of all these feeds. If an incident occurs at 3rd and Main, a Department of Transportation application may automatically, or with user intervention, select the 4th and Main traffic speed sensor to be included with the UICDS incident information. Personnel in other agencies do not have to sort through all the feeds to find the one that helps them make a decision. Rather, information experts and analysts build the set of UICDS incident knowledge so that operations personnel can quickly understand the incident and do their job of protecting their assets and services according to the ConOps.

Throughout the course of an emergency, alerts (5) are provided by various applications and become part of the UICDS incident knowledge. UICDS has adopted the Common Alerting Protocol (CAP) as its standard description of an alert. If an application disseminates CAP messages, UICDS can consume them and associate them with an incident, thus building incident knowledge. When an application wants to know what alerts are associated with an incident, it obtains the CAP UICDS Work Product and, because it is in the CAP standard format, can understand the content of the CAP message.

UICDS does not take away the mission of alerting applications. They remain the system of record and their time-critical delivery of vital messages goes unimpeded. The role UICDS plays is to be a consumer of an alert and then to notify UICDS subscriber applications that an alert has taken place. Thus, agencies and individuals that are not part of the alerting system of record know that alerts have been issued.

UICDS extends incident knowledge by allowing sensors (6) to be included in the available incident information. Using the Open Geospatial Consortium Sensor Observation Service standard format, sensor applications can identify the availability of sensor data related to the incident and publish that availability to the UICDS Sensor Work Product. Thus, UICDS points the end user application to any subscribing traffic cameras or weather sensor or chemical sensors that the contributing emergency management sensor applications are offering to support the emergency response. In this way, the UICDS incident knowledge expands and is constantly updated with the latest sensor information.

During an emergency, people and organizations are engaged in a wide variety of activities, all of which are part of the necessary knowledge about an incident captured in the UICDS Task Work Product (7). Applications that specialize in standard operating procedures (SOPs) and tracking of the performance of such procedures are the sources of data for the UICDS Task Work Product. As jobs are assigned to individuals performing roles in the response, those applications provide such data to UICDS. UICDS then relates that data about procedures, assignments, roles, and status to the incident and makes each successive update of the work product available to those applications consuming the incident. Those applications, in turn, use the task data to visualize for their end users the current status of procedures and tasking for the incident.

Sharing of information about ongoing response resources used in carrying out SOPs is accomplished through UICDS Resource Management Work Products (8). UICDS has adopted the primary emergency management resource standard, Emergency Data Exchange Language-Resource Messaging (EDXL-RM). UICDS enables the exchange of all of the EDXL-RM messages that allow applications to request resources, inquire about resources, negotiate their delivery, track their use, and eventually return or replace the resources. UICDS develops Resource Management Work Products specifically to enable the request and commitment of resources. The fractional data from the EDXL-RM exchange that UICDS tracks and makes available to other applications is the request/commit of EDXL-RM. Thus, resource management applications remain the systems of record for the resource negotiation, while UICDS shares with all applications the need for resources and the satisfaction of that need.

With people, organizations, resources, and assignments in place, the final piece of incident knowledge is the record keeping that leads to planning for the next response period. UICDS maintains the Incident Action Plan Work Product (9), which is a representation of several ICS forms that culminate in an Incident Action Plan. The purpose of this service is to support ICS forms that enable an incident to be managed at the incident commander level. This allows information sharing and reporting on the status of the incident, future requirements, and action plans to be undertaken.

All these elements of incident knowledge that are shared through UICDS add up to the UICDS Tree of Incident Knowledge. If you look at these nine information clusters, you will see all the critical information that is now shared around a conference table in an EOC. People, plans, resources, observations, alerts, responsibilities … these are the elements of incident management that are currently in silos and that become a coherent whole through the sharing of individual application data to the composite of all applications serving the end users making decisions in an emergency.

The UICDS Tree of Incident Knowledge represents Common Operational Data that can be composed by end user applications and multiple COPs into exactly the right information for the ConOps being deployed. For the first time, COD shared through UICDS can enable the "right content" to support the many complex decisions required in homeland security today.

WORKING WITH OTHER SHARING PROGRAMS AS COD SOURCES

Numerous information sharing programs have been sponsored over the years by government and the private sector. As the creator of COD through integration at the integration layer, UICDS embraces the work done by other programs and incorporates it into the UICDS sharing designs. There is enough to do without reinventing the EIS wheel, as will be highlighted in this section.

The Department of Homeland Security is currently advancing three programs in EIS, UICDS being one of them. The Integrated Public Alert and Warning System (IPAWS), created by Executive Order as the national alerting system, has been developed by FEMA (see Figure 45-8). Virtual USA, a geospatial catalog, is a program of the DHS Science and Technology Directorate, like UICDS (see Figure 45-9).

Despite their different sponsorship, these three programs are parts of the whole EIS capability. The text that follows explains, at a very high level, the integration of IPAWS and Virtual USA programs at the integration layer through UICDS. In addition, one other sharing program from the private sector, the utility industry's Common Information Model, is described. There is still work to be done on this integration; however, first steps to success have been completed and demonstrated.[6]

Gary Ham is unquestionably the most experienced technical resource for the operation of OPEN (Open Platform for Emergency Networks) as the aggregator gateway software for IPAWS. He explains how UICDS and IPAWS are mutually supportive information sharing tools when integrated at the integration layer:

> IPAWS primary function is public alerting. In support of this function it also provides private alerts between organizations and private DE wrapped message exchange between organizations. The UICDS mission is locally controlled integration of disparate systems as well as exchange between UICDS cores. Different but complementary missions. IPAWS is a central hub under FEMA control. UICDS is based on a network of distributed hubs defined by UICDS cores. A UICDS core is a natural candidate for a IPAWS COG for the purpose of public alerting.[7]

A technical review of UICDS and Virtual USA technical led to the following integration conclusion:

> "USA is currently a structured, governed catalog focused on sharing geospatial data. UICDS currently is focused on sharing emergency information in standard formats, especially incident reports and status information, on a day-to-day basis, through middleware linkages among different applications. Both components share information among all levels of government and the private sector. By connecting them operationally, the two could provide a continuum of information sharing from the local to the regional and national levels, spanning multiple types of emergency information in real time."[8]

The International Electrotechnical Commission (IEC) Common Information Model (CIM) provides the basis for enterprise interoperability and information sharing in the utility market (see Figure 45-10). The CIM allows different vendors and solutions to interoperate and share power system domain information. CIM provides a standard utility definition of the data layer, some fraction of which is needed by emergency organizations to effectively support management of utility incidents. Linking the CIM-based utility enterprise bus-based architecture with the UICDS peer-to-peer cloud architecture middleware can produce public–private sector information sharing.[9]

Figure 45-8

The IPAWS OPEN message aggregator and router interfaces with the UICDS CAP messaging service to enable two-way exchange of alert messages between UICDS-connected applications and IPAWS alert disseminators

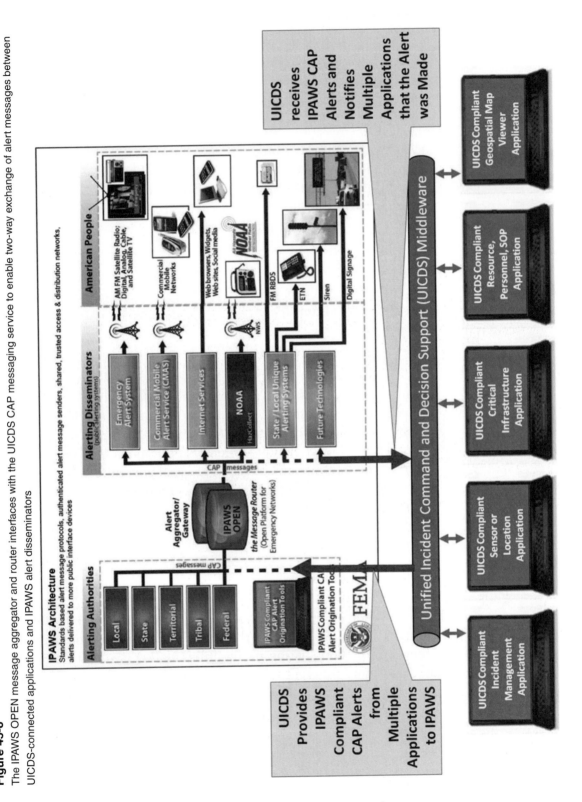

Figure 45-9

The Virtual USA geospatial information catalog interfaces to UICDS by providing the catalog data to the UICDS content management service and by consuming UICDS incident feeds for subsequent distribution to Virtual USA subscribers.

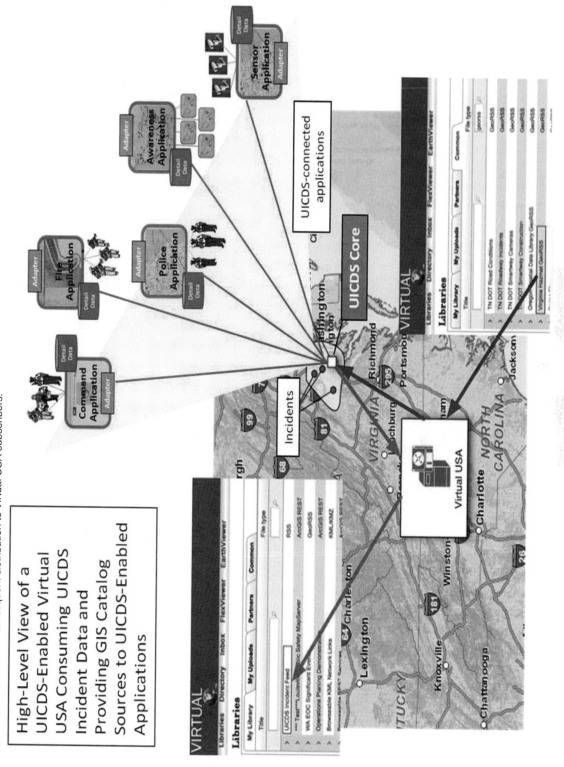

High-Level View of a UICDS-Enabled Virtual USA Consuming UICDS Incident Data and Providing GIS Catalog Sources to UICDS-Enabled Applications

Figure 45-10

The EIC CIM data sharing environment interfaces effectively with UICDS at the integration layer to promote COD between government and utilities.

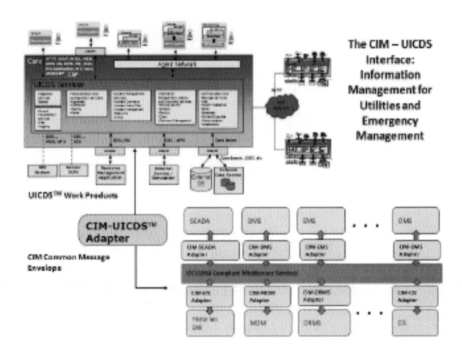

These three examples illustrate the versatility of UICDS not only to reach end user applications through data exchange standards but also to incorporate data aggregators and other data standard interfaces into the development of COD for critical incident management.

CONCLUSION

Figure 45-11 shows a high-level architectural view of UICDS with notes about many of the capabilities of the middleware to integrate applications, data, other sharing programs, and mobile apps by working at the integration layer. It does this with the goal of addressing the problem of sharing information among local, tribal, state, and federal governments, critical infrastructure owner/operators, and volunteer organizations. To accomplish the goal, UICDS developed an open architecture and a set of middleware Web services that allow commercial, government, academic, and volunteer technologies important to managing an incident and to share information.

Functionally, as middleware, UICDS operates in the background, allowing existing applications to function for their end users unimpeded. There is no new user interface, no cost for the middleware, and no training needed for the end user. UICDS supports the National

Figure 45-11

UICDS middleware integrates emergency applications, technologies, and other information sharing programs to create two-way sharing of COD among all connected applications to ensure that data seen at various presentation layer tools is current, authenticated, and shared to improve decision making and collaboration throughout an emergency.

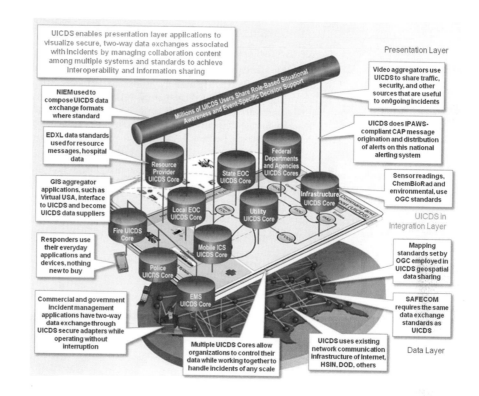

Incident Management System by creating EIS to answer key operational questions that are common to the disparate ConOps used across the many stakeholders. Supporting those different ConOps are different applications and technologies well-suited and carefully chosen to meet the needs of different missions and organizations.

UICDS enables trusted applications serving disparate organizations to interoperate by creating standardized data, called Common Operational Data. COD is transparently transferred among UICDS nodes and to the end user applications based on two-way sharing rules, content agreements, and secure authentication. UICDS also integrates with other information sharing programs or data aggregators, becoming the gateway for sharing among sharing programs. The end result is the availability of COD through UICDS on any authorized application that can compose the exact right content for its end users, visualize the data, analyze it, improve it, and further share it back to the originators and other trusted partners to ensure collaborative decision-making. This results in everyone in an incident having the same information selected and viewed in display formats that are ideal for their specific mission, decisions, and collaboration within the responding community.

NOTES

1. See www.UICDS.us.
2. http://eisalternatives.com/Conceptual_Framework.html.
3. John M. Contestabile, *Concepts on Information Sharing and Interoperability*, Johns Hopkins University Applied Physics Laboratory, 2011. Portions of that paper were presented at the IEEE Conference on Homeland Security Technology 2011as Information Sharing for Situational Understanding and Command Coordination in Emergency Management and Disaster Response, Robert I. Desourdis, Jr., and John M. Contestabile.
4. Ibid.
5. http://eisalternatives.com/uploads/Initiative_Integration_for_EIS.JPG[0].
6. http://eisalternatives.com/uploads/IPAWS-UICDS_Interface_Architecture.pdf.
7. http://grandpaham.com/category/ipaws-open/.
8. http://eisalternatives.com/uploads/vUSA-UICDS_Overview_1_03.pdf[0].
9. http://eisalternatives.com/uploads/Utility_Industry_Looking_to_UICDS_as_Link.pdf.

46

THE CHALLENGING REALITIES OF HOMELAND SECURITY TECHNOLOGY BUSINESS

Rick Wimberly

CEO, Government Selling Solutions/Galain Solutions, Inc.

David Kamien

CEO, Mind-Alliance Systems, LLC

INTRODUCTION

Charged with keeping the homeland secure, government organizations, as well as critical infrastructure, need to embrace the most effective technology. After the terror attacks of 9/11, the prospect of the government spending billions of dollars on homeland security attracted a surge of technology companies offering solutions of every kind. In recent years, interest in homeland security markets has intensified as defense contractors, faced with prospects of billions of dollars in budget cuts in military spending, look for sales opportunities outside of defense.

Recognition of the wide array of technology needs, government funding, and an ever-expanding set of creative solutions has resulted in a highly competitive homeland security information technology market. This represents both challenges and opportunities for companies looking to sell to this market.

This chapter will address opportunities in the homeland security technology space, as well as challenges of successfully introducing new technologies to government buyers. Practical approaches for evaluating, then pursuing, homeland security technology markets will be discussed.

MARKET SIZE

The greatest growth in federal contract spending commenced with the post-9/11 formation of the U.S. Department of Homeland Security (DHS) and the beginnings of the related Global War on Terrorism (GWOT). Figure 46-1 shows how homeland security has driven spending over the last decade. Large growth periods were also driven by the federal emergency response to damage from Hurricanes Katrina and Rita and the military GWOT surge in Southwest Asia (SWA Surge).

For the last few years, and into the foreseeable future, overall contract spending by agencies within the HLS establishment is declining, as shown in the figure. Following are several contributing factors:

- Achievement of desired performance levels in certain agency missions, including successful mitigation of the effects of certain threats

- Balanced workforce policies that result in some insourcing of contract services, or trading contractor personnel for government personnel

- More thoughtful, deliberative approaches to acquisition, including management approaches that accept certain threat risks, at a reduced cost

Figure 46-1

Growth in federal spending driven by HLS requirements

Source: Deltek, Inc.

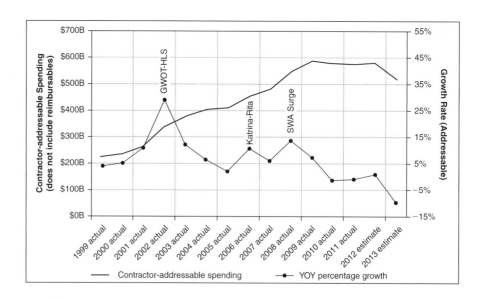

- More centralization of procurement operations, consolidation of contract vehicles, and increased acquisition professional proficiency

The bright spot is that certain types of homeland security spending are increasing. For congressional oversight purposes, the Executive Branch categorizes HLS spending into seven segments which are useful in determining the types of technologies and professional services required by the HLS establishment:

1. *Intelligence and Warning.* To detect terrorist activity, before attack; disseminate resultant warnings; identify, collect, analyze, distribute source intelligence; share information
2. *Domestic Counterterrorism.* To target transnational criminal organizations; identify, thwart, and prosecute terrorists in the United States
3. *Border and Transportation Security.* To protect border and transportation systems; reduce illicit flow of drugs, currency, weapons, and people
4. *Protecting Critical Infrastructure and Key Assets.* To unify disparate efforts to protect critical infrastructure across governments and private interests; assess and prioritize protective action based on risk; improve physical security; reduce threats and vulnerabilities in cyberspace
5. *Defending Against Catastrophic Threats.* To protect against, detect, deter, or mitigate terrorist use of weapons of mass destruction; improve decontamination techniques; develop medical countermeasures to protect the public
6. *Emergency Preparedness and Response.* To help plan, equip, train, and practice the capabilities of first responders and emergency managers; conduct agency incident management; prepare for terrorist-related threats
7. *Other.* To manage special projects related to intelligence and advanced technologies

Figure 46-2 illustrates the total expenditures and contractor-addressable spend in each of the seven segments and the agencies in the HLS establishment planning to spending the most within each segment. While contract spending in each of the named agencies is down overall from GFY2012 to GFY2013, HLS spending is resurging, especially in three areas.

Figure 46-2

HLS spending profile

Source: Deltek, Inc.

	Intelligence and Warning	Domestic Counter-terrorism	Border and Transport-ation Security	Protecting Critical Infra-structure and Key Assets	Defending Against Catastrophic Threats	Emergency Prepared-ness and Response	Other	Totals
Total segment spend	$0.8B	$5.3B	$27.1B	$24.0B	$4.7B	$6.3B	$0.6B	$23.0B
Contractor-addressable spend	$0.2B	$1.5B	$7.4B	$10.3B	$1.9B	$1.3B	$0.3B	$68.9B
Growth in contractor-addressable spend, GFY2012-2013	–6%	–2%	–6%	28%	31%	–7%	65%	11%
Agencies planning to spend the most on contracts in the segment	DHS	DHS	USDA	DoD	USDA	DoD	DHS	
	DOJ	DOJ	DHS	DOE	DoD	DOE		
				DHS	DOE	HHS		
				DOT	HHS	DHS		
				VA	DHS			
				NASA				
				SSA				

The most important of these three areas is developing and deploying the means to protect critical infrastructure and key resources (CIKR). Much of the spending within CIKR will be on cybersecurity. But physical security will also see spending on security for government facilities, public works, and government employees.

The second area is developing resources needed to defend against major threats. Besides defensive military systems, this spending area includes systems for biosecurity, food security, and enforcement of export controls.

The final area of promising growth includes investments in new technologies for threat detection, a portion of which is depicted in the Other category.

While the above 11 percent proposed growth rate is attractive, the effects of the annual appropriations process and other initiatives to manage spending make the future less certain. The 11 percent growth rate may turn out to be a smaller number. Nevertheless, not all challenges and threats to homeland security have been addressed. Substantial contract opportunities remain for industry, professional services, and academic organizations.

DIVERSITY OF NEEDS

As an indicator of technology diversity needed in homeland security, over 1,300 Information Technology and Communications products are listed in the Responder Knowledge Base (RKB), a database maintained by the DHS's Federal Emergency Management Agency (FEMA). Not all vendors doing business in the homeland security technology space are listed in the RKB database. However, for many product categories, multiple offerings from a variety of companies are listed, indicating the competitive nature of homeland security markets for information technology.

FEDERAL TECHNOLOGY PRIORITIES

At the federal level, the U.S. DHS has established a large list of active technology projects being pursued through its Science and Technology Directorate (DHS S&T). The list doesn't represent the full spectrum of interests, but it gives an example of the range of interests.

Human Factors/Behavioral Science Projects

- Actionable Indicators and Countermeasures
- Biometric Detector
- Community Perceptions of Technology Panel
- Community Resilience
- Enhancing Public Response and Community Resilience
- Future Attribute Screening Technology (FAST)
- Hostile Intent Detection—Automated Prototype
- Hostile Intent Detection—Validation of Observable Indicators of Suspicious Behavior
- Human Systems Engineering
- Human Systems Research
- Insider Threat Detection
- Mobile Biometrics System
- Multi-Modal Biometrics
- Passive Methods for Precision Behavioral Screening
- Predictive Screening
- Quantitative Psychosocial Impacts Index
- Rapid DNA
- Risk Prediction
- Violent-Intent Modeling and Simulation Project

Infrastructure Protection & Disaster Management Projects

- Advanced Surveillance
- Building Infrastructure Protection
- Blast Analysis of Complex Structures

- Blast/Projectile—Protective Measures and Design Tools
- Blast/Projectile—Unified Blast Analysis Tool Project
- Common Operating Picture (COP) Data Fusion Technologies
- Complex Event Modeling, Simulation, and Analysis (CEMSA)
- Disaster Management Support Environment (DMSE)
- Geospatial Analytics in Support of Federal Air Marshal Service Project (formerly, Suspicious Activity Reporting)
- Geospatial Location Accountability and Navigation System for Emergency Responders (GLANSER)
- Integrated Data Processing and Analysis
- Integrated Rapid Visual Tool (IRVS)
- Kentucky Critical Infrastructure Protection Institute Program (KCI)
- Law Enforcement Data Fusion
- National CIP R&D Plan
- Overhead Imagery Data
- Owner Performance Requirements (OPR)
- Physiological Health Assessment Sensor for Emergency Responders (PHASER) Project
- Rapid Mitigation and Recovery
- Recovery Transformer
- Resilient Electric Grid
- Resilient Tunnels
- Searchable Toner and Printing Ink Library
- Southeast Region Research Initiative (SERRI)
- Seismic Activity Detection Data Collection, Analysis, Alert, and Warning
- Sport-Evac Simulation
- Standard Unified Modeling Mapping Integrated Toolkit (SUMMIT)
- Underwater Surveillance Project
- Unified Incident Command and Decision Support (UICDS)
- Visual and Data Analytics

- Wide Area Surveillance
- Wild Fire Detection and Prediction

Nuclear Detection and Forensics
- Advancing Nuclear Detection Technologies
- Coordinating the Detection Architecture
- Creating Detection Standards & Evaluating Systems
- Implementing Detection Capabilities
- Increase Nuclear Forensic Capabilities

STATE AND LOCAL TECHNOLOGY PRIORITIES

Interests at the state and local levels are similar. Each year, the Center for Digital Government conducts its Digital States and Digital Cities and Counties Surveys. The 2011 surveys identified a varied list of homeland security-related priorities.

State Technology Priorities
- Communications Networks
- Interoperability
- Offender Management Systems
- Computer-Aided Dispatch
- Next Generation 9/11
- Mobility
- Corrections Health Records
- Courts Case Management

Local Technology Priorities
- Computer-Aided Dispatch
- Next Generation 9/11 Upgrades or Replacements
- Case and Eecords Management
- Multi-Agency, Integrated Systems that Allow Data-Sharing
- Mobility Hardware, Networks, and Applications
- Consolidation of Facilities, Staffing, or Services

WHY SOME MAKE IT AND OTHERS DON'T

The size and diversity of homeland security technology markets naturally attract the interest of many companies. Many, though, find pursuit of these government markets to be overly difficult for several reasons:

- *Government sales cycles are long.* Decisions are made slowly, and the procurement process can linger for months. Even the sense of urgency surrounding deployment of homeland security technologies will not necessarily circumvent the inherently slow pace of government buying cycles.
- *Procurement guidelines are very strict.* Failure to follow them properly can result in disqualification from a procurement opportunity, even if the solution offered is a very strong and cost-efficient fit.
- *Preferences for certain vendors are often established before procurements become public.* Procurement guidelines require transparency and equal access to information for all vendors, but there's a "pre-procurement" process that some companies miss. This is the time when relationships with government buyers are established, information is gleaned, and technical specifications are established. Missing the pre-procurement process can hinder a company's ability to sell its solution to the government, despite government procurement guidelines designed to create equal opportunity for all.
- *Government budgets are unpredictable.* Government establishes budgets for no more than a year at a time (sometimes less). Plus, government revenue sources fluctuate with the economy. Thus, it's difficult to project whether funds will be available. Because of budget uncertainty, even a contract award does not necessarily mean a purchase order will follow.
- *Homeland security customers are demanding.* Their missions focus on saving lives and property, and a failure to perform can be dangerous. Needs change as perceived threats change. At the same time, a change in process or user behavior required by a new technology can be difficult to implement in tradition-minded or bureaucratic organizations.
- *Communication between the sides can be inadequate.* Conventional government S&T programs are based on a reactive approach. The government agency releases a public solicitation expressing a need or requirement currently not met. (Broad agency announcements, or BAAs, and requests for proposals, or

RFPs, are the most typical solicitation vehicles.) Then potential performers react to the description in the solicitation. By trying to address the requirements, the performers' technology is "pushed" to fit the advertised need. However, often the communication between the buyers and the sellers is insufficient to provide a full understanding of either the customer's needs or the capabilities of the offered technology. For further analysis, see the Chapter 43 by Michael Hopmeier on "Technology Foraging" in this volume.

Small businesses have an additional hurdle. According to a report from the US CIO, *25 Point Implementation Plan to Reform Federal Information Technology Management* (December 2010), small businesses too rarely approach the federal government as a customer because of real and perceived barriers to contracting:

> The sales process is perceived as lengthy and complex, and, therefore, not seen as worthwhile unless done at scale. Without existing knowledge or access to specialized lawyers and lobbyists, small firms default to more traditional channels. And given their limited size, small businesses often find it difficult to bid on the large chunks of government work that require a substantial workforce across many functional capabilities . Ultimately, the government contracting process is easier to navigate by large, existing players, who in turn dominate the volume of contracts and therefore create a track record making them "less risky" and more likely to win future contracts.

A failure to understand, and mitigate, any of these factors can result in disappointing results in the pursuit of homeland security technology markets.

INCREASING CHANCES FOR SUCCESS

Although the homeland security technology market is challenging, taking six sequential steps can maximize chances of successful sales and business development efforts (see Figure 46-3).

Figure 46-3

Six steps to increase
homeland security
technology sales
success

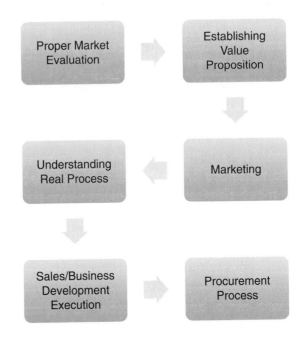

**1. Proper Market
Evaluation:
Identify the Pain**

Success selling technology products to homeland security markets begins with a proper evaluation of the market. Vendors need to answer the question, "How do we know a market for our technology offering exists in homeland security markets?"

The key to market evaluation is developing a good understanding of the pain relieved by the technology being offered. Professionals in the homeland security space are often creative and forward thinking. However, their priorities are generally defined by current problems and challenges created by events outside their control, such as immediate or imminent threats or financial constraints. In other words, their buying decisions are generally focused on the pain or challenge at hand.

The need to focus on the most painful issues at hand is partly due to tight budgets. Other reasons relate to the complexity of government procurement. Approval to move forward on a new technology initiative is generally required at a number of levels. Thus, initiative champions must "sell" their technology concepts to a large and often diverse group of people, ranging from operators to elected officials. This internal selling process becomes easier when an acknowledged problem is being addressed.

Solution providers interested in selling in the homeland security space must find ways to identify existing challenges their solutions can help relieve. Tactics to uncover this information include use of publicly available resources, professional studies, and simply asking.

Using Resources

Fortunately for would-be homeland security technology vendors, extensive information is available from public sources that point to pain points. Because of the nature of the work, the field has its areas of confidentiality and secrecy. However, most areas of focus are discussed very openly in public forums. An early case in point is the "9/11 Commission Report," which discussed, even critiqued, in great detail U.S. response to the events of 9/11.

Examples of publicly available documents that can point to homeland security technology pain points include the following:

- *Department of Homeland Security Science and Technology Directorate.* DHS S&T manages science and technology research to protect the homeland. It attempts to focus on areas where need is greatest or where the pain is acute. Its website provides deep detail of the interest in the following categories:
  - Borders and Maritime Security projects develop and transition tools and technologies to improve the security of our nation's borders and waterways without impeding the flow of commerce and travelers.
  - Command, Control, and Interoperability projects develop interoperable communication standards and protocols for emergency responders, cybersecurity tools for protecting the integrity of the Internet, and automated capabilities to recognize and analyze potential threats.
  - Homeland Security Advanced Research Projects Agency (HSARPA) focuses on homeland security research and development that could lead to significant technology breakthroughs and greatly enhance departmental operations.
  - Explosives projects develop the technical capabilities to detect, interdict, and lessen the impacts of non-nuclear explosives used in terrorist attacks against mass transit, civil aviation, and critical infrastructure.
  - Office of National Laboratories (ONL) provides a coordinated, enduring core of productive science, technology, and engineering laboratories, organizations, and institutions, which can provide the knowledge and technology required to secure the nation.
  - Science & Technology Standards address the standards needs of homeland security customers at multiple levels: department

operational components, state and local governments, and the private sector. These standards help the nation's emergency responders acquire equipment, procedures, and mitigation processes that are safe, reliable, and effective.

- *Department of Homeland Security SECURE and FutureTECH Programs.* The SECURE (System Efficacy through Commercialization Utilization, Relevance and Evaluation) Program is designed to foster partnerships between government and private companies "aligned to the needs of its (DHS) operating components, first responders and critical infrastructure/key resources owners and operators." SECURE says its partnerships can represent "large potential available markets." FutureTECH is a related program, but focused on earlier-stage development.

- *Government Accounting Office Reports.* The investigative arm of Congress regularly releases reports describing problems and challenges creating struggles for homeland security with regard to technology and acquisition. Recent GAO reports related to homeland security technology and procurement include the following:

  o *Progress Made and Work Remaining in Implementing Homeland Security* Missions 10 Years after 9/11 (http://www.gao.gov/assets/130/126861.pdf)

  o *DHS and TSA Acquisition and Development of New Technologies* (http://www.gao.gov/assets/590/585355.pdf)

  o *Billions Invested in Major Programs Lack Appropriate Oversight* (http://www.gao.gov/assets/290/283448.pdf)

  o *Improvements Could Further Enhance Ability to Acquire Innovative Technologies Using Other Transaction Authority* (http://www.gao.gov/assets/290/281442.pdf)

  o *Management of First Responder Grant Programs and Efforts to Improve Accountability Continue to Evolve* (http://www.gao.gov/assets/120/111488.pdf)

  o *DHS Faces Challenges to Successfully Consolidating Its Existing Disparate Systems* (http://www.gao.gov/assets/300/299187.pdf)

  o *Technologies to Secure Federal Systems* (http://www.gao.gov/assets/250/241678.pdf)

- *State Programs and Plans.* Most states publicly release their plans, often updated annually, for coping with issues related to homeland security. Among the technology-oriented plans are those relating to interoperability, communications, and alert systems. The reports are generally available online through websites published by governors or state public safety organizations (i.e., homeland security, emergency management).
- *Requests for Proposals (RFPs)/Requests for Information (RFIs).* RFPs and RFIs are published aggressively to encourage competition. A keyword search of "RFP and RFI databases" will reveal both past and future procurements. Searching these databases will show where governmental agencies have placed their purchasing priorities. On the federal level, procurement databases can be searched through a service offered by the U.S. government at no charge called FedBizOpps. Searches of local and state procurements can be conducted on a state-by-state or city/county-by-city/county basis or through commercially available procurement compilation services.

Other Ways to Identify and Weigh Opportunities

While review of publicly available documentation is an important aspect of market evaluation, it's not the only effort that will produce results. For example, a firm could commission a professional market study with expertise in both homeland security markets and market research studies for commercial purposes. In addition to addressing areas of interest, such studies can apply statistical models and market intelligence to estimate market size.

Another tried-and-true method is to simply ask. Even when facing demanding schedules, government officials focused on homeland security are generally open to discussing their needs.

2. Establish a Value Proposition

Once identification of pain has helped provide confidence that a real market exists for a technology solution, the next step is establishing a value proposition. This links the information gathered during the pain identification process to the values a solution can provide for eliminating the pain. Although it is important to consider value propositions in an early stage, they should be reconsidered regularly as new information becomes available—particularly information obtained through direct input from potential customers.

In addition to answering the question of "what pain is being relieved?" a number of other questions should be answered when establishing a value proposition. These are questions almost always asked by government officials when considering a purchase:

- **Can the solution be funded?**
  Funds are often not immediately available to support a technology acquisition, particularly since government establishes budgets over short periods. However, government officials interested in a homeland security technology solution may be able to obtain future funding for the project.
- **Can the proposed solution fit within current operational environments without significant change, including to human behavior?**
  While implementing change is difficult in any organization, challenges related to change are particularly acute in government environments. Government organizations are often large and unwieldy; their organizational structures are often complex; their cultures slow to change. Introduction of new products or solutions often add to the complexity. A high level of effort is often required to convince operators to adjust behavior.
- **Can the solution be sustained over a significant period at reasonable cost?**
  In addition to being concerned about tight budgets, government buyers are very cautious about ongoing costs beyond initial purchases. Since their budgets are set over a short period, they have no way of knowing whether they will receive funds in subsequent years for sustaining a purchase. Additionally, they tend to look at adopting solutions over longer terms because of challenges of navigating the idea–purchase–deployment cycle.
- **Does the solution satisfy technology security requirements?**
  Many technology solutions operate in environments connected in some way to other technology solutions. This can create security issues. Governmental agencies generally have strict security requirements for technologies placed in their technology infrastructures. Often security certifications are required.

3. Marketing: Messaging, Outreach, and Lead Generation

With pain identified and value propositions in hand, attention turns to marketing. For the purpose of this chapter, marketing is defined as activities that create awareness and identify sales/business development leads. Marketing often includes product management functions, which are not addressed here.

Messaging

Good marketing begins with good messaging. Messaging consists of written and verbal statements that quickly describe solution offerings and value propositions. Messaging is used throughout marketing and sales processes in a variety of environments and contexts:

- "Elevator pitch": A 30-second statement that describes the solution, presented succinctly enough so it could be conveyed to a stranger in a quick elevator ride
- Sales and marketing materials including written materials, advertisements, taglines/slogans
- Press releases and interviews
- Presentations
- Content: White papers, blogs, websites, social media campaigns

In fact, messaging should be cultivated and included within corporate culture via the mission statements, business plans, and regular communications throughout an organization.

Messaging should be built upon a solid "message platform" used to ensure messages are consistent, even when used in varied environments and contexts. Elements include the following:

- *Close tie to organization's strategic plan.* As messaging strategy and specific language recommendations are developed, the question must be asked, "Does each word support the Vision, Mission, Goals, and Objectives of the strategic plan?"
- *Understanding of audience.* Effective messaging is focused on what the audience *really* wants to hear and see.
- *A common vocabulary.* The same terms must be used consistently to convey the same messages to all. Important terms must be identified and defined. A dictionary, available both internally and externally, is helpful.

Investments of time and money into marketing and outreach activities can be wasted if the right information and positioning concepts are not presented clearly and creatively.

Outreach

Successfully spreading messages in homeland security technology markets requires a comprehensive approach. Many people working in diverse environments are engaged in the business of protecting the homeland. They rely on many sources to deliver their information and influence their thought. Thus, companies must rely on different sources to spread their message and consider their outreach efforts as a coordinated campaign covering a number of facets.

Events

One of the most common tactics used in marketing products to government is participation in seminars, conferences, and trade shows, as well as other events focused on homeland security. These are gathering places for decision makers who attend largely with the purpose of identifying solutions for their most pressing problems. Such events are held regularly at national and regional levels, and can be highly effective in spreading a company's message and/or identifying leads.

However, events can be costly in both time and money. Successful event endeavors require more than displaying and staffing an attractive exhibition booth. They require specific strategy including elements such as:

- *Careful selection.* As an organization enters the homeland security technology market, it can be tempting to invest in as many events as possible and build a marketing strategy around the events. The opposite should occur. Events are but one element of a strong marketing program and should be closely aligned to other marketing activities. Thus, careful decisions must be made to invest resources in events. Sending company representatives to attend and "scout" specific events before committing significant resources can help lead to smart selections. As well, consider smaller, "boutique" events such as trade shows covering homeland security for small geographic areas or finite special interests.
- *Careful messaging.* Ensure messaging is carefully crafted before attending events.
- *"Draw" activities.* For events where a company display booth will be used, consider activities and promotions that will help attract attention and encourage people to visit.
- *Document activity.* Establish systems to capture contact information and a summary of interest levels so follow-up activity can occur.

- *Active participation.* In addition to exhibiting via display booths, many conferences offer speaking opportunities for vendors either as part of the conference general sessions or for a fee.

Publications

The importance and diversity of homeland security efforts have created a wide variety of publications generating homeland security-related content. They can be identified through keyword searches that contain terms related directly to not only homeland security, but also to other public safety endeavors (i.e., law enforcement, fire services, emergency management, emergency communications such as 9-1-1, etc.).

These publications are often interested in content relating to new and innovative uses of technology designed to help protect the homeland. This is particularly true when actual use case studies can be presented. Vendors often find they are successful facilitating the conveyance of related content to pertinent publications. Even though vendors will not likely have complete control over the content, their value proposition can still be a part of a publication's editorial content.

Advertising

Advertising opportunities exist through many of the same publications mentioned, focused on delivering content related to homeland security and public safety. As well, events and homeland security-related organizations often seek sponsorships from interested vendors to help support their activities. In addition to providing advertising avenues, these sponsorships can help create goodwill with the organizations.

Viral Marketing

One of the fastest, most effective, and least expensive means for getting a message to market is through a viral marketing campaign. Although relatively inexpensive, viral marketing is not simple. A viral marketing campaign is a series of initiatives designed to create "buzz" about a company's offerings. The campaign deploys specific tactics to stimulate contagious behavior so the buzz develops a life of its own, and spreads rapidly—like a virus.

Viral marketing is well-described in Malcolm Gladwell's popular book, *The Tipping Point: How Little Things Can Make a Big Difference.*

He identifies three target areas that can work particularly well in homeland security markets:

- *Identify Mavens.* These are individuals whose opinions others regard as important. They are often the thought leaders. People look to them for insight and guidance. Having them aware and enthusiastic about an organization's solution and value proposition helps establish credibility and trust among an ever-growing number of people.
- *Ignite the Communicators.* Once Mavens are "captured," the "Communicators" need to be identified and ignited. These are the individuals who can spread the word. They don't necessarily create leading thought, but they spread it.
- *Close with the Salespeople.* With buzz beginning to spread, the "salespeople" are activated. These are individuals with something specific to gain. Most obvious would be internal business development personnel. However, others can include teaming partners, resellers, even homeland security personnel whose initiatives can benefit from an organization's technology solutions.

Special Events

Some of the more sophisticated vendors of technology for homeland security have sponsored events, held at think tanks and universities. These events focus on discussion of substantive issues and challenges, and it is frowned upon to hijack them for overt sales talk from the podium, but they serve as excellent mechanisms for senior level networking.

Lead Generation and Qualification

While marketing activities help spread a company's message, they should also help generate leads of individuals and organizations who may be interested in a company's offerings. This can be accomplished by providing methods in marketing endeavors for organizations or individuals to express their interest in a company's offerings.

For example, a website may provide a page for interested parties to initiate contact and express interest. It may also include a sign-up page for an electronic newsletter. Those who sign up may be considered leads, worthy of follow-up. An advertisement may include contact information, perhaps a stimulator to encourage an interested party to visit the company's web page. Company personnel staffing trade shows should collect contact and other information (see information objectives below) from visitors to the company's display booth.

Information Objectives

Obtaining particular information is required when exploring leads. This information will be used to, first, qualify the leads for their real potential and, second, follow up leads to help them progress through the sales cycle. Information objectives should include the following:

- *Pain to be addressed.* What is the primary need/problem to be solved and mission, objective, or main threat to be addressed?
- *Organizational information.* Type of organization and its mission, management structure, budget sources.
- *History.* Is the lead from a past, current, or new customer? Have there been performance issues? Have articles been written about the organization that relate to the solution being offered? What's the organization's reputation?
- *Decision structure.* How are decisions made within the organization? What's the approval process?
- *Hot buttons and constraints.* Typically concerns, issues, worries, biases, hazards, threats, risks, challenges, imperatives, or environmental factors (political, legislative, sociocultural, etc.). Vendors may also identify key constraints the customer may be facing with this potential acquisition (e.g., inadequate funding, vague requirements).

Lead Management

As a company pursues homeland security technology markets, qualified leads can become a valuable asset. Properly qualified and well-pursued leads evolve into real opportunities and then to closed sales. As valuable assets, they must be managed carefully. Lead generation is best considered a proactive endeavor, rather than a passive one that's simply a by-product of marketing activities. In addition to collecting leads, the endeavor should include lead management to ensure leads are followed up appropriately for exploration and pursuit.

A solid lead management program contains the following elements:

- *Information objective documentation.* Information objectives discussed above must be carefully documented and updated as new information becomes available.
- *Follow-up activities.* Even when a prospective lead expresses strong enthusiasm for the solution being offered, they must be persistently followed up. An organization cannot assume

of individuals representing various disciplines within an organization. Presentations by multiple competitors are often heard on the same day to help accommodate schedules of busy homeland security personnel. While it's unlikely that a buying decision will be made on a presentation alone, they can be important to help determine the winner of a competitive procurement.

Presentation formats and delivery preferences can vary widely. They need to be comprehensive, but a fine balance exists between providing information needed and creating positive, memorable, emotional responses that support the presenter's position.

The solution must be presented in the context of:

- National, regional, provincial, and municipal-level risk analysis (focusing on natural threats and hazards)
- The customer's political, human, and technical structures
- The current body of statutes, authorities, regulations, executive guidance and directives, and national-level strategic planning as it relates to disaster preparedness and emergency management
- The customer's current authorities

Presentations should be carefully structured to accurately present the information while conveying an understanding of customer's needs. (See "1. Proper Market Evaluation.") Effective presentations follow formats similar to the following:

Presentation Structure

1. *Brief introduction.* Emphasis on brief.
2. *Customer references.* Establish credibility up front.
3. *Problem–cause–solution–benefits.* Demonstrate a thorough understanding.
4. *Questions.* Soliciting questions midpoint helps illustrate whether the audience is engaged.
5. *Pricing.* Never leave pricing to last.
6. *Contracting.* Generate discussion that provides insight into how decisions will be made.
7. *Impressive company history points and customer case studies.* Helps end the presentation on a positive note.

Rules of Engagement

Vendors must understand that DHS program managers and other DHS staff members must follow strict rules before they meet with vendors and industry representatives. DHS program managers and other staff are encouraged to talk with industry representatives of both large and small businesses so DHS procurements reflect an understanding of the commercial marketplace and the business environment of the vendors that support DHS programs. This exchange of information, however, must take place within a framework that treats all vendors (and potential vendors) fairly and impartially.

After the agency needs are established and the requirements to satisfy those needs are developed, no exchange with industry and potential vendors are allowed without the permission and without the presence of the contracting officer. Procurement begins at the point when the agency needs are established and the description of the requirements to satisfy agency need is developed. In meetings with vendors or industry representatives, government officials are not allowed to disclose "procurement sensitive" or "source selection sensitive" information, the proposal evaluation process, or the specifics of an ongoing procurement, or discuss litigation or pending litigation. No information may be released after agency needs are established and the requirements to satisfy those needs are developed, except by the contracting officer.

Writing Proposals That Stand Out and Win

Winning proposals demonstrate the *unique value* of the solution for the customer relative to the alternatives. They explain how the offered solution provides the greatest value in light of mission and program priorities and makes the best use of the customer's current capabilities and existing resources.

Proposals should demonstrate the following:

- The vendor has applicable credentials and a contractual track record indicating it can perform the project successfully, on schedule, and within budget.
- The vendor understands the mission-level importance and technical requirements of the project.
- The vendor will apply best practices including program and project management, organizational development, strategic planning, enterprise architecture, business case analysis, funding,

systems engineering, standards development, information sharing protocol development, and so on.

- Selecting this vendor will benefit the clients from technical, programmatic, risk mitigation, and cost perspectives.

Proposals must demonstrate understanding of the project requirements, critical issues, and success criteria, including the following:

- How does the vendor demonstrate that its innovative, solutions-oriented approach satisfies all requirements?
- What are the benefits of the vendor's approach now and over the life of the program?
- How does the vendor's approach minimize schedules, cost, and technical performance risk?
- How is the vendor demonstrating value and applicability by leveraging existing infrastructure?
- Does the vendor have experience with all the technologies, conceptual frameworks, and methodologies needed to develop this solution?
- Can the vendor use photos of related projects, equipment, and systems to help authenticate contractual experience and technical approach?
- Does vendor have unique methodologies, planning, modeling, or simulation tools to support the analysis needed to design a solution?
- How does the vendor demonstrate it develops partnerships with customers and remains committed to sustainable long-term success?
- Can the vendor demonstrate experience in this country / region / client organization and preparedness to meet client requirements in a timely manner, as well as an understanding of local political and regulatory decision-making environments?
- Can the vendor highlight successful past performance with a few success stories, as well as key lessons learned and best practices?
- How well does the proposed solution help the client address their critical need?
- Does the proposal explain how the offered solution will enable information to flow in the context of a role that needs to make a decision?

- Does the explanation clarify the interdependence between tasks and information flows across organizations and show the cascading impact of potential failure?
- Which capabilities will give the best risk reduction or crisis readiness return on investment for their limited budget?
- Who are the customer decision makers, influencers, and buyers (the users, and operational, financial, IT influencers), and what are their interests?
- What information does the vendor have about competitors and their solutions?
- Has the customer provided an adequately documented concept of operation that describes how a set of capabilities or a proposed system will be employed or used to achieve desired objectives or a particular end state for a specific scenario?
- Is the vendor already capable of defining the measures of effectiveness (MoEs) required to quantify and compare potential solutions?
- What will be the key variables between alternative solutions to the identified threats and vulnerabilities?
- What key discriminators would differentiate the vendor and its approach from the competition in the eyes of the customer?

SUMMARY

Selling homeland security technology is a complex and challenging undertaking. The bureaucracy, slow pace, false starts, and occasional dead ends resulting from personnel turnover, budget reprioritization, and program termination can discourage even highly motivated sales professionals. The best technology business development professionals share a sense of higher purpose with the government officials they serve. They recognize the services, products, and solutions they are providing will save lives.

ACKNOWLEDGEMENTS

The authors would like to express their thanks to the following people for their assistance with this chapter: Ron Krakower, Deltek, Inc., and Stephen Rodriguez, President, Coldon Strategic Advisors.

FURTHER READING

Small Business Assistance—http://www.dhs.gov/xopnbiz/smallbusiness/.

Acquisition Planning and Forecast System (Contracting Opportunities)—http://www.dhs.gov/xopnbiz/opportunities/gc_1300288340710.shtm.

Department and Component Industry Communication Liaison Listing—http://www.dhs.gov/xopnbiz/opportunities/industry-communication-liaisons.shtm.

Department and Component Small Business Specialist Listing—http://www.dhs.gov/xopnbiz/smallbusiness/gc_1178570919850.shtm.

Department of Homeland Security Acquisition Regulation—http://www.dhs.gov/xopnbiz/regulations/index.shtm.

Homeland Security Acquisition Manual (which includes, as appendices, the new DHS Debriefing Guide and the DHS Market Research Guide)—http://www.dhs.gov/xopnbiz/regulations/index.shtm.

DHS Acquisition Planning and Forecast System—http://www.dhs.gov/xopnbiz/opportunities/gc_1300288340710.shtm.

Department and Component Industry Communication Liaisons—http://www.dhs.gov/xopnbiz/opportunities/industry-communication-liaisons.shtm.

Department and Component Small Business Specialists—http://www.dhs.gov/xopnbiz/smallbusiness/gc_1178570919850.shtm.

DHS's Office of Small and Disadvantaged Business Utilization (OSDBU) and Component Small Business Specialists provide active small business support and sponsors popular monthly *Vendor Outreach Sessions,* composed of a series of prearranged 15-minute appointments between DHS Small Business Specialists and representatives from small business communities. These sessions provide the small business community with an opportunity to discuss their capabilities and learn of potential procurement opportunities. Notices of upcoming *Vendor Outreach Sessions* are posted on the Small Business Central Event Listing on FedBizOpps (www.fbo.gov) and on the DHS.gov Small Business Assistance page at http://www.dhs.gov/xopnbiz/smallbusiness/.

For a number of years, DHS has hosted an annual DHS Industry Day. Industry Day activities include panel discussions from each component moderated by the respective DHS Head of Contracting Activity (HCA). The panels provide acquisition planning information for the specific component/contracting activity. This one-day event provides a forum by which the Department can communicate its requirements and increase competition by sharing useful information. Industry Day is open to representatives of both small and large businesses. DHS Industry Day notices are posted on FedBizOpps (www.fbo.gov).

DHS Acquisition Planning Forecast System (APFS) provides real-time access to the DHS Forecast of Contract Opportunities. See http://www.dhs.gov/xopnbiz/opportunities/gc_1300288340710.shtm.

Malcolm Gladwell, *The Tipping Point: How Little Things Can Make a Big Difference* (Boston: Back Bay Books, 2002).

Lorin Bristow and Rick Wimberly, *Seven Myths of Selling to Government: Secrets for Success in Government Sales Today* (Franklin, TN: Galain Solutions, Inc., 2011).

10

INTRODUCTION TO PART X: CIVIL LIBERTIES AND OTHER LEGAL ISSUES

K. A. Taipale

Founder and Executive Director of the Stilwell Center, a Senior Fellow at the World Policy Institute, and a member of the Markle Taskforce for National Security in the Information Age

In introducing the section on domestic security and civil liberties in an earlier edition of this book, I optimistically argued that security and liberty might more easily be reconciled if they were considered for purposes of public discourse and policy as dual obligations of civil society, rather than as dichotomous rivals to be traded one for the other in a zero-sum political game of balance. I posited that security and liberty ought best be considered Janus-like sides to the same social compact coin, in which securing one was not possible without securing the other: "In a liberal republic, liberty presupposes security; [and] the point of security is liberty."[1] I further argued that the prevailing metaphorical public discourse of achieving some sort of balance between security and liberty—with its smuggled assumption of a fulcrum point of perfect policy equilibrium—was misleading and might too easily foster an antagonistic Jacobin scrum in which those seeking to maintain civil liberties are simply accused of being against collective security, and those seeking security too willing to relinquish individual liberty. I concluded that essay by asserting hopefully that a better informed policy debate—one in which the particular nature of the new challenges and threats to both security and liberty were honestly examined within this framework of dual obligation—could lead to policies in which *both* improved security *and* protected liberty might be achieved. It seems I was naïve.

Instead of the hoped-for reasoned debate and resulting rational policies, partisan political and ideological motivations on the part of dissembling politicians, insatiable institutional imperatives for extended power and control by expansive government bureaucracies, and raw commercial self-interest by disingenuous individuals and private firms on the one hand, together with a hypersensitive and self-absorbed "privacy lobby" driven in large part by fundraising needs, attention-seeking desires, and a doctrinaire ideological agenda on the other, have resulted in "security theater" triumphing over real security, and "political correctness" over essential liberty. Thus, the "enhanced" pat-downs and groping of six-year-old children or elderly grandmothers with colostomy bags passes for security at airports, while an absolutist fetish for avoiding even the remotest potential for chimerical "privacy violations" prevents even the innocuous use of data or behavioral analytics to enhance security screening. In simple economic costs, more than $1 trillion has been squandered in homeland security spending since 9/11, with little to show except for the expansion of a massive homeland security industrial complex (one that eagerly supplies, at taxpayer expense, Zodiac boats with side-scanning sonar to protect rural Nebraska reservoirs from Al Qaida inspired ice-fishermen, and nine-ton armored vehicles to protect Los Angeles movie studios from terrorist film critics). The Transportation Security Administration spends $8 billion a year on a vast airport screening program with 50,000 employees that regularly humiliate the traveling public but that have never identified a single terrorist. (Although Homeland Security Secretary Napolitano absurdly claimed at the time that "the system worked," both the shoe bomber and the underwear bomber were apprehended in the act by fellow passengers, not DHS). Commercial profiteering abounds. For example, $50 million was wasted installing so-called "puffer" machines that never worked to detect explosives and had to be removed from service at airports only to be replaced now with radiation machines that, according to the GAO, also don't work against the very threat that they were intended for. These machines are banned in Europe as a potential health threat (but are supplied by a company represented by a former Secretary of DHS under a program that will cost $300 million to install and $300 million a year to operate). Meanwhile, a tetchy privacy lobby recklessly opposes even the most innocuous government actions, for example, shrilly decrying the government monitoring of information voluntarily posted to public websites that is accessible to anyone through Google, or vehemently opposing even minimal data-retention requirements in collusion with actors driven primarily to protect their own free-riding business models. The combined result to the public is little in the way of real improved security and much in the way of impaired liberty.

This is not to deny the seriousness of the threat to public safety from terrorist acts, nor the justifiable need to preempt attacks with potentially catastrophic outcomes. We face a tireless enemy sworn to destroy our economic and political way of life, whose foot soldiers and acolytes must be identified and stopped before they act. Nor is it an attempt to belittle the need to vigilantly maintain civil liberties and vigorously resist encroachments on privacy. As Benjamin Franklin noted, any compromise of essential liberty for temporary security is unacceptable.[2] Nevertheless, as I earlier posed, security and liberty are better considered complimentary values to be maximized within the constraints of each other, not simply as trump cards to be played with relish, one to obstruct the other in the petty game of partisan politics. In my earlier essay I argued that reconciling these seemingly conflicting values need not necessitate slighting one for the other, since actually there should be no inherent policy conflict at all between security and liberty within the Constitutional framework of reasonableness. Strategies that place an unreasonable burden on liberty—for example, demonizing a minority or engendering suspicion of everyone—are not just unacceptable outcomes for liberty, but provide little or no security. These strategies are ineffective at identifying terrorists and they undermine the cooperation and confidence of the populace that are needed for success. On the other hand, liberty incurs responsibility, and unfettered liberty at the expense of security against potentially catastrophic outcomes impinges not just on collective security, but also on the very foundation of liberty for all individuals and is itself, therefore, unreasonable. Reasonableness, I argued, inherently requires *effective* security strategies; that is, strategies that actually help locate, target, and preempt terrorists before they act without unduly burdening the vast majority of innocent people. Reasonableness is the essential calculus for maximizing both.

Unfortunately, through feckless promises of absolute security on the one hand and uncompromising insistence on a one-size-fits-all-lest-it-unintentionally-burden-anyone-disproportionally security model on the other, we have achieved the perfectly unreasonable—little security with much impairment of liberty in some cases and an illusion of liberty at the cost of rationality in others. In the pursuit of false security and faux liberty we have set the security bar to maximally discommode the vast majority, yet at a threshold under which the real terrorist can easily limbo. Although the terrorist may not have won, surely the rest of us will have lost if we do not revamp our approach.

NOTES

1. Thomas Powers, Can We Be Secure and Free? 151 *Public Interest* 3, 5 (Spring 2003).
2. "Those who would give up Essential Liberty to purchase a little temporary Safety, deserve neither Liberty nor Safety." Attributed to Benjamin Franklin. Benjamin Franklin, Pennsylvania Assembly: Reply to the Governor, November 11, 1755. 6 *The Papers Of Benjamin Franklin* 242 (Leonard W. Labaree, ed., 1963).

47

VIGILANCE ON TWO FRONTS: CIVIL LIBERTIES & THE HOMELAND SECURITY PROFESSIONAL[1]

Laura W. Murphy

Director, Washington Legislative Office, American Civil Liberties Union

INTRODUCTION

The introduction to the 2006 version of this chapter noted how the events of 9/11 had fundamentally transformed academic curricula in fields related to defense or security. When I started out at the ACLU, the civil liberties issues in national security were all tied up in the Cold War. The university security studies classes teaching the future deputy undersecretaries at the Department of Defense and the deputy directors at the CIA focused on things like Sovietology and mutually assured destruction.

If you look at the same programs now, the course descriptions tend to feature buzzwords like "counter-insurgency," "asymmetrical warfare," "emerging technology and security," "cyberwar," "domestic intelligence," "ethnic conflict & civil war," "counter-proliferation," and, of course, "terrorism and counterterrorism." Some of you reading this are likely in a class with one or more of these terms in the course title.

Unfortunately, even six years after the original publication of this book, one does not regularly see core courses in security studies programs at major universities with descriptions like: "counter-terrorism *and* free speech," "domestic intelligence *and* privacy," "emergency preparedness *and* the separation of powers," or "homeland security *and* civil rights."

I would argue that, much like law schools require students to take professional responsibility classes or business schools require budding executives to take a course on business ethics, security studies programs should offer a mandatory course on the civil liberties aspects of national security work. Too often, those who are responsible for keeping us safe (work that certainly merits applause) have an underdeveloped understanding of how to maintain basic constitutional freedoms at the same time—how to maintain vigilance on two fronts.

The 2006 version of this chapter offered a few thoughts on certain principles that inform the balancing act between security and liberty, and then applied these principles in the context of several specific case studies, including the debate over a national identification card, the possibility of emergency measures in response to bioterrorism and the dangers of profiling based on certain characteristics like race or ethnicity. This chapter takes the same approach, but updates the case studies to include security responses to "radicalization" and the due process questions surrounding the "targeted killing" program, which currently allows the president, without any independent review, to take lethal action against those suspected of terrorism, even American citizens.

The hope is that this chapter will spur greater interest in and awareness of the civil liberties responsibilities of the homeland security practitioner. Groups like the ACLU that monitor the national security and intelligence agencies for civil liberties violations can only cover so much ground; most often, civil liberties are protected by the conscientious security professionals who effectively spot the issue in their day-to-day work, care about the issue's ramifications, and act accordingly.

Further, the intention with the case studies presented here is not to convince the reader of the rightness of a particular position (though I certainly hope that the reader would be open to the ACLU's arguments). Rather, it is to promote critical thought about the issues at hand, and to give the security professional some inkling of what to think about when presented with a hard issue. The worst civil liberties abuses in our history often occur because individuals with power, and the best intentions, just don't know the right questions to ask.

THE DEBATE

The liberty versus security debate is both simple on the level of abstract theory and deceptively complicated when one has to apply grand concepts to everyday facts.

Security hawks tend to argue in terms such as those that follow. The quotation is from retired Lieutenant General Patrick M. Hughes, a former head of the Defense Intelligence Agency and a senior intelligence official at the Department of Homeland Security. He made the statement during a presentation at Harvard (while out of government service), and it illustrates the basic assumptions of those who believe the "war on terrorism" fundamentally changed the relationship of civil liberties to security in the United States. Lt. Gen. Hughes made these comments in the context of envisioning how 9/11 would impact America's future legal landscape.

> What I'm about to say is very arrogant—arrogant to a fault. Set aside what the mass of people think. Some things are so bad for them that you cannot allow them to have them. One of them is war in the context of terrorism in the United States. Therefore, we have to abridge individual rights, change the societal conditions, and act in ways that heretofore were not in accordance with our values and traditions, like giving a police officer or security official the right to search you without a judicial finding of probable cause. Things are changing, and this change is happening because things can be brought to us that we cannot afford to absorb. We can't deal with them, so we're going to reach out and do something ahead of time to preclude them. Is that going to change your lives? It already has.[2]

The other side of the divide argues that the choice between liberty and security is a false one (save in the most extreme scenarios), and the curtailment of liberties based on irrational or unfounded fears is, in point of fact, the goal of most extremist groups, including both Al Qaeda and many of the right-wing extremist groups.[3]

For civil libertarians (and, indeed, for most policymakers), the trick is not choosing between liberty and security as an either/or option, so much as it is identifying effective security policies that either do not infringe on constitutional rights (such as cargo screening or the explosive detection "wands" used at airports), or are so effective that the benefits of their use make it worth figuring out ways to minimize the impact on our rights (and these are rare). Obviously, security measures that are ineffective should be rejected out of hand, without any inquiry into the civil liberties implications of their use.

Following this basic logic, the 9/11 Commission proposed a bare bones test that security professionals could adopt when considering the civil liberties implications of any proposed new security policy.

> The test is a simple but important one. The burden of proof should be on the proponents of the measure to establish that the power or authority being sought would in fact materially enhance national security, and that there will be adequate supervision of the exercise of that power or authority to ensure the protection of civil liberties. If additional powers are granted, there must be adequate guidelines and oversight to properly confine their use.[4]

This chapter proposes a similar set of relevant questions that should be considered when assessing the need for, and possible danger of, new security measures or the adoption of new security technologies.

1. What is the balance between effectiveness and invasiveness? Is the policy or technology possibly effective but highly invasive of basic freedoms (e.g., strip-searching every airline passenger)? If so, reject and more narrowly tailor. Is it of marginal effectiveness but highly invasive of liberty (e.g., racial profiling)? If so, obviously reject. Finally, is it effective and only minimally invasive (e.g., passive explosive screening at airports)? That should be the goal.

2. Does the measure discriminate against individuals based on characteristics they can't change (like race, ethnicity, or other group characteristics)? Around 9/11, plenty of commentators were of the view "if you're color-blind, you're blind,"[5] and actively supported profiling Arab and Muslim Americans as potential terrorists. But this both ignores the practical problem of terrorist workarounds like the "black widows" in Chechnya,[6] and is deeply violative of core principles. The United States took this approach when we interned Japanese-Americans in World War II, and that remains a national shame (one that prompted federal legislation requiring[7] reparations payments of $20,000

to individuals who had been forced into internment camps [imprisoned] by the program).[8]

3. Is there a risk of unintended consequences? Many of the worst civil liberties violations proceed from the best of intentions, but the devil is in the details. The rapid and costly expansion of counter-terrorism agencies in the national intelligence community may superficially and temporarily assuage the fears of Americans, but the proliferation of intelligence agencies also increases the size of the information "haystack," making the terrorism "needle" much more difficult to find. Further, the sheer size of the intelligence sector makes congressional oversight and public accountability difficult as a check and balance to prevent civil liberties violations.[9]

4. Even if the answer to question one is favorable in terms of the balance between effectiveness and civil liberties, and the answers to questions two and three are "no," the homeland security practitioner needs to ask whether there is a public relations dimension to any proposal. This consideration may sound like it is a little out of left field, but Americans are finely attuned to violations of their civil liberties. Even after 9/11, government responses that did violate civil liberties (and could possibly have been more effectively formulated and presented) were shot down after public outcry.[10] Assuring an informed public response and increasing transparency about proposed or existing national security policies will serve the ends of both civil liberties and security. To that end, I would urge homeland security professionals to engage with groups like the ACLU prior to implementation of potentially controversial programs and policies to gauge the degree and scope of potential public objection.

APPLYING THESE CONSIDERATIONS

It may be helpful to explore these four questions in the context of two case studies. The first involves so-called "radicalization" policies or theories, which attempt to show how terroristic "intention forms, hardens and leads to an attack or attempted attack. ..."[11] The second looks at the presidential "targeted killing" program, in which alleged terrorism suspects are killed overseas by the U.S. government based on secret legal standards and without judicial review.

groups becoming more violent and more secretive, and it gives their abhorrent underlying ideas a perverse respectability among some.

In practice, attempts to formulate a coherent theory of "radicalization" invariably threaten these basic freedoms. In 2007, for instance, the New York Police Department published *Radicalization in the West: The Homegrown Threat*, which was quickly adopted as a comprehensive policy statement and lauded by some as providing a framework for radicalization investigations. In 2009, however, the authors of the report were forced to issue a "Statement of Clarification" noting that "the NYPD's focus on Al Qaeda inspired terrorism should not be mistaken for any implicit or explicit justification for racial, religious or ethnic profiling," and that the report was never meant to be "policy prescriptive for law enforcement."[20] Unfortunately, the statement was released to little fanfare and the report continues to be cited by academics and policymakers as "prescriptive" of policy, despite dramatic methodological deficiencies. Most notably, the report identifies a four-step "radicalization" process, but notes that not everyone passes through all of the stages and many "abandon the process at different points."[21] Furthermore, the four steps themselves encompass perfectly lawful, constitutionally protected speech and lawful assembly.[22] Indeed, only the last step, "jihadization," has any connection to prohibited *conduct*. Only there does the supposed radical begin planning for violent acts. The rest of the process involves merely an ideological evolution of the individual, which directly implicates freedom of thought and conscience, rights that deserve the highest protection under the Constitution.[23]

The report even explicitly calls for government monitoring of constitutionally protected conduct:

> The subtle and *non-criminal* nature of the behaviors involved in the process of radicalization makes it difficult to identify or even monitor from a law enforcement standpoint. Taken in isolation, individual behaviors can be seen as innocuous; however, when seen as part of the continuum of the radicalization process, their significance becomes more important. Considering the sequencing of these behaviors and the need to *identify those entering this process at the earliest possible stage* makes intelligence the critical tool in helping to thwart an attack or even prevent the planning of future plots.[24] (*emphasis added*)

If you apply the four question framework this chapter laid out in the preceding section, it becomes clear that there is significant danger in adopting any predictive "radicalization" theory as official law enforcement policy:

Balancing Liberty and Security

Although it depends on how the policy is implemented, almost any deployment of the four-part radicalization process is going to involve significant monitoring of entirely innocuous behavior. Which websites is a target visiting? Where is the individual going to worship? What coffee shops, restaurants, bookstores, or cultural centers are individuals frequenting? Not only does this type of monitoring violate the Constitution, it also threatens to "chill" or reduce perfectly lawful associational activity and speech, with relatively little in the way of added security. Indeed, this may be illustrated by the Merah case, where it does appear that Merah adopted radical beliefs and was actively monitored by the French government during this time, but that monitoring failed to tip the French authorities off to his violent intentions.

Is It Discriminatory?

Here, the answer is clearly yes. Although al Qaeda sympathizers (let alone violent operatives) are a minute fraction of the American Arab and Muslim population, a "radicalization" policy would require the government to monitor hundreds of thousands of law abiding Americans simply because of their religious or ethnic background. On this basis alone, "radicalization" theories pose significant constitutional infirmities.

Unintended Consequences

Any poorly focused intelligence policy framework runs the risk of wasting valuable resources. These resources could be used to investigate more fruitful, factual indicators of possible terrorist planning (e.g., large fertilizer purchases or the cultivation of informants that are actually party to the criminal enterprise), and to mitigate the harm of possible terrorist attacks (e.g., target-hardening[25]). Even if "radicalization" theory were constitutionally sound, it would be unwise on this basis alone: It is far too vague and over-broad a policy to provide useful guidance for law enforcement.[26] Additionally, by focusing narrowly on Salafi Islam and Al Qaeda-inspired terrorism, the radicalization framework risks diluting law enforcement focus on other forms of violent extremism (recall that before 9/11, the deadliest terrorist attack on American soil was the Oklahoma City bombing in 1996, which was carried out by white male, anti-government, right-wing zealots).[27]

Public Relations Blowback

Here again, radicalization theory poses risks, namely that the backlash against the blanket surveillance of an entire group of people based on ethnicity or religious affiliation will harm policymakers' ability to adopt more narrowly tailored aspects of the policy. For instance, there may be certain specific behavioral indicators that are agnostic with respect to ethnicity and/or religion that actually are predictive of a violent terrorist act (stockpiling weapons or attending a terrorist training camp abroad). Attempts to identify this behavior may become immediately suspect when the underlying policies that permit these investigations are poorly conceived. Further, to the extent that cooperation by the Arab and Muslim communities is valuable in preventing terrorist acts, that cooperation may be chilled if law enforcement policy fosters a climate of mistrust.

The fundamental civil liberties problem with radicalization theories has long been recognized by the Supreme Court, including in the context of left-wing revolutionary and right-wing white supremacist movements. According to the Court, the First Amendment fully applies to speech that justifies and advocates for violent action, as abhorrent and hateful as such speech may be. "The mere abstract teaching of Communist theory," the Court wrote in the early 1960s, "including the teaching of the moral propriety or even moral necessity for a resort to force and violence, is not the same as preparing a group for violent action and steeling it to such action."[28] And, in striking down the conviction of a member of the Ku Klux Klan for a speech praising violent conduct, the Court wrote, "the constitutional guarantees of free speech and free press do not permit a State to forbid or proscribe advocacy of the use of force or of law violation except where such advocacy is directed to inciting or producing imminent lawless action and is likely to incite or produce such action."[29]

Accordingly, because radicalization theory targets protected speech and conduct, and *not* imminent violent action, its risks for civil liberties outweigh any potential benefit for public safety.

Targeted Killing

On September 30, 2011, a United States unmanned aircraft killed an alleged American Al Qaeda operative, Anwar Al-Awlaki, in Yemen. Two weeks later, his 16-year-old son, Abdulrahman, who was born in Denver, was also killed in a U.S. missile attack in Yemen. The strikes were part of an extra-judicial "targeted killing" program where the president can authorize the killing of a U.S. civilian who is suspected of terrorism against the United States or its allies.

Although the scope of the president's authority to conduct this type of program is hotly disputed, only two narrow aspects of the case are addressed below.

First, part of the controversy about the program is that the decision on whether to pursue lethal action is made by the executive branch alone without any meaningful transparency.[30] The administration has not released the legal standards it applies to determine who may be killed, the process by which people are added to kill lists, or the factual basis for the strikes. In addition, although the administration claims it briefs members of the intelligence committees in Congress, oversight is still inadequate.

Second, there is no judicial review of the president's action. Attorney General Holder has stated that judicial process is unnecessary in the national security context: "The Constitution guarantees due process, not judicial process."[31] The most severe deprivation of liberty is death at the hands of the government. The Constitution forecloses the government from depriving an American citizen of life without due process, and that due process must take the form of judicial process. Review by an independent court is the only way to apply appropriate legal standards to the facts properly.

Nevertheless, for the sake of argument, assume that Attorney General Holder is correct, and the targeted killing program allows the president to kill Americans suspected of terrorism without any independent judicial review or public transparency into the program. How would that stack up under the four questions suggested earlier?

Balancing Liberty and Security

We cannot know whether there is sufficient due process in President Obama's targeted killing program, which in itself should be a clear knock against the policy. We simply do not know what legal standards the government is using, and we have no credible information one way or the other on the actual danger posed by the targets of the targeted killing program. Any time the government says "trust us" in this fashion, alarm bells go off both for civil liberties advocates and national security professionals. In addition, the program is unequivocally a danger to civil liberties. We have a fundamental right to be free of government death squads in the United States, unless there is due process of law. The president is asserting unilateral authority to abridge that right (that is, to kill you) without any independent review by a court.

Is It Discriminatory?

Not on its face, but there is a significant question of whether terrorism suspects who are not Muslim or of Middle Eastern, South Asian, or North African descent would be subject to targeted killing. The administration is asserting a blanket right to unilaterally kill any person it deems an unlawful combatant under its own views of the laws of war or the right to self-defense. This would apply, and would set a precedent for, any war (be it a conventional war with a defined geographic scope or the so-called "war on terror"), which, in and of itself, is troubling.

Unintended Consequences

Here, the dangers of the Obama administration's stated position are particularly acute. While some might trust the Obama administration's interpretation of the applicable laws, and that the administration will weigh the evidence fairly and provide appropriate "due process" through some sort of internal review mechanism, would those same people put equal faith in the Bush administration (or vice-versa)? The problem with assertions of unilateral presidential power is that they set a precedent for all subsequent presidencies. The Johnson administration set precedents for Nixon in the Vietnam War, for instance. The whole point of checks and balances, the separation of powers and independent review as the prerequisite for due process is to protect against the unintended abuse of laws and policies by future administrations.

Public Relations Blowback

The blowback against the administration's position has been severe. By many accounts, the targeted killing program has actually boosted Al Qaeda recruitment abroad, as well as tarnishing the administration's reputation at home.[32] This is especially troubling because it may impact the administration's credibility in other areas, hindering its ability to exercise the president's constitutional authority in legitimate and beneficial ways.

While the radicalization example provided previously in this section illustrates the danger in policies that target groups of individuals for special law enforcement scrutiny based on characteristics like ethnicity or religion, the targeted killing discussion shows the problem of unintended consequences of poorly constructed national security policies. Both policies illustrate the danger that public backlash will create a "Chicken Little" fear that the civil liberties "sky is falling." Because there is distrust of the government based on past overreaching, legitimate national security programs will be viewed with skepticism, or worse, this distrust could interfere with the government's ability to implement appropriate security policies.

CONCLUSION

In 2012, more than 10 years after the 9/11 attacks, there is little or no indication that the "homeland security revolution," which is so evident in today's security studies curricula, is close to slowing. The Cold War is a distant memory, and the threat of terrorism has overtaken the discipline of national security in still evolving ways. As the perceived threat has changed (moving from external terrorist attacks to fear of sleeper cells or homegrown terrorism threats) and refocused itself inward—into the "homeland"—novel and dangerous civil liberties threats have likewise come to the fore. As homeland security practitioners exercise vigilance as defenders of our security, they should remain equally vigilant to threats to our (and their) freedom.

NOTES

1. This chapter revisits and updates *Principled Prudence: Civil Liberties and the Homeland Security Practitioner*, published in the 2006 version of this handbook. Nothing in this chapter should be construed as endorsing anything counter to ACLU policy or its publicly stated positions.
2. Patrick M. Hughes, Presentation on Future Conditions: The Character and Conduct of War, 2010 and 2020 (Mar. 30, 2003).
3. Al Qaeda, for instance, desires the establishment of a pan-Arab mega-state, and the removal of what it sees as Western puppet leaders. It believes this can be achieved by forcing Western overreaction against terrorism, which will boost Al Qaeda's recruiting and further its aims. Violent right-wing extremists harbor similar aspirations—terrorism engenders overreaction, overreaction engenders support for the terrorists.
4. National Communication on Terrorist Attacks Upon the U.S., *The 9/11 Commission Report* 394–95 (2004).
5. Bill Maher, *Victory Begins at Home* (HBO television broadcast 2003).
6. The Chechen "Shahidka" or, colloquially, "black widows" are typically young female suicide bombers used by Chechen militants because of the ease with which they can avoid

CHAPTER

48

GOVERNMENT DATA MINING

Newton N. Minow[1]

Senior Counsel, Sidley Austin LL.P.

Fred H. Cate[2]

Distinguished Professor and C. Ben Dutton Professor of Law
Indiana University Maurer School of Law

INTRODUCTION

The government faces new and intense pressure to collect and use personal data. Much of that pressure reflects the conviction that greater reliance on digital data will reduce costs and enhance convenience, speed, efficiency, and accountability. Perhaps the greatest source of that pressure, however, is the fear of terrorist attacks and the widely shared view, as 9/11 Commission Vice Chairman Lee Hamilton testified before Congress in November 2005, that the inability of federal agencies to marshal and share information about suspected terrorists and their activities "was the single greatest failure of our government in the lead-up to the 9/11 attacks."[3]

This indictment has led Congress and the President to expand the authority of the government to collect personal data through mandatory disclosure, seizure, independent creation, and purchase, and contributed to fueling an apparently insatiable appetite of the government to access and retain personal data, especially the vast databases routinely maintained by the private sector. The government uses these data sets for a spectrum of data mining activities, ranging from inquiries on specified individuals and the people with whom they interact to broad searches for unusual or predetermined patterns of activities or relationships.[4]

people who meet specific criteria or otherwise present unusual patterns of activities.

Second, these technologies have exponentially increased the volume of data available about individuals and greatly reduced the financial and other obstacles to retaining, sharing, and exploiting those data in both the public and private sector. One of the most immediate challenges facing U.S. anti-terrorist activities is separating out the "signal" of useful information from the "noise" of all of that data.

Finally, the government has significant incentives to invest in data mining. Many of these incentives relate to administrative programs, where data mining can reduce costs and improve convenience, speed, and efficiency. These reflect what Professor Paul Schwartz has described as the *data processing model* of administrative control."[6] In this model, government agencies become largely information processors, substituting information-based determinations for what previously might have involved subjective judgment. These agencies now employ clerks, who feed data into computers and act on the result, rather than utilizing professionals who assess and evaluate independently. The increased reliance on personal data helps to provide services to a larger population, diminish the perceived inequality of subjective determinations, reduce the costs of litigating decisions and maintaining more skilled personnel, and enhance accountability. It is no exaggeration to say that "[i]nformation is the lifeblood of regulatory policy. ... Regulators depend on information for nearly everything they do."[7]

Many of the incentives also relate to the perceived value of data mining as a tool to combat crime and terrorist threats and protect critical infrastructure. It is in these areas that we have witnessed the greatest growth in government data mining activities. which are routinely applied to financial transactions, passenger lists, intercepted telephone calls and e-mails, visa applications and visitor fingerprints, employment data in critical industries, DNA and fingerprints collected from crime scenes and individuals who are arrested by, or cooperate with, law enforcement, and video surveillance images.

INFORMATION PRIVACY AND ITS PROTECTION FROM INTRUSION BY THE GOVERNMENT

Information privacy is protected in the United States by a variety of constitutional, statutory, administrative, and common law provisions. In this section we address the most important of these applicable to data mining. We do not, however, address the range of other international and multinational privacy laws. Many of these laws, unlike those found in the United States, apply across all sectors and create equal protection for privacy against intrusions by both the private sector and the government. In 1980, the Committee of Ministers of the Organization for Economic Cooperation and Development adopted *Guidelines on the Protection of Privacy and Transborder Flows of Personal Data*.[8] In 1995, the European Union adopted an omnibus data protection directive in 1995,[9] and proposed a draft European General Data Protection Regulation,[10] as well as a draft directive on data protection in law enforcement.[11]

Constitutional Protections

Privacy is not explicitly protected by the Constitution. The Supreme Court, however, has interpreted many of the amendments constituting the Bill of Rights to provide protection to a variety of elements of privacy, including an individual's right to be free from unreasonable searches and seizures by the government;[12] the right to make decisions about contraception,[13] abortion,[14] and other "fundamental" issues such as marriage, procreation, child rearing, and education;[15] the right not to disclose certain information to the government;[16] the right to associate free from government intrusion;[17] and the right to enjoy one's own home free from intrusion by the government,[18] sexually explicit mail,[19] radio broadcasts,[20] or other intrusions.[21]

In the context of protecting individual privacy from intrusion by the government, the Court has found protections for privacy in various amendments to the Constitution. These include:

- The First Amendment provisions for freedom of expression and association
- The Third Amendment restriction on quartering soldiers in private homes
- The Fourth Amendment prohibition on unreasonable searches and seizures
- The due process clause and guarantee against self-incrimination in the Fifth Amendment
- The Ninth and Tenth Amendment reservations of power in the people and the States
- The equal protection and due process clauses of the Fourteenth Amendment[22]

Two constitutionally based privacy protections are most applicable to information privacy: the Fourth Amendment and the protection against compelled disclosure of personal matters.

The Fourth Amendment

One of the colonists' most potent grievances against the British government was its use of general searches. The hostility to general searches found powerful expression in the Fourth Amendment. As interpreted by the Supreme Court, this provision prohibits "unreasonable" searches and seizures, requires that most searches be conducted only with a warrant issued by a court,[23] conditions the issuing of warrants on the government showing "probable cause" that a crime has been or is likely to be committed and that the information sought is germane to that crime, and generally requires that the government provide the subject of a search with contemporaneous notice of the search.[24]

The protection afforded by the Fourth Amendment, while considerable, is not absolute. The Supreme Court has determined, for example, that warrants are not required to search or seize items in the "plain view" of a law enforcement officer,[25] searches that are conducted incidental to valid arrests,[26] or searches specially authorized by the Attorney General or the President involving foreign threats of "immediate and grave peril" to national security.[27]

The Fourth Amendment applies to searches and surveillance conducted for domestic law enforcement purposes within the United States, as well as those conducted outside of the United States if they involve U.S. citizens (although not necessarily permanent resident aliens). The Fourth Amendment also applies to searches and surveillance conducted for national security and intelligence purposes within the United States, if they involve U.S. persons who do not have a connection to a foreign power.[28] The Supreme Court has not yet addressed whether the Fourth Amendment applies to searches and surveillance for national security and intelligence purposes, if they involve U.S. persons who are connected to a foreign power or are conducted wholly outside of the United States.[29] Appellate courts have found, however, that there is an exception to the Fourth Amendment's warrant requirement for searches conducted for intelligence purposes within the United States that involve only non-U.S. persons or agents of foreign powers.[30] Statutory protections, discussed below, fill some of the gaps in the Fourth Amendment's scope and impose additional restrictions on government searches and seizures.

In the areas where the Fourth Amendment does apply, what makes a search or seizure "unreasonable"? In his 1967 concurrence in *Katz v. United States,* Justice Harlan wrote that reasonableness was defined by the individual's "actual," subjective expectation of privacy and the extent to which that expectation was "one that society was prepared to recognize as 'reasonable.'"[31] The Court adopted that test for determining what was "private" within the meaning of the Fourth Amendment in 1968 and continues to apply it today, with somewhat uneven results. The Court has found "reasonable" expectations of privacy in homes,[32] businesses,[33] sealed luggage and packages,[34] and even drums of chemicals,[35] but no "reasonable" expectations of privacy in voice or writing samples,[36] phone numbers,[37] conversations recorded by concealed microphones,[38] or automobile passenger compartments,[39] trunks,[40] or glove boxes.[41]

Moreover, the Supreme Court interprets the Fourth Amendment to apply only to the collection of information, not its use. Even if information is obtained in violation of the Fourth Amendment, the Supreme Court has consistently found that the Fourth Amendment imposes no independent duty on the government to refrain from using it. "The Fourth Amendment contains no provision expressly precluding the use of evidence obtained in violation of its commands, and an examination of its origin and purposes makes clear that the use of fruits of a past unlawful search or seizure '[works] no new Fourth Amendment wrong.'"[42]

Under the Court's "exclusionary rule," illegally seized data may still be used if the government agent acted in good faith,[43] to impeach a witness,[44] or in other settings in which the "the officer committing the unconstitutional search or seizure" has "no responsibility or duty to, or agreement with, the sovereign seeking to use the evidence."[45] The Court suppresses the use of information obtained in violation of the Fourth Amendment only when doing so would have deterred the conduct of the government employee who acted unconstitutionally when collecting the information. So, for example, the Court has allowed records illegally seized by criminal investigators to be used by tax investigators on the basis that restricting the subsequent use would not deter the original unconstitutional conduct.[46] The Court wrote in 1974 that the exclusionary rule operates as "a judicially created remedy designed to safeguard Fourth Amendment rights generally through its deterrent effect, rather than a personal constitutional right of the party aggrieved."[47] If the Court finds no independent

Fourth Amendment basis for restricting the use of illegally obtained information, it goes without saying that the Court does not apply the Fourth Amendment to restrict the use of lawfully obtained information. The Fourth Amendment today thus poses no limit on the government's use of lawfully seized records, and in the case of unlawfully seized material, restricts its use only to the extent necessary to provide a deterrent for future illegal conduct.

In the case most pertinent to government projects that could involve accessing data about U.S. persons from commercial databases, in 1976 the Supreme Court held in *United States v. Miller*[48] that there can be no reasonable expectation of privacy in objects or information held by a third party. The case involved bank records, to which, the Court noted, "respondent can assert neither ownership nor possession."[49] Such documents "contain only information voluntarily conveyed to the banks and exposed to their employees in the ordinary course of business,"[50] and therefore the Court found that the Fourth Amendment is not implicated when the government sought access to them:

> The depositor takes the risk, in revealing his affairs to another, that the information will be conveyed by that person to the Government. This Court has held repeatedly that *the Fourth Amendment does not prohibit the obtaining of information revealed to a third party and conveyed by him to Government authorities, even if the information is revealed on the assumption that it will be used only for a limited purpose and the confidence placed in the third party will not be betrayed.*[51]

The Court's decision in *Miller* is remarkably sweeping. The bank did not just happen to be holding the records the government sought. Instead, the Bank Secrecy Act required (and continues to require) banks to maintain a copy of every customer check and deposit for six years or longer.[52] The government thus compelled the bank to store the information, and then sought the information from the bank on the basis that since the bank held the data, there could not be any reasonable expectation of privacy and the Fourth Amendment therefore did not apply.[53] A majority of the Supreme Court was not troubled by this end-run around the Fourth Amendment: "even if the banks could be said to have been acting solely as Government agents in transcribing the necessary information and complying without protest with the requirements of the subpoenas, there would be no intrusion upon the depositors' Fourth Amendment rights."[54]

Congress reacted to the decision by enacting modest statutory protection for customers' financial records held by financial institutions,[55] but there is no constitutional protection for financial records or any other personal information that has been disclosed to third parties. As a result, the government can collect even the most sensitive information from a third party without a warrant and without risk that the search may be found unreasonable under the Fourth Amendment.

The Court reinforced its holding in *Miller* in the 1979 case of *Smith v. Maryland*, involving information about (as opposed to the content of) telephone calls.[56] The Supreme Court found that the Fourth Amendment is not applicable to telecommunications "attributes" (e.g., the number dialed, the time the call was placed, the duration of the call, etc.), because that information is necessarily conveyed to, or observable by, third parties involved in connecting the call.[57] "[T]elephone users, in sum, typically know that they must convey numerical information to the phone company; that the phone company has facilities for recording this information; and that the phone company does in fact record this information for a variety of legitimate business purposes."[58]

As a result, under the Fourth Amendment, the use of "pen registers" (to record outgoing call information) and "trap and trace" devices (to record incoming call information) does not require a warrant because these devices only collect information about the call that is necessarily disclosed to others.[59]

Because virtually all transactions and communications, especially if they have any electronic component, require disclosing information to a third party, the scope of Fourth Amendment protection is dramatically reduced. This is especially apparent in the context of the Internet, both because anonymous transactions are technologically difficult and even the most secure, encrypted communications require the disclosure of significant communications attributes. As with information disclosed to a third party, Congress reacted to the Supreme Court's decision by creating a statutory warrant requirement for pen registers,[60] but the Constitution does not apply.

The exclusion from Fourth Amendment protection of information disclosed to (or possessed by) a third party raises significant issues when applied to government mining of commercial databases and other government efforts to aggregate personally identifiable information held in the private sector. Such information, by definition, is held by third parties, so government use of that data, under the Supreme Court's current interpretations, is unlikely to be limited by the Fourth Amendment, no matter how great the intrusion into information privacy.

Technological advances, and the development of new products and services in response to those changes, have significantly expanded the scope of the *Miller* exclusion. Today there are vastly more personal data in the hands of third parties, they are far more revealing, and much more readily accessible than was the case in the 1970s. Moreover, for the first time the government has the practical ability to exploit these huge data sets. As a result, the scope of the *Miller* decision has been greatly expanded and the balance between the government's power to obtain personal data and the privacy rights of individuals has altered.

This concern was flagged by Justice Sotomayor in her concurrence in the 2012 case of *United States v. Jones*.[61] The majority found that law enforcement officials attaching a GPS device to the bumper of a suspect's car without a warrant constituted an unlawful search. Justice Sotomayor wrote a separate opinion, in which she argued that it might be time for the Court to revisit *Miller* and the third-party doctrine:

> More fundamentally, it may be necessary to reconsider the premise that an individual has no reasonable expectation of privacy in information voluntarily disclosed to third parties. This approach is ill suited to the digital age, in which people reveal a great deal of information about themselves to third parties in the course of carrying out mundane tasks. ... I would not assume that all information voluntarily disclosed to some member of the public for a limited purpose is, for that reason alone, disentitled to Fourth Amendment protection.[62]

Protection Against Government Disclosure of Personal Matters

The Supreme Court has extended the protection of privacy from government intrusion beyond the Fourth Amendment to a more general constitutional right against government-compelled "disclosure of personal matters."[63] In 1977, the Supreme Court decided *Whalen v. Roe*, a case involving a challenge to a New York statute requiring that copies of prescriptions for certain drugs be provided to the state, on the basis that the requirement would infringe patients' privacy rights. In his opinion for the unanimous Court, Justice Stevens wrote that the constitutionally protected "zone of privacy" included "the individual interest in avoiding disclosure of personal matters. ..."[64] Nevertheless, having found this new privacy interest in nondisclosure of personal information, the Court did not apply strict scrutiny—which it typically reserves for cases involving "fundamental" interests—to the statute. Instead, applying a lower level of scrutiny, the Court found that the statute did not infringe upon the individuals' interest in nondisclosure.[65] The Court also explicitly rejected the application of the Fourth Amendment right of privacy, writing that Fourth Amendment cases "involve affirmative, unannounced, narrowly focused intrusions."[66]

The Supreme Court has never decided a case in which it found that a government regulation or action violated the constitutional privacy right recognized in *Whalen*. Lower courts have, with courts in the District of Columbia,[67] Second,[68] Third,[69] Fifth,[70] and Ninth[71] Circuits using *Whalen* to strike down government actions on the basis that they violated individuals' right in nondisclosure. Courts in the Fourth[72] and Sixth[73] Circuits have severely limited the scope of the *Whalen* nondisclosure privacy right. Even those courts that have relied on the right of nondisclosure, however, have applied only intermediate scrutiny, instead of the strict scrutiny typically used to protect fundamental constitutional rights.[74]

Other Protections for Information Privacy in the Public Sector

Most of the provisions that protect information privacy from intrusion by the government are statutory, rather than constitutional, in origin.

The Privacy Act of 1974

Congress has enacted a variety of statutory provisions limiting the power of the government to compel the disclosure of personal information and protecting against misuse of personal information possessed by the government. The broadest of these is the Privacy Act of 1974.[75] That Act requires federal agencies to store only relevant and necessary personal information and only for purposes required to be accomplished by statute or executive order; collect information to the extent possible from the data subject; maintain records that are accurate, complete, timely, and relevant; and establish administrative, physical, and technical safeguards to protect the security of records.[76] The Privacy Act also prohibits disclosure, even to other government agencies, of personally identifiable information in any record contained in a "system of records," except pursuant to a written request by or with the written consent of the data subject, or pursuant to a specific exception.[77] Agencies must log disclosures of records and, in some cases, inform the subjects of such disclosures when they occur. Under the Act, data subjects must be able to access and copy their records; each agency must establish a procedure for amendment of records; and refusals by agencies to amend their records are subject to judicial review. Agencies must publish a notice of the existence, character, and accessibility of their record systems.[78] Finally, individuals may seek legal redress if an agency denies them access to their records.

The Privacy Act is less protective of privacy than may first appear, because of numerous broad exceptions.[79] Twelve of these are expressly provided for in the Act itself. These include:

1. An agency can disclose its records to officers and employees within the agency itself, the Bureau of the Census, the National Archives, Congress, the Comptroller General, and consumer reporting agencies.[80]

2. Information contained in an agency's records can be disclosed for "civil or criminal law enforcement activity if the activity is authorized by law."[81]

3. Under the "routine use" exemption,[82] federal agencies are permitted to disclose personal information so long as the nature and scope of the routine use was previously published in the *Federal Register* and the disclosure of data was "for a purpose which is compatible with the purpose for which it was collected." According to the Office of Management and Budget (OMB), "compatibility" covers uses that are either (1) functionally equivalent or (2) necessary and proper.[83]

In addition, the Privacy Act has been subject to judicial interpretations which have created new exceptions. For example, courts have found that the following special entities do not constitute an "agency": a federally chartered production credit association, an individual government employee,[84] state and local government agencies,[85] the White House Office, and those components of the Executive Office of the

President whose sole function is to advise and assist the President,[86] grand juries,[87] and national banks.[88]

Moreover, the Privacy Act applies only to information maintained in a "system of records."[89] The Act defines "system of records" as a "group of any records under the control of any agency from which information is retrieved by the name of the individual or by some identifying number, symbol, or other identifying particular assigned to the individual."[90] As a result, the D.C. Circuit Court held that "retrieval capability is not sufficient to create a system of records. ... 'To be in a system of records, a record must ... in practice [be] retrieved by an individual's name or other personal identifier.'"[91]

In June 2008, the Government Accountability Office identified a number of weaknesses in the Privacy Act, and proposed specific corrections.[92] Those include: (1) revising the scope of the laws to cover all personally identifiable information collected, used, and maintained by the federal government, rather than just files maintained in a "system of records"; (2) setting requirements to ensure that the collection and use of personally identifiable information is limited to a stated purpose; and (3) establishing additional mechanisms for informing the public about privacy protections by revising requirements for the structure and publication of public notices.[93] To date, none of these have been adopted.

Sectoral Protections

In addition to the Privacy Act and the privacy exceptions to the Freedom of Information Act,[94] there are also many more focused privacy laws applicable to specific sectors of the government or types of government activities. Many of these apply to information, people, or settings left unprotected by the Supreme Court's interpretation of the Fourth Amendment. For example, the Right to Financial Privacy Act, enacted in response to the Supreme Court's decision in *United States v. Miller*,[95] restricts the government's access to bank records.[96]

Federal statutes prohibit the Department of Health and Human Services from disclosing Social Security records, except as "otherwise provided by Federal law" or regulation.[97] Similarly, federal law prohibits the Internal Revenue Service from disclosing information on income tax returns[98] and the Census Bureau from disclosing certain categories of census data.[99]

Some statutes protecting privacy in commercial sectors also impose limits on government access to personal information. For example, the Cable Act of 1984 prohibits cable companies from providing the government with personally identifiable information about their customers, unless the government presents a court order.[100] Stewart Baker writes that such an order can "only be obtained upon 'clear and convincing evidence' that the customer was suspected of engaging in a crime and if the order afforded the customer an opportunity to contest the government's claim."[101] The USA PATRIOT Act amended this provision to apply only to records about cable television service and not other services—such as Internet or telephone—that a cable operator might provide.[102] The Video Privacy Protection Act prohibits video rental companies from disclosing personally identifiable information about their customers unless the government presents a search warrant, court order, or grand jury subpoena.[103] The Family Education Rights and Privacy Act of 1974 contains a similar provision applicable to educational records.[104]

Electronic Surveillance

Perhaps the most significant sectoral protections for information privacy apply to electronic surveillance and other searches. Title III of the Omnibus Crime Control and Safe Streets Act of 1968, as amended by the Electronic Communications Privacy Act of 1986 (ECPA), sets forth statutory guidelines for obtaining a warrant to conduct surveillance for domestic law enforcement purposes.[105] These requirements go beyond the protections provided by the Fourth Amendment. The additional protections include: restricting the use of wiretaps to investigations of serious crimes;[106] requiring law enforcement agencies to exhaust less intrusive techniques before turning to eavesdropping;[107] limiting the duration of wiretaps and requiring procedures to minimize the interception of innocent conversations;[108] establishing a statutory suppression rule;[109] requiring detailed annual reports to be published on the number and nature of wiretaps;[110] and subjecting the entire process to judicial oversight.[111]

The USA PATRIOT Act subsequently weakened some of these protections. Even prior to that, however, courts rarely refused the government a wiretap order. Between 1968 and 2010, courts approved a total of 44,256 wiretap orders (14,549 federal and 29,707 state). Requests for wiretap orders have increased from 1,186 in 1997, to 1,491 in 2001, to 3,194 in 2010. Over the past 43 years, courts have only refused 32 wiretap orders sought by the government.[112] Each order is likely to result in the collection of many people's communications. In 2010, on

average, each order was in effect 40 days and captured the communications of 118 people.[113]

ECPA's restrictions on wiretaps are greatly weakened in the case
of pen registers and trap-and-trace devices that only seek identifying information about calls. In those situations, the government must
merely certify that the "information likely to be obtained is relevant
to an ongoing 'criminal investigation.'"[114] The USA PATRIOT Act
extended these provisions to "addressing and routing" information
about Internet communications.[115] To obtain more detailed information about communications, such as where a particular cell phone
is located, the government must obtain either a search warrant or a
special court order—known as a "section 2703(d) order." To obtain
a section 2703(d) order, the government must present "specific and
articulable facts" that the information sought is relevant to an ongoing criminal investigation.[116]

To obtain access to e-mail stored by a service provider (to which
the Fourth Amendment does not apply because the information is in
the hands of a third party), ECPA requires that the government obtain
a warrant if the e-mail has been stored for 180 days or less.[117] If the
e-mail has been stored for more than 180 days, the government need
only present a subpoena,[118] which the Federal Bureau of Investigation
(FBI), the Internal Revenue Service, and grand juries are empowered
to issue themselves.[119]

Intelligence Gathering

While the above statutes apply when the government seeks information for law enforcement purposes, Congress also has enacted a variety
of laws governing data collection for intelligence, national security, and
anti-terrorism purposes.

Foreign Intelligence Surveillance Act. The Foreign Intelligence Surveillance
Act of 1978 (FISA) governs surveillance and, since being amended in
1994, physical searches conducted within the United States for the purpose of gathering foreign intelligence.[120] FISA regulates certain electronic surveillances and physical searches in the U.S. against foreign
powers and agents of foreign powers, including U.S. persons, where
a significant purpose of the surveillance or search is to obtain foreign
intelligence information.

As amended by the USA PATRIOT Act, FISA creates a special
eleven-judge court—the Foreign Intelligence Surveillance Court.[121]

An application for surveillances and/or searches of this nature must first be approved by the Attorney General. The application sets out the facts to support a finding by the judge that there is probable cause to believe that the proposed target is a foreign power or an agent of a foreign power and describing the premises or property to be the subject of the search or surveillance.[122] Following the Attorney General's approval (or that of a designee), the application is then submitted to the Court for authorization. Each application includes "minimization procedures" as the term is defined in the Act, setting out the procedures to be employed to minimize the acquisition, retention, and dissemination of U.S. person information.[123] Surveillances and searches are authorized for a period of 90 days to target a U.S. person agent of a foreign power, and up to a year to target a foreign government.[124] In certain limited circumstances, the Attorney General may authorize electronic surveillances or physical searches without Court authorization when the means of communication or premises are used exclusively by certain foreign powers as defined in the Act (e.g., a foreign government).[125] Between 1979 and 2010, FISA judges approved 30,317 FISA warrants—all but ten that the Attorney General had sought.[126]

Congress substantially amended FISA in the Protect America Act of 2007[127] and the FISA Amendments Act of 2008.[128] The laws were enacted in response to a number of Bush Administration programs involving warrantless searches of telephone conversations. One of these programs, the Terrorist Surveillance Program, was described by administration officials as involving surveillance of communications into and out of the United States where there is a "reasonable basis to conclude that one party to the communications is a member of al Qaeda, affiliated with al Qaeda, or a member of an organization affiliated with al Qaeda."[129] Another program allegedly involved the installation by the NSA of sophisticated surveillance equipment in domestic switching facilities operated by AT&T and Verizon. The Electronic Frontier Foundation filed lawsuits alleging that the equipment was used to "intercept[] and disclos[e] to the government the contents of its customers' communications as well as detailed communications records about millions of its customers."[130]

In response to the threat of liability against government officials and private companies that participated in these programs, the Protect America Act and the FISA Amendments Act of 2008 permit the Attorney General and the Director of National Intelligence to "authorize jointly, for a period of up to one year from the effective date of the authorization, the targeting of persons reasonably believed to be located outside the United States to acquire foreign intelligence information," even if all or part of the communication occurs within the United States.[131] Applications for mass surveillance of persons reasonably believed to be located outside of the United States ("mass acquisition orders") must be submitted to the FISA Court, but the court's role is "narrowly circumscribed" and extends only to reviewing such applications to ensure compliance with procedural requirements.[132]

FISA's definition of "electronic surveillance" is amended to exclude any surveillance directed at a person reasonably believed to be located outside the United States, thereby exempting surveillance of these communications from the oversight of the FISA Court.[133] The FISA Amendments Act of 2008 effectively granted immunity to the telecommunications providers for "providing any information, facilities, or assistance" to the warrantless surveillance program.[134]

Section 215 Orders. Section 215 of the USA PATRIOT Act amended an existing FISA provision that permitted the FBI to apply to the FISA Court for a secret order requiring communications firms to disclose specified business records sought as part of a terrorism or intelligence investigation. As amended by section 215, the law now permits the Director of the FBI or a designee of the Director (not lower than the rank of Assistant Special Agent in Charge) to apply for an order requiring the production of "any tangible things (including books, records, papers, documents, and other items) for an investigation to protect against international terrorism or clandestine intelligence activities."[135]

Section 215 was amended in 2006 to require that an application establish "reasonable grounds to believe that the tangible things are relevant to an authorized investigation," but presuming relevance in the case of foreign powers, agents of foreign powers, subjects of authorized counterintelligence or counterterrorism investigations, and individual known to associate with the subjects of such investigations.[136]

The investigation of a U.S. citizen or permanent legal resident may not be "conducted solely upon the basis of activities protected by the first amendment to the Constitution," and must follow guidelines approved by the Attorney General.[137] The application for the order is made to the FISA Court. "A person who, in good faith, produces tangible things under an order pursuant to this section shall not be liable to any other person for such production. Such production shall not be deemed to constitute a waiver of any privilege in any other proceeding or context."[138]

The USA PATRIOT Act prohibits the recipient of a section 215 order from disclosing its contents or even its existence to anyone forever, "other than those persons necessary to produce the tangible things under this section."[139] Because a similar ban concerning National Security Letters (discussed below) was struck down as facially unconstitutional in 2004,[140] it is likely that the force of this provision has been weakened.

According to congressionally mandated reports by the U.S. Department of Justice Inspector General, the FBI submitted no section 215 applications in 2002 and 2003, and between 2004 and 2006, the FBI submitted 36 "pure" section 215 applications and 173 section 215 applications combined with other FISA-authorized surveillance requests.[141] All were approved by the FISA Court, although at least six other applications were withdrawn by the FBI. One reason that section 215 orders have not been more widely used is that it took an average of between 147 and 169 days to process an application.[142]

National Security Letters. The government has special authority to collect information without judicial oversight in the cases of national security investigations. Four federal statutes authorize the FBI to issue "National Security Letters" (NSLs) to telephone companies, financial institutions, internet service providers, and consumer credit agencies, which require the recipients to produce the records that the government seeks:

- Right to Financial Privacy Act (1978) (codified as amended at 12 U.S.C. § 3401(a)(5))
- Electronic Communications Privacy Act (1986) (codified as amended at 18 U.S.C. § 2709(b)(2))
- Fair Credit Reporting Act (1970) (codified as amended at 15 U.S.C. § 1681u(a))
- 1994 amendments to the National Security Act (1947) (codified as amended at 50 U.S.C. § 436(A)(1))

The government need only state that the records sought are relevant to an authorized international terrorism or counterintelligence investigation and that the investigation is not being conducted "solely on the basis of activities protected by the first amendment" (e.g., not based solely on speech, protest, association, or religious practice). No court is involved.

Originally, recipients of NSLs were prohibited from disclosing the contents or even the existence of an NSL. After that provision was declared unconstitutional under the First and Fourth Amendments,[143] Congress amended the law to prohibit a recipient of an NSL from disclosing that the FBI "has sought or obtained access to information or records" only if the Director of the FBI, or his designee, certifies that disclosure "may result" in "a danger to the national security of the United States, interference with a criminal, counterterrorism, or counterintelligence investigation, interference with diplomatic relations, or danger to the life or physical safety of any person."[144] Ninety-seven percent of NSLs examined by the Inspector General in 2007–2008, that had been issued since this provision took effect carried this certification.[145]

The 2006 amendments allow an NSL recipient to challenge the NSL itself, as well as the nondisclosure requirement. A federal court may issue an order "modifying or setting aside the request" if it finds that "compliance would be unreasonable, oppressive, or otherwise unlawful."[146] A federal court may modify or set aside a nondisclosure requirement within one year of its being imposed only if it finds that "there is no reason to believe" that disclosure will result in one of the harms asserted by the FBI.[147] Certifications by the FBI that "disclosure may endanger the national security of the United States or interfere with diplomatic relations … shall be treated as conclusive unless the court finds that the certification was made in bad faith."[148] If more than a year has passed since the FBI's certification, the Bureau must either terminate the nondisclosure requirement or recertify the need for it.[149] If the court upholds a nondisclosure requirement, the NSL recipient is precluded from filing another petition for one year.[150]

The FBI is required to inform Congress twice a year about its use of NSLs. In 2007, the DOJ Inspector General found that the FBI had substantially under-reported to Congress the number of NSLs it issued between 2003 and 2005. Instead of the 52,199 NSLs reported by the FBI, the actual figure was 143,074.[151] For 2006, the Inspector General found that the FBI issued 49,425 NSLs.[152]

Each request may seek records concerning many people. In fact, nine NSLs in one investigation sought data on 11,100 separate telephone numbers. The *New York Times* reported in September 2007 that the FBI had issued NSLs seeking data not only about the communications of identified individuals (or telephone numbers), but also of their "community of interest"—the "network of people that the target was in contact with."[153]

Executive Order 12333. Executive Order 12333, issued by President Ronald Reagan in 1981, established the basic framework under which U.S. intelligence activities are conducted today.[154] The Executive Order explicitly recognizes that "[t]imely and accurate information about the activities, capabilities, plans, and intentions of foreign powers, organizations, and persons and their agents, is essential to the security of the United States," but that intelligence gathering activities must be carried out in a "responsible manner that is consistent with the Constitution and applicable law."[155] The Executive Order restricts government surveillance of U.S. persons outside of the United States, even for foreign intelligence purposes, unless the persons involved are agents of a foreign power or the surveillance is necessary to acquire "significant information that cannot reasonably be acquired by other means."[156]

The Executive Order is implemented within each agency by procedures that require the approval of the agency head and of the Attorney General. These procedures address in detail the collection, retention, and dissemination of information about U.S. persons, and provide extensive guidance as to when and how Department of Defense (DOD) officials may engage in collection techniques such as electronic surveillance and nonconsensual physical searches, but they provide little direct guidance concerning data mining.

Attorney General's Guidelines. The Attorney General's Guidelines on General Crimes, Racketeering Enterprise and Terrorism Enterprise Investigations, first adopted in 1976 by Attorney General Edward Levi and most recently revised by Attorney General John Ashcroft in May 2002, provide guidance to FBI officials concerning surveillance and other searches, including concerning the terms under which the FBI may use publicly available sources of information. According to the Guidelines, the FBI "may draw on and retain pertinent information from any source permitted by law," including publicly available information, whether obtained directly or through services or resources (whether nonprofit or commercial) that compile or analyze such information[,] and information voluntarily provided by private entities."[157]

The Guidelines specifically authorize the FBI to carry out "general topical research, including conducting online searches and accessing online sites and forums as part of such research on the same terms and conditions as members of the public generally," but require that such research not include searches by "individuals' names or other individual identifiers."[158] The Guidelines authorize "online search activity" and "access [to] online sites and forums on the same terms and conditions as members of the public generally," without any restriction as to subject-based searches "[f]or the purpose of detecting or preventing terrorism or other criminal activities."[159] Finally, the Guidelines provide that "[f]or the purpose of detecting or preventing terrorist activities," the FBI may "visit any place and attend any event that is open to the public, on the same terms and conditions as members of the public generally."[160]

The General Crimes Guidelines are supplemented by the Attorney General's Guidelines for FBI National Security Investigations and Foreign Intelligence Collection that Attorney General John Ashcroft revised in October 2003.[161] These more recent Guidelines, large portions of which are classified, focus on guiding the activities of the FBI in "preventing, preempting, and disrupting terrorist threats to the United States."[162] The new Guidelines authorize widespread sharing of information necessary to achieve this purpose. The sections concerning how this information may be collected are classified, but given the subject of these Guidelines, it is reasonable to assume that they are no more restrictive than the General Crimes Guidelines.

The number and variety of statutes applicable to government collection and use of personal information highlight the special sensitivity in the United States of government use of personal information, but also suggest the complexity of laws in this area. Moreover, in every case, the protection for information privacy is subject to significant exemptions to accommodate other public interests.

RECOMMENDATIONS FOR REGULATING GOVERNMENT DATA MINING

Government data mining presents many potential practical risks, for example, of chilling innocent behavior and protected expression; erroneously targeting innocent people for sanction or further investigation due to errors in the data, its aggregation, or the algorithms used to analyze it; and embarrassing or harming people through inadvertent or wrongful disclosure or misuse of the data. These risks are significant, and they are inherent in any mining of personal information, especially when engaged in by the government. Recent government data mining activities by national security authorities make some of these concerns even more acute or present special issues of which legal advisors should be aware. These concerns have also been addressed in recent years by many organizations and individuals, including the Markle Foundation Task Force on National Security in the Information Age,[163] the Cantigny Conference on Counterterrorism Technology and Privacy organized by the Standing Committee on Law and National Security of the American Bar Association,[164] and two high-level national commissions whose recommendations we consider in greater detail here.

The first was the Technology and Privacy Advisory Committee (TAPAC), the "blue ribbon"[165] bipartisan independent committee appointed by then-Secretary of Defense Donald Rumsfeld in 2003 to examine privacy and security issues following the controversy over the Total Information Awareness Program. TAPAC's 2004 final report, *Safeguarding Privacy in the Fight Against Terrorism*,[166] recommended the adoption of significant incentives for using anonymized or pseudonymized data whenever possible, and systemic privacy protections and judicial oversight when that is not possible. Despite the far-reaching scope of these recommendations, they were accepted by the Department of Defense in August 2006.[167]

In 2008, the National Academy of Sciences released the long-awaited report of its Committee on Technical and Privacy Dimensions of Information for Terrorism Prevention and Other National Goals.[168] The report, *Protecting Individual Privacy in the Struggle Against Terrorists: A Framework for Assessment*, contained the conclusions of a three-year inquiry into the science of data mining and its impact on privacy, as well as a framework based on the work of the TAPAC, for evaluating the effectiveness of such programs and their consistency with U.S. privacy values.

We conclude by highlighting some of the critical issues surrounding government data mining and some of the recommended responses by these two influential commissions. We divide our assessment into two broad themes: efficacy and impact.

Efficacy

The first set of issues concern the efficacy of government data mining: how well does it work to achieve its intended objectives? Mounting evidence suggests that data mining is not effective for many of the purposes to which the government is seeking to put it, especially in the national security and law enforcement arenas. According to the NAS committee, there is good reason for skepticism. While proponents of data mining hope that "[i]mportant clues might also be found in commercial and government data bases that record a wide range of information about individuals, organizations, and their transactions, movements, and behavior," the committee stressed "success in such efforts will be extremely difficult to achieve."[169] This reflects the impediments presented by data quality issues, difficulties with data matching, and limits in data mining tools, especially when data mining in the national security setting is contrasted with data mining for commercial target marketing.

There is nearly universal agreement about the need to assess the efficacy of data mining systems. Many of the committees created to examine various aspects of government data mining and information use have proposed ways of doing so. One of the earliest proposals came from TAPAC, which recommended to the Secretary of Defense that any DOD data mining program should require a "written finding" by the "agency head" addressing the efficacy of the proposed program.[170]

The NAS committee proposed a detailed framework for government agency officials and policymakers to use in evaluating the effectiveness of proposed and existing data mining programs, especially in comparison with other tools, and to "assess whether they [the programs] are warranted in light of their likely effectiveness."[171] (The committee proposed a separate framework for evaluating the legality of programs and their impact on civil liberties, discussed below.) The key points of the committee's proposed analysis are instructive and suggest the committee's concerns about current practice with regard to government data-mining programs:

1. There should be a *clearly stated purpose* for the information-based program. …
2. There should be a *sound rational basis* for the information-based program and each of its components. …
3. There should be a *sound experimental basis* for the information-based program and each of its components. …
4. The information-based program should be *scalable*. …
5. There should be a clearly stated set of *operational or business processes* that comprehensively specify how the information-based program should operate within the organization. …

6. The information-based program should be capable of being *integrated* in practice with relevant systems and tools. ...

7. Information-based programs should be *robust.* ...

8. There must be appropriate guarantees that the data on which the information-based program depends are *appropriate* and *reliable.* ...

9. The information-based program should provide for appropriate *data stewardship.* ...

10. There should be adequate guarantees of *objectivity* in the testing and assessment of the information-based program. ...

11. There should be *on-going assessment* of the information-based program. ...

12. The effectiveness of the information-based program and its compliance with these key requirements should be *documented.* ... [172]

Despite the burden that the process of assessing efficacy clearly will present, it is essential. The argument that the perceived danger is too great to allow time for meaningful assessment is exactly backwards. As the NAS committee stressed, "[t]he policy impulse to 'do something' (by which is usually meant something new) under these circumstances is understandable, but it is simply not true that doing something new is better than nothing."[173] Doing "something," if it is the wrong thing, can seriously undermine security, divert scarce resources, and compromise public confidence, as well as endanger privacy. Assessment is critical at all times to ensure that the government is doing not merely "something," but the best thing in light of the available resources.

Impact

Data mining that involves personal data necessarily impacts personal privacy. This is the consistent conclusion of every inquiry into government data mining, from the first—the 1973 report of the then-Department of Health, Education and Welfare Advisory Committee on Automated Personal Data Systems[174]—to the most recent—the 2008 report of the NAS committee. "Collecting and examining information to inhibit terrorists inevitably conflicts with efforts to protect individual privacy. And when privacy is breached, the damage is real."[175]

To minimize the harmful impact of government data mining on individuals and assess the magnitude of that impact in light of the value that the nation has historically placed on privacy and other civil liberties, every group to consider the issue has recommended some form of legal process—in addition to the little required under current law.

For example, TAPAC recommended five new legal requirements to address the impact of government data mining on individuals and minimize it to the extent possible. The first would condition most data mining on a "[w]ritten finding by agency head authorizing data mining" that addresses the likely impact of the proposed program.[176, 177]

TAPAC's second recommendation would require "[d]ata mining of databases known or reasonably likely to include personally identifiable information about U.S. persons" to employ a series of "technical requirements," including "Data minimization,"[178] "Data anonymization,"[179] "Audit trail,"[180] "Security and access,"[181] and "Training."[182]

The third TAPAC recommendation for protecting personal privacy in government data mining would require judicial authorization from the Foreign Intelligence Surveillance Court ("FISC") for searches—or entire data mining programs—that would involve the use of "personally identifiable information" about U.S. persons.[183] That authorization would depend on "specific and articulable facts" that:

---

i.   The search will be conducted in a manner that otherwise complies with the requirements of these recommendations however enacted;

ii. The use of personally identifiable information is reasonably related to identifying or apprehending terrorists, preventing terrorist attacks, or locating or preventing the use of weapons of mass destruction;

iii. The search is likely to yield information reasonably related to identifying or apprehending terrorists, preventing terrorist attacks, or locating or preventing the use of weapons of mass destruction; and

iv. The search is not practicable with anonymized data in light of all of the circumstances.[184]

Fourth, TAPAC recommended that data mining "known or reasonably likely to include personally identifiable information about U.S. persons should be audited not less than annually to ensure compliance" with these requirements.[185]

24. *Richards v. Wisconsin*, 520 U.S. 385 (1997).

25. *Coolidge v. New Hampshire*, 403 U.S. 443 (1971).

26. *United States v. Edwards*, 415 U.S. 800 (1974).

27. 68 *American Jurisprudence 2d*, Searches and Seizures § 104 (1993); "Federal Legal Constraints on Electronic Surveillance," supra at 136, n.16.

28. *U.S. v. U.S. District Court for the Eastern District of Michigan*, 407 U.S. 297 (1972) (commonly referred to as the *Keith* decision).

29. Jeffrey H. Smith & Elizabeth L. Howe, "Federal Legal Constraints on Electronic Surveillance," *Protecting America's Freedom in the Information Age* 133 (2002).

30. See *U.S. v. Bin Laden*, 126 F. Supp. 2d 264, 271–72 (S.D.N.Y. 2000).

31. 389 U.S. 347, 361 (1967).

32. *Camara v. Municipal Court*, 387 U.S. 523 (1967).

33. *G.M. Leasing Corp. v. United States*, 429 U.S. 338 (1977).

34. *United States v. Chadwick*, 433 U.S. 1 (1977); *Arkansas v. Sanders*, 442 U.S. 753 (1979); *Walter v. United States*, 447 U.S. 649 (1980).

35. *United States v. Knotts*, 460 U.S. 276 (1983).

36. *United States v. Dionisio*, 410 U.S. 1 (1973).

37. *Smith v. Maryland*, 442 U.S. 735 (1979).

38. *United States v. White*, 401 U.S. 745 (1971).

39. *New York v. Belton*, 453 U.S. 454 (1981).

40. *United States v. Ross*, 456 U.S. 798 (1982).

41. *South Dakota v. Opperman*, 428 U.S. 364 (1976).

42. *Leon*, 468 U.S. at 906 (quoting *United States v. Calandra*, 414 U.S. 338, 354 (1974)).

43. *United States v. Leon*, 468 U.S. 897 (1984).

44. *Walder v. United States*, 347 U.S. 62 (1954).

45. *United States v. Janis*, 428 U.S. 433, 455 (1975).

46. Id.

47. *Calandra*, 414 U.S. at 354.

48. *United States v. Miller*, 425 U.S. 435 (1976).

49. Id. at 440.

50. Id. at 442.

51. Id. at 443 (citation omitted) (emphasis added).

52. 12 U.S.C. § 1829b(d); see 425 U.S. at 436; *California Bankers Assn. v. Shultz*, 416 U.S. 21 (1974).

53. 425 U.S. at 443.

54. Id. at 444.

55. Right to Financial Privacy Act, 12 U.S.C. §§ 3401–3422.

56. 442 U.S. 735 (1979).

57. Id. at 743.

58. Id.

59. Id. at 742.

60. 18 U.S.C. §§ 3121, 1841.

61. __ U.S. __, 2012 U.S. LEXIS 1063.

62. Id. at __ (Sotomayor, J., concurring).

63. *Whalen v. Roe*, 429 U.S. 589, 599–600 (1977).

64. Id. at 599–600.

65. Id. at 603–04.

66. Id. at 604, n.32.

67. *Tavoulareas v. Washington Post Company*, 724 F.2d 1010 (D.C. Cir. 1984).

68. *Barry v. City of New York*, 712 F.2d 1554 (2d Cir. 1983); *Schacter v. Whalen*, 581 F.2d 35 (2d Cir. 1978).

69. *Doe v. Southeastern Pennsylvania Transportation Authority*, 72 F.3d 1133 (3d Cir. 1995); *United States v. Westinghouse Electric Corporation*, 638 F.2d 570 (3d Cir. 1980).

70. *Plante v. Gonzalez*, 575 F.2d 1119 (5th Cir. 1978).

71. *Doe v. Attorney General*, 941 F.2d 780 (9th Cir. 1991).

72. *Walls v. City of Petersburg* 895 F.2d 188, 192 (4th Cir. 1990).

73. *J.P. v. DeSanti*, 653 F.2d 1080 (6th Cir. 1981).

74. *Doe v. Attorney General*, 941 F.2d at 796.

75. 5 U.S.C. §§ 552a(e)(1)-(5).

76. Id.

77. Id. § 552a(b).

78. Id. § 552a(e)(4).

79. Markle Foundation Task Force, *Protecting America's Freedom in the Information Age*, supra at 127, 128 (Sean Fogarty & Daniel R. Ortiz, "Limitations Upon Interagency Information Sharing: The Privacy Act of 1974"), available at http://www.markletaskforce.org/documents/Markle_Report_Part3.pdf.

80. 5 U.S.C. § 552a(b),

81. Id. § 552a (b)7

82. Id. § 552a (b)3

83. Privacy Act of 1974; Guidance on the Privacy, Act Implications of "Call Detail" Programs to Manage Employees' Use of the Government's Telecommunications Systems, 52 Fed. Reg. 12,900, 12,993 (1987) (OMB) (publication of guidance in final form).

84. *Petrus v. Bowen*, 833 F.2d 581 (5th Cir. 1987).

85. *Perez-Santos v. Malave*, 23 Fed. App. 11 (1st Cir. 2001); *Ortez v. Washington County*, 88 F.3d 804 (9th Cir. 1996).

86. *Flowers v. Executive Office of the President*, 142 F. Supp. 2d 38 (D.D.C. 2001).

87. *Standley v. Department of Justice*, 835 F.2d 216 (9th Cir. 1987).

88. *U.S. v. Miller*, 643 F.2d 713 (10th Cir. 1981). See generally Fogarty & Ortiz, supra at 128.

89. 5 U.S.C. § 552a(b).

90. Id. § 552a(a)(5).

91. *Henke v. United States DOC*, 83 F.3d 1453, 1461 (D.C. Cir. 1996) (quoting *Bartel v. F.A.A.*, 725 F.2d 1403, 1408 n.10 (D.C. Cir. 1984)).

92. U.S. Government Accountability Office, *Privacy: Congress Should Consider Alternatives for Strengthening Protection of Personally Identifiable Information* (GAO-08-795T 13–14 (2008).

93. Id. at 22.

94. 5 U.S.C. §§ 552, 552(b)(6), (b)(7)(C).

95. 425 U.S. 435.

96. 12 U.S.C. §§ 3401–3422.

97. 42 U.S.C. § 1305 (1997).

98. 26 U.S.C.§§ 6103, 7431 (1997).

99. 13 U.S.C. §§ 8–9 (1994).

100. 47 U.S.C. § 551.

101. Markle Foundation Task Force, *Protecting America's Freedom in the Information Age*, supra at 161, 167 (Stewart A. Baker, "The Regulation of Disclosure of Information Held by Private Parties"), available at http://www.markletaskforce.org/documents/Markle_Report_Part3.pdf.

102. Pub. L. No. 107–56, supra, Title II, § 211.

103. 18 U.S.C. 2710.

104. 20 U.S.C. 1232(g).

105. 18 U.S.C. §§ 2510–2522.

106. Id. § 2516.

107. Id. § 2518(3).

108. Id. § 2518(5).

109. Id. § 2518(10).

110. Id. § 2519.

111. Id. §§ 2516–19; see also *Internet Security and Privacy*, Hearing before the Senate Judiciary Com., May 25, 2000 (statement of James X. Dempsey, Senior Staff Counsel, Center for Democracy and Technology), available at http://www.cdt.org/testimony/000525dempsey.shtml.

112. Electronic Privacy Information Center, Title III Electronic Surveillance 1968–2010, http://www.epic.org/privacy/wiretap/stats/wiretap_stats.html.

113. Administrative Office of the United States Courts, *2010 Wiretap Report* 5 (2011), http://www.uscourts.gov/uscourts/Statistics/WiretapReports/2010/2010WireTapReport.pdf.

114. Id. §§ 3122–23.

115. Pub. L. No. 107–56, supra, Title II, § 216(a).

116. 18 U.S.C. § 2703(d).

117. Id. § 2703(a).

118. Id. §§ 2703(a), (b), (d).

119. *Baker*, supra at 163.

120. 50 U.S.C. §§ 1801 et seq., 1841 et seq. & 1861 et seq.

121. Id. § 1803.1

122. Id. § 1804.

123. Id. §§ 1804(a)(5), 1801(h)

124. Id. § 1805(e).

125. Id. § 1802.

126. Electronic Privacy Information Center, Foreign Intelligence Surveillance Act Orders 1979–2007, http://www.epic.org/privacy/wiretap/stats/fisa_stats.html.

127. Pub. L. No. 110–55, § 105A (2007).

128. Pub. L. No. 110–261, § 702(a) (2008).

129. Press Briefing by Attorney General Alberto Gonzalez and General Michael Hayden, Principal Deputy Director of National Intelligence (Dec. 19, 2005), available at http://www.whitehouse.gov/news/releases/2005/12/20051219-1.html.

130. *Hepting v. AT&T Corp.*, No. C-06-0672-JCS, Amended Complaint for Damages, Declaratory and Injunctive Relief (N.D. Cal. Feb. 22, 2006) ¶ 6, available at http://www.eff.org/legal/cases/att/att_complaint_amended.pdf.

131. Pub. L. No. 110–261, § 702(a) (2008) (codified at 50 U.S.C. § 105B(a)).

132. Id.

133. 50 U.S.C. § 105A.

134. 50 U.S.C. § 105B(l).

135. 50 U.S.C. § 1861.

136. USA PATRIOT Improvement and Reauthorization Act of 2005, Public Law No. 109–177, 120 Stat. 192 (Mar. 9, 2006) (codified at 50 U.S.C. § 1861(b)(2)).

137. Id.

138. Id.

139. Id.

140. *Doe v. Ashcroft*, 334 F. Supp. 2d 471 (S.D.N.Y. 2004).

141. Statement of Glenn A. Fine, Inspector General, U.S. Department of Justice, before the Senate Committee on the Judiciary concerning the FBI's Use of National Security Letters and Section 215 Requests for Business Records, Mar. 21, 2007, at 11, available at http://www.usdoj.gov/oig/testimony/0703a/final.pdf; Statement of Glenn A. Fine, Inspector General, U.S. Department of Justice, before the House Committee on the Judiciary Subcommittee on the Constitution, Civil Rights, and Civil Liberties concerning the FBI's Use of National Security Letters and Section 215 Requests for Business Records, Apr. 15, 2008, at 9, available at http://www.usdoj.gov/oig/testimony/t0804/final.pdf.

142. Id.

143. *Doe v. Ashcroft*, 334 F. Supp. 2d 471 (S.D.N.Y. 2004); *Doe v. Gonzales*, 386 F. Supp. 2d 66, 82 (D. Conn. 2005).

144. USA PATRIOT Improvement and Reauthorization Act of 2005, Pub. L. No. 109–177, 120 Stat. 192 (Mar. 9, 2006) (codified at 18 U.S.C. § 2709(c) (1)).

145. U.S. Department of Justice, Office of the Inspector General, Semiannual Report to Congress [on the] Federal Bureau of Investigation, October 1, 2007-March 31, 2008, at 3, available at http://www.usdoj.gov/oig/semiannual/0805/fbi.htm.

146. 18 U.S.C. § 3511(a).

147. Id. § 3511(b) (2).

148. Id.

149. Id. § 3511(b) (3).

150. Id.

151. U.S. Department of Justice, Office of the Inspector General, *A Review of the Federal Bureau of Investigation's Use of National Security Letters* 37–38 (2007), http://www.usdoj.gov/oig/special/s0703b/final.pdf.

152. U.S. Department of Justice, Office of the Inspector General, *A Review of the FBI's Use of National Security Letters* 9 (2008), http://www.usdoj.gov/oig/special/s0803b/final.pdf.

153. Eric Lichtblau, "F.B.I. Data Mining Reached Beyond Initial Targets," *New York Times*, Sept. 9, 2007, at A1.

154. 3 C.F.R. pt. 200.

155. Id., Preamble ¶¶ 2.1, 2.3.

156. Id., ¶ 2.4.

157. U.S. Department of Justice, Office of Legal Policy, Attorney General's Guidelines on General Crimes, Racketeering Enterprise and Terrorism Enterprise Investigations at 21–22 (2002), available at http://www.usdoj.gov/ag/readingroom/generalcrimea.htm.

158. Id. at 22.

159. Id.

160. Id.

161. U.S. Department of Justice, Office of Legal Policy, Attorney General's Guidelines for FBI National Security Investigations and Foreign Intelligence Collection (2003), available at http://www.usdoj.gov/olp/nsiguidelines.pdf.

162. Id. at 1.

163. See *Protecting America's Freedom in the Information Age*, supra; Markle Foundation, Task Force on National Security in the Information Age, *Creating a Trusted Network for Homeland Security* (2003); Markle Foundation, Task Force on National Security in the Information Age, *Mobilizing Information to Prevent Terrorism* (2006), available at http://www.markletaskforce.org/.

164. "The Cantigny Principles on Technology, Terrorism, and Privacy," *National Security Law Report*, Feb. 2005, at 14.

165. Ronald D. Lee & Paul M. Schwartz, "Beyond the 'War' on Terrorism: Towards the New Intelligence Network," 103 *Michigan Law Review* 1446, 1467 (2005).

166. U.S. Department of Defense, Technology and Privacy Advisory Committee, *Safeguarding Privacy in the Fight Against Terrorism* (2004), available at http://epic.org/privacy/profiling/tia/tapac_report.pdf. The eight members of the committee reflected an impressive array of private practice, corporate and academic experience, and philanthropic and government service. They included, in addition to Newton N. Minow, Chairman (and co-author of this chapter): Floyd Abrams, a partner in the New York law firm of Cahill Gordon & Reindel and the William J. Brennan, Jr. Visiting Professor of First Amendment Law at the Columbia Graduate School of Journalism; Zoë Baird, president of the Markle Foundation and previously senior vice president and general counsel of Aetna, Inc., and an attorney in White House and DOJ; Griffin Bell, former Managing Partner of King & Spalding, a judge on the U.S. Court of Appeals for the Fifth Circuit, and Attorney General of the United States; Gerhard Casper, President Emeritus of Stanford University and the Peter and Helen Bing Professor in Undergraduate Education at Stanford; William T. Coleman, Jr., a Senior Partner and the Senior Counselor in O'Melveny and Myers and Secretary of Transportation during the Ford Administration; Lloyd N. Cutler, founding partner of the law firm of Wilmer, Cutler & Pickering and Counsel to Presidents Clinton and Carter; and John O. Marsh Jr., Distinguished Professor of Law at George Mason University, former member of Congress, Counselor to President Ford, and the longest-serving Secretary of the Army. Id. at 93–96.

167. Letter from William J. Haynes II, General Counsel, DOD, to Carol E. Dinkins, Chair, Privacy and Civil Liberties Oversight Board, Sep. 22, 2006 (attaching a list of TAPAC's recommendations with each of those applicable to the DOD initialed by the Deputy Secretary as "approved").

168. Committee on Technical and Privacy Dimensions of Information for Terrorism Prevention and Other National Goals, National Academy of Sciences, *Protecting Individual Privacy in the Struggle Against Terrorists: A Framework for Assessment* (2008), available at http://epic.org/misc/nrc_rept_100708.pdf. The committee was chaired by William J. Perry, Michael and Barbara Berberian Professor, Stanford University and former Secretary of Defense, and Charles M. Vest, President of the National Academy of Engineering and former President of MIT.

169. Id. at 2.

170. *Safeguarding Privacy*, supra at 49–50.

171. *Protecting Individual Privacy*, supra at 48.

172. Id. at 48–51 (emphasis in original).

173. Id. at 75.

174. U.S. Department of Health, Education & Welfare, *Report of the Secretary's Advisory Committee on Automated Personal Data Systems, Records, Computer, and the Rights of Citizens* (1973).

175. *Protecting Individual Privacy*, supra at 4.

176–177. *Safeguarding Privacy*, supra at 49. TAPAC recommended applying its new legal framework to "all DOD programs involving data mining concerning U.S. persons" except for "data mining (1) based on particularized suspicion (including searches of passenger manifests and similar lists); (2) that is limited to foreign intelligence that does not involve U.S. persons; or (3) that concerns federal government employees in connection with their employment." Id. The committee noted that "these three areas are already subject to extensive regulation, which we do not propose expanding." Id. The committee also recommended that "data mining that is limited to information that is routinely available without charge or subscription to the public—on the Internet, in telephone directories, or in public records to the extent authorized by law" should be subject to only the written authorization and compliance audit requirements. Id.

The finding would have to address, in addition to the points already discussed, "that other equally effective but less intrusive means of achieving the same purpose are either not practically available or are already being used;" "the effect(s) on individuals identified through the data mining (e.g., they will be the subject of further investigation for which a warrant will be sought, they will be subject to additional scrutiny before being allowed to board an aircraft, etc.);" and "that there is a system in place for dealing with false positives (e.g., reporting false positives to developers to improve the system, correcting incorrect information if possible, remedying the effects of false positives as quickly as practicable, etc.), including identifying the frequency and effects of false positives." Id. at 50.

178. Id. (using "the least data consistent with the purpose of the data mining should be accessed, disseminated, and retained").

179. Id. ("whenever practicable data mining should be performed on databases from which information by which specific individuals can be commonly identified (e.g., name, address, telephone number, SSN, unique title, etc.) has been removed, encrypted, or otherwise obscured").

180. Id. ("data mining systems should be designed to create a permanent, tamper-resistant record of when data have been accessed and by whom").

181. Id. ("data mining systems should be secured against accidental or deliberate unauthorized access, use, alteration, or destruction, and access to such systems should be restricted to persons with a legitimate need and protected by appropriate access controls taking into account the sensitivity of the data").

182. Id. ("all persons engaged in developing or using data mining systems should be trained in their appropriate use and the laws and regulations applicable to their use").

183. Id. at 51.

184. Id. FISC authorization meeting similar requirements would be required to reidentify search results conducted with anonymized or pseudonymized personal data. Id. at 52. The recommendations also include a provision dealing with "exigent circumstances," which would allow the government to engage in data mining without FISC authorization. Id.

185. Id.

186. Id. at 50, 52–55.

187. *Protecting Individual Privacy*, supra at 54 ("The information-based program should be demonstrated to yield a rate of false positives that is acceptable in view of the purpose of the search, the severity of the effect of being identified, and the likelihood of further investigation.")

188. Id. at 55 ("The effects on individuals identified through the information-based program should be identified clearly. (e.g., they will be the subject of further investigation for which a warrant will be sought, they will be subject to additional scrutiny before being allowed to board an aircraft, and so on).")

189. Id. ("The information-based program should operate with the least personal data consistent with its objective. Only necessary data should be accessed, disseminated, or retained. … Whenever practicable, the information-based program should rely on personal data from which information by which specific individuals can be commonly identified (e.g., name, address, telephone number, SSN, unique title, etc.) has been removed, encrypted, or otherwise obscured.")

190. Id. ("The information-based program should create a permanent, tamper-resistant record of when data have been accessed and by whom. Continuous, automated analysis of audit records can help ensure compliance with applicable laws and policies. This is especially important when sensitive or potentially sensitive data are involved.")

191. Id. ("The information-based program should be secured against accidental or deliberate unauthorized access, use, alteration, or destruction. Access to such information-based program should be restricted to persons with a legitimate need and protected by appropriate access controls taking into account the sensitivity of the data.")

192. Id. at 54.

193. Id. at 56–57.

194. Id. at 56 (citation omitted).

195. *Safeguarding Privacy*, supra at 46; *Protecting Individual Privacy*, supra at 54.

risk assessment. Certification enables organizations to better plan in advance for disruptions to their supply chains and to establish necessary procedures for resilience, recovery, and continuity of essential operations after a disruptive event occurs, regardless of its origin—terrorism, piracy, cargo theft, fraud, natural emergencies, crises, disasters, accidents, etc.

The importance of applying international standards and learning from incidents in other countries is a key takeaway from the article by James Acton and Mark Hibbs about the Fukushima Nuclear Disaster. Japan's nuclear regulator did not apply those international standards that address the risks of tsunamis to nuclear power plants. The plant operator, Tepco, was also negligent because it did not follow up on geological evidence that the region surrounding the plant had been periodically flooded about once every thousand years. The Fukushima accident would have been prevented had Tepco and the nuclear safety agency followed international standards and best practices about equipping plants with more emergency electricity supplies, and protecting them to better withstand a whole range of hard-to-predict extreme hazards. The lack of transparency into safety and security measures makes it impossible to properly assess the strengths and weaknesses of their approaches to enhancing safety. If countries are serious about learning lessons from Fukushima, they need to start by opening their nuclear programs to the outside scrutiny.

The concept of societal security is a pillar of the Swedish approach to the protection of its inhabitants. This approach is based on the recognition that the threats and challenges of the twenty-first century are less about the integrity of territory than about safeguarding the critical functions of society, protecting people, and upholding fundamental values in the face of many types of threats and risks. Authors Helena Lindberg and Bengt Sundelius explain the building blocks that underpin their nation's whole-of-society approach to disaster resilience. The effort toward enhancing societal security can only be effective to the extent that partners or stakeholders outside the sphere of government become engaged and contribute. Fostering a culture of horizontal coordination and networking across jurisdictional borders is also key.

On February 27, 2010, an earthquake struck Chile and caused a tsunami which devastated coastal towns and resulted in a death toll of 524. Information sharing, communication, and coordination between government authorities broke down and hindered government response actions to such a degree that a national investigation was undertaken, which attempted to establish criminal liability for poor handling of the crisis. Nick Lavars' chapter investigates the challenge of communicating critical information between relevant government bodies to alert and advise a nation at risk. What can be taken from these events is of international relevance—the importance of a national emergency service working in cohesion with government in coordinating information, and then proceeding to provide guidance to its citizens in a state of emergency.

In his chapter on the evolution of Counterterrorism and Security in India, R.V. Raju describes key events that have shaped India's response to terrorism, challenges such as the lack of national political consensus on security issues, and high-profile projects such as the national intelligence grid (NATGRID) and the National Counter Terrorism Centre. India's experiences illuminate the cost of the lack of a national political consensus on security issues. Individual states view security issues through the prism of federalism, while politicians look at them from the point of vote banks, with elections being held for either the State assemblies or the Parliament in almost every calendar year, forgetting that these issues threaten the very existence of the country. Raju warns that it is vital that India learns to work out a minimum political consensus to build a robust security architecture which can successfully thwart terrorist attempts to destabilize the country.

In her chapter on the Hyogo Framework for Action (HFA), Margareta Wahlstrom presents progress and challenges related to strengthening disaster management and the arrangements and mechanisms that underpin it. Although early warning systems can be further improved, investments in enhancing preparedness and response are paying off, and weather-related disaster mortality is now declining. Despite a manifest commitment to disaster risk management (DRM), few countries systematically account for disaster losses and impacts or comprehensively assess their risks. Factoring DRM into national and sector planning and public investment is a particular challenge for many countries, as is the use of social protection to help vulnerable households and communities.

In the chapter on International Cooperation in Counterterrorism, Gilles De Kerchove describes what the EU is doing internally among its 27 Member States in order to enhance its strategic approach and to improve operational tools for counterterrorism. De Kerchove comments on cooperation at the international level, in particular information sharing between the different agencies involved in counterterrorism, which has progressively been strengthened over the last few years.

49

THE HYOGO FRAMEWORK FOR ACTION

Margareta Wahlstrom

UN Secretary General's Special Representative for Disaster Risk Reduction, and Head of UNISDR, the UN Office for Disaster Risk Reduction

In 2005, 168 member states endorsed the Hyogo Framework for Action (HFA): Building the resilience of nations and communities to disasters with the aim of achieving a substantial reduction of disaster losses in lives and in the social, economic, and environmental assets of countries and communities by 2015.

Today 133 national governments are reporting on their progress against the HFA's priorities. Major progress is being made in strengthening disaster management and the institutional and legislative arrangements and mechanisms that underpin it. Significant momentum in the implementation of the HFA is also being generated through the development of regional and sub-regional strategies, frameworks, plans, and programs. Although early warning systems can be further improved, investments in enhancing preparedness and response are paying off and weather-related disaster mortality is now declining.

In contrast, many governments and regional organizations find it difficult to address the underlying risk drivers. Despite a manifest commitment to disaster risk management (DRM), few countries systematically account for disaster losses and impacts or comprehensively assess their risks. As of this writing in the early spring of 2012, the United Nations International Strategy for Disaster Reduction (UNISDR) collaborates with 40 countries that have national disaster data loss bases. It is hoped this number will rise to 70 by 2013. The political and economic imperative to invest in DRM remains weak, with few countries reporting dedicated national budget lines or adequate financing for risk reduction.

Factoring DRM into national and sector planning and public investment is a particular challenge for many countries, as is the use of social protection to help vulnerable households and communities. Whereas many countries reported improvements in their legislative and institutional arrangements, and have decentralized functions to local government, this is not necessarily leading to more effective implementation. In addition, gender considerations must be better incorporated into DRM across all geographic and income regions.

The HFA is a comprehensive set of actions that a country can take to strengthen its risk governance capacities. The HFA Progress Review allows countries to reflect on their efforts to strengthen their capacities and to identify strengths and gaps. By offering a framework for analysis, it catalyzes both strategic and action-oriented planning. Where governments have made serious efforts to engage key public, civil society, and academic stakeholders in the review process, communication and consensus building have improved. Most importantly, the discussion of indicators helps generate a common language and understanding, thus fostering real dialogue.

Although the HFA Monitor does not measure risk governance capacities directly, it identifies successes and highlights challenges, irrespective of a country's starting point. The national reports do not provide in-depth reasons for progress or lack thereof, though a number of countries provide information on the underlying drivers and barriers to progress. It is also important to note that countries are addressing the HFA from very different baselines. There are enormous objective differences between, for example, the risk governance capacities of Switzerland or New Zealand and Afghanistan or Haiti. Regionally, 58 percent of the countries and territories in the Americas, 72 percent in Asia, 61 percent in Africa, 53 percent in Europe, and 28 percent in Oceania participated in the HFA Progress Review.

The number and quality of the reports and associated documentation indicate continued and increased commitment to the HFA, which now constitutes the single most important source of information on DRM at the country level. It also provides a unique insight into where governments themselves see significant achievements and identify remaining gaps.

For this review period, local and regional monitoring frameworks, with attendant indicators, have also been developed. In light of the fact that local governments often have widely differing risk governance capacities, the national averages reported by the HFA Monitor hide large discrepancies in capacities among different areas within a country. For example, there are often dramatic differences between the capacities in a strong municipal administration in a capital or large city, and those in weakly resourced localities in remote rural areas. The local monitoring framework factors local government contributions and community perspectives into national planning.

There are now over 1050 municipalities and cities that have signed up to the "Making Cities Resilient" campaign and they are committed to the Ten Essentials—a checklist that helps them monitor their progress in managing disaster risks. The Ten Essentials are aligned to the local indicators, thus allowing local progress to be highlighted. The regional framework has also aided reporting by regional inter-governmental organizations.

The global overview is based on the analysis of the interim review reports shared by the participating governments. Out of 133 countries and territories which carried out the review process, 82 have shared their interim reports.

The *2009 Global Assessment Report* (GAR09) indicated that although many countries' disaster management capacities were increasing, far less progress was being made towards addressing the underlying drivers that are increasing countries' stock of risk. The evidence to support this finding is even stronger in the *2011 Global Assessment Report* (GAR11). With notable exceptions, countries find it difficult to comprehensively assess their disaster risks and to factor risk assessment information into national planning, investment, and development decisions. However, they also highlight achievements and innovative practices that can drive change and provide political and economic incentives for DRM.

GAR09 highlighted that national efforts were mainly focused on strengthening policy, legislation, and institutional frameworks, along with boosting capacities for risk assessments, early warning, and disaster preparedness and response. In contrast, countries reported limited progress in using knowledge, innovation, and education to build a culture of resilience, as well as to address the underlying drivers of risk.

The 2009–2011 HFA Progress Review indicates improvement across all priority areas. Progress in addressing underlying risk, however, continues to be particularly challenging, and progress in some areas, such as policy development, does not automatically trigger improvements in others, such as the ability to address the underlying drivers of risk. Although global averages do not give an accurate picture of progress in any particular country, mapping global progress does highlight areas in which more effort is required.

Progress in HFA Priority Area 1 (*Ensure that disaster risk reduction is a national and local priority with a strong institutional basis for implementation*) has been consistent across the world. More than 42 of the 82 reporting countries and territories reported substantial or comprehensive achievement in this priority area. Specifically, 48 countries reported substantial achievement developing national policy and legal frameworks. Importantly, almost half of these are low- or lower-middle-income countries. A number of countries, however, also highlighted that this progress does not necessarily translate into effective DRM. This is consistent with the findings from the HFA Mid-term Review, which reported notable progress setting up institutional structures and developing plans, but limited improvements in adequate resourcing and local implementation.

The institutional arrangements for DRM in many countries have certainly evolved, from traditional single-agency civil protection of defense structures to multi-sector systems and platforms. Finding appropriate institutional arrangements, however, to ease the incorporation of DRM into development planning and public investment remains a challenge.

Currently 81 national platforms for coordination of DRM exist globally (as of March 2012). These platforms vary widely in terms of their authority, membership, and history. In some cases existing disaster management organizations have been nominated as national platforms; in other cases they are an advisory or consultative mechanism to foster cross-sector coordination and to involve civil society and academic organizations. Only 55 countries confirm that civil society and relevant development sectors are represented in their national platforms, and only 37 scored level 4 or 5 on the functioning of national multi-sector platforms for DRM.

For HFA Priority Area 2 (*Knowledge of risk at national and local level*), comprehensive risk assessments remain elusive, particularly at the local level. Just 46 of the reporting countries have undertaken national multi-hazard risk assessments that could hypothetically inform planning and development decisions. Many countries, however, faced major challenges linking these to development processes at the national and local levels. The HFA Mid-term Review also reflects that scientific assessments, useful as they are, rarely connect with assessments of community-level vulnerability and capacity.

Unfortunately, countries that reported substantial progress in this area also highlight an absence of national standards for assessing both disaster losses and risks. In particular, few countries carry out risk assessments of schools and health facilities. The overwhelming majority of countries (65 out of 82) do not collect gender-disaggregated vulnerability and capacity information.

The use of new technologies has been a key driver in the substantial progress reported on early warning. However, difficulties with all components of the early warning system, or chain, potentially limit corresponding improvements at the local level. The HFA Mid-term Review also indicated that more progress has been made on warning for major hazards than on developing relevant local systems and communicating early warning of recurrent extensive risks through appropriate channels.

HFA Priority Area 3 (*Use knowledge, innovation, and education to build a culture of safety and resilience at all levels*) continues to show limited progress. Identifying and further developing methods and tools for multi-risk assessments and cost–benefit analyses remains a particularly weak area, with only 19 of 82 countries scoring level 4 or 5. Less than a third of reporting countries rated as substantial or comprehensive their efforts to integrate risk reduction into school curricula and relevant formal training. The majority of countries reported significant gaps in developing public awareness strategies

Progress in HFA Priority Area 4 (*Reduce the underlying risk factors*) is even lower. Although countries reported a greater awareness of the need to factor DRM into planning and investment, less than a third (28 percent) rated their progress towards addressing the underlying risk drivers at 4 or 5. Countries reported difficulties addressing the risks internalized in the different development sectors, which explains why economic loss and damage continue to increase. Only 40 percent of countries, including only a quarter of low-income countries, invested in retrofitting critical public infrastructure such as schools and hospitals.

HFA Priority Area 5 (*Strengthening disaster preparedness for effective response*) has been the dominant focus of national governments for decades. This area encompasses disaster preparedness and contingency plans at all administrative levels, financial reserves and contingency mechanisms, and well-established procedures for information exchange during emergencies. More than half (46 of 82) of the countries reported substantial or comprehensive achievement developing policy, technical, and institutional capacities. It is clear that effective disaster management has contributed to the decline in weather-related disaster mortality.

report having mechanisms in place to systematically report disaster loss and impacts. The associated challenges, however, indicate that these mechanisms do not generate sufficient data, and suffer from fragmentation and limited accessibility. Where data-sharing protocols and mechanisms still do not exist, information remains scattered across various departments within the sector and does not provide a complete picture of national losses.

Producing reliable loss and impact information remains a challenge, especially after large disasters or in difficult environments, such as those encountered in Haiti and Myanmar. Moreover, this problem extends to localized losses, where most countries also reported limited data availability and difficulties connecting local disaster impact assessments with national monitoring systems and loss databases. For example, despite confirming that it systematically records disaster losses, Mauritius reported it had no quantitative data on the extent of damages caused by all hazards.

Also, as highlighted above, fewer than half of the countries undertook comprehensive multi-hazard risk assessments, and less than a quarter did so in any sort of standardized way. Many high-risk countries, such as Armenia, Colombia, Comoros, Dominican Republic, Ecuador, Guatemala, Turkey, and Viet Nam, reported little progress on multi-hazard risk assessment and identification. There are two reasons for this: in some of these countries such initiatives may have just begun; in others, such as Turkey and Colombia, it more likely reflects a growing and sophisticated understanding of the complexity of the challenge.

The European Commission has recognized this complexity and has developed and adopted guidelines for mapping and assessing risk, based on a multi-hazard and multi-risk approach. Canada is currently developing an all-hazards risk assessment framework that will become part of the country's emergency planning system. Romania has plans for an East European Multi-Risk Management Center. A number of countries also made efforts to integrate risk assessments into a range of sectors, including health, education, agriculture and transport, and water management.

UNDERSTANDING RISKS

As previously discussed, countries from all geographic and income regions reported three main obstacles to undertaking comprehensive risk assessments: limited financial resources; lack of technical capacity;

and a lack of harmonization among the instruments, tools, and institutions involved. These challenges were also reported by regional and sub-regional intergovernmental organizations.

In many countries a wide range of institutions are engaged in institute- and sector-specific assessments. Data on individual hazards and vulnerabilities are scattered across many organizations. This creates problems for the coordination and compatibility of data, and the harmonization of data collection and storage. Encouragingly, some countries are starting to overcome this fragmentation by finding new ways to organize.

In general, the practice of systematically incorporating risk assessments into recovery programs has failed to take root overall, with only limited progress since the last reporting period. Most advances have occurred in low-income countries, where 42 percent report substantial progress (level 4 or 5) in 2011, compared with 29 percent in 2009.

Where responsibility for risk assessment has been decentralized, countries reported an uneven level of progress, depending on technical capacities and resources. Some provinces and districts regularly update comprehensive assessments, while others had difficulty assessing even individual hazards. China provides one such example, reporting substantial progress against this indicator with successful disaster loss and hazard monitoring at national, provincial, and city levels. At the same time, it had significant trouble setting up similar systems at the county level.

FROM WORDS TO INVESTMENT

Unsurprisingly, given their difficulty in assessing risks and accounting for losses, countries have difficulty justifying investments in DRM. GAR09 showed that low- and middle-income countries require several hundred billion dollars of development investment per year to upgrade informal human settlements, to restore damaged ecosystems, and to provide basic needs. Furthermore, they require specific resources to strengthen risk governance capacities and thus ensure that such investment does indeed reduce risks. The assignment of dedicated resources for this purpose provides a clear indication that countries are really following through on their stated political commitment to the HFA.

In 2009–2011, many countries recognized that development investments in poverty reduction, food security, and public health reduce risks. They find it difficult, however, to quantify these investments, which are provided through diverse instruments including sector budgeting, environmental protection funds, social solidarity and development funds, compensation funds, civil society, and, in some countries (Algeria, for example), the private sector.

Most countries across all geographical and income regions reported relatively little progress towards assigning dedicated resources to strengthen their risk governance capacities.

Less than one country in five could show the percentage of their national budgets assigned to DRM, indicating that allocating dedicated resources remains the exception and not the norm. The figures provided vary from 0.005 percent (Lesotho) to 2.58 percent (Sri Lanka). Even countries such as Viet Nam and India, which have both passed legislation to allocate financial resources, found it difficult to quantify their investments. Resources allocated for DRM within sectors and for local governments are even more limited. India's 2005 DRM law requires that every national ministry integrates disaster risk reduction elements in their ongoing development programs, and local authorities are given limited responsibility for response and reconstruction. Despite these responsibilities, dedicated budgets are lacking. Costa Rica's 2006 disaster management law similarly requires that "every public institution" dedicate a specific line item in its budget for disaster risk reduction.

While global targets for DRM investment have been suggested—for example, 10 percent of response funds, two percent of development funds, and two percent of recovery funds—financial reporting systems still do not allow progress to be monitored against these targets. Less than half the countries (38 out of 82) budgeted explicitly for DRM within post-disaster recovery programs and, of these, very few could report specific amounts or percentages of recovery and reconstruction funds assigned to risk reduction.

INCORPORATING DRM INTO NATIONAL PLANNING AND INVESTMENT

If development planning and investments fail to incorporate risk reduction, a country's stock of risk will continue to grow. Yet, most countries and territories reported least progress in this area of the HFA. Antigua and Barbuda, Bolivia, Botswana, Georgia, Lesotho, Mauritius, Mexico, Monaco, occupied Palestinian Territory, Paraguay, Saint Lucia, and Togo are just some of the countries struggling to reduce underlying risk. But even countries that have attained some success, such as France, Germany, Portugal, and the United States of America, score their efforts as low in this area.

The 2009–2011 review shows little or no advance on the 2007–2009 results. Most countries continue to have difficulty integrating risk reduction into public investment planning, urban development, environmental planning and management, and social protection

Some countries have yet to recognize climate change adaptation as an important area. A number of high-income countries or territories, such as Croatia, Czech Republic, and the Turks and Caicos Islands, reported that climate change is not yet on their policy agendas and, as a result, increasing climate risk is not taken into account in DRM. The majority, however, did report the emergence or strengthening of climate change adaptation projects and programs: 72 percent globally, with a relatively equal distribution across regions and income classes.

Compared with 2007–2009, lower-middle-income countries, such as Bhutan, reported most progress in integrating disaster risk reduction into national development plans and climate change policies. Lower-middle-income countries, however, reported less substantial progress integrating risk reduction into poverty reduction strategies or other sector strategies that address the underlying drivers of risk.

Given these different starting points, it is unsurprising that those countries that reported little progress did so from very different perspectives. Some national reports (from Albania and Senegal, for example) reveal a focus on preparedness and emergency management and higher progress in HFA Priority Area 5 (strengthening disaster preparedness) than in other areas. Others, such as Peru, show a sophisticated understanding of the complexities of addressing underlying vulnerabilities and drivers of risk together with a low progress score. Namibia reported that investment into DRM, rather than response and preparedness, is difficult account for and to plan. Greater understanding appears to bring greater awareness of the magnitude of the task.

Only 38 percent of all countries and territories, relatively equally spread across income classes and regions, systematically incorporated risk reduction into national- and sector-level public investment systems. It is unclear, however, if more than a few of these are fully functioning and institutionalized systems. For example, Viet Nam reported that decisions on public investment are based on relatively limited information on hazards, climate change, and underlying vulnerabilities.

Countries reported less progress towards estimating the potential impacts on future disaster risk of large infrastructure projects—such as dams, highways and tourism developments—than they did in the previous reporting period. Less than 10 percent of lower-middle-income countries awarded themselves a score of 4 or 5. Again, this limited progress may reflect increased understanding of the complexities involved in conducting systematic assessments.

New supporting data for the current reporting period show that countries employ different types of mechanisms to assess disaster risk. While most Organisation for Economic Co-operation and Development (OECD) and other high-income countries directly assessed risks in critical infrastructure projects, low- and middle-income countries seem to rely more on pre-existing environmental impact assessments to fulfill this function.

URBAN AND LAND USE PLANNING

In the present reporting cycle, lower-middle-income countries reported significant progress in the area of urban development and land use planning compared with 2009. There remains a staggering discrepancy, however, between high- and low-income nations, with almost 70 percent of high-income countries and only 15 percent of low-income countries scoring 4 or 5.

While most (95 percent) high-income countries (and all OECD countries) invested to reduce risks in vulnerable settlements, only 60 percent of low-income countries reported such investments. This is particularly critical considering the large concentration of disaster risk in urban areas in low- and middle-income countries. But even some high-income countries had trouble developing appropriate land use plans. In Barbados, for example, this problem led to increased vulnerability for low-income groups. Barbados also had difficulties dealing with vulnerable settlements that were developed before current legislation on zoning and urban land use planning was passed. Although a lack of political will is rarely acknowledged, particularly with regard to relocation, it is implicit in many countries' descriptions of barriers to progress. Weak enforcement of plans is another reported challenge, reflecting the need for more participatory approaches to planning and development.

Low-income countries find it harder than higher-income countries to make the investments necessary to reduce urban risk. Urban drainage systems, for example, are recognized as an important tool for reducing urban risk, but less than half (46 percent) of low-income countries invested in drainage infrastructure in flood-prone areas. Less than a third (31 percent) of low-income countries took measures to counter landslide risk, compared with around 60 percent of lower- and upper-middle-income countries, and 68 percent of high-income countries. A less significant but similar trend was observed for the provision of safe land for low-income households and communities. This finding is consistent with the rapid increase in housing damage in urban areas.

Some countries have introduced hazard-resistant building regulations only recently. Syria, for example, first introduced a seismic code in 1995. Weak implementation and enforcement mechanisms are common problems in countries where most urban development is informal.

In addition, reports from several countries and territories reveal the trade-offs internalized in any decision to invest in DRM. For example, Croatia reported pressure from the construction industry to lower standards and codes to reduce overall construction costs, even in hazard-prone areas.

ENVIRONMENTAL PLANNING AND MANAGEMENT

Most countries and territories addressed the decline of regulatory ecosystem services and reported positively on provisions for protected areas legislation (77 percent), environmental impact assessments (83 percent), and climate change adaptation projects and programs (73 percent). Fewer reported payments for ecosystem services, which is still a relatively new policy area. Integrated planning, such as risk-sensitive coastal zone management, was also lacking. Overall, and except for middle-income countries, less progress was made integrating DRM into environmental policies than in 2007–2009.

More than 95 percent of lower-middle-income countries have ecosystem protection measures in place, and more than 80 percent of countries globally have mechanisms to protect and restore regulatory ecosystem services. A number of countries, however, claimed that existing laws needed stronger legislation or enforcement. For example, Sierra Leone reported that enforcement bylaws need updating to act as effective deterrents. Similarly, Indonesia points out that overlapping responsibilities and legislation on environmental and disaster management result in a lack of synergy and coordination, which hinders enforcement. Timor-Leste, along with several other countries worldwide, is hampered by protective-area legislation that does not take disaster risk into account.

SOCIAL PROTECTION

The lack of effective social protection erodes the resilience of poor households globally. Ensuring that micro-level social support and economic incentives—such as targeted welfare and employment programs and micro-business development—are in place before a disaster strikes can be an effective way to assist vulnerable households. Progress in this area since the last reporting period has been particularly significant for middle-income countries.

Different instruments scored very differently across income groups. On one hand, penetration of crop and property insurance is far higher in high- and upper-middle-income countries than in low-income countries. On the other hand, 58 percent of low-income countries use micro-insurance instruments, compared with only 25 percent of high-income countries.

Low- and lower-middle-income countries and territories such as Bolivia, Cayman Islands, Côte d'Ivoire, El Salvador, Guatemala, Indonesia, Madagascar, Maldives, and Nicaragua all reported no or little progress on the provision of social protection instruments, such as cash transfers or employment programs that can enhance households' disaster resilience.

Ecuador is one of few countries that implemented a wide range of social policy instruments as part of their disaster risk reduction strategy. As the country's Ministry for Agriculture is responsible for a number of these social development programs, they are tightly linked to livelihoods and asset protection.

Myanmar and Timor-Leste reported limited progress in the provision of social development policies (levels 2 and 1, respectively). Their analysis of constraints and challenges echoes that of many disaster-prone countries. Social protection is often limited to areas that have recently experienced disasters, such as those affected by Cyclone Nargis in Myanmar (2008) or regions suffering recurring floods in Timor-Leste.

Only 23 percent of countries globally reported the use of employment guarantee schemes. This is unsurprisingly low, given that such schemes are perceived as a large burden on national budgets, though this is being countered by evidence from successful and affordable schemes across the globe.

Conditional cash transfers, although considered more targeted and efficient, are used by only 31 percent of low-income countries, including Burundi, Kyrgyzstan, and Zambia. Of all the countries that use these instruments, more than half are middle-income countries. High-income countries tended not to use these instruments because their social welfare systems usually operate via pensions, family benefits, and other similar mechanisms.

STRENGTHENING INSTITUTIONAL AND LEGISLATIVE ARRANGEMENTS

The location within a government of authority for national policy on DRM can critically influence a country's ability to use national and sector development planning and investment to reduce its disaster risks. National DRM organizations often lack the political authority and technical capacity to engage development sectors. Timor-Leste, for example, failed to generate substantial momentum for DRM in sector ministries because of the relatively isolated and weak position of its National Disaster Management Department.

Some countries have made DRM apex bodies of presidents' and vice-presidents' offices (or placed them within existing apex bodies). These include Myanmar, where the National Disaster Preparedness Central Committee is chaired by the prime minister; Nepal, which has moved the responsibility for its National Strategy for Disaster Risk Management under the chairmanship of the prime minister; and Botswana, where the National Disaster Management Office is an apex of the vice-president's office. It is unclear, however, whether this has improved the coordination of national or sector development planning and investment.

There is little evidence of countries locating responsibility for DRM in their economic and financial planning ministries. Only the United Republic of Tanzania reported such a move, developing its Zanzibar Strategy for Growth and Reduction of Poverty for 2010–2015 through the Ministry of Finance and Economic Affairs. This has provided a strong push for DRM, from reviewing and harmonizing laws and policies to infrastructure improvements, capacity building, and community-based disaster preparation.

Several countries have spread the various functions of DRM across different levels of governance. In Nigeria, for example, a central coordinating body chaired by the vice president leads policy development, monitoring, and response; at the lower levels of governance, states set up their own emergency management agencies with responsibility for disaster prevention, education and awareness raising, and local response preparedness.

A number of countries reported major coordination challenges where DRM responsibilities are distributed across sectors. In addition, where responsibilities are spread horizontally and vertically, new laws and strategies may sit awkwardly next to outdated statutes and policies developed within sector departments. To address this challenge, Morocco, for example, has set up a working group with the Ministry of the Interior to conduct a joint revision of outdated laws and policies. As reported by Namibia, however, updating national policies and disaster management plans according to new legislation can be a slow process.

LIMITED LOCAL CAPACITY AND ACTION

The central role of local governance in DRM is now acknowledged by most countries. Across all indicators relating to decentralization, however, a failure to strengthen local governments and make progress in community participation, means that the gap between rhetoric and reality is widening.

Local capacity was identified as a key gap in delivering effective DRM. While Yemen, for example, has structurally decentralized disaster risk management and reduction, existing financial and technical resources do not match local governments' new responsibilities. This is a common experience across the globe. In Madagascar, the legal framework for decentralized risk management does not include any provisions for budget allocations or specific responsibilities and procedures. As a result, local governments find it difficult to assume their roles as designated leaders in disaster risk reduction. As discussed. dedicated budget allocations to local governments for DRM remain the exception rather than the rule. China and a handful of other countries, however, reported comprehensive achievements in this area—though much of this progress concerns response preparedness rather than DRM in a broader sense.

VERY LIMITED PROGRESS IN PUBLIC AWARENESS AND EDUCATION FOR DRM

Public awareness of risks and of how to address them is a key to strengthening accountability and ensuring that disaster risk management is implemented. Yet, only 19 countries reported substantial progress in this area, with 63 indicating weak or average progress. Anguilla, Côte d'Ivoire, Kyrgyzstan, Poland, and the Seychelles advanced least in this area, compared with all other HFA priority areas. Most countries reported significant efforts in campaigns to raise public awareness, including outreach to local governments and risk-prone communities. Despite these advances, around 60 percent of countries that rated themselves as making good overall progress, reported weak or average progress on making available information on disasters and disaster risk reduction issues.

China was a notable exception, reporting substantial and comprehensive progress on the availability of risk information, on developing a countrywide public awareness strategy, and on integrating DRM into school curricula (from primary to tertiary levels). Access to information and risk awareness drive social demand for disaster risk reduction. If countries have no established mechanism for accessing disaster risk information, their citizens will find it difficult to demand more effective risk reduction.

Almost 60 percent of countries have included DRM in the national educational curriculum. But efforts have focused more on the primary level than the secondary or tertiary levels. While few countries, however, included DRM in university and professional training, the literature analyzed for the HFA Mid-term Review in 2010 highlighted a rapid expansion of specialized DRM courses at training institutes and universities. Distance-learning courses are also becoming more popular, particularly for developing the skills and knowledge base of governmental and NGO staff.

Another area where progress has been slow is in research; in particular, research on improved multi-risk assessments and cost–benefit analyses. Three-quarters (63 out of 82) of the reporting countries reported little or average progress in this area, with only 19 countries indicating substantial progress. Furthermore, most countries curricula (85 percent) reported no research into the economic costs and benefits of disaster risk reduction.

REGIONAL PROGRESS

Disaster risks associated with major hazards are often a regional concern. Most (74 out of 82) countries participated in regional and sub-regional DRM programs and projects, and many countries also have action plans addressing trans-boundary issues.

Many regional intergovernmental organizations have successfully developed regional risk reduction frameworks. More than three-quarters (63) of the countries participated in the development of regional strategies—with the Secretariat of the Pacific Community Applied Geoscience and Technology Division (SOPAC) in the Pacific, the Association of Southeast Asian Nations (ASEAN) in South-East Asia, the Caribbean Disaster Emergency Management Agency (CDEMA) in the Caribbean, Centro de Coordinación para la Prevención de los Desastres Naturales en América Central (CEPREDENAC) in Central America, the African Union and the New Partnership for Africa's Development (NEPAD) in Africa, amongst others, all developing regional disaster risk reduction frameworks. The most recent success was provided by the Council of Arab Ministers Responsible for the Environment (CAMRE), which adopted the Arab Strategy for Disaster Risk Reduction 2020, endorsed by heads of state in January 2011. The Incheon Regional Roadmap and Action Plan on DRR through CCA in Asia and the Pacific (Incheon REMAP) initiative is another example of an innovative approach to regional learning and cooperation. Initiatives in Europe have resulted in agreement on a comprehensive strategy and implementation plan for the European Commission's support to disaster risk reduction.

Moreover, the Council of Europe has taken steps toward a joint European approach to managing risk in Member States. The South Asian Association for Regional Cooperation (SAARC) has agreed on a Comprehensive Regional Framework on Disaster Management, and has established its organizational structure. Despite this success, SAARC reported that although constitutional commitment has been attained, comprehensive or substantial achievements are still elusive.

The regional progress report of the Arab States also highlights a lack of ongoing sub-regional and regional programs that consider transboundary risks. Whereas national processes to better understand and monitor risk are underway (in Algeria, Egypt, Jordan, Morocco, Syrian and Yemen, for example), the lack of information at the regional level affects regional capacity for early warning on trans-boundary risks, particularly for multiple hazards. Regional access to national hazard analysis and loss databases has also been identified as a constraint for regional progress. The League of Arab States initiated the first review of progress on the current status of implementing disaster risk reduction in the Arab region in 2007. After encountering significant constraints in the start-up phase, the League has since seen a surge in member countries' interest in engaging in national as well as regional reporting and coordination.

Many of the existing regional frameworks and strategies remain skewed towards disaster management and HFA Priority Area 5 (strengthening disaster preparedness). The European Commission, for example, admits that its contributions have to date been mostly to HFA Priority Area 5, but points to a number of "projects fitting into a more holistic DRR approach." Similarly, the South Asian Association For Regional Cooperation (SAARC) report emphasizes achievements in response preparedness, particularly when it comes to capacity building.

Regional intergovernmental organizations also find it difficult to meaningfully engage nongovernmental actors in their processes. For example, SAARC reported that efforts to reach out to a wider audience and involve NGOs and independent experts are regularly limited by the Association's own "rigid rules and procedures," which can make it impossible to convene multi-stakeholder forums.

GLOBAL GENDER BLINDNESS

Integrating gender considerations into disaster risk reduction remains a major challenge. Only 20 percent of countries reported substantial achievement in this area in 2009. Two years on, there has been little improvement, with only 26 percent of countries reporting significant ongoing commitment to gender as a driver of progress.

Even countries that score their efforts as "significant and ongoing," such as Brazil and Saint Kitts and Nevis, provided little detail on what constitutes progress or reflects gender across the different priority areas. This limited visibility of the role of gender in DRM is confirmed by the low proportion of countries that included gender considerations in different areas of DRM.

Few risk assessments consider or generate gender-disaggregated data and few countries incorporate gender-based issues into recovery. Gender-differentiated needs and vulnerabilities remain neglected in recovery assessments, with severe consequences for safety and health, particularly of women.

These gaps are echoed in country reports. Gender aspects are "not taken into account in current risk reduction policies" in Comoros, and there is no "specific policy on gender perspectives in risk reduction" in Antigua and Barbuda. Argentina, Bolivia, British Virgin Islands, Maldives, and Nepal all reported existing gender policies but have difficulty integrating them with DRM. A large number of countries concur with the United Republic of Tanzania, which identifies the lack of appropriate knowledge of "how and where to implement gender matters" as the main barrier. Many countries, including Honduras, reported on gender-based programs and initiatives led and funded by international organizations, implying that addressing gender considerations remains a donor-driven priority rather than a government one.

Although most countries now have legislation, policies, and institutions in place to promote gender equality in employment, health, and education, progress incorporating gender considerations into DRM is much slower. Some countries, such as Egypt, appear to have difficulty promoting or even protecting the constitutional rights of women in practice. The lack of gender disaggregated data, as identified by Bahrain, also hampers understanding of how women and men differ in their vulnerability and their specific contributions to reducing disaster risk.

As is the case in many countries generally, most of the progress is focused on response and preparedness. This is an obvious and practical area in which to ensure gender equality, but does not necessarily challenge dominant gender dynamics and power relations. Nevertheless, there are exceptions in low- and lower-middle-income countries. In Zambia, for example, assessments conducted for social protection programs incorporate gender considerations and the different kinds of vulnerabilities of women and children.

Despite the hurdles, there are also encouraging and concrete examples of progress. In Ghana, a gender-based NGO was tasked by the national government to engage in a countrywide education campaign for women and humanitarian service providers. The program included raising women's awareness of their right to humanitarian support and their role in reducing disaster risk. As a result, women have become more involved in planning and implementing risk reduction activities, particularly in the vulnerable northern regions of the country.

FURTHER INFORMATION AND READING

Hyogo Framework for Action 2005–2015: Building the resilience of nations and communities to disasters: http://www.preventionweb.net/english/professional/publications/v.php?id=1037.

The Global Assessment Report 2009: http://www.preventionweb.net/english/hyogo/gar/2011/en/home/gar09.html.

The Global Assessment Report 2011: http://www.preventionweb.net/english/hyogo/gar/2011/en/home/index.html.

Mid-Term Review of the Hyogo Framework for Action (HFA): http://www.preventionweb.net/english/professional/publications/v.php?id=18197.

Towards a post–2015 framework for disaster risk reduction: http://www.preventionweb.net/english/professional/publications/v.php?id=25129&pid:24.

PreventionWeb, http://www.preventionweb.net.

Latest versions of the HFA Progress Reports: http://www.preventionweb.net/english/hyogo/gar/2011/en/hfa/reports.html.

HFA progress viewer: http://www.preventionweb.net/english/hyogo/gar/2011/en/hfa/viewer.html.

50

INTERNATIONAL HOMELAND SECURITY

Nadav Morag

Author of Comparative Homeland Security: Global Lessons *(New York: John Wiley & Sons, 2011)*

INTRODUCTION

Homeland Security, as a distinct field of policy, practice, and research, developed in the United States in the wake of the September 11, 2001 Al-Qaeda terrorist attacks on New York and the Washington, D.C. area. Given its origins and the unique nature of American laws and institutions, homeland security was, and frequently still is, viewed as an American construct and concern. Unfortunately, this approach is shortsighted for two reasons. Firstly, while other countries did not view things through a homeland security lens (in terms of bringing together previously seemingly disparate fields such as counterterrorism, emergency response, disaster preparedness, and public health, to name a few), there was and is a wealth of experience to be tapped into with respect to the knowledge other countries have in dealing with the various challenges that fall within the homeland security rubric. Israel and the United Kingdom have a long history of dealing with terrorism; Japan has a great deal of experience dealing with natural disasters, etc. While other countries have environments (human and natural), institutions, laws, and cultures that differ from those of the United States, it makes no sense for American policymakers and scholars to forgo the lessons of others, even if those lessons will need to be adapted to some degree in order to be implemented in the United States. Secondly, many homeland security threats originate overseas: whether terrorists trying to access the American homeland from abroad, carriers of the latest pandemic pathogen unwittingly bringing that agent to an American airport, or agents of dangerous organized crime syndicates infiltrating the border in order to ultimately weaken the rule of law. The current failure to understand how other countries can and cannot cope with such threats before they reach American shores represents a profound gap in American homeland security strategy. Practitioners of US diplomatic, military, and intelligence strategies have long been used to focusing on the intricate workings of other governments and societies in order to help shape U.S. strategy, yet homeland security policymakers seem to be complacently avoiding these resources when it comes to homeland security strategy.

As one of the two objectives in looking at foreign homeland security policy is to adopt best practices, understanding the criticality of looking overseas to help fashion better homeland security laws, institutions, and strategies in the United States is only the first step in the process. American scholars, analysts, and decision-makers must then undertake a meaningful analysis and application of overseas practices. Such an analysis requires obtaining the relevant data regarding policies, laws, institutions, etc. in a given country, including some sense as to whether these policies, laws, institutions, etc. are effective. It is important to note, however, that efficacy is notoriously hard to establish with respect to homeland security issues, as homeland security threats and events, such as terrorism, major disasters, etc., are often fairly rare, and hence there is not enough data to show whether certain policies are working or not. The next step is to then take these overseas laws, institutions, and strategies and analyze them by determining how they would need to be adapted in order to be applicable in the United States—given American laws, governmental structures, culture, ways of doing business, and the acuteness in the U.S. of the kind of threats that the foreign laws, institutions, and policies are designed to address. In short, it is critical to run foreign practices through an "American sieve" in order to determine what is applicable and which policies and practices will need to be adapted in order to be executable in the American context. While there may be specific tactical-level practices that may be applied as is in the United States, most strategic-level policies and laws or major institutional structures and operations will require significant adaptation in order to be implementable in the United States. That is in the nature of things given significant differences in governance, culture, and ways of doing business, even across sister democracies. The fact that differences exist across countries should not, needless to say, prevent us from adapting and then adopting tools and policies that work overseas and that can enhance American homeland security policies.

This chapter will attempt, in the limited space available, to provide a handful of "tip of the iceberg" examples of laws, institutions, and policies followed by a few countries in a number of areas within the homeland security enterprise. This will, by no means, be a comprehensive treatment of the subject area, but rather is designed to provide the reader with an *hors d'oeurve* that will hopefully whet the appetite for further exploration of global homeland security strategies and policies. We will focus here on just three areas within homeland security: counterterrorism and policing models, emergency management, and the role of the military in homeland security. Naturally, these sub-disciplines represent just a fraction of the areas that fall within the homeland security enterprise.

COUNTERTERRORISM AND POLICING MODELS

There are a number of countries that can be analyzed in terms of having experience and using novel approaches to coping with terrorism; still others that have interesting models for structuring police forces and engaging in community policing efforts in order to counteract significant criminal activity. We can look at Israel and the United Kingdom for examples of effective counterterrorism strategies, and to Canada and Japan for policing models.

Approaches to fighting terrorism, broadly speaking, fall into two rough categories. Some countries, such as the UK, view terrorism largely as a category (albeit a highly dangerous one) of criminal activity, and thus argue that terrorism has to be addressed through the tools of the criminal justice system (though frequently with special powers granted to the authorities through so-called "emergency legislation"). Other countries, such as Israel, view terrorism as a form of military aggression and argue that it has to be dealt with using a warfighting approach similar to that used against guerrilla and insurgent military threats. While these categories are not mutually-exclusive—(the UK deals with terrorism in Afghanistan using military tools, and did so in the past in Northern Ireland, and Israel sometimes deals with terrorist threats via its civilian criminal justice system as well as through the use of emergency legislation)—they are nevertheless distinct methodologies.

The UK has had to deal with modern Irish nationalist terrorism since the late eighteenth century and has, much more recently, been faced with the threat of global Jihadi movements. In keeping with the British approach that terrorism is largely an issue for the criminal justice system, the UK has employed a string of criminal laws dating back to the *Explosive Substances Act* of 1883 to cope with terrorism. Most British counterterrorism (CT) legislation historically dealt with acts of sedition and murder or existed in the form of emergency legislation granting special powers to the authorities but carrying an expiration date (though these laws were frequently renewed). During the early 1970s, in response to a dramatic increase in terrorism, the British Parliament passed a new series of emergency laws that gave the British authorities the power to outlaw organizations deemed to be terrorist groups, to try terrorism cases speedily and without juries, and to engage in pre-charge detention for up to 28 days, as well as providing broad powers of search and seizure.[1] In 2000, Parliament passed the *Terrorism Act*, which gave the UK a permanent piece of non-emergency legislation for dealing with terrorism. The law incorporated elements from previously existing emergency legislation but also gave suspects stronger protections and allowed for greater judicial scrutiny. In the wake of the 9/11 attacks, Parliament passed a series of additional CT laws that, among other things, allowed for the use of "control orders" to limit the freedom of movement of terrorism suspects; provided police with additional powers to investigate individuals, premises, and financial transactions; and made it an offense to glorify terrorism and even to be in attendance at a place used for terrorist training, even if the individual in question had not received training or if the training itself was not connected to any specific act of terrorism.[2] Additional powers afforded by this new legislation included stop-and-search powers that made it possible for the authorities to search persons and vehicles in specially designated areas without a warrant or even probable cause, gave the Home Secretary the power to intercept telephone and electronic communications data, provided police the power to arrest anyone without a warrant that they suspected to be a terrorist, and even delayed an arrested suspect's access to an attorney for up to 36–48 hours, depending on the piece of legislation being used, if there was concern that access to an attorney may interfere with the investigation and/or pending arrests.[3]

Beyond these wide-ranging legislative powers, the British CT structure and institutions are well-suited to investigating and often thwarting terrorist activity. The primary CT agencies are housed in the Home Office, which is responsible for police oversight, the domestic intelligence service (the British Security Service, a.k.a. MI–5), and a host of functions relating to security policy. MI–5 is a domestic intelligence and security service that focuses primarily on collection and analysis of intelligence and is not a law enforcement entity. In the UK, police forces are, with a few exceptions such as the British Transport Police, regionally-based and decentralized, and thus MI–5 must develop cooperative relationships with the various independent police forces. It does this primarily through the funding and training that it provides for Special Branch (SB) units. SB departments exist in every one of the UK's police forces and these consist of officers who engage primarily in CT intelligence-gathering and analysis in support of MI–5's efforts. MI–5 tasks the SBs, and the latter serve as the intelligence community's force multiplier as they are more numerous than MI–5 and know their own communities far better.[4] As MI–5 and the SBs engage primarily in the collection and analysis of intelligence, evidence-based investigations designed to build cases for the prosecution of suspected terrorists are performed nationally by the country's largest police force, the London Metropolitan Police and its Counter Terrorism Command (a.k.a. SO15). The UK thus affords an interesting example of effective coordination between police forces and intelligence agencies.

Underpinning the overall British CT approach is a strategic framework known as CONTEST (Counter Terrorism Strategy) that is based on four workstreams: Pursue, Prevent, Protect, and Prepare. *Pursue* and *Prevent* focus on reducing the threat from terrorism. The *Terrorism Act* and its more recent amendments, as well as other legislation, form part of Pursue, as do information-sharing and cooperation efforts between law enforcement and intelligence agencies, enhanced technical capacities, overseas operations (military and covert), and efforts in the realm of terrorism prosecution and post-prison supervision. Prevent focuses primarily on trying to counter the conditions that may breed homegrown terrorism within the UK, including challenging radical ideologies, increasing the resilience of communities to radicalization, addressing economic and social grievances that extremists attempt to take advantage of, disrupting the activities of radicalizers, and attempts to steer recruits to radical causes away from extremism.

The *Protect* and *Prepare* streams are designed to reduce the UK's vulnerability to attack. Protect focuses on reducing vulnerability to terrorism in the context of critical infrastructures, public places, transportation systems, hazardous materials storage and transport, and border, port, and airport security. Prepare focuses on mitigating the impact of terrorist attacks. This includes a range of policies designed to increase local and regional resilience, enhancing response and recovery efforts to terrorist incidents, and overall crisis management.[5]

Israel, as noted above, employs more of a warfighting approach to its counterterrorism policies. Israel employs wide-ranging emergency legislation, not unlike the British practice in previous years and, indeed, many of Israel's CT emergency laws have their origins in legislation passed by the British Palestine Mandate authorities prior to Israel's independence. The *Defense Regulations* and other Israeli emergency laws give military commanders in the West Bank (those parts of the West Bank not under the control of the Palestinian Authority are governed under military rule, never having been annexed to the State of Israel) and the Minister of Defense in Israel proper, the authority to prohibit meetings, establish curfews, arrest, search, and detain without judicial authorization. These powers have almost never been used within Israel but are regularly used in the West Bank (and were used in the Gaza Strip prior to Israel's withdrawal from that territory in 2005). Israel also employs regular civilian legislation such as the *Penal Law* to prosecute terrorism suspects under ordinary criminal procedures. As with the UK in previous decades, Israel is currently working on normalizing its CT legislation so that it will be of a non-emergency nature and more in keeping with democratic norms. Current Israeli emergency legislation also affords the authorities the right to detain someone for periods of up to six months at a time, subject to the review of a military court within 96 hours of the arrest, under a procedure known as *Administrative Detention*. In addition, Israeli law allows for pre-charge detention of up to twelve days for non-citizens, though only 48 hours for citizens. Detention is conceived of as a measure designed to safeguard investigations and prevent terrorist activity rather than as a measure of punishment, and people held under Administrative Detention are eventually either tried or released.

In terms of CT structures and institutions, Israel, like the UK, has a domestic intelligence and security service, the Israel Security Agency (ISA—a.k.a. *Shabak* or *Shin Bet*). Also, as with the UK, the ISA works hand in hand with the police with respect to the gathering of CT intelligence. There is one national police force in Israel and its personnel assigned to intelligence duties often interface with the ISA; though, in terrorism investigations, the ISA generally runs the investigations, relying considerably less on the police as compared with British practice. As the West Bank is governed under military rule, the ISA works with the Israel Defense Force (IDF), since the military is the law enforcement body for the West Bank while it works with the police in Israel proper (as the military have no law enforcement powers in Israel, with the exception of special situations—more on this later).

As the terrorism threat to Israel comes primarily from outside of its borders (the West Bank and Gaza Strip, Egypt's Sinai Peninsula, or Lebanon) it is easier for Israel to employ more of a warfighting approach and to view the struggle against terrorism as just another form of the endemic Arab-Israeli conflict. Israel's CT policies focus on intelligence-gathering and attempts to thwart terrorist plots before they become attacks. Doing so has been particularly critical as the terrorist threat has morphed, from the mid–1990s on, to one increasingly characterized by suicide bombings. Suicide bombing operations, in particular, need to be thwarted prior to the suicide bomber gaining access to a city because, given the nature of the weapon in question, a suicide bomber is virtually guaranteed to kill innocents once inside an urban area regardless of whether he/she reaches their designated target (and thus potentially killing even more people as the targets were chosen for this purpose). Israel has used large-scale Administrative Detentions, as well as, in a minority of cases, "targeted killings" of terrorist operatives, in order to disrupt terrorism planning and operations. In general, whether Israel, acting in a warfighting mode, is apprehending or killing suspected terrorists, the essence of the Israeli approach revolves around three key assumptions. Firstly, the number of dangerous terrorists is limited, and therefore it is possible to arrest most of them and assassinate those that are not as accessible. This also means that no matter how much rage is produced in Palestinian society as a result of aggressive Israeli counterterrorism policies, this will not translate into more terrorism because very few people possess the resourcefulness and capacity to develop expertise in some area of terrorist operations, and thus to become effective terrorists. In other words, more angry people does not equal more truly dangerous terrorists. Being a truly effective terrorist operative is a fulltime professional enterprise that requires years of training and development and cannot be the preserve of enraged amateurs desperate to strike out at Israel. Those amateurs can and do fill the ranks of the suicide bombers, but the suicide bomber without an organization behind him or her to supply the wherewithal can only be a *potential* suicide bomber. Secondly, not every terrorist has to be neutralized in order for the counterterrorism strategy to be deemed a success. Since terrorists almost always operate as part of complex organizations that involve logistic, internal security, recruitment, leadership, smuggling, bomb-making and other functions, neutralizing key individuals in one or more of these component areas of the organization can severely hobble the organization, at least temporarily. Third and last, over time an unrelenting policy of arrests can severely decrease the effectiveness of the organization, and with most of the leadership in detention lower-level operatives are left demoralized and directionless.[6]

While the UK and Israel stand out as countries having a long history of coping with terrorism, there are also some interesting policing structures and models in use by countries focused more on combatting day-to-day crime.

Canada provides a unique policing model for countries that have federal systems of government. Canada has three tiers of government: federal, provincial, and municipal, and has policing agencies for each tier, though these do not exist uniformly across the country. Unlike the United States, Canada has a federal police agency, the Royal Canadian Mounted Police (RCMP) that engages in specialized, but also run-of-the-mill, policing duties across the country. The RCMP enforces federal laws (many of which relate to smuggling, drug crimes, organized crime, fraud, immigration violations, etc.) but can also enforce provincial laws (most criminal justice legislation is provincial). The RCMP contracts with eight provinces and the country's two territories as well as the majority of the country's towns and cities and, thus, in those areas, provides policing services at the provincial and municipal levels. There are also some 150 municipal police forces, fifty tribal policing agencies, and the provinces of Quebec and Ontario have their own provincial police forces. Canada thus has a rather strange mix of law enforcement agencies but its model allows for a great deal of flexibility in using a national police agency in a variety of contexts.

Japan is arguably the world's pioneer and leader in the use of Community Policing. Community Policing can be defined as a policing approach that focuses on the provision of service to and partnership with a community on the part of law enforcement in order to proactively address public safety issues and create an environment that lessens crime and social disorder. Japan has a national police force, the National Police Agency (NPA), that enforces laws and oversees local prefect and municipal police agencies. The senior officers in these prefectural and municipal police agencies are employees of the NPA and deployed from force to force during the course of their respective careers. Consequently, while Japan has a centralized police structure and force, that centralization is primarily expressed in matters of resources, planning, and the senior command, while there is a considerable degree of decentralization and localization with respect to actual policing functions.[7]

At the heart of Japan's community policing structure are the urban neighborhood police posts (*Koban*) and the village police posts (*Chuzaisho*). Officers assigned to these posts serve as first-responders when crimes or accidents, occur, provide instruction to the local community on prevention of crime and accidents and provide administrative and social services (provide directions to visitors, handle lost and found articles, provide counseling services for residents, etc.). Japanese police are seen as multi-purpose public servants and it is not unusual for them to act as counselors for troubled individuals, couples with marital problems, people with money problems, and parents with rebellious children.[8] Japanese police interface regularly with other governmental organizations and the private sector to decrease the likelihood of criminal activity. Thus, they will lobby for the construction of pedestrian overpasses, request that the sanitation department pick up trash and abandoned items, and ask business owners not to serve children during school hours.[9] Essentially then, a *Koban/Chuzaisho* policeman (there are few such policewomen) is more like a postman than a firefighter, responding to calls and spending most of his time on a daily round consisting of low-key activities.

In criminal matters, Koban officers are tasked with documenting crime scenes and tracking down witnesses but they rarely deal with arrests. Decisions to arrest are usually made at the central police station, where the primary processing of suspects also occurs. Low crime rates in Japan, compared to other developed countries, seem to suggest that this community policing model is successful (though there is some dispute regarding the accuracy of Japanese crime data as, for example, domestic violence crimes are rarely dealt with as a police matter). Moreover, Japanese society is largely collectivist and conformist and the public is expected to cooperate with the police in reporting on irregular behavior. Overall, Japan's system of community policing is seen as a model to be considered, if not emulated, and Japan manages to have a centralized police force that is also able to focus locally and be responsive to local needs.

In a society in which the police play such a visible (and some might say, intrusive) role in daily life, it has been perhaps even more essential to ensure that there are laws in place to restrain police action and safeguard civil liberties. One example of this has been Japan's *Religious Corporation Law,* which was designed to safeguard religious organizations from state interference (such interference and, at times, religious repression, had been ongoing problems prior to the establishment of democracy in Japan in the wake of the Second World War). Under this law, the Japanese authorities were not permitted to investigate religious groups or virtually anything a religious group was doing. This wide-ranging piece of legislation was used as cover by the Japanese cult and terrorist organization *Aum Shinrikyo* and allowed it free rein to plan and execute three sarin gas attacks (the last of which was carried out against the Tokyo Subway in 1995) as well as individual acts of murder. Hence, as the Japanese example shows, intensive law enforcement does not necessarily mean greater security if laws designed to safeguard civil liberties also significantly restrict police authority. Japan too faces the classical trade-off between liberty and security.

In sum, as the above brief examples suggest, there is much to be learned from other countries with respect to their laws, strategies, and structures in the CT and policing realms.

EMERGENCY MANAGEMENT

The United Kingdom has one of the more interesting approaches to emergency management. The UK emergency response strategy is governed by the *Civil Contingencies Act 2004* (CCA). The CCA divides local first-responders into "Category 1" and "Category 2" responders. Category 1 responders are those organizations directly involved on the scene or in treating casualties, and include the local police, fire brigade, ambulance service, local hospitals, and National Health Service bodies responsible for hospital management and public health.[10] Category 2 organizations include agencies not usually directly involved in coping with an emergency but rather in dealing in the aftermath of an incident. These include public utilities (electricity, natural gas, water, sewage, telecommunications, the transport system, airports and sea-ports, etc.) and safety bodies. Category 1 and 2 agencies coordinate their activities and information flow at the local level via Local Resil-ience Forums (LRFs) and Regional Resilience Forums (RRFs). LRFs are geographically-based on police districts and act as the platform for the joint planning of local response agencies—though they do not have command authority over any of the agencies represented. The role of the LRF includes: compiling an agreed-upon risk profile for the area, planning joint approaches and operations on the part of the Cat-egory 1 responders, and developing a common strategic communica-tions policy and common interface policies with the private sector, as well as supporting the preparation of exercises and coordinating their execution.[11]

The strategic approach taken by the British to coping with emer-gency incidents is to handle them, in the first instance, at the local level. If local resources prove inadequate, then local agencies will turn to neighboring agencies for mutual aid. The military can also sometimes be brought in, but, in most cases, this will only be done at the request of local authorities. Only if an incident is so serious that it proves beyond the capacity of local and regional resources will the central government be activated, and then primarily to provide support to local first responders.

In the UK, serious emergency situations requiring central govern-ment resources are ranked on the basis of their level of seriousness (from Level 3 to Level 1). A catastrophic emergency (Level 3) is one with a significant and widespread impact, or potential impact, requir-ing immediate central government direction and possibly the use of emergency powers. This would include attacks of the scope of 9/11, or disasters such as Hurricane Katrina, or the March 2011 Japanese Earthquake and Tsunami. If a Level 3 emergency is declared, the strategic response will be led by a Cabinet Office Civil Contingen-cies Committee (known as COBR—Cabinet Office Briefing Room—after the location in which the committee meets), often with the Prime Minister as the chair. In the case of a serious emergency (Level 2) or significant emergency (Level 1), the role of central government grad-ually diminishes, with central government guidance handled at a lower decision-making echelon than Level 3 incidents and with a con-current increase in regional and local management. In Level 2 crises, the COBR coordination is handled by the Lead Government Depart-ment and Level 1 crises are generally not handled via COBR at all, but rather in the premises of the Lead Government Department.[12] In all of the above cases, the government will appoint a Government Liaison Officer (GLO) to support the police incident commander and act as a single point of contact for central government services. The central government emergency response process in the UK follows the Lead Government Department (LGD) model, wherein one department or devolved administrative unit (such as Scotland) takes overall responsibility for coordinating the central government response. The LGD will be determined by COBR on the basis of the nature of the emergency, the nature and quality of the department's access to information (in terms of whether this department normally works closely with other departments), and the availability of facilities from which to run the operation.[13] For example, in cases of terrorism, the Home Office is the LGD. A Government Liaison Team (GLT) led by a Government Liaison Officer (GLO) will be dispatched to liaise between COBR and the responders at the scene of the event. During an emergency, the LGD will act as a communications and information focal point, facilitate discussion and decision-making among the response organizations, coordinate the provision of information to the media and the public, brief strategic-level decision-makers such as Government Ministers, oversee the process of movement from immediate response to recovery, reconstruction and risk reduction, and, finally, oversee the debriefing process in terms of lessons-learned and the review of existing plans.[14]

The UK also employs a three-tiered approach to dealing with emergencies known as "Gold, Silver, and Bronze." (See Figure 50-1.) These designations have to do with roles in an emergency rather than rank and correspond to strategic, tactical, and operational approaches. The Gold level is strategic and not on-scene, and it focuses on formulating the strategy for dealing with the major incident within each response organization at the senior management level. Gold Command is only used in very large incidents (Level 3 emergencies) to make strategic decisions regarding the deployment of resources, managing populations, providing information, and restoring the status quo. In cases where central government intervention becomes necessary, the Gold Command will act as the primary liaison body with the central government and will be based away from the scene, usually in the offices of the lead governmental department, which becomes the Strategic Coordination Center (SCC). The members of Gold Command act as the Strategic Coordinating Group (SCG) and are usually made up

Figure 50-1

The United
Kingdom's three-
tiered approach
to emergency
management[15]

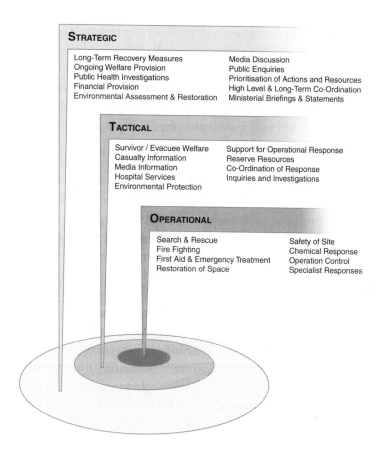

of a nominated senior member from each of the response organizations. The military is also represented at the Gold level via a military
liaison officer, posted to the SCC, who acts as a point of contact for
requests for military aid. The Gold level individual will have control
over the resources of his/her own organization but will delegate the
tactical response to his/her Silver-level counterpart. Gold Command
is responsible for determining the strategic aim of the response, establishing a policy framework for the overall management of the event,
prioritizing the requests from the Silver command, formulating and
implementing strategic communication policies vis-à-vis the media,
and directing operations focusing on the post-event recovery. The
police will normally chair the SCG but control can shift to other agencies depending on the nature of the incident.[16]

The Silver level is tactical and involves control over the incident
scene on behalf of the Silver commander's organization based on the
strategy set by the Gold commander (in cases when the Gold level

has been activated). The Silver commander will not be involved in the actual response activities, but rather will set priorities, plan tasks, and obtain needed resources, and will typically be based at an incident control point near or adjacent to the scene of the event. Silver Command provides Gold Command with feedback and intelligence regarding the event based on information that it gathers, as well as information of relevance to the Gold level received from Bronze Command.[17] The Silver commander is responsible for allocating resources and obtaining additional resources, assessing risk, ensuring the safety of response personnel, and helping determine if there is a need to activate Gold command. Finally, the Bronze commander will be responsible for the operational response in terms of managing the scene based on the tactical guidance provided by his/her Silver counterpart (the Silver commander will be activated, in many cases, at the recommendation of the Bronze commander, though all levels can be activated concurrently). As the police normally act as coordinators of the overall response at the scene, the Bronze police commander will normally focus on establishing cordons, maintaining security, controlling traffic, and generally managing the incident area. The Bronze commander is responsible for assessing the extent of the incident, providing input on helping determine whether additional levels of command (Silver and/or Gold) are needed, obtaining resources, and deciding on which tasks need to be executed. As additional resources arrive, managers will be assigned roles within the Gold, Silver, and Bronze structure.

One of the first roles of the police Bronze commander at a scene is to establish an inner cordon. The boundaries of that cordon will be decided in consultation between the police, fire service, and ambulance service, and those entering or leaving the cordoned area must report to an egress point under the authority of the Bronze commander. The Bronze commander will also set up Forward Control Points (FCP) for each agency and organize regular inter-agency coordination committees.[17]

The UK emergency management structure and approach could not, in total, be applied in the U.S. given the federal structure of the United States. The British model does, however, provide some interesting approaches, particularly in terms of the coordination of agencies and authorities at the national and local levels, and the strategic, operational, and tactical structures put in place during emergencies that might provide some more flexibility to the normally more rigid set of authorities provided to each level of government in the American system.

THE ROLE OF THE MILITARY IN HOMELAND SECURITY

Israel, Italy, France, and Canada provide a wide variety of different examples in the use of the military in support of various homeland security missions. In Israel, the military plays a wide-ranging role in homeland security. This varies from counterterrorism operations in the West Bank and Gaza Strip (as noted previously) to organizing and overseeing national preparedness and response efforts. The Israel Defense Force (IDF) was traditionally seen as fulfilling a role far beyond the function of providing security from external enemies. The military was viewed as a public service and an integrative force for the immigrant nation, and not just an armed force. During different periods of its history, the IDF was involved in agricultural enterprises, immigrant absorption, providing teaching services to disadvantaged communities, and other such public services.[19]

Apart from pitched battles within the country during Israel's War of Independence (May 1948–January 1949), the civilian sector of the country was largely exempted from military attack (though not terrorism) during Israel's first decades. Israel's wars with its Arab neighbors were confined almost exclusively to battlefield and border regions, and consequently the military was focused on defending the borders and fighting wars on enemy soil—in keeping with Israel's forward battle space doctrine that called for fighting and maneuver on enemy soil due to Israel's small size. Civil defense efforts on the part of the military were therefore limited. When Israel signed a peace treaty with its most formidable enemy, Egypt, in 1979, the Arab world effectively lost even the theoretical possibility of defeating Israel through military force because Egypt possessed, far and away, the largest and most effective Arab military force. Defeating Israel on the battlefield without Egyptian participation was therefore thought to be inconceivable. At the same time, the deployment to the Middle East of long range/high payload surface-to-surface missiles gave those local and regional neighbors of Israel that were in a declared or undeclared state of hostilities with it (Syria, Iran, Iraq under Saddam Hussein, and Hizballah in Lebanon) the option of firing missiles at the civilian population as a way of deterring Israel or undermining its war effort in the event of another Middle Eastern war. Somewhat ironically then, Israel's military supremacy on the battlefield brought less security for the civilian population because it made that population the primary target. Israel's civilian population received its first taste of this new reality during the Persian Gulf War of 1991, when Saddam Hussein's forces fired 39 SCUD missiles at Israeli cities. More recently, Israel's adversaries (namely Hizballah and Hamas) have followed the same strategy, using primarily short-range/low payload rockets. In the wake of the 1991 Gulf War, the IDF recognized that the civilian sector had come to be part of the battle space (if not, indeed, the primary battle space) and created a fourth regional command (in addition to the Northern, Central, and Southern Commands), the Home-front Command (HFC). The HFC was created to improve interagency cooperation between the military, first responders, and government ministries; to free the three IDF regional commands to focus exclusively on the frontlines; to provide military resources to the civilian sector (capabilities such as search and rescue, CBRNE detection and response, etc.); and to enable the centralization of response efforts.[20]

The HFC has five operational areas broken down into sub-areas that are geographically aligned to police districts and sub-districts respectively. In the Northern and Southern districts, which border Lebanon and the Gaza Strip respectively, the HFC does not have operational control of its units, but rather they are under the operational control of the commanding officers of the IDF Northern and Southern Commands respectively. The HFC does however have operational control of its units in the other districts. This is because the threats in the north and south of the country are more acute and require all military resources in those areas to be put at the disposal of the IDF regional commanders. The HFC also has direct control over specialist units that deal with non-conventional weapons attacks, urban search and rescue, and civilian casualty identification and management.

In peacetime, the HFC is responsible for establishing emergency procedures, supervising preparedness exercises, and monitoring the preparedness of the health system, municipalities, the transportation system, and critical infrastructures. The HFC also operates national warning systems based on air raid sirens and, as of 2011, on a system that pushes out text messages to all cell phone subscribers. In the past, the HFC also distributed gas masks and atropine injectors to the population, though the Israeli Postal Service is now responsible for this distribution. The HFC is also responsible for the preparedness of first responders within each district and sub-district, though it does not have operational command over these areas during peacetime. During periods in which Israel is facing an active wartime scenario (or potentially, a WMD terrorist attack or other mass casualty event), the Cabinet can declare a "Limited State of Emergency" whereupon the HFC is given command and control over the other response agencies. In 2007, Israel established the National Emergency Management Authority (NEMA) in order to serve as a staff and coordination center for the Ministry of Defense, which oversees the IDF as a whole (including, of course, the HFC). The creation of NEMA added an additional layer to governmental coordination efforts in civil defense and was designed to complement the more direct operational and planning role played by the HFC. The Israeli Government is also in the process of setting up a Ministry for Civil Defense (though this embryonic organization is currently housed within the Ministry of Defense). It remains to be seen however what the precise function and impact of this Ministry will be, as it is unlikely that it will have any direct command authority over the HFC or any of the civilian first responder agencies.

Italy and France employ their respective militaries in the homeland security context in a rather different way than does Israel. In Italy, in addition to the Air Force, Navy, and Army, there is a fourth military branch, the gendarmerie corps (known as the *Arma de Carabinieri*). The majority of *Carabinieri* units are responsible for law enforcement missions and the maintenance of public order, and also focus on specialized law enforcement activities such as fighting organized crime and the drug trade. In addition, the *Carabinieri* conduct military duties such as military police and security tasks as well as oversee policing deployments. They have a hybrid command in that they report to the Minister of the Interior with respect to their law enforcement and public security tasks, and to the military chain of command in the context of their military duties. There are some 5,000 *Carabinieri* stations across the country as well as mobile territorial battalions. Maritime, border policing duties, and customs enforcement are carried out by another force, the Financial Police (*Guardia di Finanza*), which, while under the authority of the Ministry of the Economy and Finance, is also a military force. Even Italy's Forestry Police is a military policing organization and, in fact, the country's National Police, which is the only civilian policing entity, was, until the early 1980s, also a military policing entity. The regular army has also been called out on a number of occasions to provide support for policing as well as disaster response.[21]

In France, the primary law enforcement and public security body in 95 percent of French territory is a military policing force, the *Gendarmerie*

Nationale. The *Gendarmerie* includes naval, helicopter, counterterrorist, riot police, and other specialized units and its mission includes the maintenance of public order, criminal investigations, intelligence-gathering, policing the roads, protecting critical infrastructure targets, responding to WMD attacks, and protecting the country's nuclear weapons (Vaultier, The Military's Role in Homeland Security in France, 2006, pp. 207–208).[22] Interestingly, and for historical reasons, even the role of firefighting is partly militarized. Military units are in charge of the firefighting units in France's two largest cities, Paris and Marseille—with army engineering units responsible for fighting fires in Paris and naval units responsible for fighting fires in Marseille.

In Canada, the military is broken down into the Regular Force and the Reserve Force. The Reserve Force consists of four components, of which three, the Primary Reserve (P Res), the Supplementary Reserve (Sup Res), and the Canadian Rangers play prominent homeland security roles. The army component of the P Res (known as the "Militia") supports regular army forces in crises. The Naval Reserve performs costal security operations that are not part of the mission of the active-duty Navy (Canada does not have a coast guard), including port security and control of shipping. The Naval Reserve operates Canada's twelve coastal defense ships and possesses port security/harbor defense units that can be deployed anywhere in the country. The Supplementary Reserve forces can be called up for periods of limited duration to supplement either the Regular Force or the P Res, and thus can serve in a homeland security capacity. Finally, the Canadian Rangers play what is perhaps the most regular and intensive homeland security role of all the reserve components, as their mission is to provide a military presence in the isolated and sparsely-settled far north of the country—areas that are so isolated that the Regular Force does not operate there.[23] Consequently, the Rangers are often the first responders when these isolated areas experience natural disasters. The Rangers, the majority of whom are volunteers, are formally tasked with reporting unusual activities, collecting data in support of military operations, conducting surveillance and sovereignty patrols, providing local expertise to reserve and regular army units, and providing local assistance to search and rescue activities. Given the geographic isolation of these areas, the Rangers are often the only government representatives in these locales. Beyond the role of the Rangers, after 9/11, the role of reservists in coping with domestic emergencies was enhanced and the government has repeatedly mobilized reservists to deal with weather crises, plane crashes, and other disasters.

As these brief examples show, many democratic countries do not shy away from taking full advantage of their respective militaries' capabilities in order to support, or even guide, the homeland security mission. Thus, the Israeli military plays a wide-ranging role in homeland security, as befitting a small country in which some tasks are simply too big for anyone but the military. Nevertheless, the use of the military to help set the "rules of the game" with respect to preparedness and response allows the creation of a common doctrine that all response agencies must employ, and this assures more consistent preparedness and response. In Italy, France, and even Canada, the military is used, in some ways, in even more day-to-day tasks than in Israel. In these countries, the military is used to carry out regular law enforcement duties or, in other cases, to augment law enforcement and rescue operations. In Canada the military is regularly used for disaster response and frequently serves as the most accessible governmental entity in isolated regions of the country.

CONCLUSION

As illustrated by the above examples, there are a variety of different ways to develop homeland security strategies, structure institutions, promulgate laws, etc. In terms of the ultimate utility of looking at other countries, homeland security policymakers in the United States (or, for that matter, other countries) need to have a full understanding of the laws, institutions, and *modus operandi* of other countries, particularly when those countries may be the source or a transit point for possible homeland security threats. National homeland security strategy, both in the U.S. and elsewhere, will thus be better informed and designed if it can factor in the strengths and weaknesses of other countries With respect to "lessons learned," American and non-American policymakers alike should take advantage of the pool of shared experience in order to fashion more efficient policies. Given the differences in laws, institutions, policies, and cultures, even across democratic countries, effective strategic-level policies will need to be modified when applied in to other countries. That modification will need to take into account these differences, but also look for creative ways to transfer such policies to other national contexts. While differences exist, there is also a surprising degree of commonality once one gets over the variations in terminology and methods of conducting day-to-day business. At the very least, the study of other countries' homeland security policies can lead policymakers to question the assumptions behind their own existing policies or to view those policies in a different light. Clearly constant introspection and evaluation are the hallmarks of relevant, responsive, and effective policymaking.

NOTES

1. Clive Walker, *The Blackstone's Guide to the Anti-Terrorism Legislation* (Oxford: Oxford University Press, 2002), 2–3.

2. *UK Terrorism Act 2006*, Part 1, Section 8.

3. UK Home Office and Northern Ireland Office, *Legislation Against Terrorism: A Consultation Paper* (London: Stationery Office, 1998), http://www.archive.official-documents.co.uk/document/cm41/4178/chap–08a.htm (accessed January 13, 2010).

4. Briefing by British CT Official, January 23, 2008.

5. Prime Minister and Home Secretary, *The United Kingdom's Strategy for Countering International Terrorism* (London: Stationery Office, 2011), 10–14.

6. Avi Dichter and Daniel L. Byman, *Israel's Lessons for Fighting Terrorism and Their Implications for the United States* (Washington, DC: The Saban Center at the Brookings Institution, 2006), 11–12.

7. Philip L. Reichel, *Comparative Criminal Justice Systems: A Topical Approach*, 2nd ed. (Upper Saddle River, NJ: Prentice Hall, 1999), 168.

8. Harry R. Dammer and Erika Fairchild, *Comparative Criminal Justice Systems*, 3rd ed. (Belmont, CA: Wadsworth, 2006), 120.

9. David H. Bayley, *Forces of Order: Policing Modern Japan*, rev. ed. (Berkeley, CA: University of California Press, 1991), 85.

10. *United Kingdom Civil Contingencies Act*, Schedule 1, Part 1, 2004.

11. UK Government, *Emergency Preparedness Guidance on Part 1 of the Civil Contingencies Act 2004, Its Associated Regulations and Non-Statutory Arrangements* (London: Stationery Office, 2005), 11.

12. Paul Cornish, *Domestic Security, Civil Contingencies and Resilience in the United Kingdom: A Guide to Policy* (London: Chatham House, 2007), 15.

13. UK Cabinet Office, *Dealing with Disaster*, 3rd ed. (London: Cabinet Office, 2003), 66.

14. Northern Ireland Central Emergency Planning Unit, *A Guide to Emergency Planning Arrangements in Northern Ireland* (Belfast: Office of the First Minister and Deputy First Minister, 2010), 23–25.

15. Nadav Morag, *Comparative Homeland Security*, figure reprinted with permission of John Wiley & Sons, Inc.

16. UK Ministry of Defense, *Operations in the UK: The Defence Contribution to Resilience* (London: Ministry of Defense, 2007), 10.5.

17. Trevor Pearce and Joyce Fortune, "Command and Control in Policing: A Systems Assessment of the Gold, Silver, and Bronze Structure," *Agency Report* 3, no. 3 (1995): 183.

18. Nadav Morag, *Comparative Homeland Security: Global Lessons* (New York: John Wiley & Sons, 2011), 306–309.

19. Yofi Tirosh, "The Legal Framework for Military Activities in Israel from the Comparative Legal Perspective," *Law and the Military* 17 (2003): 342.

20. Morag, *Comparative Homeland Security*, 212–15.

21. Ibid., 209–10, 227–34.

22. Richard Weitz, *The Reserve Policies of Nations: A Comparative Analysis* (Carlisle, PA: US Army War College, Strategic Studies Institute, 2007), 39.

23. Ibid., 59–61.

51

ISO SECURITY MANAGEMENT STANDARDS

Be prepared—Ensuring security throughout the supply chain

Captain Charles H. Piersall[1]

Chairman of ISO/TC 8, Ships and Marine Technology

INTRODUCTION

As goods move around the world, crossing boundaries through water, air, and land, they are exposed to security threats such as terrorism, piracy, cargo theft, and fraud, as well as natural emergencies, crises, and disasters which can happen at any time, such as, the tsunami and earthquake in Japan or the riots in London. Organizations around the world are increasingly implementing risk management processes to deal with uncertainty and ensure continuity of operations.

More than ever, the topics of security, security management, and safety and security of the supply chain, are riddled with buzzwords sometimes, from sources with no practical experience or understanding of the subject or of what is needed from decision makers. Along with these buzzwords, there are often attempts to create additional layering of management systems, redefining the security regime and imposing additional certification requirements. This approach not only adds confusion, but also unwarranted costs to the industry.

I will therefore begin by clarifying what we mean by "supply chain." The supply chain is not as simple as a single linking of elements in a chain. It is a complex network of multinational interconnected processes and resources that begin with the sourcing of raw materials and end with the delivery of products and services to consumers. It incorporates many links and nodes, which may be tailored to meet the needs of a particular organization or industry, as well as government regulatory requirements. In many cases there will be multiple supply chains differing with participants in multiple contracts for goods and services. *Supply chains* include banks, other sources of finance, insurers, producers, suppliers, manufacturers, distributors, wholesalers, vendors, logistics providers, transporters, regulators, and consumers, to name a few. The supply chain includes facilities, plants, offices, warehouses, and branches, and can be both internal and external to an organization. If we look at this broad understanding, it is easy to see that virtually everyone has a supply chain—from small and large companies down to the individual household shopping for groceries, utilities, and goods.

This clarification of supply chains matters, because today companies and governments need to be able to move product components smoothly across borders. Products are being made in global production chains that span the world. Standards play an important role, because if one component of the product is not of high quality, or is technologically not compatible with the rest, then the final product may itself be undermined. Today very few products are made exclusively in a single country. An International Standard can be seen as an embodiment of the collective know-how of the international community in any particular field. Almost by definition, an international standard is the outcome of multilateral cooperation. Participation in the process itself—or simply the use of the final product—is a form of technology transfer. Again, virtually everyone has a supply chain—companies, governments, and even individuals.

If we look at a "tailored supply chain" definition, which focuses only on those portions of the overall "chain" which match specific areas of responsibility and authority or direct interest, the customs/border protection control chain is the most widely known, understood, and enforced. Their supply chain segment basically starts with packing containers at the point of origin and ends with clearance of Customs at the port of destination.

The World Customs Organization's (WCO) Customs Guidelines on Integrated Supply Chain Management states:

> In the interest of supply chain security and the integrated Customs control chain, in particular to ensure a fully secure movement from packing of the container to its final destination, Customs should apply a seal integrity program as detailed in the revised Guidelines to Chapter 6 of the General Annex to the Revised Kyoto Convention. Such seal integrity programs include procedures for recording the affixing, changing and verification of seal integrity at key points, such as modal change.[2]

ISO'S SOLUTION TO THE SUPPLY CHAIN SECURITY PROBLEM

The International Standards Organisation (ISO) 28000 family of standards provides specifications and guidelines for supply chain security. The ISO 28000 family comprises a series of standards to help organizations successfully plan for and recover from, any disruptive event.

The core standard, ISO 28000:2007, *Specification for security management systems for the supply chain,* serves as an umbrella management system that enhances overall security performance, while reducing financial burden. *ISO 28000 is the only published and certifiable "all hazards" voluntary industry International Security Management Systems Standard for the total supply chain.* It takes a holistic, risk-based approach to managing risks associated with any disruptive incident in the supply chain—before, during, and after the event—and assists the implementer in necessary planning to take appropriate actions to help ensure the supply chain's viability and continued operation. The leadership of any organization has a duty to its stakeholders to plan for the organization's survival.

The management system framework established by ISO 28000 is a generic standard applicable in all sectors, for all size organizations, private or public, and can be used to cover all aspects of security: risk assessment, emergency preparedness, business continuity, sustainability, recovery, resilience, and/or disaster management, whether relating to terrorism, piracy, theft, fraud, earthquakes, or other natural or man-made disruptions.

According to the ISO 28000:2007 standard, risk assessment

> ... shall consider the likelihood of an event and all of its consequences which shall include:
>
> a) physical failure threats and risks...
>
> b) operational threats and risks...
>
> c) natural environmental events (storm, floods, earthquakes, etc.)[3]...
>
> d) factors outside of the organization's control...
>
> e) stakeholder threats and risks such as failure to meet regulatory requirements or damage to reputation or brand...
>
> h) a threat to continuity of operations.[4]

Organizations are realizing more and more that to be resilient, it is not enough to focus on internal processes. If their suppliers are unable to deliver, or customers unable to purchase, the ability of an organization to achieve its objectives would be compromised. As organizations seek assurance that their suppliers, and the extended supply chain in general, have planned for and taken steps to prevent and mitigate the threats and hazards to which they may be exposed, there is a strong demand for standards and best practice.

Organizations may tailor an approach compatible with their existing operating systems. Those who have already adopted a process approach to management systems may be able to use their existing system as a foundation for implementing an ISO 28000 security management system based on ISO 28000. There are two other well known and widely implemented generic certifiable management systems standards—ISO 9001 (Quality Management Systems) and ISO 14001 (Environmental Management Systems). Table 51-1 provides a side-by-side comparison among the sections of the three management standards. ISO 28000 is a risk-based management systems standard, and therefore follows more closely with the risk-based approach of ISO 14001. It also follows the ISO Guide 73 (Risk management—Vocabulary).[5]

Table 51-1

Corresponding Sections of ISO 28000:2007 Compared with ISO 14001:2004 and ISO 9001:2000.

ISO 28000:2007		ISO 14001:2004		ISO 9001:2000	
Supply chain security management system requirements (title only)	4	Environmental management system requirements (title only)	4	Quality management system requirements (title only)	4
General requirements	4.1	General requirements	4.1	General requirements	4.1
Security management policy	4.2	Environmental policy	4.2	Management commitment	5.1
				Quality policy	5.3
				Continual improvement	8.5.1
Security risk assessment and planning (title only)	4.3	Planning (title only)	4.3	Planning (title only)	5.4
Security risk assessment	4.3.1	Environmental aspects	4.3.1	Customer focus	5.2
				Determination of requirements related to the product	7.2.1
				Review of requirements related to the product	7.2.2
Legal, statutory, and other security regulatory requirements	4.3.2	Legal and other requirements	4.3.2	Customer focus	5.2
				Determination of requirements related to the product	7.2.1
Security management objectives	4.3.3	Objectives, targets, and programme(s)	4.3.3	Quality objectives	5.4.1
				Quality management system planning	5.4.2
				Continual improvement	8.5.1
Security management targets	4.3.4	Objectives, targets, and programme(s)	4.3.3	Quality objectives	5.4.1
				Quality management system planning	5.4.2
				Continual improvement	8.5.1
Security management programme(s)	4.3.5	Objectives, targets and programme(s)	4.3.3	Quality objectives	5.4.1
				Quality management system planning	5.4.2
				Continual improvement	8.5.1
Implementation and operation (title only)	4.4	Implementation and operation (title only)	4.4	Product realization (title only)	7
Structure, authority, and responsibilities for security management	4.4.1	Resources, roles, responsibility, and authority	4.4.1	Management commitment	5.1
				Responsibility and authority	5.5.1
				Management representative	5.5.2
				Provision of resources	6.1
				Infrastructure	6.3
Competence, training, and awareness	4.4.2	Competence, training, and awareness	4.4.2	(Human resources) General	6.2.1
				Competence, awareness, and training	6.2.2

(*Continued*)

Table 51-1

Corresponding
Sections of ISO
28000:2007
Compared with ISO
14001:2004 and
ISO 9001:2000.
(*Continued*)

ISO 28000:2007		ISO 14001:2004		ISO 9001:2000	
Communication	4.4.3	Communication	4.4.3	Internal communication	5.5.3
				Customer communication	7.2.3
Documentation	4.4.4	Documentation	4.4.4	(Documentation requirements) General	4.2.1
Document and data control	4.4.5	Control of documents	4.4.5	Control of documents	4.2.3
Operational control	4.4.6	Operational control	4.4.6	Planning of product realization	7.1
				Determination of requirements related to the product	7.2.1
				Review of requirements related to the product	7.2.2
				Design and development planning	7.3.1
				Design and development inputs	7.3.2
				Design and development outputs	7.3.3
				Design and development review	7.3.4
				Design and development verification	7.3.5
				Design and development validation	7.3.6
				Control of design and development changes	7.3.7
				Purchasing process	7.4.1
				Purchasing information	7.4.2
				Verification of purchased product	7.4.3
				Control of production and service provision	7.5.1
				Validation of processes for production and service provision	7.5.2
				Preservation of product	7.5.5
Emergency preparedness, response, and security recovery	4.4.7	Emergency preparedness and response	4.4.7	Control of nonconforming product	8.3
Checking and corrective action (title only)	4.5	Checking (title only)	4.5	Measurement, analysis and improvement **(title only)**	8
Security performance measurement and monitoring	4.5.1	Monitoring and measurement	4.5.1	Control of monitoring and measuring devices	7.6
				General (measurement, analysis, and improvement)	8.1
				Monitoring and measurement of processes	8.2.3

ISO 28000:2007		ISO 14001:2004		ISO 9001:2000	
				Monitoring and measurement of product	8.2.4
				Analysis of data	8.4
System evaluation	4.5.2	Evaluation of compliance	4.5.2	Monitoring and measurement of processes	8.2.3
				Monitoring and measurement of product	8.2.4
Security related failures, incidents, nonconformances, and corrective and preventive action	4.5.3	Nonconformity, corrective action, and preventive action	4.5.3	Control of nonconforming product	8.3
				Analysis of data	8.4
				Corrective action	8.5.2
				Preventive action	8.5.3
Control of records	4.5.4	Control of records	4.5.4	Control of records	4.2.4
Audit	4.5.5	Internal audit	4.5.5	Internal audit	8.2.2
Management review and continual improvement	4.6	Management review	4.6	Management commitment	5.1
				Management review (title only)	5.6
				General	5.6.1
				Review input	5.6.2
				Review output	5.6.3
				Continual improvement	8.5.1

Each of the three systems standards shown in Table 51-1 follow the concept of continuous improvement based on the ISO plan-do-check-act (PDCA) management system methodology:

Plan — establish objectives and make plans (analyze your organization's situation, establish your overall objectives, set your interim targets, and develop plans to achieve them).

Do — implement your plans (do what you planned).

Check — measure your results (measure/monitor how far your actual achievements meet your planned objectives).

Act — correct and improve your plans and how you put them into practice (correct and learn from your mistakes to improve your plans in order to achieve better results next time).

This PDCA process applied to the ISO 28000 Security Management Systems standard, together with ISO 28002 on Resilience, to improve preparedness and resilience is shown in Figure 51-1.

Figure 51-1

Security
management
systems elements
Plan–Do–Check-Act
(PDCA) methodology

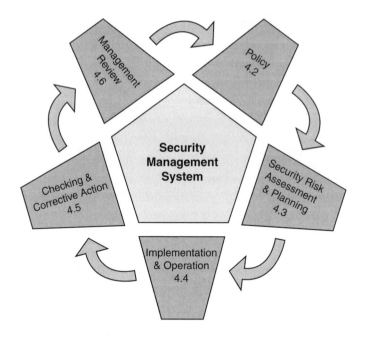

The ISO 28000 family

- **ISO 28000:2007,** *Specification for security management systems for the supply chain*—the overall "umbrella," certifiable, management systems standard for supply chain security.

- **ISO 28001:2007,** *Best practices for implementing supply chain security, assessments and plans*—designed to assist industry in meeting requirements for Authorised Economic Operator (AEO) programme.

- **ISO 28002:2011,** *Development of Resilience in the Supply Chain—Requirements with guidance for use.* This standard provides additional focus on resilience. It supports the strong demand as firms are looking for assurance that their suppliers and the extended supply chain have planned for steps to prevent and mitigate the threats and hazards to which they are exposed. As part of the ISO 28000 management system, the ISO 28002 standard emphasizes the need for an ongoing, interactive process to prevent, respond to, and assure continuation of an organization's core operations after a major disruptive event.

- **ISO 28003:2007,** *Requirements for bodies providing audit and certification of supply chain security management systems*—guidance for accreditation and certification bodies.
- **ISO 28004:2007,** *Guide for implementing ISO 28000*—assists users in implementation.
  - **Additional ISO 28004 parts** were developed subsequent to the publication of the standard in order to provide additional useful guidance.
    - **Part 1**—will renumber the basic published ISO 28004: 2007—Guide for implementing ISO 28000—assist users in implementation(no change in content).
    - **Part 2**—for use in medium and small seaport operations [in support of request from the International Maritime Organization (IMO)].
    - **Part 3**—for specific guidance for small- to—medium-sized enterprises (SMEs) to implement ISO 28000.
    - **Part 4**—for specific guidance for organizations seeking to incorporate requirements contained in ISO 28001 for Authorised Economic Operators. The security best practices contained in ISO 28001 were carefully developed in cooperation with the World Customs Organization (WCO). Published as Publically Available Specification (PAS) in 2010.
- **ISO 28005,** *Electronic port clearance (EPC)*—provides for computer-to-computer data transmission.
  - Handle data related to a ship's clearance into or out of a port, port state controlled area, and related reporting.
  - This standard is consistent with requirements from International Maritime Organization (IMO) and WCO.
  - Based on EU Project MarNIS; IMO Facilitation (FAL) Requirements.
  - XML format employed (allows data to be displayed in many forms).
  - Areas already using XML format: SafeSeaNet (EU Directive), PortNet, United States Coast Guard early Notification Of Arrival and Departure (USCG eNOA/D); Ports in Norway, Singapore, Hong Kong, Sweden, Valparaiso, and some in the USA; United Nations Economic Commission of Europe (UN/ECE).

- Refers to two existing standards: ebXML (Electronic business, ISO/TS15000 series) and MSML (Maritime Safety Markup Language—ISO 22853).

ISO 28005 has been broken into two parts:

1. **ISO 28005-1,** *Implementation of a Maritime Single Window System)* **(Message structures), publication expected in 2012.**
   I.   Establishes the EPC structure and requirements
   II. Promotes the adoption of a single approval message
   III. Will not conflict with existing Custom Authority systems

2. **ISO 28005-2: 2011,** *Core data elements*
   I. Contains the definition of core data elements for use in Electronic Port Clearance (EPC) messages.
   II. Will align with the World Customs Organization V3 guidelines that are currently awaiting approval. Inclusion of the US Customs and Border Protection's 10+2 data elements is under review.

- **ISO 28007 Guidelines and the certification of Private Marine Security Companies (PMSC) providing contracted armed security personnel (PCASP) on board ships (and pro forma contract).**
  As an action relating to piracy and armed robbery against ships taken by the 90th session of the IMO Maritime Safety Committee (MSC 90), the Committee agreed that ISO should be entrusted with the development of a standard for the use of armed guards, as set out in (MSC 90/28) and clearly stated that the IMO did not support self-certification or self-regulation.[6] This high priority item has active support and participation by many flag states, national bodies, as well as Interpol and the European Commission.

- **ISO 20858:2007,** *Ships and marine technology—Maritime port facility security assessments and security plan development* . While not a member of the ISO 28000 family, this standard is closely related regarding security in the maritime sector. It provides for uniform implementation of IMO's International Ship and Port Facility Security (ISPS) Code. ISO 20858 has been used both as a teaching tool and by port facility operators that want to document their full compliance with the IMO's ISPS Code.

WHO'S USING ISO 28000? EXAMPLES OF RECENT, DIVERSE ISO 28000 CERTIFICATIONS

The ISO 28000 series has already experienced considerable success. Numerous businesses and organizations in diverse sectors (e.g., logistics, forwarders, software, transportation (all modes), pharmaceutical, electronics, IT, etc.) are certified or in the process of obtaining certification to ISO 28000 by third-party independent auditors. This section provides a few examples to illustrate the widely diverse industries implementing and certifying to ISO 28000.

DP World was first to certify to ISO 28000. This international system underpins all of DP World's internal and external security initiatives and activities. They have dedicated strategic security resources focused on implementation of their corporate security policy across their entire network of container terminals and have committed to certify ISO 28000 in their more than 60 global marine terminals in 31 countries across six continents. ISO 28000 complements all international security legislative codes at DP World.

- DP World is the only global marine terminal operator to have achieved simultaneous ISO 28000 certification and C-TPAT membership. Its European terminals were certified as Authorised Economic Operators (AEO) by the European Union. Additionally, they also have the largest number of terminals participating in the U.S. anti-terrorist Container Security Initiative (CSI), which screens containers at ports of origin supported by U.S. Customs officers stationed at participating terminals. DP World is a principal partner in the U.S.-led Secure Freight Initiative, and is a partner in the U.S. Mega ports initiative (container scanning program).
- Recent terminal certification examples are:
  - Cochin International Container Transshipment Terminal (ICTT) at Vallarpadam has been certified under the ISO 28000 as the only container terminal in India to be certified in port security.
  - Callao, Peru, the largest and most modern container terminal on the west coast of South America, is the first terminal operator on the South American west coast and only the second company in Peru to earn ISO 28000 certification.
  - Saigon Premier Container Terminal (SPCT) in Ho Chi Minh City, Vietnam, is the first terminal in Vietnam to be certified ISO 28000 compliant.

○ Tarragona, a marine terminal in the Catalan region of northeastern Spain capable of receiving mega ships with a nominal capacity of over 13,800 TEU (twenty foot equivalent container units) was the fortieth DP World facility to certify to ISO 28000. Flemming Dalgaard, Senior Vice President and Managing Director, Europe & Russia, DP World, said:

> This is an important milestone in our programme to achieve ISO 28000 security certification at every one of our network of container terminals across six continents. We regard security as a baseline service for our customers and DP World Tarragona's achievement adds further strength to our global operations. We congratulate DP World Tarragona's management and staff for their commitment and hard work in achieving this important certification.

Oscar Rodriguez, General Manager, DP World Tarragona, said:

> Securing the ISO 28000 certification is the latest of our initiatives to consistently deliver superior services to our customers. DP World Tarragona serves a significant industrial hinterland and provides a crucial gateway and supply chain hub for customers wanting to access the surrounding Catalan region and on to Madrid. In turn, DP World Tarragona connects Spain's vast market to the Mediterranean region and beyond.[7]

Port of Houston Authority, USA, one of the world's largest ports, was the first port authority in the world to become certified to ISO 28000.

YCH Group, Singapore, is the first end-to-end supply chain management company in the world to be certified to ISO 28000. YCH Group is the leading integrated end-to-end supply chain management and logistics partner to some of the world's largest consumer electronics, chemical, and healthcare companies, including Canon, Dell, Moet-Hennessy, ExxonMobil, B. Braun, LVMH, Royal Friesland Campina, and Motorola.

Improvements to supply chain security processes at YCH used to be cyclical and based on scheduled reviews, but now it is a continual process requiring commitment from all departments within YCH. More importantly, YCH CEO, Dr Robert Yap took the lead in driving ISO 28000:2007 implementation across all levels at YCH. Upon receiving the ISO 28000 certification, Dr. Yap commented

> "Entrusting a company to manage your supply chain is akin to depositing money in a bank—our customers entrust us with the security management of their goods and it is an imperative that we are accountable to them. Being the first end-to-end SCM provider to be certified ISO 28000: 2007 is a great affirmation of our commitment to our customers in the region and a testament to our leadership position in the Asia Pacific's logistics industry. This certification will give customers greater peace of mind and reinforce the trust they have in the security management system and measures that we have in place to secure their billions of inventory flowing through our hubs daily.[8]

YCH has an effective security management system that can continually assess its security processes to protect its business interests and ensure compliance to global regulatory requirements. In addition, YCH has also been able to reduce supply chain variability and enhance greater supply chain velocity and visibility. Dr. Lye Wei Moon, Vice President of Operations Excellence at YCH commented:

> As part of our security excellence journey at YCH, we are happy to have received this endorsement for our ongoing efforts to enhance supply chain security. This builds on YCH's foundation of years of security excellence and reinforces the trust that customers have in the security management system that we have implemented at our facilities and in our overall operations.[9]

The benefits gleaned from the ISO 28000: 2007 certification will enable better monitoring of freight flow, aid in combating smuggling, and allow YCH to respond to the threat of piracy and terrorist attacks, as well as to create a safe and secure international supply chain regime.

The standard takes a pragmatic and business-centric approach to risk management as a critical component of effective management. Invariably, the standard also ensures that key business decisions are based on a process of proactive and effective risk assessment.

> Singapore is well known for its excellence in the logistics sector and has maintained [a] leadership position as a logistics and supply chain management nerve centre for the region. As we continue to build on our capabilities, it is extremely encouraging for YCH, a local company, to strengthen its security management capabilities and to achieve the ISO 28000:2007 Specifications for Security Management Systems for the Supply Chain certification. This shows that local companies are aspiring to supply chain management excellence, regionally and globally.[10]

The ISO 28000: 2007 certification has enabled YCH to scale its security management system to manage all of the company's specific security needs in a realistic, sustainable, and cost-effective manner across its network of facilities throughout the Asia–Pacific region. YCH was also the first end-to-end supply chain management provider to be accredited with the Secure Trade Partnership (STP) certification by Singapore Customs.

YCH India is certified to the Transported Asset Protection Association (TAPA) A-class and is ISO 28000-compliant for its security systems. YCH India provides customized supply chain solutions for electronics, consumer goods, chemicals/healthcare, and automotive industries in India. Its clientele includes Dell, ACER, TPV, General Mills, HCL, and others.

TNT Express, Asia regional head office in Singapore is the first express integrator to achieve certification to ISO 28000.

DB Schenker, the world's second-largest forwarder, obtained certification to ISO 28000 for its regional head office for the Asia–Pacific sector in Singapore, along with its local office and operations at Singapore Changi airport. Klaus Eberlin, Chief Operating Officer for Asia-Pacific, views the ISO standard as a "kind of umbrella standard that encompasses elements like the TAPA programmes. ISO 28000 extends beyond physical aspects of security to elements like information flow and financial data."[11]

"Before implementing ISO 28000, we had different security programmes, which were developed based on customer, industry or customs demands," says Mr. Roman Lüth, Director of Dangerous Goods, Security & Safety, Competence Centre Chemicals at DB Schenker Asia Pacific. "ISO 28000 was the missing link in managing all these programmes, and acts as an overarching system to control the different security processes. It also provides a flexible framework that can easily be integrated with other security initiatives such as Singapore's Secure Trade Partnership (STP) or STP-Plus guidelines, Transported Asset Protection Association (TAPA) standards, or Customs-Trade Partnership Against Terrorism (C-TPAT) programmes."

Achieving ISO 28000 certification gave DB Schenker's Asia Pacific operations a clearly recognizable boost in terms of corporate branding, competitiveness, and marketability. "Because this is an internationally-accepted standard for supply chain security, it gives us bigger business opportunities," says Mr. Lüth. "Tenders by multinational companies, for example, are getting more detailed in their requirements for information on security-related issues. With ISO 28000 compliance, we are able to provide such information readily. Furthermore, being ISO 28000 certified gets us more recognition among business partners."

This has brought about many benefits. "Having to carefully analyse each individual step in the system, identify the potential risks, assess how important it was to address each one and take steps to reduce risks in vulnerable areas, helped us to learn a lot and even develop other standards and management systems," says Mr. Lüth. As training and implementation sessions involved the entire company, "we realised that ISO 28000 is an overall approach to supply chain security, one that involves not just Operations, but Finance, Human Resources, and all the other departments." He noted, "We are all now more aware and careful about security risks, which definitely benefits our customers and the company."[12]

Asian Terminals is a port operator, developer, and investor in the Philippines, and the first marine terminal to obtain certification to ISO 28000 in the country.

CTS Logistics–China, a logistics and manufacturing company providing kitting assembly of turnkey management of consumer electronics, IT, and telecommunication products, has successfully implemented ISO 28000.

Banner Plasticard—Philippines, which offers design and printing of cards, personalization, embossing, encoding, thermal printing, wrapping, crating, and palletizing, is certified to ISO 28000.

DHL Express has certified ISO 28000 in Spain. DHL Express is part of the world's leading logistics group, Deutsche Post DHL The express sector is one of the major drivers of global trade and excellently positioned to capitalize on this through services which meet customers' domestic and international transport requirements, anywhere around the world.

Sony Electronics, a leading provider of audio/video electronics and information technology products for the consumer and professional markets, is ISO 28000 certified. Sony has played a key role in the development of Blu-ray, Disc, CD, DVD, and Super Audio CD technologies. The company is noted for a wide range of consumer audio-visual products, high-definition televisions, digital cameras, camcorders, and personal stereos. Sony is an innovator in the IT arena with its personal computers, as well as in high-definition professional broadcast and video equipment.

Ken Wheatley, Senior Vice President, Sony Electronics and the immediate past president of the International Security Management Association, the worldwide organization of Chief Security Officers, talks about the security challenges faced by corporations today and how ISO 28000 can help.

While some organizations have unique threats and vulnerabilities based on their industry or location, the challenges for most are quite similar. Some particular areas of concern are:

- Protecting intellectual property
- Securing IT systems with the growing emergence of cloud computing
- Product counterfeiting
- Financial fraud
- Money laundering
- Business continuity and corporate resilience in the face of earthquakes, tsunamis, floods, fires, political and economic upheaval, terrorist acts
- And, of course, the global supply chain.

With a global economy and just-in-time manufacturing, organizations and countries cannot afford the types of disruption caused by a ship piracy event. If, for example, critical construction materials, parts, or machinery are delayed for weeks or months, without a back-up plan in place, a major infrastructure project in a country can come to a grinding halt, potentially leading to an increase in unemployment.

So standards, like ISO 28000 and ISO 28002 (development of resilience in the supply chain), help companies assess the vulnerabilities in their operations that then lead to designing and building-in the processes and systems necessary to mitigate the impact of an event.[13]

Pantos Logistics, Seoul, Korea, a major air freight company, with 83 offices in 35 countries, has recently certified to ISO 28000.

Professional training for security and other practitioners based on ISO 28000 is also being conducted for both supply chain business operators and customs officers. Each day more companies in a wide variety of sectors are certifying to ISO 28000.

THE ROAD AHEAD

Clearly, the standard is rapidly gaining ground since it was first published in 2007. The reason for this is simple: there is a need for unambiguous international guidance to help tackle the vulnerabilities of the supply chain and world trade in all sectors. ISO 28000 is just that. It is no surprise, therefore, that more and more industries are turning towards ISO 28000. In addition to all of the examples mentioned, there are also additional transportation, pharmaceutical, health care, high tech, and many other global industries and government organizations in the process of implementing and certifying to ISO 28000.

Bankers Exposed to Supply Chain Risk

The banking institutions of the globe are on high alert. Operational risk is beyond the historical threats of fraud and rogue traders. The "new norm," as we say in standardization, covers many other significant business disruptions. On its website, the Basel Committee on Banking Supervision endorses updated principles on how banks should protect themselves from risks not directly linked to lending or market movements. Banks should bolster their defenses against losses that require lenders to hold reserves against risks including natural disasters, computer hacking, malicious software, systems failures, theft, fraud, terrorism, and unauthorized trading.[14]

The Basel Committee states in their "Principles for Sound Management of Operational Risk (Section on Mitigation and Control)" that one of the weak links for banks, or any business, is outsourcing—the use of a third party to perform activities on behalf of the business. Outsourcing can involve transaction processing or business processes. While outsourcing can help manage costs, provide expertise, expand product offerings, and improve services, it also introduces risks that management should address. There are a tremendous number of outsourced services containing inherent risks, from the critical information systems infrastructure in the banking industry to the supply chain risk of the major global firms that the banks themselves are investing in for the continued commerce of the world.

One key aspect of this area of risk has to do with the sense of risk mitigation that usually occurs with a company's use of a "service contract" with a vendor or service provider, which may never be audited or tested to find out how a supplier would respond or behave during a major incident that impacts their particular area of supply chain operations.

How ISO 28000 Can Help Bankers

ISO 28000:2007 specifies the requirements for a security management system, including those aspects critical to security assurance of the supply chain. Security management is linked to many other aspects of business management. Aspects include all activities controlled or influenced by organizations that impact on supply chain security. These other aspects should be considered directly, where and when they have an impact on security management, including transporting these goods along the supply chain. A key companion to the certifiable ISO 28000 is the newly published ISO 28002 on resilience.

In what businesses are major banks major investors? Are these companies ISO 28000 certified to be more business resilient throughout their supply chains?

In giving advice to bankers, it can be stated that regardless of the legal documents agreed upon with suppliers, you can bet that they have their own supply chains where you have not done any due diligence. Can you trust that all of your suppliers have gone down another layer or two to ensure their own survivability for a myriad of risks? Adopting an international management system such as ISO 28000, will help bankers develop planning which is more adaptive to their enterprise and will improve business resilience.

In ISO 28000 and 28002, there is a focus on integrated risk management, continuity of operations, resilience (by confirming that the right resources are in the right place at the right time, despite staff constraints or fluctuating demands for highly skilled talent), regulatory compliance, privacy, and data protection (to help safeguard and manage the organization's most valuable assets: data, information, systems, and people).

Any significant business disruption to the enterprise could be fatal, but if a budget were created to devote resources for security, how would funding be allocated among the topics listed above?

Just as in other businesses, banks should have business resiliency and continuity plans in place to ensure an ability to operate on an ongoing basis and limit losses in the event of severe business disruption. Banks are exposed to disruptive events, some of which may be severe and result in an inability to fulfill some or all of their business obligations. Incidents that damage or render inaccessible the bank's facilities, telecommunication, or information technology infrastructures, or an event that affects human resources, can result in significant financial losses to the bank, as well as broader disruptions to the financial system.

To provide resiliency against this risk, a bank should establish business continuity plans commensurate with the nature, size, and complexity of their operations. Such plans should take into account likely or plausible scenarios to which the bank may be vulnerable.

Continuity management should incorporate business impact analysis, recovery strategies, testing, training, and awareness programs, as well as communication and crisis management programs. A bank should identify critical business operations, key internal and external dependencies, and appropriate resilience levels. Plausible disruptive scenarios should be assessed for their financial, operational, and reputational impact, and the resulting risk assessment should be the foundation for recovery priorities and objectives. A bank should periodically review and test its continuity plans to ensure contingency strategies remain consistent. The Basel Committee states "ISO 28000 is the only published and certifiable international supply chain securitmanagement plan. It may be worth reading."[15]

ISO 28000 SUPPORTS REGIONAL, DOMESTIC, AND SECTOR-SPECIFIC PROGRAMS

World trade currently benefits from several government-to-business supply chain security-related initiatives. Most are customs related;

some are sector specific; some are regional; and some are bilateral agreements. *The U.S. Customs Trade Partnership Against Terrorism (C-TPAT)*[16] was created for companies to improve the security against terrorism of their customs-related supply chains segments. The Authorised Economic Operator (AEO)[17] program enables certain companies to play their part in the SAFE framework of WCO (World Customs Organization).[18]

Although these two programs find their roots in the SAFE framework of standards, the approaches differ. The USA only allows importers to participate in C-TPAT, whereas the European AEO program is open to all operators in the supply chain. The European AEO program also differs in that it has a wider scope, as it encompasses other customs procedures that relate to compliance with all customs legislation, including customs duties.

Each of the generic programs in Figure 51-2 is aimed principally at satisfying Customs and Border Protection requirements. Each of these listed programs is implemented and sustained by individual company or government management systems.

The WCO SAFE framework is part of the future international customs model designed to support secure trade. SAFE sets out a range of standards to guide international customs administrations towards a

Figure 51-2

How ISO 28000 is being used around the world.

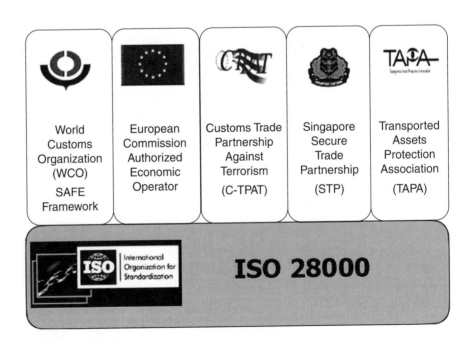

harmonized approach based on customs-to-customs cooperation and customs-to-business partnerships. SAFE is based on four core elements, two pillars, and seventeen standards. The four core elements are:

- Harmonization of the advance electronic cargo information.
- Each country that joins SAFE commits to employing a consistent risk management approach to address security threats.
- On request of the customs administration of the receiving nation, the customs administration of the sending nation will perform an outbound inspection of high-risk containers and cargo.
- Definition of benefits that customs will provide to businesses that meet minimal supply chain security standards and best practices.[19]

AEOs

An AEO is defined as: *"a party involved in the international movement of goods in whatever function that has been approved by or on behalf of a national Customs administration as complying with WCO or equivalent supply chain security standards. Authorised Economic Operators include inter alia manufacturers, importers, exporters, brokers, carriers, consolidators, intermediaries, ports, airports, terminal operators, integrated operators, warehouses and distributors."*[20]

The essence of the AEO concept can be found in the customs-to-business partnerships. Operators can be accredited by customs as AEOs when they prove to have high quality internal processes that will prevent goods in international transport from being tampered with. Standards for this include that the operators will

- Ensure the integrity of the information; i.e., what is said to be in a container really is in the container and nothing else, more, or less
- Ensure the integrity of its employees, that they will not put goods in a container that should not be there
- Secure access to its premises, to prevent unauthorized persons from putting goods in the container

As a result, customs will trust the operator and perform fewer or no inspections on goods imported or exported by or via the AEO. This is of great benefit to the mover of the goods, as goods are available more quickly, resulting in lower transport costs. Customs also benefits, as scarce inspection capacity can be targeted better at cargo of unknown and potentially unsafe operators.

European
Commission
Regulation for
AEO Guidelines
(TAXUD/2006/1450)[21]

- Aim: To provide security of the international supply chain
- Explain the route to achieve AEO status
- Demonstrates internal customs controls and procedures are efficient and compliant
- Results in reduced interventions and delay

Table 51-2

AEO Alignments with
ISO 28000

AEO "Risks"	ISO 28000 "Requirements"
Compliance (I.2.2.1)	Policy (4.2)
Internal control systems (I.2.3.3)	Risk assessment (4.3.1)
Flow of goods (I.2.3.4)	Legal requirements (4.3.2)
Information security (I.2.3.7)	Security objectives (4.3.3)
Physical security (I.2.5.3)	People competence (4.4.4)
Cargo units (I.2.5.4)	Document and data control (4.4.5)
Logistical processes (I.2.5.6)	Operational controls (4.4.6)
Incoming/storage of goods (I.2.5.7/8)	Emergency preparedness (4.4.7)
Production/loading of goods (I.2.5.9/10)	Corrective actions (4.5.3)
Security requirements – partners (I.2.5.11)	Audits (4.5.5)
Personnel security (I.2.5.12)	Management review (4.6)

WCO and the European Union have acknowledged the benefit of ISO 28000 as a "stepping stone" to AEO Certification. Table 51-2 shows the alignment between the sections of the two documents.

U.S. C-TPAT

C-TPAT is a voluntary U.S. government–business initiative to build cooperative relationships that strengthen and improve overall international supply chain and border security against terrorism. U.S. Customs and willing members of the trade community collaborate to better secure the international supply chain to the United States in support of the homeland security mission. The initiative serves to insure that C-TPAT partners improve the security of their supply chains pursuant to C-TPAT security criteria while providing incentives and benefits to include expedited processing of C-TPAT shipments to C-TPAT partners. The initiative encompasses

- Security systems and procedures
- Physical inspections

- Access controls
- Education training and awareness
- Review performance of service providers
- Maintenance of comprehensive records

TAPA[22]

TAPA provides a forum of about 600 companies that unites global manufacturers, logistics providers, freight carriers, law enforcement agencies, and other stakeholders with the common aim of reducing losses from international supply chains.

The transportation of high value, high risk, and / or high demand cargo has become a challenge for industry due to the rapid increase in cargo theft. These goods have become prime targets of thieves in the distribution network when stored in warehouses and in transit.

While government programs such as C-TPAT focus on keeping dangerous items out of the supply chain, TAPA focuses mainly on the issue of theft. But because the concerns are interrelated, TAPA and government agencies work together in confronting these challenges. TAPA consists of three regional branches:

1. TAPA EMEA (Europe, Middle East, and Africa)
2. TAPA AMERICAS
3. TAPA APAC (Asia Pacific)

TAPA FSR (Freight Security Requirements) Certification

One method to ensure the security of the goods in an organization's supply chain is by implementing the TAPA Freight Security Requirements (FSR). Businesses storing high-value goods such as pharmaceuticals, clothing, tobacco, retail, and high-tech equipment in warehouses and distribution centers implement this standard to safeguard those warehouses, as well as those of their transportation providers. TAPA certification assessment includes an audit of elements across an organization, such as, access control, employee checks, perimeter security, intrusion security devices, monitoring systems, high-value storage areas, and transit delays. The TAPA audit process will also look for any areas of concern in warehouses, distribution centers, and consolidation facilities, as well as helping organizations to specify minimum security measures for drivers.

TAPA TSR (Trucking Security Requirements) Certification

Trucking Security Requirements (TSR) have been established to address the nature by which high-tech products and materials are transported by road. The TSR specifies the minimum acceptable security standards for assets traveling throughout the supply chain and the methods to be used in maintaining those standards. In contradiction to the FSR, TSR is a compliance program and is carried out by a self-assessment program. The TSR outlines the processes and specifications for suppliers to attain TAPA compliance to the TSR on their transport operations. It is the intention of TAPA members to select suppliers which meet or exceed TAPA TSR compliance requirements. Successful implementation of the TSR is dependent upon suppliers and buyers working in concert to accurately interpret, adopt, and audit against these requirements.

TAPA PSR (Parking Security Requirements) Certification

The standards for secure parking are to have an auditable security level and to promote secure parking to support protecting valuable goods and drivers during transport on the road.

TACSS (TAPA Air Cargo Security Standards) Certification

The tenth anniversary of 9/11 reminded everyone involved in aviation of the importance of security measures. The air cargo supply chain is a complex process with goods passing through many hands. Around the world, there has been a demand for more extensive screening of cargo goods prior to allowing them on board aircraft. Better measures are needed, from initial security checks at the departure station until the moment that goods leave the aircraft.

TACSS is the first security standard that has been developed specifically for air cargo. The program is based on a risk assessment model which ensures the implementation of appropriate levels of security. It sets out a set of stringent requirements that integrates specific security equipment with equally strict procedural rules. It is based on a risk assessment to ensure implementation of the right level of security. It addresses secure screening and verification of cargo goods being transported to identify any explosives in a shipment, and enhances data intelligence in the supply chain to improve the screening and security flow.

STP (Singapore Secure Trade Partnership): Boosting Supply Chain Security with ISO 28000[23]

The ISO 28000 Security Management Systems for the Supply Chain standard is applicable to businesses of all sizes. Be it in manufacturing, service, storage or transportation, any company that wishes to establish a security management system can implement ISO 28000 and seek certification with an accredited third party certification body.

With a well-managed security program in place, companies can expect improvements such as better inventory management, reduction in loss through theft, improved supply chain visibility, and business resilience with reduced supply risk. In turn, all this translates into a better business reputation.

ISO 28000 also complements other government and international customs security initiatives, including Singapore's Secure Trade Partnership (STP). While the ISO 28000 standard specifies the requirements for implementation of a security management system, the STP guidelines spell out the operational and process requirements which companies in the supply chain should adopt to enhance security.

To help companies implement ISO 28000, a project under the Standards Implementation for Productivity (SIP) initiative was developed. Led by the Singapore Manufacturers' Federation, seven companies in four industry clusters took part in the project, which ran from June 2009 through October 2009. The companies cut across the manufacturing, logistics, trading, and services industries. Under the project, companies have to review their supply chain framework and risk profiles and implement the proposed improvements.

IMO ISPS Code (International Maritime Sector— Government Specific)

The International Maritime Organization (IMO)[24] International Ship and Port Facility Security Code (ISPS Code) is a comprehensive set of measures to enhance the security of ships and port facilities, developed in response to the perceived threats to ships and port facilities in the wake of the 9/11 attacks in the United States. The ISPS Code is implemented through chapter XI–2 Special measures to enhance maritime security in the International Convention for the Safety of Life at Sea (SOLAS), 1974. The Code has two parts, one mandatory and one recommendatory.

In essence, the Code takes the approach that ensuring the security of ships and port facilities is a risk management activity and that, to determine what security measures are appropriate, an assessment of the risks must be made in each particular case. The purpose of the Code is to provide a standardized, consistent framework for evaluating risk, enabling governments to offset changes in threat with changes in vulnerability for ships and port facilities through determination of appropriate security levels and corresponding security measures. Most countries around the world implement and enforce the ISPS Code and companies track and monitor the integrity of cargo containers moving around the world using technologies such as RFID and GPS.

Mutual Recognition and Support

The ISO 28000 series indeed assists in implementing governmental and international customs agency security initiatives, including the World Customs Organization's Framework of Standards to Secure and Facilitate Global Trade, the EU Authorised Economic Operators Programme, the U.S. Customs Trade Partnership against Terrorism, and the Singapore Secure Trade Partnership. The ISO 28000 likewise supports the Industry Transported Assets Protection Program. The ISPS Code industry implementation is supported by ISO standards, but as it is sector specific it is not shown in Figure 51-2.

Most members of WCO have acceded to the SAFE framework and it can be expected that the majority of customs administrations will introduce AEO or similar programs. The importance of coordinated, similar, programs lies in the fact that the ultimate goal is to get all national programs mutually recognized, meaning that AEO accreditations have the same value everywhere. As a result, customs-driven secure supply chains can be established, as all parts of the chain from origin (place of packing of the container) to destination (place of unpacking of the container) are deemed to be safe, albeit under different AEO programs. This would greatly facilitate customs concerns for global trade and would also facilitate support. Customs will also recognize AEOs' compliance with other intergovernmental security requirements, such as IMO and ICAO, as constituting compliance with the applicable customs-identified best practices.

International trade accreditation schemes that many airlines and shipping companies are likely to hold and that match AEO certification include: an internationally recognized security and/or safety certificate issued on the basis of international conventions; a relevant International Standard of the International Organisation for Standardization, in particular ISO 28000 and ISO 9001, although others may also apply; a European Standard of the European Standards Organisations; and other internationally recognized security and/or safety certificates issued by organizations such as the Transported Asset Protection Association.

Example European
Commission
(EC) Regulations
Supporting ISO
28000

- **EC TAXUD/2006/1450—*AUTHORISED ECONOMIC OPERATORS GUIDELINES*[25]** *states* "The legislation ensures automatic recognition of safety and security standards for Regulated Agents. As laid down in Article 14k(3) of CCIP, security & safety criteria shall also be deemed to me met if the applicant, established in the Community ... is the holder of any of the following: ... an International Standard of the International Organisation for Standardisation ... "

- **EC No 1875/2006 of 18 December 2006**, under TITLE IIA "AUTHORISED ECONOMIC OPERATORS"; *CHAPTER 1 Procedure for granting the certificates,* Section 3, Conditions and criteria for granting the AEO certificate, *Article 14k, section 1 states* "If the applicant, established in the Community, is the holder of an internationally recognised security and/or safety certificate issued on the basis of international conventions, of a European security and/or safety certificate issued on the basis of Community legislation, of an International Standard of the International Organisation for Standardisation, or of a European Standard of the European Standards Organisations, the criteria provided for in paragraph 1 shall be deemed to be met to the extent that the criteria for issuing these certificates are identical or correspond to those laid down in this Regulation."

- **EC No 73/2010 of 26 January 2010**, laying down requirements on the quality of aeronautical data and aeronautical information for the single European sky *Article 2:*

  1. This Regulation shall apply to EATMN (European air traffic management network) systems, their constituents and associated procedures involved in the origination, production, storage, handling, processing, transfer and distribution of aeronautical data and aeronautical information;
  2. This Regulation shall apply to the following parties: (a) air navigation service providers;

(b) operators of those aerodromes and heliports, for which IFR or Special-VFR procedures have been published in national aeronautical information publications;
(c) public or private entities providing, for the purposes of this Regulation:
(i)   services for the origination and provision of survey data;
(ii) procedure design services;
(iii) electronic terrain data;
(iv) electronic obstacle data.

3. This Regulation shall apply up to the point where the aeronautical data and/or aeronautical information are delivered by the aeronautical information service provider to the next intended user, defined: (a) in the case of distribution by physical means, as the point after which the aeronautical data and/or aeronautical information has been delivered to the organisation responsible for providing the physical distribution service; (b) in the case of automatic distribution through the use of a direct electronic connection between the aeronautical information service provider and the entity receiving the aeronautical data and/or aeronautical information, as either:

   – the point after which the next intended user accesses and extracts aeronautical data and/or aeronautical information held by the aeronautical information service provider, or;

   – the point after which the aeronautical data and/or aeronautical information is delivered, by the aeronautical information service provider, into the next intended user's system.

- **ANNEX VII, Quality, safety and security management requirements referred to in Article 10, Part C: Security Management Objectives**[26]
  1. The security management objectives shall be:
     - to ensure the security of aeronautical data aeronautical information received, produced or otherwise employed so that it is protected from interference and access to it is restricted only to those authorised;
     - to ensure that the security management measures of an organization meet appropriate national or international requirements for critical infrastructure and business continuity, and international standards for security management, including the ISO standards referred to in Annex III points (22) and (23).
  2. Regarding the ISO standards, the relevant certificate issued by an appropriately accredited organisation, shall be considered as a sufficient means of compliance. The parties referred to in Article 2(2) shall accept the disclosure of the documentation related to the certification to the national supervisory authority upon the latter's request."
- **Annex III, Point 23**: International Organisation for Standardisation, ISO 28000:2007: – Specification for security management systems for the supply Chain. It is noteworthy that EC No 73/2010 prescribes the use of ISO 28000 for aviation – single European sky!

AUDIT, ACCREDITATION, AND CERTIFICATION

ISO 28000, as mentioned, is a generic ISO management systems standard. Two other ISO management systems standards that are universally known are ISO 9001 (Quality Management) and ISO 14001 (Environmental Management). One of the significant attributes of an ISO management systems standard is the requirement for auditing the system. ISO 28000 requires that the organization shall establish, document, implement, maintain, and continually improve an effective security management system for identifying security threats, assessing risks, and controlling and mitigating their consequences. The organization will establish an audit program and shall insure that audits of the security management system are carried out at planned intervals, in order to:

a) determine whether or not the security management system:
  1) conforms to planned arrangements for security management and resilience;
  2) has been properly implemented and maintained;
  3) is (are) effective in meeting the organization's security management policy and objectives;
b) review the results of previous audits and the actions taken to rectify non-conformances;
c) provide information on the results of audits to management;
d) verify that the security equipment and personnel are appropriately deployed.

The audit program, including any schedule, shall be based on the results of threat and risk assessments of the organization's activities, and the results of previous audits. The audit procedures shall cover the scope, frequency, methodologies, and competencies, as well as the responsibilities and requirements for conducting audits and reporting results. Where an organization chooses to outsource any process that affects conformity with these requirements, the organization shall ensure that such processes are controlled. The necessary controls and responsibilities of such outsourced processes shall be identified within the security management system. Where possible, audits shall be conducted by personnel independent of those having direct responsibility for the activity being examined. Organizations using ISO management systems standards may (1) make a self-determination and self-declaration of conformity or (2) seek certification/registration of conformity by an accredited independent third party organization.

Recognizing the fact that any disruption within the supply chain may have impact resulting in disruption throughout the chain, and that consequences may be grave, government regulatory requirements as well as the necessity of avoiding disruption to trade are demanding necessary insurances of integrity, security, safety, and resilience to recover and maintain continuity of operations. Thus, to gain acceptance and to have confidence in adequacy of security policy, planning, and execution in an organization the use of independent accredited third party auditing and certification is the norm. In other words: "trust, but verify." It is highly recommended that the third party should be "accredited." Anyone can give you a certification, but how good is it? What is the knowledge and reputation of the certifier? It's all about "brand name" as several senior industry executives have stated. There must be confidence in the quality of the certification.

It is important to note that not all whom profess to be qualified auditing firms are accredited. Who did the accreditation of the certification bodies? How well trained are the auditing personnel? Remember, your certification is only as good as the reputation of the certifier and how they were accredited!

INTERNATIONAL ACCREDITATION FORUM (IAF)[27]

Accreditation is the independent evaluation of conformity assessment bodies against recognized standards to ensure their impartiality and competence. Through the application of national and international standards, government, procurers, and consumers can have confidence in the calibration and test results, inspection reports and certifications provided. The IAF, in consultation with ISO, uses the ISO/IEC 17021:2011 (Conformity Assessment) as the principal standard in this process.

Accreditation bodies are established in many countries with the primary purpose of ensuring that conformity assessment bodies are subject to oversight by an authoritative body.

Accreditation bodies, which have been evaluated by peers as competent, sign arrangements that enhance the acceptance of products and services across national borders, thereby creating a framework to support international trade through the removal of technical barriers. These arrangements are managed by the International Accreditation Forum (IAF) in the fields of management systems, products, services, personnel and other similar programs of conformity assessment, and the International Laboratory Accreditation Cooperation (ILAC), in the field of laboratory and inspection accreditation. Both organizations, ILAC and IAF work together and coordinate their efforts to enhance the accreditation and the conformity assessment worldwide.

Role of IAF

The primary purpose of IAF is twofold. First, to ensure that its accreditation body members only accredit bodies that are competent to do the work they undertake and are not subject to conflicts of interest. The second purpose of the IAF is to establish mutual recognition arrangements, known as Multilateral Recognition Arrangements (MLA), between its accreditation body members, which reduces risk to business and its customers by ensuring that an accredited certificate may be relied upon anywhere in the world.

The MLA contributes to the freedom of world trade by eliminating technical barriers to trade. IAF works to find the most effective way of achieving a single system that will allow companies with an accredited conformity assessment certificate in one part of the world to have that certificate recognized elsewhere in the world. The objective of the MLA is that it will cover all accreditation bodies in all countries in the world.

IAF Membership

Accreditation body membership of IAF is open to organizations that conduct and administer programs by which they accredit bodies for certification/registration of quality systems, products, services, personnel, and/or environmental management systems of similar programs of conformity assessment.

These organizations must declare their intention to join the IAF Multilateral Recognition Agreement (MLA), recognizing the equivalence of other members' accreditations to their own. IAF Association Members are organizations or associations that represent a similar group of entities internationally or within an economy or region. These entities are associated with programs by IAF Accreditation Body Members supporting IAF objectives.

IAF Members may grant Special Recognition status to organizations that share a common objective with the Corporation. Organizations granted Special Recognition status may be represented and participate at any IAF Members meeting[28] but are not eligible to vote. Special Recognition status may also be granted to regional groupings where the implementation of the IAF's multilateral recognition arrangement is promoted. Therefore, regional groups of Accreditation Bodies that operate a Regional Multilateral Recognition Arrangement based upon the equivalence of accreditations to IAF MLA, are eligible for Special Recognition status in IAF. For example, in the U.S., the organization is ANAB (ANSI–ASQ National Accreditation Board); in the UK, it is UKAS (United Kingdom Accreditation Service).

Integrated Audits

Integrated audits eliminate the duplication of work by synergizing several standards into one management system and save time and money by having systems simultaneously audited against multiple standards. The integrated solutions approach was established to provide customers with maximum output for minimum input. As standards tend to share certain common requirements and management principles, there is an inevitable overlap. By selecting multiple services from an accredited certifier, however, you can rest assured that wherever possible audits will be conducted simultaneously, saving you time and money. Integrated management systems are suitable for all kind of organizations. They are highly effective for management strategy, as well as for companies seeking continuous improvement and growth. A single system that integrates the operation of two or more management systems is not only an effective way to acquire additional ISO certification or to use the current certification to meet more than one standard, but it's also an efficient tool for strengthening your organization. Simultaneous auditing of two or more management systems is the first step on the path to achieving a fully integrated management system.

Potential benefits obtained from a single system that integrates the operation of two or more management systems are: internal streamlining; consistency with company policy, management system goals and targets, and stakeholder expectations; elimination of duplication among internal audits for improved business efficiency; audit efficiency; only one audit per year; reduced auditing time for common elements and personnel; shorter compliance time for each division; cost efficiency; reduction in audit man-days leads to reduced costs; and lower costs due to higher overall performance feedback.

CONCLUSION

The benefits gleaned from the ISO 28000: 2007 certification will enable organizations to better plan in advance for disruptions to their supply chains and to establish necessary procedures for resilience, recovery, and continuity of essential operations after a disruptive event occurs, regardless of its origin—terrorism, piracy, cargo theft, fraud, natural emergencies, crises, disasters, accidents, etc. Certification provides the essential framework to assist organizations of all sizes, in all sectors, across all borders by any mode of transport to develop their prioritized total supply chain security management plan that looks both upstream (starting with raw materials and financing) and downstream (ending with the final consumer).

The ISO 28000 standard, coupled with the supportive ISO 28002, takes a pragmatic and business-centric approach to risk management as a critical component of effective management. Invariably, the ISO 28000 also ensures that key business decisions are based on a process of proactive and effective risk assessment.

The ISO 28000 family of supporting standards offers additional assistance and guidance for specific applications; such as, requirements for auditors and certifiers, small-to-medium business applications, and small ports; obtaining AEO certification; uniform industry implementation of regulatory requirements, and the like. These standards have additionally proven to be indispensable to those conducting supply chain security training and education programs.

There are many regional or other supply chain security standards which cover the specific range of the supply chain as viewed by customs authorities' responsibilities. The supportive relationships between the most widely known of these and the ISO 28000 has been discussed. European Union Directives and regulations which reference the ISO supply chain security standards have been presented for ready reference.

The importance of third party independent certification for ISO 28000 to provide confidence and assurance of credible implementation in an organization has been discussed. What is most important, however, is not just getting a certificate—it is all about brand name, Thus, the formal international accreditation process has been highlighted to focus on accredited certifiers and auditors.

Another critical ingredient to a successful supply chain security management program is training, at all levels—in the organization, for auditors, and for government personnel. There are many organizations engaging in supply chain security training, and training for ISO 28000 in particular. Again, be selective in your decision—pick a "brand name" and be sure you understand the qualifications and experience of their instructors.

Decide at what levels in your organization you want instructors from an external source and at what organizational level you want to train internally. A well-trained staff on developing and implementing your plan will be crucial. You will need expert advice, but you cannot simply "contract out" your security management.

Recognizing the financial and resource costs associated with certifying as well as the maintenance of the certification, the concept of integrated audits was introduced in this chapter as a means of taking full advantage of management systems already accredited within an organization. Coordinating and integrating these plans together with the supply chain security and resilience planning in the ISO 28000 series may well be the best cost–benefit approach within an organization.

To provide the reader with an appreciation of the range and depth of organizations across many sectors, a number of distinguished examples have been cited, together with a limited discussion relevant to each case.

Finally, the job is not done! There are additional critical security issues which are under development as additions to the ISO 28000 family. For example, anti-piracy standards determining criteria for: contractor acceptance/selection for armed security guards in ports andarmed guards on board ships; design features for anti-piracy in new ships, modifications of existing fleets, or suggested guidance for change in operating plans and procedures. Additionally, security issues which may develop as the Arctic region accommodates changes in transport routes will need to be addressed.

RESOURCES AND SUGGESTED READING

CAPT. Charles Piersall, "All hazards risk management approach to supply chain security—the ISO 28000 series," ANSI Homeland Security Standards Panel 10th Annual Plenary Meeting, Arlington, VA, 2011–11–09.

CAPT. Charles Piersall, "Be prepared—Ensuring security and resilience throughout the supply chain," Special Report, ISO *Focus+*, February 2011.

CAPT. Charles Piersall, "Supply Chain Security Management Update—ISO 28000 Series," Organization for Security and Cooperation in Europe (OSCE), Counter Terrorism Network Newsletter, Special Bulletin, Vienna, Austria 26 July 2010.

DP World Press Release—"New milestone for DP World as Spanish Terminal wins ISO 28000 certification," published January 15, 2012.

"Ensuring Security in and Facilitating International Trade, ISO 28000 Series Standards Update," IMO Facilitation Committee document FAL37/8/3 submitted by ISO, July 2011.

E. E. Mitropoulos, Secretary General IMO, "Guest View," ISO Focus, January 2005.

Michel Danet, Secretary General WCO, "Guest View," ISO Focus, October 2007.

"ISO 28000 Training for Women Port Managers," World Scene, ISO Focus+, February 2012.

ISO Press Release—"New suite of ISO supply chain management standards to reduce risks of terrorism, piracy and fraud," 2007-10-25.

ISO Press Release—"Are you ready? New ISO standard for ensuring resilience throughout the supply chain," 2011–08–18.

Ornulf Rodseth, Head of Norway Delegation to ISO/TC8, Marintek, SINTEF, "Development of an e-Navigation strategy implementation plan," ISO comment on IMO Navigation Subcommittee-NAV57/6, May 2011.

Paul Lightburn, Manager Intermodal Products LRQA, "ISO Supply chain security standards," Presentation to Chartered Institute of Logistics and Transport (UK), 2011.

NOTES

1. Captain Charles H. Piersall has been Chairman of ISO/TC 8, Ships and marine technology, for 17 years. He coordinates ISO's efforts on supply chain security. He is a retired U.S. Navy Captain with over 56 years of distinguished maritime service and industry leadership—first as a senior naval officer and then as an industry executive. He is recognized worldwide as a leader in the field of international maritime and supply chain security standards. In addition to the highest military awards and honors, Capt. Piersall has received numerous high-level awards for his contributions to international standardization including the ANSI Astin-Polk International Standards Medal. and the US Coast Guard's Distinguished Public Service Award. Under his leadership, ISO/TC 8 received ISO's highest award—the Lawrence D. Eicher Leadership Award.

2. www.wcoomd.org/files/1 … /safe … /safe_package_II.pdf, accessed August 10, 2012.

3. While the chance of an earthquake in one location may be small, the chance of an earthquake impacting your supply chain is substantially higher. Even a low probability threat can have consequences. Though millions of people may never experience an earthquake, each year there are about 18 earthquakes of magnitude 7.0 or larger worldwide—their impact can be considerable.

4. ISO 28000:2007(E), *Specification for security management systems for the supply chain*, Section 4.3.

5. ISO 28000:2007, Annex A.

6. IMO MSC90/28.

7. www.spct.vn (2011).

8. www.ych.com (2008).

9. Ibid.

10. Remarks made by Mr. Teo Nam Kuan, Group Director of Quality & Standards for SPRING (an agency under the Ministry of Trade and Industry responsible for helping Singapore enterprises grow and building trust in Singapore products and services). As the enterprise development agency, SPRING works with partners to help enterprises in financing, capability and management development, technology and innovation, and access to markets. As the national standards and accreditation body, SPRING develops and promotes an internationally-recognized standards and quality assurance infrastructure. SPRING also oversees the safety of general consumer goods in Singapore.

11. *SPRINGnews* July 2011.

12. Ibid.

13. ISO *Focus+* November/December 2011.

14. www.bis.org/bcbs, accessed August 10, 2012.

15. www.bis.org/publ/bcbs 195;pdf accessed August 10, 2012.

16. http://www.cbp.gov/xp/cgov/trade/cargo security/ctpat, accessed August 10, 2012.

17. http://ec.europa.eu/taxation customs/customs/policy issues/customs security/aeo/index en.htm, accessed August 10, 2012.

18. www.osce.org/atu. "OSCE CTN Newsletter Speciall Bulletin Enhancing Container and Supply Chain Security, July 2012."

19. http://ec.europa.eu/taxation customs/customs/policy issues/customs security/aeo/index en.htm, accessed August 10, 2012.

20. Ibid.

21. CAPT. Charles Piersall, "ISO Supply Chain Security Standards—Current Status," OSCE Workshop Integrated Approach to Supply Chain Security for the Mediterranean Region, Valletta, MALTA, 2009-12-16.

22. http://www.tapaemea.com/about-tapa/tapa-worldwide.html.

23. *World Customs Journal*, volume 1, number 2, september 2007.

24. www.imo.org.

25. CAPT. Charles Piersall, "ISO Supply Chain Security Standards—Current Status," OSCE Workshop Integrated Approach to Supply Chain Security for the Mediterranean Region, Valletta, MALTA, 2009-12-16.

26. http://eur-lex.europa.eu/LexUriServ/LexUriServ.do?uri=OJ:L:2010:023:0006:01:EN:HTM.

27. www.iaf.nu.

28. www.iaf.nu/articles/IAF_Membership_/33.

52

WHY FUKUSHIMA WAS PREVENTABLE

James M. Acton and Mark Hibbs

Reprinted with permission by the publisher, from **Why Fukushima Was Preventable**, *by James M. Acton and Mark Hibbs (Washington, D.C.; Carnegie Endowment for International Peace, 2012).* *www.carnegieendowment.org*

Public sentiment in many states has turned against nuclear energy following the March 2011 accident at Japan's Fukushima Daiichi Nuclear Power Station. The large quantity of radioactive material released has caused significant human suffering and rendered large stretches of land uninhabitable. The cleanup operation will take decades and may cost hundreds of billions of dollars.

The Fukushima accident was, however, preventable. Had the plant's owner, Tokyo Electric Power Company (TEPCO), and Japan's regulator, the Nuclear and Industrial Safety Agency (NISA), followed international best practices and standards, it is conceivable that they would have predicted the possibility of the plant being struck by a massive tsunami. The plant would have withstood the tsunami had its design previously been upgraded in accordance with state-of-the-art safety approaches.

The methods used by TEPCO and NISA to assess the risk from tsunamis lagged behind international standards in at least three important respects:

- Insufficient attention was paid to evidence of large tsunamis inundating the region surrounding the plant about once every thousand years.
- Computer modeling of the tsunami threat was inadequate. Most importantly, preliminary simulations conducted in 2008

that suggested the tsunami risk to the plant had been seriously underestimated were not followed up and were only reported to NISA on March 7, 2011.

- NISA failed to review simulations conducted by TEPCO and to foster the development of appropriate computer modeling tools.

At the time of the accident, critical safety systems in nuclear power plants in some countries, especially in European states, were—as a matter of course—much better protected than in Japan. Following a flooding incident at Blayais Nuclear Power Plant in France in 1999, European countries significantly enhanced their plants' defenses against extreme external events. Japanese operators were aware of this experience, and TEPCO could and should have upgraded Fukushima Daiichi.

Steps that could have prevented a major accident in the event that the plant was inundated by a massive tsunami, such as the one that struck the plant in March 2011, include:

- Protecting emergency power supplies, including diesel generators and batteries, by moving them to higher ground or by placing them in watertight bunkers;
- Establishing watertight connections between emergency power supplies and key safety systems; and
- Enhancing the protection of seawater pumps (which were used to transfer heat from the plant to the ocean and to cool diesel generators) and/or constructing a backup means to dissipate heat.

Though there is no single reason for TEPCO and NISA's failure to follow international best practices and standards, a number of potential underlying causes can be identified. NISA lacked independence from both the government agencies responsible for promoting nuclear power and also from industry. In the Japanese nuclear industry, there has been a focus on seismic safety to the exclusion of other possible risks. Bureaucratic and professional stovepiping made nuclear officials unwilling to take advice from experts outside of the field. Those nuclear professionals also may have failed to effectively utilize local knowledge. And, perhaps most importantly, many believed that a severe accident was simply impossible.

In the final analysis, the Fukushima accident does not reveal a previously unknown fatal flaw associated with nuclear power. Rather, it underscores the importance of periodically reevaluating plant safety in light of dynamic external threats and of evolving best practices, as well as the need for an effective regulator to oversee this process.

INTRODUCTION

The accident at Fukushima Daiichi Nuclear Power Station on March 11, 2011, has put safety concerns front and center of the ever-contentious debate about nuclear energy. With large quantities of radioactivity released into the environment, over three hundred thousand residents evacuated from the vicinity of the plants,[1] and a cleanup operation that will take decades and cost tens, if not hundreds of billions of dollars, critics have argued that nuclear power is too dangerous to be acceptable. But are they right? Can nuclear power be made significantly safer? The answer depends in no small part on whether nuclear power plants are inherently susceptible to uncommon but extreme external events or whether it is possible to predict such hazards and defend against them.

To date, there have been three severe accidents at civilian nuclear power plants. Two of these led to significant releases of radiation, which averages out to about one major release every seven thousand five hundred years of reactor operation. The International Atomic Energy Agency's (IAEA's) International Nuclear Safety Group believes that if best practices are implemented, major releases of radiation from existing nuclear power plants should occur about fifteen times less frequently.[2] Indeed, improvement on this scale is probably necessary for nuclear power to gain widespread social and political acceptance.

It is clear that the two major nuclear accidents before Fukushima—Chernobyl in 1986 and Three Mile Island in 1979 (which involved extensive damage to nuclear fuel but a relatively small release of radiation)—were preventable. In each case the cause was inadequate operator training and flaws in reactor design, exacerbated by inadequate understanding of potential risks. Better training and better design (areas in which the global nuclear industry has made significant strides) should prevent a recurrence of similar events.

By contrast, the Fukushima accident—superficially at least—appears to be very different. The plant was hit by a massive earthquake and then a tsunami, triggering a chain of events that led to fuel melting and a significant off-site release of radiation. The accident has reinforced public sentiment worldwide—from Japan to Switzerland, and Germany to India—that nuclear power is unacceptably risky.

One year after the Fukushima accident, however, a picture is emerging that suggests that the calamity was not simply an "act of god" that could not be defended against. There is a growing body of evidence that suggests the accident was the result of failures in regulation and nuclear plant design and that both were lagging behind international best practices and standards. Had these been heeded and applied, the risks to the Fukushima Daiichi Nuclear Power Station would likely have been recognized and effective steps to prevent a major accident could have been taken. In this sense, we believe the Fukushima accident—like its predecessors—was preventable.

THE ACCIDENT SEQUENCE

On March 11, 2011, at 2:46 pm local time, Japan was struck by a magnitude 9.0 earthquake, centered in the Pacific Ocean about 80 kilometers east of the city of Sendai, that set a powerful tsunami in motion.[3] This was the largest earthquake ever recorded in Japan and, according to the United States Geological Survey, the fourth largest recorded worldwide since 1900.[4]

Three of the six reactor units at Fukushima Daiichi Nuclear Power Station (units 1, 2, and 3) were operating at the time and are shown schematically in figure 52-1.

Figure 52-1

Highly simplified schematic diagram of a boiling water reactor defining key terms used in this report. Many important components, including those for converting steam to electricity, are not shown. Not drawn to scale.

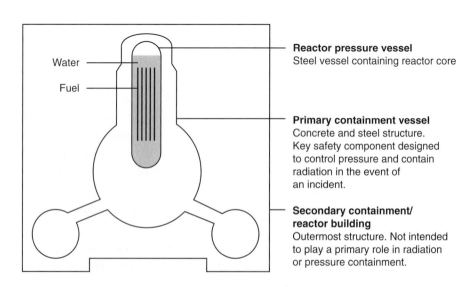

Water

Fuel

Reactor pressure vessel
Steel vessel containing reactor core

Primary containment vessel
Concrete and steel structure. Key safety component designed to control pressure and contain radiation in the event of an incident.

Secondary containment/ reactor building
Outermost structure. Not intended to play a primary role in radiation or pressure containment.

When the earthquake hit, these units automatically "scrammed," that is, control rods were inserted into the reactor cores to suppress nuclear fission. Nonetheless, the reactors still required cooling—as all reactors do immediately after shutdown, since the highly radioactive material accumulated during operation continues to decay and produce heat.

With the reactor shut down and the plant no longer generating electricity, the post-shutdown cooling systems at the Fukushima Daiichi reactors, like at all currently operating power reactors, required an alternative electricity supply (although there was one system in each reactor that did have limited functionality in the absence of a power supply).[5] Because all six external power lines from Japan's grid to the plant were destroyed by the earthquake, the on-site emergency diesel generators began operating. With electricity still available, cooling appeared to proceed normally in units 2 and 3 before the tsunami arrived. In unit 1, for reasons that are not yet known, the temperature and pressure of the core dropped unexpectedly quickly. In order to avoid damage to the reactor vessel and in keeping with the plant's operating procedure, operators turned the emergency cooling system on and off repeatedly to slow the rate of cooling. The system happened to be disabled at the time all electrical power to the plant was lost following the tsunami.[6] Had it been operating, the subsequent accident sequence may have unfolded more slowly at unit 1.[7]

About forty-five minutes after the earthquake, the station was inundated by a series of tsunami waves that caused serious damage. Eleven of the twelve emergency diesel generators in service at the time failed (one connected to unit 6 worked) as they required water cooling, which was no longer possible because the tsunami had destroyed the sea water pumps. This resulted in the complete loss of AC power from both internal and external sources for units 1–5, a situation that is known as a station blackout. The plants were equipped with DC batteries to compensate for the station blackout; however, the batteries in units 1 and 2 were flooded and rendered inoperable. The batteries in unit 3 continued to function for about thirty hours—far beyond their eight-hour design life. In addition, the power distribution buses that would have allowed an external power source to be connected to the plant were also swamped and extensively damaged.[8] The seawater pumps and their motors, which were responsible for transferring heat extracted from the reactor cores to the ocean (the so-called "ultimate heat sink") and also for cooling most of the emergency diesel generators, were built at a lower elevation than the reactor buildings. They were flooded and completely destroyed. Thus, even if electricity had been available to drive the emergency cooling systems, there would have been no way of dissipating the heat.

Over the next three days, one by one, the three reactors that had been operating when the earthquake struck lost core cooling capability, resulting in a loss of coolant accident: without cooling, the water in the reactor pressure vessels boiled, uncovering the fuel, which subsequently melted. In this situation, there was a risk that the "corium" (the molten mix of fuel and reactor components) could burn through the steel reactor pressure vessel and the concrete and steel primary containment vessel into the earth below, thus increasing the likely quantity of radiation released into the environment. Simulations by the plant's owner, Tokyo Electric Power Company (TEPCO), performed with extremely conservative assumptions, suggest that even in the absolute worst case where corium burned through the reactor pressure vessels in all three of the damaged units at Fukushima Daiichi, it would not have completely penetrated the containment (although in unit 1 it could have come within 37 centimeters, or 15 inches, of the outer steel lining).[9] Other simulations suggest that although fuel may have melted and collected at the base of the pressure vessel, it did not burn through.[10] It bears emphasizing, however, that the exact extent of the damage will only be known when the pressure vessels and primary containments can be observed directly, several years from now.

A large quantity of radioactivity from the damaged fuel escaped into the environment. As cooling water evaporated and turned into steam, pressure inside the primary containment grew, creating leaks that allowed radiation to escape. More radiation was deliberately released when, after some delays, workers "vented" the containments to try to reduce the internal pressure. Yet more radiation was released by a series of explosions that occurred in the reactor buildings of units 1, 3, and 4 in the four days following the tsunami. As the reactors overheated and the fuel melted, highly flammable hydrogen was generated (mostly by a reaction between steam and zirconium "cladding" that surrounds the fuel). It built up in the reactor buildings of units 1 and 3 before eventually exploding. Hydrogen may also have caused an explosion in unit 4 after it migrated there from unit 3 along their common venting system.[11]

In its June 2011 report to the IAEA explaining the accident, the Japanese government estimated that the quantity of radiation released into the atmosphere by the accident was about 15 percent of the radiation released from Chernobyl. That accident resulted in the permanent evacuation of over 200,000 people and is ultimately likely to result in thousands of "excess" cancer cases.[12] For many days, Soviet authorities were unable to prevent the uninterrupted release of large amounts of radiation after a severe explosion inside the reactor core directly exposed its burning fuel to the environment. By contrast, at Fukushima considerably more of the fuel inventory in the cores was contained, and Japanese authorities were able to far more quickly and effectively limit the accident's impact to human health. In any case, the quantity of radiation released by the Fukushima accident has proved controversial and estimates may change as more information becomes available. A much smaller quantity of radiation was released into the Pacific Ocean, most of it in the form of overflow of contaminated water that had been used to cool the reactors.

On December 16, 2011, Japanese officials announced that the plant had been brought into a state of "cold shutdown." This declaration attracted criticism from some reactor safety experts on the grounds that it gives the false impression that the damaged Fukushima Daiichi units now pose no more risk than any undamaged reactor after shutdown. While there is certainly some truth to this criticism, the declaration is reasonable if it is understood to be a judgment call on the part of the plant's owner and officials that the remains of the plant cores are now being stably cooled, that radioactive emissions have been brought down to near acceptable levels, and that, barring an unforeseen accident, the status quo can be maintained indefinitely.

Nonetheless, complete remediation of the site is likely to take three or four decades, and the biggest challenge will probably be removing all the melted fuel. The road to complete recovery will be an extremely long and expensive one.

IDENTIFYING KEY QUESTIONS

There is still much to be learned about the accident sequence, including the actions of the plant operators to mitigate it. In contrast to the report by an IAEA fact-finding mission (which was highly complimentary of the plant operators), an interim report by a commission appointed by the Japanese government to investigate the accident expressed direct and significant criticism of plant operators in units 1 and 3 for delays in implementing emergency cooling procedures.[13] The commission, however, stopped short of asserting that a swifter response would have prevented the explosions in those units, withholding judgment until more information becomes available. The actions of the operators will undoubtedly come under considerable scrutiny in the months ahead. In assessing these actions, it is necessary to keep two points in mind.

First, the accident progressed extremely quickly. The table below shows estimates, by both the Japanese regulator, the Nuclear and Industrial Safety Agency (NISA), and TEPCO of the length of time that passed after the earthquake until (i) fuel became exposed, (ii) fuel started to melt, and (iii) molten fuel started to damage the reactor pressure vessels. At unit 1, it appears that the emergency cooling system became inoperative immediately after the tsunami and fuel damage began two or three hours later (that is, three or four hours after the earthquake).[14] However, the operators were flying blind for much of that time. All instrumentation in the main control room of units 1 and 2 was lost following the tsunami, and it was almost three hours before some instrumentation had been restored and the operators had reason to suppose that

Table 52-1

The Accident's Quick Progression

		Fuel Assemblies Exposed	Fuel Assemblies Damaged	Reactor Pressure Vessel Damaged
Unit 1	NISA	2	3	5
	TEPCO	3	4	15
Unit 2	NISA	75	77	80
	TEPCO	75	77	109
Unit 3	NISA	41	44	79
	TEPCO	40	42	66

Approximate Time After Earthquake (in Hours)

Note: NISA's and TEPCO's estimates of the time after the earthquake at which (i) fuel became exposed, (ii) fuel was damaged, and (iii) molten fuel started to damage the reactor pressure vessel for each of the three units at Fukushima Daiichi Nuclear Power Station that were in operation at the time of the accident.
Source: The Federation of Electric Power Companies of Japan (FEPC), "Update to Information Sheet Regarding the Tohoku Earthquake," June 10, 2011, available at http://michelekearneynuclearwire.blogspot.com/2011/06/fepc-update-toinformation-sheet_10.html.

the emergency cooling system had failed.[15] By the time operators could reasonably have known there was a problem, fuel damage was already imminent.

The accident progressed somewhat more slowly in units 2 and 3. The emergency cooling systems in those units failed after about seventy and thirty-five hours, respectively, and in each case fuel damage began about seven or eight hours later (that is, about seventy-seven and forty-three hours, respectively, after the earthquake).[16]

Second, the conditions at the plant site confronting plant operators were truly appalling. The IAEA report notes:

> [d]uring the initial response, work was conducted in extremely poor conditions, with uncovered manholes and cracks and depressions in the ground. Work at night was conducted in the dark. There were many obstacles blocking access to the road such as debris from the tsunami and rubble that was produced by the explosions that occurred in Units 1, 3 and 4. All work was conducted with respirators and protective clothing and mostly in high radiation fields.[17]

To regain instrumentation, operators had to scour the plant for cables and batteries (including from their own cars) that they hooked up to the control panel (in the dark in one case—there was no lighting on unit 2's side of the control room it shared with unit 1).[18] Communication between the on-site emergency control center and each control room was limited to a single wired telephone line. The off-site nuclear emergency response headquarters had to be evacuated because it was so underprepared.[19] The periodic explosions at the site were not just dangerous but also hampered relief efforts. For instance, a cable and a hose that had been laid to supply power and water to unit 2 were destroyed by fragments from the explosion in unit 1.[20] Finally, workers must have been under extraordinary physical and psychological stress. Indeed, during the early stages of the accident, many of them would not have known whether their families had survived the disasters.

These two observations have important implications for assessing the Fukushima Daiichi accident. Given the short time that might be available for operators to take action in the event of a station blackout and the extraordinary stress under which they are likely to be working, actions to be taken after an extreme external event and measures to prevent fuel damage must be prepared in advance, must have been practiced extensively, and must rely only on local resources if they are to have a realistic chance of success. None of these criteria was met at Fukushima Daiichi.[21]

As a result, we believe it would be unfair to apportion significant blame for the accident on the actions the operators took (or failed to take) after the tsunami, as the official investigation committee has done. Furthermore, given the potential challenges of a complete loss of AC power, it is clear that prevention is the best form of management. To this end, the key questions raised by the accident are why was the tsunami hazard at Fukushima Daiichi so dramatically underestimated? And could changes in plant design (resulting from effective safety reviews) have prevented a severe accident in the event that a tsunami struck the plant? The answers to these questions help shed light on whether the accident could have been prevented.

UNDERESTIMATING THE THREAT

The Fukushima Daiichi Nuclear Power Station was not designed to withstand a tsunami even half the size of the one that ultimately struck the Japanese coast in March 2011.

According to the official licensing documents, Fukushima Daiichi's design basis tsunami was estimated to have a maximum height of 3.1 meters above mean sea level.[22] Given this, TEPCO decided to locate the seawater intake buildings at 4 meters above sea level and the main plant buildings at the top of a slope 10 meters above sea level (figure 52-2).[23] In 2002, on the basis of a new methodology for assessing tsunami safety developed by the Japan Society of Civil Engineers, TEPCO voluntarily reevaluated the tsunami hazard and adopted a revised design-basis tsunami height of 5.7 meters. Yet, NISA neither updated the licensing documents to reflect this change nor reviewed TEPCO's analysis. Given that the revised design-basis tsunami was now 1.4 meters above the seawater pumps, such a review should have been conducted.[24]

The maximum height of the tsunami that actually hit the plant is not known exactly since the sea-level gauge at the plant was destroyed. However, TEPCO and the Japan Society of Civil Engineers, using computer modeling to re-create the observed pattern of flooding at

Figure 52-2

Simplified cross-section through one of the reactors at Fukushima Daiichi showing the approximate location of critical components damaged by the tsunami. Not drawn to scale.

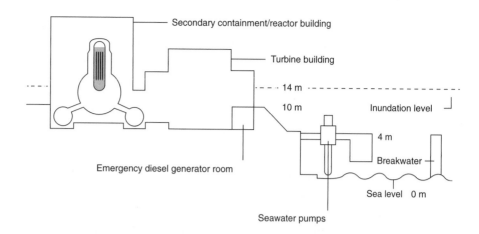

the plant, have estimated that just before it made landfall, the tsunami had a height of 13.1 meters, over twice the revised design basis.[25] Once the tsunami had "run up" the slope on which the main buildings of the plant sit, it reached 14–15 meters above sea level in many areas and, in a few places, more than 17 meters.[26]

The size of the tsunami at Fukushima Daiichi was the result of a number of factors conspiring together. A tsunami actually consists of a series of waves. In this case, more than about 10 kilometers from the coast, the largest of these had a height of only about 6 meters. However, as it approached the shoreline, earlier waves reflected from the land "reinforced" it (an effect properly known as "constructive interference"), ultimately producing a tsunami of over 13 meters.[27] This phenomenon dramatically increased the tsunami height in the vicinity of the plant. (For comparison, at Fukushima Daiini Nuclear Power Station, about 12 kilometers south of Fukushima Daiichi, the tsunami height was 9 meters.[28] At Iwaki, about 40 kilometers south of Fukushima Daiichi, it was only 1 meter.[29]) Although this effect was well understood and had been predicted in advance, the height of the tsunami was underestimated because simulations assumed a considerably smaller earthquake than the one that actually struck on March 11.

The earthquake that preceded the tsunami exceeded the seismic design basis of the plant at units 2, 3, and 5.[30] TEPCO and NISA have stated that no critical safety-related equipment—such as emergency diesel generators, seawater pumps, and cooling systems—was damaged in the earthquake, although it seems that this claim cannot be conclusively verified until the plant can be inspected much more closely than is currently possible.[31] Though the tsunami led to most—if not all—of the damage, the underestimation of the seismic hazard provides evidence of systemic problems in disaster prediction and management.

PREDICTING DISASTER

Because the underlying geophysical phenomena are extremely complicated, accurate hazard assessment for earthquakes and tsunamis is exceedingly challenging. But it is becoming increasingly evident that there were significant flaws in the methodology used to assess hazards to the Fukushima Daiichi plant.

An earthquake offshore of the Miyagi region, where the epicenter of the March 11 earthquake was located, had been long anticipated.[32] For example, as recently as January 11, 2011, the Headquarters for Earthquake Research Promotion (a Japanese government–funded organization set up after the 1995 Kobe earthquake to improve seismic modeling) repeated a long-standing prediction that in that region there was a 99 percent probability of a magnitude 7.5 earthquake within thirty years.[33] But when the earthquake actually arrived, its magnitude caught seismologists by surprise. The Great East Japan Earthquake on March 11, 2011, was actually a magnitude 9.0 event. This significant underestimation, in spite of Japan's considerable investments in seismology, is a sobering warning against overconfidence in hazard prediction.

Indeed, even within the last fifteen years, there are a number of other examples of beyond-design-basis earthquakes and floods at nuclear plants. In December 1999, for example, a storm surge caused flooding at two reactors at the Blayais Nuclear Power Plant in France. The Indian Ocean tsunami of December 26, 2004, flooded seawater pumps at the Madras Atomic Power Station in India.[34] On July 16, 2007, an earthquake exceeded the design basis of TEPCO's Kashiwazaki-Kariwa Nuclear Power Station in Niigata Prefecture. Just five and a half months after the Fukushima accident, on August 23, 2011, an earthquake on the East Coast of the United States marginally exceeded the design basis of the North Anna Nuclear Generating Station in Virginia.[35] This series of events illustrates how difficult hazard prediction is. However, the fact that all operating units were brought successfully into cold shutdown suggests that, for most beyond-design-basis events, plant safety margins are probably sufficient to compensate for this difficulty.

Notwithstanding the intrinsic difficulties of hazard prediction, the approach to hazard prediction for Fukushima Daiichi appears to have been at variance, in three important areas, with both international best practices and, in some cases, with Japanese best practices.

First, there appears to have been insufficient attention given by TEPCO and NISA to historical evidence of large earthquakes and tsunamis. Best practice, as promulgated by the IAEA, requires the collection of data on prehistorical and historical earthquakes and tsunamis in the region of a nuclear power plant in order to protect the plant against rare extreme seismic events that may occur only once every ten thousand years.[36] Historical data was used in assessing plant safety. The original design-basis tsunami for Fukushima Daiichi of 3.1 meters was chosen because a 1960 earthquake off the coast of Chile created a tsunami of that height on the Fukushima coast.[37] However, greater attention should have been paid to evidence from further back in history. Over the last decade or so, evidence of much larger tsunamis in and around Miyagi has emerged. Japanese researchers have discovered layers of sediment that appear to have been deposited by tsunamis and have concluded that the region had been inundated by massive tsunamis about once every one thousand years.[38] They have attributed the most recent of these events—in 869 AD—to a magnitude 8.3 earthquake. More generally, given the historical record of tsunamis in Japan, TEPCO and NISA should have been much more conservative in defining the design-basis tsunami. For instance, one compilation of historical tsunamis in and around Japan lists twelve events since 1498 having a maximum amplitude of more than 10 meters, six of which had a maximum amplitude of over 20 meters.[39]

Of course, such "red flags" are much easier to spot with the benefit of hindsight than they are ahead of a disaster. The challenge of sifting through and evaluating the stream of potentially relevant geophysical studies to extract data important to nuclear power plant safety should not be underestimated. Perhaps not surprisingly, there has been a fairly bitter debate within Japan about whether academia did not provide suitable warnings or whether it did and industry and regulators ignored them. Nonetheless, Japan has a historical legacy of severe tsunamis; it does appear that heeding this record, especially as it relates to the area around the plant, would have led to an upward revision of the design basis for Fukushima Daiichi Nuclear Power Station and perhaps consequently to infrastructural improvements to better defend the installation.

Second, there appear to have been deficiencies in tsunami modeling procedures, resulting in an insufficient margin of safety at Fukushima Daiichi. A nuclear power plant built on a slope by the sea must be designed so that it is not damaged as a tsunami runs up the slope. In 2002, the Japan Society of Civil Engineers developed a detailed methodology for determining the maximum run-up of a tsunami.[40] This methodology prompted TEPCO, voluntarily, to revise the design-basis tsunami at Fukushima Daiichi from 3.1 meters to 5.7 meters. However, in at least one important respect, TEPCO does not appear to have implemented the relevant procedures in full.

In keeping with international best practices, the Japan Society of Civil Engineers methodology requires computer modeling based on detailed site-specific data.[41] Yet, a report by the IAEA prepared following its expert mission to Japan from May 25 to June 2, 2011, notes that "[i]t seems also that [TEPCO's] calculation of the run up have [sic] not considered the specific and detailed arrangements of plant layout."[42] In other words, TEPCO's simulations to determine how far above sea level a tsunami would reach were inadequate.

Moreover, whatever calculation TEPCO did perform seems questionable. During its mission to Japan the IAEA was told by TEPCO that, according to its calculations, a 5.7 meter tsunami would not run up "significantly" above that height. However, preliminary results from a 2008 study by TEPCO (that was not reported to the IAEA and is discussed further below) reportedly indicated that a 9 meter tsunami could have a run-up of over 15 meters.[43] Indeed, on March 11, a 9 meter tsunami did flood the neighboring Fukushima Daiini Nuclear Power Station, which is built on a 12 meter slope.[44] These observations raise important questions about whether even a 5.7 meter tsunami (like the one TEPCO believed the plant could withstand) would have caused serious damage to Fukushima Daiichi Nuclear Power Station. Given that such a tsunami might have run up higher than anticipated, it is possible it could have damaged vulnerable low-lying components such as the seawater pumps.

Improved modeling of tsunami run-up—had it been heeded— might have provided information that could have prompted TEPCO to take mitigating action in advance of the accident on March 11, even if that modeling had assumed a smaller tsunami than the one that actually inundated the plant. Specifically, it would probably have warned TEPCO that its tsunami defenses were inadequate. Enhanced defenses would have widened safety margins at the plant and might have mitigated the consequences of a tsunami that was larger than the plant was designed to withstand.

Not only did TEPCO not implement the Japan Society of Civil Engineers methodology in full, but the methodology itself is flawed because it focuses exclusively on evaluating run-up on the grounds that "other phenomena are less important than that of the water level."[45] "Other phenomena," which include the hydrodynamic force of the tsunami and the effects of any debris and sediment it may be carrying, can cause extensive damage to a nuclear power plant. International best practices, as promulgated by the IAEA, requires such phenomena to be considered, as does the U.S. Nuclear Regulatory Commission.[46] The failure to consider them at Fukushima may have given plant operators a false sense of the safety margins at the plant in the event of a beyond-design-basis tsunami.

To be fair, it appears that there were no suitable tools available in Japan for TEPCO to analyze the full range of effects of a tsunami. But given the prevalence of tsunamis in Japan, NISA should have encouraged the development of such instruments in keeping with international standards.

Since the IAEA mission it has emerged that, in 2008, TEPCO did in fact perform some preliminary computer modeling that tentatively suggested the tsunami hazard to the plant had been severely underestimated.[47] TEPCO stated that, at the time, it was not convinced of the simulations' reliability and intended to pursue them further in collaboration with the Japan Society of Civil Engineers.[48] This follow-up appears not to have taken place. TEPCO informed NISA of its results only three years later on March 7, 2011.

These simulations assumed a repeat of the 869 AD earthquake.[49] Because this event was larger than the earthquake on which previous simulations were based, the resulting tsunami was predicted to be higher. Given the new simulations were based on an actual historical earthquake, they should have been followed up on immediately. Had the results been verified, TEPCO may have been able to take corrective action in time to avert the disaster of March 11, 2011.

Further evidence of NISA's insufficiently conservative strategy for assessing safety margins comes from its approach to seismic safety. Following the 2006 publication of new earthquake safety guidelines and the 2007 earthquake that affected the Kashiwazaki-Kariwa station, the seismic design basis for all Japanese nuclear power plants was reevaluated and at some, including Fukushima Daiichi, it was increased. Under a process known as back checking, no work was required at plants—including Fukushima—that already met the revised guidelines. The problem with this approach is that it narrows margins of safety and could lead to "cliff edge" effects in the event of a beyond-design-basis earthquake. Indeed, there was clearly some concern about this problem among Japanese utilities. For instance, when Chubu Electric Power Company chose to expand the seismic design basis for its Hamaoka Nuclear Power Plant (actually prior to 2006), it did undertake physical improvements at the plant, even though they were not required under the back-checking process, in order to widen safety margins and hence mitigate the consequences of a beyond-design-basis earthquake.[50]

Third, a fundamental principle of nuclear safety is the existence of an effective and independent regulator to set safety rules and to ensure compliance with them. Japan's regulators, however, appear to have been inattentive to tsunami risks. NISA's guidelines for reviewing nuclear power plant safety were set by a separate body, the Nuclear Safety Commission (the two bodies will be merged as part of an ongoing regulatory reform). Remarkably, the basic guidelines, *The Regulatory Guide for Reviewing Safety Design of Light Water Nuclear Power Reactor Facilities* (last updated in 1990), do not mention tsunami safety specifically. The issue is captured only by a catch-all clause about ensuring safety in the event of "other postulated natural phenomena than [an] earthquake."[51] An official methodology to assess tsunami safety was only developed as late as 2002, and tsunami safety was finally mentioned explicitly for the first time in a 2006 revision to a specific guide dealing with seismic safety.

By contrast, computer modeling of tsunami safety was called for as early as the first IAEA guide on flooding hazards at coastal nuclear power plants published in 1983.[52] (And indeed utilities, including TEPCO, had carried out such studies even before then.[53]) Moreover, the Japan Society of Civil Engineers' methodology that was developed in 2002 appears to have been employed solely by Japanese utilities and not by NISA's technical support agency, the Japan Nuclear Energy Safety Organization, for review purposes.

A senior NISA official has confirmed to us that NISA neither "commissioned nor reviewed" numerical studies of tsunami run-up at

Fukushima Daiichi.[54] NISA's failure to update the licensing documents for the plant when TEPCO voluntarily changed the design-basis tsunami from 3.1 to 5.7 meters is yet more evidence of its inattention to tsunami safety. In short, NISA appears to have failed in its responsibilities to review compliance with tsunami safety standards and also to update them in light of both emerging new evidence and evolving international standards.

Had international standards and best practices been followed, the scale of the natural disaster on March 11, 2011, might have been predicted, giving TEPCO the opportunity to enhance plant defenses. We say "might" rather than "would" because while it is often possible after the fact to point to indicators of an impending disaster, we also recognize that, in practice, hazard prediction is challenging. In any case, the accident sequence dramatically demonstrated that the plant was not equipped to cope with the events of March 11. Could the plant have been better prepared? Could prior actions by TEPCO and regulators have prevented a severe accident?

A MISSED OPPORTUNITY

In theory, during the decade before the accident, NISA might have urged or required TEPCO to significantly strengthen the design of the Fukushima Daiichi Nuclear Power Station. NISA had been reviewing the safety of unit 1 related to a TEPCO request to extend its operating lifetime. Just a few weeks before the accident, NISA gave unit 1 the green light to operate for an additional ten years.

Japan is a densely populated, highly industrialized country with few energy natural resources. Beginning in the 1990s, and especially thereafter in response to the realities of global climate change, Japan's government and industry planned to significantly increase the country's reliance on nuclear energy. An important component of Japan's nuclear strategy was to extend the operating lifetime of a score of reactors that by 2012 would be at least thirty years old and that produce about a third of Japan's nuclear electricity.[55] Fukushima Daiichi unit 1 began operating in March 1971. Under Japanese rules, to operate it beyond an initial forty-year period, TEPCO required the approval of regulators. Japanese regulations do not impose an absolute legal limit on the operating lifetimes of the country's nuclear power plants. Under an agreement between regulators and plant owners, before the end of a plant's thirtieth year of licensed operation, a so-called "soundness assessment" is carried out to determine whether it can continue operating for a longer period, foreseen by owners to be as long as sixty years. The assessment is mainly focused on equipment and structures having a safety function and specifically addresses aging issues. A plant deemed sound enough would be eligible to be operated for an additional ten or more years, on the basis of a "long-term maintenance plan" that would include component monitoring. The focus is on selected equipment that may suffer age-related degradation and failure, not on safety weaknesses related to the design or configuration of the installation.

Japan is not unique in concentrating attention on the status of aging equipment during reactor lifetime extension examinations. This is also the case in other advanced nuclear programs. In fact, IAEA peer reviews of some countries' national regulatory systems have criticized that procedures for extending the lifetime of older reactors have neglected other safety issues and are too specifically focused on plant aging.

In February 2011, just one month prior to the Fukushima accident, NISA granted TEPCO a ten-year operating license extension for unit 1 after a technical review and some modifications that were carried out the year before.[56] The license extension was permitted on the basis that TEPCO would monitor the condition of critical components during the term of the extended license.[57] It was not based on a reevaluation of the tsunami safety of the plant and did not require that TEPCO take significant actions to increase tsunami resistance of the installation before the unit began operating under its extended license. In the view of one senior Japanese executive, it would have been "difficult to detect the vulnerability of [the plant's] design to a tsunami using this system."[58]

Japan's nuclear regulatory guidelines themselves made clear neither what level of protection against a tsunami threat was required nor what steps TEPCO should undertake to protect the plant from a tsunami. When Japan's Nuclear Safety Commission in 2006 included tsunami risk for the first time in its guidelines for nuclear power plant seismic safety, the requirement for tsunamis was loosely worded: "Safety functions of facilities shall not be affected by a tsunami which could be appropriately postulated to occur even if rarely during the operation period of the facility."

After the Fukushima accident, the chairman of the Nuclear Safety Commission stated that the body's seismic safety guidelines should be revised to reflect a "dramatic improvement of the present measures for ensuring safety."[59] The Japanese government is currently in the process of revising its requirements for nuclear power plant life extension. Draft legislation containing far more stringent requirements and procedures has been approved by the cabinet[60] and submitted to Japan's national parliament for its consideration.[61]

HOW COULD THE PLANT HAVE BEEN PROTECTED?

Though Japan was quite slow to adopt firm regulations for protection against the tsunami threat, it was not for lack of knowledge of proper guidelines and review processes. Japan, like many other advanced countries, requires periodic safety reviews to assess and update the safety status of nuclear installations at ten-year intervals. According to executives and safety experts with many years of experience in nuclear power programs outside of Japan and at the IAEA, and who have knowledge of Japan's nuclear power program, Japanese industry and government would have been familiar with, and in some cases participants in, international efforts to review the safety of nuclear power plants concerning severe externally caused events. On the basis of this activity, TEPCO and Japanese regulators should have taken well-understood and straightforward engineering measures to better protect the Fukushima Daiichi Nuclear Power Station before the accident occurred.

According to these experts, on the basis of international knowledge accumulated during the four-decade operating lifetime of the Fukushima Daiichi Nuclear Power Station and put into practice at nuclear power plants elsewhere, TEPCO, encouraged by Japanese regulators, could have taken some or all of the following actions to have protected the plants against a tsunami:

- Moving emergency diesel generators and other emergency power sources to higher ground on the plant site.
- Establishing watertight connections between emergency power supplies and the plant.
- Building dikes and seawalls to protect against a severe tsunami.
- Installing emergency power equipment and cooling pumps in dedicated, bunkered, watertight buildings or compartments.
- Assuring that seawater-supply infrastructure is robust and providing additional robust sources to serve as the plants' ultimate heat sink.

When the Fukushima Daiichi station was constructed, the emergency diesel generators and emergency batteries were installed on the floor inside the plant building to afford protection against earthquakes. Ventilation ducts in the compartments where this equipment was located were not waterproofed. Moving this emergency power equipment to higher ground, safety experts said, would not have increased its vulnerability to seismic shock, provided it was fixed to a platform designed to resist earthquakes.[62]

The value of taking such action was demonstrated by upgrades that one Japanese utility, Japan Atomic Power Company (JAPC), was in the process of carrying out when the tsunami struck Japan's east coast. JAPC's Tokai-2 plant is located about 100 miles south of Fukushima, and the tsunami that ravaged Fukushima also caused flooding at Tokai–2. Prior to the tsunami, JAPC had partially implemented plans to erect a wall to prevent tsunami water from flooding two pits at the plant where seawater pumps were located and to make the pump rooms watertight. The wall was erected before the tsunami occurred. Water entered one of the pits because spaces where pipes penetrated into the pit had not yet been made watertight before the accident. In that pit, a seawater pump that provided cooling for an emergency diesel generator was damaged and unable to function, forcing JAPC to shut down the generator. But no flooding occurred at the other pit where pipe penetrations had been made watertight.[63] This saved the cooling pumps for two more diesel generators. Had JAPC not carried out these upgrades, it would almost certainly have lost all three emergency diesel generators, potentially resulting in a much more serious accident.

Within just a few weeks after the accident at Fukushima, Japanese nuclear power plant owners began announcing concrete plans to make widespread and significant plant design changes and other upgrades.[64] In April 2011, for example, Chubu Electric Power Company, Japan's third-largest utility company, initiated work on surveys, measurements, and ground clearance to erect an 18-meter-high seawall to defend its Hamaoka nuclear power plant against a tsunami; construction is expected to be completed by the end of 2012.[65] Separately, the company plans to waterproof the diesel generator rooms and the seawater pumps, install pumps in the basement of the buildings, double the plant's connections to the electricity grid, and add another set of emergency diesel generators behind the main plant building at an elevation of 25 meters above sea level. On site, spare equipment for the seawater pumps will be stored in a bunkered facility and heavy earth-moving equipment will maintained.[66] Similar measures are being undertaken or considered at other nuclear power stations in Japan.[67] And according to Japanese executives and officials, shortly after the accident NISA ordered nuclear power plant owners to erect seawalls around their coastal installations with a minimum height of 15 meters.[68]

Some senior Japanese government and industry experts interviewed for this paper privately concurred that, had TEPCO and regulators taken these steps before, a severe accident with significant off-site radiation releases could have been avoided. Said one nuclear industry executive: "If the occurrence of the tsunami was assumed, I believe that it would have been possible to take technical measures" to prevent a severe accident. But before the accident the will to make these changes was not there.

INTERNATIONAL BEST PRACTICES

During the four decades that the Fukushima Daiichi Nuclear Power Station was in operation, nuclear safety authorities and nuclear power plant owners in several countries were establishing requirements and configuring nuclear power plants in ways that could potentially have saved the Fukushima Daiichi nuclear station from disaster had they been heeded. In particular, some regulatory bodies outside of Japan reassessed the safety of installations in the event of extreme flood hazards, a station blackout, and the loss of the ultimate heat sink. In the view of safety experts participating in such assessments, had Japan acted on these developments, the plant could have survived the tsunami that struck in March 2011.

Defense Against a Station Blackout

Compared to some nuclear power plants in other countries, the units at Fukushima Daiichi were considerably less protected against a loss of internal and external AC power on the site. In addition to the lack of waterproofing and bunkering that proved fatal to the emergency power supplies at Fukushima Daiichi, most of this equipment was water cooled, not air cooled as is the case for more modern nuclear power plants. The water-cooled diesel generators required a cooling water system connected to the ultimate heat sink.

There are ample instances of international review processes that have led to upgrades that can help protect nuclear power plants against station blackouts. For example, in the United States beginning in 1988, the Nuclear Regulatory Commission required that a nuclear power plant withstand a complete loss of AC power for between four and eight hours, depending on specific conditions. It then instituted a program to improve plants' protection against station blackouts, and after 9/11, made further improvements, mandating so-called B.5.b measures. However, little information about post-9/11 measures has been made public, and the extent to which these measures have significantly reduced risk associated with a station blackout at a nuclear power plant in the United States is subject to debate.

Some senior European nuclear safety experts expressed the view that the Fukushima Daiichi units in fact likely met the U.S. station blackout criteria. Unit 1 featured an isolation condenser and units 2 and 3 were equipped with reactor core isolation cooling systems using turbine-driven pumps.[69] In many plants in the United States, one expert said, the on-site AC power supply is not stronger than that at Fukushima Daiichi.

Despite this, one Japanese executive asserted that, compared to Japan, the post-9/11 reinforcement of power supply systems in the United States was considerable. Compared to the United States and Europe, he said, "In Japan there has been no large-scale reinforcement [of power supplies] against a station blackout."[70] One U.S. safety expert said that after 9/11 the U.S. government had encouraged Japan to implement similar measures, and that post-Fukushima inspections at some U.S. nuclear power plants demonstrated that those plants had made B.5.b upgrades that might have saved the reactors at Fukushima Daiichi.[71]

In Germany, the requirements to protect a nuclear power plant against a station blackout are specified in the regulatory document KTA 3701.[72] Over the years these requirements have been amended and they now compel owners to provide for several layers of redundancies in emergency diesel generators and batteries including, for all plants, a group of bunkered generators.

According to an assessment last year by Germany's Reactor Safety Commission, "the electricity supply of the German nuclear power plants is more robust throughout than Fukushima [Daiichi]. All German plants have at least one additional standby grid connection and more emergency diesel generators, with at least two of them being protected against external impacts."[73] Most German power reactors have at least four emergency diesel generators, plus additional diesel generators that are designed to expressly cope with external events.[74]

The situation in some nuclear power plants in some other European countries is similar.[75] Each of the two-unit Doel-3/4 nuclear power plants in Belgium, for instance, is equipped with three backup diesel generators in the case of loss of off-site AC power, plus three more in bunkers. The older Doel-1/2 plant, built during the 1970s on a site located on a coastal estuary, is outfitted with four first-level diesel generators in the case of loss of off-site power, plus two more emergency diesel generators should these fail. These generators are not bunkered but are located in a separate "emergency systems building," that has been upgraded to be protected against external events.[76]

Each unit at the three-unit Olkiluoto Nuclear Power Station in Finland, to give another example, is equipped with four emergency diesel generators necessary for a safe shutdown in all postulated conditions. Each emergency diesel generator is in a fireproofed compartment located well above the design-basis flood level calculated for the plant. There is also an air-cooled gas-turbine power plant backing up the emergency diesel generators. That power plant is located above the design-basis flood level for the station, is in a separate building, and features two separate generator units, each having two gas turbines. Each of the four gas turbines can supply more than enough power for all three nuclear power plants at Olkiluoto.[77]

In the aftermath of the accident at Fukushima, Japanese experts have drafted new, revised, and more stringent requirements for coping with a station blackout at a nuclear power plant.[78]

Loss of Ultimate Heat Sink

The March 11 tsunami disabled seawater pumps and all associated electrical and mechanical equipment at Fukushima Daiichi. Without an alternate heat sink, the plant was left without a way to cool its reactors. As it turns out, this absence of an alternate heat sink is a problem in other countries as well. Unlike the case for hardware defenses against a station blackout, post-Fukushima examinations by European Union country regulators testify to an absence of national requirements for providing backup alternate heat sinks to cope with a severe external event.

For German nuclear power plants, for example, "there is no requirement in the regulations for a diverse [alternate] heat sink."[79] The French nuclear safety authority noted in its report that, "in France, no power reactor with the exception of the [reactor] at Flammanville-3 now under construction has an alternate heat sink" such as the water table, a lake, or cooling tower.[80] Alternate heat sinks in nuclear power plants in some other countries are, according to stress test reports, only partially available or have not been qualified under national nuclear safety regulations.[81] At one Swiss nuclear power plant, featuring a boiling water reactor with some design features similar to that at Fukushima, regulators after March 2011 found that, in case of a failure of the primary riverine heat sink, at the time of the Fukushima accident, the plant would have needed an alternate heat sink. Regulators ordered a mobile pump–based system installed at the plant in 2011 and, for the longer term, they "required the installation of a new heat sink as a full-scale alternative to the river water supply."[82]

But several owners of nuclear power plants in these countries, in consultation with regulators well before the accident in Japan, had provided alternate heat sinks that would be available in the case of a severe external event. These include the Borssele nuclear power plant in the Netherlands, which in the case of the loss of the main riverine heat sink is served by a system designed to be redundant and hardened against the impact from external events that vents steam via relief valves. It is also served by eight deep water wells designed to be seismic and flood resistant.[83] Several nuclear power plants in Switzerland prior to the Fukushima accident were equipped with groundwater wells and, in one case, with an emergency cooling tower. River water pumping and intake equipment for the Swiss and Dutch plants is also designed to maximize reliability in case of postulated severe external events.[84] The United Kingdom's one pressurized water reactor, Sizewell B, has a reserve ultimate heat sink in the form of an air-cooled heat exchanger that is designed to remove decay heat from the core after shutdown should the primary seawater-cooled heat sink become disabled. This reserve system is situated in a separate building from the seawater pumps, enhancing redundancy (although the EU-mandated stress test on this reactor did identify some potential flooding vulnerabilities that need to be rectified).[85]

Particularly noteworthy are measures taken by Taiwan to protect its nuclear power plants against a severe tsunami by taking advantage of the physical geography of the plant layout. Like Japan, a number of reactors on Taiwan are located on the Pacific coast and the plant sites are vulnerable to extreme seismic events. To avoid the loss of the ultimate heat sink in the first place, the two-unit Chinshan boiling water reactor nuclear power station, built during the 1970s to essentially the same design as Fukushima Daiichi units 2 and 3, was designed to withstand a tsunami having a maximum amplitude of 10.73 meters above sea level. The plant was therefore built at 12 meters. In addition to emergency diesel generators located inside the plant and above the level of the postulated design-basis tsunami, two gas turbine electricity generators are available at an elevation of 22 meters. In the case of the loss of the primary heat sink, for emergency cooling, two water reservoirs were installed at an elevation of 62 meters. At Kuosheng, another site on Taiwan hosting two older boiling water reactors, the nuclear power plant was constructed at an elevation of 12 meters above sea level, above the design-basis tsunami of 10.28 meters. Two emergency gas turbine generators were installed at 22 meters, and two water reservoirs are located at 90 meters.[86] By comparison, the physical geography of the Fukushima Daiichi site is more level, and critical equipment to provide the heat sink and emergency power was located at elevations too low to afford severe tsunami protection.

Protection Against Severe Flooding

NISA and TEPCO failed to heed relevant warnings from elsewhere in the world about the risk from flooding. In December 1999, a storm surge at high tide exceeded the design-basis flood scenario for the Blayais Nuclear Power Station in France, causing flooding at two units and a partial loss of power. The storm also resulted in the loss of some telecommunications links and road access to the site. Examination by French authorities revealed that dikes were too low and that rooms containing emergency equipment were insufficiently protected from flooding.

Recognizing that the Blayais event represented a systemic failure in hazard assessment, all nineteen nuclear power stations in France were thereafter ordered by regulators to identify all phenomena that could cause a flood, and to reassess site-specific flood management protection with regard to loss of off-site power, communications, and heat sinks. Some plants were required to raise dikes and walls. All had to waterproof building substructures, plant areas where floodwater could intrude, and rooms containing emergency equipment. Finally, plants' safety was reassessed for the postulated case that a combination of extreme natural phenomena could simultaneously threaten any given plant. Upgrading of the French plants was carried out over seven years in a program monitored by regulators and at a cost of 110 million euros to the plants' owner, Electricité de France.[87]

Between 1999 and 2001 the Blayais event was also studied at the Nuclear Energy Agency of the Organization for Economic Cooperation and Development, of which Japan is a member.[88] The Blayais incident led some other countries to reassess the safety of their own plants against flooding, resulting in plant owners and regulators adopting measures to significantly improve protection.[89] For example, analysis of the flooding at Blayais was included in a reassessment of the defense against external events at Belgium's seven nuclear power plants undertaken in 2006-2007. It made some recommendations to upgrade the plants, not all of which had been implemented by the time of the Fukushima accident. By contrast, according to Japanese industry officials, Japanese safety experts were aware of the Blayais event but they did not rigorously reexamine the flood protection situation at the country's own nuclear power plants.[90]

Protection against flooding and other external events are assessed during the periodic safety review process for many nuclear power plants worldwide. The Doel-1/2 nuclear power plants mentioned above were not originally designed to cope with a station blackout or a loss of ultimate heat sink in the case of a design-basis earthquake. But after an initial periodic safety review for these plants was carried out during the 1980s, a separate building was built to house additional cooling sources and emergency diesel generators and to protect these in the case of an external event. Other upgrades at Doel-1/2 were also required after the periodic safety review to better manage decay heat removal. These reviews considered specific scenarios where more than one external cause resulted in a severe event; thereafter, the height of the design-basis flood was increased from 9.13 meters to 9.35 meters (still well below the height of the river embankment built at the plant site at just over 12 meters).

Tsunami Risk Assessment

Finally, a growing divergence between their practices and evolving international standards should have alerted NISA and TEPCO to potential problems in their approach to tsunami risk assessments. In 2003, the IAEA published a safety guide on flood hazards for nuclear power plants, which contains guidance concerning all factors that must be considered in assessing the risk from tsunamis.[91] The Japanese methodology did not meet this guidance since it focused only on evaluating tsunami run-up and ignored other salient factors such as the effect of debris.

The IAEA more forcefully injected itself into the issue of tsunami safety following a December 2004 tsunami that ravaged many seacoast areas in the Indian Ocean and shut down a nuclear power plant in India. A revision of the 2003 safety guide was developed with the participation of the World Meteorological Organization incorporating updated criteria and recommendations and integrating meteorological and hydrological hazards. A specific project, mainly supported by Japan and the United States, was launched in relation to tsunami hazard assessment methodologies.

Japan participated actively in the implementation of the project, but the IAEA findings were not translated into practice in time to protect Fukushima Daiichi from the tsunami in 2011. Nonetheless, given Japan's participation in the project, it should have been well aware of how far its own practice was lagging behind international standards, and this should have prompted remedial actions.

WHY WEREN'T THESE PRACTICES AND ACTIONS CARRIED OUT AT FUKUSHIMA DAIICHI?

There is no simple answer to the question of why there were major safety deficiencies in the protection against tsunamis at Fukushima Daiichi and other Japanese nuclear power plants. On the basis of information provided by Japanese government and industry experts for this paper, there appears to be no consensus in Japan about what were the most important contributory factors and, in the most general sense, who was to "blame" for the accident. This paper does not intend to provide conclusive answers to these questions.

Regulatory Quality and Independence

It has been frequently asserted, including well before the accident, that NISA's lack of independence from the Ministry of Economy, Trade and Industry's Agency for Natural Resources and Energy, the government body responsible for promoting nuclear power, deterred NISA from asserting its authority to make rules, order safety improvements, and enforce its decisions.

During the 1990s and 2000s, Japan's nuclear program was punctuated by several incidents that foreign nuclear regulators interpreted as a signature for a lack of effective and persistent oversight. These included a fatal criticality accident at a nuclear fuel production complex at Tokai in 1999, which the IAEA said was caused by "human error and serious breaches of safety principles."[92] The U.S. Nuclear Regulatory Commission reported internally that the cause of the Tokai accident was "inadequate regulatory oversight."[93] In 2002, top management executives at TEPCO resigned after the company and NISA confirmed that, for over a decade, nuclear power plant personnel systematically ignored regulatory procedures in failing to report engineering plant changes and falsifying installation status reports to regulators. In response to these events, Japanese industry and government made changes that were intended to restore public confidence in Japan's nuclear power program, but the relationship between NISA and the Japanese government, on the one hand, and that between NISA and industry, on the other, was not fundamentally challenged.

Following the Fukushima accident, there has been much more extensive domestic and international criticism of the Japanese regulatory system. This criticism has largely focused on NISA's lack of independence from government. But NISA's lack of independence from industry is perhaps even more problematic. Japan has put new rules in place to prevent the practice of *amakudari* ("descent from heaven") in which senior regulators are appointed as senior executives in major utilities. Yet, a lesser-known practice—*amaagari* ("ascent to heaven")—in which industry safety experts are employed by NISA's technical support agency, the Japan Nuclear Energy Safety Organization, is also troublesome.[94] To be clear, it would be both impractical and problematic for Japanese regulators not to use industry experts. However, until now, a comparative lack of independent expertise in Japan may have rendered NISA overreliant on them. Most obviously, industry experts on loan to the regulator may be reluctant to criticize their employers. Even those who have severed their formal association with industry may be less able or less willing than experts without much nuclear industry expertise to "think outside the box" and identify new potential safety issues. Solving this problem will require a large and long-term investment in human resources.

Japan's regulatory system is currently being reorganized and a new, more powerful regulator under the Environment Ministry will be constituted in the spring of 2012. Establishing the formal independence of Japan's regulatory body however will not result in stronger nuclear oversight if Japanese regulators will not assert themselves. Persons with many years of experience in Japan's nuclear energy program have suggested to us that regulatory deficiencies in Japan were ultimately rooted in the lack of accountability in Japan's "nuclear culture" and in low tolerance in Japanese society for challenging authority.

Ignoring Safety Threats

The U.S. Nuclear Regulatory Commission concluded that the 1999 criticality event at Tokai happened because during licensing of the facility, regulators "incorrectly concluded that there was 'no possibility of criticality accident occurrence due to malfunction and other failures."' The "resultant belief that a criticality accident was not credible," the commission said, complicated management of the accident and may have led to radiation exposure of personnel.[95] NISA and TEPCO likewise played down the threat of a tsunami and also, more broadly, the threat that an external event could cause a severe accident at a nuclear power plant.

When the era of commercial nuclear power generation began nearly a half century ago, safety experts initially were most concerned about the possibility that a serious accident would be caused by a sequence of events unfolding inside the plant—such as that leading to the Three Mile Island accident in the United States in 1979 and to the explosion at Chernobyl in 1986. Only gradually did concern become focused on the possibility that an extreme external event could cause a reactor to fail. And in some nuclear programs over time specific threat assessments for external events have changed. In Germany, for example, during the 1970s regulators and industry designed nuclear power reactors to withstand the impact from an F-104 jet aircraft because during the 1960s 292 of the Luftwaffe's 916 F-104s had crashed. Germany's reactors were not explicitly designed to withstand the impact of a crash of a passenger jet. After 9/11, German regulators and industry focused on defining, and then addressing, the threat of a severe accident caused by terrorists aiming a passenger jet into a reactor.[96]

Japan's attitude to the threat of external events was extremely selective. On the one hand, Japan's entire industrial and engineering culture is highly informed by the danger of seismic activity, and Japan has firm and robust technical requirements for all its civil engineering structures, including nuclear power plants. By contrast, Japan has been much slower to appreciate the potential danger of some other external events, especially tsunamis. A government-appointed investigation committee, headed by Yotaro Hatamura, Professor Emeritus at the University of Tokyo, explained in an interim report from December 2011, that

in the past, risks of tsunamis were not fully considered in the context of severe accident[s dealing] with incidents exceeding design standards. ... The risk of [a] tsunami exceeding design basis [was] not considered. Therefore no preparation was made for eventualit[ies] such as "simultaneous and multiple losses of power" and "[station blackout] including DC power supplies."

No operational manuals were in place for recovering instrumentation equipment and power supplies, [primary containment vessel] venting, etc., in such conditions. Staff education was not organized for such [an] eventuality and equipment and materials for such recovering operations were not ready for use. … TEPCO did not take precautionary measures in anticipation that a severe accident could be caused by a tsunami such as the one [in March 2011]. Neither did the regulatory authorities.[97]

Why this should be the case might be explained at least in part by deficits in regulatory quality and independence as discussed above. Some Japanese government officials interviewed for this paper asserted that NISA had no authority to impose tsunami-related standards and plant design modifications on nuclear power plant owners. Some industry executives claimed instead that NISA did have this authority. If Hatamura's above analysis is correct, the point may be moot. Neither NISA nor TEPCO were inclined to force the issue of tsunami safety because they didn't believe an extreme tsunami was a serious threat. One foreign expert involved in peer reviews of Japan's nuclear regulatory system said that the lack of clarity in defining responsibilities of industry and regulators has permitted both sides to assert that the other was amiss in fulfilling its responsibilities.[98]

Risk Assessment

One apparent difference between Japan's nuclear culture and that in many other countries is its attitude toward risk. This may account in part for Japan's reluctance to embrace methodologies that examined external events in risk-informed and probabilistic ways.

In numerous countries outside Japan, plant-specific probabilistic safety assessments routinely estimate the contribution of both internal and external events to core damage frequency—a common yardstick for nuclear power plant safety. In some of these countries, regulators required owners to design their installations to withstand a thousand-year flood event, and probabilistic methods were used to calculate the height of that flood. After the Blayais event in France, some countries imposed the requirement that nuclear power plants withstand a ten-thousand-year flood. European regulations for some events require that a one-million-year event is considered. IAEA guidelines encourage including both external and internal events in plant-specific probabilistic safety assessments.

According to Japanese government and industry officials, most Japanese safety rules follow from deterministic assessments. Regulations do not require probabilistic safety assessments to demonstrate that plants are protected against the threat of severe external events. Japanese experts said that especially after a severe earthquake damaged the Kashiwazaki-Kariwa Nuclear Power Station in 2007, plant-specific seismic probabilistic safety assessments in Japan have been carried out on an experimental basis but as of the date of the Fukushima accident, the results had not been used by owners or regulators in decisions about making design modifications.[99] In the view of one Japanese executive, the bottom line was that Japan's "utilization of risk information was insufficient, and the risk of [a station blackout] was not widely recognized by the management."[100]

Still more broadly, Japanese nuclear officials and executives said the reluctance of authorities to reevaluate tsunami risk may reflect a more general Japanese cultural bias against open discussion of worst-case scenarios or contingencies for which Japanese society and its authorities may be unprepared. While earthquake safety is a subject that has generated wide public interest and debate in Japan for many decades, before the Fukushima accident tsunami safety was never singled out for intensive public or media scrutiny.

When public and political pressure was brought to bear on the Japanese government to take effective action in response to the accident, NISA quickly reacted by requiring reactors in Japan to erect 15-meter-high seawalls. According to Japanese experts in both government and industry, NISA's order, as well as the decision by Chubu Electric Power Company to erect an 18-meter wall at Hamaoka, was made under political duress, not on the basis of the application of a scientific methodology to identify a design-basis tsunami at any specific location.

Ultimately, in the view of some Japanese experts queried for this paper, the accident at Fukushima Daiichi was an expression of supreme overconfidence by decisionmakers that Japan's nuclear power program would never suffer a severe accident. The station blackout condition is covered by the 1990 safety guide established by Japan's Nuclear Safety Commission, which states that "nuclear reactor facilities shall be designed such that safe shutdown and proper cooling of the reactor after shutting down can be ensured in case of a short-term total AC power loss." According to a senior Japanese nuclear executive, "short-term" was interpreted to mean thirty minutes or less. A long-term loss of power was not included in the design basis of nuclear power plants, meaning that their owners did not have to demonstrate that it would be prevented. (In practice, Japanese power plant operators provided emergency power supplies for a longer period, but most emergency DC batteries at Fukushima Daiichi did not survive the tsunami.)

Another illustration of this excessive confidence is that, unlike nearly all other power reactor owners worldwide, Japanese utilities face unlimited liability in the event of an accident. This provision was apparently implemented at the request of plant owners, who wanted to demonstrate their confidence in the safety of their power plants to local populations.

One executive said that, compared to the United States and Europe, in Japan there is less concern about station blackout risk because of the great reliability of the Japanese power supply system. "We fundamentally believed that if we lost off-site power, we would be back up on the grid in no more than about half an hour," he said. Compared to the United States and Europe, he also said, Japan's nuclear program was not convinced that there was a direct relationship between nuclear safety and nuclear security. For this reason, he said, "Japan was negligent in evaluating the approaches taken by the U.S. after 9/11 from the viewpoint of nuclear safety."

Corporate and Nuclear Culture

Some safety experts in Japan suggested that the lack of concerted attention to tsunami safety at Fukushima over several decades may have been less an expression of general Japanese safety culture deficiencies and at least partially attributable to deficiencies in TEPCO's management culture.[101] A few suggested that TEPCO tolerated or encouraged the practice of covering up problems. They described TEPCO's concealment of actions from regulators prior to 2002 as a systematic effort to bypass rules and procedures that require plant owners to provide regulators detailed documentation of plant activities and to obtain regulatory approvals for actions that have little or no safety significance.

In many other nuclear programs, a so-called in-service inspection rule permits nuclear power plant owners to repair or replace equipment having little safety significance without having to shut down the plant and obtain regulatory approval for such actions. In one case, however, the results of a leak-tightness examination for a reactor containment—clearly a safety-significant issue—were falsified at Fukushima Daiichi.[102] It must also be said that personnel at other utility companies likewise engaged in these deceptive practices, albeit apparently to a lesser degree.

More generally, some nuclear industry executives and officials in Japan have blamed bureaucratic and professional stovepiping, as well as insularity and elitism attributed to Japan's nuclear energy sector, for the unwillingness of nuclear professionals to take advice from experts outside the nuclear field. That, they said, might partly explain why Japanese nuclear installations are well protected against earthquakes but may be far more vulnerable to tsunamis.

The generally low priority awarded to tsunami safety in Japan's nuclear program is reflected in funding arrangements for risk research. An official from NISA noted that much of the agency's funding was devoted to earthquake safety, thereby marginalizing tsunami safety. In 2005, Japan's leading nuclear safety research center, the Japan Atomic Energy Research Institute, was merged with another government agency, the Power Reactor and Nuclear Fuel Development Corporation, to form the Japan Atomic Energy Agency. Some Japanese experts assert that the merger inhibited support and funding for pioneering investigation into tsunami-related nuclear risk.

As one government official said, "there are many tsunami experts in Japan," but their findings as a rule have "not been taken seriously" by industry and government agencies responsible for making rules on nuclear safety issues. This is borne out by the Japanese commission's investigation, which noted that no tsunami experts were involved in drafting the tsunami-related safety clauses in the 2006 guidelines on seismic safety.[103] In a similar vein, Japanese media reports asserted that TEPCO's top management ignored warnings from Japanese experts that tsunamis were a serious safety threat.[104]

For nuclear safety decisionmaking, the most significant tsunami awareness in Japan may be local. In 1979, the Tohoku Electric Power Company relocated the site for its three-unit Onagawa Nuclear Power Station prior to construction in light of tsunami concerns. The March 2011 earthquake and tsunami devastated the town of Onagawa, located about 75 miles north of Fukushima. The event knocked out four of five power lines connecting the power station to the grid. Unlike at Fukushima Daiichi, where turbine buildings hosting emergency diesel generators suffered a direct assault from the tsunami, the Onagawa station was better protected. According to Japanese safety officials and the plant owner, it escaped serious damage because prior to construction, a civil engineer employed by the owning utility company, having personal local knowledge of tsunami dangers, insisted that the plant site be moved to higher ground and farther back from the seacoast.[105]

One official suggested that because decisionmaking for the Onagawa nuclear plant project at Tohoku Electric Power Company involved local personnel, top management there may have been more receptive to making costly siting changes. But that knowledge may be underutilized elsewhere. The lack of follow-through by TEPCO at Fukushima prior to March 2011, despite voluntary initiatives its staff undertook beginning in 2002 to investigate tsunami risk, may have reflected a high concentration of decisionmaking and lack of local knowledge at corporate headquarters in Tokyo.[106]

CONCLUSION

The combined earthquake and tsunami that struck the Fukushima Daiichi Nuclear Power Station was not simply the Japanese nuclear power program's bad luck, nor was the event an unpredictable act of god that the power reactors at the site—or nuclear power–generating infrastructure in general—could not possibly have withstood.

Intensive investigation of nuclear safety issues in nuclear power programs worldwide in the aftermath of the accident in Japan has revealed potential vulnerabilities of many reactors to extreme external events. In France alone, regulators will issue about one hundred new rules, and plant owner Electricité de France will implement scores of actions at 58 plants concerning issues such as the possible loss of power and loss of heat sinks during extreme events[107] costing an estimated 10 billion euros.[108]

But in Japan, which unlike some other countries did not systematically revisit issues critical to tsunami safety during the last two decades, the weaknesses—in hazard assessment and in plant design—were greater. Had the plant's owner, TEPCO, and the Japanese regulator, NISA, heeded timely warnings and good practices elsewhere about the dangers discussed above, they might have realized that the tsunami threat to Fukushima Daiichi had been underestimated and that they could have defended the plant against the natural forces that fatally crippled three reactors at the site without such advance preparations.

Accurate hazard prediction is extremely challenging. It is always possible, after the fact, to spot indicators of an impending disaster that, in this case, included evidence for massive tsunamis inundating the region once every one thousand years. However, the clearest warning signs of potential risk before the accident were procedural: Japan's methodology for assessing tsunami risks lagged markedly behind international standards, TEPCO did not even implement that methodology in full, and NISA showed little concern about the risks from tsunamis. Given Japan's historical legacy of tsunamis, this last point—NISA's inattention to tsunamis—should have warned the Nuclear Safety Commission (which was supposed to act as a check on NISA) that potential risks might have been underestimated.

Akira Omoto, a member of Japan's Atomic Energy Commission, said that a Gedankenexperiment to identify what engineering design attributes could have "saved Fukushima" might conclude that these included—as our foregoing treatment suggests—"protection against natural hazards" and "plant capability against [a station blackout] and against isolation of the ultimate heat sink."[109]

Regardless of a certain homogenization of nuclear safety practices and standards among advanced nuclear programs worldwide during the last half century, significant differences remain in the safety approaches among nuclear programs in Japan, Europe, and the United States. In general, European regulators appear to have most consistently and expressly required nuclear power plants to undergo expensive engineering modifications to enhance safety. In the United States, one European regulator said, the approach is not to enhance safety but to maintain it. There, decisions to make engineering upgrades at nuclear power plants—especially significant and costly ones—are routinely based on calculations of costs and benefits and safety margins. This approach is based on a so-called "backfit rule," which in the view of some safety experts and regulators discourages safety upgrades requiring expensive engineering changes at U.S. nuclear power plants.

Japan has no such "backfit rule," but regulators have not routinely required making hardware modifications at nuclear power plants. Post-Fukushima draft amendments to Japan's nuclear safety law and atomic energy act include provisions giving Japan's new regulatory body the express authority to require power plant owners to make hardware upgrades.[110] In view of concerns about tsunami protection, TEPCO began reinvestigating the matter in 2002 but as of March 2011 its investigations had not been brought to a conclusion such that management and regulators were motivated to make engineering modifications that might have saved three units at Fukushima Daiichi.

Given that Japanese industry and government during the 2000s had been exposed to expert doubt that Japanese nuclear power plants were fit to cope with tsunami risk, had decisionmakers then taken the tsunami threat seriously, NISA and TEPCO could have made some or all of the hardware upgrades discussed in this paper well before regulators gave TEPCO a green light to operate the oldest of six reactors at Fukushima Daiichi for an extended ten-year term just weeks before the accident. In the absence of clear regulatory authority and the political will to require these modifications, such a decision would have had to be predicated upon TEPCO's understanding that the nuclear power station, without these modifications, was not adequately defended against a severe tsunami. In the absence of evidence of any decisions by TEPCO to order those upgrades to be carried out prior to the accident, we must assume that before March 2011 the company did not conclude that the tsunami risk was unacceptably high.

A former IAEA safety official with many years of experience in assessing the safety of nuclear power plants against extreme events said that the failure of NISA and TEPCO to make sure that Fukushima Daiichi Nuclear Power Station had been better prepared for what happened in March 2011 raised questions about Japan's political will to effectively enforce a growing international consensus that an array of potential external threats must be addressed. Measures to improve resistance to flooding, a loss of the ultimate heat sink, and a station blackout could have been identified in a straightforward manner and in accordance with internationally recognized methodologies as recommended by the IAEA. Indeed, immediately after the accident, Japan's nuclear power plant owners announced plans to take steps that experts interviewed for this paper said could have averted a severe accident with significant off-site radiation releases.

It would be wrong to conclude that the accident at Fukushima revealed a fatal and uncovered intrinsic risk associated with nuclear power technology and infrastructure. With appropriate foresight by Japan's authorities and industry, it appears that the accident could have been avoided or prevented. At the time of the accident, it appears that Japanese industry and government were taking tentative steps toward what might have emerged as a consensus view that Japan's nuclear power plants were not prepared to cope with an extreme tsunami. But they had not overcome impediments inhibiting TEPCO and NISA from taking effective action sooner.

External threats to nuclear installations are dynamic. In recent years, threats due to natural causes have been augmented by threats from sabotage and terrorism. In the future, they will include local threats resulting from global climate change. In the aftermath of the Fukushima disaster, Japan, as well as all other nuclear power–generating countries, should make sure that nuclear power plants can withstand all such threats, including multi-threat scenarios that the Fukushima accident dramatically underscored were credible but until then had not been considered in the threat assessments of many nuclear programs worldwide.

NOTES

1. Reconstruction Unit Secretariat, "Report on the Number of Evacuees Across the Country, Prefectural and Other Refugees," February 1, 2012, www.reconstruction.go.jp/topics/20120201zenkoku-hinansyasu.pdf.

2. International Nuclear Safety Advisory Group, "Basic Safety Principles for Nuclear Power Plants," 75-INSAG–3 Rev. 1, 1999, www-pub.iaea.org/MTCD/publications/PDF/P082_scr.pdf, para 27.

3. The description of the accident presented in this section is largely drawn from the IAEA report on Fukushima, except where otherwise stated. IAEA, "IAEA International Fact Finding Expert Mission of the Fukushima Dai-ichi NPP Accident Following the Great East Japan Earthquake and Tsunami," June 16, 2011, www-pub.iaea.org/MTCD/meetings/PDFplus/2011/cn200/documentation/cn200_Final-Fukushima-Mission_Report.pdf.

4. U.S. Geological Survey, "Largest Earthquakes in the World Since 1900," http://earthquake.usgs.gov/earthquakes/world/10_largest_world.php.

5. The systems with limited functionality in the absence of power were an isolation condenser (in unit 1) and a reactor core isolation cooling (RCIC) system (in units 2 and 3). An isolation condenser takes steam from the reactor core, passes it through a tank of water to cool and condense it, and then feeds it back as water into the reactor pressure vessel. The flow is gravity driven (i.e., no pumps are needed). The system in unit 1 had a thermal capacity of about eight hours. RCICs use steam from the core to drive a turbine and pump that replenishes the water in the pressure vessel. Although electricity is not required to drive pumps in either an isolation condenser or an RCIC, it is needed for instrumentation and to open and close the valves used for control. Moreover, RCICs will only function if the steam is above a certain pressure. In addition to an IC or RCIC, all units at Fukushima Daiichi contained various cooling systems that did require electricity. One of these, the HPCI (high-pressure coolant injection) system was activated in unit 3 (where some battery power was available) after the RCIC in that unit had failed.

6. Institute of Nuclear Power Operators (INPO), "Special Report on the Nuclear Accident at the Fukushima Daiichi Nuclear Power Station," INPO 11–005, revision 0, November 2011, www.nei.org/filefolder/11_005_Special_Report_on_Fukushima_Daiichi_MASTER_11_08_11_1.pdf, 14.

7. According to one experienced nuclear power regulator, the fail-safe position for the relevant valves was closed, i.e., the isolation condenser was designed to be disabled in the event that control of the valves was lost. In this case, the state of the valves just prior to station blackout may have been immaterial. Personal communication, February 2012.

8. TEPCO, "Fukushima Daiichi Nuclear Power Station: Response After Earthquake," June 18, 2011, www.tepco.co.jp/en/press/corp-com/release/betu11_e/images/110618e15.pdf, 4.

9.   Justin McCurry, "Fukushima Fuel Rods May Have Completely Melted," *Guardian*, December 2, 2011, www.guardian.co.uk/world/2011/dec/02/fukushima-fuel-rodscompletely-melted.

10. INPO, "Special Report on the Nuclear Accident at the Fukushima Daiichi Nuclear Power Station," 9–10.

11. TEPCO, "Fukushima Nuclear Accident Analysis Report," summary of interim report, December 2, 2011, www.tepco.co.jp/en/press/corp-com/release/betu11_e/images/111202e13.pdf, 10.

12. This includes 1.6×10^{17} Bq of I−131 and 1.5×10^{16} Bq of Cs−137 leading to a total emission of 7.6×10^{17} Bq I−131 equivalent. By comparison, the total emission from Chernobyl was 5.2×10^{18} Bq I−131 equivalent. Nuclear Emergency Response Headquarters, Government of Japan, "Report of the Japanese Government to the IAEA Ministerial Conference on Nuclear Safety: The Accident at TEPCO's Fukushima Nuclear Power Stations," June 2011, available from www.iaea.org/newscenter/focus/fukushima/japan-report, VI–1.

13. Investigation Committee on the Accidents at Fukushima Nuclear Power Stations of Tokyo Electric Power Company, "Executive Summary of the Interim Report," December 26, 2011, http://icanps.go.jp/eng/111226ExecutiveSummary.pdf, 7–9. For a good discussion of the effects of the Chernobyl accident see David Bodansky, *Nuclear Energy: Principles, Practices and Prospects*, second edition (New York: Springer, 2004), 426–36.

14. Investigation Committee on the Accidents at Fukushima Nuclear Power Stations of Tokyo Electric Power Company, "Executive Summary of the Interim Report," 7.

15. Ibid. See also TEPCO, "Fukushima Daiichi Nuclear Power Station," 2–5.

16. The RCIC (see note 5) in unit 2 failed at about 1 pm on March 14. The HPCI in unit 3 was stopped at 2:42 am on March 13. TEPCO, "Fukushima Daiichi Nuclear Power Station," 26 and 36.

17. IAEA, "IAEA International Fact Finding Expert Mission of the Fukushima Daiichi NPP Accident Following the Great East Japan Earthquake and Tsunami," 30.

18. TEPCO, "Fukushima Daiichi Nuclear Power Station," 2.

19. Investigation Committee on the Accidents at Fukushima Nuclear Power Stations of Tokyo Electric Power Company, "Executive Summary of the Interim Report," 4.

20. TEPCO, "Fukushima Daiichi Nuclear Power Station," 17. For other examples see 26 and 30.

21. Investigation Committee on the Accidents at Fukushima Nuclear Power Stations of Tokyo Electric Power Company, "Executive Summary of the Interim Report," 4–7.

22. IAEA, "IAEA International Fact Finding Expert Mission of the Fukushima Daiichi NPP Accident Following the Great East Japan Earthquake and Tsunami," 74.

23. Contrary to some media reporting there is not a proper sea wall at Fukushima Daiichi. There is a shallow breakwater around the plant, but it was apparently not designed to play any role in tsunami protection and is not regulated by NISA. Its role was simply to create a calm harbor for shipping.

24. IAEA, "IAEA International Fact Finding Expert Mission," 75.

25. Masafumi Matsuyama, "Outline of Tsunami Evaluation Technology," Nuclear Civil Engineering Committee, November 2, 2011, http://tinyurl.com/6qpuko9, 42.

26. TEPCO, "Report on Investigation Results Regarding Tsunami Generated by the Tohoku-Taiheiyou-Oki Earthquake in Fukushima Daiichi and Daini Nuclear Power Stations," vol. 2 [outline], July 8, 2011, www.tepco.co.jp/en/press/corp-com/release/betu11_e/images/110708e18.pdf, 3.

27. Matsuyama, "Outline of Tsunami Evaluation Technology," 51–70.

28. TEPCO, "Report on Investigation Results Regarding Tsunami Generated by the Tohoku-Taiheiyou-Oki Earthquake in Fukushima Daiichi and Daini Nuclear Power Stations," 2.

29. Japan Weather Association, "Overview of the Tsunami caused by the 2011 off the Pacific coast of Tohoku Earthquake (bulletin report)," March 29, 2011, www.jwa.or.jp/static/topics/20110329/touhokujishin110329.pdf. For an alternative slightly different data set provided by the Japan Meteorological Office see Japan Meteorological Agency, Monthly Report on Earthquakes and Volcanoes (edition on disaster prevention), March 2011, www.seisvol.kishou.go.jp/eq/2011_03_11_tohoku/tsunami_jp.pdf.

30. IAEA, "IAEA International Fact Finding Expert Mission," 70. Because of local geology, the ground motion at units 1, 4, and 6 was less severe than at units 2, 3, and 5.

31. IAEA, "IAEA International Fact Finding Expert Mission," 71. It should be noted that damage to non-critical equipment can prove very problematic. For instance, highly radioactive water drained out of a pit at the plant and into the Pacific Ocean through a crack that was, presumably, created by the earthquake. David Batty, "Radioactive Water From Japan's Fukushima Plant is Leaking Into the Sea," *Guardian*, April 2, 2011, www.guardian.co.uk/world/2011/apr/02/japanfukushima-radioactive-water-leaking-sea.

32. Denis Normile, "Devastating Earthquake Defied Expectations," *Science*, vol. 331, no. 6023 (2011): 1375–1376.

33. Nuclear Emergency Response Headquarters, Government of Japan, "Report of the Japanese Government to the IAEA Ministerial Conference on Nuclear Safety," III-3 and III–16.

34. See Nuclear Power Corporation, "Impact of Tsunami that struck Kapakkam on 26 December, 2004," press releases, www.dae.gov.in/press/tsunpcil.htm.

35. U.S. Nuclear Regulatory Commission, "North Anna Earthquake Summary," www.nrc.gov/about-nrc/emerg-preparedness/virginia-quake-info/va-quake-summary.pdf.

36. For example, IAEA, Site Evaluation for Nuclear Installations, NS-R-3 (Vienna: IAEA, 2003), www-pub.iaea.org/MTCD/publications/PDF/Pub1177_web.pdf, paras. 3.2, 3.6(a), and 3.24–3.38.

37. IAEA, "IAEA International Fact Finding Expert Mission," 74.

38. K. Minoura, F. Imamura, D. Sugawara, Y. Kono and T. Iwashita, "The 869 Jogan Tsunami Deposit and Recurrence Interval of Large-Scale Tsunami on the Pacific Coast of Northeast Japan," *Journal of Natural Disaster Science*, vol. 23, no. 2 (2001), www.jsnds.org/contents/jnds/23_2_3.pdf, 83–88. See also K. Satake, Y. Sawai, M. Shishikura, Y. Okamura, Y. Namegaya, and S. Yamaki, "Tsunami Source of the Unusual AD 869 Earthquake off Miyagi, Japan, Inferred From Tsunami Deposits and Numerical Simulation of Inundation," paper presented to American Geophysical Union, Fall Meeting 2007, December 2007, http://adsabs.harvard.edu/abs/2007AGUFM.T31G..03S.

39. Ludger Mohrbach et al., "Earthquake and Tsunami in Japan on March 11, 2011 and Consequences for Fukushima and Other Nuclear Power Plants," VGB Power Tech (Germany), April 1, 2011, www.vgb.org/vgbmultimedia/News/Fukushimav15VGB.pdf.

40. The Tsunami Evaluation Subcommittee and the Nuclear Civil Engineering Committee, Japan Society of Civil Engineers (JSCE), "Tsunami Assessment Method for Nuclear Power Plants in Japan," February 2002, www.jsce.or.jp/committee/ceofnp/Tsunami/eng/JSCE_Tsunami_060519.pdf.

41. JSCE, "Tsunami Assessment Method for Nuclear Power Plants in Japan," 61.

42. IAEA, "IAEA International Fact Finding Expert Mission," 75.

43. "TEPCO Warned of Big Tsunami 4 Days Prior to March 11," *Asahi Shimbun*, August 25, 2011, http://ajw.asahi.com/article/0311disaster/quake_tsunami/AJ201108257639.

44. TEPCO, "Report on Investigation Results Regarding Tsunami Generated by the Tohoku-Taiheiyou-Oki Earthquake in Fukushima Daiichi and Daini Nuclear Power Stations," 1–2.

45. JSCE, "Tsunami Assessment Method for Nuclear Power Plants in Japan," 3.

46. For IAEA guidance see IAEA, Flood Hazard for Nuclear Power Plants on Coastal and River Sites, IAEA Safety Standard Series, NS-G-3.5, (Vienna: IAEA, 2003), www-pub.iaea.org/MTCD/publications/PDF/Pub1170_web.pdf, paras. 11.21-22.3. For a description of U.S. practice see IAEA, Meteorological and Hydrological Hazards in Site Evaluation for Nuclear Installations, SSG-18, (Vienna: IAEA, 2011), www-pub.iaea.org/MTCD/publications/PDF/Pub1506_web.pdf, 120–26.

47. "TEPCO Warned of Big Tsunami 4 Days Prior to March 11."

48. TEPCO, "Fukushima Nuclear Accident Analysis Report," 2–4.

49. TEPCO, "Fukushima Nuclear Accident Analysis Report," 4.

50. Personal communication, July 2011.

51. Nuclear Safety Commission of Japan, "Regulatory Guide for Reviewing Safety Design of Light Water Nuclear Power Reactor Facilities," NSCRG: L-DS-I.0, August 30, 1990, www.nsc.go.jp/NSCenglish/guides/lwr/L-DS-I_0.pdf, para. 2.(2).

52. IAEA, Design Basis Flood for Nuclear Power Plants on Coastal Sites, Safety Series 50-SG-S10B (Vienna: IAEA, 1983), 26.

53. IAEA, "IAEA International Fact Finding Expert Mission," 75.

54. E-mail communication from senior NISA official, August 25, 2011.

55. "Japan's Uncertain Nuclear Energy Outlook in 2012," Institute for Energy Economics Japan (IEEJ) Energy Brief, January 31, 2012, www.siew.sg/energyperspectives/alternative-energies/japans-uncertain-nuclear-energy-outlook–2012.

56. World Nuclear Association, "Nuclear Power in Japan," February 2012, www.worldnuclear.org/info/inf79.html.

57. Hiroko Tabuchi, Norimitsu Onishi, and Ken Belson, "Japan Extended Reactor's Life, Despite Warning," *New York Times*, March 21, 2011, www.nytimes.com/2011/03/22/world/asia/22nuclear.html?_r=2&pagewanted=all.

58. Personal communication, January 2012.

59. "To Chairman of Special Committee for the Nuclear Safety Standards and Guides, Chairman of the Nuclear Safety Commission, About the Examination of the Regulatory Guides for Safety Review (Direction)," 43rd Session of the Nuclear Safety Commission of Japan, Document no. 1, www.nsc.go.jp/NSCenglish/geje/doc_dis/2011_43rd/2011_0616_43th_doc1.pdf.

60. Mari Yamaguchi, "Japan Cabinet OKs Bill to Cap Nuke Reactor Life," Associated Press, January 31, 2012, www.google.com/hostednews/ap/article/ALeqM5jZtFBo8gzMIAnhRe2JwCmPdslsbw?docId=d575cdf0ba5c402a8ead3083b623a8d0.

61. Personal communication, January 2012.

62. Personal communication, November 2011.

63. "Receipt of a Report Regarding a Legally Reportable Event that Occurred at the Tokai-Daini Power Station, Owned by Japan Atomic Power Company," News Release, Ministry of Economy, Trade and Industry (METI), September 2, 2011, www.atomdb.jnes.go.jp/content/000119422.pdf.

64. "Reactor Operators Accelerate Anti-Tsunami Defenses," Asahi Shimbun, March 30, 2011, http://ajw.asahi.com/article/0311disaster/fukushima/AJ201103313751.

65. "Overview of Seawall Construction Work and Installation Schedule," Chubu Electric Power Company, Incorporated, www.chuden.co.jp/english/corporate/ecor_releases/erel_pressreleases/__icsFiles/afieldfile/2011/12/16/111101.pdf.

66. World Nuclear News, "Hamaoka Protection Plans," July 22, 2011, www.worldnuclear-news.org/RS_Hamaoka_protection_plans_2207112.html.

67. Atoms in Japan, "Power Utilities Announce Earthquake and Tsunami Measures Following Fukushima NPS Crisis," April 3, 2011, www.jaif.or.jp/english/aij/member/2011/2011-04-03a.pdf.

68. Personal communication, January 2012.

69. See note 5 for explanation.

70. Personal communication, January 2012.

71. Personal communication, January 2012.

72. "Übergeordnete Anforderungen an die elektrische Energieversorgung in Kernkraftwerken" (General Requirements for Electrical Energy Supply in Nuclear Power Plants), Kerntechnische Ausschuss (German Nuclear Safety Standards Commission/KTA) 6/99, www.kta-gs.de/d/regeln/3700/3701.pdf.

73. "Plant-Specific Safety Review (RSK-SÜ) of German Nuclear Power Plants in the Light of the Events in Fukushima–1 (Japan)," (translation of Chapter 1 of the RSK statement entitled "Anlagenspezifische Sicherheitsüberprüfung (RSK-SÜ) deutscher Kernkraftwerke unter Berücksichtigung der Ereignisse in Fukushima-I [Japan]"), www.rskonline.de/English/downloads/memrskstnuezusammenfassungreven.pdf.

74. According to German safety experts, currently operating German pressurized water reactors have four emergency diesel generators plus four more to cope with external events. Pressurized water reactors shut down since 2011 have four emergency diesel generators (some of which are protected against external hazards) plus between one and three more emergency diesel generators designed to cope with external events. Operating German boiling water reactors have five emergency diesel generators (some of which are protected against external hazards) plus one more expressly designed to cope with external events. Boiling water reactors shut down since 2011 have between four and six emergency diesel generators (some of which are protected against external events) and some of these have up to two additional emergency diesel generators which are protected against external events.

75. Personal communication.

76. Federal Agency for Nuclear Control, "Belgian Stress Tests, National Report for Nuclear Power Plants," December 23, 2011, www.ensreg.eu/sites/default/files/National_report_Master_2011.12.29.pdf.

77. Tomi Routamo (ed.), "European Stress Tests for Nuclear Power Plants, National Report, Finland," Radiation and Nuclear Safety Authority, December 30, 2011, www.ensreg.eu/sites/default/files/EU_Stress_Tests_-_National_Report_-_Finland.pdf.

78. Personal communication, January 2012.

79. Federal Ministry for the Environment, Nature Conservation, and Nuclear Safety, "EU Stresstest National Report of Germany, Implementation of the EU Stress Tests in Germany," www.ensreg.eu/sites/default/files/EU_Stress_test_national_report_Germany.pdf.

80. Autorité de Sûreté Nucléaire, "Complementary Safety Assessments of the French Nuclear Power Plants (European Stress Tests)," December 2011, www.ensreg.eu/sites/default/files/120106%20Rapport%20ASN%20ECS%20-%20ENG%20validated.pdf.

81. Routamo (ed.), "European Stress Tests for Nuclear Power Plants, National Report, Finland."

82. Swiss Federal Safety Inspectorate, "EU Stress Test: Swiss National Report, ENSI Review of the Operators' Reports," http://static.ensi.ch/1326182677/swissnational-report_eu-stress-test_20111231_final.pdf.

83. Ministry of Economic Affairs, Agriculture and Innovation, "Netherlands' National Fukushima Stress Test for the Borssele Nuclear Power Plant," December 2011, www.ensreg.eu/sites/default/files/NetherlandsNatRep-StressTest2011-sec-v2.pdf.

84. Swiss Federal Safety Inspectorate, "EU Stress Test: Swiss National Report, ENSI Review of the Operators' Reports."

85. EDF Energy, "EU Stress Test, Sizewell B," www.edfenergy.com/about-us/energygeneration/nuclear-generation/documents/sizewell-b-stress-test.pdf, 66.

86. Wen-Chun Teng, "Safety Re-assessment of Taiwan's Nuclear Power Plants After Fukushiima Daiichi Accident," presentation at the 26th Japanese-Sino Seminar on Nuclear Safety, Tokyo, Japan, July 26–27, 2011, www.aec.gov.tw/www/english/international/files/sino25–02.pdf.

87. Eric de Fraguier, "Lessons Learned from 1991 Blayais Flood," RIC 2010 External Flood and Extreme Precipitation Hazard Analysis for Nuclear Plant Safety Session, March 11, 2010, www.nrc.gov/public-involve/conference-symposia/ric/slides/th35defraguierehv.pdf.

88. International Nuclear Information System (INIS), "Results of study and reference list regarding the Blayais nuclear power plant accident," www.google.com/url?sa=t&rct=j&q=&esrc=s&frm=1&source=web&cd=3&ved=0CDIQFjAC&url=http%3A%2F%2Fjolisfukyu.tokai-sc.jaea.go.jp%2Fird%2Fsanko%2Ffile07.xls&ei=xjcYT9LhDY-CtQawqP3mDQ&usg=AFQjCNGm28eaR-IRKmbFVfgxOJ95h7wEiw&sig2=phQrE8LWTQoHh0ojtNxwog.

89. Personal communication, January 2012.

90. Personal communication, January 2012, with reference to the article, "Why Were Regulations on Station Blackout Delayed?" in the January 2012 edition of the *Journal of the Atomic Energy Society of Japan*, which documented that the author had found few references to the Blayais event in Japanese nuclear safety literature and official reports.

91. International Atomic Energy Agency, "Flood Hazard for Nuclear Power Plants on Coastal and River Sites."

92. World Nuclear Association, "Tokaimura Criticality Accident," July 2007, www.world-nuclear.org/info/inf37.html.

93. Division of Fuel Cycle Safety and Safeguards, Office of Nuclear Material Safety and Safeguards, Nuclear Regulatory Commission, "NRC Review of the Tokai-Mura Criticality Accident," April 2000, www.nrc.gov/reading-rm/doc-collections/commission/secys/2000/secy2000-0085/attachment1.pdf.

94. Norimitsu Onishi and Ken Belson, "Culture of Complicity Tied to Stricken Nuclear Plant," *New York Times*, April 20, 2011, www.nytimes.com/2011/04/27/world/asia/27collusion.html?pagewanted=all.

95. Division of Fuel Cycle Safety and Safeguards, Office of Nuclear Material Safety and Safeguards, Nuclear Regulatory Commission, "NRC Review of the Tokai-Mura Criticality Accident."

96. Federal Office for Radiation Protection, "Sicherheit deutscher Atomkraftwerke gegen gezielten Absturz von Grobflugzeugen mit vollem Tankinhalt" (Safety of German Nuclear Power Plants Against a Deliberate Crash of Large, Fully Fueled Aircraft), www.rskonline.de/downloads/snabsturzgroflugzeugen111001.pdf. In the view of some European safety officials, German nuclear power plant owners' efforts to protect existing nuclear power plants against air crashes relied upon methods—such as use of smoke generators to disguise the location of critical infrastructure—which are unreliable and intended primarily to increase public acceptance.

97. *Investigation Commission on the Accidents at Fukushima Nuclear Power Plant Station, Provisional Report*, December 26, 2011, Executive Summary of the Interim Report, 16–18, http://icanps.go.jp/eng/111226ExecutiveSummary.pdf.

98. Personal communication, February 2012.

99. Personal communication, January 2012.

100. Personal communication, November 2011.

101. One safety official said that TEPCO had apparently disguised a track record of common-cause failures in equipment problems at its nuclear power plants by repairing equipment found to be faulty and then not recording the flaws. The practice became apparent, he said, when data from other Japanese utilities became available, documenting that they had experienced repeated failures in similar equipment but had kept records of the failures.

102. "TEPCO Admits Leaktightness Test Falsification," *Nuclear Engineering International*, November 3, 2002, www.neimagazine.com/story.asp?storyCode=2017707.

103. Investigation Commission on the Accidents at Fukushima Nuclear Power Plant Station, Provisional Report, December 26, 2011, Executive Summary of the Interim Report, 14.

104. For example, "TEPCO Ignored Latest Research on Tsunami," *Asahi Shimbun*, March 25, 2011, http://ajw.asahi.com/article/0311disaster/fukushima/AJ201103253443.

105. "Japanese Nuclear Plant Survived Tsunami, Offers Clues," Reuters, October 19, 2011, www.reuters.com/article/2011/10/20/us-japan-nuclear-tsunamiidUSTRE79J0B420111020.

106. Personal communication, January 2012.

107. "Complementary Safety Assessments of the French Nuclear Power Plants (European Stress Tests)."

108. Max Colchester, "EDF Pegs Nuclear Upgrade Cost at $13 Billion," *Wall Street Journal*, January 3, 2012, http://online.wsj.com/article/SB10001424052970203550304577138392366526910.html.

109. Omoto also included more robust accident management procedures, supported by design provisions, more advanced systems for hydrogen management, and enhanced enabling systems (such as for back up air supply for valves) as potentially contributing to "saving" the plant in such a case. We excluded these considerations from this paper. Officials from a leading government nuclear safety agency told us that currently the Fukushima accident is not well enough understood to estimate whether improved accident management would have stabilized the reactors without fuel melting and significant off-site releases.

110. "Japan's Uncertain Nuclear Energy Outlook in 2012."

53

WHOLE-OF-SOCIETY DISASTER RESILIENCE: THE SWEDISH WAY

Helena Lindberg

Director General, the Swedish Civil Contingencies Agency

Bengt Sundelius

Professor of Government, Swedish National Defense College

INTRODUCTION

After the 9/11 terror attacks in 2001, in the United States it became clear to the world that a new national security paradigm was needed. Gone was the era when a strong military capacity could be the primary resource to defend territorial borders and protect the well-being of a nation's citizens, property, or critical functions. This was reinforced by the terror bombings in Madrid (2004) and London (2005). More recent events, such as the massive volcanic ash cloud from Iceland (2010) and the earthquake in combination with the tsunami in Japan, displayed our vulnerabilities to disruption and destruction. Furthermore, these events have shown that another significant trend, globalization, has brought an intended, but also unforeseen coupling of systems that has created high levels of interdependence and new vulnerabilities.

Sweden has also had to recover from several dramatic security challenges in recent years. In 2004, over 500 Swedish citizens died in the waves of the tsunami in Southeast Asia. During the suddenly escalating Lebanon conflict of 2006, over 8,000 citizens were hastily, but successfully, evacuated out of harm's way. Days before Christmas 2010, the first suicide bomber in the Nordic region, exploded his bomb, luckily prematurely, near a crowded shopping street in the city center of Stockholm. Our neighbor, Norway, experienced a terrible mass murder in July 2011 undertaken by a solo terrorist.

One fundamental element of good governance is the responsibility to be able to manage everyday accidents and emergencies, but also to build the capacity to prevent, manage and recover from complex mega-disasters. So-called "Black Swan" events that are surprising and consequently can be expected to occur in Sweden and in other nations, and in many colors, in the future.[1]

SOCIETAL SECURITY

The concept of societal security is a pillar of the Swedish approach to the protection of our inhabitants. This is an acknowledgement of the fact that the threats and challenges of the twenty-first century are less about the integrity of territory than about safeguarding the critical functions of society, protecting people, and upholding fundamental values from many types of threats and risks. The threat from an armed attack by a state with the intent to capture and hold territory is very low today in our vicinity. Instead massive loss of life, damage to the socioeconomic system, and impairment of the capacity for rules-based democratic governance can be caused by failing critical societal functions. Societal security suggests an all-hazards approach, as many harmful consequences are similar regardless of whether an event is caused by ill-will, nature, or accident.

In Sweden, the government and the parliament have identified three components to be a baseline of the official objectives for societal security:

- Protect our population
- Maintain our fundamental values
- Secure the functionality of our society

If life and property cannot be safeguarded, then it is not a society where people can live. If a government cannot uphold key values, it will be a society where no one will want to live. Similarly, if a government cannot create and sustain resilient critical functions people will not have confidence in their leaders and in the long run an unstable society will emerge. It is an obligation of good governance to prepare for the unthinkable and to allocate the necessary resources to minimize the impact on people and on our democratic societies from catastrophic events, such as antagonistic attacks, man-made accidents, or natural disasters.

Societies and all its stakeholders, from individuals to government entities, private corporations, and nongovernmental organizations are challenged by a new and still evolving security context. As a result, Sweden has embarked on a course to create tools that can facilitate a *"whole-of-society"* approach for societal security. This resembles the strategies of a *"whole-of-community"* approach being pursued in the U.S. by the Obama administration.[2] This concept indicates a more inclusive approach than the previously advocated *"whole-of-government approach"* which is too narrow in scope. The effort toward enhancing societal security can only be effective to the extent that partners or stakeholders outside the sphere of government become engaged and contribute. Most importantly, individuals must be mobilized in a more direct manner than was presumed in the whole-of-government approach.

Another building block that underpins the whole-of-society approach is the concept of *disaster resilience*. The notion of resilience, usually described as a capacity to "withstand" or "bounce back" in the face of a disturbance, can be applied to citizens, organizations, technological systems, and societies as a whole.[3] It includes proactive mitigation, as well as speedy response and recovery, and relies on the ability among a range of interdependent stakeholders to share information and take coordinated action. An element of prevention could also be inferred, as for example terrorists and organized crime could be influenced to choose an alternative target if a nation is perceived to have a high degree of resilience.

The ambiguous concept of resilience is increasingly used by academics and includes several components, such as human, societal, organizational, political, and transnational contexts. A working definition of resilience is:

> *"Resilience is the capacity of a social system (e.g., an organization, city, or society) to proactively adapt to and recover from disturbances that are perceived within the system to fall outside the range of normal and expected disturbances."*[4]

The rapid rise of the use and popularity among practitioners of the term resilience may be driven by several factors. One driver is a better understanding of the nature of the security landscape, where uncertainty and complexity are key features. Another driver is shrinking national budgets that make it impossible to allocate huge sums of money to prevent certain scenarios or substantially minimize risk.

Disaster resilience is about shared risks, but also about shared costs. In a situation where governments have to manage a growing spectrum of harmful events with shrinking budgets, the issue of "cost transfer" has become increasingly critical. Doing more with less may be less of a challenge if more stakeholders are contributing to the effort. Ultimately, shared efforts will benefit all stakeholders in society. However, there should also be an element of doing things smarter with fewer resources. In contrast, the alternative of doing less with less offers no viable way forward. One needs to examine and learn from how different nations have handled this dilemma of finding less costly but still effective measures to enhance societal security.

Achieving a whole-of-society approach will require fostering a culture of horizontal coordination and networking across jurisdictional borders. Government reform is the stepchild of crisis. On both sides of the Atlantic, bureaucratic and political stakeholders have decided upon institutional reforms and shifts in strategic thinking concerning the security challenges for the twenty-first century. In the U.S. a whole new policy area emerged after the 9/11 attack, with the centerpiece being the new Department of Homeland Security (DHS) that became operational in 2003. In the European Union (EU), there are now several organizational entities such as a Home Affairs Commissioner and a counterterrorism coordinator. The most recent EU treaty, the 2009 Lisbon Treaty, includes a solidarity clause that requires and necessitates increased cooperation by the twenty-seven member states of the EU in the face of various attacks or disasters. In essence, an EU societal security policy area is being created and cultivated. This evolving field can be seen as a counterpart to the U.S. Homeland Security policy area. It would seem important that these distinct but clearly interrelated enterprises are in harmony.

For the future, it is essential that a strong transatlantic bond is forged in this area of societal security. The threats facing nations in the transatlantic basin in the foreseeable future are mainly nonmilitary and nonterritorial in nature and primarily directed against critical societal functions. The main stakeholders are the U.S., EU and member state entities. NATO has an important role, but it is more supportive in character, since most relevant policy areas and assets are outside its domain of responsibility. This theme was explored most convincingly by a group of scholars in the 2010 report, *Shoulder to Shoulder: Forging a Strategic U.S.-EU Partnership.*[5]

THE ENGINE THAT DRIVES THE ENTERPRISE IN SWEDEN

In Sweden there is broad political support for a "whole-of-society" approach on disaster resilience. A key reform was the creation of the Swedish Civil Contingencies Agency (MSB) in 2009 with the aim of building resilience across sectors and levels of government—reaching from the individual to society as a whole. The new agency replaced the Swedish Rescue Services Agency (SRSA), the Swedish Emergency Management Agency (SEMA), and the National Board of Psychological Defense (SPF). It was the result of Government Bill 2007/08:92 "Stronger emergency preparedness—for safety's sake."[6] The goal was to give coordinated support to society in the area of civil contingency management leading to enhanced emergency management capability at home and abroad by harnessing efficiency and effectiveness synergies.

An additional organizational innovation was a new crisis coordination secretariat in the prime minister's office that serves the needs of the Swedish cabinet offices (comparable to the U.S. White House staff). It was given three main tasks: operating a 24/7 situational awareness center, maintaining a strategic analysis cell, and creating a training and exercise unit for the staff of the ministries.

The trigger for these reforms was the tsunami of late 2004. Although the geographical location was far from Swedish territory, the dramatic loss of over 500 Swedish lives in a matter of hours[7] made clear that future challenges to societal security required a more nimble system. A government commission examined the response and recovery efforts and made recommendations for sweeping reforms. For Sweden, this devastating experience resembled that of the U.S., where reports by the 9/11 Commission noted a *failure of imagination* and the reports investigating the response to Hurricane Katrina highlighted a *failure of initiative.*[8]

MSB's mandate is a concrete expression of a widened policy field for crisis and disaster management, integrating across sectors, across the internal and the external divide, the risks and the threats, as well as the different management phases, before, during and after incidents. MSB is both an engine and a champion to create and facilitate a whole-of-society approach with diverse, and sometimes unevenly motivated, stakeholders.

The Swedish emergency preparedness system is primarily built on the principle of assigned responsibility, which means that whoever is responsible for an activity in normal conditions should maintain that corresponding responsibility during major emergencies. Coordination takes place across sector and jurisdictional boundaries and levels of authority, but MSB will not take over the direct responsibility of primary stakeholders. Coordination among many and diverse stakeholders is a key instrument for MSB to build a common capacity for effective action under the pressures of a diverse set of threats and risks.

The hardest obstacles to overcome for a whole-of-society approach to societal security are conceivably the deeply rooted mental gaps that tend to separate distinct professions with different training and backgrounds. Such gaps complicate close cooperation and smooth coordination, which in turn reduces effectiveness. Gaps in understanding exist between most professional areas, but can be exemplified by the following relationships:

- Between security and safety professionals
- Between civil and military professionals
- Between different civil authorities
- Between public authorities and the private sector
- Between the public domain and volunteer associations
- Between levels of authority
- Among individuals

All of these groups have in common the necessity to cooperate and coordinate before, during, and after an event to achieve the best results for society. Some key factors contributing to these mental gaps are that each category, over time, created their own terminology, ways of organizing, procurements of sector-specific technological solutions, and perhaps most importantly, established idiosyncratic education and training systems that foster sectoral approaches. Thus far, our systems have been better at accommodating interblocking stovepipes than interlocking networks.

Security and Safety Professionals

In general, a gap exists between safety and security professionals. One difference is the way that these groups work with information. Security officials are used to working with closed information systems to manage classified intelligence material, which they see little necessity to share outside a trusted few. Safety officials on the other hand are accustomed to using open information and may not even see a need for "intelligence-based" information. With threats becoming more complex, where an event at first can be difficult to define as an apparent "normal" accident or as a terrorist attack, robust cooperation between, for example, police forces and emergency responders needs to be developed well in advance. Emergency responders or local police can also be effective as additional eyes and ears to discover suspicious activities. Another example is to have trusted information systems so that the police and intelligence communities can provide intelligence to the public health community of impending threats in a timely fashion. This would create a better opportunity for health professionals and hospital systems to prepare if there are indications that CBRN (Chemical, Biological, Radiological, and Nuclear) materials could be used in an attack. As the security environment develops, it is necessary to foster greater understanding between the circles of security and safety professions to ensure the ability to connect the dots in time. [9]

Civil and Military Sector

In many ways, the gap between the civilian and the military sector can be among the easiest to overcome, as awareness is high of the need for closer coordination in planning and in operations in field missions abroad. An example was when MSB dispatched resources in the response phase of the Haiti earthquake using military strategic airlift capacity. The military is also highly standardized from an international perspective when it comes to planning, procurement, and exercises. It perhaps helps that the military has a centralized decision-making hierarchy. The question here is mainly about on whose terms coordination is pursued, as the military machine can overwhelm the more fragmented civilian resources.

Civil–Civil Coordination

Surprisingly civil–civil coordination may be one of the most complex areas. The primary reason is that the roles and responsibilities in the complex civilian sphere are often less clear cut and sometimes even overlapping. As threats and risks evolve, rules and routines may be missing or outdated. Jurisdictional lines can be viewed as complimentary or as competing. Some resistance to being coordinated can be detected, and one reason is probably that interactions for the purpose of modifying behaviors can be highly sensitive among proud professionals.

To foster joint capacity and a common outlook between civilian agencies in Sweden MSB supports six coordination arenas for stakeholder agencies in societal security. Of these six areas, five are thematically organized (see Figure 53-1) and one is territorially based (primarily for regional authorities that work together with the many autonomous municipalities).

These arenas are used to cooperate and collaborate for various purposes, for example, exchanging information on risk and vulnerability assessments and standardization processes, setting science and technology priorities and sharing results, and coordinating exercises and training activities. To support such activities, every year MSB provides these stakeholders with capacity building grants amounting to about 1 billion Swedish crowns ($150 million USD).

Public–Private Partnerships

Society cannot reach effective security solutions without engaging the private sector through public–private partnerships (PPP). The private sector is crucial, as it operates or owns most of the critical infrastructure in many nations. There was a rich tradition of PPP in Sweden during the Cold War days. At that time, cooperation and coordination were

Figure 53-1

"Coordination Areas" planning and preparedness. (Swedish Civil Contingencies Agency)

Swedish Civil Contingencies Agency

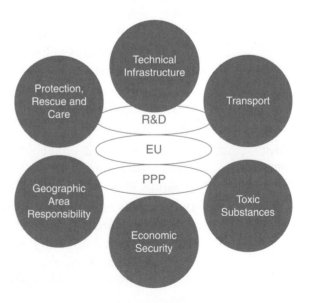

"Coordination Areas" Planning and Preparedness

smooth, as it was mutually understood that if total war would occur through a Soviet invasion there would be no more free enterprise. After that threat was dissolved much was lost in terms of incentives for continuing this close relationship through networking and nurturing trust. Adding to this, business practices and corporate ownerships changed. Today, privatization has gone very far in Sweden, as it has in other free market economies. Most companies have, or are part of, global supply chains that operate with just-in-time deliveries. These practices, however efficient, may not be the most resilient, which was felt by those companies that were dependent on deliveries from Japan after the earthquake and tsunami in 2011.

In Sweden, recent advances in terms of forging trusted relationships with key industry stakeholders have been uneven. In some sectors lost ground has been recaptured and progress has been made, like the well-functioning cooperation between the major players (public and private) in the financial sector, focusing on different aspects of business continuity. There is also a forum for information exchange on the security of critical SCADA (Supervisory Control And Data Acquisition) systems, which includes key operators of critical infrastructure. Those and other examples constitute "islands of excellence" from which lessons can be drawn. MSB seeks to extend the web of resilience to other sectors.

By creating a trusted environment for information sharing in normal times there is a stronger basis for common action when the extraordinary strikes. But besides trust, PPP requires practical frameworks for cooperation. Roles and responsibilities have to be clarified (joint training can provide a useful tool) and issues like financial (and other) incentives, market distortions, and liabilities have to be addressed. Those are all difficult questions for which there appears to be no universal recipe for success. Sweden is far from alone in struggling with these urgent issues. A useful step would be a more systematic international exchange of best practices.

Public Domain and Volunteer Associations

Sweden has a strong tradition of engaging volunteer associations in security enhancing work. But often the more traditional defense voluntary associations are not totally "in tune" with our new security demands and needs. In Sweden, this tradition of active voluntary organizations involve close to 500,000 people.[10] Many organizations were formed in the early twentieth century and most had a focus on supporting society before and during warlike situations. Many had, and still have, the task to support the armed forces either directly or indirectly. As the military has broadened its scope of activities to cover national tasks other than confronting armed attacks, as well as supporting civilian authorities in times of extreme emergency situations, so have many voluntary organizations.

MSB supports many voluntary organizations; independent, non-profit associations that recruit and train volunteers for community resilience tasks. As societies grow more diverse due to increasing migration flows, it is important to incorporate organizations representing various religious communities. MSB promotes such dialogues, since these organizations often are influential at the local level and reach many foreign-born individuals in Sweden. Over ten percent of the population is foreign born, and many are youngsters. This requires an understanding of many languages, and insights into various cultures and religions.

Between Levels of Authority

There are also mental gaps between the different levels of authority—the local, the regional, the national/supra-national (EU), and the international. The principle is that events shall be managed at the lowest level possible, but if one level is overwhelmed, the next level must be ready to step in and support efforts. This principle of subsidiarity is also a guiding element for the relationship between the EU and its member states in the civil protection field. To an extent, it may clash with another EU principle, that of solidarity among the member states and the peoples of the Union. U.S. readers should be quite familiar with the dilemmas of multilevel governance for emergency management.

Among Individuals

Making the individual a central component of societal security and resilience is critical. Without individual preparedness it will be quite difficult to achieve a whole-of-society approach with a strong level of disaster resilience. Individuals and families are often the ones affected most directly by a crisis, or are present on-site before first responders or other official representatives. Individuals should be viewed as assets. Furthermore, new social media technologies in the hands of citizens could be utilized by government agencies to receive and transmit information in a more timely manner. Earlier and better information is a driver towards more effective decision making.

In recent years, the government has emphasized the responsibility of the individual to be prepared for crises. MSB's task and challenge is to analyze what, more precisely, is included in this responsibility.

What services, and how quickly, can individuals expect services from the authorities on a local, regional, or national level to meet their demands before, during, and after a crisis or a major accident? How should cost sharing be balanced among the individuals, insurance providers, infrastructure owners and operators, and tax-funded government bodies at different levels?

MSB has developed several tools and channels to inform individuals about the benefits of being well prepared and conscious of risks and threats in society. Strategies for communication and education are different depending on the target group. MSB has identified two key groups that are particularly exposed and vulnerable: children and the elderly.

School systems provide an arena where MSB can disseminate information on a national level about safety issues. This audience includes not only children, teenagers, and their teachers, but also parents and other relatives. A central strategy of the work with schools is to offer education and training for teachers, aiding them in instilling a safety culture among their students.

Elderly people are another important target group. The elderly are over-represented in the statistics for many types of accidents, mostly at home. Major economic costs are associated with the elderly falling and dying. Because the number of elderly people is expected to increase by more than 25 percent in the coming decade this is a priority group. Extensive cooperation has been established between authorities, such as local health authorities, county councils, county administrative boards, municipalities, and organizations for the elderly.

A highly useful tool that exposes weaknesses and offers a way to achieve a whole-of-society approach is exercises. MSB leads the planning and the execution of exercises as well as the vital evaluation processes. An exercise was conducted in 2011 that involved thousands of participants in different organizations on all societal levels (local, regional, and national). It featured a nuclear accident scenario, which required close coordination and cooperation between many societal stakeholders. The exercise took place just a month before the real situation in Fukushima and sensitized the participants to the inherent challenges faced when confronted by real-world disasters. Increasingly used in these exercises are social media of different types. These are becoming more important to be able to rapidly collect information for situational awareness. Social media are also tools for meaning-making, to explain what the situation is about and what actions the government is taking. The new generation that is taking full advantage of increasingly sophisticated information technologies needs to be reached. In this recent exercise, the primary decision makers at the national level were overwhelmed by the impact of the pressures from the new media, as one could later witness in the rapidly evolving Japanese disaster.

TOWARDS AN ALL-HAZARDS PLUS APPROACH

MSB is involved with the entire spectrum of threats and risks to society—from everyday accidents to major disasters—and at all levels of society. MSB policies concern efforts to address issues before, during, and after the occurrence of accidents, emergencies, and disasters. Although the geo-political environment in the near-abroad is stable and an armed attack by another state against Swedish sovereignty is believed to be improbable, the possibility cannot be ignored in the future. This contingency is therefore included in the planning activities.

MSB provides the government with a nationally aggregated risk and vulnerability assessment. By law, all government entities are obligated since 2006 to produce and submit a risk and vulnerability analysis to MSB. The purpose is to guide investments and for MSB and other relevant departments to make informed decisions about scarce resources to build capacity and provide smart resilience.

A danger would be to equate all-hazards only with saving scarce resources, as the same capabilities can be used for several types of events. It must be recognized that an *all-hazards plus* approach is necessary, as certain antagonistic scenarios demand unique prevention, response, and recovery capabilities. One example would be an event involving weapons of mass destruction, which highlights the need for specialized prevention efforts and stockpiling pre-existing resources for response and recovery efforts. This all-hazards plus approach is different from the counterterrorism plus strategy used in the early years in the homeland security arena in the U.S. The immense investment in counterterrorism measures was then also used for other types of threats, where different solutions may have been more cost-effective. There also needs to be an understanding that all threats cannot be prevented or deterred. Resources need to also be allocated for early warning, response, and recovery efforts. Thus, the emphasis is on resilience in the Swedish approach.

Communicating the value of resilience is an implied acknowledgement that all threats and risks cannot be deterred or prevented. Accidents, disasters, and crises will happen. Establishing a risk-free society is in fact not possible or even desirable. The foundation of a resilient society is having prepared individuals, families, and communities. Therefore, motivating a private will among individuals to make reasonable investments in self-preparedness is a major public leadership challenge for the future.

Risk analyses are needed and the relationship between risk, threat, and basic societal values needs to be examined. Perceptions and social constructions of risk and threats are important additions to traditional methods of analyzing these phenomena. Methods for constructing national or regional risk maps with clear indications of consequences, including economic and social costs, are being developed. Comparative studies of national methodologies and profiles are needed. The EU Commission has initiated such a process and many governments are in the midst of putting together such risk maps. These need to be problematized and more firmly founded in research.

FLOW SECURITY

A central notion that characterizes the novel environment of the twenty-first century is flow security. Globalization is a force that has transformed how people, corporations, and societies organize and function. Technological developments have been transformational in their development of economies and ways of doing business.

Societies are tightly interconnected by flows of information, energy, computer signals, people and goods. For society to be prosperous, it is important to enable safe, secure, and efficient critical flows. If critical functions, such as transportation, energy, healthcare systems, agriculture, communications, and financial systems are debilitated, it can have consequences for all in society and on several continents simultaneously. This is a message advocated by Swedish Minister for Foreign Affairs, Carl Bildt.

> In this age of accelerating globalisation, the true security of our societies, or its citizens, economy and state institutions, is to a very large extent a function of the security of the flows across borders, of the securities of all of those flows of persons, goods, capital, energy, information, whether it be digital or otherwise, that flows across nations, regions and the globe; that is the core of the process of globalisation. To secure all of these flows all the way naturally requires a high degree of collaboration; national security is no longer enough.[11]

Thus, the traditional goals of ensuring territorial integrity and national sovereignty must be complemented with securing critical functions in society. These are linked by shared transnational or even global inter-dependencies that must not be transformed into vulnerability traps. Examples are the deliberate denial of critical metals or components, or simply interruptions in access due to various types of disasters.

Globalized flows are not always beneficial and desired. The flow of narcotics, weapons, trafficked persons, cyber intrusions and compu-ter viruses are examples of the dark side of globalization that requires more focused attention. Those working outside the law are more apt to take advantage of these flows than government regulators or political decision makers. Multilateral legal frameworks or regimes are needed to keep up with the rapidly evolving networks of positive and negative flows across national boundaries.

Certain flow enablers are highly critical, such as the maritime ship-ping lanes and harbors and the air transport system. However, a pri-mary enabler at the center of most globalized transactions is the cyber backbone that involves continental cables and central nodes. The cyber infrastructure links nations, companies, and citizens around the world and helps us channel information and goods more efficiently, but it also generates vulnerabilities. If the global digital infrastruc-ture is ruptured, it will have grave consequences for the financial sys-tems and for the command of critical infrastructure control systems in many industries.

The institutional design of government, however, is slow to adapt to this changing context for security. There is an historical legacy that separates agencies and departments operating in either the domestic or the international sphere. Failing to address jurisdictional, organi-zational, and even mental barriers to national and international organizational cooperation will be at our peril. Organized crime and terrorists, for example, maneuver in the trans-border sphere, which challenges outdated organizational structures. Exploring new ways to cooperate on planning, information exchange, training, and response is critical for the future. The new security sphere can be character-ized by the convergence of the domestic and international (security) arenas. The strategic setting is interdependent, as consequences in one country can have their origins far from that country's territorial border. The merging of the international and domestic settings into an operational sphere of "intermestics" will require individual and institutional rethinking to break mental, legal, and organizational stovepipes.

Globalization fueled by rapid technological developments has given rise to trans-boundary threats that may overwhelm our national prevention, protection, response, and recovery systems. These threats cannot be dealt with in a one-by-one manner. Isolation is not a solution for Sweden. A successful response will require a networked approach. In addition, the unconventional and trans-national nature of crises demands a multilateral response. This requires capacity to quickly combine and allocate resources, share expertise, information and disaster logistics, and synchronize crisis decision making. It demands a coordinated approach among international partners across continents. A critical task is being able to quickly and accurately diagnose a rapidly unfolding incident. The processes to achieve such shared sense making under difficult circumstances must begin long before the need becomes imminent.

It is impossible to predict what the next catastrophe will entail. However, we can safely assume that events are likely to provide consequences beyond what we have experienced so far. Some events may not even have a geographically defined impact zone, but can be felt across the globe. In particular, events that affect global arteries, such as the cyber-system, shipping lanes and air transport systems, will display our interdependent vulnerabilities. It is imperative to create tools to overcome the present status of vulnerability surpluses in combination with capacity deficits regarding foreseeing and meeting novel trans-boundary threats.

SWEDEN'S HOLISTIC PHILOSOPHY—A BALANCING ACT

The objective for society is to be able to prevent, respond to, and recover from unexpected high consequence events, thus having a high degree of disaster resilience. To achieve those objectives, three major components and three central values need to be delicately calibrated. The three building components require having a mix of highly trained individuals embedded in flexible organizational structures and drawing upon supportive technical systems. The solution resides in the combinational effects rather than in one or the other of these components. In addition, three central values need to be incorporated and skillfully balanced: security, efficiency and privacy/integrity (see Figure 53-2).

Figure 53-2

A holistic
perspective.
(Swedish Civil
Contingencies
Agency)

**GOAL: To be able to prevent, respond to and recover from unexpected high
consequence events we need highly educated and trained individuals in flexible
organizational structures with supportive technical systems.**

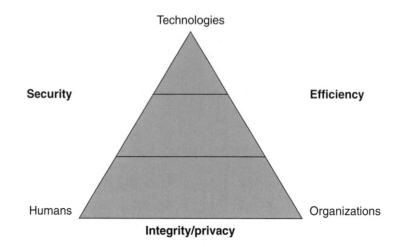

If security is the dominant value that underpins the societal security system it can have side-effects such as wasteful spending. Absolute security cannot be achieved, or will only result in making for an inhospitable society where few would like to live. Efficiency is an important value as it is an integral part of successful economic development. In the long term a nation without economic prosperity and growth will not be able to afford the level of security it desires. A foundation for a democratic society is respect for individual privacy and integrity. Carefully crafted temporary encroachments may be needed at times for security purposes at the expense of privacy and integrity. However, finding the right mix of these fundamental values is highly important in order to provide good economic and societal conditions for economic growth, citizen approval, and security. There is a continuous public debate on this balancing act in Sweden.

COOPERATION IN THE NORDIC AREA AND IN THE NEAR-ABROAD

Close cooperation in the area of societal security has existed for decades in the Nordic region, in spite of different role positions during the Cold War. Denmark, Iceland, and Norway belong to NATO, while Finland and Sweden have remained outside any military alliances. The former Minister of Foreign Affairs of Norway, T. Stoltenberg, was commissioned by his former Nordic colleagues to present a report with recommendations for more intense security collaboration in the region. His report was tabled in 2009 and it has generated a number of initiatives in the area of societal security.[12] One such innovation was the 2011 Nordic Solidarity Declaration,[13] which complemented the Solidarity Clause of the EU Lisbon Treaty.

Another recent step was to solidify deeper cooperation through the Nordic Declaration at Haga in 2009.[14] In this political statement, the ministers responsible for societal security agreed to further develop emergency management cooperation within specific areas. It is interesting to note that overall responsibility for societal security falls under three different ministries, Defense (Denmark and Sweden), Justice (Iceland and Norway), and Internal Affairs (Finland). This is an example that it is possible to bridge gaps between different ministries and professional groups and achieve notable results.

Several expert working groups for various concrete tasks were established at the Haga meeting and these are obligated to report annually to the ministers. In 2011, a working group addressing vulnerabilities and prospects for shared operational readiness in the cyber domain was added by the Nordic Foreign Ministers as the first step in making their solidarity pledge more concrete.

Enhanced cooperation in the Baltic Sea Region is also a centerpiece of regional capacity building for societal security. In 2009, an EU Strategy for the Baltic Sea Region was adopted that has four focus areas, one of them being safety and security.[15] Enhancing maritime surveillance and domain awareness through coupling the many national systems is a priority task. Facilitating closer cooperation of national emergency management systems leading to a more coordinated response in a transboundary disaster is another priority. Furthermore, MSB is involved in a project together with its regional counterparts (including EMERCOM of Russia) within the framework of the Council of Baltic Sea States (CBSS) to develop a regional risk assessment that can inform future planning for societal security. Within the purview of an agreement on cooperation on emergency prevention, preparedness, and response large-scale exercises are held between Norway, Sweden, Finland, and Russia in the Barents Region every other year.

The Arctic region is an area of increasing strategic importance as climate change over time will allow for new and increased activities, such as tourism (especially cruise ships), economic activity (fishing, transport routes, and oil and mineral exploration), and military movements. The Arctic Council that Sweden chairs until 2013, signed in 2011 its first binding agreement on "Cooperation on Aeronautical and Maritime Search and Rescue (SAR) in the Arctic."[16] This vast region around the North Pole is set to experience increasing trans-boundary activity, making common capacity building important. An agreement on mutual assistance in the case of oil spills in the Arctic will most likely be concluded in the near future. Also the U.S., Canada, and Russia are important participants in these multilateral arrangements.

DEVELOPING THE COMMON EU CAPACITY

The reality of trans-boundary risks is increasingly pushing European member states to deepen their cooperation and tighten the web of resilience across the Union. The internal market allows people, goods, and information to travel rapidly across national borders. Since the end of the 1980s, large sums have been invested in establishing so called Trans-European Networks for transport, energy, and telecommunications, which provide effective linkages between the EU's 500 million inhabitants. The recent economic crisis is also pushing member states towards closer financial integration.

As the chains of interdependence grow increasingly strong across the European homeland, there has been a renewed focus on the need for joint risk and threat assessment, as well as more developed instruments for "pooling and sharing" in crises and disasters. In 2009, during the Swedish Presidency of the EU, the Stockholm Program was presented, defining the common agenda for justice and home affairs over the next five years. An important component in this new work program was the call for a European Internal Security Strategy (ISS) and an action plan which would help define the area of European internal (societal) security and identify strategic priorities for the future. One of the key actions was the development by 2014 of "a coherent risk management policy, linking threat and risk assessments to decision making."[17]

In response to this, EU member states are currently involved in a joint effort to develop risk assessments at a national level, which will feed into a broad overview of major risks at a European level. Sweden has provided the Commission with a first report, identifying 24 different risks, some of which are considered serious enough to entail a possible need for European or international assistance.

EU capacity for managing risks and crises has been considerably boosted over the past few years, but is still marked by a lack of overall coherence. Within the Commission and among EU agencies there are currently a number of sector crisis centers and early warning systems focused *inter alia* on civil protection, health threats (pandemics, CBRN), nuclear security, food safety, migration, and critical infrastructure protection. With the new EU Lisbon Treaty and the creation of the External Action Service (EEAS), additional bodies for crisis response and EU coordination have emerged, increasing the possibilities for duplication and unclear divisions of responsibility.

One of the most advanced of these EU crisis centers, the so called European Response Center (ERC), is currently hosted by the Commissioner for International Cooperation, Humanitarian Aid and Crisis Response, Kristalina Georgieva. The ERC provides risk monitoring, training, and coordination of member states' resources across a wide risk spectrum, covering both EU-internal and external crises. In order to allow for a swift response, member states have agreed to organize their response capacities in pre-defined modules which are placed in a common pool. Since 2009, there has also been an increasing focus on the development of policies for disaster prevention and resilience within member states and non-EU countries.

Despite the raised ambitions for EU cooperation in risk and crisis management there is still untapped potential. The squeezing of national budgets will, over time, require more developed positions and policies on the pooling of resources. The concept of solidarity, which appears in a number of different sections of the Lisbon Treaty, may need to be more sharply defined to match future challenges such as the consequences of climate change and the growing cost of disasters. Article 222 (the Solidarity Clause) in the EU treaty states, in no uncertain terms, the political will to move towards closer integration of policies and instruments for cross-border cooperation and security in the EU:

> The Union and its Member States shall act jointly in a spirit of solidarity if a Member State is the object of a terrorist attack or the victim of a natural or man-made disaster. The Union shall mobilise all the instruments at its disposal, including the military resources made available by the Member States, to:
>
> - prevent the terrorist threat in the territory of the Member States; protect democratic institutions and the civilian population from any terrorist attack; assist a Member State in its territory, at the request of its political authorities, in the event of a terrorist attack;
> - assist a Member State in its territory, at the request of its political authorities, in the event of a natural or man-made disaster.[18]

So far EU member states have not revealed any lack of political will to support each other "in a spirit of solidarity" in situations of need. There are, however, still a number of hurdles of a practical, legal, or administrative nature that make cross-border assistance complicated in the EU and even more so in a Euro-Atlantic context. Some of those hurdles became apparent in the management of Hurricane Katrina in 2005. One of the more useful tools to pinpoint obstacles for international assistance is exercises. The topic of assistance across the Atlantic was recently explored at the National Level Exercise (NLE) 2011 in the U.S., but more narrowly focused and smaller exercises to identify problems and discuss constructive ways forward are needed.

EURO-ATLANTIC COOPERATION

The Euro-Atlantic strategic setting of entangled interdependencies, where critical functions and nodes rely on the actions of others, creates a necessity for a well functioning U.S. and EU partnership. Future trans-boundary crisis management in the transatlantic domain should not risk becoming "a failure of coordination." It is imperative to secure in advance an ability to act effectively and legitimately in concert within this new policy domain of the transatlantic partnership.

Although it is not necessary for the same institutional and strategic concept to be embraced on both sides of the Atlantic, it is important that efforts are, at a minimum, mutually reinforcing and not inter-blocking. It is also necessary to view homeland security, or societal security, as an activity rather than as the policy domain of a specific department, ministry, agency, or directorate.

While much has been achieved to put institutions and policies in place to make our domestic societies more safe and secure and to enhance the capacity for alleviating complex emergencies in distant places, we must not neglect to address our shared transatlantic space. "The responsibility to protect" has been established as a guiding principle for engagement by governments on behalf of suffering populations in non-EU countries. By the same logic, the governments around the Euro-Atlantic basin have a shared responsibility to protect their populations and their open democracies and economies. This is a core element of good governance, and something expected from the leaders of these nations by the voters. A Europe and North America, "whole and free" but suffering from societal vulnerability surpluses, would not be in line with the governing principle of the responsibility to protect.

As Dr. Cecilia Malmström, the EU Commissioner for Home Affairs and a former member of the Swedish Cabinet, has stated, the transatlantic community is in this enterprise together.

> Besides addressing global security we need to focus much more on cooperation on internal security. An attack on Baltimore is as much an attack on Berlin or Brussels. Our societies are so open and interlinked that no matter if an attack occurs in Europe or the U.S. we are both paying the price. So only by working together will we be able to counter terrorism. Only by working together will we be able to fight the cyber threat.[19]

The nature and origins of U.S. and EU developments within this complex and emerging policy area can be summarized as follows:

U.S. Homeland Security	EU Societal Security
• Instant reaction to 9/11	• Gradual developments over time
• Terrorism was the impetus, but now an all-hazards approach	• From looking to the East (Soviet Union and Warsaw Pact) to an all-hazards approach
• Clear decision in 2002 to create Department of Homeland Security (operational 2003)	• No formal decision (but irreversible step by step)
• Organizational focus	• Network-based cooperation
• Ample resources available	• Fragmented resources
• Domestic focus, but increasingly international outlook	• National focus, but an expanding multilevel and multisector EU approach

A vitalized and more coherent partnership in societal/homeland security needs to be forged between the EU institutions, the member states, and the U.S. A natural arena to establish and legitimize a new and critically important dimension of the partnership for a secure transatlantic community is the regular EU–U.S. summits. More concrete activities with joint working groups and task forces could be created to give these summits more of an analytical and cumulative underpinning. Considering the importance of enhancing the security of our own societies, it would be timely to launch an EU–U.S. Transatlantic Cooperative Security Working Group or Task Force to advance the discussion on societal security across all sectors.

Some important pioneering efforts exist in specialized sectors, such as in science and technology, cybersecurity, and civil protection. In addition to specialized transatlantic working groups, some of these cooperative arrangements are also regulated in Memoranda of Understanding (MoUs) or similar legal foundations. There are biannual high-level meetings between the EU and the U.S. in the area of Justice and Home Affairs, where, for example, DHS Secretary Napolitano meets with EU counterparts such as Commissioner Malmström and Commissioner Reading (EU Vice President and Commissioner for Justice). However, these meetings usually deal with the immediate and near-term affairs. At the 2010 EU–U.S. Summit, an EU–U.S. Working Group on Cybersecurity and Cybercrime was formed to discuss issues such as cyber incident management, public–private partnerships, awareness raising, and combatting cybercrime. An EU–U.S. cybersecurity table-top exercise, Cyber Atlantic, was organized in November 2011 with the aim to strengthen collaboration in the area of incident management and response.

Some DHS and EU agencies have signed formal agreements to cooperate within their silos of excellence. In 2009 DHS, for example, signed a Cooperative Work Arrangement with FRONTEX, the EU's border management agency, to share best practices on integrated border management, information sharing, risk analysis, training, and research and development.[20] The EU Directorate-General for Humanitarian Aid and Civil Protection (DG ECHO) signed an administrative arrangement with the U.S. Federal Emergency Management Agency in November 2011 to create a framework for sharing information in areas such as risk assessments, lessons learned, and exercises.[21] In 2010, the EU Commission and the Directorate for Science and Technology at DHS signed an implementing arrangement to cooperate in the field of homeland/civil security research. This can facilitate academic networks across the Atlantic that are competitive in funding opportunities within the EU's next Framework Program "Horizon 2020" and the DHS grant awarding process.[22]

All these examples of activities, working groups, and signed agreements are valuable, but insufficient if long-term and emerging vulnerabilities are to be addressed together. The suggested EU–U.S. Transatlantic Cooperative Security Working Group or Task Force, comprised of strategic policy planners, would serve as a cross-sector forum for strategic deliberations about threats, vulnerabilities, and response and recovery capacities that cut across sectors and borders.

It would complement existing professional work within established but stovepiped fora. It would provide the needed holistic and strategic perspective on what sectors and areas are working smoothly and where more attention is needed.

This is a relatively immature policy area lacking a developed professional corps to manage such a wide field of cross-sector and multilevel issues. Flow security is a shared concern that cuts across many sectors and stakeholder interests. Novel tools to meet these challenges need to be developed together and with a holistic perspective. How can a shared approach allow effective use of assets, as well as balancing core values such as privacy and civil liberties?

To further foster a shared understanding of the challenges and opportunities for cooperation, a common strategic executive training curriculum could be developed for senior leaders' transatlantic workshops in the societal security area. Education and training to cope with the unexpected and consequential is obligatory for advancements in the military sphere, why not for leaders in public service and business executives? Various NATO training programs have considerable experience and could inspire similar investments in strategic leadership for an all-hazards approach to security.

The task for an EU–U.S. Transatlantic Cooperative Security Work Group or Task Force would be to turn our shared values and preferences regarding security into action plans. Concepts have to be operationalized and transformed into concrete activities with deadlines and measurable effects. Academics and think tanks should be well placed to contribute ideas and expertise to such work. The time is overdue to turn the homeland security and societal security continental enterprises into interlocking work packages that transcend the Euro-Atlantic space.

NOTES

1. Taleb, N. Nassim, (2007) *The Black Swan: The Impact of the Highly Improbable*. Random House, New York.

2. A Whole Community Approach to Emergency Management: Principles, Themes, and Pathways for Action. FDOC 104–008–1 / December 2011. Federal Emergency Management Agency (FEMA). http://www.fema.gov/library/file;jsessionid=741676596316FFFCE0BDA5D4D6C84050.WorkerLibrary?type=publishedFile&file=whole_community_dec2011__2_.pdf&fileid=19b11000–1d02–11e1-a2c1–001cc456982e.

3. For an excellent in-depth study of the concept of resilience and its applications see *Designing Resilience: Preparing for Extreme Events*, by L.K.Comfort, A. Boin, and C.C. Demchak (eds.). Pittsburgh: University of Pittsburgh Press, 2010.

4. Ibid. p.9.

5. *Shoulder to Shoulder: Forging a Strategic U.S. – EU Partnership* (2010) Ed. by Daniel S. Hamilton. Washington D.C.: Johns Hopkins University Center for Transatlantic Relations.

6. Government Bill: Stärkt krisberedskap – för säkerhets skull, Prop. 2007/08:92 (2008). http://www.regeringen.se/sb/d/10393/a/101151.

7. With a population of 9 million, over 500 deaths would be comparable to a loss of 15000 lives in a few hours in the U.S.

8. *The 9/11 Commission Report* (2004) Final Report of the National Commission on Terrorist Attacks Upon the United States. http://www.9–11commission.gov/report/911Report.pdf; *The Federal Response to Hurricane Katrina: Lessons Learned.* February 2006, White House; *A Failure of Initiative.* Final Report of the Select Bipartisan Committee to Investigate the Preparation and Response to Hurricane Katrina. (2006) U.S. House of Representatives.

9. *New Information and Intelligence Needs in the 21st Century Threat Environment* (2008). Report No. 70. The Henry L. Stimson Center, Washington D.C. http://www.stimson.org/images/uploads/research-pdfs/SEMA-DHS_FINAL.pdf.

10. http://www.forsvarsmakten.se/sv/Forband-och-formagor/Frivilligorganisationer/

11. Speech by Swedish Foreign Minister Carl Bildt (December 2010) The Changing Nature of Regional Security Issues. The 7th IISS Regional Security Summit, the Manama Dialogue. http://www.iiss.org/EasySiteWeb/getresource.axd?AssetID=50249&type=full&servicetype=Attachment.

12. Nordic Cooperation on Foreign and Security Policy. Proposals presented to the extraordinary meeting of Nordic foreign ministers in Oslo on 9 February 2009. Thorvald Stoltenberg. http://www.mfa.is/media/Frettatilkynning/Nordic_report.pdf.

13. The Foreign Ministers of Denmark, Finland, Iceland, Norway, and Sweden met in Helsinki on 5 April 2011 for their biannual meeting to discuss matters of common interest in the area of foreign affairs and security policy including a Nordic declaration on solidarity. http://www.regjeringen.no/upload/UD/Vedlegg/Nordisk%20samarbeid/Deklarasjon_nordisk_utenriksministermote_Helsingfors050411_vedtatt_versjon.pdf.

14. Haga-deklarationen: Nordiskt ministermöte rörande samhällsskydd och beredskap Stockholm 27 april 2009. (Text of the Haga Declaration, in Swedish). https://www.msb.se/Upload/Om%20MSB/Internationellt/Deklaration%20Haga-deklarationen%20slutlig%20(4)%5b1%5d.pdf.

15. Communication from the Commission to the European Parliament, The Council, The European Economic and Social Committee and the Committee of the Regions concerning the European Union Strategy for the Baltic Sea Region. Brussels 10.6.2009. COM(2009) 248 final. http://eur-lex.europa.eu/LexUriServ/LexUriServ.do?uri=CELEX:52009DC0248:EN:NOT.

16. Agreement on Cooperation on Aeronautical and Maritime Search and Rescue in the Arctic, signed April 2011. http://www.arctic-council.org/index.php/en/about/documents/category/20-main-documents-from-nuuk?download=73:arctic-search-and-rescue-agreement-english.

17. See "The EU Internal Security Strategy in Action: Five steps towards a more secure Europe," COM(2010) 673 final, Brussels 22.11.2010.

18. Consolidated Version of The Treaty on The Functioning of The European Union, 9.5.2008, Official Journal of the European Union C 115/47. http://eurlex.europa.eu/LexUriServ/LexUriServ.do?uri=OJ:C:2008:115:0047:0199:EN:PDF.

19. Cecilia Malmström, Member of the European Commission responsible for Home Affairs. The EU Internal Security Strategy – What does it mean for the United States? Discussion organized by The Center for Transatlantic Relations Washington DC, 8 December 2010. http://europa.eu/rapid/pressReleasesAction.do?reference=SPEECH/10/739&format=HTML&aged=0&language=en&guiLanguage=en.

20. Press Release Frontex: Frontex and the US Department of Homeland Security http://frontex.europa.eu/news/-frontex-and-the-us-department-of-homeland-security-FOVAKa.

21. Administrative Arrangement between the U.S. Department of Homeland Security Federal Emergency Management Agency and The Directorate-General for Humanitarian Aid and Civil Protection of the European Commission (November 2011) http://www.fema.gov/pdf/about/offices/iad/us_aa_eu_signed.pdf.

22. Implementing Arrangement between the Government of the United States of America and the European Commission for cooperative activities in the field of homeland/civil security research (November 2010). http://www.dhs.gov/xlibrary/assets/sandt-implementing-arrangement.pdf.

54

EVOLUTION OF COUNTERTERRORISM AND SECURITY IN INDIA

R.V. Raju

Former Director General of the National Investigation Agency of India

> "Who lives if India dies? Who dies if India lives?"
> —Jawaharlal Nehru[1]

India's federal polity has clearly demarcated subjects that shall be the exclusive preserve of the central government and the state governments, as well as subjects over which both the central and state governments would have concurrent jurisdictions. These subjects figure in Lists I, II, and III of the Seventh Schedule of the Indian Constitution. These Lists are called the Central List, the State List, and the Concurrent List, respectively. Public order and police figure as item numbers 1 and 2 of the State List. At the time of the promulgation of the Indian Constitution, the problems confronting the nation on the law and order front could be tackled by the criminal laws that were then in use, and the police machinery that was available to the central government and the governments in the states. The Indian Army was used to tackle the Naga insurgency in the Northeast. The controversial Armed Forces (Special Powers) Act, 1958, was passed to empower the Armed Forces to tackle armed militancy in the Northeast, as the state government was found incapable of tackling militancy in the region.[2]

Terrorism as we know it today raised its head in India in the early 1980s, in the North and the Northeast. The borders were porous, and hostile neighbors provided material support to the militants. Their initial targets were members of the security forces and noncombatants. However, it was not until the assassination of Prime Minister Indira Gandhi by her Sikh bodyguards in October of 1984, that India enacted an anti-terror law, the controversial Terrorist and Disruptive Activities (Prevention) Act (TADA) in 1987, with a sunset clause that it would be in force for two years from 24 May, 1987.[3] This law was given an extension every two years until 1995. The assassination of Mrs. Gandhi was a direct consequence of Operation Blue Star in June of 1984. This Army operation took place in the Golden Temple in Amritsar, the holiest shrine of the Sikhs, which had been taken over by heavily armed Sikh militants. The operation led to damage to the buildings and deaths of hundreds of militants and devotees who were trapped in the Temple.

The TADA provided for admission of confessions, made before senior police officers of the rank of Superintendent of Police and above, as evidence in courts of law. In normal cases, the Indian Evidence Act bars confessions made before police officers from being used in trials. This special provision was made in the TADA, as witnesses were not willing to depose against terrorists in the courts. The TADA also provided for detention of accused persons in police custody for up to two months, compared with the normal provision of 15 days and for in-camera trial. The final report of the investigation could be filed in the court within a year's time, as opposed to the normal period of 90 days, and during this period the accused would continue in judicial custody.

The National Security Guard Act was passed by the Indian Parliament in September of 1986, "to provide for the constitution and regulation of an armed force of the Union for combatting terrorist activities with a view to protecting States against internal disturbance and for matters connected therewith."[4] According to the official website of the National Security Guard, the agency was set up with the specific purpose "to tackle all facets of terrorism in the country. Thus the primary role of this Force is to combat terrorism in whatever form it may assume in areas where activity of terrorists assumes serious proportions, and the State Police and other Central Police Forces cannot cope up [sic] with the situation. The NSG is a Force specially equipped and trained to deal with specific situations and is therefore, to be used only in exceptional situations."[5] Though the operational division of the NSG consisted of officers and men drawn from the Indian Army, officers and men were also taken on deputation from the paramilitary forces and the states, and it was headed by a senior police officer. One of the NSG's important tests came in May of 1988, when the Golden Temple was once again occupied by militants. But this time, the Punjab police, led by the redoubtable police officer KPS Gill, together with the NSG, tired out the militants by means of a protracted siege denying them essentials, and calling on them to surrender. The ploy finally succeeded.

After the assassination of Prime Minister Indira Gandhi, the security detail of the prime minister was reorganized. A special force was created for the proximate security of the prime minister due to the incessant terrorist threats to his person. This force was called the Special Protection Group (SPG), and it was given statutory authority by an Act of Parliament, called the SPG Act, 1988.[6] This Act ensured that there was no interference, either political or administrative, in the matter pertaining to the prime minister's proximate security.

Throughout the 1980s, India faced terrorist attacks in its North and East. Moreover, Tamil militancy in Sri Lanka's Northeast region had its own impact on South India, with thousands of Sri Lankan Tamils pouring into the State of Tamil Nadu, and the various Tamil militant groups setting up base there.

Punjab and Delhi bore the brunt of the terrorist attacks unleashed by Sikh militants, though the Chief of the Army Staff at the time of the Blue Star operation in the Golden Temple, General A K Vaidya, was killed by Sikh militants in Pune in August, 1986.[7] While some of the sensational terrorist cases were investigated by India's premier investigation agency, the Central Bureau of Investigation (CBI), most of such cases were handled by the local or state police, which were ill equipped to tackle these cases. Police and law and order were state subjects according to the Indian Constitution, and as such, terrorist cases occurring in different states were registered in the local police stations and investigated by very junior officers. Very little, if any, use of forensic tools was made during investigations by the state police officers, and in most cases, such assistance was hardly available. The focus was invariably on maintaining law and order and providing security to VIPs, with investigations taking a backseat.

According to Mr. P. Chidambaram, India's Home Minister who was addressing an elite gathering of India's security bosses on the occasion of the Intelligence Bureau's Centenary Endowment lecture in December 2009, the over 13,000 police stations in the country were functioning as islands. And, while there was better connectivity, there was no single system of data storage, data sharing, or accessing data. There was "no system under which one police station [could] talk to another directly."[8] There was "no record of crimes or criminals that [could] be accessed by a Station House Officer, except the manual records relating to that police station." Indian police were grossly under-staffed, with about 142 policemen for every hundred thousand citizens, compared with 250 in Western countries. The police were badly equipped, with the majority of them armed with the obsolete .303 Royal Enfield rifles, without modern communication equipment or bulletproof jackets or helmets to take on heavily armed terrorists.[9]

Thus, at the end of the 1980s, Punjab, Delhi, and the Northeast of India were severely affected by terrorism, and terrorist attacks had taken place in other parts of India as well. India's counterterrorist architecture consisted of a highly proficient group to protect the person of the prime minister, giving him proximate security; a group to take on terrorists in exceptional circumstances like kidnappings and hijackings; and a law to deal with terrorist cases. But by and large, the police set-up in the States was not yet geared to take on the terrorists in India.

The Kashmiri insurgency, backed by training, funding, and material support from Pakistan, broke into the open in 1988–89 in the beautiful valley of Kashmir in North India. Selected killings of police personnel and well-known people like judges and politicians belonging to the minority community, as well as explosions in public places, heralded the commencement of this phase of the insurgency. Two books by eminent Pakistani Academic/Diplomat Hussain Haqqani and journalist Arif Jamal explain how the Pakistani military ruler, General Zia Ul-Haq, had planned to divert funds and arms received from foreign powers for the jihad in Afghanistan to conduct a jihad in Kashmir for its "liberation" and amalgamation with Pakistan.[10] What is important here is the fact that the Jammu & Kashmir police, like the other police forces in the states of India, was totally unprepared to face terrorists armed with sophisticated AK 47s, rocket propelled guns, universal machine guns/Pika guns, grenades, and sophisticated communication equipment. The early years of militancy in Kashmir, therefore, saw the Indian Army and the paramilitary forces like the Border Security Force and the Central Reserve Police Force being used to tackle militant attacks in the valley of Kashmir. The Rashtriya Rifles, a subsidiary force of the Indian Army, was introduced in Kashmir during this phase of militancy. Ambushes and militant attacks with car bombs and other improvised explosive devices became common, and though the Armed Forces neutralized hundreds of armed militants and suffered losses themselves, there were also serious charges of human rights violations in the valley.

As mentioned earlier, police is a State subject, firmly under the control of the state governments. While everyone watched what was happening in the Punjab and in Jammu & Kashmir with concern, it did not strike any of the state governments that terrorism might spread to other parts of India. Each state government thought that their state was safe, and that terror would not ever find any place in their region. The extremist communist groups like the Peoples' War of Andhra Pradesh had not grown into the menace that they have now become. In view of this, no attempt was made to draw lessons from the events in Punjab, Jammu & Kashmir, or the Northeast by any of the state police organizations. The only Indian security organization that made a serious study of militancy and terrorism was the Intelligence Bureau, which had some of the best police minds in India. But they only had an advisory role, sending warning signals to the central Ministry of Home Affairs (MHA) and the state governments on the basis of their intelligence reports and analytical assessments.

According to certain official reports, there were Pakistani attempts to link the Sikh militants with a pan-Indian extremist Islamic movement and the Students' Islamic Movement of India, spreading this militant extremism across India.[11] The demolition of the Babri Masjid, a three-hundred year old monument credited to the first Mughal Emperor of India, in December of 1992 by fanatical Hindu right-wing mobs brought a paradigm change in the situation, especially after communal riots broke out in the wake of the Masjid's destruction targeting minority Muslims in places like Bombay.[12]

The destruction of the Masjid and the subsequent riots targeting Muslims in Bombay (currently known as Mumbai) and other places led to radicalization of sections of the minority youth, and have been cited as causative factors for the serial Mumbai blasts that took place in March 1993, killing over 250 innocent people. This was the most devastating terrorist attack to take place in India up to that time, and easily one of the worst in the world. Subsequent investigations revealed a nexus between terrorism and organized crime, the latter being led by the notorious Mumbai Don Dawood Ibrahim, currently based in Pakistan, whose smuggling network was used to bring into Mumbai huge quantities of RDX and a large number of AK 56 rifles.[13]

While Jammu & Kashmir saw an escalation of cross-border terrorism, there were terrorist attacks in other parts of India as well. These included the assassinations of former Prime Minister Rajiv Gandhi by a suicide bomber of the Liberation Tigers of Tamil Eelam, a terrorist group of Sri Lanka, near Chennai in South India in May 1991;[14] the assassination of Chief Minister Beant Singh of Punjab by terrorists of the Babbar Khalsa International[15] in August 1995; the Coimbatore blasts of February 1998;[16] the attack on scientists in the Indian Institute of Science in December 2005;[17] attacks on local trains in Mumbai in July 2006;[18] and attacks in crowded markets[19] and religious places in different cities of India. Even though there was a highly professional group with statutory powers for the proximate security of the prime minister, the shortsightedness of Indian politicians came through in the fact that the law was made applicable only to serving prime ministers. The SPG Act was introduced in the Parliament when Rajiv Gandhi was the prime minister, as he was facing threats from several terrorist groups. Though there were voices in Parliament which asked that the law be made applicable to former prime ministers as well, they were ignored, due to the pervasive belief that Rajiv Gandhi would continue as prime minister for a long time to come. He was, however, defeated in the elections held in 1989, and the SPG cover given to him was withdrawn. Had the SPG cover been provided to him when he was on election tour in May 1991, the suicide bomber would not have had the opportunity to attack him.

In May 1995, the TADA lapsed due to the sunset clause incorporated in the law. This was due to serious and well-founded allegations of misuse of the law against minority community members, as well as general opposition to the law.[20] The expiration of TADA was followed by the passing of the Prevention of Terrorism Act (POTA) in 2002, amidst widespread opposition, by the right wing Bharatiya Janata Party Government.[21] The POTA incorporated some safeguards, however, as soon as the United Progressive Alliance Government took over the reins of the central government in May 2004, one of its first acts was to withdraw the POTA. Thus, though India continued to face serious terrorist problems, there was no consistency in government thinking about having a law to tackle it. On top of it all, the Supreme Court of India, while disposing of the appeal of the accused in the assassination of Rajiv Gandhi by a suicide bomber, held, in its order of May 1999, that the assassination had not been a "terrorist act" as defined in the TADA which was the law that had been applied in the case![22] To think that it was the first human bomb used to assassinate a political leader who was a former prime minister, and that nine police officers, including the district superintendent of police perished in the bomb attack along with Rajiv Gandhi, and yet it was not deemed to be a terrorist act! It took over eight years following the assassination for the Supreme Court to confirm the conviction in the case and uphold the death sentences handed down to four of the twenty-six accused who had faced trial. In one of these cases, the death has since been commuted to a life sentence. In the case of the other three, there are fierce discussions in the media that they have been wrongly convicted and should be set free, although due process of law had been clearly observed in both letter and spirit throughout the trial and appeal process.

Later in 1999, an Indian Airlines flight from Kathmandu on the way to Lucknow was hijacked by Pakistani terrorists in order to secure the release of Maulana Masood Azhar and Omar Sheikh (later involved in the killing of U.S. journalist Daniel Pearl) from Indian prisons. The flight was stopped for refueling in Amritsar for a short while, but the Indian Crisis Management Group fumbled and miserably failed to dispatch the NSG to tackle the terrorists. The government finally had to buckle under public/media pressure and release three hard core terrorists, including Masood Azhar and Sheikh Omar, one a Pakistani and the other a Briton of Pakistani origin. Masood Azhar was to later form the Jaish-e-Mohammad, a terrorist outfit responsible for the attack on the Indian Parliament on 13 December 2001, and the Jammu & Kashmir Legislative Assembly earlier in October of that year,[23] while Omar Saeed Sheikh was held in Pakistan for the murder of journalist Daniel Pearl.[24]

Thus despite being subjected to terrorist attacks in Punjab, Jammu & Kashmir, India's financial capital Mumbai, and several Indian cities, as well as on iconic Indian targets, India did not have a consistent counterterrorism policy or architecture to fight terrorists. State police organizations continued to be neglected, and no expertise was built either for investigation of terrorist crimes or to fight terrorist attacks, with only a few honorable exceptions.

Historically, Indian borders have been notoriously porous, and this fact has helped in pushing in militants into J&K and other border regions. A fence has now been built at the borders—including in J&K, except where the terrain is not suitable for fencing—to prevent cross-border movement of terrorists. While this has not completely stopped militant movement, there has been some positive check on movement into India. The Border Security Force, the Sashastra Seema Bal, the Indo-Tibetan Border Police, and the Assam Rifles guard the various borders of India. The Central Industrial Security Force has been trained to guard sensitive installations and industrial complexes, including airports, most of which have come under terrorist attacks or threats.

The southern state of Andhra Pradesh had been bedevilled by the extremist communist movement, Peoples' War Group (PWG), since the early eighties. There were strong indications of the Sri Lankan Tamil militant group LTTE colluding with the Peoples' War, training them in launching improvised explosive devices,[25] and supplying them with sophisticated AK47 assault rifles.[26] A study of casualties inflicted on Indian security forces by the PWG since 1989, when this collusion was suspected, would show the increase in casualties among security forces due to the extensive use of IEDs by this group. The PWG developed deep roots in the state. The primary causes for the rise of the extremist communist movements like the PWG are lack of governance and land reforms. The Andhra Police have an exclusive force, the Greyhounds, set up to fight the PWG in its own backyard. This force was trained in jungle warfare, like the PWG, and learned to survive in jungles for days and weeks at a time. The strength of the Greyhounds was the intelligence network that the Andhra police had developed exclusively to deal with the PWG.[27] Political governments, including the Congress party and the Telugu Desom, attempted to enter into talks with the group, but were unsuccessful, as the group only believed in displacing the democratically elected government through the use of guns. Participation in the talks was used as a tactic by the PWG to gain time to consolidate or replace resources, or to escape the net drawn by the Greyhounds to trap and eliminate them.[28] The PWG succeeded in killing scores of politicians, including members of Parliament and ministers of the government of Andhra Pradesh. There was a murderous attempt on the life of Chandra Babu Naidu, then Chief Minister of Andhra Pradesh, who survived the attempt by a whisker.[29] The Andhra Police has succeeded in driving out the bulk of the PWG from Andhra, but they have spread to other states from where they are directing the movement. The states of Chhatisgarh, Jharkhand, Orissa, Maharashtra, Madhya Pradesh, Bihar, and West Bengal are seriously or partially affected by Naxal trouble.

The other exception to the development of expertise in dealing with terrorism is the Jammu & Kashmir police. This organization was drawn into the mainstream to fight militancy after being kept out for over three years from 1990 to 1993. The J&K police rapidly developed local sources, and based on pinpointed information, began targeting and eliminating militant leaders. There were threats to the force and members of their families. But the police leadership, with firm grounding in the state, rose to the occasion and devised means to protect their men who fought the terrorists. The Special Operations Group (SOG) of the J&K police became the lead agency in the campaign against terrorism,[30] and soon the army and the paramilitary forces were vying with each other to partner with the SOG. Bulletproof jackets, vehicles, and the best arms were made available to the force to take on the militants. The SOG generated its own information, and soon allegations of human rights violations started emerging against officers of the SOG, which had to be countered. While individual aberrations in the conduct of the SOG have taken place and been dealt with, by and large the SOG has distinguished itself as an outstanding operational unit in all major cities and towns of Jammu & Kashmir. The Union Home Ministry gave generous funds to the J&K police under modernization grants, which enabled the police to upgrade their police stations, other police buildings, police housing,[31] and vital equipment needed to take on the militants.

The Lashkar-e-Taiba's (LeT) assault on India's financial capital of Mumbai on 26 November 2008 was perhaps the most devastating terrorist attack in the world, after 9/11. In this assault, 10 men of the LeT, armed with sophisticated AK 47s, grenades, improvised explosive devices, and communication equipment, including mobile phones with Indian SIM cards, landed in a dinghy near Colaba on the Mumbai coast. Working in pairs, the terrorists went about mowing down civilians at different sites, including iconic hotels like the Taj and Oberoi. They held the nation hostage for some 60 hours, by which time about 166 persons, including several foreigners, had been killed.[32] The operation was shown live on TV, and reflected poorly on the preparedness of Indian security agencies and their ability to quickly counter the raiders. This happened despite warnings from the Americans that a seaborne jihadi assault on Mumbai was in the offing.[33] Later investigations established that the LeT assault team had hijacked an Indian fishing vessel, Kuber, the crew of which, excluding the captain, were killed. The captain was forced to navigate the vessel until it approached the Mumbai coast. Thereafter, the captain's throat was slit and his body abandoned in the Kuber itself.[34] The terrorists used a dinghy to cover the remaining distance to the coast. The arrest in the United States of David Coleman Headley, aka Daood Gilani, a U.S. citizen of Pakistani origin, for conducting surveillance of targets in Mumbai for the LeT's attacks in November 2008, and for surveillance of the Jyllands Posten newspaper office in Denmark, selected as a target by the jihadis for publishing cartoons of the Prophet of Islam, brought out links to the Pakistani spy agency, the ISI, in the Mumbai attacks and the planned attacks in Denmark.[35] Both the U.S. federal agency and the National Investigation Agency of India have filed charge sheets in the courts against the ISI officers and others for the Mumbai attacks of November 2008.[36]

There were dozens of landing points for fishing vessels in Mumbai where there were no police posts to conduct any checks.[37] One recalls the ease with which sophisticated arms and explosives were landed on the Indian coast in early 1993 by the Dawood Ibrahim network, just before the Mumbai serial blasts of March 1993. From March 1993 to November 2008, there were still no police posts in place to check the unmanned landing points for fishing vessels. It was only following Mumbai's 26/11 attack that certain measures were taken to upgrade coastal security in India, including additional patrolling by the Indian Navy and Indian Coast Guard (ICG) aircraft and ships. A new force, called the Marine Police, would patrol the 12 nautical mile area of India's territorial waters. Radar was to be set up all along the coast, which would detect ships at between 30 to 50 nautical miles. Through the use of this technology, as well as shipborne and airborne radar, details about the crew, cargo, movement, last port of call, and next port of call of these ships would be obtained through the Automatic Identification System (AIS).This system is triggered by radar pulses from the aforementioned sources. According to a report,[38] "the coastal radar chain was to have an optronic sensor which would enable the display of TV-like images of ships and fishing vessels in India's territorial waters. Any vessel not triggering an AIS response on the radar screen would be immediately stopped and searched." Additional trained manpower, patrol ships, and boats, along with fishermen all along the coast have been brought into this security grid adding muscle to the coastal security. But the implementation of this network will take time, and already three years have gone by since the Mumbai attack. In the meantime, two abandoned ships, MV Wisdom and MV Pavit, recently floated into the Mumbai coast undetected, questioning the efficacy of the various measures that have been put in place to date.[39]

For the first time, after seeing the rampaging terrorists destroy life and property in Mumbai, the states, which used to jealously guard their rights under the Constitution, kept quiet as the new National Investigation Agency (NIA) Act was passed and some teeth were added to the Unlawful Activities (Prevention) Act (UAPA) by an amendment in the Parliament just weeks after the 26/11 attack.[40] According to the new Act, the Ministry of Home Affairs could direct the NIA to take over any terror-related case from any state without that state government's consent, though police and police work, including investigation, are state subjects under the Constitution. This Act was passed not by amending the Constitution, which would have been the right way of doing it, but by invoking Article 253 of the Constitution, which empowers Parliament to make laws for the whole or any part of the territory of India in order to implement any treaty, agreement, or convention with any other country or countries, or to ratify decisions made at any international conference. Sooner or later, one or more state governments may challenge this Act on the ground that it was against the federal spirit of the Constitution. The amended UAPA gives police the ability to keep an accused person in custody for 30 days, compared with the normal 15 days, and charges could be brought against the accused within 180 days, as opposed to the normal 90 days. However, confessions made by accused before police officers, even of superior rank, are not admissible in courts.

In short, the anti-terror architecture in the country consists of the amended law to deal with terrorists, which is not as strong as the TADA or POTA were. India has an agency exclusively to deal with terrorist cases, but it cannot *suo moto* take up terrorist cases; it can take up cases only when the Ministry of Home Affairs directs it to do so by a written order. The foundations of the UAPA are weak, as it was not passed by amending the Constitution, and therefore the MHA itself is not sure which cases it should transfer to the NIA! After the NIA was set up in January of 2009, there have been several major terrorist incidents, in Pune and Mumbai, and a few in Delhi. Only one of these cases was given to the NIA for investigation. Following India's 26/11, at which time the counterterrorist force NSG took several hours to reach Mumbai from Delhi, it was decided to set up NSG hubs in Mumbai, Chennai, Hyderabad, and Kolkata.[41]

There are anti-terrorist units in most states, and some of them are doing exceptionally well, like the West Bengal unit. Whether these anti-terror units can take on the terrorists in an urban or rural setting remains to be seen. The Maharashtra Police have set up a separate unit, called Force I, to fight the terrorists. They have been equipped with modern weapons and armor to defend them against terrorist fire, but they do not have any field exposure. It would be a good idea if such units trained alongside Jammu & Kashmir's Special Operation Groups, which have been fighting terrorists over the last fifteen years, and have been coming out on top.

The NIA has been organizing regional conferences to create coordination between themselves and these anti-terrorist units in the states. Officers of other relevant agencies, including the Narcotics Control Bureau, Customs, and Central Excise have also been participating in these conferences.[42] Intelligence sharing has become more effective, with the Multi-Agency Centre in the Intelligence Bureau having been reactivated and the subsidiary centers in the states doing similar work.

In the meantime, two of Home Minister P. Chidambaram's pet projects are taking shape, though not as originally envisaged by him. One of these projects is the NATGRID, or national intelligence grid. This agency was to bring together 21 different databases, including banking, insurance, immigration, income tax, telephone, rail and road travel, credit card accounts, passport and visa records, pan card details, voter card details, land records, and drivers' license records, and provide access to 11 security agencies, including the newly created National Investigation Agency. This would be of significant assistance to these agencies during investigation of cases, though its usefulness for preventing terrorist attacks is questionable. After much debate, the Home Ministry was able to allay fears expressed by other sections of the government in regard to privacy of individuals, following which the Cabinet Committee of Security (CCS) cleared the first two phases of the project. The next two phases of the project will be cleared after the proposal is resubmitted to the CCS, and some changes in existing laws may be required.

But the most important counterterrorism project of the Home Minister, the setting up of the National Counter Terrorism Centre (NCTC), has had a checkered growth. In the Intelligence Bureau Centenary Endowment Lecture in December 2009, Mr. Chidambaram announced the ambitious NCTC project, setting a timetable of one year to get it going. But after three years, there is a much more modest NCTC than he had envisioned set up within the Intelligence bureau, which has powers of arrest, searches, and seizure under the provisions of existing laws, in addition to its functions of coordinating the collection and dissemination of intelligence. This has invited severe criticism from the government's coalition ally, the Trinamool Congress, as well as the opposition, and the Centre's operationalization, which was to begin on 1 March 2012, has been put on hold. It is doubtful if it will be put into action unless this provision of arrest, searches, and seizure is given up as demanded by the opposition, and even the government's ally in the name of preserving the federal structure of the Constitution.

Thus, India has the Army, the Border Security Force, the Indo-Tibetan Border Force, the Sashastra Seema Bal, the Assam Rifles, and the Navy and Coast Guard to guard its land and maritime boundaries. India has so far not faced any terrorist attack from the sky other than hijackings of aircraft, which took place due to failure at checkpoints. The Rashtriya Rifles, which is a subsidiary of the Indian Army, the CRPF, and the state police forces perform counterterrorism and insurgency duties in states like Jammu & Kashmir, which are affected by terrorism. The National Security Guards, Rashtriya Rifles, and Special Operations Groups aided by the CRPF in states like Jammu & Kashmir take on terrorists when there are encounters in built-in areas. The Central Industrial Security Force protects vital installations that are under terrorist threat. The Intelligence Bureau, the Research & Analysis Wing, Military Intelligence, the CID Special Branch in the states, and the District Special Branch provide the intelligence back up to the men in the field. New units like the National Investigation Agency, the NATGRID, and the NCTC set up in the wake of the Mumbai terrorist attacks, are yet to prove their mettle. The NCTC is already mired in controversy. The NSG hubs have started functioning from Mumbai, Chennai, Hyderabad, and Kolkata, but skeptics point out the traffic snarls in these cities, and claim it would take hours for the NSG to reach a given point where their services may be required, even within the cities in which they are stationed. Only a fresh crisis triggered by terrorists would allow us to measure the success of the steps taken so far, and whether the anti-terror law currently in operation would be sufficient to give legal cover to the steps to counter terror that have been taken.

One serious problem that security planners face in India is the lack of a national political consensus on security issues, whether these issues deal with jihadist terror or Naxalite terror. Individual states view security issues through the prism of federalism, while politicians look at them from the standpoint of vote banks, with elections being held for either the state assemblies or the Parliament in almost every calendar year, forgetting that these issues threaten the very existence of the country. It is vital that India learns to work out a minimum political consensus to build a robust security architecture which can successfully thwart any terrorist attempt to destabilize the country, and the earlier this is done, the better.

ENDNOTES

1. During an address to the youth on 29 March, 1930 in connection with Gandhiji's Salt Satyagraha: http://www.mkgandhi-sarvodaya.org/articles/1salt_satya.htm, (first accessed on 09/02/2012).

2. http://mha.nic.in/pdfs/armed_forces_special_powers_act1958.pdf, (accessed 03/02/2012).

3. http://www.satp.org/satporgtp/countries/india/document/actandordinances/Tada.htm (accessed 02/10/2012).

4. http://mha.nic.in/pdfs/NSG%20Act1986.pdf, (accessed 08/12/2012).

5. http://www.nsg.gov.in/organisation_history.php, (accessed 02/10/2012).

6. http://spg.nic.in/spgact.htm (accessed 02/10/2012).

7. http://www.hindu.com/2007/09/01/stories/2007090155000500.htm (accessed 02/11/2012).

8. http://static.indianexpress.com/frontend/iep/docs/Chidambaram-speech.pdf, (accessed 02/12/2012).

9. http://indiatoday.intoday.in/story/Overhauling+the+police/1/24793.html (accessed 02/11/2012).

10. Hussain Haqqani, *Pakistan: Between Mosque And Military; Jihad without Borders*, p. 273 published by the Carnegie Endowment For International Peace, Washington D.C. and Arif Jamal, *Shadow War: The Untold Story of Jihad in Kashmir*. pp. 109–110 Vij Books, 4675-A, 21 Ansari Road, Darya Ganj New Delhi–110002.

11. http://www.satp.org/satporgtp/countries/india/terroristoutfits/simi.htm accessed 02/12/2012.; http://maloykrishnadhar.com/simi-the-open-and-hidden-faces-of-indian-jihad (accessed 02/13/2012). Mr. Maloy Krishna Dhar retired as Joint Director in the Intelligence Bureau.

12. http://www.enotes.com/india-modern-reference/india-modern, (accessed 02/13/2012).

13. http://qspace.library.queensu.ca/bitstream/1974/1938/1/Singh_Tarun_P_200906_LLM.pdf (accessed 02/14/2012).

14. http://www.asiantribune.com/news/2005/05/22/india-remembers-rajiv-gandhi-who-was-killed-ltte-human-bomb (accessed 02/15/2012).

15. http://www.indianexpress.com/news/beant-singh-assassination-six-found-guilty/207274/ first (accessed 02/14/2012).

16. http://www.rediff.com/news/1998/feb/14blast.htm (accessed 02/15/2012).

17. http://www.rediff.com/news/2005/dec/28bang.htm (accessed 02/15/2012).

18. http://www.rediff.com/news/2006/jul/11train.htm, (accessed 03/10/2012).

19. http://news.bbc.co.uk/2/hi/south_asia/4388292.stm, (accessed 03/10/2012).

20. http://indiatoday.intoday.in/story/1985-TADA+is+passed+in+Parliament:+Strong+arm+of+the+law/1/76383.html (accessed 02/15/2012).

21. http://www.asianage.com/india/nda-cleared-draconian-potasays-congress–472 (accessed 03/10/2012).

22. http://www.frontlineonnet.com/fl1611/16110970.htm (accessed 02/15/2012).

23. http://www.satp.org/satporgtp/countries/india/states/jandk/terrorist_outfits/jaish_e_mohammad_mujahideen_e_tanzeem.htm (accessed 03/02/2012).

24. http://news.bbc.co.uk/2/hi/uk_news/1804710.stm (accessed 03/03/2012).

25. http://www.psci.unt.edu/jbooks/TerrorBib_files/National-Separatist%20Terrorism/Joshi-On%20the%20Razor's%20Edge.pdf (accessed 03/03/2012).

26. Uncivil Wars Pathology of Terrorism in India by Ved Marwah, pages 325–326

27. http://naxalwatch.blogspot.in/2008/09/andhra-greyhounds-to-train-cobra-squads.html, (accessed 03/03/2012).; http://naxalwatch.blogspot.in/2005/12/greyhounds-police-surround-naxal.html (accessed 03/03/2012).

28. http://naxalwatch.blogspot.in/2005/12/greyhounds-police-surround-naxal.html, (accessed 03/09/2012).

29. http://www.financialexpress.com/news/naidu-survives-but-naxals-challenge-must-be-met/94318/0 (accessed 03/03/2012).

30. http://www.frontlineonnet.com/fl1510/15100650.htm (accessed 03/09/2012).

31. http://www.dailypostindia.com/news/13431-j-k-police-strengthening-its-infrastructure-dgp.html, (accessed 03/09/2012).

32. http://www.guardian.co.uk/world/mumbai-terror-attacks (accessed 03/10/2012).

33. http://www.propublica.org/article/david-headley-homegrown-terrorist (accessed 03/10/2012).

34. (http://www.thehindu.com/news/national/article2672239.ece (accessed 03/10/2012).

35. http://abcnews.go.com/Politics/mumbai-terror-attack-trial-chicago-man-david-headley/story?id=13695812#.T1s44oHrplw (accessed 03/10/2012).

36. http://articles.economictimes.indiatimes.com/2011–05–10/news/29528349_1_isi-role-major-sameer-ali-david-coleman-headley, accessed03/10/2012. and http://www.satp.org/satporgtp/countries/india/states/jandk/terrorist_outfits/lashkar_e_toiba_lt2011.htm, (accessed 03/10/2012).

37. http://maritimeindia.org/article/coastal-security-deep-water (accessed 03/10/2012).

38. http://maritimeindia.org/article/coastal-security-deep-water (accessed 03/10/2012).

39. http://www.dnaindia.com/mumbai/slideshow_first-pictures-after-mv-wisdom-mt-pavit-runs-aground-at-juhu-beach_1571388#top, (accessed 03/10/2012).

40. (http://indiatoday.intoday.in/story/Toughening+the+law/1/24801.html (accessed 03/11/2012).

41. http://www.thehindu.com/news/states/other-states/article2465070.ece (accessed 16/03/2012).

42. As the first Director General of the NIA, the author organized several such conferences. This practice continued until his death in 2012.

55

156 CHILEANS DEAD: HOW THE IMPACT OF THE 2010 TSUNAMI COULD HAVE BEEN MINIMIZED

Nick Lavars

Journalist, The Santiago Times

INTRODUCTION

Early on Saturday the 27th of February 2010, a magnitude-8.8 earthquake struck the central and southern region of Chile, affecting over eight million Chileans. The epicenter of the earthquake was located off the coast, 105 kilometers northeast of Chile's second largest city, Concepción. It caused damage to many of the country's highways, railways, airports, and seaports as a result of ground shaking that lasted more than three minutes. An ensuing tsunami devastated coastal towns south of Santiago, destroying 81,000 homes and significantly damaging 109,000[1] more as series of waves engulfed more than 500 kilometers of coastline. According to figures released by the government, the official death toll from the disaster stands at 524.[2]

In his inauguration speech only two weeks later on March 12th, President-elect Sebastián Piñera acknowledged the reconstruction process would take years and not months. However, slow progress has meant that many remain homeless some two years later. Therefore, the ramifications of that morning are never too far from the minds of the Chilean population. With the day-to-day lives of many still affected by the tragedy, it not only brings into question the progress of reconstruction, but is a constant reminder of how the damage could have been minimized. Many government officials, both past and present, have been openly critical of former President Michele Bachelet's handling of the catastrophe. Following the disaster, national prosecutor Sabas Chahuán appointed Regional Attorney Solange Huerta to lead an investigation into the emergency response actions taken by government authorities. In an attempt to establish criminal liability, Huerta would collect valuable information and testimonies from the Chilean Navy and government officials.

This chapter explores the difficulties in collaborating information across different ministries with efficiency and the consequences when this breaks down. It investigates the challenge of communicating critical information between relevant government bodies to alert and advise a nation at risk. Chile's handling of the 2010 earthquake and tsunami has been subject to criticism, polarizing the nation on the issue of accountability. What can be taken from these events is the importance of a national emergency service working in cohesion with a government in coordinating information, and then proceeding to provide guidance to its citizens in a state of emergency.

SATURDAY FEBRUARY 27th, 2010

At 3:34 a.m. local time, a magnitude-8.8 earthquake struck off the shore of central Chile, 335 kilometers southwest of Santiago. 35 kilometers[3] deep at its epicenter, the earthquake delivered intense ground shaking throughout the country's most densely populated regions. Ranking as the sixth strongest earthquake[4] ever recorded by a seismograph, it lasted for approximately three minutes, with tremors being felt in the Argentine city of Buenos Aires and as far north as Peru. A series of aftershocks followed, with some recorded as a high as magnitude 6.9,[5] causing residents of southern towns to leave their homes and sleep on the street in fear of their lives.

At 5:10 a.m., President Michele Bachelet arrived at ONEMI (National Emergency Service Office) where, aware of the immediate danger of a tsunami, she convened with ONEMI director Carmen Fernández to assess the situation. A video of the two in the office during the hours following the earthquake was broadcast by Chilean television station *Canal 13* on March, 5th. As demonstrated by the footage, there appeared to exist a severe communication breakdown between ONEMI and SHOA (Hydrographic and Oceanographic Service), a department of the Chilean Navy.

At approximately 3:50 a.m., around 15 minutes after the earthquake, the first waves of the tsunami began to hit the coastal towns of Constitución, San Antonio, and Pichilemu. Based on eyewitness accounts, waves varied in height between 2.6 and 11.2 meters.[6]

Chile is a country prone to earthquakes as it is situated at the junction of three tectonic plates: the Nazca Plate, the South American Plate, and the Antarctic Plate.[7] Native people of Chile are well educated in what to do in the event of an earthquake and immediately move to higher ground in case of a tsunami. This ability to move to higher ground meant that the least urbanized of the coastal towns would be the ones with the best chance of survival, leaving inhabitants of the larger cities such as Concepción reliant on a warning that would come, but come too late.

Professor Alfonso Campusano, Director of the Center for Oceanic Study from Andres Bello University was on Juan Fernandez Island off Chile's coast participating in a search of a seventeenth century shipwreck when the tsunami struck.

> I was not in the village, but in the Hostería el Pangal, a few kilometers from town on a small cliff by the sea. There was no warning whatsoever. Fortunately a colleague went to the balcony to smoke a cigarette and noticed that the sea had retreated uncharacteristically. Knowing that I was an oceanographer he awoke me straight away. I then proceeded to lead an evacuation of the 40 people who were there at the time.

Bachelet told the press[8] that the first confirmation of the tsunami she received was a phone call from residents of Juan Fernandez Island saying it had been hit by the waves. 156 deaths have been directly attributed to the tsunami.[9]

In the days that followed the disaster, Chile's status as a nation ill-prepared to deal with a catastrophe of this stature became apparent. In the aftermath, at the El Manzano prison in the city of Concepción, more than 200 inmates escaped via a crumbled wall. Authorities initially were able to recapture around 60 of the prisoners[10] with many not located until more than a year later.[11]

As the nation fell into disarray, Bachelet signed a decree on Sunday February 29th, which deployed 10,000 military troops to the city of

Concepción in an attempt to re-establish order. Curfews were imposed as looters clashed with police in frustration about food shortages and power outages. Water cannons and tear gas were used, as looters not only took to ransacking supermarkets for necessities, but department stores for plasma televisions and other electrical goods. The first night of military enforcement saw 160 people arrested and a 22-year old man shot dead.[12, 13]

WHERE DID IT GO WRONG?

ONEMI Director for the region of the Bio Bio, Jorge Henríquez Cárcamo, was asleep with his wife when the earthquake struck. As his wife gathered their three children, he maintained his composure and attempted to gauge the intensity of the fierce shaking. Amid buckling furniture and items crashing to the floor around him, Henríquez—with skills acquired through his training—calculated the intensity of the quake in accordance with the Mercalli scale. In San Pedro de La Paz, only two miles off the coast of Concepción, Henríquez then immediately acknowledged the likelihood of a consequent tsunami. As soon as the ground stopped shaking and knowing that communication networks could collapse at any moment, he promptly picked up the phone and dialed the ONEMI central office in Santiago.

A staff member on duty at the ONEMI Early Warning Center (CAT) received the call in which Henríquez reported the quake was of intensity X to XI on the Mercalli scale. Henríquez's information was refuted and he was told that information ONEMI had received measured it at only grade VII. "Look 'conchetumadre,'" Henriquez said, "this is an earthquake and it is grade X to XI."[14]

This conversation did not surface again until at a dinner meeting in April 2011, when Henríquez shared his version of events with Carmen Fernández, who had resigned as Director of ONEMI only days after the disaster. Fernández told investigators:

> I felt my legs buckle underneath me when I was told. I was never informed that the head of the regional ONEMI had advised the central office of the level of intensity and so close to the coast. If that information had circulated that morning then there probably would have been very different choices made.[15]

In actual fact, what prevented ONEMI from raising a tsunami alert and evacuating coastal regions was the law. According to Supreme Decree No. 26 of January 11, 1966, only SHOA possesses the authority to issue a tsunami alert. It is then up to ONEMI to implement evacuation plans. This exclusive power of the Chilean Navy is one of the main arguments wielded by ONEMI as to why they did not raise an alert that morning.

However, for years ONEMI has been training its regional coastal authorities on evacuation procedures through a document titled "Plan Accemar."[16] The plan stipulates under what conditions to expect a tsunami in the aftermath of an earthquake. According to the government document, among other things, the earthquake must measure greater than 7.5 on the Richter scale; the rupture zone must be located underneath a seabed; and the movement must be vertical, not just lateral. However it can take 10 to 15 minutes for these measurements to be made and data to be relayed back to ONEMI, which as demonstrated, can be enough time for waves to strike the coastline. Huerta's investigation states, "People living close to locations where earthquakes are known to occur have discovered that waves of a tsunami can envelop the coast only minutes after the quake strikes."[17]

As ONEMI awaited the evaluation of the situation by SHOA, waves were engulfing the coast and destroying homes. Despite having received information from its own regional director, Henríquez, ONEMI was left powerless to alert the nation—highlighting a critical flaw in Chile's emergency response system.

Approximately ten minutes after the earthquake, at 3:44 a.m., Vindell Hsu, a geologist from the Pacific Tsunami Warning Center (PTWC) in Hawaii, dispatched the first data regarding the earthquake and its magnitude to SHOA in Valparaiso. "Once we determined the location and magnitude, which we recorded at 8.5 (Richter scale), we realized it was an earthquake with a high potential for a tsunami."[18]

Meanwhile, Mario Andina, Head of the Oceanographic Department for SHOA, and his colleagues took to their posts at the headquarters of the National Tidal Wave Warning System (SNAM). Andina was yet to receive the information on the earthquake from PTWC and therefore ordered his people to their monitoring instruments. Tidal indicators stationed along the coast to detect variations in sea level were rendered useless, as the earthquake had severed fiber optic cables relaying the data back to SNAM. Andina quickly realized that under these circumstances, devoid of the typical instruments, he would be forced to make his decision on whether to raise the tsunami alarm based on information from U.S. agencies such as PTWC.

In the central ONEMI office at 3:50 a.m., duty manager Osvaldo Malfanti Torres, together with radio operator Rafael López Meza, finished collating the reports from different regions regarding the strength of the earthquake. They then began to distribute information by radio to the network of civil protection. However, perhaps due to the manic situation, critical information like the initial report from Henríquez was not included. The result of this omission was the official recording of the earthquake in Bio Bio at only VIII Mercalli.

Communications had been cut between ONEMI and the regions of Maule and Bio Bio, meaning that reported sightings of the destructive waves on the coast were not received. Had this not been the case, Malfanti would have been able to bypass SHOA and raise the alert himself.

After receiving ONEMI's radio transmission, Andina at SNAM pieced together the information and calculated the likely epicenter. It was in these moments that the information came through to SHOA from PTWC. Andina reviewed the information and concluded that the earthquake was magnitude 8.5 on the Richter scale, locating the epicenter on land northeast of Concepción but only kilometers from the coastline. With this data, Andina determined there was high probability of a tsunami and prepared his team to launch the alert. It was at exactly this time, 3:50 a.m. that the first waves began to strike the coast in San Antonio, Pichilemu, and Constitución. This area would be the "sacrifice zone," in that it could not have possibly been alerted in time, even if a proper warning procedure had been executed.

At 3:51 a.m., Andina was prepared to launch the alert via the Genmercalli network through radio, fax, and email. In line with government protocol, the alert would first be issued to ONEMI in order to disseminate the emergency plan to the network of civil protection. Seventy receivers made up of various naval installations, port authorities, and maritime governorates were issued the alert by SHOA, which included estimated wave arrival times along the coast. Due to widespread communication breakdown, of the seventy intended recipients, only eight received the warning.

SHOA had assumed that all intended recipients had received the warning. An officer on duty at SHOA explained the urgency of the situation.

> We have to receive confirmation of each recipient. The first one I checked with was in Valparaiso and then amid the chaos I was sent to do something else. We were left with the idea that if the warning had been received in Valparaiso, then it had been received in all locations.[19]

As a means of confirming the alert had been received and response enacted, Andina then took to the radio and contacted the CAT. "Atento Omega Cero (radio code of ONEMI). ... Atento Omega Cero de SHOA ... Alerta de tsunami en curso (tsunami alert in progress),"[20] he broadcast.

This message was somehow interpreted by staff in the ONEMI office as the Navy having determined the epicenter was on land. ONEMI specialists then assumed that as the epicenter was on land, there was no chance of a consequent tsunami and did not proceed to disseminate the alarm. This assumption proved to be devastatingly incorrect. There is no recording of the radio transmission, but determining whether or not it was clear remains futile. It would be the mistake of the ONEMI staff to assume that the epicenter on land could not result in a tsunami. Malfanti confirmed this judgemental error in his administrative summary of the events. "The information received from SHOA indicating the epicenter was on land, we proceeded to rule out the chance of a tsunami."[21]

Paolo Marini Pakarati, who joined the emergency effort after the quake struck, reiterated this conclusion. "The data transmitted by the Navy with regard to the earthquake's epicenter did not correspond with what is technically required to generate a tsunami."[22] As did ONEMI officer and head of the CAT early warning center, Johaziel Jamett Paz. "To generate a tsunami, the epicenter of the earthquake should be on a seabed."[23]

At 3:55 a.m., as waves began to hit the coastal town of Talcahauno, Vindell Hsu picked up the phone to contact the naval office of SHOA, attempting to confirm that the officers on duty had received his warning of the tsunami. "I tried to converse with the Chilean on the other end of the phone, they replied with something that was not English and that I did not understand."[24]

Fortunately, present in at the PWTC facility at the time was geophysicist Victor Sardiña of Cuban origin. Upon realizing the language complications, he picked up the phone himself and called SHOA. Speaking with oceanographic specialist, Corporal Jorge Araya in Spanish, Sardiña again attempted to confirm that SHOA had received their information of an 8.5 Richter earthquake. According to Sardiña's official testimony, Araya confirmed that SHOA had received the information.[25] Geophysicist Hsu also wanted to know if there had been any reported sightings of waves, as he was aware that Chile had only 12 tidal gauges along its 4,000-mile coastline. In his opinion, it was entirely possible that waves could strike before the instruments detected them. Corporal Araya promised to raise the tsunami alert if SHOA received such information. By this time, waves were already engulfing the coast in Constitución and Talcahuano.

Following the unclear radio transmission from Andina, ONEMI requested clarification from SHOA via fax. Andina ordered a fax to be sent with the heading "Tsunami Alert." SHOA began attempting to send the fax at 3:55 a.m., but problems with the telephone lines meant it didn't reach CAT until 4:07, following five or six unsuccessful attempts. The fax was received by shift manager, Malfanti, who interpreted it as a notice of readiness and an alert of the possibility of a tsunami, with SHOA to alert ONEMI if there were waves moving toward the coast. Malfanti then dismissed the alarm on the basis that the fax clarified his assumption there was no risk of a tsunami, predominantly because the epicenter was on land.

In fact, what the fax dictated was that the earthquake met the requirements for a tsunami alarm to be issued under the SHOA Technical Standing Order (OPT1).[26]

The earthquake was of sufficient magnitude to generate a tsunami. It is still unknown whether or not it actually has. The possibility of occurrence will be informed in due course and the estimated wave arrival times are as follows. (11 locations along coastline from Puerto Montt to Arica attached).[27]

In line with this, ONEMI was obligated by law to inform the country that it was at risk and that coastal regions should be evacuated. An untrained reader could be forgiven for misinterpreting the fax, given the ambiguity of the phrase "The possibility of occurrence." However, the staff of ONEMI, particularly the shift manager on duty at CAT, ideally would have been trained to recognize the danger of the tsunami in line with OPT1. Malfanti would confirm the confusion upon receiving the fax in his internal summary: "On the format of the fax, I do not know if there is a particular format established between SHOA and ONEMI in order to raise a tsunami warning."[28]

The head of CAT, Johaziel Jamett said in the same summary: "I want to emphasize that the fax from SHOA, in the case that it was an intended alert, does not correspond to the format established by the Navy and their interior processes."[29]

If the radio transmission from Andina at 3:51 a.m. was unclear and the intention remained unclear after reception of the fax, then it was Malfanti's duty to contact SHOA for clarification. ONEMI Director Carmen Fernández confirmed this as part of the emergency procedure in her declaration to the prosecution."In the case that doubt exists, immediately SHOA should be contacted to clarify the risk of a tsunami. After the necessary clarifications have been made, then proceed to implement the alarm."[30]

Malfanti made no call to SHOA after receiving the fax. He did not realize it was a tsunami alert that obligated him to immediately issue a warning. His superior, Johaziel Jamett, after reaching ONEMI minutes later, would review the actions taken by his subordinate and would not amend the error.

At 4:15 a.m., 41 minutes after the earthquake, as waves continued to strike Chile's coast, Malfanti informed ONEMI chief of staff Pedro Salamanca that there was no risk of tsunami. Salamanca has just arrived at the CAT and informed then Deputy Interior Minister Patricio Rosende, who was the first political authority to intervene at ONEMI, that SHOA had ruled out a tsunami. Together they re-read the fax and were left confused. They interpreted it as an alert to enlist resources only if required and not grounds to warn and evacuate the population. The confusion arose as a result of the consistency of the warning system with that used for other types of natural disasters—disasters that can be assessed as they develop, such as forest fires or volcanic activity. In these cases, ONEMI first initiates a "yellow alert," at which point the situation is monitored until it develops into a "red alert." However SHOA utilizes only a "tsunami alert" and a "tsunami alarm." However the difference is merely semantic, as both should initiate the evacuation of coastal regions.

In accordance with OPT1, SHOA can issue an early warning based purely on seismological magnitude, the epicenter, and the depth of the fracture if they indicate imminent threat of destructive waves. This was unbeknownst to the staff of ONEMI, who were under the assumption that dramatic change in sea level was a requirement, as shown by Malfanti's statement. "The fax would have contained data on abnormalities in the sea and data from oceanographers [in order to alert the public]."[31]

Unaware of the protocol of the naval division, ONEMI specialists concluded that the "tsunami alert" that arrived by fax was equivalent to a "yellow alert." Jamett demonstrated this in his statement. "There are two systems, one is an alarm and the other is an alert. What the SHOA should have issued, if it had assurance there would be a tsunami, should have been an alarm and not an alert."[32]

Contrary to this, the Maritime Department of the region of San Antonio had received the same alert issued by SHOA. They proceeded to act in accordance with protocol of the navy and ordered the departure of boats, indicating a conflicting reception of the transmission.

Those who were in the CAT that morning said that after reading the fax, Jamett ordered a radio call to SHOA to clarify the situation and that everyone heard the Navy say that the epicenter was on land. SHOA denies that this happened.

At 4:51 a.m., an hour and seven minutes after the earthquake, Commander of SHOA Mariano Rojas Bustos stood in the center of the SNAM facility and asked aloud: "How are we to cancel?"[33] Met with silence from Lieutenant Andina and Lieutenant Commander Andrés Enríquez Olavarría, Rojas took this as approval and issued orders to cancel the alert. Putting the cancellation into process he radioed ONEMI at 4:56 a.m. and then dispatched messages via the Genmercalli network at 5:10 a.m. This decision would prove to be a lethal one. More than one hour after this decision was made, at least 32 people were swept away by waves in Talcahuano and Dichato. At the same time this fatal decision was made, Director Carmen Fernández arrived at the ONEMI office and reviewed the information, including the 4:07 fax from SHOA. Upon citing the heading "Tsunami Alert" she told Rosende that an evacuation might have to be ordered. In this moment, the radio transmission came through from SHOA ruling out the tsunami and canceling the alarm. The order of Commander Rojas had already been carried out.

With what appeared to be a common misconception that morning, Lt. Andina was convinced that the first wave of a tsunami was the most destructive. When they began to collect satellite data of tidal marks, Corporal Jorge Araya analyzed the graphs and interpreted them as displaying normalization of the sea level. The first wave had not been lethal and the risk was vanishing, thought Andina. This is the only explanation for SHOA canceling the alert.

Lieutenant Commander Andrés Enríquez had been head of the Department of Oceanography of SHOA until January 31, 2010, less than a month before the earthquake. Rojas himself was no expert on oceanography, so he therefore called on Enríquez, Andina, and Service Oceanographer Cecillia Zelaya for assistance that morning.

Zelaya had arrived at ONEMI at around 5 a.m. and begun compiling a folder of all data collected regarding the earthquake. It was at this moment that she realized the alert had been canceled, being under the impression that evacuation was still taking place. Zelaya, head of the Tsunami Section for SHOA, was the only one present that morning that had a university education in oceanography and short courses on tsunamis, yet no one informed her that the status of the situation had changed. She found it odd that the alert had been canceled, given the magnitude of the earthquake, and knew that it was possible for large intervals between waves. After looking at the graphs herself that had led Rojas to cancel the alarm, she instantly recognized the error that had been made. She approached Enríquez to alert him of her different interpretation of the data and her recommendation that the alert be raised to alarm status. Zelaya's findings were dismissed. She never directly discussed this with Commander Rojas, as she was informed she should respect the chain of command and report to Enríquez, the officer reporting to Rojas.

As Commander Rojas was canceling the alert, the PTWC in Hawaii issued its second bulletin regarding the danger of tsunami. The tsunami warning center had received the same data via the same satellite that had reached SHOA in Valparaiso. Yet the geophysicists in the Pacific had interpreted it very differently.

A tsunami warning is in effect for Chile and Peru ... Sea level readings indicate a tsunami was generated ... Authorities should take appropriate action in response to this possibility ... Arrival times may differ and the initial wave may not be the largest. A tsunami is a series of waves and the time between successive waves can be five minutes to one hour.[34]

A later technical investigation of the Navy led by Vice-Admiral Enrique Larrañaga would deem the cancelation of the alarm incorrect. Larrañaga recommended the dismissal of Commander Rojas based on his ignorance of the second bulletin from PTWC.

At 5:40 a.m., President Michelle Bachelet gave her first press conference from the ONEMI offices and gave no mention of the ongoing tsunami risk. She did so, according to her official testimony, because Commander Rojas had withdrawn the alert and SHOA had ruled out the chance of a tsunami.

> Upon arriving at the ONEMI office I was not shown nor was I made aware of the tsunami alert fax sent from SHOA at 4:07 a.m. It was indicated to me only that SHOA had ruled out the alert and all subsequent communication between ONEMI and SHOA had dismissed the likelihood of a tsunami.[35]

Following this statement, Bachelet was informed that the Directorate of Meteorology had reports of the tsunami on Juan Fernandez Island. She contacted SHOA seeking confirmation, but the technical department of the Navy insisted that tidal variations were of no more than 18 to 20 cm in the area. Soon after, speaking to a seismologist from the University of Chile, Carlos Aranda, she was told that there had already been a tsunami and the risk had passed, the same ill-fated assumption made by Lt. Andina.

Over an hour later, at 6:55 a.m., Bachelet returned to speak to the press indicating that there had been reports of large waves, but it was not determined if it was a tsunami.

> We have received information from police that there has been waves of great proportion. I do not know if we call this a tsunami. According to information that the Navy gives us there is no further risk of tsunami.

At 8:01 a.m., Commander Rojas finally spoke directly with Bachelet. At this time the final wave had struck the coastal town of Dichato one hour and 20 minutes prior, killing 12 Chileans. The disaster was consummated.

WHO ASSUMES RESPONSIBILITY?

Around two weeks after the disaster, on March 12, 2010, President Sebastián Piñera entered office, taking on the task of reconstruction. He acknowledged immediately the monumental task he was faced with, and announced it would be a matter of years before it was completed. Slow progress has meant that many victims of the tsunami and earthquake remain homeless, living in tents or temporary housing projects known as "media-aguas." On a regular basis, the reconstruction process would be drawn into the media spotlight, bringing with it the events of that morning and the issue of accountability.

Members of the current administration have been critical of Bachelet and her cabinet. Interior Minister Rodrigo Hinzpeter told the press that he believes ultimately the blame falls with the former president. "When you are part of a team and simply say 'that day was not my responsibility, there was nothing for me to do,' is perhaps not the way I think these situations should be handled."[36]

Current Minister for Public Works and presidential candidate Laurence Golborn was also outspoken. "The leadership was in crisis. When there are decisions to be made which will have important implications on the lives of citizens, that is where you would like to see the true resilience of particular people."[37]

These attacks on Bachelet as a president were refuted by members of her cabinet, particularly Francisco Vidal, who labels the attacks as motivated by political agenda. "That is the opinion of a candidate who has decided from today to enter the presidential campaign. His comments comparing his pathetic behaviour as a minister during the rescue of the miners and a catastrophe which affected eight million Chileans foreshadow what will be his political strategy."[38]

Attorney for the Western Metropolitan Area, Solange Huerta, was appointed by National Prosecutor Sabas Chahuán to lead an investigation into the events of that morning. Ultimately, it would lead to the indictment of eight government officials, but not Bachelet herself. The former president was cleared of liability, as at the point of her first press conference she was acting purely on information relayed to her upon arriving at ONEMI. Her second press conference took place 15 minutes after the last wave had struck the town of Dichato. Her public intervention would have no effect on the amount of lives lost.

The National Civil Protection Plan is the legal document that dictates responsibilities of government authorities in the case of an emergency. According to the plan, the role of the president is purely to act as a

33. Centro de Investigacion Periodistica, *Tsunami paso a paso: los escandalosos errores y omisiones del SHOA y la ONEMI,* http://ciperchile.cl/2012/01/18/tsunami-paso-a-paso-los-escan-dalosos-errores-y-omisiones-del-shoa-y-la-onemi (Jan. 18, 2012).

34. Pacific Tsunami Warning Centre, *Tsunami Bulletin Number 002,* http://ciperchile.cl/wp-content/uploads/Bolet%C3%ADn–02.pdf (Feb. 27, 2012).

35. Veronica Michelle Bachelet, *Declaracion Voluntaria,* Pg 2. http://ciperchile.cl/wp-content/uploads/Declaracion-Bachelet.pdf (Dec. 28, 2010).

36. The Santiago Times, *Chile's former officials attempt to wash hands of tsunami blame* http://www.santiagotimes.cl/chile/politics/23402-chiles-former-officials-attempt-to-wash-hands-of-tsunami-blame (Feb. 14 2012).

37. The Santiago Times, *Scrutiny for Chile's former admin days before tsunami anniversary* http://www.santiagotimes.cl/chile/politics/23430-scrutiny-for-chiles-former-admin-days-before-tsunami-anniversary (Feb. 20, 2012).

38. The Santiago Times, *Scrutiny for Chile's former admin days before tsunami anniversary* http://www.santiagotimes.cl/chile/politics/23430-scrutiny-for-chiles-former-admin-days-before-tsunami-anniversary (Feb. 20, 2012).

39. The Santiago Times, *Emails reveal officials ignored Chile's faulty emergency system* http://www.santiagotimes.cl/chile/politics/23470-emails-reveal-officials-ignored-chiles-faulty-emergency-system (Feb. 28, 2012).

40. The Santiago Times, *Weekend quake reveals distrust of Chile's emergency systems,* http://www.santiagotimes.cl/chile/environment/23613-weekend-quake-reveals-chiles-distrust-of-emergency-systems (Mar. 27, 2012).

41. El Mercurio, *Onemi y U. de Chile adoptan medidas para enfrentar nuevas emergencias* http://diario.elmercurio.com/2012/03/28/nacional/nacional/noticias/BA89C610–0D99–471B-AF21-BB93A52F00F9.htm?id=%7BBA89C610–0D99–471B-AF21-BB93A52F00F9%7D (Mar. 27, 2012).

42. The Santiago Times, *Weekend quake reveals distrust of Chile's emergency systems,* http://www.santiagotimes.cl/chile/environment/23613-weekend-quake-reveals-chiles-distrust-of-emergency-systems (Mar. 27, 2012).

56

INTERNATIONAL COOPERATION IN COUNTERTERRORISM

Gilles De Kerchove

European Union Counterterrorism Coordinator

INTRODUCTION

At the beginning of 2011, the Al Qaeda narrative quite literally collapsed. The Arab Spring has shown the irrelevance of Al Qaeda's message to the hopes and aspirations of the people in the Arab world. At the same time, the death of Osama Bin Laden is a further expression of the degree to which core Al Qaeda has been weakened. The physical resurrection of Bin Laden is impossible. We need to ensure that his ideas also are safely entombed, and with them the terrorist organizations they have spawned. We do now have the opportunity for a real push forward in the counter-narrative against Al Qaeda's ideology. Even though successful reforms will reduce the terrorist risk in the long term, terrorists might take advantage of destabilization in the region in the short and medium terms.

The terrorist threat remains significant and is becoming more diverse. Violent radicalization continues to take place, both through personal contact and via the Internet. Terrorist groups are changing in composition and leadership. Regional Al Qaeda affiliates, such as Al Qaeda in the Islamic Maghreb or Al Qaeda in the Arabian Peninsula, are getting stronger. Self-radicalized "lone wolves" are getting involved in terrorist activities. EU nationals are traveling to hotspots such as Afghanistan or Somalia for fighting or training before returning to Europe.

On Christmas Day, 25 December 2009, terrorists tried to bring down the Northwest Airlines Flight from Schiphol to Detroit during its final descent. In October 2010, two parcel bombs hidden in printer cartridges sent via air freight from Yemen to the U.S. were intercepted at Dubai and at the UK's East Midlands Airport. Responsibility was claimed by an Al Qaeda affiliate in the Arabian Peninsula.

The terrorist threat is thus evolving and taking advantage of our vulnerabilities. Only an integrated strategic and global approach can get us ahead of it. Terrorism is indeed a global threat that knows no borders, and which must be countered globally. We are all potential targets, and we must work together to combat terrorism effectively.

IMPORTANCE OF A STRATEGIC APPROACH, INCLUDING THE RESPECT OF HUMAN RIGHTS

Having a counterterrorism strategy is vital. It prevents erratic ups and downs, including overreaction in the direct aftermath of an attack—a temptation that many unfortunately fall prey to too often—and "counterterrorism fatigue" in between attacks, equally unhelpful and based on the paradoxical belief that when there have been no attacks there is no threat. The EU Counter-Terrorism Strategy gives all actors a common reference, allows regular monitoring, and provides transparency with parliamentarians and the public, which helps to increase acceptance of counterterrorism measures.

It is important to make a clear distinction between policy strictly related to counterterrorism (information exchange, law enforcement cooperation, etc.) and counterterrorism-relevant activities, like promoting integration, or fighting discrimination, which could help to address conditions conducive to radicalization and recruitment to terrorism. It is often counterproductive to add the counterterrorism label to the latter activities.

The Global Counter-Terrorism Strategy, adopted by the United Nations General Assembly in 2006, expresses the shared view of the international community that "effective counter-terrorism measures and the protection of human rights are not conflicting goals, but complementary and mutually reinforcing." We can only be successful in the fight against terrorism in the long run if we stay true to our core values: international law, human rights, and the rule of law. Perceived violations of human rights and the rule of law, and discrimination and repression by government agencies in the fight against terrorism, provide grievances which can be misused to justify political violence. Even when such policies are intended to fight terrorism, they in fact give rise to conditions conducive to it spreading. Promoting human rights is one of our most effective weapons against terrorism. To act otherwise would undermine the very legitimacy of our own fight and thereby its effectiveness.

I will first describe what the EU is doing internally among its 27 Member States in order to enhance its strategic approach and to improve operational tools for counterterrorism, then comment on cooperation at the international level. Much has already been done: cooperation, in particular information sharing, has been improved between the different agencies involved in counterterrorism. European and international counterterrorism cooperation has progressively been strengthened over the last few years.

EU ACHIEVEMENTS

In recent years, Member States and the European institutions have continued to implement the EU Counter-Terrorism Strategy[1] and have made great efforts to fight terrorism under its four main pillars: prevent, protect, pursue, and respond.

The Lisbon Treaty, adopted in 2007, has removed a number of legal barriers that had separated Justice and Home Affairs from other aspects of EU policy. Under the Lisbon Treaty, significant counterterrorism issues are now being addressed using the regular community method, with majority voting, co-legislation by the European Parliament, and oversight by the European Court of Justice. This allows the EU to come up with a better-coordinated approach, combining different policy fields like transport and security or internal and external aspects.

Prevent

Addressing violent radicalization has been at the heart of EU counterterrorism policy, but it is also the most difficult aspect. We have collected best practices of the work of some of the Members States on such issues as training of religious leaders, the role of local authorities, community policing, deradicalization of youth, and the Internet. But we still need to understand better the process of how people become radicalized into violence. We also need to improve the way we counter the Al Qaeda narrative, especially on the Internet.

Civil society and communities play a crucial role in making the overall approach successful. This is because violent radicalization is best contained at a level closest to the most susceptible individuals.

Also victims and victims' organizations have powerful voices that need to be heard.

Most importantly, in the Arab world, people are calling for dignity, democracy, freedom, economic opportunity, and the rule of law. This is not the message of the terrorists, whose ideology and means have been rejected by the very people they claim to represent.

On 9 September 2011, the Radicalization Awareness Network, an EU-wide umbrella platform for practitioners involved in countering violent radicalization and extremism was inaugurated by Commissioner Malmstrōm. The purpose of the network is to identify good practices and to promote exchange of information in different fields of countering violent radicalization and extremism.

Protect and Respond

The protection of our citizens and infrastructure is the second objective of the Counter-Terrorism Strategy. Measures have been taken to reduce our vulnerability to terrorist attacks, for instance in regard to border control, transport security measures, critical infrastructure protection, and in the field of cybersecurity.

To minimize the impact of any attack, we have to increase the resilience of our critical infrastructure, and the resilience of society. The more a society is willing to accept risks, the less its government is pushed to adopt intrusive counterterrorism measures that restrict freedom and privacy.

The use of new technologies by malicious actors remains an issue of concern. The number of attacks in the field of cybercrime or espionage rose significantly in 2011. Cyberattacks could cause huge damage, with a direct impact on such things as nuclear power plants or air traffic control. Reports of a modified version of the Stuxnet worm demonstrate that information technology, and critical infrastructures in general, remain highly vulnerable. The EU is committed to close international cooperation, which is a central element in enhancing cybersecurity. There is growing consensus in the EU on the need to increase preparedness, to adopt a strategy to bring together all relevant players, and to start defining a code of conduct on how to behave in cyberspace. Member States are working on a future pan-European exercise to take place in 2012, and the EU and the U.S. are working on a roadmap towards joint and synchronized transcontinental cyber-exercises in 2013. As terrorists have the intention to become active in the cyberdomain, preparedness against terrorist-motivated cyberattacks has to be part of a cyberstrategy.

Since 2006, the European Programme for Critical Infrastructure Protection (EPCIP) has constituted a framework for increasing critical infrastructure protection capability across all EU Member States through funding of relevant projects. The EU is also continuing its work on maritime and aviation security. For instance, new legislation aiming at improving the security of high risk air cargo has been adopted, introducing special measures for high risk cargo and a risk-based approach to cargo security.

Security-related research is also important: it can increase both security and freedom ("privacy by design"). The challenge is for the internal security community to develop a culture of forward planning to identify its real needs—otherwise the choices will be made either by what the industry wants to supply or what scientists want to develop. For the period 2007–2013, 1.4 billion Euros have been allocated to support research and technological development in the security field. Eight-hundred million Euros are already being spent on 203 projects, bringing together more than 1500 participants, including subject matter experts coming from large industries, research centers, academia, and the user community, including first responders, border guards, and law enforcement.

We have started to strengthen public–private partnerships, and we need to do this even more; counterterrorism, like customs, should learn from those actually running businesses how to design measures for maximum effect with minimum impact on the public. For example, the Yemen parcel-bomb plot of October 2010 led to many surprises: terrorists exploited the different rules that existed for screening of passengers and their luggage, compared to those for cargo.

In the autumn of 2010, as an additional overall measure, EU Members States agreed on an information sharing mechanism on changes in the national threat level, allowing system-wide distribution of the information that the threat level in a Member State had changed.

Pursue

Regretably, the EU has extensive experience with terrorism going back well before the rise of Al Qaida. We promote a criminal justice approach in our response. Terrorists should be investigated, prosecuted, and convicted according to the normal rules of criminal law. Regular criminal courts have a strong track record in fighting terrorism. Law enforcement investigations have been crucial in gaining information about terrorist networks and disrupting plots. Fair trials in regular criminal courts have put hundreds of terrorists behind bars. Treating terrorists as criminals and not "warriors" takes the false glamour out of terrorism. A public court hearing provides visible justice to the victims and their families, whose rights are specifically recognized by the UN Strategy. Indefinite detention of terrorist suspects without trial is not only against our values and unlawful, it also provides propaganda arguments to terrorists.

The EU has developed the most comprehensive criminal justice response anywhere to the fight against terrorism, which could serve as a successful model for others around the world. There is now a common definition and criminalization of terrorist offenses, including before an attack occurs. The 2002 Framework Decision on combatting terrorism, which defines terrorist offenses, was amended in 2008 to include public provocation to commit a terrorist offense, recruitment, and training for terrorism. Cross-border cooperation in investigations and prosecutions has been strengthened, going far beyond traditional mutual legal assistance by innovating instead around the principle of mutual recognition.

EUROPOL and EUROJUST provide platforms for real time cooperation and strategic and operational exchanges among law enforcement and judicial authorities. Cooperation between EUROPOL and EUROJUST has been strengthened. Modern cooperation mechanisms have been created with interested non-EU countries.

INTERNATIONAL COOPERATION

The EU is working together with partners bilaterally and in the context of international and regional organizations. The better internal counterterrorist arrangements are, the greater the potential for effective external international cooperation. Increasingly, the EU is providing counterterrorism capacity building assistance to non-EU countries. Cooperation between EU and non-EU countries on counterterrorism is complementary to the counterterrorism cooperation between Member States and these countries.

The European External Action Service (EEAS) led by the High Representative became fully operational on 1 January 2011. The reforms introduced under the Lisbon Treaty allow significant improvements in the overall coherence between the EU's internal and external policies. Security expertise in EU delegations around the world is being strengthened as a matter of priority.

Increasingly, the EU is addressing the internal–external link: working with non-EU countries in mitigating transnational security threats to the EU and its citizens. The European Commission is working with countries around the world on the criminal justice and law enforcement cooperation aspects of the fight against terrorism (the external dimension of Freedom, Justice, and Security).

Following the collapse of the Iron Curtain and the opening of Eastern Europe, the EU developed vast experience with the colossal task of developing security and judicial systems that respect the rule of law and human rights. While the EU continues to work with and assist partners globally in this respect, this has to be taken to another level. We need now to build on our existing work with Sahel countries and Pakistan, providing assistance to enhance their law enforcement and criminal justice systems so that they can better investigate and prosecute terrorist offenses. If they so wish, the EU stands ready to assist the emerging democratic governments of the Arab world in the reform of their security and judicial sectors, in line with internationally accepted norms of human rights and the rule of law. We must also be aware of the risk that disappointment about the expected improvement in the situation in the Arab world might lead to an increase in radicalization.

The EU has started the complex task of integrating development assistance and security. The EU recently adopted a comprehensive Strategy for the Sahel, where it is obvious that security is a necessary prerequisite for development. The risk of kidnapping has made it too dangerous for development workers to operate in most places. Conversely, there will not be any lasting security without development. Otherwise, there are virtually no economic alternatives for young people, except smuggling, other crimes, and collaborating with the terrorists. This twin approach—development with security—should be taken up elsewhere.

The UN provides an essential framework for international cooperation in counterterrorism, and the EU is fully committed to supporting that key role. To have a real impact, counterterrorism cooperation and norms must be as universal as possible. All countries should ratify and implement the UN's conventions and protocols relating to counterterrorism, as well as the relevant UN Security Council resolutions. In recent years, the rate of ratification of these instruments has gone up. The EU is funding relevant UN projects, for example in the criminal justice field by UNODC. The EEAS has also supported the

UN in a project to encourage the countries of Central Asia to develop a regional approach to the comprehensive implementation of the UN Global Counter-Terrorism Strategy, including its human rights aspects.

The inauguration of the Global Counterterrorism Forum "GCTF" by the U.S. Secretary of State and Turkish Foreign Minister in New York in September 2011 was a step forward in international cooperation on counterterrorism. The GCTF has 30 founding members (29 countries plus the EU, with the UN as an observer). It is intended to provide a unique action-oriented platform for senior counterterrorism policymakers and experts from around the world to work together to identify urgent needs, devise solutions, and mobilize resources for addressing key challenges. It has regional working groups dealing with Southeast Asia, the Sahel, and the Horn of Africa/Yemen (co-chaired by the EU), and thematic working groups on criminal justice/rule of law and countering violent extremism.

EU–U.S. COUNTERTERRORISM COOPERATION

The U.S. is a key partner for the EU in the fight against terrorism. Both sides face similar threats, and there are significant interconnections: The 9/11 perpetrators were from Hamburg; the Detroit Christmas day bomber was on a flight from Amsterdam; foreign fighters from both the U.S. and the EU are traveling to and from conflict zones. The EU and the U.S. have shared values and are committed to working together on many aspects of counterterrorism, such as aviation security, countering violent extremism, and terrorist financing. An EU–U.S. legal framework for operational judicial and law enforcement cooperation has been established with Mutual Legal Assistance and Extradition Agreements. There are U.S. liaison officers and cooperation agreements with EUROPOL, EUROJUST, and FRONTEX. There is also regular ministerial level dialogue on Justice and Home Affairs (JHA) issues. An EU–U.S. working group on Countering Violent Extremism is cooperating and sharing best practices, for example, workshops on Pakistan and Somalia have taken place, which looked also at how these issues affect transnational communities.

Challenges in the EU–U.S. relationship relate to data and information collection and sharing. The Passenger Name Record (PNR) and TFTP agreements allow for large scale information sharing. The necessary common data protection principles have been developed and a data protection agreement is under negotiation.

Another challenge in the EU–U.S. relationship is the approach regarding the international legal framework used for the fight against terrorism. Since 2006, taking into account the fact that action against international terrorism raises important legal questions, a semi-annual dialogue with the U.S. Department of State Legal Adviser has taken place on counterterrorism and international law, where international legal principles of the fight against terrorism are discussed. The dialogue has the objective of furthering an improved mutual understanding of our respective legal frameworks, and developing common ground from which we can work more effectively on combatting terrorism. In 2009, the EU created a framework to help the U.S. close the Guantanamo Bay detention camp "against the background" of a thorough review of U.S. counterterrorism policies, consistent with the rule of law and international law in the expectation that the underlying policy issues would be addressed.

CONCLUSION

Terrorism will remain a long-term challenge with no quick or easy solutions. While there have been successes, steady progress and close attention is necessary. Close international cooperation remains crucial. Upholding human rights and the rule of law are crucial to our long-term success. The promotion and protection of human rights is essential for all components of the EU's own Counter Terrorism Strategy and the UN Global Counter-Terrorism Strategy. Ahead of the upcoming review of the UN Strategy, we should reflect on how best human rights and the rule of law can be mainstreamed into all counterterrorism measures and capacity building efforts. EU and its Member States are determined to play their full part.

NOTE

1. See "The European Union Counter Terrorism," 30 November 2005, doc no. 14469/4/05 and "the European Union Action Plan on Combating Terrorism," update 2011, 25 November 2011, doc no.17594/11.

AFTERWORD

HOMELAND SECURITY—THE ORGANIZATIONAL CHALLENGE

Terrorist attacks, catastrophic natural disasters, contagious diseases, and economic collapses over the last decade have repeatedly served to remind us that the risks we face globally are rapidly evolving. As a result, organizations need to develop new, and more interconnected, risk management criteria to remain current.

The success or failure of our efforts to protect society depends on the efficacy and effectiveness of organizations. The objective of Homeland Security will only be realized when people and organizations come together to accomplish collectively what they cannot do individually. We must continue to learn about and understand the functions and dysfunctions of multi-organizational efforts, domestically and internationally, to manage shared risks—how they work and don't work—and how they can be changed.

Orchestrating a concerted effort to build safer, more secure, and more resilient nations, communities, and enterprises is a major global challenge. Yet today there is a critical need for expertise, wisdom, and leadership to enable organizations from all parts of society to manage risks collaboratively. The success of a homeland security enterprise will be determined by its ability to interact with and coordinate networks of organizations to overcome security challenges, not by the sum of its own individual actions.

The unity of effort required in order for society to manage catastrophic risks collectively and to make communities and enterprises secure and resilient does not spontaneously result from massive spending, good intentions, or high-level policy documents that emphasize the need for "whole of nation," "whole of government," or "whole community" preparedness.

To better integrate risk management efforts across companies, value chains, communities, regions, and nations, leaders must commit to a collaborative risk management paradigm and purposefully transform their enterprises' organizational cultures. This requires designing a shared vision of the future and then realizing it through successive approximation, continual learning, innovation, and improvements—creating a flexible and responsive infrastructure, designed for nimble response, regardless of source. Leaders must have the courage to periodically pause and question the sacred assumptions of the existing order, battle complacency, address conflict born of self-centered political interests, and abandon outdated modes of organization and management.

The *McGraw-Hill Homeland Security Handbook* reflects the reality that the world of risk management has changed and is shifting to a collaborative paradigm. Those who understand this and can add value will play important roles in the years to come in addressing some of the most significant problems facing our society today. We congratulate the contributors to this book for recognizing the importance of leadership and the design of effective inter-organizational dynamics in advancing the vital mission of homeland security.

David A. Nadler
Vice Chairman, Marsh & McLennan Companies
Chairman, Board of Advisors, Elliott School of International Affairs, George Washington University

Alex Wittenberg
Partner, Oliver Wyman Director, Oliver Wyman Risk Institute

INDEX

1993 World Trade Center attack, 878
2006 Quadrennial Defense Review, 180
2011 Defense Authorization bill, 143
2011 Nordic Solidarity Declaration, 1311
311 call center
    provision of transportation triage by,
        623–624
    use of during Hurricane Gustav
        evacuation, 629–630
3i model, 294–295
9-1-1 centers. *See* PSAPs
9/11 attacks
    assumptions made during, 212–213
    dismissal of possibility of, 227
    economic impact of, 9–10
    evolution of threat vectors following,
        497–498
    government response to, 493–496
    history of aviation terrorism preceding,
        490–492
    incident management following,
        659–662
    inconsistency of communication during,
        240
    information sharing failures, 214–215,
        222–223
    initial perceptions of, 878–879
    lack of information sharing preceding,
        143–144
    organizational confusion during,
        210–211
    role of globalization in, 493
9/11 Commission Act of 2007, implementing
    recommendations of, 81

9/11 Commission, formation of, 495
9/11 Commission Report, 150–151

A

A-Space, 155, 157
Abbas, Abu, 126, 135
Abdulmutallab, Umar Farouk, 161, 498,
    511, 521
    information on prior to Christmas Day
        attack, 968–970
Abdulqader, Mufid, prosecution and
    conviction of, 113–114
Abqaiq, attack on Saudi Aramco facility at,
    14
Academic Centers of Excellence, 818–819
Acadis Readiness Suite, 381–382
Access control
    securing less obvious entrances, 749
    use of to mitigate risk, 482
    vehicular, 748
Accidental threats, 86
    threats to water systems of, 465–467
ACEIR, 818–819
Achille Lauro
    civil suit following, 135
    hijacking of, 122, 126
    legislation following hijacking, 128
Acquisitions, traditional *vs.* technology
    foraging process for, 1022–1023
Action Plan (TISP), 524
    alerts, information sharing, and
        situational awareness, 544–546
    characterization of regional all-hazards
        threats, 537–538

Action Plan (TISP) *(Cont.)*
  considerations for development of,
    536–537
  continuity of operations and business,
    554–557
  determining financial and other resource
    needs, 579–580
  developing framework for regional
    resilience, 531–532
  exercises, education, and training,
    577–579
  identification of infrastructure
    interdependencies, 538–541
  implementation of, 580–581
  legal and liability considerations,
    574–575
  multi-step process for development of,
    532–536
  obtaining resources for activities of,
    582–583
  recovery and long-term restoration
    challenges, 551–554
  regional response challenges,
    546–551
  risk assessment and management,
    543–544
  roles, responsibilities, authorities and
    decision making, 541–543
  societal challenges, 572–574
  stakeholder collaboration and
    empowerment, 586
Actionable information, 224
Active engagement, 723
Active technology push process, 1022
Adaptability deficiencies, 207, 230–231
  prevention of, 231
Administrative Detention (Israel), 1200
Adversarial responses, identification and
    assessment of consequences of,
    359

AEDPA
  allowance of civil actions by, 136
  material support provisions in,
    129–131
  Patriot Act modifications of FTO
    designations, 134
  provisions of regarding CBR agents,
    132
Afghan Arabs, role of in Afghan-Soviet war,
    7–9
Afghan Mission Network (AMN), 181
Afghanistan
  planned attack on American drinking
    water distribution in, 472
  United States war in, 10–11
Afghan–Soviet war, role of Osama bin Laden
    in, 7–9
African Union and the New Partnership for
    Africa's Development (NEPAD),
    1190
Aggregators, 1056
Ahmed, Farooque, 22
Air cargo security, 510–511
Airborne hazards, 789–790
  emergency procedures for, 790–791
Aircraft destruction, attempts at post-9/11,
    499–500
Airline hijackings, 1327
  history of, 490–491
  post-9/11, 499
Airport facilities
  attacks against, 500–501
  regional resilience planning for,
    570–572
Airport Security Plans (ASPs), 503
Al Awlaki, Anwar, 15
Al Qaeda. *See also* Jihadi terrorists
  bioweapons programs of, 63–65
  collapse of the narrative of, 1357
  designation of as FTO, 103

evolution of, 6, 19

exploration of chemical-biological
weapons by, 24–25

finances of, 99–100

founding of, 9

geopolitical perceptions of, 35

resurgence of, 5–6

role of globalization in 9/11 attacks, 493

suicide bombing attacks of, 878

support of terrorist campaigns on surface
transportation, 24

thousand cuts strategy of, 15–18

Al Qaeda in the Arabian Peninsula. *See*
AQAP

Al Qaeda in the countries of the Islamic
Magrheb. *See* AQIM

Al-Arian, Sami, prosecution of, 110–111

Al-Awlaki, Anwar, 1127

Al-Hazmi, Nawaf, 157

Al-Mihdhar, Khalid, 157

Al-Moayad, Mohammed Ali Hasan,
prosecution and conviction of,
113–114

Aldawsari, Khalid, 159, 167

Alertness deficiencies, 207, 217–218

prevention of, 218–219

All hazards, definition of, 527

All hazards approach to societal security,
1296–1297

All-hazards approach to disaster resilience,
527–528

All-hazards approach to emergency planning,
826. *See also* Whole-of-community
approach

All-hazards emergency management, 83, 598

resource allocation for counterterrorism,
337–338

All-hazards emergency preparedness,
drinking water vulnerabilities,
462

All-hazards planning, 86, 655

All-hazards plus approach, 1306–1307

All-hazards readiness, 379–382

All-hazards threat environment,
characterization of for Action Plan
development, 537–538

All-of-nation approach. *See* Whole-of-nation
approach

Allocation of resources. *See also* Resource
allocation

impact of terrorism on, 335–336

Alternative generation table, 344–345

American National Standards Institute. *See*
ANSI

American Society of Civil Engineers (ASCE),
assessment of condition of U.S.
infrastructure, 440–441

Analyst Toolbox, 289

Analysts

functions of in fusion centers, 307–308

role of in fusion centers, 288–289

role of in intelligence-led policing,
295–296

Analytic transformation, 173

Analytical risk assessment, 496

use of in aviation security, 514

ANSI, 764

ANSI–ASQ National Accreditation Board
(ANAB), 1246

Anthrax letters, 63

emergency procedures for, 794

Anti-Hijacking Act of 1974, 123

Anti-Terrorism and Arms Export Control Act
of 1989, 125–126

Antihijacking convention of The Hague,
127

Antiterrorism and Effective Death Penalty Act
of 1996. *See* AEDPA

Antiterrorist Assistance (ATA) program,
budgeting for, 144

Applied Center of Excellence for
  Infrastructure Resilience.
  See ACEIR
AQAP, 13, 1357
  thousand cuts strategy of, 15–18
AQIM, 34, 1357
  designation of as FTO, 103
Arab Bank of Jordan, civil suits against, 136
Arab Spring, 1357
  effect of on al Qaeda, 5–6, 19
Arab Strategy for Disaster Risk Reduction
  2020, 1190
Arctic Council, 1311
Arizona, insider attack on wastewater system
  in, 469
Armed Forces (Special Powers) Act (India),
  1321
Army of Islam, designation of as FTO, 104
Arnaout, Enaam, prosecution of, 111–112
Arts, Entertainment, and Recreation services,
  842
Ashqar, Abdelhaleem
  conviction of, 119
  prosecution of, 112
Asian Terminals (Philippines), certification to
  ISO 28000 standards, 1229
Assembly areas, establishment of in
  evacuation plans, 783–784
Assessment of options in crisis situations
  authorization, 728–729
  judgment, 730–731
  prohibitions, 729
  risk, 729–730
Assets, use of vulnerability–consequence
  tables for risk analysis, 347
Association of Southeast Asian Nations
  (ASEAN), 1190
Assumption, 207
  deficiencies in planning and execution
  due to, 211–213

paraphrasing and, 229–230
  prevention of, 213
Asymmetrical warfare, terrorism as, 888–889
At-risk populations, consideration of in
  regional resilience plans, 546–547
Attack trees, 346–347
Attitude, 207
  deficiency of superiority, 225–226
Attorney General's Guidelines, intelligence
  gathering under, 1152–1153
Aum Shinrikyo, 1204
  use of bioweapons by, 64
Australia, cyber attack on wastewater utility
  in, 475
Authorised Economic Operators (EU),
  1225, 1234
  accreditation, 1235
  definition of, 1235
  guidelines, 1236
  support of by ISO 28000 standards,
  1240
Aviation and Transportation Security Act
  (ATSA), 493
Aviation security, 26–27
  approaches to passenger screening,
  504–508
  bag screening, 502
  cargo in international distribution stream,
  510–511
  evolution of post 9/11, 497
  generic threats, 497–498
  insider threats, 508–509
  layered, 518–519
  legislation related to, 127–128
  new threat vectors, 498–501
  personal screening, 502
  prohibited items list, 501–502
  psychological battle of, 489–490
  public education and civil liberties,
  511–514

separating functions of, 503
shared responsibility for, 514–518
Azhar, Masood, 1327
Azzam, Abdullah, 9

B

BAAs, 1021
Babbar Khalsa International, assassination
    of Chief Minister Beant Singh by,
    1326
Babri Masjid, destruction of and subsequent
    riots, 1325
Bachelet, President Michele, activities
    of surrounding 2010 disaster,
    1338–1340
Backflow prevention program, use of for
    risk mitigation by water utilities,
    483
Backup power, necessity of, 645
Bag screening, 502
Baker, Shukri Abu, prosecution and
    conviction of, 113–114
Baltic Sea Region, collaboration in, 1311
Baltimore. *See also* Maryland
    communication interoperability in,
        664–665
    use of talkgroups by first responders in,
        661–662
Bank records
    government access to, 1140–1141
    Right to Financial Privacy Act, 1145
Bank Secrecy Act, 1140–1141
Banking industry
    applicability of ISO 28000 standards to,
        1232–1233
    supply chain risk of, 1231–1232
Banner Plasticard (Philippines), certification
    to ISO 28000 standards, 1229
Barriers, use of to mitigate risk, 481
Base map layers, 991–992

Basel Committee on Banking Supervision,
    1231–1232
Baseline Capabilities Assessment, 280
*Baseline Capabilities for State and Major Urban
    Area Fusion Centers,* 289
Baseline corporate security, 747–748
Baseline risk, assessment of, 359
Basque separatists (ETA), surface
    transportation attacks by, 23
BCM, role of in operational resilience, 802
Behavior Detection Officers of TSA, 505–506
Behavior patterns, identifying system
    structures and, 866–867
Behavioral research
    applying lessons learned to risk
        communication, 409–410
    role of in terror risk management, 415
    technology projects, 1087
Benefit–cost analysis, 356–357
Benevolence International Foundation (BIF),
    prosecution of executive director of,
    111–112
Berman, Rep. Howard, 125
Best practices
    collaboration, 328–330
    foreign homeland security policy, 1196
    fusion centers, 311
    nuclear power industry, 1254,
        1273–1279
    verification, 216
Bin Laden, Osama
    analysis of economic impact of 9/11
        attacks, 9–10
    death of, 5
    role of in Afghan-Soviet war, 7–9
    support of terrorist campaigns on surface
        transportation, 24
Biological attacks, 24–25
    distinguishing from chemical attacks, 787
    modeling of using GIS, 1005–1006

Biological weapons, 59
  capability of terrorists to produce and
    deliver, 62–64
  intent of terrorists to use, 64–65
  vulnerability to and consequences of,
    65–67
Biological Weapons Convention (BWC),
  62
Biometric IDs, support for, 514
Biosurveillance system, use of for
    detection and tracking of
    outbreaks, 645–646
Bioterrorism, forecasting the threat of,
    62–67
Bioterrorism Act of 2002, 462, 485
Bipartisan WMD Terrorism Research
    Center, 67
Black Swan events, 1296
Black widows, 1129–1130
Bleeding wars, role of al Qaeda in,
    10–12
Bologna train station bombing, 23
Bomb search team, 774
Bomb squads
  collaboration of with hazmat teams,
    643–644
  measuring response time of, 648
Bomb threats, emergency procedures for,
    796–798
Bombings, casualties from attacks on surface
    transportation, 23
Border security
  advances in information technology,
    951–952
  homeland security spending for,
    1085
  provision of Patriot Act regarding,
    135
  use of complex event processing in,
    944

Boston Logan International Airport, use of
    SPOT program at, 505–506
Boumediene v. Bush, 141
BP Oil Spill. *See* Deepwater Horizon
Brazil, First Commando of the Capital gang
    in, 39
Breivik, Anders Behring, 1122–1123
  intent of to use bioweapons, 65
Bridges
  effect of condition of on performance,
    440
  embedding resilience into, 817
  use of rapid construction on following
    earthquakes, 454–455
Brisbane floods, case study of GIS technology
    use following, 1012–1014
British counterterrorism
  CONTEST strategic framework,
    1199–1200
  legislation, 1198
  structure and institutions, 1199
Broad Agency Announcements. *See* BAAs
Bronze Command (U.K.), responsibilities
    of in emergency response, 1208
Budget appropriations
  aviation security and, 516–517
  counterterrorism spending, 144–145
  disaster risk management and,
    1173–1174
  readiness and, 387
Build back better, 827
Bush Administration
  creation of Department of Homeland
    Security by, 73–74
  detainee of policies, 139–140
  executive orders related to information
    sharing, 153
  homeland security policy documents of,
    75–77
  post 9/11 war on Iraq, 11–12

post-9/11 national security strategies of, 887

pre-9/11 counterterrorism activities, 144

Terrorist Surveillance Program of, 1148

Bush, George W. *See also* Bush Administration

initial perceptions of 9/11 attacks, 878

Business continuity

consideration of in regional resilience plan, 554–557

consideration of supply chain in planning, 848

coordinating with emergency and crisis management, 765

information sharing and, 177

ISO 28000 standards and, 1233

messaging system for, 856

NFPA 1600, 764-765

standards applicable to, 803–805

Business Continuity Management. *See* BCM

Business Crime Reduction Team (UK), 849

lessons learned, 854–856

strategy of, 850–851

Business optimization, use of technology for, 957

Business partnerships, use of to build resilience, 851–853

Business Process Management (BPM), use of in collaborative efforts, 329

C

C-TPAT, 1234, 1236–1237

Cabinet Office Civil Contingencies Committee (U.K.). *See* COBR

Cable Act of 1984, 1146

CAD/RMS, 986–987

use of by first responders, 639

CAEP

challenges to evacuation, 614–615

designation and communication of pick-up points, 619–621

evacuation of pets, 624–625

evacuation timeline, 626–628

full-scale exercise of, 628–629

lessons learned, 630–634

logic model, 615–618

objectives for the development of, 612

planning cycle, 629

process flow, 622

provision of transportation assistance, 618

reentry planning, 632–633

tri-modal evacuation model, 618–619

triage model for transportation, 621–624

Calculated Priority Risk Index. *See* CPRI

Calculated Risk Specific Readiness, 393–394

California

case study of GIS technology use for wildfires in, 1015–1016

effect of Northridge Earthquake on water systems in, 464–465

Camacho, Marcos, 39

Cameras

use of CCTV networks for critical infrastructure, 640–641

use of for risk mitigation for water utilities, 480

use of in surface transportation security, 28

Campaign to build and sustain preparedness, 84

Canada, role of military in homeland security, 1212

Canadian policing model, 1202

Canadian Rangers, 1212

Capabilities

cost-effectiveness of development of, 94–95

integration of management system standards with requirements, 90–91

mission area focus of *National Preparedness System*, 88

Capacity *vs.* capability, 368–369

CAPPS, 492, 494–495

selection of 9/11 terrorists by, 492

Carabinieri (Italy), 1211

Care providers

preparedness planning for, 675–676

psychological consequences of terrorism events and, 675

Cargo aircraft

printer bombs, 499

security of in international distribution stream, 510–511

Caribbean Disaster Emergency Management Agency (CDEMA), 1190

Carnegie Mellon's CERT Resilience Management Model. *See* CERT-RMM

CARRI, 821–822, 826

Community Resilience System Initiative of, 829 (*See also* CRS)

definition of community resilience, 828

Catastrophic events, 80

homeland security spending for, 1085–1086

CBR agents

delivering decision-relevant risk communication, 411–412

emergency procedures for attacks involving, 786–788, 790–791

risk communication regarding decontamination, 406

U.S. legislation regarding, 132

CCTV

use of by first responders, 664

use of for transportation system security, 642

use of integrated networks to secure infrastructure, 640–641

Census Bureau, disclosure of information by, 1145

Center for Advancing Microbial Risk Assessment (CAMRA), 930

Center for Maritime, Island and Remotes and Extreme Environment Security (MIREES), 931

Center for Risk and Economic Analysis of Terrorism Events (CREATE), 930

Center of Excellence for Awareness & Location of Explosives-Related Threats (ALERT), 931

Center of Excellence for Zoonotic and Animal Disease Defense (ZADD), 930

Center of Excellence in Command, Control and Interoperability (C2I), 932

Centers of Excellence, 818–819

provision of research needs by, 929–932

Central America, criminality in, 39–40

Central List (India), 1321

Centro de Coordinación para la Prevención de los Desastres Naturales en América Central, 1190

CERT-RMM, 807–809

Challenge interviews, 505, 508, 514

Chechen black widows, 1129–1130

Chemical, biological, and radioactive (CBR) agents. *See* CBR agents

Chemical attacks, 24–25

distinguishing from biological attacks, 787

modeling of using GIS, 1005–1006

recognizing physical evidence of, 786–787

use of countermeasures for by water utilities, 482

Chemical storage security, 751

Chemicals, effects of accidental infiltration of in water systems, 466

Chernobyl, 1255

Chicago, planned attacks on drinking water system, 471–472

Chidden, psychological responses to terrorism, 671

Chile

2010 earthquake and tsunami, 1337

description of 2010 disaster, 1338–1340

investigation of events surrounding 2010 disaster, 1348–1349

miscommunications surrounding 2010 disaster, 1340–1348

natural disaster planning in following 2010 disaster, 1350–1352

China

contamination of drinking water supply in, 478

effect of petrochemical plant explosion on water systems in, 467

Cho, Seung Hui, 202, 223–224

Christchurch, NZ earthquakes

role of Student Volunteer Army in, 1040–1041

use of Tomnod.com for damage mapping, 1039

Christmas Bomber, 967–970, 1357–1358. *See also* Underwear bomber

Chuzaisho officers (Japan), 1203

CIKR, 439

homeland security spending for protection of, 1085–1086

role of fusion centers in protection of, 280

CISSO, 156

Citizen involvement, risk communication and, 402–403

Citizen self-help, 511–512

City Assisted Evacuation Plan. *See* CAEP

Civil and military sectors, coordination in planning between, 1301

Civil Contingencies Act 2004 (U.K.), 849, 1204–1205

Civil Defense Act, 597

Civil defense system, 655

evolution of, 597–598

Civil liberties

aviation screening procedures and, 512–513

concerns regarding predictive radicalization theory policies, 1125–1127

concerns regarding suspicious activity reporting, 159

concerns regarding targeted killing policy, 1127–1129

information sharing concerns, 163

Japanese laws to safeguard, 1204

security *vs.*, 1119–1120

Civil suits, use of by victims of terrorist acts, 135–137

Civil–civil coordination

arenas for stakeholder agencies in society security, 1302

difficulties of, 1301

Classified Information Sharing and Safeguarding Office. *See* CISSO

Clean Water Act, 462

Climate change, 441

increasing strategic importance of Arctic region due to, 1311–1312

preparedness planning for, 86, 93

Closed-circuit television. *See* CCTV

Cloud computing, 963–967

CNN, use of crowdsourcing by, 1037

Coastal Hazards Center of Excellence (CHC), 931

Coastal zone management, 1185

COBR (U.K.), responsibilities of during emergency response, 1205–1206

COD, 1050
  creation of by UICDS, 1071–1074
  integration of alternate sources of in UICDS, 1076–1080

COG
  plans, 644–645
  role of in operational resilience, 802

Coimbatore blasts, 1326

Cold War, terrorism during, 33

Collaboration
  best practices, 328–330
  cross-sector, multi-jurisdiction, 528
  efforts of DHS, 327–328
  encouragement of between businesses, 850–851
  failure due to lack of, 241–242
  Google Hack response, 326–327
  Haiti disaster response, 325–326
  importance of information sharing for, 180
  interagency, 323–324
  leader–lawyer relationships during disasters, 712–713
  meta-leadership and, 696–699
  Nordic region, 1310–1312
  public–private partnerships in evacuation planning, 631–633
  safety and security professionals, 1300–1301

Collaborative risk management, information sharing and, 171–172

Columbine
  information sharing failures, 224
  lessons learned from, 202

Commercial databases, government mining of, 1141–1142

Common Information Model (CIM), 1076
  integration of with UICDS, 1077, 1080

Common Operational Data. *See* COD

Commonwealth Fusion Center, 296

Communication
  importance of for collaboration, 328–329
  inconsistency of, 240
  logic of creating content of, 407
  operational plans for scheduled events, 655–656

Communication deficiencies, 207, 228
  paraphrasing, 229–230
  prevention of, 229

Communications services, 842
  corporate planning for, 780
  redundant systems for, 645
  use of messaging system for business resilience, 856
  use of radio systems during large scale events, 660–662

Communities of interest, 158, 192

Community
  definition of, 526, 828
  regional resilience planning considerations, 572–574

Community and Regional Resilience Institute. *See* CARRI

Community Leaders Working Group (CRS), 829

Community organizations
  management of psychological consequences of events by, 675
  preparedness planning for, 675–676

Community Records services, 842

Community resilience, 649, 828–829
  assessment of, 834–840
  building, 820–822

Community Resilience System Initiative.
    See CRS
Community service areas, 842–845
    use of in resilience assessment,
        836–840
Complacency, 207, 217–218
    deficiency of, 219–220
    prevention of, 221
Complex event processing (CEP), 953, 958
    embedding of into predictive analytic
        solutions, 956–957
    scorecards of, 963–964
Compliance, operational resilience and,
        805–806
Components, identification of, 866
Comprehensive National Cybersecurity
        Initiative, information sharing
        emphasis in, 174–176
CompStat, 647–648
Computational general equilibrium analyses,
        448
Computer Assisted Passenger Prescreening
        System. *See* CAPPS
Computer-aided dispatch and records
        management systems. *See*
        CAD/RMS
Conceptual lenses, use of in multiple frame
        analysis of homeland security,
        881–883
Conciliatory counterterrorism, 892
Concurrent List (India), 1321
Condition and performance of infrastructure,
        439–441
Conditional cash transfers, 1187
Confirmatory bias, 343
Conflict, collaboration and, 330
Consensus building, 833–834
Consistency deficiencies, 208, 239–240
    prevention of, 240
Consolidated watch list, 495

Constitutional privacy protections,
        1137–1138
    Fourth Amendment, 1138–1142
Constitutive elements, identification of,
        866
Consumption, infrastructure independence
        and increase in, 445–446
Container Security Initiative (CSI), 1225
CONTEST strategic framework (U.K.),
        1199–1200
Context enhanced cloud environments,
        966
Contextual awareness, 726–727
Contingency planning, progress of HFA
        member states regarding,
        1177–1178
Continuity management. *See* Business
        continuity
Continuity of government. *See* COG
Continuity of operations. *See* COOP
Continuous improvement, 1218. *See also*
        PDCA process
Contractual compliance, 805
Contraflow mechanism, 626–627
Control orders, 1198
Controlled Unclassified Information (CUI),
        153
Controlled Unclassified Information
        framework, 156
Convention for the Suppression of Financing
        of Terrorism, 123
COOP
    plans, 644–645
    role of in operational resilience, 802
Coordinated incident management,
        529–530
    meta-leadership and, 696–699
Coordination Areas planning and
        preparedness (Sweden), 1302
Core capabilities, 84–86

Core capacity, 439

Corporate emergency management
    critical resources, 772
    critiques, audits, and evaluations, 799
    incident command system, 775–779
    management commitment and policy,
        768
    mitigation, 770–771
    notification and escalation procedures,
        780–781
    program development, 766–767
    protective actions, 781–785
    threat assessment, 769–770
    training, drills, and exercises, 798–799
    vulnerability assessment, 770

Corporate security, 771
    baseline processes for, 747–748
    building perimeters and interior security,
        749
    concealment areas, 748–749
    crisis management, 754–758
    critical utilities and chemicals, 751
    development of overseas contacts,
        760–761
    emergency planning, 751–753
    information requirements and sources,
        758–760
    loading docks, 750
    lobbies, 749
    mail rooms, 750
    perimeter lighting, 748
    risk assessments, 745–747
    underground parking garages, 750
    vehicular access control, 748
    windows and exterior glass, 750

Cosa Nostra, 34

Cost transfer, 1298

Cost-effectiveness analysis, preparedness
    capabilities, 94–95

Cost–benefit analysis, 356–357

Council of Arab Ministers Responsible for the
    Environment (CAMRE), 1190

Council of Baltic Sea States (CBSS), 1311

Counter Terrorist Security Advisors (CTSAs,
    UK), 849–850

Counter-Terrorism Strategy (EU), 1358
    pillars of, 1359–1362

Counterterrorism
    approaches to resource allocation for,
        337–339
    British structure of, 1199
    classification of options for, 891–892
    communicating about risks of,
        397–399
    comparison of with other risk
        applications, 341–342
    cooperation between EU and non-EU
        countries on, 1362–1364
    EU–U.S. cooperation, 1364–1365
    evolution of in India, 1327–1334
    fusion of with crime fighting efforts,
        641–642
    integration of resource allocation with
        risk management, 357–362
    Israeli emergency legislation for, 1200
    Israeli structures and institutions,
        1200–1201
    Jammu & Kashmir police efforts,
        1328–1329
    legislation in the U.K., 1198
    network governance and strategies for,
        894
    resilience and, 813–815
    role of fusion centers in, 283–286
    strategies of to prevent and deter
        terrorism, 884

Counterterrorism conventions (U.S.), 118

Counterterrorism efforts, information sharing
    among partners, 172–173

Counterterrorism fatigue, 1358

Counterterrorism laws, implementation and
        challenges, 143–146
Counterterrorism programs, U.S. funding of,
        143–145
CPRI, 377–379, 391–393
    use of to measure readiness, 383–384
Crescent City. *See* New Orleans
Crime Act of 1994, material support
        definitions in, 130
Crime analysis, use of GIS technology for,
        993–996
Crime fighting, fusion of with
        counterterrorism efforts, 641–642
Crime globalization, 38–40, 1308
Crime prevention
    business continuity and, 850
    use of strategies in counterterrorism
        efforts, 884
Criminal armies, wars and, 37–38
Criminal justice view of homeland
        security and terrorism, 883–887,
        1361–1362
Criminal middle class, 41–42
Criminal organizations, evolution of,
        34–35
Criminal prosecution of terrorists, 139
Criminals *vs.* terrorists, 883–884
Crisis action planning, 169
Crisis attorneys
    GAIN model for, 718–726 (*See also*
        GAIN model)
    importance of listening skills for, 725
    perception of as obstacles, 714–715
    PREP model for, 716–718
    relationship of with leaders, 712–713
    SOAP model for, 726–732
Crisis coordination secretariat (Sweden),
        1299
Crisis leadership
    ability to follow, 694–696

    characteristics of meta-leaders,
        685–688
    demands of, 680–682
    diagnosing objective reality of events,
        688–692
    engagement of extended networks,
        696–699
    engaging followers, 692–694
    five-dimension meta-leadership
        model, 682, 684–685
    legal and ethical questions of,
        711–712
    unity of purpose, 699–701
Crisis management
    coordinating with business continuity
        and emergency management, 765
    corporate security and, 754–758
    human resources programs, 484
Crisis management teams (CMTs),
        754–755
    communication and, 755–756
    designation of, 752
    human resources and, 755–756
    security and, 757–758
Crisis negotiators, 725
Crisis planning
    lack of imagination during,
        226–227
    role of fusion centers in, 312–313
Crisis teams, group dynamics of,
        719–722
CrisisCommons, 1043
    use of during 2011 crisis in Japan, 1038
    wiki, 1035
Critical assets
    identification of, 358
    identification of dependencies and
        interdependencies, 538–541
    national network of, 649
    securing, 751

Critical infrastructure, 526–527
    analyzing interdependence of,
        447–449
    definitions of, 438–439
    EU efforts to increase resilience of,
        1360–1361
    factors contributing to interdependence,
        445–447
    information sharing and protection of,
        174–176, 1303
    institutional interdependence,
        449–452
    interdependencies among, 443–445
    mapping of, 643
    modifying interdependency of,
        453–455
    operational risk concepts and challenges,
        802–806
    policies regarding vulnerability of,
        439–442
    reconstitution of after an evacuation,
        632–633
    requirements for corporate emergency
        planning, 769
    role of information technology in, 452
    security of, 437–438
    use of CCTV networks to secure,
        640–641
    use of GIS technology for operational
        decision support, 993
    use of GIS technology for protection of,
        1007–1009
    vulnerability assessments of, 642–643
Critical infrastructure and key resources.
    See CIKR
Critical infrastructure index, 379
Critical Infrastructure Protection Board,
    450–451
Critical operational capability areas (COCs),
    289–290

Cross-discipline information sharing, 254.
    See also Information sharing
Cross-system linkages, creation of by meta-
    leaders, 696–699
Crowd
    gathering of situational awareness data
        by, 1037–1038
    making sense of data, 1038–1039
    trusting information from, 1044–1045
Crowd sentiment detection, 1046–1047
CrowdFlower, 1036
Crowdsensing, 1036
Crowdsourcing
    concerns regarding use of, 1044–1045
    definition, 1035
    harnessing the power of, 1041–1044
    use of by first responders, 1036
    use of by fusion centers, 310–311
    use of for risk communication,
        431–432
    use of to inform the public, 1040
CRS, 821–822, 826
    assessment of resilience, 834–840
    Awareness and Engagement Planning
        Matrix, 834
    community engagement, 833–834
    development of, 829
    forming the leadership team,
        831–833
    overview of, 830–831
    piloting, 840
Cryptosporidium spp.
    infiltration of Milwaukee drinking
        water supply, 465–466
    influence diagram for predicting
        risks from, 414
CTS Logistics (China), use of ISO 28000
    standards by, 1229
Cuba, designation of as terrorist regime,
    124–125

Culture
 pervasive readiness and changes in,
  387
 psychological responses to terrorism
  and, 671–672
 security, 362
Customer Relationship Management (CRM),
  1102
Cyber attacks
 EU development of strategy to address,
  1360
 infrastructure policy and, 442–443
 use of against water systems, 475
 vulnerability of infrastructure to, 452
Cyber interdependent infrastructure, 444
Cyber security
 consideration of in regional resilience
  plans, 557–558
 globalization and, 1308
Cyberspace, defense of, 323–324

D

Dams, regional resilience planning for,
  565–567
Data
 capture of for information sharing,
  255
 cooperative EU–U.S. agreement on
  protection of, 1364–1365
 disaster loss, 1179–1180
 fractional, 1065
 standards-based exchanges of for SAR,
  278–280
 use of crowd to make sense of,
  1038–1039
Data analysis
 challenges to information sharing, 162
 definition of, 288
 information sharing and, 173
Data fusion domain, 953

Data mining
 definition of, 1134–1135
 efficacy of, 1154–1156
 impact of, 1156–1160
 legal questions regarding,
  1135–1136
 Privacy Act of 1974, 1143–1145
 recommendations for regulating,
  1153–1154
Data processing model of administrative
  control, 1136
DB Schenker, certification to ISO 28000
  standards, 1228–1229
Death on the High Seas Act, 135
Decision analysis techniques, 352–353
Decision makers
 relationships of with fusion centers,
  297–298
 role of in intelligence-led policing,
  295
Decision making
 biases influencing perception of risk,
  342–344
 Canadian Q850 risk management
  process, 401
 coordinated incident management
  and, 529–530
 framework for counterterrorism,
  336–337
 perspectives on disaster decisions,
  713
 role of uncertainty in, 713–714
 urgency and, 714
Decision tree models, 354–355
Decontamination standards
 creating channels for risk
  communication, 406
 delivering decision-relevant risk
  communication, 411–412
 managing risks, 415–416

Deepwater Horizon, 598
    "Path to Tragedy" report, 203–204
    case study of GIS usage, 1011–1012
    demands of crisis leadership following
        spill, 680–681
    failures due to complacency, 220
    information sharing failures, 218
    lack of proactive risk mitigation, 815
Defense Regulations (Israel), 1200
Deficiencies in planning, 195–197. *See also*
        Strategic planning failures; specific
        deficiencies
Deficiency, definition of, 209
Delegation of responsibility, 208
    deficiency of, 246–248
Deliberate planning, 169
Department of Defense (U.S.), collaboration
        of with U.S. Department of State,
        327
Department of Energy (U.S.), national
        laboratories, 929
Department of Homeland Security.
        See DHS
Department of State (U.S.), collaboration of
        with U.S. Department of Defense, 327
Deradicalization, 49
Deregulation, financial crimes and, 41
Detail complexity, 863
Detainee Treatment Act (DTA) of 2005,
        139, 141
Detection, use of GIS for, 1008
Detention policies
    Bush administration, 139–140
    non-criminal detention, 141–143
    Obama administration, 140
Detention Policy Task Force, 140
Deterrence
    perceptions of, 881
    theory of, 884
    U.S. foreign policy and doctrine of, 890

DG ECHO, administrative arrangement of
        with FEMA, 1316
DHL Express, certification to ISO 28000
        standards in Spain, 1230
DHS
    bureaucratic structure of, 893–894
    changes in mission of, 895
    collaboration efforts of, 327–328
    Cooperative Work Arrangement of with
        FRONTEX, 1316
    creation of, 73–74, 494
    HSEEP, 906 (*See also* HSEEP)
    importance of relationships for vendors,
        1107
    national laboratories, 929
    National Preparedness System, 88
    Office of Emergency Communications,
        663
    PS-Prep program of, 805
    quadrennial review, 81–82
    rules of engagement for vendors, 1109
    Science and Technology Directorate
        (*See* S&T Directorate)
    Standing Information Needs, 299
    technology projects of, 1087–1089
    Traveler Redress Inquiry Program,
        495
    US-VISIT program, 949–951
    USCIS (*See* USCIS)
    use of NIEM by, 278
    Virtual Social Media Networking Group,
        1044
Digital infrastructure. *See also* Cyberspace
    protection of, 323–324
Digitization of information, use of crowd
    for, 1039
Director of National Intelligence. *See* DNI
Dirty bombs
    delivering decision-relevant risk
        communication, 411–412

recognition of physical evidence of, 786–787

risk communication regarding, 406

Disaster loss data, 1179–1180

Disaster management

all-hazards planning, 655

assessment of options by attorneys, 728–731

decision making perspectives, 713

information sharing and, 177–180

key concepts, 595–597

large-scale events, 659–662

legal and ethical questions of, 711–712

preparedness planning and, 529

role of volunteers in, 630–631

technology projects, 1087–1089

use of GIS technology for, 998

Disaster mitigation, resilience as, 815–816

Disaster preparedness. *See also* Preparedness

Chile, 1350–1352

deficiencies in, 195–197

planning cycle for, 629

progress of HFA member states, 1177

Disaster recovery (DR), operational resilience and, 802

Disaster Relief Act of 1950, 596

Disaster resilience, 526. *See also* Resilience

Action Plan implementation, 580–581

cyber security and IT system resilience, 557–558

measuring, 583–585

whole-of-society approach to in Sweden, 1297–1298

Disaster response. *See also* Response

crowdsourcing tasks, 1035

evolution of, 597–599

Disaster risk management. *See* DRM

Disasters

categories of, 595–596

leader–lawyer relationships during, 712–713

outcomes of, 838

presidential declarations of, 596–597, 599

role of uncertainty in decision making during, 713–714

use of crowd sentiment detection during, 1046–1047

Disclosure deficiencies, 208, 232

prevention of, 232–233

Disclosure of personal matters, government-compelled, 1142–1143

Discriminatory security policies, 1120

radicalization, 1125

targeted killing, 1128

Discussion-based exercises, 906. *See also* Exercises

Diseases

biosurveillance system for, 645–646

detection of contamination of drinking water supplies, 477

emergence and evolution of, 60

threats to from drinking water and wastewater utilities from, 464

Dispatch systems, GIS technology in, 986–987

Dispatches, necessity for clarity of, 228

Disregard for event independence, 343

Dissemination of information, 208. *See also* Information sharing

deficiency of, 234–236, 240

preventing failure of, 236

District Model, 370

Risk-Specific Readiness measures, 383–384

use of to reduce fragmentation, 374–376

DNI, 152
  information sharing of, 154–155
Doe v. Gonzalez, 134
DOJ, use of NIEM by, 278
Domestic counterterrorism effort
  homeland security spending for, 1085
  information sharing among partners,
    172–173
Domestic crime, distinction of terrorism from,
    883–884
Domestic Security Advisory Council, 159
Domestic surveillance
  creating channels for risk communication,
    404–405
  delivering decision-relevant risk
    communication, 411
  managing risks, 415
Donations, solicitation of by social media,
    1039–1040
DP World, certification to ISO 28000
    standards, 1225–1226
Drills
  corporate emergency management,
    798–799
  HSEEP, 906
  use of for preparedness improvement,
    645
  use of GIS in, 1001–1004
Drinking water systems
  disruptions in, 461
  effects of vandalism on, 468–469
  emergency response plans for, 484–485
    (*See also* ERPs)
  insider attacks on, 469
  intentional or accidental contamination
    of, 477–479
  physical assault on components of,
    473–474
  terrorist attacks on, 470–473
  threats to from accidents, 465–467

  threats to from natural disasters,
    464–465
  vulnerability assessment of, 462, 479–480
DRM
  environmental planning and
    management, 1185–1186
  HFA priority of, 1173–1174
  incorporating in national planning and
    investment, 1182–1184
  integration of gender considerations into,
    1191–1192
  justifying investments in, 1181–1182
  limited local capacity and action, 1188
  progress of HFA member states
    regarding, 1176–1177
  public awareness and education for,
    1188–1189
  regional progress, 1189–1191
  social protection, 1186–1187
  strengthening institutional and
    legislative arrangements,
    1187–1188
  urban and land use planning,
    1184–1185
Drug cartels, 34
  criminal armies of, 37–38
Dual-use equipment, export of by terrorist
    regimes, 123–125
Duration, definition of for CPRI, 378
Dynamic sensor data, 992–993
Dynamic situations, determining objective
    reality of, 688–692
Dynamically complex systems, 864
  mass transit systems, 870–871

E

E-Borders, 961
E-mail
  privacy of, 1147
  use of for risk communication, 431–432

E-Verify system, 944, 947–949

Early warning systems, 1177

European Union, 1312–1313

gaps and challenges in, 1178–1180

Earthquakes. *See also* Natural disasters

case study of use of GIS technology in Japan, 1012

Chile, 1337 (*See also* Chile)

damage to infrastructure during, 441

effect of Northridge Earthquake on water systems, 464–465

Great Eastern (Japan), 431, 1264–1265

Haiti disaster response, 325–326

infrastructure interdependence and, 445

performance of lifelines following, 440

use of social media and crowdsourcing following, 1037–1039

Economic index, measurement of in Priority Risk Index, 379

Economic interdependent infrastructure, 444

Economic models, analysis of interdependent infrastructure, 448

Economic services, 842–843

Economic targets, jihadi attacks on, 15–18

Economics

financial crimes, 40–41

role of in Afghan-Soviet war, 8

Economy

effect of bleeding wars on, 10–12

effect of war on oil on, 13–14

impact of terrorist attacks on, 9–10

thousand cuts strategy and, 15–18

Education initiatives

disaster risk management, 1188–1189

inclusion of in regional resilience planning, 572–574

Educational services, 843

EIS, 1051–1052

conceptual interoperability model of, 1053–1054

creation of by UICDS, 1049

national doctrine for, 1067–1068

operational questions for, 1069–1070

programs for, 1076

two-way exchange of information among applications, 1056–1058

El-Mezain, Mohammad, prosecution and conviction of, 113–114

Elashi, Ghassan, prosecution and conviction of, 113–114

Electric power, terrorist attacks on infrastructure, 442–443

Electronic Communications Privacy Act of 1986. *See* EPCA

Electronic surveillance

FISA definition of, 1149

privacy protections, 1146–1147

Elevated threat, 428

Emergency alerts, developing a regional system for, 544–546

Emergency call handling, use of GIS technology for, 986–987

Emergency exercises

goal of, 910

importance of, 905

Emergency information sharing. *See* EIS

Emergency management

all-hazards planning, 655

coordinating with business continuity and crisis management, 765

corporate program development, 766–767

definition of, 763

developing an effective system for, 601–602

future of in the U.S., 602–604

historical use of technology in, 1050–1051

Emergency management *(Cont.)*
importance of history of, 594
importance of public–private
partnerships in, 649–650
incorporation of public health with,
530
information sharing and, 177–180
key concepts, 595–597
large-scale events, 659–662
legal and ethical questions of, 711–712
NFPA 1600, 764–765 *(See also* NFPA
standards)
policy and politics, 599–601
risk mitigation strategies for water
utilities, 483
United Kingdom approach to,
1204–1208
use of GIS technology for, 998
water utilities, 486–487
whole-of-community approach,
826–827 *(See also* Whole-of-
community approach)
Emergency Management Accreditation
Program (EMAP), management
system standards of, 91
Emergency manager
community, 828–829
corporate, 773
Emergency operational responses
standard, 658
water utilities, 485–486
Emergency Operations Centers. *See* EOCs
Emergency planning
education, 753
elements of, 751–753
role of fusion centers in, 312–313
Emergency preparedness, 910. *See also*
Preparedness
assigned responsibility for in Sweden,
1300

deficiencies in, 195–197
homeland security spending for, 1085
local level, 637–638
mass casualty events, 646
necessity of backup power and
communications, 645
Emergency procedures
airborne hazards, 790–791
bomb threats, 796–798
detection and assessment, 785–787
determination of protective actions,
788–789
distinguishing between indoor and
outdoor release, 787–788
fires and explosions, 792
radiological incidents, 790–791
suspicious packages or letters,
792–796
Emergency response plans. *See* ERPs
Emergency response teams, 773–775
Emergency Support Functions. *See* ESFs
Emergency wireless calls, 987
Emergent properties, 867
EMI, efforts to define emergency
management education programs,
919
Employment guarantee schemes, 1187
Energy sector
effect of failure in on water systems,
467
regional resilience planning for,
562–563
technology interdependence,
452–453
Energy services, 843
Engagement Working Group (EWG), 818
Engineering models, analysis of infrastructure
interdependence using, 448
Enterprise resilience, information sharing
and, 177

Enterprise Risk Management. *See* ERM

Enterprise service bus (ESB), 955–956
    use of in collaborative efforts, 329

Enterprise Social Media, 967–969

Enterprise-scale messaging, 955

Environmental change, 93

Environmental hazards, regional resilience
    and management of, 530

Environmental planning and management,
    risk reduction and, 1185–1186

Environmental regulations, requirements of
    for corporate emergency planning,
    768

Environmental risk communication, creating
    appropriate channels for, 400–403

EOCs
    corporate emergency planning for,
      779
    exercise to test functional performance
      of, 914–916
    regional integration of, 548
    use of during prolonged events, 657
    use of UICDS by, 1062

EPCA
    restrictions on e-mail access by
      government, 1147
    restrictions on electronic surveillance,
      1146–1147

EPCIP (EU), 1361

Equality model of passenger screening,
    504, 506–507

ERM, role of in operational resilience, 802

Ernest N. Morial Convention Center,
    611–612

ERPs, 484, 779–780
    preparation and maintenance of by
      water utilities, 462–463
    water utility planning, 484–485

Error of the third kind, 875

ESFs, 632, 654

ESSENCE biosurveillance system, 645–646

Ethnic profiling, 496, 1120

Ethnicity, psychological responses to
    terrorism and, 671–672

EU–U.S. Transatlantic Cooperative
    Security Work Group, proposal
    for, 1314–1316

Euro-Atlantic cooperation, 1314–1317

EUROJUST, 1362

European Commission
    regulations supporting ISO 28000,
      1241–1243
    support of disaster risk reduction,
      1190

European External Action Service (EEAS),
    1362–1364

European Internal Security Strategy, 1312

European Programme for Critical
    Infrastructure Protection.
    See EPCIP

European Response Center (ERC), 1313

European Union (EU). *See also* specific
    countries
    Authorised Economic Operators
      program, 1225, 1235–1236, 1240
    cooperation on counterterrorism with
      non-EU countries, 1362–1364
    Cooperative Work Arrangement
      between U.S. DHS and FRONTEX,
      1316
    Counter-Terrorism Strategy, 1358
    crisis response and coordination,
      1312–1314
    Directorate-General for Humanitarian
      Aid and Civil Protection (*See* DG
      ECHO)
    Lisbon Treaty, 1298, 1311, 1313–1314,
      1359
    partnership with U.S. in fighting
      terrorism, 1364–1365

EUROPOL, 1362

Evacuation plans
    collaboration with industry partners,
        631–633
    corporate, 781–783
    development of a timeline for, 626–628
    development of for City of New Orleans,
        612–613 (*See also* CAEP)
    development of for regional resilience,
        546–551
    triage model for transportation, 621–624
    use of logic model to create, 615–618

Evacuation team, 773–774

Evacuteer.org, 630–631

Event stream processing, 953

Event tree models, 354–355
    use of for risk analysis of infrastructure
        interdependence, 448

Event-driven architectures (EDA), 944

Event-Enabled Architecture, 960–961

Events, perception of risk of and personal
    bias, 342–343

Events (IT)
    importance of, 957–958
    role of in data fusion model, 953

Ex ante disaster decisions, 713

Ex post disaster decisions, 713

Exclusionary rule, application of to
    information privacy, 1139–1140

Executive Order 12333, intelligence
    gathering under, 1152

Executive Order 12947, 129

Exercises. *See also* Training
    assessment of information sharing,
        260
    corporate emergency management,
        798–799
    design layout for, 909
    design objectives, 907
    design principles, 908–911

design steps, 910
importance of for emergency personnel,
    905
importance of for preparedness, 665
New Orleans City Assisted Evacuation
    Plan, 628–629
operational and communication plans,
    655
use of for preparedness against cyber
    attacks, 1360
use of for preparedness improvement,
    645
use of for whole-of-society
    preparedness, 1305–1306
use of GIS in, 1001–1004

Explosions, emergency procedures for,
    792

Explosive Substances Act of 1883 (U.K.),
    1198

Explosives, use of on aircraft, 491

Explosives-sniffing dogs, use of in surface
    transportation security, 28

Export Administration Act of 1979,
    counterterrorism amendment to,
    124–125

External Action Service (EEAS), 1313

Extreme weather conditions, 339, 394.
    See also Natural disasters
    calculating risk for, 384–386
    threats to water systems due to,
        464–465

Exxon Valdez oil spill, 203–204

F

Facebook. *See also* Social media
    use of for risk communication, 431–432

Failure
    definition of, 209
    use of probabilistic risk analysis for
        predicting, 340

Failure impact analysis, use of diagnostic mapping for, 265

Failure modes and effects analysis and critical items lists. *See* FMEA/CIL

Failure to improve, 208, 245–246
  use of holistic interoperability to prevent, 246

Failures in response, 195–197

False alarms, complacency and, 217–218

Family issues, consideration of in regional resilience planning, 572–574

FARC, 34

Fariz, Hatem Naji, prosecution of, 111

Fault trees, 346–347

FBI
  Field and Regional Intelligence Groups, 276
  field office self-assessments, 280–281
  mission of post-9/11 attacks, 895
  responsibility for investigating terrorism, 885
  role of in information sharing, 156

Federal Air Marshal Service (FAMS), 492
  changes to post-9/11, 502–503
  citizen self-help and, 511–512

Federal Aviation Act, Section 1115, 127

Federal Aviation Administration (FAA)
  Airport Improvement Program, 517
  mandatory passenger screening, 492

Federal Bureau of Investigation. *See* FBI

Federal Disaster Assistance Act, 597

Federal Emergency Management Agency. *See* FEMA

Federal Flight Deck Officers (FFDO) program, 494

Federal Resource Allocation Criteria policy, 280

Federal threat information, use of fusion centers to process, 290–291

Federalism, 92

FEMA, 73–74, 602. *See also* DHS
  administrative arrangement of with DG ECHO, 1316
  attorneys (*See* Crisis attorneys)
  Comprehensive Preparedness Guide (CPG-101), 179
  core capabilities Framework documents, 88–89
  creation of, 598
  Emergency Management Institute, 919 (*See also* EMI)
  hazards, 339
  IS-139 course, 906
  national preparedness assessment efforts, 94
  regional model of, 375–376
  SALT performance standard of, 716
  Strategic Foresight Initiative, 603
  whole-of-community approach of, 371–372, 825–826 (*See also* Whole-of-community approach)

Fenwick, Rep. Millicent, 124

Financial criminal crises, 40–41

Financial interdependence, 444

Financial needs, regional resilience planning considerations, 579–580

Financial networks of terrorists, disrupting, 100–101

Financial services, 843

Fire stations, use of GIS technology to analyze locations for, 996–998

Firefighters
  militarization of in France, 1212
  use of GIS technology by, 988

Fires, emergency procedures for, 792

Firescope, development of incident command system by, 654

First Amendment rights, profiling and, 1123

First Commando of the Capital, 39–40

First responders
    basic responses for, 657–658
    challenges of for WMD events, 662
    coordination of activities, 658–659
    incident command procedures,
        653–654
    inclusion of public works personnel as,
        484
    interoperable communications for,
        639–640, 662–665
    necessity of personal protective
        equipment for, 644
    preparedness of, 76, 638–639
    psychological effects of terrorist events
        on, 669–670
    responsibilities of in United Kingdom,
        1204–1205
    role of French military as, 1211–1212
    use of crowdsourcing by, 1036
    use of GIS technology by, 987–990
FirstNet, 664
FISA
    amendments to, 1147–1148
    protections under, 1147
FISA Amendments Act of 2008,
        1148–1149
Five-dimension meta-leadership model,
        682
    characteristics of meta-leaders,
        685–688
    design, concept, and practice,
        684–685
    diagnosing objective reality of
        situations, 688–692
    leading across the system, 696–699
    leading the base, 692–694
    leading up, 694–696
Floods. *See also* Natural disasters
    effect of on water systems, 464
Flow security, 1307–1309

FMEA/CIL
    advantages and disadvantages of,
        349–350
    use of for risk analysis, 348–349
Food Supply and Distribution services, 843
Foreign homeland security policy, adopting
        best practices from, 1196
Foreign intelligence, Patriot Act provisions
        regarding sharing of, 133
Foreign Intelligence Surveillance Act of 1978.
        See FISA
Foreign policy, terrorism as a tool of, 889
Foreign Relations Authorization Act, material
        support definitions in, 130
Foreign Sovereign Immunity Act (FSIA),
        amendment of to allow civil suits,
        136
Foreign terrorist organizations. *See* FTOs
Fort Dix plot, role of information sharing in
        investigation of, 159, 167
Fort Hood attack
    lack of information sharing prior to,
        161
    praise of by jihadi terrorists, 16
Fourth Generation Warfare, 6
Fractional data, 1065
Fragmentation
    public safety, 373–374
    use of District Model in Indiana to
        address, 374–376
France, role of military in homeland security
        of, 1211–1212
Fraud, financial crimes and, 41
French terrorists, surface transportation
        attacks by, 23
FSR certification (TAPA), 1237
FTOs
    collateral attack of the designation,
        105–106
    designation and renewal of, 131

designation process, 103–104

judicial review of designations,
106–105

legislation regarding, 129–131

material support statutes targeting,
101–103

modification of designation of by
Patriot Act, 134

prosecution and convictions of financiers
of, 110–114

Fukushima Daiichi nuclear facility

accident sequence, 1256–1259

actions that would have prevented
disaster, 1271–1273

contributory factors to 2011 disaster,
1279–1286

failure of emergency vents at, 815–816

hazard assessment at, 1264–1269

investigation of accident at, 1260–1262

lack of resiliency planning at, 1254

soundness assessment, 1269–1270

tsunami hazard assessment at,
1262–1264

Full-Scale Exercise of HSEEP, 906

Functional Exercise of HSEEP, 906

Functional interdependence, 444

Funding, 803

challenges of for fusion centers,
304–305

Fusion Center Guidelines, 287

Fusion centers, 156, 158–159, 175, 276

adoption of NSI by, 301–302

assessment of, 293

balancing federal and local priorities,
303–304

Baseline Capabilities document, 289

best practices, 311

capabilities of, 309–310

comparison of with JTTFs and HIDTAs,
314–316

customers of, 297–298

definition of COCs for, 289–290

horizontal information sharing between,
298–301

hub-and-spoke systems of in Maryland,
641–642

Indiana, 377

information sharing by, 176, 280–281

involvement of private sector in,
305–307

organizational structure of, 298

planning, 312–313

recommendations for future directions,
316–317

role of analysts in intelligence-led
policing, 295–296

role of in counterterrorism, 283–286

role of in national preparedness,
290–293

scope of, 302–303

staffing of, 307–308

sustainable funding for, 304–305

training of staff for, 308–309

use of crowdsourcing by, 310–311

use of GIS technology for intelligence
analysis, 1006–1007

Fusion Liaison Officer (FLO) program,
306–307

Fusion process

capability areas, 292–293

definition of, 287

evolution of, 287–290

intelligence-led policing and, 294

FutureTECH program, 1094

G

Gadahn, Adam, 16

GAIN model, 718–719

active engagement, 723

group dynamics, 719–722

GAIN model *(Cont.)*
    individual requirements, 723–724
    negotiation, 724–726
Game theory models, 354
Games exercise of HSEEP, 906
Gandhi, Indira, assassination of, 1322
Gandhi, Rajiv, assassination of,
        1326–1327
Gendarmerie Nationale (France), 1211–1212
Gender, consideration of in disaster risk
        reduction, 1191–1192
General Crime Guidelines, intelligence
        gathering under, 1152–1153
General public, information sharing with,
        160
Geographic analysis, use of GIS for, 1005
Geographic information systems. *See* GIS
        technology
Geographic interdependence, 444
Geospatial predictive analysis, 308
GIS technology, 983–984
    Brisbane floods case study, 1012–1014
    California wildfires case study, 1015–1016
    crime analysis using, 993–996
    Deepwater Horizon case study,
        1011–1012
    emergency call handling, 986–987
    evolution of, 984–986
    HAZUS, 1003–1004
    Japan earthquake/tsunami case study,
        1012
    mobile, 1009–1010
    situational awareness using, 990–993
    Tuscaloosa tornadoes case study,
        1016–1017
    use of by first responders, 987–990
    use of for emergency/disaster
        management, 998
    use of for fire/rescue station location,
        996–998
    use of for hazard and risk analysis,
        998–1001
    use of for intelligence analysis,
        1004–1007
    use of in response exercises,
        1001–1004
Global Assessment Reports, 1175
Global Counter-Terrorism Strategy (U.N.),
        1358–1359
Global Counterterrorism Forum (GCTF),
        1364
Global gender blindness, 1191–1192
Global positioning systems (GPS), 986
Global war on terrorism (GWOT). *See also*
        Terrorism
    civil liberties *vs.* security in the U.S.,
        1119–1120
    diversionary effects of, 35
Globalization
    evolution of criminal organizations and,
        34–35
    flow security, 1307–1309
    growth of criminal bourgeoisie, 41
    role of in 9/11 attacks, 493
    transnational terrorism and, 890–891
Goals, measuring success of, 647–648
Gold Command (U.K.), responsibilities of in
        emergency response, 1206–1208
Golden chain, 9
Golden Temple
    occupation of by militants 1988, 1323
    Operation Blue Star, 1322
Google Hack, collaborative response to,
        326–327
Google Person Finder, 1037
Government
    effect of politics on emergency
        management, 599–601
    historical role of in disaster management,
        594

location of authority for DRM,
    1187–1188
need for improved cooperation of with
    private sector, 817–818
procurement process, 1092, 1104–1111
reform of in response to crisis, 1298
response of to 9/11 attacks, 493–496
role of ISE in changing culture of, 277
science and technology strategy of,
    1021
secrecy of regarding threats and
    vulnerabilities, 820
understanding buying process of,
    1102–1103
Government data mining
    efficacy of, 1154–1156
    impact of, 1156–1160
    recommendations for regulating,
        1153–1154
Government intelligence, deficiency of
    sharing, 222–224
Government lawyers
    GAIN model for, 718–726 (*See also*
        GAIN model)
    leader requirements of, 715–716
    perception of as obstacles, 714–715
    PREP model for, 716–718
    SOAP model for, 726–732
Government Liaison Officer (U.K.),
    responsibilities of during emergency
    response, 1206
Government-compelled disclosure of
    personal matters, 1142–1143
Governmental organizations, infrastructure
    interdependence and, 449–451
Gradual progression of exercises, 908–909
Graduate-level homeland security
    education, 925–926
    integration of critical thinking skills in,
        927–928

lines of inquiry for, 926–927
roles and objectives for, 927
Great Eastern earthquake (Japan), warning
    systems used following, 431
Green energy, 453–454
Green's Exercise Alternatives for Training
    Emergency Management Command
    Center Staffs, 908–909
Green, Walter, 908–909
Gross domestic product (GDP), assessing
    contribution of infrastructure to,
    437–438
Group dynamics
    attorney's role within the team, 722
    awareness of by crisis attorneys, 719
    time and timing for successful
        integration, 720–721
    unhealthy, 721–722
Guantanamo Bay, Cuba
    review of detainee cases, 140–141
    rights of detainees in, 139

H
H-Hour timelilne, 626–628
Haiti
    collaborative response to 2010 earthquake
        in, 325–326
    crowd mapping of, 1036, 1038
    use of the crowd to translate and geo-
        locate messages, 1038–1039
Hamas
    civil suit against, 137
    designation of as FTO, 104
    finances of, 99–100
    use of short-range/low payload rockets
        in Israel, 1210
Hamdan v. Rumsfeld, 139–140
Hamdan, Salim, 140
Hammoud, Mohammed, prosecution of,
    112

Hardened Unit Load Devices (HULDs), 511

Harris, Eric, 202, 224

Hasan, Nidal, 16, 161

Hazard analysis
  early warning systems and, 1178–1180
  use of GIS technology for, 998–1001

Hazard Vulnerability Assessment (HVA),
      612–613. *See also* Risk assessment

Hazard/Threat Identification and Risk
      Assessment. *See* HIRA

Hazardous treatment chemicals, release of
      into water system, 474–475

Hazards, 595–596

Hazmat teams, collaboration of with bomb
      squads, 643–644

HAZUS (Hazards U.S.), 1003–1004

Headley, David, 161

Health risk communications, creating
      appropriate channels for, 400–403

Healthcare
  integrated dashboard for use during mass
      casualty events, 646
  regional resilience planning for, 567–570

Healthcare industry, collaboration with in
      evacuation planning, 631–632

HFA, 1173. *See also* DRM
  Progress Review, 1174–1178

HIDTAs
  comparison of fusion centers and,
      314–316
  partnership of with fusion centers, 281

Hierarchical governance, 894

Hierarchical leadership, 703

High Intensity Drug Trafficking Areas.
      See HIDTAs

Higher education
  graduate-level homeland security
      curricula, 925–928
  undergraduate homeland security
      curricula offerings, 920–925

HIPAA, permitted disclosure, 232–233

HIRA, 382
  quantification of risk using, 376–379

Hizballah
  designation of as FTO, 104
  evolution of, 34
  finances of, 99–100
  use of short-range/low payload
      rockets in Israel, 1210

Holder v. Humanitarian Law Project,
      106–109

Holistic interoperability, 198
  continuum of, 199–201
  infrastructure interdependencies and,
      527–528
  ISP frameworks, 257
  quality control and enhancement,
      245–246
  Swedish perspective of, 1309–1310

Holy Land Foundation for Relief and
      Development, civil suit against,
      113–114, 137

Homefront Command (Israel), role of in
      homeland security efforts,
      1210–1211

Homegrown violent extremism (HVE),
      814
  increasing threat of, 286

Homeland security
  advancing role of fusion centers in,
      316–317
  building a theory of using multiple
      frame analysis, 881–883
  comparison of with EU societal security,
      1315
  complexity of, 863–865
  conflict in federal control over other
      governmental levels, 92
  contract spending post-9/11,
      1084–1086

criminal justice view, 883–887

definition of, 879–880

evolution of, 637–638

existing curricula offerings in higher education, 919–920

framework for, 71–72

future of technology for, 960–969

holistic review of, 865–866

international experience in, 1195–1197

international relations view of, 887–892

Maryland (*See* Maryland)

national strategy for, 79–80

network governance of, 894

operational risk in, 802–806

organizational design/public administration perspective of, 893–898

policy documents, 75–77

PPD-8 emphases for, 83

pursuing technology contracts for, 1089–1091

refinement in definition of, 72

role of Canadian military in, 1212

role of French military in, 1211–1212

role of information sharing in, 170–171

role of Israeli material in, 1210–1211

role of Italian military in, 1211

selection of risk analysis techniques, 357–362

strategic position documents, 72–75

systems thinking for, 862–863

technical goal of organizations, 953

technology market evaluation, 1092–1095

use of scenario analysis to analyze risks for, 353–354

Homeland Security Act of 2002, 74, 152

information sharing provisions in, 152

Homeland Security Advisory System. *See* HSAS

Homeland security education

future challenges and opportunities, 932–934

graduate-level curricula for, 925–928

research needs, 928–932

undergraduate curricula for, 920–925

Homeland Security Exercise Evaluation Program. *See* HSEEP

Homeland Security Information Network (HSIN), 157, 300–301

Homeland Security Management System, 80

Homeland Security Presidential Directive 5, 75

Homeland Security Presidential Directive 8 (HSPD-8), 75–76. *See also* specific policies

implementation of, 77

replacement of by PPD-8, 82

Homeland Security Presidential Directives (HSPDs), information sharing provisions in, 153–154

Homeland Security Studies and Analysis Institute, 928

Homeland Security Systems Engineering and Development Institute, 928

Homeland Security/Defense Education Consortium. *See* HSDEC

Homeland Security/Defense Education Consortium Association. *See* HSDECA

Horizon 2020, 1316

Horizontal goals, use of vertical command/action structures for, 832

Horizontal information sharing, 298–301

Hospitality industry, role of in preparedness, 631

Hospitals
    patient surge due to mass casualty
        events, 646
    regional resilience planning for,
        567–570
Housing services, 843–844
HSAS, 291, 425
    failures of, 426–427
    information sharing obstacles of, 430
    psychological impact of threat levels,
        429
HSDEC, 918
HSDECA, accreditation efforts for homeland
    security education, 919
HSEEP, 906
HSPD-8, inclusion of public works personnel
    as first responders, 484
Human factor analysis
    lack of following 9/11 attacks, 496
    use of in aviation security, 497
Human factors
    consideration of in regional resilience
        planning, 572–574
    technology projects, 1087
    technology use for passenger screening
        and, 506–507
Human resources, crisis management teams
    and, 755–756
Human rights, respect for in counterterrorism
    strategies, 1358
Human-caused threats, 86
Humanitarian Law Project v. Gonzales, 102
Hurricane Betsy, 611
Hurricane Gustav
    lessons learned, 630–634
    successful use of the CAEP during,
        629–630
Hurricane Katrina, 607–609
    communication failures, 240–241
    community recovery from, 837–838

    controversy surrounding evacuation
        during, 712
    effect of on water systems, 465
    evacuation failures due to complacency,
        220
    failure of response due to lack of proper
        prioritization, 244
    lack of situational awareness following,
        177–179
    lessons learned, 630–634
    use of Baltimore City USAR team
        following, 648
Hussein, Saddam, 11
Hydrographic and Oceanographic Service
    (Chile). *See* SHOA
Hyogo Framework for Action. *See* HFA

I
IAF
    accreditation bodies of, 1245
    membership, 1246
    role of, 1245–1246
    Special Recognition Status, 1246
IALEIA
    Analyst Toolbox, 289
    Law Enforcement Analytic Standards, 288
Ibrahim, Dawood, 1325
ICS
    9/11 attacks, 659–662
    corporate emergency management,
        775–779
    incident communications plan, 655–656
    organizational structure of, 654–655
IEDs, use of in surface transportation attacks,
    23
IEEPA, 131
ILAC, 1245
Imagination deficiencies, 207, 226–227
    prevention of, 227–228
Immigration and Nationality Act

criteria for FTO designations, 103–104

FTO provisions, 131

material support definitions in, 130

Imminent threat, 428

IMO, 128

International Ship and Port Facility Security Code, 1239–1240

Implementation Plan for Presidential Policy Directive 8: National Preparedness, 84

Improvised explosive devices. *See* IEDs

In Re Terrorist Attacks on September 11, 2001, 137

Incheon Regional Roadmap and Action Plan, 1190

Incident command (IC)

coordination of activities, 658–659

corporate emergency planning and, 775–779

perception of government lawyers, 714

standardized procedures for, 653–654

Incident command system. *See* ICS

Incident Command System (ICS), 487

Inconsistency, 208

failures due to, 239–240

India

evolution of border security in, 1327–1328

terrorist attacks in, 1322–1327

terrorist campaigns targeting surface transportation in, 23–24

Indian Evidence Act, 1322

Indian Institute of Science, terrorist attacks at, 1326

Indiana Department of Homeland Security (IDHS)

creation of, 373

District Model of, 374–376

Indicators, risk modeling, 449

Individuals, disaster preparedness responsibilities of, 1304–1305

Individuals and Family services, 844

Ineffective communication, 409–410

Influence diagram

use of in analysis of interdependence, 447

use of to predict risk, 413–414

Influential individuals, 55

Influenza pandemics, repercussions of, 60

Information Analysis and Infrastructure Protection (IAIP), 451

Information assurance (IA), use of risk analysis for, 340–341

Information dissemination analysis, use of diagnostic mapping for, 265

Information flows

acknowledgment of, 245

collaboration and, 328–329

mapping, 257

mapping of, 260–261

needed improvements in, 254

restriction of due to relationship conflicts, 242

use of visualization for modeling and planning, 262–268

Information objectives, 1101

Information privacy, 1136–1137

constitutional protections, 1137–1143

electronic surveillance, 1146–1147

intelligence gathering, 1147–1153

Privacy Act of 1974, 1143–1145

recommendations for regulating government data mining, 1153–1154

sectoral protections of, 1145–1146

Information sharing, 865, 1051–1052

accountability for, 192

assessment of progress on initiatives, 160–161

balance of with safeguarding, 162

Information sharing *(Cont.)*
  classification system and security
      clearances, 163–165
  communication and, 229
  conceptual interoperability model of,
      1053–1054
  critical infrastructure, 174–176
  cultural initiatives, 158
  data analysis for, 173
  data analytic challenges, 162–163
  disclosure issues, 232–233
  dissemination failures, 234–236
  effective, 254–255
  European Union mechanism for,
      1361
  failures of due to assumptions,
      211–213
  failures of due to lack of intelligence
      sharing, 221–224
  funding challenges, 165
  fusion centers and mission partners,
      280
  fusion process, 287
  holistic interoperability continuum,
      199–201
  horizontal, 298–301
  importance of in local preparedness
      efforts, 641–642
  lack of preceding 9/11 attacks,
      143–144
  major initiatives from 2001 to 2011,
      151–160
  measuring progress, 166
  mechanism and entities, 174–176
  mechanisms for, 157
  military approach to, 180–181
  national doctrine for, 1067
  national intelligence reform, 172–174
  operational questions for, 1069–1070
  privacy and civil liberties concerns, 163

  processes for, 256
  protocols, 179
  provisions in Patriot Act regarding,
      133
  regional resilience and, 530–531,
      544–546
  role of fusion centers in, 284–286
  role of in homeland security,
      170–171
  role of leadership and management in,
      185
  role of NTAS in, 430
  role of PM-ISE in, 276–277
  state, local, and tribal entities, 158–159
  terrorism-related, 150–151
  tools for, 1076–1080
  with the private sector, 165
  with the private sector and the general
      public, 159–160
Information Sharing and Access Interagency
      Policy Committee. *See* ISA IPC
Information Sharing and Analysis Centers
      (ISACs), 159, 450
Information Sharing Council (ISC),
      establishment of, 272
Information Sharing Environment. *See* ISE
Information sharing planning. *See* ISP
Information sharing protocols, 179
  formulating for mass transit security,
      873
Information technology (IT)
  advances in, 953–954
  advances in for border security,
      951–952
  advances in for homeland security,
      944
  adversary classes, 341
  collaboration and, 325
  emerging secure technologies, 975–977
  Google hack and response, 326–327

historical use of in emergency
management, 1050–1051

regional resilience planning for,
557–558

role of in critical infrastructure, 452

system architecture, 958–960

vision for the future, 977–978

vision for the future—scenario,
979–982

Infragard program, 159

Infrastructure

assessing the contribution of to GDP,
437–438

assessing vulnerability of to intentional
attack, 441–442

building resilience of, 816–820

definition of, 438

identification of dependencies and
interdependencies of, 538–541

interdependencies, 527 (*See also*
Interdependent infrastructure)

policies regarding condition and
performance of, 439–441

public perception of threats to,
451–452

reconstitution of following an
evacuation, 632–633

reducing vulnerability by modifying
interdependency of, 453–455

technology projects for the protection of,
1087–1089

terrorism and policy, 442–443

TISP regional resilience Action Plan,
524

Insider attacks, effects of on water utilities,
469–470

Insider threats to aviation security,
508–509

Insight deficiencies, 208, 233–234

prevention of, 234

Inspection deficiencies, 208, 236
prevention of, 236–237

Institute of Brilliant Failures, 704

Institutional interdependence, governmental
organizations, 449–451

Insurance industry, community risk
mitigation and, 821

Integrated audits, 1246–1247

Integrated health and medical dashboard,
646

Integrated Public Alert and Warning
System. *See* IPAWS program

Intellectual capital, importance of in
collaborative environments,
329–330

Intelligence

homeland security spending for,
1085

IRTPA definition of, 172

use of GIS for analysis of, 1004–1007

Intelligence collection

Israeli approach to, 1200–1201

role of in protecting public surface
transportation, 30

United Kingdom approach to, 1199

Intelligence community (IC), use of
crowdsourcing by, 310–311

Intelligence Community Directive (ICD)
501, 155

Intelligence Community Information
Sharing Strategy, 155

Intelligence Liaison Officer, 158

Intelligence organizations, culture of, 896

Intelligence Reform Act of 2004, 128
material support definitions in, 130

Intelligence Reform and Terrorism
Prevention Act of 2004. *See* IRTPA

Intelligence sharing deficiencies, 207,
221–224

prevention of, 224–225

Intelligence-led policing
  customer service and, 298
  definitions of, 294–295
  role of data analysis in, 288
  role of fusion centers in, 316–317
Intelligent adversary models, 354–356
Intellipedia, 155, 157
Interagency collaboration, 323–324
  DHS and, 328
Interagency information sharing, 180
Interagency Threat Assessment and
      Coordination Group. *See* ITACG
Interconnectedness, 444
Interdependencies, 820
  analysis of, 447–449
  Euro-Atlantic, 1314–1317
  factors contributing to, 445–447
  globalization of flow and, 1308
  infrastructure security and, 437–438
  institutional, 449–452
  reducing vulnerability by modification of,
      453–455
  technology, 452–453
Interdependent infrastructure, 443–444
  categories of, 444–445
  definition of, 438–439
  holistic approach to resilience of,
      527–528
  mechanisms of, 445
Interdiction and disruption, 87
Interim National Preparedness Goal,
      76–77
Intermestics, 1308–1309
Internal Revenue Service, disclosure of
      information by, 1145
International Accreditation Forum. *See* IAF
International Association of Law Enforcement
      Intelligence Analysts. *See* IALEIA
International Emergency Economics Powers
      Act. *See* IEEPA

International Fire Code (IFC), emergency
      planning for, 769
International Laboratory Accreditation
      Cooperation. *See* ILAC
International Maritime Organization.
      See IMO
International privacy laws, 1137
International relations view of homeland
      security and terrorism, 887–892
International Security and Development
      Cooperation Act of 1985, Sec. 551,
      127–128
International Standards Organisation.
      See ISO
International terrorism. *See also* Terrorism
  changes in goals of, 491
  use of international treaties to counter,
      122–123
International trade accreditation, 1240
Interoperability, 444
  communications technology,
      662–665
  emergency information system,
      1053–1054
  statewide, 639–640
Interoperable communication, 76,
      662–665
INTERPOL, global databases of,
      961–963
Interrelationships, identification of, 866
Intrusion detection, use of to mitigate risk,
      482
Iowa, effect of 1993 floods on water
      systems in, 464
IPAWS program, 1076–1078
Iran
  civil suits against, 136–137
  designation of as terrorist regime,
      124–125
Iran-Contras scandal, 125

Iraq
   designation of as terrorist regime,
      124–126
   destruction of water pipeline in, 474
   United States war in, 11–12
   use of SCUD missiles against Israel, 1210
Irish Republican Army (IRA), surface
      transportation attacks by, 23
Irish Republican Movement, understanding
      factionalization and loyalties in,
      54–56
IRTPA, 152–153, 172
   constitutional challenges to, 106–109
   DNI, 154
   information sharing provisions in,
      152
   Program Manager for the Information
      Sharing Environment (*See* PM-ISE)
ISA IPC, membership of, 274–275
ISE, 174
   attributes of, 272
   background of, 271–272
   mission partners, 275–276
   Privacy Policies of, 277
   purpose and scope, 273–275
   role of in changing government culture,
      277
   SAR initiative of (*See* NSI)
ISE-PM, 172
ISO 20858:2007 ships and marine technology
      standard, 1224
ISO 28000 standards, 1222–1224
   alignment of European AEO program
      with, 1236
   auditing organizational systems for
      compliance, 1243–1244
   certification to, 1244–1245
   certified organizations, 1225–1231
   comparison of with ISO 14001 and ISO
      9001, 1218–1221

coordination of with other accrediting
      organizations, 1240–1243
   international use of, 1234
ISO 28000:2007 supply chain management
      standard, 1217–1218
ISP, 224–225
   adaptability of, 230–231
   developing protocols for, 183–185
   Mind-Alliance Systems' methodology
      for, 259–261
   national policy, 186–188
   necessity of beyond technology,
      182–183
   omissions during, 213–215
   process requirements, 254–255
   role of fusion centers in, 312–313
   roles and perspectives of participants,
      258–259
   software requirements, 261–268
   systematic framework for, 255–257
ISPS Code (IMO), 1239–1240
Israel
   counterterrorism emergency legislation,
      1200
   counterterrorism structures and
      institutions, 1200–1201
   military aggression conception of
      terrorism, 1197, 1201
   model for aviation passenger screening,
      505–506
   role of military in homeland security,
      1209–1211
   terrorism experience of, 1195
Israel Defense Force (IDF), 1201
   regional commands of, 1210
   role of in homeland security,
      1209–1211
Israel Security Agency (ISA), 1200–1201
Istanbul, planned attack on drinking water
      system, 472

ITACG, 156, 159
Italy
    attacks on surface transportation, 23–24
    contamination of bottled water in, 478
    role of military in homeland security,
        1211

J

Jammu & Kashmir police (India),
        counterterrorism efforts of,
        1328–1329
Japan
    accident sequence at Fukushima Daiichi
        plant, 1256–1259
    Aum Shinrikyo cult in, 64, 1204
    case study of GIS technology use
        following earthquake/tsunami,
        1012
    Community Policing model of,
        1202–1204
    Fukushima disaster, 1255 (*See also*
        Fukushima Daiichi nuclear facility)
    natural disaster experience of, 1195
    Tokyo subway attacks, 24
    use of CrisisCommons to compile data
        during 2011 crises, 1038
    use of Google People Finder following
        tsunami in, 1037, 1039
    warning systems used in following
        Great Eastern earthquake, 431
Jarrah, Ziad, 283
JDL data fusion model, 952–953
Jealousy, 208
    deficiency of, 240–241
    prevention of, 241
Jemaah Islamiya, designation of as FTO,
        103
Jihad, financiers of during Afghan-Soviet
        war, 9
Jihadi terrorists, 24. *See also* Al Qaeda

attacks on Saudi Arabian oil facilities by,
        12–14
    recidivism of, 51
Joint Directors of laboratories. *See* JDL data
        fusion model
Joint Terrorism Task Forces. *See* JTTFs
Joint-planning, role of information sharing,
        171
JTTFs, 156
    comparison of fusion centers and,
        314–316
Judgment, 730–731
Just-in-time training, 909
Justice and Home Affairs, 1364

K

Kashmiri insurgency, 1324
Katz v. United States, 1139
Key performance indicators. *See* KPIs
Key stakeholders, 827
    coordination of counterterrorism efforts
        of, 871
    definition of, 526
    engagement of regional resilience
        Action Plan, 534
    leveraging participation of, 867–868
Klebold, Dylan, 202, 224
Klinghoffer, Leon, 126
    civil suit brought by family of, 135
Knowledge sharing, 324
Known Shipper Program, 510
Known travelers, 519
Koban officers (Japan), 1203
KPIs, use of to measure public safety
        performance, 388–389
Kurdistan Workers' Party. *See* PKK

L

Land use planning, risk reduction and,
        1184–1185

Large-scale events, incident management of, 659–662

Lashkar-e Taiba
    2008 attacks on Mumbai, 161, 1329–1330
    designation of as FTO, 103

Law enforcement. *See also* First responders
    benefits of fusion centers for, 295–296
    Canadian model of, 1202
    customer service and, 298
    intelligence-led policing, 294
    Japanese Community Policing model, 1202–1204
    nature of in India, 1323–1324
    predictive, 962–963
    role of French military in, 1211–1212
    role of Italian gendarmerie corps in, 1211
    use of GIS technology for geospatial intelligence, 988–990

Law Enforcement Analytic Standards, 288

Law Enforcement Online (LEO), 157, 300–301

Lawyers
    mission preparation and readiness (PREP), 716–718
    producing substantive advice in crisis (SOAP), 726–732
    relationship of with leaders, 712–713
    social-behavioral elements for effective advice in crisis (GAIN), 718–726

Lead generation and qualification, 1100

Lead Government Departments (U.K.), responsibilities of during emergency response, 1205–1206

Lead management programs, 1101–1102

Leaders
    corporate crisis management teams, 755
    disaster negotiations, 724–726
    getting the best from lawyers, 733–734
    relationship of with lawyers, 712–713
    requirements of from lawyers, 715–716
    role of in group development, 719
    successful collaboration and, 330

Leadership
    deficiency of insight of, 233–234
    forming a whole-of-community team, 832–833
    meta-leaders (*See* Meta-leaders)
    role of in information sharing, 192
    role of information sharing in, 185

League of Arab States, review of disaster risk reduction efforts by, 1190–1191

Legal attachés (LEGATs), 127

Legal compliance, 805

Legislation (U.S.)
    aviation and maritime security, 127–128
    exportation, 123
    provisions allowing civil suits by terror victims, 135–137

Levees, regional resilience planning for, 565–567

Liberation Tigers of Tamil Eelam (LTTE). *See* Tamil Tigers

Library of National Intelligence, 157

Libya
    civil suits against, 136
    export of dual-use equipment by, 123–125

Life Safety Code, 769

Lifelines
    engineering models to analyze infrastructure interdependence, 448
    performance of, 440

Lighting, use of to mitigate risk, 481

Linde, John, 136

Liquid bomber plot, 498, 506–507, 521

Lisbon Treaty (EU), 1298, 1359
    Solidarity Clause of, 1311, 1313–1314
Loading dock security, 750
Lobby access security, 749
Local capacity, disaster risk management and,
    1188
Local government services, 844
    technology priorities of, 1089
Local preparedness, 637–638, 648, 665–666
    assurance of backup power and
        communications, 645
    critical infrastructure mapping,
        642–643
    importance of information sharing,
        641–642
    importance of public–private
        partnerships in, 649–650
    measuring goal success, 647–648
    planning, 644–645
    planning for mass casualty events, 646
    responsibility of airport security in
        case of proximity attacks, 515
    transportation system security, 642
    use of CCTV networks, 640–641
    use of drills and exercises to improve,
        645
    use of interoperable communications,
        639–640
Local Resilience Forums (U.K.), 1205
Local, State, Tribal, and Federal Preparedness
    Task Force, report of, 95–96
Logic model for evacuation planning,
    615–618
Logical interdependence, 444
London Metropolitan Police, Counter
    Terrorism Command (SO15), 1199
London Transport bombings, 23
Lone wolves, 814, 1357
Long networks, infrastructure
    interdependence and, 446

Long-arm statute, 126–127
Long-term restoration, consideration of
    challenges to, 551–554
Longer-term threats, 93
    preparedness planning for, 86
Loss data, 1179–1180
Loss-recovery curve, use of to evaluate
    service area resilience, 836–838
Louisiana, effect of Hurricane Katrina on
    water systems in, 465
LTTE. *See* Tamil Tigers

M

Madrid commuter train bombings, 23–24
Magnitude/severity element of CPRI,
    definition of, 377
Mail room security, 750
Major events, preparedness for, 78
Making Cities Resilience campaign, 1175
Man-made accidental disasters, 598. *See also*
    Deepwater Horizon
Man-made accidental hazard, 595
Man-made deliberate disasters, 598. *See also*
    9/11 attacks; Terrorist attacks
Man-made deliberate hazard, 596
Man-portable air-defense systems
    (MANPADS), availability of for
    proximity attacks, 500
Management
    operational risk assessment, 802–803
    role of in corporate emergency
        management, 768
    role of in information sharing, 192
    role of information sharing in, 185–186
Management system standards
    integrating of capabilities requirements
        with, 90–91
    ISO 28000 family, 1217–1225
Maritime domain awareness, importance of
    information sharing in, 174

Maritime security, legislation related to, 128

Markle Task Force for National Security, 151, 160

Maryland
core capacities of, 639–646
measuring goal success, 647–648

Mass acquisition orders, 1149

Mass casualty events, 646

Mass transit security, systems thinking applied to, 868–874

Mass violence, psychological consequences of, 668–669

Master Street Address Guide (MSAG), 986

Material support, legislative definitions of, 129–130

Material support and resources, definition of, 103

Material support statutes, 129
18 U.S.C. sections 2339A and 2339B, 101–111

Matrix organizations, 330

Maximum of maximum approach to emergency planning, 826

Mayfield v. U.S., sneak and peek provisions of Patriot Act, 134–135

Mechanisms of interdependence, 445

Media
monitoring of emergencies by, 658
regional resilience planning and utilization of, 575–577
role of in regional resilience, 531

Medical Institution Evacuation Plan (MIEP), 631–632

Medical response, 76

Medical treatment, corporate planning for, 785

Memorandums of understanding (MoUs), 529

Memorial availability of events, 343

Mental health specialists, role of following terrorism events, 674

Merah, Mohammed, 1122–1125

Message layer products, 954–955

Message routers, 1055–1056

Messaging for marketing, 1097

Messaging system for business resilience, 856

Meta-events, 80

Meta-leaders
ability of to follow, 694–696
characteristics of, 685–688, 701–704
engagement of extended networks by, 696–699
engaging followers, 692–694
unity of purpose, 699–701

Meta-leadership, 679–680
diagnosing objective reality of crisis situations, 688–692
five dimension model of, 682, 684–685
origins and extensions of model, 682–684
outcome and effect of, 699–701
permission to fail, 703–704

Methodology, integrating risk management and counterterrorism resource allocation, 357–362

Mexico
accidental contamination of sewage system in, 476–477
criminal insurrection in, 37–38
drug cartels in, 34

MGive platform, 1039, 1043

MI-5, 1199

Michigan, planned attack on water bottling plant in, 472

Military
collaboration and cooperation of with civilian partners, 181, 1301
response of to WMD events, 662

Military *(Cont.)*

role of in French homeland security, 1211–1212

role of in Israeli homeland security, 1209–1211

role of in Italian homeland security, 1211

use of in counterterrorist efforts, 889–892

Military Commissions Acts, trying of terrorist cases under, 140–141

Mineta Transportation Institute, 30

Ministry for Civil Defense (Israel), 1211

Mission areas, 87

detail complexity of, 863

information sharing as a core capability, 180

Mission assurance resource allocation

counterterrorism, 337–338

natural disasters, 339

Mission preparation and readiness model. *See* PREP model

Mitigation, 80, 85–87, 595. *See also* Capabilities

corporate emergency planning, 770–771

definition of, 527

PPD-8 definition of capabilities for, 83

pre-disaster, 604

regional resilience and, 528–529

resilience and, 815–816

role of in emergency management, 763

use of GIS technology for, 1008

Mitigation of risk, 480–481

physical means of for water utilities, 480–482

use of operational measures for water utilities, 482–483

Mobile GIS technology, 1009–1010

Modes of communication, use of for terror alerts, 431–432

Mohammed, Khalid Sheikh, 141, 878

Money laundering, provisions in Patriot Act regarding, 133–134

Moscow Metro bombing, 23

Move up and cover, GIS technology for, 987

MSB (Sweden), facilitation of whole-of-society approach by, 1299–1300

Mujahedin, role of in Afghan-Soviet war, 7–8

Multi-sensor data fusion, 953

Multi-tenant cloud centers, 964–966

Multiagency interoperability, 199–201. *See also* Holistic interoperability

Multilateral Recognition Arrangements (MLA), 1245–1246

Multinational privacy laws, 1137

Multiple frame analysis, use of to build a theory of homeland security, 881–883

Mumbai

1993 terrorist attacks in, 1325

2006 terrorist attacks on trains in, 1326

2008 Lashkar-e Taiba attacks on, 161, 1329–1330

commuter train bombings, 23

Munich massacre, 491

Muslim separatists, surface transportation attacks by, 23

Muslim world, condemnation of Afghan-Soviet war, 8

Muslim-majority countries. *See also* specific countries

al Qaeda's focus on, 5–6

globalization and transnational terrorism, 891

Mutual aid agreements, 371, 395, 529

use of by water utilities for risk mitigation, 483–484

N

NASA, use of probabilistic risk analysis by, 340

NATGRID (India), 1332

National Academy of Sciences, recommendations regarding government data mining, 1154–1160

National Business Crime Forum (UK), 853

National Center for Border Security and Immigration (NCBSI), 931

National Center for Food Protection and Defense (NCFPD), 930

National Center for the Study of Preparedness and Catastrophic Event Response (PACER), 930

National Civil Protection Plan (Chile), 1348–1349

National Consortium for the Study of Terrorism and Responses to Terrorism (START), 930

National Counter Terrorism Centre (India), 1332–1333

National Counterterrorism Center. See NCTC

National Criminal Intelligence Sharing Plan. See NCISP

National Critical Infrastructure Protection Plan, information sharing emphasis in, 174–176

National Defense Authorization for Fiscal Year 2012, non-criminal detention provisions of, 142

National Disaster Recovery Framework, 88

National Emergency Management Authority (Israel), 1211

National Emergency Service Office (Chile). See ONEMI

National Flood Insurance Program, 604

National Governor's Association. See NGA

National hierarchy, 373

National Incident Management Systems. See NIMS

National Information Exchange Model. See NIEM

National information sharing planning policy, 186–188

National Infrastructure Advisory Council. See NIAC

National Infrastructure Protection Center (NIPC), 450

National Infrastructure Protection Plan, 76, 442

National Integration Center. See NIC

National intelligence reform, information sharing, 172–174

National interoperability, 664–665. See also Interoperability

National Investigation Agency Act (India), 1331

National laboratories, 929

National Network of Fusion Centers. See Fusion centers

National planning, incorporating DRM into, 1182–1184

National Police Agency (Japan), 1203

National preparedness
    assessment of, 78
    leadership and management of expectations, 90–93
    performance assessment, 93–95
    pervasive readiness and, 372
    policy evolution, 89–90
    PPD-8 emphases for, 83
    role of fusion centers in, 290–293
    vision, 79

National preparedness goal
    HSPD-8, 75
    implementation of and updates to, 77
    PPD-8 requirements for, 84

National Preparedness Goal (2005), 77–78

National Preparedness Goal First Edition,
national preparedness goal, 85–89
National Preparedness Guidance, 77
National Preparedness Guidelines (2007), 78
National Preparedness Standards. *See* NFPA standards
National Preparedness System, mission area components, 88
National Public Safety Advisory Council. *See* NPSPAC
National resilience, 394. *See also* Resilience
government's role in building, 811–813
infrastructure investments and, 816–820
National Response Framework, 88, 442, 654
information sharing doctrine, 1067
National Response Plan, 76
National security
definition of, 887
evolution of technologies for, 61
homeland security and, 887–892
intelligence related to, 172
refining definition of, 80–82
National Security Agency, SNIP, 973–974
National Security Guard Act (India), 1322
National security information, classification of, 163–164
National Security Letters, 134, 1150–1152
National Security Staff (NSS), 274
National Security Strategy (2010), 82
information sharing emphasis in, 174
objectives of, 888
National Strategy for Homeland Security (2002), 74–75, 888
National Strategy for Homeland Security (2007), 79–80

National Strategy for Information Sharing, 174
National Strategy for Information Sharing, 289
National Strategy for Maritime Security, information sharing emphasis in, 174–176
National Strategy to Secure Cyberspace, information sharing emphasis in, 174–176
National Terrorism Advisory System. *See* NTAS
National Transportation Security Center of Excellence (NTSCOE), 931–932
Nationwide Public Safety Broadband Network, 664
Nationwide Suspicious Activity Reporting (SAR) initiative. *See* NSI
NATO
comprehensive approach action plan of, 180–181
NNEC initiatives of, 181
Natural disasters, 368, 394, 598. *See also* specific disaster events
infrastructure security and, 441
threats to drinking water and wastewater utilities, 464–465
use of all-hazards approach to, 339
use of crowdsourcing and social media in, 1039–1040
Natural Environment services, 844
Natural hazards, 595
Natural threats, 86
Naturally occurring disease, threat of, 59–60
NCISP, 288
definition of intelligence-led policing, 294
NCTC, 152
data analysis at, 173
role of in information sharing, 155

Ndrangheta, 34

Near-miss events, 343

Needs Medical Resources population, 615
triage model for transportation of, 621–624

Negotiation, importance of in crisis situations, 724–726

Nepal, destruction of water distribution system in, 474

Nerve gas, use of in terrorist attacks and plots, 24–25

Network approach to emergency management, 601–602

Network Enabled Capability (NNEC) initiatives, 181

Network governance structures, 894

Network theory, use of to analyze infrastructure interdependence, 448

New Jersey fusion center, 296

New Orleans
311 call center, 623–624, 629–630
challenges to evacuation, 614–615
development of City Assisted Evacuation Plan, 609–610 (*See also* CAEP)
effect of Hurricane Katrina on water systems in, 465
lessons learned from Hurricanes Katrina and Gustav, 630–634
mindset in pre-Katrina, 610–611
triggers for evacuation of, 613

New York, planned attack on drinking water system, 471–472

NFPA standards, 764–765, 769

NGA, role of in establishment of fusion centers, 286

NIAC, Final Report and Recommendations on Intelligence Information Sharing, 175–176

NIC, 396

NIEM, 276
case study, 278

NIMA, 76

NIMS, 75, 396
emergency preparedness of water utilities, 486–487
Form 205, 655–656
information sharing doctrine, 1067
resource typing (*See* Resource typing)
standardized incident command procedures of, 653–654
support of by UICDS, 1049

NISA (Japan), 1253
insufficient disaster planning by, 1264–1269
lack of design review of Fukushima plant by, 1262

No Fly lists, 495

Non-criminal detention
background of policies, 139
law, 141
policies, 141–143

Non-state actors
capability of terrorists to produce and deliver, 62
intent of to use bioweapons, 64–65
U.S. legislation focusing on, 128–129

Nondisclosure rights, 1143

Nordic Declaration at Haga (2009), 1311

North America, criminality in, 37–38

North Korea, designation of as terrorist regime, 124–125

North, Oliver, 125

Northern Alliance, 11

Northridge Earthquake, effect of on water systems, 464–465

NPSPAC, use of interoperability frequencies of, 663–664

NSI, 156, 159, 276, 278–280
adoption of by fusion centers, 301–302

NTAS, 160, 291, 425, 427–428
  information sharing and, 430
  psychological impact of threat levels,
    429
Nuclear and Industrial Safety Agency (Japan).
    See NISA
Nuclear detection and forensics technology
    projects, 1089
Nuclear power industry
  accident sequence at Fukushima Daiichi
    plant, 1256–1259
  beyond-design-basis events and,
    1264–1265
  critical safety system best practices,
    1254
  defense against a station blackout,
    1273–1275
  investigation at Fukushima Daiichi plant,
    1260–1262
  loss of ultimate heat sink, 1275–1277
  protection against severe flooding,
    1277–1278
  public sentiment following Fukushima
    disaster, 1253
  seismic safety, 1267–1268
  tsunami risk assessment, 1278–1279
  use of probabilistic risk analysis by,
    339–340

O
Oak Ridge National Laboratory, CARRI, 821
Obama Administration
  civil liberties concerns of targeted killing
    policy of, 1127–1129
  detainee policies of, 140–141
  executive orders related to information
    sharing, 153
  homeland security strategy of, 880
  refinement of homeland security strategy,
    80–81

Occupational Safety and Health
    Administration. See OSHA
Odeh, Abdulrahman, prosecution and
    conviction of, 113–114
Office of Domestic Preparedness (ODP)
    toolkit, 358–359
Office of Infrastructure Protection (DHS),
    Engagement Working Group, 818
Office of Management and Budget (U.S.).
    See OMB
Ohio
  insider attack on water system in, 469
  malevolent attack on wasterwater system
    in, 476
Oil, 12–14
Omar, Sheikh, 1327
OMB
  partnership of with ISE and NSS,
    273–275
  pre-9/11 counterterrorism budget cuts,
    144
Omission, 207
  deficiency of, 213–215
  prevention of during information-sharing
    planning, 215
Omnibus Crime Control and Safe Streets Act
    of 1968, 1146
Omnibus Diplomatic Security and
    Antiterrorism Act of 1986, 128
One Situational Picture Real-Time EmergencY
    system. See OSPREY
ONEMI (Chile), 1338
  activities of surrounding 2010 earthquake
    and tsunami, 1341
  ranking of 2010 earthquake intensity by,
    1340
Open Services Gateway (OSG) architecture,
    954
Open Services Gateway Initiative (OSGI),
    956

Operation "TIPS," 1130

Operation Aurora, collaborative response to, 326–327

Operation Blue Star, 1322

Operational context, determination and communication of by meta-leaders, 688–692

Operational continuity, consideration of in regional resilience plan, 554–557

Operational coordination, role of information sharing, 171

Operational decision support, use of GIS technology for, 993

Operational emergency response (U.K.), 1205–1206
  Bronze command, 1208

Operational measures, use of to mitigate risk for water utilities, 482–483

Operational planners, tasks of, 259

Operational plans, 655–656

Operational resilience
  challenges to, 802–804
  framework for integrating capabilities to manage risk, 806–809
  risk management capabilities, 802

Operational responses, water utilities, 485–486

Operational risk, definition of, 809

Operations-based exercises, 906. *See also* Exercises

Optimal readiness, measurement of, 384–386

Options
  assessment of in crisis situations, 728–731
  generation of in crisis situations, 727–728

Organization of the Islamic Conference (OIC), condemnation of Afghan-Soviet war, 8

Organizational compliance, 806

Organizational culture, 895

Organizational deficiencies, 207, 209–211
  prevention of, 211

Organizational design view of homeland security and terrorism, 893–898

Organized crime
  effect of war on terror on, 36
  nexus of with terrorism in India, 1325
  partnerships of with legal world, 42
  transnational nature of, 1308

OSHA, 29 CFR 1910 standards, 768

OSPREY, mapping of critical infrastructure using, 643

Outreach, use of by technology vendors for marketing, 1098

Overseas Security Advisory Council (OSAC), 746, 760–761

P

P/CR/CL protections, 277
  fusion centers, 313–314

Pain points, identifying for technology sales, 1093–1095

Pakistan
  crowd mapping of during floods in, 1036
  planned attacks on drinking water supply in, 472–473

Palestine Liberation Organization (PLO), civil suits against, 135–136

Palestinian extremists, surface transportation attacks by, 24

Palestinian Islamic Jihad (PIJ), prosecution of alleged financiers of, 110–111

Pan Am 103, 491

Pandemics, repercussions of, 60

Pantos Logistics (Korea), certification to ISO 28000 standards, 1231

Paradigms, 880

Paraphrasing of information, 207
  deficiency of, 229–230
  prevention of, 230
Paris, planned attack on drinking water
    system, 472
Partiya Karkeran Kurdistan. *See* PKK
Passenger Name Record (PNR), 1364
Passenger risk analysis, 496
Passenger screening
  future of, 519–520
  implementation of by FAA, 492
  technological solutions *vs.* risk
    management, 504–508
Passenger self-help, 511–512
Pathogens
  aerosolization of, 64
  weaponization of, 62–64
Patriot Act, 152
  amendment of Cable Act by, 1146
  amendments to FISA of, 1147–1148
  information sharing provisions in, 152
  provisions of, 133–135
  Section 215 Orders, 1149–1150
  weakening of privacy protections by,
    1146–1147
Pattern-based data mining, 1135
PCQ, 943, 946–949
PDCA process, 1221–1222
PDD 63, 438, 441
  infrastructure interdependencies, 443–444
  institutional interdependencies, 450
Pearl Harbor, 61
  assumptions made, 212
  deficiencies, 205–209 (*See also* specific
    deficiencies)
  deficiency of insight of leaders, 233
  failure due to attitude, 225
  failure due to inability to delegate
    responsibility, 247
  failure due to lack of flexibility, 231

failure due to lack of intelligence sharing,
    222
  failure due to lack of proper
    prioritization, 243
  failure due to poor communication, 228
  failure to remain alert, 217–218
  information sharing failures due to
    omission, 214
  organizational deficiencies, 210
  preparedness deficiencies, 237–239
  responsibility for, 196–197
Pearl, Daniel, 1327
Pen registers, 1141, 1147
Penal Law (Israel), use of to prosecute
    terrorists, 1200
Pennsylvania
  contamination of drinking water supply
    in, 478–479
  insider attack on drinking water system
    in, 469
People's War Group (PWG)
  success of Andhra Pradesh Greyhound
    police force in combating, 1328
  support of by Tamil Tigers, 1328
Perceptual filters, 881
Performance assessment, national
    preparedness, 93–95
Performance measures, use of public safety
    KPIs, 388–389
Performance throughput
  enterprise service bus (ESB), 955–956
  message bus, 954–955
Perimeter security
  airports, 499–500, 515
  controlled access, 749
  lighting, 748
  use of to mitigate risk, 481
Personal data, mining of, 1133–1134
Personal protective equipment, 785
  necessity of for first responders, 644

Personal relationships, failures in
communication due to, 241–242

Personal screening, 502

Personnel, importance of for risk assessment
and management, 362

Pervasive readiness, 369–371

all-hazards readiness, 379–380

budgets and performance measures,
386–389

collecting data, 381–382

framework for, 371–372

importance of structure for measurement
of, 372–374

measuring, 382–384

optimizing, 384–386

quantification of risk, 376–379

regional planning using District Model,
374–376

Pets, evacuation plans for, 624–625

Philippines, terrorist attack on drinking water
supplies in, 472

Phone records, government access to, 1141

Physical interdependence, 444

Physical security, use of to mitigate risks for
water utilities, 480–482

Piracy, 39

PKK, 34

Holder v. Humanitarian Law Project case,
106

planned attack on drinking water system,
472

Plan-do-check-act management system
methodology. *See* PDCA process

Planning. *See also* ISP

critical nature of, 644–645

deficiencies in, 195–197

Planning cycle, 629

Planning frameworks, 84

Planning scenarios, inclusion of in Interim
National Preparedness Goal, 76

Platform-as-a-service (PAAS), 966

Plume models, 993

PM-ISE, 156, 271–272

measuring progress on information
sharing, 166

role of, 273–275

sharing and safeguarding of information
by, 276–277

Poison gas, use of in terrorist attacks and
plots, 24–25

Police intelligence operations, role of
in protecting public surface
transportation, 30

Policies and procedures, use of for
mitigation of risk by water
utilities, 483–484

Policy, infrastructure vulnerability, 439–442

Population, infrastructure interdependence
and concentration of, 446–447

Population index, 379

Port Authority of New York and New Jersey,
ACEIR, 818–819

Port of Houston Authority, certification to
ISO 28000 standards, 1226

Post-Katrina Emergency Reform Act of 2006,
implementation of, 77

Poster-Reporter-Message algorithm, 1046

Posttraumatic stress disorder (PTSD),
668–669

POTA (India), 1326

Potential threats, identification and
assessment of, 358–359

PPD-8, 82–85, 180

implementation plan, 84

mission areas for national preparedness,
292

national preparedness goal, 85

Pre-crisis planning, 254. *See also* ISP

Predictive Analysis and Staging System
(PASS), 970–973

Predictive analytics solutions, complex event processing and, 956–957

Predictive law enforcement, 962–963

PREP model, 716–718

Preparedness, 72, 595, 665–666. *See also* National preparedness

assessing national levels of, 93–94

challenges to policy and operations, 90–95

cost effectiveness of capabilities development, 94–95

deficiencies in, 195–197, 208, 237–239

definition of, 78

holistic interoperability continuum, 199–201

HSPD-8 national goal, 75–77

PPD-8 emphases for, 83

prevention of deficiencies, 239

psychological consequences of terrorism, 672

regional resilience, 528–529

role of hospitality industry in, 631

use of GIS for, 1008

Preparedness fatigue, 611

Preparedness index, 379

Presidential Decision Directive 63. *See* PDD 63

Presidential disaster declarations, 596

Presidential Policy Directive 8 National Preparedness. *See* PPD-8

Prevention, 76, 85–87. *See also* Capabilities

EU efforts towards, 1359–1360

PPD-8 definition of capabilities for, 83

use of GIS for, 1008

Prevention of Terrorism Act. *See* POTA

Prevention, Protection, and Mitigation Frameworks, 88

Preventive detention, 138

PRI, 379

Primary Reserve forces (Canada), 1212

Primary vehicular access controls, 748

Principle of subsidiarity, 1304

Printer bombs, 499, 510–511, 814, 1358

Prioritization of critical needs, 208

deficiency in, 243–244

meta-leadership and, 694–696

risk communication and, 407

risk/expected-cost ranking, 244

Priority Risk Index. *See* PRI

Privacy

civil rights, and civil liberty protections (*See* P/CR/CL protections)

constitutional protections, 1137–1143

fusion centers, 313–314

information sharing concerns, 163

intelligence gathering, 1147–1153

role of ISE in maintaining, 277

Privacy Act of 1974, 1143–1145

Privacy by design, 1361

Private sector, 526

emergency management and NFPA 1600, 764–765 (*See also* NFPA standards)

emergency management program development, 766–767

homeland security education efforts of academia, 918

information sharing business continuity, 177

information sharing with, 159–160, 165

involvement of in fusion centers, 305–307

need for improved cooperation of government with, 817–818

Private Sector Preparedness Accreditation and Certification Program. *See* PS-Prep

Probabilistic risk analysis (PRA), 350–352

advantages and disadvantages of, 352

use of by nuclear power industry, 339–340

Probability of risk, definition of for CPRI, 377

Problem-solving process, role of information sharing in, 171

Procurement process, 1092, 1104–1107
importance of relationships, 1107
presentations, 1107–1108
rules of engagement, 1109
writing proposals for, 1109–1111

Producing substantive advice in crisis. *See* SOAP model

Professional responders. *See* First responders

Program Manager for the Information Sharing Environment. *See* PM-ISE

Program planning logic model, 615–618

Project Bioshield Act of 2004, 132

Protect America Act of 2007, 1147

Protection, 85–87. *See also* Capabilities
PPD-8 definition of capabilities for, 83
use of GIS for, 1009

Protective actions, 781–785
determination of, 788–789

Provision of advice, 731–732

Proximity attacks, 500
local airport security responsibility in case of, 500

PS-Prep, 805

PSAPs
dispatch of first responders by, 653
GIS technology in dispatch systems for, 986–987
situational awareness of, 657

PSR certification (TAPA), 1238

Psychological warfare, terrorism as, 889

Psychology of terrorism, 489–490, 668
developing and evaluating interventions, 673–674

effects of events on different populations, 670–672
heterogeneity of involvement, 52–54
replication and retesting of research, 50
responses to events, 668–669
strategies for preparedness and response, 672
terrorist recidivism, 50–52
understanding of terrorist engagement and disengagement, 54–56

Psychopathy, terrorism and, 47

Public alerts
effective risk communication, 426
NTAS, 428

Public awareness of DRM, 1188–1189

Public bid procurements, 1104–1105

Public domain and volunteer organizations, 1303–1304

Public education, aviation security and efforts at, 511–512

Public Health and Bioterrorism Preparedness and Response Act, 132

Public health organizations, incorporation of in emergency management, 530

Public Health services, 844

Public information
developing regional procedures for, 575–577
provision of through CCTV networks, 641

Public Information Officers (PIOs), use of crowdsourced information by, 1038

Public relations
civil liberties and security policies, 1121
radicalization theory and First Amendment rights, 1126
targeted killing policies, 1128–1129
use of social media and crowdsourcing for, 1040

Public safety
    budgets and performance measures,
       386–389
    data-driven approach to, 370–371
    ecosystems, 389–391
    fragmentation of community, 373–374
    use of mobile GIS technology for,
       1009–1010
Public Safety and Security services,
    844–845
Public safety answering points. *See* PSAPs
Public surface transportation
    casualties from bombings, 23
    chemical and biological attacks on, 24–25
    role of employees and passengers in
       security, 29–30
    security model for, 26
    terrorist attacks on, 21–22
    terrorists' use of train derailment, 25–26
Public trust
    credibility of risk communication, 426
    exploitation of by terrorists, 397
    ineffective communication and loss of,
       409–410
    information sharing and, 176
    loss of, 186
    risk management communication and,
       402, 404–405
Public–private partnerships
    building community resilience through,
       820–822
    creating a trusted environment for in
       Sweden, 1302–1303
    cross-sector, multi-jurisdiction
       collaboration through, 528
    importance of in emergency management,
       649–650
    regional resilience Action Plan
       implementation, 581–582
    role of in evacuation planning, 631–633

    strengthening of in the European Union,
       1361
Publications, use of by technology vendors
    for marketing, 1099

Q

QRAS (Quantitative Risk Assessment
    System), risk modeling using, 340
Quadrennial homeland security review
    (QHSR), 81
Qualitative information, 407–408
Quality control, failure of, 245–246
Quantification of risk, 376–379
Quantitative information, 407

R

Racial profiling, 496, 1120
    Israeli model of passenger screening,
       505–506
Radicalization, 1357
    case study, 1122–1125
    civil liberty concerns of predictive theory
       policies, 1125–1126
    efforts to address in the U.K., 1199
    predictive model of, 1130
    prevention of, 1359–1360
    process of, 1124, 1131
Radicalization Awareness Network (EU),
    1360
Radio over IP, use of for emergency
    communications, 663
Radio systems, 639–640
    use of during large scale events,
       660–662
Radiological incidents
    accident sequence at Fukushima Daiichi
       plant, 1256–1259
    emergency procedures for, 791
    exposure modeling of using GIS, 1005
Rahstriya Rifles, 1324

Rail lines, hardening against attack, 642

Rail systems, systems thinking applied to security of, 868–874

Random passenger screening, 28

Rapid recovery, technologies for, 454–455

Rasul v. Bush, 139

Ratcliffe's 3i model, 294–295

RDR Guide (TISP)

    definitions of terms used in, 525–527

    fundamental principles underlying, 527–531

    purpose and scope of, 525

Readiness

    all-hazards, 379–380

    budgets and performance measures, 386–389

    capability *vs.* capacity, 368

    collecting data on, 381–382

    cycle, 380

    importance of structure for measurement of, 372–374

    measuring, 382–384

    optimizing, 384–386

    State of Indiana approach to, 369–371 (*See also* Pervasive readiness)

Readiness exercises. *See also* Exercises

    importance of for emergency personnel, 906

Reasonable expectation of privacy

    data mining and, 1134

    United States v. Miller, 1140–1141

Recidivism of terrorists, 50–52

Recovery, 76, 85–87, 595. *See also* Capabilities

    community strategies for, 838

    consideration of challenges to, 551–554

    PPD-8 definition of capabilities for, 83

    technologies for, 454–455

    use of GIS for, 1009

Redundant communications, 645

Reentry planning, 632–633

Regional all-hazards threat environment, characterization of for Action Plan development, 537–538

Regional Catastrophic Planning program (FEMA), 179

Regional interoperability, 639–640

Regional planning, Indiana's District Model, 374–376

Regional resilience

    Action Plan (TISP), 524 (*See also* Action Plan (TISP))

    Action Plan implementation, 580–581

    air and seaports, 570–572

    all-hazards regional approach to, 527–528

    assessment, planning and mitigation for, 528–529

    coordinated incident management and decision making, 529–530

    cyber security and IT systems, 557–558

    dam and levee systems, 565–567

    energy sector, 562–563

    financial and other resource needs, 579–580

    funding efforts towards, 582–583

    hospitals and healthcare, 567–570

    information and media considerations, 575–577

    legal and liability considerations, 574–575

    measuring, 583–585

    multi-jurisdictional organizational structures for, 541–543

    multi-step process description, 532–534

    partnerships, 581–582

    societal challenges, 572–574

    stakeholder collaboration and empowerment, 586

    transportation systems, 559–561

    water and wastewater systems, 563–565

Regional Resilience Forums (U.K.), 1205

Regional risk assessment, 543–544

Regional risk reduction frameworks, 1189–1191

Regional stakeholders, information sharing of with states, 280–281

Regionalism, effect of on terrorist engagement and disengagement, 55–56

Regions, definition of, 526

Regulations
applicability of to corporate emergency planning, 768
operational risk and resilience, 803–805

Regulatory compliance, 805

Reid, Richard, 498, 511, 521

Relationship deficiencies, 208, 241–242
prevention of, 243

Religious Corporation Law (Japan), 1204

Renewable energy, decoupling of, 453–454

Reporting deficiencies, 208, 245
prevention of, 245

Repressive counterterrorism options, 892

Request for Information process. See RFI process

Request for Proposals. See RFPs

Requirements pull process, 1022

Rescue stations, use of GIS technology to analyze locations for, 996–998

Research needs, 928–932
disaster risk management, 1189
security-related, 1361

Resilience
as a counterterrorism imperative, 813–815
as disaster mitigation, 815–816
assessment of, 834–840
building a culture of, 585–586
business continuity planning and, 850, 1233 (See also Business continuity)
capabilities, 83

communicating the value of, 1306–1307
community, 649, 820–822
definition of, 368
government's role in building, 811–813
infrastructure, 816–820
measuring, 583–585
pervasive readiness and, 371–372
public safety ecosystems and, 389–391
role of supply chain management in, 1218
Sweden's whole-of-society approach to, 1297–1298
TISP regional Action Plan, 524

Resilience Benefits Working Group (CRS), 829

Resilience Capacity Index, use of to assess community resilience, 836

Resource allocation
approaches to for counterterrorism, 337–339
collaborative environments and, 329
counterterrorism decision making framework, 336–337
impact on of terrorism, 335–336
integration of with risk management for counterterrorism, 357–362

Resource typing, 396

Response, 85–87, 595. See also Capabilities
capability vs. capacity, 368–369
community-oriented, 672
coordination of activities, 658–659
EU measures targeting, 1360–1361
PPD-8 definition of capabilities for, 83
role of government in, 597–599
use of GIS for, 1009

Response exercises, use of GIS in, 1001–1004

Restoration, consideration of challenges to, 551–554

RFI process, standardization of for horizontal information sharing, 299

RFPs, 1021
    determining purchasing priorities from, 1095

Ricin, use of in terrorist attacks and plots, 24–25

Right to Financial Privacy Act, 1145

Risk
    assessment of options in crisis situations, 729–730
    biases influencing perception of, 342–343
    identifying and assessing, 88

Risk analysis, 342–343, 412–413
    benefit–cost analysis, 356–357
    decision analysis techniques, 352–353
    fault trees, 346–347
    game theory models, 354
    information assurance, 340–341
    infrastructure interdependence, 447–449
    intelligent adversary models, 354–356
    probabilistic risk analysis, 350–352
    quantifying risk, 376–379
    risk matrices, 347–348
    scenario analysis, 353–354
    selection of techniques, 357–362
    systems engineering techniques, 344–345
    terminology, 345
    use of all-hazards approach for natural disasters, 339
    use of GIS technology for, 998–1001
    use of in all-hazards plus approach, 1307
    use of influence diagrams for, 413–414

use of probabilistic risk analysis for, 339–340

Risk Analysis Management for Critical Asset Protection (RAMCAP), 480

Risk assessment
    annual updates of, 612
    corporate security, 745–747
    Japanese nuclear culture attitude toward, 1282–1284
    obstacles to, 1179–1181
    performance of by HFA member states, 1176–1177
    preventing preparedness failures, 239
    psychological, 52
    trusted travelers program, 513–514
    use of in aviation security, 496

Risk Assessment Methodology for Water (RAM-W), 479

Risk communication, 398–399
    creating appropriate channels for, 400–408
    definition of, 397
    delivery of decision-relevant information, 407–412
    future of, 432–433
    information sharing and, 430
    managing risks well, 412–416
    modes of, 431–432
    principles of, 426
    psychological impact of threat alerts, 429
    regional resilience and, 530–531, 575–577
    responding to terrorism, 425
    strategy for the content of, 419–421

Risk governance, national differences in, 1174

Risk management, 815
    Canadian Q850 decision-making process, 401

Risk management *(Cont.)*
definition of, 527, 809
development of EU strategy for, 1312–1314
development of regional strategy for, 543–544
identification of alternatives, 360
integration of with counterterrorism resource allocation, 357–362
ISO 28000:2007 definition, 1218
model of aviation passenger screening, 504
resource allocation for counterterrorism, 337–338
Risk mitigation, water utilities, 480–484
Risk rating, assignment of based on CPRI, 377–378
Risk-Specific Readiness (RSR), 383–384
RISSNET, 157, 300–301
Roving wiretap provision of Patriot Act, 133
Royal Canadian Mounted Police (RMCP), 1202
Russia, attacks on surface transportation, 23–24

S
S&T Directorate (DHS)
technology needs of, 1093
use of technology foraging by, 1020
Safe Drinking Water Act, 461–462
SAFE framework (WCO), 1234–1235
support of by ISO 28000 standards, 1240
Safeguarding information, balance of with information sharing, 162
Safety and security professionals, information needs of, 1300–1301
Safety risk communications, creating appropriate channels for, 400–403
Saffir–Simpson Hurricane Wind Scale, modifications to since 2005, 612–613

Salafi Jihad Movement, geopolitical perceptions of, 35
Salah, Muhammad
conviction of, 119
prosecution of, 112
Salesforce Chatter, 1046
SALT performance standard, 716, 735–736
provision of advice consistent with, 731–732
Samjhauta Express bombing, 23
San Bruno fire
solicitation of blood donations through social media, 1039–1040
use of crowd sentiment detection during, 1046–1047
use of Twitter during, 1039
SAR, 159, 172
ISE role in, 274
role of private sector security personnel in, 306
use of for horizontal information sharing, 300
use of standards-based data exchanges for, 278–280
Saudi Arabia
al Qaeda attacks on oil facilities in, 12–14
civil suit against following 9/11, 136–137
threat of attack on drinking water system in, 472
Savings and loan collapses, role of deregulation in, 41
SBU systems, use of for horizontal information sharing, 300–301
Scenario analysis, 353–354
evacuation plans, 783
infrastructure interdependence, 447–448

School systems, role of in disaster
preparedness in Sweden, 1305
Scotland, contamination of drinking water
supply in, 478
Screening
baggage, 502
cargo, 510–511
implementation of by FAA, 492
personal, 502
use of in aviation security model,
26–27
Screening of Passengers by Observation
Techniques program. *See* SPOT
program
Screening Partnership Program (SPP), 494
Seaports, regional resilience planning for,
570–572
Search-and-rescue operations, case study of
GIS technology use for, 1016–1017
Search-and-rescue team, 774–775
Searches. *See also* Unreasonable searches and
seizures
FISA Act provisions for, 1148
Secondary screening, 502
Secretariat of the Pacific Community
(SOPAC), 1190
Section 215 orders, 1149–1150
Sector Coordinating Councils, 159
Sector crisis centers (EU), 1312–1313
Sector Information Needs process, 176
SECURE Program, 1094
*Securing the Homeland: Strengthening the
Nation*, 73
Security
application of systems thinking to, 873
aviation (*See* Aviation security)
baseline measures, 748–751
civil liberties *vs.*, 1119–1120
consultants, 746–747
corporate crisis management, 754–758

critical infrastructure, 437–438
development of a coordinated
responsibility structure for,
514–518
development of contacts, 760–761
dual use/daily use equipment
philosophy, 638–639
emergency planning, 751–753
layers of, 518–519
mitigation of risk for water utilities,
480–482
model of for surface transportation,
26–29
policies regarding infrastructure
vulnerability, 439–442
privacy by design, 1361
risk assessments, 745–747
role of in operational resilience, 802
role of surface transportation employees
and passengers in, 29–30
strategy of a thousand cuts and cost of,
16–18
supply chain management, 1217–1218,
1232–1233
threat assessment by, 758
transportation systems, 642
Security and Emergency Management System
(SEMS), 479
Security clearances, information sharing and,
165
Security policies
civil liberties considerations, 1120
relevant questions for, 1120–1121
transnational evolution of, 1298
Security Self Assessment Tool for Small and
Very Small Systems, 479
Security threat assessments (STA), 509
Security tunnels, 519
See Something Say Something campaign, 160,
511

Seismic safety of nuclear power plants, 1267–1268

Self-knowledge, importance of for meta-leaders, 685–688

Seminar exercise of HSEEP, 906

Sense-making, 726–727

Sensitive But Unclassified systems. *See* SBU systems

Sensors, 963

Service areas, 842–845
  use of in community resilience assessment, 836–840
  use of loss-recovery curve to assess resilience of, 836–838

Service-oriented architectures (SOA), 944
  enterprise service bus in, 955–956
  importance of events in, 957–958
  use of in collaborative efforts, 329

Services Component Architecture (SCA), 954

Seventh Schedule of the Indian Constitution, Lists of, 1321

Sewage and Water Board of New Orleans (SWBNO), 465

Shabak. See Israel Security Agency

Shadow Lake Fire
  use of VOST for public relations help following, 1040
  use of VOST to filter data regarding, 1038

Shahzad, Faisal, 22, 307, 814

Shared responsibility, risk communication and, 400–401

Shared Responsibility, Pooled Resources, 327

Shared Space, 301, 306

Shelter-in-place team, 774

Sheltering in place, corporate procedures for, 784–785

Shin Bet. See Israel Security Agency

SHOA (Chile), 1338
  activities of surrounding 2010 earthquake and tsunami, 1341–1348

Shoe bomber, 498, 521
  role of passenger self-help in stopping, 511

Sikh militants
  assassination of PM Indira Gandhi by, 1322
  terrorist attacks by, 1323

Silver Command (U.K.), responsibilities of in emergency response, 1207–1208

Singapore Secure Trade Partnership. *See* STP

Singh, Beant, assassination of, 1326

Situation awareness technology solutions, 956–957

Situational awareness, 188
  definition of, 990
  failures of, 223, 236, 245
  PSAPs, 657
  regional resilience and, 530–531, 544–546
  reporting of by fusion centers, 309
  systems thinking and, 871
  use of CCTV networks for, 640–641
  use of crowdsourcing and social media for, 1037–1038
  use of GIS technology for, 990–993

Situational priorities, determination of by meta-leaders, 694–696

Size-up, use of GIS technology for, 987–990

Slowly emerging threats, 92–93

Small businesses, competing for government technology contracts, 1091

Smallpox, 66

Smallpox vaccination
  creating channels for risk communication, 403–404
  delivering decision-relevant risk communication, 410–411

managing risks, 415

SME business community, formation of business crime reduction team for, 849

Smith v. Maryland, 1141

SO15, 1199

SOAP model
assessment, 728–731
options, 727–728
provision of advice, 731–732
sense-making, 726–727

Social media, 1034–1035
costs of monitoring, 1044
credibility assessment tool, 1046
exploitation of by terrorists, 1045
harnessing, 1041–1044
policies regarding, 1044
reliability of information from, 1037
use of for risk communication, 431–432
use of to inform the public, 1040
use of to organize volunteers, 1040–1041
use of to solicit donations, 1039–1040

Social protection, disaster risk management and, 1186–1187

Social resilience, 399

Social Security records, privacy of, 1145

Social-behavioral elements for effective advice in crisis. *See* GAIN model

Societal challenges, regional resilience planning for, 572–574

Societal security (Sweden), 1296–1299
comparison of with U.S. homeland security, 1315
cooperation in the Nordic area and near-abroad, 1310–1312

Sole source procurements, 1104

Solid Waste Management services, 845

Somalia, piracy in, 39

Sony Electronics, certification to ISO 28000 standards by, 1230–1231

South America, criminality in, 39–40

South Asian Association for Regional Cooperation (SAARC), risk reduction efforts of, 1190

South Yemen, designation of as terrorist regime, 124–125

Sovereign immunity, terrorist acts and, 136–137

SoVI, use of to assess community resilience, 836

Soviet Union, role of bin Laden in Afghan-Soviet war, 7–9

Space planning, 771

Spain, attacks on surface transportation, 23–24

Spatial interdependence, 444

Special Branch units of U.K police forces, 1199

Special events
sponsoring of by technology vendors, 1100
use of GIS technology for vulnerability analysis, 1011

Special events index, 379

Special Operations Group (India), 1329

Special populations
consideration of in regional resilience plans, 547
Needs Medical Resources, 615

Special Protection Group (India), 1323

Specific information flow, 200–201

SPG Act (India), 1323

SPOT program, 505–506

Sri Lanka, destruction of water distribution system in, 474

Stafford Act
assessment of options in crisis situations, 728
interpretation of, 724–725

Stakeholders, 827
 coordination of counterterrorism efforts
  of, 870–871
 definition of, 526
 engagement of regional resilience Action
  Plan, 534
 leveraging participation of, 867–868
Standard emergency operations, 658
Standards
 applicability of to corporate emergency
  planning, 768
 operational risk and resilience, 803–805
Standards Implementation for Productivity
 (SIP) initiative, 1239
Standing Information Needs (U.S. DHS),
 299
State and local fusion centers. *See* Fusion
 centers
State List (India), 1321
State of Indiana, approach to readiness. *See*
 Pervasive readiness
State of Louisiana contraflow plan, 626–627
State sponsors list, 123–126
States
 criminalized, 38–40
 information sharing of with regional
  stakeholders, 280–281
 technology priorities of, 1089
Statewide interoperability, 639–640
Static situations, meta-leadership in, 688
Statistical modeling, 308
Stavropol train bombing, 23
Sterile zones
 insider threats and, 508–509
 use of by terrorists, 499
Stockholm Program, 1312
Storm damage recovery, case study of GIS
 technology use for, 1016–1017
STP, integration of ISO 28000 standards with,
 1239

Strategic Coordinating Group (U.K.),
 1206–1207
Strategic emergency response (U.K.),
 1205–1206
 Gold Command, 1206–1208
Strategic intelligence, deficiency of sharing,
 222–224
Strategic Intent for Information Sharing,
 155
Strategic National Risk Assessment, 86, 88
Strategic planners, tasks of, 259
Strategic planning failures, 197–198
Strategy for Homeland Defense and Civil
 Support (U.S. DOD), 180
Strategy for the Sahel (EU), 1363
Strategy of a thousand cuts, 15–18
Structure, critical importance of for readiness
 and resilience, 372–374
Student Volunteer Army (SVA), organization
 of, 1040–1041
Subject matter expert business community.
 See SME business community
Subject Matter Working Group (CRS), 829
Subject-based data mining, 1134–1135
Subprime crisis
 effect of on organized crime, 36
 role of deregulation in, 41
Subways
 bombing of, 23
 nerve gas attack on, 25
Sudan
 civil suit against, 137
 designation of as terrorist regime,
  124–125
Suicide bombers, 1201
 human factors analysis of, 507–508
 psychological characteristics of, 53–54
 use of by Tamil Tigers to assassinate
  Rajiv Gandhi, 1326–2437
Suicide hijacking, 227. *See also* 9/11 attacks

Supervisory deficiencies, 207, 216
    prevention of, 216–217
Supplementary Reserve forces (Canada),
    1212
Supply chain, 1215–1216
    ISO solution to security problems of,
        1217–1224
    security management, 1232–1233
Suppression of the Financing of Terrorism
    Act, 109–110
Surface transportation
    attacks on, 447
    casualties from bombings, 23
    terrorist attacks on, 21–22
Surveillance
    creating channels for risk communication,
        404–405
    delivering risk communication
        information, 411
    electronic, 1146–1147
    FISA Act provisions for, 1148
    Fourth Amendment protections, 1138,
        1142
    managing risks, 415
    transportation system security and,
        642
    unfocused, 1131
    use of to mitigate risk, 482
Suspicious Activity Reporting. *See* SAR
Suspicious packages or letters
    emergency procedures for, 794–796
    general characteristics, 792–794
Swarming attack, 448
Swedish Civil Contingencies Agency. *See* MSB
Synergies, importance of for counterterrorism
    mission assurance, 362
Syria, export of duel-use equipment by,
    123–125
System and Network Interdisciplinary
    Program (SNIP), 973–974

System architecture requirements, 958–960
System of records, definition of, 1145
System planning frameworks, 84
System plans and modeling, use of for risk
    mitigation by water utilities, 483
System redundancy and backups, use of for
    risk mitigation by water utilities,
    482
System structures, identifying and leveraging,
    866–867
Systematic Alien Verification for Entitlements
    (SAVE) program, 945
Systems engineering techniques, alternative
    generation table, 344–345
Systems thinking, 862
    application of to mass transit security,
        868–874
    fundamentals of, 866–867
    leveraging stakeholder participation,
        867–868
    understanding emergence and
        unintended consequences, 867

T

Tabletop exercises
    EU–U.S. Cyber Atlantic, 1316
    HSEEP, 906
    sample emergency preparedness scenario,
        910–914
TACSS certification (TAPA), 1238
Tactical emergency response (U.K.), 1205
    Silver command, 1207–1208
Tactical failures, 198–199
TADA (India)
    enactment of, 1322
    lapse of, 1326
Tailgating, 749
Tailored supply chain, 1216
Taliban, United States war on Afghanistan
    and, 11

Talkgroups, 661–662

Tamil militants, terrorist attacks in India by, 1323

Tamil Tigers (LTTE)
assassination of PM Rajiv Gandhi by, 1326–1327
evolution of, 34
Holder v. Humanitarian Law Project case, 106
support of PWG by, 1328
surface transportation attacks by, 23–24

TAPA, 1237
Air Cargo Security Standards (TACSS) certification, 1238
Freight Security Requirements (FSR) certification, 1237
Parking Security Requirements (PSR) certification, 1238
support of by ISO 28000 standards, 1240
Trucking Security Requirements (TSR) certification, 1238

TAPAC
recommendations of regarding data mining efficacy, 1154–1156
recommendations of regarding data mining impact, 1156–1160

Target capabilities, evolution of to core capabilities, 85–86

Target capabilities list, inclusion of in Interim National Preparedness Goal, 76–77

Target hardening, 884, 1131
rail lines, 642

Target levels of capability, 78

Targeted killing
case study, 1127
civil liberties concerns of, 1127–1129
use of in Israeli counterterrorism efforts, 1201

Technological threats, 86

Technology
diversity of needs for homeland security, 1086–1087
establishing a value proposition for, 1095–1096
federal priorities for, 1087–1089
future role of in incident command, 660
government buying process for, 1102–1103
government procurement process, 1092, 1104–1111
historical use of in emergency management, 1050–1051
homeland security market evaluation, 1092–1095
human factors and, 506–507
information sharing and, 182–183, 200
interoperable communications, 662–665 (*See also* Interoperable communication)
marketing of, 1096–1102
pursuing of government contracts for, 1089–1091
sales and business development, 1103–1104
state priorities for, 1089
use of for aviation passenger screening, 504

Technology and Privacy Advisory Committee. *See* TAPAC

Technology foraging (TF)
description of, 1019–1021
down-select to projects, 1029
goals of, 1022–1023
implementation of, 1030–1031
lessons learned, 1031
process, 1025–1029
technical approach, 1024–1025

Technology interdependencies, 452–453

Technology push process, 1021–1022

Telecommunications, attacks and disruptions of infrastructure, 443

Telecosm, 971–975

Ten Essentials checklist, 1175

TEPCO, 1253

    design of Fukushima Daiichi Nuclear Power Station, 1262

    insufficient disaster planning by, 1264–1269

    request of to extend Fukushima plant's operating lifetime, 1269–1270

Territories, criminalized, 38–40

Terror risk communication. *See also* NTAS

    creating appropriate channels for, 403–408

    delivery of decision-relevant information, 409–412

    managing risks well, 415–416

    modes of, 431–432

Terrorism

    appearance of in India, 1321–1322

    changes in goals of, 491

    corporate security risk assessments, 745–747

    criminal conception of, 883–887, 1197, 1361–1362

    definitions of, 667

    developing an understanding of, 45–46

    disengagement from, 49

    distinction of from domestic crimes, 883–884

    economic disruption, 814

    effect of on direct and indirect victims of, 670

    effective risk communication, 425

    emotional consequences of, 668

    evolution of, 1357–1358

    impact of on resource allocation, 335–336

    infrastructure security policies, 442–443

    legal responses to, 892

    local nature of, 886

    network conception of, 893–898

    new risks of, 399–400

    planning and exercises, 865

    post-attack psychological interventions, 673–674

    psychological consequences of, 668–669

    response structure in U.K., 1206

    use of Indian National Security Guard to combat, 1322–1323

    use of international treaties to counter, 122–123

    warfare conception of, 887–892, 1200

Terrorism Act (U.K.), 1198

Terrorism Liaison Officer, 158

Terrorism list, 123–126

Terrorism psychology, 47–49

Terrorism-related information sharing, impetus to improve, 150–151

Terrorist and Disruptive Activities (Prevention) Act. *See* TADA

Terrorist attacks

    detection and assessment, 785–787

    detection of smaller-scale, 814

    determination of protective actions, 788–789

    distinguishing between chemical and biological attacks, 786–787

    distinguishing between indoor and outdoor release, 787–788

    economic impact of, 9–10

    procedures for airborne hazards, 790–791

    procedures for radiological incidents, 791

    surface transportation, 21–23

Terrorist attacks *(Cont.)*
  targeting of Americans in aviation attacks, 491
  thousand cuts strategy, 15–18
  water utilities, 470–473
Terrorist campaigns, attacks on surface transportation, 23
Terrorist financing, 125
  legislation regarding, 129–131
  prosecuting, 100–101
  provisions in Patriot Act regarding, 133–134
  successful prosecution of, 112–114
  unsuccessful prosecutions, 110–112
Terrorist Financing Statute, 109–110
Terrorist Identities Datamart Environment. *See* TIDE
Terrorist networks, organization of, 897–898
Terrorist organizations. *See also* specific groups
  evolution of, 34–35
  finances of, 99–100
  material support statutes targeting, 101–110 (*See also* FTOs)
  understanding factionalization and loyalties in, 54–56
Terrorist recidivism, 50–52
Terrorist Screening Center, 156
Terrorist Surveillance Program, 1148
Terrorist Watch lists, 495
Terrorist watchlisting
  enhancement to system for, 157
  role of NCTC in, 155
Terrorists
  airport bombings by, 500–501
  attacks of in India, 1322–1327
  capability of to produce and deliver bioweapons, 62–64
  exploitation of social media by, 1045
  heterogeneity of involvement, 52–54

intent of to use bioweapons, 64–65
Israeli approach to, 1201–1202
legislation regarding prosecution and detention of, 138–143
psychological methods of, 397
recruitment and radicalization of, 813
role of context in ideology behavior of, 48
targeting of aviation by, 490
Terrorists *vs.* criminals, 883–884
TFTP agreements, 1364
The Infrastructure Security Partnership. *See* TISP
Thousand cuts strategy of al Qaeda, 15–18
Threat alerts. *See also* Risk communication
  cost of response, 430–431
  modes of communication for, 431–432
  psychological impact of, 429
Threat and Hazard Identification and Risk Assessment, 88
Threat assessment. *See also* Risk assessment
  analysis of interdependence, 447–449
  corporate emergency management, 769–770
  corporate security, 758–760
  Fukushima Daiichi Nuclear Power Station, 1262–1264
  role of in community resilience assessment, 836
Threat conditions, information sharing during, 255
Threat detection, homeland security spending for, 1086
Threat information, use of fusion centers to process, 290–291
Threat levels
  HSAS, 427
  information sharing regarding, 1361
  NTAS, 428

Threat tables, 347

Threat-specific emergency procedures
    airborne hazards, 790–791
    bomb threats, 796–798
    chemical *vs.* biological attacks,
        786–787
    detection and assessment, 785–786
    determination of protective actions,
        788–789
    fires and explosions, 792
    indoor *vs.* outdoor release, 787–788
    radiological incidents, 790–791
    suspicious packages or letters,
        792–796

Threats
    evolution of post 9/11, 497–501
    identification and assessment of,
        358–359
    measures and procedures to address,
        869
    trans-boundary, 1307–1309

Three Mile Island, 1255

TIBCO
    messaging products, 954
    Predictive Business Solutions of, 952

TIDE, 155

Tiered reentry process, 633

Timeline for hurricane evacuation,
    626–628

Times Square bombing attempt, 814

Timing and context, 55

TISP, 524
    Regional Disaster Resilience Guide,
        524 (*See also* RDR Guide)

TNT Express, certification to ISO 28000
    standards, 1228

Tohu bohu, 33

Tokyo Electric Power Company.
    See TEPCO

Tokyo subway attacks, Japan, 24

Tomnod.com, 1039

Tornadoes, 394. *See also* Natural disasters
    case study of GIS technology use
        following, 1016–1017

Total Information Awareness Program,
    1154

Toxins, detection of in drinking water
    supplies, 477

Training
    corporate emergency management,
        798–799
    definition of in AEDPA, 130
    definition of in material support statutes,
        103, 106–107, 109
    effect of on alertness, 233–234
    emergency management and, 604
    evacuteers, 631
    fusion center personnel, 308–309, 313
    importance of for improved
        information sharing, 182–185,
        260–261
    information sharing, 260
    preparedness, 88
    preventing complacency with, 221
    privacy, 277
    regional resilience planning and,
        577–579
    risk communications, 410
    role of in all-hazards readiness, 379
    role of in calculated risk specific
        readiness, 383, 393–394
    role of in effective collaboration, 328
    supervisor attitudes, 226
    terrorist training camps, 25, 99–100
    use of for mitigation of risk by water
        utilities, 483–484

Trains
    bombing of, 23
    derailment of, 25–26
    securing, 642

Trans-boundary threats, 1307–1309
  developing the common EU capacity to
    address, 1312–1314
Trans-European Networks, 1312
Transformational leadership, 703
Transit police, role of in protecting public
    surface transportation, 30
Transit systems
  systems thinking applied to security of,
    868–874
  terrorist attacks on, 442–443
Transnational terrorism, 890–891
Transportation assistance, inclusion of in
    evacuation planning, 618
Transportation infrastructure
  improving condition of, 440
  regional resilience planning for,
    559–561
Transportation security, homeland security
    spending for, 1085
Transportation Security Administration.
    See TSA
Transportation services, 845
Transportation systems. *See also* specific forms
    of transportation
  securing, 642
Transportation Worker Identification
    Credential Program. *See* TWIC
    program
Transportation workers, insider threats from,
    508–509
Transported Assets Protection Association.
    See TAPA
Trap and trace devices, 1141, 1147
Travel advisories, 128
Travel document fraud, 961–962
Tri-modal evacuation model,
    618–619
Triage model for evacuation transportation,
    621–624

Trust
  credibility of risk communication,
    426
  importance of for risk management,
    402
  information sharing and, 176, 185–186
  necessity of in whole-of-community
    approach, 833
  role of in fusion center partnerships,
    311
  role of in successful collaboration,
    329–330
  terrorists misuse of, 397
Trusted travelers, 513–514, 519
Trusted volunteers. *See also* VOST
  use of by professional responders,
    1042
  use of for public relations support,
    1040
TSA
  bag screening by, 502
  Behavior Detection Officers, 505–506
  creation of, 493–494
  incorporation of FAMS into, 502
  prohibited items list of, 501–502
  regulatory functions of, 503
  VIPR teams of, 28
TSR certification (TAPA), 1238
Tsunamis. *See also* Natural disasters
  case study of use of GIS technology in
    Japan, 1012
  Chile, 1337 (*See also* Chile)
  failure of TEPCO and NISA to assess risk
    from, 1253–1254
  hazard prediction and historical
    information, 1264–1269
  use of crowdsourcing and social media,
    1039–1040
  use of Twitter to send fake warnings
    about, 432

Tuscaloosa tornadoes, case study of GIS
        technology use following,
        1016–1017
Tweak the Tweet syntax, 1038
TweetDeck, 1040
TWIC program, 509
Twitpics, exploitation of by terrorists during
        Mumbai bombings, 1045
Twitter. *See also* Social media
    #SMEM, 1043
    use of for risk communication,
        431–432

U

U.S. Citizenship and Immigration Service.
        See USCIS
U.S. Customs Trade Partnership Against
        Terrorism. *See* C-TPAT
U.S. Department of Justice. *See* DOJ
U.S. Federal Air Marshal Service (FAMS),
        492
U.S. National Academy of Sciences, red book
        reports, 402–403, 413
U.S. Northern Command, partners, 918
U.S. State Department, Antiterrorist
        Assistance (ATA) program, 144
U.S. Transportation Security Administration.
        See TSA
UCore standard, 1066–1067
UICDS, 1049–1050
    aggregators, 1056
    Agreement and Profile Services,
        1070–1071
    architecture, 1058–1060
    Core Web services, 1062–1063
    creation of COD by, 1071–1074
    data exchange standards of, 1055,
        1065–1066
    data sharing, 1064–1065
    end users, 1068

information sharing operational
        questions, 1069–1070
    integration of alternate sources of COD,
        1076–1080
    message router, 1055–1056
    objectives of, 1052–1053, 1068–1069
    real-world deployment of, 1060–1062
    schematic diagram of, 1081
    Tree of Incident Knowledge,
        1074–1076
    two-way information sharing
        capabilities of, 1056–1058
    Work Products, 1066–1067
Uncertainty
    role of in disaster decision making,
        713–714
    sense-making and, 726
Undergraduate homeland security education
    areas of focus for, 922–925
    core academic areas, 920–921
    program outcomes, 921
Underground parking garages, securing,
        750
Underwear bomber, 161, 498, 521, 967–970
    role of passenger self-help in stopping,
        511
Undetected plots, thwarting, 869
Unfunded Mandates Reform Act (UMRA),
        517
Ungar, Yaron, 136
Unified Incident Command and Decision
        Support. *See* UICDS
Uniform Fire Code (UFC), emergency
        planning for, 769
Unintended consequences, 867
    radicalization theory, 1125–1126
    risks of for security policies, 1121
    targeted killing policy, 1128
UNISDR, 1173
United Flight 93, passenger effort on, 511

United Kingdom
    attacks on surface transportation in,
        23–24
    business practices in, 847–848
    counterterrorism legislation of, 1198
    criminal conception of terrorism,
        1197–1198
    emergency management approach,
        1204–1208
    terrorism experience of, 1195
United Kingdom Accreditation Service
    (UKAS), 1246
United National Strategy for Disaster
    Reduction. *See* UNISDR
United Nations
    counterterrorism treaties of, 122
    framework for international cooperation
        in counterterrorism, 1363–1364
United Stated v. Afshari, 105
United States
    al Qaeda's response to 2008 economic
        collapse, 15
    bleeding wars, 10–12
    counterterrorism treaties of, 122–123
    Department of Homeland Security, 73–74
    economic impact of 9/11 attacks on,
        9–10
    partnership of with EU in fighting
        terrorism, 1364–1365
    threat of terrorist attacks on surface
        transportation in, 22
United States v. Hammoud, 112
United States v. Jones, 1142
United States v. Miller, 1140
Unity of purpose, 699–701
Unlawful Activities (Prevention) Act (India),
    1331
Unreasonable searches and seizures
    information privacy issues, 1138–1142
    Katz v. United States, 1139

Untested assumptions, use of emergency
    exercises to overcome, 906–907
Urban neighborhood police posts (Japan),
    1203
Urban planning, risk reduction and,
    1184–1185
Urban search and rescue teams. *See* USAR
    teams
Urgency, role of in disaster decision making,
    714
US-VISIT program, 944, 949–951
USA Patriot Act. *See* Patriot Act
USAR teams, 648
USCIS, 944
    challenges, 945–946
    E-Verify system, 947–949
    PCQ, 946–949
    Person Centric Query, 943
    program overview, 945
    prospective architecture, 945
User Agreements, 529
Ushahidi Crowdmap, 1036
Utilities, water systems. *See* Water systems

V

Value propositions, establishing for
    technology solutions, 1095–1096
Values hierarchy, 352–353
Vandalism, effects of on drinking water
    supplies, 468–469
Vehicular access controls, 748
Vendor–vendor resilience, 851–854
Verification deficiencies, 207, 215
    prevention of, 216
Vertical command/action structures, use of to
    achieve horizontal goals, 832
Vertical evacuation, 611
Victims of terrorism, psychological reactions
    of, 670
Video Privacy Protection Act, 1146

Village police posts (Japan), 1203

Vinas, Bryant, 22

Violent Crime Control and Enforcement Act of 1994, material support statutes of, 101–110, 129

Violent radicalization
efforts to address in the U.K., 1199
prevention of, 1359–1360
process of, 1124, 1131

Viral marketing, 1099–1100

Virginia Tech mass shootings, 202
communication failures, 232
effective collaboration preceding, 243
Emergency Response Plan, 227
failure due to inability to delegate responsibility, 247–248
failure due to lack of preparedness, 238
information dissemination failures, 235–236
information sharing failures, 188–189, 223–224

Virtual Operations Support Team. *See* VOST

Virtual USA, 1076–1077, 1079

Visa lookout system, sharing of, 133

Visual information flow mapping, 262–268

Visual Intermodal Prevention and Response (VIPR), 28

Visual surveillance, use of to mitigate risk, 482

Voice over IP (VoIP), use of for emergency communications, 663

Voluntary Private Sector Preparedness Accreditation and Certification Program. *See* PS-Prep

Voluntary standards, 768

Volunteers. *See also* Crowd
coordination of with the public domain, 1303–1304
crowdsourcing tasks of, 1036 (*See also* VOST)
role of in disaster management, 630–631

VOST
use of for public relations support, 1040
use of for trusted information, 1044–1045
use of to filter data during Shadow Lake Fire, 1038

Vulnerability
bioweapons and, 65–67
cyber attacks on critical infrastructure, 452
identification and assessment of, 359
infrastructure interdependencies and, 538–541
policies related to infrastructure, 439–442
proximity attacks, 500
reduction of by modifying interdependency, 453–455
use of HIRA to quantify risk, 376–379
use of vulnerability–consequence tables for risk analysis, 347

Vulnerability assessment
corporate emergency management, 770
critical infrastructure, 642–643
drinking water utilities, 462
tools, 479–480
use of GIS technologies for, 992, 998–1001, 1007–1009
water utilities, 479–480

Vulnerability Self-Assessment Tool (VSAT), 479

Vulnerable populations
disaster preparedness of, 1305
psychological effects of terrorist events on, 670

W

War on oil, role of al Qaeda in, 12–14

War on terrorism. *See also* Terrorism
civil liberties *vs.* security in the U.S., 1119
diversionary effects of, 35–36

Warfare
  chemical-biological, 24–25
  criminal armies and, 37–38
  economic, 9–18
  Fourth Generation, 6
  terrorism as, 887–892
Warning systems, 780
  homeland security spending for, 1085
Warning time, definition of for CPRI, 378
Warnings, developing a regional system for, 544–546
Warrantless searches, protection of under FISA and Protect America Act, 1148–1149
Washington, DC
  planned attack on drinking water system, 471–472
  potential release of hazardous chemicals into water system, 474–475
Wastewater systems
  disruptions in, 461
  emergency response plans for, 484–485 (*See also* ERPs)
  insider attack on, 469–470
  intentional or accidental contamination of, 475–477
  physical assault on components of, 473–474
  regional resilience planning for, 563–565
  terrorist attacks on, 470–473
  threats to from accidents, 465–467
  threats to from natural disasters, 464–465
  use of cyber attack against, 475
  vulnerability assessment of, 479–480
Water and Wastewater Agency Response Network (WARN), 483–484
Water Pollution Control Act, 462
Water services, 845

Water systems
  emergency operational responses, 485–486
  emergency preparedness planning, 462–463
  emergency response plans for, 484–485 (*See also* ERPs)
  intentional attacks on, 468–470
  regional resilience planning for, 563–565
  terrorist attacks on, 443, 461, 470–473
  threats to from accidents, 465–467
  types of malevolent attacks on, 473–479
  vulnerability assessment of, 479–480
WCO
  Customs Guidelines on Integrated Supply Chain Management, 1216–1217
  SAFE framework, 1234–1235, 1240
Weapons of mass destruction. *See* WMD
Western nations. *See also* specific countries
  terrorist attacks on surface transportation in, 22
Whalen v. Roe, 1143
What-if factor (WIF), 848
White collar organized crime (WCOC), 41
Whole community, defining, 827
Whole community resilience, information sharing and, 177–180
Whole of government approach, 82
Whole-of-community approach, 371–372, 649–650. *See also* CRS
  assessment of community resilience, 834–840
  benefits of, 826–827
  homeland security, 72
  implementing, 840–841
  national preparedness, 84
Whole-of-nation approach, national preparedness, 84

Whole-of-society approach, 1297
    overcoming mental gaps, 1300
Wholes, identification of, 866
Wikileaks, 162, 174, 965
    response of Obama Administration to,
        276–277
Wildfires
    case study of GIS technology use for,
        1015–1016
    coordination required to control,
        653–654
    use of social media and crowdsourcing
        during, 1039–1040
Wiretaps, 1146–1147
Witt, James Lee, 598
WMD
    challenges of emergency response, 662
    role of Israeli HFC in the event of an
        attack, 1210–1211
    spending to defend against, 1085
    U.S. legislation regarding, 132

Workforce services, 845
Workshop exercise of HSEEP, 906
World Customs Organization. *See* WCO
Worst-case scenario
    planning for, 644–645
    preparing for, 226–228, 237–239

Y
Yakuza recession, role of deregulation in, 41
YCH Group (Singapore), certification to ISO
        28000 standards, 1226–1228
Yousef, Ramzi, 878

Z
Zambia, attack on water pipeline in, 474
Zawahiri, Ayman, 63
Zayed, Mohammed Mohsen Yahya,
        prosecution and conviction of,
        113–114
Zazi, Najibullah, 307
Zetas, 38